# Television Specials

---

## 3,201 Entertainment Spectaculars, 1939–1993

---

by VINCENT TERRACE

McFarland & Company, Inc., Publishers
*Jefferson, North Carolina, and London*

**British Library Cataloguing-in-Publication data are available**


**Library of Congress Cataloguing-in-Publication Data**

Terrace, Vincent.
   Television specials : 3,201 entertainment spectaculars,
1939–1993 / by Vincent Terrace.
    p.  cm.
   Includes index.
   ISBN 0-89950-966-5 (lib. bdg. : 50# alk. paper)
   1. Television specials — United States — Encyclopedias.
I. Title.
PN1992.8.S64T37   1995
791.45′75′0973 – dc20                   94-7225
                                          CIP

Manufactured in the United States of America

*McFarland & Company, Inc., Publishers*
  *Box 611, Jefferson, North Carolina 28640*

# TABLE OF CONTENTS

# ACKNOWLEDGMENTS

The author would like to thank the following people for their help in making this book possible: Nicole Galiardo, Barry Gillam, Steven Lance, Debbie Milano, James Robert Parish, and Robert "Bob" Reed.

# PREFACE

Specials have been around since the early days of television. Prior to 1954, however, they appeared infrequently and were often unnoticed. They were usually considered to be just something that preempted a regular program that week. In 1954 everything changed when then NBC president Sylvester "Pat" Weaver introduced what he called "Spectaculars" — lavish, color entertainment programs that added a new dimension to the medium. As the new phenomenon caught on, both ABC and CBS jumped on the bandwagon (although they refused to copy NBC's terminology) and called them "Specials" (NBC eventually used the term "Specials" also).

Whether they were called "Spectaculars," "Specials," or "One Shots," a whole new world of entertainment found its way onto the small screen. "Peter Pan" flying, adaptations of Broadway plays and books, and big-name stars appearing on television for the first time were all a part of what could be called the golden age of television specials. As production costs rose and ratings became more important for advertising dollars, the networks cut back on the number of lavish specials in the mid–1960s. The years that followed produced many specials, but the quality and lavish production values were absent from many.

*Television Specials* is the first book to provide facts on specials. It is an alphabetical listing of 3,201 programs (2,249 numbered entries with 952 shows contained within these titles) broadcast from 1939 through the 1992-93 season. All entries are listed alphabetically and contain the following information: casts, credits (music, producer, writer, and director), formats, dates, networks, and running times. In many cases the entries listed here are the only source of such information that is currently available to the general public.

One may discover in this reference work countless facts — from Arnold Schwarzenegger's performance on a variety special, to Valerie Bertinelli's dramatic debut on "The Secret Life of Charles Dickens," to who competed on "The Battle of the Network Stars," and who performed on "Circus of the Stars."

There are Christmas specials (1947–92), the Charlie Brown Peanuts specials, the specials of well-known celebrities (for example, Ann-Margret, Bob Hope, Lynda Carter, and Perry Como) and celebrity documentary specials (for example, Marilyn Monroe and Elvis Presley).

Excluded from this book are news specials, noncelebrity documentaries, sports, religious projects, awards, beauty pageants, and parades. Specials for celebrities have been set up to provide easy access to the information. Under the main title listing (for example, "Alan King Specials"), one finds a chronological listing of the shows hosted by or starring that performer. Other credits (for example, guesting on a program) will not appear here, but will be in the index.

This book provides a complete reference source to information that is available for the first time—the only source needed for 54 years of television specials.

# TELEVISION SPECIALS

**The ABC Afterschool Special.** An alphabetical listing of 128 outstanding specials that were broadcast on a monthly basis. See individual titles for information: Alexander, All That Glitters, The Almost Royal Family, The Amazing Cosmic Awareness of Duffy Moon, Amy and the Angel, Andrea's Story: A Hitchhiking Tragedy, Are You My Mother? Backwards: The Riddle of Dyslexia, Between Two Loves, Blind Sunday, The Bridge of Adam Rush, But It's Not My Fault! Can a Guy Say No? The Celebrity and the Arcade Kid, The Cheats, Cindy Eller: A Modern Fairy Tale, Class Act: A Teacher's Story, The Color of Friendship, The Crazy Comedy Concert, Cyrano, Daddy Can't Read, Daddy, I'm Their Mama Now; Date Rape, The Day My Kid Went Punk, Dear Lovey Hart: I Am Desperate, A Desperate Exit, Dinky Hocker, Divorced Kids' Blues, Don't Touch, A Family Again, A Family of Strangers, Fawn Story, First the Egg, Francesca, Baby; Gaucho, Getting Even, The Gift of Amazing Grace, Girlfriend, The Great Love Experiment, The Gymnast, The Hand-Me-Down Kid, Have You Ever Been Ashamed of Your Parents? The Heartbreak Winner, The Hero Who Couldn't Read, Hewitt's Just Different, A Home Run for Love, The Horrible Honchos, I Want to Go Home, In the Shadow of Love, The Incredible, Indelible, Magical, Physical Mystery Trip; It Isn't Easy Being a Teenage Millionaire, It Must Be Love ('Cause I Feel So Dumb!), It's a Mile from Here to Glory, It's No Crush, I'm in Love; It's Only Rock 'n' Roll, Just a Regular Kid, Just Tipsy, Honey; The Kid Who Wouldn't Quit, Last of the Curlews, The Late Great Me, The Less Than Perfect Daughter, The Magical Mystery Trip Through Little Red's Head, Make Believe Marriage, A Matter of Time, Me and Dad's New Wife, Michel's Mixed-Up Musical Bird, Mighty Moose and the Quarterback Kid, Mom and Dad Can't Hear Me, Mom's on Strike, A Movie Star's Daughter, My Dad Can't Be Crazy, Can He? My Dad Lives in a Downtown Hotel, My Mom's Having a Baby, My Mother Was Never a Kid, No Greater Gift, One of a Kind, One Too Many, Out of Step, Over the Limit, The Perfect Date, The Pinballs, P.J. and the President's Son, Please Don't Hit Me, Mom; Private Affairs, Pssst! Hammerman's After You! A Question About Sex, The Rag Tag Champs, Rookie of the Year, Run, Don't Walk; The Runaways, Santiago's America, Santiago's Ark, Sara's Summer of the Swans, Seasonal Differences, The Secret Life of T. K. Dearing, The Seven Wishes of a Rich Kid, The Seven Wishes of Joanna Peabody, The Shaman's Last Raid, She Drinks a Little, The Skating Rink, Sometimes I Don't Love My Mother, A Special Gift, Starstruck, Stoned, Stood Up, Summer Switch, Supermom's Daughter, Taking a Stand, Tattle, Teen Father, The Terrible Secret, Terrible Things My Mother Told Me, Testing Dirty, The Toothpaste Millionaire, Torn Between Two Fathers, Tough Girl, A Town's Revenge, The Unforgivable Secret, A Very Delicate Matter, Very Good Friends, Wanted: The Perfect Guy, The Wave, What Are Friends For? Where Do Teenagers Come From? Which Mother Is Mine? William, The Woman Who Willed a Miracle.

**1 The ABC All-Star Spectacular.** Variety, 60 min., ABC, 9/15/85. A celebration of ABC's fall 1984-85 season wherein its stars perform while attending a lavish party. *Hosts:* Gavin MacLeod, Patricia Klous, Bernie Kopell, Ted Lange, Jill Whelan. *Guests:* Joan Collins, Tony Danza, Linda Evans, John Forsythe, Brian Keith, Emmanuel Lewis, Marie Osmond, Emma Samms, Cybill Shepherd, Robert Urich, Ben Vereen, Robert Wagner, Eli Wallach, Bruce Willis.

*Music:* Lenny Stack. *Producer:* Dick Clark. *Writer:* Robert Arthur. *Director:* Jeff Margolis.

## 2 ABC Presents a Royal Gala.

Variety, 90 min., ABC, 5/25/88. A star-studded musical performance for England's Prince Charles and Princess Diana. Taped at the London Palladium. *Hosts:* John Ritter, David Frost. *Guests:* Belinda Carlisle, Phil Collins, Elton John, Gloria Estefan, Art Garfunkel, James Taylor, Robin Williams. *Announcer:* Charlie O'Donnell. *Music:* Alyn Ainsworth. *Producer:* David Frost. *Writer:* Stephen Pouliot. *Director:* Jeff Margolis.

## 3 ABC Presents Tomorrow's Stars.

Variety, 2 hrs., ABC, 6/17/78. A showcase for talented new performers. Celebrity guests and studio audience members vote to determine the best new acts. *Host:* John Ritter. *Guests:* The Captain and Tennille, Norm Crosby, Florence Henderson, Charles Nelson Reilly, Joan Rivers, Cheryl Tiegs, Dick Van Patten. *Producers:* Marty Pasetta, Dan Lewis. *Director:* Marty Pasetta.

## The ABC Weekend Special.

A series of specials geared to children. See the following titles for information: The Adventures of Con Sawyer and Hucklemary Finn, The Adventures of Teddy Ruxpin, All the Money in the World, The Amazing Bunjee Venture, Arthur the Kid, The Baby with Four Fathers, The Big Hex of Little Lulu, Choose Your Own Adventure, Columbus Circle, The Contest Kid, The Contest Kid Strikes Again, Cougar! The Day the Kids Took Over, A Different Twist, The Dog Days of Arthur Kane, The Escape of a One-Ton Pet, The Ghost of Thomas Kempe, The Girl with ESP, The Haunted Mansion Mystery, The Haunted Trailer, Henry Hamilton, Graduate Ghost; Homer and the Wacky Doughnut Machine, Horatio Alger Updated, If I'm Lost, How Come I Found You? Jeeter Mason and the Magic Headset, The Joke's on Mr. Little, The Legend of Lochnager, Little Lulu, Mayday! Mayday! Miss Switch to the Rescue, The Mouse on the Motorcycle, My Dear Uncle Sherlock, The Notorious Jumping Frog of Calaveras County, The Nunundaga, The $1,000 Bill, Otherwise Known as Sheila the Great, The Parsley Garden, Portrait of Grandpa Doc, Ralph S. Mouse, The Ransom of Red Chief [1977 version], The Red Room Riddle, The Revenge of Red Chief, Runaway Ralph, Scruffy, The Secret World of Og, Soup and Me, Soup for President, Stanley, the Ugly Duckling; Trouble River, Valentine's Second Chance, The Winged Colt, Zack and the Magic Factory.

## 4 ABC's Silver Anniversary Celebration.

Variety, 4 hrs., ABC, 1/31/78. A lavish celebration in which hundreds of ABC-TV stars, past and present, gather to honor the American Broadcasting Company on the occasion of its twenty-fifth anniversary. *Guests include:* Edie Adams, John Astin, Ernest Borgnine, Tom Bosley, Paul Burke, Charo, Chuck Connors, Robert Conrad, Howard Cosell, Richard Crenna, Billy Crystal, Patty Duke, Barbara Eden, Vince Edwards, Norman Fell, John Forsythe, Redd Foxx, David Hedison, Katherine Helmond, Ron Howard, Kate Jackson, Bernie Kopell, Cheryl Ladd, Hal Linden, Paul Lynde, Gavin MacLeod, Fred MacMurray, Kristy McNichol, Barry Manilow, Penny Marshall, Pamela Sue Martin, Vic Morrow, Harriet Nelson, Rick Nelson, Hugh O'Brian, Patti Page, Donna Reed, John Ritter, Jaclyn Smith, Robert Stack, Toni Tennille, Danny Thomas, Marlo Thomas, Karen Valentine, John Wayne, Anson Williams, Cindy Williams, Henry Winkler. *Music:* Lenny Stack. *Producer:* Dick Clark. *Writers:* Robert Arthur, Bill Lee, Stuart Bloomberg, Phil Hahn. *Director:* Perry Rosemond.

**5 Abe Lincoln in Illinois.**
Drama, 90 min., NBC, 2/5/64. Set between 1830 and 1860. Follows Abraham Lincoln from backwoods law practice to presidency. Based on Robert E. Sherwood's historical drama. Broadcast on "Hallmark Hall of Fame." *Cast:* Jason Robards, Jr. (Abe Lincoln), Kate Reid (Mary Todd), James Broderick (Joshua Speed), Burt Brinckerhoff (William Herndon), Mildred Trases (Ann Rutledge), Hiram Sherman (Judge Bowling Greene), Roy Poole (Seth Gale), Staats Cotsworth (Crimm), Nan McFarland (Nancy Greene), Jack Bittner (Stephen Douglas), Tom Slater (Robert Lincoln). *Producer-Director:* George Schaefer. *Writer:* Robert Hartung.

**6 Academy Award Songs.**
Variety, 60 min., NBC, 3/15/60. Celebrities perform songs that have won an Oscar for best song. *Host:* Jane Wyman. *Guests:* Nat King Cole, The Four Aces, Gogi Grant, Elsa Lanchester, Kay Starr, Tex Ritter. *Music:* Tutti Camarata. *Producer:* Hubbell Robinson. *Choreographer:* Hermes Pan.

**7 The Academy of Country Music's Greatest Hits.** Variety, 2 hrs., NBC, 2/16/93. A look at the first performances of country music's greatest stars: Clint Black, Garth Brooks, Naomi and Wynonna Judd, Tanya Tucker, Jerry Lee Lewis, Reba McEntire, George Strait, Tammy Wynette, Lorrie Morgan, Hank Williams, Jr., Gary Morris, Vince Gill, Dwight Yoakam, Buck Owens. *Producer-Director:* Gene Weed.

**8 Academy of Country Music's 20th Anniversary Reunion.** Variety, 60 min., NBC, 2/18/86. A Hollywood celebration of the greatest moments and memories from 20 years of the Academy of Country Music. *Hosts:* Tammy Wynette, Glen Campbell. *Guests:* Alabama, Claude Akins, Eddy Arnold, Debby Boone, Johnny Cash, Charlie Daniels, Donna Fargo, Janie Fricke, Larry Gatlin, Mickey Gilley, Charles Haid, Waylon Jennings, Johnny Lee, Patsy Montana, The Oak Ridge Boys, Patti Page, Charlie Rich, John Schneider, Charlene Tilton. *Announcer:* Ron Martin. *Music:* Tom Burner. *Producer:* Dick Clark. *Writer:* Richard Oliver. *Director:* Gene Weed.

**9 Accent on Love.** Variety, 60 min., NBC, 2/28/59. A musical revue based on the theme of love. *Host:* Louis Jourdan. *Guests:* Marge and Gower Champion, Danny Costello, Jaye P. Morgan, Mike Nichols and Elaine May, The Ray Charles Singers, Ginger Rogers. *Music:* Tutti Camarata. *Producer:* Joseph Cates. *Writers:* Mel Brooks, Mel Tolkin. *Directors:* Gower Champion, Joseph Cates.

**10 Ace Hits the Big Time.** Comedy, 60 min., CBS, 4/2/85. A musical comedy that focuses on Horace "Ace" Hobart, a 16-year-old from New Jersey, as he attempts to adjust to his new neighborhood and school (Marshall High) in Manhattan. Musical numbers revolve around Ace's fantasies about and confrontations with two street gangs: The Purple Falcons and the Piranhas. Aired as a "CBS Schoolbreak Special." *Cast:* Rob Stone (Ace Hobart), Julie Akin (Nora Hobart), Karen Petrasek (Raven), Kelly Britt (Ms. Dupar), Tony Longo (Mario), Anthony Barrile (Slick), James LeGros (Freddy), Lance Slaughter (J.D.). *Music:* Misha Segal. *Lyrics:* Harriet Schock. *Producer:* Martin Tahse. *Writer:* Linda Elstad. *Director:* Robert C. Thompson.

**11 Addie and the King of Hearts.** Drama, 60 min., CBS, 1/25/76. The fourth in a series of acclaimed dramas about the Mills family and their life in a small Nebraska town during the 1940s (see also The Easter

Promise, The House Without a Christmas Tree, and The Thanksgiving Treasure). The story details 13-year-old Addie Mills' efforts to understand the emotion of love when she discovers that her widowed father, James, is dating Irene Davis, the local beautician. Her adolescent shock, jealousy, and shattered security later teach her that love has many faces and that telling them apart is a function of growing up. *Cast:* Lisa Lucas (Addie Mills), Jason Robards (James Mills), Mildred Natwick (Grandma Mills), Diane Ladd (Irene Davis), Richard Hatch (Mr. Davenport), Christina Hart (Kathleen Tate). *Music:* Arthur Rubinstein. *Producer:* Alan Shayne. *Writer:* Gail Rock. *Director:* Joseph Hardy.

## 12 The Admirable Crichton.

Comedy-Drama, 90 min., NBC, 5/2/68. A turn-of-the-century satire, based on the play by J. M. Barrie, that follows a group of people who set up a community on a tropical island after a shipwreck. Aired on the "Hallmark Hall of Fame." *Cast:* Bill Travers (Crichton), Virginia McKenna (Lady Mary), Laurance Naismith (Lord Loam), Carrie Nye (Lady Catherine), Janet Munro (Tweeny), Richard Easton (Ernest), Pamela Brown (Lady Brockelhurst). *Producer-Director:* George Schaefer. *Writer:* Robert Hartung.

## 13 The Adventures of a Two-Minute Werewolf.

Comedy, 30 min., ABC, 2/23 and 3/2/85. Following a sixteenth viewing of the classic *Wolfman* movie, 13-year-old Walt Cribbens, an avid horror-film fan, discovers that he has begun to turn into a werewolf—an affliction that lasts for periods of two minutes. The story relates his misadventures as he attempts to cope with the situations that occur and discover a reason for its happening. (It is explained that Walt has inherited the affliction from his mother, Wilma, and that they are both of the

friendly werewolf variety.) *Cast:* Barrie Youngfellow (Wilma Cribbens), Knowl Johnson (Walter Cribbens), Julia Reardon (Cindy Deardorf), Lainie Kazan (Madame Zola), Melba Moore (Ms. Lopez). *Music:* Rupert Holmes. *Producer:* Jane Startz. *Writer:* Pamela Pettler. *Director:* Mark Cullingham.

## 14 The Adventures of Candy Claus.

Cartoon, 30 min., Syndicated, 12/87. When a young girl discovers that Santa Claus receives no gifts for Christmas, she and her parents decide to make him a gift—a rag doll. When Santa receives the doll, his touch brings it to life. The doll, whom Santa names Candy, becomes the daughter he and Mrs. Claus never had. The story relates Candy's first adventures in Santa Claus Town. *Voices:* Robyn Moore (Candy Claus/Mrs. Claus), Keith Scott (Santa Claus). *Music:* Guy Gross. *Producer:* Louis Carbo. *Director:* Yoram Gross.

## 15 The Adventures of Con Sawyer and Hucklemary Finn.

Comedy, 30 min., ABC, 9/7 and 9/14/85. A variation on the Mark Twain stories *The Adventures of Tom Sawyer* and *Adventures of Huckleberry Finn*. The adventures of Connie "Con" Sawyer and her friend, "Huckle" Mary Finn, two mischievous preteens who live in modern-day Mississippi. The story itself relates the girls' efforts to foil a robbery. Aired as an "ABC Weekend Special." *Cast:* Drew Barrymore (Con Sawyer), Brandy Ward (Hucklemary Finn), Pat Richardson (Pamela Sawyer), James Naughton (Captain Sawyer), James Rebhorn (Charlie Riley), M. Emmet Walsh (Rocco), Alan North (Skeezer), Terri Hanauer (Sarah). *Music:* Paul Chihara. *Producers:* Diane Silver, Doro Bachrach. *Writers:* Anne Elder, Cynthia Chenault. *Director:* Joan Darling.

## 16 The Adventures of Huckleberry Finn.

Cartoon, 60 min., CBS,

11/26/82. An animated adaptation of the novel by Mark Twain. The adventures of Huckleberry Finn, the homeless boy, and his friend, Jim, the runaway slave (of Miss Watson on Jackson Island), as they travel on a raft down the Mississippi River. *Voices:* Simon Hinton (Huckleberry Finn), Alistair Duncan (Jim), Barbara Frawley (Widow Douglas/Miss Watson). *Producer:* Walter J. Hucker. *Writer:* John Palmer. *Director:* Paul McAdam.

**17 The Adventures of Teddy Ruxpin.** Cartoon, 30 min., ABC, 11/30 and 12/7/85. The adventures of Teddy Ruxpin, a lovable Illiop (bear-like animal); Grubby, a caterpillar; Newton Gimmick, an inventor; and Prince Arin, as they battle evil in their quest to see the world. Filmed in a newly developed computer technology called Animagic, which helps costume characters come alive. Aired as an "ABC Weekend Special." *Voices:* Phil Baron, Katie Leigh, Tony Pope, Will Ryan, Russi Taylor, B. J. Ward. *Producer:* Neal Simmons. *Writer:* Ken Forsee. *Director:* Lee Bernhardi.

**18 The Adventures of Tom Sawyer.** Cartoon, 60 min., Syndicated, 1/89. The story, set on the Mississippi River in 1846, follows the adventures of Tom Sawyer and his friend, Huck Finn, as they become involved with the evil Injun Joe (here accused of stealing money) and rescue the beautiful Becky Thatcher from certain death in a cave. Adapted from the novel by Mark Twain. *Voices:* Simon Hinton (Tom Sawyer), Scott Higgins (Huck Finn), Jane Harder (Becky Thatcher), Michael Tate (Injun Joe), Jane Harder (Aunt Polly). *Producer:* Tom Stacey. *Writer:* Joel Kane. *Director:* Warwick Gilbert.

**19 After Hours: From Janice, John, Mary and Michael,** with Love. Variety, 60 min., CBS, 12/8/76. The first of three specials that highlight the musical talents of CBS soap opera stars (see the following two titles also). *Stars:* Janice Lynde and John McCook ("The Young and the Restless"), Michael Nouri and Mary Stuart ("Search for Tomorrow"). *Music:* John Berkman. *Producer:* John Conboy. *Director:* William E. Glenn.

**20 After Hours: Getting to Know Us.** Variety, 60 min., CBS, 5/26/77. Stars from various CBS soap operas showcase their musical talents in a primetime special. (See previous and next entry.) *Stars:* Michael Allinson ("Love of Life"), Meg Bennett and David Hasselhoff ("The Young and the Restless"), Kathryn Hays ("As the World Turns"), Don Stewart and Tudi Wiggins ("The Guiding Light"). *Music:* Nick Perito. *Producer-Director:* Bob Henry.

**21 After Hours: Singin', Swingin' and All That Jazz.** Variety, 60 min., CBS, 12/6/77. The third of three primetime specials (see two prior titles) that showcase the musical talents of various CBS soap opera stars. *Stars:* Keith Charles and Don Hastings ("As the World Turns"), Beau Kayzer, Victoria Mallory, John McCook ("The Young and the Restless"). *Music:* Marvin Laird. *Producer:* John Conboy. *Director:* William E. Glenn.

**22 Ah! Wilderness.** Comedy, 90 min., NBC, 4/28/59. A "Hallmark Hall of Fame" presentation about Richard Miller, the son of a Connecticut newspaper publisher, and his attempts to court a girl (Muriel McComber) against the wishes of her father. Based on the play by Eugene O'Neill. *Cast:* Lee Kinsolving (Richard Miller), Abigail Kellogg (Muriel McComber), Helen Hayes (Essie Miller), Lloyd Nolan (Nat Miller),

Burgess Meredith (Sid Davis), Betty Field (Lily), Nicholas Pryor (Arthur). *Producer-Director:* George Schaefer. *Writer:* Robert Hartung.

### 23 Ain't Misbehavin'. Musical, 2 hrs., NBC, 6/21/82.

A television adaptation of the 1978 Broadway musical with the original cast repeating their roles. The play, set in a re-created nightclub stage of the 1930s, salutes the career of Thomas "Fats" Waller through renditions of 31 blues and bop songs associated with the entertainer-composer. *Performers:* Nell Carter, Andre DeShields, Ken Page, Armelia McQueen, Charlaine Woodward. *Music:* Luther Henderson, Al Aarons, Garrett Brown, Marshall Royal, Roger Hogan. *Musical Staging:* Richard Faria. *Producers:* Alvin Cooperman, Buddy Bregman. *Writer:* Richard Malby, Jr. *Director:* Don Mischer.

### 24 Air Supply in Hawaii.

Variety, 60 min., HBO, 1/23/83. A concert by the Australian rock group Air Supply (Russell Hitchcock, Graham Russell, Rex Goh, David Moyse, David Green, Frank Smith, Ralph Cooper). *Producer:* Don Arden, Danny O'Donovan. *Director:* Mike Mansfield.

### 25 Alabama ... My Home's in Alabama. Variety, 60 min., CBS, 11/28/86.

A profile of and performances by the country and western group Alabama (Randy Owen, Jeff Cook, Teddy Gentry, Mark Henndon). *Guests:* The Charlie Daniels Band, Naomi and Wynonna Judd, Willie Nelson. *Producers:* Dick Clark, Dale Morris. *Writer:* Fred Tatashore. *Director:* Gene Weed.

### 26 Alan King Specials. A

chronological listing of comedian Alan King's satirical specials. All are 60 minutes in length and present sketches that poke fun at contemporary life. Alan King was the host of each show.

**1 Comedy Is King** (NBC, 4/9/68). *Guests:* Charlie Callas, Linda Lavin, Kenneth Mars, Liza Minnelli, Connie Stevens. *Producer:* Michael Ross. *Writers:* Larry Markes, Marty Farrell, Alan King. *Director:* Walter C. Miller.

**2 The Alan King Show** (ABC, 1/16/69). *Guests:* Jack Carter, Shirley Jones, Linda Lavin, Tony Randall, Nipsey Russell, Leslie Uggams. *Music:* Norman Paris. *Producer:* Alan King. *Writers:* Marty Farrell, Tom Whedon, David Axelrod. *Director:* Walter C. Miller.

**3 Alan King and His Buddy** (ABC, 5/19/69). *Co-host:* Buddy Hackett. *Guests:* Linda Lavin, Karen Morrow. *Producer:* Alan King. *Writers:* Herb Sargent, Bob Ellison, John Boni, Alan King. *Director:* Kenneth Johnson.

**4 Alan King Looks Back in Anger — A Review of 1972** (ABC, 1/3/73). *Guests:* Rona Barrett, Jerry Brown, Nancy Dussault, Anne Meara, Larry Storch, Jack Weston. *Producer:* Alan King. *Writers:* Herb Sargent, Bob Ellison, John Boni, Norman Steinberg, Alan King. *Director:* Kenneth Johnson.

**5 Alan King in Las Vegas, Part I** (ABC, 2/5/73). *Guests:* Totie Fields, Joey Heatherton, Pamela Mason. *Producers:* Lawrence D. Savadore, Alan Landsburg. *Director:* Kenneth Johnson.

**6 Alan King in Las Vegas, Part II** (ABC, 5/7/73). *Guests:* Phil Harris, George Kirby, Cliff Perlman. Same credits as special number 5.

**7 Alan King's Energy Crisis** (ABC, 4/8/74). *Guests:* James Coco, Cass Elliot, Barbara Feldon, Morgan Freeman, Jack Klugman, Shimen Ruskin, David Steinberg, Sid Stone. *Producers:* Alan King, Rupert Hitzig. *Writers:* Norman Steinberg, Howard Albrecht, Sol Weinstein, Chevy Chase, Herb Sargent, Alan King. *Director:* Dave Wilson.

**8 Alan King's Final Warning** (ABC, 4/12/77). *Guests:* Angie Dickinson, Don Knotts, Linda Lavin, Abe Vigoda.

*Producers:* Alan King, Rupert Hitzig. *Writers:* George Bloom, Harry Crane, Bill Persky, Alan King. *Director:* Bill Persky.

**9 Alan King's Second Final Warning** (ABC, 5/13/78). *Guests:* Arlene Golonka, Darryl Hickman, Elliott Reid, Bella Bruck, Phoebe Dorin, Ed Barth. *Music:* Elliot Lawrence. *Producers:* Alan King, Rupert Hitzig. *Writers:* Jeffrey Barron, Harry Crane, Bob Comfort, Alan King. *Director:* Rocco Urbisci.

**10 Alan King's Third Annual Final Warning** (ABC, 5/24/79). *Guests:* Hal Linden, Gavin MacLeod. *Producers:* Alan King, Rupert Hitzig. *Director:* Don Mischer.

**11 Alan King's Thanksgiving Special** (ABC, 11/26/80). *Guests:* Angie Dickinson, McLean Stevenson, Dick Van Patten. *Producers:* Alan King, Rupert Hitzig. *Writers:* Jeffrey Barron, Howard Albrecht, Sol Weinstein, Richard Marcus. *Director:* Bill Davis.

**12 An Evening with Alan King at Carnegie Hall** (HBO, 6/6/87). *Producers:* Alan King, Daniel A. Bohr.

**27 Alexander.** Drama, 60 min., ABC, 4/4/73. After many years on the road, Alexander Foster, a whimsical 75-year-old gentleman and world traveler, returns to his family estate, Wildwood Manor, in New England. Shortly after, he befriends three children (Sue, Tom, and Raymond), who become fascinated by stories of his experiences (which unfold as Alexander opens his Scrapbook of Life and plays out each fanciful adventure — as a sailor, clown, concert pianist, and mountain climber). Alexander's stories leave the children with an important legacy — that they, too, can be anything they set out to become — from cowboy to president of the United States. Aired as an "ABC Afterschool Special." *Cast:* Red Buttons (Alexander Foster), Jodie Foster (Sue), Kerry MacLane (Tom), Robbie Rist (Raymond), Helen Kleeb (Emily), John Lupton (Mr. Adams), Nancy Jeris

(Mrs. Adams). *Music:* Gary William Friedman. *Producer:* Henry Jaffe. *Writers:* Larry Spiegel, Jan Hartman. *Director:* Mel Ferber.

**28 ALF Loves a Mystery.** Preview, 30 min., NBC, 9/11/87. An elaborate preview of NBC's new Saturday morning 1987 schedule where ALF and Benji Gregory (costars of "ALF") search an old mansion for hidden treasure. Clips from the new series ("ALF Tales," "Fraggle Rock" and "The New Archies") are interspersed into the story. *Cast:* Benji Gregory (Kid Cameron), Paul Fusco (Voice of ALF), Shannen Doherty (Lady in Red), Jackee Harry (Countess), Betty White (Aunt Harriet), Mary Wickes (Agatha Megpeace), Heidi Zeigler (Jo Hardy), Donny Ponce (Frank Hardy). *Music:* Misha Segal. *Producer-Writers:* Bradley Wigor, Joseph Mauer. *Director:* Tony Singletary.

**29 The Alfred G. Graebner Memorial High School Handbook of Rules and Regulations.** Comedy, 60 min., CBS, 6/12/84. A "CBS Schoolbreak Special" about the trials and tribulations of first-year high school students as they learn the importance of retaining individuality amid peer pressure of high school life that is not usually covered by a school handbook. *Cast:* Kelly Wolf (Julie Ross), Fisher Stevens (Gary Gordon), Elizabeth Halvorsen (Nat Landis), Martha Gehman (Izzy Otis), Johann Carlo (Consuela Fabian), Karl Unterholzner (Tony Lambert), Suzy Snyder (Candy Barnett), Jenn Thompson (Dawn Fumpmeister). *Producers:* Frank Doelger, Mark Silverman. *Writer:* Marjorie Rosen. *Director:* Mark Cullingham.

**30 Alice in Wonderland.** Fantasy, 90 min., NBC, 10/23/55. A television adaptation of the Lewis Carroll story about a young girl and her adventures in a fantasy world called Wonderland. Aired on the "Hallmark Hall of Fame." See also "Alice Through the Looking Glass." *Cast:* Gillian Barber (Alice), Martyn Green (White Rabbit), Noel Leslie (Caterpillar), Michael Enserro (Fish Footman), Bobby Clark (Duchess), Burr Tillstrom (Cheshire Cat), Ian Martin (Tweedledum), Don Hanmer (Tweedledee), Robert Caspar (March Hare), Mort Marshall (Mad Hatter), Alice Pearce (Doormouse), Tom Bosley (Knave of Hearts), Hiram Sherman (King of Hearts), Ronald Long (Queen of Hearts), Elsa Lanchester (Red Queen), Eva LaGallienne (White Queen), Reginald Gardiner (White King), Don Somers (Red King), Karl Swenson (Humpty Dumpty). *Producers:* Maurice Evans, Jack Royal. *Writers:* Florida Friebus, Eva LeGallienne. *Director:* George Schaefer.

## 31 Alice Through the Looking Glass.

Fantasy, 60 min., NBC, 11/6/66. A musical adaptation of the classic by Lewis Carroll in which Alice attempts to become Queen of Wonderland by making a visit to the royal castle. Her object: To avoid Jabberwock, a flame-breathing monster that rules the land. *Cast:* Judi Rolin (Alice), Roy Castle (Lester the Jester), Robert Coote (Red King), Richard Denning (Alice's father), Jimmy Durante (Humpty Dumpty), Nanette Fabray (White Queen), Ricardo Montalban (White King), Agnes Moorehead (Red Queen), Jack Palance (Jabberwock), Tom Smothers (Tweedledum), Dick Smothers (Tweedledee). *Music:* Harper McKay. *Songs:* Moose Charlap, Elsie Simmons. *Writer:* Albert Simmons.

## 32 All Commercials—A Steve Martin Special.

Comedy, 60 min., NBC, 9/30/80. A series of sketches and blackouts that spoof television commercials. *Host:* Steve Martin. *Guests:* Antonio Fargas, Julieann Griffin, Robert Klein, Julie McWhirter, The Nitty Gritty Dirt Band, Louis Nye, Anne Lockhart, Pat Proft, Paul Reubens,

Avery Schreiber. *Music:* Bob Rozario. *Producer:* Joseph Cates. *Director:* Walter C. Miller.

## 33 All Creatures Great and Small.

Drama, 90 min., NBC, 2/4/75. An adaptation of the autobiographical novel by James Herriot which tells of Herriot's early career as a veterinarian in Yorkshire, England, in 1937 when he became the assistant to Siegfried Farnon, an eccentric vet. Aired on the "Hallmark Hall of Fame." *Cast:* Simon Ward (James Herriot), Anthony Hopkins (Siegfried Farnon), Lisa Harrow (Helen), Brian Stirner (Tristan), T. P. McKenna (Soames), Jane Collins (Connie). *Producers:* David Susskind, Duane C. Bogie. *Writer:* Hugh Whitemore. *Director:* Claude Whatham.

## 34 All I Could See from Where I Stood.

Drama, 90 min., PBS, 11/10/77. The story of a young girl (Sara) as she attempts to cope with her mother's addiction to alcohol. *Cast:* Season Hubley (Sara Blakemore), Louise Latham (Mary Blakemore), Richard Gilliland (Mark Taylor), Biff McGuire (Sara's father), Phyllis Thaxter (Mark's mother), Jack Murdock (Mark's father). *Producer:* Barbara Schultz. *Writer:* Elizabeth Clark. *Director:* Burt Brinckerhoff.

## 35 All in Fun.

Variety, 30 min., CBS, 10/2/52. A simple program of music and songs featuring top performers of the era. *Host:* Tom Ewell. *Guests:* Johnny Desmond, Betty Ann Grove, The Honeydreamers, Jonathan Lucas. *Music:* Alvy West. *Producer:* Richard Lewine. *Writer:* George Axelrod. *Director:* John Peyser.

## 36 All in the Family 20th Anniversary Special.

Comedy, 90 min., CBS, 2/16/91. Memorable moments from the long-running series "All in the Family." Taped on the original Bunker household set. *Host:*

Norman Lear. *Guests:* Carroll O'Connor, Rob Reiner, Jean Stapleton, Sally Struthers. *Producers:* Norman Lear, Mark E. Pollack. *Writer-Director:* David Jackson.

## 37 All Night Strut! Variety, 90 min., PBS, 12/25/88.

A song and dance revue that recalls the American swing music of the 1930s and 1940s. *Host:* Maxene Andrews. *Guests:* Katherine Buffaloe, Janet Hubert, Lance Roberts, Jim Walton. *Producer:* John Grant. *Writer:* Harry Zimbler. *Director:* Philip Byrd.

## 38 All-Star Celebration: The '88 Vote. Comedy, 2 hrs., ABC, 10/15/88.

A collection of comedy skits, musical numbers, and filmed segments that are designed to encourage the public to vote. *Stars:* Roseanne Barr, William F. Buckley, Jr., George Carlin, Billy Crystal, Whoopi Goldberg, the Rev. Jesse Jackson, Martin Mull, Paul Rodriguez, Jerry Seinfeld, Tom Selleck, Judy Tenuta, Lily Tomlin, Robin Williams, Stevie Wonder. *Music:* Steve Thoma. *Producers:* Ted Steinberg, Rocco Urbisci, Neal Marshall. *Director:* Ellen Brown.

## 39 The All-Star Comedy Hour. Comedy, 60 min., ABC, 4/6/62.

A comical survey of the various styles of humor. *Host:* Johnny Carson. *Guests:* Mel Brooks, Dr. Joyce Brothers, Buddy Hackett, Carl Reiner, Kaye Stevens. *Music:* Les Brown. *Producer-Director:* Coby Ruskin. *Writers:* Sydney Zelenka, Will Glickman, Sidney Reznick.

## 40 All-Star Gala at Ford's Theater. Variety, 60 min., ABC, 10/24/87.

A command performance for President Ronald Reagan and his wife, Nancy. The program is a fund-raiser to help obtain money to preserve historic Ford's Theater. Taped June 21, 1987. *Host:* Bea Arthur. *Guests:* Mikhail Baryshnikov, Cab Calloway, Glen Campbell, David Copperfield, Norm Crosby, Don Johnson, Maureen McGovern, David Sanborn. *Announcer:* Dick Tufeld. *Music:* Elliot Lawrence. *Producer:* Frankie Hewitt. *Writer:* Frank Slocum. *Director:* Joseph Cates.

## 41 The All-Star Gong Show Special. Comedy, 60 min., NBC, 4/26/77.

A primetime, special one-hour version of the daily 30-minute talent show wherein unusual acts are judged by a celebrity panel. *Host:* Chuck Barris. *Panel:* Jamie Farr, Arte Johnson, Jaye P. Morgan. *Guests:* Ray Charles, Aretha Franklin, Rosey Grier, Tony Randall, Ben Vereen. *Music:* Milton Delugg. *Producer:* Chuck Barris. *Director:* John Dorsey.

## 42 The All-Star Party.

Elaborate black-tie celebrity parties that honor selected entertainers. All are 60 minutes and presented on behalf of Variety Clubs International, the "show-business charity." For each show, the honoree was the guest of honor.

**1 All-Star Party for Lucille Ball** (CBS, 1/29/84). *Guests:* Lucie Arnaz, Desi Arnaz, Jr., Joan Collins, Sammy Davis, Jr., Cary Grant, Monty Hall, Shelley Long, Dean Martin, Carl Reiner, Burt Reynolds, John Ritter, Frank Sinatra, James Stewart. *Music:* Nelson Riddle. *Producer:* Paul W. Keyes. *Director:* Dick McDonough.

**2 All-Star Party for Carol Burnett** (CBS, 12/12/82). *Guests:* Lucille Ball, Tim Conway, Bette Davis, Sammy Davis, Jr., Monty Hall, Glenda Jackson, Steve Lawrence, Jim Nabors, Jack Paar, Burt Reynolds, Tom Selleck, Beverly Sills, James Stewart. *Music:* Nelson Riddle. *Producer:* Paul W. Keyes. *Director:* Dick McDonough.

**3 All-Star Party for Joan Collins** (CBS, 12/2/87). *Host:* Monty Hall. *Guests:* James Stewart, Tony Bennett, Michele Lee, Lynn Redgrave, Michael York, Brian Keith, Art Linkletter, Clint Eastwood, Rich Little, Bea Arthur,

Robin Leach. *Music:* Nick Perito. *Producer:* Paul W. Keyes. *Director:* Dick McDonough.

**4 All-Star Party for Clint Eastwood** (CBS, 12/15/86). *Host:* Lucille Ball. *Guests:* Sammy Davis, Jr., Roberta Flack, Cary Grant, Merv Griffin, Monty Hall, Bob Hope, Marsha Mason, Don Rickles, James Stewart. *Music:* Nick Perito. *Producer:* Paul W. Keyes. *Director:* Dick McDonough.

**5 All-Star Party for "Dutch" Reagan** (CBS, 12/8/85). (President Ronald Reagan was given the nickname "Dutch" by his father at his birth in 1911.) *Host:* Frank Sinatra. *Guests:* Chuck Connors, Angie Dickinson, Gary Collins, Eydie Gorme, Peter Graves, Merv Griffin, Monty Hall, Charlton Heston, Steve Lawrence, Rich Little, Dean Martin, Mary Ann Mobley, Nancy Reagan, Burt Reynolds, Cliff Robertson, Susan Sullivan, Ben Vereen. Same credits as party number 4.

**6 All-Star Party for Burt Reynolds** (CBS, 12/10/84). *Guests:* Loni Anderson, Dom DeLuise, Jackie Gleason, Monty Hall, Madeline Kahn, Brian Keith, Jack Lemmon, Anne Murray, Pat O'Brien, Dolly Parton, Jerry Reed, Charles Nelson Reilly, Dinah Shore, James Stewart. Same credits as party number 4.

**7 All-Star Party for Frank Sinatra** (CBS, 12/11/83). *Guests:* Foster Brooks, Carol Burnett, Richard Burton, Vic Damone, Cary Grant, Monty Hall, Florence Henderson, Julio Iglesias, Howard Keel, Steve Lawrence, Michele Lee, Ricardo Montalban, Bob Newhart, Dionne Warwick. *Music:* Nelson Riddle. *Producer-Writer:* Paul W. Keyes. *Director:* Dick McDonough.

**43 All-Star Salute to Ford's Theater.** Variety, 60 min., CBS, 6/25/86. A star-studded fundraiser to help support Washington, D.C.'s historic Ford's Theater. *Host:* Jaclyn Smith. *Guests:* Louie Anderson, Paul Anka, Victor Borge, Sandy Duncan, Joel

Gray, Freddie Roman, Tommy Tune. *Special Guests:* President Ronald Reagan and his wife, Nancy. *Music:* Elliot Lawrence. *Producer:* Frankie Hewitt. *Writer:* Frank Slocum. *Director:* Joseph Cates.

**44 The All-Star Salute to Mother's Day.** Variety, 2 hrs., NBC, 5/10/81. A lavish special wherein celebrity guests perform in honor of their mothers and mothers everywhere. *Hosts:* Ed McMahon, Jayne Kennedy. *Guests:* Claude Akins, Melissa Sue Anderson, Foster Brooks, Dr. Joyce Brothers, Charlie Callas, Diana Canova, Judy Canova, David Copperfield, Jamie Lee Curtis, Bob Denver, Eva Gabor, Zsa Zsa Gabor, Bobbie Gentry, Shecky Greene, Michele Lee, Janet Leigh, Barbara Mandrell, Irlene Mandrell, Louise Mandrell, Yvette Mimieux, Jim Nabors, Donald O'Connor, Debbie Reynolds, Don Rickles, Ginger Rogers, Brooke Shields, Richard Simmons, Rip Taylor, Bobby Vinton, Anson Williams, Cindy Williams. *Announcer:* Jayne Kennedy. *Music:* George Wyle. *Producer:* Bob Stivers. *Writers:* Lyla Oliver Noah, Dorian Kane. *Director:* Bruce Gowers.

**45 All-Star Salute to Our Troops.** Variety, 2 hrs., CBS, 4/3/91. A live telecast of the homecoming celebration for troops returning home from the Persian Gulf War (to Andrews Air Force Base, Camp Springs, Maryland). *Guests:* Louie Anderson, Glenn Ford, Charlton Heston, Jennifer Holliday, Sophia Loren, Howie Mandell, Barbara Mandrell, Gary Morris, K. T. Oslin, Tony Orlando, The Radio City Music Hall Rockettes, Lynn Redgrave, George C. Scott, Ray Stevens, Richard Thomas, Randy Travis. *Producers:* Roger Ailes, Gary Smith. *Writers:* Rita Cash, Marty Farrell, Bob Arnott. *Director:* Dwight Hemion.

**46 All-Star Salute to Women's Sports.** Variety, 90 min., ABC, 3/2/78.

A celebrity salute to women in sports, coupled with an auction to augment the Women's Sports Foundation. *Host:* Billy Jean King. *Guests:* Bill Cosby, Suzy Chaffee, Phyllis Diller, Alan King, Harvey Korman, Helen Reddy, Cathy Rigby, McLean Stevenson. *Producer:* Carolyn Raskin.

### 47 All-Star Swing Festival.
Music, 60 min., NBC, 11/29/72. A Peabody Award–winning special that features performances from the top names in jazz music. Taped at New York's Lincoln Center. *Host:* Doc Severinsen. *Performers:* Count Basie, Duke Ellington, Ella Fitzgerald, Dizzy Gillespie, Benny Goodman, Bobby Hackett, Lionel Hampton, Gene Krupa, Willie Smith. *Producers:* Burt Rosen, David Winters. *Writer:* Donald Ross. *Director:* Grey Lockwood.

### 48 All-Star Tribute to Elizabeth Taylor.
Variety, 60 min., CBS, 12/1/77. A celebrity party in honor of Elizabeth Taylor on behalf of the Variety Clubs International's children's charities. *Host:* Elizabeth Taylor. *Guests:* Robert Blake, Debby Boone, Henry Fonda, Frank Gorshin, Monty Hall, Bob Hope, Rock Hudson, James Lydon, Roddy McDowall, Dick Martin, Paul Newman, Carroll O'Connor, Dan Rowan. *Music:* Nelson Riddle. *Producer:* Paul W. Keyes. *Writers:* Paul W. Keyes, Marc London, Bob Howard. *Director:* Dick McDonough.

### 49 All-Star Tribute to General Jimmy Doolittle.
Variety, 2 hrs., Syndicated, 8/86. A ninetieth birthday celebration for Jimmy Doolittle, an aviation pioneer (best remembered for the first U.S. air raid on Japan in April 1942). *Host:* Glen Campbell. *Guests:* George Burns, Johnny Carson, Andy Gibb, Charlton Heston, Bob Hope, Jack Jones, Shirley Jones, Audrey Landers, The Lennon Sisters, Kenny Loggins, Loretta Lynn,

Brooke Shields. *Special Guest:* President Ronald Reagan. *Music:* Bob Alberti. *Producer:* Bob Hope. *Writers:* Gene Perret, Fred S. Fox, Seaman Jacobs, Gig Henry, Robert L. Mills. *Director:* Bob Wynn.

### 50 All-Star Tribute to John Wayne.
Variety, 60 min., ABC, 11/26/76. A star-studded tribute to John Wayne under the auspices of Variety Clubs International. *Host:* Frank Sinatra. *Guest of Honor:* John Wayne. *Guests:* Charles Bronson, John Byner, Glen Campbell, Sammy Davis, Jr., Angie Dickinson, Monty Hall, Bob Hope, Ron Howard, Lee Marvin, Maureen O'Hara, James Stewart, Claire Trevor, Henry Winkler. *Music:* Nelson Riddle. *Producer:* Paul W. Keyes. *Writers:* Paul W. Keyes, Marc London. *Director:* Dick McDonough.

### 51 All-Star Tribute to Kareem Abdul-Jabbar.
Variety, 60 min., NBC, 5/12/89. Stars salute the NBA great on behalf of the Variety Clubs International's children's charities. *Guest of Honor:* Kareem Abdul-Jabbar. *Guests:* Billy Crystal, Angie Dickinson, Danny Glover, Whoopi Goldberg, Herbie Hancock, Jackee Harry, Gladys Knight, Martin Mull, Joan Van Ark, Bruce Willis. *Music:* Dennis McCarthy. *Producers:* Pierre Cossette, Kareem Abdul-Jabbar. *Writer:* Buz Kohan. *Director:* Walter C. Miller.

### 52 All That Glitters.
Drama, 60 min., ABC, 1/25/90. An "ABC Afterschool Special" about a group of high school students who turn a class project — making cookies — into a profitable business for charity. *Cast:* Nancy Balbirer (Veronica), Scott Allegrucci (Mike), Jason Andrews (Vag), Tovah Feldshuh (Mrs. Garr), Marc Price (Chris Derby), Nile Lanning (Lori). *Music:* Coati Mundi. *Producer:* Eve Silverman. *Writer:* D. J. MacHale. *Director:* Steven Schachter.

**53 All the Kids Do It.** Drama, 60 min., CBS, 4/24/84. A reality drama about a motivated 16-year-old (Buddy Elder), an Olympic high-diving hopeful, who learns, not a moment too soon, the painful consequences of diving while under the influence of alcohol. A "CBS Schoolbreak Special." *Cast:* Scott Baio (Buddy Elder), Leslie Hope (Linda), George Dzundza (Mr. Elder), Frances Lee McCain (Mrs. Elder), Jeremy Licht (Matt Elder), Geoffrey Blake (Lon), Danny DeVito (Used car salesman). *Music:* Randy Edelman. *Producers:* Henry Winkler, Roger Birnbaum. *Writer:* Paul W. Cooper. *Director:* Henry Winkler.

**54 All the Money in the World.** Comedy, 30 min., ABC, 3/19/83. When Quentin Stowe, a 13-year-old farm youth (in Cedarville) saves the life of a leprechaun named Flan, he is granted three wishes. The story relates the problems that arise when Quentin wishes for all the money in the world and it creates an international banking crisis. Aired as an "ABC Weekend Special." *Cast:* Nyles Harris (Quentin Stowe), Dick Beals (Flan), Kim Hamilton (Mrs. Stowe), Hal Williams (George Stowe), Laura Tubelle (Roselynn), Lee Patterson (President), Mabel King (Mrs. Trussker). *Music:* John Cacavas. *Producer:* Robert Chenault. *Writers:* Glen Olson, Rod Baker. *Director:* Marc Daniels.

**55 All the Way Home.** Drama, 90 min., NBC, 12/1/71. An adaptation of the Pulitzer Prize story about the grief shared by a family after the father is killed in an accident. Aired on the "Hallmark Hall of Fame." *Cast:* Joanne Woodward (Mary), Richard Kiley (Jay), Eileen Heckart (Aunt Hannah), Pat Hingle (Ralph), James Woods (Andrew), Betty Garde (Aunt Sadie), Barney Hughes (Joel), Shane Nickerson (Rufus). *Producer:* David Susskind. *Writer:* Ted Mosel. *Director:* Fred Coe.

**56 All Things Bright and Beautiful.** Variety, 60 min., Syndicated, 11/69. A musical celebration of Thanksgiving. *Host:* Burl Ives. *Guests:* Kellie Flanagan, Randy Sparks and the Backporch Majority. *Producer:* Ernest D. Glucksman. *Writer-Director:* Barry Shear.

**57 All-Time Greatest TV Censored Bloopers.** Comedy, 60 min., NBC, 2/1/85. A first-time airing of bloopers from television and feature films. *Host:* Dick Clark. *Guests:* Tim Conway, Deidre Hall, Bob Keeshan, Dick Martin. *Producers:* Dick Clark, Al Schwartz. *Writer:* Ken Shapiro. *Director:* Lee Miller.

**58 Allan Sherman's Funnyland.** Comedy, 60 min., NBC, 1/18/65. An hour of music and satirical comedy sketches. *Host:* Allan Sherman. *Guests:* Angie Dickinson, Jack Gilford, Lorne Greene, The Ray Charles Singers. *Producer:* Roger Gimbel. *Writers:* Allan Sherman, David Vern, Bill Idelson, Sam Bobrick, Roger Price. *Director:* Greg Garrison.

**59 The Almost Royal Family.** Comedy, 60 min., ABC, 10/24/84. An "ABC Afterschool Special" about the Hendersons, a New York City family who inherit an unclaimed island between New York State and Canada. Their efforts to give up the comforts of city life and establish a home on the primitive island are the focal point of the story. *Cast:* Garrett M. Brown (John Henderson), Mary Elaine Monte (Helen Henderson), Sarah Jessica Parker (Suzanne Henderson), Fred Koehler (Jimmy Henderson), Christine Langer (Natalie). *Music:* Bruce Coughlin. *Producer:* Jane Starte. *Writer:* Jeffrey Kindley. *Director:* Claude Kerven.

**60 Amahl and the Night Visitors.** Operetta, 60 min., NBC, 12/24/51 (1st staging), 4/13/52 (2nd staging),

12/20/53 (3rd staging), 12/19/54 (4th staging), 12/2/55 (5th staging), 12/24/58 (6th staging). A Christmas opera, composed especially for television by Gian-Carlo Menotti, about Amahl, a crippled boy who joins the three Wise Men as they journey to Bethlehem on the eve of the first Christmas. Aired as the first "Hallmark Hall of Fame" and restaged seven additional times (see the following two titles also). *Cast:* Chet Allen (Amahl, 1st staging), William McIver (Amahl, 2nd through 5th stagings), Kirk Jordan (Amahl, 6th staging), Rosemary Kuhlmann (Mother), Andrew McKinley (King Kaspar), Leon Lishner (King Melchior), David Aiken (King Balthazar). *Music:* Thomas Shippers (first five stagings), Herbert Grossman (6th staging). *Producer:* Samuel Chotzinoff. *Director:* Kirk Browning.

## 61 Amahl and the Night Visitors. Operetta, 60 min., NBC, 12/25/63. The seventh staging of the Christmas opera by Gian-Carlo Menotti. The story of a crippled boy (Amahl) who journeys with the three Wise Men to Bethlehem on the eve of the first Christmas. *Cast:* Kurt Yaghiijian (Amahl), Martha King (Mother), Richard Cross (King Melchior), Willis Patterson (King Balthazar), John McCullom (King Kaspar). *Music:* Herbert Grossman.

## 62 Amahl and the Night Visitors. Operetta, 60 min., NBC, 12/24/78. The eighth staging of the Gian-Carlo Menotti story about Amahl, a crippled boy who joins the three Wise Men on the road to Bethlehem on the eve of the first Christmas. *Cast:* Robert Sapolsky (Amahl), Teresa Stratas (Mother), Giorgio Tozzi (King Kaspar), Nico Castel (King Melchior), Willard White (King Balthazar). *Conductor of the London Philharmonic Orchestra:* Jesus Lopez-Cobos. *Production Supervisor:* Gian-Carlo Menotti.

## 63 The Amazing Bunjee Venture. Cartoon, 30 min., ABC, 3/24 and 3/31/84. While in the garage investigating their father's newest invention, a time machine, youngsters Karen and Andy Winsborrow are swept back in time to the prehistoric era. The story relates their adventures as they befriend Bunjee, an elephant-like creature, and seek to find a way back home. Aired as an "ABC Weekend Special." *Voices:* Frank Welker (Bunjee), Nancy Cartwright (Karen), Robbie Lee (Andy), Michael Rye (Mr. Winsborrow and Narrator), Linda Gary (Mrs. Winsborrow). *Producer:* Doug Patterson. *Writer:* Doug Marmorstein. *Director:* Don MacKinnon.

## 64 The Amazing Cosmic Awareness of Duffy Moon. Comedy, 60 min., ABC, 2/4/76. Duffy Moon is an undersized but multitalented sixth grader. When his schoolmates tease him about his height, he enrolls in a mailorder self-improvement course. Duffy finds inspiration from the course and with his friend, Peter Finley, establishes an odd-job company called Duffy Moon, Inc. The story follows Duffy's efforts to overcome the devious efforts of Boots McAfee, a pretty, fellow sixth grader who runs Help Is Here, as she attempts to put him out of business. An "ABC Afterschool Special." *Cast:* Ike Eisenmann (Duffy Moon), Lance Kerwin (Peter Finley), Alexa Kenin (Boots McAfee), Jim Backus (Dr. Flamel), Jerry Van Dyke (Mr. Finley), Sparky Marcus (Brian Varner), Jane Connell (Aunt Peggy). *Music:* Joe Weber. *Producer:* Daniel Wilson. *Writer:* Thomas Baum. *Director:* Larry Elikann.

## 65 America. Variety, 60 min., CBS, 9/10/70. A star-studded musical tour of the United States. *Host:* Glenn Ford. *Guests:* Mac Davis, John Hartford, Mark Lindsey, Bill Medley, Gary Puckett, Connie Stevens. *Music:* Eddie Karam. *Producer-Director:* Steve

Binder. *Writers:* Phil Hahn, Jack Hanrahan.

**66 America Censored.** Documentary, 60 min., CBS, 5/28/85. An informative and entertaining look at censorship in American television, movies, comedy, and music over the last 60 years. Much of the footage used is seen for the first time by the public, and the program itself is a visual history of how the public's standards have changed over the years and how once taboo themes are now accepted. Highlights include "the naughty bits" from the first censored film, "Fatama, the Belly Dancer"; David O. Selznick's battle with the Hays Office for two years over Clark Gable's use of the word "damn" in *Gone with the Wind*; and innocent footage of a "topless" six-year-old Shirley Temple (footage that was cut from the film *Curly Top*). Host John Denver was once personally involved in censorship when the lyrics to his song "Rocky Mountain High" were misinterpreted and the recording was banned from a number of radio stations. *Host:* John Denver. *Announcer:* Don Carney. *Music:* Don Great. *Producer:* Andrew Solt. *Writer:* Gerald Gardner. *Director:* Andrew Solt.

**67 America Comes to Graceland.** Documentary, 60 min., Syndicated, 8/15/93. A tour of Graceland, the mansion in Memphis, Tennessee, that was home to Elvis Presley. Friends and celebrities comment on the king of rock and roll music. *Hosts:* Lisa Hartman, Mac Davis. *Guests:* James Brown, Elton John, George Klein, Jerry Schilling, Naomi Stiers, J. D. Sumner, Michelle Wright, Dwight Yoakam. *Producers:* Rick Ray, Dee Ray, Stephen Pouliot. *Writer:* Robynn Lee. *Director:* J. D. Hansen.

**68 America Pauses for Springtime.** Variety, 60 min., CBS, 3/30/59. A musical salute to the spring of 1959. *Host:* Burgess Meredith. *Performers:*

Marge and Gower Champion, Genevieve, Keye Luke, Robert Merrill, Jean Ritchie, Herb Shriner, Jane Wyman. *Music:* Harry Sosnik. *Producer:* Barry Wood. *Director:* Sid Smith.

**69 America Pauses for the Merry Month of May.** Variety, 60 min., CBS, 5/18/59. A sequel to the above special in which celebrities perform songs associated with the month of May. *Host:* Burgess Meredith. *Performers:* Marian Anderson, Russell Arms, Molly Bee, Larry Blyden, Art Carney, Carol Haney, Connie Russell. *Music:* Harry Sosnik. *Producer:* Barry Wood. *Director:* Sid Smith.

**70 America Picks the #1 Songs.** Variety, 2 hrs., ABC, 5/28/86. The program, which looks at America's favorite songs over the past 30 years, is constructed to allow viewers to call in (via special 900 numbers) and vote for their favorites in three separate decades (1955–65, 1965–75, 1975–85). The nominated songs (seen on film or tape), 1955–65: "Rock Around the Clock" (Bill Haley and the Comets), "My Prayer" (The Platters), "Hound Dog" (Elvis Presley), "Mack the Knife" (Bobby Darin), "You've Lost That Lovin' Feelin'" (The Righteous Brothers); 1965–75: "Satisfaction" (The Rolling Stones), "Yesterday" (The Beatles), "Respect" (Aretha Franklin), "I Heard It Through the Grapevine" (Marvin Gaye), "Bridge Over Troubled Water" (Simon and Garfunkel); 1975–85: "Billie Jean" (Michael Jackson), "Every Breath You Take" (The Police), "All Night Long" (Lionel Richie), "Time After Time" (Cyndi Lauper), "What's Love Got to Do with It" (Tina Turner). The winners: 1955–65 ("Hound Dog"), 1965–75 ("Bridge Over Troubled Water"), 1975–85 ("What's Love Got to Do with It"). *Hosts:* Barbara Mandrell, Frankie Avalon, Dick Clark, Tony Orlando. *Performers:* Air Supply, Roberta Flack, The Four Tops, The Kingston Trio, Mr. Mister, Tony Orlando and

Dawn (reunited for this event), The Kenny Ortega Dancers, Frankie Valli. *Announcer:* Charlie O'Donnell. *Music:* Peter Matz. *Producer:* Dick Clark. *Director:* Jeff Margolis.

## 71 America Salutes Richard Rodgers: The Sound of His Music. Variety, 2 hrs., CBS, 12/9/76.

A retrospective that traces the musical career of composer Richard Rodgers. *Cast:* Gene Kelly (Oscar Hammerstein II), Henry Winkler (Lorenz Hart). *Performers:* Diahann Carroll, Vic Damone, Sammy Davis, Jr., Sandy Duncan, Lena Horne, Cloris Leachman, Peggy Lee, John Wayne. *Music:* Ian Fraser. *Producers:* Gary Smith, Dwight Hemion. *Writers:* Buz Kohan, Ted Strauss. *Director:* Dwight Hemion.

## 72 America Salutes the Queen. Variety, 3 hrs., NBC, 11/29/77.

A music and comedy salute to Queen Elizabeth on the occasion of her silver jubilee. Taped at the London Palladium. *Host:* Bob Hope. *Performers:* Julie Andrews, Paul Anka, Harry Belafonte, The Brotherhood of Man, Tommy Cooper, Alan King, Cleo Laine and the Johnny Dankworth Orchestra, Rich Little, Shirley MacLaine, Yoko Morishita, Rudolph Nureyev. *Music:* Jack Parnell. *Producers:* Gary Smith, Dwight Hemion. *Director:* Dwight Hemion.

## 73 America — The Great Mississippi. Variety, 60 min., Syndicated, 7/87.

A program of music and songs that celebrate the Mississippi River. *Hosts:* The Serendipity Singers (John Ross, Laura McKenzie, Jodie Scott, Andy Hooper, Holly Setlock). *Guests:* Charley Pride, B. J. Thomas, Charlene Tilton, Dottie West. *Music:* John Ross. *Producer:* Paul Sharratt. *Writer:* Laura McKenzie. *Director:* David Stanton.

## 74 America, You're On. Com-

edy, 60 min., ABC, 11/24/75. A topical comedy-variety special in which twelve performers, portraying a cross section of Americans, air their views on current events. *Cast:* Susan Bay (Judy Daniels), Michael Bell (Bill Kenyon), Vivian Bonnell (Viola May Johnson), Randall Carver (Stanley Jenks), Barbara Cason (Mildred Moffett), Jay Gerber (Fred Dobbs), Bruce Kirby (Charles Ralston), Susan Lawrence (Sandi Kelly), Pamela Myers (Margaret Campbell), Guy Raymond (Wallace Kirkeby), Ray Vitte (Carlyle Green II), Yvonne Wilder (Lola Redondo), Ian Wolfe (Harley Dibble). *Music:* Elaine Laron. *Producers:* Bernard Rothman, Jack Wohl. *Writers:* Bob Arnott, Jeffrey Barron, Coslough Johnson, Jonathan King. *Director:* Bill Hobin.

## 75 American Bandstand's 25th Anniversary Special. Music,

2 hrs., ABC, 2/4/77. A retrospective recalling 25 years of the Saturday afternoon series "American Bandstand." *Host:* Dick Clark. *Guests:* Chuck Berry, David Brenner, The Captain and Tennille, Chubby Checker, Barry Manilow, Tony Orlando, Johnnie Ray, Jim Stafford, Frankie Valli and the Four Seasons, Stevie Wonder. *Music:* H. B. Barnum. *Producers:* Dick Clark, Bill Lee. *Writers:* Robert Arthur, Bill Lee. *Director:* Barry Glazer.

## 76 American Bandstand's 33⅓ Celebration. Music, 3 hrs.,

ABC, 12/1/85. The program recalls the music and performers who have appeared on "American Bandstand" over the past 33⅓ years. *Host:* Dick Clark. *Guests:* Frankie Avalon, Burt Bacharach, Laura Branigan, Chubby Checker, Dion, Fabian, Crystal Gayle, Kenny Loggins, Madonna, Johnny Mathis, Marie Osmond, Bobby Rydell, Rick Springfield, Donna Summer, Dionne Warwick. *Music:* Lenny Stack. *Producer:* Dick Clark. *Writer:* Robert Arthur. *Director:* Barry Glazer.

**77 American Bandstand's 40th Anniversary Special.** Music, 2 hrs., ABC, 5/13/92. A tribute to "American Bandstand," America's longest-running variety program (1952–89) with live performances and clips from past shows. *Host:* Dick Clark. *Guests:* Paula Abdul, Alabama, Roseanne and Tom Arnold, Pat Boone, Boyz II Men, Garth Brooks, Neil Diamond, Gloria Estefan, George Foreman, Evander Holyfield, Richard Lewis, Little Anthony and the Imperials, Reba McEntire, Don McLean, Barry Manilow, Johnny Mathis, John Mellencamp, Miami Sound Machine, Pat Sajak, Pauly Shore, Spinal Tap, Luther Vandross, Vanna White. *Producers:* Dick Clark, Larry Klein. *Writers:* Barry Adelman, Robert Arthur. *Director:* Barry Glazer.

**78 American Cowboy.** Variety, 60 min., CBS, 2/10/60. A music and comedy salute to the American cowboy. *Host:* Fred MacMurray. *Guests:* Edie Adams, Carol Burnett, Hans Conried, Wally Cox. *Music:* Charles Sanford. *Producer:* Max Liebman. *Writers:* Joe Stein, Lucille Fallen, Norman Barasch, Carroll Moore. *Director:* Bill Hobin.

**79 The American Dance Machine Presents a Celebration of Broadway Dance.** Variety, 60 min., Showtime, 6/81. A re-creation of some of Broadway's greatest dance numbers (for example, from *Finian's Rainbow, George M, Carousel, Shenandoah,* and *The Boyfriend*). *Host:* Gwen Verdon. *Guests:* The American Dance Machine, Wayne Cilento, Janet Eilber, John Jones, Lee Roy Reams. *Producers:* James Lipton, Mike Gargiulo. *Director:* Philip Gay.

**80 American Eyes.** Drama, 60 min., CBS, 3/27/90. A "CBS Schoolbreak Special" about a Korean teenager (John Henderson), who was adopted

as an infant by an American family (the Hendersons), as he struggles with his cultural identity. *Cast:* Jason Scott Lee (John Henderson), David Ogden Stiers (Jack Henderson), Concetta Tomei (Elizabeth Henderson), Kelly Hu (Emily Owens), Deborah Tucker (Missy), Una Kim (Kim), Christa Denton (Rachel). *Music:* Dan Kwamoto. *Producer:* Cynthia Cherbak. *Writers:* Cynthia Cherbak, Elizabeth Hansen, Herb Stein. *Director:* Herb Stein.

**81 American Film Institute Comedy Special.** Comedy, 60 min., NBC, 7/15/87. Four short stories, scripted by new writers, are presented as part of the AFI's sponsorship of a comedy workshop to discover tomorrow's comedy writers. **The Stories:** "Blue Suits." The adventures of a starving artist turned hotshot businessman. *Cast:* Jason Bateman (Paul Henderson), Geoffrey Lewis (Bill Henderson), Beverly Archer (Mom Henderson), Edward Winter (Mr. Sterling). "Gwendolyn." The romantic misadventures of Gwendolyn Jones, a child psychologist. *Cast:* Telma Hopkins (Gwendolyn Jones), Glynn Turman (Eric), Clint Holmes (Pete), Susan Ruttan (Marian), Joel Brooks (Franklin). "The Rec Room." A spoof of "This Is Your Life," wherein unsuspecting people are surprised on a television show called "The Rec Room." *Cast:* John Larroquette (Skip Distance), Annie Golden (Mary), Jean Kasem (April), Orson Bean (Father Sean), Meshach Taylor (Virgil), Mabel King (Grandmother). "Five Corners." Incidents in the lives of a family who run a luncheonette in the Bronx. *Cast:* Timothy Williams (Vincent), Kaye Ballard (Mrs. Pagano), Robert Costanzo (Big Vin). *Host:* Dick Van Dyke. *Comedy Setups:* David Leisure. *Music:* Terry Kirkman. *Producers:* Sam Denoff, Aaron Ruben. *Director:* Peter Baldwin. *Writers:* Richard Day ("Blue Suits"), Delle Chatman ("Gwendolyn"), Leslie Fuller ("The Rec Room"), Michael Sardo ("Five Corners").

## 82 The American Film Institute Salutes.

A chronological listing of 21 testimonial dinners honoring selected entertainment figures with an AFI (American Film Institute) Life Achievement Award. Nelson Riddle composed the theme; George Stevens, Jr., is the producer. On each show, the honoree appeared as the guest of honor.

**1 AFI Salute to John Ford** (CBS, 4/2/73). *Host:* Danny Kaye. *Guests:* Charlton Heston, Jack Lemmon, Maureen O'Hara, Gregory Peck, Frank Sinatra, James Stewart, John Wayne.

**2 AFI Salute to James Cagney** (CBS, 3/20/74). *Host:* Frank Sinatra. *Guests:* Mae Clark, Doris Day, Kirk Douglas, Frank Gorshin, Charlton Heston, Jack Lemmon, Shirley MacLaine, Ronald Reagan, George C. Scott, George Segal, Cicely Tyson, John Wayne.

**3 AFI Salute to Orson Welles** (CBS, 2/19/75). *Host:* Frank Sinatra. *Guests:* Edgar Bergen, Ingrid Bergman, Peter Bogdanovich, Johnny Carson, Joseph Cotten, Charlton Heston, Janet Leigh, Dennis Weaver, Natalie Wood.

**4 AFI Salute to William Wyler** (CBS, 3/14/76). *Guests:* Eddie Albert, Henry Fonda, Greer Garson, Audrey Hepburn, Charlton Heston, Myrna Loy, Merle Oberon, Gregory Peck, Walter Pidgeon, Jimmy Stewart, Barbra Streisand.

**5 AFI Salute to Bette Davis** (CBS, 3/21/77). *Host:* Jane Fonda. *Guests:* Olivia de Havilland, Peter Falk, Geraldine Fitzgerald, Henry Fonda, Paul Henreid, Celeste Holm, Joseph L. Mankiewicz, Martin Manulis, Liza Minnelli, George Stevens, Jr., Robert Wagner, Natalie Wood, William Wyler.

**6 AFI Salute to Henry Fonda** (CBS, 3/15/78). *Guests:* Jane Alexander, Lucille Ball, Richard Burton, Bette Davis, Kirk Douglas, Jane Fonda, Peter Fonda, James Garner, Lillian Gish, Charlton Heston, Ron Howard, Jack Lemmon, Dorothy McGuire, Fred MacMurray, Marsha Mason, Lloyd Nolan, Gregory Peck, Barbara Stanwyck, James Stewart, Richard Widmark, Billy Dee Williams.

**7 AFI Salute to Alfred Hitchcock** (CBS, 3/12/79). *Guests:* Ingrid Bergman, Sean Connery, Henry Fonda, Charlton Heston, John Houseman, Janet Leigh, Anthony Perkins, Jimmy Stewart.

**8 AFI Salute to Jimmy Stewart** (CBS, 3/16/80). *Host:* Henry Fonda. *Guests:* Frank Capra, Charlton Heston, Gene Kelly, Jack Lemmon, Walter Matthau, Princess Grace of Monaco.

**9 AFI Salute to Fred Astaire** (CBS, 4/18/81). *Host:* David Niven. *Guests:* Cyd Charisse, Barrie Chase, Bob Fosse, Audrey Hepburn, Gene Kelly, Charlton Heston, Eleanor Powell, James Stewart.

**10 AFI Salute to Frank Capra** (CBS, 4/4/82). *Host:* James Stewart. *Guests:* Richard Benjamin, Art Buchwald, Claudette Colbert, Bette Davis, Peter Falk, Charlton Heston, Bob Hope, Jack Lemmon, Hal Linden, Fred MacMurray, Steve Martin, Burgess Meredith, Bette Midler, Donna Reed, Telly Savalas, Lionel Stander, Donald Sutherland.

**11 AFI Salute to John Huston** (CBS, 3/9/83). *Host:* Lauren Bacall. *Guests:* Robert Blake, Jeff Bridges, Zsa Zsa Gabor, Charlton Heston, Sam Jaffe, Stacy Keach, James Mason, Jack Nicholson, Ray Stark, Max Von Sydow.

**12 AFI Salute to Lillian Gish** (CBS, 4/17/84). *Host:* Douglas Fairbanks, Jr. *Guests:* Sally Field, John Houseman, John Huston, Jennifer Jones, Mary Martin, Robert Mitchum, Colleen Moore, Jeanne Moreau, Eva Marie Saint, Mary Steenburgen, Richard Thomas, Lily Tomlin, Richard Widmark.

**13 AFI Salute to Gene Kelly** (CBS, 5/7/85). *Host:* Shirley MacLaine. *Guests:* Mikhail Baryshnikov, Leslie Caron, Cyd Charisse, Betty Comden, Adolph Green, Gregory Hines, Donald O'Connor, Debbie Reynolds, Fred

Astaire, Betty Garrett, Kathryn Grayson. **14 AFI Salute to Billy Wilder** (NBC, 4/26/86). *Host:* Jack Lemmon. *Guests:* Don Ameche, Lucille Ball, Carol Burnett, Johnny Carson, Richard Chamberlain, Tony Curtis, Ted Danson, Angie Dickinson, Charles Durning, Linda Evans, Sally Field, John Forsythe, Whoopi Goldberg, Audrey Hepburn, Jessica Lange, Shelley Long, Walter Matthau, Fred MacMurray, Gregory Peck, Ginger Rogers, Sylvester Stallone, James Stewart.

After 41 years and 54 films, the AFI honors one of the most distinguished careers in Hollywood history with clips from her greatest films

**Ad for "The AFI Salute to Elizabeth Taylor."**

**15 AFI Salute to Barbara Stanwyck** (ABC, 5/29/87). *Host:* Jane Fonda. *Guests:* Ann-Margret, Eve Arden, Linda Evans, John Forsythe, Bonita Granville Wrather, John Huston, Shirley MacLaine, Fred MacMurray, Walter Matthau, Robert Wagner.

**16 AFI Salute to Jack Lemmon** (CBS, 5/30/88). *Host:* Julie Andrews. *Guests:* Melvyn Douglas, Shirley MacLaine, Steve Martin, Walter Matthau.

**17 AFI Salute to Gregory Peck** (NBC, 3/21/89). *Host:* Audrey Hepburn. *Guests:* Lauren Bacall, Angie Dickinson, Jane Fonda, Jennifer Jones, Anthony Quinn, Jimmy Smits, Dean Stockwell, Richard Widmark, Henry Winkler.

**18 AFI Salute to David Lean** (ABC, 4/21/90). *Guests:* Chevy Chase, Goldie Hawn, Angelica Huston, Peter O'Toole, Gregory Peck, Omar Shariff, Steven Spielberg.

**19 AFI Salute to Kirk Douglas** (CBS, 5/23/91). *Host:* Michael Douglas. *Guests:* Lauren Bacall, Dana Carvey, Tom Cruise, Danny DeVito, Angie Dickinson, Richard Harris, Karl Malden, Patricia Neal, Jean Simmons, Sylvester Stallone.

**20 AFI Salute to Sidney Poitier** (NBC, 4/4/92). *Host:* Harry Belafonte. *Guests:* Dan Aykroyd, Kirstie Alley, Bill Cosby, Tony Curtis, Morgan Freeman, Danny Glover, Louis Gossett, Jr., Lee Grant, James Earl Jones, Quincy Jones, Stanley Kramer, Gregory Peck, Rod Steiger, Denzel Washington, Richard Widmark, Shelley Winters.

**21 AFI Salute to Elizabeth Taylor** (ABC, 5/5/93). *Host:* Carol Burnett. *Guests:* Michael Caine, Dennis Hopper, Angela Lansbury, Roddy McDowall, Michael York.

# 83 The American Film Institute's 10th Anniversary Special.

Tribute, 90 min., CBS, 11/21/77. The AFI salutes its tenth anniversary by showcasing scenes, selected by its 35,000 members, from American motion pictures. Taped at the John F. Kennedy Center for the Performing Arts in Washington, D.C. *Host:* Charlton Heston. *Guests:* Lauren Bacall, Henry Fonda, Henry Mancini, Sidney Poitier, Lily Tomlin. *Music:* Henry Mancini. *Producer:* George Stevens, Jr. *Writers:* Rod Warren, Larry McMurty. *Director:* Marty Pasetta.

**84 An American Saturday Night.** Variety, 60 min., ABC, 5/4/91. Live and taped segments are combined to showcase the performances of guest celebrities. *Host:* Richard Lewis. *Guests:* Christie Brinkley, Julie Brown, David Cassidy, Phil Collins, Dana Delany, Shelley Duvall, Teri Garr, Billy Joel, Kurt Russell, Katey Sagal. *Producers:* Ken Ehrlich, Michael Hirsh, Jeff Androsky. *Director:* Lou Horvitz.

**85 The American West of John Ford.** Tribute, 60 min., CBS, 12/5/71. The program salutes film director John Ford through interviews and clips from his western motion pictures. *Hosts:* Henry Fonda, Jimmy Stewart, John Wayne. *Guest of Honor:* John Ford. *Producer:* Don Ford. *Director:* Dennis Sanders.

**86 America's All-Star Tribute to Elizabeth Taylor.** Tribute, 60 min., ABC, 3/9/89. A lavish celebration for actress Elizabeth Taylor as she is honored for her showbusiness career. *Host:* Charles Bronson. *Guest of Honor:* Elizabeth Taylor. *Guests:* June Allyson, Beau Bridges, Carol Burnett, Bob Hope, Roddy McDowall, Vera Miles, Margaret O'Brien, Mickey Rooney, Robert Stack, Stevie Wonder. *Music:* Lenny Stack. *Producer-Director:* Marty Pasetta. *Writers:* Stephen Pouliot, Ken Welch, Mitzie Welch.

**87 America's All-Time Favorite Movies.** Audience Participation, 60 min., ABC, 10/16/88. A call-in program (via a 900 number) wherein viewers choose their favorite comedies, dramas, adventure, and horror films. *Host:* Jerry Lewis. *Guests:* Linda Blair, Olympia Dukakis, James Earl Jones. *Music:* Lenny Stack. *Producer:* Dick Clark. *Writers:* Barry Adelman, David Forman. *Director:* Bill Davis.

**88 America's Sweetheart: The Mary Pickford Story.** Documentary, 75 min., Syndicated, 1977. A profile of silent screen actress Mary Pickford. *Narrator:* Henry Fonda. *Special Commentary:* Gene Kelly. *Music:* David Fanshawe. *Producers:* Matty Kemp, Michael Small. *Writer-Director:* John Edwards.

**89 America's Tribute to Bob Hope.** Variety, 60 min., NBC, 3/5/88. A music and comedy celebration of the opening of the Bob Hope Cultural Center in Palm Springs. *Hosts:* Lucille Ball, Diahann Carroll, Vic Damone, John Forsythe. *Guest of Honor:* Bob Hope. *Guests:* Ann-Margret, George Burns, Phyllis Diller, Dolores Hope, Alan King, Barbara Mandrell, Donald O'Connor, Nancy Reagan, President Ronald Reagan, Dinah Shore, O. J. Simpson, Danny Thomas. *Music:* Ian Fraser. *Producers:* Gary Smith, Dwight Hemion. *Writer:* Buz Kohan. *Director:* Dwight Hemion.

**90 Amy and the Angel.** Drama, 60 min., ABC, 9/22/82. Amy Watson is a teenage girl who is suffering from low self-esteem caused by taunts from a group of snobbish classmates. When Amy thinks a handsome new boy at school has lost interest in her because of an incident caused by the snobs, her condition worsens. Amy is about to take poison when Oliver, an angel, appears and courts her in an effort to help her. However, it is not until Amy wishes that she was never born that Oliver hits upon the idea to grant her wish—to show her how much she contributes to the lives of her friends and family. Aired as an "ABC Afterschool Special." *Cast:* Helen Slater (Amy Watson), Albert Macklin (Oliver), David Huddleston (Edgar Watson), Gail Strickland (Mrs. Watson), Concetta Tomei (Mrs. Mixner), Hansford Rowe (St. Peter), James Earl Jones (Gabriel), Hermione Gingold (Pincus). *Producer:* Frank Doelger. *Writer:* Bruce Harmon. *Director:* Ralph Rosenblum.

## 91 Amy Grant: Headin' Home for the Holidays.

Variety, 60 min., NBC, 12/21/86. A Christmas special in which singer Amy Grant heads home for Montana to spend the holidays with her husband, Gary Chapman, and several celebrity guests. *Host:* Amy Grant. *Guests:* Ed Begley, Jr., Art Garfunkel, Dennis Weaver. *Music:* Brown Bannister. *Producers:* Gary Smith, Dwight Hemion. *Writer:* Carleton Cuse. *Director:* Dwight Hemion.

## 92 Anastasia.

Drama, 90 min., NBC, 3/17/67. When it is learned that the children of Czar Nicholas II of Russia are reported to have been killed (1926), a group of conspirators persuade an amnesiac girl to pose as Anastasia, the czar's daughter who survived. Their plan: to prove she is really Nicholas's child and collect the money she will inherit. Based on the 1954 Broadway play by Marcelle Maureth. Aired on the "Hallmark Hall of Fame." *Cast:* Julie Harris (Anastasia), Lynn Fontanne (Dowager Empress), Charles Gray (Bounine), Robert Burl (Dr. Senensky), George Irving (Chernov), David Hurst (Petrovini), Paul Roebling (Prince Paul). *Producer-Director:* George Schaefer. *Writer:* John Edward Friend.

## 93 ...And Beautiful.

Variety, 60 min., Syndicated, 9/69. The first of two programs (see next title) that spotlight the performances of black entertainers. *Host:* Della Reese. *Guests:* The Blossoms, Jerry Butler, The Donald McKayle Dancers, Redd Foxx, Little Dion, Wilson Pickett. *Music:* H. B. Barnum. *Producer:* William H. Barnett. *Writers:* William H. Barnett, Hugh Robertson. *Director:* Hugh Robertson.

## 94 ...And Beautiful, II.

Variety, 60 min., Syndicated, 9/70. A sequel to the prior title that spotlights black singers and musicians. *Guests:* Louis Armstrong, B. B. King, Cannonball Adderley Quintet, Count Basie, Duke Ellington, Billie Holliday, Mahalia Jackson, Nina Simone, Sly and the Family Stone, Bessie Smith. *Producer:* William H. Barnett. *Writers:* William H. Barnett, Hugh Robertson. *Director:* Hugh Robertson.

## 95 ...And Debbie Makes Six.

Variety, 60 min., ABC, 1/19/67. Actress Debbie Reynolds and her five male guests in a series of music, songs, and comedy sketches. *Host:* Debbie Reynolds. *Guests:* Bobby Darin, Frank Gorshin, Bob Hope, Jim Nabors, Donald O'Connor. *Music:* Nelson Riddle. *Producer:* Joe Layton. *Writers:* Milt Rosen, Gerald Gardner, Dee Caruso, Billy Barnes, Bob Rodgers. *Director:* Walter C. Miller.

## 96 Andrea's Story: A Hitchhiking Tragedy.

Drama, 60 min., ABC, 12/7/83. An "ABC Afterschool Special" that explores the dangers of hitchhiking as seen through the experiences of Andrea Cranston, a teenage girl who accepts a ride from a stranger and is raped. *Cast:* Michele Greene (Andrea Cranston), Carrie Snodgress (Mrs. Cranston), Matt Clark (Phil Cranston), Moosie Drier (David), Robert DoQui (Sgt. Corbett). *Music:* Misha Segal. *Producer:* Martin Tahse. *Writer:* Paul W. Cooper. *Director:* Robert Mandel.

## 97 Androcles and the Lion.

Musical, 90 min., NBC, 11/15/67. A musical based on the fable about Androcles, a meek Christian tailor who crosses the path of an injured lion and removes a painful thorn from its paw. Later, when Androcles and a group of Christians are captured by the Romans and destined to be eaten by lions in the Coliseum, his life is spared by the lion who recognizes him as the friend who helped him in a time of need. *Cast:* Norman Wisdom (Androcles), Inga Swenson (Lavinia), Noel Coward (Cae-

**Debbie Reynolds**

sar), Ed Ames (Ferrovius), Geoffrey Holde (Lion), John Cullum (Captain), Patricia Rutledge (Magaera). *Music Directors:* Jay Blackton, Robert Russell Bennett. *Music and Lyrics:* Richard Rodgers. *Producer:* Marc Merson. *Writer:* Peter Stone (adapted from the George Bernard Shaw play). *Director:* Joe Layton.

**98 The Andy Griffith — Don Knotts — Jim Nabors Show.** Variety, 60 min., CBS, 10/7/65. An hour of music and comedy that showcases the talents of three of CBS's biggest stars: Andy Griffith and Don Knotts (of "The Andy Griffith Show"), and Jim Nabors (of "Gomer Pyle, USMC"). *Music:* Alan Copeland. *Pro-

*ducers:* Richard O Linke, Alan Handley, Bob Wynn. *Writer:* Aaron Ruben. *Director:* Alan Handley.

## 99 The Andy Griffith Show Reunion. Retrospective, 60 min., CBS, 2/10/93.

Andy Griffith, Don Knotts, Ron Howard, Jim Nabors, George Lindsey, and Jack Dodson, the original cast members of "The Andy Griffith Show" (CBS, 1960–68) gather to pay tribute to the series via clips. *Producers:* Andy Griffith, Andrew Solt. *Writer-Director:* Andrew Solt.

## 100 Andy Williams Specials.

A chronological listing of singer Andy Williams' television specials. All are 60 minutes and feature music, songs, and light humor. Andy Williams hosted each show.

**1 The Andy Williams Special** (NBC, 5/4/62). *Guests:* Ann-Margret, Andy Griffith, Dick Van Dyke. *Music:* Henry Mancini. *Producer-Writers:* Bud Yorkin, Norman Lear. *Director:* Bud Yorkin.

**2 The Andy Williams Special** (NBC, 10/15/63). *Guests:* Joey Bishop, The Osmond Brothers, Lee Remick. *Music:* Dave Grusin. *Producer-Director:* Bud Yorkin.

**3 The Andy Williams Special** (NBC, 10/29/63). *Guests:* Carl Ballantine, Ernest Borgnine, Jane Wyman. Same credits as special number 2.

**4 The Andy Williams Special** (NBC, 11/12/63). *Guests:* Buddy Ebsen, Peggy Lee. Same credits as special number 2.

**5 The Andy Williams Special** (NBC, 11/26/63). *Guests:* Phil Harris, The Osmond Brothers, Lawrence Welk. Same credits as special number 2.

**6 The Andy Williams New Year's Eve Special** (NBC, 12/31/63). *Guests:* The Good Time Singers, Fred MacMurray, The Nick Castle Dancers. Same credits as special number 2.

**7 The Andy Williams St. Patrick's Day Special** (NBC, 3/17/64). *Guests:* The Good Time Singers, Andy Griffith, The Nick Castle Dancers, Maureen O'Hara. Same credits as special number 2.

**8 Love, Andy** (NBC, 11/6/67). *Guests:* Erroll Garner, Claudine Longet, Henry Mancini. *Music:* Henry Mancini. *Producer:* Jack Good. *Director:* Rita Gillespie.

**9 The Andy Williams Christmas Show** (NBC, 12/13/67). *Guests:* Claudine Longet, The Osmond Brothers. *Music:* Dave Grusin. *Producer-Director:* Bud Yorkin.

**10 Andy Williams Kaleidoscope Company** (NBC, 4/28/68). *Guests:* Burt Bacharach, Ray Charles, Cass Elliot, Art Garfunkel, Paul Simon. *Music:* Jimmie Haskell. *Producers:* Andy Williams, Bob Henry. *Writers:* Mason Williams, Allan Blye. *Director:* Bob Henry.

**11 The Andy Williams Christmas Special** (NBC, 12/19/68). *Guests:* Claudine Longet, The Osmond Brothers. Same credits as special number 10.

**12 The Andy Williams Magic Lantern Show Company** (NBC, 5/4/69). *Guests:* Aretha Franklin, Claudine Longet, Roger Miller. *Music:* Jimmie Haskell. *Producers:* Andy Williams, Jack Good. *Writers:* Chris Bearde, Bob Einstein, Larry Murray. *Director:* Art Fisher.

**13 The Andy Williams Special** (NBC, 1/2/71). *Guests:* Petula Clark, Bill Hayes, Flip Wilson. *Music:* Nick Perito. *Producers:* Andy Williams, Alan Handley. *Writers:* Marty Farrell, Milt Rosen. *Director:* Alan Handley.

**14 The Andy Williams Christmas Special** (NBC, 12/14/71). *Guests:* The Lennon Sisters, Claudine Longet, The Williams Family (Andy, his wife, Claudine, and their children Noelle, Christian, and Bobby; Andy's sister, Janie; Andy's brothers, Don, Dick, and Bob; and Andy's parents). Same credits as special number 13.

**15 The Andy Williams Christmas Special** (NBC, 12/13/73). *Guests:* The Williams Family (see special number 14). *Music:* Mike Post. *Producer:* Andy Williams. *Writers:* John McGreevey,

Claudine Longet. *Director:* Norman Campbell.

**16 The Andy Williams Christmas Show** (NBC, 12/11/74). *Guests:* Claudine Longet, Danielle Longet, The Williams Family. Credits same as special number 15.

**17 Andy Williams' Early New England Christmas** (CBS, 12/7/82). *Guests:* James Galway, Dorothy Hamill, Aileen Quinn, Dick Van Patten. *Music:* Ray Charles. *Producers:* Bob Banner, Andy Williams. *Writer:* Phil Kellard. *Director:* Sterling Johnson.

**18 Andy Williams and the NBC Kids Search for Santa** (NBC, 12/20/85). *Guests* (child stars from NBC shows): Tempestt Bledsoe, Lisa Bonet, Mindy Cohn, Casey Ellison, Ami Foster, Cherie Johnson, Keshia Knight Pulliam, Joey Lawrence, Matthew Lawrence, Soleil Moon Frye, Alfonso Riberio, Malcolm-Jamal Warner. *Music:* Ian Fraser. *Producer:* Pierre Cossette. *Writer:* Buz Kohan. *Director:* Dwight Hemion.

**19 Andy Williams and the NBC Kids: Easter in Rome** (NBC, 4/17/87). *Guests:* Topo Gigio, Pope John Paul II. *Kids:* Kim Fields, Joey and Matthew Lawrence, Danny Ponce, Tina Yothers. *Music:* Ian Fraser. *Producer:* Pierre Cossette. *Writer:* Buz Kohan. *Director:* Walter C. Miller.

## 101 Animals Are the Funniest People. Comedy, 60 min., NBC, 11/24/83. A lighthearted look at animals and the unusual and sometimes crazy things they do. *Hosts:* Bill Burrud, Loretta Swit. *Guests:* Dick Clark, Brooke Shields. *Producers:* Dick Clark, Bill Burrud. *Writer:* Barry Miller. *Director:* Lee Miller.

## 102 The Animalympics. Cartoon, 30 min., NBC, 2/1/80. A spoof of the 1980 Winter Olympics and television coverage of such events as seen through the antics of the reporters and participants who are portrayed as animals. *Voice Cast:* Gilda Radner

(Barbara Warblers and Brenda Springer), Billy Crystal (Rugs Turkell), Harry Shearer (Keen Hacksaw). *Music:* Jimmie Haskell. *Producer-Director:* Steve Lisberger.

## 103 The Anita Bryant Spectacular. Variety, 2 hrs., Syndicated, 3/80. A lavish, star-studded tribute to the United States via music and songs. *Host:* Anita Bryant. *Guests:* Tex Beneke, Pat Boone, Chapter 5, Bob Hope, The Imperials, Lulu Roman, The West Point Glee Club, Efrem Zimbalist, Jr. *Announcer:* Eddie King. *Music:* Ralph Carmichael. *Producers:* Bob Cawley, Rena Winters.

## 104 Ann-Margret Specials. A chronological listing of actress Ann-Margret's music and comedy specials. All are 60 minutes in length. Ann-Margret hosted each show.

**1 The Ann-Margret Show** (CBS, 12/11/68). *Guests:* Jack Benny, Bob Hope, Danny Thomas. *Music:* Billy Goldenberg. *Producer:* Burt Rosen. *Writers:* Robert Wells, Larry Alexander, Marc Ray. *Director:* David Winters.

**2 Ann-Margret: From Hollywood with Love** (CBS, 12/6/69). *Guests:* Lucille Ball, Dean Martin, Larry Storch. *Music:* Lenny Stack. *Producers:* Roger Smith, Allan Carr, Burt Rosen. *Writers:* Bill Angelos, Buz Kohan, Gail Parent, Kenny Solms. *Director:* David Winters.

**3 Ann-Margret—When You're Smiling** (NBC, 4/4/73). *Guests:* George Burns, The Firm of Hodges, James, and Smith; Bob Hope, The Walter Painter Dancers. *Music:* Henry Mancini. *Producers:* Roger Smith, Joseph Cates, Allan Carr. *Director:* Art Fisher.

**4 Ann-Margret Olsson** (NBC, 1/23/75). *Guests:* The Osmonds, The Rob Iscove Dancers, Tina Turner. *Producers:* Roger Smith, Allan Carr. *Writer:* Marty Farrell. *Director:* Dwight Hemion.

**105 Anne Murray: The Sounds of London.** Variety, 60 min., CBS, 2/15/85. A musical tour of London with singer Anne Murray. *Host:* Anne Murray. *Guests:* Bananarama, Bruce Murray, Miss Piggy, Dusty Springfield. *Music:* Pat Riccio, Jr. *Producer:* Leonard T. Rambeau. *Writer:* Alan Thicke. *Director:* Dwight Hemion.

**106 Anne Murray's Caribbean Cruise.** Variety, 60 min., CBS, 1/19/83. A musical hour set on the world's largest cruise ship, the SS *Norway*, as it tours the Caribbean. *Host:* Anne Murray. *Guests:* Eddie Rabbitt, Jose Luis Rodriguez, Richard Simmons. *Music:* Rick Wilkins. *Producers:* Gary Smith, Dwight Hemion. *Writer:* Alan Thicke. *Director:* Dwight Hemion.

**107 Anne Murray's Ladies' Night.** Variety, 60 min., Syndicated 5/79. Anne Murray and her guests (all female) perform songs written, for the most part, by women. *Host:* Anne Murray. *Guests:* Carroll Baker, Salome Bey, Charity Brown, Shirley Eikhard, Mary Hartt, Gloria Kay, Marilyn McCoo, Mary Ann McDonald, Colleen Peterson, Phoebe Snow. *Music:* Rick Wilkins. *Producer-Writer:* Alan Thicke. *Director:* J. Edward Shaw.

**108 Anne Murray's Winter Carnival from Quebec.** Variety, 60 min., CBS, 3/30/84. A songfest celebrating Quebec's 1984 Winter Carnival.

**Ann-Margret**

**5 Ann-Margret Smith** (NBC, 11/20/75). *Guests:* Sid Caesar, Michel Legrand, Roger Smith. *Music:* Jack Parnell. *Producers:* Roger Smith, Allan Carr. *Writers:* Buz Kohan, Michael Abrams. *Director:* Dwight Hemion.

**6 Ann-Margret ... Rhinestone Cowgirl** (NBC, 4/26/77). *Guests:* Chet Atkins, Perry Como, Bob Hope, Minnie Pearl. *Music:* Bill Walker. *Producers:* Roger Smith, Allan Carr. *Writer:* Buz Kohan. *Director:* Dwight Hemion.

**7 Ann-Margret's Hollywood Movie Girls** (ABC, 5/3/80). *Guests:* George Burns, Dom DeLuise, Danny DeVito, Dean Paul Martin, Roger Moore, Bill Saluga. *Music:* Ian Fraser. *Producers:* Gary Smith, Dwight Hemion. *Writers:* Buz Kohan, Marty Farrell. *Director:* Dwight Hemion.

*Host:* Anne Murray. *Guests:* Glen Campbell, Claude Leveille, Dionne Warwick. *Music:* Pat Riccio, Jr. *Producer:* Leonard T. Rambeau. *Writer:* Alan Thicke. *Director:* Dwight Hemion.

### 109 Annie and the Hoods.

Variety, 60 min., CBS, 11/27/74. Actress Anne Bancroft and her male guests perform various skits and musical numbers. See also "Annie, the Woman in the Life of a Man." *Host:* Anne Bancroft. *Guests:* Alan Alda, Jack Benny, Mel Brooks, Tony Curtis, Robert Merrill, Carl Reiner, Gene Wilder. *Music:* Elliot Lawrence. *Producer:* David J. Cogan. *Writers:* Gary Belkin, Martin Charnin, Bob Ellison, Thomas Meehan, Gail Parent, Bob Randall, Kenny Solms. *Director:* Martin Charnin.

### 110 Annie Get Your Gun.

Musical, 2 hrs., NBC, 11/27/57. A television adaptation of the Broadway play about Phoebe Anne Oakley Moses (1860–1926), better known as Annie Oakley, a sharpshooting hillbilly who made a name for herself with Buffalo Bill Cody's Wild West Tent Show. The play itself revolves around Annie's rivalry with Frank Butler, the star marksman she adores and would eventually marry (in 1876). Based on the 1946 musical by Irving Berlin and Dorothy and Herbert Fields. See the following title also. *Cast:* Mary Martin (Annie Oakley), John Raitt (Frank Butler), William O'Neal (Buffalo Bill), Reta Shaw (Dolly Tate), Patricia Morrow (Jessie Oakley), Jan Skidmore (Nellie Oakley), Donald Burr (Charles Davenport), Zachary Charles (Sitting Bull), Robert Nash (Pawnee Bill), Stuart Hodes (Wild Horse). *Music:* Louis Adrian. *Producer:* Richard Halliday. *Director:* Vincent J. Donehue.

### 111 Annie Get Your Gun.

Musical, 2 hrs., NBC, 3/19/67. A second television adaptation of the 1946 Broadway play by Irving Berlin and

Dorothy and Herbert Fields. See the prior title for storyline information. *Cast:* Ethel Merman (Annie Oakley), Bruce Yarnell (Frank Butler), Rufus Smith (Buffalo Bill), Jerry Orbach (Charles Davenport), Beany Venuta (Dolly Tate), Harry Bellaver (Sitting Bull), Jack Dabdoub (Pawnee Bill), Tony Catanzaro (Wild Horse), Wayne Hunter (Tommy Keller). *Producer:* Clark Jones. *Directors:* Clark Jones, Jack Sydow.

### 112 Annie, the Woman in the Life of a Man.

Variety, 60 min., CBS, 2/18/70. Music, songs, and sketches that feature actress Anne Bancroft as the woman in the lives of various men. See also "Annie and the Hoods." *Host:* Anne Bancroft. *Guests:* Jack Cassidy, Lee J. Cobb, Robert Merrill, Arthur Murray, Dick Shawn, Dick Smothers, David Susskind. *Music:* Elliot Lawrence. *Producer:* Martin Charnin. *Writers:* Robert Bellwood, Thomas Meehan, Herb Sargent, Judith Viorst. *Director:* Walter C. Miller.

### 113 Another Evening with Fred Astaire.

Variety, 60 min., CBS, 11/4/59. A lively hour of music and songs that is a sequel to the 1958 special "An Evening with Fred Astaire" (listed separately). *Host:* Fred Astaire. *Guests:* Barrie Chase, The Bill Thompson Singers, The Jonah Jones Quartet, Ken Nordine. *Announcer:* Art Gilmore. *Music:* David Rose. *Producer:* Fred Astaire. *Director:* Bud Yorkin.

### 114 The Anthony Newley Show.

Variety, 60 min., ABC, 8/23/71. An hour of music and songs. *Host:* Anthony Newley. *Guests:* Diahann Carroll, Liza Minnelli. *Music:* Ian Fraser. *Producer:* Jackie Barnett. *Writers:* Sid Green, Dick Hills. *Director:* Tony Charmoli.

### 115 Anything for Laughs.

Comedy, 60 min., ABC, 5/1/85. Highlights of twenty years of Chuck Barris–produced television programs. Outrageous moments from "The Gong Show," "The Newlywed Game," "The Dating Game," "Operation: Entertainment," "The $1.98 Beauty Show," and "The Chuck Barris Rah Rah Show." *Host:* Chuck Barris. *Guests:* Bob Eubanks, Jamie Farr, Arte Johnson, Jim Lange, Jaye P. Morgan. *Announcer:* Dick Tufeld. *Music:* Milton DeLugg. *Producers:* Chuck Barris, Budd Granoff. *Writer:* Bob Booker. *Director:* John Dorsey.

**116 Anything Goes.** Musical, 60 min., NBC, 10/2/50. An adaptation of the Broadway musical about Reno Sweeney, a nightclub singer, as she tries to help a man (Billy Crocker) romance an English heiress (Hope Harcourt) who is being forced to marry a man she does not love (Sir Evelyn Oakleigh). See the following title also. *Cast:* Martha Raye (Reno Sweeney), John Conte (Billy Crocker), Kathryn Mylrole (Hope Harcourt), Fred Wayne (Sir Evelyn Oakleigh), Billy Lynn (the Reverend Dr. Moon), Helen Raymond (Mrs. Harcourt), Gretchen Hauser (Babe). *Music:* Harry Sosnik. *Producer-Director:* Richard Berger. *Writer:* John W. Ledon.

**117 Anything Goes.** Musical, 60 min., NBC, 2/28/54. A second television adaptation of the 1934 Broadway play by Guy Bolton, P. G. Wodehouse, Howard Lindsay, and Russell Crouse, with the music and lyrics of Cole Porter. See the prior title for storyline information. *Cast:* Ethel Merman (Reno Sweeney), Frank Sinatra (Billy Crocker), Arthur Gould Porter (Sir Evelyn Oakleigh), Bert Lahr (the Reverend Dr. Moon), Sheree North (Babe). *Music:* Al Goodman. *Producers:* Leland Hayward, Jule Styne. *Writer:* Herbert Baker. *Director:* Peter Barnum.

**118 The Apollo Hall of Fame.** Variety, 2 hrs., NBC, 8/4/93. A concert that honors the rich heritage of New York's Apollo Theater by paying tribute to some of its members. *Host:* Bill Cosby. *Honorees:* Sam Cooke, Ella Fitzgerald, Billie Holliday, The Ink Spots, Richard Pryor. *Performers:* Bryan Adams, B. B. King, Jeff Beck, Ben E. King, Thelma Carpenter, Ray Charles, Eric Clapton, The Cleftones, Mark Curry, Al Green, Buddy Guy, Brian McKnight, Teddy Pendergrass, Smokey Robinson, Diana Ross, Shai Regina Belle, Robin Williams. *Music:* Harold Wheeler. *Producers:* Leon B. Denmark, Charles Range, Ken Ehrlich. *Writer:* Ken Ehrlich. *Director:* Stan Lathan.

**119 Applause.** Musical, 2 hrs., CBS, 3/15/73. A musical version of the film *All About Eve*. The story of Eve Harrington, a sugar-coated aspiring actress with a heart of iron who schemes her way into the confidence, life, and performances of a Broadway star (Margo Channing). *Cast:* Lauren Bacall (Margo Channing), Penny Fuller (Eve Harrington), Larry Hagman (Bill Sampson), Robert Mandan (Howard Benedict), Sarah Marshall (Karen Richards), Rod McLennan (Buzz Richards). *Music:* Robert Farnam. *Producers:* Richard Rosenbloom, Lawrence Kasha, Joseph Kipness. *Writers:* Betty Comden, Adolph Green. *Directors:* Ron Field, Bill Foster.

**120 Aqua Varieties.** Variety, 60 min., ABC, 2/26/65. Music and comedy from the winter variety show at the Fontainebleau Hotel in Miami Beach, Florida. *Hosts:* Gordon and Sheila MacRae. *Guests:* The Aqua Maids, Barney Cipriani, Raul Garcia, Henry LaMothe, The Mitchell Trio, Vic Zoble. *Music:* Richard Haymond. *Writer:* Selma Diamond.

**121 Archy and Mehitabel.** Musical, 2 hrs., Syndicated, 5/16/60. Archy, a pensive roach with a flair for free verse, attempts to reform Mehitabel, a flamboyant cat with a penchant for free love. Based on the comedy *The Life and Times of Archy and Mehitabel* by Don Marquis. *Cast:* Eddie Bracken (Archy), Tammy Grimes (Mehitabel), Jules Munshin (Tyrone T. Tattersall), Sondra Lee (Rusty), Michael Kermoyan (Big Bill). *Music:* Maurice Levin. *Producer:* Jack Kuney. *Directors:* Ed Greenberg, Bob Blum.

## 122  Are You My Mother?

Drama, 60 min., ABC, 3/5/86. Brittany Gordon, now sixteen years old, has been raised by her grandparents in Connecticut since she was told at a young age that her mother had died. When Brittany comes to Hollywood to work on a music video with her father, Chet, her life changes. While logging documentary film footage of homeless people, she sees a woman who resembles her mother—the mother she has only known through photographs. Chet sees her also and each launches an independent search to find the woman (who is schizophrenic and wants nothing to do with either of them). Aired as an "ABC Afterschool Special." *Cast:* Michael York (Chet Gordon), Beth Miller (Brittany Gordon), Belinda Balaski (Anna Gordon), Sheree North (Madelyn), Marian Mercer (Sister Regina), Tyra Ferrell (Tracy). *Music:* Michael Franks. *Producer:* Joanne A. Curley. *Writer:* Jeanne Betancourt. *Director:* Joseph Manduke.

## 123  Aretha Franklin: Duets.

Variety, 60 min., Fox, 5/9/93. Aretha Franklin, the "Queen of Soul Music," performs her solo hits and her greatest hits with some of her famous friends: "Chain of Fools" (with Rod Stewart, Elton John, and Smokey Robinson), "Spirit in the Dark" (with Elton John), "People Get Ready" (with Rod Stewart), "Since You've Been Gone" (with Bonnie Raitt), "Just to See Her" (with Smokey Robinson), "Coming Out of the Dark" (with Gloria Estefan). *Host:* Aretha Franklin. *Guests:* En Vogue,

Gloria Estefan, Elton John, Bonnie Raitt, Smokey Robinson, Rod Stewart. *Cameos:* Candice Bergen, Whoopi Goldberg, Lena Horne. *Music:* Leon Pendarois. *Producer-Writer:* Ken Ehrlich. *Director:* David Grossman.

## 124  Arsenic and Old Lace. A

chronological listing of the television adaptations (as specials), of the comical play by Joseph Kesselring. The story of Abby and Martha Brewster, two spinster sisters who delight in poisoning elderly men they interview as potential boarders.

**1 Arsenic and Old Lace** (60 min., CBS, 4/11/49). *Cast:* Josephine Hull (Abby Brewster), Ruth McDevitt (Martha Brewster), Boris Karloff (Jonathan Brewster), William Prince (Mortimer Brewster), Bert Freed (Teddy Brewster). *Music:* Cy Feurer. *Producer:* Garth Montgomery. *Director:* Marc Daniels.

**2 Arsenic and Old Lace** (90 min., CBS, 1/5/55). *Cast:* Helen Hayes (Abby Brewster), Billie Burke (Martha Brewster), Boris Karloff (Jonathan Brewster), John Alexander (Teddy Brewster), Orson Bean (Mortimer Brewster), Peter Lorre (Dr. Einstein), Edward Everett Horton (Mr. Witherspoon), Patricia Breslin (Elaine Harper). *Producer:* Martin Manulis. *Writers:* Howard Lindsay, Russell Crouse. *Director:* Herbert Swope.

**3 Arsenic and Old Lace** (90 min., NBC, 2/5/62). *Cast:* Dorothy Stickney (Abby Brewster), Mildred Natwick (Martha Brewster), Boris Karloff (Jonathan Brewster), Tony Randall (Mortimer Brewster), Tom Bosley (Teddy Brewster), George Voskovec (Dr. Einstein), Dody Heath (Elaine Harper). *Producer-Director:* George Schaefer. *Writer:* Robert Hartung. *Note:* Aired on the "Hallmark Hall of Fame."

**4 Arsenic and Old Lace** (2 hrs., ABC, 4/2/69). *Cast:* Helen Hayes (Abby Brewster), Lillian Gish (Martha Brewster), Fred Gwynne (Jonathan Brewster), David Wayne (Teddy Brewster), Bob Crane (Mortimer Brewster), Jack Gilford (Dr. Einstein), Sue Lyon (Elaine Harper), Billy DeWolfe (Mr. Witherspoon). *Producer:* Hubbell Robinson. *Writer:* Luther Davis. *Director:* Robert Scheerer.

**125 Art Carney Meets Peter and the Wolf.** Children, 60 min., NBC, 5/3/59. An updated version of the *Peter and the Wolf* story wherein a young boy, lost in the woods, meets a wolf who, with the sympathetic help of Art Carney, tries to prove he is not as bad as people make him out to be. Characters are the Bil and Cora Baird Puppets. *Cast:* Art Carney (Himself), Bil and Cora Baird (Voices). *Music:* Paul Weston. *Producer:* Burt Shevelove. *Writer:* A. J. Russell. *Director:* Dick Feldman.

**126 Art Carney Meets the Sorcerer's Apprentice.** Children, 60 min., NBC, 4/5/59. The story of Cicero, a magician whose sorcery backfires. With the exception of Cicero, all characters are the Bil and Cora Baird puppets. *Cast:* Art Carney (Cicero), Bil and Cora Baird (Voices). *Music:* Paul Weston. *Producer:* Burt Shevelove. *Writer:* A. J. Russell. *Director:* Seymour Robbie.

**127 The Art Carney Show.** Variety, 60 min., NBC, 11/4/59. A program of music, songs, and comedy sketches. *Host:* Art Carney. *Guests:* David Doyle, Betty Garrett, Gloria Vanderbilt, Dick Van Dyke. *Producer:* David Susskind. *Writers:* Larry Gelbart, Sheldon Keller. *Director:* Burt Shevelove.

**128 Arthur Godfrey Specials.** A chronological listing of humorist Arthur Godfrey's television specials. All specials are 60 minutes in length and feature music, songs, and light humor. Arthur Godfrey hosted each show, unless noted otherwise.

**1 The Arthur Godfrey Show** (CBS, 9/16/59). *Guest:* Johnny Nash. *Music:* Dick Hyman. *Producer:* Charles Andrews. *Director:* Bill Hobin.

**2 The Arthur Godfrey Show** (CBS, 5/6/60). *Guest:* Jackie Gleason. *Music:* Dick Hyman. *Producer:* Charles Andrews. *Director:* Michael Zeamer.

**3 The Arthur Godfrey Show** (CBS, 5/19/61). *Guests:* Erroll Garner, Buddy Hackett, The McGuire Sisters, Johnny Nash. *Music:* Dick Hyman. *Producer:* Charles Andrews. *Director:* Michael Zeamer.

**4 Arthur Godfrey in Hollywood** (CBS, 11/10/62). *Guests:* Pat Buttram, June Foray, Jerry Hausner. *Music:* John Scott Trotter. *Producer:* Perry Lafferty. *Writer:* Hal Kanter. *Director:* Perry Lafferty.

**5 Arthur Godfrey and the Sounds of New York** (CBS, 2/1/63). *Guests:* Phil Foster, The Jonah Jones Quartet, Chita Rivera, Linda Scott. *Music:* John Parker. *Producer-Director:* Perry Lafferty. *Writers:* George Foster, Saul Ilson.

**6 Arthur Godfrey Loves Animals** (CBS, 3/18/63). *Guests:* Mel Blanc, Shari Lewis, Paul Lynde. *Music:* John Parker. *Producer-Director:* Perry Lafferty.

**7 The Arthur Godfrey Thanksgiving Special** (NBC, 11/28/63). *Guests:* Orson Bean, Tony Bennett, Ray Kirchner, Carol Lawrence, Shari Lewis, Liza Minnelli, Bill Starr.

**8 Arthur Godfrey's Portable Electric Medicine Show** (NBC, 3/28/72). A series of ecology-based sketches combining music, song, and comedy. *Guests:* Ken Berry, Jack Cassidy, Dom DeLuise, The Establishment, Barbara Feldon, Teresa Graves, Arte Johnson, Carol Lawrence, Tom Patchett, Jay Tarses. *Producer:* Marty Pasetta. *Writers:* Buz Kohan, Bill Angelos, Tom Patchett, Jay Tarses. *Director:* Marty Pasetta.

**9 The Arthur Godfrey Special** (Syndicated, 8/79). A salute to Arthur Godfrey on the occasion of his fiftieth year in broadcasting. *Guest of Honor:* Arthur

Godfrey. *Guests:* Steve Allen, Eddy Arnold, Annette Funicello, Jo Anne Worley. *Music:* Pat Valentino. *Producer:* Dick Foster. *Director:* Sterling Johnson.

### 129 The Arthur Murray Party for Bob Hope. Variety, 2 hrs. (two 60 min. segments), NBC, 3/15 and 3/22/60. Dance instructors Arthur and Kathryn Murray host a lavish music and comedy party honoring comedian Bob Hope. *Hosts:* Arthur and Kathryn Murray. *Guest of Honor:* Bob Hope. *Guests:* Cliff Arquette, Tony Bennett, Johnny Carson, Gloria DeHaven, Alan King, Dorothy Lamour, Jayne Mansfield, Ethel Merman, Jane Russell, Earl Wilson. *Music:* Ray Carter.

### 130 Arthur the Kid. Comedy, 30 min., ABC, 1/3/81. Hoping to become big-name outlaws, Maurice, Phil, and Sutcliffe, three bungling old west outlaws, advertise for a "boss" in the *Medicine Bow Gazette.* The story relates their adventures when Arthur Fosket, a ten-year-old boy answers the ad and proceeds to make them famous. An "ABC Weekend Special." *Cast:* Dennis Dimster (Arthur), Marvin Kaplan (Sutcliffe), Graham Jarvis (Phil), Charles Hyman (Maurice), Richard O'Brien (Sheriff). *Producer:* Robert Chenault. *Writers:* Jim Carlson, Terrence McDonnell. *Director:* Arthur Lubin.

### 131 As Caesar Sees It. Comedy, 30 min., Syndicated, 11/25/62. A somewhat funny look at life as seen through the eyes of comedian Sid Caesar. Two additional specials, featuring the same format, cast, and credits, aired in syndication on 12/15/62 and 1/5/63. *Host:* Sid Caesar. *Regulars:* Jane Connell, Gordon Conwell, Jim Dooley, Norman Douglas, Andrew Duncan, Edward Ryder, Paul Sand. *Producer:* Leo Morgan. *Writers:* Marvin Marx, Hugh Wedlock, Marty Roth. *Director:* David Brown.

### 132 Astaire Time. Variety, 60 min., CBS, 9/25/60. A lively hour of music, song, and dance. *Host:* Fred Astaire. *Guests:* Barrie Chase, Count Basie, The Earl Twins, Joe Williams. *Announcer:* Ken Nordine. *Music:* David Rose. *Producer:* Fred Astaire. *Director:* Greg Garrison.

### 133 At This Very Moment. Variety, 60 min., ABC, 4/1/62. An entertainment benefit for the American Cancer Society/Eleanor Roosevelt Cancer Fund. *Host:* Burt Lancaster. *Guests:* Harry Belafonte, Richard Chamberlain, Jimmy Durante, Connie Francis, Greer Garson, Charlton Heston, Bob Hope, Lena Horne, Rock Hudson, Paul Newman, Jack Paar, Edward G. Robinson, Dinah Shore, Danny Thomas, Joanne Woodward. *Producer:* Michael Abbott. *Writers:* Arnold Peyser, Lois Peyser. *Director:* Richard Schneider.

### 134 Audrey Hepburn Remembered. Documentary, 65 min., PBS, 8/16/93. A tribute to actress Audrey Hepburn (1929–93) through clips of her films (for example, *Roman Holiday, Breakfast at Tiffany's, Funny Face, My Fair Lady, Two for the Road,* and *Robin and Marian*) and the remembrances of her friends and family. *Host:* Roger Moore. *Guests:* Richard Brown, Blake Edwards, Sean Ferrer, Elizabeth Taylor, Connie Wald, Billy Wilder. *Music:* Michael Bacon. *Writer-Producers:* Suzette Winter, Gene Feldman. *Director:* Gene Feldman.

### 135 Babes in Toyland. Musical, 90 min., NBC, 12/18/54. During the Christmas season a young girl (Joan) becomes lost in a department store. She finds comfort from a Santa Claus, who tells her the story of an imaginary land where storybook characters come to life. As the girl dreams, the viewer is transported to Toyland where the adventures of Tommy Tucker are depicted as he attempts to romance Jane

Piper against the wishes of Silas Barnaby, a villain who wants the lovely girl for himself. *Cast:* Wally Cox (Toymaker Grumino), Dave Garroway (Santa Claus), Ellen Barrie (Joan), Dennis Day (Tommy Tucker), Barbara Cook (Jane Piper), Jack E. Leonard (Silas Barnaby), Karin Wolfe (Ann Piper). *Dancers:* Rod Alexander, Bambi Linn. *Music:* Charles Sanford. *Producer-Director:* Max Liebman. *Writers:* Neil Simon, William Friedberg, Fred Sardy.

**136 Babies Having Babies.** Drama, 60 min., CBS, 3/4/86. A compassionate "CBS Schoolbreak Special" about teenage pregnancy as told from the viewpoint of four pregnant teenagers gathered for a counseling session. *Cast:* Renee Estevez (Maxene), Claudia Wells (Lisa), Jill Whelan (Mary Pat), Lori Loughlin (Kelly), Akoshua Busia (Brenda), Nona White (Mrs. Chapman). *Producers:* Martin Sheen, William Greenblat. *Writers:* Katherine Montgomery, Jeffrey Auerbach. *Director:* Martin Sheen.

**137 The Baby with Four Fathers.** Comedy, 30 min., ABC, 3/31/79. The story, set in New York in 1946, relates the adventures of four boys (Billy D'Amico, "Baldy" Egan, "Vinnie the Doctor," and "Horse"), members of the Loring Place Gang, and the problems they encounter when they find an abandoned baby girl—and decide to "adopt" her. Aired as an "ABC Weekend Special." *Cast:* Al Billera (Billy), Patrick Piccininni (Baldy), Albert Ferrara (Vinnie), Eric Gurry (Horse), Rex Everhart (Paddy O'Brien). *Producer-Writer-Director:* William P. D'Angelo.

**138 The Baby-sitter.** Comedy, 25 min., NBC, 9/5/48. An original musical comedy about the experiences of a timid baby-sitter and the problems that arise when the precocious child he is minding talks him into taking her to a nightclub to see her sister, a singer, perform. *Cast:* Johnny Bradford (Baby-sitter), Bambi Linn (Child), Eugenie Baird (Child's sister). *Producer-Writer-Director:* John Gaunt.

**139 The Bachelor.** Comedy, 90 min., NBC, 7/15/56. A romantic comedy about an account executive (Larry) with three beautiful girlfriends (Robin, Marion, Leslie) and his efforts to keep each girl from learning of the others' existence. *Cast:* Hal March (Larry), Jayne Mansfield (Robin), Carol Haney (Marion), Julie Wilson (Leslie), Georgann Johnson (Francesca), Harry Holcombe (Wainwright). *Music and Lyrics:* Steve Allen. *Producer-Director:* Joseph Cates. *Writers:* Arne Rosen, Coleman Jacoby.

**140 Backbone of America.** Comedy, 60 min., NBC, 12/29/53. The comical escapades of an advertising executive (Ben) as he seeks the perfect family for an upcoming campaign called "The Typical American Family." *Cast:* Wendell Corey (Ben Bruce), Yvonne DeCarlo (Victoria Johnson), Thomas Mitchell (Fred Tupple), Gloria Talbott (Janet), Gene Lockhart (Uncle Cedric), Lee Patrick (Ethel), Regis Toomey (Bill Carmody), Sammy Ogg (Wallie). *Writer:* Robert E. Sherwood.

**141 Backwards: The Riddle of Dyslexia.** Drama, 60 min., ABC, 3/7/84. Brian Ellsworth is a teenager who can't read or write. He is frustrated and ashamed, but is unaware that he suffers from an undiagnosed case of dyslexia. Brian's teachers acknowledge his basic intelligence and, so far, he has masked his reading problems by memorizing. Embarrassed to ask for help, Brian defensively takes on the role of a smart alec. Ultimately, he gives himself away when he writes a jumbled and backward message on the school's hallway walls. Brian's teacher, Miss Tomas, feels Brian needs help, especially after it is discovered that Brian's father has a similar reading problem. Brian is diagnosed with dyslexia. The story follows Brian as he struggles to overcome his disability. *Cast:* River Phoenix (Brian Ellsworth), Madge Sinclair (Miss Tomas), Judy Farrell (Barbara Ellsworth), Leaf Phoenix (Robby Ellsworth), Bo Caprall (Walter Ellsworth). *Producers:* John D. Backe, Philip D. Fehrle. *Writer:* Arthur Heinemann. *Director:* Alex Grashoff.

### 142 The Ballad of Louie the Louse. Comedy, 60 min., CBS, 10/17/59.

Louie is a heartless loan shark who lives off the misery of others. When a newspaper reporter believes that Louie has died, he writes a story that praises Louie as a hero. Louie's efforts to reform and live up to that reputation are the focal point of the story. *Cast:* Phil Silvers (Louie), Eddie Albert (Paul Hughes), Betsy Palmer (Tina Adams), Pert Kelton (Begger Mary). *Music:* Gordon Jenkins. *Producer-Writer:* Nat Hiken. *Director:* Greg Garrison.

### 143 Banjo the Woodpile Cat. Cartoon, 30 min., ABC, 5/1/82.

Banjo, a mischievous little cat, forsakes the comfort of the family woodpile for life in the big city. His adventures with Crazylegs, a street-smart alleycat, and Zazu, the lead singer of the swinging Cat Sisters Variety Show, are depicted as Banjo learns the value of friendship. *Voices:* Scatman Crothers (Crazylegs), Beah Richards (Zazu), Sparky Marcus (Banjo). *Music:* Robert F. Brunner. *Producers:* Don Bluth, John Pomeroy, Gary Goldman. *Director:* Don Bluth.

### 144 The Barbara McNair and Duke Ellington Special. Variety, 60 min., Syndicated, 2/68.

An hour of music and songs with Barbara McNair and Duke Ellington. *Music:* Ralph Carmichael. *Producer:* Jackie Barnett. *Director:* Dick Ross.

### 145 Barbara Mandrell: Something Special. Variety, 60 min., CBS,

1/9/85. An hour of music and songs with country and western singer Barbara Mandrell. *Host:* Barbara Mandrell. *Guests:* Roy Acuff, Lee Greenwood, Bert Remsen, The Voices of Inspiration. *Music:* Dennis McCarthy. *Producers:* Barbara Mandrell, Don Mischer. *Writer:* R. C. Bagnon. *Director:* Don Mischer.

### 146 Barbara Mandrell: The Lady Is a Champ. Variety, 60 min., HBO, 11/27/83.

A concert by country and western singer Barbara Mandrell; taped at Nashville's Tennessee Performing Arts Center. *Host:* Barbara Mandrell. *Guests:* The New Life Singers, The Scott Salmon Dancers. *Music:* Dennis McCarthy. *Producers:* Barbara Mandrell, Ken Dudney. *Director:* Jack Regas.

### 147 Barbara Mandrell's Christmas ... A Family Reunion. Variety, 60 min., CBS, 12/22/86.

Barbara, her sisters (Louise and Irlene), and their families gather for a musical celebration of Christmas. *Hosts:* Barbara Mandrell, Louise Mandrell, and Irlene Mandrell. *Guests:* The Do-Rights (singers), The Scott Salmon Dancers. *Music:* Dennis McCarthy. *Producers:* Barbara Mandrell, Don Mischer. *Writers:* Mitzie Welch, Ken Welch. *Director:* Don Mischer.

### 148 A Barbi Doll for Christmas. Variety, 60 min., Syndicated, 12/78.

A country and western program of Christmas music and songs with singer-actress Barbi Benton. *Host:* Barbi Benton. *Music:* Bill Walker. *Producers:* Jim Owens, Chet Hagan. *Writers:* Frank Slocum, Chet Hagan. *Director:* Ivan Curry.

### 149 Barbra Streisand Specials.

A chronological listing of the variety specials hosted by singer-actress Barbra Streisand. All are 60 minutes except where noted. Barbra Streisand hosted each show, unless noted otherwise.

**1 My Name Is Barbra** (CBS, 4/29/65). Barbra's first television special; a solo hour of songs. *Music:* Peter Matz. *Producers:* Martin Erlichman, Richard Lewine. *Writer:* Robert Emmett. *Director:* Dwight Hemion.

**2 Color Me Barbra** (CBS, 3/30/66). A one-woman concert by Barbra Streisand. Taped in color (and partially at the Philadelphia Museum of Art with one camera. Two of the three cameras CBS had broke down shortly before taping; the technology was so new that there were no replacement parts to repair the other cameras). *Music:* Peter Matz. *Producers:* Martin Erlichman, Richard Lewine. *Writer:* Robert Emmett. *Director:* Dwight Hemion.

**3 Barbra Streisand: A Happening in Central Park** (CBS, 9/15/68). Videotaped highlights of Barbra's one-woman concert in New York's Central Park. *Music:* Mort Lindsay. *Producer:* Martin Erlichman. *Producer-Director:* Robert Scheerer.

**4 Barbra Streisand and Other Musical Instruments** (CBS, 11/2/73). The program features a cast of international musicians playing their national instruments. *Guest:* Ray Charles. *Musical Material:* Ken Welch, Mitzie Welch. *Producers:* Martin Erlichman, Gary Smith, Dwight Hemion. *Director:* Dwight Hemion.

**5 Barbra Streisand—Putting It Together: The Making of the Broadway Album** (40 min., HBO, 1/11/86). A behind-the-scenes look at Barbra as she records her landmark album, *The Broadway Album.* Taped 7/25/85. *Guests:* William Friedkin, David Geffen, Sydney Pollack, Stephen Sondheim. *Producer:* Barbra Streisand. *Director:* William Friedkin.

**6 Barbra Streisand: One Voice** (70 min., HBO, 12/27/86). *Host:* Robin Williams. *Star:* Barbra Streisand. *Barbra's Band:* Randy Waldman, Jim Cox, Mike Fisher, Niles Steiner, John Pierce, Dan Sawyer, Chad Whackman. *Producers:* Barbra Streisand, Martin Erlichman, Marilyn Bergman, Gary Smith, Dwight Hemion. *Director:* Dwight Hemion.

**150 Barefoot in Athens.** Drama, 90 min., NBC, 11/11/66. A television adaptation of Maxwell Anderson's Pulitzer Prize–winning story about the early life of Greek philosopher Socrates (470–399 B.C.). Aired on the "Hallmark Hall of Fame." *Cast:* Peter Ustinov (Socrates), Geraldine Page (Xantippe), Anthony Quayle (Pausanius), Salome Jens (Theodote), Eric Berry (Meletos). *Producer-Director:* George Schaefer. *Writer:* Robert Hartung.

**151 Barefoot in the Park.** Comedy, 2 hrs. 20 min., HBO, 3/21/82. A television adaptation of the Neil Simon Broadway play about the trials and tribulations of the Bratters, newlyweds struggling to make a life for themselves in New York City. *Cast:* Bess Armstrong (Corie Bratter), Richard Thomas (Paul Bratter), Barbara Barrie (Mabel Banks), Hans Conried (Victor Velasio), James Cromwell (Harry Pepper). *Producer:* Michael Brandman. *Writer:* Neil Simon. *Director:* Harvey Medlinsky.

**152 The Barretts of Wimpole Street.** Drama, 60 min., CBS, 6/8/55. A television adaptation of the 1930 play by Rudolf Besier. The story of the meeting, courtship, and marriage of poets Elizabeth Barrett and Robert Browning. (The title refers to Elizabeth's home on Wimpole Street in London.) *Cast:* Geraldine Fitzgerald (Elizabeth Barrett), Robert Douglas (Robert Browning), Sir Cedric Hardwicke (Edward Barrett), Joan Elan (Henrietta Barrett), Jerry Barclay (Octavius Barrett), John Irving (Septimus Barrett), William Schallert (Alfred Barrett). *Announcer:* Bob Lemond. *Music:* Don Ray. *Producer:* Fletcher Markle. *Writer:* Vincent McConnor. *Director:* James Sheldon.

### 153 Barry Manilow: Big Fun on Swing Street.

Variety, 60 min., CBS, 3/7/88. Singer Barry Manilow combines the music of the 1940s with the sounds of the 1980s to create "Swing Street" music. *Host:* Barry Manilow. *Guests:* Stanley Clarke, Phyllis Hyman, Kid Creole and the Coconuts, Carmen MacRae, Dana Robbins, Diane Schuur, Tom Scott. *Music:* Eddie Arkin. *Producers:* Barry Manilow, Jack Feldman, Bruce Sussman. *Choreographer:* Kevin Carlisle.

### 154 Barry Manilow — One Voice.

Variety, 60 min., ABC, 5/19/80. An hour of music and song. *Host:* Barry Manilow. *Guest:* Dionne Warwick. *Music:* Artie Butler. *Producer-Writers:* Ernest Chambers, Barry Manilow. *Director:* George Schaefer.

### 155 The Barry Manilow Special.

Variety, 60 min., ABC, 3/2/77. Music, songs, and light comedy with singer Barry Manilow in his first television special. See also "The Second Barry Manilow Special" and "The Third Barry Manilow Special." *Host:* Barry Manilow. *Guests:* Lady Flash, Penny Marshall. *Music:* Gerald Alters. *Producer:* Miles Lourie. *Writers:* Alan Thicke, Barry Manilow, Susan Clark, Don Clark, Steve Binder, Ron Pearlman. *Director:* Steve Binder.

### 156 Baryshnikov in Hollywood.

Variety, 60 min., CBS, 4/21/82. A musical that takes Mikhail Baryshnikov from his final ballet appearance of the season to his introduction to life in the fast lane of the Hollywood movie studios. Although exhausted, Mikhail signs a contract with a fast-talking agent (Dom DeLuise) who envisions him not as a dancing star, but as a great actor. Mikhail receives acting lessons, makes a screen test, and appears in an all-dancing, no-talking version of the famous silent film *The Sheik*, with Mikhail in the Rudolph Valentino role and Bernadette Peters as the harem maiden he rescues. *Host:* Mikhail Baryshnikov. *Guests:* Dom DeLuise, Shirley MacLaine, Charles Nelson Reilly, Bernadette Peters, Orson Welles, Gene Wilder. *Music:* Peter Matz. *Producer:* Sherman Krawitz. *Writers:* Buz Kohan, Bob Arnott. *Director:* Don Mischer.

### 157 Baryshnikov on Broadway.

Variety, 60 min., ABC, 4/24/80. A tribute to the American musical theater, featuring Russian-born ballet star Mikhail Baryshnikov. *Host:* Mikhail Baryshnikov. *Guests:* Nell Carter, Liza Minnelli. *Music:* Ian Fraser. *Producers:* Sherman Krawitz, Gary Smith, Dwight Hemion. *Writer:* Fred Ebb. *Director:* Dwight Hemion.

### 158 The Bat.

Mystery, 60 min., NBC, 3/31/60. The story of Cornelia Van Gorder, a wealthy spinster, and her efforts to protect herself from "The Bat," a mysterious killer who is seeking a hidden fortune in her home. Based on the story by Mary Roberts Rinehart and Avery Hopwood. Aired on "The Dow Hour of Great Mysteries." *Cast:* Helen Hayes (Cornelia Van Gorder), Margaret Hamilton (Lizzie Arlen), Jason Robards, Jr. (Lieutenant Anderson), Bethel Leslie (Dale Ogden), Sheppard Strudwick (Dr. Wells), Karl Light (Richard Fleming). *Narrator:* Joseph N. Welch. *Producer:* Robert Saudek. *Writer:* Walter T. Kerr. *Director:* Paul Nickell.

### 159 Battle of the Bands.

Variety, 60 min., ABC, 7/29/93. Performances by professional bands (who never had a major label recording contract) from across the nation (the winning band receives a recording contract). Taped at the Wiltern Theater in Los Angeles. *Hosts:* Adam Curry, Holly Robinson. *Bands:* B.L.U., Dox Haus Mob, Flesh 'n' Blood, Noise Boys, 2 Skinee J's, Wake. *Producers:* Dick Clark, Al Schwartz, Arthur Smith.

*Writer:* Barry Adelman. *Director:* Jeff Margolis.

## 160 Battle of the Network Stars.

A chronological listing of the 19 specials that aired on ABC from 11/13/76 to 12/10/88. Stars from ABC, CBS, and NBC compete in a series of athletic events to determine which network is best on the athletic field. Roone Arledge and Don Ohlmeyer produced the first 16 specials; Barry Frank and Bill Garnett produced specials 17 and 18; and Robert Bagley and Vin DiBona produced the last special. All are two hours in length.

**1 Battle of the Network Stars** (11/13/76). *Host:* Howard Cosell. *ABC Team:* Gabe Kaplan (Captain), Darleen Carr, Lynda Carter, Farrah Fawcett, Richard Hatch, Robert Hegyes, Ron Howard, Hal Linden, Penny Marshall, John Schuck. *CBS Team:* Telly Savalas (Captain), Adrienne Barbeau, Gary Burghoff, Kevin Dobson, Pat Harrington, Bill Macy, Lee Meriwether, Mackenzie Phillips, Loretta Swit, Jimmie Walker. *NBC Team:* Robert Conrad (Captain), Melissa Sue Anderson, Karen Grassle, Tim Matheson, Ben Murphy, Barbara Parkins, Joanna Pettet, Kevin Tighe, Bobby Troupe, Demond Wilson.

**2 Battle of the Network Stars** (2/28/77). *Host:* Howard Cosell. *ABC Team:* Gabe Kaplan (Captain), LeVar Burton, Darleen Carr, Richard Hatch, Lawrence Hilton-Jacobs, Ron Howard, Hal Linden, Kristy McNichol, Penny Marshall, Jaclyn Smith. *CBS Team:* Telly Savalas (Captain), Sonny Bono, Kevin Dobson, Mike Farrell, David Groh, Linda Lavin, Lee Meriwether, Rob Reiner, Loretta Swit, Marcia Wallace. *NBC Team:* Robert Conrad (Captain), Elizabeth Allen, Lynda Day George, Carl Franklin, Karen Grassle, Dan Haggerty, Art Hindle, Kurt Russell, Jane Seymour, W. K. Stratton.

**3 Battle of the Network Stars** (11/4/77). *Hosts:* Howard Cosell, Telly Savalas. *ABC Team:* Gabe Kaplan (Captain), Fred Berry, Billy Crystal, Chris DeRose, Victor French, Cheryl Ladd, Kristy McNichol, Penny Marshall, Suzanne Somers, Parker Stevenson. *CBS Team:* Jimmie Walker (Captain), Adrienne Barbeau, Valerie Bertinelli, Kevin Dobson, Jamie Farr, Caren Kaye, James MacArthur, James Vincent McNichol, Loretta Swit, Lyle Waggoner. *NBC Team:* Dan Haggerty (Captain), Robert Conrad, Elinor Donahue, Patrick Duffy, Peter Isacksen, Lance Kerwin, Donna Mills, Belinda J. Montgomery, Michelle Phillips, Larry Wilcox.

**4 Battle of the Network Stars** (5/7/78). *Hosts:* Howard Cosell, Bruce Jenner, Suzanne Somers. *ABC Team:* Gabe Kaplan (Captain), Debby Boone, Daryl Dragon, Kene Holliday, Steve Landesberg, Parker Stevenson, Toni Tennille, Cheryl Tiegs. *CBS Team:* Tony Randall (Captain), Kevin Dobson, James MacArthur, Denise Nicholas, Mackenzie Phillips, Victoria Principal, Bo Svenson, Jimmie Walker. *NBC Team:* Richard Benjamin (Captain), Rhonda Bates, Jane Curtin, Dennis Dugan, Melissa Gilbert, Dan Haggerty, Arte Johnson, Lance Kerwin, Larry Wilcox.

**5 Battle of the Network Stars** (11/18/78). *Hosts:* Howard Cosell, Frank Gifford. *ABC Team:* Gabe Kaplan (Captain), Debby Boone, Billy Crystal, Joyce DeWitt, Richard Hatch, Maren Jensen, Robert Urich, Robin Williams. *CBS Team:* McLean Stevenson (Captain), Valerie Bertinelli, LeVar Burton, Lou Ferrigno, Patricia Klous, David Letterman, Tim Reid, Charlene Tilton. *NBC Team:* Robert Conrad (Captain), Joseph Bottoms, William Devane, Pamela Hensley, Brianne Leary, Wendy Rastatter, William Shatner, Caskey Swaim.

**6 Battle of the Network Stars** (5/7/79). *Host:* Howard Cosell. *ABC Team:* Dick Van Patten (Captain), Scott Baio, Billy Crystal, Richard Hatch, Donna Pescow, Susan Richardson, Toni Tennille, Robert Urich. *CBS Team:* Jamie

Farr (Captain), Catherine Bach, Valerie Bertinelli, Patrick Duffy, Jamie Farr, Lou Ferrigno, Leif Garrett, Victoria Principal, Gary Sandy. *NBC Team:* Robert Conrad (Captain), Todd Bridges, Mary Crosby, Jane Curtin, William Devane, Greg Evigan, Brianne Leary, Larry Wilcox.

**7 Battle of the Network Stars** (11/2/79). *Hosts:* Howard Cosell, Billy Crystal. *ABC Team:* Dick Van Patten (Captain), Willie Aames, Diana Canova, Joanna Cassidy, Max Gail, Robert Hays, Kristy McNichol, Shelley Smith. *CBS Team:* Edward Asner (Captain), Valerie Bertinelli, Gregory Harrison, Kathryn Leigh Scott, Judy Norton-Taylor, Jan Smithers, Allen Williams. *NBC Team:* Robert Conrad (Captain), Greg Evigan, Gil Gerard, Melissa Gilbert, Erin Gray, Randi Oakes, Sarah Purcell, Patrick Wayne.

**8 Battle of the Network Stars** (5/4/80). *Hosts:* Howard Cosell, Joyce DeWitt. *ABC Team:* Cathy Lee Crosby (Captain), Scott Baio, Robyn Douglass, Robert Hays, Grant Goodeve, Kent McCord, Caroline McWilliams, Joan Prather. *CBS Team:* Chad Everett (Captain), Jonelle Allen, Catherine Bach, Gregory Harrison, Sherman Hemsley, Gary Sandy, Charlene Tilton, Joan Van Ark. *NBC Team:* William Devane (Captain), Gil Gerard, Karen Grassle, Pamela Hensley, Brian Kerwin, Randi Oakes, Sarah Purcell, Larry Wilcox.

**9 Battle of the Network Stars** (12/5/80). *Hosts:* Howard Cosell, Cathy Lee Crosby. *ABC Team:* John Davidson (Captain), Willie Aames, Scott Baio, Phyllis Davis, Donna Dixon, Max Gail, Ann Jillian, Susan Richardson. *CBS Team:* Jamie Farr (Captain), Gregory Harrison, Diane Ladd, Donna Mills, Judy Norton-Taylor, Tom Selleck, Joan Van Ark, Robert Walden. *NBC Team:* Arte Johnson (Captain), Byron Allen, John Beck, Greg Evigan, Erin Gray, Judy Landers, Sarah Purcell, Cristina Raines.

**10 Battle of the Network Stars** (5/8/81). *Hosts:* Howard Cosell, Erin Gray. *ABC Team:* Robert Urich (Captain), Scott Baio, Melanie Chartoff, Jeff Conaway, Linda Evans, Jenilee Harrison, Ann Jillian. *CBS Team:* Tom Selleck (Captain), Danielle Brisebois, Gregory Harrison, Michele Lee, Leigh McCloskey, Judy Norton-Taylor, Tim Reid, Charlene Tilton. *NBC Team:* Barbara Mandrell (Captain), Woody Brown, Melissa Gilbert, Brian Kerwin, Louise Mandrell, Randi Oakes, Skip Stevenson, Michael Warren.

**11 Battle of the Network Stars** (11/20/81). *Hosts:* Howard Cosell, Lee Majors. *ABC Team:* Scott Baio (Captain), Douglas Barr, Cathy Lee Crosby, Donna Dixon, Telma Hopkins, Ann Jillian, Sam J. Jones, Andrew Stevens. *CBS Team:* Pernell Roberts (Captain), Mimi Kennedy, Lorenzo Lamas, Jared Martin, Donna Mills, Tim Reid, Charlene Tilton, Berlinda Tolbert. *NBC Team:* Gabe Kaplan (Captain), Maud Adams, Melissa Gilbert, Mark Harmon, Randi Oakes, Cristina Raines, Fred Willard.

**12 Battle of the Network Stars** (5/7/82). *Hosts:* Howard Cosell, Randi Oakes. *ABC Team:* William Shatner (Captain), Douglas Barr, Joan Collins, Lydia Cornell, John Davidson, Telma Hopkins, John James, Heather Thomas. *CBS Team:* Pernell Roberts (Captain), Catherine Bach, Danielle Brisebois, Audrey Landers, Brian Mitchell, Joan Van Ark, Robert Walden, Tom Wopat. *NBC Team:* Daniel J. Travanti (Captain), Debbie Allen, Mark Harmon, Nancy McKeon, Joe Piscopo, Cristina Raines, Lynn Redgrave, Bruce Weitz.

**13 Battle of the Network Stars** (10/1/82). *Hosts:* Debbie Allen, Howard Cosell. *ABC Team:* William Shatner (Captain), Stephen Collins, Helen Hunt, John James, Heather Locklear, Kathy Maisnik, Heather Thomas, Demond Wilson. *CBS Team:* Kevin Dobson (Captain), Bruce Boxleitner, Delta Burke, Byron Cherry, Christopher Norris, Jameson Parker, Penny Peyser,

Joan Van Ark. *NBC Team:* Daniel J. Travanti (Captain), Dean Butler, Tina Gayle, Melissa Gilbert, Ricky Schroder, Leigh Taylor-Young, Betty Thomas, Michael Warren.

**14 Battle of the Network Stars** (5/4/83). *Hosts:* Howard Cosell, Morgan Fairchild. *ABC Team:* John James (Captain), Scott Baio, Rachel Dennison, Lisa Eilbacher, Heather Locklear, Randi Oakes, Jeffrey Scott, Adrian Zmed. *CBS Team:* Tom Wopat (Captain), John Beck, Danielle Brisebois, Audrey Landers, Denise Miller, Billy Moses, Tracy Nelson, Ted Shackelford. *NBC Team:* Bruce Weitz (Captain), Peter Barton, Meredith Baxter Birney, David Birney, Nancy McKeon, Mr. T, Cynthia Sikes, Betty Thomas.

**15 Battle of the Network Stars** (11/3/83). *Hosts:* Robert Conrad, Howard Cosell, Donna Mills. *ABC Team:* William Shatner (Captain), Shari Belafonte-Harper, Daniel Hugh Kelly, Heather Locklear, Ben Murphy, Geoffrey Scott, Heather Thomas, Jill Whelan. *CBS Team:* William Devane (Captain), Ana Alicia, Rosalind Chao, Charles Frank, William R. Moses, Martha Smith, Andrew Stevens, Joan Van Ark. *NBC Team:* Mr. T (Captain), Edward Albert, Teri Copley, Melinda Culea, Chad Everett, Charles Haid, Vicki Lawrence, Cynthia Sikes.

**16 Battle of the Network Stars** (5/3/84). *Hosts:* Scott Baio, Debby Boone, Howard Cosell. *ABC Team:* John James (Captain), Shari Belafonte-Harper, Pamela Bellwood, James Darren, C. Thomas Howell, Ted Lange, Heather Locklear, Shawn Weatherly. *CBS Team:* William Devane (Captain), Richard Dean Anderson, Abby Dalton, Sarah Douglas, William R. Moses, Douglas Sheehan, Charlene Tilton, Celia Weston. *NBC Team:* Flip Wilson (Captain), Ellen Bry, Kim Fields, Michael J. Fox, Charles Haid, Mark Harmon, Vicki Lawrence, Lisa Whelchel.

**17 Battle of the Network Stars** (12/20/84). *Hosts:* Shari Belafonte-Harper, Howard Cosell. *ABC Team:* William Shatner (Captain), Douglas Barr, Mary Cadorette, Tony Danza, Tony LoBianco, Heather Locklear, Tracy Scoggins, Brenda Vaccaro. *CBS Team:* William Devane (Captain), Constance McCashin, Jennifer O'Neill, Tim Reid, Douglas Sheehan, Deborah Shelton, Parker Stevenson, Charlene Tilton. *NBC Team:* Mark Harmon (Captain), Jane Badler, Teri Copley, Kim Fields, Michael J. Fox, Stepfanie Kramer, James B. Sikking, Marc Singer.

**18 Battle of the Network Stars** (5/23/85). *Hosts:* Joan Van Ark, Dick Van Dyke. *ABC Team:* Tony Danza (Captain), Deborah Adair, Mary Cadorette, Jack Coleman, Patricia Klous, Ted McGinley, Emma Samms, Michael Spound. *CBS Team:* Lorenzo Lamas (Captain), Lucie Arnaz, Mary Frann, Jenilee Harrison, Doug McKeon, William R. Moses, Jennifer O'Neill, Dack Rambo. *NBC Team:* Bubba Smith (Captain), Lisa Bonet, Erin Gray, Nancy McKeon, Patricia McPherson, Keil Martin, Ken Olin, Philip Michael Thomas.

**19 Battle of the Network Stars** (12/10/88). *Hosts:* Shari Belafonte-Harper, Howard Cosell. *ABC Team:* John Davidson (Captain), Rebeca Arthur, Allyce Beasley, Olivia D'Abo, Brian Robbins, Rob Stone, JoAnn Willette, Brian Wimmer. *CBS Team:* Lorenzo Lamas (Captain), Kristin Alfonso, Steve Kanaly, Daphne Maxwell Reid, Jack Scalia, Nicollette Sheridan, William Sanderson. *NBC Team:* Greg Evigan (Captain), Teri Copley, Clifton Davis, Deidre Hall, Dawnn Lewis, Blair Underwood, Malcolm-Jamal Warner, Tina Yothers.

**161 Battle of the Video Games.** Game, 60 min., Syndicated, 8/83. Four three-member celebrity teams play video games for charity. Each round pits one member from each team in a specific game (for example, Ms. Pac-Man). The winner scores ten points (the second highest scorer receives five points and three points are awarded for third place). The two highest scoring teams compete in a final round—a game of Pac-Man (which involves the best players on each team). The highest scoring team wins $5,000 for its charity; $2,500 is awarded to the second place team; $1,500 for third place; and $1,000 for last place. *Hosts:* Jayne Kennedy, Anson Williams. *Gold Team:* Scott Baio, Heather Locklear, Denise Miller. *Blue Team:* Philip McKeon, Lynn Redgrave, Jackie Zeman. *Red Team:* Todd Bridges, Mindy Cohn, Deney Terio. *Gray Team:* Lou Ferrigno, Jenilee Harrison, Michael Young. *Commentator:* Marty Cohan. *Music:* Dan Elliott. Producer: Gary Hunt. *Writer:* Randy Wilson. *Director:* Al Footnick.

## 162  Be My Valentine, Charlie Brown. Cartoon, 30 min., CBS, 1/28/75.

The program focuses on several of the Peanuts characters: Sally, who thinks Linus's purchase of a box of candy is for her, when in reality it is for his homeroom teacher; Lucy, who seeks Schroeder's attention; and Charlie Brown, who begins a vigil by his mailbox, hoping to receive a valentine. *Voices:* Duncan Watson (Charlie Brown), Stephen Shea (Linus), Melanie Kohn (Lucy), Greg Felton (Schroeder), Lynn Mortensen (Sally), Linda Ercoli (Violet), Bill Melendez (Snoopy). *Music:* Vince Guaraldi. *Producers:* Lee Mendelson, Bill Melendez. *Writer:* Charles M. Schulz. *Director:* Phil Roman.

## 163  The Beach Boys Specials.

A chronological listing of the variety specials hosted by the world-famous Beach Boys (Al Jardine, Bruce Johnson, Mike Love, Brian Wilson and Carl Wilson).

**1 The Beach Boys Special** (60 min., NBC, 8/5/76). *Hosts:* The Beach Boys. *Guests:* Dan Aykroyd, John Belushi. *Producer:* Lorne Michaels. *Writers:* Alan Zweibel, Dan Aykroyd, John Belushi, Lorne Michaels. *Director:* Gary Weis.

**2 The Beach Boys in Concert** (2 hrs., HBO, 11/11/80). *Hosts:* The Beach Boys. *Producers:* Howard K. Grossman, Rick Melling. *Director (as credited):* Keefe.

**3 The Beach Boys 20th Anniversary Special** (2 hrs., Syndicated, 5/81). *Host:* Scott Muni. *Guests:* Glen Campbell, Daryl Dragon, Andy Williams. *Producers:* Howard K. Grossman, Andrew Holmes. *Director:* Richard Melling.

**4 D.C. Beach Party** (60 min., Showtime, 9/15/84). *Hosts:* The Beach Boys. *Guests:* Julio Iglesias, Ringo Starr. *Producer:* Neal Marshall. *Director:* Tom Trbovich.

**5 The Beach Boys—25 Years Together** (90 min., ABC, 3/13/87). *Hosts:* The Beach Boys. *Guests:* Glen Campbell, Belinda Carlisle, Ray Charles, Patrick Duffy, The Everly Brothers, Gloria Loring, Jeffrey Osborne, Joe Piscopo, Paul Shaffer, Three Dog Night. *Producers:* Tom Hulett, Marty Pasetta. *Writers:* David Forman, David Leaf. *Director:* Marty Pasetta.

**6 The Beach Boys: An American Band** (2 hrs., Syndicated, 9/87). *Performers:* The Beach Boys. *Producers:* John Pesinger, Michael Wiese, Malcolm Leo, Bonnie Peterson. *Writer-Director:* Malcolm Leo.

**7 The Beach Boys: Endless Summer** (60 min., Syndicated, 6/89). *Hosts:* The Beach Boys. *Band Members:* Ed Carter, Jeffrey Foskett, William Hinsche, Mike Kowalski, Mike Meros. *Dancers:* Aurorah Allain, Leslie Cook, Jamilah Lucas, Trish McFarland, Regan Panto, Darrell Wright. *Music Director:* Glen Jordan. *Producer:* Steve Binder. *Writer:* Buddy Sheffield. *Director:* Gary Halvorson.

## 164 The Bear Who Slept Through Christmas. Cartoon, 30 min., NBC, 12/17/73.

Ted E. Bear is a young cub who has never seen Christmas. Curious about it, but always in hibernation when it occurs, he decides to travel to the big city and stay awake for the big event. The story relates his efforts, despite ridicule from his peers. *Voices:* Tom Smothers (Ted E. Bear), Barbara Feldon (Patti Bear), Arte Johnson (Professor Von Bear), Robert Holt (Santa Claus), Kelly Lange (Lady Weather Bear). *Music:* Doug Goodwin. *Producers:* Norman Sedawie, David DePatie, Friz Freleng. *Writers:* John Barrett, Larry Spiegel. *Directors:* Hawley Pratt, Gerry Chiniquy.

**165 Beat of the Brass.** Variety, 60 min., CBS, 4/22/68. A solo concert performance by Herb Alpert and the Tijuana Brass. *Host:* Herb Alpert. *Producers:* Alfred D. Scipio, Jack Haley, Jr. *Writer:* Tom Mankiewicz. *Director:* Jack Haley, Jr.

**166 The Beatles at Shea Stadium.** Variety, 60 min., ABC, 1/17/67. An edited-for-television version of the August 1965 concert by the Beatles at New York's Shea Stadium. *Performers:* The Beatles, The Discoteque Dancers, Brenda Holloway, The King Curtis Orchestra, Sounds, Inc. *Producer:* Robert H. Precht.

**167 The Beatles Forever.** Variety, 60 min., NBC, 11/24/77. A Thanksgiving Day special that salutes the music of the Beatles. *Guests:* Diahann Carroll, Ray Charles, Anthony Newley, Bernadette Peters, Tony Randall, Mel Tillis, Paul Williams. *Music:* Larry Grossman. *Producer:* Syd Vinnedge. *Writers:* Sheldon Keller, Richard Albrecht, Casey Keller. *Director:* Jon Scoffield.

**168 The Beatrice Arthur Special.** Variety, 60 min., CBS, 1/19/80. A variety outing that spotlights the singing, acting, and comedic talents of Beatrice Arthur (in her first music and comedy television special). *Host:* Beatrice Arthur. *Guests:* Wayland Flowers, Rock Hudson, Melba Moore. *Music:*

Bob Rozario. *Producer:* Saul Ilson. *Writers:* Hal Goldman, Saul Ilson, Jeffrey Barron. *Directors:* Jeff Margolis, Howard Morris.

**169 Beauty and the Beast.** Fantasy, 90 min., NBC, 12/3/76. An adaptation of Madame Leprince de Beaumont's classic 1756 text about a beautiful young woman (Belle) and the hideous beast who loves her. When Belle's father offends the Beast, Belle agrees to live in the Beast's castle to save her father's life. Unknown to Belle, the Beast is a handsome prince under the spell of a fairy. The Beast is taken by Belle's lovely ways, but she cannot bring herself to accept his marriage proposal. The story follows Belle as she learns that simple virtues and human values are the qualities that make one truly beautiful. Aired on the "Hallmark Hall of Fame." *Cast:* George C. Scott (The Beast), Trish Van Devere (Belle), Bernard Lee (Edward), Virginia McKenna (Lucy), Patricia Quinn (Susan), Michael Harbour (Anthony), William Relton (Nicholas). *Music:* Ron Goodwin. *Producer:* Thomas Johnson. *Writer:* Sherman Yellen. *Director:* Fielder Cook.

**170 Beauty and the Beast.** Cartoon, 60 min., CBS, 11/25/83. An animated adaptation of the classic 1756 text by Madame Leprince de Beaumont; see the prior title for story. *Voices:* Janet Waldo (Beauty/Jacqueline/Queen), Linda Gary (Erwina), Robert Ridgely (Beast/Prince), Paul Kirby (Narrator/Gerard), Alan Young (Rene), Stacy Keach, Sr. (Merchant). *Music:* Dean Elliott. *Producers:* Joe Ruby, Ken Spears. *Writers:* Steve Gerber, Martin Pasko. *Director:* Ruby Larriva.

**171 Bedrooms.** Comedy, 60 min., HBO, 2/14/84. Four adult vignettes about the trials and tribulations of love and marriage: "Laura and Bill," "Betty, Alan and Riva," "David, Loretta and Nancy," and "Nick and Wendy." *Hosts:* Joseph Bologna, Renee Taylor. *Cast:* Joseph Bologna (Bill/David), Louise Lasser (Betty/Loretta), Renee Taylor (Riva/Wendy), Demi Moore (Nancy), Jane Curtin (Laura), Rudy DeLuca (Alan). *Music:* Ray Ellis. *Producers:* Alvin Perlmutter, Renee Taylor. *Writer-Directors:* Joseph Bologna, Renee Taylor.

### 172 Bedtime Story. Comedy,
30 min., ABC, 11/21 and 11/22/72. An epilogue to the special "Let's Celebrate" (see entry). Two scenes (15 minutes each) that feature the conversations between a man and his wife as they prepare for bed. *Cast:* Lawrence Pressman (Husband), Melodie Johnson (Wife). *Producer-Writers:* Saul Ilson, Ernest Chambers. *Directors:* Hy Averback, Michael J. Kane.

### 173 Belafonte, New York.
Variety, 60 min., CBS, 11/20/60. An hour of folk songs and music. *Host:* Harry Belafonte. *Guest:* Gloria Lynne. *Music:* Robert DeCormier. *Producer:* Phil Stein. *Director:* Norman Jewison.

### 174 A Bell for Adano. Drama,
2 hrs., NBC, 11/11/67. A "Hallmark Hall of Fame" presentation about Major Victor Joppolo, the military governor of Adano, as he attempts to establish a democracy in the conquered Italian town. *Cast:* John Forsythe (Victor Joppolo), Kathleen Widdoes (Tina), Murray Hamilton (Sergeant Borth), Tom Skerritt (Trapani), Peter Brandon (Captain Purvis). *Producer:* Leland Hayward. *Writer:* Roger O. Hirson. *Director:* Mel Ferber.

### 175 The Belle of Amherst.
Drama, 90 min., PBS, 12/29/76. A portrait of American poet Emily Dickinson based on her poems, notes, and letters. The one-woman show was recorded before a live audience. *Cast:* Julie Harris (Emily Dickinson). *Producers:* Mike Merrick, Don Gregory.

*Writer:* William Luce. *Director:* Charles S. Dubin.

### 176 The Belle of 14th Street.
Variety, 60 min., CBS, 10/11/67. The program re-creates the music and comedy of vaudeville at the turn of the century. *Host:* Barbra Streisand. *Guests:* Lee Allen, Susan Alpern, John Bubbles, Jason Robards, Smith and Dale. *Music:* Mort Lindsey. *Producers:* Martin Erlichman, Joe Layton. *Writer:* Robert Emmett. *Directors:* Joe Layton, Walter C. Miller.

### 177 The Belles of St. Mary's.
Drama, 90 min., CBS, 10/27/59. St. Mary's is a poor and decaying parochial school. The story follows the efforts of a group of nuns to convince a millionaire to help pay for needed repairs. *Cast:* Claudette Colbert (Sister Benedict), Robert Preston (Father O'Malley), Charlie Ruggles (Horace Bogardus), Nancy Marchand (Sister Michael). *Producer:* David Susskind. *Writer:* Irving Gaynor Neiman.

### 178 Ben Vereen—His Roots.
Variety, 60 min., ABC, 3/2/78. An hour of music and songs in which performer Ben Vereen traces his musical roots. *Host:* Ben Vereen. *Guests:* Debbie Allen, Louis Gossett, Jr.; Cheryl Ladd. *Music:* Ian Fraser. *Producers:* Jerrold H. Kushnick, Gary Smith, Dwight Hemion. *Writer:* Michael Kagan. *Director:* Dwight Hemion.

### 179 Benny Goodman: Let's Dance—A Musical Tribute.
Tribute, 90 min., Syndicated, 3/86. A musical tribute to Benny Goodman, the legendary "King of Swing." Taped at New York's Marriott Marquis Hotel. *Guest of Honor:* Benny Goodman. *Guests:* Louis Bellson, Rosemary Clooney, Red Norvo, Bobby Short, Frank Sinatra, Carrie Smith, Slam Stewart, Teddy Wilson. *Announcer:* John Bartholomew Tucker. *Music:* Dick Hyman. *Producer:* Jack Sameth.

*Writer:* Michael Winship. *Director:* William Cose.

## 180 Berkeley Square. Drama, 90 min., NBC, 2/5/59.

Peter Standish, a modern-day American, is whisked back in time when he moves into a mansion on Berkeley Square in London. His experiences in eighteenth-century England are depicted on this "Hallmark Hall of Fame" presentation. *Cast:* John Kerr (Peter Standish), Jeannie Carson (Kate Pettigrew), Edna Best (Anne Pettigrew), Janet Munro (Helen Pettigrew), John Colicos (Tom Pettigrew). *Producer-Director:* George Schaefer. *Writer:* Theodore Apstein.

## 181 The Bert Convy Special— There's a Meeting Here Tonight.

Variety, 60 min., Syndicated, 2/81. An hour of music, songs, and comedy sketches. *Host:* Bert Convy. *Guests:* Lynn Anderson, Carol Burnett, Conrad Janis, Steve Lawrence, Rich Little, George Segal, Dick Shawn. *Music:* Bob Rozario. *Producers:* Jack Barry, Dan Enright. *Writers:* Al Rogers, Ray Jessel. *Director:* Bill Foster.

## 182 The Best Christmas Pageant Ever. Comedy, 60 min., ABC, 12/5/83.

Grace Bradley is a harried housewife who has been given the job of directing the annual Christmas play for the local Sunday School. When the six meanest kids in town, the Herdman kids, hear about the play, they muscle in and take over the main roles of Mary, Joseph, and the Wise Men. Grace's efforts to save the play—and teach the Herdmans the true meaning of the holiday—is the focal point of the story. *Cast:* Loretta Swit (Grace Bradley), Jackson Davies (Bob Bradley), Megan Hunt (Imogene Herdman), Glen Reid (Ralph Herdman), Teri Dean (Gladys Herdman), Jason Micus (Leroy Herdman), Beau Heaton (Claude Herdman), Shane Punt (Ollie Herdman), Janet Wright (Helen Armstrong), Anthony Holland (the Reverend Hopkins). *Producer:* Merrill Karpf. *Writer:* Barbara Robinson. *Producer-Director:* George Schaefer.

## 183 Best Foot Forward. Musical, 90 min., NBC, 11/20/54.

Gale Joy is a fading movie star who accompanies a student (Bud Hooper) to his Junior Prom. Complications set in when she is recognized at the dance, stripped practically naked by souvenir-seeking students, and takes refuge in the men's dormitory—a situation that threatens the expulsion of several students. The efforts of all concerned to straighten out the situation and return the school to normal are the focal point of this adaptation of the Broadway play by John Cecil Holm. *Cast:* Marilyn Maxwell (Gale Joy), Bob Cummings (Jack Haggerty), Charlie Applewhite (Bud Hooper), Hope Holliday (Minerva), Jeannie Carson (Helen Twitterton), Harrison Miller (Dutch), Arte Johnson (Chuck), James Komack (Hunk), Howard St. John (Dean Reeber). *Music:* Charles Sanford. *Producer-Director:* Max Liebman. *Writers:* Neil Simon, Will Glickman, Fred Saidy, William Friedberg, William Jacobson.

## 184 Best Legs in the 8th Grade. Comedy, 60 min., HBO, 10/7/84.

A bittersweet comedy about an unplanned reunion between Mark Fisher, a nerd-turned-lawyer, and Leslie Applegate, his former high school heartthrob, when they meet by chance at a health spa. (The title refers to Leslie, who was voted the girl with the best legs in eighth grade.) *Cast:* Tim Matheson (Mark Fisher), Kathryn Harrold (Leslie Applegate), Annette O'Toole (Rachel Blackstone), Jim Belushi (St. Valentine). *Music:* Lee Holdridge. *Producers:* Michael Lepiner, Marcia Lewis. *Writer:* Bruce Feirstein. *Director:* Tom Patchett.

## 185 The Best Little Special in Texas. Variety, 60 min., Syndicated,

7/82. A country music jamboree celebrating the premiere of the movie *The Best Little Whorehouse in Texas* (which stars Dolly Parton, Burt Reynolds, and Jim Nabors). *Host:* Jerry Reed. *Guests:* Amanda Blake, Dom DeLuise, Charles Durning, Jim Nabors, Dolly Parton, Burt Reynolds, The Statler Brothers, Mel Tillis, Tanya Tucker. *Producer-Writers:* Bob Booker, Jack Thompson. *Director:* Jack Regas.

## 186 The Best of Anything.
Comedy, 60 min., NBC, 3/4/60. A live special that spoofs award shows and ceremonies through a series of satirical comedy sketches. *Host:* Art Carney. *Guests:* Beatrice Arthur, Betty Garrett, Roddy McDowall. *Music:* Bernard Green. *Producer:* David Susskind. *Writers:* Larry Gelbart, Sheldon Keller. *Director:* Burt Shevelove.

## 187 Best of Country Music '92.
Variety, 2 hrs., ABC, 12/10/92. A salute to country music's top songs and singers of 1992. *Hosts:* Clint Black, Mary-Chapin Carpenter. *Guests:* Brooks and Dunn, Billy Dean, Billy Ray Cyrus, Vince Gill, Alan Jackson, Lorrie Morgan, Sawyer Brown, Shenandoah, Marty Stuart, Pam Tillis, Randy Travis, Ricky Van Shelton. *Producer:* Don Weiner. *Director:* Gary Halverson.

## 188 The Best of Disney: 50 Years of Magic.
Variety, 2 hrs., ABC, 5/20/91. A look at the Disney entertainment empire on the occasion of the fiftieth anniversary of the Disney Studios in Burbank, California. The program features clips from Disney films and television series, and never before seen footage of behind-the-scenes activities at Disney theme parks. *Hosts:* Harry Connick, Jr.; Annette Funicello, Teri Garr, Daryl Hannah, Neil Patrick Harris, Shelley Long, Dick Van Dyke. *Producers:* Don Mischer, David Goldberg. *Director:* Don Mischer.

## 189 The Best of Disney Music.
Variety, 60 min., CBS, 2/3/93 and 5/21/93. Two 60-minute specials that present songs from over sixty years of Disney's animated feature films— from *Silly Symphonies*, to *The Three Little Pigs*, to *Aladdin*. *Hosts:* Angela Lansbury (2/3/93), Glenn Close (5/21/93). *Guests:* Branford Marsalis (2/3/93), Placido Domingo (5/21/93). *Music:* Glen Roven. *Producers:* Don Mischer, Phil Savenick, Harry Arends. *Writers:* Buz Kohan, Mark Saltzman. *Director:* Don Mischer.

## 190 The Best of Friends.
Drama, 60 min., Syndicated, 8/81. A television adaptation of Ernest Hemingway's *Three Day Blow*. The story of a love triangle that develops between three friends during a holiday in Colorado when Marge Adams leaves her husband, Nick, and makes a play for their friend, Bill. *Cast:* Carol Lynley (Marge Adams), Peter Graves (Nick Adams), Alex Cord (Bill), George Sawaya (River man), Jim Skags (Man at bar). *Producer:* Robert Halmi. *Writer:* Venable Herndon. *Director:* Ron Satlof.

## 191 The Best of SCTV.
Comedy, 2 hrs., ABC, 9/21/88. Clips of eight years of SCTV (Second City Television, 1976–84) are shown as SCTV studio owner Guy Caballero (Joe Flaherty) and his station manager Edith Prickley (Andrea Martin) face a congressional committee to defend their station's right to have its license renewed. *Cast:* John Candy, Joe Flaherty, Don Lake, Eugene Levy, Andrea Martin, Rick Moranis, Catherine O'Hara, Martin Short, Betty Thomas. *Producers:* Andrew Alexander, Joe Flaherty, Patrick Whitley. *Writers:* John Candy, Joe Flaherty, Andrea Martin, Catherine O'Hara, Eugene Levy, Martin Short, Rick Moranis, Harold Ramis. *Directors:* Jim Blake, Paul Flaherty.

## 192 The Best of the Hollywood Palace.
Variety, 60 min., ABC,

11/25/92. Also "More of the Best of the Hollywood Palace," 5/11/93. A compilation of clips from "The Hollywood Palace" (ABC, 1964–70) that showcases the top names in show business. *Host:* Suzanne Somers. *Producers:* Peggy Sandvig, Malcolm Leo, David Fairfield. *Writers:* Sam Denoff, Marc Sheffler, Malcolm Leo. *Director:* Malcolm Leo.

**193 The Best on Record.** Variety, 60 min., NBC, 5/18/65. Performances by the winners of the 1964 Grammy Awards. *Host:* Dean Martin. *Guests:* Woody Allen, Louis Armstrong, Eddy Arnold, Tony Bennett, Godfrey Cambridge, Carol Channing, Petula Clark, Sammy Davis, Jr.; Arthur Fiedler, Jack Jones, Steve Lawrence, Peter Sellers, Frank Sinatra. *Music:* Les Brown.

**194 Bette Midler — Art or Bust.** Variety, 60 min., HBO, 8/18/84. A solo concert by Bette Midler ("The Divine Miss M"). *Host:* Bette Midler. *Music:* Bob Kaminsky, Bob Martino. *Producers:* Thomas Schlamme, Peter Kauff, Bob Meyrowitz. *Writers:* Bette Midler, Jerry Blatt. *Director:* Thomas Schlamme.

**195 Bette Midler — Ol' Red Hair Is Back.** Variety, 60 min., NBC, 12/7/77. An hour of music, songs, and light comedy. *Host:* Bette Midler. *Guests:* Dustin Hoffman, Emmett Kelly. *Producers:* Aaron Russo, Gary Smith, Dwight Hemion. *Writers:* Buz Kohan, Jerry Blatt, Pat McCormick, Rod Warren, Bette Midler. *Director:* Dwight Hemion.

**196 The Bette Midler Show.** Variety, 60 min., HBO, 6/19/76. Music and songs coupled with light comedy. *Host:* Bette Midler. *Guests:* The Dick York Band, The Harlettes (Sharon Redd, Ula Hedwig, Charlotte Crossley). *Producer:* Aaron Russo. *Writers:* Bruce Vilanche, Jerry Blatt. *Director:* Tom Trbovich.

**197 Bette Midler's Mondo Beyondo.** Variety, 60 min., HBO, 3/19/88. A spoof of public access cable programs with Mondo Beyondo, a rather bizarre woman who hosts "The Mondo Beyondo Show" and presents various variety acts. *Host:* Bette Midler (as Mondo Beyondo). *Guests:* David Gale, Bill Irwin, The Kipper Kids, Pat Oleszko, The Yes/No People, Paul Zaloom. *Music:* Marc Shaiman. *Producers:* Martin von Haselberg, Fred Berner. *Writers:* Jerry Blatt, Bette Midler. *Director:* Thomas Schlamme.

**198 Between Two Loves.** Drama, 60 min., ABC, 10/27/82. Susan Adams plays sixth chair, the lowest rung in the violin section of her high school orchestra. She does not take her music seriously until her teacher, Henry Forbes, tells her that with practice she could win a college scholarship. Susan takes his advice and improves dramatically. The story follows Susan's dilemma when her teacher enters her in a contest that pits her against her boyfriend, Doug Henshaw, the orchestra's first chair violinist. An "ABC Afterschool Special." *Cast:* Karlene Crockett (Susan Adams), Lance Guest (Doug Henshaw), Robert Reed (Henry Forbes), Barbara Tarbuck (Mrs. Adams), Michelle LaMar (Pam Schultz). *Music:* Al Allen. *Producer:* Martin Tahse. *Writer:* Paul W. Cooper. *Director:* Robert C. Thompson.

**199 A Beverly Hills Christmas.** Variety, 60 min., Fox, 12/22/87. A program of Christmas music and songs from Beverly Hills. *Host:* James Stewart. *Guests:* Lucille Ball, The Bronson Brothers, George Burns, The Caroling Company, Lee Greenwood, Walter Matthau, Jeffrey Osborne, Alison Porter, Burt Reynolds. *Producers:* Earl Durham, Mark Shaw. *Writer:* Anita Doohan. *Director:* Woody Fraser.

**200 The Big Band and All That Jazz.** Variety, 60 min., NBC,

11/29/72. The program features performances by jazz personalities. *Host:* Doc Severinsen. *Guests:* Count Basie, The Dave Brubeck Quartet, Duke Ellington, Ella Fitzgerald, Dizzy Gillespie, Benny Goodman, Bobby Hackett, Lionel Hampton, Gene Krupa, Teddy Wilson. *Producers:* Burt Rosen, David Winters. *Writer:* Donald Rosen. *Director:* Grey Lockwood.

## 201 Big Henry and the Polka Dot Kid. Drama, 60 min., NBC, 11/9/76.

The story follows the adventures of a ten-year-old boy named Luke and his blind dog, Dan. *Cast:* Ned Beatty (Big Henry), Chris Barnes (Luke Baldwin), Estelle Parsons (Edwina Kemp), Barry Corbin (Stokey Andrews). *Music:* Carl Davis. *Producers:* George A. Heinemann, Linda Gottlieb. *Writer:* W. W. Lewis. *Director:* Richard Marquand.

## 202 The Big Hex of Little Lulu. Comedy, 30 min., ABC, 1/16 and 1/23/81.

The misadventures of Little Lulu, a young girl with a knack for finding mischief. The story itself relates Lulu's efforts to raise money for hockey uniforms by tricking her reluctant-to-help friend, Tubby, into believing he is hexed — and the curse can only be lifted if he contributes to the fund. An "ABC Weekend Special." See also "Little Lulu." *Cast:* Lauri Hendler (Little Lulu), Annrae Walterhouse (Gloria), Robbie Rist (Iggie), Kevin King Cooper (Tubby), Lulu Baxter (Anne), Billy Jacoby (Alvin), Frances Bay (Madame Zarona). *Music:* Tommy Leonetti. *Producers:* Robert Chenault, Ann Elder. *Writers:* Ann Elder, Cindy Leonetti. *Director:* Robert Chenault.

## 203 The Big Sell. Comedy, 60 min., CBS, 10/9/60.

Comedy sketches that spoof "The Great American Salesman." *Cast:* Jackie Gleason, Phil Harris, T. C. Jones, Jack Lescoulie. *Producer:* Jack Philbin. *Writers:* A. J. Russell, Sydney Zelenka, Walter Stone. *Director:* Frank Bunetta.

## 204 The Big Stuffed Dog. Comedy, 60 min., NBC, 2/8/80.

Petey Pearson is a young boy who is looking forward to visiting his grandfather. Petey is very attached to his five-feet-tall Snoopy dog and insists on taking it with him, especially since he will be flying alone. At the airport Petey finds that he cannot board the plane with the dog and must send it to the plane's baggage section. A reluctant Petey gives up Snoopy and boards the plane — but the dog does not reach its intended destination. A series of vignettes follow depicting how people's lives are affected by contact with Snoopy. *Cast:* Rossie Harris (Petey), Noah Beery (Grandfather), Sydney Penny (Lily), Robert Ginty (Petey's father), Gordon Jump (Crazy), Denise Nicholas (Nurse Reilly), Sharon Spelman (Petey's mother), Mildred Dunnock (Old Woman), Abe Vigoda (Carnival pitchman). *Music:* Ed Bogas, Judy Munsen. *Producer:* Karen Crommie. *Writers:* Charles M. Schulz, Karen Crommie. *Director:* Robert Feust.

## 205 The Big Time. Variety, 90 min., NBC, 2/27/55.

A lavish musical revue featuring music, songs, dances, and comedy sketches. *Hosts:* Milton Berle, Ray Bolger, Martha Raye. *Guests:* Rod Alexander, The Bil and Cora Baird Puppets, Fred Clark, Brenda Forbes, Sylvia Lewis, Bambi Linn. *Music:* Charles Sanford. *Producer-Director:* Max Liebman.

## 206 Bill Cosby Specials.

A chronological listing of comedian Bill Cosby's television specials. All feature sketches and monologues tailored to Bill Cosby's unique comedy wit. All are 60 minutes each. Bill Cosby hosted each show.

**1 The Bill Cosby Special** (NBC, 3/20/68). *Guests:* Sheldon Leonard, Janice Robinson. *Producers:* Bill Persky, Sam Denoff, Bill Hobin. *Writers:* Bill Persky, Sam Denoff. *Director:* Bill Hobin.

**2 Bill Cosby Does His Own Thing** (NBC, 2/9/69). *Guests:* The Art Reynolds Singers, The Donald McKayle Dancers. *Music:* Jack Elliott. *Producers:* Roy Silver, Bruce Campbell. *Writers:* Frank Burton, Ed Weinberger. *Director:* Seymour Berns. *Note:* Although this is Bill Cosby's second special, his 1968 special was overlooked, and this is considered "The First Bill Cosby Special" for a trio of specials that aired in 1969 and 1970.

**3 The Second Bill Cosby Special** (NBC, 3/11/69). *Guests:* The Art Reynolds Singers. *Producer:* Roy Silver. *Director:* Seymour Berns. *Note:* Also known as "A Special Bill Cosby Special."

**4 The Third Bill Cosby Special** (NBC, 4/1/70). *Guest:* Roberta Flack. *Producer:* Marvin Miller. *Writers:* Ed Weinberger, Bill Cosby. *Director:* Vantile Whitfield.

**5 The Bill Cosby Special, Or?** (NBC, 3/2/71). *Guests:* Johnny Brown, John Denver, Billy Eckstein, Herb Edelman, Dizzy Gillespie, Bill Henderson, Burgess Meredith, Nancy Wilson. *Producers:* William H. Cosby, Jr., Marvin Miller. *Writers:* Bill Cosby, Michael Elias, Frank Shaw, Sid Green, Dave Hill, Ray Jessel. *Director:* Ivan Dixon.

**6 Cos: The Bill Cosby Comedy Special** (CBS, 11/10/75). *Guests:* Loretta Lynn, Tony Randall, Karen Valentine. *Music:* Milton DeLugg. *Producer:* Joseph Cates. *Writers:* Larry Markes, Tony Geiss, June Reisner. *Director:* Walter C. Miller.

## 207 Billy Crystal: A Comic's Line. Comedy, 60 min., HBO, 2/10/84.

A comical depiction of the problems Billy Crystal faces from his friends and family as he prepares for a solo concert on television. *Cast:* Billy Crystal (Himself), Norman Friedman (Billy's father), Paul Garner (Uncle Lou), Jeannie Linero (Billy's mother), David Steinberg (Casting director), Toni Nero (Billy's girlfriend), Twyla Littlejohn (Cheerleader), Cathy Lee Crosby (Herself), Johnny Yune (Himself). *Producers:* Buddy Morra, Larry Brezner. *Writers:* Billy Crystal, Rocco Urbisci. *Director:* Bruce Gowers.

## 208 Billy Joel — A TV First.

Variety, 60 min., HBO, 7/24/83. A solo concert by singer Billy Joel in his first television special. *Host:* Billy Joel. *Producers:* Frank Weber, Jeff Schock, Rick London, Jon Small. *Director:* Jay Dubin.

## 209 Billy Joel from Leningrad, USSR. Music, 60 min., HBO, 10/24/87.

Highlights of Billy Joel's musical tour of the USSR. Taped over three nights in August 1987 at the V. I. Lenin Sports and Concert Complex in Leningrad. *Host:* Billy Joel. *Billy's Band:* Liberty DeVitto (drums), Doug Stegmeyer (bass), Dave LeBolt (keyboards), Russell Javors (guitar), Kevin Dukes (guitar), Mark Rivera (sax), Peter Hewett, George Simms (backup vocal). *Producers:* Frank Weber, Rick London. *Director:* Wayne Isham.

## 210 The Billy Joel Special.

Music, 90 min., ABC, 6/15/88. A network version of the prior Billy Joel title that adds additional footage not seen on the cable version as it chronicles Billy's 1987 tour of the Soviet Union. *Host:* Billy Joel. *Guests:* Christie Brinkley, Alexa Ray. *Producer:* Frank Weber.

## 211 The Billy Ray Cyrus Special: Dreams Come True. Variety, 60 min., ABC, 2/17/93.

A concert by country singer Billy Ray Cyrus that features selections from his album *Some Gave All.* *Host:* Billy Ray Cyrus. *Guests:* Mary-Chapin Carpenter, Kathy Mattea, Dolly Parton. *Producers:* Jack McFadden, Anthony Eaton. *Director:* Jeff Margolis.

**Bing! . . . A 50th Anniversary Gala** *see* **Bing Crosby Specials**

## 212 Bing Crosby and Carol Burnett — Together Again for the First Time. Variety, 60 min., NBC, 12/17/69.

An hour of music, songs, and light comedy as Carol Burnett jumps networks (from CBS) to join Bing for a holiday special. *Hosts:* Carol Burnett, Bing Crosby. *Guests:* Roy Clark, Juliet Prowse. *Music:* John Scott Trotter. *Producers:* Nick Vanoff, William O. Harbach. *Writers:* Sheldon Keller, Kenny Solms, Gail Parent. *Director:* Grey Lockwood.

**Bing Crosby and Friends** *see* **Bing Crosby Specials**

**Bing Crosby and His Friends** *see* **Bing Crosby Specials**

**Bing Crosby and the Sounds of Christmas** *see* **Bing Crosby Specials**

**Bing Crosby — Cooling It** *see* **Bing Crosby Specials**

## 213 Bing Crosby Specials.

A chronological listing of singer-actor Bing Crosby's television specials. Each is 60 minutes in length (except where noted) and each is a program of music, songs, and light comedy. Bing Crosby hosted each show.

**1 The Bing Crosby Special** (CBS, 1/3/54). *Guests:* Jack Benny, Sheree North. *Music:* John Scott Trotter. *Producer-Writer:* Bill Morrow. *Director:* Fred DeCordova.

**2 The Bing Crosby Special** (CBS, 4/25/54). *Guests:* Buddy Cole, Joanne Gilbert, The Wiere Brothers. *Music:* John Scott Trotter. *Producer-Writer:* Bill Morrow. *Director:* Leslie Goodwins.

**3 Bing Crosby and His Friends** (CBS, 1/12/58). *Guests:* Kathryn Grant, Howard Keel, Fred MacMurray, Guy Madison, Dean Martin, Dennis O'Keefe, Randolph Scott. *Music:* Buddy Cole. *Producer:* Cecil Baker. *Writer:* Joe Quillan. *Director:* Seymour Berns.

**4 The Bing Crosby Special** (ABC, 10/2/58). *Guests:* Mahalia Jackson, Dean Martin, Patti Page. *Music:* Buddy Cole. *Producer:* Bill Colleran. *Writer:* Bill Morrow. *Director:* Seymour Berns.

**5 The Bing Crosby Special** (ABC, 3/2/59). *Guests:* Dennis Crosby, Philip Crosby, James Garner, Tom Hanson, Jo Stafford, Thelma Tadlock. *Music:* Nelson Riddle. *Producer-Director:* Bill Colleran. *Writer:* Bill Morrow.

**6 The Bing Crosby Special** (ABC, 9/29/59). *Guests:* Louis Armstrong, Joe Bushkin, Peggy Lee, George Shearing, Frank Sinatra, Paul Smith, Jane Turner. *Music:* Axel Stordahl. *Producers:* Sammy Cahn, Bill Colleran. *Writer:* Bill Morrow. *Director:* Bill Colleran.

**7 The Bing Crosby Special** (ABC, 2/29/60). *Guests:* Perry Como, Dennis Crosby, Lindsay Crosby, Philip Crosby, Elaine Dunne, Sandy Stewart. *Music:* Vic Schoen. *Producer-Director:* Walter O. Harbach. *Writers:* Sheldon Keller, Saul Ilson, Herb Sargent, James Elson.

**8 The Bing Crosby Special** (ABC, 10/5/60). *Guests:* Rosemary Clooney, Dennis Crosby, Lindsay Crosby, Philip Crosby, Johnny Mercer. *Music:* Nelson Riddle. *Producer-Director:* William O. Harbach. *Writers:* Herb Sargent, Sheldon Keller, Saul Ilson, James Elson.

**9 The Bing Crosby Special** (ABC, 3/22/61). *Guests:* Maurice Chevalier, Hugh Lambert, Carol Lawrence. *Music:* Nelson Riddle. *Producer-Director:* William O. Harbach. *Writers:* Bill Morrow, George Foster, Saul Ilson.

**10 The Bing Crosby Springtime Special** (ABC, 5/14/62). *Guests:* Edie Adams, Pete Fountain, Bob Hope, Tom and Dick Smothers. *Music Director:* David Rose.

**11 The Bing Crosby Christmas Show** (ABC, 12/14/62). *Guests:* Mary Martin, Andre Previn, The UN Children's Choir. *Music:* Andre Previn. *Producer:* Nick Vanoff. *Writers:* Bill Morrow, Max Wilk. *Director:* Norman Abbott.

**12 The Bing Crosby Special** (NBC, 11/7/63). *Guests:* Buddy Ebsen, Andre Previn, Caterina Valente, The Young Americans. *Music:* Andre Previn. *Producer-Director:* Nick Vanoff. *Writers:* Bill Morrow, Max Wilk.

**13 The Bing Crosby Special** (CBS, 2/15/64). *Guests:* Rosemary Clooney, Kathryn Crosby, Peter Gennaro, Bob Hope, Dean Martin, Frank Sinatra. *Music:* John Scott Trotter. *Producer-Director:* Nick Vanoff. *Writers:* Howard Leeds, Sid Dorfman, Bob Rodgers, Bill Morrow.

**14 The Bing Crosby Special** (NBC, 10/23/68). *Guests:* Jose Feliciano, Bob Hope, Diana Ross and the Supremes, Stella Stevens. *Producer:* Ray Charles. *Writers:* Bill Morrow, Hal Fimberg. *Director:* Marc Breaux.

**15 Bing Crosby and Carol Burnett — Together Again for the First Time** (NBC, 12/17/69). See title for information.

**16 Bing Crosby — Cooling It** (NBC, 4/1/70). *Guests:* Dean Martin, Bernadette Peters, Flip Wilson. *Music:* Nick Perito. *Producer:* Bob Finkel. *Writers:* Buz Kohan, Bill Angelos. *Director:* Art Fisher.

**17 Bing Crosby's Christmas Show** (NBC, 12/16/70). *Guests:* Joe Besser, Harry Crosby, Kathryn Crosby, Mary Crosby, Nathaniel Crosby, The Doodletown Pipers, Melba Moore, Jack Wild. *Music:* Nick Perito. *Producer:* Bill Angelos. *Writers:* Buz Kohan, Bill Angelos, Rod Warren. *Director:* Marty Pasetta.

**18 Bing Crosby and the Sounds of Christmas** (NBC, 12/14/71). *Guests:* Mary Costa, Harry Crosby, Kathryn Crosby, Mary Crosby, Nathaniel Crosby, Robert Goulet, The Mitchell Boys Choir. *Music:* Ray Charles. *Producer:* Bob Finkel. *Writers:* Buz Kohan, Bill Angelos. *Director:* Ray Klaussen.

**19 Christmas with the Bing Crosbys** (NBC, 12/10/72). *Guests:* Harry Crosby, Kathryn Crosby, Mary Crosby, Nathaniel Crosby, David Hartman, Sally Struthers, Edward Villella. *Music:* Nick Perito. *Producer:* Bob Finkel. *Writers:* Buz Kohan, Bill Angelos. *Director:* Marty Pasetta.

**20 Bing Crosby's Sun Valley Christmas Show** (NBC, 12/9/73). *Guests:* John Byner, Harry Crosby, Kathryn Crosby, Mary Crosby, Nathaniel Crosby, Michael Landon, Connie Stevens. *Music:* Nick Perito. *Producer:* Bob Finkel. *Writers:* Buz Kohan, Bill Angelos. *Director:* Art Fisher.

**21 Bing Crosby and Friends** (CBS, 10/9/74). *Guests:* Pearl Bailey, Sandy Duncan, Bob Hope. *Music:* Peter Matz. *Producer:* Bob Finkel. *Writers:* Harry Crane, George Bloom, Mitzie Welch, Ken Welch. *Director:* Marty Pasetta.

**22 Christmas with the Bing Crosbys** (NBC, 12/15/74). *Guests:* Harry Crosby, Kathryn Crosby, Mary Crosby, Nathaniel Crosby, Mac Davis, Karen Valentine. *Music:* Peter Matz. *Producer:* Bob Finkel. *Writers:* Buz Kohan, Bill Angelos. *Director:* Marty Pasetta.

**23 Merry Christmas, Fred, from the Crosbys** (CBS, 12/3/75). *Special Guest:* Fred Astaire. *Guests:* Joe Bushkin, Harry Crosby, Kathryn Crosby, Mary Crosby, Nathaniel Crosby, The Young Americans. *Music:* Ian Fraser. *Producers:* Gary Smith, Dwight Hemion. *Writer:* Buz Kohan. *Director:* Dwight Hemion. *Note:* The format has Fred Astaire dropping by to discuss a new record album with Bing. The visit inspires reminiscences and family fun as Fred joins Bing, his wife, Kathryn, and their children, Harry, Mary Frances, and Nathaniel for Christmas.

**24 Bing Crosby's White Christmas** (CBS, 12/1/76). *Guests:* Harry Crosby, Kathryn Crosby, Mary Crosby, Nathaniel Crosby, Bernadette Peters. *Music:* Peter Knight. *Producer:* Frank Konigsberg. *Writer:* Herbert Baker. *Producer-Director:* Norman Campbell.

**25 Bing! ... A 50th Anniversary Gala** (90 min., CBS, 3/20/77). *Guests:* Paul Anka, Pearl Bailey, Rosemary

Clooney, Harry Crosby, Kathryn Crosby, Mary Crosby, Nathaniel Crosby, Sandy Duncan, Bob Hope, The Mills Brothers, Donald O'Connor, Martha Raye, Debbie Reynolds, Bette Midler, Anson Williams. *Music:* Nick Perito. *Producer:* Frank Konigsberg. *Writer:* Buz Kohan. *Director:* Marty Pasetta. *Note:* The program celebrates Bing Crosby's fifty years in showbusiness.

**26 Bing Crosby's Merrie Olde Christmas** (NBC, 11/30/77). *Guests:* Stanley Baxter, David Bowie, Harry Crosby, Kathryn Crosby, Mary Crosby, Nathaniel Crosby, Ron Moody, Twiggy. *Music:* Ian Fraser. *Producer:* Frank Konigsberg. *Writer:* Buz Kohan. *Director:* Dwight Hemion.

**Bing Crosby's Merrie Olde Christmas** *see* **Bing Crosby Specials**

**Bing Crosby's White Christmas** *see* **Bing Crosby Specials**

**214 Biography of a Boy.** Variety, 60 min., ABC, 8/3/60. A musical songfest in which the songs of the 1920s are sung as a man (Merv Griffin) reminisces about his youth. *Host:* Merv Griffin. *Guests:* Lauri Peters, June Valli. *Music:* Glenn Osser.

**215 The Black Arrow.** Cartoon, 60 min., Syndicated, 1/89. The story, set in England in the mid-1500s, dramatizes the famous War of the Roses, which divided England and placed it in a civil war—the rich against the poor—for thirty years. Based on the story by Robert Louis Stevenson. *Voices:* Bob Baines, Claire Crowther, Philip Hinton, Graham Matters, Lloyd Morris. *Music:* Mark Isaacs. *Producer:* Tom Stacey. *Writer:* Paul Leadon. *Director:* Alex Nicholas.

**216 Black Beauty.** Cartoon, 60 min., CBS, 10/28/78. An animated adaptation of Anna Sewell's cherished tale of Black Beauty, a proud but gentle horse, as he learns the perils of life lived at the mercy of human masters. *Voices:* Cathleen Cordell, Alan Dinehart, Mike Evans, David Gregory, Barbara Stevens, Alan Young, Cam Young. *Music:* Australian Screen Music. *Producer:* Neil Balnaves. *Writer:* Kimmer Ringwald. *Director:* Chris Cuddington.

**217 Blind Alleys.** Drama, 60 min., Syndicated, 9/85. A powerful drama about the problems of a troubled interracial marriage as seen through the eyes of Kenji Sato, a bitter and disillusioned Japanese American, and his American wife, Fran, when he returns after a three-year absence to attend the wedding of his daughter, Amy. *Cast:* Pat Morita (Kenji Sato), Cloris Leachman (Fran Sato), June Angela (Amy Sato), Frederic Kimball (Woody), Dean Norris (Peter Brockway), Nada Rowand (Clara Brockway), Charles Werner Moore (Art Brockway). *Music:* Peter Bell, Peter Johnson. *Producers:* Charles Kravetz, Lisa Schmidt. *Writers:* David Hwang, Frederic Kimball. *Directors:* David Wheeler, Bill Coswell.

**218 Blind Sunday.** Drama, 60 min., ABC, 4/21/76. A sensitive "ABC Afterschool Special" about the friendship between a sightless girl (Eileen) and a sighted boy (Jeff) and his attempts to strengthen their relationship by spending a day blindfolded. *Cast:* Jewel Blanch (Eileen), Leigh McCloskey (Jeff), Betty Beaird (Mrs. Hays), Robert Ridgely (Jeff's father), Corbin Bernsen (Lifeguard), Cindy Eilbacher (Marge), Debi Storm (Pam), Steve Tanner (Erik). *Music:* Michel Legrand. *Producer:* Daniel Wilson. *Writers:* Arthur Barron, Fred Pressburger. *Director:* Larry Elikann.

**219 Blithe Spirit.** Fantasy, 90 min., NBC, 5/12/46. The story of a novelist (Charles) and his efforts to live with two wives — his second wife, Ruth, and the spirit of Elvira, his first, who appears and speaks only to him. Based on the 1941 play by Noel Coward. *Cast:* Philip Tonge (Charles Condomine), Carol Goodner (Ruth Condomine), Lenore Corbett (Elvira Condomine), Alexander Clark (Dr. Bradman), Valerie Cossart (Mrs. Bradman), Doreen Lang (Edith). *Producer-Director:* Edward Sobol.

**220 Blithe Spirit.** Fantasy, 90 min., CBS, 1/14/56. A second television adaptation of Noel Coward's 1941 Broadway play about a novelist with two wives — Ruth, his second wife, and the spirit of Elvira, his first wife, who has come back to haunt him. *Cast:* Noel Coward (Charles Condomine), Claudette Colbert (Ruth Condomine), Lauren Bacall (Elvira Condomine), Mildred Natwick (Madame Arcati), Marion Ross (Edith), Philip Tonge (Dr. Bradman), Brenda Forbes (Mrs. Bradman). *Producers:* Charles Russell, Lance Hamilton, Richard Lewine. *Writer:* Noel Coward. *Directors:* Noel Coward, Fred DeCordova.

**221 Blithe Spirit.** Fantasy, 90 min., NBC, 12/7/66. A third television adaptation of Noel Coward's play about a novelist whose second marriage is threatened by the ghost of his first wife. Aired on the "Hallmark Hall of Fame." *Cast:* Dirk Bogarde (Charles Condomine), Rosemary Harris (Elvira Condomine), Rachel Roberts (Ruth Condomine), Ruth Gordon (Madame Arcati). *Producer-Director:* George Schaefer. *Writer:* Noel Coward.

**222 Blockheads.** Comedy, 60 min., HBO, 11/24/82. The program features performances by the country's top ventriloquists. *Host:* Mariette Hartley. *Ventriloquists:* Jay Johnson, Chris Kirby, Terry Rogers, Bruce D. Schwartz, Willie Tyler. *Music:* Bob Rosengarden. *Producers:* Michael Brandman, Susan Masters. *Writer:*

Howard Kiperberg. *Director:* Henry Polonsky.

**223 Blondes vs. Brunettes.** Variety, 60 min., ABC, 5/14/84. A light-hearted comedy special that attempts to dispel the myths about personality traits of blondes and brunettes. *Hosts:* Joan Collins, Morgan Fairchild. *Guests:* Elizabeth Ashley, Catherine Bach, Pamela Bellwood, Dr. Joyce Brothers, Phyllis Diller, Kerry Millerick, Rita Moreno, Brooke Shields. *Music:* Fred Tahler. *Producers:* Claude Ravier, Steve Binder. *Writers:* Rod Warren, George Beckerman, Don Novello, David Scott Jones, Buz Kohan, Lisa Medway. *Directors:* Steve Binder, Sterling Johnson.

**224 Blondie.** Music, 60 min., HBO, 4/19/83. A solo rock concert by the group Blondie (Deborah Harry, Clem Burke, James Destri, Nigel Harrison, Chris Stern, Eddie Martinez). *Producers:* Shep Gordon, Ken Weinstock, Stan Harris. *Director:* Stan Harris.

**225 Blondie and Dagwood.** Cartoon, 30 min., CBS, 5/15/87. The first animated television adaptation of the Depression-era comic about marrieds Blondie and Dagwood Bumstead and their children, Cookie and Alexander. The updated (to 1987) story finds Blondie taking a job when Dagwood is fired from his job as an architect from the J. C. Dithers Construction Company. *Voices:* Loni Anderson (Blondie Bumstead), Frank Welker (Dagwood Bumstead), Ellen Gerstel (Cookie Bumstead), Ike Eisenman (Alexander Bumstead), Alan Oppenheimer (J. C. Dithers), Russi Taylor (Cora Dithers), Laurel Page (Tootsie), Jack Angel (Mr. Beasley/Herb Woodley), Pat Fraley (Daisy). *Music:* Rob Walsh. *Producers:* Margaret Loesch, Lee Gunther, Hank Saroyan. *Writers* (based on the comic by Dean Young and Stan Drake): Bob Smith, Barry O'Brien. *Director:* Mike Joens.

**226 Blondie and Dagwood: Second Wedding Workout.** Cartoon, 30 min., CBS, 11/1/89. A second Blondie animated special (see "Blondie and Dagwood") in which Dagwood Bumstead struggles to complete a building project in order to receive a bonus to pay for Blondie's twentieth wedding anniversary gift. Based on the comic strip by Dean Young and Stan Drake. *Voices:* Loni Anderson (Blondie Bumstead), Frank Welker (Dagwood Bumstead), Ellen Gerstel (Cookie Bumstead), Ike Eisenman (Alexander Bumstead), Alan Oppenheimer (J. C. Dithers), Russi Taylor (Cora Dithers). *Producers:* Bruce L. Paisner, Hank Saroyan. *Writers:* Barry O'Brien, Bob Smith. *Director:* Bob Shellhorn.

**227 Bloomer Girl.** Musical, 90 min., NBC, 5/28/56. The story, set in Cicero Falls, New York, in 1850, tells of young Elvinia Applegate and her crusade for women's rights. Based on the Broadway play. *Cast:* Barbara Cook (Elvinia Applegate), Keith Andes (Jeff Calhoun), Paul Ford (Horatio Applegate), Nydia Westman (Serena Applegate), Paula Stewart (Julie), Elsie Rhodes (Octavia), Jack Russell (Joshua), Danny Scholl (Ebenezer), Paul McGrath (Governor). *Songs:* Harold Arlen, E. Y. Harburg.

**228 The Blue Ribbon Christmas Eve Musical.** Variety, 30 min., CBS, 12/24/52. A Christmas Eve program of music and songs sponsored by Pabst Blue Ribbon Beer. *Host:* Gene Lockhart. *Guest:* Maria Tallchief (a ballerina). *Music:* David Rose.

**229 Bob and Ray and Jane, Laraine and Gilda.** Comedy, 90 min., NBC, 10/24/81. The program, set at the Finley Quality Network, spoofs television programs and commercials via comedy sketches. *Cast:* Jane Curtin, Bob Elliott, Ray Goulding, Laraine Newman, Gilda Radner. *Guest:* Willie Nelson. *Music:* Tom Malone. *Producer:* Lorne Michaels. *Writers:* Bob Elliott, Ray Goulding, Al Franken, Tom Davis, Jean Doumanian. *Director:* Dave Wilson.

**230 Bob Dylan in Concert.** Music, 55 min., HBO, 6/21/86. Highlights of Bob Dylan's 1986 True Confessions Tour. Taped at the Sydney, Australia, Entertainment Center in February 1986. *Host:* Bob Dylan. *Band:* Tom Petty (guitar/vocals), Mike Campbell (guitar), Stan Lynch (drums), Benmont Tench (keyboards), Howie Epstein (bass). *Producer:* Elliott Rabinowitz. *Director:* Gillian Armstrong.

**231 The Bob Goulet Show Starring Robert Goulet.** Variety, 60 min., ABC, 4/7/70. A fancy title for a simple program of music, songs, and comedy with singer Robert Goulet and his guests. *Host:* Robert Goulet. *Guests:* Diahann Carroll, The Clara Ward Gospel Singers, Bob Denver, Bob Hope. *Music:* Joe Guerico, Bill Reddie. *Choreography:* Claude Thompson.

**Bob Hope Buys NBC** *see* **Bob Hope Specials**

**Bob Hope: Don't Shoot, It's Only Me** *see* **Bob Hope Specials**

**Bob Hope for President** *see* **Bob Hope Specials**

**Bob Hope Goes to College** *see* **Bob Hope Specials**

**Bob Hope in Moscow** *see* **Bob Hope Specials**

**Bob Hope in Who Makes the World Laugh?** *see* **Bob Hope Specials**

**Bob Hope on Campus** *see* **Bob Hope Specials**

**Bob Hope on the Road to China** *see* **Bob Hope Specials**

**Bob Hope — On the Road with Bing** *see* **Bob Hope Specials**

**Bob Hope Presents the Stars of Tomorrow** *see* **Bob Hope Specials**

**232 Bob Hope Specials.** A chronological listing of 269 variety specials hosted by Bob Hope from 4/9/ 50 to 5/14/93. Specials with formats that differ from the usual hour of music, songs, monologues, and comedy sketches are referred to here but listed in detail elsewhere in the book. Les Brown is the musical director except where noted. Jack Hope (1950– 64), George Hope (1964–68), Mort Lachman (1968–70), and Bob Hope (1968–92) were the producers.

Bob first appeared on television in the summer of 1948 as the host of a 90- minute special broadcast from Madison Square Garden in New York. Bob, attired in an airman's uniform, hosted a salute to the men and women of the U.S. armed forces. Jerry Colonna and Jack Dempsey were the guests. Bob is famous for his Christmas shows, which were filmed at various military bases overseas (a tradition he began in 1941; his first telecast USO show was in 1950 during the Korean War). "Thanks for the Memory" is Bob's theme song (which he first sang with Shirley Ross in the film *The Big Broadcast of 1938*). All are 60 minutes in length (except where noted) and broadcast by NBC. All shows were hosted by Bob Hope, except where noted otherwise.

**1 The Bob Hope Show** (90 min., 4/9/50). *Guests:* Douglas Fairbanks, Jr., Beatrice Lillie, Dinah Shore. *Music:* Charles Sanford.

**2 The Bob Hope Show** (5/27/50). *Guests:* Bill Hayes, Michael Kid, Peggy Lee, Beatrice Lillie, Frank Sinatra, Arnold Stang. *Music:* Charles Sanford.

**3 The Bob Hope Show** (9/14/50). *Guests:* Lucille Ball, Bob Crosby, The Jack Cole Dancers, Dinah Shore. *Music:* Al Goodman.

**4 The Bob Hope Show** (11/26/50). *Guests:* The Hugh Hatter Dancers, Judy Kelly, Marilyn Maxwell, The Tailor Maids, Jimmy Wakeley. *Note:* The first of Bob's overseas tour shows (Bob relates how he and his troupe entertained GIs on their 25,000-mile tour of the Pacific bases in Japan and Korea).

**5 The Bob Hope Christmas Show** (12/24/50). *Guests:* Betty Bruce, Bob Cummings, Robert Maxwell, Lily Pons, Eleanor Roosevelt, The St. John's Cathedral Boys Choir.

**6 The Bob Hope Show** (4/8/51). *Guests:* Sid Caesar, Eddie Cantor, Imogene Coca, Jimmy Durante, Faye Emerson, Jinx Falkenberg, Rex Harrison, Tex McCary, Janis Paige, Lili Palmer.

**7 The Bob Hope Show** (10/14/51). *Guests:* Jerry Colonna, Dinah Shore.

**8 The Bob Hope Show** (11/25/51). *Guests:* William Bendix, Lina Romay.

**9 The Bob Hope Show** (3/9/52). *Guests:* Anna Maria Alberghetti, Martha Stewart.

**10 The Bob Hope Show** (4/26/52). *Guests:* The Bell Sisters, Fred MacMurray, Gale Robbins.

**11 The Bob Hope Show** (6/15/52). *Guest:* Paul Douglas.

**12 The Bob Hope Show** (10/12/52). *Guests:* The Clark Brothers, Connie Haines, Fred MacMurray.

**13 The Bob Hope Show** (11/9/52). *Guests:* Rosemary Clooney, The Four Step Brothers, Bill Goodwin.

**14 The Bob Hope Christmas Show** (12/7/52). *Guests:* The Esquire Calendar Girls, Frances Langford, Tony Martin.

**15 The Bob Hope Show** (1/4/53). *Guests:* Jack Buchanan, Don Cherry, Marilyn Maxwell.

**16 The Bob Hope Show** (2/1/53). *Guests:* Nelson Eddy, Margaret Whiting.

**17 The Bob Hope Show** (3/1/53). *Guests:* Robert Alda, George Jessel, Constance Moore.

**18 The Bob Hope Show** (3/22/53). *Guests:* Bud Abbott and Lou Costello, Eddie Cantor, Dean Martin and Jerry Lewis, Donald O'Connor. *Note:* Aired as the one hundredth telecast of "The Colgate Comedy Hour."

**19 The Bob Hope Show** (3/29/53). *Guest:* Rosemary Clooney.

**20 The Bob Hope Show** (4/19/53). *Guests:* Phil Harris, Marilyn Maxwell.

**21 The Bob Hope Show** (5/24/53). *Guests:* The Castro Sisters, Gloria De-Haven, Don McNeill.

**22 The Bob Hope Show** (6/14/53). *Guests:* Rosemary Clooney, Frankie Laine, Randy Merriman, Bess Myerson.

**23 The Bob Hope Show** (10/20/53). *Guests:* Gloria DeHaven, Phil Harris. *Note:* Music and comedy were centered around the Ohio sesquicentennial anniversary celebration.

**24 The Bob Hope Show** (11/17/53; Bob's first color special). *Guests:* Arlene Dahl, Fred MacMurray, Janis Paige.

**25 The Bob Hope Christmas Show** (12/14/53). *Guest:* Gale Storm.

**26 The Bob Hope Show** (1/26/54). *Guests:* Cass Daley, Zsa Zsa Gabor, Tony Martin.

**27 The Bob Hope Show** (2/16/54). *Guests:* Jerry Colonna, Gloria De-Haven, Nelson Eddy.

**28 The Bob Hope Show** (3/16/54). *Guests:* Jack Benny, Cass Daley, David Niven, Janis Paige.

**29 The Bob Hope Show** (4/13/54). *Guests:* Jack Benny, Rosemary Clooney, Jimmy Durante.

**30 The Bob Hope Show** (5/11/54). *Guests:* Dorothy Lamour, Sheldon Leonard, Edmond O'Brien.

**31 The Bob Hope Show** (6/1/54). *Guests:* Jack Benny, Cass Daley, Zsa Zsa Gabor, Marilyn Maxwell.

**32 The Bob Hope Show** (10/12/54). *Guests:* David Niven, Jose Greco, Marilyn Maxwell.

**33 The Bob Hope Show** (12/7/54). *Guests:* Maurice Chevalier, Doreen Dawne, Liana Dayde, Jerry Desmond, Shirley Eaton, Beatrice Lillie, Moira Lister.

**34 The Bob Hope Christmas Show** (1/9/55). *Guests:* Jerry Colonna, Anita Ekberg, William Holden, Peter Leeds, Hedda Hopper, Robert Strauss, Margaret Whiting.

**35 The Bob Hope Show** (2/1/55). *Guests:* Shirley Jones, Roy Rogers and Dale Evans, Line Renaud, The Sons of Pioneers, Trigger (Roy's horse).

**36 The Bob Hope Show** (3/1/55). *Guests:* Vivian Blaine, Jimmy Durante, David Niven.

**37 The Bob Hope Show** (4/26/55). *Guests:* Ralph Edwards, Line Renaud, Lloyd Nolan, Lassie.

**38 The Bob Hope Special** (5/24/55). *Guests:* Bing Crosby, Don Hartman, Jane Russell.

**39 The Bob Hope Show** (10/4/55). *Guests:* Wally Cox, Janis Paige, Jane Russell.

**40 The Bob Hope Show** (11/15/55). *Guests:* Jeanne Crain, Betty Hutton.

**41 The Bob Hope Show** (12/27/55). *Guests:* Betty Grable, James Mason, Joan Rhodes.

**42 The Bob Hope Show** (2/7/56). *Guests:* Diana Dors, Nancy Crompton.

**43 The Bob Hope Show** (2/28/56). *Guests:* Douglas Fairbanks, Jr., Line Renaud, Jean Wallace, Cornel Wilde.

**44 The Bob Hope Show** (3/21/56). *Guests:* Vivian Blaine, Dick Foran, Greer Garson.

**45 The Bob Hope Show** (5/1/56). *Guests:* Pearl Bailey, George Gobel, Kathryn Grayson, George Sanders.

**46 The Bob Hope Show** (5/22/56). *Guests:* Pearl Bailey, Vic Damone, Leo Durocher, Ken Murray, Kim Novak.

**47 The Bob Hope Show** (90 min., 6/17/56). *Guests:* Steve Allen, Dorothy Lamour, Betty Grable, Marilyn Maxwell, Jane Russell, George Sanders, Ed Sullivan. *Note:* The program promotes Bob's new film, *That Certain Feeling.*

**48 The Bob Hope Chevy Show** (10/

24/56). *Guests:* Desi Arnaz, Lucille Ball, James Cagney, Diana Dors, William Frawley, Don Larsen, Vivian Vance.

**49 The Bob Hope Chevy Show** (11/18/56). *Guests:* Steve Allen, Milton Berle, Perry Como, Joan Davis, Julie London, John Cameron Swayze.

**50 The Bob Hope Chevy Christmas Show** (12/28/56). *Guests:* Jerry Colonna, Charley Cooley, The Del Rubio Triplets, Hedda Hopper, Peggy King, Peter Leeds, Mickey Mantle, Carol Morris, Ginger Rogers.

**51 The Bob Hope Chevy Show** (1/25/57). *Guests:* Eddie Fisher, Betty Grable, Harry James, Jack Kirkwood, Dan Rowan and Dick Martin.

**52 The Bob Hope Chevy Show** (3/10/57). *Guests:* Rosemary Clooney, Wally Cox, Lana Turner.

**53 The Bob Hope Chevy Show** (4/8/57). *Guests:* Janis Paige, Natalie Wood, Frank Sinatra.

**54 The Bob Hope Show** (5/6/57). *Guests:* Sonny James, George Jessel, Shelley Winters.

**55 The Bob Hope Show** (10/6/57). *Guests:* Gary Crosby, Eddie Fisher, Marie McDonald, Ann Miller. *Note:* Filmed at the Nouasseur Air Depot in Morocco as a tribute to American GIs.

**56 The Bob Hope Show** (11/24/57). *Guests:* Francis X. Bushman, Joan Caulfield, Jimmy Durante, Rhonda Fleming, Sheree North, Danny Thomas.

**57 The Bob Hope Show** (1/19/58). *Guests:* Alan Gifford, Hedda Hopper, Carol Jarvis, Irving Kupcinet, Peter Leeds, Jayne Mansfield.

**58 The Bob Hope Show** (2/6/58). *Guests:* Wally Cox, Dorothy Malone, Doris Singleton, Nick Todd.

**59 The Bob Hope Show** (3/2/58). *Guests:* Bing Crosby, Anita Ekberg, Robert Wagner, Natalie Wood.

**60. Bob Hope in Moscow** (4/5/58). *Guests:* Yuri Durov, David Oistrakh, Popov, David Raikin, Galina Ulanova, The Ukraine State Dancers. *Note:* Filmed on location in Russia and features native talent as Bob's guests.

**61 The Bob Hope Buick Show** See Roberta (9/19/58). *Guests:* Anna Maria Alberghetti, Howard Keel, Janis Paige.

**62 The Bob Hope Buick Show** (10/15/58). *Guests:* Joan Crawford, Marion Ryan, Robert Strauss.

**63 The Bob Hope Buick Show** (11/21/58). *Guests:* Wally Cox, Betty Grable, Randy Sparks, Gloria Swanson.

**64 The Bob Hope Buick Christmas Show** (1/16/59). *Guests:* Molly Bee, Jerry Colonna, Elaine Dunn, Hedda Hopper, Gina Lollobrigida, Randy Sparks. *Note:* Filmed at ten overseas military bases as a tribute to U.S. GIs.

**65 The Bob Hope Buick Show** (2/6/59). *Guests:* Wally Cox, Ray Farrell, Alan Gifford, Dorothy Malone, Doris Singleton, Mike Todd.

**66 The Bob Hope Buick Show** (2/10/59). *Guests:* Carol Haney, Peter Lawford, Maureen O'Hara, Danny Thomas.

**67 The Bob Hope Buick Show** (3/13/59). *Guests:* Chuck Connors, Gail Davis, Fess Parker, Julie London, Guy Mitchell.

**68 The Bob Hope Buick Show** (4/15/59). *Guests:* Jack Benny, Milton Berle, Jerry Colonna, Ginger Rogers, Dodie Stevens.

**69 The Bob Hope Buick Show** (5/15/59). *Guests:* Rosemary Clooney, Joan Collins, Wendell Corey.

**70 The Bob Hope Buick Show** (10/8/59). *Guests:* The Crosby Brothers, Dean Martin, Natalie Wood.

**71 The Bob Hope Buick Show** (11/9/59). *Guests:* Mary Britt, Zsa Zsa Gabor, Patti Page. *Music Director:* David Rose.

**72 The Bob Hope Buick Show** (12/12/59). *Guests:* Rhonda Fleming, Ernie Kovacs. *Music Director:* David Rose.

**73 The Bob Hope Buick Christmas Show** (1/13/60). *Guests:* Jerry Colonna, Frances Langford, Steve McQueen, Jayne Mansfield, Patti Thomas, Tony

Romano. *Music Director:* Skinnay Ennis.

**74 The Bob Hope Buick Show** (2/22/60). *Guests:* Wally Cox, Troy Donahue, Michelle Gordon, Ross Hunter, Millie Perkins, Ginger Rogers. *Music Director:* David Rose.

**75 The Bob Hope Buick Show** (4/22/60). *Guests:* Joan Caulfield, James Garner, Patti Page. *Music Director:* David Rose.

**76 The Bob Hope Buick Show** (10/3/60). *Guests:* Bobby Darin, Joan Crawford, Patti Page. *Music Director:* David Rose.

**77 The Bob Hope Buick Show** (10/22/60). *Guests:* Perry Como, Lisa Davis, Peter Leeds, Ginger Rogers, Herb Vigran. *Music Director:* David Rose. *Note:* The program spoofs politics with songs written by Sammy Cahn and Jimmy Van Heusen.

**78 The Bob Hope Show** (11/16/60). *Guests:* Neile Adams, Steve McQueen, Kay Starr. *Music Director:* David Rose.

**79 The Bob Hope Show** (12/12/60). *Guests:* Jimmy Durante, Polly Bergen. *Music Director:* David Rose.

**80 The Bob Hope Buick Christmas Show** (1/11/61). *Guests:* Anita Bryant, Jerry Colonna, Zsa Zsa Gabor, Janis Paige, Andy Williams. *Music Director:* David Rose. *Note:* Bob's annual overseas tour; filmed at Caribbean military bases.

**81 The Bob Hope Buick Sports Awards Show** (2/15/61). *Guests:* Dana Andrews, Lucille Ball, Julie London, Jayne Mansfield, Dean Martin, Ronald Reagan, Ginger Rogers, Jane Russell, Tuesday Weld, Jane Wyman. *Music Director:* David Rose. *Note:* A comical awards show wherein sports editors select the top athletes.

**82 The Bob Hope Buick Show** (4/12/61). *Guests:* James Darren, Phil Harris, Patti Page. *Music Director:* David Rose.

**83 The Bob Hope Buick Show** (5/13/61). *Guests:* James Garner, Julie London, Juliet Prowse. *Music Director:* David Rose.

**84 The World of Bob Hope** (10/29/61). *Narrator:* Alexander Scourby. *Special Guest:* Bob Hope. *Guests:* Monty Brice, Jack Hope, Jimmy Saphier, Louis Shurr. *Music Director:* David Rose. *Note:* A look at the life of comedian Bob Hope.

**85 The Bob Hope Show** (12/31/61). *Guests:* James Garner, Nancy Kwan, Danny Thomas. *Music Director:* David Rose.

**86 The Bob Hope Christmas Show** (1/24/62). *Guests:* Anita Bryant, Jerry Colonna, Jayne Mansfield, Dorothy Provine. *Music Director:* David Rose. *Note:* Filmed at U.S. Air Force bases in the Arctic.

**87 The Bob Hope Show** (2/27/62). *Guests:* Steve Allen, Bing Crosby, Joan Collins, Jack Paar, Joanie Sommers. *Music Director:* David Rose.

**88 The Bob Hope Show** (3/22/62). *Guests:* Fabian Forte, Piper Laurie, Ethel Merman, Maximilian Schell. *Music Director:* Skinnay Ennis.

**89 The Bob Hope Show** (4/25/62). *Guests:* Dorothy Lamour, Janis Paige, Frank Sinatra. *Music Director:* Skinnay Ennis.

**90 The Bob Hope Show** (10/24/62). *Guests:* Lucille Ball, Bing Crosby, Juliet Prowse. *Music Director:* Skinnay Ennis.

**91 The Bob Hope Show** (11/29/62). *Guests:* Jack Benny, Bobby Darin, Ethel Merman. *Music Director:* Skinnay Ennis.

**92 The Bob Hope Christmas Show** (1/16/63). *Guests:* Jerry Colonna, Peter Leeds, Janis Paige, Lana Turner. *Note:* Filmed at U.S. military bases in the Orient.

**93 The Bob Hope Show** (3/13/63). *Guests:* Edie Adams, Robert Goulet, Brenda Lee, Frank Sinatra. *Deb Stars:* Sandra Bettin, Sandy Descher, Mimsey Farmer, Laurel Goodwin, Joan Freeman, Susan Hart, Sheila James, Karyn Kupcinet, Lori Martin, Patricia McCormack, Roberta Shore, Lana Wood. *Note:* The program spotlights the 1963 Hollywood Deb Stars.

**94 The Bob Hope Show** (4/14/63). *Guests:* Lucille Ball, Dean Martin, Martha Raye.

**95 The Bob Hope Show** (9/27/63). *Guests:* James Garner, Dean Martin, Barbra Streisand, Tuesday Weld.

**96 The Bob Hope Show** (10/25/63). *Guests:* Beryl Davis, Tommy Davis, Don Drysdale, Andy Griffith, Connie Haines, Sandy Koufax, Martha Raye, Jane Russell.

**97 The Bob Hope Christmas Show** (1/17/64). *Guests:* Anita Bryant, John Bubbles, Jerry Colonna, Philip Crosby, Tuesday Weld.

**98 The Bob Hope Show** (2/14/64). *Guests:* Anne Bancroft, Sergio Franchi, Janet Leigh, Julie London.

**99 Her School for Bachelors** (3/20/64). See title for information.

**100 The Bob Hope Show** (4/17/64). *Guests:* Jack Jones, Groucho Marx, Tony Randall, Martha Raye.

**101 Have Girls—Will Travel** (10/16/64). See title for information.

**102 The Bob Hope Show** (11/20/64). *Guests:* Richard Chamberlain, Annette Funicello, Trini Lopez, Donald O'Connor, Stella Stevens.

**103 The Bob Hope Show** (9/29/65). *Guests:* Douglas Fairbanks, Jr., Beatrice Lillie, Dinah Shore, Andy Williams.

**104 The Bob Hope Show** (10/20/65). *Guests:* Phyllis Diller, James Garner, Carol Lawrence, The Wee Five.

**105 The Bob Hope Show** (11/3/65). *Guests:* Jack Jones, Martha Raye, Tony Randall.

**106 Russian Roulette** (11/17/65). See title for information.

**107 The Bob Hope Show** (12/15/65). *Guests:* Jack Benny, Bing Crosby, Janet Leigh, Mickey Rooney, Nancy Wilson.

**108 The Bob Hope Christmas Show** (1/19/66). *Guests:* Anita Bryant, Jerry Colonna, Jack Jones, The Nicholas Brothers, Kaye Stevens.

**109 The Bob Hope Show** (3/16/66). *Guests:* Phyllis Diller, Pete Fountain, Jonathan Winters.

**110 The Bob Hope Show** (9/28/66). *Guests:* Lucille Ball, Madeleine Carroll, Joan Caulfield, Joan Collins, Jerry Colonna, Arlene Dahl, Phyllis Diller, Anita Ekberg, Rhonda Fleming, Joan Fontaine, Signe Hasso, Hedy Lamarr, Dorothy Lamour, Peter Leeds, Paul Lynde, Marilyn Maxwell, Vera Miles, Virginia Mayo, Janis Paige, Jane Russell. *Note:* Format pokes fun at the fairer sex.

**111 Murder at NBC** (10/19/66). See title for information.

**112 The Bob Hope Show** (11/16/66). *Guest:* Bing Crosby. *Note:* Officially titled "A Bob Hope Comedy Special Starring Bing and Me" (Bing Crosby is Bob's solo guest).

**113 The Bob Hope Special** (1/18/67). *Guests:* Anita Bryant, Vic Damone, Phyllis Diller, Joey Heatherton.

**114 The Bob Hope Special** (2/15/67). *Guests:* Tony Bennett, Shirley Eaton, Carol Lawrence, Jill St. John.

**115 The Bob Hope Special** (9/20/67). *Guests:* Phyllis Diller, Jimmy Durante, Jack Jones, Kaye Stevens, Dan Rowan and Dick Martin.

**116 The Bob Hope Special** (10/16/67). *Guests:* Eydie Gorme, Steve Lawrence, Debbie Reynolds.

**117 Shoot-In at NBC** (11/8/67). See title for information.

**118 The Bob Hope Special** (11/29/67). *Guests:* David Janssen, Jack Jones, Shirley Jones, Elke Sommer. *Note:* Taped at the UCLA campus in California.

**119 The Bob Hope Christmas Special** (12/14/67). *Guests:* Don Adams, Ernest Borgnine, Wally Cox, Phil Silvers.

**120 The Bob Hope Special** (1/18/68). *Guests:* Phil Crosby, Elaine Dunn, Barbara McNair, Raquel Welch. *Note:* Highlights of Bob's Christmas program for servicemen overseas.

**121 The Bob Hope Special** (2/12/68). *Guests:* Pearl Bailey, Bing Crosby, Barbara Eden.

**122 The Bob Hope Special** (3/20/68). *Guests:* Anne Bancroft, Arnold Palmer, Lou Rawls, Jill St. John.

**123 The Bob Hope Special** (4/9/68). *Guests:* Fernando Lamas, Janet Leigh, Pat Harrington, Jr., Eddie Mayehoff, J. Carrol Naish.

**124 For Love or Money** (4/11/68). See title for information.

**125 A Special Bob Hope Special** (9/25/68). An hour long comedy in which Bob Hope plays Gaylord Goodfellow, a political candidate, and Irving, a cab driver who is his exact double. The story follows Irving's adventures when Gaylord drops out of the running and Irving is chosen to secretly replace him—and keep his promise to marry six women. *Cast:* Bob Hope (Gaylord/Irving), Carroll Baker (First Would Be Wife), Cyd Charisse (Second Would Be Wife), Angie Dickinson (Third Would Be Wife), Zsa Zsa Gabor (Fourth Would Be Wife), Jill St. John (Fifth Would Be Wife), Vikki Carr (Sixth Would Be Wife).

**126 The Bob Hope Special** (10/14/68). *Guests:* John Davidson, Bob Fosse, Jeannie C. Riley, Gwen Verdon.

**127 The Bob Hope Special** (11/27/68). *Guests:* Glen Campbell, Barbara McNair, Juliet Prowse, Sergio Mendes and Brasil '66. *Note:* A college concert from the University of Southern California. There is no "live" music due to a musicians' strike at the time of taping.

**128 The Bob Hope Christmas Special** (12/19/68). *Guests:* Nancy Ames, Glen Campbell, Jerry Colonna, Carol Lawrence, Janet Leigh, Stella Stevens. *Note:* A spoof of "Mission: Impossible," wherein Bob Hope plays an agent who has been assigned to find Santa Claus, who has been kidnapped on Christmas Eve.

**129 The Bob Hope Special** (1/16/69). *Guests:* Ann-Margret, Linda Bennet, Penny Plummer, Rosey Grier, The Golddiggers, Honey, Ltd. *Note:* Highlights of Bob's annual Christmas show for servicemen overseas.

**130 The Bob Hope Special** (2/17/69). *Guests:* George Burns, Bing Crosby, Lisa Miller, Martha Raye, Diana Ross and the Supremes.

**131 The Bob Hope Special** (3/19/69). *Guests:* Cyd Charisse, Ray Charles, Nancy Sinatra.

**132 The Bob Hope Special** (4/17/69). *Guests:* Maureen Arthur, Tina Louise, Jack Nicklaus, Patti Page, Jane Wyman, Sergio Mendes and Brasil '66.

**133 The Bob Hope Special** (9/22/69). *Guests:* Marty Allen, Steve Allen, Shelly Berman, Red Buttons, Sid Caesar, Johnny Carson, Jack Carter, Jerry Colonna, Wally Cox, Bill Dana, Richard Deacon, George Gobel, Shecky Greene, Buddy Hackett, Jack E. Leonard, Pat Paulsen, Nipsey Russell, Soupy Sales, Phil Silvers, Dick Smothers, Tom Smothers, Danny Thomas.

**134 The Bob Hope Special** (10/13/69). *Guests:* Jimmy Durante, Tom Jones, Barbara McNair, Donald O'Connor.

**135 Roberta** (11/6/69). See title for information.

**136 The Bob Hope Special** (11/24/69). *Guests:* Eydie Gorme, Steve Lawrence, Virni Lisi, Danny Thomas.

**137 The Bob Hope Special** (12/6/69). *Guests:* John Davidson, Michele Lee, Laura Miller, Janis Paige, Ann Shoemaker.

**138 The Bob Hope Christmas Special** (12/18/69). *Guests:* Anthony Newley, Elke Sommer, Andy Williams.

**139 The Bob Hope Special** (90 min., 1/14/70). *Guests:* Ursula Andress, Johnny Bench, The Golddiggers, Jennifer Hosten, Gloria Loring, Bobbi Martin, Yvonne Ormes. *Note:* The first of a two-part special (see following title) that highlights Bob's Christmas tour to servicemen overseas.

**140 The Bob Hope Special** (1/15/70). *Guests:* Suzanne Charny, The Golddiggers, Teresa Graves, Romy Schneider, Connie Stevens. *Note:* The concluding part of Bob's 1970 overseas Christmas show.

**141 The Bob Hope Special** (2/16/70). *Guests:* Ray Bolger, Johnny Cash, Bing Crosby, Raquel Welch.

**142 The Bob Hope Special** (3/18/70). *Guests:* Perry Como, Tony Curtis, Barbara Eden.

**143 The Bob Hope Special** (4/13/70). *Guests:* Ann-Margret, Jerry Colonna, Wally Cox, Phyllis Diller, Buddy Greco.

**144 The Bob Hope Special** (10/5/70). *Guests:* Edie Adams, Kaye Ballard, Ruth Buzzi, Imogene Coca, Phyllis Diller, Nanette Fabray, Totie Fields, Zsa Zsa Gabor, Virginia Graham, Teresa Graves, Sheila MacRae, Minnie Pearl, Irene Ryan, Connie Stevens, Nancy Walker, Jo Anne Worley. *Note:* The program pokes fun at Women's Lib.

**145 The Bob Hope Special** (11/16/70). *Guests:* Lucille Ball, George Burns, Tom Jones, Danny Thomas.

**146 The Bob Hope Christmas Special** (12/7/70). *Guests:* Jack Benny, Engelbert Humperdinck, Dorothy Lamour, Elke Sommer.

**147 The Bob Hope Special** (90 min., 1/14/71). *Guests:* Ursula Andress, Johnny Bench, Lola Falana, The Golddiggers, Bobbi Martin. *Note:* Highlights of Bob's Christmas show for servicemen overseas.

**148 The Bob Hope Special** (2/15/71). *Guests:* Petula Clark, Bing Crosby, Teresa Graves, Jo Anne Worley.

**149 The Bob Hope Special** (4/5/71). *Guests:* Wally Cox, Sammy Davis, Jr., Shirley Jones, Lee Marvin.

**150 Bob Hope's 22nd Anniversary Special** (9/13/71). *Guests:* Edie Adams, Dr. Joyce Brothers, Imogene Coca, Linda Cristal, Angie Dickinson, Phyllis Diller, Nanette Fabray, Zsa Zsa Gabor, Sue Lyon, Barbara McNair, Rose Marie, Phyllis Newman, Martha Raye, Jill St. John, Sally Struthers, Jacqueline Susann, Edy Williams, Jo Anne Worley. *Note:* The program celebrates Bob's twenty-second year on NBC with a parody of the movie *Planet of the Apes*.

**151 The Bob Hope Special** (11/7/71). *Guests:* Jack Benny, The Osmond Brothers, Debbie Reynolds.

**152 The Bob Hope Christmas Special** (12/9/71). *Guests:* Barbara Eden, Robert Goulet, Lee Marvin, Smokey Robinson and the Miracles.

**153 The Bob Hope Special** (1/17/72). *Guests:* Don Ho, Jim Nabors, Charley Pride, Jill St. John, Sunday's Child. *Note:* Highlights of Bob's 1971 overseas Christmas show for GIs.

**154 The Bob Hope Special** (3/13/72). *Guests:* Dyan Cannon, Eva Gabor, Elke Sommer, Connie Stevens. *Note:* A spoof of Academy Award–winning movies.

**155 The Bob Hope Special** (4/10/72). *Guests:* Ingrid Bergman, Shirley Jones, Barbara McNair, Ray Milland. *Note:* A comical salute to the 1972 Oscar-nominated movies.

**156 The Bob Hope Special** (4/27/72). *Guests:* Glen Campbell, Dorothy Lamour, Carol Lawrence, Sugar Ray Robinson.

**157 The Bob Hope Special** (10/5/72). *Guests:* Karen and Richard Carpenter, David Cassidy, Peter Leeds, Alexis Smith, Mark Spitz.

**158 The Bob Hope Christmas Special** (12/10/72). *Guests:* Phyllis Diller, Gloria Loring, Elke Sommer.

**159 The Bob Hope Special** (90 min., 1/17/73). *Guests:* Lola Falana, Redd Foxx, Roman Gabriel, Belinda Green, Dolores Hope. *Note:* Highlights of Bob's overseas Christmas show for GIs.

**160 The Bob Hope Special** (2/8/73). *Guests:* Jack Benny, Red Buttons, Jerry Colonna, George Foreman, Jan Murray, Tony Randall, Don Rickles.

**161 The Bob Hope Special** (3/7/73). *Guests:* Pete Fountain, Phil Harris, Al Hirt.

**162 The Bob Hope Special** (4/19/73). *Guests:* Milton Berle, Glen Campbell, Joey Heatherton, The Supremes, Doodles Weaver.

**163 The Bob Hope Special** (9/26/73). *Guests:* Ann-Margret, John Denver, The Jackson Five, Bobby Riggs.

**164 The Bob Hope Special** (11/13/73). *Guests:* Karen and Richard Carpenter, Redd Foxx, Don Rickles.

**165 The Bob Hope Christmas Show** (12/9/73). *Guests:* Lucille Ball, Shirley Jones, Marie Osmond.

**166 The Bob Hope Special** (1/24/74). *Guests:* Dyan Cannon, Burt Reynolds, Dionne Warwick.

**167 The Bob Hope Special** (9/25/74). *Guests:* Glen Campbell, Carol Channing, Jackie Gleason.

**168 The Bob Hope Christmas Special** (12/15/74). *Guests:* Dyan Cannon, Dean Martin, Olivia Newton-John.

**169 Bob Hope Presents the Stars of Tomorrow** (3/5/75). *Note:* The program spotlights ten up-and-coming performers.

**170 Bob Hope on Campus** (4/17/75). *Guests:* Aretha Franklin, John Wayne, Flip Wilson. *Note:* Taped on the campus of the University of Southern California.

**171 A Quarter Century of Bob Hope on Television** (2 hrs., 10/24/75). *Guests:* Bing Crosby, Frank Sinatra, John Wayne. *Note:* Highlights of Bob's 25 years on NBC.

**172 Bob Hope's Christmas Party** (12/14/75). *Guests:* Angie Dickinson, Redd Foxx, Marie and Donny Osmond.

**173 The Bob Hope Comedy Special** (2/13/76). *Guests:* Glen Campbell, Roy Clark, Raquel Welch, Telly Savalas, Andy Williams, Flip Wilson.

**174 Joys (A Bob Hope Special)** (3/5/76). See title for information.

**175 Bob Hope's Bicentennial Star Spangled Spectacular** (90 min., 7/4/76). *Guests:* The Captain and Tennille, Sammy Davis, Jr., Marie and Donny Osmond, Debbie Reynolds. *Note:* Sketches that relate how television might have been over the last 200 years.

**176 Texaco Presents Bob Hope's World of Comedy** (2 hrs., 10/29/76). *Guests:* Lucille Ball, Norman Lear, Don Rickles, Neil Simon.

**177 Texaco Presents Bob Hope's Comedy Christmas Special** (90 min., 12/13/76). *Guests:* Dyan Cannon, Lola Falana, Kate Jackson, Neil Sedaka, John Wayne.

**178 Texaco Presents Bob Hope's All-Star Comedy Spectacular from Lake Tahoe** (90 min., 1/21/77). *Guests:* Ann-Margret, Charo, Mac Davis, Sammy Davis, Jr., Dean Martin.

**179 Texaco Presents Bob Hope's All-Star Comedy Tribute to Vaudeville** (90 min., 3/25/77). *Guests:* Jack Albertson, Lucille Ball, The Captain and Tennille, Bernadette Peters.

**180 Bob Hope — On the Road with Bing** (2 hrs., 10/28/77). *Note:* An affectionate tribute to Bing Crosby (who starred with Bob in a number of "Road" pictures).

**181 Bob Hope's Christmas Special** (12/19/77). *Guests:* Perry Como, Mark Hamill, Olivia Newton-John.

**182 Texaco Presents Bob Hope's All-Star Tribute to the Palace Theater** (90 min., 1/8/78). *Guests:* George Burns, Sammy Davis, Jr.; Eydie Gorme, Carol Lawrence, Steve Lawrence, Marie and Donny Osmond.

**183 Texaco Presents the Bob Hope Special from Palm Springs** (2/13/78). *Guests:* Phyllis Diller, Telly Savalas, Raquel Welch, Andy Williams.

**184 Bob Hope's All-Star Comedy Spectacular from Australia** (90 min., 4/15/78). *Guests:* Charo, Barbara Eden, Florence Henderson.

**185 Happy Birthday, Bob** (3 hrs., 5/29/78). *Guests:* Ann-Margret, Lynn Anderson, Pearl Bailey, Lucille Ball, Johnny Carson, Charo, Kathryn Crosby, Redd Foxx, Dorothy Lamour, Carol Lawrence, Fred MacMurray, Marie and Donny Osmond, Don Rickles, Red Skelton, David Soul, Danny Thomas, Fred Travalena. *Note:* A salute to Bob Hope on his seventy-fifth birthday.

**186 The Bob Hope Special** (10/18/78). *Guests:* Charo, Howard Cosell, Joe DiMaggio, Reggie Jackson, Danny Kaye, Billy Martin, Steve Martin. *Note:* A comical salute to the seventy-fifth anniversary of the World Series.

**187 Bob Hope's All-Star Christmas Show** (12/22/78). *Guests:* Andy Gibb, Red Skelton, Dionne Warwick.

**188 The Bob Hope Special** (1/28/79). *Guests:* Debby Boone, Pat Boone, Sammy Davis, Jr.; Debbie Reynolds.

**189 The Bob Hope Special** (3/2/79).

*Guests:* Chris Evert-Lloyd, Ron Howard.

**190 The Bob Hope Special** (5/14/79). *Guests:* Richard Burton, Leif Garrett, Susan George, Leslie Uggams, Raquel Welch. *Note:* A music and comedy salute to the 1920s and 1930s.

**191 Bob Hope's All-Star Birthday Party** (90 min., 5/30/79). *Guests:* Lucie Arnaz, Diahann Carroll, Charo, Robert Klein, Don Knotts. *Note:* A seventy-sixth birthday celebration for Bob.

**192 Bob Hope on the Road to China** (3 hrs., 9/16/79). *Guests:* Mikhail Baryshnikov, Crystal Gayle, Shields and Yarnell. *Note:* The first variety show to be shown for the People's Republic of China.

**193 Bob Hope on Campus** (2 hrs., 11/19/79). *Guests:* Erik Estrada, Melissa Manchester, Joe Namath, Tony Randall, Tanya Tucker, Dionne Warwick.

**194 The Bob Hope Christmas Special** (12/13/79). *Guests:* Kathryn Crosby, Angie Dickinson, Bonnie Franklin, Adam Rich.

**195 Bob Hope: Hope, Women and Song** (1/21/80). *Guests:* Bea Arthur, Debby Boone, Diahann Carroll, Shirley Jones. *Note:* Bob recalls the songs he made famous in a career that spans vaudeville, Broadway, radio, and feature films.

**196 Bob Hope's Overseas Christmas Tours, Part 1** (3 hrs., 2/3/80). Bob Hope hosts film and videotape highlights of his annual USO Christmas tours to servicemen stationed overseas.

**197 Bob Hope's Overseas Christmas Tours, Part 2** (3 hrs., 2/10/80). Videotape and film highlights of Bob Hope's overseas Christmas tours to servicemen—a tradition he began during World War II; the concluding segment of a two-part special (see prior listing).

**198 The Starmakers** (3/17/80). A musical-comedy in which Miles Baudac, a down on his luck talent agent, and Ace Robbins, a wealthy but naive Texan, team to find an "11," the most

beautiful girl in the world—for a television series, "Levitt's Lovelies," a program about a fashion designer and two models. *Cast:* Bob Hope (Miles Baudac), Robert Urich (Ace Robbins), Bernadette Peters (Sally), Linda Gray (Wendy Trousdale), Robert Guillaume (The Singer), Elaine Joyce (Candy Cinnamon), Conrad Janis (Roman Lear), and Gallagher.

**199 Bob Hope's All-Star Comedy Birthday Party** (90 min., 5/28/80). *Guests:* Loni Anderson, Tai Babilonia, Andy Gibb, Barbara Mandrell, Diana Ross, Alan B. Shepard. *Note:* Bob's seventy-seventh birthday celebration.

**200 Bob Hope's All-Star Look at TV's Prime Time Wars** (9/6/80). *Guests:* Willie Aames, Claude Akins, Loni Anderson, Cathy Lee Crosby, Howard Duff, Barbara Eden, Erik Estrada, Gil Gerard, Charlotte Rae, Brooke Shields, Stella Stevens, Danny Thomas, Larry Wilcox. *Note:* Sketches that satirize the fall 1980 television season.

**201 Bob Hope for President** (11/1/80). *Guests:* Johnny Carson, Sammy Davis Jr., Angie Dickinson, Lou Ferrigno, Gerald R. Ford, Harvey Korman, Jayne Kennedy, Paul Lynde, Gary Owens, Stefanie Powers, Tony Randall, Vidal Sassoon, Brooke Shields, Toni Tennille, Jonathan Winters. *Note:* Sketches that revolve around Bob Hope's mythical campaign for president of the United States.

**202 The Bob Hope Christmas Special** (12/16/80). *Guests:* Loni Anderson, Larry Gatlin, Loretta Swit.

**203 Bob Hope's 30th Anniversary TV Special** (2 hrs., 1/18/81). *Guests:* Ann-Margret, Lucille Ball, Milton Berle, George Burns, Sammy Davis, Jr.; Douglas Fairbanks, Jr.; Eydie Gorme, Steve Lawrence, Marie Osmond, Brooke Shields, Danny Thomas, Tanya Tucker, Robert Urich.

**204 Bob Hope's Funny Valentine** (2/11/81). *Guests:* Dr. Joyce Brothers, Cathy Lee Crosby, Phyllis Diller, Barbara Mandrell, Charlene Tilton.

**205 Bob Hope's Spring Fling of Comedy and Glamour** (4/13/81). *Guests:* Loni Anderson, Donna Dixon, Morgan Fairchild, Melissa Manchester, Jill St. John, Brooke Shields.

**206 Bob Hope's All-Star Comedy Birthday at West Point** (2 hrs., 5/25/81). *Guests:* Glen Campbell, Dolores Hope, Sugar Ray Leonard, Mary Martin, Marie Osmond, George C. Scott, Brooke Shields, Robert Urich. *Note:* A birthday celebration for Bob Hope (born May 29) at the U.S. Military Academy at West Point.

**207 Bob Hope's All-Star Comedy Look at the Fall Season: It's Still Free and Worth It!** (9/27/81). *Guests:* Loni Anderson, Cathy Lee Crosby, Barbara Eden, Linda Evans, Kelly Lange, Bruce Jenner, Merlin Olsen, Cheryl Tiegs.

**208 Bob Hope Presents a Celebration with Stars of Comedy and Music** (2 hrs., 10/22/81). *Guests:* Pearl Bailey, Debby Boone, Foster Brooks, George Bush, Glen Campbell, Sammy Davis, Jr.; Gerald R. Ford, Alexander Haig, Henry Kissinger, Gordon MacRae, Thomas "Tip" O'Neill, Jr.; Tony Orlando, Nancy Reagan, Ronald Reagan, Mark Russell, Danny Thomas, Pierre Trudeau, Margaret Truman, Caspar Weinberger. *Note:* Bob and his guests celebrate the dedication of the Ford Presidential Museum in Grand Rapids, Michigan.

**209 Bob Hope's Stand Up and Cheer for the National Football League's 60th Year** (2 hrs., 11/22/81). *Guests:* Susan Anton, Michael Conrad, Howard Cosell, George Gobel, Don Knotts, Barbara Mandrell, Olivia Newton-John, O. J. Simpson, Elizabeth Taylor, Betty White.

**210 The Bob Hope Christmas Special** (12/20/81). *Guests:* Loni Anderson, Phyllis Diller, Olivia Newton-John.

**211 Bob Hope's Women I Love—Beautiful but Funny** (2 hrs., 2/28/82). *Bob's Girls:* Loni Anderson, Ursula Andress, Ann-Margret, Bea Arthur, Pearl Bailey, Carroll Baker, Lucille Ball, Anne Bancroft, Ingrid Bergman, Debby Boone, Dyan Cannon, Diahann Carroll, Charo, Petula Clark, Rosemary Clooney, Imogene Coca, Joan Collins, Jeanne Crain, Joan Crawford, Cathy Lee Crosby, Phyllis Diller, Diana Dors, Shirley Eaton, Barbara Eden, Linda Evans, Nanette Fabray, Morgan Fairchild, Bonnie Franklin, Zsa Zsa Gabor, Greer Garson, Betty Grable, Teresa Graves, Linda Gray, Florence Henderson, Shirley Jones, Dorothy Lamour, Carol Lawrence, Beatrice Lillie, Virna Lisi, Gina Lollobrigida, Dorothy Malone, Jayne Mansfield, Mary Martin, Marie Osmond, Janis Paige, Lilli Palmer, Bernadette Peters, Martha Raye, Dolores Reade, Debbie Reynolds, Ginger Rogers, Barbara Rush, Jill St. John, Romy Schneider, Brooke Shields, Dinah Shore, Alexis Smith, Elke Sommer, Stella Stevens, Barbra Streisand, Sally Struthers, Elizabeth Taylor, Charlene Tilton, Lana Turner, Tuesday Weld, Shelley Winters, Jane Wyman. *Note:* A salute to the women Bob has worked with for 32 years on television.

**212 Bob Hope Laughs with the Movie Awards** (3/28/82). *Guests:* George Burns, Andy Gibb, Ann Jillian, Lee Marvin. *Note:* A satirization of the 1982 Oscar nominees (*Atlantic City, Raiders of the Lost Ark, Reds,* and *Chariots of Fire*).

**213 Bob Hope's Stars Over Texas** (5/3/82). *Guests:* Morgan Fairchild, Larry Gatlin, Jack Lemmon, Dottie West.

**214 Bob Hope's All-Star Birthday at Annapolis** (2 hrs., 5/25/82). *Guests:* Christie Brinkley, James Coburn, Charlton Heston, Bernadette Peters, Brooke Shields, Larry Holmes, Roger Staubach. *Note:* Bob Hope, born May 29, 1903, celebrates his seventy-ninth birthday at the U.S. Naval Academy at Annapolis.

**215 Bob Hope's Star-Studded Spoof of the New TV Season—G Rated—With Glamour, Glitter and Gags** (10/3/82). *Guests:* Billy Barty, Linda Evans, Julie Ann Haddock, Ricky

Schroder, Tom Selleck, Brooke Shields, Elizabeth Taylor.

**216 Bob Hope's Pink Panther Thanksgiving** (2 hrs., 11/21/82). *Guests:* Julie Andrews, Dean Martin, Dudley Moore, Bernadette Peters, Robert Preston, Willie Nelson, Robert Wagner. *Note:* An all-star spectacular that celebrates the twentieth anniversary of the Pink Panther films with comedy skits and film clips.

**217 The Bob Hope Christmas Special** (12/20/82). *Guests:* Loni Anderson, Brooke Shields, Andy Williams.

**218 Bob Hope's All-Star Super Bowl Party** (1/29/83). *Guests:* Lola Falana, Ann Jillian, Audrey Landers, Merlin Olsen, Don Rickles.

**219 Bob Hope's Road to Hollywood** (2 hrs., 3/2/83). *Guests:* Lucille Ball, George Burns, Rosemary Clooney, Rhonda Fleming, Dorothy Lamour, Virginia Mayo, Martha Raye, Jane Russell, Jill St. John. *Note:* The program salutes, via clips, Bob Hope's film career.

**220 Bob Hope in Who Makes the World Laugh?** (4/20/83). *Guests:* Erma Bombeck, Skip Stephenson, Jonathan Winters. *Note:* Live performances and vintage clips of comedians at work.

**221 Happy Birthday, Bob!** (3 hrs., 5/23/83). *Guests:* Lucille Ball, Christie Brinkley, George Burns, Lynda Carter, Kathryn Crosby, Phyllis Diller, Dolores Hope, Ann Jillian, Loretta Lynn, Barbara Mandrell, Dudley Moore, Ronald and Nancy Reagan, Tom Selleck, Brooke Shields, George C. Scott, Flip Wilson. *Note:* An eightieth birthday celebration for Bob Hope.

**222 Bob Hope's Salute to NASA— 25 Years of Reaching for the Stars** (90 min., 9/19/83). *Guests:* Perry Como, John Denver, Olivia Newton-John, Marie Osmond.

**223 Bob Hope Goes to College** (2 hrs., 11/23/83). *Guests:* Irene Cara, Morgan Fairchild, Eddie Rabbitt, Bonnie Tyler, Dionne Warwick, Vanessa Williams. *Note:* Comedy from college campuses across the country.

**224 Bob Hope's Merry Christmas Show** (12/19/83). *Guests:* Catherine Bach, John Forsythe, Brooke Shields.

**225 Bob Hope's USO Christmas in Beirut** (2 hrs., 1/15/84). *Guests:* Cathy Lee Crosby, Vic Damone, Ann Jillian, George Kirby, Brooke Shields. *Note:* Highlights of Bob's twenty-third USO Christmas tour for servicemen overseas.

**226 Bob Hope's Wicki-Wacki Special from Waikiki** (2/27/84). *Guests:* Loni Anderson, Mr. T, Tom Selleck.

**227 Bob Hope in Who Makes the World Laugh? Part 2** (4/4/84). *Guests:* Lucille Ball, George Burns, Mickey Rooney. *Note:* A tribute to American comedians via live performances and film clips. A sequel to Bob's special of April 20, 1983 (number 220).

**228 Bob Hope's Super Birthday Special** (2 hrs., 5/28/84). *Guests:* Red Buttons, Johnny Cash, June Carter Cash, Dick Cavett, Dolores Hope, Placido Domingo, David Letterman, Mr. T, John Ritter, Twiggy. *Note:* An eighty-first birthday celebration for Bob Hope; taped at the New Orleans World's Fair.

**229 Bob Hope's Hilarious, Unrehearsed Antics of the Stars** (9/28/84). *Guests:* Lucille Ball, Milton Berle, Angie Dickinson, Lee Marvin. *Note:* Outtakes from Bob's previous specials are presented.

**230 Ho Ho Hope's Christmas Hour** (12/16/84). *Guests:* Shirley Jones, Joey Lawrence, Mary Lou Retton, Brooke Shields.

**231 Bob Hope Lampoons Television 1985** (2/24/85). *Guests:* George Burns, Elvira (Cassandra Peterson), Morgan Fairchild, Hal Linden, Donna Mills, Mr. T.

**232 Bob Hope's Comedy Salute to the Soaps** (4/15/85). *Guests:* Morgan Brittany, Diahann Carroll, Deidre Hall, Joan Van Ark.

**233 Bob Hope's Happy Birthday Homecoming** (5/23/85). *Guests:* Michael Caine, Chevy Chase, Phyllis Diller, Duran Duran, Crystal Gayle,

Charlton Heston, Julio Iglesias, Spike Milligan, Bernadette Peters, Brooke Shields. *Music Director:* Allyn Ferguson. *Note:* An eighty-second birthday celebration for Bob Hope, who returns to the land of his birth, England, for a royal celebration. Taped on May 14, 1985 (Bob's birthday is May 29), at London's Lyric Theatre.

**234 Bob Hope Buys NBC** (9/17/85). *Guests:* Lucille Ball, Milton Berle, George Burns, Johnny Carson, Lynda Carter, Phyllis Diller, Elvira (Cassandra Peterson), Gerald R. Ford, Michael J. Fox, Dolores Hope, Michael Landon, Dean Martin, Mr. T, Tom Selleck, Danny Thomas. *Note:* Program revolves around Bob Hope as he stages a telethon to buy NBC, his adopted network.

**235 The Bob Hope Christmas Show** (12/15/85). *Guests:* Barbara Eden, Emmanuel Lewis, Brooke Shields, Raquel Welch.

**236 Bob Hope's All-Star Super Bowl Party** (1/25/86). *Guests:* Susan Akin, Diahann Carroll, Donna Mills, Don Rickles.

**237 Bob Hope's Royal Command Performance from Sweden** (3/19/86). *Guests:* Boy George, Glen Campbell, Scott Grimes, Shirley Jones, Emmanuel Lewis, Omar Sharif, Liv Ullmann. *Music Director:* Bob Alberti. *Note:* A music and comedy concert for Sweden's King Carl XVI Gustaf and Queen Silvia.

**238 Bob Hope's High-Flying Birthday** (2 hrs., 5/26/86). *Guests:* Patty Andrews, Mac Davis, Sammy Davis, Jr.; Dolores Hope, Don Johnson, Barbara Mandrell, Phylicia Rashad, Brooke Shields, Elizabeth Taylor. *Note:* An eighty-third birthday celebration for Bob Hope. Taped aboard the carrier USS *Lexington* in Pensacola, Florida.

**239 Bob Hope Lampoons the New TV Season** (9/15/86). *Guests:* George Burns, Morgan Fairchild, Ann Jillian, Tony Randall, Danny Thomas.

**240 Bob Hope's Bagful of Christ-**
**mas Cheer** (12/21/86). *Guests:* Crystal Gayle, Donna Mills, Brooke Shields.

**241 From Tahiti: Bob Hope's Tropical Comedy Special** (2/23/87). *Guests:* Susan Akin, Morgan Brittany, John Denver, Howard Keel, Jonathan Winters.

**242 Bob Hope with His Beautiful Easter Bunnies and Other Friends** (4/19/87). *Guests:* Lynda Carter, Stepfanie Kramer, Gloria Loring, Vanna White. *Note:* An hour of music and song geared to springtime.

**243 Bob Hope's High-Flying Birthday Extravaganza** (2 hrs., 5/25/87). *Guests:* Lucille Ball, Glen Campbell, Kirk Cameron, Phyllis Diller, Dolores Hope, Don Johnson, Emmanuel Lewis, Barbara Mandrell, Phylicia Rashad, President Ronald Reagan, Brooke Shields. *Note:* A celebration of Bob Hope's eighty-fourth birthday at Pope Air Force Base in North Carolina.

**244 NBC Investigates Bob Hope** (9/17/87). See title for information.

**245 The Bob Hope Christmas Show — A Snow Job in Florida** (12/19/87). *Guests:* Morgan Fairchild, Reba McEntire, Tony Randall, Brooke Shields.

**246 Bob Hope's USO Christmas from the Persian Gulf: Around the World in Eight Days** (90 min., 1/9/88). *Guests:* Barbara Eden, Joely Fisher, Tricia Fisher, Lee Greenwood, Michelle Royer (Miss USA, 1987), Connie Stevens. *Note:* A chronicle of Bob Hope's thirty-first USO Christmas tour — his first since 1983.

**247 Happy Birthday, Bob** (3 hrs., 5/16/88). *Guests:* ALF, Steve Allen, Lucille Ball, Milton Berle, George Burns, Kirk Cameron, Diahann Carroll, Bert Convy, Sammy Davis, Jr.; Angie Dickinson, Phyllis Diller, John Forsythe, Dolores Hope, Ann Jillian, Jack Jones, Stepfanie Kramer, Dorothy Lamour, Michael Landon, Jay Leno, Shelley Long, Reba McEntire, Donald O'Connor, Marie Osmond, Tony Randall, Don Rickles, Brooke Shields,

**Ad for "Bob Hope's Fun Birthday Spectacular from Paris"**

Dinah Shore, James Stewart, Danny Thomas, Leslie Uggams, Betty White, Jonathan Winters. *Note:* An elaborate celebration of Bob Hope's eighty-fifth birthday and his fiftieth year with NBC.

**248 Stand By for HNN—The Hope News Network** (9/8/88). *Guests:* Phyllis Diller, Morgan Fairchild, Tony Randall, Brooke Shields. *Note:* The special finds Bob as the owner of the all news Hope News Network with him and his guests spoofing news programs.

**249 Bob Hope's Jolly Christmas Show** (12/19/88). *Guests:* Orel Hershiser, Don Johnson, Florence Griffith Joyner, Dolly Parton.

**250 Bob Hope's Super Bowl Party** (1/21/89). *Guests:* George Burns, Sammy Davis, Jr.; Shelley Long, Tiffany.

**251 Bob Hope's Easter Vacation in the Bahamas** (3/25/89). *Guests:* LaToya Jackson, Barbara Mandrell, Tony Randall, Andy Williams.

**252 Bob Hope's Fun Birthday Spectacular from Paris** (2 hrs., 5/24/89). *Guests:* Bea Arthur, Sid Caesar, Linda Evans, John Forsythe, Dolores Hope, Louis Jourdan, Melissa Manchester, Brooke Shields, Randy Travis. *Note:* Bob celebrates his eighty-sixth birthday in Paris.

**253 Bob Hope's Love Affair with Lucy** (90 min., 9/23/89). *Guests:* George Burns, Kirk Cameron, Danny Thomas, Betty White. *Note:* A tribute to Lucille Ball via clips of Bob's movie and television appearances with her.

**254 Bob Hope's Christmas in Hawaii** (12/16/89). *Guests:* Barbara Eden, The Judds.

**255 Bob Hope Lampoons Show Business** (2/17/90). *Guests:* Michael Crawford, Norm Crosby, Morgan Fairchild, John Forsythe.

**256 Bob Hope's Spring Fling of Comedy and Glamour from Acapulco** (4/8/90). *Guests:* Kirk Cameron, Phyllis Diller, Ann Jillian.

**257 Bob Hope's USO Road Tour to the Berlin Wall and Moscow** (90 min.,

5/19/90). *Guests:* Rosemary Clooney, Dolores Hope, LaToya Jackson, Brooke Shields, Yakov Smirnoff.

**258 Bob Hope: Don't Shoot, It's Only Me** (9/15/90). *Guests:* Milton Berle, George Burns, Dolores Hope, Henry Kissinger, Frances Langford, Gloria Loring, Connie Stevens, Danny Thomas.

**259 Bob Hope's 1990 Christmas Show** (12/15/90). *Guests:* Loni Anderson, Dixie Carter, Joan Van Ark.

**260 Bob Hope's Christmas Cheer from Saudi Arabia** (90 min., 1/12/91). *Guests:* Johnny Bench, Khrystyne Haje, Dolores Hope, Ann Jillian, Marie Osmond, The Pointer Sisters.

**261 Bob Hope's Yellow Ribbon Celebration** (90 min., 4/5/91). *Guests:* Clint Black, Delta Burke, Clint Holmes, Ann Jillian, Patti LaBelle, Ed McMahon, Gerald McRaney, Marie Osmond, Brooke Shields, James Stewart. *Note:* Bob, who visited the American troops in the Persian Gulf in December 1990, carries out his promise to give them a welcome home celebration by throwing a party from his home in Palm Springs.

**262 Bob Hope and Friends ... Making New Memories** (90 min., 5/1/91). *Guests:* Kirk Cameron, Shannen Doherty, Jennie Garth, Kathy Ireland, Brooke Shields.

**263 Bob Hope's Star Studded Comedy Special of the New Season** (90 min., 9/12/91). *Guests:* Roseanne Arnold, Garth Brooks, Dorothy Lamour, Angela Lansbury, Burt Reynolds, Debbie Reynolds, Jane Russell.

**264 Bob Hope's Cross-Country Christmas Show** (12/18/91). *Guests:* Macaulay Culkin, Dolores Hope, Carolyn Sapp (Miss America, 1992), Reba McEntire.

**265 Bob Hope and Other Young Comedians** (3/14/92). *Guests:* Milton Berle, Phyllis Diller, Betty White. *Note:* Established performers appear with new hopefuls (Jeff Cesario, Pam Stone, Max Alexander, Carol Leifer,

**Ad for "Bob Hope's 1990 Christmas Show from Bermuda"**

Jeff Foxworthy, John Henton, Jeff Dunham).

**266 Bob Hope's America: Red, White and Beautiful—The Swimsuit Edition** (90 min., 5/16/92). *Guests:* Dolores Hope, Elle MacPherson, Dolly Parton, Loretta Swit. *Note:* A comedy and music salute to American beauties and the women of courage in the armed services.

**267 Bob Hope Presents the Ladies of Laughter** (11/28/92). *Guests:* Crystal Bernard, Phyllis Diller, Rue Mc-Clanahan. *Featured Comediennes:* Margaret Cho, Wendy Liebman, Kathleen Madigan, Carol Siskind, Anita Wise.

**268 Bob Hope's Four-Star Christmas Fiesta** (12/19/92). *Guests:* Clint Black, Dolores Hope, Phylicia Rashad. *Note:* Bob's Christmas special from San Antonio.

**269 Bob Hope: The First 90 Years** (5/14/93). *Hosts:* Paula Abdul, Lucie Arnaz, Roseanne and Tom Arnold, Walter Cronkite, Angela Lansbury, Paul Reiser, Betty White. *Guest of Honor:* Bob Hope. *Guests:* Milton Berle, Garth Brooks, George Burns, Kirk Cameron, Johnny Carson, Chevy Chase, Rosemary Clooney, Whoopi Goldberg, Phil Hartman, Florence Henderson, Dolores Hope, Ann Jillian, Dorothy Lamour, Jay Leno, Michael Richards, Tom Selleck, Garry Shandling, Brooke Shields, Dave Thomas, Raquel Welch. *Note:* A tribute to Bob Hope on the occasion of his ninetieth birthday (born 5/29) and his fifty-ninth year with NBC; clips are used to recall Bob's career in radio, vaudeville, movies, and on television.

**Bob Hope's Funny Valentine** *see* **Bob Hope Specials**

**Bob Hope's Love Affair with Lucy** *see* **Bob Hope Specials**

**Bob Hope's Pink Panther Thanksgiving** *see* **Bob Hope Specials**

**Bob Hope's Road to Hollywood** *see* **Bob Hope Specials**

**Bob Hope's Salute to NASA** *see* **Bob Hope Specials**

**Bob Hope's Spring Fling to Comedy and Glamour** *see* **Bob Hope Specials**

**Bob Hope's Stars Over Texas** *see* **Bob Hope Specials**

**Bob Hope's Women I Love** *see* **Bob Hope Specials**

**233 The Bob Newhart 19th Anniversary Special.** Comedy, 60 min., CBS, 11/23/91. A reunion of "The Bob Newhart Show" cast with clips and remembrances from the CBS show (1972–78). *Cast:* Bob Newhart, Suzanne Pleshette, Bill Daily, Peter Bonerz, Jack Riley. *Producers:* George Zaloom, Les Mayfield. *Writers:* Michael Mahler, Mark Egan, Mark Solomon.

**234 The Bobbie Gentry Special.** Variety, 60 min. (each), Syndicated, 5/71 and 7/71. An hour of country and western music with singer Bobbie Gentry and her guests. *Host:* Bobbie Gentry. *Guests* (5/71): John Hartford, Richie Havens, Billy Rose, The Staple Singers, Ian and Sylvia Tyson. *Guests* (7/71): Fannie Flagg, Bobby Goldsboro, Rick Nelson, Joe South, The Sugar Shoppe. *Music Director:* Bill Walker.

**235 The Bobby Sherman Special.** Variety, 60 min., ABC, 6/4/71. A program of music and songs with then teen idol Bobby Sherman. *Host:* Bobby Sherman. *Guests:* The Fifth Dimension, Rip Taylor. *Producers:* Ward Sylvester, Burt Rosen. *Writers:* Burt Rosen, Frank D. Glucksman. *Director:* Jorn Winther.

## 236 The Bobby Van and Elaine Joyce Special.
Variety, 60 min., CBS, 12/17/73. Music, songs, and comedy with singer-dancer Bobby Van and his wife, actress Elaine Joyce. *Host:* Bobby Van, Elaine Joyce. *Guest:* Richard Thomas. *Music:* Buster Davis. *Producer:* Arne Rosen. *Writers:* George Bloom, Robert Hilliard, Woody Kling. *Director:* Bill Davis.

## 237 Bogart.
Documentary, 60 min., NBC, 4/23/67. A profile of actor Humphrey Bogart through film clips and the memories of coworkers. *Host-Narrator:* Charlton Heston. *Guests:* Ingrid Bergman, Stanley Kramer, Ida Lupino, Joseph L. Mankiewicz, Michael Romanoff. *Music:* Nelson Riddle. *Producer:* Sherman Grinberg. *Producer-Writer-Director:* Marshall Flaum. *Note:* The special was reedited (deleting Charlton Heston and adding Joseph Campanella as the host-narrator) and syndicated in September 1987.

## 238 Bonnie and the Franklins.
Variety, 60 min., CBS, 1/2/82. A musical comedy hour in which actress Bonnie Franklin (then star of "One Day at a Time") "writes" her autobiography in song and dance — with help from her friends and family. *Host:* Bonnie Franklin. *Guests:* Gene Castle, Michele Lee, Joe Namath, Lee Roy Reams. *Music:* Gerald Alters. *Producer:* Marilyn Shapario. *Writers:* Sam Hart, Mitzie Welch. *Director:* Tony Charmoli.

## 239 Boop Oop a Doop.
Documentary, 75 min., PBS, 4/15/89. The program traces the history of Betty Boop, cartoon land's most enduring sex symbol. *Narrator:* Steve Allen. *Guests:* Helen Kane, Mae Questel (voice of Betty Boop). *Producer-Director:* Vernon P. Becker. *Cartoon Producer:* Max Fleischer. *Cartoon Director:* Dave Fleischer.

## 240 The Booth.
Comedy-Drama, 90 min., ABC, 10/9/85. Three stories, by prominent writers, of people whose lives change during their lunch in a restaurant booth. **Story 1:** "Bread." A young producer (Ted) attempts to lure an aged but famous actress (Rosa) back to the Broadway stage. **Story 2:** "The 75th." A melodramatic segment about Arthur and Amy, the last surviving members of their high school graduating class who meet on the occasion of the seventy-fifth anniversary of their graduation. **Story 3:** "Death at Dinner." The complications that result when a man with a weak heart attempts to romance a vibrant young woman during lunch. *Cast, Story 1:* Dame Judith Anderson (Rosa Monterey), Peter Coyote (Ted Steadman), Mary Kay Place (Sara Aaronson). *Cast, Story 2:* Barnard Hughes (Arthur Silverstein), Mildred Natwick (Amy Chamberlain). *Cast, Story 3:* James Coco (Man), Teri Garr (Woman), Rene Auberjonois (Waiter). *Music:* Denny Crockett, Ike Egan. *Producers:* Merrill K. Karpf, George Schaefer. *Story 1 Writer:* James Prideaux. *Story 2 Writer:* Israel Horowitz. *Story 3 Writer:* Rose Goldberg. *Director:* George Schaefer.

## 241 The Boots Randolph Show.
Variety, 60 min., NBC, 9/5/72. An hour of country and western songs with singer Boots Randolph. *Host:* Boots Randolph. *Guests:* Chet Atkins, Barbara McNair, Doc Severinsen, The Star Spangled Dancers, Gordie Tapp, Today's Children. *Music:* Bill Walker. *Producers:* Roy A. Smith, Bill Williams. *Writers:* Bill Wingford, Jim Carlson. *Director:* Joseph Hostettler.

## 242 Born Yesterday.
Comedy, 90 min., NBC, 10/28/56. The story of a wealthy junk dealer (Harry Brock) and the complications that ensue when he hires a writer (Paul Verrall) to "educate" his sassy girlfriend (Billie Dawn). Based on the play by Garson Kanin and broadcast on the "Hallmark Hall of Fame." *Cast:* Mary Martin (Billie

Dawn), Paul Douglas (Harry Brock), Arthur Hill (Paul Verrall), Harry Oliver (Senator Hedges), Otto Hulett (Ed Devery), Laura Pierpont (Mrs. Hedges), Belle Flower (Helen). *Producer:* George Schaefer. *Writer-Director:* Garson Kanin.

### 243 The Borrowers. Fantasy, 90 min., NBC, 12/14/73.

The Clocks are an inches-high family who live beneath the floorboards of a Victorian country home. Their efforts to escape capture when they are discovered by an eight-year-old boy are the focal point of the story. Aired on the "Hallmark Hall of Fame." *Cast:* Eddie Albert (Pod Clock), Tammy Grimes (Homily Clock), Karen Pearson (Arriety Clock), Judith Anderson (Aunt Sophy), Dennis Larson (Tom), Beatrice Straight (Mrs. Crampfurl), Barnard Hughes (Mr. Crampfurl). *Music:* Rod McKuen. *Producer:* Duane C. Bogie. *Writer:* Jay Presson Allen. *Director:* Walter C. Miller.

### 244 Bradymania. Retrospective, 60 min., ABC, 5/19/93.

Clips are used to recall "The Brady Bunch," which ran on ABC from 1969 to 1974. The program also tries to explain the show's impact on American culture. Original cast members appear and clips are seen from Brady Bunch television movies and the stage show, "The Real Live Brady Bunch." *Host:* Florence Henderson. *Guests:* Ann B. Davis, Christopher Knight, Michael Lookinland, Susan Olsen, Barry Williams. *Music:* Peggy Sandvig. *Producers:* Malcolm Leo, Bonnie Peterson. *Writers:* Malcolm Leo, Allen Rucker. *Director:* Malcolm Leo.

### 245 The Brass Are Coming. Variety, 60 min., NBC, 10/29/69.

An hour of music with Herb Alpert and the Tijuana Brass. *Host:* Herb Alpert. *Guests:* George Burns, Petula Clark. *Producers:* Frank Peppiatt, John Aylesworth. *Writers:* Frank Peppiatt, John Aylesworth, George Yanok. *Director:* Bill Davis.

### 246 Breadwinner. Drama, 30 min., HBO, 4/9/87.

The story of a college student (Joey) who relinquishes his college fund to find a part-time job to help support his family following his father's layoff from a steel mill. *Cast:* Lance Kerwin (Joey Brennan), Pat Hingle (Frank Brennan), Quinn Cummings (Cathy Brennan), Lee Meriwether (Mary Brennan), Ken Swofford (Paul Gates), Tommy Bush (Ben Crowley). *Music:* Chris Stone. *Producers:* Ellwood E. Kieser, Mike Rhodes. *Writer:* Tim McGinn. *Director:* Mike Rhodes.

### 247 Breck's Golden Showcase. Anthology, 60 min., CBS, 12/6/61–4/30/62.

The overall title for a series of five specials sponsored by Breck Shampoo. For information on each of the specials that aired, see the following titles: "The Devil and Daniel Webster," "The Four Poster," "The Picture of Dorian Gray," "Saturday's Children," and "Tonight in Samarkand."

### 248 The Bridge of Adam Rush. Drama, 60 min., ABC, 10/23/74.

Following the death of his father and the subsequent remarriage of his mother (Rebecca) to a poor farmer (Tom), 12-year-old Adam Rush suddenly finds his comfortable life disrupted when he is forced to live on his stepfather's farm. The story, set in the 1880s, follows Adam's efforts to prove himself to Tom by helping him build a bridge to get their livestock to market—a project that becomes a bridge of respect and understanding between them. Aired as an "ABC Afterschool Special." *Cast:* Lance Kerwin (Adam Rush), James Pritchett (Tom), Barbara Anders (Rebecca), Karen Sedore (Elizabeth), Kay Belleran (Jody). *Producer:* Daniel Wilson. *Writer:* Lee Kalcheim. *Director:* Larry Elikann.

**249 Brief Encounter.** Drama, 60 min., NBC, 3/26/61. A romantic story about two married strangers (Laura and Alec) who meet and fall in love during a summer holiday. The program marks the dramatic television acting debut of Dinah Shore. *Cast:* Dinah Shore (Laura Jesson), Ralph Bellamy (Dr. Alec Harvey), Howard St. John (Albert Godby), Collette Lyons (Myrtle Bagot), Arte Johnson (Stanley), Bennye Getteys (Miss Waters), Jacqueline DeWitt (Dolly). *Producers:* Dean Whitmore, Bob Finkel. *Writer:* Joseph Shrank. *Director:* Dean Whitmore.

**250 Brief Encounter.** Drama, 90 min., NBC, 11/12/74. A "Hallmark Hall of Fame" adaptation of the Noel Coward play about two married people (Anna and Alec) who meet by chance and fall in love. The special marks the American television debut of Sophia Loren. *Cast:* Sophia Loren (Anna Jesson), Richard Burton (Alec Harvey), Jack Hedley (Graham), Rosemary Leach (Mrs. Gaines), Gwen Cherell (Dolly). *Music:* Cyril Ornadel. *Producer:* Duane C. Bogie. *Writer:* John Bowen. *Director:* Alan Bridges.

**251 Brigadoon.** Musical Fantasy, 90 min., ABC, 10/15/66. Tommy Albright and Jeff Douglas, two Americans lost on the Scottish moors, come across Brigadoon, a strange village that appears for only one day every 100 years. Their experiences in the mythical village and Tommy's romance with Fiona MacLaren are the focal point of the 1947 musical by Alan Jay Lerner and Frederick Loewe. *Cast:* Robert Goulet (Tommy Albright), Peter Falk (Jeff Douglas), Sally Ann Howes (Fiona MacLaren), Marlyn Mason (Meg Brockie), Thomas Carlisle (Charley Dalrymple), Linda Howe (Jeannie MacLaren), Rhys Williams (Andrew MacLaren), Edward Villella (Harry Beaton). *Music:* Irwin Kostel. *Producers:* Norman Rosemont, Fielder

Cook. *Writer:* Ernest Kinoy. *Director:* Fielder Cook.

**252 Brigitte Bardot.** Variety, 60 min., NBC, 12/3/68. A bilingual hour of song and travel as actress Brigitte Bardot tours France. *Host:* Brigitte Bardot. *Guests:* Sacha Distel, Serge Gainsbourg. *Music:* Francis Lai. *Producer:* Bob Zagury. *Directors:* Eddie Mathlon, Francois Reichenbach.

**253 Broadway.** Drama, 60 min., CBS, 5/4/55. A television adaptation of the 1926 Broadway play by Philip Dunning and George Abbott about a nightclub dancer (Billie Moore) who becomes involved with the murder of a gangster ("Scar" Edwards). *Cast:* Piper Laurie (Billie Moore), Joseph Cotten (Dan McCorn), Gene Nelson (Roy Lane), Akim Tamiroff (Nick Vardis), Keenan Wynn (Steve Crandall), Martha Hyer (Pearl), Frank Marth ("Scar" Edwards). *Music:* Alfredo Antonini. *Producer:* Felix Jackson. *TV Adaptation:* Philip Dunning. *Director:* Franklin Schaffner.

**254 The Broadway of Lerner and Loewe.** Variety, 60 min., NBC, 2/11/62. A tribute to composers Alan Jay Lerner and Frederick Loewe. *Performers:* Richard Burton, Robert Goulet, Stanley Holloway. *Music:* Franz Allers. *Producer-Director:* Norman Jewison.

**255 Broadway Sings the Music of Jule Styne.** Variety, 90 min., PBS, 12/1/89. A tribute to composer Jule Styne with celebrities performing his songs. *Host:* Jule Styne. *Performers:* Patti Austin, Sammy Cahn, Diahann Carroll, Carol Channing, Betty Comden, Vic Damone, Adolph Green, Mariette Hartley, Maurice Hines, Fran Jeffries, Jack Jones, Larry Kerts, Jack Klugman, Arthur Laurents, Linda Lavin, Hal Linden, Melissa Manchester, Phyllis Newman, Jeffrey Osborne, Ann Reinking, Chita Rivera,

Rex Smith. *Music:* Don Pippin. *Producer:* Jac Venza. *Writer:* Robert L. Freedman. *Directors:* Joe Layton, Gary Halvorson.

### 256 Brooke Shields: Pretty Baby.

Documentary, 30 min., ABC, 7/16/80. A profile of model-actress Brooke Shields — from her controversial 1978 role (at age 12) in *Pretty Baby* to her newest role as a sex symbol (at age 15) in *Endless Love* (the program aired on the night before the movie opened in theaters). Brooke herself appears to talk about her film roles (*Endless Love*, for example, was originally rated "X" but was later edited for an "R" rating) and how she is an "R"-rated actress living a "PG" life. The program also explores Brooke's controversial television commercial for Calvin Klein jeans (which was considered too suggestive and pulled). *Host:* Geraldo Rivera. *Guests:* Karen Hirsch, Jon Peters, Teri Shields, Frank Zaparelli. *Producer:* Michael Smith.

**Brooke Shields**

### 257 Brown Sugar.

Documentary, 60 min., PBS, 2/8/86. The program recalls (via film clips, stills, and interviews) the personal and professional lives of black female entertainers. *Host:* Billy Dee Williams. *Producers:* Donald Bogle, Jeorg Klebe. *Writer-Director:* Donald Bogle.

### 258 Bruce Willis: The Return of Bruno.

Music, 60 min., HBO, 2/7/87. A "rockumentary" spoof wherein "Moonlighting" star Bruce Willis portrays his alter ego, rock star Bruno Radolini. *Host:* Bruce Willis. *Guests:* The Bee Gees, Dick Clark, Elton John, Mavis Staples, The Temptations. *Music:* Robert Kraft. *Producers:* Bruce Willis, Paul Flattery. *Writers:* Paul Flattery, Bob Hari, Bruce Willis, Bruce DiMattia. *Director:* Jim Yukich.

### 259 The Buddy Greco Show.

Variety, 60 min., Syndicated, 2/69. A musical celebration of Valentine's Day. *Host:* Buddy Greco. *Guests:* The Backporch Majority, Jackie DeShannon, Elaine Dunn, The James Hibbard

Dancers, Sal Mineo, Ted Neely, Marie Wilson. *Music Director:* Ralph Carmichael.

## 260 Buddy Hackett — Live and Uncensored. Comedy, 60 min., HBO, 7/10/83. Comedian Buddy Hackett performs his adults only, uncensored nightclub act (from Resorts International in Atlantic City, N.J.). *Music:* Ron Ponzio. *Producers:* Ken Weinstock, Buddy Hackett. *Writer:* Buddy Hackett. *Director:* Christopher Kelly.

## 261 The Budweiser Showdown. Contest, 60 min., Syndicated, 8/89. The program, sponsored by Budweiser Beer, features a talent contest in which amateur rock groups compete for a recording contract and a guest spot in a beer commercial. *Hosts:* Patti Austin, Lou Rawls. *Announcer:* Joe Graham. *Producer:* Gary Firth. *Producer-Director:* Gary Menotti.

## 262 Bugs Bunny: All-American Hero. Cartoon, 30 min., CBS, 5/14/81. A rabbit's eye view of our nation's glorious past as related by Bugs Bunny as he attempts to help his nephew, Clyde, prepare for an American history test. *Voices:* Mel Blanc (as Bugs Bunny, Clyde Bunny, Tweety Pie, Yosemite Sam, Sylvester). *Producer:* Hal Geer. *Writers:* Friz Freleng, John Dunn, David Detiege. *Directors:* Friz Freleng, David Detiege.

## 263 The Bugs Bunny Easter Special. Cartoon, 30 min., CBS, 4/7/77. The story finds Bugs desperately seeking to find a replacement for the Easter Rabbit, who is bedridden with a cold and unable to make his traditional Sunday morning rounds. *Voices:* Mel Blanc (as Bugs Bunny, Daffy Duck, Yosemite Sam, Foghorn Leghorn, Pepe LePew), June Foray (Granny). *Music:* Harper McKay, Carl Stalling, Milt Franklyn. *Producer:* Hal Geer.

*Directors:* Friz Freleng, Robert McKimson, Gerry Chiniquy, Chuck Jones.

## 264 Bugs Bunny in Space. Cartoon, 30 min., CBS, 9/6/77. A compilation of Bugs Bunny in space scenes culled from previous cartoons. *Voices:* Mel Blanc. *Producer:* Hal Geer. *Directors:* Chuck Jones, Friz Freleng.

## 265 The Bugs Bunny Mystery Special. Cartoon, 30 min., CBS, 10/15/80. Bugs Bunny attempts to prove he is innocent of a daring daytime bank robbery — despite the efforts of special agent Elmer Fudd to convict him of the charge. *Voices:* Mel Blanc (as Bugs Bunny, Elmer Fudd, Yosemite Sam, Wile E. Coyote, Tweety Pie, Sylvester, Porky Pig). *Producer:* Hal Geer. *Writers:* Jack Enyart, Hal Geer. *Directors:* Friz Freleng, Chuck Jones, Gerry Chiniquy.

## 266 The Bugs Bunny Thanksgiving Diet. Cartoon, 30 min., CBS, 11/17/79. Bugs Bunny's attempts to help his friends (Porky Pig, Yosemite Sam, Tweety Pie, Sylvester, and Wile E. Coyote) who are seeking a special diet to avoid those Thanksgiving Day pounds. *Voices:* Mel Blanc, June Foray. *Music:* Carl Stalling, Milt Franklyn, Harper McKay. *Producer:* Hal Geer. *Writers:* Jack Enyart, Warren Foster, Michael Maltese, Tedd Pierce, John Dunne. *Directors:* Hal Geer, Chuck Jones, Friz Freleng, Robert McKimson.

## 267 Bugs Bunny's Bustin' Out All Over. Cartoon, 30 min., CBS, 5/21/80. An animated special composed of three vignettes. In the first, Bugs Bunny recalls his childhood where an infant Elmer Fudd is seen with his popgun waiting for the opening of "Wabbit Season." In the second episode, Bugs welcomes springtime and has an encounter with Marvin the

Martian. The third segment revolves around Wile E. Coyote who, after 30 years, finally captures the elusive Road Runner. *Voices:* Mel Blanc. *Music:* Dean Elliott. *Producer:* Hal Geer. *Writer:* Chuck Jones. *Directors:* Chuck Jones, Phil Monroe.

## 268 Bugs Bunny's Howl-O-Ween Special. Cartoon, 30 min., CBS, 10/30/77.

New animation with excerpts from old movie cartoons are used to tell how Bugs Bunny falls into the clutches of the evil witch, Hazel, while trick or treating. *Voices:* Mel Blanc. *Music:* Harper McKay, Carl Stalling, Milt Franklin. *Producer:* Hal Geer. *Writers:* Cliff Roberts, Tedd Pierce, Warren Foster, Michael Maltese, John Dunne. *Directors:* Robert McKimson, Chuck Jones, Friz Freleng, Abe Levitow, Maurice Noble, David Detiege.

## 269 Bugs Bunny's Looney Christmas Tales. Cartoon, 30 min., CBS, 11/13/79.

Bugs Bunny spins three yuletide yarns: "A Christmas Carol" (Bunny style) with Porky Pig as Bob Cratchit; Yosemite Sam as Ebenezer Scrooge; and Tweety Pie as Tiny Tim. The second tale relates Wile E. Coyote's attempts to catch himself a Christmas dinner—the Road Runner. In the final story, the Tasmanian Devil poses as Santa Claus and drops in on Bugs and his nephew Clyde—seeking to satisfy his voracious appetite. *Voices:* Mel Blanc, June Foray. *Music:* Harper McKay, Carl Stalling, Milt Franklin. *Producer:* Hal Geer. *Writers:* Friz Freleng, John Dunne, Chuck Jones, Tony Benedict. *Directors:* Bill Perez, David Detiege, Art Vitello, Tony Benedict.

## 270 Bugs Bunny's Mad World of Television. Cartoon, 30 min., CBS, 9/6/85.

A compilation of scenes from various Bugs Bunny cartoons that explore the antics of "that silly wabbit." *Voices:* Mel Blanc. *Music:* Carl Stal-

ling, Milt Franklin, Harper McKay. *Producer:* Hal Geer. *Writers:* David Detiege, John Dunne, Jack Enyart, Warren Foster, Hal Geer, Chuck Jones. *Directors:* Friz Freleng, Chuck Jones, Robert McKimson.

## 271 Bugs Bunny's Valentine. Cartoon, 30 min., CBS, 2/14/79.

The story follows Bugs Bunny as he attempts to romance the electric rabbit at the dog track when he is shot by Elmer (Fudd) Cupid's love arrow—and falls head over heels in love with it. *Voices:* Mel Blanc. *Music:* Harper McKay, Carl Stalling, Milt Franklin. *Producer:* Hal Geer. *Writers:* Warren Foster, Hal Geer, Michael Maltese, Sid Marcus, Tedd Pierce. *Directors:* Jim Davis, Hal Geer, Friz Freleng, Chuck Jones, Robert McKimson.

## 272 Bulova Watch Time with Pat Boone. Variety, 60 min., ABC, 4/20/61.

An hour of music and songs; sponsored by Bulova Watches. *Host:* Pat Boone. *Guests:* Fabian, The Kingston Trio, Johnny Mercer, Dorothy Provine, Joanie Sommers. *Music:* Vic Schoen. *Producer-Director:* Norman Jewison. *Writers:* Herb Sargent, Saul Ilson.

## 273 The Burl Ives Thanksgiving Special. Variety, 60 min., Syndicated, 11/68.

A holiday program of music and song. *Host:* Burl Ives. *Guests:* The Backporch Majority, Lionel Hampton, Randy Sparks.

## 274 Burlesque. Drama, 60 min., NBC, 4/24/49.

A television adaptation of the Broadway play by George Manker Watters and Arthur Hopkins about Skid Johnson, a second-rate comic, and his wife and stage partner, Bonny, and their attempts to make the big time. *Cast:* Bert Lahr (Skid Johnson), Vicki Cummings (Bonny Johnson). *Producer:* Owen Davis. *Director:* Vic McLeod.

**275 Burlesque.** Drama, 60 min., CBS, 3/17/55. A second television adaptation of the 1927 Broadway play about a showbusiness couple and their attempts to make the big time. *Cast:* Dan Dailey (Skid Johnson), Marilyn Maxwell (Bonny Johnson), Jack Oakie (Bozo), Joan Blondell (Gussie), Dick Foran (Harvey Howell), Helen Stanley (Sylvia Marco), Jack Benny (Himself). *Music:* David Rose. *Producer:* Nat Perrin. *Writers:* Martin Fyne, David Friedkin. *Director:* Seymour Berns.

**276 Burley-Q.** Comedy, 60 min., Showtime, 5/81. A re-creation of the burlesque-like comedy of the 1920s. *Stars:* Arte Johnson, Louis Nye. *Producers:* Seymour Berns, Ann O'Brien, Gerry Rochon. *Director:* Gerry Rochon.

**277 Burnett "Discovers" Domingo.** Variety, 60 min., CBS, 1/27/84. Songs and comedy skits with Carol Burnett and Placido Domingo. *Music:* Peter Matz. *Producers:* Marty Pasetta, Kenny Solms. *Writers:* Kenny Solms, Mitzie Welch. *Director:* Marty Pasetta.

**278 The Burning Court.** Mystery, 60 min., NBC, 4/24/60. A "Dow Hour of Great Mysteries" presentation about a man who discovers that his wife is the reincarnation of a seventeenth-century witch. *Cast:* Barbara Bel Geddes (Marie Stevens), George C. Scott (Gordon Cross), Robert Lansing (Edward Stevens), Anne Seymour (Mrs. Henderson). *Producer:* Robert Saudek. *Writer:* Kelly Roos.

**279 Burt and the Girls.** Variety, 90 min., NBC, 12/8/73. A program of light conversation and improvisational skits. *Host:* Burt Reynolds. *Guests:* Carol Burnett, Nancy Dussault, Nanette Fabray, Jaye P. Morgan, Bernadette Peters, JoAnn Pflug, Della Reese, Joyce Van Patten. *Music:* John Rodby. *Producers:* Jack Wohl, Bernard Rothman, Fred Tatashore.

*Writers:* Charles Bloom, James Hampton, Jack Wohl, Bernard Rothman, Fred Tatashore. *Director:* Art Fisher.

**280 Burt Bacharach Specials.** A chronological listing of composer Burt Bacharach's specials. All are 60 minutes each and feature music and songs. Burt Bacharach was the host for each special.

**1 The Burt Bacharach Special** (CBS, 3/14/71). *Guests:* Tom Jones, Rudolph Nureyev, Barbra Streisand. *Music:* Peter Matz. *Producers:* Gary Smith, Dwight Hemion. *Writers:* Marty Farrell, Bob Ellison. *Director:* Dwight Hemion.

**2 Burt Bacharach: Close to You** (ABC, 4/23/72). *Guests:* Carol Burnett, Rex Harrison, Isaac Hayes, The Rob Iscove Dancers. *Music:* Jack Parnell. *Producers:* Gary Smith, Dwight Hemion. *Writers:* Bob Ellison, Herb Sargent, Bryan Blackburn. *Director:* Dwight Hemion.

**3 The Magical Music of Burt Bacharach** (Syndicated, 5/72). *Guests:* Sacha Distel, Joel Grey, Dionne Warwick. *Music:* Jack Parnell. *Producers:* Gary Smith, Dwight Hemion. *Writers:* Bob Willson, Herb Sargent, Bryan Blackburn. *Director:* Dwight Hemion.

**4 Burt Bacharach!** (ABC, 11/15/72). *Guests:* Vikki Carr, Sammy Davis, Jr.; Anthony Newley, The Paddy Stone Dancers. *Music:* Jack Parnell. *Producers:* Gary Smith, Dwight Hemion. *Writers:* Herb Sargent, Marty Farrell. *Director:* Dwight Hemion.

**5 Burt Bacharach in Shangri-La** (ABC, 1/27/73). *Guests:* Chris Evert, The Fifth Dimension, Richard Harris, The Jamie Rogers Dancers, Bobby Van. *Music:* Jack Parnell. *Producers:* Gary Smith, Dwight Hemion. *Writers:* Marty Farrell, Marc Ray. *Director:* Dwight Hemion.

**6 Burt Bacharach — Opus Number 3** (ABC, 2/28/73). *Guests:* Bette Midler, Gilbert O'Sullivan, Peter Ustinov, Stevie Wonder. *Music:* Jack Parnell. *Producers:* Gary Smith, Dwight Hemion.

*Writers:* Marty Farrell, Marc Ray. *Director:* Dwight Hemion.
**7 The Burt Bacharach Special** (NBC, 1/10/74). *Guests:* Sandy Duncan, Jack Jones, Roger Moore, The Harlem Globetrotters. *Music:* Jack Parnell. *Producer:* Gary Smith, Dwight Hemion. *Writer:* Marty Farrell. *Director:* Dwight Hemion.

**281 Burt Reynolds' Late Show.** Variety, 90 min., NBC, 10/13/73. A late night program (11:30 P.M.–1:00 A.M.) of performances by country and western entertainers. *Host:* Burt Reynolds. *Guests:* Glen Campbell, Bobby Goldsboro, Roger Miller, Jim Nabors, Dolly Parton, Minnie Pearl, Charlie Rich, Rusty Richards, Dinah Shore, Mel Tillis, Porter Wagoner. *Music:* John Rodby. *Producers:* Bernard Rothman, Jack Wohl, Fred Tatashore. *Writers:* James Hampton, Fred Tatashore, Jack Wohl, Bernard Rothman. *Director:* Art Fisher.

**282 Bus Stop.** Comedy, 2 hrs., HBO, 8/22/82. The story, set at Grace's Diner (30 miles from Kansas City), follows the romance between a second-rate saloon singer (Cherie) and a love-sick cowboy (Bo) who pursues her. Based on the play by William Inge and taped in May 1982 at the Garrison Theater at Claremont College in California. *Cast:* Margot Kidder (Cherie), Tim Matheson (Bo Decker), Joyce Van Patten (Grace), Marilyn Jones (Thelma Duckworth), Pat Hingle (Dr. Gerald Lyman), Claude Akins (Sheriff Will Masters). *Producers:* Peter H. Hunt, John Thomas Lenox. *Director:* Peter H. Hunt.

**283 Bush Doctor.** Drama, 60 min., Syndicated, 1/82. When he is unable to save the life of his daughter, an American surgeon (Dr. Robert Marshall) flees to Africa to escape his past. The story follows Marshall as he rediscovers the meaning of his profession when he is asked to help a group of children injured in a bus accident. *Cast:* Hugh O'Brian (Robert Marshall), Katherine Justice (Samantha), Jack Hedley (Dr. James Stone), Mildred Awiti (Rebecca). *Music:* Rod Levitt. *Producer:* Robert Halmi. *Writer:* Robert Janes. *Director:* Ron Satlof.

**284 But He Loves Me.** Drama, 60 min., CBS, 3/5/91. A "CBS Schoolbreak Special" about a pretty teenage girl (Cassie) who falls in love with the most popular boy in school (Charlie) and her struggles to cope with his abusive and violent behavior toward her. *Cast:* Kelli Williams (Cassie McBride), Donovan Leitch (Charlie Taylor), Season Hubley (Cassie's mother), Douglas Barr (Cassie's father). *Producers:* George McQuilkin, Nicky Noxon, Noel Resnick. *Writer:* Betty Birney. *Director:* Strath Hamilton.

**285 But It's Not My Fault!** Drama, 60 min., ABC, 3/2/83. Craig Foster is a 16-year-old boy who wants to be a part of the crowd, but he is ignored by the neighborhood boys he admires. To become accepted he first lets the guys hold a recording session in his parents' garage; he next "borrows" electronic equipment from the school; and finally pays for a session at the local video arcade. When Craig's newfound friends claim they have no money to go to a dance, Craig steals an elderly woman's purse to get some. Craig is arrested and sent to juvenile hall when his parents, who are away for the weekend, cannot be reached. The story follows Craig as he learns a lesson while facing two long days in detention with some tough boys. Aired as an "ABC Afterschool Special." *Cast:* Billy Warlock (Craig Foster), Jay Varela (Victorio Baca), Ray Anthony Williams (Ahmaad), Michael Carmine (Vato Loco), Al White (Fred Carver), Ken Kimmons (Uncle Paul), Jeri Arredondo (Annie). *Music:* John Maxwell Anderson. *Producer:* Virginia Carter. *Writer:* Jeri Taylor. *Director:* Victor Lobl.

## 286 Caesar and Cleopatra.

Comedy, 90 min., NBC, 3/5/56. The story, set in 48 B.C., recounts the lives of Caesar and Cleopatra, not as the famous lovers they were, but in Caesar's role as instructor to Cleopatra, the fledgling ruler of Egypt. Based on the play by George Bernard Shaw; see also the following title. *Cast:* Sir Cedric Hardwicke (Caesar), Claire Bloom (Cleopatra), Patrick Macnee (Lucius), Jack Hawkins (Rufio), Judith Anderson (Flatateeta), Cyril Richard (Britannus), Farley Granger (Apollodorus), Thomas Gomez (Pothinus). *Music:* George Bassman. *Producers:* Anthony Quayle, Donald Davis, Dorothy Mathews. *Writer:* Joseph Schrank. *Director:* Kirk Browning.

## 287 Caesar and Cleopatra.

Comedy, 90 min., NBC, 2/1/76. A "Hallmark Hall of Fame" presentation of the play by George Bernard Shaw that examines Caesar's role as instructor to Cleopatra, the fledgling ruler of Egypt in 48 B.C. *Cast:* Sir Alec Guinness (Caesar), Genevieve Bujold (Cleopatra), Margaret Courtenay (Flatateeta), Clive Francis (Apollodorus), Michael Bryant (Britannus), Gareth Thomas (Achillas). *Producers:* Louis Judd, David Susskind. *Writer:* Audrey Mass. *Director:* James Cellan Jones.

## 288 Calamity Jane. Musical,

90 min., CBS, 11/12/63. A musical recounting of Calamity Jane, a tomboyish woman of the old west who earned her living as a stagecoach driver. *Cast:* Carol Burnett (Calamity Jane), Art Lund (Wild Bill Hickok), Beryl Towbin (Katie Brown), Bernie West (Henry Miller), Mark Harris (Francis Fryer), Cathryn Damon (Adelaide Adams), Don Chastain (Danny Gilmartin). *Music Director:* Harry Zimmerman. *Music:* Earl Flatt. *Producers:* Bob Banner, Joe Hamilton. *Writer:* Phil Shuken. *Directors:* Dick Altman, Ernest Flatt.

## 289 California Girl. Documen-

tary, 60 min., ABC, 4/26/68. A lighthearted film and videotape look at the life of the teenage California girl (specifically the girls who find fun and sun at the beaches). Sponsored by Revlon. *Narrator:* Sally Field. *Producer:* Lester Cooper. *Writer:* Arthur Holch. *Directors:* Jonathan Donald, Arthur Holch.

## 290 California Girls. Docu-

mentary, 60 min., ABC, 9/17/88. California girls are thought of as living in bikinis and spending all their time on the beach. The program challenges that myth by profiling several women who are California girls—but also career women who bear little resemblance to the typical stereotype. *Host:* Lorenzo Lamas. *The Women:* Hope Carlton, Kathleen Egan, Vickie Fishbeck, Rebecca Foster, Rosalyn Keithly, Dian Parkinson, Melissa Proud, Michelle Spolar, Ellen Stohl. *Producers:* Eric Schotz, Carol Sherman. *Writer:* Lou DeCosta. *Directors:* Jeff Androsky, Dan Weyand.

## 291 Call Me Back. Drama, 60

min., NBC, 1/16/60. A one-character play that focuses on Tom O'Neill, a man who lost his family (through divorce), his job, and his friends (who shun him). Engulfed by loneliness, he sits by the telephone with a bottle of liquor, trying desperately to make contact with the world he once knew. *Cast:* Art Carney (Tom O'Neill). *Producers:* Robert Alan Arthur, David Susskind. *Writer:* Tony Webster. *Director:* Tom Donovan.

## 292 Can a Guy Say No?

Drama, 60 min., ABC, 2/12/86. Scott Tauscher is a clean-cut and ambitious 16-year-old who feels that he is the last male virgin. Hoping to resolve this situation, Scott becomes more aggressive with his girlfriend, Alix, who is not ready to go all the way. When Alix breaks off their relationship, Scott casts off his old look and adopts the look of "a swinger." He then makes a play for Paula Finkle, a gorgeous girl who has earned a reputation for being easy. When Scott learns that Paula has been subconsciously using sex as a way of gaining approval and he confronts the truth of his situation, he loses interest in her sexually, but develops a strong friendship with her. The story shows some of the pressures young people are experiencing from their peers and from advertisements which put great emphasis on "sex appeal." Aired as an "ABC Afterschool Special." *Cast:* Steve Antin (Scott Tauscher), Heather Langencamp (Paula Finkle), Khrystyne Haje (Alix Shuman), Christa Denton (Kerry Tauscher), Brooke Bundy (Mrs. Finkle), Beau Bridges (Mr. Tauscher), Sharon Spelman (Mrs. Tauscher). *Music:* Garry Sherman. *Producer:* Diana Kerew. *Writer:* Judy Engles. *Director:* Thomas Schlamme.

## 293  Can I Save My Children?

Drama, 90 min., ABC, 10/17/74. En route to spend a holiday with an old friend (Clay), Diana Hansen and her children, Melanie and Peter, are stranded in the wilderness when their small plane crashes. The tense story relates their struggles as they attempt to reach civilization. *Cast:* Diane Baker (Diana Hansen), Tammi Bula (Melanie Hansen), Todd Gross (Peter Hansen), Jack Ging (Harry Hansen), David Hedison (Clay Hollinger), Jack Riley (Braddock), Ken Tobey (Doug), Pat Cranshaw (Matthew). *Producers:* Stanley L. Colbert, Lee Miller. *Writers:* A. Roy Moore, Jonah Royston, Norman Hudis. *Director:* Walter C. Miller.

## 294  Candid Camera Specials.

A chronological listing of specials based on the long-running series "Candid Camera" (1948–56; 1960–67; 1974–80). People caught in the act of being themselves by hidden cameras are the format of the series and its specials. Allen Funt hosted the series from 1948 to 1956; he was then joined by the fol-

lowing cohosts: Arthur Godfrey (1960–61), Durward Kirby (1961–66), Bess Myerson (1966–67), John Bartholomew Tucker (1974–75), Phyllis George (1975–76), JoAnn Pflug (1976–77), and Betsy Palmer (1977–80). Allen Funt produced the series and specials and Sid Ramin composed the theme, "Smile, You're on Candid Camera." Allen's son, Peter Funt, became coproducer with Allen in 1988 (at which time Allen also directed and wrote his specials). Credits are listed only on those specials where Allen was not in charge of the entire production. Allen Funt was the host unless otherwise noted.

**1 The Candid Camera Special** (60 min., NBC, 10/22/81). *Cohosts:* Loni Anderson, Valerie Harper. *Guests:* Wilt Chamberlain, Carol Doda. *Producers:* Allen Funt, Barbara Ferris, David Yarnell. *Director:* Louis J. Horvitz.

**2 Candid Camera Looks at the Difference Between Men and Women** (60 min., NBC, 11/19/83). *Cohost:* Stephanie Zimbalist.

**3 Candid Camera: The First 40 Years** (CBS, 2/17/87). *Guests:* George Burns, Pam Dawber, Fannie Flagg, Kristy McNichol, Paul Newman, Rhea Perlman, Dinah Shore, Danny Thomas, Dr. Ruth Westheimer. *Producers:* Allen Funt, Bob Henry. *Director:* Bob Henry.

**4 The Candid Camera Christmas Special** (60 min., CBS, 12/16/87). *Guests:* Mary Hart, Florence Henderson, Steve Landesberg, Martin Mull, Sarah Purcell, Lynn Redgrave. *Producers:* Allen Funt, Rudi Godlan. *Director:* Rudi Godlan.

**5 Candid Camera: Eat! Eat! Eat!** (60 min., CBS, 1/27/89). *Guests:* Jason Bateman, Justine Bateman, Shari Belafonte-Harper, Peter Funt, Wil Shriner.

**6 Candid Camera on Wheels** (60 min., CBS, 5/17/89). *Cohost:* Peter Funt. *Guests:* Mario Andretti, Kristian Alfonso, Elliott Gould, Edie McClurg, Geraldo Rivera, Pia Zadora.

The One, The Only,
The Original
Candid Camera

**Hosted by Allen Funt.**

From runaway luggage
to motel mayhem,
you never know
where Allen will pop up.

Guests: Julie McCullough(Growing Pains), Peter Funt,
Fred Willard, Payne Stewart, Mitzi McCall & Charlie Brill.

**☞8PM☺2WCBS-TV**    A CBS SPECIAL PRESENTATION

**Ad for "Candid Camera on Vacation"**

**7 Candid Camera Funny Money** (60 min., CBS, 1/3/90). *Cohost:* Peter Funt. *Guests:* Paul Anka, Susan Anton, Ron Carey, Fred Willard.

**8 Candid Camera on Vacation** (60 min., CBS, 4/6/90). *Cohost:* Peter Funt. *Guests:* Charlie Brill, Mitzi McCall, Julie McCullough, Fred Willard.

**9 Candid Camera Goes to the Doctor** (30 min., CBS, 9/27/90). *Guests:* Victoria Jackson, Peter Funt.

**10 Candid Camera ... The Sporting Life** (30 min., CBS, 11/17/90). *Guests:* Julie Brown, Peter Funt.

**11 Candid Camera ... Crazy Cooks and Comedy Kitchen Capers** (60 min., CBS, 2/16/91). *Cohosts:* Allen Funt and Peter Funt. *Guest:* Khrystyne Haje.

**295 Candida.** Comedy, 105 min., The Entertainment Channel, 1/2/83. An adaptation of George Bernard Shaw's 1894 play about Candida, a clever woman caught in a comic love triangle between her macho husband (James) and the romance of a fanciful young poet (Eugene). *Cast:* Joanne Woodward (Candida Morell), Ron Paraday (James Morell), Eugene Marchbanks (Tait Campbell), Jane Curtin (Proserpine Garnett), Ronald Bishop (Mr. Burgess). *Music:* Paul Posnak. *Producer:* Arnold H. Huberman. *Director:* Alex Barker.

**296 The Canine Hall of Fame.** Variety, 60 min., NBC, 9/12/78. A humorous look at man's best friend — both real and imaginary — from Lassie to Snoopy. *Host:* Joe Garagiola. *Guests:* Anne Meara, Jerry Stiller. *Music:* Dick Hyman. *Producer:* George A. Heinemann. *Writers:* Charles Andrews, Tony Geiss. *Director:* Lloyd Gross.

**297 A Capitol Fourth.** A chronological listing of the music specials that celebrate the Fourth of July. The programs are broadcast from Washington, D.C., and feature the music of the National Symphony Orchestra (conducted by Mstislav Rostropovich, 1981–89; Erich Kunzel, 1990–93). All are 90 minutes and broadcast on July 4.

**1 A Capitol Fourth 1981.** *Host:* Pearl Bailey.

**2 A Capitol Fourth 1982.** *Host:* Pearl Bailey. *Note:* A repeat of the 1981 broadcast.

**3 A Capitol Fourth 1983.** *Hosts:* Leontyne Price, Slugger Willie Stargell.

**4 A Capitol Fourth 1984.** *Hosts:* James Galway, Robert Merrill.

**5 A Capitol Fourth 1985.** *Host:* E. G. Marshall. *Guests:* Gweneth Bean, Lucille Beer, Alexander and Nina Bern-

stein, Leonard Bernstein, Clemma Dale, Kurt Ollman, Charles Walker.
**6 A Capitol Fourth 1986.** *Host:* E. G. Marshall. *Guests:* Henry Mancini, Sarah Vaughan.
**7 A Capitol Fourth 1987.** *Host:* E. G. Marshall. *Guests:* Roberta Flack, Marvin Hamlisch, Jean-Pierre Rampal, Jon Vickers.
**8 A Capitol Fourth 1988.** *Host:* E. G. Marshall. *Guest:* Tony Bennett.
**9 A Capitol Fourth 1989.** *Host:* E. G. Marshall. *Guests:* Pearl Bailey, James Galway, Henry Mancini, Peter Nero.
**10 A Capitol Fourth 1990.** *Host:* Beverly Sills. *Guests:* Simon Estes, Henry Mancini.
**11 A Capitol Fourth 1991.** *Host:* E. G. Marshall. *Guests:* Tony Bennett, Cab Calloway, Diahann Carroll, Bill Cosby, Joel Grey.
**12 A Capitol Fourth 1992.** *Host:* E. G. Marshall. *Guests:* James Galway, Patti LaBelle, Henry Mancini, Julia Migenes.
**13 A Capitol Fourth 1993.** *Host:* E. G. Marshall. *Guests:* Johnny Cash, June Carter Cash, Mary-Chapin Carpenter, Rita Moreno, Peter Nero.

**298 The Captain and Tennille in Hawaii.** Variety, 60 min., ABC, 5/5/78. An hour of music and song from Hawaii. *Hosts:* Daryl Dragon ("The Captain"), Toni Tennille. *Guests:* Don Knotts, Kenny Rogers, David Soul, Melissa and Louisa Tennille. *Music:* Lenny Stack. *Producer:* Bill Lee. *Director:* John Moffitt.

**299 The Captain and Tennille in New Orleans.** Variety, 60 min., ABC, 4/3/78. An hour of music, songs, and comedy from New Orleans. *Hosts:* Daryl Dragon, Toni Tennille. *Guests:* John Byner, Fats Domino, Hal Linden, Melissa and Louisa Tennille. *Music:* Lenny Stack. *Producer:* Bill Lee. *Director:* John Moffitt.

**300 The Captain and Tennille Songbook.** Variety, 60 min., ABC,

3/26/79. An hour of music and songs. *Hosts:* Daryl Dragon, Toni Tennille. *Guests:* Glen Campbell, Ella Fitzgerald, B. B. King. *Music:* John Beal. *Producers:* Daryl Dragon, Bruno Cicotti. *Writers:* Ernest Chambers, Allyn Warner, Toni Tennille. *Director:* Jeff Margolis.

**301 The Captain and Tennille Special.** Variety, 60 min., ABC, 8/23/76. An hour of music, songs, and dances with the Captain and Tennille in their first television special (see also the prior three titles). *Hosts:* Daryl Dragon, Toni Tennille. *Guests:* Billy Barty, Milton Frome, Joan Lawrence, Dave Shelley, Melissa Tennille. *Music:* Lenny Stack. *Producers:* Alan Bernard, Dick Clark, Mace Neufeld. *Writers:* Stephen Spears, Thad Mumford, John Boni, Lennie Ripps, Bob Sand, April Kelly. *Directors:* Tony Charmoli, Bob Henry.

**302 Captain Brassbound's Conversion.** Comedy, 60 min., NBC, 5/2/60. The story of a woman (Lady Cicely), who sees only good in people, and her efforts to reform Captain Brassbound, a man who is feared by everyone. Based on the play by George Bernard Shaw; aired on the "Hallmark Hall of Fame." *Cast:* Greer Garson (Lady Cicely Waynflete), Christopher Plummer (Captain Brassbound), Loring Smith (Captain Hamlin Kearney), George Rose (Drinkwater), Liam Raymond (Rankin), Loring Smith (Sir Howard Hallam). *Producer-Director:* George Schaefer.

**303 Captain EO – Backstage.** Variety, 60 min., ABC, 5/15/88. Songs by Michael Jackson and a behind-the-scenes look at the artistic and technological processes that created *Captain EO*, the 3-D musical motion picture space adventure. *Host:* Whoopi Goldberg. *Starring:* Michael Jackson. *Producer-Director:* Muffett Kaufman. *Writers:* Jeff Walker, Joshua Alper,

Douglas Ross, Mathew Cohen, Muffett Kaufman.

## 304 Carly Simon — Coming Around Again. Variety, 60 min., HBO, 7/25/87. A concert by the sultry singer Carly Simon. Taped in Massachusetts on 6/9/87. *Host:* Carly Simon. *The Band:* Rick Marotta, Jimmy Ryan, Robbie Kilgore, Robbie Condor, Michael Beeker. *Background Vocals:* Lenny Gross, Frank Simms, Kay Tiller, Holly McCracken, Sherry Colin. *Music Director:* Tom T-Bone Wolk. *Producers:* Tommy Mottola, Al Smith, Brian Doyle. *Directors:* Jeb Brian, Tony Mitchell.

## 305 Carly Simon: My Romance. Variety, 60 min., HBO, 2/13/90. A concert by Carly Simon (featuring songs from her album, *My Romance*). Taped in a New York theater designed to look like a 1940s nightclub on Valentine's Day. *Host:* Carly Simon. *Guest:* Harry Connick, Jr. *Music:* Tommy T-Bone Wolk. *Producer:* Brian Doyle. *Director:* Jeb Brian.

## 306 Carnegie Hall: The Grand Reopening. Variety, 2 hrs., CBS, 4/21/87. A music and song special that celebrates America's greatest concert stage, New York's Carnegie Hall, on the occasion of its reopening after a multimillion dollar face-lift. *Host:* Isaac Stern. *Guests:* Leonard Bernstein, Lena Horne, Robert Klein, Zubin Mehta, Liza Minnelli, Jessye Norman, John Rubinstein, Frank Sinatra, Benita Valente, James D. Wolfensohn. *Producers:* Don Mischer, Jan Cornell, David J. Goldberg. *Writer:* Sara Luckinson. *Director:* Gary Halvorson.

## 307 Carol and Company. Variety, 60 min., CBS, 10/9/66. An hour of music and comedy. *Host:* Carol Burnett. *Guests:* Ken Berry, Frank Gorshin, Rock Hudson. *Music:* Harry Zimmerman. *Producers:* Bob

Banner, Joe Hamilton. *Writers:* Bill Angelos, Buz Kohan. *Director:* Clark Jones.

## 308 The Carol Burnett Show: A Reunion. Retrospective, 2 hrs., CBS, 1/10/93. Carol Burnett and her television family from "The Carol Burnett Show" (CBS, 1967–78) take a trip down memory lane via clips from the show. Taped on CBS's Stage 23 (where the original series was also taped). *Host:* Carol Burnett. *Cast:* Harvey Korman, Vicki Lawrence, Tim Conway, Lyle Waggoner. *Producers:* Carol Burnett, Harvey Korman, Robert Wright. *Writers:* Buz Kohan, Roger Beatty, Tim Conway, Jenna McMahon, Harry Cauley, Kenny Solms, Ken and Mitzie Welch. *Director:* Dave Powers.

## 309 Carol, Carl, Whoopi and Robin. Comedy, 60 min., ABC, 2/10/87. A series of comedy skits that highlight the unique talents of Carol Burnett, Carl Reiner, Whoopi Goldberg, and Robin Williams. *Music:* Peter Matz. *Producers:* Marcy Carsey, Tom Werner, Stephanie Sills, Dick Clair, Jenna McMahon. *Writers:* Jim Evering, Ken and Mitzie Welch, Dick Clair, Jenna McMahon, Chris Durang. *Directors:* Harvey Korman, Roger Beatty.

## 310 Carol Channing and 101 Men. Variety, 60 min., ABC, 11/16/67. An hour of music, song, and comedy in which singer-actress Carol Channing is assisted by 101 male guests (most of whom are the U.S. Air Force Academy Chorale). *Host:* Carol Channing. *Guests:* Eddy Arnold, The Association, Walter Matthau, The U.S. Air Force Academy Chorale. *Music:* Ray Charles. *Producers:* Alan Handley, Bob Wynn. *Writer:* Milt Rosen. *Director:* Alan Handley.

## 311 Carol Channing and Pearl Bailey on Broadway. Variety, 60

min., ABC, 3/16/69. A musical variety hour that spotlights the talents of Carol Channing and Pearl Bailey. *Stars:* Carol Channing, Pearl Bailey. *Producer-Writers:* Saul Ilson, Ernest Chambers. *Director:* Clark Jones.

### 312 Carol Channing Proudly Presents the Seven Deadly Sins.

Variety, 60 min., ABC, 4/14/69. A lighthearted look at the seven deadly sins: avarice, envy, gluttony, lust, pride, sloth, and wrath. *Host:* Carol Channing. *Guests:* Carol Burnett, Danny Thomas. *Producers:* Saul Ilson, Ernest Chambers. *Writers:* Saul Ilson, Ernest Chambers, Al Gordon, Hal Goldman. *Director:* Clark Jones.

### 313 Carol Channing's Mad English Tea Party.

Variety, 60 min., NBC, 9/9/70. Rapid-fire sketches and blackouts that spoof great names in British history. Taped in England. *Host:* Carol Channing. *Guests:* Art Carney, Sir John Gielgud, Fred MacMurray, Sir Ralph Richardson. *Producers:* Saul Ilson, Ernest Chambers. *Writers:* Ron Friedman, Saul Ilson, Ernest Chambers. *Director:* Colin Clews.

### 314 Carol for Another Christmas.

Drama, 90 min., ABC, 12/28/64. A contemporary version of Charles Dickens's *A Christmas Carol* in which Daniel Grudge, a modern-day isolationist, and his idealistic nephew, Fred, "see" through the ghosts of Christmas Past, Future, and Present a world headed for H-Bomb annihilation. *Cast:* Sterling Hayden (Daniel Grudge), Ben Gazzara (Ben Grudge), Peter Sellers (The Imperial Me; King of Individualists), Eva Marie Saint (Lieutenant Gibson), Steve Lawrence (Ghost of Christmas Past), Pat Hingle (Ghost of Christmas Present), Robert Shaw (Ghost of Christmas Future), Britt Ekland (Mother), Percy Rodrigues (Charles). *Music:* Henry Mancini. *Producers:* Edgar Rosenberg, Joseph Mankiewicz. *Writer:* Rod Serling. *Director:* Joseph Mankiewicz.

### 315 Carol + 2.

Variety, 60 min., CBS, 1/15/67. A sequel to "Carol and Company" (see entry) which again features Carol Burnett and her guests in a variety of comedy skits. *Host:* Carol Burnett. *Guests:* Lucille Ball, Zero Mostel. *Music:* Harry Zimmerman. *Producers:* Bob Banner, Nat Hiken. *Writer:* Nat Hiken. *Director:* Marc Breaux.

### 316 Carousel.

Musical, 2 hrs., ABC, 5/7/67. When unemployed carnival barker Billy Bigelow discovers that his wife, Julie, is pregnant, he unsuccessfully attempts a robbery to acquire money for his family. Rather than face imprisonment, he kills himself. After serving sixteen years in purgatory, Billy is allowed to return to earth for one day to perform a good deed and exonerate himself. His efforts to help his daughter Louise are the focal point of the third act of the three-act play by Ferenc Molnar. *Cast:* Robert Goulet (Billy Bigelow), Mary Grover (Julie Jordan), Linda Howe (Louise Jordan), Marlyn Mason (Carrie Pipperidge), Pernell Roberts (Jigger), Charlie Ruggles (Starkeeper), Patricia Neway (Nettie Fowler). *Music:* Jack Elliott. *Producer:* Norman Rosemont. *Writer:* Sidney Michaels. *Director:* Paul Bogart.

### 317 The Carpenters.

Variety, 60 min., ABC, 12/8/76. An hour of song with Karen and Richard Carpenter (sister and brother) in their first television special. *Hosts:* Karen and Richard Carpenter. *Guests:* Victor Borge, John Denver. *Music:* Eddie Karam. *Producer:* Jerry Weintraub. *Writers:* Jim Mulligan, Ray Jessel, Ronny Graham, April Kelly, George Geiger, Rich Eustis, Al Rogers. *Director:* Bill Davis.

### 318 The Carpenters.

Variety, 60

min., ABC, 5/16/80. A salute to American songwriters. *Hosts:* Karen and Richard Carpenter. *Guests:* John Davidson, Ella Fitzgerald. *Music:* Nelson Riddle. *Producer:* Jerry Weintraub. *Writer:* Rod Warren. *Director:* Bob Henry.

### 319 The Carpenters at Christmas. Variety, 60 min., ABC, 12/9/77. A musical holiday special with the Carpenters. *Hosts:* Karen and Richard Carpenter. *Guests:* Harvey Korman, Kristy McNichol. *Music:* Billy May. *Producer:* Jerry Weintraub. *Writers:* Bill Larkin, Stephen Spears. *Director:* Bob Henry.

### 320 The Carpenters ... Space Encounters. Variety, 60 min., ABC, 5/17/78. An hour of music and songs highlighted by laser effects. *Hosts:* Karen and Richard Carpenter. *Guests:* Charlie Callas, John Davidson, Suzanne Somers. *Music:* Peter Knight. *Producer:* Jerry Weintraub. *Writers:* Bill Larkin, Stephen Spears, Tom Sawyer. *Director:* Bob Henry.

### 321 Cartoon All-Stars to the Rescue. Cartoon, 30 min., ABC, CBS, Fox, NBC, Syndicated, TBS, 4/21/90. A multibroadcast, antidrug abuse special aimed at children. The story relates the efforts of Saturday morning cartoon characters to rescue a 14-year-old boy (Michael) from the dangers of a life with drugs. *Cast:* Jason Marsden (Michael). *Voices:* Don Messick (Papa Smurf), Danny Goldman (Brainy Smurf), Lorenzo Music (Garfield), Frank Welker (Baby Kermit/Slimer), Jim Cummings (Winnie the Pooh/Tigger), Russi Taylor (Huey/Dewey/Louie/Baby Gonzo), Laurie O'Brien (Miss Piggy), Townsend Coleman (Michaelangelo), Jeff Bergman (Daffy Duck/Bugs Bunny), Paul Fusco (ALF). *Producers:* Roy Disney, Buzz Potamkin. *Writers:* Duane Poole, Tom Swale.

### 322 The Case Against Milligan. Drama, 60 min., CBS, 1/26/75. An historical drama, based on an actual case, about President Lincoln's suspension of the constitutional right of habeas corpus during the Civil War. *Cast:* Richard Basehart (Lambdin P. Milligan), Alice Drummond (Sarah Milligan), Tim Kirkpatrick (Moses Milligan), Fred Stuthman (Abraham Lincoln), Glenn Zachar (Lou Milligan), Brooks Rogers (Justice Davis), Henderson Forsythe (Bowles). *Narrator:* Joel Fabiani. *Producers:* Joel Heller, Jack Willis. *Writer:* Loring Mandel. *Director:* Jan Kadar. *Music:* Lee Holdridge.

### 323 A Case of Libel. Drama, 90 min., PBS, 5/12/86. A television adaptation of Henry Denker's 1963 courtroom drama about Boyd Bendix, a self-appointed and self-righteous Red Menace watchdog, who is accused of libeling Dennis Corcoran, a one-time World War II correspondent he feels is a drunken, yellow-bellied degenerate and a Communist sympathizer. *Cast:* Edward Asner (Robert Sloane), Daniel J. Travanti (Boyd Bendix), Gordon Pinsent (Dennis Corcoran), Charlotte Blunt (Anita Cochran), Chris Wiggins (Colonel Douglas), Larry Reynolds (Judge). *Producer:* Gladys Rackmill. *Writer:* Henry Denker. *Director:* Eric Till.

### 324 Casey Kasem: Rock and Roll Goldmine. Documentary, 60 min., Syndicated, 7/1/89. Radio disc jockey Casey Kasem traces a three-year period of rock and roll music (1960–63) via rare recordings of the era's artists. *Producers:* Ron Ziskin, Shukai Ghalayini. *Writers:* Joel Parks, Sam Grossman. *Director:* Joel Parks.

### 325 Casper's First Christmas. Cartoon, 30 min., NBC, 12/18/79. Just prior to Christmas, Casper, the Friendly Ghost, and his friend, Hairy Scarey, are evicted from their old, battered house.

The story follows their efforts to find new lodgings in time to celebrate Christmas. *Voices:* Julie McWhirter (Casper), John Stephenson (Hairy Scarey and Doggie Daddy), Hal Smith (Santa Claus), Daws Butler (Quick Draw McGraw/Snagglepuss/Augie Doggie/Huckleberry Hound/Yogi Bear/Boo Boo Bear). *Music:* Hoyt Curtin. *Producers:* William Hanna, Joseph Barbera. *Directors:* Ray Patterson, George Gordon, Carl Urbano.

### 326  The Cat and the Canary.

Mystery, 60 min., NBC, 9/27/60. Shortly after a will makes Annabelle West, a distant cousin of the West family, sole heiress to the family fortune, a second will is found that disqualifies Annabelle if she is found to be mentally incompetent. The story relates the family's attempts to drive Annabelle insane and claim the fortune. Based on the Broadway play by John Willard; aired on "The Dow Hour of Great Mysteries." *Cast:* Collin Wilcox (Annabelle West), Andrew Duggan (Paul Jones), Sarah Marshall (Cicily Sillsby), Telly Savalas (Hendricks), George Macready (Roger Crosby), Hortense Alden ("Mammy" Pleasant). *Producer:* Robert Saudek. *Writers:* William Roos, Audrey Roos. *Director:* William A. Graham.

### The Cat in the Hat *see* Dr. Seuss' The Cat in the Hat

### 327  Cat on a Hot Tin Roof.

Drama, 2 hrs. 30 min., Showtime, 8/19/84. The story, set in a Mississippi Delta plantation house, focuses on the Pollitts, a wealthy Southern family divided by hypocrisy and malice: "Big Daddy," the patriarch, is dying and about to lose control of his family; Brick, his son, a former football hero, is having marital difficulties with his sexually frustrated wife, Maggie; and Gooper, Brick's brother, and his wife, Mae, are scheming to inherit the family plantation. Based on the play by Tennessee Williams. *Cast:* Jessica Lange (Maggie Pollitt), Tommy Lee Jones (Brick Pollitt), Rip Torn (Big Daddy Pollitt), Kim Stanley (Big Mama Pollitt), David Dukes (Gooper Pollitt), Penny Fuller (Mae Pollitt), Ami Foster (Polly), Fran Bennett (Sookey), Jake Jundef (Buster), Macon McCalman (Reverend Tooker), Neta-Lee Noy (Sunnie). *Music:* Tom Scott. *Producers:* Lou LaMonte, Phyllis Geller, Elizabeth Ashley, Alan Pierce, Marilyn Larson. *Writer:* Tennessee Williams. *Director:* Jack Hofsiss.

### 328  Caterina Valente from Heidelberg.

Variety, 60 min., Syndicated, 4/20/75. An hour of music and song from Germany with singer Caterina Valente. *Host:* Caterina Valente. *Guests:* Nick Castle, Silvio Francesco. *Music:* John Berkman. *Producer:* Eric von Aro. *Writers:* Wolfgang Francke, Nick Castle. *Director:* Michael Pfleghar.

### 329  Cathy.

Cartoon, 30 min., CBS, 5/15/87. A television adaptation of the comic strip about a single girl's search for happiness. The story itself relates Cathy's efforts to find Mr. Right. Created by Cathy Guisewite. See also the following two titles. *Voices:* Kathleen Wilhoite (Cathy Andrews), Allison Argo (Andrea), Shirley Mitchell (Mom), William L. Guisewite (Dad), Robert F. Paulsen (Irving). *Music:* James Lee Stanley. *Producer:* Lee Mendelson. *Writer:* Cathy Guisewite. *Director:* Evert Brown.

### 330  Cathy's Last Resort.

Cartoon, 30 min., CBS, 11/11/88. A sequel to the "Cathy" special that finds the stress-ridden career woman seeking to get away from it all by vacationing at a tropical resort called Passion Paradise—but where Cathy goes, mishap follows. *Voices:* Kathleen Wilhoite (Cathy Andrews), Robert F. Paulsen (Irving), William L. Guisewite (Dad), Allison Argo (Andrea), Shirley Mitchell

(Mom). *Music:* James Lee Stanley. *Producers:* Lee Mendelson, Bill Melendez. *Writer:* Cathy Guisewite. *Director:* Evert Brown.

### 331 Cathy's Valentine.
Cartoon, 30 min., CBS, 2/10/89. A third "Cathy" special (see prior two titles) that relates Cathy's efforts to win her the love of her boyfriend, Irving, for Valentine's Day. *Voices:* Kathleen Wilhoite (Cathy Andrews), Robert F. Paulsen (Irving), Shirley Mitchell (Mom), William L. Guisewite (Dad), Susan Silo (Janet), Allison Argo (Andrea). *Music:* James Lee Stanley. *Producers:* Lee Mendelson, Bill Melendez. *Writer:* Cathy Guisewite. *Director:* Evert Brown.

### 332 CBS Comedy Bloopers.
Comedy, 30 min., CBS, 5/23/90. Outtakes from various CBS comedy shows produced for the 1989-90 season. *Host:* Mary Frann. *Announcer:* Stan Freberg. *Music:* Chris Stone. *Producer-Writer-Director:* Joie Albrecht.

### 333 CBS Library: Animal Talk.
Drama, 60 min., CBS, 3/4/80. A drama, aimed at children, that dramatizes scenes from three famous novels: Jack London's *Call of the Wild*, Sterling North's *Rascal*, and Mel Eliss's *Flight of the White Wolf*. Cast: Anthony Newley (Dr. John Dolittle), Lance Kerwin (Rus), Keith Michell (Sterling North), John Quade (Mathewson), Spencer Milligan (Thornton), Billy Jacoby (Oscar), Arthur Space (Mr. Shadwick), Lois Phillips (Mrs. Clagg), Richard Kennedy (Mr. Clagg), Hugh Gillin (Judge). *Music:* Charles Alexander. *Producer:* Diane Asselin. *Writer:* Kimmer Ringwald. *Director:* Paul Asselin.

### 334 CBS: On the Air.
Retrospective, 9 hrs. 30 min., CBS, 3/26 to 4/1/78. A lavish production in which the Columbia Broadcasting System celebrates 50 years of radio and television broadcasting. *Sunday, March 26* (2 hrs.) *Hosts:* Walter Cronkite, Mary Tyler Moore. *Guests:* Alfred Hitchcock, Bob Keeshan, Telly Savalas, Jean Stapleton. *Monday, March 27* (60 min.). *Host:* Mary Tyler Moore. *Guests:* Bea Arthur, Lucille Ball, George Burns, Arthur Godfrey. *Tuesday, March 28* (60 min.). *Hosts:* Walter Cronkite, Mary Tyler Moore. *Guests:* Alan Alda, Garry Moore, Phil Silvers. *Wednesday, March 29* (60 min.). *Host:* Mary Tyler Moore. *Guests:* Buddy Ebsen, Danny Kaye, the animated "Peanuts" characters, Cicely Tyson, Dick Van Dyke. *Thursday, March 30* (60 min.). *Host:* Mary Tyler Moore. *Guests:* Ellen Corby, Kami Cotler, Will Geer, Michael Learned, Mary Elizabeth McDonough, Richard Thomas, Ralph Waite. *Friday, March 31* (60 min.). *Host:* Mary Tyler Moore. *Guests:* Eve Arden, Lauren Bacall, Bert Convy, Richard Crenna, Bonnie Franklin, Linda Lavin, Jim Nabors. *Saturday, April 1* (2 hrs., 30 min.). *Hosts:* Walter Cronkite, Mary Tyler Moore. *Guests:* Bea Arthur, Edward Asner, Ken Berry, Carol Burnett, Art Carney, Andy Griffith, Valerie Harper, Sherman Hemsley, Art Linkletter, Jim Nabors, Carroll O'Connor, Tony Randall, Esther Rolle, Isabel Sanford, Danny Thomas. *Music Director:* Elliot Lawrence. *Producers:* Alexander H. Cohen, Lee Miller. *Writer:* Hildy Parks. *Directors:* Clark Jones, Sid Smith.

### 335 CBS Salutes Lucy — The First 25 Years.
Tribute, 2 hrs., CBS, 11/28/76. Film and videotape highlights that recall Lucille Ball's 25 years of series, specials, and guest appearances on CBS. *Guest of Honor:* Lucille Ball. *Guests:* Desi Arnaz, Sr.; Milton Berle, Carol Burnett, Richard Burton, Johnny Carson, Sammy Davis, Jr.; Gale Gordon, Bob Hope, Danny Kaye, Dean Martin, James Stewart, Danny Thomas, Vivian Vance, Dick Van Dyke, John Wayne. *Music:* Peter Matz. *Producers:* Gary Morton,

Sheldon Keller. *Writer:* Sheldon Keller.

### CBS Schoolbreak Special/ CBS Afternoon Playhouse/CBS Children's Mystery Theater/CBS Library.

CBS's answer to ABC's "Afterschool Special"; a series of outstanding programs first broadcast as the "CBS Afternoon Playhouse," then the "CBS Children's Mystery Theater." See the following titles for information: Ace Hits the Big Time, The Alfred G. Graebner Memorial High School Handbook of Rules and Regulations, All the Kids Do It, American Eyes, Babies Having Babies, But He Loves Me, Contract for Life, Crosses on the Lawn, The Day the Senior Class Got Married, Dirkham Detective Agency, Drug Knot, The Emancipation of Lizzie Stern, An Enemy Among Us, The Exchange Student, 15 and Getting Straight, The Fourth Man, Frog Girl, Gambler, The Girl with the Crazy Brother, God, the Universe and Hot Fudge Sundaes; The Great Gilly Hopkins, The Haunting of Harrington House, Have You Ever Tried Talking to Patty?, Hear Me Cry, Help Wanted, Home Sweet Homeless, I Think I'm Having a Baby, The Incredible Book Escape, Journey to Survival, Just Pals, Juvi, Lies of the Heart, Little Miss Perfect, Maggie's Secret, Me and Mr. Stenner, My Dissident Mom, My Past Is My Own, Mystery at Fire Island, No Means No, Portrait of a Teenage Shoplifter, Revenge of the Nerd, The Shooting, Soldier Boys, Student Court, A Tale of Four Wishes, The Treasure of Alpheus T. Winterborn, Two Teens and a Baby, The War Between the Classes, Welcome Home, Jellybean; Words to Live By, The Wrong Way Kid, The Year of the Gentle Tiger, The Zertigo Diamond Caper.

### 336 Celebrate the Miracles.

Tribute, 60 min., Syndicated, 12/28/88. A musical tribute to children who have overcome serious injuries or medical problems. The stories of four children, who experienced and overcame heartbreaking tragedies, are profiled, followed by a musical tribute to each one. *Hosts:* Marilyn McCoo, Merlin Olsen. *Guests:* Debbie Gibson, The Jets, The Oak Ridge Boys. *Music:* Sam Cardon. *Producers:* Mick Shannon, Joseph Lake. *Writer:* J. Scott Iverson. *Director:* John Hesse.

### 337 Celebrate the Spirit: Disney's All-Star Fourth of July Spectacular.

Variety, 2 hrs., CBS, 7/4/92. Music and songs coupled with a fireworks display from Disney World and Disneyland. *Host:* John Ritter. *Guests:* Mary-Chapin Carpenter, Billy Ray Cyrus, Celine Dion, Kriss Kross, Los Lobos, Martina McBride, Shanice. *Producers:* Don Weiner, Michael Petok. *Writer:* Stephen Pouliot. *Director:* Gary Halvorson.

### 338 Celebration.

Variety, 60 min., Showtime, 1/81. A musical tribute to singer-songwriter Dorsey Burnette. *Performers:* Glen Campbell, Duane Eddy, Kris Kristofferson, Tanya Tucker. *Producer:* Don Davis.

### 339 A Celebration at Ford's Theater.

Variety, 60 min., NBC, 2/2/78. A music and song salute celebrating the first ten years of performances on the stage of historic Ford's Theater in Washington, D.C. *Host:* Lorne Greene. *Guests:* The Acting Company, Roderick Cook, Henry Fonda, Delores Hall, Linda Hopkins, John Houseman, Bill Schustidk, Alexis Smith, James Whitmore. *Producer:* Joseph Cates. *Writer:* Frank Slocum. *Director:* Gilbert Cates.

### 340 Celebration: The American Spirit.

Variety, 90 min., ABC, 1/25/76. Stars from the entertainment world pay tribute to the glory and vitality of the American spirit through song, dance, and humor. *Performers:*

Don Adams, The American Folk Ballet, James Caan, Ray Charles, Pat Cooper, Howard Cosell, Clifton Davis, Sandy Duncan, Steve Forrest, Andy Griffith, Don Ho, Gabriel Kaplan, Jack Lemmon, Trini Lopez, Shirley MacLaine, Anne Meara, The Osmonds, Helen Reddy, Frank Sinatra, Jim Stafford, The Texas Boys Choir, Dionne Warwick, James Whitmore, Andy Williams, Robert Young. *Music:* Jack Elliott, Allyn Ferguson. *Producer-Directors:* Herman Rush, Marty Pasetta. *Writers:* Marty Farrell, Marc London.

## 341 Celebrities: Where Are They Now? Human Interest, 60
min., ABC, 5/16/85. An update on the lives of Anita Bryant, Diahann Carroll, Angela Cartwright, Hal Linden, Linda Lovelace, Liza Minnelli, Fess Parker, Teddy Pendergrass, Samantha Smith, Tiny Tim, and Billy Dee Williams. *Host:* Ed Asner. *Producers:* Dick Clark, Al Schwartz. *Writer:* Robert Arthur. *Director:* Al Schwartz.

## 342 The Celebrity and the Arcade Kid. Comedy, 60 min., ABC,
11/9/83. While in a video arcade, young celebrity Kyle Rhoades encounters video game whiz Johnny Grant—his exact look-alike, and devises a plan to escape from the limelight. The story relates Kyle and Johnny's experiences when they agree to change places and live like the other for a brief time. Aired as an "ABC Afterschool Special." *Cast:* Darnell Williams (Kyle and Johnny), Shelley Fabares (Fran Brogliatti), Roxie Roker (Aunt Helen), Hal Williams (Tony Grant), Debbi Morgan (Jennifer Sanders), Dick Sargent (Lew Shorr). *Producer:* Virginia L. Carter. *Writer:* Michael McGreevey. *Director:* Fern Field.

## 343 Celebrity Challenge of the Sexes. A chronological listing of
the five challenges that aired on CBS

from 4/17/77 to 4/19/80. The specials pit celebrities in various athletic contests to determine which is the better sex (the program is actually CBS's version of ABC's "Battle of the Network Stars"; see entry. All programs are two hours in length and produced by Howard Katz, Rudy Tellez, and Ken Weinstock.
**1 Celebrity Challenge of the Sexes 1** (4/17/77). *Hosts:* Phyllis George, Vin Scully. *Female Team:* Penny Marshall (Captain), Cathy Lee Crosby, Lola Falana, Farrah Fawcett, Susan Howard, Roz Kelly, Kristy McNichol, Stefanie Powers, Connie Stevens, Brenda Vaccaro, Cindy Williams. *Male Team:* Rob Reiner (Captain), Edward Asner, Lloyd Bridges, Robert Conrad, Bill Cosby, Redd Foxx, Elliott Gould, Dan Haggerty, Gabriel Kaplan, Tony Randall, O. J. Simpson, McLean Stevenson.
**2 Celebrity Challenge of the Sexes 2** (11/20/77). *Hosts:* Flip Wilson, Brent Musburger. *Female Team:* Valerie Perrine (Captain), Linda Blair, Lola Falana, Farrah Fawcett, Phyllis George, Kristy McNichol, Susan Saint James, Suzanne Somers, Elke Sommer, Leslie Uggams. *Male Team:* McLean Stevenson (Captain), LeVar Burton, David Cassidy, Robert Conrad, James Farentino, James Franciscus, Steve Garvey, Tab Hunter, Bruce Jenner, Gabriel Kaplan, Jack Klugman, Dick Van Patten.
**3 Celebrity Challenge of the Sexes 3** (2/25/79). *Hosts:* Buddy Hackett, Tom Brookshier. *Female Team:* Carol Wayne (Captain), Valerie Bertinelli, Quinn Cummings, Joyce DeWitt, Jayne Kennedy, Brianne Leary, Donna Pescow, Susan Richardson, Suzanne Somers, Connie Stevens, Tanya Tucker. *Male Team:* Ted Knight (Captain), Scott Baio, Dirk Benedict, Gary Coleman, Sammy Davis, Jr.; Patrick Duffy, Erik Estrada, Lou Ferrigno, Dan Haggerty, Gavin MacLeod, Carl Reiner.
**4 Celebrity Challenge of the Sexes 4** (10/20/79). *Host:* Tom Brookshier.

*Female Team:* Phyllis George (Captain), Catherine Bach, Barbi Benton, Charo, Lola Falana, Elaine Joyce, Martina Navratilova, Joan Rivers, Toni Tennille. *Male Team:* Bill Cosby (Captain), LeVar Burton, Richard Dawson, Michael Douglas, Redd Foxx, Gallagher, Leif Garrett, Howard Hesseman, Charlie Pride.

**5 Celebrity Challenge of the Sexes 5** (4/19/80). *Host:* Tom Brookshier. *Female Team:* Victoria Principal (Captain), Catherine Bach, Cathy Lee Crosby, Melissa Gilbert, Erin Gray, Jayne Kennedy, Connie Needham, Judy Norton-Taylor, Lani O'Grady, Sarah Purcell, Connie Sellecca, Brooke Shields, Joan Van Ark. *Male Team:* Robert Conrad (Captain), Ira Angustain, Scott Baio, Jamie Farr, Leif Garrett, Gil Gerard, Andy Gibb, Kevin Hooks, Jay Johnson, Steve Kanaly, Vic Tayback, Tom Wopat.

**344 Celebrity Daredevils.** Adventure, 2 hrs., ABC, 1/16/83. Well-known celebrities risk their lives by performing dangerous stunts. *Studio Host:* William Shatner. *Location Hosts:* Bert Convy, Cathy Lee Crosby, Jill St. John. *Movie Studio Host:* Army Archerd. *Performers:* Christopher Atkins, Barbi Benton, Linda Blair, Chuck Connors, Kirk Douglas, Marty Feldman, Anthony Geary, Gloria Loring, Eddie Mekka, Jim Nabors, Dana Plato, Christopher Reeve, Burt Reynolds, John Schneider, Elke Sommer, Bo Svenson, Betty Thomas, Bruce Weitz, Adam West. *Producer:* Bernard Rothman. *Writers:* Robert Stivers, Bunny Stivers. *Director:* Tony Verna.

**345 The Celebrity Football Classic.** Game, 60 min., NBC, 11/16/79. Top-name celebrities compete in a game of flag football for charity. *Color Commentator:* Burt Reynolds. *Field Announcer:* Tim Conway. *Celebrity Interviewer:* Marilu Henner. *Field Commentator:* Chick Hearn. *Players:* Anne Archer, Adrienne Barbeau, Le-Var Burton, Diana Canova, Joanna Cassidy, Wilt Chamberlain, Charo, Cathy Lee Crosby, Billy Crystal, Jamie Lee Curtis, William Devane, Joyce DeWitt, David Doyle, Lola Falana, Norman Fell, Cyndy Garvey, Steve Garvey, Grant Goodeve, Fred Grandy, Richard Hatch, Bo Hopkins, Ken Howard, Jayne Kennedy, Harvey Korman, Ted Lange, Hal Linden, Kent McCord, Ed McMahon, Penny Marshall, Donna Mills, John Ritter, Wayne Rogers, Connie Sellecca, Shelley Smith, Laurette Spang, Lauren Tewes, Robert Urich. *Music:* Eddie Karam. *Producers:* Bert Convy, Merrill Grant. *Director:* Bill Davis.

**346 Center Stage: Cyd Charisse.** Variety, 60 min., Syndicated, 9/67. A solo concert performance by actress-dancer Cyd Charisse. *Host:* Cyd Charisse. *Music:* Ralph Carmichael. *Producer:* Jackie Barnett. *Director:* Tony Charmoli.

**347 Challenge of the Super Heroes.** Adventure, 60 min., NBC, 1/16/79. A live-action adventure that pits the Super Heroes against the Super Villains in a story that finds the heroes struggling to stop the villains from destroying the world with their Doomsday Machine. *Super Heroes:* Adam West (Batman), Burt Ward (Robin), Garrett Craig (Captain Marvel), Danuta (Black Canary), William Nuckols (Hawkman), Howard Murphy (Green Lantern), Rod Haase (The Flash), Barbara Joyce (Huntress). *Super Villains:* Frank Gorshin (The Riddler), Jeff Altman (Weather Wizard), Charlie Callas (Sinestro), Gabriel Dell (Mordru), Mickey Morton (Solomon Grundy), Howard Morris (Dr. Sivana), Aleshia Brevard (Giganta).

**348 The Changing Scene.** Variety, 60 min., ABC, 9/11/70, 12/10/70, 1/7/71, 4/14/71. A series of four 60-minute specials of fast-paced music, songs, and comedy that explore the rapidly changing American scene. *Host:* Gene Kelly (9/11 and 12/10/70), Engelbert Humperdinck (1/7/71), Robert Culp (4/14/71). *Guests* (9/11 and 12/10/70): Barbara Eden, Arte Johnson, The Kevin Carlisle Dancers, The Mike Curb Congregation, Jud Strunk, Yvonne Wilder. *Guests* (1/7/71): Don Adams, Barbara Eden, The Kevin Carlisle Dancers, The Mike Curb Congregation, The Osmond Brothers, Jud Strunk, Yvonne Wilder. *Guests* (4/14/71): Johnny Brown, John Denver, Barbara Eden, Robert Goulet, Bernie Kopell, The Mike Curb Congregation. *Music:* Gene DiNovi. *Producers:* Burt Sugarman, Pierre Cossette. *Writers:* Jeffrey Barron, Ron Friedman, Gene Moss, Mickey Rose, James F. Thurman. *Producer-Director:* Robert Scheerer.

### 349 Charley's Aunt. Comedy,
2 hrs., The Entertainment Channel, 2/6/83. An adaptation of the 1892 play by Brandon Thomas. The story follows Fancourt Babberly, an English lord inveigled into portraying the aunt of his friend, Charley, a Yale undergraduate, so he can act as a chaperone while Charley entertains his proper young lady (as was the tradition in the 1890s). *Cast:* Charles Grodin (Fancourt Babberly), James Widdoes (Charley Wykham), Efrem Zimbalist, Jr. (Francis Chesney), Anne Francis (Dona Lucia D'Alvadorez), Joyce Bulifant (Ela Delahay), Vincent Gardenia (Stephen Spettigue), Ilene Graff (Kitty Spettigue). *Producers:* Herb Rogers, Richard Carrothers, Dennis Hennessey. *TV Adaptation:* Ron Friedman. *Director:* William Asher.

### 350 A Charlie Brown Celebration. Cartoon, 60 min., CBS,
5/24/82. An anthology type of special wherein some of Peanuts creator Charles Schulz's favorite newspaper strips are set to animation. *Voices:* Casey Carlson, Shannon Cohn, Chris-

topher Donohoe, Kristen Fullerton, Brent Hauer, Michael Mandy, Bill Melendez, Cindi Reilly, Rocky Reilly. *Music:* Ed Bogas, Judy Munson. *Producers:* Lee Mendelson, Bill Melendez. *Director:* Bill Melendez.

### 351 A Charlie Brown Christmas. Cartoon, 30 min., CBS, 12/9/65.
The story relates Charlie Brown's unsuccessful efforts to relate the commercialism of Christmas to his friends, who are eagerly awaiting the big day. *Voices:* Peter Robbins (Charlie Brown), Tracy Stafford (Lucy), Christopher Shea (Linus), Cathy Steinberg (Sally), Bill Melendez (Snoopy). *Music:* Vince Guaraldi. *Producers:* Lee Mendelson, Bill Melendez. *Writer:* Charles M. Schulz. *Director:* Bill Melendez.

### Charlie Brown "Peanuts" Specials. See the following titles for
information: Be My Valentine, Charlie Brown; A Charlie Brown Celebration, A Charlie Brown Christmas, A Charlie Brown Thanksgiving, Charlie Brown's All Stars, Happy Anniversary, Charlie Brown; Happy New Year, Charlie Brown; He's Your Dog, Charlie Brown; Is This Goodbye, Charlie Brown; It Was a Short Summer, Charlie Brown; It's a Mystery, Charlie Brown; It's an Adventure, Charlie Brown; It's Arbor Day, Charlie Brown; It's Christmas Time Again, Charlie Brown; It's Flashbeagle, Charlie Brown; It's Magic, Charlie Brown; It's the Easter Beagle, Charlie Brown; It's the Girl in the Red Truck, Charlie Brown; It's the Great Pumpkin, Charlie Brown; It's Your First Kiss, Charlie Brown; Life Is a Circus, Charlie Brown; Play It Again, Charlie Brown; She's a Good Skate, Charlie Brown; Snoopy Come Home, Snoopy—The Musical, Snoopy's Getting Married, Charlie Brown; Snoopy's Musical on Ice, Snoopy's Reunion, Someday You'll Find Her, Charlie Brown; There's No Time for Love, Charlie Brown; This Is America, Charlie Brown; What a Nightmare,

Charlie Brown; What Have We Learned, Charlie Brown?; Why, Charlie Brown, Why?; You Don't Look 40, Charlie Brown; You're a Good Man, Charlie Brown; You're a Good Sport, Charlie Brown; You're in Love, Charlie Brown; You're Not Elected, Charlie Brown; and You're the Greatest, Charlie Brown.

### 352 A Charlie Brown Thanksgiving. Cartoon, 30 min., CBS, 11/20/73. The story focuses on Charlie Brown's well-intentioned efforts to organize a Thanksgiving feast for his friends. *Voices:* Todd Barbee (Charlie Brown), Robin Kohn (Lucy), Stephen Shea (Linus), Hilary Momberger (Sally), Christopher Defaria (Peppermint Patty), Jimmy Ahrens (Marcie), Robin Reed (Franklin), Bill Melendez (Snoopy). *Music:* Vince Guaraldi. *Producers:* Lee Mendelson, Bill Melendez. *Writer:* Charles M. Schulz. *Director:* Bill Melendez.

### 353 Charlie Brown's All Stars. Cartoon, 30 min., CBS, 6/8/66. Charlie Brown is a pitcher for the All Stars, a Little League baseball team that has a record of 999 straight losses. The story relates Charlie Brown's efforts to keep from losing the one-thousandth consecutive game. *Voices:* Peter Robbins (Charlie Brown), Christopher Shea (Linus), Sally Dryer (Lucy), Glenn Mendelson (Schroeder), Ann Altieri (Frieda), Chris Doran (Pig-Pen), Bill Melendez (Snoopy). *Music:* Vince Guaraldi. *Producers:* Bill Melendez, Lee Mendelson. *Writer:* Charles M. Schulz. *Director:* Bill Melendez.

### 354 Charo. Variety, 30 min., ABC, 5/24/76. Spanish entertainer Charo in her first television special: a program of music, song, and light comedy. *Host:* Charo. *Guest:* Mike Connors. *Announcer:* David Michaels. *Music:* Frank DeVol. *Producers:* Saul Ilson, Ernest Chambers. *Writers:* Bob Booker, George Foster, Jeffrey Barron,

Reuben Carson, Sybil Adelman. *Director:* Jack Regas.

### 355 Charo. Variety, 70 min., Showtime, 6/79. An electrifying one-woman concert by Charo from the Sahara Hotel in Las Vegas. *Host:* Charo. *Producer:* Don Davis.

### 356 The Cheats. Drama, 60 min., ABC, 3/30/89. Holly, Beth, and Robin are three close friends who attend the exclusive Braidon Academy for Girls. When the girls are faced with what they believe will be a tough final exam, they foolishly steal a copy of the test. The story relates how the "crime" affects their lives. Aired as an "ABC Afterschool Special." *Cast:* Heather McAdam (Holly Mitchell), Dana Behr (Beth Davis), Elsie Hillario (Robin Archer), Daphne Maxwell Reid (Judith Daniels), Christine Langer (Lynnie Ryan), Mona Clark (Mrs. Lederer). *Producers:* Judith Stoia, Lisa Schmid. *Writer:* Caryl Rivers. *Director:* Fred Barzak.

### 357 Cher. Variety, 60 min., CBS, 2/12/75. An hour of music and song with singer Cher in her first television special. *Host:* Cher. *Guests:* Elton John, Bette Midler, Flip Wilson. *Producers:* George Schlatter, Lee Miller. *Writers:* Digby Wolfe, Don Reo, Allan Katz, Iris Rainer, Pat Proft, Bo Kaprall, David Panich, Ron Pearlman, Nick Arnold, John Boni, Ray Taylor, Billy Barnes, Earl Brown. *Director:* Art Fisher.

### 358 Cher—A Celebration at Caesar's Palace. Variety, 90 min., Showtime, 4/21/83. A solo performance by Cher as she performs her nightclub act at Caesar's Palace in Las Vegas. *Host:* Cher. *Music:* Garry Scott. *Producer-Director:* Art Taylor.

### 359 Cher and Other Fantasies. Variety, 60 min., NBC, 4/3/79. A lively hour of music and song in

**Ad for "Cher at the Mirage"**

which Cher and her guests live out their fantasies. *Host:* Cher. *Guests:* Lucille Ball, Elliott Gould, Andy Kaufman, Bill Saluga. *Music:* Earl Brown. *Producers:* George Schlatter, Lee Miller. *Writers:* Digby Wolfe, Don Reo. *Director:* Art Fisher.

**360 Cher at the Mirage.** Variety, 60 min., CBS, 2/4/91. A musical special based on Cher's "Heart of Stone" tour (which was taped during the summer of 1991 at the Mirage Hotel in Las Vegas). *Host:* Cher. *Singers:* Pattie Darcy, Darlene Love, Edna Wright. *Guest:* John Elgin Kenna (a Cher impersonator). *Music:* Gary Scott. *Producers:* Bill Sammeth, Joe DeCarlo, Richard Baskin. *Producer-Director:* Marty Callner.

**361 Cher ... Special.** Variety, 60 min., ABC, 4/3/78. An hour of music and songs. *Host:* Cher. *Guests:* Dolly Parton, Rod Stewart. *Producers:* Raymond Katz, Sandy Gallin. *Writers:*

Buz Kohan, Patricia Resnick, Rod Warren. *Director:* Art Fisher.

**362 Cheryl Ladd ... Looking Back — Souvenirs.** Variety, 60 min., ABC, 5/19/80. Rock, folk, and gospel sequences that showcase the musical, comedic, and dramatic talents of actress Cheryl Ladd. *Host:* Cheryl Ladd. *Guests:* The Charlie Daniels Band, Jeff Conaway, Joyce DeWitt. *Music:* Peter Matz. *Producers:* Cheryl Ladd, Henry Jaffe. *Writer:* Rod Warren. *Director:* Don Mischer.

**363 Cheryl Ladd: Scenes from a Special.** Variety, 60 min., ABC, 3/31/82. A fast-paced hour of music and comedy. *Host:* Cheryl Ladd. *Guests:* Billy Barty, Carol Burnett, Patty Maloney, Rick Springfield. *Music:* John Scott Trotter. *Producers:* Henry Jaffe, Brian Russell. *Writer:* Jack Wohl. *Director:* Don Mischer.

**364 The Cheryl Ladd Special.** Variety, 60 min., ABC, 4/3/79. The program finds the lovely star of "Charlie's Angels" returning to her hometown in South Dakota for a musical get-together at a tavern called Ma's Place. *Host:* Cheryl Ladd. *Guests:* Waylon Jennings, Ben Vereen. *Music:* Larry Grossman. *Producers:* Gary Smith, Dwight Hemion. *Director:* Dwight Hemion.

**365 The Chevrolet Golden Anniversary Show.** Variety, 60 min., CBS, 11/3/61. Songs and sketches drawn from the ranks of showbusiness over the last fifty years. Sponsored by Chevrolet. *Host:* James Arness. *Guests:* Art Carney, Allen Case, Nanette Fabray, Tony Randall, Eileen Rogers. *Music:* Harry Zimmerman. *Producers:* Barry Wood, Burt Shevelove. *Writers:* Larry Gelbart, Gary Belkin. *Director:* Sid Smith.

### 366 The Chevy Chase National Humor Test.

Comedy, 60 min., NBC, 5/10/79. Various sketches that are designed to test American humor. *Host:* Chevy Chase. *Guests:* Milton Berle, Dr. Joyce Brothers, Pam Dawber, Hugh Hefner, Martin Mull. *Producer:* Terry Hughes. *Director:* Tom Trbovich.

**Cheryl Ladd**

### 367 The Chevy Chase Show.

Variety, 60 min., NBC, 5/5/77. An hour of comedy with Chevy Chase in his first television special. *Host:* Chevy Chase. *Guests:* Dr. Joyce Brothers, Tim Conway. *Repertoire Company:* Brian Doyle-Murray, Edie McClurg, Wendie Jo Sperber, Bunny Summers, Bill Zuckert. *Announcer:* Dick Tufeld. *Music:* Alan Copeland. *Producers:* Martin Erlichman, Bob Finkel. *Writers:* Chevy Chase, Stuart Birnbaum, Brian Doyle-Murray, Thomas Leopold. *Director:* Art Fisher.

### 368 A Child's Christmas in Wales.

Drama, 60 min., PBS, 12/23/87. A television adaptation of the 1954 Dylan Thomas poem about a kindly grandfather (Geraint) who delights his grandson (Thomas) with memories of his Christmases as a youth in a small Welsh town. *Cast:* Denholm Elliott (Geraint), Jesse McBreaty (Geraint, young), Mathonwy Reeves (Thomas), Glynis Davies (Mother), Helen Beavis (Aunt Bessie), Cullum McGeachie (Jim). *Music:* Lewis Natole. *Producers:* Michael McMillan, Joseph Pierson. *Writer:* Peter Kreutzer. *Director:* Don McBrearty.

### 369 The Chipmunks—Rockin' Through the Decades.

Tribute, 30 min., NBC, 1/29/90. A live-action and animated special that looks at the 32-year history of the Chipmunks (Alvin, Theodore, and Simon), three singing rodents created by Ross Bagdasarian. *Host:* Will Smith. *Guests:* Shelley Duvall, Little Richard,

Kenny Loggins, Richard Moll, Markie Post, Raven-Samone, Ben Vereen. *Producer-Writers:* Ross Bagdasarian, Janice Karman. *Producers:* Cliff Ruby, Walt Kubiak.

## 370 The Chocolate Soldier.

Comedy, 90 min., NBC, 6/4/55. A comic opera based on George Bernard Shaw's 1894 play *Arms and the Man.* When he discovers that his cook wagon is in the direct line of fire, Captain Bumerli, a cowardly Swiss army pastry chef who carries chocolate in his holsters instead of pistols, flees the battlefield. In an attempt to avoid capture by the Bulgarians, he climbs up a trellis and into the bedroom of Nadina, the fiancée of a famed war hero. Nadina shelters Bumerli and later helps him escape. The story relates Bumerli's efforts to win Nadina's love when he returns one year later to court her (and save her from a loveless marriage to Major Alexius Spiridoff). *Cast:* Eddie Albert (Bumerli), Rise Stevens (Nadina), Akim Tamiroff (Major Ludek), David Atkinson (Alexius Spiridoff), George Ebeling (General Masakroff). *Music:* Charles Sanford. *Producer:* Max Liebman. *Writers:* Neil Simon, William Friedberg, Will Glickman, Oskar Strauss. *Director:* Jeffrey Hayden.

## 371 Choose Your Own Adventure: The Case of the Silk King. Adventure, 30 min., ABC, 12/12 and 12/19/92. An "ABC Weekend Special" about the adventures of Tina and Sean, orphaned teenage siblings, as they search for their uncle in Bangkok. *Cast:* Soleil Moon Frye (Tina), Chad Allen (Sean), Charles Haid (Uncle). *Also:* Michael Locking, Pat Morita, Suchai Thilua. *Producer:* George McQuilkin, Nicky Weaver Noxon. *Writer:* Marc Scott Zicree. *Director:* Burt Brinckerhoff.

## 372 Christmas Around the World. Variety, 90 min., NBC, 12/19/

76. The program explores the various Christmas celebrations from around the world. *Guests:* Vikki Carr, William Conrad, Gene Kelly, Marcel Marceau, Marilyn McCoo, Billy Davis, Jr.; Liv Ullmann, Dick Van Dyke, Jonathan Winters. *Music:* Ed Bogas. *Producer-Writer-Director:* Lee Mendelson, Karen Crommie.

## 373 Christmas Calendar.

Documentary, 60 min., PBS, 12/15/88. A Yuletide special that traces the history of Christmas, which is believed to have begun in Germany 750 years ago (the Christmas tradition of a tree was begun in the 1500s). The program also traces the origins of the most beloved Christmas song, "Silent Night" (which was written on December 24, 1818). The special is heightened by host Loretta Swit as she shares an old-fashioned European Christmas with her German friends. *Cast:* Loretta Swit (Host/Narrator), Reinhart Schmidt (Father), Theresia Schmidt (Mother), Barry Sharon (Son), Felicia Sharon (Daughter). *U.S. Producer:* Thomas Boggalt. *German Producer:* Klaus Weber. *Writer:* Hildegarde Schroeder. *Director:* Jochen Richter.

## 374 A Christmas Carol. A chronological listing of six television adaptations of the Charles Dickens classic, *A Christmas Carol* (excluded are series episode parodies, animated adaptations, and television movies). The story itself focuses on Ebenezer Scrooge, a mean and miserly businessman, who comes to see his faults one Christmas Eve when he is visited by the ghosts of Christmas Past, Present, and Future. See also "Carol for Another Christmas."

**1 A Christmas Carol** (60 min., DuMont, 12/25/47). *Cast:* John Carradine, Barnard Hughes, Eva Marie Saint, Somer Alder, Sam Fertig, Helen Stenberg, Jonathan Marlowe. *Producer-Director:* James L. Caddigan.

**2 A Christmas Carol** (60 min., NBC,

12/19/48). *Cast:* Dennis King (as Scrooge). The program marks the television debut of Bing Crosby (who sang "Silent Night" with the Bob Mitchell Boys Choir in a segment filmed especially for the program).

**3 A Christmas Carol** (60 min., ABC, 12/24/48). *Cast:* The Rufus Rose Marionettes portray all characters in a show produced by Leonard Steinman.

**4 A Christmas Carol** (30 min., NBC, 12/25/51). *Cast:* Ralph Richardson (Scrooge), Norman Barr (Bob Crachit), Robert Hay Smith (Tiny Tim), Margaret Phillips (Mrs. Crachit), Melville Cooper (Ghost of Christmas Past), Arthur Treacher (Ghost of Christmas Present), Malcolm Keen (Marley's Ghost), Alan Napier (Ghost of Christmas Future). *Music:* Harry Sosnik. *Producer:* Fred Coe. *TV Adaptation:* David Swift. *Director:* Gordon Duff. *Note:* Gypsy Raine, who portrayed Mrs. Fezziwig, is Charles Dickens's great-granddaughter.

**5 A Christmas Carol** (60 min., CBS, 12/23/54). *Cast:* Fredric March (Scrooge), Basil Rathbone (Marley), Bob Sweeney (Bob Crachit), Queenie Leonard (Mrs. Crachit), Christopher Cook (Tiny Tim), Ray Middleton (Ghost of Christmas Present), Sally Fraser (Ghost of Christmas Past), Bonnie Franklin (Child), Judy Franklin (Child), Janine Perreau (Belinda). *Music:* Bernard Herrmann. *Producer-Director:* Ralph Levy. *TV Adaptation:* Maxwell Anderson.

**6 A Christmas Carol** (90 min., The Entertainment Channel, 12/82). *Cast:* Richard Hilger (Scrooge), Marshall Borden (Charles Dickens), Catherine Burns (Mrs. Dickens), John Patrick Martin (Bob Crachit), Jonathan Fuller (Ghost of Christmas Past), Peter Thoemke (Ghost of Christmas Present), Stephen D'Ambrose (Ghost of Christmas Future), Sara Hennessey (Mamie), Oliver Cliff (John Dickens). *Music:* Dick Whitbeck. *Producer:* Donald Schoenbaum. *TV Adaptation:* Barbara Field. *Director:* Paul Miller.

**375 A Christmas Dream.** Musical, 60 min., NBC, 12/16/84. The story of a sidewalk Santa who tries to rekindle the Christmas spirit in a depressed latchkey youngster. *Cast:* Mr. T. (Santa Claus), Emmanuel Lewis (Youngster), David Copperfield (Toy store manager), Maureen McGovern (Singer), Willie Tyler and Lester (Doorman and his ventriloquist's dummy). *Also:* Tai Babilonia, Randy Gardner, and the Radio City Music Hall Rockettes. *Music:* Elliot Lawrence. *Producer:* Joseph Cates. *Writer:* Frank Slocum. *Director:* Sid Smith.

**376 A Christmas Eve Musicale.** Variety, 45 min., CBS, 12/24/52. A Christmas Eve program of music, song, and dance highlighted by a reading of the Nativity story. *Host:* Gene Lockhart. *Guest:* Maria Tallchief (a ballerina). *Music:* David Rose. *Producer-Director:* Bob Banner.

**377 Christmas in Disneyland.** Variety, 60 min., ABC, 12/8/76. The story of a Scrooge-like character who finds the true meaning of Christmas at Disneyland. *Cast:* Art Carney (Gramps/Dr. Wunderbar), Glen Campbell (Grandpa Jones/Disneyland visitor), Sandy Duncan (Tour Guide), Terri Lynn Wood (Terri), Brad Savage (Brad). *Music:* Jack Elliott, Allyn Ferguson. *Producer-Director:* Marty Pasetta. *Writer:* Buz Kohan.

**378 Christmas in Washington.** A chronological listing of the 11 variety specials broadcast during December of each year. The programs, consisting of Christmas music and songs, are each 60 minutes and broadcast by NBC. George Stevens, Jr., Dwight Hemion, and Gary Smith are the producers; Ian Fraser is the musical director: Buz Kohan is the writer; and Dwight Hemion is the director.

**1 Christmas in Washington** (12/13/ 82). *Guests:* Diahann Carroll, Barbara Mandrell, Nancy Reagan, President

**Ad for "Christmas in Washington"**

Ronald Reagan, John Schneider, The Shiloh Baptist Church Choir, Dinah Shore.

**2 Christmas in Washington** (12/15/83). *Guests:* Julio Iglesias, Nancy Reagan, President Ronald Reagan, The Shiloh Baptist Choir, Leslie Uggams, The U.S. Naval Academy, Andy Williams.

**3 Christmas in Washington** (12/16/84). *Host:* Hal Linden. *Guests:* Nell Carter, Roger Mudd, The Osmond Brothers, Donny Osmond, Marie Osmond, Nancy Reagan, President Ronald Reagan.

**4 Christmas in Washington** (12/15/85). *Host:* Tom Brokaw. *Guests:* Pat Boone, Natalie Cole, Amy Grant, Emmanuel Lewis, Viktoria Mullova, Nancy Reagan, President Ronald Reagan, The U.S. Naval Academy Glee Club.

**5 Christmas in Washington** (12/20/86). *Host:* John Forsythe. *Guests:* Mac Davis, Nancy Reagan, President Ronald Reagan, The U.S. Navy Glee Club.

**6 Christmas in Washington** (12/21/87). *Host:* Barbara Mandrell. *Guests:* The Brunson Brothers, Jack Jones, Marilyn McCoo, Nancy Reagan, President Ronald Reagan, The U.S. Naval Academy Glee Club.

**7 Christmas in Washington** (12/21/88). *Host:* James Stewart. *Guests:* Kathleen Battle, Vikki Carr, Shirley Jones, Garry Morris, Nancy Reagan, President Ronald Reagan, The U.S. Naval Academy Glee Club.

**8 Christmas in Washington** (12/18/89). *Guests:* Barbara Bush, President George Bush, Diahann Carroll, Vic Damone, James Galway, Olivia Newton-John, Michael W. Smith, Take 6, The U.S. Naval Academy Glee Club.

**9 Christmas in Washington** (12/19/90). *Host:* John Denver. *Guests:* Barbara Bush, President George Bush, Aretha Franklin, Barbara Hendricks,

Reba McEntire, The U.S. Naval Academy Glee Club.

**10 Christmas in Washington** (12/18/ 91). *Guests:* Anita Baker, Barbara Bush, President George Bush, Vince Gill, Johnny Mathis, Anne Murray, The U.S. Naval Academy Glee Club.

**11 Christmas in Washington** (12/19/ 92). *Hosts:* Julie Andrews, Neil Diamond. *Guests:* Barbara Bush, President George Bush, Peabo Bryson, Midori (violinist), The Soul Children Singers.

## 379 Christmas Legend of Nashville. Tribute, 90 min., Syndicated, 12/82. A tuneful yuletide salute to the country stars of the past. *Hosts:* Pat Boone, Dottie West. *Guests:* Alabama, Bobby Bare, John Conlee, David Frizzell, Grandpa Jones, Jim Owens, Minnie Pearl, George Strait. *Music:* Bill Walker. *Producers:* Chet Hagan, Peter Birch. *Writer:* Chet Hagan. *Director:* Reg Dunlap.

## 380 A Christmas Memory. Drama, 60 min., ABC, 12/21/66. A television adaptation of novelist Truman Capote's sensitive Christmas memory, which he wrote in 1956. The story, set in a small Alabama town, tells of Capote's desperately lonely childhood, and one Christmas memory he shared with his aunt, Sookie, a gentle and eccentric spinster who raised him. See also "The Thanksgiving Visitor," the sequel story. *Cast:* Truman Capote (Narrator), Geraldine Page (Aunt Sookie), Donnie Melvin (Truman as a boy). *Music:* Meyer Kupferman. *Producer-Director:* Frank Perry. *Writer:* Eleanor Perry.

## 381 A Christmas Present. Variety, 50 min., CBS, 12/25/48. A live program of holiday songs, music, and stories. The program was scheduled to run for sixty minutes with the last ten minutes devoted to Gypsy Rose Lee as Cinderella's Fairy Godmother. Miss Lee failed to appear and the broadcast ended ten minutes early. *Host:* Jan

Murray. *Guests:* Lyn Duddy, Edith Fellows, Georgia Gibbs, Bob Howard, The Six Talley Beatty Dancers (from the Katherine Dunham Troupe). *Music:* Bob Grant. *Producer:* Paul Feigay. *Director:* Alex Leftwich.

## 382 A Christmas Sampler. Music, 60 min., Syndicated, 12/17/87. A program of yuletide music with the Mormon Tabernacle Choir. *Host:* Hal Linden. *Music Conductor:* Jerrold Ottley. *Music Composer:* Roger Lambson. *Organist:* Richard Leendick. *Producers:* Jack Adamson, Margaret Smoot, Al Henderson. *Writers:* Maurine J. Ward, Margaret Smoot. *Director:* J. Scott Iverson.

## 383 Christmas Snow. Drama, 60 min., NBC, 12/20/86. A poignant Yuletide story about a kind-hearted widow (Gertrude) and her adopted children (Amy and Wally) who face eviction from her candy store by a Scrooge-like landlord (Reginald Snyder). *Cast:* Katherine Helmond (Gertrude Mutterance), Sid Caesar (Reginald Snyder), Melissa Hart (Amy Mutterance), Kimble Joyner (Wally Mutterance), Howard Storey (Policeman), Lillian Carlson (Mrs. Wilmot). *Producer:* Marian Rees. *Writer:* Suzanne Clauser. *Director:* Gus Trikonis.

## 384 A Christmas Song. Variety, 60 min., DuMont, 12/25/50. A musical play about how the Christmas spirit affects the people who live in a lower-class apartment house on New York's Lower East Side. *Cast:* Harold Brown, Gordon Dilworth, Beverly Hanis, Joe Helgesen, Lois Hunt, Stephen Kennedy, Margery Myer, Norman Scott, Jon Silo. *Music:* Robert Russell Bennett. *Producer:* Paul Rosen. *Writer:* Barbara Boothe. *Director:* Larry White.

## Christmas Special ... With Love, Mac Davis *see* Mac Davis Specials

**385 Christmas Startime with Leonard Bernstein.** Variety, 60 min., NBC, 12/22/59. An hour of Christmas music and readings. *Host:* Leonard Bernstein. *Guests:* Marian Anderson, The St. Paul's Cathedral Boys Choir of London. *Music:* Tutti Camarata. *Producer:* Hubbell Robinson.

**386 Christmas with Lorne Greene.** Variety, 30 min., NBC, 12/17/66. A yuletide program in which host Lorne Greene and the 45-member UNICEF Children's Choir reflect on what makes Christmas special as they take an imaginary trip to nineteenth-century England and the era of Charles Dickens. *Host:* Lorne Greene. *Music:* Peter Matz. *Producer:* Gary Smith, Dwight Hemion. *Writer:* Sheldon Keller. *Director:* Dwight Hemion.

**Christmas with the Bing Crosbys** *see* **Bing Crosby Specials**

**387 Christmas with the Stars.** Variety, 60 min., NBC, 12/25/53. A Christmas Day program of music and songs. *Host:* Jimmy Powers. *Guests:* Eddie "Rochester" Anderson, Victor Borge, Rosemary Clooney, Mel Ferrer, Arthur Fiedler and the Boston Pops Orchestra, Eddie Fisher, Helen Hayes, Bob Hope, Tony Martin, Tyrone Power, Rosalind Russell. *Music Director:* Axel Stordahl. *Producer:* Joseph Santley. *Writer:* Howard Teichmann.

**388 Cinderella.** Ballet, 90 min., NBC, 4/29/57. The Royal Ballet of Great Britain performs the story of a mistreated girl (Cinderella) whose dream to become beautiful and attend a lavish ball is granted by her fairy godmother. *Cast:* Margot Fonteyn (Cinderella), Michael Somes (Prince Charming), Julia Farrow (Fairy Godmother), Frederick Ashton and Kenneth MacMillan (Ugly Stepsisters), Alexander Grant (Jester). *Music:* Sergei Prokofiev. *Music Director:* Robert Irving. *Choreography:* Frederick Ashton.

**389 Cinderella.** Musical, 90 min., CBS, 1/18/67. A musical version of the classic story about a degraded girl whose dream to become beautiful and attend a lavish ball is granted by her fairy godmother. *Cast:* Lesley Ann Warren (Cinderella), Ginger Rogers (Queen), Walter Pidgeon (King), Jo Van Fleet (Stepmother), Celeste Holm (Fairy Godmother), Stuart Damon (Prince Charming), Pat Carroll (Prunella), Barbara Ruick (Esmerelda). *Music Director:* John Green. *Music and Lyrics:* Richard Rodgers, Oscar Hammerstein II. *Producer-Director:* Charles S. Dubin. *Writer:* Joseph Schrank.

**390 Cinderella.** Ballet, 2 hrs., Syndicated, 6/28/81. The story of Cinderella, a young girl dominated by her evil stepsisters who is granted a special wish — to be elegant and attend a lavish ball. Choreographed in 1948, "Cinderella" marked the first full-length English ballet done in classic nineteenth-century style. This version, by Frederick Ashton, is a delightful three-act ballet that is stylish in presentation and a blend of tender romance and gentle music. Taped at the London Royal Opera House in 1979 and first presented on American television in 1981. *Cast:* Leslie Collier (Cinderella), Anthony Dowell (Prince Charming), Lois Rutland and Adrian Reid (Evil Stepsisters), Monica Mason (Fairy Godmother), Leslie Edwards (Cinderella's father), Jennifer Penney (Fairy Spring), Merle Park (Fairy Summer), Pippa Wylde (Fairy Winter), Merle Park (Fairy Autumn), Wayne Sleep (Jester). *Host:* Jim Dale. *Conductor of the Royal House Orchestra:* Ashley Lawrence. *Producers:* Paul Noble, Doris Bergman. *Directors:* Brian Large, Norman Ross.

## 391 Cinderella at the Palace.

Variety, 2 hrs., CBS, 11/2/78. Marlene Ricci, a showbusiness newcomer, is the Cinderella of the title. She performs with established stars at Caesar's Palace in Las Vegas. Repeated on 8/16/79 as "Las Vegas Palace of Stars." *Host:* Gene Kelly. *Star:* Marlene Ricci. *Guests:* Paul Anka, Ann-Margret, Sammy Davis, Jr., Merv Griffin, Tom Jones, Elaine Joyce, Don Knotts, Frank Sinatra, Rip Taylor, Jimmie Walker, Andy Williams. *Music:* Nick Perito. *Producers:* Gary Smith, Dwight Hemion. *Writers:* Harry Crane, Norm Liebman, Marty Farrell. *Director:* Bob Henry.

## 392 Cindy Eller: A Modern Fairy Tale.

Drama, 60 min., ABC, 10/9/85. A modern adaptation of the Cinderella tale. Cindy Eller is a very pretty 15-year-old girl who has come to live with her stepmother (Janet) and her stepsisters (Liza and Laura) following her father's remarriage. Cindy has no friends and seems to live in her own dream world; and she is constantly being put down by Liza and Laura. One day Cindy meets Martha Dermody, a shopping cart lady, who possesses magical powers. As Cindy and Martha become friends, Cindy tells her that she likes Greg Prince, a handsome boy at school — a boy that both Liza and Laura also like. When Greg's mother throws an elegant party and invites Liza, Laura, and Cindy, Cindy refuses to go, feeling she is not as glamorous as her stepsisters. Martha steps in and Cindy finds herself living a fairy tale when she attends the dance and wins the affections of Greg. Aired as an "ABC Afterschool Special." *Cast:* Kyra Sedgwick (Cindy Eller), Kelly Wolf (Liza Eller), Jennifer Grey (Laura Eller), Pearl Bailey (Martha Dermody), Melanie Myron (Janet Eller), Grant Show (Greg Prince), Sylvia Miles (Sweet Susie), Stephen Keep (Mr. Eller). *Music:* Joe Bickley. *Producer:* Joseph Feury. *Writer:* Jeffrey Kindley. *Director:* Lee Grant.

## 393 Circus, Lions, Tigers and Melissas Two.

Variety, 60 min., NBC, 5/21/77. "Little House on the Prairie" costars Melissa Sue Anderson and Melissa Gilbert host a program that features performances by circus acts from around the world. *Producer-Directors:* Gilbert Cates, Joseph Cates. *Writer:* Frank Slocum.

## 394 Circus of the Stars.

A chronological listing of the 17 "Circus of the Stars" specials broadcast from 1/10/77 through 11/27/92. Each program features showbusiness personalities performing circus acts (all are two hours in length and broadcast on CBS).

**1 Circus of the Stars** (1/10/77). *Host:* John Forsythe. *Ringmasters:* Jean-Pierre Aumont, Jack Cassidy, George Hamilton, Bernadette Peters. *Performers:* Marty Allen, Ed Asner, Billy Barty, Karen Black, Claudia Cardinale, Lynda Carter, Gary Collins, David Doyle, Peter Fonda, Rosey Grier, Joey Heatherton, David Janssen, Janet Leigh, Rue McClanahan, Peter Marshall, Mary Ann Mobley, Pat Morita, David Nelson, Valerie Perrine, Deborah Raffin, Wayne Rogers, Jean Stapleton, Bobby Van, Abe Vigoda.

**2 Circus of the Stars** (12/5/77). *Hosts-Ringmasters:* Lucille Ball, Telly Savalas, Cindy Williams, Michael York. *Performers:* Marty Allen, Lucie Arnaz, George Burns, Lynda Carter, Gary Collins, Robert Conrad, Lola Falana, Peter Fonda, Richard Hatch, Earl Holliman, Jack Klugman, Tony LoBianco, James Vincent McNichol, Kristy McNichol, Penny Marshall, Lee Meriwether, Mary Ann Mobley, David Nelson, Valerie Perrine, Mackenzie Phillips, Deborah Raffin, Richard Roundtree, Susan Saint James, Tom Sullivan, Abe Vigoda, Betty White, Paul Williams.

**3 Circus of the Stars** (6/20/79). *Ringmasters:* Lauren Bacall, Sammy Davis, Jr., Jerry Lewis, Anthony Newley, Bernadette Peters. *Performers:* Marty Allen, Dirk Blocker, Foster

Brooks, Charlie Callas, Gary Collins, Cathy Lee Crosby, Jamie Lee Curtis, Jamie Farr, Buddy Hackett, Tony Lo-Bianco, Carol Lynley, Eddie Mekka, Lee Meriwether, Mary Ann Mobley, David Nelson, Ken Norton, Valerie Perrine, Michelle Phillips, Bob Seagren, Martin Sheen, Betty White.

**4 Circus of the Stars** (12/16/79). *Ringmasters:* Erik Estrada, Douglas Fairbanks, Jr., Lola Falana, Mariette Hartley, Loretta Swit. *Performers:* Leslie Aletter, Marty Allen, Loni Anderson, Bob Barker, Barbi Benton, Candy Clark, Gary Collins, Cathy Lee Crosby, Quinn Cummings, Vince Edwards, Jamie Farr, Marjoe Gortner, Richard Hatch, Richard Kiel, Lee Meriwether, Mary Ann Mobley, David Nelson, John Schneider, Bob Seagren, Brooke Shields, Elke Sommer, Trish Stewart, Vic Tayback, Rip Taylor, Charlene Tilton.

**5 Circus of the Stars** (12/14/80). *Ringmasters:* Lloyd Bridges, Rock Hudson, Angela Lansbury, Valerie Perrine. *Performers:* Marty Allen, Scott Baio, Barbi Benton, Gil Gerard, Marjoe Gortner, Linda Gray, Richard Hatch, Jayne Kennedy, Ted Lange, Michele Lee, Mary Elizabeth McDonough, David Nelson, Randi Oakes, Dana Plato, Joan Rivers, Wayne Rogers, Bob Seagren, Connie Sellecca, Brooke Shields.

**6 Circus of the Stars** (12/13/81). *Ringmasters:* Linda Evans, Elliott Gould, Bob Newhart, Brooke Shields. *Performers:* Marty Allen, Catherine Bach, Jamie Lyn Bauer, Todd Bridges, Danielle Brisebois, Mike Connors, Britt Ekland, Greg Evigan, Jamie Farr, Steven Ford, Marjoe Gortner, Brodie Greer, Pat Harrington, Jr., Tab Hunter, Sally Kellerman, Eddie Mekka, David Nelson, Randi Oakes, Dana Plato, William Shatner, Andrew Stevens.

**7 Circus of the Stars** (12/5/82). *Ringmasters:* Scott Baio, Morgan Fairchild, Vincent Price, Martha Raye, Debbie Reynolds, Mickey Rooney,

Isabel Sanford. *Performers:* Leslie Aletter, Marty Allen, Jamie Lyn Bauer, Barbi Benton, Tracy Bregman, Linda Blair, Lindsay Bloom, Todd Bridges, Danielle Brisebois, Darleen Carr, Didi Conn, Robert Culp, Missy Gold, Marjoe Gortner, Brodie Greer, Judy Landers, Gloria Loring, Jean Marsh, Roddy McDowall, Eddie Mekka, Anita Morris, David Nelson, Bob Newhart, Ethan Phillips, Adam Rich, Ricky Schroder, Peter Scolari, Brooke Shields, Betty Thomas.

**8 Circus of the Stars** (12/18/83). *Ringmasters:* Beverly D'Angelo, Louis Gossett, Jr., Ann Jillian, Robert Preston, Dottie West. *Performers:* Marty Allen, Douglas Barr, Linda Blair, Foster Brooks, Charlie Callas, Tony Curtis, Phyllis Diller, Jamie Farr, Missy Gold, Tracey Gold, Andre Gower, Judy Landers, Michele Lee, Kari Michaelsen, Judy Norton-Taylor, Bruce Penhall, Lynn Redgrave, Tracy Scoggins, Peter Scolari, Brooke Shields, Morgan Stevens, Herve Villechaize, Pia Zadora.

**9 Circus of the Stars** (12/2/84). *Ringmasters:* Gary Collins, Jamie Farr, Merv Griffin, Brooke Shields. *Performers:* Kyle Aletter, Lindsay Bloom, Tim Conway, Ted Knight, Marcy Lafferty, Emmanuel Lewis, Patricia McPherson, Lee Meriwether, Brian Mitchell, Tracy Nelson, Judy Norton-Taylor, Randi Oakes, Ken Olandt, Tony Randall, Ricky Schroder, Peter Scolari, George Segal, William Shatner.

**10 Circus of the Stars** (12/8/85). *Host:* Burt Lancaster. *Ringmasters:* Bea Arthur, Dick Clark, Merv Griffin. *Performers:* Willie Aames, Lucie Arnaz, Christopher Atkins, Danielle Brisebois, Nell Carter, Candy Clark, Cathy Lee Crosby, Phyllis Diller, Ami Foster, Deidre Hall, Scott Hamilton, Mary Hart, Lauri Hendler, Telma Hopkins, Perry King, Ronn Lucas, Lara Jill Miller, Tony O'Dell, Alfonso Riberio, Pernell Roberts, Ricky Schroder, Lana Turner, Cory Yothers, Tina Yothers, Kim Zimmer.

**11 Circus of the Stars** (12/9/86). *Ringmasters:* Dick Clark, Barbara Eden, Merv Griffin, Dionne Warwick. *Performers:* Lisa Aliff, Douglas Barr, Leslie Bega, Clifton Davis, Shannen Doherty, Nicole Eggert, Britt Ekland, Ami Foster, Scott Grimes, Dorothy Hamill, Mary Hart, Lorenzo Lamas, Greg Louganis, Anita Morris, Pat Petersen, Jane Powell, Ernie Reyes, Jr., Alfonso Riberio, Deborah Shelton, Krista Tesreau, Alan Thicke, Dee Wallace.

**12 Circus of the Stars** (12/15/87). *Host:* Kirk Douglas. *Ringmasters:* Delta Burke, Merv Griffin, Cesar Romero. *Performers:* Heidi Bohay, Carol Channing, Candy Clark, Tony Dow, Nicole Eggert, Glenn Ford, Ami Foster, Marla Gibbs, Marjoe Gortner, Andre Gower, Tony Griffin, Katherine Kelly Lang, Terry Ann Lynn, Pat Morita, Bronson Pinchot, Juliet Prowse, Ernie Reyes, Jr., Richard Simmons.

**13 Circus of the Stars** (11/25/88). *Ringmasters:* Bea Arthur, Martin Mull. *Performers:* Louie Anderson, Rebeca Arthur, Steve Burton, John Byner, Khrystyne Haje, Mary Hart, Christopher Hewett, Harvey Korman, Heather Langencamp, Matthew Lawrence, Anita Morris, Tom Poston, Cathy Rigby, Emma Samms, O. J. Simpson, Gordon Tomson, Krista Tesreau, Marsha Warfield.

**14 Circus of the Stars** (11/22/89). *Ringmasters:* Stacy Keach, Barbara Mandrell, Leslie Nielsen. *Performers:* Willie Aames, Kristen Alfonso, Rebeca Arthur, Mayim Bialik, Karen Black, Maureen Flannigan, Jennie Garth, Deidre Hall, Telma Hopkins, Omri Katz, Allan Kayser, David Leisure, Mario Lopez, Jamie Luner, Julie McCullough, Allen Rachins, Lynn Redgrave, Vonni Ribisi, Tracy Scoggins, Alex Trebek, Ben Vereen, Fred Willard.

**15 Circus of the Stars** (11/21/90). *Ringmasters:* Richard Crenna, Whoopi Goldberg, Robert Urich, Joan Van Ark. *Performers:* Rebeca Arthur, Linda Blair, Morgan Brittany, Da-ve Choden, Dick Clark, Wendy Cox, Ann Jillian, Bill Kirchenbauer, Richard Simmons, David Soul, Lisa Marie Todd, Dick Van Patten.

**16 Circus of the Stars** (11/29/91). *Ringmasters:* Dixie Carter, Leslie Nielsen. *Performers:* Susan Anton, Julie Brown, Gabrielle Carteris, Sherman Hemsley, William Katt, Alfonso Riberio, Paul Rodriquez, Tracy Scoggins, Jay Thomas, Charlene Tilton, Jerry Van Dyke, Tom Wopat.

**17 Circus of the Stars and Sideshow** (11/27/92). *Ringmasters:* Loni Anderson, Alan Thicke. *Performers:* Harry Anderson, Julie Brown, Patrick Duffy, Alice Ghostley, Brian Austin Green, Sally Kirkland, Linda Purl, Alfonso Riberio, Emma Samms, Richard Simmons, Sinbad, Meshach Taylor, Judy Tenuta, Robert Torti, Weird Al Yankovic.

**395 City vs. Country.** Variety, 60 min., ABC, 12/21/71. A music and comedy battle between Danny Thomas (representing the city) and Tennessee Ernie Ford (representing country). Stars from the fields of comedy and country music appear to support their team captains. *Hosts:* Tennessee Ernie Ford, Danny Thomas. *Comedy Guests:* Jack Benny, Milton Berle, Joey Bishop, Andy Griffith, George Lindsey, Sid Melton, Phil Silvers. *Music Guests:* Sammy Davis, Jr., Florence Henderson, Dean Martin, Anne Murray. *Cameos:* James Brolin, Howard Cosell. *Music:* Harper McKay. *Producer:* Ronald Jacobs. *Director:* Jack Donohue.

**396 Class Act: A Teacher's Story.** Drama, 60 min., ABC, 3/18/87. The story of an English teacher (Sam) who uses soccer to motivate a group of malcontents at Westview High School. Aired as an "ABC Afterschool Special." *Cast:* Ron Leibman (Sam Greene), Lisa Vidal (Gloria Rodriquez), Thomas Davis, Jr. (Otis Schneider), Kelly Neal

(Reggie Franklin), Pat Cooper (Coach Corsini), Susan Wilder (Mrs. Hopkins), Charlene Cheslak (Blade Gilbert). *Producers:* Fran Sears, Alan Cohen. *Writer:* Mardee Kravitt. *Director:* Kevin Hooks.

## 397 Class of '67. Variety, 60

min., NBC, 9/10/66. A song and dance review of the American college scene. *Host:* George Hamilton. *Guests:* Don Adams, Jack Burns, Trudy Desmond, The Doodletown Pipers, Lada Edmund, Jr., Peter Nero, Avery Schreiber, Nancy Sinatra. *Music:* Peter Matz.

## 398 Classic Creatures: Return of the Jedi. Documentary, 60

min., CBS, 11/21/83. A behind-the-scenes look at how the "creatures" from the film, *Return of the Jedi*, were created and made to come to life. *Hosts:* Carrie Fisher, Billy Dee Williams. *Music:* John Williams. *Producers:* Robert Guenette, Sidney Ganis, Howard Kazanjian. *Writers:* Robert Guenette, Greg O'Neill.

## 399 A Claymation Christmas Celebration. Cartoon, 30 min., CBS,

12/15/87. Animated clay figures (created through a process called claymation) sing and dance renditions of traditional Christmas songs. *Voices:* Tim Conner (Herb), Johnny Counterfit (Rex). *Singers:* Ron Tinsley, Dan Sachs, Jim Stienberger, Pat Harryman, Reid Stewart, Greg Black, Joni Miller, Amy Miller, Deborah Miller, Bernadette Coughlin, Roxy Ragozzino. *Music:* Patric J. Miller. *Producer:* David Altschul. *Writer:* Ralph Liddle. *Director:* Will Vinton.

## 400 Claymation Comedy of Horrors Show. Cartoon, 30 min.,

CBS, 5/29/91. Schemer Wilshire and his buddy Sheldon Snail, characters created through a process called claymation, encounter the supernatural as they search the castle of Dr. Frankenswine

for secret formulas that can make them a fortune. *Voices:* Tim Conner, Brian Cummings, Krisha Fairchild, Todd Tolces. *Producers:* Will Vinton, Paul Diener. *Writers:* Barry Bruce, Mark Gustafson, Ryan Holznagel. *Director:* Barry Bruce.

## 401 Close Ties. Drama, 1 hr. 45

min., The Entertainment Channel, 3/6/83. A stage play that presents a touching and insightful look at the problems of growing up and growing old as seen through the eyes of a family spending one last summer together in the Berkshires. *Cast:* Shelley Hack (Anna), Kim Darby (Evelyn), Ann Dusenberry (Connie), Joyce Ebert (Bess), Christopher Guest (Ira), Alan Oppenheimer (Watson), Anne Seymour (Josephine). *Music:* Jerry Frankel. *Producer:* Harlan P. Kleiman. *Writer:* Elizabeth Diggs. *Director:* Arvin Brown.

## 402 Clown Alley. Variety, 60

min., CBS, 11/9/66. A tribute to circus clowns. *Host:* Red Skelton. *Guests:* Billy Barty, Amanda Blake, Jackie Coogan, Audrey Meadows, Robert Merrill, Vincent Price, Martha Raye, Bobby Rydell. *Music:* Jack Lloyd. *Producers:* Red Skelton, Bill Hobin. *Writers:* Dave O'Brien, Mort Greene, Red Skelton. *Director:* Bill Hobin.

## 403 Clownaround. Variety, 60

min., CBS, 3/26/72. A tribute to circus clowns and comedians. *Host:* Ed Sullivan. *Guests:* Lucie Arnaz, George Carlin, Chuck McCann, Tiny Tim. *Music:* Moose Charlap. *Producers:* Robert H. Precht, Robert Alan Arthur. *Writer:* Alvin Cooperman. *Director:* John Moffitt.

## 404 Club Date: Peanuts Hucko. Music, 30 min., PBS, 8/84.

Half an hour of Dixieland music with Peanuts Hucko and his band: Peanuts Hucko (clarinet), Eddie Miller (tenor sax), John Best (trumpet), Carl Fontana (trombone), Joe Guarnieri (piano), Ray Leatherwood (bass), Danny Pucillo (drums), Louise Tobin (vocals). *Producers:* Bill Pivoritto, Paul Marshall. *Director:* Paul Marshall.

### 405 Clue: Movies, Murder and Mystery. Documentary, 60 min., CBS, 9/17/86. An exploration of whodunits and crime detection via clips from movies and television shows. *Host-Narrator:* Martin Mull. *Guests:* Peter Falk, Angela Lansbury, Mickey Spillane. *Music:* Kevin Kiner. *Producers:* Peter Guber, Jon Peters, Andrew Solt. *Writer:* Theodore Strauss. *Director:* Andrew Solt.

### Color Me Barbra *see* Barbra Streisand Specials

### 406 The Color of Friendship.
Drama, 60 min., ABC, 11/11/81. The story focuses on the relationship between David Bellinger, a white teenager, and Joel Garth, the only black student in his class at Nichols Junior High. The program stresses the friendship that develops between them and how under difficult circumstances (racial prejudice) their friendship knows no color boundaries. Aired as an "ABC Afterschool Special." *Cast:* Chris Barnes (David Bellinger), James Bond III (Joel Garth), Mary Alice (Mrs. Garth), Katherine Houghton (Miss James), Eric Schiff (Beany), Cleavon Little (Community leader). *Music:* Webster Lewis. *Producer:* Diana Kerew. *Writer:* Johnny Dawkins. *Director:* Stan Lathan.

### 407 Columbus Circle. Comedy, 30 min., ABC, 11/23/85. The misadventures of Leslie, Jimmy, Jo, Noah, Tracy, and Sarah, five fun-loving kids who form the Columbus Circle Gang. The story itself finds the gang attempting to play a practical joke on their new and snobbish neighbor, Mr. Waterford. Aired on the "ABC Weekend Special." *Cast:* Pam Potillo

(Leslie Thorton), Peter Smith (Jimmy Jo Abernathy), Jason Late (Noah Green), Chrissy Stevens (Tracy Carbone), Kathleen Sisk (Sarah Peterson), Ron Parady (Mr. Waterford), C. D. Barnes (Gardner Waterford), Jennifer Bassey (Mrs. Waterford), Nancy Walker (Dolores Fantasia Rockefeller), Peggy Cass (Big Millie). *Music:* Howard Goodall. *Producer:* Frank Doelger. *Writer:* Bruce Harmon. *Director:* Claude Kerven.

### 408 Come with Me—Lainie Kazan. Variety, 60 min., Syndicated, 11/71. A solo concert performance by singer Lainie Kazan. *Host:* Lainie Kazan. *Music:* Alyn Ainsworth. *Producers:* Jason G. Brent, Lawrence Schiller. *Director:* Lawrence Schiller.

### 409 The Comedy Club Special. Comedy, 2 hrs., ABC, 9/29/88. New comedy talent is profiled. Acts were chosen from eight of North America's "most fertile laugh centers": The Punchline (Atlanta), Zanie's (Chicago), Comedy Works (Philadelphia), Comedy Connection (Boston), Caroline's (New York), Holy City Zoo (San Francisco), Yuk Yuk's (Toronto), The Comedy Club (Los Angeles). *Host:* Dudley Moore. *Guests:* Lily Tomlin, Jackie Mason. *New Comics:* Richard Belzer, Tim Cavanaugh, Blake Clark, Ellen Degeneres, Gilbert Gottfried, Don Irrera, Carol Leifler, Emo Philips, Peter Pitofsky, Pam Stone, Judy Tenuta. *Producer:* George Schlatter. *Writers:* Chris Langham, Bruce Vilanch, George Schlatter. *Director:* Don Hoyer.

### Comedy Is King *see* Alan King Specials

### 410 The Comedy of Ernie Kovacs. Comedy, 60 min., ABC, 4/10/68. The program recalls the comedy genius of Ernie Kovacs via film clips from his various television shows.

*Host:* Edie Adams. *Producer:* Milt Hoffman. *Director:* Joseph Behar.

## 411 The Comedy Store's 20th Birthday. Comedy, 60 min., NBC, 9/24/92.

Onstage performances by many of the comedians who got their start at the Comedy Store in Hollywood, California, on the occasion of its 20th anniversary. *Guests:* Jeff Altman, Louie Anderson, Richard Belzer, Sandra Bernhard, Jim Carrey, Charles Fleischer, Arsenio Hall, Steve Landesberg, David Letterman, Craig T. Nelson, Tamayo Otsuki, Paul Rodriguez, Bob Saget, George Schlatter, Garry Shandling, Pauly Shore, Yakov Smirnoff, James Stephens III, Tim Thomerson, Jimmie Walker, Damon Wayans. *Producers:* Mitzi Shore, Marty Callner, Michael W. Becker. *Writers:* Peter Howard Shore, Mitzi Shore, Marty Callner. *Director:* Peter Howard Shore.

## 412 The Comics. Comedy, 60 min., NBC, 11/8/65.

Performances by the country's top comedians. *Host:* Danny Thomas. *Guests:* Tim Conway, Bill Cosby, Spike Jones, Jr., Martha Raye, The Three Stooges (Moe Howard, Larry Fine, Joe DeRita). *Music:* Harper McKay. *Producer-Director:* Alan Handley. *Writers:* Hugh Wedlock, Jr., Allan Manings.

## 413 Command Performance.

Variety, 60 min., ABC, 1/19/89. An all-star music and comedy salute to President George Bush. *Hosts:* Harry Hamlin, Jane Seymour. *Guests:* Rosemary Clooney, Clifton Davis, Michael Feinstein, LaToya Jackson, Shirley Jones, Robert Klein, Bobby Rydell, James Stewart. *Music:* Elliot Lawrence. *Producers:* Frankie Hewitt, Joe Cates. *Writer:* Frank Slocum. *Director:* Joe Cates.

## Como Country ... Perry and His Nashville Friends *see* Perry Como Specials

## 414 Compleat Gilbert and Sullivan: Patience. Opera, 2 hrs., PBS, 7/3/85.

A television adaptation of Gilbert and Sullivan's 1881 opera that lampoons Britain's aesthetic literary-artistic movement of the nineteenth century. The story, set in and around Bucolic Castle, centers on the romantic yearnings of Reginald Bunthorne, a foppish poet who is in love with a charming dairymaid named Patience. *Host:* Douglas Fairbanks, Jr. *Cast:* Derek Hammond-Stroud (Reginald Bunthorne), Sandra Dugdale (Patience), John Fryatt (Archibald Grosvenor), Anne Collins (Lady Jane), Shirley Chapman (Lady Angela), Patricia Hay (Lady Ella), Donald Adams (Colonel Calverley). *Music Director of the London Symphonic Orchestra:* Alexander Faris. *Producers:* George Walker, Judith DePaul. *Director:* Dave Heather. *Writer:* John Cox.

## 415 Compleat Gilbert and Sullivan: Ruddigore. Opera, 2 hrs., PBS, 4/3/85.

A television adaptation of Gilbert and Sullivan's 1887 opera. The story, set in the nineteenth-century fishing village of Rederring, relates the efforts of the lord of Ruddigore Castle to have his curse — which compels him to commit a crime each day or die — lifted. The program features the music of the London Symphony Orchestra and the Ambrosian Opera Chorus. *Host:* Douglas Fairbanks, Jr. *Cast:* Vincent Price (Sir Despard), Keith Michell (Robin), Sandra Dugdale (Rose), John Treleaven (Richard), Ann Howard (Mad Margaret), Donald Adams (Roderick), Johanna Peters (Dame Hannah), Paul Hudson (Adam). *Music Director:* Alexander Faris. *Producers:* George Walker, Judith DePaul. *Writers:* William Gilbert, Sir Arthur Sullivan. *Director:* Barrie Gavin.

## 416 Compleat Gilbert and Sullivan: The Sorcerer. Opera, 2

hrs., PBS, 6/5/85. In the gardens of Sir Marmaduke Poindextre's home, the village of Cloverleigh gathers to celebrate the betrothal of Marmaduke's son, Alexis, to the aristocratic Aline Sangazure. Alexis wants to share his euphoria, so he asks the sorcerer John Wellington Wells to administer a secret love potion to the entire village. The story follows the chaos that results. Based on the Gilbert and Sullivan operetta about romantic mixups in a genteel English village. *Host:* Douglas Fairbanks, Jr. *Cast:* Clive Revill (John Wellington Wells), Alexander Oliver (Alexis Poindextre), Nan Christie (Aline Sangazure), David Kernan (Dr. Daly), Donald Adams (Sir Marmaduke Poindextre), Nuala Willis (Lady Sangazure). *Conducting the London Symphonic Orchestra:* Alexander Faris. *Producers:* George Walker, Judith DePaul. *TV Staging:* Stephen Pinlott. *Director:* Dave Heather.

### 417 The Confessions of Dick Van Dyke. Variety, 60 min., ABC, 4/10/75. A lighthearted look at the funny side of fear through music and comedy sketches. *Host:* Dick Van Dyke. *Guests:* Moosie Drier, David Doyle, Michele Lee, Cliff Pellow, Stacy Van Dyke. *Producers:* Byron Paul, Bill Persky, Sam Denoff. *Writers:* Norman Barasch, Carroll Moore, Bill Persky, Sam Denoff. *Director:* Marc Breaux.

### 418 A Connecticut Yankee. Musical Comedy, 90 min., NBC, 3/12/55. The story of Martin Barret, a Connecticut man who, after suffering a head injury, is propelled back in time — to sixth-century England and the court of King Arthur. His experiences, as he incorporates his knowledge of the twentieth century in a primitive time, are the focal point of this adaptation of Mark Twain's *A Connecticut Yankee in King Arthur's Court. Cast:* Eddie Albert (Martin Barret), Janet Blair (Sandy), Leonard Elliott (Merlin the Magician), Gale Sherwood (Morgan Le Fay), Boris Karloff (King Arthur), John Conte (Sir Kay). *Music Director:* Charles Sanford. *Music Composer:* Richard Rodgers. *Lyrics:* Lorenz Hart. *Producer:* Max Liebman. *Writers:* William Friedberg, Neil Simon, Will Glickman, Al Schwartz. *Directors:* Max Liebman, Bill Hobin.

### 419 The Connie Francis Show. Variety, 60 min., ABC, 9/13/61. A charming hour of music, song, and comedy with singer Connie Francis in her first (and only) television special. *Host:* Connie Francis. *Guests:* Bea Arthur, Art Carney, Eddie Foy, Jr., Tab Hunter. *Music:* Mitch Leigh. *Producer-Director:* Greg Garrison.

### 420 The Contest Kid. Comedy, 30 min., ABC, 9/16/78. Harvey Small is a young boy who enjoys entering — and winning — giveaway contests. The story follows the misadventures that occur when Harvey enters a contest sponsored by the *Suburban Gentleman Magazine* and wins one month's attendance by a gentleman's gentleman named Hawkins. Aired as an "ABC Weekend Special"; see also the following title. *Cast:* Patrick Petersen (Harvey Small), John Williams (Hawkins), Pat Stevens (Mrs. Small), William Bogert (Mr. Small), Olivia Barash (Charlotte Cooper), Ronnie Scribner (Woody). *Music:* Tommy Leonetti. *Producer:* Robert Chenault. *Writers:* Jim Carlson, Terrence McDonnell. *Director:* Harvey Laidman.

### 421 The Contest Kid Strikes Again. Comedy, 30 min., ABC, 10/17/79. A sequel to "The Contest Kid" (see prior title). The further adventures of Harvey Small, a young boy with a knack for winning giveaway contests. In the second story Harvey wins a flock of chickens in a contest and creates havoc when he decides to keep them on an elegant estate to help his friend, an underpaid butler, avoid starvation. Aired as an "ABC Weekend

Special." *Cast:* Patrick Petersen (Harvey Small), Alan Napier (Butler), Olivia Barash (Charlotte Cooper), Pat Stevens (Mrs. Small), William Bogert (Mr. Small). *Producer:* Robert Chenault. *Writers:* Jim Carlson, Terrence McDonnell. *Director:* Harvey Laidman.

## 422 Contract for Life: The S.A.D.D. Story. Drama, 60 min., CBS, 12/11/84.

A "CBS Schoolbreak Special" that relates how the Contract for Life, Students Against Drunk Drivers, came into being (when a high school health teacher loses two students in separate car accidents, he devises a "contract" to be signed between the students and their parents to help ensure the young people a safe trip home after a night out with their friends). *Cast:* Stephen Macht (Bob Anastas), Anne Gee Byrd (Mrs. Shaw), Estee Chandler (Lucy Wilson), Robert Chestnut (David Shaw), Timothy Gibbs (Jimmy Matthews), Linda Kaye Henning (Carol Anastas). *Music:* Misha Segal. *Producer:* Paul Deason. *Writer:* Peter Silverman. *Director:* Joseph Pevney.

## 423 The Corn Is Green. Drama, 90 min., NBC, 1/8/56.

The story, set in a Welsh mining town in the early 1900s, relates the efforts of a schoolteacher (Miss Moffat) to transform a brilliant student (Morgan Evans) into an outstanding citizen. Based on the play by Emlyn Williams and broadcast on the "Hallmark Hall of Fame." *Cast:* Eva LaGallienne (Miss Moffat), John Kerr (Morgan Evans), Joan Lorring (Bessie Watty), Carmen Matthews (Miss Ronberry), Melville Cooper (Squire), Gwilym Williams (John Jones), Eva Leonard-Boyne (Mrs. Watty), Noel Leslie (Old Tom), David Cole (Glyn Thomas). *Producer:* Maurice Evans. *Writer:* Arthur Arent. *Director:* George Schaefer.

## Cos: The Bill Cosby Comedy

## Special *see* Bill Cosby Specials

## 424 Cotton Club '75. Variety, 90 min., NBC, 11/23/74.

A review that re-creates the famed Cotton Club. *Performers:* Franklyn Ajaye, Jonelle Allen, Ray Charles, Billy Daniels, Johnny Dankworth, Clifton Davis, Redd Foxx, Rosey Grier, Cleo Laine, Buddy Rich, Jimmie Walker. *Music:* Phil Moore. *Producers:* Burt Reynolds, Henry Jaffe. *Writers:* Bob Booker, George Foster. *Director:* Mark Warren.

## 425 Cougar! Drama, 90 min. (total), ABC, 1/7, 1/14, 1/21/83.

During a fierce storm, a flash flood uproots a house and sends it swirling down the Mississippi River. Soon after, the house slams into a mud bar. The occupants, a young sister and brother (Sarah and Albie Bright), discover that a mountain lion had at some point entered their house and is now trapped by a tree branch in another room. The story relates the children's efforts to escape—a situation that is compounded when two ruthless kidnappers happen upon the scene. Aired as three 30-minute "ABC Weekend Specials." *Cast:* Kim Hauser (Sarah Bright), Matthew Vipond (Albie Bright), Richard Donat (Reuben Bright), Caroline Yeager (Ruth Bright), Angus MacInnes (Rafe), Wayne Best (Spider). *Producer:* Diana Kerew. *Producer-Director:* Stephen H. Foreman.

## 426 A Country Christmas 1979. Variety, 60 min., CBS, 12/2/79.

A country music celebration of Christmas. *Performers:* Barbi Benton, Roy Clark, George Gobel, Loretta Lynn, Minnie Pearl, David Soul. *Music:* Jack Elliott, Allyn Ferguson. *Producers:* Marty Pasetta, Buz Kohan. *Writer:* Buz Kohan. *Director:* Marty Pasetta.

## 427 A Country Christmas 1980. Variety, 60 min., CBS, 12/1/80.

A holiday special featuring performances by country and western artists.

*Host:* Minnie Pearl. *Guests:zzz* Lynn Anderson, Debby Boone, Glen Campbell, Loretta Lynn, The Oak Ridge Boys, Tanya Tucker, Tom Wopat. *Music:* Jack Elliott. *Producers:* Marty Pasetta, Buz Kohan. *Writer:* Buz Kohan. *Director:* Marty Pasetta.

### 428 A Country Christmas 1981.

Variety, 60 min., CBS, 12/9/81. A Christmas special featuring country and western entertainers performing with their families. *Performers:* Roy Clark, David Frizzell, Minnie Pearl, Charlie Pride, Jerry Reed, John Schneider, Dottie West, Shelley West. *Music:* Jack Elliott. *Producers:* Marty Pasetta, Buz Kohan. *Writer:* Buz Kohan. *Director:* Marty Pasetta.

### 429 Country Comes Home.

Variety, 2 hrs., CBS, 4/1/81. A gala presentation wherein country and western artists perform. *Performers:* Roy Acuff, Chet Atkins, Bill Anderson, Bobby Bare, Glen Campbell, Hoagy Carmichael, Johnny Cash, June Carter Cash, Ray Charles, Roy Clark, Larry Gatlin, Crystal Gayle, George Jones, Doug Kershaw, Loretta Lynn, Minnie Pearl, Charley Pride, Jeannie C. Riley, The Statler Brothers, Tanya Tucker, Kitty Wells, Hank Williams, Jr., Tammy Wynette, Faron Young. *Announcer:* Dan Hoffman. *Music:* Bill Walker. *Producers:* Joseph Cates, Chet Hagan. *Writers:* Frank Slocum, Chet Hagan. *Director:* Walter C. Miller.

### 430 Country Comes Home.

Variety, 2 hrs., CBS, 4/10/82. Performances by country and western entertainers. *Host:* Glen Campbell. *Performers:* Roy Acuff, Chet Atkins, Alabama, Rosie Carter, Johnny Cash, June Carter Cash, Roy Clark, Crystal Gayle, Earl Klugh, Kris Kristofferson, Loretta Lynn, Taffy McElroy, John McEuen, Anne Murray, Jimmy C. Newton, The Oak Ridge Boys, Billy Swan, Hank Thompson, Mel Tillis,

Don Williams, Boxcar Willie. *Announcer:* Dick Tufeld. *Music:* Bill Walker. *Producers:* Joseph Cates, Chet Hagan. *Writers:* Frank Slocum, Chet Hagan. *Director:* Walter C. Miller.

### 431 Country Comes Home.

Variety, 2 hrs., CBS, 5/3/84. Performances by country and western artists. *Hosts:* Glen Campbell, Charley Pride. *Performers:* Chet Atkins, Alabama, Asleep at the Wheel, Roy Clark, Lacey J. Dalton, The Charlie Daniels Band, Jimmy Dickens, Tennessee Ernie Ford, David Frizzell, Johnny Gimble, Mickey Gilley, Lee Greenwood, Waylon Jennings, Charlie McCoy, Barbara Mandrell, Willie Nelson, The Oak Ridge Boys, Minnie Pearl, Hargus "Pig" Robbins, Buddy Spicher, Shelley West. *Music:* Bill Walker. *Producers:* Joseph Cates, Chet Hagan. *Writers:* Frank Slocum, Chet Hagan. *Director:* Stan Harris.

### 432 Country Galaxy of Stars.

Variety, 2 hrs., Syndicated, 10/81. Performances by country and western entertainers. *Hosts:* Mel Tillis, Sylvia. *Guests:* Lynn Anderson, Foster Brooks, Roy Clark, Larry Gatlin, Terry Gibbs, Mickey Gilley, Loretta Lynn, Barbara Mandrell, Irlene Mandrell, Louise Mandrell, The Oak Ridge Boys, Eddie Rabbitt, R. G. Springfield, Conway Twitty, Tammy Wynette. *Music:* Bill Walker. *Producers:* Walter E. Bartlett, Dick Thrall, Jim Owens. *Writers:* Barry Galvin, Pat Galvin. *Director:* Steve Womack.

### 433 The Country Girl.

Drama, 90 min., NBC, 2/5/74. The story of three people: Frank Elgin, a matinee idol drowning in self-pity and alcohol; Georgie, his long-suffering wife; and Bernie Dodd, an ambitious director. Aired on the "Hallmark Hall of Fame." *Cast:* Jason Robards, Jr. (Frank Elgin), George Grizzard (Bernie Dodd), Shirley Knight Hopkins (Georgie

Elgin), Larry Haines (Phil Cook), John Lithgow (Paul Unger), Lisa Pelikan (Nancy). *Producer:* David Susskind. *Writer:* Sidney Carroll (based on the play by Clifford Odets). *Director:* Paul Bogart.

### 434 Country Gold — The First 50 Years. Variety, 60 min., ABC, 10/16/80. A salute to country and western music. *Host:* Dennis Weaver. *Guests:* Lynn Anderson, Johnny Cash, June Carter Cash, The Carter Sisters, Roy Clark, Larry Gatlin, Merle Haggard, Waylon Jennings, Loretta Lynn, Barbara Mandrell, Mel Tillis, Ernest Tubb, Don Williams. *Music Director:* Bill Walker.

### 435 A Country Music Celebration: The 30th Anniversary of the Country Music Association. Variety, 2 hrs., CBS, 2/23/88. A musical celebration by country and western artists on the occasion of the thirtieth anniversary of the Country Music Association. *Performers:* Roy Acuff, Alabama, Eddy Arnold, Sawyer Brown, T. Graham Brown, Rosanne Cash, Rodney Crowell, Charlie Daniels, Holly Dunn, Larry Gatlin, Lee Greenwood, Emmylou Harris, The Judds, Kris Kristofferson, Loretta Lynn, Reba McEntire, Barbara Mandrell, Ronnie Milsap, Bill Monroe, Willie Nelson, K.T. Oslin, Buck Owens, Minnie Pearl, Ray Price, Ricky Skaggs, Tanya Tucker, Hank Williams, Jr., Dwight Yoakam, Faron Young. *Music:* Bill Walker. *Producer:* Robert H. Precht. *Writer:* Donald Epstein. *Director:* Walter C. Miller.

### 436 A Country Music Celebration: The 35th Anniversary of the Country Music Association. Variety, 2 hrs., CBS, 2/6/93. Country and western entertainers perform in honor of the Country Music Association's thirty-fifth anniversary. Taped January 13, 1993, at the Grand

Ole Opry House in Nashville, Tennessee. *Performers:* Alabama, John Anderson, Clint Black, Suzy Bogguss, Brooks and Dunn, Sam Bush, Glen Campbell, Mary-Chapin Carpenter, Rodney Crowell, Charlie Daniels, Bob Dylan, Vince Gill, Emmylou Harris, Alan Jackson, Wynonna Judd, Patti LaBelle, Little Texas, Lyle Lovett and the Large Band, Delbert McClinton, Reba McEntire, Ronnie Milsap, Lorrie Morgan, Willie Nelson, Mark O'Connor, Lee Roy Parnell, Dolly Parton, Kenny Rogers, Ricky Skaggs, Marty Stuart, Pam Tillis, Travis Tritt, Trisha Yearwood. *Music Directors:* David Briggs, Bergen White. *Producers:* Irving Waugh, Walter C. Miller. *Writer:* Donald K. Epstein. *Director:* Walter C. Miller.

### 437 Country Music Hall of Fame 25. Variety, 2 hrs., CBS, 5/20/92. Performances by country and western artists on the occasion of the Country Music Hall of Fame's twenty-fifth anniversary. Taped April 1, 1993, at the Grand Ole Opry House in Nashville, Tennessee. *Performers:* Chet Atkins, Clint Black, Suzy Bogguss, Clarence "Gatemouth" Brown, Sam Bush, Mary-Chapin Carpenter, The Chieftains, Governor Jimmie Davis, Jerry Douglas, Joe Ely, Bela Fleck, Vince Gill, Johnny Gimble, Emmylou Harris, Alan Jackson, Garrison Keillor, Alison Krauss, Patty Loveless, Barbara Mandrell, Kathy Mattea, Edgar Meyer, Gary Morris, The Nashville Bluegrass Band, Mark O'Connor, Riders in the Sky, Kenny Rogers, Don Schlitz, Ricky Skaggs, Marty Stuart, Pam Tillis, Randy Travis, Travis Tritt, Tanya Tucker, Ricky Van Shelton, Hank Williams, Jr., Wynonna Judd. *Special Guests:* Roy Acuff, Eddy Arnold, Bela Fleck, Loretta Lynn, Kitty Wells. *Producers:* Fred Rappoport, Walter C. Miller, Bill Ivey. *Writers:* Walter C. Miller, Bill Ivey, Fred Rappoport, Loree Gold. *Director:* Walter C. Miller.

### 438 Country Music Hit Parade. Variety, 60 min., NBC, 2/25/73.
Performances by country and western entertainers from the Grand Ole Opry House in Nashville, Tennessee. *Host:* Tennessee Ernie Ford. *Guests:* Lynn Anderson, Eddy Arnold, Donna Fargo, Loretta Lynn, Charlie McCoy, Anne Murray. *Music:* Milton DeLugg. *Producers:* Joseph Cates, Walter C. Miller. *Writer:* Chet Hagan. *Director:* Walter C. Miller.

### 439 County Music Hit Parade. Variety, 60 min., CBS, 11/28/75.
Music and songs from the Grand Ole Opry in Nashville, Tennessee. *Host:* Roy Clark. *Guests:* Donna Fargo, Freddy Fender, Dolly Parton, Charlie Rich, Johnny Rodriguez, Tanya Tucker. *Music:* Milton DeLugg. *Producer:* Joseph Cates. *Writer:* Chet Hagan. *Director:* Walter C. Miller.

### 440 Country Music Hit Parade. Variety, 90 min., NBC, 5/3/77.
The top twenty country and western songs are performed by the artists who made them popular. *Host:* Jimmy Dean. *Guests:* Donna Fargo, Freddy Fender, Larry Gatlin, Crystal Gayle, Jan Howard, George Jones, Ray Stevens, Mel Tillis, Don Williams, Tammy Wynette. *Music:* Bill Walker. *Producer:* Joseph Cates. *Writers:* Frank Slocum, Chet Hagan, Joseph Cates. *Director:* Walter C. Miller.

### 441 Country Music, USA.
Variety, 60 min., HBO, 9/6/82. A salute to country and western music. *Host:* Roy Clark. *Guests:* Lacey J. Dalton, Merle Haggard, Johnny Lee, Ronnie Milsap, Charlie Rich. *Music:* Rodney Lay. *Producer:* Dick Howard. *Director:* Marty Callner.

### 442 Country Night of Stars.
Variety, 2 hrs., NBC, 5/23/78. A program of country and western music. *Hosts:* Tennessee Ernie Ford, Charlie Pride. *Guests:* Bill Anderson, Jimmy Dean, Freddy Fender, George Jones, Barbara Mandrell, Anne Murray, Johnny Paycheck, Jeannie C. Riley, Tom T. Hall, Conway Twitty. *Music:* Bill Walker. *Producers:* Gilbert Cates, Joseph Cates. *Writers:* Chet Hagan, Frank Slocum. *Director:* Ivan Cury.

### 443 Country Night of Stars II. Variety, 2 hrs., NBC, 5/30/78.
A sequel to the above special; an additional two hours of country and western music. *Hosts:* Eddy Arnold, Crystal Gayle. *Guests:* Helen Cornelius, Lester Flatt, Pee Wee King, Roger Miller, Patti Page, Ray Price, Eddie Rabbitt, Dottie West. *Music:* Bill Walker. *Producers:* Gilbert Cates, Joseph Cates. *Writers:* Chet Hagan, Frank Slocum. *Director:* Ivan Cury.

### 444 Country Rock '82. Variety, 60 min., HBO, 12/11/82.
Performances by country and western entertainers. *Performers:* Rosanne Cash, The Charlie Daniels Band, The Oak Ridge Boys. *Producers:* Jim Halsey, Dick Howard. *Director:* Art Fisher.

### 445 Country Stars of the 70s.
Variety, 2 hrs., NBC, 10/16/79. Performances by the top names in country and western music. *Host:* Dolly Parton. *Performers:* Lynn Anderson, Glen Campbell, Johnny Cash, Roy Clark, Freddy Fender, Eddie Rabbitt, Charlie Rich, Ray Stevens, The Statler Brothers, Mel Tillis, Dottie West. *Music:* Bill Walker. *Producers:* Joseph Cates, Gilbert Cates. *Writers:* Chet Hagan, Frank Slocum. *Director:* Stan Harris.

### 446 Country Top 20. Variety, 90 min., Syndicated, 6/81.
A survey of the top twenty country and western hits for the first six months of 1981. See also the following title. *Host:* Dennis Weaver. *Guests:* Alabama, The Gatlin Brothers, Larry Gatlin, The Oak Ridge Boys, John Schneider, T. G. Shepherd, Sylvia, Conway Twitty, Dottie West,

Shelley West. *Music:* Al Capps. *Producers:* Bob Banner, Sam Riddle. *Writer:* Emil Davidson. *Director:* Tim Kiley.

### 447 Country Top 20. Variety,
2 hrs., Syndicated, 12/81. A survey of the top twenty country and western hits for the final six months of 1981. See also the above title. *Hosts:* Charly McClain, Roger Miller. *Guests:* John Conlee, Gail Davies, Crystal Gayle, Johnny Lee, Eddie Rabbitt, Eddie Raven, Joe Stampler, Sylvia, Hank Williams, Jr. *Music:* Al Capps. *Producers:* Bob Banner, Sam Riddle. *Writer:* Emil Davidson. *Director:* Tim Kiley.

### 448 A Couple of Dons. Comedy, 60 min., NBC, 9/8/73. A series of
comedy skits tailored to the talents of Don Adams and Don Rickles. *Hosts:* Don Adams, Don Rickles. *Guests:* Jan Arvan, Karene Frederick, The Tom Hansen Dancers, The Jackson Sisters, Sally Kellerman, Allison McKay, George Segal. *Producer:* Joseph Scandore. *Writers:* Bob Ellison, Woody Kling, Robert Hilliard, Lloyd Garver, Pat McCormick. *Director:* Robert Scheerer.

### 449 The Court-Martial of General George Armstrong
Custer. Drama, 90 min., NBC, 12/1/77. A "Hallmark Hall of Fame" dramatization of what might have happened had the cavalry commander survived to stand trial for the Indian massacre of his troops at the 1876 Battle of Little Bighorn. *Cast:* James Olson (George Custer), Ken Howard (Major Gardiner), Brian Keith (Allan Jacobson), Blythe Danner (Elisabeth Custer), Stephen Elliott (General Schofield), Richard Dysart (President Grant), William Daniels (Major Reno), J. D. Cannon (General Sherman). *Producer:* Norman Rosemont. *Writer:* John Gay. *Director:* Glenn Jordan.

### 450 The Cradle Song. Comedy-
Drama, 90 min., NBC, 5/6/56. The story relates the comical and touching reactions of several nuns to the prospect of what to do with a baby left at their convent gate, with a note attached asking them to care for it. Aired on the "Hallmark Hall of Fame." *Cast:* Evelyn Varden (Vicaress), Judith Anderson (Prioress), Siobhan McKenna (Sister Joanna), Deirdre Owens (Teresa), Barry Jones (Doctor), Tony Franciosa (Antonio), Kate Harrington (Sister Tornera), Katherine Raht (Sister Inez), Jeanne Tobey (Sister Sagrario), Mildred Trases (Sister Marcella). *Producer-Director:* George Schaefer. *Writer:* James Costigan.

### 451 The Crazy Comedy Concert. Comedy, 60 min., ABC, 6/5/74.
A lighthearted look at classical music as seen through the antics of a janitor who conducts an imaginary orchestra and a cleaning lady who falls in love with him at first sight and sound. Aired as an "ABC Afterschool Special." *Cast:* Tim Conway (Janitor), Ruth Buzzi (Cleaning Lady). *Producers:* William Hanna, Joseph Barbera. *Writer:* Duane C. Poole. *Director:* Alan Handley.

### 452 The Crazy World of
Benny Hill. Comedy, 2 hrs., Syndicated, 2/23/89. A compilation of skits from the British-produced "Benny Hill Show" that highlights the comic genius of one of England's top comics. Produced by Thames television especially for American television. *Host-Star:* Benny Hill. *Regulars:* Lorraine Doyle, Louise English, Hills Angels (dancers), Jon-Jon Keefe, Henry McGee, Alison Marsh, Rebecca Marsh, Bob Todd, Sue Upton, Gerald Wells, Jade Westbrook, Jennie Lee Wright. *Vocalists:* The Ladybirds. *Music:* Ronnie Aldrich. *Producer-Director:* Dennis Kirkland. *Writer:* Benny Hill.

**453 Crescendo.** Variety, 90 min., CBS, 9/27/57. A kaleidoscope of American music as seen through the eyes of Mr. Sir, a visiting Englishman whose skepticism about American culture is changed when he is introduced to a wide variety of American music styles. *Cast:* Rex Harrison (Mr. Sir). *Guests:* Louis Armstrong, Eddy Arnold, Diahann Carroll, Carol Channing, Benny Goodman, Mahalia Jackson, Sonny James, Stubby Kaye, Peggy Lee, Ethel Merman, Lizie Miles, Turk Murphy, Dinah Washington. *Music:* Paul Weston. *Producer:* Paul Gregory. *Writers:* Peter Ustinov, Leslie Stevens. *Director:* Bill Colleran.

**454 The Cricket in Times Square.** Cartoon, 30 min., ABC, 4/24/73. The story of Chester C. Cricket, a Connecticut cricket who possesses the ability to make any tune sound like a violin solo. His adventures as he travels to New York and becomes a Broadway star are depicted. *Voices:* Les Tremayne (Chester C. Cricket/Harry the Cat/Father/Music Teacher), Mel Blanc (Tucker the Mouse), June Foray (Mother). *Violinist:* Israel Baker. *Producer-Writer-Director:* Chuck Jones.

**455 Crimes of the Century.** Documentary, 60 min., ABC, 11/5 and 11/12/88. A two-part special that dramatizes some of the most notorious cases on record (for example, the largest cash robbery in America; the 1970 explosion of a terrorist bomb in New York; and the case of the richest man ever tried for murder). *Host:* Mike Connors. *Producers:* Don Ohlmeyer, Linda Jonsson, Vin DiBona. *Writers:* David Israel, Peter S. Greenberg. *Director:* Robert Katz.

**456 Crosses on the Lawn.** Drama, 60 min., CBS, 4/13/93. Springdale is a small, job-hungry town. When STB Industries opens a new plant in town, the citizens are elated with the prospect of jobs. The story relates the conflicts that arise when STB imports minority workers to fill 1,000 jobs. Aired as a "CBS Schoolbreak Special." *Cast:* Justin Whalen (Chaz Havelik), Michael Warren (Andre Dyson), Monica Creel (Tina Kosloski), Rugg Williams (Chris Hawkins), Art Evans (Tucker Hawkins), Nick Angotti (Marv Havelik), Valorie Armstrong (Sandy Myerson), Gloria Carlin (Lorraine Havelik). *Music:* Lee Curreri. *Producers:* William Greenblat, Martha Humphreys. *Writer-Director:* Alan L. Gansberg.

**457 Crown Matrimonial.** Drama, 90 min., NBC, 4/3/74. The story, set in England in 1936, dramatizes the abdication of Edward VIII. Aired on the "Hallmark Hall of Fame." *Cast:* Greer Garson (Queen Mary), Peter Barkworth (Edward), Anna Cropper (Mary), Barbara Atkinson (Margaret), Amanda Reiss (Duchess of York). *Producer:* David Susskind. *Writer:* Royce Ryton. *Director:* Alan Bridges.

**458 A Cry of Angels.** Drama, 90 min., NBC, 12/15/63. A "Hallmark Hall of Fame" presentation that dramatizes the life of composer George Handel. *Cast:* Walter Slezak (George Handel), Maureen O'Hara (Susanna Cibber), Hermione Gingold (Caroline), Hurd Hatfield (Frederick), Douglas Rain (Charles). *Music:* Herbert Grossman. *Producer-Director:* George Schaefer. *Writer:* Sheldon Yellen.

**459 Crystal.** Variety, 60 min., CBS, 12/4/80. A country and western special that spotlights the musical talents of Crystal Gayle. *Host:* Crystal Gayle. *Guests:* The Charlie Daniels Band, Eddie Rabbitt, Dionne Warwick. *Music:* Lenny Stack. *Producer:* Robert Precht. *Writer:* Ann Martin. *Director:* Sterling Johnson.

**460 A Crystal Christmas.** Variety, 60 min., Syndicated, 12/87. A program of Christmas music and songs from Nashville and Sweden (where Crystal Gayle celebrates a Swedish Christmas). *Host:* Crystal Gayle. *Guests:* Tai Babilonia, Michael Damian, John Davidson, Randy Gardner, David Hasselhoff. *Music:* Bill Walker. *Producers:* Bill Gatzimos, Dick Arlett. *Writer:* Cort Casady. *Director:* Stan Harris.

**461 Crystal Gayle in Concert.** Variety, 60 min., HBO, 10/23/82. A concert in which the country and western star mixes rock tunes and Nashville hits with pop tunes and blues standards. Taped live at the Hamilton Palace in Canada. *Star:* Crystal Gayle. *Host:* Murray Langston. *Music:* Charles Cochran. *Backup Vocalists:* Patti Leatherwood, Cindy Richardson, Jennifer Kimball. *Producer:* Lewis Chesler. *Director:* Stan Harris.

**462 The Crystal Gayle Special.** Variety, 60 min., CBS, 12/12/79. The country star's first television special, which traces her wide range of musical talents from country and blues to the music of the 1960s. *Host:* Crystal Gayle. *Guests:* Judy Collins, Doug Henning, B. B. King, The Statler Brothers. *Music:* Lenny Stack. *Producers:* Bill Gatzimos, Robert Precht. *Writers:* Martin A. Ragaway, Donald Epstein. *Director:* Russ Petranto.

**463 The Crystal Light National Aerobic Championship.** Contest, 60 min., Syndicated, 4/86. Highlights of the National Aerobics finals, featuring choreographed exercise routines, mixed pairs, and individual categories. Sponsored by Crystal Light soft drink mix and taped in Burbank, California, on December 14, 15, 1985. *Hosts:* Cathy Lee Crosby, Ed Marinaro. *Music:* Dan Slider. *Producer:* Howard Schwartz. *Writer:* Larry Strawhater. *Director:* Bob Bowker.

**464 The Crystal Light National Aerobic Championship.** Contest, 60 min., Syndicated, 4/87. Sixty aerobic finalists from across the country compete in choreographed exercise routines featuring mixed pairs, team, and individual categories. Sponsored by Crystal Light soft drink mix. *Hosts:* Teri Austin, Alan Thicke. *Guests:* Allison Brown (1986 champion), Raquel Welch. *Finalists:* Mona Hartman, Jeff Vandiver, Kim Wells. *1987 Winner:* Jeff Vandiver. *Music:* Dan Slider. *Producer:* Howard Schwartz. *Director:* Jack Regas.

**465 Culture Club in Concert.** Variety, 60 min., HBO, 4/28/84. A concert by the rock group Culture Club: Boy George (lead singer), Roy Hay (drummer), John Moss (drummer), Mickey Craig (bass), and Helen Terry (singer). *Producers:* Tessa Watts, Hugh Symonds. *Director:* Keefe (as credited on the screen).

**466 Curtain's Up.** Variety, 60 min., Syndicated, 6/85. The program compares the stages of Broadway and London via clips of shows that played in both cities. *Host:* Tony Randall. *Music:* Bruce Hanifan. *Producer:* Charlotte Schiff-Jones. *Writer:* John Crowley. *Director:* Rudi Goldman.

**467 The Cyd Charisse Special.** Variety, 60 min., Syndicated, 5/67. A solo concert performance by singer-dancer Cyd Charisse. *Host:* Cyd Charisse. *Music:* Ralph Carmichael. *Producer:* Jackie Barnett. *Director:* Dick Ross.

**468 Cyndi Lauper in Paris.** Music, 60 min., HBO, 6/20/87. A solo concert by singer Cyndi Lauper. Taped in Paris at the Le Zenith Concert Hall in March 1987. *Host:* Cyndi Lauper. *Band:* Sterling Campbell (drummer), Keith Jenkins (bass), Rick Derringer (guitar), David Rosenthal (keyboards). *Producers:* David Wolff, John Diaz. *Director:* Andy Morahan.

**469 Cyrano de Bergerac.** A chronological listing of television specials based on the classic comedy by Edmond Rostand. The story tells of Cyrano de Bergerac, a seventeenth-century French nobleman who, despite his large nose, attempts to romance the lovely Roxane, a woman who wants nothing to do with him.

**1 Cyrano de Bergerac** (2 hrs., NBC, 10/17/55). *Cast:* Jose Ferrer (Cyrano de Bergerac), Claire Bloom (Roxane), Christopher Plummer (Christian), Jacques Aubuchon (Ragueneau), Edith King (Mother Marguerite), Will Kuluva (Cutpurse), Sarah Marshall (Orange girl), Patricia Wheel (Sister Martha). *Producer:* Jose Ferrer. *Writers:* Donald Davis, Dorothy Matthews. *Director:* Kirk Browning.

**2 Cyrano de Bergerac** (90 min., NBC, 12/6/62. Aired on the "Hallmark Hall of Fame"). *Cast:* Christopher Plummer (Cyrano de Bergerac), Hope Lange (Roxane), Donald Harron (Christian), George Rose (Raqueneau), John Colicos (Comte de Guiche), William Hutt (Le Bret). *Producer-Director:* George Schaefer. *Writer:* Robert Hartung.

**3 Cyrano de Bergerac** (2 hrs. 30 min., PBS, 2/6/74). *Cast:* Peter Donat (Cyrano de Bergerac), Marsha Mason (Roxane), Marc Singer (Christian), Robert Mooney (Ragueneau), Elizabeth Huddle (Duenna), Earl Boen (Le Bret), Paul Shenar (De Guiche). *Producer:* Jac Venza. *Directors:* William Ball, Bruce Franchini.

**4 Cyrano** (Cartoon, 60 min., ABC, 3/6/74. Aired as an "ABC Afterschool Special"). *Voices:* Jose Ferrer (Cyrano de Bergerac), Joan Van Ark (Roxane), Kurt Kaszner (Raqueneau), John Stephenson (Richelieu), Martyn Green (Comte de Guiche), Joan Connell (Duenna). *Producers:* William Hanna, Joseph Barbera. *Writer:* Harvey Bullock. *Director:* Charles A. Nichols.

**470 Daddy Can't Read.** Drama, 60 min., ABC, 3/16/88. A topical "ABC Afterschool Special" about adult illiteracy as seen through the experiences of Bill Watson, a muffler plant foreman, who refuses to learn how to read (feeling embarrassed), and the efforts of his daughter, Alison, to change her stubborn father's mind. *Cast:* Edward Albert (Bill Watson), Cheryl Arutt (Alison Watson), Marcia Strassman (Mary Watson), Cathy Rigby (Lenore Luellen), Joey Travolta (Bobby), Richard Roundtree (Jason). *Producers:* Gilbert Moses, Efrem Schaffer. *Writer:* Chris Whitesell. *Director:* Gilbert Moses.

**471 Daddy, I'm Their Mama Now.** Drama, 60 min., ABC, 3/3/82. The story of Retta Rollins, a 13-year-old girl who finds the responsibility is hers of raising her two brothers, Johnny and Roy, when their mother dies and their father, Shorty, a country singer, devotes his full time to building his career. Aired as an "ABC Afterschool Special." *Cast:* Mallie Jackson (Retta Rollins), Trey Wilson (Shorty Rollins), Jason Hervey (Roy Rollins), Jason Lively (Johnny Rollins), Betty Beaird (Brendelle), Eric Taslitz (Arthur). *Music:* Misha Segal. *Producer:* Martin Tahse. *Writer:* Durrell Royce Crays. *Director:* Jeff Bleckner.

**472 Daffy Duck's Easter Show.** Cartoon, 30 min., NBC, 3/5/80. The mischievous mallard celebrates Easter in three sketches. In the first, Daffy seeks to outfox Sylvester the cat for a golden egg laid by Prissy the hen; the second story finds Daffy attempting to protect a chocolate factory from intruders; in the finale, Daffy attempts to hitchhike north for the winter. *Voices:* Mel Blanc (Daffy Duck). *Music:* Harper McKay. *Producer:* Hal Geer. *Writers:* Friz Freleng, Tony Benedict, John Dunn. *Director:* Friz Freleng.

**473 Daffy Duck's Thanks-for-Giving Special.** Cartoon, 30 min., NBC, 11/20/80. Daffy Duck's

Thanksgiving treat to his fans—a sequel to his 1953 cartoon, *Duck Dodgers in the 24½ Century*—a fowl spoof of Buck Rogers. *Voices:* Mel Blanc (Daffy Duck). *Music:* Dean Elliot, Milt Franklyn, Carl Stalling. *Producer:* Hal Geer. *Writers:* Chuck Jones, Mike Maltese. *Director:* Chuck Jones.

**474 Damn Yankees.** Musical Comedy, 2 hrs., NBC, 4/8/67. A television adaptation of the novel *The Year the Yankees Lost the Pennant* by Douglas Wallop. The story of Joe Boyd, a middle-aged man who sells his soul to the Devil (Mr. Applegate) to become the world's greatest baseball player (as 22-year-old Joe Hardy with the Washington Senators team). *Cast:* Jerry Lanning (Joe Hardy), Lee Remick (Lola), Phil Silvers (Mr. Applegate), Linda Lavin (Gloria), Jim Backus (Mr. Van Buren), Ray Middleton (Joe Boyd), Fran Allison (Meg Boyd), Bob Dishy (Rocky), Lee Goodman (Linville), Joe Garagiola (Announcer). *Producer:* Alvin Cooperman. *Producer-Director:* Kirk Browning.

**475 Dan Haggerty Goes to the Circus.** Variety, 60 min., NBC, 5/30/78. Dan Haggerty, the star of NBC's "The Life and Times of Grizzly Adams," hosts a series of performances by world-famous circus acts. *Host:* Dan Haggerty. *Producer-Director:* Milt Altman. *Writer:* Daniel Segal.

**476 Dangerfield's.** Comedy, 60 min., HBO, 5/2/87. Performances by comedians at Dangerfield's, a club owned by Rodney Dangerfield. *Host:* Rodney Dangerfield. *Guests:* Jeff Altman, Roseanne Barr (Arnold), Stan Kenton, Jerry Seinfeld. *Producer:* Kathy Lymberopoulos. *Writer:* Rodney Dangerfield. *Director:* Walter C. Miller.

**477 The Dangerous Christmas of Red Riding Hood.** Musical Comedy, 60 min., ABC, 11/28/65. With Christmas approaching and the animals in the zoo preparing for the holiday, Mr. Lone T. Wolf finds himself ostracized from the festivities because of an incident from his past—the story of Little Red Riding Hood as we know it. The story relates Mr. Wolf's attempts to prove that the story is a complete fairy tale; that Little Red mistook his actions as he attempted to make friends with her, not harm her. *Cast:* Liza Minnelli (Little Red), Vic Damone (Woodsman), Cyril Ritchard (Grandmother). *Music Score:* Jule Styne, Bob Merrill. *Producers:* Richard Lewine, Jim Stanley, Dorothy Dicker. *Writer:* Robert Emmett. *Director:* Sid Smith.

**478 The Danny Kaye Special.** Variety, 60 min., CBS, 11/6/61. An hour of music, songs, and comedy. See also "An Hour with Danny Kaye." *Host:* Danny Kaye. *Guests:* Phyllis Avery, Alice Backes, Jesslyn Fax, Barry Livingston, James Milhollin. *Music:* David Rose. *Producers:* Bud Yorkin, Norman Lear. *Writers:* Norman Lear, Hal Kanter. *Director:* Bud Yorkin.

**479 The Danny Kaye Special.** Variety, 60 min., NBC, 11/11/62. An hour of music, songs, and comedy. See also the prior title and "The Enchanted World of Danny Kaye." *Host:* Danny Kaye. *Guest:* Lucille Ball. *Producer:* Jess Oppenheimer. *Writers:* Herbert Baker, Sylvia Fine, Ernest Chambers. *Director:* Greg Garrison.

**480 Danny Thomas Specials.** A chronological listing of the variety specials hosted by Danny Thomas. All are 60 minutes in length.
**1 The Danny Thomas Special** (NBC, 11/13/64). *Guests:* Semina DeLaurentis (singer), Juliet Prowse, Piccola Pupa (singer), Dick Van Dyke. *Music:* Frank DeVol. *Producer:* George Schlatter. *Writers:* Garry Marshall, Jerry Belson, Harry Crane, Bob Mott. *Director:* Alan Handley.

**2 The Danny Thomas Special** (NBC, 12/10/64). *Guests:* Joey Bishop, Jimmy Durante, Eddie Fisher. *Music:* Frank DeVol. *Producer:* George Schlatter. *Writers:* Harry Crane, Carl Kleinschmitt, Dale McRaven. *Director:* Alan Handley.

**3 The Danny Thomas TV Family Reunion** (NBC, 2/14/65). See entry for details.

**4 The Danny Thomas Special** (NBC, 4/23/65). *Guests:* Guy Apollo (singer), Mel Brooks, Andy Griffith, Carl Reiner, The Stoneman Family (singers), Mary Tyler Moore. *Cameos:* Walter Brennan, George Burns, Bing Crosby, Bill Dana, George Gobel, Bob Hope, Don Knotts, Rich Little, Dick Van Dyke. *Music:* Frank DeVol. *Producer:* George Schlatter. *Writers:* Dale McRaven, Carl Kleinschmitt, Harry Crane. *Director:* Alan Handley.

**5 The Danny Thomas Special: The Comics** (NBC, 11/8/65). *Guests:* Tim Conway, Bill Cosby, Martha Raye, The Three Stooges (Moe Howard, Larry Fine, Joe De Rita). *Music:* Harper McKay. *Producer:* George Schlatter. *Writers:* Bill Persky, Sam Denoff. *Director:* Alan Handley.

**6 The Wonderful World of Burlesque** (NBC, 12/8/65). *Guests:* Lucille Ball, Jimmy Durante, Shirley Jones, Sheldon Leonard, Jerry Lewis. *Music:* Frank DeVol. *Producer-Director:* Alan Handley. *Writers:* Hugh Wedlock, Jr., Allan Manings.

**7 Danny Thomas: My Home Town** (NBC, 2/6/66). Danny and his guests utilize the costumes and sets of MGM Studios for a series of comical adventures. *Guests:* Mitzi Gaynor, Jim Nabors, Sonny and Cher. *Music:* Harper McKay. *Producer:* Alan Handley, Bob Wynn. *Writer:* Milt Rosen. *Director:* Alan Handley.

**8 Danny Thomas Goes Country and Western** (NBC, 3/13/66). *Guests:* Eddy Arnold, Pat Buttram, The Doodletown Pipers, Kay Starr, Bobby Vinton. *Music:* Harper McKay. *Producers:* Alan Handley, Bob Warren. *Writers:* Pat Buttram, Milt Rosen. *Director:* Alan Handley.

**9 The Danny Thomas Special: The Road to Lebanon** (NBC, 4/20/66). A spoof of the Bob Hope–Bing Crosby "Road" pictures wherein Bing Crosby travels to Lebanon to sign Danny Thomas as a costar in "The Road to Lebanon." *Guests:* Claudine Auger, Bing Crosby, Hugh Downs, Sheldon Leonard. *Music:* Earle Hagen. *Producers:* Alan Handley, Bob Wynn. *Writers:* Garry Marshall, Jerry Belson. *Director:* Alan Handley.

**10 The Wonderful World of Burlesque II** (NBC, 12/11/66). *Guests:* Don Adams, Carol Channing, Bill Cosby, Robert Culp, Phil Harris, Dean Martin, Wayne Newton, Mickey Rooney. *Music:* Harper McKay. *Producers:* Danny Thomas, Alan Handley. *Writers:* R. S. Allen, Harvey Bullock. *Director:* Alan Handley.

**11 Guys 'n' Geishas** (NBC, 2/10/67). See entry for details.

**12 The Danny Thomas Special** (NBC, 4/12/67). Patterned after an old-fashioned block party, the program presents music, songs, and guests, all representing America's melting-pot heritage. *Guests:* Vic Damone, Sammy Davis, Jr., Dennis Day, Jimmy Durante, Myron Floren, Ricardo Montalban, Jane Powell, Lawrence Welk. *Music:* Harper McKay. *Producers:* Alan Handley, Bob Wynn. *Writers:* Pat McCormick, Ron Clark, Ray Singer. *Director:* Alan Handley.

**13 The Wonderful World of Burlesque III** (NBC, 9/11/67). *Guests:* Cyd Charisse, Nanette Fabray, Tennessee Ernie Ford, Phil Silvers. *Music:* Harper McKay. *Producers:* Danny Thomas, Alan Handley. *Writer:* Sheldon Keller. *Director:* Alan Handley.

**14 The Royal Follies of 1933** (NBC, 12/11/67). See entry for details.

**15 Danny Thomas: America I Love You** (NBC, 1/8/68). *Guests:* Polly Bergen, The Jack Regas Dancers, Van

Johnson, Louis Prima, Andy Williams. *Music:* Harper McKay. *Producers:* Alan Handley, Milt Rosen. *Writer:* Milt Rosen. *Director:* Alan Handley.

**16 The Danny Thomas Special** (NBC, 2/26/68). Highlights of Danny's nightclub act; taped in Lake Tahoe, Nevada. *Music:* Walter Popp. *Producers:* Alan Handley, Milt Rosen. *Writers:* Danny Thomas, Milt Rosen. *Director:* Alan Handley.

**17 Danny Thomas Looks at Yesterday, Today and Tomorrow** (NBC, 1/28/70). Skits that spoof the past, present, and future of mankind. *Guests:* Angela Cartwright, Carol Channing, Tim Conway, Bob Hope, Marjorie Lord, Juliet Prowse, Dionne Warwick. *Music Directors:* Harper McKay, Allan Davies. *Producers:* Danny Thomas, Bob Wynn, Norman Abbott. *Writers:* Jack Elinson, Norman Paul. *Director:* Norman Abbott.

**18 City vs. Country** (ABC, 12/21/71). See entry for details.

**481 The Danny Thomas TV Family Reunion.** Comedy, 60 min., NBC, 2/14/65. The first reunion program of a television cast after the original series faded from the scene. A series of skits that reunite Danny Thomas and his "Make Room for Daddy" television family. *Host:* Danny Thomas. *Danny's TV Family:* Angela Cartwright, Hans Conried, Rusty Hamer, Marjorie Lord, Amanda Randolph. *Featured:* The Ray Charles Singers. *Music:* Frank DeVol. *Producer:* George Schlatter. *Writers:* Ray Singer, Dick Chevellet, Jack Elinson. *Director:* Alan Handley.

**482 The Darin Invasion.** Variety, 60 min., Syndicated, 10/71. Music and songs with singer Bobby Darin and his guests. *Host:* Bobby Darin. *Guests:* George Burns, Pat Carroll, The Poppy Family, Linda Ronstadt. *Producers:* Burt Rosen, David Winters, Philip Wedge, Jorn Winther, Ernest D. Glucksman. *Writer:* Alex

Barris. *Director:* Jorn Winther.

**483 The Datchet Diamonds.** Mystery, 60 min., NBC, 9/20/60. Cyril Paxton is a handsome British con artist who suddenly loses Lady Luck, his money, and his beautiful fiancée, Daisy, who has given up on him. The mystery centers on the changes in his life when he picks up the wrong valise and discovers he is in possession of stolen gems—the Datchet Diamonds. Aired on "The Dow Hour of Great Mysteries." *Cast:* Rex Harrison (Cyril Paxton), Tammy Grimes (Daisy Strong), Robert Fleming (Laurance), Alice Ghostley (Charlotte), David Hurst (Baron), Reginald Denney (Inspector Ireland), Melville Cooper (Franklyn). *Producer:* Robert Saudek. *Writer:* Walter T. Kerr. *Director:* Gower Champion.

**484 Date Rape.** Drama, 60 min., ABC, 9/15/88. A reality story that opens the seventeenth season of "The ABC Afterschool Special" (which also moves it from its customary Wednesday afternoon time to Thursday afternoons). The drama examines the shame and pain of date rape as seen through the experiences of Samantha Matian, a high school girl who is sexually attacked by the high school heartthrob (Gary). She remains silent. Several days later, when she realizes that Gary will most likely do it to someone else, she decides to report it. *Cast:* Danielle Von Zerneck (Samantha "Sam" Matian), John Karlen (Joe Farrell), Patricia Kalember (Maria Acero), Reed Edward Diamond (Gary Farrell), John Savage (Bernie Morton), Gabrielle Carteris (Cecile), Sarah Inglas (Amanda), Nile Lanning (Katherine). *Music:* Steve Margoshes. *Producer:* Patricia Depew. *Writers:* David Harmon, Donald McDonald. *Director:* Jesus S. Trevino.

**485 A Date with Debbie.** Variety, 60 min., ABC, 12/27/60. A delightful hour of music, comedy, and song with singer-actress Debbie Reynolds in her first television special. *Host:* Debbie Reynolds. *Guests:* Walter Brennan, Carleton Carpenter, Carl Reiner, Charlie Ruggles. *Music:* Nelson Riddle. *Producer-Director:* Bill Colleran. *Writers:* Carl Reiner, Joe Stein.

**486 Dateline.** Tribute, 90 min., NBC, 12/13/54. A program of music and song in which the Overseas Press Club dedicates its Memorial Building in Manhattan in the name of the men and women who have given their lives in the cause of the free press. *Host:* John Daly. *Guests:* Fred Allen, Marian Anderson, Sid Caesar, Milton Caniff, Perry Como, Eddie Fisher, Bob Hope, Elsa Maxwell, Martha Raye, Richard Rodgers, Carl Sandburg, Robert E. Sherwood. *Music:* Harry Sosnik. *Producers:* John Daly, Fred Coe. *Director:* Fred Coe.

**487 Dave's Place.** Variety, 60 min., NBC, 11/18/60. A personal tour of NBC's Rockefeller Center headquarters in New York City by humorist Dave Garroway (host of "The Today Show"). *Host:* Dave Garroway. *Guests:* Sid Gould, Helen Halpin, Al Kelly, The New York Winwood Quintet, Cliff Norton, Bernie West, The Joe Wilder Jazz Sextet. *Music:* Joe Wilder. *Producers:* Dave Garroway, Norman Kahn. *Writers:* Lester Colodny, I. A. Lewis, Andy Rooney. *Director:* Lynwood King.

**488 David Bowie: Glass Spider Tour.** Music, 60 min., ABC, 6/3/88. Highlights of David Bowie's 1987 "Glass Spider Tour" concert. Taped in Sydney, Australia. *Special Guest Star:* Charlie Sexton. *Performers:* David Bowie and the Glass Spider Band: Carlos Alomar, Alan Childs, Richard Cottle, Peter Frampton, Erdal Kizilcay, Carmine Rojas. *Singers/Dancers:* Melissa Hurley, Viktor Manoei, Constance Marie, Stephen Nichols, Craig

Allen Rothwell. *Producer:* Anthony Eaton. *Director:* David Mallet.

**489 David Bowie — Serious Moonlight.** Variety, 60 min., HBO, 2/12/84. A concert by David Bowie that was taped in Vancouver during Bowie's 1983 concert tour. *Host:* David Bowie. *Band:* Carlos Alomar, Steve Elson, Stan Harrison, David LeBolt, Lenny Pickett, Carmine Rojas, Frank Simms, George Simms, Earl Slick, Tony Thompson. *Producer:* Anthony Eaton. *Director:* David Mallet.

**490 The David Soul and Friends Special.** Variety, 60 min., ABC, 8/18/77. The star of ABC's "Starsky and Hutch" in his only television special; an hour of music, songs, and comedy. *Host:* David Soul. *Guests:* Dick Clark, Lynne Marta, Ron Moody, Donna Summer. *Producers:* Dick Clark, Robert Arthur. *Writers:* Phil Hahn, Robert Arthur. *Directors:* Perry Rosemond, Steve Turner.

**491 The Day My Kid Went Punk.** Comedy, 60 min., ABC, 10/21/87. Terry Warner is a gifted young musician who decides to change his drab image and become "one of the guys." He goes punk (a red-moussed, spiked mohawk haircut and black leather) and the story relates his misadventures as he tries to become someone he is not. Aired as an "ABC Afterschool Special." *Cast:* Christina Belford (Louise Warner), Bernie Kopell (Tom Warner), Jay Underwood (Terry Warner), Albert Hague (Professor Steinberg), Roxie Roker (Phyllis Brooks), James Noble (Max Smiley), Craig Bierko (Carl Warner). *Music:* John Debney. *Producers:* Norman G. Brooks, Fern Field. *Writer-Director:* Fern Field.

**492 The Day the Kids Took Over.** Comedy, 30 min., ABC, 9/20 and 9/27/86. Two land developers plan to bulldoze a swampland area where all the kids in town play. The kids protest, but the mayor, R. Van Winkle, and the town council ignore their pleas. Shortly before he is able to finalize the plan, Mayor Van Winkle trips and bumps his head. When he awakens, he sees that the kids have taken over the jobs formerly held by adults and that adults act like children. The story follows Van Winkle as his dream about a topsy-turvy world shows him first-hand what it is like to be a kid and constantly told what to do. Aired as two segments of "The ABC Weekend Special." *Cast:* Lou Jacobi (Mayor Van Winkle), Eddie Barth (Mateo), Pierre Epstein (Timmons), Carol-Jean Lewis (Bryant), Joey Grasso (Erik Linderman), Senta Moses (Rebecca), Julie Reardon (Sylvia Van Winkle), Ward Saxton (Stan Van Winkle). *Music:* Howard Goodall. *Producer:* Frank Doelger. *Writer:* Bruce Harmon. *Director:* John Fox.

**493 The Day the Senior Class Got Married.** Drama, 60 min., CBS, 3/5/85. Dr. Womer is a consumer economics teacher. He feels that his students have had too much theory and not enough practical application. With the help of a computer he pairs off his students as make-believe marriage partners to help them understand first-hand how economic facts can affect the marriage. The story relates the lessons the students learn. Aired as a "CBS Schoolbreak Special." *Cast:* Paul Dooley (Dr. Womer), Robin Morse (Lori Banks), Steve Monarque (Garrick Hamilton), Laura Galusha (April Sullivan), Lionel Chute (Bobby D'Angelo), Peter Kluge (Paul Tucker), Vicki Lewis (Diane Kaplan), Johann Carlo (Mary Judson). *Music:* Steve Margoshes. *Producer:* Louise Goodsill. *Writer:* Charles Purpora. *Director:* Sandy Tung.

**494 Day-to-Day Affairs.** Comedy, 50 min., HBO, 2/4/85. A series of comedy sketches that satirize man's attempts to cope with life's everyday problems. *Performers:* James Coco, Geena Davis, Jack Gilford, Madeline Lee, Ron Leibman, Robert Morse, Daniel Stern, Joyce Van Patten, Jessica Walter. *Music:* Mark Snow. *Producer:* Michael Brandman. *Writers:* Marty Farrell, Jules Feiffer. *Director:* Noam Pitlik.

**495 Daytime Lovers ... A Soap Opera Special.** Profile, 60 min., Syndicated, 8/86. A look at daytime serial romances—on and off the set with clips from shows and interviews with their stars. *Host:* Kim Zimmer. *Guests:* Joyce Becker, Brian Bloom, Martha Burns, Kate Collins, Andrea Evans, John LeClerc, A Martinez, Patricia Pease, Frank Runyon, Charles Shaughnessy, Ellen Wheeler, John Wheeler. *Producer:* Richard Perrin. *Writers:* Jason Bonderoff, Rick Ganside. *Director:* Richard Phillips.

**D.C. Beach Party** *see* **Beach Boys Specials**

**496 Deadly Game.** Drama, 2 hrs., HBO, 7/23/82. Howard Trapp is an American salesman conducting business in Switzerland. During a snowstorm he finds shelter in a remote cabin occupied by three eccentric, retired criminal lawyers who entertain themselves by conducting trials. To pass the time, Trapp decides to join them and becomes a man accused of killing his employer. The tense drama follows Trapp's desperate efforts to prove his innocence when he discovers that their "game" is becoming all too real. Based on the novel by Freidrich Durrematt. *Cast:* George Segal (Howard Trapp), Trevor Howard (Gustave Kummer), Robert Morley (Bernard Laroque), Emlyn Williams (Emile Carpeau). *Producers:* Mort Abrahams, Edie Landau, Ely Landau, Hillard Elkins. *Director:* George Schaefer.

**497 Dean Martin Celebrity Roasts.** A chronological listing of the comical tributes (roasts) to celebrities hosted by Dean Martin. Greg Garrison is the producer and director of the specials, each of which is 60 minutes in length (except where noted).

**1 Dean Martin Celebrity Roast: Bob Hope** (NBC, 10/31/74). *Guest of Honor:* Bob Hope. *Guests:* Neil Armstrong, Johnny Bench, Jack Benny, Milton Berle, Foster Brooks, Charlie Callas, Howard Cosell, Phyllis Diller, President Gerald Ford, Zsa Zsa Gabor, the Reverend Billy Graham, Rich Little, Don Rickles, Sugar Ray Robinson, Ginger Rogers, Nipsey Russell, Mark Spitz, Jimmy Stewart, John Wayne, Flip Wilson.

**2 Dean Martin Celebrity Roast: Telly Savalas** (NBC, 11/15/74). *Guest of Honor:* Telly Savalas. *Guests:* Ernest Borgnine, Foster Brooks, Howard Cosell, Angie Dickinson, Phyllis Diller, Peter Graves, Alex Karras, George Kennedy, Steve Lawrence, Darren McGavin, Don Rickles, Richard Roundtree, Rowan and Martin, Nipsey Russell, Robert Stack, Shelley Winters.

**3 Dean Martin Celebrity Roast: Jackie Gleason** (NBC, 2/27/75). *Guest of Honor:* Jackie Gleason. *Guests:* Milton Berle, Foster Brooks, Sid Caesar, Art Carney, Phyllis Diller, Frank Gorshin, Gene Kelly, Audrey Meadows, Nipsey Russell, Danny Thomas.

**4 Dean Martin Celebrity Roast: Joe Garagiola** (NBC, 5/25/76). *Guest of Honor:* Joe Garagiola. *Guests:* Hank Aaron, Yogi Berra, Red Buttons, Charlie Callas, Jack Carter, Norm Crosby, Pat Henry, Shirley Jones, Gabe Kaplan, Mickey Mantle, Willie Mays, Stan Musial, Nipsey Russell, Orson Welles.

**5 Dean Martin Celebrity Roast: Redd Foxx** (NBC, 11/26/76). *Guest of Honor:* Redd Foxx. *Guests:* Marty Allen, Steve Allen, Milton Berle, Norm Crosby, Joe Garagiola, Isaac Hayes, George Kirby, LaWanda Page, Don Rickles, Nipsey Russell, Isabel Sanford, Liz Torres, Abe Vigoda, Jimmie Walker, Orson Welles, Slappy White.

**6 Dean Martin Celebrity Roast: Danny Thomas** (NBC, 12/15/76). *Guest of Honor:* Danny Thomas. *Guests:* Lucille Ball, Milton Berle, Red Buttons, Ruth Buzzi, Charlie Callas, Charo, Howard Cosell, Dena Dietrich, Gene Kelly, Don Knotts, Harvey Korman, Jan Murray, Jimmie Walker, Orson Welles.

**7 Dean Martin Celebrity Roast: Angie Dickinson** (NBC, 2/8/77). *Guest of Honor:* Angie Dickinson. *Guests:* Eve Arden, Joey Bishop, Foster Brooks, Red Buttons, Ruth Buzzi, Scatman Crothers, Earl Holliman, Jackie Mason, LaWanda Page, Juliet Prowse, Rex Reed, Cathy Rigby, James Stewart, Jimmie Walker, Orson Welles, Cindy Williams.

**8 Dean Martin Celebrity Roast: Gabe Kaplan** (NBC, 2/21/77). *Guest of Honor:* Gabe Kaplan. *Guests:* Johnny Bench, Milton Berle, Red Buttons, Charlie Callas, Charo, Howard Cosell, Billy Crystal, Joe Garagiola, Alice Ghostley, George Kirby, Nipsey Russell, Abe Vigoda, Jimmie Walker, Orson Welles.

**9 Dean Martin Celebrity Roast: Ted Knight** (NBC, 3/2/77). *Guest of Honor:* Ted Knight. *Guests:* Edward Asner, Foster Brooks, Red Buttons, Jack Carter, Scatman Crothers, Georgia Engel, Harvey Korman, Gavin MacLeod, Julie McWhirter, Jackie Mason, LaWanda Page, James Stewart, Willie Tyler and Lester, Jimmie Walker, Orson Welles, Paul Williams.

**10 Dean Martin Celebrity Roast: Peter Marshall** (NBC, 5/2/77). *Guest of Honor:* Peter Marshall. *Guests:* Joey Bishop, Foster Brooks, Red Buttons, Jack Carter, Wayland Flowers and Madame, Zsa Zsa Gabor, Jackie Gayle, Paul Lynde, Rose Marie, Vincent Price, Rip Taylor, Karen Valentine, Jimmie Walker, Orson Welles.

**11 Dean Martin Celebrity Roast: Dan Haggerty** (NBC, 11/2/77). *Guest of Honor:* Dan Haggerty. *Guests:* Foster Brooks, Red Buttons, William Conrad, Jackie Gayle, Pat Harrington, Jr.,

Rich Little, Marilyn Michaels, Roger Miller, Harry Morgan, LaWanda Page, Denver Pyle, Abe Vigoda, Jimmie Walker, Orson Welles.

**12 Dean Martin Celebrity Roast: Frank Sinatra** (NBC, 2/7/78; 2 hrs.). *Guest of Honor:* Frank Sinatra. *Guests:* Milton Berle, Ernest Borgnine, George Burns, Red Buttons, Ruth Buzzi, Charlie Callas, Dom DeLuise, Peter Falk, Redd Foxx, Gene Kelly, Jack Klugman, Rich Little, LaWanda Page, Ronald Reagan, Don Rickles, Telly Savalas, James Stewart, Orson Welles, Jonathan Winters.

**13 Dean Martin Celebrity Roast: Jack Klugman** (NBC, 3/17/78). *Guest of Honor:* Jack Klugman. *Guests:* Milton Berle, Joey Bishop, Foster Brooks, Dr. Joyce Brothers, Red Buttons, Ruth Buzzi, Phyllis Diller, Robert Guillaume, Katherine Helmond, Abbe Lane, Dick Martin, Kay Medford, Tony Randall, Connie Stevens.

**14 Dean Martin Celebrity Roast: Jimmy Stewart** (NBC, 5/10/78). *Guest of Honor:* Jimmy Stewart. *Guests:* Eddie Albert, June Allyson, Lucille Ball, Milton Berle, Foster Brooks, George Burns, Red Buttons, Ruth Buzzi, Henry Fonda, Greer Garson, Janet Leigh, Rich Little, LaWanda Page, Tony Randall, Don Rickles, Mickey Rooney, Orson Welles, Jesse White.

**15 Dean Martin Celebrity Roast: George Burns** (NBC, 5/17/78; 90 min.). *Guest of Honor:* George Burns. *Guests:* Milton Berle, Red Buttons, Ruth Buzzi, Jack Carter, Dom DeLuise, Phyllis Diller, Gene Kelly, LaWanda Page, Ronald Reagan, Don Rickles, Connie Stevens, James Stewart, Abe Vigoda, Frank Welker, Orson Welles.

**16 Dean Martin Celebrity Roast: Betty White** (NBC, 5/31/78). *Guest of Honor:* Betty White. *Guests:* Milton Berle, Phyllis Diller, Georgia Engel, Bonnie Franklin, Dan Haggerty, John Hillerman, Allen Ludden, Peter Marshall, LaWanda Page, Abe Vigoda, Jimmie Walker, Orson Welles.

**17 Dean Martin Celebrity Roast:**

**Joan Collins** (NBC, 2/23/84). *Guest of Honor:* Joan Collins. *Guests:* Bea Arthur, Anne Baxter, Milton Berle, Red Buttons, Dom DeLuise, Angie Dickinson, Phyllis Diller, John Forsythe, Zsa Zsa Gabor, Rich Little, Gavin Macleod, Don Rickles.

**18 Dean Martin Celebrity Roast: Mr. T** (NBC, 3/14/84). *Guest of Honor:* Mr. T (Lawrence Tero). *Guests:* Red Buttons, Nell Carter, Gary Coleman, Howard Cosell, Bob Hope, Ann Jillian, Rich Little, Billy Martin, George Peppard, Don Rickles, Ricky Schroder, Orson Welles.

**19 Dean Martin Celebrity Roast: Michael Landon** (12/7/84). *Guest of Honor:* Michael Landon. *Guests:* Dick Butkus, Victor French, Melissa Gilbert, Lorne Greene, Pat Harrington, Jr., Rich Little, Maureen Murphy, Merlin Olsen, Don Rickles, Dick Shawn, Bubba Smith, Vic Tayback, Orson Welles.

## 498 Dean Martin Specials (1957-61).
A chronological listing of singer Dean Martin's early variety specials. All are 60 minutes in length and broadcast by NBC. Credits for these specials are as follows: David Rose (Music), Hubbell Robinson and Jack Donohue (Producers), Herbert Baker and Robert O'Brien (Writers), and Jack Donohue (Director). Each show was hosted by Dean Martin.

**1 The Dean Martin Show** (10/6/57). *Guests:* Joel Grey, James Mason.

**2 The Dean Martin Show** (2/2/58). *Guests:* Frank Sinatra, Danny Thomas.

**3 The Dean Martin Show** (11/22/58). *Guests:* Bing Crosby, Phil Harris.

**4 The Dean Martin Show** (3/22/59). *Guests:* Gisele MacKenzie, Donald O'Connor.

**5 The Dean Martin Show** (5/4/59). *Guests:* Bob Hope, Mae West.

**6 The Dean Martin Show** (11/3/59). *Guests:* Mickey Rooney, Frank Sinatra.

**7 The Dean Martin Show** (1/12/60). *Guests:* Nanette Fabray, Fabian Forte, Andre Previn.

**8 The Dean Martin Show** (11/1/60). *Guests:* Don Knotts, Dorothy Provine, Frank Sinatra.

**9 The Dean Martin Show** (5/3/61). *Guests:* Andy Griffith, Tony Martin.

## Dean Martin Specials (Celebrity Roasts, 1974–84) *see* Dean Martin Celebrity Roasts

## 499 Dean Martin Specials (1975–83).

A chronological listing of the variety specials hosted by Dean Martin, in addition to his famous "Celebrity Roasts." All are 60 minutes in length.

**1 Dean Martin's Christmas in California** (NBC, 12/14/75). *Guests:* Georgia Engel, Freddy Fender, Michael Learned, Dionne Warwick. *Music:* Les Brown. *Producer-Director:* Greg Garrison.

**2 Dean Martin's Red Hot Scandals of 1926** (NBC, 11/8/76). Music and comedy set against the background of the 1920s. *Guests:* Hermione Baddeley, Dom DeLuise, Georgia Engel, The Golddiggers, Abe Vigoda, Jonathan Winters. *Music:* Les Brown. *Producers:* Greg Garrison, Lee Hale. *Writers:* Mike Marmer, Stan Burns. *Directors:* Greg Garrison, Robert Sidney.

**3 Dean Martin's Red Hot Scandals, Part 2** (NBC, 4/4/77). A sequel to the above special; additional music and comedy from the 1920s. *Guests:* Hermione Baddeley, Dom DeLuise, Georgia Engel, The Golddiggers, Charles Ryan, Abe Vigoda, Jonathan Winters. *Music:* Les Brown. *Producers:* Greg Garrison, Lee Hale. *Writers:* Mike Marmer, Stan Burns. *Directors:* Greg Garrison, Stan Burns.

**4 Dean Martin's Christmas in California** (NBC, 12/18/77). *Guests:* Crystal Gayle, The Golddiggers, Linda Lavin, Mireille Mathieu (singer), Jonathan Winters. *Music:* Van Alexander. *Producers:* Greg Garrison, Lee Hale. *Directors:* Greg Garrison, Hugh Lambert.

**5 The Dean Martin Christmas Special** (NBC, 12/16/80). *Guests:* Erik Estrada, Andy Gibb, Beverly Sills, Mel Tillis. *Music:* Van Alexander. *Producers:* Greg Garrison, Lee Hale. *Writer:* Bill Box. *Director:* Greg Garrison.

**6 Dean Martin's Comedy Classics** (NBC, 5/12/81). Highlights (via clips) of Dean Martin's television series (1965–74) and his celebrity roasts. *Guests:* Dom DeLuise, Bob Newhart, Frank Sinatra, Orson Welles. *Music:* Lee Hale. *Producers:* Greg Garrison, Lee Hale. *Writer:* Bill Box. *Directors:* Greg Garrison, Jonathan Lucas.

**7 Dean Martin's Christmas at Sea World** (NBC, 12/10/81). *Guests:* Lynn Anderson, Charlie Daniels, Buck Owens, T. G. Shepherd. *Music:* Les Baxter. *Producers:* Greg Garrison, Jonathan Lucas, Lee Hale. *Writer:* Bill Box. *Director:* Lee Hale.

**8 Dean Martin at the Wild Animal Park** (NBC, 4/18/82). Music, songs, and comedy set against the background of San Diego's Wild Animal Park. *Guests:* Barbi Benton, Dom DeLuise, Jerry Reed. *Music:* Les Baxter. *Producers:* Greg Garrison, Lee Hale. *Writer:* Bill Box. *Director:* Greg Garrison.

**9 Dean Martin in London** (Showtime, 11/8/83). A comedy concert by Dean Martin from the Apollo Victoria Theatre in London. *Producers:* Greg Garrison, Lee Hale, Janet Tighe. *Director:* Greg Garrison.

## 500 Dear Lovey Hart: I Am Desperate.

Comedy-Drama, 60 min., ABC, 5/19/76. Carrie Wasserman and Skip Custer are sophomores at Lincoln High School. Skip is the editor of the school's newspaper, the *Lincoln Log*, and Carrie is "Dear Lovey Hart," the columnist for advice to the lovelorn. Carrie does not take the job seriously and begins to write flip answers to questions to boost circulation. The story deals with the trials of growing up and taking responsibility for one's actions when Carrie learns that her answers have caused more harm than good. Aired as an "ABC Afterschool Special." *Cast:* Susan Lawrence (Carrie Wasserman), Meegan King (Skip Custer), Elyssa Davalos (Linda), Barbara Timko (Susan), Del Hinkley (Mar), Bebe Kelly (Bernice), Al Eisenmann (Jeff Wasserman), Stephen Liss (Marty), Benny Medina (Bob). *Music:* Glen Paxton. *Producer:* Martin Tahse. *Writer:* Bob Rodgers. *Director:* Larry Elikann.

**501 Dear Mr. Gable.** Tribute, 60 min., NBC, 3/5/68. The program traces the life and career of actor Clark Gable. The title song, sung by Judy Garland, comes from the 1938 feature film *Broadway Melody of 1938. Narrator:* Burgess Meredith. *Music:* Gerald Fried. *Producer:* Irwin Rosten. *Writer:* Nicholas Nixon.

**502 Dearest Enemy.** Musical, 90 min., NBC, 11/26/55. A television adaptation of the Rodgers and Hart musical about a group of American Revolutionary women who helped the Continental Army by making ammunition (while pretending to put up preserves). *Cast:* Anne Jeffreys (Betsy Burke), Robert Sterling (John Copeland), Cyril Ritchard (General Howe), Cornelia Otis Skinner (Mrs. Murray). *Music:* Charles Sanford. *Producers:* Max Liebman, Bill Hobin. *Writers:* William Friedberg, Neil Simon. *Director:* Max Liebman.

**503 Death of a Porn Queen.** Documentary, 60 min., PBS, 6/9/87. The moving and tragic story of Colleen Applegate, a Farmington, Minnesota, farm girl who became the adult film actress Shauna Grant. The program traces her life from 1982 (when she became a model) to her suicide in March 1984. *Host:* Judy Woodruff. *Guests:* Karen and Philip Applegate, Wendy Applegate, Jerry Butler, Bobby Hollander, Mike Marsell, Laurie Smith,

Jim South. *Producers:* Michael Sullivan, Andy Greenspan, Janet McFadden. *Director:* Paul Henschel.

**504 Death of a Salesman.** Drama, 2 hrs., CBS, 5/8/66. A television adaptation of the 1949 play by Arthur Miller. The story relates the downfall of Willy Loman, a once successful traveling salesman who, after years of struggle, comes to realize that he is a failure in life. *Cast:* Lee J. Cobb (Willy Loman), Mildred Dunnock (Linda Loman), James Farentino (Happy Loman), George Segal (Biff Loman), Bernie Kopell (Howard Wagner), Edward Andrews (Charley), Albert Dekker (Ben Loman), Karen Steele (Letta). *Producer:* David Susskind. *Director:* Alex Segal.

**505 The Debbie Allen Special.** Variety, 60 min., ABC, 3/5/89. An hour of music, song, and comedy with actress-dancer Debbie Allen. *Host:* Debbie Allen. *Guests:* Michael Adams, Paula Brown, Whoopi Goldberg, Robert Guillaume, Little Richard, Barbara Montgomery, Phylicia Rashad, Philip Michael Thomas. *Music:* Barry Fasman. *Producers:* Raymond Katz, Norman Nixon. *Director:* Debbie Allen.

**506 Debbie Reynolds and the Sound of Children.** Variety, 60 min., NBC, 11/6/69. The program features actress-singer Debbie Reynolds in musical numbers surrounded by children. *Host:* Debbie Reynolds. *Producers:* Alan Handley, Bob Wynn, Dorothy Kingsley. *Writers:* Dorothy Kingsley, Portia Nelson. *Director:* Marc Breaux.

**507 Debby Boone ... One Step Closer.** Variety, 60 min., NBC, 4/26/82. A musical comedy about a company of singers and dancers preparing to open on Broadway. Taped at a theater in Detroit where Debby and the cast are actually preparing a Broadway-bound adaptation of *Seven Brides for Seven Brothers*. *Host:* Debby Boone. *Cast:* Debby Boone, Jeff Calhoun, Linda Hoinxt, Wendy Hutton, Shawn Newman, Michael Regan, Jeff Reynolds, Lara Teeter, Carmen Willingham. *Guests:* James Low, Dionne Warwick. *Music:* Peter Matz. *Producer-Director:* Steve Binder. *Writers:* Norman Martin, Lois Weldon, Steve Binder.

**508 Debby Boone ... The Same Old Brand New Me.** Variety, 60 min., NBC, 6/23/80. An hour of music, songs, and comedy with singer Debby Boone in her first television special. *Host:* Debby Boone. *Guests:* Greg Evigan, Jose Ferrer, Bob Hope, Gene Kelly. *Music:* Don Costa. *Producers:* Don Henley, Jack Spina. *Writer:* Buz Kohan. *Director:* Marty Pasetta.

**509 Dennis the Menace: Mayday for Mother.** Cartoon, 30 min., NBC, 5/8/81. Dennis Mitchell, the mischievous young boy, attempts to overcome numerous setbacks as he struggles to make a special gift for his mother for Mother's Day. *Voices:* Joey Nagy (Dennis Mitchell), Kathy Garver (Alice Mitchell), Bob Holt (Henry Mitchell), Larry D. Mann (George Wilson), Elizabeth Kerr (Martha Wilson), Nicole Eggert (Margaret). *Music:* Joe Raposo. *Producers:* Friz Freleng, David DePatie. *Creator-Writer:* Hank Ketchum. *Directors:* Bob Richardson, Bob Leonardi.

**510 The Desert Song.** Operetta, 90 min., NBC, 5/7/55. The story, set in French Morocco, relates the exploits of Pierre Birbeau, the son of the governor who is secretly the Red Shadow, a Robin Hood of the Sierra, and his efforts to win the heart of Margot Bonvalet, a woman he loves but who is engaged to another man. *Cast:* Nelson Eddy (Pierre/Red Shadow), Gale Sherwood (Margot Bonvalet), John Conte (Paul Fontaine), Otto Kruger (General Birbeau), Salvatore Baccoloni (Ali Ben Ali), Viola Essen (Azzuri). *Music:* Charles Sanford. *Producers:* Max Liebman, Bill Hobin. *Writers:* William Friedberg, Neil Simon, Will Glickman. *Director:* Max Liebman.

**511 The Desilu Revue.** Variety, 60 min., CBS, 12/25/59. A one-hour review, broadcast as a special segment of "Desilu Playhouse," that spotlights members of the Desilu Workshop for aspiring performers. (Lucille Ball and Desi Arnaz established Desilu Studios, which in turn produced "The Desilu Playhouse.") *Host:* Lucille Ball. *Guests:* Desi Arnaz, John Bromfield, Spring Byington, Rory Calhoun, William Demarest, William Frawley, Hedda Hopper, George Murphy, Hugh O'Brian, Ann Sothern, Vivian Vance. *Aspiring Performers:* Jerry Antes, Majel Barrett, Bob Barron, Janice Carroll, Carole Cook, Georgine Darcy, Dick Kallman, Marilyn Lovell, Fran Martin, Gary Menteer, Johnny O'Neill, Bob Osborne, Roger Perry, Howie Storm, Mark Tobin, Mark Trevis. *Music:* Walter Kent, Walton Farrer. *Producer:* Lucille Ball. *Writers:* Bob Schiller, Bob Weiskopf. *Director:* Claudio Guzman.

**512 A Desperate Exit.** Drama, 60 min., ABC, 9/17/86. An "ABC Afterschool Special" that explores teen suicide. Charlie Curtis is seventeen years old, intelligent, good-looking, popular, and appears certain to win a college scholarship. But he commits suicide. Why? That is the question his best friend, Jed, seeks to answer as he begins an investigation and finds a side of Charlie he never knew—a boy who was compulsive about being perfect and afraid of failure. More upsetting to Jed is that all the clues to Charlie's unhappiness were there—but he did not recognize them. *Cast:* Malcolm-Jamal Warner (Charlie), Rob Stone

(Jed), Nadia DeLeye (Dominique), Penelope Sudrow (Iris). *Producer-Director:* Martin Tahse. *Writer:* Linda Elstad.

## 513 The Desperate Hours.

Drama, 2 hrs., ABC, 12/13/67. The story of a middle-class family (the Hilliards) held hostage by three escaped convicts (Glen Griffin, Hank Griffin, and Sam Robish). Based on the Broadway play by Joseph Hayes. *Cast:* Arthur Hill (Dan Hilliard), Teresa Wright (Eleanor Hilliard), Yvette Mimieux (Cindy Hilliard), Michael Kearney (Ralphie Hilliard), George Segal (Glen Griffin), Barry Primus (Hank Griffin), Michael Conrad (Sam Robish), Dolph Sweet (Jesse Bard), Ralph Waite (Lieutenant Fredericks). *Producer:* Dan Melnick. *Writer:* Clive Exton. *Director:* Ted Kotcheff.

## 514 The Devil and Daniel Webster.

Drama, 60 min., NBC, 2/14/60. An adaptation of the 1939 Broadway play by Stephen Vincent Benet and Douglas Moore. Lawyer Daniel Webster's courtroom battle against the Devil, who is seeking the soul of Jabez Stone, a farmer who agreed to exchange his soul for seven years of wealth, then reneged on the deal. *Cast:* Edward G. Robinson (Daniel Webster), David Wayne (Devil), Tim O'Connor (Jabez Stone), Betty Lou Holland (Dorcus Stone), Royal Beal (Justice Hawthorne), Howard Freeman (Pinkham). *Producer:* David Susskind. *Writer:* Phil Reisman, Jr. *Director:* Tom Donovan.

## 515 The Devil's Disciple.

Drama, 90 min., NBC, 11/20/55. The story, set in Yankee, New Hampshire, during the American Revolution, relates an incident in the life of Dick Dudgeon, a local sinner who sheds his evil ways to help a poor, belabored servant girl when no one else does. Based on the play by George Bernard Shaw and broadcast on the "Hallmark Hall of Fame." *Cast:* Maurice Evans (Dick Dudgeon), Ralph Bellamy (Pastor Anderson), Teresa Wright (Judith), Dennis King (Burgoyne), Jada Rowland (Essie), Margaret Hamilton (Mrs. Dudgeon), Logan Ramsey (Christy). *Producers:* Jack Rayel, Maurice Evans. *Writer:* S. Mark Smith. *Director:* George Schaefer.

## 516 The Devil's Web.

Thriller, 90 min., ABC, 2/24/75. The story of Elizabeth "Bessy" Morne, a nurse who uses occult powers to cure a paralyzed girl (Charlotte Harrow). Also known as "Nurse Will Make It Better." *Cast:* Diana Dors (Elizabeth Morne), Linda Liles (Charlotte Harrow), Andrea Marcovicci (Ruth Harrow), Cec Linder (Edgar Harrow), Michael Culver (Simon Burns). *Music:* Laurie Johnson. *Producer:* John Cooper. *Writer:* Brian Clemens. *Director:* Shaun O'Riordan.

## 517 The Diahann Carroll Show.

Variety, 60 min., NBC, 4/5/71. A lively hour of music and song. *Host:* Diahann Carroll. *Guests:* Harry Belafonte, Tom Jones, Donald Sutherland. *Music:* Nelson Riddle. *Producer:* Carolyn Raskin. *Writers:* Bill Richmond, Ed Haas. *Director:* Mark Warren.

## 518 Dial a Deadly Number.

Thriller, 90 min., ABC, 11/18/75. The story of Dave Adams, a poor American actor in London who masquerades as a psychiatrist and becomes involved with two sisters, one of whom is a murderer. *Cast:* Gary Collins (Dave Adams), Gemma Jones (Helen Curry), Linda Liles (Ann), Beth Morris (Sally), Cavan Kendall (Tim). *Music:* Laurie Johnson. *Producer-Director:* Ian Fordyce. *Writer:* Brian Clemens.

## 519 Dial "M" for Murder.

Drama, 90 min., NBC, 4/25/58. A suspense melodrama about a tennis star (Tony Wendice) who marries for money then plots to have his wife, Margot, murdered. Aired on the "Hallmark Hall of Fame." See also the following title. *Cast:* Maurice Evans (Tony Wendice), Rosemary Harris (Margot Wendice), John Williams (Inspector Hubbard), Anthony Dawson (Captain Lesgate), William Windom (Max Halliday), Felix Deebank (Lionel), Richard Bouler (Sergeant O'Brien). *Producer-Director:* George Schaefer. *Writer:* Frederick Knott.

### 520 Dial "M" for Murder.

Drama, 2 hrs., ABC, 11/15/67. The story of a man who marries for money then plots to have his wife murdered. See the prior title also. *Cast:* Lawrence Harvey (Tony Wendice), Diane Cilento (Margot Wendice), Cyril Cusak (Inspector Hubbard), Hugh O'Brian (Max Halliday), Nigel Davenport (Captain Lesgate). *Producer:* David Susskind. *Writer:* Frederick Knott. *Director:* John Llewellyn Moxey.

### 521 Diana Ross Specials.

A chronological listing of the variety specials hosted by singer Diana Ross. All are 60 minutes except where noted.

**1 Diana Ross and The Supremes and The Temptations on Broadway** (NBC, 11/9/69). *Guests:* The Supremes, The Temptations. *Producer:* George Schlatter. *Writers:* Sheldon Keller, Billy Barnes, Earl Brown. *Directors:* Grey Lockwood, George Schlatter.

**2 Diana** (NBC, 4/18/71). *Guests:* Bill Cosby, The Jackson Five, Danny Thomas. *Producer:* Berry Gordy, Jr. *Writers:* Martin A. Ragaway, Jack Wohl, Mark Shekter, Tom Patchett, Jay Tarses, Bernard Rothman. *Director:* Kip Walton.

**3 Diana** (CBS, 3/2/81). *Guests:* Larry Hagman, Michael Jackson, The Joffrey Ballet, Quincy Jones. *Music:* Johnny Harris. *Producer-Director:* Steve Binder. *Writers:* Diana Ross, Steve Binder, Buz Kohan.

**4 Diana Ross in Concert** (HBO, 75 min., 7/27/82). *Guests:* The Eddie Kendrix Singers. *Music:* The Caesar's

Palace Orchestra (directed by Joe Guerico). *Producer:* Michael Fuchs. *Producer-Director:* Marty Callner.

**5 Diana Ross in Central Park** (2 hrs., Syndicated, 2/85). Highlights of Diana's July 1983 concert in New York's Central Park. *Music:* Joe Guerico. *Producers:* Diana Ross, Greg Sills. *Director:* Steve Binder.

**6 Diana Ross ... Red Hot Rhythm and Blues** (ABC, 5/20/87). *Guests:* John David Bland, Etta James, Little Richard, Bernadette Peters, Marty Schiff, Dick Shawn, Billy Dee Williams, Wolfman Jack. *Music:* Tom Bahler. *Producers:* Diana Ross, Gary Halvorson. *Writers:* Diana Ross, Lanie Robertson. *Directors:* Joe Layton, Gary Halvorson.

### 522 The Diary of Anne Frank.

Drama, 2 hrs., ABC, 11/26/67. The story, set in Nazi-occupied Amsterdam during World War II, relates the experiences of Anne Frank, a 13-year-old Jewish girl, hiding in a warehouse with her family, as she records her two-year ordeal in her diary. Based on Anne Frank's book, *Anne Frank: The Diary of a Young Girl.* The novel was also staged as a 1980 television movie with Melissa Gilbert as Anne Frank. *Cast:* Diane Davilla (Anne Frank), Max Von Sydow (Otto Frank), Lilli Palmer (Edith Frank), Theodore Bikel (Mr. Van Daan), Viveca Lindfors (Mrs. Van Daan), Marisa Pavan (Margot), Donald Pleasence (Mr. Dussel). *Music:* Emmanuel Verdi. *Producer:* David Susskind. *Writer:* James Lee. *Director:* Alex Segal.

### 523 Dick Cavett's Backlot USA.

Documentary, 60 min., CBS, 4/5/76. A nostalgic look at the golden age of filmmaking. *Host:* Dick Cavett. *Guests:* Gene Kelly, Mickey Rooney, John Wayne, Mae West. *Music:* Ian Fraser. *Producers:* Gary Smith, Dwight Hemion. *Writers:* Buz Kohan, Marty Farrell. *Director:* Dwight Hemion.

## 524 Dick Clark's Good Ol' Days: From Bobby Sox to Bikinis.

Variety, 2 hrs., NBC, 10/11/77. A review of the music of the 1950s and 1960s. *Hosts:* Frankie Avalon, Annette Funicello. *Guests:* The Beach Boys, Dr. Joyce Brothers, The Captain and Tennille, Angela Cartwright, Dick Clark, Noreen Corcoran, Johnny Crawford, Elinor Donahue, Evel Knievel, Snooky Lanson, Mickey Mantle, Jerry Mathers, Cubby O'Brien, O. J. Simpson, Connie Stevens, Brian Wilson. *Producers:* Dick Clark, Bill Lee, Al Schwartz. *Writers:* Robert Illes, James Stein. *Director:* Jeff Margolis.

## 525 Dick Van Dyke and the Other Woman, Mary Tyler Moore.

Variety, 60 min., CBS, 4/13/69. The program reunites Dick Van Dyke and his costar from "The Dick Van Dyke Show," Mary Tyler Moore, for an hour of music, song, and comedy. *Host:* Dick Van Dyke. *Guest:* Mary Tyler Moore. *Music:* Jack Elliott, Allyn Ferguson. *Producers:* Byron Paul, Bill Persky, Sam Denoff. *Writers:* Bill Persky, Sam Denoff, Arnold Kane. *Director:* Dean Whitmore.

## 526 Dick Van Dyke Meets Bill Cosby.

Comedy, 60 min., CBS, 3/26/72. Specially written comedy skits designed to showcase the comedic talents of Dick Van Dyke and Bill Cosby. *Hosts:* Bill Cosby, Dick Van Dyke. *Music:* Nelson Riddle. *Producers:* Byron Paul, Saul Ilson, Ernest Chambers. *Writers:* Hal Goldman, Al Gordon, Ron Friedman. *Director:* Bill Foster.

## 527 The Dick Van Dyke Special.

Variety, 60 min., CBS, 4/11/67. An hour of music and comedy with Dick Van Dyke in his first solo television special. *Host:* Dick Van Dyke. *Guests:* Ann Morgan Guilbert, Phil Erickson. *Music:* Earle Hagen. *Producers:* Byron Paul, Jack Donohue.

*Writers:* Pat McCormick, Ron Friedman, Dick Van Dyke. *Director:* Jack Donohue.

## 528 The Dick Van Dyke Special.

Variety, 60 min., CBS, 4/7/68. An hour of music, song, and comedy. *Host:* Dick Van Dyke. *Guests:* Michel Legrand, Carl Reiner, Jerry Van Dyke. *Music:* Irwin Kostel. *Producer:* Byron Paul. *Writers:* Jerry Belson, Garry K. Marshall. *Directors:* Jerry Paris, Dean Whitmore.

## 529 A Different Twist.

Comedy, 30 min., ABC, 2/1/86. Christi Bay is a pretty 12-year-old girl who has aspirations to be an actress. When she learns that her screen idol, Phil Gray, is going to direct a local production of *Oliver*, she rushes over for an audition—only to find that all roles are billed "For Boys Only." With the help of her girlfriend, Lizabeth, Christi changes her look and pretends to be a boy (Chris Bayton). Christi auditions for and gets the role of Oliver. The story relates Christi's predicament—whether or not to reveal her identity if she is going to enjoy her part in the play. Aired as an "ABC Weekend Special." *Cast:* Allison Smith (Christi/Chris), Peter Gallagher (Phil Gray), Pamela Potillo (Lizabeth), Brian Bloom (Tony Dispirito), Michele Shay (Miss Cartwright). *Producers:* Jane Startz, Terry Benes. *Writer:* Dianne Dixon. *Director:* Mark Cullingham.

## 530 Dinah Shore Specials (1954–57).

A chronological listing of the variety specials hosted by singer-actress Dinah Shore from 11/23/54 to 6/16/57. All are 60 minutes in length, (except where noted), broadcast by NBC, and have the following credits in common: Harry Zimmerman (Music Director), Bob Banner (Producer-Director).

**1 The Dinah Shore Show** (30 min., 11/23/54). A salute to General Motors on the occasion of its production of its

50 millionth car. *Guest:* George Gobel.
**2 The Dinah Shore Special** (10/7/56). *Guests:* Dizzy Dean, Frank Sinatra, The Skylarks.
**3 The Dinah Shore Special** (11/4/56). *Guest:* Betty Grable.
**4 The Dinah Shore Special** (12/2/56). *Guests:* Joel Grey, Shirley MacLaine.
**5 The Dinah Shore Special** (12/2/56). *Guests:* Dale Evans, Donald O'Connor, Roy Rogers.
**6 The Dinah Shore Special** (1/14/57). *Guests:* Art Carney, Perry Como, Count Basie, Stubby Kaye.
**7 The Dinah Shore Special** (3/24/57). *Guests:* Pat Boone, Dan Dailey, Shirley MacLaine.
**8 The Dinah Shore Special** (4/21/57). *Guests:* Dean Martin, Hugh O'Brian.
**9 The Dinah Shore Special** (5/19/57). *Guests:* Art Carney, Betty Hutton, Boris Karloff.
**10 The Dinah Shore Special** (6/16/57). *Guests:* Nanette Fabray, Fred MacMurray.

## 531 Dinah Shore Specials

**(1961–63).** A chronological listing of the Dinah Shore specials broadcast from 10/6/61 to 5/12/63. All are 60 minutes long, broadcast by NBC, and have the following credits in common: Frank DeVol (Music Director), George Schlatter (Producer), Dean Whitmore (Director). Dinah Shore hosted each show.
**1 The Dinah Shore Special** (10/6/61). *Guests:* Nanette Fabray, Al Hirt's

Dinah Shore

Jazz Group, George Montgomery (Dinah's husband).
**2 The Dinah Shore Special** (11/3/61). *Guests:* Dean Martin, Donald O'Connor.
**3 The Dinah Shore Special** (12/29/61). *Guests:* George Burns, Nat King Cole, Ginger Rogers.
**4 The Dinah Shore Special** (2/23/62). *Guests:* George Chakiris, Vince Edwards, Big Tiny Little, Keely Smith.
**5 The Dinah Shore Special** (6/1/62). *Guests:* Vic Damone, Rita Moreno, Robert Preston.
**6 Dinah Shore's One Woman Show** (10/14/62). A one-woman show in which Dinah gets her wish—"To do one show in which I can just sing and sing and sing." She is accompanied by pianist Ticker Freeman and The Even Half Dozen Singers.

**7 The Dinah Shore Special** (11/11/
62). *Guests:* James Garner, Dean Martin.
**8 The Dinah Shore Special** (12/9/
62). *Guests:* Bessie Griffin and the
Gospel Pearls, Gerry Mulligan's Jazz
Quartet featuring saxophonist Ben
Webster, Frank Sinatra.
**9 The Dinah Shore Special** (12/30/
62). *Guests:* Cyd Charisse, Jack Lemmon.
**10 The Dinah Shore Special** (2/17/
63). *Guests:* Bud and Travis (folk
singers), Bing Crosby, Al Hirt.
**11 The Dinah Shore Special** (3/17/
63). *Guests:* Ella Fitzgerald, Joan
Sutherland.
**12 The Dinah Shore Special** (5/12/
63). *Guests:* Georgia Brown, The Chad
Mitchell Trio, Sam Fletcher, Barbra
Streisand.

## 532 The Dinah Shore Purex Specials (1964–65).

A chronological listing of the variety specials hosted
by Dinah Shore and sponsored by
Purex (also known as "The Purex
Dinah Shore Special"). All are 60
minutes and broadcast by NBC.
**1 The Dinah Shore Purex Special**
(10/17/64). A comical look at the world
of the teenager. *Guests:* George Gobel,
David Janssen, Rose Marie, Missy
Shore (Dinah's daughter). *Music:* Pete
King. *Producers:* Henry Jaffe, Roger
Gimbel. *Writers:* Bob Carroll, Jr.,
Madelyn Davis, Frank Peppiatt, John
Aylesworth. *Director:* Clark Jones.
**2 The Dinah Shore Purex Special**
(11/18/64). Skits based on problems
found in the average American home.
*Guests:* Polly Bergen, Buddy Ebsen,
Hugh O'Brian, The Sixtee Dancers.
*Music:* Pete King. *Producer-Director:*
Charles Andrews. *Writers:* Charles
Andrews, Bob Carroll, Jr.
**3 The Dinah Shore Purex Special**
(2/15/65). A musical salute to the
Peace Corps. *Guest:* Harry Belafonte.
*Music:* Robert Emmett Dolan. *Producers:* Henry Jaffe, Charles Andrews.
*Director:* Charles Andrews.

**4 The Dinah Shore Purex Special**
(3/17/65). Music and songs in the first
program to be broadcast from the
newly constructed Los Angeles Music
Center Pavilion. *Guests:* Laurindo
Almeida (classical guitarist), John Butler (ballet dancer), Joao Gilberto (bosa
nova expert), Bob Hope, Henry Mancini, Jimmy Smith (jazz organist),
Maria Tallchief (ballet dancer), The
UCLA Chorus. *Music:* Robert Emmett
Dolan. *Producers:* Henry Jaffe, Carolyn Raskin. *Writers:* Mort Lachman,
Art Weingarten. *Director:* Clark Jones.

## 533 Dinah Shore Specials (1969–74).

A chronological listing of
the last variety specials hosted by
Dinah Shore.
**1 The Dinah Shore Special – Like
Hep** (60 min., CBS, 4/13/69). A fast-
paced hour of music and comedy.
*Guests:* Lucille Ball, Dick Martin,
Della Reese, Dan Rowan. *Producer:*
Carolyn Raskin. *Writers:* Chris
Bearde, Coslough Johnson. *Director:*
Marc Breaux.
**2 How to Handle a Woman** (60
min., NBC, 10/20/72. A lighthearted
salute to women via music and comedy
sketches. *Guests:* Jack Benny, Sonny
Bono, Marty Brill, Cher, Nancy Dussault, Bob Hope, Burt Reynolds.
*Music:* John Rodby. *Producers:* Saul
Ilson, Ernest Chambers. *Writers:*
Howard Albrecht, Sol Weinstein,
George Yanok, Mark Shekter, Dick
Clair, Jenna McMahon, Saul Ilson,
Ernest Chambers. *Director:* Marty
Pasetta.
**3 Dinah in Search of the Ideal Man**
(60 min., NBC, 11/18/73). *Cast:* Dinah
Shore (Host), Burt Reynolds (Host),
Don Knotts (Super Lover), Telly
Savalas (Decision Maker), Edward
Asner (Know-it-all), McLean Stevenson (Agreeable Milquetoast), Peter
Graves (Mr. Super Memory), Ricardo
Montalban (Ideal Dancer), Andy
Griffith (Mr. Already Married), Mike
Douglas (Mr. Velvet Voice), Danny
Thomas (Confidant). *Music:* John

Rodby. *Producers:* Henry Jaffe, Rich Eustis, Al Rogers. *Writers:* Ray Jessel, Frank Shaw, Harry Lee Scott, Bob Comfort, Barbara Feldon, Rich Eustis, Al Rogers. *Director:* Jack Regas.
**4 Dinah Won't You Please Come Home!** (60 min., NBC, 4/7/74). Dinah leads the audience in a musical tour of her home town of Nashville, Tennessee. *Guests:* James Arness, Jack Benny, Glen Campbell, The Fisk Jubilee Singers, Isaac Hayes. *Producer:* Henry Jaffe. *Director:* Jack Regas.

**534 Dinky Hocker.** Drama, 60 min., ABC, 12/12/79. An "ABC After-school Special" about an overweight teenage girl (Dinky Hocker) and her desperate attempts to control her urges for food. *Cast:* Wendie Jo Sperber (Susan "Dinky" Hocker), June Lockhart (Helen Hocker), Alan Oppenheimer (John Hocker), Jon Walmsley (Tucker Woolf). *Music:* Kenyon Hopkins. *Producer:* Robert Guenette. *Writer:* Howard Rayfield. *Director:* Tom Blank.

**535 Dinosaur!** Documentary, 60 min., CBS, 11/5/85. A fascinating look at the dinosaurs with an attempt to discover how they lived and why they perished. Incorporates clips from movies, art, and specially created scenes for the program. *Host-Narrator:* Christopher Reeve. *Music:* Peter Scherer, John Holbrook. *Producers:* Robert Guenette, Steven Paul Mark. *Writer:* Steven Paul Mark. *Director:* Robert Guenette.

**536 Dionne Warwick in London.** Variety, 60 min., Syndicated, 2/27/88. A concert by Dionne Warwick from London's Royal Albert Hall. *Host:* Dionne Warwick. *Guests:* Peter Allen, Rita Coolidge, Gregory Hines. *Music:* Ettore Stratta, Joe Kloess. *Producer:* Paul Barnes-Taylor. *Writer:* Patrick Malynn. *Director:* David G. Hillier.

**537 The Dionne Warwick Special.** Variety, 60 min., CBS, 9/17/69. An hour of music, song, and comedy with singer Dionne Warwick in her first television special. *Host:* Dionne Warwick. *Guests:* Burt Bacharach, Glen Campbell, George Kirby. *Music:* Jack Elliott, Allyn Ferguson. *Producers:* Pierre Cossette, Burt Sugarman. *Writers:* Robert Wells, Sandy Krinski, Bob Jacobs, John Bradford. *Director:* Robert Wells.

**538 Dirkham Detective Agency.** Comedy, 60 min., CBS, 1/25/83. David, Theodora, and Jake are three preteen children who fancy themselves as detectives and who run the Dirkham Detective Agency in their neighborhood. They have assignments, like finding lost dogs and getting cats out of trees—but not assignments like detectives on television. One day they get a chance to act out their fantasies when the local veterinarian, Dr. Arthur, hires them to recover two dog-napped poodles. Broadcast as a "CBS Children's Mystery Theater Special." *Cast:* Bobby Fite (David), Mara Hobel (Theodora), Leo O'Brien (Jake), Sally Kellerman (Zoe), Gordon Jump (Dr. Arthur), Stuart Margolin (Happy Jack), John Quade (Frankie). *Music:* John Cacavas. *Producers:* S. Bryan Hickox, Jay Daniel. *Writer:* Chuck Menville. *Director:* Stuart Margolin.

**539 The Disappearance of Aimee.** Drama, 2 hrs., NBC, 11/17/76. A "Hallmark Hall of Fame" presentation based on the mysterious six-week disappearance of evangelist Aimee Semple McPherson in 1926. It examines both sides of the story: Aimee's claim that she was kidnapped and brought to Mexico, and her mother's claim that she ran off with a married man. *Cast:* Faye Dunaway (Aimee McPherson), Bette Davis (Minnie Kennedy), James Sloyan (Asa Keyes), James Woods (Joseph Ryan), John Lehne (Captain

Cline), Lelia Goldoni (Emma Shaffer). *Music:* Steve Byrne. *Producer:* Thomas W. Moore. *Writer:* John McGreevey. *Director:* Anthony Harvey.

**540 Disney Goes to the Academy Awards.** Documentary, 60 min., ABC, 3/23/86. A tribute to Disney's Oscar-winning films. *Host:* Tony Danza. *Producer:* Andrew Solt. *Writers:* Elayne Boosler, Sam Cerlin, Andrew Solt. *Director:* Andrew Solt.

**541 Disney World — A Gala Opening — Disneyland East.** Variety, 90 min., NBC, 10/29/71. Ceremonies marking the opening of Disney World in Florida. *Guests:* Julie Andrews, Glen Campbell, Buddy Hackett, Bob Hope, Jonathan Winters. *Music:* Dave Grusin. *Producer-Director:* Robert Scheerer.

**542 Disney World's 20th Anniversary Celebration.** Variety, 60 min., CBS, 10/25/91. A music and comedy salute to Disney World in Orlando, Florida, on the occasion of its twentieth anniversary (the story itself revolves around host Michael Eisner, chief executive officer of the Walt Disney Company, and his superefficient secretary, Laverne, seeking a host for the special). *Host:* Michael Eisner. *Guests:* Tim Allen, Garth Brooks, Carol Burnett, Kathie Lee Gifford, Whoopi Goldberg, Amy Grant, Goldie Hawn, Patti LaBelle, Angela Lansbury, Steve Martin, Bette Midler, Eddie Murphy, Park Overall (as Laverne), Dolly Parton, Regis Philbin, Robin Williams. *Producers:* Gary Smith, Dwight Hemion. *Director:* Dwight Hemion.

**543 Disneyland's All-Star Comedy Circus.** Comedy, 60 min., NBC, 12/11/88. Stars from various NBC shows perform comical circus acts. *Host:* Rue McClanahan. *Guests:* Kim Fields, Benji Gregory, Dian Parkinson,

Donny Ponce, Countess Vaughn, Tina Yothers. *Music:* Anthony Martinelli, Brian Banks. *Producer:* Saul Ilson. *Writers:* Jeffrey Barron, Saul Ilson, Turk Pipkin. *Director:* Stan Harris.

**544 Disneyland's Summer Vacation Party.** Variety, 2 hrs., NBC, 5/23/86. A presummer party of music, song, and comedy from Disneyland. *Party Hosts:* Mindy Cohn, Kim Fields, Scott Valentine, Malcolm-Jamal Warner. *Guests:* Adam Ant, The Bangles, Chubby Checker, Culture Club, ELO, The Fabulous Thunderbirds, The 5th Dimension, Jay Leno, Kenny Loggins, Miami Sound Machine, Oingo Boingo, The Pointer Sisters, The Righteous Brothers, Paul Rodriguez, Jerry Seinfeld, Sha Na Na, Garry Shandling. *Music:* John Debney. *Producer-Director:* Marty Pasetta. *Writers:* Kenny Solms, Ann Elder, Tom Perew.

**545 Disneyland's 25th Anniversary.** Variety, 60 min., CBS, 3/6/80. A music and comedy tour of Disneyland in Anaheim, California, on its silver anniversary. *Host:* Danny Kaye. *Guests:* Annette Funicello, Michael Jackson, Donny Osmond, Adam Rich. *Music:* Dennis McCarthy. *Producers:* Gary Smith, Dwight Hemion. *Writer:* Buz Kohan. *Director:* Dwight Hemion.

**546 Disneyland's 30th Anniversary Celebration.** Variety, 2 hrs., NBC, 2/18/85. A star-studded celebration of Disneyland (in Anaheim, California) on the event of its thirtieth anniversary. The fast-paced, well-produced special incorporates clips from the "Disneyland" series and "The Mickey Mouse Club." *Hosts:* Drew Barrymore, John Forsythe. *Guests:* Alabama, Debbie Allen, Peter Allen, Harry Anderson, Julie Andrews, Roy Clark, Mindy Cohn, Kim Fields, Annette Funicello, David

Hasselhoff, Julian Lennon, Marie Osmond, The Pointer Sisters, Donna Summer, Tina Yothers. *Announcer:* Jack Wagner. *Music:* Lenny Stack. *Producer-Director:* Marty Pasetta. *Writer:* Buz Kohan.

**547 Disney's Christmas Fantasy on Ice.** Variety, 60 min., CBS, 12/19/92. An ice extravaganza performed to Christmas music and against the background of Sun Valley, Idaho, and at Disneyland in Anaheim, California. *Host:* Bronson Pinchot. *Ice Skaters:* Brian Boitano, Kurt Browning, Kitty and Peter Carruthers, Ekaterina Gordeeva, Sergei Grinkov, Scott Hamilton, Nancy Kerrigan, Katarina Witt. *Producers:* Kimber Rickabaugh, Paul Miller. *Writers:* Bruce Vilanch, Bill Prady. *Director:* Paul Miller.

**548 Disney's Christmas on Ice.** Variety, 60 min., CBS, 12/21/90. A live-action music and comedy special featuring ice skaters Peggy Fleming, Katarina Witt, Tai Babilonia, Randy Gardner, Robin Cousins, Scott Hamilton, Caryn Kadavy, Judy Blumberg. *Host:* Peggy Fleming. *Producer-Director:* Don Ohlmeyer. *Writer:* Barbara Allen.

**549 Disney's DTV Doggone Valentine.** Music, 60 min., NBC, 2/13/87. A Disney music video saluting man's best friend via clips from Disney films coupled with rock music. Hosted by Mickey and Minnie Mouse. *Voices:* Les Perkins, Lisa St. James, Russi Taylor. *Announcer:* J. J. Jackson. *Music:* John Debney. *Producer-Director:* Andrew Solt. *Writers:* Susan F. Walker, Jim Milio, Andrew Solt.

**550 Disney's DTV Monster Hits.** Cartoon, 60 min., NBC, 10/30/87. Classic Disney cartoon footage is coupled with contemporary songs that reflect a Halloween theme. *Announcer:* J. J. Jackson. *Producer-Writer-Director:* Andrew Solt.

**551 Disney's DTV Valentine.** Cartoon, 60 min., NBC, 2/14/86. The program combines contemporary music with classic Disney animation as it takes a lighthearted look at love and Valentine's Day. The program, hosted by Professor Ludwig Von Drake, Donald Duck, Chip and Dale, and Jiminy Cricket, features the music of Madonna, Elvis Presley, Lionel Richie, Elton John, Stevie Wonder, Whitney Houston, Huey Lewis and the Playboys, and the Eurythmics. *Announcer:* Paul Frees. *Special Music:* John Debney. *Producer-Director:* Andrew Solt. *Writers:* Jim Milio, Phillip Savenick, Andrew Solt, Susan F. Walker.

**552 Disney's Fluppy Dogs.** Cartoon, 60 min., ABC, 11/27/86. Seeking adventure, five Fluppy Dogs (Stanley, Ozzie, Tippi, Bink, and Dink) leave their enchanted kingdom with a magic key that unlocks interdimensional doors. One door leads them to the world of humans where they befriend ten-year-old Jamie and his neighbor, Claire. The story relates Jamie and Claire's efforts to rescue the Fluppy Dogs from Wagstaff, an eccentric who collects exotic animals. *Voices:* Susan Blu (Tippi and Bink), Marshall Efron (Stanley), Cloyce Morrow (Mrs. Bingham), Lorenzo Music (Ozzie), Jessica Pennington (Claire), Michael Rye (Wagstaff), Hal Smith (Dink), Carl Stevens (Jamie). *Music:* Shirley Walker. *Producer-Director:* Fred Wolf. *Writer:* Haskell Barkin.

**Disney's Fourth of July Spectacular** *see* **Celebrate the Spirit: Disney's All-Star Fourth of July Spectacular**

**553 Disney's Golden Anniversary of Snow White.** Variety, 60 min., NBC, 5/22/87. A celebration of the film *Snow White and the Seven*

*Dwarfs* on the occasion of its fiftieth birthday. The program also shows the technical advances Walt Disney originated to create his dream movie. Scenes from the movie are interspersed with a story in which an evil witch tries to destroy the film by putting a spell on Grumpy. *Cast:* Dick Van Dyke (Host), Jane Curtin (Witch), Sherman Hemsley (Magic Mirror), Linda Ronstadt (Singer), Adrianne Caselotti (Voice of Snow White). *Cameos:* Christopher Hewett, Jean Kasem, Stepfanie Kramer, Richard Moll, Lindsay Wagner. *Music:* Michael Miller. *Producer:* Brad Lachman. *Writers:* Jack Burns, Daniel Helfgott. *Director:* Louis J. Horvitz.

**554 Disney's Great American Celebration.** Variety, 2 hrs., CBS, 7/4/91. Fourth of July festivities from Disneyland and Disney World. *Hosts:* Robert Guillaume, Connie Sellecca. *Guests:* Steven Banks, The C & C Music Factory, Tevin Campbell, Sheena Easton, The Kentucky Headhunters, Barbara Mandrell. *Producers:* Brad Lachman, Garry Bormet. *Writer:* Bill Prady. *Director:* Michael Dimich.

**555 Disney's Magic in the Magic Kingdom.** Variety, 60 min., NBC, 2/12/88. An hour of magic and illusion from Disneyland. *Host:* George Burns. *Guests:* Harry Anderson, Lance Burton, Morgan Fairchild, The Miami Sound Machine, Markie Post, Princess Tenko, John Ratzenberger. *Producer:* Brad Lachman.

**556 Disney's Totally Minnie.** Live Action/Animation, 60 min., NBC, 3/25/88. Live action is combined with animation (clips from Disney films) to relate the search of an awkward man (Maxwell Dweeb) for his ideal girl. *Starring:* Robert Carradine as Maxwell Dweeb. *Voice of Minnie Mouse:* Russi Taylor. *Guests:* Elton John, Suzanne Somers, Philip Michael Thomas, Vanna White. *Music:* Bob Eston. *Producers:*

Joie Albrecht, Scott Garen. *Writers:* Joie Albrecht, Scott Garen, Jack Weinstein. *Director:* Scott Garen.

**557 The Divine Garbo.** Documentary, 60 min., PBS, 6/5/90. A tender tribute to actress Greta Garbo (1905-90) that examines her life and career. *Host-Narrator:* Glen Close. *Music:* Mark Governor. *Producer:* Ellen M. Krauss. *Writer:* David Ansen.

**558 Divorced Kids' Blues.** Drama, 60 min., ABC, 3/4/87 (Network; 3/6/87, New York). An "ABC Afterschool Special" that explores divorce as seen through the eyes of Diane Sherman, the sensitive daughter of an artistic mother (Gina) and a jazz musician father (Paul). *Cast:* Ronnee Blakley (Gina Sherman), Ken Sylk (Paul Sherman), Lauri Hendler (Diane Sherman), Steve Mailer (Mickey Sherman), Linda Wasserman (Tracy), David Margulies (Justin), Kristen Jones (Young Diane; flashback). *Music:* Paul Allen Levi. *Producers:* Linda Marlmestein, Dorothy Gilbert Goldstein. *Writer:* Donald Margulies. *Director:* Art Wolff.

**559 Doc and Gladys Celebrate.** Variety, 3 hrs., NBC, 1/1/77. The first special of 1977. A lengthy program of music, songs, and comedy that celebrates the new year (broadcast from 1 to 4 A.M.) on New Year's Day. *Hosts:* Gladys Knight, Doc Severinsen. *Guests:* The Bay City Rollers, Elvin Bishop, Jeff Kutash and the Dancin' Machine, Loretta Lynn, Orleans, The Pips, Jim Stafford, Fred Travalena. *Announcer:* Wolfman Jack. *Producer:* Burt Sugarman. *Producer-Director:* Stan Harris.

**560 The Dog Days of Arthur Cane.** Comedy, 30 min., ABC, 2/18 and 2/25/84. When Arthur Cane and his friend, James, an exchange student from Africa, are skateboarding, Arthur scoffs at the supposed magical powers

**Dolly Parton**

of James's amulet. Later that night Arthur recites the amulet's inscription: "If all you care about is you, the next thing you see beneath a full moon is what you will be." Unfortunately, the first thing Arthur sees is what he becomes—a shaggy dog. The story relates Arthur's adventures as he befriends a blind musician (Tyree) and learns about love and caring. As Arthur's selfish attitude begins to change, he reverts to his normal self. Aired as two segments of the "ABC Weekend Special." *Cast:* Ross Harris (Arthur Cane), John Scott Clough (Tyree), Linda Kaye Henning (Mrs. Cane), Alex Henteloff (Duane), Nyles Harris (James), Vivian Bonnell (Gertie), Bandit (Arthur the Dog). *Music:* Misha Segal. *Producer:* Martin Tahse. *Writers:* Glen Olson, Rod Baker. *Director:* Robert Thompson.

**561 A Doll's House.** Drama, 90 min., NBC, 11/15/59. A "Hallmark Hall of Fame" adaptation of the play by Henrik Ibsen. The story of Nora Helmer, a childlike woman searching for her own identity, who fails to recognize that her husband treats her like an ornament—a "doll" for his house. *Cast:* Julie Harris (Nora Helmer), Christopher Plummer (Torvald Helmer), Jason Robards (Dr. Rank), Hume Cronyn (Nils Krogstad), Eileen Heckart (Kristine Linden), Richard Thomas (Ivor). *Producer-Director:* George Schaefer. *Writer:* James Costigan.

**562 Dolly and Carol in Nashville.** Variety, 60 min., CBS, 2/14/79. A Valentine's Day program of music and song with Dolly Parton and Carol Burnett from Nashville. *Hosts:* Carol Burnett, Dolly Parton. *Guests:* The B.C.M. Choir, The Joe Layton Dancers. *Music:* Peter Matz. *Producers:* Joe Hamilton, Ken Welch, Mitzie Welch, Joe Layton. *Director:* Roger Beatty.

**563 Dolly in Concert.** Variety, 80 min., HBO, 6/19/83. Dolly Parton's first solo concert. Taped in London, England. *Host:* Dolly Parton. *Musicians:* Eddie Anderson, Walt Cunningham, Joe McGuffie, Michael Rhodes, Tom Rutledge, Jim Salestrom, Mike Seves. *Backup Vocalists:* Anita Ball, Richard Dennison. *Orchestrations:* Gregg Perry. *Producers:* Stan Harris, Garry Blye. *Director:* Stan Harris.

**Dolly Parton: Christmas at Home** *see* **Dolly Parton ... Home for Christmas**

**564 Dolly Parton ... Home for Christmas.** Variety, 60 min., ABC, 12/21/90. Singer-actress Dolly Parton returns to her home in the Smoky Mountains (Sevierville, Tennessee) to join her family for an hour of memories and Christmas music. The program, which reflects the screen title here, is also known as "Dolly Parton: Christmas at Home." *Host:* Dolly Parton. *Music:* Vernon Ray Bunch. *Producers:* Dolly Parton, Sandy Gallin, Jim Morey, Walter C. Miller. *Writer:* Buz Kohan, Buddy Sheffield. *Director:* Walter C. Miller.

**565 Dom DeLuise and Friends.** Comedy, 60 min., ABC, 2/16/83. An hour of comedy sketches featuring friends of comedian Dom DeLuise. *Host:* Dom DeLuise. *Guests:* Mel Brooks, Angie Dickinson, John Forsythe, Gene Kelly, Dean Martin, Burt Reynolds, Orson Welles. *Producers:* Greg Garrison, Lee Hale. *Writers:* Bill Box, Jay Burton, Stan Daniels, Rich Eustis, Marty Feldman, David Panich, Al Rogers, Robert Sidney. *Director:* Greg Garrison.

**566 Dom DeLuise and Friends, Part 2.** Comedy, 60 min., ABC, 2/23/84. A sequel to the above title; an additional hour of comedy vignettes. *Host:* Dom DeLuise. *Guests:* Carol Arthur, Scott Baio, Ruth Buzzi, Charlie Callas, Zsa Zsa Gabor, Dean Martin, Marian Mercer, Telly Savalas, Shelley Winters. *Producers:* Greg Garrison, Lee Hale. *Writers:* Bill Box, Greg Garrison, Tom Waldron, Howard Albrecht, Jay Burton. *Director:* Greg Garrison.

**567 Dom DeLuise and Friends, Part 3.** Comedy, 60 min., ABC, 5/21/85. A third special featuring the friends of comedian Dom DeLuise. (The Bo Derek segment showcases Bo's equestrian skills.) *Host:* Dom DeLuise. *Guests:* Bo Derek, Charles Durning, Ann Jillian, Jim MacGeorge, Marian Mercer, Ricardo Montalban, Orson Welles. *Producers:* Greg Garrison, Lee Hale. *Writers:* Bill Box, Jay Burton, Tom Perew, Robert Sidney, Dom DeLuise. *Director:* Greg Garrison.

## 568 Dom DeLuise and Friends, Part 4.

Comedy, 60 min., ABC, 5/17/86. A fourth comedy special featuring Dom DeLuise and his guests in various comedy sketches. *Host:* Dom DeLuise. *Guests:* Lyle Alzado, Loni Anderson, Red Buttons, Mark Gastineau, Dean Martin, Elke Sommer, Joan Van Ark. *Producers:* Greg Garrison, Lee Hale. *Writers:* Howard Albrecht, Dom DeLuise, Sol Weinstein. *Director:* Greg Garrison.

## 569 The Don Adams Special: Hooray for Hollywood.

Comedy, 60 min., CBS, 2/26/70. A comical spoof of the motion picture industry. *Host:* Don Adams. *Guests:* Edie Adams, Charlton Heston, Don Rickles. *Music:* Jack Elliott, Allyn Ferguson. *Producers:* Nick Vanoff, William O. Harbach. *Writers:* Don Adams, Gerald Gardner, Dee Caruso. *Director:* Grey Lockwood.

## 570 Don Knotts Nice Clean, Decent, Wholesome Hour.

Variety, 60 min., CBS, 4/3/70. As the title implies, an hour of wholesome songs and comedy sketches. *Host:* Don Knotts. *Guests:* Andy Griffith, Juliet Prowse, Andy Williams. *Music:* Pete Rugolo. *Producers:* Frank Peppiatt, John Aylesworth. *Writers:* Bill Dana, Jerry Mayer, Don Knotts. *Director:* Grey Lockwood.

## 571 The Don Knotts Special.

Variety, 60 min., CBS, 10/26/67. An hour of music and comedy with comedian Don Knotts in his first television special. *Host:* Don Knotts. *Guests:* Andy Griffith, Juliet Prowse, Roger Williams. *Music:* Alan Copeland. *Producer-Writer:* Aaron Ruben. *Director:* Jack Donohue.

## 572 Don Rickles—Alive and Kicking.

Comedy, 60 min., CBS, 12/12/72. An hour of music and comedy with the Master of Insults. *Host:* Don Rickles. *Guests:* Don Adams, Johnny Carson, Harvey Korman, Anne Meara, Bob Newhart, Carroll O'Connor, Juliet Prowse. *Music:* Peter Matz. *Producer:* Joseph Scandore. *Writers:* Arne Rosen, Arthur Julian, Elias Davis, David Pollock. *Directors:* Hy Averback, Dick McDonough.

## 573 The Don Rickles Special.

Comedy, 60 min., CBS, 1/19/75. An hour of comedy sketches with the Master of Insults in his second television special. *Host:* Don Rickles. *Guests:* Jack Klugman, Steve Landesberg, Dean Martin, Jaye P. Morgan, Bob Newhart, Helen Reddy, Frank Sinatra, Loretta Swit, John Wayne. *Music:* Nelson Riddle. *Producers:* Joseph Scandore, Herbert F. Solow. *Writers:* Paul W. Keyes, Marc London, Bob Howard, Bob O'Brien, Terry Hart. *Director:* Bill Foster.

## 574 Donahue: The 25th Anniversary.

Retrospective, 2 hrs., NBC, 11/15/92. A salute to the Phil "Donahue" show on the occasion of its twenty-fifth year on the air (premiered in Dayton, Ohio, on 11/6/67). Highlights of clips from nearly 6,000 episodes are showcased. *Host:* Phil Donahue. *Guests:* Larry King, David Letterman, Maury Povich, Sally Jessy Raphael, Geraldo Rivera, Joan Rivers, Diane Sawyer, Barbara Walters, Oprah Winfrey. *Producer:* Jack Haley, Jr. *Director:* Gary Halvorson.

## 575 Donald Duck's 50th Birthday.

Variety, 60 min., CBS, 11/13/84. A live action and animated salute to Walt Disney's Donald Duck on the occasion of his fiftieth birthday. *Host:* Dick Van Dyke. *Guests:* Ed Asner, Anthony Daniels (as C-3PO), Bruce Jenner, Cloris Leachman, Clarence Nash (voice of Donald Duck), John Ritter, Kenny Rogers, Donna Summer, Andy Warhol, Henry Winkler. *Music:* Paul J. Smith. *Producer-Director:* Andrew Solt. *Writers:* Peter Elbling, Andrew Solt.

**Marie and Donny Osmond**

## 576 The Donald O'Connor

**Special.** Variety, 60 min., NBC, 10/11/60. The program highlights three facets of Donald O'Connor's talents: as a singer, dancer, and comedian. *Host:* Donald O'Connor. *Guests:* Mitzi Gaynor, Sidney Miller, Andre Previn. *Producer:* Donald O'Connor. *Writers:* Al Goodman, Larry Klein, Sidney Miller, Mel Diamond. *Director:* Greg Garrison.

## 577 The Donna Summer

**Special.** Variety, 60 min., ABC, 1/27/80. A musical showcase for Donna Summer, "the Queen of Disco." *Host:* Donna Summer. *Guests:* Pat Ast, Robert Guillaume, Debralee Scott, Twiggy. *Music:* Michael Warren. *Producer-Writer:* Ernest Chambers. *Director:* Don Mischer.

### 578 The Donny and Marie Christmas Special.
Variety, 60 min., ABC, 12/14/79. A Christmas celebration with Donny and Marie Osmond. *Hosts:* Donny Osmond, Marie Osmond. *Guests:* Erik Estrada, Adam Rich, Cindy Williams. *Music:* Bob Rozario. *Producer:* Alan Osmond. *Director:* Walter C. Miller.

### 579 The Donny and Marie Osmond Show.
Variety, 60 min., ABC, 11/16/75. An hour of music and song with brother and sister singers Donny and Marie Osmond. *Hosts:* Donny Osmond, Marie Osmond. *Guests:* Bob Hope, Paul Lynde, Lee Majors, Kate Smith. *Music:* Jack Elliott. *Producers:* Raymond Katz, Sid and Marty Krofft. *Writers:* Chet Dowling, Sandy Krinski, Bob Arnott, Chuck McCann. *Director:* Art Fisher.

### 580 Don't Get Me Started.
Comedy, 60 min., HBO, 8/9/86. The program combines stand-up comedy with a parody on musicals wherein Billy Crystal (as Fernando) attempts to organize a show featuring an array of guests (all impersonated by Crystal). Taped at Hofstra University. *Cast:* Billy Crystal (Host/Fernando/Buddy/Sandy), Rob Reiner (Marty DiBergi, the filmmaker), Eugene Levy (Morty Arnold, the producer), Christopher Guest (Chip), Brother Theodore (Himself). *Music:* Mark Shaiman. *Producers:* Buddy Morra, Larry Brenton,

Billy Crystal. *Writer-Directors:* Billy Crystal, Paul Flaherty.

### 581 Don't Touch. Drama, 60 min., ABC, 11/6/85.

While baby-sitting for six-year-old Molly Stewart, a teenager (Karen Anderson) notices that Mike Rivers, a trusted friend of the Stewarts, pays excessive attention to Molly. When sudden changes in Molly's behavior become apparent to Karen, she realizes that from her own personal experience, Molly is a victim of child molestation. The story relates Karen's efforts to help Molly and her parents when she brings the incident to their attention. Aired as an "ABC Afterschool Special." *Cast:* Kelly Wolf (Karen Anderson), Niki Scalera (Molly Stewart), Lenny Von Dohlen (Mike Rivers), Blair Brown (Joan Stewart), John Glover (Mr. Stewart), Lisa Bonet (Carrie), Deborah Mooney (Mrs. Anderson), Joey Lawrence (Joey). *Music:* Garry Sherman. *Producer:* Diana Kerew. *Writer:* Jeanne Betancourt. *Director:* Beau Bridges.

### 582 The Door Is Always Open. Tribute, 2 hrs., Syndicated, 10/85.

A musical tribute to Sue Brewer (1934–81), whose Nashville home was a gathering place for aspiring country and western performers. *Host:* Waylon Jennings. *Guests:* Jessi Colter, Little Jimmy Dickens, George Jones, Kris Kristofferson, Roger Miller, Willie Nelson, Web Pierce, Hank Williams, Jr. *Producers:* Jack Thompson, Waylon Jennings. *Writers:* Jack Thompson, Tom C. Armstrong. *Director:* Norman Abbott.

### 583 Dorf's Family Stump.

**Ad for "Don't Touch"**

Comedy, 60 min., CBS, 4/18/91. A comic look at life as seen through the eyes of Derk Dorf, an offbeat, four-feet tall, badly toupeed man with an exaggerated walk and Scandinavian accent. *Starring:* Tim Conway as Derk Dorf. *Guests:* Ruth Buzzi, Billie Jean King, Harvey Korman, Cathy McAuley, Joe Namath, Tom Poston, Bob Uecker. *Producer:* Joe Hamilton. *Writers:* Roger Beatty, Tim Conway, Tom Egan. *Director:* Roger Beatty.

### 584 Doris Day: A Sentimental Journey. Documentary, 60 min., PBS, 5/26/90.

A profile of Doris Mary Anne Kappelhoff, better known as Doris Day, from her childhood in Cincinnati to her early years as a big-band singer to her career as an actress in motion pictures. The program incorporates rare film footage of Doris with the Les Brown Band. Doris herself recalls her experiences. *Host:* Roger Ebert. *Guests:* Kirstie Alley, Kaye Ballard, Les Brown, Rosemary Clooney, Clint Eastwood, Ross Hunter, Terry Melcher, Tony Randall, Betty White. *Producer:* Glen DuBose.

### 585 Doris Day Today. Variety, 60 min., CBS, 2/19/75.

An hour of music, song, and light comedy with

**Doris Day**

singer-actress Doris Day. *Host:* Doris Day. *Guests:* Tim Conway, John Denver, Rich Little. *Music:* Tommy Oliver. *Producer:* George Schlatter. *Writers:* Digby Wolfe, George Schlatter. *Director:* Tony Charmoli.

**586 The Doris Mary Anne Kappelhoff Special.** Variety, 60 min., CBS, 3/14/71. A lively hour of music and song with Doris Mary Anne Kappelhoff, better known as singer-actress Doris Day. *Host:* Doris Day. *Guest:* Perry Como. *Music:* Jimmie Haskell. *Producers:* Don Gerson, Terry Melcher, Saul Ilson, Ernest Chambers. *Writers:* Saul Ilson, Ernest Chambers, Gary Belkin, Alex Barris. *Director:* Bill Foster.

**587 Dorothy Hamill in**

**Romeo and Juliet on Ice.** Ballet, 60 min., CBS, 11/25/83. An elaborate ice ballet based on the classic story of the ill-fated lovers by William Shakespeare. *Cast:* Dorothy Hamill (Juliet), Brian Pockor (Romeo), Toller Cranston (Tybalt), Richard O'Neil (Friar Laurence), Val Bezic (Paris), Gord Crossland (Capulet). *Conducting the London Symphonic Orchestra:* Andre Previn. *Producers:* Dwight Hemion, Gary Smith. *Choreography:* Rob Iscove. *Director:* Rob Iscove.

**588 Dorothy Hamill Presents Winners.** Tribute, 60 min., ABC, 4/28/78. Dorothy Hamill, the 1976 Olympic figure skating medalist, salutes other award winners. *Host:* Dorothy Hamill. *Guests:* Bruce Jenner, Hal Linden. *Music:* Eddie Karam. *Producer:* Jerry Weintraub. *Writers:* Frank Peppiatt, John Aylesworth, Barry Adelman, Barry Silver. *Director:* Stan Harris.

**589 The Dorothy Hamill Special.** Variety, 60 min., ABC, 11/17/76. A musical hour with ice skating star Dorothy Hamill. *Host:* Dorothy Hamill. *Guests:* Gene Kelly, Jim McKay, Carrie Weber. *Music:* Ian Fraser. *Producer:* Jerry Weintraub. *Writer:* Buz Kohan. *Director:* Dwight Hemion.

**590 The Dorothy Hamill Winter Carnival Special.** Variety, 60 min., ABC, 3/2/77. Music and songs from the site of the 1977 Winter Carnival in Quebec. *Host:* Dorothy Hamill. *Guests:* Beau Bridges, Karen Carpenter, Richard Carpenter. *Music:* Ian Fraser. *Producer:* Jerry Weintraub. *Writers:* Rich Eustis, Al Rogers. *Director:* Bill Davis.

**591 Dorothy Hamill's Corner of the Sky.** Variety, 60 min., ABC, 4/22/79. Champion figure skater Dorothy Hamill returns to her hometown for a nostalgic hour of music and song. *Host:* Dorothy Hamill. *Guests:* Professor Irwin Corey, Gary Frank, Henry Gibson, Sally Kellerman, Avery Schreiber. *Music:* Dennis McCarthy. *Producer:* Jerry Weintraub. *Director:* Steve Binder.

**592 Dorothy in the Land of Oz.** Cartoon, 30 min., CBS, 12/10/81. A sequel to *The Wizard of Oz* that follows the further adventures of Dorothy and her friends Jack Pumpkin Head and Tic Toc the Tin Man as they battle Tyrone, the Terrible Toy Maker, as he seeks to gain control of Winkle Country, a community in Oz. Originally broadcast as "Thanksgiving in the Land of Oz" on 11/25/80. *Voices:* Sid Caesar (Wizard of Oz), Mischa Bond (Dorothy), Robert Ridgely (Jack), Joan Gerber (Tic Toc), Lurene Tuttle (Aunt Em), Robert Ridgely (Tyrone), Joan Gerber (Osmo, Queen of Oz), Charles Woolf (Uncle Henry). *Music:* Stephen Lawrence. *Producer:* Robert L. Rosen. *Writer:* Romeo Muller. *Director:* Charles Swenson.

**593 The Double Kill.** Thriller, 90 min., ABC, 2/18/75. The story of Hugh Briant, the Amerian husband of a wealthy British woman (Clorissa), who blackmails a captured burglar into killng his wife. *Cast:* Gary Collins (Hugh Briant), Penelope Horner (Clorissa Briant), James Villars (Paul), Stuart Wilson (Max Burns), Peter Bowles (Lucas), John Flanagan (Michael Player). *Music:* Laurie John-

son. *Producer:* Cecil Clarke. *Writer:* Brian Clemens. *Director:* Ian Fordyce.

**594 Doug Henning's World of Magic.** A chronological listing of the six specials hosted by magician Doug Henning. Each program, broadcast on NBC, features an hour of magic and illusion. Peter Matz provides the music; Jerry Goldstein and Walter C. Miller are the producers; Buz Kohan and Doug Henning the writers, and Walter C. Miller the director.
**1 Doug Henning's World of Magic I** (12/23/76). *Guests:* Joey Heatherton, Michael Landon.
**2 Doug Henning's World of Magic II** (12/15/77). *Guests:* Glen Campbell, Sandy Duncan.
**3 Doug Henning's World of Magic III** (2/15/80). *Guests:* Barbi Benton, Bill Cosby, Melba Moore.
**4 Doug Henning's World of Magic IV** (2/15/81). *Guests:* Marie Osmond, Ricky Schroder, Robert Shields, Lorene Yarnell.
**5 Doug Henning's World of Magic V** (2/14/82). *Guests:* Cherish Alexander, Billy Crystal, Debby Henning, Bruce Jenner, Ann Jillian, Orson Welles.
**6 Doug Henning: Magic on Broadway** (11/14/82). *Guests:* Erik Estrada, Debby Henning, Andrea McArdle, Tony Randall, Ann Reinking, Allison Smith.

**The Dow Hour of Great Mysteries.** The overall title for a series of seven mystery specials sponsored by the Dow Chemical Corporation. For information, see the following titles: The Bat, The Burning Court, The Cat and the Canary, The Datchet Diamonds, The Great Impersonation, Inn of the Flying Dragon, and The Woman in White.

**595 Dr. Jekyll and Mr. Hyde.** Musical, 90 min., NBC, 3/7/73. A musical adaptation of the 1886 novel by Robert Louis Stevenson. The story of

Henry Jekyll, a doctor who develops a potion that changes human personality and transforms him into an evil being he names Edward Hyde. See also "The Strange Case of Dr. Jekyll and Mr. Hyde." *Cast:* Kirk Douglas (Dr. Jekyll/ Mr. Hyde), Michael Redgrave (Danvers), Susan Hampshire (Isabel), Donald Pleasence (Smudge), Susan George (Anne), Stanley Holloway (Poole), Judy Bowker (Tupenny). *Music-Lyrics:* Lionel Bart, Mel Mandell, Norman Sacks. *Producer:* Burt Rosen. *Writer:* Sherman Yellen. *Director:* David Winters.

## 596 Dr. Seuss' Horton Hears a Who.

Cartoon, 30 min., CBS, 3/19/ 70. A television adaptation of the children's story by Dr. Seuss finds Horton the Elephant attempting to save the microscopic land of Whoville from the villainous Wickersham Brothers and Vlad Vlad-i-koff, the black-bottomed eagle. *Narrator:* Hans Conried. *Music:* Eugene Poddany. *Producers:* Theodor Geisel, Chuck Jones. *Writer:* Theodor Geisel. *Director:* Chuck Jones.

## 597 Dr. Seuss' How the Grinch Stole Christmas.

Cartoon, 30 min., CBS, 12/18/66. The Grinch is a crotchety creature who hates Christmas. The story follows the Grinch as he tries to erase the holiday from the tiny town of Whoville by stealing all the material symbols of its Yuletide celebration. The first of the Dr. Seuss books (written by Theodor Geisel) to be adapted to television. *Narrator:* Boris Karloff. *Music:* Albert Hague. *Producers:* Chuck Jones, Theodor Geisel. *Writer:* Theodor Geisel. *Director:* Chuck Jones.

## 598 Dr. Seuss on the Loose.

Cartoon, 30 min., CBS, 10/15/73. A trilogy of allegorical classics by Dr. Seuss: "The Sneetches," "Green Eggs and Ham," and "The Zax." Snobbery is the basis of "The Sneetches." It is the story of star-bellied Sneetches, who boast stars in their middles, as they ostracize the plain-bellied Sneetches, who were not similarly endowed. "Green Eggs and Ham" focuses on the foolishness of prejudging something without first giving it a try (as seen through Joe, who refuses to eat green eggs prepared by his friend Sam). "The Zax" tells the tale of stubbornness when a south-going Zax encounters a north-going Zax in the middle of the path across the prairie to the Prax, and neither will yield the right-of-way to the other. *Narrator:* Hans Conried. *Voices:* Bob Holt, Allan Sherman, Paul Winchell. *Music:* Dean Elliott. *Producers:* Friz Freleng, Theodor Geisel. *Writer:* Theodor Geisel. *Director:* Hawley Pratt.

## 599 Dr. Seuss' The Cat in the Hat.

Cartoon, 30 min., CBS, 3/10/71. A whimsical tale about a reckless cat (who wears a hat) and his mischievous friends: Thing One, Thing Two, and a goldfish named Karlos K. Krinklebein. *Voices:* Allan Sherman (Cat), Daws Butler (Fish), Pamelyn Ferdin (Girl), Tony Frazier (Boy), Gloria Camacho (Mother). *Music:* Dean Elliott. *Producers:* Friz Freleng, Theodor Geisel. *Writer:* Theodor Geisel. *Director:* Hawley Pratt.

## 600 Dr. Seuss' The Hoober-Bloob Highway.

Cartoon, 30 min., CBS, 2/19/75. The story, the first written especially for television by Theodor "Dr. Seuss" Geisel, tells the tale of the Hoober-Bloob Highway, an imaginary thoroughfare through which new creatures are dispatched to the world after having been briefed on the pros and cons of earthbound living by Mr. Hoober-Bloob, the chief dispatcher. *Voices:* Bob Holt. *Music:* Dean Elliott. *Producers:* Friz Freleng, Theodor Geisel. *Writer:* Theodor Geisel. *Director:* Alan Zaslove.

## 601 Dr. Seuss' The Lorax.

Cartoon, 30 min., CBS, 2/14/72. An

ecology story about an endangered species called the Truffula Tree (its silken tufts can be knitted into all-purpose thneeds). As the trees are destroyed to build factories, the gnome-like Lorax begins a crusade to save one of nature's wonders. *Narrator:* Eddie Albert. *Voices:* Bob Holt (Lorax/Once-Ler), Harlen Carraher (Boy). *Music:* Dean Elliott. *Producers:* David H. DePatie, Friz Freleng, Theodor Geisel. *Writer:* Theodor Geisel. *Director:* Hawley Pratt.

**602 Dream Girl.** Comedy, 90 min., NBC, 12/11/55. A feminine version of *The Secret Life of Walter Mitty* that tells of Georgina Allerton, the manager and part owner of a bookstore, who daydreams herself into exciting adventures. Aired on the "Hallmark Hall of Fame." *Cast:* Vivian Blaine (Georgina Allerton), Hal March (Clark Redfield), Evelyn Varden (Lucy Allerton), Edmond Ryan (George Hand), Priscilla Morrill (Clair), Kathleen Mansfield (Miss Delehanty). *Producer:* Maurice Evans. *Writer:* S. Mark Smith. *Director:* George Schaefer.

**603 Drug Knot.** Drama, 60 min., CBS, 9/10/86. A powerful "CBS Schoolbreak Special" about Doug Dawson, a self-destructive teenager. *Cast:* Tracy Nelson (Lori), David Toma (Himself), Dermot Mulroney (Doug Dawson), Mary Ellen Turner (Helen Dawson), Lawrence Pressman (Jack Dawson), David Faustino (Jack Dawson). *Music:* Robert dela Garza. *Producer:* Arnold Shapiro. *Writer:* David Villaire. *Director:* Anson Williams.

**604 The Drunkard.** Comedy-Drama, 87 min., The Entertainment Channel, 9/7/82. The story, first staged in 1844, details one man's bout with alcoholism and his attempts to save his soul. *Cast:* Tom Bosley (Lawyer Cribbs), Marcia McClain (Mary), Erick Devine (Edward), Charita Bauer

(Mrs. Wilson), Lenny Wolpe (William), Cindy Rosenthal (Julia), Patricia Carr-Bosley (Agnes). *Music:* Barry Manilow. *Music Director:* Richard A. Schacher. *Producer-Director:* Jeffrey B. Moss. *Writer:* Bro Herold.

**605 Duke Ellington ... We Love You Madly.** Tribute, 90 min., CBS, 1/13/73. A musical tribute to jazz great Duke Ellington. *Guests:* Count Basie, Ray Charles, James Cleveland, Sammy Davis, Jr., Billy Eckstein, Roberta Flack, Aretha Franklin, Quincy Jones, Paula Kelly, Peggy Lee, Sarah Vaughan, Joe Williams. *Music:* Quincy Jones. *Producers:* Bud Yorkin, Quincy Jones. *Director:* Stan Harris.

**606 The      Dumb-Waiter.** Drama, 60 min., ABC, 5/12/87. A one-act play about two hit men (Gus and Ben) who arrive at a deserted café to get further information on their target. The story focuses on the perplexity that confronts the duo as they wait and receive a series of baffling food orders via the dumb-waiter. *Cast:* Tom Conti (Gus), John Travolta (Ben). *Music:* Judith Gruber-Stitzer. *Producers:* Scott Bushnell, Robert Altman. *Writer:* Harold Pinter. *Director:* Robert Altman.

**607 Eagle in a Cage.** Drama, 90 min., NBC, 10/20/65. An original "Hallmark Hall of Fame" drama that relates incidents in Napoléon's last years—from the Battle of Waterloo (1815) to his attempted escape to France from his exile on St. Helena. *Cast:* Trevor Howard (Napoléon), James Daly (Dr. O'Meara), Pamela Franklin (Betsy Balcombe), George Rose (Cipriani), Richard Waring (Bertrand), William Smithers (Gourgaud), Basil Langton (Hudson Lowell). *Producers:* George Schaefer, Robert Hartung. *Writer:* Millard Lampell. *Director:* George Schaefer.

**608 Early Days.** Drama, 60 min., PBS, 4/18/86. The lucid insights and conversations of Sir Richard Kitchen, a former British cabinet minister who is now elderly and lives under the watchful eye of his daughter and philandering son-in-law. *Cast:* Sir Ralph Richardson (Richard Kitchen), Sheila Ballantyne (Mathilda), Marty Cruickshank (Gloria), Edward Judd (Bristol), Gerald Flood (Benson), Peter Machin (Steven). *Music:* Alan Price. *Producer:* Terence Donovan. *Writer:* David Storey. *Director:* Anthony Page.

**609 Earth, Wind and Fire in Concert.** Music, 60 min., HBO, 9/7/82. A concert by the group Earth, Wind and Fire (Johnny Graham, Anthony Wollfolk, Philip Bailey, Roland Bautista, Fred White, Larry Dunn, Ralph Johnson, Verdone White, Maurice White). *Producers:* Maurice White, Michael Schultz, Gloria Schultz. *Director:* Michael Schultz.

**610 The Eartha Kitt Show.** Variety, 30 min., Syndicated, 9/69. A solo concert by singer Eartha Kitt. *Host:* Eartha Kitt. *Music:* Matt Robinson. *Producer:* Charles Arden. *Director:* Scott Ward.

**611 The Easter Bunny Is Comin' to Town.** Fantasy, 60 min., ABC, 4/6/77. Sunny the baby bunny lives in Kidville, a town on Big Rock Mountain that is populated by children. When Sunny discovers that three wacky hens, the Hendrews Sisters, are laying beautiful eggs, he decides to spread the word. His joyous journey is cut short when he discovers the town of Town. Children are outlawed in Town and it is ruled by seven-year-old King Bruce, the only child, under the domination of his mean aunt, Lilly Longtooth. The story relates Sunny's efforts to bring the holiday spirit to the people of Town. The animated story, filmed in animagic (dimensional stop-motion photography) gives logical but fantasy explanations of many Easter customs (for example, egg rolling, jelly beans, and chocolate bunnies). *Voices:* Skip Hinnant (Sunny), James Spies (King Bruce), Meg Sargent (Lilly Longtooth), Ron Marshall (Hallelujah Jones), Robert McFadden (Chugs). *Narrator:* Fred Astaire. *Music Director:* Bernard Hoffer. *Music and Lyrics:* Maury Laws and Jules Bass. *Producer-Directors:* Arthur Rankin, Jr., Jules Bass. *Writer:* Romeo Muller.

**612 Easter Parade of Stars.** Variety, 30 min., CBS, 4/13/54. A program of Easter music and songs. *Performers:* Robin Chandler, Buff Cobb, Irene Dunne, Eva Gabor, Phyllis Kirk, Denise Lor, Rex Marshall, Nancy Olson, Roxanne, Ann Rutherford. *Producer:* Martin Manulis. *Director:* Byron Paul.

**613 The Easter Promise.** Drama, 90 min., CBS, 3/26/75. The third of four specials about the Mills family and life in Nebraska during the 1940s (see also: "Addie and the King of Hearts," "The House Without a Christmas Tree," and "The Thanksgiving Treasure"). The story focuses on Addie, the 12-year-old daughter of widower James Mills, and her experiences with Constance Payne, a visiting actress who overcomes great difficulties due to Addie's caring and understanding. The title is derived from a promise Constance made to Addie, but was unsure of keeping: to spend Easter with her family. *Cast:* Jason Robards (James Mills), Lisa Lucas (Addie Mills), Mildred Natwick (Grandmother Mills), Jean Simmons (Constance Payne), Elizabeth Wilson (Mrs. Coyle), Franny Michael (Cora Sue), Lori Ann Rutherford (Linda), Vicki Schreck (Terry). *Music:* Arthur Rubinstein. *Producer:* Alan Shayne. *Writer:* Gail Rock. *Director:* Paul Bogart.

## 614 An Echo of Theresa.
Thriller, 90 min., ABC, 1/15/73. While honeymooning in London, an American couple is suddenly plunged into a nightmare world when the husband (Brad) witnesses an event that triggers memories hidden deep in the recesses of his mind. Imagining himself as someone else and married to a woman named Theresa, he believes his wife (Suzy) is an enemy and plots to kill her. The story depicts the conflict that ensues when the past and present merge into one. *Cast:* Paul Burke (Brad Hunter), Polly Bergen (Suzy Hunter), Meriel Brooke (Theresa), William Job (Trasker), Roger Hume (Dr. Korner), Dinsdale Landen (Matthew Earp). *Music:* Laurie Johnson. *Producer:* Cecil Clarke. *Writer:* Brian Clemens. *Director:* Peter Jeffries.

## 615 Echoes of the Sixties.
Variety, 60 min., NBC, 7/25/79. Film clips are used to recall the sights and sounds of the 1960s. *Hosts:* John Ritter, Suzanne Somers, Twiggy. *Producers:* Sandra Allyn, William Allyn. *Director:* Kevin Billington.

## 616 Ed McMahon and Company.
Variety, 60 min., Showtime, 8/80. A lively hour of music, song, dance, and comedy with Ed McMahon and his guests. *Host:* Ed McMahon. *Guests:* The Association, Richard Dawson, Phyllis Diller, Frank Gorshin, Shecky Greene, Abbe Lane, Jerry Lewis, Dinah Shore, The Texas Cowgirls. *Producer:* Jerrold T. Brandt, Jr.

## 617 Ed McMahon and His Friends . . . Discover Wet at Cypress Gardens.
Comedy, 60 min., NBC, 3/12/72. Various comedy sketches set against the background of Florida's Cypress Gardens. *Host:* Ed McMahon. *Guests:* Liz Allen, The Burgundy Street Singers, Bob Newhart, The Stingers. *Producer:* John Tuzee. *Writers:* Ron Pedderson, Joan Tuzee. *Director:* Dick Matt.

## 618 Ed Sullivan's Broadway.
Variety, 90 min., CBS, 3/16/73. A look at the past, present (1973), and future of Broadway. *Host:* Ed Sullivan. *Guests:* Jack Cassidy, Julie Harris, Lou Jacobi, Michele Lee, Ethel Merman, Marilyn Michaels, Frank Sinatra, Jr., Gwen Verdon, Hattie Winston, Sam Wright. *Music:* Ray Bloch. *Producer:* Robert H. Precht. *Directors:* Ron Field, Dan Smith.

## 619 The Eddie Fisher Special.
Variety, 60 min., Syndicated, 5/69. An hour of music and songs with singer Eddie Fisher and his guests. *Host:* Eddie Fisher. *Guests:* The Roy Castle Singers and Dancers, Connie Stevens. *Music:* Jack Parnell. *Producer:* Jackie Barnett. *Director:* Tony Charmoli.

## 620 The Eddie Rabbitt Special.
Variety, 60 min., NBC, 7/10/80. An hour of music, songs, and comedy sketches with singer Eddie Rabbitt in his first television special. *Host:* Eddie Rabbitt. *Guests:* Stockard Channing, Emmylou Harris, Wendy Holcombe, Jerry Lee Lewis. *Music:* Dennis McCarthy. *Producers:* Gary Smith, Dwight Hemion. *Writers:* Rod Warren, Cort Casady, Ed Hider. *Director:* Dwight Hemion.

## 621 The Edgar Bergen and Charlie McCarthy Show.
Variety, 30 min., CBS, 11/23/50 (first special), 4/30/51 (second special). Ventriloquist Edgar Bergen and his dummy, Charlie McCarthy, star in a television version of their popular radio series. The comedy stems from the antics of Charlie McCarthy and Edgar's other dummies Mortimer Snerd and Effie Klinker (Charlie wore a monocle over his right eye and always appeared in formal dress [including a top hat]; Effie was an unattractive old maid; and Mortimer was a bucktoothed country bumpkin). *Hosts:* Edgar Bergen and Charlie McCarthy. *Guests:* (11/13/50): Diana Lynn, Jim

Backus, Pat Patrick. *Guests (4/30/51):* Dorothy Kirsten, The Wiere Brothers. *Music:* Ray Noble. *Producer:* Edgar Bergen. *Writer:* Zeno Klinker. *Director:* Alan Dinehart.

**622 The Edsel Show.** Variety, 60 min., CBS, 10/7/57. An hour of music, songs, and comedy sponsored by the Ford Motor Company in an effort to promote what turned out to be one of the biggest flops in automotive history, the 1957 Edsel. *Host:* Bing Crosby. *Guests:* Louis Armstrong, Rosemary Clooney, Lindsay Crosby, The Four Preps, The Norman Luboff Choir, Frank Sinatra. *Music:* Tutti Camarata. *Producer-Writer:* Bill Morrow. *Director:* Seymour Berns.

**623 Eleanor Roosevelt Diamond Jubilee Plus One.** Tribute, 60 min., NBC, 10/7/60. An all-star celebration for former First Lady Eleanor Roosevelt on the occasion of her seventy-sixth birthday. *Guest of Honor:* Eleanor Roosevelt. *Guests:* Lucille Ball, Jack Benny, General Omar Bradley, George Burns, Carol Channing, Irene Dunne, Jimmy Durante, Bob Hope, Senator John F. Kennedy, Paul Newman, Vice President Richard Nixon, Simone Signoret, Joanne Woodward. *Producer:* Michael Abbott. *Writer:* Reginald Rose. *Director:* Dick Schneider.

**624 Elizabeth Taylor in London.** Variety, 60 min., CBS, 10/6/63. A personalized tour of London as seen through the eyes of actress Elizabeth Taylor. *Host:* Elizabeth Taylor. *Music Director:* John Barry. *Music Conductor:* Johnnie Spence. *Producer-Director:* Sid Smith. *Writers:* Louis Solomon, S. J. Perelman.

**625 Elizabeth the Queen.** Drama, 90 min., NBC, 1/31/68. The story, set in the 1500s, relates the stormy affair between Queen Elizabeth I, the shrewdly intelligent and dedicated ruler

of England, and the Earl of Essex, an ambitious and impetuous member of her court. Aired on the "Hallmark Hall of Fame." *Cast:* Judith Anderson (Queen Elizabeth I), Charlton Heston (Earl of Essex), Alan Webb (Sir Francis Bacon), Michael Allinson (Sir Walter Raleigh), Harry Townes (Sir Robert Cecil), Anne Rogers (Penelope). *Producer-Director:* George Schaefer. *Writer:* John Edward Friend.

**626 Elton John in Central Park.** Variety, 60 min., HBO, 7/27/82. Videotaped highlights of a concert given by Elton John in New York's Central Park. *Host:* Elton John. *Producers:* Danny O'Donovan, Mike Mansfield, John Reid, Hilary Stewart. *Director:* Mike Mansfield.

**627 Elton John: In Concert.** Variety; 90 min., ABC, 2/3/77. Highlights of a 1977 concert by Elton John in Scotland. *Host:* Elton John. *Producer:* John Reid. *Director:* David Bell.

**628 Elvis.** Variety, 60 min., NBC, 12/3/68. Elvis Presley's first television special; an informal hour wherein Elvis, surrounded by musicians and fans, sings his most famous songs. The program, sponsored by the Singer Sewing Machine Company, is officially titled "Singer Presents Elvis." *Host:* Elvis Presley. *Guests:* The Blossoms, Barbara Burgess, D. J. Fontana, Alan Fortas, Susan Henning, Charles Hodge, Lance LeGault, Scotty Moore, Jaime Rogers, Claude Thompson. *Music:* Billy Goldenberg. *Producers:* Bob Finkel, Steve Binder. *Writers:* Allan Blye, Chris Bearde. *Director:* Steve Binder.

**629 Elvis: His Life and Times.** Documentary, 2 hrs., Syndicated, 8/15/93. A look back on the life of Elvis Presley (1935-77) through archival footage and comments from family, friends, and musicians. *Hosts:* Mac Davis, Lisa Hartman. *Guests:* Chet

Atkins, Richard Egan, D. J. Fontana, Marion Keisker, George Klein, Wink Martindale, Ulysses S. Mayhorn, Sam Phillips, Priscilla Presley, the Reverend Frank Smith, Gordon Stoker, Gladys Tipler, Jim Tipler. *Producers:* Rick Ray, Dee Ray, Stephen Pouliot. *Writer:* Robynn Lee. *Director:* J. D. Hansen.

**630 Elvis Memories.** Tribute, 60 min., Syndicated, 1/85. A fond remembrance of Elvis Presley (1935–77) through rare film footage and the recollections of friends and family. *Host:* George Klein. *Guests:* Ginger Alden, Chet Atkins, Dick Clark, Donna Douglas, Mickey Gilley, Al Green, Merle Haggard, Barbara Mandrell, Wink Martindale, Jerry Reed, Charlie Rich, Jerry Schilling, Cybill Shepherd, Hank Snow. *Producers:* Alan Johnson, Wallace Johnson.

**631 Elvis: One Night with You.** Variety, 60 min., HBO, 1/5/85. An informal jam session in which Elvis Presley reminisces about his early years as a performer. The session was originally taped as part of an NBC special called "Elvis" (see entry) but only a small portion of it aired. The HBO version presents the unedited taped version of the session, which marked Elvis's return to live performing after a seven-year absence. *Host:* Elvis Presley. *Guests:* The Blossoms, Barbara Burgess, D. J. Fontana, Alan Fortas, Susan Henning, Charles Hodge, Lance LeGault, Scotty Moore, Jaime Rogers, Claude Thompson. *Producers:* Joseph Rascoff, Steve Binder. *Writers:* Allan Blye, Chris Bearde. *Director:* Steve Binder.

**632 Elvis Remembered: Nashville to Hollywood.** Tribute, 60 min., NBC, 2/8/80. A salute to Elvis Presley by film and record industry colleagues. *Hosts:* Larry Gatlin, Barbara Mandrell. *Guests:* Jack Albertson, Bill Bixby, Merle Haggard, The Jordan-aires, Jerry Lee Lewis, Mary Ann Mobley, Sheree North, Roy Orbison, Carl Perkins, Charlie Rich, Nancy Sinatra, Stella Stevens, Dottie West. *Music:* Bill Walker. *Producers:* Gil Cates, Joseph Cates. *Writer:* Chet Hagan. *Director:* Ivan Curry.

**633 Elvis: The Echo Will Never Die.** Documentary, 60 min., Syndicated, 8/86. The program examines the way Elvis Presley lived and the way he died. *Host-Narrator:* Casey Kasem. *Guests:* Ursula Andress, Sammy Davis, Jr., Tom Jones, B. B. King. *Music:* Mike Jeffrey. *Producers:* Peter Barton, Jeff Melby. *Writer:* William Stover. *Director:* Paul Barton.

**634 Elvis: The Great Performances.** Retrospective, 2 hrs., CBS, 4/24/92. A compilation of clips from movies and television specials that showcase the musical performances of Elvis Presley. *Host:* Priscilla Presley. *Producers:* Andrew Solt, Jerry Schilling. *Writer-Director:* Andrew Solt.

**635 Elvis's Graceland.** Documentary, 60 min., Syndicated, 8/87. A very moving tribute to Elvis Presley by Priscilla Beaulieu Presley (Elvis's exwife) as she tours the house and grounds of Graceland, his Memphis estate. The program also features comments by Elvis's friends. *Host:* Priscilla Presley. *Guests:* Elwood David, Joe Esposito, George Klein. *Music:* Donald Pomeranz. *Producers:* Joseph Roscoff, Steve Binder. *Writer:* Buz Kohan. *Director:* Steve Binder.

**636 The Emancipation of Lizzie Stern.** Drama, 60 min., CBS, 1/22/91. A "CBS Schoolbreak Special" about a 16-year-old girl (Lizzie Stern) and her battle to be legally declared an adult after her mother (Donna) announces she is remarrying and the family is moving to another state. *Cast:* Tammy Lauren (Lizzie Stern), Karen

Valentine (Donna Stern), Adrianna Petrich (Sandy Stern), Sean Tant (Matthew Stern), Dennis Parlato (Jeffrey), John Haymes Newton (Jason). *Music:* Brent Havens. *Producer-Writer-Director:* Susan Rohrer.

**637 Emily, Emily.** Drama, 90 min., NBC, 2/7/77. A "Hallmark Hall of Fame" presentation about a retarded boy's growth into maturity as seen through the eyes of Emily Ward, a graduate student in psychology, who gives the boy a chance for fulfillment in the outside world. *Cast:* Pamela Bellwood (Emily Ward), Thomas Hulce (Freddie Putnam), John Forsythe (Niles Putnam), James Farentino (Joe Crane), Karen Grassle (Terry). *Producers:* Henry Jaffe, Michael Jaffe. *Writer:* Allen Sloane. *Director:* Marc Daniels.

**638 Emmanuel Lewis: My Very Own Show.** Variety, 60 min., ABC, 2/13/87. How a network variety special is produced is seen through the experiences of "Webster" star Emmanuel Lewis as he plans for his first (and only) television special. *Host:* Emmanuel Lewis. *Guests:* Debbie Allen, Rene Auberjonois, Shelly Berman, Sammy Davis, Jr., Frank Gorshin, Bob Hope, Victoria Jackson, Paul Rodriguez, Siegfried and Roy. *Music:* Tom Chase, Steve Rucker. *Producer:* George Schlatter. *Writers:* Bob Arnott, George Schlatter. *Director:* Paul Miller.

**639 The Enchanted World of Danny Kaye.** Children, 60 min., CBS, 2/20/72. An animagic (puppets brought to life) version of the Hans Christian Andersen fable *The Emperor's New Clothes* (about a vain emperor and an invisible wardrobe of clothes created for him by a tailor). *Host:* Danny Kaye. *Voices:* Robert McFadden, Cyril Ritchard, Gary Shapiro, Allen Swift. *Producer-Directors:* Arthur Rankin, Jr., Jules Bass. *Writer:* Romeo Muller.

**640 An Enemy Among Us.** Drama, 60 min., CBS, 7/21/87. A contemporary drama about AIDS and its effect on a small community as seen through the eyes of Scott Fischer, a teenager who is infected with the HIV virus. A "CBS Schoolbreak Special." *Cast:* Dee Wallace (Jan Fischer), Stephen Macht (Jack Fischer), Danny Nucci (Scott Fischer), Tammy Lauren (Karen), Robin Gammell (Tom), Gail Strickland (Kay), Gladys Knight (Dr. Donna Robinson). *Music:* Misha Segal. *Producers:* Joseph Maurer, Bradley Wigor. *Writer:* Joseph Maurer. *Director:* Arthur Allan Seidelman.

**641 The Engelbert Humperdinck Special.** Variety, 60 min., ABC, 12/2/69; Syndicated 8/71 and 8/73. An hour of music, songs, and light comedy. *Host:* Engelbert Humperdinck. *Guests* (12/2/69): Barbara Eden, Jose Feliciano, Tom Jones, Dionne Warwick. *Guests* (8/71): Kaye Ballard, Gina Lollobrigida, Lou Rawls, Roger Whittaker. *Guests* (7/73): Buddy Greco, Dusty Springfield, Jonathan Winters. *Music:* Jack Parnell. *Producer:* Colin Clews. *Writers:* Sheldon Keller, Bryan Blackburn, Tony Hawes. *Directors:* Colin Clews (12/2/69), Ian Fordyce (8/71 and 7/73).

**642 Entertaining the Troops.** Documentary, 90 min., PBS, 3/11/89. The program blends archival footage with interviews to salute World War II performers. *Guests:* Maxene Andrews, Mel Blanc, Bob Hope, Dorothy Lamour, Frances Langford, Tony Romano, Patti Thomas. *Producer-Writer-Director:* Robert Mugge.

**643 Entertainment 1955.** Variety, 90 min., NBC, 3/27/55. NBC-TV's first color special to emanate from the network's new $3.7 million Burbank studios. A live program of music, comedy, and dramatic vignettes with remote pickups from New York. *Host:* Fred Allen. *Guests:* Pat Carroll, Buddy

**Engelbert Humperdinck**

Hackett, Bob Hope, Dinah Shore, Jimmy Durante, Leontyne Price, Judy Holliday, Cesar Romero, Ralph Edwards, Adolph Zukor, Sylvester "Pat" Weaver, Robert Sarnoff. *Producer-Director:* Jack Rayel. *Writer:* Charles Isaacs.

**644 Eric.** Drama, 2 hrs., NBC, 11/10/75. A courageous battle against terminal illness as seen through the eyes of Eric Swensen, a college athlete who is stricken by leukemia, but who refuses to give up the fight for life. Aired on the "Hallmark Hall of Fame." *Cast:* John Savage (Eric Swensen), Patricia Neal (Lois Swensen), Claude Akins (Stanley Swensen), Sian Barbara Allen (Marilyn), Mark Hamill (Paul), Nehemiah Persoff (Dr. Duchesnes). *Music:* Dave Grusin. *Producers:* Lee Rich, Philip Capice. *Writers:* Carol Evan McKeand, Nigel McKeand. *Director:* James Goldstone.

**645 The Ernie Kovacs Special.** Comedy, 30 min., ABC, 1/23/62. A series of outlandish comedy vignettes that were taped one week prior to Ernie Kovacs's untimely death in a car accident. While intended to be an episode of "The Ernie Kovacs Show," it was instead run as a special tribute to "The Master" (as Ernie was called for his comedy innovations). *Host:* Ernie Kovacs. *Regulars:* Jolene Brand, Maggie Brown, Bobby Lauher, Joe Mikolas. *Producer-Writer-Director:* Ernie Kovacs.

**646 Errol Flynn: Portrait of a Swashbuckler.** Documentary, 60 min., Syndicated, 3/87. A profile of screen actor Errol Flynn (1909–59). *Host-Narrator:* Christopher Lee. *Guests:* John Huston, David Niven, Hal Wallis. *Producers:* David Kellogg, Mark Massari. *Director:* Craig Haffner.

## 647 The Escape of a One-Ton Pet.

Comedy-Drama, 30 min., ABC, 1/7, 1/14, 1/21/78. Shortly after her bull, Percy, wins a blue ribbon at a county fair, Pru Miller, a spirited teenage girl who raised the animal, learns that her pet can never father calves. When she discovers that her father has decided to sell the bull to a butcher shop, Pru takes matters into her own hands and loads her beloved Percy onto a truck and takes to the open road. The three-part story relates Pru's adventures as she tries to protect her one-ton pet. Aired as an "ABC Weekend Special." *Cast:* Stacy Swor (Pru Miller), James Callahan (Dusty Miller), Michael Morgan (Jamie), Richard Yniquez (Stino Montez), Roxanna Bonilla-Giannini (Angela Montez). *Producers:* Thomas W. Moore, Jean Moore. *Writers:* Arthur Heinemann, George Lefferts. *Director:* Richard Bennett.

## 648 Esther Williams Aqua Spectacular.

Variety, 90 min., NBC, 9/29/56. An entertainment spectacular that features actress Esther Williams in music, song, comedy, and in vignettes that showcase her aquatic skills. *Host:* Esther Williams. *Guests:* Don Adams, Fran Allison, Red Barber, Peter Lawford, Jonathan Lucas Dancers, Arnold Stang. *Music:* Gerald Dolin. *Producer-Director:* Greg Garrison. *Writer:* Gordon Auchincloss.

## 649 Esther Williams at Cypress Gardens.

Variety, 60 min., NBC, 8/8/60. A musical showcase that spotlights Esther Williams as she performs in water and on dry land at Cypress Gardens in Florida. *Host:* Esther Williams. *Guests:* Joey Bishop, Fernando Lamas. *Music:* Paul Weston. *Producer-Writers:* Jack Brooks, Milt Rosen. *Directors:* Alan Handley, Roy Montgomery.

## 650 E.T. and Friends — Magical Movie Visitors.

Documentary, 60 min., CBS, 12/14/82. A nostalgic look at the history of aliens in motion pictures. *Host:* Robin Williams. *Music:* William Loose. *Producer-Directors:* Andrew Solt, Malcolm Leo. *Writers:* Peter Elbing, Andrew Solt, Malcolm Leo.

## 651 Eunice.

Comedy-Drama, 90 min., CBS, 3/15/82. A special based on the series of sketches originally performed on "The Carol Burnett Show," 1974–78. The program is a seriocomic slice of American life as seen through the eyes of a middle-class family: Eunice Higgins, who is frustrated and envious; Ed Higgins, her feckless husband; and Thelma Harper, her crotchety mother. The story reunites the characters in a four-act teleplay that spans 25 years in Eunice's life. Act 1, set in 1955, introduces Eunice and her brother, Philip, and details Eunice and Ed's bumbling courtship. 1963 is the setting for act 2, where Eunice dreams of becoming an actress when her brother, a successful writer, returns home for a visit. Act 3 is set in 1973 and shows how Eunice's dreams begin to fall apart with her drifting into and becoming an alcoholic. It is 1978 when act 4 begins and it depicts Eunice's efforts to cope with her sharp-tongued, social climbing sister, Ellen. *Cast:* Carol Burnett (Eunice Higgins), Harvey Korman (Ed Higgins), Vicki Lawrence (Thelma Harper), Ken Berry (Philip Harper), Betty White (Ellen). *Music:* Peter Matz. *Producer:* Joe Hamilton. *Writers:* Dick Clair, Jenna McMahon. *Director:* Harvey Korman.

## 652 Evel Knievel's Death Defiers.

Variety, 60 min., CBS, 1/31/77. Evel Knievel and other daredevils perform death-defying feats from the Amphitheater in Chicago and from Lincolnshire Resort in Illinois. *Hosts:* Jill St. John, Telly Savalas. *Guests:* Joe Gerlach, Orvall Kisseburg, Evel Knievel, Dave Merrifield, Ron Phillips, Karl Wallenda. *Music:* Nick Perito.

*Producer-Director:* Marty Pasetta. *Writers:* Don Clark, Susan Clark.

## 653 An Evening at the Moulin Rouge.

Variety, 60 min., HBO, 1/22/83. Variety acts from the Moulin Rouge Night Club in Paris. *Host:* George Peppard. *Music:* Georges Bessario. *Producers:* Gary Smith, Dwight Hemion, Jack Cellcio. *Director:* David Niles.

## An Evening with Alan King at Carnegie Hall *see* Alan King Specials

## 654 An Evening with Carol Burnett.

Variety, 60 min., CBS, 2/24/63. An hour of music, songs, and comedy. *Host:* Carol Burnett. *Guest:* Robert Preston. *Producer:* Bob Banner. *Writer:* Igor Peshkowsky. *Director:* Ernest Chambers.

## 655 An Evening with Carol Channing.

Variety, 60 min., CBS, 2/18/66. Actress-singer Carol Channing in a lively hour of music and song. *Host:* Carol Channing. *Guests:* George Burns, David McCallum. *Music:* David Rose. *Producer-Director:* Bud Yorkin.

## 656 An Evening with Diana Ross.

Variety, 90 min., NBC, 3/6/77. The program traces the life and career of Diana Ross through music and song. *Host:* Diana Ross. *Music:* Billy Goldenberg. *Producer:* Joe Layton. *Writer:* Bill Dyer. *Director:* Norman Campbell.

## 657 An Evening with Fred Astaire.

Variety, 60 min., CBS, 10/17/58. Dancer Fred Astaire's first television special; an hour of music, singing, and dancing. See also the sequel special, "Another Evening with Fred Astaire." *Host:* Fred Astaire. *Guests:* Barrie Chase, The Jonah Jones Quartet, Ken Nordine, The Bill Thompson Singers. *Announcer:* Art Gilmore. *Music:* David Rose. *Producer-Director:*

Bud Yorkin. *Choreographer:* Hermes Pan.

## 658 An Evening with Jimmy Durante.

Variety, 60 min., NBC, 9/25/59. A program of music, song, and comedy sketches. *Host:* Jimmy Durante. *Guests:* Bobby Darin, Gisele MacKenzie, Sal Mineo, Ginny Tiu, Lawrence Welk. *Music:* Roy Bargy. *Producer:* Charles Isaacs. *Director:* Dick McDonough.

## An Evening with John Denver *see* John Denver Specials

## 659 An Evening with Julie Andrews and Harry Belafonte.

Variety, 60 min., NBC, 11/9/69. A solid hour of songs with actress Julie Andrews and singer Harry Belafonte. *Hosts:* Julie Andrews, Harry Belafonte. *Music:* Michel Legrand. *Producer-Director:* Gower Champion. *Writer:* Robert Emmett.

## 660 An Evening with Robin Williams.

Comedy, 85 min., HBO, 3/12/83. A program of adult-oriented comedy routines. *Host:* Robin Williams. *Music:* John Sebastian. *Writer:* Robin Williams. *Producer-Director:* Don Mischer.

## 661 An Evening with the Statler Brothers.

Variety, 2 hrs., Syndicated, 12/81. A musical salute to the 1950s. *Hosts:* The Statler Brothers. *Guests:* Chet Atkins, Brenda Lee, Barbara Mandrell, Conway Twitty. *Music:* Bill Walker. *Producers:* Walter Burnett, Dick Thrall. *Writers:* Bill Galvin, Pat Galvin, Howard Reid, Don Reid. *Director:* Steve Womack.

## 662 The Everly Brothers Reunion Concert.

Variety, 60 min., HBO, 1/14/84. The program reunites the Everly Brothers in a concert together for the first time in ten years. *Hosts:* Don Everly, Phil Everly. *Musicians:*

Mark Griffiths, Graham Jarvis, Martin Jenner, Albert Lee. *Producers:* Stephanie Beknett, Alan Yentob, Anthony Wall. *Director:* Rick Gardner.

**Everything You Always Wanted to Know About Jack Benny and Were Afraid to Ask** *see* **Jack Benny Specials**

**663 Everything You Ever Wanted to Know About Monsters . . . But Were Afraid!** Documentary, 60 min., CBS, 10/23/81. A fascinating look at monsters—both in movies (via film clips) and real life (undocumented reports of real sightings). *Host-Narrator:* Charles Osgood. *Producers:* Joel Heller, Virginia Grey. *Writers:* Joel Heller, Charles Osgood. *Director:* Vern Diamond.

**664 The Exchange Student.** Drama, 60 min., CBS, 1/22/85. A "CBS Schoolbreak Special" about the friendship between two girls: Julie Johnson, an American high school girl, and Maneka Desai, an exchange student from India, and how they learn to accept each other's values and customs. *Cast:* Paige Price (Julie Johnson), Neeta Puri (Maneka Desai), Josh Hamilton (Todd Johnson), Lauren Tom (Kim), Kathryn Grody (Amy Johnson), Roxanne Chang (Teri), Peter Blake Barton (Mike Johnson). *Music:* Glen Roven. *Producer:* Jane Startz. *Writer:* Barry Dantzscher. *Director:* Michael Tsohiyuki Uno.

**665 The Eyes Have It.** Thriller, 90 min., ABC, 1/14/74. A suspense story about a group of blind students who find themselves in the midst of an assassination plot. *Cast:* Sinead Cusack (Sally), Dennis Waterman (Frank), Alun Armstrong (Mike), Peter Vaughan (Anderson), William Marlowe (Jeffries), Leslie Schofield (Moore). *Music:* Laurie Johnson. *Producer:* Cecil Clarke. *Writer:* Terence Feely.

*Director:* Shaun O'Riordan.

**666 Fabian's Good Time Rock and Roll.** Variety, 2 hrs., Syndicated, 12/85. The program recalls the heyday of rock and roll music. Taped at Riverfront Plaza in Baton Rouge, Louisiana. *Host:* Fabian Forte. *Guests:* Frankie Avalon, Chubby Checker, Lou Christie, The Coasters, The Crystals, Bo Diddley, Lesley Gore, Little Anthony and the Diamonds, The Platters, Bobby Rydell, Del Shannon. *Producers:* Sheldon Saltzman, Fabian Forte. *Director:* Arthur Forrest.

**667 The Fabulous Fifties.** Variety, 2 hrs., CBS, 1/31/60. A music, comedy, and song salute to the 1950s. *Performers:* Julie Andrews, Shelly Berman, Betty Comden, Henry Fonda, Jackie Gleason, Rex Harrison, Elaine May, Mike Nichols, Suzy Parker, Eric Sevareid. *Music Directors:* Alfredo Antonini, Franz Allers, John Lesko, Jay Blackton. *Producers:* Leland Hayward, Marshall Jamison. *Writers:* Max Wolk, A. J. Russell, Stephen Sondheim. *Director:* Norman Jewison.

**668 The Fabulous Fordies.** Variety, 60 min., NBC, 3/7/72. A music and comedy tribute to the 1940s. *Host:* Tennessee Ernie Ford. *Guests:* Frank Gorshin, Betty Grable, Dick Haymes, Maureen O'Hara. *Producers:* Bob Wynn, Digby Wolfe. *Writer:* Digby Wolfe. *Director:* Bob Wynn.

**669 The Fabulous Funnies.** Comedy, 60 min., NBC, 2/12/68. A salute to the comic strips found in the daily newspapers. *Host:* Carl Reiner. *Guests:* Ken Berry, Jack Burns, Avery Schreiber. *Music:* John Scott Trotter. *Producers:* Lee Mendelson, George Schlatter. *Writers:* Bill Persky, Sam Denoff, Lee Mendelson, George Schlatter. *Director:* Gordon Wiles.

**670 Faeries.** Cartoon, 30 min., CBS, 2/25/81. In the fantastic world of

Faerie, the King performs a feat of magic that conjures life into his own Shadow. For a time all is well as the Shadow becomes the King's friend and constant companion. But, through a tragic miscalculation, the Shadow's power proceeds to grow while the King's strength begins to fade. Soon the Shadow, now turned evil, forms alliances with the evil creatures of the realm and begins to take control of Faerie Land. When it is learned that faerie fate decrees that only a mortal can save the kingdom, Oisin, a young hunter, is captured by the faeries and put under an enchanted spell by Princess Niamh, the King's beautiful daughter. The story follows Oisin's efforts, assisted by Puck—a fun-loving, shape-shifting Pixie—to find and destroy the Shadow. *Voices:* Hans Conried (Faerie King/Shadow/Narrator), Craig Schaeffer (Oisin), Morgan Brittany (Princess Niamh), Frank Welker (Puck), Bob Arbogast (Kobold). *Producers:* Thomas W. Moore, Jean Moore Edwards, Anne Upson. *Writer:* Christopher Gore. *Director:* Fred Hellmich.

**671 Fair Game.** Drama, 30 min., Syndicated, 4/23/88. When Charlie Barker is cut from the all-male running team to make room for a girl, he decides to get even by joining the girls' hockey team. The story relates his experiences as he attempts to join the girls' hockey team—first as a joke—but later to play seriously with them. *Cast:* Jordan Marder (Charlie Barker), Kathleen Sisk (Sarah), Mitchell Marchand (Ubba), Mara Hobel (Patty Corbin), Paul Avery (Principal), Sharon Chatten (Coach Kelly), Ken Kliban (Coach Durala). *Music:* Steve Hoskins. *Producer-Writer-Director:* Gene McPherson.

**672 Fame.** Comedy, 90 min., NBC, 11/30/78. An original comedy by Arthur Miller that relates the absurdities of being famous as seen through the experiences of Meyer Shine, a noted playwright who is having difficulty accepting fame. Aired on the "Hallmark Hall of Fame." *Cast:* Richard Benjamin (Meyer Shine), Jose Ferrer (Francesco), Raf Vallone (Driver), Robert Alda (Concierge), Shera Danese (Lucia), Linda Hunt (Mona), Nipsey Russell (Vinnie). *Producers:* Joseph Cates, Gilbert Cates. *Writer:* Arthur Miller. *Director:* Marc Daniels.

**673 A Family Again.** Drama, 60 min., ABC, 10/15/88. A moving story about a teenage girl (Lindsey) who struggles to come to terms with the accidental death of her older sister (Beth). Aired as an "ABC Afterschool Special." *Cast:* Tonya Crowe (Lindsey), Michael Tucker (Jeremy), Jill Eikenberry (Clare), Judith Barsi (Billie), Rob Stone (Chris), Rhea Perlman (Aunt Dee), Pamela Segall (Jill), Sherilyn Fenn (Beth), Ricki Lake (Carmen). *Music:* Randy Edelman. *Producers:* Jeffrey White, Henry Winkler, Ann Daniel. *Writer-Director:* Camille Thomasson.

**674 Family Night with Horace Heidt.** Variety, 60 min., Syndicated, 8/71. An hour of music and songs with bandleader Horace Heidt. *Host:* Horace Heidt. *Guests:* Pete Condoli, Mary Ford, John Gary, Barbara Hines, Al Hirt, Red Nichols, Lee Tully, Gretchen Wyler. *Music:* Horace Heidt. *Producers:* Jerry Browne, Horace Heidt. *Director:* Dick McDonough.

**675 A Family of Strangers.** Drama, 60 min., ABC, 9/24/80. A sensitive "ABC Afterschool Special" about two single parents (Dominic and Marie) who marry. Dominic is a widower with two daughters (Ginger and Rose Ann) who resent the intrusion of a new mother and her 12-year-old daughter (Carrie) into their lives. The story focuses on their struggles to become a family. *Cast:* Danny Aiello

(Dominic Ginetti), Maria Tucci (Marie Mills), Lauri Hendler (Carrie Mills), Laura Dean (Ginger Ginetti), Mara Hobel (Rose Ann Ginetti).

**676 The Family Sing.** Musical Comedy, 30 min., DuMont, 8/17/48. Music and songs are presented in a situation comedy format wherein the musically inclined Barton family sing and entertain from their home. *Cast:* Grace Albert (Mother), Elliott Sullivan (Father), Diana Donnewirth (Daughter), Mickey Carroll (Son), Bertha T. Powell (Daughter). *Guest:* Margaret Irving. *Announcer:* Jack Rayel. *Producers:* Arthur Ehrlich, Sheelagh K. O'Malley. *Writer:* George Rosen. *Director:* Carl Beier.

**677 A Family Tree.** Comedy, 30 min., PBS, 10/18/87. The story of a young woman (Kara) and her misadventures as she struggles to impress her future in-laws (the Fletchers) when she meets them for the first time. *Cast:* Rosanna Arquette (Kara Dimly), John Stockwell (Maxwell Fletcher), Hope Lange (Frances Fletcher), Robert Ridgely (Marlin Fletcher), Tracy Brooks Swope (Allison). *Music:* Tito Larriva. *Producer:* Phyllis Geller. *Writers:* Beth Henley, Budge Threlkeld. *Director:* Jonathan Demme.

**678 Fanfare.** Variety, 90 min., NBC, 11/7/54. A lavish, color production featuring music, songs, and comedy sketches. *Performers:* Steve Allen, Judy Holliday, Dick Shawn, Frank Sinatra, Jacques Tati. *Music:* Charles Sanford. *Producers:* Max Liebman, Bill Hobin.

**679 The Fantastic Funnies.** Tribute, 60 min., CBS, 5/15/80. A salute to the 85-year history of comic strips via live action and animation. *Host:* Loni Anderson. *Guests:* Brad Anderson, Dik Browne, Keene Curtis, Cathy Guisewite, Johnnie Hart, Howard Hesseman, Hank Ketchum, Mell

Lazarus, John Cullen Murphy, Russell Myers, Patricia Patts, John Raymond, Charles Schulz, Morrie Turner, Mort Walker, Dean Young. *Music:* Ed Bogas, Judy Munsen. *Producers:* Lee Mendelson, Karen Crommie. *Writer-Director:* Lee Mendelson.

**680 The Fantastic Miss Piggy Show.** Variety, 60 min., ABC, 9/17/82. An hour of music, songs, and comedy featuring the Muppet character Miss Piggy. *Voice of Miss Piggy:* Frank Oz. *Guests:* George Hamilton, Andy Kaufman, John Ritter. *Music:* Joe Raposo. *Producer-Director:* Jim Henson. *Writers:* Buz Kohan, Henry Beard.

**681 The Fantasticks.** Musical, 90 min., NBC, 10/18/64. A television adaptation of the off–Broadway musical about an illusion-filled romance between a young man (Matt) and girl (Luisa). Aired on the "Hallmark Hall of Fame." *Cast:* John Davidson (Matt), Susan Watson (Luisa), Ricardo Montalban (El Gallo), Bert Lahr (Hucklebee), Stanley Holloway (Bellamy). *Music/Lyrics:* Tom Jones, Harvey L. Schmidt. *Producer-Director:* George Schaefer. *Writer:* Robert Hartung.

**682 The Farmer's Daughter.** Comedy-Drama, 60 min., NBC, 1/14/62. The story, set in Washington, D.C., follows events in the life of Katrin Holstrom, a Swedish farm girl who comes to work as a housekeeper for Congressman Glen Morley. Based on the Loretta Young feature film of the same title. Aired on "Theater '62." *Cast:* Lee Remick (Katrin Holstrom), Peter Lawford (Glen Morley), Charles Bickford (Clancy), Cornelia Otis Skinner (Mrs. Morley), Jerome Cowan (Finley), Milton Selzer (Adolph), Murray Hamilton (Nordick). *Producer:* Fred Coe. *Writer:* Thomas W. Phipps. *Director:* Fielder Cook. *Note:* The film was also adapted to television as a series called "The Farmer's Daughter" (ABC, 1963–66) with Inger Stevens as Katy and William Windom as Glen.

## 683 The Fat Albert Christmas Special.

Cartoon, 30 min., CBS, 12/18/77. A modern-day version of the Nativity. With Christmas approaching, Fat Albert and his friends, Mushmouth, Bill, Dumb Donald, Weird Harold, Russell, and Rudy, fear losing their beloved clubhouse, a ramshackle old shed, that is in danger of being destroyed by its owner, the mean old Tyrone. To compound their troubles, Fat Albert and the gang stumble upon a young boy named Michael, his unemployed father, and his pregnant mother, all of whom are stranded by a disabled car with no place to go. The kids shelter the family in their clubhouse — and, just like the ancient Christmas story, a child is born. The program concludes with Tyrone giving Fat Albert and the gang the shed when it is revealed that Tyrone, a widower, is only mean to mask his grief of loneliness. Based on characters created by Bill Cosby. *Voices:* Bill Cosby (Fat Albert/Bill/Mush Mouth/Dumb Donald/Weird Harold), Jan Crawford (Russell), Eric Suter (Rudy). *Other Voices:* Erika Carroll, Gerald Edwards, Lane Vaux. *Music:* Yvette Blais, Jeff Michael. *Producers:* William H. Cosby, Jr., Lou Scheimer, Norm Prescott. *Writers:* Bill Danch, Jim Ryan. *Director:* Hal Sutherland.

## 684 The Fat Albert Halloween Special.

Cartoon, 30 min., CBS, 10/24/77. Fat Albert and his friends attempt to stop a troublemaker (Devery) from pulling a prank to scare the neighborhood's old people on Halloween. *Voices:* Bill Cosby, Jan Crawford, Gerald Edwards, Eric Suter. *Music:* Yvette Blais, Jeff Michael. *Producers:* William H. Cosby, Jr., Norm Prescott, Lou Scheimer. *Writers:* Bill Danch, Jim Ryan. *Director:* Hal Sutherland.

## 685 Favorite Songs.

Variety, 60 min., NBC, 11/26/64. A musical song-fest that features selections based on a Reader's Digest poll of its readers' favorite songs. *Hosts:* Eydie Gorme, Dean Martin. *Guests:* The Bitter End Singers, The Nick Castle Dancers, Juliet Prowse, Nipsey Russell, Jill St. John, Allan Sherman. *Music:* Jerry Fielding. *Choral Director:* Dick Williams. *Choreography:* Nick Castle.

## 686 Fawn Story.

Drama, 60 min., ABC, 10/22/75. Jenna and Toby McVey are a sister and brother who live on a farm. One day they find an injured doe and bring it home. As they nurse the doe, named Lady by Jenna, authorities tell them that they are in conflict with the law (which forbids private citizens from holding wild animals in captivity, regardless of the situation). Despite the urging of their father to set the doe free, Jenna and Toby refuse. The authorities step in. In an attempt to subdue the doe, it is shot with a tranquilizer dart that causes it to die. Jenna and Toby are burning with resentment; then, motivated by genuine concern, they begin a letter-writing campaign to change the law to allow citizens to hold wild animals when it is in the best interest of the animals. Aired as an "ABC Afterschool Special." *Cast:* Kristy McNichol (Jenna), Poindexter (Toby), Med Flory (John), Karen Oberdiear (Louise), Gordon Jump (Forest Ranger). *Music:* Lauren Rubin, Mike Lewis. *Producers:* Alan Landsburg, Laurence Savadore. *Writer:* Tony Kayden. *Director:* Larry Elikann.

## 687 The Fear Is Spreading.

Thriller, 90 min., ABC, 2/25/75. A desperate struggle for survival as seen through the experiences of Tracy Loxton, an American journalist on a routine assignment in England, who is taken hostage by two prison escapees. Also known as "The Crazy Kill." *Cast:* Tandy Cronyn (Tracy Loxton), Denholm Elliott (Dr. Frank Henson), Anthony Valentine (Garrard), Claire Nielsen (Hiliary). *Music:* Laurie Johnson. *Producers:* Cecil Clarke, Ian Fordyce.

*Writer:* Dennis Spooner. *Director:* Dennis Vance.

## 688 Feathertop.

Musical, 60 min., ABC, 10/19/61. When Madame Eau Charme, a social-climbing witch, fails to receive an invitation to the governor's ball, she becomes angered and plots a dreadful revenge against the governor. She brings a scarecrow (named Feathertop) to life and sets him on a quest to break the heart of Julie Balfour, the governor's beloved daughter. *Cast:* Jane Powell (Julie Balfour), Hugh O'Brian (Feathertop), Hans Conried (Governor Balfour), Cathleen Nesbitt (Madame Eau Charme). *Musical Score:* Mary Rodgers. *Lyrics:* Martin Charnin. *Producer:* Tony Charmoli. *Writer:* John Marsh. *Director:* Dean Whitmore.

## 689 Feliciano — Very Special.

Variety, 60 min., NBC, 4/27/69. An hour of music and song with singer-guitarist Jose Feliciano. *Host:* Jose Feliciano. *Guests:* Burt Bacharach, Glen Campbell, Dionne Warwick, Andy Williams. *Music:* Jimmie Haskell. *Producer-Director:* Bob Henry.

## 690 Fellini: A Director's Notebook.

Documentary, 60 min., NBC, 4/11/69. Federico Fellini's first television film, a complex personal documentary fantasy that, in a series of vignettes, follows Fellini's symbolic journey through Rome, Italy. *Narrators:* Marina Borato, Federico Fellini, Frank Wolff. *Music:* Nino Rota. *Producer:* Peter Goldfarb. *Writer-Director:* Federico Fellini.

## 691 Festival of Magic.

Variety, 90 min., NBC, 5/27/57. Guest magicians perform their most amazing feats. The first 90-minute television program to be devoted to the subject of magic. *Host:* Ernie Kovacs. *Guests:* Cardini, Milbourne Christopher, Robert Harbin, Li King Si, June Merlin, Rene Septembre, Sorcar. *Music Director:* George Bassman.

## 692 Festival of Music.

Variety, 90 min., NBC, 1/30/56. A lavish production that features performances by opera and concert artists. *Performers:* Marian Anderson, Jussi Bjoerling, Zinka Milanov, Jan Peerce, Roberta Peters, Gregor Piatigorsky, Arthur Rubinstein, Isaac Stern, Rise Stevens, Renata Tebaldi, Blanche Thebom, Leonard Warren. *Music:* Max Rudolf. *Producer:* Sol Hurok.

## 693 15 and Getting Straight.

Drama, 60 min., CBS, 3/28/89. A "CBS Schoolbreak Special" that dramatizes the plight of teens addicted to drugs and alcohol as seen through the counseling of three addicts: Susan, Jeff, and Patti. *Cast:* Drew Barrymore (Susan), Tatum O'Neal (Kim), Corey Feldman (Jeff), Stefanie Nichols (Patti), David Birney (Dr. DeVito), Darleen Carr (Eleanor Prosky), Shirley Jo Finney (Mrs. Jackson). *Music:* Jimmie Haskell. *Producers:* Joanna Lee, Richard David. *Writer-Director:* Joanna Lee.

## 694 The Fifth Dimension Special: An Odyssey in the Cosmic Universe of Peter Max.

Variety, 60 min., CBS, 5/21/70. An hour of music and song with the Fifth Dimension. *Hosts:* The Fifth Dimension (Marilyn McCoo, Billy Davis, Jr., Florence LeRue, Lamonte McLemore, Ron Townson). *Guests:* Glen Campbell, Joey Heatherton, Arte Johnson, Flip Wilson. *Music:* Ray Knight. *Producer:* Robert H. Precht. *Writers:* Phil Hahn, Jack Hanrahan. *Director:* John Moffitt.

## 695 The Fifth Dimension Traveling Show.

Variety, 60 min., ABC, 8/18/71. A program of music and songs with the Fifth Dimension. *Hosts:* The Fifth Dimension (Marilyn McCoo, Billy Davis, Jr., Florence LeRue, Lamonte McLemore, Ron Townson).

*Guests:* Karen Carpenter, Richard Carpenter, Dionne Warwick. *Producers:* Burt Rosen, Ernest D. Glucksman. *Director:* Jorn Winther.

### 696 Fifth of July. Drama, 2 hrs. 30 min., Showtime, 10/14/82. A television adaptation of Lanford Wilson's 1978 drama about Ken Talley, Jr., a disabled, homosexual Vietnam veteran struggling to cope with a family he loves and fears. *Cast:* Richard Thomas (Ken Talley, Jr.), Swoosie Kurtz (Gwen Landis), Helen Stenborg (Aunt Sally), Joyce Reehling Christopher (June Talley), Jonathan Hogan (John Landis), Jeff Daniels (Jed), Cynthia Nixon (Shirley). *Music:* John Adams. *Producers:* Jac Venza, Sam Paul. *Writer:* Lanford Wilson. *Directors:* Marshall W. Mason, Kirk Browning.

### 697 The 50th Presidential Inaugural Gala. Variety, 2 hrs., ABC, 1/19/85. President Ronald Reagan and his wife Nancy are honored by celebrities two days before his inauguration for a second term. *Guests:* Pearl Bailey, Mikhail Baryshnikov, The Beach Boys, Larry Gatlin and the Gatlin Brothers, Crystal Gayle, Charlton Heston, Emmanuel Lewis, Rich Little, Dean Martin, Mr. T, Lou Rawls, Jill St. John, Tom Selleck, Frank Sinatra, James Stewart, Donna Summer, Elizabeth Taylor, Robert Wagner, Efrem Zimbalist, Jr., Stephanie Zimbalist. *Music:* Nelson Riddle. *Producers:* Gary Smith, Dwight Hemion, Frank Sinatra. *Writer:* Buz Kohan. *Directors:* Dwight Hemion, Frank Sinatra.

### 698 50 Years of Country Music. Variety, 3 hrs., NBC, 1/22/78. A review of country and western music over the past 50 years. Taped at the Grand Ole Opry House in Nashville. *Hosts:* Glen Campbell, Roy Clark, Dolly Parton. *Guests:* Chet Atkins, Johnny Cash, Ray Charles, Crystal Gayle, Merle Haggard, Loretta Lynn, The Statler Brothers, Mel Tillis, Ernest

Tubb. *Music:* Bill Walker. *Producers:* Joseph Cates, Gilbert Cates, Chet Hagan. *Writers:* Frank Slocum, Chet Hagan, Joseph Cates. *Director:* Walter C. Miller.

### 699 50 Years of Television: A Golden Celebration. Documentary, 2 hrs., CBS, 11/26/89. A look at television's past via clips from shows. *Hosts:* Walter Cronkite, Kermit the Frog, John Larroquette, Miss Piggy, Carl Reiner, Jane Seymour. *Announcer:* Gary Owens. *Music:* Tom Scott. *Producers:* John Moffitt, Pat Tourk Lee. *Writers:* Richard Rosen, Phil Savenick, Harry Arends. *Director:* John Moffitt.

### 700 File It Under Fear. Thriller, 90 min., ABC, 10/9/73. The story of a rural community that is rocked by a series of library murders. *Cast:* Maureen Lipman (Liz), Richard O'Callaghan (George), James Grout (Superintendent Cramer), Jan Francis (Gillian), Richard Pendrey (Gerry). *Music:* Laurie Johnson. *Producer:* John Sichel. *Writer:* Brian Clemens. *Director:* Bill Hays.

### 701 The File on Devlin. Drama, 90 min., NBC, 11/21/69. A drama of international intrigue in which the United States and Russia become involved in a search to find Lawrence Devlin, a British spy who disappeared under mysterious circumstances. Based on the novel by Catherine Gaskin and broadcast on the "Hallmark Hall of Fame." *Cast:* Elizabeth Ashley (Sally Devlin), Judith Anderson (Elisabeth Devlin), David McCallum (Kenneth Canfield), Helmut Dantine (Hans Raedler), Donald Moffat (Hywood), Laurence Naismith (Lord Pomeroy). *Producer-Director:* George Schaefer. *Writers:* Michael Dyne, Edward Essex.

### 702 The First Christmas Snow. Cartoon, 30 min., CBS, 12/15/

79. While tending his flock, Lucas, an orphaned shepherd boy, is struck by lightning during a fierce storm. Found by a nun (Sister Theresa), Lucas is brought to her convent and nursed back to health. Lucas, however, has been left blinded by the accident. As Christmas approaches, young Lucas, who had been entertained by tales of the season by Sister Theresa, expresses a desire to participate in a Nativity play. The story relates the miracle that occurs when, on Christmas Day, it begins to snow (as on the very first Christmas Day) and Lucas receives his gift of sight. *Voices:* Angela Lansbury (Sister Theresa), Cyril Ritchard (Father Thomas), David Kelley (Lucas). *Music:* Maury Laws. *Producer-Directors:* Arthur Rankin, Jr., Jules Bass. *Writer:* Julian P. Gardner.

**703 The First Easter Rabbit.** Cartoon, 30 min., CBS, 3/19/78. The program explains the traditions of Easter and how the Easter Rabbit came into being. *Voices:* Burl Ives (Great Easter Bunny), Robert Morse (Sunny, the First Easter Rabbit), Stan Freberg (Flops), Paul Frees (Zero and Spats), Joan Gardner (Mother), Don Messick (Whiskers), Dina Lynn (Glinda). *Music:* Maury Laws. *Producer-Directors:* Arthur Rankin, Jr., Jules Bass. *Writer:* Julian P. Gardner.

**704 The First 50 Years.** Documentary, 4 hrs. 30 min., NBC, 11/21/76. The National Broadcasting Company celebrates its first 50 years in radio and television in a lavish program that showcases NBC's history through photos, recordings, and film clips. *Hosts:* Jack Albertson, Milton Berle, David Brinkley, Johnny Carson, Angie Dickinson, Joe Garagiola, Bob Hope, Gene Kelly, Jerry Lewis, Dean Martin, Don Meredith, Gregory Peck, Freddie Prinze, George C. Scott. *Narrator:* Orson Welles. *Music:* Jack Elliott. *Producers:* Greg Garrison, Lee Hale, Chet Hagan. *Writers:* Abby Mann, Jess Op-

penheimer, Mike Marmer, Orson Welles. *Director:* Greg Garrison.

**705 The First Nine Months Are the Hardest.** Comedy, 60 min., NBC, 1/24/71. A warm-hearted look at pregnancy as seen through the eyes of three showbusiness couples as they endure the long wait. *Cast:* Dick Van Dyke (Obstetrician), Ken Berry and Jackie Joseph (First Couple), James Farentino and Michele Lee (Second Couple), Sonny and Cher (Third Couple). *Music:* Ray Charles. *Producer-Writers:* Bill Persky, Sam Denoff. *Director:* Clark Jones.

**706 First the Egg.** Drama, 60 min., ABC, 3/6/85. Sara White is a carefree high school student who shuns responsibility. As part of a Marriage and Family Life class, Sara is teamed with a fellow student (David) and made the parent of an egg, which must be treated as if it were a real child. The story follows Sara as she learns the meaning of serious responsibility. Aired as an "ABC Afterschool Special." *Cast:* Justine Bateman (Sara White), James McNichol (David Hannah), Mary Wickes (Helen Crandell), Elizabeth Huddle (Sara's mother), Jack Riley (Sarah's father), Chris Hebert (Robbie White). *Music:* Douglas Timm. *Producer:* Martin Tahse. *Writer:* Margaret Rosen. *Director:* Robert Thompson.

**707 Five Finger Discount.** Drama, 60 min., NBC, 11/1/77. The story of a pretty 13-year-old girl (Corny) who shoplifts to impress a group of students and become one of their group. *Cast:* Dawn Lyn (Corny), Dana Laurita (Angela), Nancy Malone (Jenna), Elizabeth Allen (Sergeant Juden), Harriet Nelson (Mrs. Summerland), Peter Donat (David). *Music:* Charles Bernstein. *Producer:* Nancy Malone. *Writer:* Jerry McNeely. *Director:* Richard Bennett.

## 708 Five Stars in Springtime.
Variety, 60 min., NBC, 6/1/57. A musical salute to the spring of 1957. *Host:* Clayton "Bud" Collyer. *Guests:* Nat King Cole, The Honeydreamers, Gordon MacRae, Rick Nelson, Patti Page, June Valli, Andy Williams. *Music:* Harry Sosnik. *Producer-Director:* Joseph Cates.

## 709 Flesh and Blood.
Drama, 2 hrs., NBC, 1/26/68. An intense portrait of an American family engulfed by dark shades of morality, memories, and time. Originally intended as a Broadway play, but debuted on television. *Cast:* Edmond O'Brien (Harry), Kim Stanley (Della), E. G. Marshall (John), Suzanne Pleshette (Nona), Kim Darby (Faye), Robert Duvall (Howard). *Producer-Director:* Arthur Penn. *Writer:* William Hanley.

## 710 The Flintstones 25th Anniversary Celebration.
Variety, 60 min., CBS, 5/20/86. A live-action and animated retrospective that recalls 25 years of "The Flintstones" (ABC, 1960–66). *Hosts:* Tim Conway, Harvey Korman. *Guests:* Joseph Barbera, Jane Curtin, Susan Saint James, Telly Savalas, Sting, Vanna White. *Music:* Hoyt Curtin, Tom Worrant, Ron Jones. *Producers:* William Hanna, Joseph Barbera. *Writers:* John Ludin, Charles Howell, Tom Ruegger. *Director:* Robert Guenette.

## 711 Flip Wilson Specials.
A chronological listing of the music, comedy, and song specials hosted by comedian Flip Wilson. All are 60 minutes in length.

**1 Flip Wilson ... Of Course** (NBC, 10/18/74). *Guests:* Richard Pryor, Martha Reeves, Peter Sellers, Lily Tomlin. *Music:* George Wyle. *Producers:* Monte Kay, Lorne Michaels. *Director:* Tim Kiley.

**2 The Flip Wilson Special** (NBC, 12/11/74). *Guests:* Diahann Carroll, Freddie Prinze, Paul Williams. *Music:*

George Wyle. *Producers:* Monte Kay, Jack Burns. *Director:* Bill Foster.

**3 The Flip Wilson Special** (NBC, 2/27/75). *Guests:* William Conrad, Sammy Davis, Jr., Helen Reddy. *Music:* George Wyle. *Producers:* Monte Kay, Jack Burns. *Director:* Bill Davis.

**4 The Flip Wilson Special** (NBC, 5/7/75). *Guests:* Cher, Richard Pryor, McLean Stevenson. *Music:* George Wyle. *Producers:* Monte Kay, Jack Burns. *Director:* Bill Hobin.

**5 Travels with Flip** (CBS, 10/15/75). See title for details.

**6 The Flip Wilson Comedy Special** (NBC, 11/11/75). *Guests:* Ruth Buzzi, George Carlin, The Pointer Sisters. *Music:* George Wyle. *Producers:* Monte Kay, Jack Burns. *Director:* Stan Lathan.

## 712 Fol-De-Rol.
Variety, 60 min., ABC, 2/27/72. A program of music, song, and comedy set against the background of a medieval fair. *Host:* Ann Sothern (as the Queen). *Guests:* Cyd Charisse, Howard Cosell, Milt Kamen, The Krofft Puppets, Rick Nelson, Mickey Rooney, Yma Sumac. *Music:* Charles Fox. *Producer:* Digby Wolfe. *Writers:* David Robinson, Lester Pine, Jerry Mayer, Dennis Klein, Digby Wolfe. *Director:* Tony Charmoli.

## 713 Folk Sound U.S.A.
Variety, 60 min., CBS, 6/16/60. An hour of folk music and songs. *Performers:* Casey Anderson, Mildred Anderson, Joan Baez, Lester Flatt, John Lee Hooker, Earl Scruggs, Peter Yarrow. *Music:* Tom Scott. *Producer-Writer:* Robert Herridge. *Director:* Mel Ferber.

## 714 The Follies of Suzy.
Variety, 90 min., NBC, 10/23/54. A Max Liebman color spectacular that features "The Parisian Pixie," Jeanmarie, in a series of romantic vignettes. Jeanmarie is a French ballerina that exists only in the mind of a young playwright (Steve

Allen). Through his daydreams viewers are treated to three stories set in various times in American history. *Host:* Steve Allen. *Cast:* Steve Allen, Tom Avera, Harrison and Eliot (dance team), Jeanmarie, Cliff Norton, Connie Russell, Paul Whiteman. *Music:* Charles Sanford. *Producers:* Max Liebman, Bill Hobin. *Writers:* William Friedberg, Fred Saidy, Neil Simon, Will Glickman, William Jacobson. *Director:* Max Liebman.

## 715 For Love or Money.

Comedy, 60 min., NBC, 4/11/68. The story of Jack Hastings, an American tourist who becomes involved in a political revolution during a vacation in a South American country. A Bob Hope Special. *Cast:* Bob Hope (Jack Hastings), Janet Leigh (Carol Van Dyke), Fernando Lamas (Fernando), J. Carrol Naish (Rafael), Pat Harrington, Jr. (Morales), Eddie Mayehoff (Carlson), Kathleen Freeman (Miss Angela). *Music:* Les Brown. *Producers:* Bob Hope, Jess Oppenheimer. *Writer:* Dean Hargrove. *Director:* Jess Oppenheimer.

## 716 The Ford 50th Anniversary Show.

Variety, 2 hrs., CBS, 6/15/53. The program, which marks the fiftieth anniversary of the Ford Motor Company, salutes the people who have helped to make America great (for example: explorers, inventors, entertainers, military leaders). *Guests:* Marian Anderson, Charles Correll, Wally Cox, Eddie Fisher, Freeman Gosden, Howard Lindsey, Mary Martin, Ethel Merman, Edward R. Murrow, Frank Sinatra, Dorothy Stickney, Lowell Thomas, Rudy Vallee, Teddy Wilson. *Music:* Bernard Green. *Producer:* Leland Hayward. *Writers:* Frederick Lewis Allen, Agnes Rogers, Howard Teichmann. *Director:* Clark Jones.

## 717 Four for Tonight.

Variety, 60 min., NBC, 2/24/60. The program spotlights the talents of four performers. Also known as "Star Parade." *Performers:* Tammy Grimes, Beatrice Lillie, Tony Randall, Cyril Ritchard. *Music:* Franz Allers. *Producer:* Robert Saudek. *Writer:* Larry Gelbart. *Directors:* Grey Lockwood, Herb Ross, William A. Graham.

## 718 The Four Poster.

Drama, 60 min., NBC, 7/25/55. A two-character play in which a husband and wife recall 35 years of married life. *Cast:* Hume Cronyn (Husband), Jessica Tandy (Wife). *Producers:* Fred Coe, Hume Cronyn. *Writer:* Jan DeHartung. *Director:* Clark Jones.

## 719 The Fourth Man.

Drama, 60 min., CBS, 10/16/90. A "CBS Schoolbreak Special" about Joey Martelli, a star in the classroom but a dud in sports, who turns to track and steroids to become the son his athletic father always wanted. *Cast:* Peter Billingsley (Joey Martelli), Lyle Alzado (John Martelli), Adrienne Barbeau (Mary Martelli), Nicole Eggert (Heidi), Mei Hunt (Mrs. Wiu), Ken Medlock (Coach). *Music:* John Tesh. *Producer-Writer-Director:* Joanna Lee.

## 720 The 4th of July Spectacular.

Variety, 2 hrs., Syndicated, 7/4/89. A holiday celebration at Walt Disney World in Florida. *Stars:* Gretchen Elizabeth Carlson, The New Kids on the Block, the New Mouseketeers, Sandi Patti, Willard Scott, The Temptations. *Announcer:* John Gabriel. *Music:* David Clydsdale. *Producers:* Don Ohlmeyer, Linda Jonsson. *Writer-Director:* Don Ohlmeyer.

## 721 The Fourth Wise Man.

Drama, 60 min., ABC, 3/30/85. An Easter parable of spiritual fulfillment based on Henry Van Dyke's nineteenth-century short story *The Other Wise Man*. When Artaban, a prosperous doctor, sees a star in the skies that he interprets to mean a new king is coming to rule the world, he sells his possessions to buy three precious stones (a ruby, a sapphire, and a pearl) to present to the Messiah. The story, set at the time of the Nativity, relates his adventures as he sets out in search of Christ. *Cast:* Martin Sheen (Artaban), Alan Arkin (Orontes), Eileen Brennan (Judith), Ralph Bellamy (Abgarus), Sydney Penny (Shamar), Charlie Steen (Maximus), Lance Kerwin (Passhur), Harold Gould (Rabbi), Richard Libertini (Tigranes). *Music:* Jerry Goldsmith. *Producers:* Ellwood Kieser, Michael Rhodes. *Writer:* Tom Fontana. *Director:* Michael Rhodes.

### 722 Fox Preview. Variety, 30 min., Fox, 4/1/87.

The first program to air in primetime on the newly established Fox Broadcasting Corporation (which premiered 4/5/87). The program was a sneak preview of the Fox Saturday ("Werewolf," "Karen's Song," "Down and Out in Beverly Hills," "The New Adventures of Beans Baxter") and Sunday evening shows ("Married . . . with Children," "The Tracey Ullman Show," "Duet," "21 Jump Street," and "Mr. President"). *Host:* Mary Ruth Carleton. *Producers:* Erik Sorenson, Peggy Holter. *Writer-Director:* Peggy Holter.

### 723 The Fox/MTV Guide to Summer '92. Variety, 60 min., Fox, 6/7/92; MTV, 6/20/92.

A look at the hottest people, places, and events of the summer of 1992; taped at Lake Havasu in Arizona. *Hosts:* Cindy Crawford, Tommy Davidson. *Guests:* Paula Abdul, The Black Crowes, Tim Burton, Jennie Garth, Genesis, Guns 'n Roses, Michael Keaton, Kriss Kross, Bruce Springsteen, U2. *Producers:* Linda Corradina, Lauren Lazin.

### 724 Frances Langford Presents. Variety, 60 min., NBC, 3/15/59.

An hour of music, songs, and comedy in which singer Frances Langford presents top-name performers. The program is actually two unsold 30-minute pilots that were reedited to form a 60-minute special. *Host:* Frances Langford. *Guests:* Edgar Bergen, Jerry Colonna, The Four Freshmen, Bob Hope, Julie London, Hugh O'Brian, Tony Romano, George Sanders. *Music Director:* David Rose. *Music and Lyrics:* Earl Brent, Bobby Troup. *Producer:* Charles Wick. *Writers:* Rip Van Ronkel, Glenn Wheaton, Monte Manheim, Dann Cahn, Si Rose, Zeno Klinker. *Director:* Ed Hillie.

### 725 The Frances Langford Show. Variety, 60 min., NBC, 5/1/60.

A program of music, song, and comedy with singer Frances Langford. *Host:* Frances Langford. *Guests:* Don Ameche, Mary Costa, Bob Cummings, Hermione Gingold, Johnny Mathis, The Three Stooges. *Music:* Ray Heindorf. *Producer:* Charles Wick. *Writer-Director:* Frank Tashlin.

### 726 Francesca, Baby. Drama, 60 min., ABC, 10/6/76.

The story follows Francesca James, a 15-year-old girl, whose mother (Lillian) is an alcoholic, as she tries to cope with the problem through Alateen, a national organization designed to help teenagers with alcoholic parents. Aired as an "ABC Afterschool Special." *Cast:* Carol Jones (Francesca James), Melendy Britt (Lillian James), Dennis Bowen (Bix), Tara Talboy (Kate), Peter Brandon (Gordon), Doney Oatman (Patty), Jody Britt (Louise). *Music:* Hod David. *Producer:* Martin Tahse. *Writer:* Bob Rodgers. *Director:* Larry Elikann.

### 727 Frank, Liza, and Sammy: The Ultimate Event. Concert, 90 min., Showtime, 5/20/89.

Frank Sinatra, Liza Minnelli, and Sammy Davis, Jr., perform separately and together in a December 1988 concert at the Fox Theater in Detroit. *Hosts:* Sammy Davis, Jr., Liza Minnelli, Frank Sinatra. *Music Directors:* Frank

Sinatra, Jr., Billy LaVorgner, Morty Stevens. *Producers:* George Schlatter, Gary Necessary. *Director:* George Schlatter.

## 728 Frank Sinatra, Jr., with Family and Friends. Variety, 60 min., CBS, 10/19/69. Music, songs, and comedy with Frank Sinatra, Jr., his friends, and family. *Host:* Frank Sinatra, Jr. *Guests:* Jack Benny, Sammy Davis Jr., The Doodletown Pipers, Arte Johnson, Jack E. Leonard, Frank Sinatra, Nancy Sinatra. *Music Directors:* Billy Strange, Jack Tillar. *Producers:* M. J. Rivkin, Harvey Bernhard. *Writers:* Marc London, David Panich. *Director:* Alex Grashoff.

## 729 Frank Sinatra Specials.
A chronological listing of the variety specials hosted by singer-actor Frank Sinatra. Frank Sinatra hosted each show, except where noted otherwise.
**1 The Frank Sinatra Timex Show** (60 min., ABC, 10/9/59). *Guests:* Bing Crosby, Jimmy Durante, Mitzi Gaynor, Dean Martin. *Music:* Nelson Riddle. *Producers:* Sammy Cahn, Jimmy Van Heusen. *Writer:* John Bradford. *Director:* Bill Colleran.
**2 The Frank Sinatra Timex Show** (60 min., ABC, 12/13/59). *Guests:* Ella Fitzgerald, Hermione Gingold, The Hi-Lo's, Peter Lawford, Juliet Prowse, The Red Norvo Combo. *Music:* Nelson Riddle. *Producers:* Sammy Cahn, Jimmy Van Heusen. *Writer:* John Bradford. *Director:* Bill Colleran.
**3 The Frank Sinatra Timex Show** (60 min., ABC, 2/15/60). *Guests:* Mary Costa, Barbara Heller, Lena Horne, Juliet Prowse, Eleanor Roosevelt. *Music:* Nelson Riddle. *Producers:* Sammy Cahn, Jimmy Van Heusen. *Writer:* Johnny Bradford. *Director:* Richard Dunlap.
**4 The Frank Sinatra Timex Show** (60 min., ABC, 5/12/60). *Guests:* Joey Bishop, Sammy Davis, Jr., Peter Lawford, Elvis Presley, The Tom Hanson Dancers. *Music:* Nelson Riddle. *Producers:* Sammy Cahn, Jimmy Van Heusen. *Writer:* John Bradford. *Director:* Richard Dunlap.
**5 The Frank Sinatra Show** (60 min., NBC, 11/24/65). A one-man show in which Frank sings the songs that mean something to him. *Music Directors:* Nelson Riddle, Gordon Jenkins. *Producers:* Dwight Hemion, Gary Smith. *Director:* Dwight Hemion.
**6 Frank Sinatra: A Man and His Music** (60 min., CBS, 5/15/66). *Music Directors:* Nelson Riddle, Gordon Jenkins. *Producers:* Dwight Hemion, Carolyn Raskin. *Writers:* Sheldon Keller, Glenn Wheaton. *Director:* Dwight Hemion.
**7 Frank Sinatra: A Man and His Music, Part 2** (60 min., CBS, 12/7/66). *Guest:* Nancy Sinatra. *Music Directors:* Nelson Riddle, Gordon Jenkins. *Producers:* Dwight Hemion, Carolyn Raskin. *Writers:* Sheldon Keller, Glenn Wheaton. *Director:* Dwight Hemion.
**8 Frank Sinatra: A Man and His Music, Part 3** (60 min., NBC, 11/13/67). *Guests:* Ella Fitzgerald, Antonio Carlos Jobim. *Music:* Nelson Riddle. *Producer:* Robert Scheerer. *Writer:* Sheldon Keller. *Director:* Michael Pfagharl.
**9 Sinatra** (60 min., CBS, 11/5/69). *Music:* Don Costa. *Producers:* Frank Sinatra, Carolyn Raskin. *Writer:* Sheldon Keller. *Director:* Tim Kiley.
**10 Magnavox Presents Frank Sinatra** (60 min., NBC, 11/18/73). *Guest:* Gene Kelly. *Producer:* Howard W. Koch. *Writer:* Fred Ebb. *Director:* Marty Pasetta.
**11 Sinatra: The Main Event** (60 min., ABC, 10/13/74). *Host:* Howard Cosell. *Star:* Frank Sinatra. *Orchestra:* Woody Herman. *Music Director:* Bill Miller. *Producers:* Jerry Weintraub, Roone Arledge. *Director:* Bill Carruthers.
**12 Sinatra and Friends** (60 min., ABC, 4/21/77). *Guests:* Tony Bennett, Natalie Cole, John Denver, Loretta Lynn, Dean Martin, Robert Merrill,

Leslie Uggams. *Music:* Nelson Riddle. *Producer-Writers:* Paul W. Keyes, Marc London. *Director:* Bill Davis.

**13 Sinatra: The First 40 Years** (2 hrs., NBC, 1/30/80). A black-tie party for Frank Sinatra on his sixty-fourth birthday — and fortieth year in show-business. Taped at Caesar's Palace in Las Vegas. *Guests:* Paul Anka, Lucille Ball, Tony Bennett, Milton Berle, Charlie Callas, Lillian Carter, Sammy Davis, Jr., Glenn Ford, Cary Grant, Harry James, Gene Kelly, Rich Little, Dean Martin, Robert Merrill, Don Rickles, Frank Sinatra, Jr., Nancy Sinatra, Tina Sinatra, Red Skelton, Dionne Warwick, Orson Welles, William B. Williams. *Music Director of the Caesar's Palace Orchestra:* Don Costa. *Producer-Writer:* Paul W. Keyes. *Director:* Clark Jones.

**14 Sinatra: The Man and His Music** (60 min., NBC, 11/22/81). *Guests:* Count Basie and His Orchestra. *Music Director:* Don Costa. *Producers:* Paul W. Keyes, Joe Kay. *Writer:* Paul W. Keyes. *Director:* Clark Jones.

**15 Sinatra: Concert for the Americas** (90 min., Showtime, 11/82). *Music:* Buddy Rich. *Producers:* George Huncher, Jerry Harrison. *Writer:* Gary Belkin. *Director:* Walter C. Miller.

**16 Sinatra 75: The Best Is Yet to Come** (2 hrs., CBS, 12/16/90). A star-studded celebration in honor of Frank's seventy-fifth birthday. *Guests:* Tony Bennett, Rosemary Clooney, Harry Connick, Jr., Tony Danza, Ella Fitzgerald, Eydie Gorme, Quincy Jones, Gene Kelly, Steve Lawrence, Sophia Loren, Shirley MacLaine, Roger Moore, Paul Newman, Tom Selleck, Jo Stafford, Barbra Streisand, Robert Wagner. *Producers:* George Schlatter, Tina Sinatra. *Writers:* Buz Kohan, George Schlatter. *Director:* Jeff Margolis.

**730 Frankenstein.** Drama, 3 hrs., ABC, 1/16 and 1/17/73. A two-part television adaptation of the 1818 novel by Mary Shelley. The story, set in Ger-

many, relates the efforts of Dr. Victor Frankenstein to create life from the dead — and the horror that results when his creature, possessed of an abnormal brain, becomes a killer. *Cast:* Robert Foxworth (Dr. Victor Frankenstein), Susan Strasberg (Elizabeth), Bo Svenson (The Monster), Heidi Vaughn (Agatha), Robert Gentry (Henri Clerval), Philip Bourneuf (Alphonse), John Karlen (Otto), Willie Aames (William). *Music:* Robert Cobert. *Producer:* Dan Curtis. *Writers:* Sam Hall, Richard Landau. *Director:* Glenn Jordan.

**731 Frankie Avalon's Easter Special.** Variety, 60 min., Syndicated, 4/69. A musical celebration of Easter. *Host:* Frankie Avalon. *Guests:* The Burgundy Street Singers, Jan Daley, Joey Forman, Jose Greco, The James Hibbard Dancers, Nana Lorca, Joanie Sommers.

**732 Fred Astaire: Change Partners and Dance.** Documentary, 60 min., Syndicated, 5/80. The program traces dancer Fred Astaire's film and television career via clips. See the following title also. *Narrator:* Joanne Woodward. *Guests:* Leslie Caron, Barrie Chase, Bob Fosse, Eugene Loring, Hermes Pan. *Producers:* George Page, Jac Venza. *Writer:* John L. Miller. *Director:* David Heeley.

**733 Fred Astaire: Puttin' on the Top Hat.** Documentary, 60 min., Syndicated, 5/80. A sequel to the above special that traces Fred Astaire's Broadway career (where he danced with his sister, Adele) to his years with RKO (1933–39) where he danced with Ginger Rogers. *Narrator:* Joanne Woodward. *Guests:* Adele Astaire, Hal Borne, Gene Kelly, Rudolph Nureyev, Hermes Pan, Ginger Rogers. *Producers:* Jac Venza, George Page. *Writer:* John L. Miller. *Director:* David Heeley.

**734 The Fred Astaire Special.**
Variety, 60 min., NBC, 5/9/60. An hour
of music, song, and dance. *Host:* Fred
Astaire. *Guests:* Barrie Chase, The
Jonah Jones Quartet. *Announcer:* Ken
Nordine. *Music:* David Rose.

**735 The Fred Astaire Special.**
Variety, 60 min., NBC, 2/7/68. An hour
of music, song, and dance. *Host:* Fred
Astaire. *Guests:* Barrie Chase, Art
Garfunkel and Paul Simon, Sergio
Mendes and Brasil '66. *Music:* Neal
Hefti. *Producers:* Fred Astaire, Gil
Rodin. *Director:* Robert Scheerer.

**736 Fred Waring: Way Back
Home.** Variety, 60 min., Syndicated,
10/67. A musical concert by bandleader Fred Waring and His Pennsyl-
vanians. *Host:* Fred Waring. *Producers:* David Fein, James Stanley.
*Director:* Lew Schwartz.

**737 Fred Waring's U.S.
Chorus.** Variety, 60 min., Syndicated, 11/24/88. A patriotic music and
song salute to America by Fred Waring's U.S. Chorus (a choral group of
young people selected from auditions
throughout the country). *Host:* Fred
Waring. *Announcer:* Kathleen Padelko.
*Music Director:* Len Thomas. *Producers:* Neal Faust, John Grant. *Director:* Charles Gudeman.

**738 Free to Be ... A Family.**
Variety, 60 min., ABC, 12/14/88. A
television first—a satellite link between
the United States and Russia in which
American and Russian children, who
had been pen pals over the past year,
meet via a satellite link (in New York's
Hard Rock Cafe and in a Moscow television studio). The program attempts
to show that children of both worlds
are the same, despite the misconcep-
tions that both countries have about
each other. *U.S. Host:* Marlo Thomas.
*Soviet Host:* Tatiana Vadeneyeva.
*Guests:* Bon Jovi, Whoopi Goldberg,
Jim Henson's Muppets, Penn and

Teller, Carly Simon, Lily Tomlin,
Robin Williams. *Music:* Paul Jacobs.
*Producers:* Marlo Thomas, Christopher
Cerf. *Writers:* Norman Stiles, Sarah
Durkee, Christopher Cerf. *Director:*
Gary Halvorson.

**739 Freedom Festival '89.**
Variety, 60 min., CBS, 7/3/89. A
musical salute to liberty and freedom at
Philadelphia's Independence Hall.
*Host:* Patrick Duffy. *Guests:* Frankie
Avalon, Nell Carter, Hal Holbrook,
Ann Jillian, Peter Nero, The Oak
Ridge Boys. *Music:* Lenny Stack. *Pro-
ducer:* Dick Clark. *Writer:* Barry Adel-
man. *Director:* Louis J. Horvitz.

**740 Friends and Nabors.**
Variety, 60 min., CBS, 10/12/66. A pro-
gram of music, songs, and comedy
sketches. *Host:* Jim Nabors. *Guests:*
Tennessee Ernie Ford, Andy Griffith,
Marilyn Horne, Shirley Jones, Ronnie
Schell. *Music:* Alan Copeland. *Pro-
ducers:* Richard O. Linke, Saul Ilson,
Ernest Chambers. *Writers:* Saul Ilson,
Ernest Chambers. *Director:* Stan
Harris.

**741 Frog Girl: The Jennifer
Graham Story.** Drama, 60 min.,
CBS, 10/17/89. A fact-based "CBS
Schoolbreak Special" about high
school student Jennifer Graham whose
refusal to dissect a frog in biology class
led to passage of a bill that protects
animals' rights and allows students to
choose whether or not to dissect an
animal in tenth grade. *Cast:* Ellen Dun-
ning (Jennifer Graham), Ivette Soler
(Keri), Sally Kemp (Mrs. Burns), Kurt
Fuller (Mr. Webster), Kerrie Keane
(Mrs. Graham), Ira Heiden (Charlie),
Rain Pryor (Student). *Producers:*
David Eagle, David Horowitz. *Writers:*
Harry Longstreet, Renee Longstreet.
*Director:* Harry Longstreet.

**From Hollywood with Love:
The Ann-Margret Special** *see*
**Ann-Margret Specials**

**742 From the Heart.** Variety, 60 min., NBC, 9/10/89. The program celebrates the accomplishments of handicapped artists. *Guests:* Lauren Bacall, Mikhail Baryshnikov, Zina Bethune, Ellen Burstyn, Judy Collins, Michael Douglas, Crystal Gayle, Jim Henson, Sen. Edward Kennedy, Ted Kennedy, Jr., Melissa Manchester, Marsha Mason, Kenny Rogers, Michael Tucker. *Music:* Ian Fraser. *Producers:* Gary Smith, Dwight Hemion, Michael B. Seligman. *Writers:* Buz Kohan, Marty Farrell, Gary Smith. *Director:* Dwight Hemion.

**743 The Front Page.** Comedy-Drama, 90 min., ABC, 1/31/70. The relationship between Walter Burns, the editor of a small-town newspaper, and Hildy Johnson, his ace reporter, who constantly threatens to quit and look for a job in New York. The story itself, based on the 1928 play by Ben Hecht and Charles MacArthur, relates Hildy's efforts to get a scoop on Earl Williams, a convict who escaped from prison hours before his scheduled execution. *Cast:* Robert Ryan (Walter Burns), George Grizzard (Hildy Johnson), Estelle Parsons (Mollie Malloy), Susan Watson (Peggy), John McGiver (Mayor), Vivian Vance (Mrs. Grant). *Narrator:* Helen Hayes.

**744 Frosty the Snowman.** Cartoon, 30 min., CBS, 12/7/69. One Christmas Eve a group of children build a snowman with "a corncob pipe, button nose, and two eyes made out of coal." When a gust of wind blows the stovepipe hat off the head of a magician named Professor Hinkle, young Karen finds the hat and places it on top of the snowman. The hat brings the snowman, named Frosty, to life. The story relates Frosty's adventures as he struggles to get to the North Pole before spring arrives and he melts. Complicating his task is Professor Hinkle, who wants his hat back. Based on the song of the same title by Jack Rollins and Steve Nelson. See also the following title. *Voices:* Jackie Vernon (Frosty), Billy De Wolfe (Professor Hinkle), June Foray (Karen), Paul Frees (Santa Claus). *Narrator:* Jimmy Durante. *Music:* Jules Bass. *Producer-Directors:* Arthur Rankin, Jr., Jules Bass. *Writer:* Romeo Muller.

**745 Frosty's Winter Wonderland.** Cartoon, 30 min., CBS, 12/7/79. A sequel to the above special. To alleviate Frosty's loneliness, the youngsters who made Frosty create a Mrs. Frosty (Crystal the Snowgirl) to be his companion during the long, cold nights and during the summer, when Frosty must return to the North Pole to avoid melting. *Voices:* Jackie Vernon (Frosty), Shelley Winters (Crystal), Dennis Day (Parson), Paul Frees (Jack Frost), Shelley Hines and Eric Stern (children). *Narrator:* Andy Griffith. *Music:* Maury Laws. *Producer-Directors:* Arthur Rankin, Jr., Jules Bass. *Writer:* Romeo Muller.

**746 Full Moon Over Brooklyn.** Drama, 60 min., NBC, 5/6/60. Incidents in the life of railroad worker Milton Barker as he crosses New York Harbor each night aboard the floats that connect two freight lines. *Cast:* Art Carney (Milton Barker), Elaine Stritch (Carmenita), Frank McHugh (Hobbs), Robert Webber (Dawes), Barbara Barrie (Ellen). *Producer:* David Susskind. *Writer:* Irving Gaynor Neiman. *Director:* Jack Smight.

**747 Fun Fair.** Variety, 60 min., NBC, 5/3/60. A music and comedy salute to the American County Fair. *Host:* Celeste Holm. *Guests:* Jaye P. Morgan, Margaret Hamilton, Marion Marlowe, Peter Palmer. *Music:* Tutti Camarata. *Producer:* Hubbell Robinson.

**748 Fun for 51.** Variety, 60 min., CBS, 12/31/50. A New Year's Eve celebration to welcome in the new year

(1951). *Host:* Ed Sullivan. *Guests:* Joey Adams, Ben Blue, Abe Burrows, Jean Carroll, Arthur Godfrey, Judy Lynn, Jan Murray, Ken Murray. *Music:* Ray Bloch. *Producer:* Marlo Lewis. *Director:* John Wray.

### 749 The Funniest Joke I Ever Heard.

Comedy, 60 min., ABC, 5/21/84 (first special), 11/27/84 (second special). Celebrities and ordinary people relate their favorite jokes and stories. *Hosts* (5/21/84): Heather Thomas, Robert Urich. *Hosts* (11/27/84): Priscilla Barnes, Robert Urich. *Guests* (5/21/84): George Burns, Dom DeLuise, Anthony Geary, John Hillerman, Jack Lemmon, Rich Little, Barbara Mandrell, Brooke Shields, Jimmy Stewart. *Guests* (11/27/84): Victor Borge, Ernest Borgnine, Morgan Brittany, Mike Connors, Shecky Greene, Kathie Lee Johnson, Martin Mull, Martin Sheen. *Music:* Merlyn Davis. *Producers:* Dick Clark, Phil Hahn. *Writer:* Donald Davis. *Director:* Phil Hahn.

### 750 Funny.

Comedy, 60 min., ABC, 1/19/86. A potpourri of comedy, including clips from shows, monologues by aspiring comedians, and clips of well-known comedians at work. *Hosts:* Karen Baldwin, Mary Donnelly. *Guests:* Steve Allen, Milton Berle, Red Buttons, Tim Conway, Bill Cosby, Phyllis Diller, Gallagher, Jan Murray, Richard Pryor. *Music:* Johnny Harris. *Producer:* George Schlatter. *Writers:* Bob Arnott, Gene Farmer, George Schlatter. *Director:* Bob Wynn.

### 751 Funny Faces.

Comedy, 60 min., HBO, 3/8/83. An hour of mime with host Red Skelton and his guest Marcel Marceau. *Music:* Ian Bernard. *Producer:* Riff Markowitz. *Director:* J. Edward Shaw.

### 752 Funny Girl to Funny Lady.

Variety, 60 min., ABC, 3/9/75. A solo concert by Barbra Streisand as she sings the songs associated with her career. Broadcast live from Washington, D.C. *Host:* Dick Cavett. *Star:* Barbra Streisand. *Music:* Peter Matz. *Producers:* Ray Stark, Gary Smith. *Writer:* Herb Sargent. *Director:* Dwight Hemion.

### 753 A Funny Thing Happened on the Way to Hollywood.

Comedy, 60 min., NBC, 5/14/67. A music and comedy spoof of the tinseled world of Hollywood. *Host:* Jack Paar. *Guests:* Judy Garland, Bob Newhart. *Music:* Jose Melis. *Producer:* Jack Haley, Jr. *Writers:* Bob Howard, Jack Paar, Sheldon Keller, David Lloyd. *Director:* Hal Gurnee.

### 754 The Funny Women of Television.

Tribute, 90 min., NBC, 10/24/91. A look at the funny women of television via clips of the series they appeared on. The program is divided into four segments: "The Ladies of 1,000 Faces" (featuring the diverse characters played by Imogene Coca, Carol Burnett, and Gilda Radner); "The Battle of the Sexes" (showcasing spats from "I Love Lucy" to "The Honeymooners" to "Roseanne"); "The Homemakers" (the roles of mothers in sitcoms); and "Working Women" (pays homage to "The Mary Tyler Moore Show," "That Girl," and "Murphy Brown"). *Hosts:* Mary Tyler Moore ("Ladies of 1,000 Faces"), Lily Tomlin ("Battle of the Sexes"), Betty White ("Homemakers"), Tracey Ullman ("Working Women"). *Guests:* Candice Bergen, Carol Burnett, Jasmine Guy, Marlo Thomas. *Producers:* Jack Haley, Jr., Michael B. Seligman, Phil Savenick. *Writers:* Buz Kohan, Rhea Kohan. *Director:* Louis J. Horvitz.

### 755 Funny, You Don't Look 200!

Variety, 60 min., ABC, 10/12/87. A series of sketches that examine the effects of the U.S. Constitution on our daily lives. *Host:* Richard Dreyfuss.

*Guests:* Hamilton Camp, Jill Eiken-berry, Emilio Estevez, Michael J. Fox, John Gielgud, Whoopi Goldberg, Goldie Hawn, Jeffrey Kramer, Judd Nelson, Randy Newman, Rhea Perl-man, Ally Sheedy, Barbra Streisand, Lily Tomlin, Lucy Webb, Henry Wink-ler, James Woods, Carmen Zapata. *Music:* Humme Mann. *Producers:* Judith Rutherford James, Richard Dreyfuss. *Writers:* Jessica Teich, Bruce Vilanch, Scott Garen, Richard Drey-fuss, Judith Rutherford Jones, Chris-topher Chase. *Director:* Jim Yukich.

### 756 The Funtastic World of Hanna-Barbera Arena Show.

Variety, 90 min., NBC, 6/25/81. Various life-sized Hanna-Barbera characters (for example, Huckleberry Hound, Fred Flintstone, Top Cat) per-form at the Perth Entertainment Center in Australia. *Host:* Michael Landon. *Guests:* The Yabba Dabba Doo Singers and Dancers. *Voices:* Henry Corden, Sammy Davis, Jr., Allan Melvin, Don Messick, Arnold Stang, John Stephenson, Janet Waldo. *Music:* Dominic Frontiere. *Producers:* Thomas Sarnoff, George M. Cohan. *Writer:* Bob Ogle. *Director* (stage show): Keith MacKenzie. *Director* (host segment): Harry Crane.

### 757 Gabriel Kaplan Presents the Future Stars.

Variety, 60 min., ABC, 4/14/77. The program spotlights the performances of up-and-coming performers in comedy, music, magic, and sports. *Host:* Gabriel Kaplan. *Per-formers:* Dick Arthur, Steve Bluestein, Amber Jim, Richard Lewis, Ann Meyers, Millsenblum, Paul Mooney, Stormin' Norman and Suzy. *Pro-ducers:* Dick Clark, Bill Lee. *Director:* Lee H. Bernhardi.

### 758 Gabriel Kaplan Presents the Small Event.

Variety, 60 min., ABC, 10/23/77. A spoof of big-event television specials. *Host:* Gabriel Kap-lan. *Guests:* Sid Caesar, Fred Willard, Cindy Williams. *Cameos:* Robert Hegyes, Lawrence-Hilton Jacobs, Pat Morita, Ron Palillo, John Travolta, John Sylvester White, Henny Young-man. *Music:* George Wyle. *Producers:* Gabriel Kaplan, Eric Cohen. *Writers:* Eric Cohen, David Panich, Gabriel Kaplan, Peter Gallay, Ray Taylor. *Director:* Bill Davis.

### 759 Gambler.

Drama, 60 min., CBS, 12/6/88. A "CBS Schoolbreak Special" about a high school athlete (Jimmy) who suffers from a compul-sion to gamble. *Cast:* Nicholas Kallsen (Jimmy), Jill Schoelen (Amy), Troy Winbush (Ty), George Dzundza (Father), Jennifer Warren (Mother), Lawrence Cook (Coach Hunt), Eugenie Ross-Leming (Counselor Ter-rana). *Music:* Brad Fiedel. *Producers:* Joseph Sern, Roger Singer. *Writer:* Barton Randall. *Director:* Roger Singer.

### 760 Game Show Biz.

Docu-mentary, 60 min., Syndicated, 9/87. A behind-the-scenes look at game shows, past and present, with a focus on how they are produced, how to become a contestant, and the off-stage lives of their hosts. *Host:* Wink Martindale. *Guests:* Ralph Andrews, Chris Bearde, Bill Carruthers, John Davidson, Bob Eubanks, Ronnie Greenberg, Jim Lange, Jack Narz, Jim Perry, Bob Synes, Peter Tomarken, Vanna White, Jay Wolpert. *Announcer:* Gary Owens. *Music:* Shaun Phillips, Dan Walker. *Producers:* Wink Martindale, Kevin Meagher. *Writer-Director:* Kevin Meagher.

### 761 The Gangsters: A Golden Age.

Documentary, 2 hrs., Syndi-cated, 8/20/89. The program recalls the history of the gangster era via news-reel footage, reenactments, and pro-files of notorious criminals. *Host:* Patrick O'Neal. *Music:* Michael Stahl. *Producer:* Lou Reda. *Writer:* Norman Stahl. *Director:* Don Horan.

**762 Garfield Cartoons.** A chronological listing of Garfield specials presented by CBS. Each of the 30-minute programs is based on the comic strip created by Jim Davis and each revolves around the antics of Garfield, a lazy, self-centered, pasta-loving cat. Other characters are Jon Arbuckle, Garfield's owner, a quiet artist; Lyman, Jon's roommate; and Odie, Lyman's dog.

**1 Here Comes Garfield** (10/25/82). Garfield's efforts to spring Odie from the dog pound. *Voices:* Lorenzo Music (Garfield), Sandy Kenyon (Jon), Henry Corden (Hubert), Hal Smith (Reba and Skinny), Hank Garrett (Fast Eddie and Fluffy), Angela Lee (Little girl). *Music:* Desiree Goyette, Ed Bogas. *Vocals:* Lou Rawls, Desiree Goyette. *Producers:* Jay Poynor, Lee Mendelson, Bill Melendez. *Writer:* Jim Davis. *Director:* Phil Roman.

**2 Garfield on the Town** (10/28/83). Garfield's adventures in the big city when he becomes separated from Jon while en route to the vet. *Voices:* Lorenzo Music (Garfield), Thom Huge (Jon), Desiree Goyette (Girl cat), Julie Payne (Dr. Wilson), Sandi Huge (Garfield's mother), George Wendt (Raoul), Lindsay Workman (Garfield's grandfather), Gerry Berger (Muhammad Ali Cat). *Credits:* Same as program 1.

**3 Garfield in the Rough** (10/26/84). Garfield's adventures when he, Jon, and Odie decide to go camping in the mountains. *Voices:* Lorenzo Music (Garfield), Thom Huge (Jon), Gregg Berger (Odie), Hal Smith (Dicky Beaver), Orson Bean (Billy Rabbit), Desiree Goyette (Girl cats), George Wendt (Ranger). *Music:* Desiree Goyette, Ed Bogas. *Producers:* Jay Poynor, Phil Roman. *Writer:* Jim Davis. *Director:* Phil Roman.

**4 Garfield in Paradise** (5/27/86). Garfield, Jon, and Odie's misadventures on a tropical island resort called Paradise World. *Voices:* Lorenzo Music (Garfield), Thom Huge (Jon), Gregg Berger (Odie), Wolfman Jack (High Rama Lama), Desiree Goyette (Princess Owooda), Julie Payne (Mai Tai), Frank Nelson (Hotel Clerk). *Music:* Desiree Goyette, Ed Bogas. *Producer:* Jay Poynor. *Producer-Writer:* Jim Davis. *Director:* Phil Roman.

**5 Garfield Goes Hollywood** (5/8/87). Garfield's efforts to win $1,000 and a trip to Hollywood by auditioning for the television show "Pet Search" (on WBOR-TV). *Voices:* Lorenzo Music (Garfield), Thom Huge (Jon), Gregg Berger (Odie), Nino Tempo (Herbie), Frank Welker (M.C.). *Music:* Desiree Goyette, Ed Bogas. *Producer-Director:* Phil Roman. *Writer:* Jim Davis.

**6 A Garfield Christmas** (12/21/87). Garfield and Jon's adventures as they spend an old-fashioned Christmas with Jon's farm family. *Voices:* Lorenzo Music (Garfield), Thom Huge (Jon), Gregg Berger (Odie), Pat Carroll (Grandma), Pat Harrington (Dad), Julie Payne (Mom). *Credits:* Same as for program number 5.

**7 Garfield – His Nine Lives** (Special 60 min. episode, 11/22/88). The program traces the nine lives of Garfield from prehistoric cat to his easy life as the pet of Jon. *Voices:* Lorenzo Music (Garfield), Thom Huge (Jon), Gregg Berger (Odie). *Additional Voices:* Carolyn Davis, Desiree Goyette, Sandi Huge, Heather Kerr, Hal Smith, Nino Tempo, Frank Welker, Lindsay Workman. *Credits:* Same as for program number 5.

**8 Garfield's Babes and Bullets** (5/23/89). A take-off on the Sam Spade detective character that finds Garfield as Sam Spayed, a feline flatfoot seeking to solve the murder of a wealthy widow's husband. *Voices:* Lorenzo Music (Garfield), Thom Huge (Jon & Thug), Gregg Berger (Odie and Burt), Desiree Goyette (Tanya), Julie Payne (Kitty), Lindsay Workman (Prof. O'Felix). *Credits:* Same as for program number 5.

**9 Garfield's Thanksgiving Special** (11/22/89). Garfield's efforts to lose weight – by going on a diet just as

Thanksgiving approaches. *Voices:* Lorenzo Music (Garfield), Thom Huge (Jon), Gregg Berger (Odie), Julie Payne (Dr. Liz Wilson), Pat Carroll (Grandma). *Credits:* Same as for program number 5.

**10 Garfield's Feline Fantasies** (5/18/90). A spoof of *The Maltese Falcon* and *Indiana Jones*, wherein Garfield daydreams that he is a soldier of fortune in the Middle East and assigned to recover the Banana of Bombay, the source for the old banana peel sight gag. *Voices:* Lorenzo Music (Garfield), Thom Huge (Jon), Gregg Berger (Odie/Walter), Julie Payne (Nadia), Frank Welker (Fat Guy/Rameet). *Music:* David Benoit, Desiree Goyette. *Producer:* Phil Roman. *Writer:* Jim Davis. *Directors:* Phil Roman, John Sparey, Bob Nesler.

**11 Garfield Gets a Life** (5/8/91). *Voices:* Lorenzo Music (Garfield), Thom Huge (Jon), Gregg Berger (Odie), Julie Payne (Library Girl), Frank Welker (Lorenzo/Gunner), June Foray (Mona). *Music:* David Benoit, Desiree Goyette. *Vocals:* Lou Rawls, B. B. King, The Temptations. *Producers:* Jim Davis, Phil Roman. *Writer:* Jim Davis. *Director:* John Sparey.

**763 Garry Shandling—Alone in Las Vegas.** Comedy, 60 min., ABC, 9/24/88. The program follows comedian Garry Shandling as he prepares for and gives his Las Vegas show. *Host:* Garry Shandling. *Guests:* Joe Behr, Zane Buzby, Susan Dear, Sandy Hackett, Bob Perlove, Lee Walsh. *Producers:* Rocco Urbisci, Garry Shandling. *Writers:* Mark Sotkin, Garry Shandling. *Director:* William Dear.

**764 The Gathering Storm.** Drama, 90 min., NBC, 11/29/74. A biographical drama based on the life of Sir Winston Churchill (here, from 1936 to 1940). Based on Churchill's World War II memories and broadcast on the "Hallmark Hall of Fame." *Cast:* Richard Burton (Winston Churchill), Virginia McKenna (Clemmie Churchill), Ian Bannen (Adolf Hitler), Robert Hardy (Von Ribbentrop), Robin Bailey (Chamberlain), Ian Ogilvy (Edward VIII), Clive Francis (Randolph Churchill). *Producer:* Duane C. Bogie. *Writer:* Colin Morris. *Director:* Herbert Wise.

**765 Gaucho.** Drama, 60 min., ABC, 10/25/78. The story of a youth (Gaucho) who unwittingly becomes involved with the underworld when he takes a job as an errand boy to earn money to fulfill his mother's dream of leaving New York's Barrio and returning to Puerto Rico. Aired as an "ABC Afterschool Special." *Cast:* Panchito Gomez (Gaucho), Alma Beltran (Mama Campos), Philip R. Allen (Jim Raddigan), Ralph James Torres (Pacheko), Amy Stryker (Denise). *Music:* Glenn Paxton. *Producer:* Martin Tahse. *Writer:* Arthur Heinemann. *Director:* Robert Liberman.

**766 Gene Kelly Specials.** A chronological listing of variety specials hosted by singer-dancer-actor Gene Kelly. All are 60 minutes in length.

**1 The Gene Kelly Pontiac Special** (CBS, 4/24/59). *Guests:* Claude Bussy, Cherylene Lee, Liza Minnelli, Carl Sandburg. *Music:* Nelson Riddle. *Producer:* Joseph Cates, Saul Chaplin. *Director:* Joseph Cates.

**2 The Gene Kelly Show** (NBC, 11/21/59). *Guests:* Carol Lawrence, Donald O'Connor. *Music:* Jeff Alexander. *Producer:* Robert Wells. *Writers:* Robert Wells, Sidney Miller. *Director:* Sidney Miller.

**3 Gene Kelly, New York, New York** (CBS, 2/14/66). *Guests:* Woody Allen, Gower Champion, Damita Jo Freeman, Tommy Steele. *Producer:* Robert Wells. *Writers:* Johnny Bradford, Woody Allen. *Director:* Charles S. Dubin.

**4 Gene Kelly's Wonderful World of**

Girls (NBC, 1/14/70). *Guests:* The American Follies Bergere Girls, Ruth Buzzi, Diane Davis, Barbara Eden, Barbara Fuller, Chanin Hale, Cynthia Lindsay, Kay Medford. *Producer:* Greg Garrison. *Writers:* Stan Daniels, Ray Jessel, Norm Liebman. *Director:* Danny Daniels.

**5 Gene Kelly ... An American in Pasadena** (CBS, 3/13/78). *Guests:* Lucille Ball, Cyd Charisse, Gloria DeHaven, Betty Garrett, Kathryn Grayson, Janet Leigh, Liza Minnelli, Frank Sinatra, Cindy Williams. *Music:* Jack Elliott. *Producers:* Marty Pasetta, Frank Konigsberg. *Writer:* Buz Kohan. *Director:* Marty Pasetta.

**767 General Electric's All-Star Anniversary.** Variety, 2 hrs., ABC, 9/29/78. The program recalls the music, song, and comedy of the past 100 years. *Host:* John Wayne. *Guests:* Lucille Ball, Albert Brooks, Henry Fonda, Pat Hingle, Bob Hope, Cheryl Ladd, Michael Landon, Penny Marshall, Donny and Marie Osmond, Charley Pride, John Ritter, Red Skelton, Suzanne Somers, Jimmy Stewart, Elizabeth Taylor, Leslie Uggams, Jimmie Walker, James Whitmore, Cindy Williams, Henry Winkler. *Music:* Nelson Riddle. *Producers:* Paul W. Keyes, Bob Howard. *Writers:* Paul W. Keyes, Bob Howard, Jeffrey Barron, Monty Aidem. *Director:* Dick McDonough.

**768 The General Foods 25th Anniversary Show.** Variety, 60 min., CBS, 3/28/54. The program salutes the General Foods Corporation on its twenty-fifth anniversary, with memorable highlights from Broadway shows. *Guests:* Jack Benny, Edgar Bergen, Yul Brynner, Jan Clayton, Rosemary Clooney, Florence Henderson, Gordon MacRae, Mary Martin, Tony Martin, Groucho Marx, Patricia Morison, Ezio Pinza, John Raitt, Ed Sullivan. *Music Director:* Harry Sosnik. *Music Arranger:* Nathan Scott. *Producer-Director:* Ralph Levy. *Writers:*

Goodman Ace, Nat Hiken, Sam Perrin, George Balzer, Bernie Smith, Robert Dwan.

**769 The General Motors 50th Anniversary Show.** Variety, 2 hrs., NBC, 11/17/57. Music, songs, dances, and comedy geared to the pursuit of happiness as the General Motors Corporation celebrates its fiftieth year. *Host-Narrator:* Kirk Douglas. *Guests:* June Allyson, Pat Boone, Ernest Borgnine, Eddie Bracken, Carol Burnett, Claudette Colbert, Hans Conried, Dan Dailey, Helen Hayes, Howard Keel, Steve Lawrence, Bambi Linn, Peg Lynch, Dean Martin, Cyril Ritchard, Chita Rivera, Dinah Shore, Kent Smith. *Music:* Bernard Green. *Producer:* Jess Oppenheimer. *Writer:* Helen Deutsch. *Director:* Charles S. Dubin.

**770 George Burns Specials.** A chronological listing of the variety specials hosted by comedian George Burns. George Burns hosted each show, except where noted otherwise.

**1 George Burns in the Big Time** (60 min., NBC, 11/17/59). A music and comedy salute to vaudeville. *Guests:* Jack Benny, Eddie Cantor, Bobby Darin, George Jessel, The Kingston Trio. *Music:* Jeff Alexander. *Producer:* Hubbell Robinson. *Writer:* Max Benoff. *Director:* Dick Darley.

**2 The George Burns Special** (60 min., CBS, 12/1/76). *Guests:* Johnny Carson, Madeline Kahn, Walter Matthau, The Osmonds, Chita Rivera. *Music:* Jack Elliott, Allyn Ferguson. *Producer:* Irving Fein. *Writers:* Fred S. Fox, Seaman Jacobs, Elon Packard. *Director:* Bill Hobin.

**3 The George Burns One-Man Show** (60 min., CBS, 11/23/77). *Guests:* Ann-Margret, The Captain and Tennille, Bob Hope, Gladys Knight and the Pips. *Music:* Jack Elliott, Allyn Ferguson. *Producer:* Irving Fein. *Writers:* Elon Packard, Fred S. Fox, Seaman Jacobs. *Director:* Stan Harris.

**4 George Burns in Nashville??** (60 min., NBC, 4/13/81). *Guests:* Roy Acuff, Larry Gatlin, Loretta Lynn, Minnie Pearl, Ben Smathers, The Stoney Mountain Cloggers. *Music:* Bill Walker. *Producer:* Irving Fein. *Writers:* Fred S. Fox, Seaman Jacobs, Hal Goldman. *Director:* Walter C. Miller.

**5 George Burns Early, Early, Early Christmas Show** (60 min., NBC, 11/16/81). *Guests:* Ann-Margret, Hans Conried, The Hawkins Family, Bob Hope, The Playboy Playmates. *Music:* Jack Elliott. *Producer:* Irving Fein. *Writers:* Fred S. Fox, Seaman Jacobs, Hal Goldman. *Director:* Walter C. Miller.

**6 George Burns' 100th Birthday Party** (60 min., NBC, 5/4/82). Actually a music and comedy celebration of George's eighty-third birthday. *Guests:* Milton Berle, Debby Boone, Johnny Carson, Andy Gibb, Goldie Hawn, Bob Hope, George Jessel, Gregory Peck, Helen Reddy, Don Rickles, Jimmy Stewart. *Music:* Jack Elliott, Allyn Ferguson. *Producer:* Irving Fein. *Writers:* Fred S. Fox, Seaman Jacobs, Hal Goldman. *Director:* Stan Harris.

**7 George Burns and Other Sex Symbols** (60 min., NBC, 11/8/82). *Guests:* Linda Evans, Bernadette Peters, John Schneider. *Music:* Peter Matz. *Producer:* Irving Fein. *Writers:* Fred S. Fox, Seaman Jacobs, Hal Goldman. *Director:* Walter C. Miller.

**8 George Burns Celebrates 80 Years in Show Business** (90 min., NBC, 9/19/83). *Host:* John Forsythe. *Guest of Honor:* George Burns. *Guests:* Ann-Margret, Milton Berle, Red Buttons, Johnny Carson, Jack Carter, Carol Channing, Phyllis Diller, Larry Gatlin, Billy Graham, Shecky Greene, Buddy Hackett, Bob Hope, Bernadette Peters, Don Rickles, Jimmy Stewart, Danny Thomas, Fred Travalena, Dionne Warwick. *Music:* Peter Matz. *Producer:* Irving Fein. *Writers:* Seaman Jacobs, Fred S. Fox, Hal Goldman. *Director:* Walter C. Miller.

**9 George Burns: An Hour of Jokes and Songs** (60 min., HBO, 1/22/84).

*Music:* Ian Bernard. *Producer:* Riff Markowitz. *Writer:* George Burns. *Director:* Jerome Shaw.

**10 George Burns' How to Live to Be 100** (60 min., NBC, 9/17/84). *Guests:* Catherine Bach, Diahann Carroll, Bob Hope, Arte Johnson. *Music:* Peter Matz. *Producer:* Irving Fein. *Writers:* Fred S. Fox, Seaman Jacobs, Hal Goldman, Harvey Berger. *Director:* Walter C. Miller.

**11 George Burns' 90th Birthday Party — A Very Special Special** (60 min., CBS, 1/17/86). *Host:* John Forsythe. *Guest of Honor:* George Burns. *Guests:* Steve Allen, Ann-Margret, Milton Berle, Red Buttons, Diahann Carroll, Carol Channing, Chevy Chase, Bill Cosby, Billy Crystal, John Denver, Bob Hope, President Ronald Reagan, Don Rickles, Joan Rivers, Kenny Rogers, Jimmy Stewart, Danny Thomas. *Music:* Peter Matz. *Producers:* Irving Fein, Walter C. Miller. *Writer:* Hal Goldman. *Director:* Walter C. Miller.

**12 George Burns' 95th Birthday Party** (60 min., CBS, 2/1/91). *Guests:* Steve Allen, Ann-Margret, Milton Berle, Red Buttons, Richard Lewis, Melissa Manchester, Carl Reiner, Kenny Rogers, Bob Saget, Ben Vereen. *Music:* Peter Matz. *Producers:* Irving Fein, Walter C. Miller. *Writers:* Hal Goldman, Jeffrey Barron. *Director:* Walter C. Miller.

**771 George Carlin at Carnegie Hall.** Comedy, 60 min., HBO, 1/8/83. Comedian George Carlin's adult-oriented show at Carnegie Hall. *Host:* George Carlin. *Producers:* Gerald Hemanza, Brenda Carlin. *Writer:* George Carlin. *Director:* Steven J. Santos.

**772 The George Jones Special.** Variety, 75 min., HBO, 3/9/83. A country and western program of music, songs, and dances. *Host:* George Jones. *Guests:* Jessi Colter, Emmylou Harris, Tanya Tucker. *Music:* Bill

Walker. *Producers:* Rick Howard, Jim Halsey. *Director:* Marty Callner.

**773 The George Kirby Special.** Comedy, 60 min., ABC, 12/18/70. An hour of music, songs, and comedy sketches. *Host:* George Kirby. *Guests:* Joe Higgins, Lainie Kazan, The Lighthouse, The Mills Brothers, The Poppy Family. *Music:* Ralph Carmichael. *Producer:* Jackie Barnett. *Director:* Kip Walton.

**774 George M!** Variety, 90 min., NBC, 9/12/70. A television adaptation of the Broadway musical about the life and songs of George M. Cohan, Broadway's "Yankee Doodle Dandy." While adapted from the stage show, the program is actually a rehearsal for *George M!* with the actors appearing as themselves as well as the characters they play. *Cast:* Joel Grey (George M. Cohan), Bernadette Peters (Josie Cohan), Red Buttons (Sam Harris), Jack Cassidy (Jerry Cohan), Nanette Fabray (Nellie Cohan), Blythe Danner (Agnes), Anita Gillette (Ethel). *Music:* Elliot Lawrence. *Producers:* Joseph Cates, Martin Charnin. *Writer:* Martin Charnin. *Directors:* Walter C. Miller, Martin Charnin.

**775 George Schlatter's Comedy Club Special.** Comedy, 2 hrs., ABC, 9/29/88. The program spotlights stand-up comics from around the country. *Host:* Dudley Moore. *Comics:* Richard Belzer, Tim Cavanaugh, Blake Clark, Barry Crimmins, Will Dust, Todd Glass, Gilbert Gottfried, Fred Greenlee, Tom Kinney, Ben Kurkland, Carol Leifler, Laura Lyness, Norm McDonald, Jackie Mason, Emo Philips, Peter Pitofsky, Larry Reed, Daniel Rosen, Jim Samuels, Margaret Smith, Pam Stone, Judy Tenuta, Jimmy Tingle, Lily Tomlin, Dennis Wolfberg, Bob Zany. *Music:* Thomas Chase, Steve Rucker. *Producers:* George Schlatter, Maria Schlatter. *Director:* Don Hoyer.

**776 The George Segal Show.** Comedy, 90 min., NBC, 10/26/74. A series of comedy sketches that spoof everyday life. *Host:* George Segal. *Guests:* Teresa Brewer, Buck Henry, David Steinberg, Maxine Weldon. *Producers:* Alan D. Courtney, Herb Sargent. *Writer:* Herb Sargent. *Director:* John Moffitt.

**777 The Gershwin Years.** Variety, 90 min., CBS, 1/15/61. A musical salute to composer George Gershwin. *Host:* Richard Rodgers. *Guests:* Maurice Chevalier, Pat Harrington, Jr., Florence Henderson, Ron Husmann, Julie London, Ethel Merman, Frank Sinatra. *Music:* Joe Layton. *Producers:* Leland Hayward, Marshall Jamison. *Writer:* A. J. Russell. *Director:* Norman Campbell.

**778 Get High on Yourself.** Variety, 60 min., NBC, 9/20/81. A public service special that seeks to generate feelings of self-respect among viewers (as explained by Cathy Lee Crosby: "We want to show that you can get high just by being yourself"). *Stars:* Muhammad Ali, Scott Baio, Carol Burnett, Burt Convy, Cathy Lee Crosby, John Davidson, Julius Erving, Leif Garrett, Andy Gibb, Linda Gray, Rosey Grier, Dorothy Hamill, Mark Hamill, Gregory Harrison, Robert Hays, Bob Hope, Darrow Igus, Kate Jackson, Bruce Jenner, Magic Johnson, Cheryl Ladd, Kelly Lange, Johnny Lee, Kristy McNichol, Paul Newman, Stefanie Powers, Joan Prather, Victoria Principal, Burt Reynolds, John Schneider, Cheryl Tiegs, John Travolta, Robert Wagner, Henry Winkler, Natalie Wood. *Music Guests:* Andre Crouch, Al Jarreau, Ted Nugent, Peaches and Herb, Sylvia. *Producers:* Cathy Lee Crosby, David Tate. *Director:* Ann Lee Lacy.

**779 Getting Even: A Wimp's Revenge.** Comedy-Drama, 60 min., ABC, 3/19/86. Jeffrey Childs is the wimp of the title, the constant target of a bully named Dewey Belasco. The only time Jeffrey is fearless is when he is a character in the cartoon he draws, "The Revenge of the Incredible Dr. Rancid and His Youthful Assistant, Jeffrey." One day, when Jeffrey finds his two friends, Bix and Candy, standing up for him, he realizes that, like in his drawings, he must face up to the real Dewey. The story relates Jeffrey's attempts to face his worst fear. Aired as an "ABC Afterschool Special." *Cast:* Jon Rothstein (Jeffrey Childs), Eddie Castrodad (Dewey Belasco), Tisha Ford (Candy Richardson), Pia Scala (Lana), Joey Grasso (Bix), Alexander Burgos (Danny), Adolph Caesar (Dr. Rancid), Marisa Berenson (Liz Childs), Michael Storm (Spencer Childs). *Producer:* Jane Startz. *Writers:* David Hoffman, Leslie Daryl Zerg. *Director:* James Scott.

**780 Getting the Last Laugh.** Comedy, 60 min., ABC, 2/26/85. The program offers humorous tips on how to get revenge on the things that annoy us in everyday life (for example, traffic jams, long lines, inefficient workers). *Hosts:* Sandahl Bergman, Kerry Millerick, Fred Willard. *Guests:* Rona Barrett, Barbara Billingsley, Arthur Hill, Shirley Jones, Jerry Mathers, Ray Parker, Jr., Danny Thomas. *Music:* Stacy Widelitz, Wendy Fraser. *Producers:* Alan Landsburg, Woody Fraser. *Writers:* Shelley Ross, Fred Willard. *Director:* Bob Fraser.

**781 The Ghost of Thomas Kempe.** Comedy, 30 min., ABC, 11/3 and 11/10/79. After moving into a charming Victorian home, 12-year-old James Harrison discovers that he has an unseen roommate—the ghost of Thomas Kempe, a seventeenth-century sorcerer. The story relates the ghost's efforts to get a reluctant James to become his apprentice—and James's efforts to lure the ghost back to its resting place. Aired as an "ABC Weekend

Special." *Cast:* Shane Sinutko (James Harrison), Madelyn Cain (Mrs. Harrison), Tara Talboy (Helen Harrison), Bob Sampson (Mr. Harrison), Garrett O'Connor (Bert Ellison), Henry Sutton (Father Hanover). *Producers:* Robert Chenault, Tom Armistead. *Writers:* Glen Olson, Rod Baker. *Director:* Robert Chenault.

**782 Giant in a Hurry.** Documentary, 60 min., CBS, 7/21/49. A look at the growth of television from 1931 to 1949. *Host:* Abe Burrows. *Music:* Milton DeLugg. *Producer-Director:* Paul Nickell, John Peyser. *Writer:* Stanley Silverman.

**783 Gideon.** Drama, 90 min., NBC, 3/26/71. A seriocomic version of the Old Testament tale of Gideon, the Hebrew who was chosen by the Angel of the Lord to perform one of God's miracles. The story, based on Paddy Chayefsky's 1961 Broadway play, relates Gideon's efforts to save his people from idolatry by winning an impossible battle against the Midianites. Broadcast on the "Hallmark Hall of Fame." *Cast:* Peter Ustinov (Gideon), Arnold Moss (Joash), Little Egypt (Oprah), Eric Christmas (Shillem), Booth Colman (Hezekiah), Harry Davis (Abimerech). *Producer-Director:* George Schaefer. *Writer:* Robert Hartung.

**784 The Gift of Amazing Grace.** Drama, 60 min., ABC, 11/19/86. The Williams family have a long tradition as gospel singers, but Grace, the young daughter of the family, is painfully aware that her singing voice is awful and so she just mouths the words during church services. When the family appear on a televised talent show and are awarded a recording contract, Grace faces a dilemma: hurting the family by quitting or staying and continuing to be upset because of her inability to sing well. The story focuses on how the family's mutual love allowed Grace's amazing gift of talent to shine through and help the family achieve its goal. An "ABC Afterschool Special." *Cast:* Tempestt Bledsoe (Grace), Della Reese (Aunt Faith), Sam Wright (Morris), Juanita Fleming (Paulette), Jennifer Leigh Warren (Charlotte), Kasi Lemmons (Subaya), Vernel Bagneris (Joe Witherspoon). *Music:* Harold Wheeler. *Producers:* Fred Berner, Thomas Schlamme. *Writer:* Jerry Blatt. *Director:* Thomas Schlamme.

**785 Gift of the Magi.** Musical, 60 min., CBS, 12/9/58. A musical adaptation of the O. Henry story about a poor, newlywed couple (Jim and Della) who sell their cherished possessions (Della her hair; Jim his watch) in an attempt to give the other a Christmas gift (combs for her hair; a bob for his watch). *Cast:* Gordon MacRae (Jim), Sally Ann Howes (Della), Howard St. John (Mr. Spiegel), Bibi Osterwald (Madame Safronie), Sally Gracie (Ethel), Tammy Grimes (Hazel), Mildred Trases (Clara). *Music Director:* Hal Hastings. *Orchestrations:* Don Walker. *Music and Lyrics:* Richard Adler. *Producers:* Albert Selden, George Schaefer. *Writer:* Wilson Lehr. *Director:* George Schaefer.

**786 The Ginger Rogers Show.** Variety, 60 min., CBS, 10/15/58. A lively hour of music, song, dance, and light comedy. *Host:* Ginger Rogers. *Guests:* The Ritz Brothers. *Music:* Nelson Riddle. *Producers:* Bob Banner, Joe Hamilton. *Writer:* Joe Stein. *Director:* Bob Banner.

**787 Girl Friends and Nabors.** Variety, 60 min., CBS, 10/24/68. Music, songs, and comedy sketches with Jim Nabors and four special female guests. *Host:* Jim Nabors. *Guests:* Carol Burnett, Vikki Carr, Mary Costa, Debbie Reynolds. *Music:* Joe Guerico. *Producer:* Richard O. Linke. *Writers:* Martin A. Ragaway, Bernard Rothman. *Director:* Jack Donohue.

**788 The Girl Who Couldn't Lose.** Drama, 90 min., ABC, 2/13/75. When Jane Darwin, a painfully plain 26-year-old single who is a chronic dreamer becomes a contestant on the game show "Lucky 13," she puts her knowledge of many subjects (being a librarian) to use and begins winning, in addition to prizes, the attention of her opponent (Mark Linden). The story relates Jane's dilemma: should she deliberately lose the championship to keep Mark or win the contest and possibly lose him. *Cast:* Julie Kavner (Jane Darwin), Jack Carter (Jackie Leroy), Frank Stell (Mark Linden), Fritzi Burr (Florence Darwin), Milton Selzer (Charlie Darwin), Beverly Sanders (Susan Miller), Candace Azzara (Rosalie), Dennis Dugan (Andy Martin), Oliver Clark (Judd Moore). *Music:* Al Kasha, Joel Hirschhorn. *Producers:* Ira Marmek, Lila Garrett. *Writers:* Lila Garrett, Sanford Krinski. *Director:* Mort Lachman.

**789 The Girl with ESP.** Comedy, 30 min., ABC, 10/27/79. Laura Hoffman is the middle child of an inventor father and writer mother. Her older sister, Jill, has dancing talents and her young brother, Dennis, is a genius at math. Laura feels average and unnoticed until one day she envisions the disappearance of Dennis and realizes she has ESP. Laura's visions enable the family to find Dennis and Laura learns an important lesson: she is loved for herself, not because she has ESP. Aired as an "ABC Weekend Special." *Cast:* Rachel Longaker (Laura Hoffman), Tracy Bregman (Jill Hoffman), Adam Starr (Dennis Hoffman), Barbara Sharma (Mrs. Hoffman), Michael Griswold (Mr. Hoffman). *Producer:* Robert Chenault. *Writers:* Cindy Leonetti, Ann Elder. *Director:* Gerald Mayer.

**790 The Girl with the Crazy Brother.** Drama, 60 min., CBS, 1/30/90. A "CBS Schoolbreak Special" about

Dana McCallister, a high school transfer student who struggles to fit into her new surroundings, despite the increasingly bizarre behavior of her schizophrenic brother, Bill. *Cast:* Patricia Arquette (Dana McCallister), William Jayne (Bill McCallister), Shelby Leverington (Mrs. McCallister), Stan Ivar (Mr. McCallister), Dulcie Hunt (Sheila), Jordan Brady (Ian Quinn), Jennifer Nash (Joanie), Lisa Ann Cabasa (Chelsea). *Music:* Charles Judge. *Producer:* William Greenblat. *Writer:* Barry Dantscher. *Director:* Diane Keaton.

**791 Girlfriend.** Drama, 60 min., ABC, 4/15/93. After Trevor Tate, a Fillmore High School student is killed by a stray bullet, a teacher (Jo Delancey), assigns her class a project to work on a commemorative mural. She teams two girls—one black (La Christa) and one white (Lynda) as partners on the project. The girls become friends, despite ridicule from La Christa's friends, who do not approve of her "white girlfriend." The story relates how La Christa and Lynda's friendship bonds when they find a common ground in their power of art, and in their friendship. Aired as an "ABC Afterschool Special." *Cast:* Samaria Graham (La Christa), Rinnan Henderson (Lynda), Larry Gilyard, Jr. (Trevor Tate), Kia Joy Goodwin (Jo Delancey), Karina Arroyave (Lourdes), Joseph D'Onofrio (Anthony), Torrance Harvey (Jay), Liana Pai (Kim). *Music:* Anton Sanko. *Producer:* Kate Forte. *Writer:* Casey Kurtti. *Director:* Lloyd Kramer.

**792 The Gisele MacKenzie Show.** Variety, 60 min., Syndicated, 10/60. A lively hour of music and songs with singer Gisele MacKenzie. *Host:* Gisele MacKenzie. *Guests:* Jack Kane and His Music Makers, Snooky Lanson, Jack Regas. *Music:* Jack Kane. *Producer-Director:* Stan Harris. *Writers:* Frank Peppiatt, John Aylesworth, Stan Harris.

**793 Give My Regards to Broadway.** Variety, 60 min., NBC, 12/6/59. A musical salute to Broadway. *Host:* Jimmy Durante. *Guests:* Ray Bolger, Eddie Hodges, Jane Powell, Jimmie Rodgers. *Music:* Axel Stordahl. *Producer:* Charles Isaacs. *Writers:* Charles Isaacs, Fred S. Fox, Irving Elison, Benedict Freeman, Danny Simon. *Director:* Dick McDonough.

**794 Give Us Barabbas!** Drama, 90 min., NBC, 3/24/61. A "Hallmark Hall of Fame" period drama that explores the reason for Pontius Pilate's decision to free the thief, Barabbas, and crucify Jesus Christ. The story also explores the evolution of Barabbas from criminal to man of awakening conscience. *Cast:* James Daly (Barabbas), Kim Hunter (Mara), Dennis King (Pontius Pilate), Robinson Stone (Phineas), Leonardo Cimino (Caleb), Toni Darnay (Mary), Keir Dullea (Elisha), Ludwig Donath (Joseph). *Producer-Director:* George Schaefer. *Writer:* Henry Denker.

**795 Gladys Knight and the Pips: Midnight Train to Georgia.** Variety, 60 min., NBC, 6/21/74. A concert by Gladys Knight and the Pips. *Host:* Gladys Knight. *Guests:* Tom T. Hall, Lou Hudson, Elizabeth Knight. *Producers:* Burt Sugarman, Stan Harris. *Director:* Stan Harris.

**796 Gladys Knight and the Pips with Ray Charles.** Variety, 60 min., Syndicated, 8/87. Gladys Knight and the Pips join Ray Charles for a concert at the Greek Theater in Los Angeles. *Producers:* Michael J. Fuchs, Neal Marshall, Susan Solomon, Marty Callner. *Director:* Marty Callner.

**797 The Glass Menagerie.** Drama, 2 hrs., CBS, 12/8/66. A television adaptation of the Tennessee Williams play about the Wingfields, a poor family living in a St. Louis tenement: Amanda, the mother, a once glamorous Southern belle who dwells on her past; Tom, her restless son, who works in a warehouse; and Laura, her crippled, lonely daughter who lives in a dream world of the small glass animals she collects. The focal point is Tom's efforts, goaded by his mother, to find a gentleman caller for Laura. *Cast:* Shirley Booth (Amanda Wingfield), Hal Holbrook (Tom Wingfield), Barbara Loden (Laura Wingfield), Pat Hingle (Jim O'Connor). *Producers:* David Susskind, Jacqueline Babbin. *Writers:* Paul Boules, Tennessee Williams. *Director:* Michael Elliott.

## 798 Glen Campbell and Friends: The Silver Anniversary. Variety, 60 min., HBO, 7/16/84.
A concert by Glen Campbell on the anniversary of his twenty-five years in showbusiness. Taped in Toronto, Canada. *Host:* Glen Campbell. *Guests:* Johnny Cash, Kris Kristofferson, Anne Murray, Willie Nelson, Kenny Rogers. *Backup Vocalists:* Deborah Grieman, Bruce Murray. *Producer:* Anthony Eaton. *Directors:* Bill Davis, Bruce Gowers.

## 799 Glen Campbell . . . Down Home — Down Under.
Variety, 60 min., CBS, 5/20/76. An hour of music and songs taped in Australia. *Host:* Glen Campbell. *Guest:* Olivia Newton-John. *Music:* Dennis McCarthy. *Producers:* Gary Smith, Dwight Hemion. *Writers:* Buz Kohan, Ray Taylor. *Director:* Dwight Hemion.

## 800 The Glen Campbell Special: The Musical West. Variety,
60 min., NBC, 3/8/74. A musical tour of the American West. *Host:* Glen Campbell. *Guests:* Burl Ives, Michele Lee, John Wayne. *Music:* Jack Parnell. *Producers:* Gary Smith, Dwight Hemion. *Director:* Dwight Hemion.

## 801 Glenn Ford's Summertime, U.S.A. Variety, 60 min., Syndicated, 9/73. A music and comedy salute to the summer of 1973. *Host:* Glenn Ford. *Guests:* Pancho Gonzales, Micki King, Don Knotts, Dianne Lennon, Janet Lennon, Kathy Lennon, Peggy Lennon, Jim McKay, Ken Roberts, Bill Toomey.

## 802 The Glory of Easter.
Documentary, 30 min., Syndicated, 3/25/89. A history of Easter, a tradition that began hundreds of years before the birth of Christ — as a pagan tradition to celebrate spring. *Host:* Princess Lynn Von Furstenberg. *Producers:* Salvatore Rondenilli, Diane Brandis. *Director:* Marco Fragale.

## 803 Go! Variety, 60 min., ABC,
4/23/67. An hour of music and song featuring top-name personalities. *Host:* Ryan O'Neal. *Guests:* Eddie "Rochester" Anderson, The David Winters Dancers, Donna Douglas, Noel Harrison, Herman's Hermits, Brian Hyland, Peter Noone, John Cameron Swayze, Rudy Vallee, Abigail Van Buren. *Producers:* Bernie Orenstein, Saul Turteltaub. *Writers:* Bernie Orenstein, Saul Turteltaub, Al Burton. *Director:* Bob Henry.

## 804 God, the Universe and Hot Fudge Sundaes. Drama, 60
min., CBS, 4/1/86. A tender drama about faith. The story follows Alfie Newton, a teenage girl, as she attempts to understand why God chose to make her sister, Francie, terminally ill and bound to a wheelchair. Aired as a "CBS Schoolbreak Special." *Cast:* Roxana Zal (Alfie Newton), Melanie Gaffin (Francie Newton), Millie Perkins (Virginia Newton), Jim Haynie (Alfred Newton), Amy Resnick (Tyler), Beau Dremann (Kurt Rosen), Jere Burns (Brother Vinnie). *Music:* James Di Pasquale. *Producer-Writer:* Cynthia Cherbak. *Producer-Director:* Leslie Hill.

**805 Going Platinum.** Variety, 60 min., Showtime, 5/2/80 to 11/12/80. A series of six specials that feature solo performances by recording stars whose records sales have gone platinum. Producers for the specials were Jackie Barnett and Neil Marshall. Director was Phil Squyres.

**1 Going Platinum with the Beach Boys** (5/2/80).

**2 Going Platinum with Smokey Robinson** (5/15/80).

**3 Going Platinum with Journey** (8/8/80).

**4 Going Platinum with Stephen Sills** (9/6/80).

**5 Going Platinum with Charlie Daniels** (10/11/80).

**6 Going Platinum with Charley Pride** (11/12/80).

**806 The Golden Boys of Bandstand.** Variety, 60 min., Syndicated, 6/86. A nostalgic concert by Fabian, Frankie Avalon, and Bobby Rydell, three teen idols of the 1950s and 1960s and frequent performers on television's "American Bandstand." *Host:* Beverly Sills. *Performers:* Frankie Avalon, Fabian Forte, Bobby Rydell. *Producers:* Michael Styer, Dick Fox, Phillip Byrd. *Director:* Clark Santee.

**807 The Golden Child.** Opera, 90 min., NBC, 12/16/60. The story, set in a California gold-mining camp on Christmas Eve in 1849, relates the incident of a Mexican who claims to have found gold nuggets as big as a man's fist. The problems that ensue as greed rears its ugly head are the focal point of this "Hallmark Hall of Fame" presentation. *Cast:* Patricia Neway (Martha), Brenda Lewis (Sara), Jerome Hines (Captain Sutter), Stephen Douglass (Martin), Judy Sanford (Rachel), Enrico Di Giuseppe (Miguel), David Lloyd (Ed), Patricia Brooks (Annabelle). *Music:* Philip Bezawson. *Music Director:* Peter Herman Adler. *Music Conductor:* Herbert Grossman. *Li-*

*bretto:* Paul Engle. *Producer:* George Schaefer. *Writer-Director:* Robert Hartung.

**808 Goldie and Liza Together.** Variety, 60 min., CBS, 2/19/80. A musical variety showcase for Goldie Hawn and Liza Minnelli, who sing, dance, and act. *Hosts:* Goldie Hawn, Liza Minnelli. *Music:* Johnny Harris. *Producers:* George Schlatter, Don Mischer, Fred Ebb. *Writer:* Fred Ebb. *Director:* Don Mischer.

**809 Goldie and the Kids: Listen to Me.** Variety, 60 min., ABC, 5/8/82. An unusual variety special that features actress Goldie Hawn in song and conversation rapping with twelve children on various aspects of life. *Host:* Goldie Hawn. *Guest:* Barry Manilow. *Children:* Allison Balson, Betsy Chasse, LaShana Dendy, Danielle Freas, Heather Haase, Jaffrey Jacquet, Nicky Katt, Eric Krakoff, Chez Lester, Pamela Segall, Eric Taslitz, Jane Tushman. *Music:* Ian Fraser. *Producers:* Goldie Hawn, Gary Smith, Dwight Hemion. *Writer:* Buz Kohan. *Director:* Dwight Hemion.

**810 The Goldie Hawn Special.** Variety, 60 min., CBS, 3/1/78. A lively hour of music, songs, and comedy. *Host:* Goldie Hawn. *Guests:* George Burns, Shaun Cassidy, John Ritter. *Music:* Jack Elliott. *Producer:* George Schlatter. *Writer:* Digby Wolfe. *Director:* Don Mischer.

**811 Good Evening, Captain.** Variety, 60 min., CBS, 8/21/81. A primetime special celebrating the twenty-fifth anniversary of the "Captain Kangaroo" television series. *Host:* Bob Keeshan ("Captain Kangaroo"). *Guests:* Cosmo F. Allegretti, Lumpy Brannum, Todd Bridges, Ja'net DuBois, Mike Farrell, Kim Fields, Ted Lange, Barbara Mandrell, LaWanda Page, Jean Stapleton. *Music:* George

Wyle. *Producers:* Bob Keeshan, Bob Henry. *Writers:* Buz Kohan, Rod Warren. *Director:* Bob Henry.

**812 The Good Fairy.** Comedy, 90 min., NBC, 2/5/56. A "Hallmark Hall of Fame" presentation about a movie theater usherette (Lu) who thinks of herself as a good fairy and her attempts to make the people she tends happy. *Cast:* Julie Harris (Lu), Walter Slezak (Max), Cyril Ritchard (Konrad), Roddy McDowall (Waiter), Florida Friebus (Karoline), Paul Lynde (Dr. Metz), Temple Texas (Blonde), Harry Ellerbee (Clerk). *Producer:* Maurice Evans. *Writer:* Jean Kerr. *Director:* George Schaefer.

**813 The Good Old Days of Radio.** Documentary, 60 min., PBS, 3/10/76. A nostalgic look at the golden age of radio through stills and audio recordings of its most famous shows and performers. *Host:* Steve Allen. *Announcer:* Bill Baldwin. *Music:* Les Brown. *Producer:* Loring d'Usseau. *Writers:* Hal Kanter, Don Bresnahan. *Director:* Marty Pasetta.

**814 Good Times.** Variety, 90 min., NBC, 1/2/55. A musical comedy revue featuring the Max Liebman–created team of Judy Holliday, Steve Allen, and Dick Shawn performing with guests in a series of music and comedy sketches. *Hosts:* Steve Allen, Judy Holliday, Dick Shawn. *Guests:* Rod Alexander, Bambi Linn, The Ritz Brothers. *Music:* Charles Sanford. *Producer-Director:* Max Liebman.

**815 Good Vibrations from Central Park.** Variety, 60 min., ABC, 8/19/71 and 8/23/73. Videotaped highlights of live concert performances in New York's Central Park. *Performers* (8/19/71): The Beach Boys, Boz Scaggs, Carly Simon, Kate Taylor, Ike Turner, Tina Turner. *Performers* (8/23/73): The Eagles, Melissa Manchester, John Sebastian, Sly and the

Family Stone, The Temptations. *Producers:* John Moffitt, Ron Delsener. *Director:* John Moffitt.

**816 The Gordon MacRae Show.** Variety, 60 min., Syndicated, 7/71. An hour of music and songs. *Host:* Gordon MacRae. *Guests:* Rich Little, Barbara McNair. *Music:* Norman Leyden.

**817 Gotta Sing, Gotta Dance.** Documentary, 60 min., HBO, 1/15/84. A review of the movie musicals—from their beginnings to the 1980s. *Narrator:* John Harlan. *Music:* Curt Roush. *Producer:* Ellen M. Krauss. *Director:* Thomas Royal.

**818 Grace Kelly: An American Princess.** Documentary, 60 min., PBS, 3/16/88. A moving special that traces the life of Grace Kelly (1929–82) from her childhood in Philadelphia, to her career as a Hollywood movie actress, to her reign as princess of Monaco. *Host-Narrator:* Richard Kiley. *Guests:* Rita Gam, Alec Guinness, Louis Jourdan, Stanley Kramer, James Stewart. *Music:* Dan Pinsky. *Producers:* Ron Dediliver, Gene Feldman, Suzette Winter. *Writers:* Gene Feldman, Suzette Winter. *Director:* Gene Feldman.

**819 Grammy Legends.** Tribute, 2 hrs., CBS, 12/11/90. The program honors artists in the music field. *Hosts:* Larry Gatlin, Oprah Winfrey, Stevie Wonder, James Woods. *Honored:* Johnny Cash, Aretha Franklin, Billy Joel, Quincy Jones. *Guests:* Tevin Campbell, John Carter, Rosanne Cash, June Carter Cash, Karen Clark, Andrae Crouch, Sandra Crouch, Rodney Crowell, Dion DiMucci, Siedah Garrett, Dizzy Gillespie, Lionel Hampton, Ice T and Quincy D, James Ingram, Glenn Jones, Big Daddy Kane, Eddie Kendricks, Cha Ka Khan, Ben E. King, Richard Marx, John Cougar Mellencamp, Smokey Robinson, David

**The Gordon MacRae Special.** *From left to right:* **Gordon MacRae, Barbara McNair, Rich Little.**

Ruffin, Frankie Valli and the Four Seasons, Dwight Yoakam, Joe Zawinul. *Producers:* Pierre Cossette, Ken Ehrlich, Walter C. Miller. *Writer:* Buz Kohan. *Director:* Walter C. Miller.

## 820 The Grammy Lifetime Achievement Awards. Tribute, 2 hrs., CBS, 12/9/87. The program honors six entertainers with the Grammy Lifetime Achievement Award. *Hosts:* Beverly Sills, Dionne Warwick. *Honored:* Roy Acuff, Benny Carter, Ray Charles, Fats Domino, B. B. King, Isaac Stern. *Guests:* Louis Bellson, Ed Bradley, Roy Clark, Joe Cocker, Natalie Cole, Charlie Daniels, Emmylou Harris, Hank Jones, Stanley Jordan, Cleo Laine, Carmen MacRae, Ronnie Milsap, Bill Monroe, James Moody, Minnie Pearl, Itzhak Perlman, David Sanborn, Paul Shaffer, Ricky Skaggs. *Music:* Elliot Lawrence. *Producer:*

Pierre Cossette, Tisha Fein, Ken Ehrlich. *Writers:* Ken Ehrlich, David Forman, Bill Ivey. *Director:* Walter C. Miller.

## 821 Grammy Living Legends. Tribute, 2 hrs., CBS, 11/24/89. A salute to Liza Minnelli, Willie Nelson, Smokey Robinson, and Andrew Lloyd Webber. *Guests:* Gene Autry, Michael Bolton, Sarah Brightman, Clarence Clemons, Harry Connick, Jr., Emmylou Harris, Heavy D and the Boyz, Kenny G and the New Kids on the Block, Kris Kristofferson, Angela Lansbury, Patti LuPone, Roger Miller, Buster Poindexter, Dwight Yoakam. *Music:* Jack Elliott. *Producers:* Pierre Cossette, Walter C. Miller, Ken Ehrlich. *Writers:* Steve Pond, David Forman. *Director:* Walter C. Miller.

## 822 The Grand Opening of Euro Disney. Variety, 2 hrs., CBS,

4/11/92. The ceremonies surrounding the opening of the Euro Disney Park in Paris, France. *Hosts:* Melanie Griffith, Don Johnson. *Reporter:* Pat O'Brien. *Guests:* Cher, Gloria Estefan, The Four Tops, The Gypsy Kings, Angela Lansbury, Olympic skaters Isabelle Duchesnay, Paul Duchesnay, Miami Sound Machine, The Temptations, Tina Turner. *Producers:* Don Mischer, David J. Goldberg. *Director:* Don Mischer.

## 823 Grandpa, Will You Run with Me?

Variety, 60 min., NBC, 4/3/83. The program explores how the very young and the very old appreciate and enjoy each other's company. Celebrities appear with children and offer personal reminiscences and variety performances that reflect the show's theme. *Host:* George Burns. *Guests:* Jack Albertson, Lloyd Bridges, Scatman Crothers, Quinn Cummings, Mac Davis, Erik Estrada, Andy Gibb, Dorothy Hamill, Nancy Marchand, Martin Mull, Kenny Rogers. *Music:* Vernon Ray Bunch. *Producer:* Ken Ehrlich. *Writer:* Rod Warren, Ken Ehrlich. *Director:* Tom Trbovich.

## 824 The Great American Laugh-Off.

Comedy, 90 min., NBC, 10/22/77. The program features performances by guest comics. *Host:* Nancy Bleiweiss. *Comics:* Ed Bluestone, Wayland Flowers and Madame, Jim Giovanni, The Graduates, Ben Powers, Bill Rafferty, Lenny Schultz, Michael Sklar, Toad the Mime, Robin Williams. *Producer:* George Schlatter. *Writers:* Donna Schuman, Judy Roche, Digby Wolfe. *Director:* Don Mischer.

## 825 The Great American Music Celebration.

Variety, 60 min., Syndicated, 6/76. A celebration of 200 years of American music and song. *Host:* Lorne Greene. *Producers:* George Paris, Buddy Bregman. *Writer:* John Bradford. *Director:* Buddy Bregman.

## 826 The Great American Music Video.

Drama, 30 min., Syndicated, 3/19/88. The story of a high school rock band (Passages) as they prepare to tape a music video — but lack harmony when it comes to selecting the type of music to play. The program is rather primitive considering it was made in 1988: closeups are uncentered and choppy; pans are off-center and hand-held camera shots are jumpy. The only saving grace the show has is star Allison Smith's ("Kate and Allie") vocal segments (even then, the camera work is very sloppy). *Cast:* Allison Smith (Martina), Danny John (Royal), David Collum (Digby), David Deblanger (Ruby). *Music:* Tom G. Robertson, Michael Haven. *Producer-Director:* Tom G. Robertson. *Writer:* D. W. Melay.

## 827 Great Catherine.

Drama, 60 min., NBC, 5/2/48. A romantic adventure revolving around a beautiful empress and an English sea captain. *Cast:* Gertrude Lawrence (Empress), David Wayne (Sea Captain), Joan McCracken (Varinka), George Matthews (Guard), Cathleen Cordell (Fiancee), Erik Rhodes (Count Chamberlain), Katherine Sergeva (Princess). *Producers:* Lawrence Langner, Theresa Helburn. *Writer:* George Bernard Shaw. *Director:* Fred Coe.

## 828 Great Circuses of the World.

Variety, 60 min., ABC, 2/26/89. Highlights of various circus acts from around the world. *Host:* Mary Hart. *Announcer:* Dick Tufeld. *Music:* Bob Gerardi. *Producer-Writer-Director:* Joe Cates.

## 829 The Great Gilly Hopkins.

Drama, 60 min., CBS, 1/9/81. The story of Gilly Hopkins, an unwanted foster child, as she searches for a home and love. Aired as a "CBS Afternoon Playhouse." *Cast:* Tricia Cast (Gilly Hopkins), Conchata Ferrell (Mamie Trotter), Edith Atwater (Mrs. Rutherford), Tyne

Daly (Catherine Ellis).
*Producer:* Joseph Bar-
bera. *Writer:* Charles
Pratt. *Director:* Jeff-
rey Hayden.

## 830 The Great
Heep. Cartoon, 60
min., ABC, 6/7/86.
While en route to their
new jobs on the peace-
ful mining planet
Biitu, "Star Wars"
droids R2-D2 and
C-3PO and merchant
explorer Mungo Bao-
bab are captured by
the Great Heep, a
mechanical behemoth
created by the Empire
to take control of
Biitu and turn it into a
wasteland. The story
relates the trio's
efforts to escape from
the Heep and save
Biitu from destruc-
tion. *Voices:* Anthony
Daniels (C-3PO),
Long John Baldry
(Great Heep), Win-
ston Reckert (Mungo Baobab),
Graeme Campbell (Admiral Screed),
Melleny Brown (Darva), Noam Xyl-
berman (Fidge). *Music:* Patricia Cullen. *Producers:* Miki Herman, Lenora
Hume. *Writer:* Ben Burtt. *Director:*
Clive A. Smith.

**Mary Hart**

## 831 The Great Impersona-
tion. Mystery, 60 min., NBC, 11/15/
60. A "Dow Hour of Great Mysteries"
presentation about a German plot to
substitute one of their own for a captured English scientist. *Cast:* Keith
Michell (Baron Von Ragastein/Domi-
ney), Eva Gabor (Stephanie), Jeanette
Sterke (Rosamund). *Producer:* Fred
Coe.

## 832 The Great Ladies of
Country. Variety, 80 min., Showtime, 3/6/80 and 3/1/81. Two specials
that spotlight the performances of
established country and western entertainers. *Host:* Tom T. Hall. *Guests*
(3/6/80): Janie Frickie, Barbara Mandrell, Dottie West. *Guests* (3/1/81):
Lynn Anderson, Lacey J. Dalton,
Donna Fargo. *Producers:* Michael
Clark, Roger Galloway. *Director:* Bay-
ron Binkley.

## 833 The Great Love Experi-
ment. Drama, 60 min., ABC, 2/8/84.
Maude Harris is a 16-year-old girl who
wears plain, shapeless dresses and her
hair in braids. She thinks of herself as
not being pretty and is in awe of the
popular students in her class. Larry
Meadows is the school's star quarterback and his girlfriend, Jen, is the head
cheerleader. When Larry shows Jen an

experiment he is conducting with mice on how love and affection shape behavior patterns, Jen convinces him — and two of the school's other most popular boys — to conduct the same experiment, but in secret, on Maude. Maude is shocked by all the attention she suddenly receives from the "in" group and seems to relish her new-found friends. The story focuses on the results of the experiment — when Maude finds out she was just being used, but also on the efforts of the four "experimenters" to convince her that, as a result of the experiment, she is now their friend, not the nobody she thought she was. Aired on the "ABC Afterschool Special." *Cast:* Tracy Pollan (Jen Robbins), Kelly Wolf (Maude Harris), Peter Kowanko (Dolph Krager), Scott Renderer (Larry Meadows), Esai Morales (Miguel Rados), Jenny Grey (Carol Durate). *Producer:* Doro Bachrach. *Writer:* Jeffrey Kindley. *Director:* Claudia Weill.

## 834 Great Movie Stunts: *Raiders of the Lost Ark.* Documentary, 60 min., CBS, 10/5/81. The program describes how the special effects were done for the film *Raiders of the Lost Ark. Host-Narrator:* Harrison Ford. *Producer-Writer:* William Kronick. *Director:* Robert Guenette.

## 835 The Great Sebastians.
Comedy-Drama, 90 min., NBC, 4/1/57. The story of a second-rate mind-reading act (The Great Sebastians) who become involved in political intrigue when they are invited by General Zandek to perform at a party for Communist officials in Prague. *Cast:* Lynn Fontanne (Essie Sebastian), Alfred Lunt (Rudi Sebastian), Akim Tamiroff (General Otakar Zandek), Anne Francine (Colonel Bradocova), Arny Freeman (Josef), Simon Oakland (Sergeant Javorsky), Lisa Ferrady (Vlastar Habova), Eugenia Rawls (Sophie Cerny).

## 836 The Great Stand-Ups: 60 Years of Laughter. Documentary, 60 min., HBO, 2/11/84. A nostalgic look at the stand-up comics — from vaudeville to radio to television. *Narrator:* Carl Reiner. *Producers:* Stuart Smiley, Robert Weide. *Writer:* Phil Berger. *Director:* Robert Weide.

## 837 Great Television Moments: What We Watched.
Documentary, 2 hrs., ABC, 2/6/93. A nostalgic look at the various types of programs that have aired on television over the past 40 years. *Hosts:* Candice Bergen, Richard Chamberlain, Louis Gossett, Jr., Marlo Thomas, Barbara Walters. *Producers:* Grant Tinker, Allan Burns, Michael Hirsh. *Writers:* Joel Lipman, Michael Hirsh. *Director:* Michael Hirsh.

## 838 The Great Waltz. Musical, 90 min., NBC, 11/5/55. A television adaptation of the Moss Hart operetta about the attempts of Johann Strauss, Jr., to overcome the machinations of his father, who is jealous of his son's ability to compose waltzes. *Cast:* Keith Andes (Johann Strauss, Jr.), Henry Sharp (Johann Strauss, Sr.), Patrice Munsel (Resi Ebsteder), Jarmila Novotna (Mme. Baranska), Bert Lahr (Hans Ebsteder), Lee Goodman (Ferdi), Mia Slavenska (Solo Ballerina), Sam Schwartz (Conductor). *Music:* Charles Sanford. *Producer-Director:* Max Liebman. *Writers:* William Friedberg, Neil Simon.

## 839 The Green Pastures.
Drama, 90 min., NBC, 10/17/57. The story, set in the deep South, relates incidents from the Bible (seen in a series of vignettes) as a Sunday School teacher preaches to her students. Based on Roark Bradford's book, "Ol' Man Adam An' His Chillun'," and broadcast on the "Hallmark Hall of Fame." *Cast:* William Warfield (De Laud), Eddie "Rochester" Anderson (Noah), Earle Hyman (Adam), Frederick O'Neal

(Moses), Terry Carter (Gabriel), Estelle Hemsley (Mrs. Deshee), Rosetta Le-Noire (Noah's wife), Sheila Guyse (Zaba). *Music:* Leonard DePaur. *Producer-Director:* George Schaefer.

**840 Gregory Peck: A Living Biography.** Documentary, 90 min., ABC, 3/31/77. The program traces the career of actor Gregory Peck. *Host-Narrator:* Peter Lawford. *Producers:* Andrew W. Solt, Ronald Lyon. *Writer:* Andrew W. Solt. *Director:* Ronald Lyon.

**841 The Grinch "Grinches" the Cat in the Hat.** Cartoon, 30 min., ABC, 5/20/82. A Dr. Seuss cartoon about the Cat in the Hat as he attempts to use psychology to make the foul-tempered Grinch nice. *Voices:* Mason Adams, Joe Eich, Bob Holt, Frank Welker. *Music:* Joe Raposo. *Producers:* David DePatie, Friz Freleng. *Writer:* Theodor Seuss Geisel. *Director:* Bill Perez.

**842 Grownups.** Drama, 1 hr. 45 min., Showtime, 11/25/85. The story focuses on the strained relationship of a middle-class New York family as seen through the eyes of Jake, a writer for the *New York Times*, who is caught up in a domestic cold war with other family members: his wife and daughter (Louise and Edie), Jack and Helen (his parents), and Marilyn, Jake's overbearing sister. *Cast:* Charles Grodin (Jake), Marilu Henner (Louise), Kerry Segal (Edie), Jean Stapleton (Helen), Martin Balsam (Jack), Paddy Campanaro (Marilyn). *Producers:* Michael Mirandman, Iris Merlis. *Writer:* Jules Feiffer. *Director:* John Madden.

**843 The Guardsman.** Comedy, 60 min., CBS, 3/2/55. A television adaptation of the play by Ferenc Molnar. The story, set in Vienna at the turn of the century, tells of a young actor who poses as a dashing guardsman to court his own wife and test her fidelity.

*Cast:* Claudette Colbert (Wife), Franchot Tone (Actor), Reginald Gardiner (Critic), Mary Boland (Mama), Mary Grace Canfield (Liesl), Harry Worth (Stage manager). *Music:* David Broekman. *Producers:* Felix Jackson, Martin Manulis. *Writer:* Felix Jackson. *Director:* Paul Nickell.

**844 Guys 'n' Geishas.** Comedy, 60 min., NBC, 2/10/67. The story, set (and filmed) in Japan, tells of a singer who falls for a beautiful Japanese girl, and a comedian who becomes involved with a wacky thief trying to steal a valuable scroll. *Cast:* Danny Thomas (Comedian), Jack Jones (Singer), Jonathan Winters (Thief), Romi Yamada (Girl). *Music:* Harper McKay. *Producers:* Bob Wynn, Alan Handley. *Writer:* Sheldon Keller. *Director:* Alan Handley.

**845 The Gymnast.** Drama, 60 min., ABC, 10/29/80. The experiences of Ginny Coker, a 16-year-old girl, as she attempts to transform her raw talent as a gymnast (at the Wade Gymnastics School in Oregon) into world-class competitive form. Aired as an "ABC Afterschool Special." *Cast:* Holly Gagnier (Ginny Coker), Zina Bethune (Leslie Wade), Jack Knight (Paul Coker), Patrick Gorman (Jack Peters), Kari Markussen (Karla Murtaugh), Kelly Gallagher (Liz Dupre), D. J. Sydney (Coleen Coker). *Producer:* Joseph Barbera. *Writer:* Durrell Royce Crays. *Director:* Larry Elikann.

**846 Gypsy in My Soul.** Variety, 60 min., CBS, 1/10/76. A salute to the theatrical chorus. *Host:* Shirley MacLaine. *Guest:* Lucille Ball. *Music:* Donn Trenner. *Producers:* William O. Harbach, Cy Coleman, Fred Ebb. *Writer:* Fred Ebb. *Director:* Tony Charmoli.

**847 Hagar the Horrible.** Cartoon, 30 min., CBS, 11/1/89. A television adaptation of the comic strip about an outrageous Viking named Hagar, his wife, Helga, their daughter, Honi, and their son, Hamlet. The story follows Hagar's efforts to regain control of his family after a two-year absence (due to a ravaging expedition). *Voices:* Peter Cullen (Hagar), Lainie Kazan (Helga), Lydia Cornell (Honi). *Additional Voices:* Jeff Doucette, Donny Most, Josh Rodine, Hank Saroyan, Frank Welker. *Music:* Sven Liback. *Producers:* William Hanna, Joseph Barbera, Bruce L. Paisner. *Writer:* Douglas Wyman. *Director:* Ray Patterson.

## 848 Hal Linden's Big Apple.

Variety, 60 min., ABC, 6/1/80. A musical tour of New York City. *Host:* Hal Linden. *Guests:* Shecky Greene, Robert Guillaume, The Rockettes. *Producers:* Jerry Levy, Paul Tush. *Writers:* Stan Hart, Mitzie Welch. *Director:* Dick Feldman.

## 849 Half a Lifetime.

Drama, 60 min., HBO, 7/20/86. An adult drama about four high school friends, now in their thirties, who gather for an evening of cards. They begin to discuss their lives — what they have done and what they hope to accomplish. *Cast:* Gary Busey (Bart Winninger), Saul Rubinek (Sam Spaulding), Nick Mancuso (Toby), Keith Carradine (J.J.). *Music:* John Mills-Cockell. *Producer:* Louis A. Stroller. *Writer:* Stephen Metcalfe. *Director:* Daniel Petrie.

## The Hallmark Hall of Fame.

Hoping to present a special Christmas Eve program, NBC hired Gian-Carlo Menotti to compose "Amahl and the Night Visitors," an opera about a crippled boy who joined the Three Wise Men on the road to Bethlehem. As Christmas Eve 1951 approached, the program was still without a sponsor (no advertiser seemed willing to pay the $150,000 NBC was asking) — until the president of Hallmark Greeting Cards decided to sponsor the program. Although it was too late to sell Christmas

cards, Hallmark decided to sponsor the program as a thankyou for all the people who did send Hallmark cards. Sarah Churchill was chosen to convey a brief thankyou and "Amahl and the Night Visitors" aired without commercial interruption. Viewers responded, flooding the NBC switchboard with congratulations all night long. Thus was born the "Hallmark Hall of Fame," an outstanding collection of top-quality productions which, since 1951, have totaled over 260 programs. One hundred and sixty-five episodes were produced as a weekly series (1/6/52–6/26/55; although 4 of these productions were 2-hour specials) and 98 episodes, which are listed below, were produced as a series of specials (10/23/55–12/17/78). The episodes produced after this date, for PBS and CBS, are television movies and not included here. For information on the 102 specials that were produced, please see the following titles:

**1951:** Amahl and the Night Visitors.

**1953:** Hamlet.

**1954:** King Richard II, Macbeth.

**1955:** Alice in Wonderland, Dream Girl, The Devil's Disciple.

**1956:** The Corn Is Green, The Good Fairy, The Taming of the Shrew, The Cradle Song, Born Yesterday, Man and Superman, The Little Foxes.

**1957:** The Lark, There Shall Be No Night, The Yeoman of the Guard, The Green Pasteurs, On Borrowed Time, Twelfth Night.

**1958:** Hans Brinker or the Silver Skates, Little Moon of Alban, Dial "M" for Murder, Johnny Belinda, Kiss Me Kate.

**1959:** Berkeley Square, Ah! Wilderness, Winterset, A Doll's House, The Hallmark Hall of Fame Christmas Festival.

**1960:** The Tempest, Captain Brassbound's Conversion, Shangri-La, Macbeth, The Golden Child.

**1961:** Time Remembered, Give Us Barabbas, The Joke and the Valley, Victoria Regina.

**1962:** Arsenic and Old Lace, Teahouse of the August Moon, Cyrano de Bergerac.

**1963:** Pygmalion, The Patriots, A Cry of Angels.

**1964:** Abe Lincoln in Illinois, Little Moon of Alban (restaged), The Fantasticks.

**1965:** The Magnificent Yankee, The Holy Terror, Eagle in a Cage, Inherit the Wind.

**1966:** Lamp at Midnight, Barefoot in Athens, Blithe Spirit.

**1967:** Anastasia, Soldier in Love, A Bell for Adano, St. Joan.

**1968:** Elizabeth the Queen, The Admirable Crichton, A Punt, a Pass and a Prayer, Pinocchio.

**1969:** Teacher, Teacher; The File on Devlin, The Littlest Angel.

**1970:** A Storm in Summer, Neither Are We Enemies, Hamlet.

**1971:** The Price, Gideon, The Snow Goose, All the Way Home.

**1972:** Love! Love! Love!; Harvey, The Hands of Cormac Joyce, The Man Who Came to Dinner.

**1973:** The Borrowers, You're a Good Man, Charlie Brown; The Small Miracle, Lisa, Bright and Dark.

**1974:** The Country Girl, Crown Matrimonial, Brief Encounter, The Gathering Storm.

**1975:** Eric, Valley Forge, The Rivalry, All Creatures Great and Small.

**1976:** Caesar and Cleopatra, Truman at Potsdam, The Disappearance of Aimee, Beauty and the Beast, Peter Pan.

**1977:** Emily, Emily; The Last Hurrah, The Court-Martial of General George Armstrong Custer, Have I Got a Christmas for You.

**1978:** Fame, Return Engagement, Stubby Pringle's Christmas, Taxi.

**850 The Hallmark Hall of Fame Christmas Festival.** Variety, 60 min., NBC, 12/13/59. A holiday program that is divided into four parts: (1) Dick Button in "The Ice Prin-cess," an ice skating fantasy narrated by Hiram Sherman with music by John Morris. (2) A performance by the Obernkirchen Children's Choir from Germany. (3) "The Borrowed Christmas," Joseph Schrank's adaptation of Ludwig Bemelman's story of a financier who tries to overcome his cynicism about Christmas (with Walter Slezak as Mr. Really Big, Jules Munshin as the Manager, Alice Pearce as Miss Talmey, and David Francis as Billy). (4) "The Nativity Story," with the narration of Judith Anderson and the music of Vaughn Williams, Cecil Cope, Bohuslao Martinu, Benjamin Britten, and Zoltan Kodaly. *Producer-Director:* George Schaefer. *Writer:* Carl Beller.

**851 Halloween Is Grinch Night.** Cartoon, 30 min., ABC, 10/29/77. A Dr. Seuss cartoon about the adventures of a small boy and his encounter with the foul-tempered Grinch when a howling night wind whisks him from his home in Whoville and lands him on the peak of Mt. Crimpit (the Grinch's home). *Voices:* Hans Conried (The Grinch), Jack DeLeon, Henry Gibson, Gary Shapiro, Hal Smith, Irene Tedrow. *Music:* Joe Raposo. *Producers:* Theodor Geisel, Friz Freleng, David DePatie. *Writer:* Theodor Geisel. *Director:* Gerald Baldwin.

**852 The Halloween That Almost Wasn't.** Comedy, 30 min., ABC, 10/30/79. As Halloween approaches, the Witch decides to retire and thus cancel Halloween. The story follows the efforts of Frankenstein, Dracula, the Wolfman, the Mummy, and the Zombie to convince the Witch to save their favorite holiday by flying over the moon on her broomstick. *Cast:* Mariette Hartley (Witch), Judd Hirsch (Dracula), John Schuck (Frankenstein), Jack Riley (Wolfman), Henry Gibson (Igor), Bob Finch (Mummy), Josip Elic (Zombie). *Producer:* Richard

Barclay. *Writer:* Gaby Monet. *Director:* Bruce Bilson.

**853 Hamlet.** Drama, 2 hrs., NBC, 4/26/53. The first television adaptation of the Shakespeare play about a young prince's struggle of conscience over the prospect of taking revenge against his father's killer. Broadcast as a two-hour special during the regular series of the "Hallmark Hall of Fame." *Cast:* Maurice Evans (Hamlet), Barry Jones (Polonius), Sarah Churchill (Ophelia), Ruth Chetterton (Queen Gertrude), Joseph Schildkraut (King Claudius). *Producer:* Albert McCleery. *Director:* George Schaefer.

**854 Hamlet.** Drama, 2 hrs., NBC, 11/17/70. A lavish "Hallmark Hall of Fame" adaptation of the play by William Shakespeare. After seeing his father's ghost, a young prince (Hamlet) has reason to believe that his father, the king, was murdered by his uncle Claudius. The story relates his struggle of conscience as he contemplates revenge. *Cast:* Richard Chamberlain (Hamlet), Michael Redgrave (Polonius), Margaret Leighton (Gertrude), John Gielgud (Ghost), Richard Johnson (Claudius), Ciaran Madden (Ophelia). *Music:* John Addison. *Producer:* George Schaefer. *Writer:* John Barton. *Director:* Peter Wood.

**855 The Hand-Me-Down Kid.** Drama, 60 min., ABC, 10/5/83. Ari Jacobs is a pretty 12-year-old girl who has always been the recipient of the castoff items of her older sister (Liz). Ari loves Liz, but Liz rarely has a kind word for her. One day Ari borrows Liz's bike without her permission. While Ari is helping an old lady in the park the bike is stolen. The story follows Ari's efforts to find the bike and something even more important — self-respect and a closer relationship with her sister. Aired as an "ABC Afterschool Special." *Cast:* Tracey Gold (Ari Jacobs), Cheryl Arutt (Liz Jacobs), Sara Botsford (Mrs. Jacobs), Terrance O'Quinn (Mr. Jacobs), Martha Plimpton (Rhona), Corey Parker (Eddie), Evan Mirand (Bucky), Alan North (Otto Rhinehart). *Music:* Howard Goodall. *Producer:* Frank Doelger. *Writer:* Judy Engles. *Director:* Robert Mandel.

**856 The Hands of Cormac Joyce.** Drama, 90 min., NBC, 11/17/72. A "Hallmark Hall of Fame" presentation about Cormac Joyce, a proud fisherman off the Irish coast, as he struggles to save his land from an approaching storm when other villagers scurry for the mainland. *Cast:* Stephen Boyd (Cormac Joyce), Colleen Dewhurst (Mollie Joyce), Dominick Guard (Jackie Joyce), Cyril Cusak (Mr. Reese), Lynette Ford (Ellis Connelley), Deryck Barnes (Pat Connelley). *Producer:* Fred L. Engel. *Writers:* S. S. Schweitzer, Leonard Wibberly. *Director:* Fielder Cook.

**857 Hans Brinker or the Silver Skates.** Musical, 90 min., NBC, 2/9/58. The story of a young boy and his efforts to compete in a local ice skating competition — despite the fact that his family is poor and he must share a pair of wooden skates with his sister. Aired on the "Hallmark Hall of Fame." *Cast:* Tab Hunter (Hans Brinker), Peggy King (Rychie Van Gleck), Basil Rathbone (Dr. Boekman), Jarmila Novotna (Dame Brinker), Carmen Matthews (Merrouw Van Gleck), Dick Button (Peter Van Gleck). *Music:* Franz Allers. *Producer-Director:* George Schaefer. *Writer:* Sally Benson.

**858 Hansel and Gretel.** Musical, 60 min., NBC, 4/27/58. A musical version of the German fairy tale about a brother and sister who encounter unknown danger from a witch when they become lost in the woods. *Cast:* Red Buttons (Hansel), Barbara Cook (Gretel), Rise Stevens (Mother), Rudy Vallee (Father), Hans Conried (Witch),

Stubby Kaye (Town Crier), Will Able (Eenie), Paula Lawrence (Meenie), Shai K. Ophir (Miney), Sondra Lee (Moe). *Music Director:* Glenn Osser. *Music and Lyrics:* Alec Wilder, William Engvick. *Producers:* David Susskind, Paul Bogart. *Writer:* Frank Yasha. *Director:* Paul Bogart.

## 859 Happy Anniversary and Goodbye. Comedy, 60 min., CBS, 11/19/74. A series of skits that revolve around the misadventures of newlyweds Norma and Malcolm Michaels. *Cast:* Lucille Ball (Norma Michaels), Art Carney (Malcolm Michaels), Nanette Fabray (Fay Lucas), Peter Marshall (Greg Carter), Don Porter (Ed Murphy), Arnold Schwarzenegger (Rico), Rhodes Reason (Doug), Louisa Moritz (Terry), Doria Cook (Linda). *Music:* Nelson Riddle. *Producer:* Gary Morton. *Writers:* Arne Rosen, Arthur Julian. *Director:* Jack Donohue.

## 860 Happy Anniversary, Charlie Brown. Cartoon, 60 min., CBS, 1/9/76. The program combines live action with animation (clips from Charlie Brown specials) to salute Charles M. Schulz on the occasion of the twenty-fifth anniversary of his Peanuts comic strip. *Host:* Carl Reiner. *Voices:* Duncan Watson (Charlie Brown), Lynn Mortensen (Lucy), Gail M. Davis (Sally), Stuart Brotman (Peppermint Patty), Liam Martin (Linus), Bill Melendez (Snoopy). *Music:* Vince Guaraldi. *Producers:* Lee Mendelson, Warren L. Lockhart. *Writer:* Bill Melendez. *Director:* Lee Mendelson.

## 861 Happy Anniversary 007: 25 Years of James Bond. Documentary, 60 min., ABC, 5/13/87. The life and times of James Bond, Ian Fleming's handsome British secret agent, are recalled in a wealth of film clips from the first cinema Bond (1962's *Dr. No* with Sean Connery) to 1987's *The Living Daylights* (with Timothy

Dalton). The other cinema Bonds are George Lazenby and Roger Moore. Barry Nelson played James Bond in a 1954 episode of "Climax." *Host-Narrator:* Roger Moore. *Producer-Director:* Mel Stuart. *Writer:* Richard Schickel.

## 862 Happy Birthday. Comedy, 90 min., NBC, 6/25/56. While in a bar, Addie, a spinster librarian, and Paul, a bank teller, meet by chance. To Paul, Addie is simply just another girl, but to Addie, Paul is the man of her dreams. The story, adapted from the Broadway play by Anita Loos, relates Addie's attempts to make Paul notice her. *Cast:* Betty Field (Addie), Harry Nelson (Paul), Tina Louise (Maude), William Harrigan (Mr. Bemis), Luella Gear (Emma), Wynne Gibson (Gail), G. Albert Smith (Judge).

## 863 Happy Birthday, America. Variety, 90 min., NBC, 7/4/76. A music and comedy salute to America on her two hundredth birthday. *Host:* Paul Anka. *Guests:* Jim Backus, Gordon Cooper, Sandy Duncan, Dale Evans, Evel Knievel, Gloria Loring, Roy Rogers, Mark Spitz, Meredith Wilson. *Producer-Director:* Marty Pasetta. *Writer:* Hal Kanter.

## Happy Birthday, Bob *see* Bob Hope Specials

## 864 Happy Birthday, Bugs: 50 Looney Years. Tribute, 60 min., CBS, 5/9/90. A celebration of Bugs Bunny's fiftieth year in showbusiness. *Guests:* Harry Anderson, Army Archerd, Allyce Beasley, Milton Berle, Pierce Brosnan, Kirk Cameron, Bill Cosby, Phil Donahue, Morgan Fairchild, Joe Garagiola, Debbie Gibson, Whoopi Goldberg, John Goodman, Valerie Harper, Mary Hart, Hulk Hogan, Tommy Lasorda, John Lithgow, Little Richard, Martin Mull, Chuck Norris, Louis Nye, George Peppard,

Maury Povich, Sally Jessy Raphael, Geraldo Rivera, Joan Rivers, Pat Sajak, Fred Savage, John Schneider, Peter Scolari, Jane Seymour, William Shatner, Vanna White, Cindy Williams. *Producers:* Gary Smith, Dwight Hemion. *Writers:* Jack Burns, Robert Cohen, Marty Farrell, Buz Kohan. *Director:* Dwight Hemion.

## 865 Happy Birthday, Hollywood. Variety, 3 hrs., ABC, 5/18/87.

A gala celebration of Hollywood on the occasion of its one hundredth birthday. *Guests:* Debbie Allen, June Allyson, Bea Arthur, Ed Asner, Lucille Ball, Gene Barry, Drew Barrymore, Hinton Battle, Shari Belafonte-Harper, Shandahl Bergman, Milton Berle, Tom Bosley, Morgan Brittany, Gregg Burge, Carol Burnett, Leslie Caron, Lynda Carter, Sid Caesar, Cyd Charisse, James Coburn, Dabney Coleman, Mike Connors, Bert Convy, Don Correia, Arlene Dahl, Tony Danza, Sammy Davis, Jr., William Devane, Angie Dickinson, Nancy Dussault, Barbara Eden, Morgan Fairchild, Alice Faye, John Forsythe, Bonnie Franklin, Mary Frann, Richard Gere, Gil Gerard, Lillian Gish, Louis Gossett, Jr., Robert Goulet, Ellen Greene, Deidre Hall, Gregory Harrison, Mary Hart, Florence Henderson, Charlton Heston, Dustin Hoffman, Bob Hope, Jill Ireland, Van Johnson, Shirley Jones, Ruby Keeler, Sally Kellerman, Jayne Kennedy, Stepfanie Kramer, Patti LaBelle, Dorothy Lamour, Michele Lee, Janet Leigh, Shari Lewis, Gloria Loring, Lorna Luft, Marilyn McCoo, Roddy McDowall, Joseph Maher, Tony Martin, Ann Miller, Donna Mills, Joe Namath, Bob Newhart, Donald O'Connor, Maureen O'Sullivan, Nia Peeples, Bernadette Peters, Ali Porter, Jane Powell, Stefanie Powers, Luise Rainer, Sheryl Lee Ralph, Lou Rawls, Lee Roy Reams, Debbie Reynolds, Alfonso Riberio, John Ritter, Ginger Rogers, Cesar Romero, Eva Marie Saint, Jill St. John, Telly Savalas, Tracy Scoggins, William Shatner, Martin Sheen, Jaclyn Smith, Robert Stack, Lionel Stander, Susan Sullivan, Loretta Swit, Alan Thicke, Lana Turner, Joan Van Ark, Dick Van Dyke, Robert Wagner, Dee Wallace-Stone, Betty White, Jesse White, Esther Williams, Treat Williams, Henry Winkler, Loretta Young. *Announcer:* Charlie O'Donnell. *Music:* Elliot Lawrence. *Producer:* Alexander H. Cohen. *Writer:* Hildy Parks. *Director:* Jeff Margolis.

## 866 The Happy Days Reunion. Comedy, 90 min., ABC, 3/3/92.

A nostalgic look back at the Cunninghams (Howard, Marion, Richie and Joanie) of the 1974–84 television series "Happy Days." Original cast members appear and film clips are used as they recall their experiences. *Guests:* Scott Baio, Tom Bosley, Ron Howard, Pat Morita, Donny Most, Marion Ross, Anson Williams, Henry Winkler. *Producers:* Malcolm Leo, Bonnie Peterson. *Writers:* Malcolm Leo, Sam Denoff, Marc Sheffler. *Director:* Malcolm Leo. *Note:* Erin Moran, who played Joanie, does not appear (due to a misunderstanding between the actress and the producers).

## 867 Happy Endings. Comedy, 60 min., ABC, 4/10/75. Four skits that satirize contemporary American life. Story 1: Big Joe and Kansas. *Cast:* James Earl Jones (Big Joe), Alan King (Kansas). *Writer:* Neil Simon. Story 2: A Commercial Break. *Cast:* Lauren Bacall (Catherine), Robert Preston (Harry). *Writer:* Peter Stone. Story 3: I'm with Ya, Duke. *Cast:* Alan King (Sam), Nancy Andrews (Nurse Carswell), John Cunningham (Dr. MacIntyre). *Writer:* Herb Gardner. Story 4: Kidnapped. *Cast:* Art Carney (Al), Elizabeth Wilson (Edna), Lisa Rochelle (Penny), Jimmy Fields (Buddy). *Writer:* Jules Feiffer. *Producers:* Alan King, Rupert Hitzig, John Gilroy. *Director:* Robert Moore.

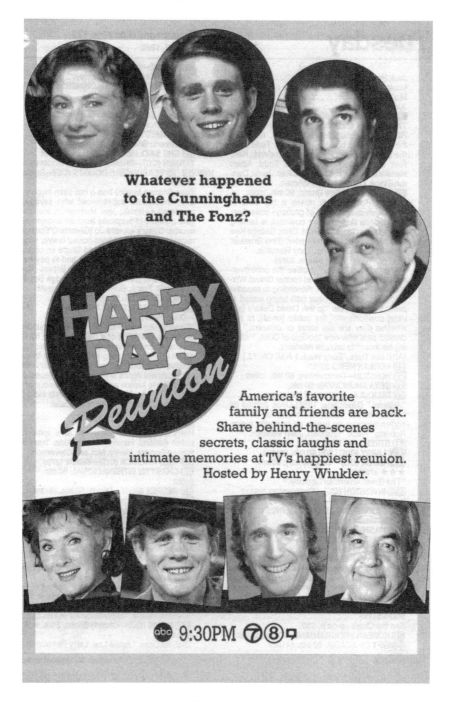

**Whatever happened to the Cunninghams and The Fonz?**

**HAPPY DAYS Reunion**

America's favorite family and friends are back. Share behind-the-scenes secrets, classic laughs and intimate memories at TV's happiest reunion. Hosted by Henry Winkler.

abc 9:30PM ⑦⑧

Ad for "Happy Days Reunion"

**868 Happy New Year, Charlie Brown.** Cartoon, 30 min., CBS, 1/1/86. The program relates Charlie Brown's efforts to get through a tough homework assignment (reading *War and Peace*) so he can attend Marcie and Peppermint Patty's New Year's Eve party. *Voices:* Chad Allen, Christie Baker, Elizabeth Ann Frazer, Jason Mendelson, Aaron Menebaun, Jeremy Miller. *Music:* Desiree Goyette, Ed Bogas. *Producers:* Lee Mendelson, Bill Melendez. *Writer:* Charles M. Schulz. *Directors:* Sam Jaimes, Bill Melendez.

**869 Happy Times Are Here Again.** Variety, 60 min., Syndicated, 10/72. The program recalls the music of the late 1800s and early 1900s. *Hosts:* Fred and Mickie Finn. *Guests:* Dave Garroway, Fay McKay. *Music:* The Mickie Finn Band.

**870 Harlow: The Blonde Bombshell.** Documentary, 60 min., TNT, 8/15/93. A look at the life and career of Jean Harlow (1911–37), one of Hollywood's legendary sex symbols of the 1930s (the sexy, bra-less bad girl of the movies). Intimate details about Jean's personal life (she was married three times) are given as well as a good sampling of clips from her films (including *Hell's Angels, Reckless, Riffraff, Saratoga*). *Host:* Sharon Stone.

**871 Harry and Lena.** Variety, 60 min., ABC, 3/22/70. An hour of music and songs with Harry Belafonte and Lena Horne. *Hosts:* Harry Belafonte, Lena Horne. *Music:* Alfred Brown. *Producer:* Chris Schultz. *Director:* Kirk Browning.

**872 Harry Anderson's Sideshow.** Variety, 60 min., NBC, 10/30/87. An offbeat program of magic, illusion, and comedy set against a carnival background. *Host:* Harry Anderson. *Cohost:* Deidre Hall. *Cast:* Emma Samms (Human Flower), Deidre Hall (Talking Head), Marsha Warfield (Human Bomb), Peter Scolari (Diminutive Duke), John Astin (Tommy Trio), Phil Procter (Barker), Jay Johnson (Man in Audience). *Also:* Eva Fay Anderson, Sandra Asbury-Johnson, Bernard Depa, Katlyn Miller, Turk Pipkin. *Music:* Lloyd Cooper. *Theme Song:* Richard Sherman, Robert Sherman. *Theme Vocal,* "Canvas, Sawdust and Dreams": Mel Torme. *Producers:* Harry Anderson, Jay Johnson. *Writers:* Harry Anderson, Grover Silcox, Turk Pipkin, Jay Johnson. *Director:* Bruce Gowers.

**873 Harry Belafonte in Concert.** Variety, 60 min., HBO, 10/12/85. A concert by singer Harry Belafonte. *Host:* Harry Belafonte. *Guests:* Dick Cavett, Marge Champion, Bill Cosby, Lee Grant, Alan King. *Music:* Richard Cummings. *Producers:* Harry Belafonte, Anthony Eaton. *Director:* Bruce Gowers.

**874 Harvey.** Comedy, 90 min., CBS, 9/22/58. The misadventures that befall Elwood P. Dowd, an aging bachelor and dedicated drinker whose problems stem from his friend and companion, Harvey, an invisible six-feet-tall white rabbit. Based on the Broadway play by Mary Chase. *Cast:* Art Carney (Elwood P. Dowd), Marion Lorne (Veta Simmons), Elizabeth Montgomery (Miss Kelly), Larry Blyden (Dr. Sanderson), Charlotte Rae (Myrtle Mae Simmons), Loring Smith (Dr. Chumley), Fred Gwynne (E. J. Lofgren), Jack Weston (Wilson). *Producer:* David Susskind. *Writers:* Jacqueline Babbin, Audrey Gellen. *Director:* George Schaefer.

**875 Harvey.** Comedy, 90 min., NBC, 3/22/72. A "Hallmark Hall of Fame" adaptation of the play by Mary Chase. The story of dedicated drinker Elwood P. Dowd and his friend and companion, Harvey, an invisible, six-feet-tall white rabbit who causes

Elwood much trouble. *Cast:* James Stewart (Elwood P. Dowd), Helen Hayes (Veta Simmons), John McGiver (Dr. Chumley), Arlene Francis (Mrs. Chumley), Marion Hailey (Myrtle Mae Simmons), Madeline Kahn (Miss Kelly), Richard Mulligan (Dr. Sanderson), Fred Gwynne (E. J. Lofgren), Jesse White (Wilson). *Producer:* David Susskind. *Writers:* Jacqueline Babbin, Audrey Gellen. *Director:* Fielder Cook.

**876  A Hatful of Rain.** Drama, 2 hrs., ABC, 3/3/68. The problems of drug addiction as seen through the experiences of Johnny Pope, a war veteran whose increasing habit is causing him to lose his family. Based on the Broadway play by Michael Gazzo. *Cast:* Michael Parks (Johnny Pope), Sandy Dennis (Celia Pope), Peter Falk (Polo Pope), Herschel Bernardi (John Pope, Sr.), John Ryan (Church), Don Stroud ("Mother"). *Producers:* David Susskind, Robert Arden, Alan Shayne. *Writer:* Michael Gazzo. *Director:* John Llewellyn Moxey.

**877  The Haunted Mansion Mystery.** Drama, 30 min., ABC, 9/10 and 9/17/83. After hearing rumors that a mansion is haunted by an old miser who disappeared with $1 million in cash, an adventurous girl (Angel) and boy (Billy) decide to solve the mystery. The story relates their dangerous quest when they find a secret room in the basement of the mansion and become trapped by a cave-in. Aired in two parts on the "ABC Weekend Special." *Cast:* Tristine Skyler (Angel Wilson), Christian Slater (Billy Beak), Paul Hecht (Mr. Wilson), Cheryl Giannini (Mrs. Beak), Jonathan Ward (Junior), Thom Barbour (Jeremiah Cleary). *Producer:* Jane Startz. *Writers:* Glen Olson, Rod Baker. *Director:* Larry Elikann.

**878  The Haunted Trailer.** Comedy, 30 min., ABC, 3/26/77. Shortly after Sharon Adams, a college-bound student, purchases a used motor home, she and her sister, Mary Alice "Mickey" Adams, discover that the home is haunted by a group of pesky poltergeists led by one Clifford Treadwell. The story relates Sharon's efforts to rid her home of the ghosts by finding them another house to haunt. Aired as an "ABC Weekend Special." *Cast:* Lauren Tewes (Sharon Adams), Monie Ellis (Mickey Adams), Murray Matheson (Clifford Treadwell), Eddie Bracken (Mr. Simpson), Stu Gilliam (Sheriff), Sara Seeger (Woman in car). *Music:* Ray Ellis. *Producers:* Allen Ducovny, William Beaudine, Jr. *Writer:* Robert Specht. *Director:* Ezra Stone.

**879  The Haunting of Harrington House.** Comedy, 60 min., CBS, 9/8/81. The story of Polly Ames, an adventurous 14-year-old girl who teams with Diogenes Chase, a retired teacher, to solve the strange happenings at Harrington House, a spooky residential hotel that is populated by some strange guests. A "CBS Afternoon Playhouse." *Cast:* Dominique Dunne (Polly Ames), Roscoe Lee Browne (Diogenes Chase), Phil Leeds (Uncle Max), Edie Adams (Madame Zenia), Vito Scotti (Marco Roselli), James Callahan (Walter Ames). *Music:* Don Heckman. *Producers:* Paul Asselin, Diane Asselin. *Writer:* Chris Manheim. *Director:* Murray Golden.

**880  Have Girls—Will Travel.** Comedy, 60 min., NBC, 10/16/64. The story, set in the old west, tells the tale of Horatio Lovelace, a marriage broker, as he peddles his ladies to prospective husbands. In the episode itself, set in the town of Golden Gulch, Horatio finds himself in a jam when three of his girls change their minds about marrying three mean and unkempt brothers. Aired as a "Bob Hope Special." *Cast:* Bob Hope (Horatio Lovelace), Rhonda Fleming (Purity), Jill St. John (Earth), Marilyn Maxwell (Charity), Bruce Cabot (Sheriff), Aldo Ray (Moose), Rod Cameron (Tiny),

Sonny Tufts (Monk). *Cameos:* Lucille Ball, Jack Benny, Richard Deacon. *Music:* Joe Lilley. *Producer:* Mort Lachman. *Writers:* Alex Gottlieb, Robert Hamner. *Director:* Fred De-Cordova.

## 881 Have I Got a Christmas for You. Drama, 60 min., NBC, 12/16/77.

A "Hallmark Hall of Fame" presentation about a group of Jewish people who become on-the-job substitutes for Christians wishing to spend Christmas Eve with their families. *Cast:* Milton Berle (Morris Glickstein), Adrienne Barbeau (Marcia Levine), Alex Cord (Sam Levine), Sheree North (Adele Serkin), Harold Gould (Leo Silver), Jim Backus (Kevin Grady), Jack Carter (Sidney Wineberg), Steve Allen (Marvin Kaplan), Jayne Meadows (Rita). *Producers:* Gilbert Cates, Joseph Cates. *Writer:* Jerome Cooper-smith. *Director:* Marc Daniels.

## 882 Have You Ever Been Ashamed of Your Parents?

Drama, 60 min., ABC, 3/16/83. The story of Fran Davies, a teenage girl who is forced to reevaluate family relationships and the meaning of self-pride when her father loses his job and her mother is forced to accept a position as a cook in the home of Fran's wealthy friend, Andrea Fairchild. Aired as an "ABC Afterschool Special." *Cast:* Kari Michaelsen (Fran Davies), Jennifer Jason Leigh (Andrea Fairchild), Marion Ross (Mrs. Davies), Don Billett (Mr. Davies), Carol Lawrence (Mrs. Fairchild), James Karen (Mr. Fairchild), Hallie Todd (Brenda), Julie Piekarski (Sarah), Shawn Schepps (Eva Marie). *Producers:* Paul Asselin, Diane Asselin. *Writer:* Chris Manheim. *Director:* Harry Harris.

## 883 Have You Ever Tried Talking to Patty? Drama, 60 min., CBS, 1/14/86.

A tender "CBS School-break Special" about Patty Miller, a pretty but deaf high school girl, as she struggles to be accepted by others. *Cast:* Mary Vreeland (Patty Miller), Michael Durrell (Nick Miller), Robin Pierson Rose (Diane Miller), Khrystyne Haje (Brianne Corey), Mark Patton (Chris Jenson), Heather Langenkamp (Erica), Rob Estes (Billy), Kathleen Wilhoite (Paulie), Deedee Pfeiffer (Queenie). *Music:* Artie Butler. *Producer:* Diane Asselin. *Director:* Daniel Petrie.

## 884 HBO Presents Emo.

Comedy, 60 min., HBO, 3/28/87. A cable concert by comedian Emo Philips. *Host:* Emo Philips. *Voice Characterizations:* Frank Buxton. *Music:* David Spear. *Producers:* C. Winston Simone, Sam Ellis. *Writer:* Emo Philips. *Director:* Cynthia L. Spears.

## 885 Hear Me Cry. Drama, 60 min., CBS, 10/16/84.

Craig Parsons and David Goldman are high school students. Craig is awkward and quiet; David is outgoing, athletic, and popular. While working on a class project, the youths, who seemingly have little in common, discover an alarming common ground—despair. Craig's parents are divorced and he is trying to compete with an outgoing older stepbrother for his father's attention; the death of David's older brother puts pressure on him to fulfill the high expectations his parents had for their other son. The stress David and Craig feel begins to show when Craig's grades begin to fall and David's football game is off—but no one recognizes the signs that tragedy is about to happen when the boys decide to resolve their problems through suicide. This tragic "CBS Schoolbreak Special" is designed to show viewers how to recognize the symptoms of suicide in adolescents. *Cast:* Robert MacNaughton (Craig Parsons), Lee Montgomery (David Goldman), Elinor Donahue (Mrs. Parsons), Bibi Besch (Mrs. Goldman),

David Spielberg (Dr. Goldman), Carmen Zapata (Mrs. Battaglia). *Producer-Writer-Director:* Joanna Lee.

**886 Heartbeat.** Music, 60 min., HBO, 1/17/87. A music video featuring Don Johnson as a documentary filmmaker injured in Central America. Based on his album, *Heartbeat.* *Cast:* Angela Alvarado, David Carradine, Don Johnson, Maria Johnson, Willie Nelson, Chadd Phinney, Paul Shaffer, Lori Singer. *Music:* Michel Rubini. *Producers:* Don Johnson, Danny Goldberg. *Writers:* Gil Evans, Francis Delia. *Director:* John Nicolella.

**887 Heartbreak House.** Comedy, 2 hrs., Showtime, 4/16/85. The story of a retired, slightly mad ex–sea captain whose household is anything but shipshape, being populated by his nurse, a philandering son-in-law who boasts of deeds never done, and a giant of capitalism who is virtually penniless. Based on the 1920 comedy of manners by George Bernard Shaw. *Cast:* Rex Harrison (Captain Shotover), Amy Irving (Ellie Dunn), Rosemary Harris (Hesione), Jan Miner (Nurse Guinness), Dana Ivey (Lady Utterword), Tom Aldredge (Mazzini), Bill Moor (Randall). *Producers:* Harold Thau, Howard K. Grossman, John H. Williams. *Writers:* Anthony Page, Rex Harrison. *Director:* Anthony Page.

**888 The Heartbreak Winner.** Drama, 60 min., ABC, 2/13/80. Maggie MacDonald is a teenage figure skater whose hopes for an Olympic gold medal are shattered when she is diagnosed with an arthritic knee. The story focuses on Maggie's efforts to accept reality and see her efforts achieved by coaching a friend, Cindy, for the Olympic medal. An "ABC Afterschool Special." *Cast:* Melissa Sherman (Maggie MacDonald), Tammy Taylor (Cindy), Chris Hagan (Bobby), Mark James (Joey Taylor), Philip Charles MacKenzie (Dr. LaFleur). *Producer:*

Martin Tahse. *Director:* Bruce Malmuth.

**889 Heaven Will Protect the Working Girl.** Variety, 90 min., NBC, 3/25/56. Music, songs, and sketches that salute the working girl, past and present. *Host:* Tony Randall. *Guests:* Janet Blair, Bob Carroll, Helen Gallagher, Tammy Grimes, Patricia Hammerlee, Bert Lahr, Connie Russell, Nancy Walker. *Music:* Charles Sanford. *Producers:* Max Liebman, Bill Hobin. *Director:* Max Liebman.

**890 Hedda Gabler.** Drama, 90 min., CBS, 9/20/63. A television adaptation of the 1890 play by Henrik Ibsen about a ruthless and destructive woman (Hedda Gabler) and her attempts to find a life of excitement away from her boring husband and his family. *Hedda Gabler* was also adapted to television as an episode of "Masterpiece Playhouse" (7/23/50) with Jessica Tandy as Hedda, and "The U.S. Steel Hour" (1/5/54) with Tallulah Bankhead in the title role. *Cast:* Ingrid Bergman (Hedda Gabler), Michael Redgrave (George Tesman), Trevor Howard (Eilert Lovborg), Ralph Richardson (Judge Brack), Beatrice Varley (Berta), Dilys Hamlett (Thea Elvsted). *Producers:* David Susskind, Lars Schmidt. *Writer:* Philip Reisman. *Director:* Alex Segal.

**891 Hedda Hopper's Hollywood.** Variety, 60 min., NBC, 1/10/60. A behind-the-scenes look at Hollywood with celebrity gossip columnist Hedda Hopper. *Host:* Hedda Hopper. *Guests:* Lucille Ball, Stephen Boyd, Francis X. Bushman, John Cassavetes, Gary Cooper, Bob Cummings, Janet Gaynor, Hope Lange, Don Murray, Ramon Novarro, Anthony Perkins, Debbie Reynolds, James Stewart, Gloria Swanson. *Producer:* Michael Abbott. *Writer:* Sumner Locke Elliott. *Director:* William Corrigan.

**892 Hee Haw's 20th Birthday Party.** Variety, 2 hrs., Syndicated, 6/9/88. A twentieth-anniversary celebration of the television series "Hee Haw." *Host:* Roy Clark. *Guests:* Highway 101, George Jones, Loretta Lynn, Barbara Mandrell, Louise Mandrell, Buck Owens, Charley Pride, Kenny Rogers, Ricky Skaggs, Ray Stevens, Sweethearts of the Rodeo, Tanya Tucker, Conway Twitty. *Series Regulars:* Roy Acuff, Cathy Baker, Gunilla Hutton, Linda Jenner, George Lindsey, Charlie McCoy, Irlene Mandrell, The Nashville Edition, Minnie Pearl, Mary Ann Rogers, Lulu Roman, Misty Rowe, Gailard Sartain, Shotgun Red, Jeff Smith, Mike Snider, Roni Stoneman, Gordie Tapp, Dub Taylor. *Music:* Charlie McCoy. *Producers:* Sam Louvollo, Marsha Minro. *Writers:* Barry Adelman, John Aylesworth, Frank Peppiatt, Bud Weingard. *Director:* Bob Boatman.

**893 Heidi.** Musical, 90 min., NBC, 10/1/55. A musical adaptation of Johanna Spyri's classic story of a lovable Swiss orphan named Heidi and her eccentric grandfather's efforts to protect her from the evils of civilization. *Cast:* Jeannie Carson (Heidi), Wally Cox (Peter), Elsa Lanchester (Frau Rottenmeier), Richard Eastham (Grandfather), Natalie Wood (Klara Sesseman), Jo Van Fleet (Aunt Dete), Robert Clary (Eric), The Schmeed Trio (Yodelers). *Music Director:* Charles Sanford. *Music:* Clay Warnick, Carolyn Leigh. *Producers:* Max Liebman, Bill Hobin. *Director:* Max Liebman.

**894 The Heiress.** Drama, 60 min., CBS, 2/13/61. The story, based on the novel *Washington Square* by Henry James, tells of Catherine Sloper, the unattractive and shy daughter of a wealthy surgeon; and Morris Townsend, a handsome fortune hunter who dates her when he learns that she will inherit a large sum of money after her father's death. *Cast:* Julie Harris (Catherine Sloper), Barry Morse (Dr. Austin Sloper), Farley Granger (Morris Townsend), Muriel Kirkland (Lavinia Penniman), Barbara Robins (Mrs. Montgomery), Suzanne Stoors (Marion Almond), Mary Van Fleet (Maria). *Music:* Robert Cobert. *Producer:* David Susskind. *Writers:* Jacqueline Babbin, Audrey Gellen. *Director:* Marc Daniels.

**895 The Helen Reddy Special.** Variety, 60 min., ABC, 5/22/79. An hour of music, song, and light comedy. *Host:* Helen Reddy. *Guests:* Jane Fonda, Elliott Gould. *Music:* Lenny Stack. *Producers:* Jeff Wald, Bill Lee, John Moffitt. *Director:* John Moffitt.

**896 Help Wanted.** Drama, 60 min., CBS, 10/12/82. Max and Jessy are the children of Jim and Fran Welsh. When Jim loses his job and is unable to find work, he contemplates selling their home and moving into an apartment. The story focuses on Max and Jessy's efforts to help their father by devising a plan to earn money. A "CBS Afternoon Playhouse." *Cast:* Kevin Dobson (Jim Welsh), Dee Wallace (Fran Welsh), K. C. Martel (Max Welsh), Melanie Gaffin (Jessy Welsh), Tricia Cast (Trisha), Arlene Golonka (Hilda), Raymond Singer (Mike), Christoff St. John (Teddy). *Music:* Joe Lazenti. *Producer-Director:* Stephen Gyllenhaal. *Writer:* Elizabeth Clark.

**897 Henry Fonda and the Family.** Comedy, 60 min., CBS, 2/6/62. A series of comedy sketches based on the statistically oriented American family. *Host:* Henry Fonda. *Guests:* Dan Blocker, Verna Felton, Paul Lynde, Carol Lynley, Flip Mark, Michael J. Pollard, Dick Van Dyke, Cara Williams. *Music:* David Rose. *Producers:* Bud Yorkin, Norman Lear. *Writers:* Norman Lear, Toni Koch. *Director:* Bud Yorkin.

**898 Henry Fonda as Clarence Darrow.** Drama, 90 min., PBS, 3/17/75. A one-man drama in which Henry Fonda portrays Clarence Darrow and contemplates his life and times. *Starring:* Henry Fonda as Clarence Darrow. *Producers:* Mike Merrick, Don Gregory. *Writer:* David W. Rintels. *Director:* John Rich.

**899 The Henry Fonda Special.** Variety, 60 min., CBS, 4/18/73. Sketches based on the theme as to how Americans get away from the pressures of life by taking on the outdoors and sports. *Host:* Henry Fonda. *Guests:* Johnny Bench, Foster Brooks, Tim Conway, John Davidson, Sammy Davis, Jr., Don Knotts, Cathy Rigby, Leslie Uggams. *Producers:* Bill Carruthers, Joel Stein. *Director:* Bill Carruthers.

**900 Henry Hamilton, Graduate Ghost.** Comedy, 30 min., ABC, 12/8 and 12/15/84. The story of Henry Hamilton, the ghost of a Civil War soldier, who descends upon the lives of a modern-day family (the Landrys) to teach them to believe in themselves and their dreams. Aired in two parts as an "ABC Weekend Special." *Cast:* Steve Nevil (Henry Hamilton), Belinda Balaski (Margaret Landry), Elizabeth Lyn Fraser (Pam Landry), Christian Jacobs (Kurt Landry), John Lawlor (Paul Landry), Marissa Mendenhall (Therese Landry), Phyllis Applegate (Evelyn Sherman), Stu Gilliam (George Sherman). *Producers:* Fern Field, Norman G. Brooks. *Writers:* Jim Carlson, Terrence McDonell. *Director:* Noam Pitlik.

**901 Henry Winkler Meets William Shakespeare.** Children, 60 min., CBS, 3/20/77. With the assistance of an actor playing William Shakespeare, actor Henry Winkler attempts to familiarize young people with some of the bard's best-known works (which are seen in excerpt form).

*Cast:* Henry Winkler (Himself), Tom Aldredge (William Shakespeare), George Ede (Falstaff), Kevin Kline (Petruchio), Robert Phelps (Tybalt), Jordan Clarke (Mercutio), Bruce Bouchard (Katharine), Erik Frederickson (Fencer). *Elizabethan Players:* Stephan Brennan, Bill McIntyre, William Sadler, Bruce Weitz. *Dueling Scene Players:* David Blessing, Bruce Bouchard, Stephan Brennan, Bill McIntyre, William Sadler, Franklin Seales, Bruce Weitz. *Producer:* Daniel Wilson. *Writer:* Lee Kalcheim. *Director:* Jeff Bleckner.

**902 Her School for Bachelors.** Comedy-Drama, 60 min., NBC, 3/20/64. When Monte Collins, editor-publisher of *Bachelor* magazine, becomes the target of an attack by Diane Westcott, a schoolteacher running for Congress, he decides to become part of the campaign by secretly backing her. Complications arise when word leaks out and Diane is touted as running a school for bachelors. The program, broadcast as a "Bob Hope Special," relates Monte's efforts to help Diane win the election. *Cast:* Bob Hope (Monte Collins), Eva Marie Saint (Diane Westcott), Linda Hope (Miss November), Louis Nye (Jack Roberts), Cass Daley (Patsy Willis), Jackie Coogan (Customer). *Music:* Joe Lilley. *Producer:* Mort Lachman. *Writers:* Alex Gottlieb, Robert Hamner. *Director:* Fred DeCordova.

**903 Herb Alpert and the Tijuana Brass.** Variety, 60 min., ABC, 10/13/74. An hour of music and song with Herb Alpert and the Tijuana Brass (John Pisano, Bob Findley, Dave Frishberg, Steve Schaeffer, Lani Hall, Vince Charles, Julius Wechter). *Host:* Herb Alpert. *Guests:* Jim Henson's Muppets. *Producers:* Gary Smith, Dwight Hemion. *Writers:* Frank Peppiatt, John Aylesworth. *Director:* Dwight Hemion.

## Here Comes Garfield see Garfield Specials

### 904 Here Comes Peter Cottontail. Cartoon, 60 min., ABC, 4/4/71.

An animated musical that follows the efforts of the Easter Bunny, Peter Cottontail, to deliver more eggs than Irontail, an evil rabbit who is seeking Peter's job. *Voices:* Casey Kasem (Peter Cottontail), Vincent Price (Irontail), Danny Kaye (Mr. Sassafrass), Iris Rainer (Donna), Joan Gardner (Bonnie Bonnet), Greg Thomas and Jeff Thomas (Children). *Music:* Maury Laws. *Producers:* Jules Bass, Arthur Rankin, Jr. *Writer:* Romeo Muller. *Directors:* Arthur Rankin, Jr., Jules Bass.

### 905 Here It Is, Burlesque!

Documentary, 90 min., HBO, 7/25/80. An adult-oriented musical comedy revue of the history of burlesque (the program contains nudity). *Hosts:* Morey Amsterdam, Ann Caprio, Pinky Lee. *Stripper:* Tami Roche. *Producer:* Michael Brandman. *Director:* Marty Callner.

### 906 Here's Edie. Variety, 30 min., ABC, 4/8/62; 1/20/63; 3/17/63.

Music, songs, and light comedy in a series of three specials that eventually led to the series "Here's Edie" (ABC, 1963–64). *Host:* Edie Adams. *Guests* (4/8/62): Andre Previn, Dick Shawn. *Guests* (1/20/63): Laurindo Almeido, Stan Getz, The Rogert Wagner Chorale. *Guests* (3/17/63): Hoagy Carmichael, Hank Henry, Dick Martin, Dan Rowan. *Music:* Peter Matz. *Producer-Director:* Barry Shear. *Writer:* David Cox.

### 907 Here's TV Entertainment. Variety, 2 hrs., Syndicated, 1/85.

A lively revue of the history of variety series and specials. *Hosts:* Carol Burnett, Dick Clark, Bob Hope, Marie Osmond, Ben Vereen, Dionne Warwick. *Music:* Ian Fraser. *Producers:* Gary Smith, Dwight Hemion. *Writer:* Buz Kohan. *Director:* Dwight Hemion.

### 908 The Hero Who Couldn't Read. Drama, 60 min., ABC, 1/9/84.

Freddie Ellis is a star high school athlete who can not read and does not worry about his grades. His teachers have given him the easier courses and his girlfriend, Cynthia, writes his term papers. When a new teacher (Mr. Simpson) suspects something is wrong because Freddie's present classroom performance contradicts his past record, Freddie admits that he can not read. Mr. Simpson's efforts to help a reluctant Freddie (who is too proud to accept help) to learn to read are the focal point of this "ABC Afterschool Special." *Cast:* Eric Wallace (Freddie Ellis), Clarence Williams III (Mr. Simpson), Lynn Hamilton (Mrs. Ellis), James Carroll Jordan (Mike Chapman), Arthur Taxier (Coach Jefferies), Renee Jones (Cynthia Beale), Kareem Abdul-Jabbar (Himself). *Producer-Director:* Robert Chenault. *Writers:* Johnny Dawkins, Adoley Odunton.

### 909 Heroes and Sidekicks — Indiana Jones and the Temple of Doom. Documentary, 60 min., CBS, 11/27/84.

The program explores the functions and values of screen heroes and sidekicks in motion pictures and on television. *Host-Narrator:* William Shatner. *Music:* John Williams, William Loose, Jack Tillar. *Producers:* Sid Ganis, Frank Marshall, Robert Guenette. *Writer-Director:* Robert Guenette.

### 910 He's Your Dog, Charlie Brown. Cartoon, 30 min., CBS, 2/14/68.

Charlie Brown's efforts to curtail the antics of his mischievous dog, Snoopy. *Voices:* Peter Robbins (Charlie Brown), Gail DeFaria (Peppermint Patty), Christopher Shea (Linus), Bill Melendez (Snoopy). *Music:* Vince

Guaraldi. *Producers:* Lee Mendelson, Bill Melendez. *Writer:* Charles M. Schulz. *Director:* Bill Melendez.

## 911 Hewitt's Just Different.

Drama, 60 min., ABC, 10/12/77. A sensitive "ABC Afterschool Special" that focuses on Hewitt Calder, a 16-year-old mentally retarded adolescent, and his 12-year-old friend, Willie Arthur. The drama centers on Hewitt's attempts to make friends with the other neighborhood kids and prove that he is a person too. *Cast:* Perry Lang (Hewitt Calder), Moosie Drier (Willie Arthur), Doney Oatman (Tally), Gloria Stroock (Mrs. Arthur), Peggy McCay (Mrs. Calder), Russell Johnson (Mr. Calder), Peter Brandon (Mr. Arthur), Christopher Maleki (Palumbo). *Producer:* Daniel Wilson. *Writer:* Jan Hartman. *Director:* Larry Elikann.

## 912 Hi, I'm Glen Campbell.

Variety, 60 min., NBC, 7/7/76. An hour of music, songs, and comedy sketches. *Host:* Glen Campbell. *Guests:* Sammy Cahn, Carrie Campbell, Wesley Campbell, Natalie Cole, Harvey Korman, Dick Martin, Don Rickles, McLean Stevenson, Lawrence Welk. *Music:* Dennis McCarthy. *Producers:* Burt Sugarman, Nick Sevano. *Director:* Stan Harris.

## 913 High Button Shoes.

Musical Comedy, 90 min., NBC, 11/24/56. The story of a charming confidence man (Harrison Floy) and his efforts to con a young couple (Sara and Henry Longstreet) into believing that they will make a remarkable profit from the sale of their family property. *Cast:* Hal March (Harrison Floy), Nanette Fabray (Sara Longstreet), Don Ameche (Henry Longstreet), Joey Faye (Mr. Pontdue), Jack Collins (Uncle Willie), Janet Ward (Nancy). *Music:* Jule Styne, Sammy Cahn. *Producer-Director:* Joseph Cates. *Writer:* Stephen Longstreet.

## 914 High Thor.

Musical, 90 min., CBS, 3/10/56. A musical adaptation of Maxwell Anderson's 1937 Broadway play about a ghost of a sixteenth-century Dutch girl (Lise) who comes to the aid of a man (Van Dorn) who is struggling to keep his mountain, High Thor, from a group of people seeking to buy it. *Cast:* Bing Crosby (Van Dorn), Julie Andrews (Lise), Nancy Olson (Judith), Everett Sloane (DeWitt), Hans Conried (Biggs), Lloyd Corrigan (Skimmerhorn), John Picaroll (Captain).

## 915 Hizzoner!

Drama, 60 min., PBS, 5/21/86. A one-man show in which Tony LoBianco portrays Fiorello LaGuardia, the mayor of New York City for 12 years. The program, set in the last days of LaGuardia's term in 1945, relates the mayor's political and personal experiences through anecdotes. *Cast:* Tony LoBianco (Fiorello LaGuardia). *Narrator:* Ed Koch (the Mayor of New York). *Music:* John Adams. *Producer:* Joan Konner. *Writer:* Paul Shyre. *Director:* Gary Halvorson.

## 916 H.M.S. *Pinafore*.

Comedy, 30 min., NBC, 1/14/60. A southern-twang adaptation of the Gilbert and Sullivan operetta about the life of Sir Joseph Porter, Lord of the British Admiralty. *Cast:* Tennessee Ernie Ford (Sir Joseph Porter), Richard Wessler (Captain Corcoran), Chet Fisher (Ralph Rackstraw), Donna Cooke (Josephine), Susan Lovell (Little Buttercup), Ken Harp (Dick Redeye), Joanne Burgan (Hebe), Don Kent (Bob Beckett). *Music:* Harry Geller. *Producer:* Cliff Stone. *Director:* Selwin Touber. *Choreographer:* Ward Ellis.

## 917 The Hobbit.

Cartoon, 90 min., NBC, 11/27/77. A musical adaptation of J. R. R. Tolkien's fantasy novel about Bilbo Baggins, a middle-earth world Hobbit, as he begins a quest to find a treasure buried deep in the heart of Lonely Mountain. *Voices:* Orson Bean (Bilbo Baggins), Richard Boone (Smaug), Hans Conried (Thorin Oakenshield), John Huston (Gandalf), Otto Preminger (The Elvenking), Cyril Ritchard (Elrond). *Music:* Maury Laws. *Lyrics:* Jules Bass. *Balladeer:* Glen Yarbrough. *Producer-Directors:* Arthur Rankin, Jr., Jules Bass. *Writer:* Jules Bass.

**918 Hockey Night.** Drama, 90 min., HBO, 4/1/85. Kathy Yerrow is a 14-year-old girl just relocated to the small town of Parry Sound with her mother (Alice) and sister (Laura) following her parents' separation. Kathy finds the town to be dull with nothing to do—until her friend, Evelyn, tells her that the only school activity is the hockey team, but it is a team for boys only (Kathy previously played hockey as a goalie at her old school for the Scarborough Hawks). Kathy tries out for and makes the team (the Parry Sound All-Stars), but the team's sponsors feel the coach's decision to add a girl is wrong. The story relates Kathy's efforts to remain on the team, despite the objections that exist. *Cast:* Megan Follows (Kathy Yerrow), Gail Youngs (Alice Yerrow), Ingrid Beniger (Evelyn), Yannick Bisson (Speak Kozak), Rick Moranis (Coach), Sean McCann (Mr. Kozak). *Music:* Fred Mollin. *Producer-Writer:* Martin Harbury. *Director:* Paul Shapin.

**919 Holiday.** Variety, 90 min., NBC, 6/9/56. The story, which places Johann Strauss's music in the Elmer Rice play *The Grand Tour*, tells of Nell Valentine, a New England schoolteacher who falls for a man she later discovers is an embezzler. *Cast:* Doretta Morrow (Nell Valentine), Keith Andes (Ray Brinton), Kitty Carlisle (Adele), Tammy Grimes (Cafe singer), George Irving (Mr. Coogan), Anthony Eisley (Mr. Montgomery), Bambi Linn and Rod Alexander (Urchins). *Music Director:* Charles Sanford. *Music:* Clay

Warnick, Mel Pahl. *Lyrics:* Edgar Eager. *Producers:* Max Leibman, Bill Hobin. *Directors:* Max Leibman, Charles S. Dubin.

**920 Holiday Greetings from The Ed Sullivan Show.** Variety, 2 hrs., CBS, 12/20/92. Clips (of guests performing Christmas songs culled from "The Ed Sullivan Show," CBS, 1948–71), coupled with live performances of traditional holiday songs. *Host:* Bob Newhart. *Guests:* Paul Anka, Kermit the Frog and Miss Piggy (Muppets), Dick Martin, Johnny Mathis, Della Reese, Roy Rogers and Dale Evans. *Producers:* Andrew Solt, Susan F. Walker. *Writers:* Peter Elbling, Andrew Solt. *Directors:* Jeff Margolis, Andrew Solt.

**921 Holiday in Las Vegas.** Variety, 60 min., NBC, 11/16/57. A musical revue from Las Vegas. *Host:* Ann Sothern. *Guests:* Vic Damone, Sammy Davis, Jr., Mickey Hargitay, Jayne Mansfield, Tony Randall. *Music:* David Rose. *Producer:* Jack Rayel. *Writers:* Mel Tolkin, Neil Simon, Lucille Kallen. *Director:* Kirk Browning.

**922 Holiday in Spring.** Variety, 30 min., DuMont, 1/30/48. A television showcase for the new 1948 spring fashions as seen through the fantasies of a businessman. Music and songs (by Jerry Wayne) were interspersed as the Conover Models showcased the fashions. *Cast:* Phyllis Jean Creore, Wilma Drake, Sterling Oliver, Jerry Wayne. *Narrator:* Adelaide Halwey. *Music:* Nathaniel Shilkret. *Producer:* Ed Cornez. *Director:* Raymond E. Nelson.

**923 Holiday Star Revue.** Variety, 2 hrs., ABC, 11/25/48. A program of variety acts from ABC's Ritz Theater. The two-hour program cost ABC $25,000 to produce, $5,000 of which was paid to the host. *Host:* George Jessel. *Guests:* Morey Amsterdam, the Bil and Cora Baird Puppets, Connee Boswell, Paul Draper, Paul and Grace Hartman, Phil Regan, Phil Silvers, Ethel Smith. *Announcer:* Andre Baruch. *Orchestra:* Paul Whiteman. *Producer-Director:* Burk Crotty.

## 924 The Hollywood Deb Stars of 1966. Variety, 60 min., ABC, 1/9/66. Comedy skits are coupled with an award honoring Walt Disney and the presentation of twelve beautiful actresses who are hoping to become stars. *Hosts:* Steve Allen, Jayne Meadows. *Skit Players:* Tim Conway, Tim Herbert, Louis Nye. *Walt Disney Award Accepter:* Maurice Chevalier. *Deb Stars:* Sherry Alberoni, Trudi Ames, Phyllis Elizabeth Davis, Sally Field, Linda Foster, Helen Funai, Shelby Grant, Peggy Lipton, Beverly Lunsford, Cheryl Miller, Melody Patterson, Edy Williams. *Introducing the Deb Stars:* Jackie Cooper, Troy Donahue, Buddy Ebsen, Nanette Fabray, Ben Gazzara, Dean Jones, Vic Morrow, Ryan O'Neal, Robert Reed, Roger Smith, Jerry Van Dyke, Ray Walston.

## 925 Hollywood Legends: Marilyn Monroe. Documentary, 60 min., Syndicated, 7/88. A profile of actress Marilyn Monroe (1926–63) from her unstable childhood, her days as a model, to her success as a film star. *Narrator:* Richard Widmark. *Guests:* Celeste Holm, Robert Mitchum, Don Murray, Sheree North, Shelley Winters. *Producers:* Ron DeVillier, Gene Feldman. *Directors:* Gene Feldman, Suzette Winter.

## 926 Hollywood Melody. Variety, 60 min., NBC, 3/19/62. A music and comedy salute to the movie musical. *Host:* Donald O'Connor. *Guests:* Richard Chamberlain, Nanette Fabray, Shirley Jones, Howard Keel, Yvette Mimieux, Juliet Prowse. *Music:* David Rose. *Producer:* Arthur Freed.

## 927 Hollywood, My Home

Town. Documentary, 60 min., NBC, 1/7/62. A showcase for the home movies of stars filmed by Ken Murray. *Host-Narrator:* Ken Murray. *Music Score:* George Stole. *Orchestrations:* Calvin Jackson, Fred Katz, Gerald Wilson. *Producer-Director:* William Martin. *Writer:* Ken Murray.

## 928 Hollywood Out-Takes. Documentary, 60 min., NBC, 3/27/77. A humorous look at flubs from motion pictures nominated for a 1977 Academy Award. *Host:* Marilyn Beck. *Guests:* Jenny Agutter, David Carradine, Blake Edwards, Bob Evans, William Holden, Bob Hope, Talia Shire, Sylvester Stallone, Burt Young. *Music:* Milton DeLugg. *Producer-Director:* Dick Schneider. *Writers:* Gene Perret, Bill Richmond.

## 929 Hollywood Sings. Variety, 60 min., NBC, 4/3/60. A revue of the Hollywood movie musicals of the past with re-creations of famous songs. *Host:* Boris Karloff. *Guests:* Eddie Albert, Tammy Grimes, The James Starbuck Singers and Dancers. *Music:* Franz Allers. *Choreographer:* James Starbuck.

## 930 Hollywood Stars' Screen Tests. Variety, 60 min., NBC, 10/5/84. The program spotlights the never before seen screen tests of famous stars. *Host:* George Peppard. *Guests:* Byron Allen, Anne Baxter, Morgan Brittany, Imogene Coca, Pia Lindstrom, Jane Russell. *Producers:* Dick Clark, Lee Miller. *Writer:* Rod Warren. *Director:* Lee Miller.

## 931 Hollywood: The Gift of Laughter. Documentary, 3 hrs., ABC, 5/16/82. A compilation of movie clips that celebrate sixty years of Hollywood comedy. *Hosts:* Carol Burnett, Dom DeLuise, Jack Lemmon, Walter Matthau, Richard Pryor, Burt Reynolds. *Music:* Fred Karlin. *Producers:* David L. Wolper, Jack Haley, Jr. *Writer-Director:* Jack Haley, Jr.

## 932 Hollywood: The Selznick Years.

Documentary, 60 min., NBC, 3/21/69. A review of the career of movie titan David O. Selznick. See also "Theater '62." *Host-Narrator:* Henry Fonda. *Guests:* Ingrid Bergman, Joseph Cotten, George Cukor, Joan Fontaine, Janet Gaynor, Katharine Hepburn, Alfred Hitchcock, Rock Hudson, Dorothy McGuire, Gregory Peck, King Vidor. *Producer-Writer-Director:* Marshall Flaum.

## 933 Hollywood's Children.

Documentary, 60 min., PBS, 1/21/89. A retrospective of Hollywood child stars from the 1920s to the 1980s. *Narrator:* Roddy McDowall. *Guests:* Diana Serra Carey, Jackie Coogan, Edith Fellows, Peggy Ann Garner, Bonita Granville, Julie Ann Haddock, Arthur Jacobson, Spanky McFarland, Louis Malle, Dickie Moore. *Producers:* Diane Ehrichman, Gene Feldman, Suzette Winter. *Writer-Director:* Gene Feldman.

## 934 Hollywood's Most Sensational Mysteries.

Documentary, 60 min., NBC, 2/4/84. The program chronicles the true and, in some cases, still unsolved crimes from Hollywood's past. Actual film clips and newsreel footage are combined with dramatic reenactments to tell of the unusual circumstances surrounding the deaths of such stars as James Dean, Marilyn Monroe, John Belushi, Sal Mineo, Lana Turner, and Freddie Prinze. *Host:* Ben Gazzara. *Cast:* Pati Blankenship (Marilyn Monroe), Lois Hamilton (Lana Turner), Angus Duncan (William Desmond Turner), Frank Annese (John Stompanato), Leslie Landon (Cheryl Crane), Kathy Maisnik (Mabel Normand), Joe Nesnow (Mickey Cohen), Nathan Adler (Jerry Geisler). *Producer-Director:* Perry Rosemond. *Writer:* Michael Alan Eddy.

## 935 Hollywood's Private Home Movies.

Variety, 60 min., ABC, 5/22/83. A somewhat nostalgic look at the actual home movies of famous Hollywood celebrities (including Brooke Shields, Bob Hope, Jayne Mansfield, Marilyn Monroe, Dean Martin, Pat Boone, Elvis Presley). *Host:* Bill Cosby. *Guests:* Ann-Margret, Ken Murray, Don Rickles. *Producers:* Dick Clark, Al Schwartz. *Writer:* Robert Arnott. *Director:* Al Schwartz.

## 936 Hollywood's Private Home Movies II.

Variety, 60 min., ABC, 11/24/83. A sequel to the previous special in which more home movies of Hollywood celebrities are seen. *Host:* Tim Conway. *Guests:* Ray Anthony, Anthony Geary, Rose Marie, Mr. T, Ken Murray, Marie Osmond, Patrick Wayne. *Producers:* Dick Clark, Al Schwartz. *Writer:* Robert Arnott. *Director:* Al Schwartz.

## 937 The Holy Terror.

Drama, 90 min., NBC, 4/7/65. A "Hallmark Hall of Fame" presentation based on the life and work of Florence Nightingale. The story, set in 1856, relates the incidents that occurred in her life following the Crimean War—when she gained notoriety—but wanted only to return to her nursing work in London. *Cast:* Julie Harris (Florence Nightingale), Denholm Elliott (Sidney Herbert), Torin Thatcher (Dr. Poole), Kate Reid (Aunt Mai), Leueen MacGrath (Fanny Nightingale), Alan Webb (Mr. Nightingale), Brian Bedford (Billy Sims). *Producer-Director:* George Schaefer. *Writer:* James Lee.

## 938 Home for Easter.

Variety, 60 min., Syndicated, 4/15/90. A celebration of Easter from Australia. *Host:* Helen Reddy. *Guests:* Patrick Macnee, The Serendipity Singers (John Ross, Laura McKenzie, Holley Setlock, Will Tremont, Julie Scott, Wally Mulso), Paul Williams, Tom Wopat.

*Music:* John Ross. *Producer:* Paul Sharrott. *Writer:* Laura McKenzie. *Director:* David L. Stanton.

## 939 A Home Run for Love.

Drama, 60 min., ABC, 10/11/78. The program is filmed in black and white and set in 1947. One day, while listening to a Brooklyn Dodgers baseball game on the radio, a lonely young boy named Sammy Greene befriends Davy Henderson, an elderly black cook in Sammy's mother's roadside inn. When Sammy discovers that Davy is a Dodgers fan also, the two become close friends. Shortly after Davy takes Sammy to see his first baseball game, Davy becomes gravely ill. Having acquired the winning ball from that game, Davy makes a lone journey from his home in New Jersey to Ebbets Field in Brooklyn to get Jackie Robinson, Davy's favorite player, and the rest of the team to autograph the game ball for his ailing friend. Because of his age (12) Sammy is not permitted to see Davy. The heartwarming "ABC Afterschool Special" relates Sammy's efforts to sneak into Davy's room and present him with his priceless treasure. *Cast:* Charles Lampkin (Davy Henderson), Ronnie Scribner (Sammy Greene), Anne Gee Byrd (Esther Greene), Flicka Huffman (Sara Greene), Niva Ruschell (Henrietta Barnes), J. Jay Saunders (Eliot Barnes), John La Fayette (Jackie Robinson), Red Barber (Dodgers Announcer). *Music:* Glenn Paxton. *Producer:* Martin Tahse. *Writer:* Arthur Heinemann. *Director:* Robert Liberman.

## 940 Home Sweet Homeless.

Drama, 60 min., CBS, 3/29/87. A moving "CBS Schoolbreak Special" about a widowed mother (Susan) who loses her job, then her home, and is forced to scratch out an existence with her three sons in the family car. *Cast:* Linda Kelsey (Susan Palmer), Ross Harris (Jeff Palmer), Chance Michael Corbitt (Johnny Palmer), Michael James Faus-

tino (Jimmy Palmer), Kelly Dunn (Jenny), Alfonso Riberio (Buddy). *Music:* Misha Segal. *Producers:* Stephen Saigenbaum, Roxanne Captor. *Writer:* Kathryn Montgomery. *Director:* Kevin Hooks.

## 941 The Homemade Comedy Special.

Comedy, 60 min., NBC, 4/8/84. The program spotlights comedy videos made by ordinary people. *Hosts:* Angie Dickinson, Michael J. Fox. *Theme Music:* Marc Tanner, Jon Reede, Marc Greene. *Producers:* Julie Brandon, Bob Perlowe, Greg Sills, Pamela Lundquist. *Writers:* Kenny Solms, Martha Williamson. *Director:* Marty Pasetta.

## 942 Homer and the Wacky Doughnut Machine.

Comedy, 30 min., ABC, 4/30/76. The problems that occur when Homer, a mechanically inclined boy, attempts to save his uncle's faltering coffee shop by perfecting an automatic doughnut-making machine. Aired as an "ABC Weekend Special." *Cast:* Michael LeClaire (Homer), David Doyle (Uncle Ulysses), Jesse White (Mr. Gabby), Tara Talboy (Kelly). *Producer:* Robert Chenault. *Writer:* Mark Fink. *Director:* Larry Elikann.

## 943 The Honeymooners Anniversary Celebration.

Comedy, 2 hrs., Syndicated, 10/85. A celebration of one of America's best-loved sitcoms, "The Honeymooners," with clips from the "lost" episodes (filmed live in the 1950s and available to television stations as a syndicated package of 75 episodes). *Hosts:* Art Carney, Jackie Gleason, Audrey Meadows, Joyce Randolph. *Music:* Kevin Kiner. *Producer-Writers:* Andrew Solt, Susan F. Walker. *Director:* Andrew Solt.

## 944 The Honeymooners Anniversary Special.

Comedy, 60 min., CBS, 11/12/90. A look back at "The Honeymooners" with two long-lost sketches from "The Jackie Gleason Show": "The Lost Baby" (10/11/52) and "The Quiz Show" (10/18/52), which were the third and fourth sketches performed. *Host:* Audrey Meadows. *Guests:* Art Carney, Frank Marth, George O. Petrie, Joyce Randolph. *Music:* Daniel May. *Producers:* George Zaloom, Les Mayfield. *Writer-Director:* Peyton Reed.

**945 The Honeymooners Reunion.** Comedy, 60 min., NBC, 5/13/85. Highlights of the funniest moments from rediscovered episodes of "The Honeymooners"—episodes, produced from 1952 through 1957, that had not been seen since their original, live telecasts on "The Jackie Gleason Show." *Host:* Jackie Gleason. *Guests:* Bob Hope, Audrey Meadows. *Music:* Bob Alberti. *Producer-Director:* Andrew Solt. *Writers:* Theodore Strauss, Andrew Solt.

**946 The Honeymooners Reunion Specials.** A chronological listing of the four 60-minute ABC specials that brought "The Honeymooners" back to television in 1976, 1977, and 1978. The cast and credits for each episode are exactly the same. *Cast:* Jackie Gleason (Ralph Kramden), Audrey Meadows (Alice Kramden), Art Carney (Ed Norton), Jane Kean (Trixie Norton). *Music Composer and Conductor:* Jackie Gleason. *Producers:* Jack Philbin, Ed Waglin. *Writers:* Walter Stone, Robert Hilliard. *Director:* Jackie Gleason. *Announcer:* Johnny Olsen.
**1 The Honeymooners Second Honeymoon** (2/2/76). The Kramdens and Nortons are reunited to help Ralph and Alice celebrate their twenty-fifth wedding anniversary.
**2 The Honeymooners Christmas** (11/28/77). Ralph's efforts to direct a stage play of *A Christmas Carol* for his fraternity, the Raccoon Lodge.
**3 The Honeymooners Valentine Special** (2/13/78). Ralph believes Alice is having an affair with another man and is planning to kill him when he overhears a conversation and, as usual, jumps to the wrong conclusion. With the help of Ed Norton, Ralph goes "undercover" and learns the awful truth: Alice had planned on surprising him with a new suit for Valentine's Day.
**4 The Honeymooners Christmas Special** (12/10/78). Ralph, famous for his get-rich-quick schemes, attempts still another one: gambling his and Ed's life savings on lottery tickets in an attempt to win $1 million.

**The Hoober-Bloob Highway** *see* **Dr. Seuss' The Hoober-Bloob Highway**

**947 Hooray for Love.** Variety, 60 min., CBS, 10/2/60. A music and comedy salute to love. *Host:* Art Carney. *Guests:* Alice Ghostley, Kenneth Nelson, Janis Paige, Jane Powell, Tony Randall. *Producer:* David Susskind. *Writers:* Woody Allen, Larry Gelbart. *Director:* Burt Shevelove.

**948 Horatio Alger Updated: Frank and Fearless.** Drama, 30 min., ABC, 2/12 and 2/19/83. The story is set in the 1940s and tells of Jasper Kent, a courageous boy who is forced from his home by an evil stepmother and her bullying son, and his attempts to outwit a group of villainous kidnappers to rescue a young child and regain his family heritage. Aired as an "ABC Weekend Special." *Cast:* Thor Fields (Jasper Kent), Blake Brocksmith (Nicholas Thorne), Denise Ferguson (Mrs. Thorne), James Edmond (Mr. Kent), James B. Douglas (Tom Keller), Beth Downey (Margaret Hanson), Ian Heath (Harry Fitch). *Producer:* Diana Kerew. *Writer:* Bruce Harmon. *Director:* Stephen Foreman.

**949 The Horrible Honchos.** Comedy-Drama, 60 min., ABC, 3/9/77.

Minnow is a very pretty girl and the leader of a group of kids who call themselves "The Horrible Honchos." Hollis is eleven years old and the new boy in town. Minnow impulsively decides that Hollis is no good and dictates that no Honcho can associate with him. As the days pass, the other Honchos discover that Hollis is really a nice kid, but peer pressure forces them to continue Minnow's campaign of harassment. Soon, Minnow is attracted by Hollis's pleasing personality, but she is forced to conceal her feelings so as not to appear as an indecisive leader. The story relates Minnow's efforts to right her wrong — and save face — by placing her life in jeopardy — and where only Hollis can save her. Aired as an "ABC Afterschool Special." *Cast:* Kim Richards (Minnow), Christian Juttner (Hollis), Tara Talboy (Louise), Billy Jacoby (Ivan), Christopher Maleki (C.C.), Larry Haddon (Hollis' father), Davey Davison (Hollis' mother). *Music:* Joe Webber. *Producers:* Daniel Wilson, Fran Sears. *Writer:* Thomas Baum. *Director:* Larry Elikann.

**950 The Horrible Secret.**
Drama, 30 min., Syndicated, 9/87. A reality drama about the sexual abuse of children. The sensitive story, set in a small Maryland town in 1943, tells of a cheerful girl (Tracy) who is sexually molested by an older man, and the torment she conceals when she keeps the experience a secret. Based on a true story. *Cast:* Jennifer East (Tracy Vinelli), Lynn Ritchie (Mrs. Vinelli), Steven McNaughton (Mr. Vinelli), Will Sahlein (Mr. Conley), Diane Danzi (Herself). *Producer-Director:* Tom G. Robertson. *Writers:* Tom G. Robertson, Diane Danzi.

**951 The Horror of It All.**
Documentary, 60 min., PBS, 2/23/83. A look at the history of horror films, via film clips, from the 1920s to the 1960s. *Narrator:* Jose Ferrer. *Guests:* Dana Andrews, Martine Beswick,

Robert Bloch, John Carradine, Roger Corman, Curtis Harrington, Gloria Stuart. *Producer-Director:* Gene Feldman. *Writers:* Gene Feldman, Suzette Winter.

**Horton Hears a Who** *see* **Dr. Seuss' Horton Hears a Who**

**952 A Hot Summer Night with Donna.** Variety, 60 min., HBO, 10/22/83. A concert by Donna Summer, the "Queen of Disco." *Host:* Donna Summer. *Guests:* Musical Youth. *Music:* Jeff Lamas. *Backup Vocalists:* Dara Bernard, Mary Ellen Bernard. *Producers:* Susan Mano, Len Epand. *Director:* Brian Grant.

**953 Hotel 90.** Comedy, 60 min., CBS, 3/26/73. Comedy sketches, songs, and dance routines set against the background of Hotel 90, a luxurious but mythical hotel. *Cast:* Alan Alda, Diahann Carroll, Tim Conway, Donna McKechnie, Sally Struthers, Joyce Van Patten. *Music:* Peter Matz. *Producers:* Arne Rosen, Ed Simmons, George Sunga. *Writers:* Ed Simmons, Bill Richmond, Arne Rosen. *Director:* Robert Scheerer.

**954 Hotpoint Holiday.** Variety, 60 min., CBS, 11/24/49. A Thanksgiving program of music and songs sponsored by Hotpoint Appliances. *Host:* Rudy Vallee. *Guests:* Carol Bruce, Mary Raye, The Three Rockets, The Upstarts. *Announcer:* Ken Roberts. *Music:* Guy Lombardo. *Producer:* Barry Wood. *Director:* Herbert Sussan.

**955 An Hour of Musical Entertainment with Paul Anka.** Variety, 60 min., Syndicated, 11/67. Music and songs with singer Paul Anka. *Host:* Paul Anka. *Guest:* Hanna Aroni. *Music:* Marty Paich. *Producer:* Jackie Barnett. *Director:* Dick Ross.

**956 An Hour with Danny Kaye.** Variety, 60 min., CBS, 10/30/60.

Music and songs coupled with light comedy. *Host:* Danny Kaye. *Guest:* Louis Armstrong. *Music:* Ray Heindorf. *Producer:* Sylvia Fine. *Writers:* Sylvia Fine, Hal Kanter. *Director:* Norman Jewison.

## 957 An Hour with Robert Goulet. Variety, 60 min., CBS, 11/19/64. An hour of music, songs, and comedy skits. *Host:* Robert Goulet. *Guests:* Leslie Caron, Ed Sullivan, Terry Thomas, Earl Wilson. *Music:* David Rose. *Producer:* Norman Rosemont. *Writer:* Arthur Alsberg. *Director:* Clark Jones.

## 958 The House Next Door. Comedy, 60 min., NBC, 11/15/63. The story of George Warren, an easterner who purchases a home in fashionable Waverly Hills, California, unaware that his neighbor is Ernie Santee, a notorious big-time mobster. The program marks Bob Hope's first role in a television play. *Cast:* Bob Hope (George Warren), Kathryn Crosby (Ginny Warren), Jill St. John (Bunky), Harold J. Stone (Ernie Santee), Jesse White (Marvin), Jerome Cowan (Mr. Bryant), Doris Singleton (Mrs. Bryant), Leo Gordon (Biggie), Frank Albertson (Morgan), Jimmy Boyd (Jerry). *Music:* Les Brown. *Producer-Director:* Jack Arnold. *Writers:* Albert E. Lewin, Burt Styler.

## 959 The House Without a Christmas Tree. Drama, 90 min., CBS, 12/3/72. The first of four specials about the Millses, a family living in Nebraska during the 1940s (see also "Addie and the King of Hearts," "The Easter Promise," and "The Thanksgiving Treasure"). The story of Addie Mills, a precocious tomboy; James, her stern, widowed father; and her compassionate grandmother. Christmas means little to James since the death of his wife, but to Addie it is a joyous occasion. Shown are Addie's efforts to convince her unsentimental father that, with Christmas Day approaching, their house needs a Christmas tree. *Cast:* Jason Robards (James Mills), Lisa Lucas (Addie Mills), Mildred Natwick (Grandmother), Alexa Kenin (Carla Mae), Kathryn Walker (Miss Thompson), Gail Dusome (Gloria Cott), Brady MacNamara (Billy Wild). *Producer:* Alan Shayne. *Writer:* Eleanor Perry. *Director:* Paul Bogart.

## 960 How Bugs Bunny Won the West. Cartoon, 30 min., CBS, 11/15/78. Live action is interspersed with clips from various Bugs Bunny cartoons to spoof the western genre and show how Bugs tamed, settled, and won the West. *Host:* Denver Pyle. *Voices:* Mel Blanc (as Bugs Bunny, Daffy Duck, Porky Pig, Yosemite Sam). *Music:* Harper McKay, Carl Stalling, Milt Franklyn, Bill Lava. *Producer-Director:* Hal Geer. *Writers:* Marc Sheffler, Hal Geer, Ted Pierce, Warren Foster, Michael Maltese.

## 961 How the Beatles Changed the World. Documentary, 60 min., NBC, 11/22/77. A special aimed at teenagers to show how the British rock group, the Beatles, affected the world's music and life-styles. *Host-Narrator:* David Frost. *Guests:* David Clayton-Thomas and Blood, Sweat and Tears, Richie Havens, Melissa Manchester, Melanie, Frankie Valli. *Producers:* Charles Andrews, Ken Greengrass. *Writer:* Charles Andrews. *Director:* Jean-Christopher Averty.

## How the Grinch Stole Christmas see Dr. Seuss' How the Grinch Stole Christmas

## 962 How to Be a Man. Variety, 60 min., CBS, 5/29/85. A lighthearted look at the role of men in the 1980s via music, songs, and comedy sketches. *Host:* Bob Keeshan. *Guests:* Susan Anton, Scott Baio, Mary Cadorette, John Denver, Rick Derringer,

Howard Hesseman, Hal Linden, Melba Moore, Rex Smith. *Music:* Garry Sherman. *Producers:* Bob Keeshan, Jim Hirschfeld. *Writers:* Emily Adams, Jason Daniels, David Axelrod, Jonathan Day, Leslie Fuller, Sean Kelly, Harold Kimmel, Larry Levin. *Director:* Robert Nigro.

**963 How to Eat Like a Kid.** Variety, 60 min., NBC, 9/22/81. A lighthearted look at being a youngster through music, songs, and comedy sketches. *Host:* Dick Van Dyke. *The Kids:* Earl Hoffman, Rachel Jacobs, Billy Jacoby, Sunshine Lee, Arlene McIntyre, Christine Murrill, Georg Olden, Ricky Segall, Rebecca Wolfe, Kimberly Woodward. *Music:* Daniel Troob. *Producer-Writer:* Judith Kahan. *Director:* Robert Scheerer.

**How to Handle a Woman** *see* **Dinah Shore Specials**

**964 How to Survive the 70s and Maybe Even Bump into Happiness.** Variety, 60 min., CBS, 2/22/78. Music and comedy sketches that probe the problems facing people in the 1970s and how to overcome them. *Host:* Mary Tyler Moore. *Guests:* Caitlin Adams, Candace Azzara, Ed Barth, Allen Case, Gino Conforti, Michael Durrell, Steve Landesberg, Alan Oppenheimer, Henry Polic II, Beverly Sanders. *Music:* Jack Elliott. *Producer-Director:* Bill Persky. *Writers:* Bill Persky, Phil Hahn, April Kelly, Tom Sawyer, Sam Bobrick.

**965 Howdy Doody and Friends.** Variety, 60 min., NBC, 9/5/72. The program reunites "Buffalo" Bob Smith and Lew "Clarabelle" Anderson for a series of skits that were originally performed on the series "Howdy Doody" (NBC, 1947–60). *Cast:* Bob Smith (Buffalo Bob Smith), Lew Anderson (Clarabelle), Bob Smith (Voice of Howdy Doody). *Producer:*

Florence Small. *Writers:* Lan O'Kun, Jon Surgal, Jack Ainob. *Puppeteers:* Paul Ritts, Carl Harms.

**966 The Howie Mandel Special.** Comedy, 50 min., HBO, 5/16/86. An adult-oriented comedy concert by comedian Howie Mandel. *Host:* Howie Mandel. *Producers:* Howie Mandel, Jonathan Krane. *Writer:* Howie Mandel. *Director:* Jerry Kramer.

**967 The Human Voice.** Drama, 60 min., ABC, 5/4/67. A one-character drama about a middle-aged woman's attempts to overcome the emotional and psychological stresses of ending a long love affair. The program relates her side of a telephone conversation with her lover. *Cast:* Ingrid Bergman (The Woman). *Producers:* David Susskind, Lars Schmidt. *Writer:* Clive Exton. *Director:* Ted Kotcheff.

**I Believe in Music** *see* **Mac Davis Specials**

**968 I Hear America Singing.** Variety, 90 min., CBS, 12/17/55. A musical salute to America. *Performers:* Nat King Cole, Eddie Fisher, Ella Fitzgerald, Debbie Reynolds, Red Skelton, Bobby Van. *Music:* Axel Stordahl. *Producer:* Ken Murray. *Writer:* Jean Holloway. *Director:* Paul Harrison.

**969 I, Leonardo: A Journey of the Mind.** Drama, 60 min., CBS, 4/26/83. The program, filmed on location in Italy, France, and New York City, chronicles Leonardo da Vinci's lifelong search for learning and knowledge. *Host:* Walter Cronkite. *Narrator:* Richard Burton. *Cast:* Frank Langella (Leonardo), Joseph Maher (Giorgio Vasari), Jeremiah Sullivan (Niccolo Machiavelli), Louis Turenne (Bernadino Corio), David Bryant (Cesare da Sesto). *Producers:* Chandler Cowles, Helen Kristt Radin. *Writer:* Chandler Cowles. *Director:* Lee R. Bobker.

**Ad for "I Love Lucy: The Very First Show"**

**970 I Love Liberty.** Variety, 2 hrs., ABC, 3/21/82. Music, songs, comedy skits, and dramatic vignettes that salute America. *Guests:* Desi Arnaz, Jr., Christopher Atkins, LeVar Burton, Patty Duke, Jane Fonda, Anthony Geary, Barry Goldwater, Valerie Harper, Gregory Hines, Judd Hirsch, Geri Jewell, Burt Lancaster, Michele Lee, Hal Linden, Kristy McNichol, Melissa Manchester, Walter Matthau, Mary Tyler Moore, Helen Reddy, Christopher Reeve, Kenny Rogers, Martin Sheen, Madge Sinclair, Rod Steiger, Barbra Streisand, Dick Van Patten, Dionne Warwick, Robin Williams. *Music:* Peter Matz. *Producers:* Norman Lear, Bud Yorkin. *Writers:* Richard Alfieri, Rita Mae Brown, Rick Mitz, Arthur Allan Seidelman, Norman Lear. *Director:* Bill Carruthers.

**971 I Love Lucy: The Very First Show.** Comedy, 60 min., CBS, 3/30/90. The first airing of the original pilot film for the series "I Love Lucy." The pilot film, thought lost for 40 years, was filmed in March 1951 and found in 1990 when the wife of a guest in the pilot (Pepito, a Spanish clown) discovered a copy among her late husband's possessions. Lucille Ball and Desi Arnaz play Lucy and Ricky Ricardo (not Lucy and Larry Lopez as reported in *TV Guide* and other printed sources). Ricky is a bandleader and Lucy is his wacky wife, who is seeking to break into show-business. Fred and Ethel Mertz are not a part of the program. The only other difference is that Lucy and Ricky live in an apartment much more modern than the one owned by Fred and Ethel in the series. *Host:* Lucie Arnaz. *Guests:* Bob Carroll, Jr. and Madelyn Pugh ("I Love Lucy" writers). *Producer:* Bud Grant. *Writers:* Jane Milmore, Billy Van Zandt. *Director:* David Steinberg.

**972 I Love You.** Variety, 60 min., NBC, 2/14/78. A Valentine's Day special in which celebrities offer their opinions on the subject of love. *Guests:* Paul and Anne Anka, Edgar Bergen, Ernest Borgnine, Angie Dickinson, Phyllis Diller, Norman Fell, Steve and Cindy Garvey, Will Geer, Melissa Gilbert, Bill Hayes, Audra Lindley, Paul Lynde, Marilyn McCoo and Billy Davis, Jr., Ed McMahon, Kristy and Jimmy McNichol, Johnny Mathis, Tony and Elaine Orlando, Don Rickles, Telly Savalas, Susan Seaforth, Doc Severinsen. *Producer:* Ken Weinstock.

**973 I Think I'm Having a Baby.** Drama, 60 min., CBS, 3/3/81. A sensitive drama about teenage uncertainties concerning love, friendship, and sex that focuses on Laurie, a beautiful teenage girl who, as the result of a romantic interlude, fears she is pregnant. Her efforts to find help and cope with the situation are the focal point of the program. A "cbs Afternoon Playhouse." *Cast:* Jennifer Jason Leigh (Laurie), Helen Hunt (Phoebe), Tracey Gold (Carrie), David Birney (Mr. Fenning), Ally Sheedy (Cathy), Shawn Stevens (Peter), Bobbi Block (Marsha), Shane Sinutko (Steven). *Music:* Bob Cobert. *Producer:* Joseph Stern. *Writer:* Blossom Elfman. *Director:* Arthur Allan Siedelman.

### 974 I Want to Go Home.
Drama, 60 min., ABC, 2/13/85. A poignant "ABC Afterschool Special" about Mary and Tommy Sanders, two children of divorce who become victims of parental kidnapping when their mother abducts them and attempts to begin a new life with them. *Cast:* Lindsay Crouse (Louise Sanders), John Getz (Thomas Sanders), Maddie Corman (Mary Sanders), Seth Green (Tommy Sanders), Laurie Heineman (Sharon Sanders), Marge Redmond (Judge Bard). *Music:* Jonathan Tunick. *Producer:* Diana Kerew. *Writer:* Jeanne Betancourt. *Director:* Alex Grashoff.

### 975 The Ice Capades 50th Anniversary Special.
Variety, 2 hrs., ABC, 12/27/90. A special television edition of the Ice Capades that salutes the troupe's fiftieth year. *Host:* Peter Scolari. *Guests:* Bobby Berosini and His Orangutans, Michael Feinstein, Elizabeth Manley and Brian Orser (skaters), Pia Zadora. *Music Directors:* Kevin Nadeau, Dell Hake. *Producers:* Marty Pasetta, Thomas Scallen, Willy Bietak. *Writer:* Garry Bormet. *Director:* Marty Pasetta.

### 976 The Ice Capades with Jason Bateman and Alyssa Milano.
Variety, 2 hrs., ABC, 12/28/89. Music, songs, and comedy featuring Ice Capades skaters. *Hosts:* Jason Bateman, Alyssa Milano. *Guests:* The Bob Mack Trio, Christopher Hewett,

Doc Severinsen, Leslie Uggams, Steve Wheeler. *Ice Skating Stars:* Bob and Julie, Jean Pierre Boulais, Angelo D'Agostino, Angelique Doud, Brad Doud, Simone Grigoreseu, David Jamison, Kitty Kelly, Kristan and Chip, Kevin Parker, David Wilson. *Music Directors:* Kevin Nadeau, Dell Hake. *Producers:* Marty Pasetta, Thomas Scallen, Willy Bietak. *Writer:* Bruce Vilanch. *Director:* Marty Pasetta.

### 977 The Ice Capades with Kirk Cameron.
Variety, 2 hrs., ABC, 12/29/88. Music, songs, and comedy skits featuring ice skating stars. *Host:* Kirk Cameron. *Guests:* Allyce Beasley, Scott Hamilton, Rita Moreno, Debbie Thomas. *Ice Skating Stars:* Andrea Beatty, Chris Beatty, Kitty Carruthers, Peter Carruthers, Richard Dalley, Tom Dickson, Carol Fox, Tricia Klocke, Leanne Knight, Jeff LaBrake, Catarina Lindgren, Staci McMullin, Elizabeth Manley, J. P. Martin, Steve Taylor, Kirk Wyss. *Music:* Kevin Nadeau, Artie Hake. *Producers:* Marty Pasetta, Thomas Scallen, Willy Bietak. *Writer:* Bruce Vilanch. *Director:* Marty Pasetta.

### 978 If I Had a Chance.
Variety, 20 min., NBC, 8/14/47. Celebrities appear to tell of the careers they would have chosen if they were given a second chance. *Guests:* Carol Brooks, Russ Case, Jessica Dragonnette, Ben Grauer, Robert Lieb. *Announcer:* Roger Bowman. *Producer-Director:* Roger Muir.

### 979 If I'm Lost, How Come I Found You?
Comedy, 30 min., ABC, 9/30 and 10/7/78. Quacky Quackenbush is a 12-year-old boy living in an orphanage. When he becomes dissatisfied with life there, he runs away to live with his slightly eccentric aunt, Maggie. Maggie runs a rooming house and has been arrested on several occasions for shoplifting health food. Jerry and Clem are amateur bank robbers who decide to use the rooming house as a hideout.

The story relates the close relationship that develops between Quacky and Jerry — both runaways until they find each other. Aired in two parts as an "ABC Weekend Special." *Cast:* Moosie Drier (Quacky), Irene Tedrow (Aunt Maggie), Ron Soble (Jerry), Ron Feinberg (Clem), Judson Pratt (Sheriff). *Music:* Tommy Leonetti. *Producer:* Robert Chenault. *Writers:* Jim Carlson, Terrence McDonnell. *Director:* Arthur Lubin.

### 980 If It's a Man, Hang Up.

Thriller, 90 min., ABC, 5/5/75. The story of Suzy Martin, a beautiful fashion model who is tormented by an anonymous phone caller. *Cast:* Carol Lynley (Suzy Martin), Paul Angelis (Terry Cleeves), Tom Conti (Bruno Varella), Gerald Harper (Greg Miles), Susan Holderness (Betty), David Gwillim (Henry Venner). *Music:* Laurie Johnson. *Producer:* Ian Fordyce. *Writer:* Brian Clemens. *Director:* Shaun O'Riordan.

### 981 I'm a Fan.

Variety, 60 min., CBS, 1/25/72. Music, songs, and comedy sketches that poke fun at the avid sports aficionado. *Hosts:* Carol Channing, Dick Van Dyke. *Guests:* MacIntyre Dixon, Donna McKechnie, Brandon Maggart, Karen Morrow, Trisha Noble, Mary Louise Wilson. *Music:* Leroy Holmes. *Producer:* Alexander H. Cohen. *Writers:* Bob Ellison, Carolyn Leigh. *Director:* Clark Jones.

### 982 I'm Sooo Ugly.

Drama, 30 min., Syndicated, 2/80. Marcy is a preteenage girl who believes she is ugly and will never be loved by anyone. The story relates her attempts to change her attitude when she meets a boy with a similar problem (he feels he's too short) and realizes that she is not alone in her feelings. *Cast:* Jenny Feeback (Marcy), Diane Schuranberd (Tracy), Barbara Britton (Marcy's mother). *Producer-Writer-Director:* Tom Robertson.

### 983 I'm the Girl He Wants to Kill.

Thriller, 90 min., ABC, 3/18/74. The story of Ann Rogers, a beautiful secretary who becomes the target of a jeweler determined to stop her from linking him to two murders. *Cast:* Julie Sommars (Ann Rogers), Robert Lang (The Man), Mark Tanner (Tony Selby). *Music:* Laurie Johnson. *Producer:* John Sichel. *Writer:* Brian Clemens. *Director:* Shaun O'Riordan.

### 984 In Performance at the White House.

Variety, 60 min., PBS, 3/25/87. A celebration of the music of Richard Rodgers and the lyrics of Lorenz Hart. *Host:* Nancy Reagan. *Guests:* Vic Damone, Marvin Hamlisch, Liza Minnelli, President Ronald Reagan, Bobby Short. *Music Director:* Marvin Hamlisch. *Producer:* John Musilli. *Director:* David Deutsch.

### 985 In Performance at the White House.

Variety, 60 min., PBS, 3/31/88. A salute to Broadway with a selection of songs from various shows. *Host:* Marvin Hamlisch. *Guests:* Pearl Bailey, Larry Kent, Judy Kuhn, Pamela Myers, Jerry Orbach, Nancy Reagan, President Ronald Reagan. *Music:* Marvin Hamlisch. *Producer:* John Musilli. *Director:* David Deutsch.

### 986 In the Shadow of Love: A Teen AIDS Story.

Drama, 60 min., ABC, 9/19/91. Katie and Lisa are reporters for their high school newspaper. While working on a story involving AIDS among teens, Katie learns that her boyfriend, Wayne, has tested HIV positive. Katie's efforts to reexamine her life-style and deal with the situation are the focal point of this "ABC Afterschool Special." *Cast:* Jennifer Dundas (Katie), Lisa Vidal (Lisa), Suzanne Douglas (Sammy), James R. O'Connor (Wayne), Harvey Fierstein (Andrew), Jung Park (June), Nicole White (Louise). *Producer:* Judith Stone. *Writer:* Gordon Rayfield. *Director:* Consuelo Gonzalez.

## 987 Inaugural Eve Gala Performance. Variety, 2 hrs. 30 min., CBS, 1/19/77.

A music, song, and comedy salute to President-Elect Jimmy Carter and Vice President–Elect Walter Mondale on the eve of their inauguration. *Guests:* Jack Albertson, Muhammad Ali, Dan Aykroyd, Warren Beatty, Leonard Bernstein, Chevy Chase, Bette Davis, Redd Foxx, Aretha Franklin, Loretta Lynn, Shirley MacLaine, Elaine May, Paul Newman, Mike Nichols, Jack Nicholson, Carol O'Connor (voice only), Freddie Prinze, Linda Ronstadt, Robert Shaw, Beverly Sills, Paul Simon, Jean Stapleton, John Wayne, Joanne Woodward. *Music:* Donn Trenner. *Producers:* James Lipton, Bob Wynn. *Director:* Marty Pasetta.

## 988 The Incredible Book Escape. Fantasy, 60 min., CBS, 6/3/80.

While in a library reading room, a young girl named P. J. becomes trapped when the library closes. Shortly after, four storybook characters come to life and befriend her. The story relates P. J.'s experiences as she and the characters (seen in animated form) devise a plan of escape. (The characters she meets: Myra, a little girl who can become whomever or whatever she imagines herself to be; a determined ghost in a shed on a New England farm; a liberated princess with a practical answer to any problem; and Melvin Spitznagle, an aspiring young inventor.) A "CBS Afternoon Playhouse." *Cast:* Quinn Cummings (P. J.). *Voices:* Penelope Sudrow (Myra), George Gobel (The Ghost), Tammy Grimes (Princess), Sparky Marcus (Melvin Spitznagel), Ruth Buzzi (Mrs. Page), Hans Conried (Professor Mickimecki), Arte Johnson (Lord Garp), June Foray (Melvin's mother), Jack Angel (Melvin's father). *Music:* Larry Wolff. *Producer:* Nick Bosustow. *Writer:* George Arthur Bloom. *Animation Director:* Sam Weiss. *Live Action Director:* Seth Pinsker.

## 989 The Incredible, Indelible, Magical, Physical, Mystery Trip. Fantasy, 60 min., ABC, 10/24/73.

A musical fantasy in which a live action brother and sister (Joey and Missey) become animated to learn about themselves by taking a trip through the human body. An "ABC Afterschool Special." *Cast:* Kim Richards (Missey), Michael Link (Joey), Hal Smith (Uncle Carl). *Voices:* Kathy Buck (Missey), Peter Broderick (Joey), Len Maxwell (Everything else). *Music and Lyrics:* Edward Newmark. *Producers:* David H. DePatie, Friz Freleng. *Writer:* Larry Spiegel. *Animation Director:* Herbert Klynn. *Live Action Director:* Jim Gates.

## 990 Inger Stevens in Sweden. Documentary, 60 min., ABC, 1/25/65.

Inger Stevens, the star of ABC's "The Farmer's Daughter," returns to the land of her birth for a personal tour of the old and new Sweden. *Host:* Inger Stevens. *Guests:* Bob Beskow, Ingemar Johansson, King Gustav, Max Von Sydow. *Producer:* Herbert Sussan. *Writer:* Jean Holloway. *Director:* Don Taylor.

## 991 Inherit the Wind. Drama, 90 min., NBC, 11/18/65.

A reenactment of the historic Scopes Trial (the 1925 case in which Clarence Darrow defended a schoolteacher accused of teaching the then taboo theory of evolution by Charles Darwin). Based on the play by Jerome Lawrence and Robert E. Lee; aired on the "Hallmark Hall of Fame." *Cast:* Melvyn Douglas (Henry Drummond), Ed Begley (Matthew Brady), Murray Hamilton (E. K. Hornbeck), Diane Baker (Rachel Brown), Burt Brinckerhoff (Bert Cates), John Randolph (the Reverend Brown), Joanna Roos (Mrs. Brady), Leora Thatcher (Mrs. Krebs). *Producer-Director:* George Schaefer.

## 992 Inn of the Flying Dragon. Mystery, 60 min., NBC, 10/18/60. A

"Dow Hour of Great Mysteries" presentation about a traveler who is mistaken for a spy when he stops for the night at a French inn called the Flying Dragon. *Cast:* Farley Granger (Richard Beckett), Hugh Griffith (Captain Harmonville), Barry Morse (Count St. Alyre). *Producer:* Robert Saudek. *Writer-Director:* Sheldon Reynolds.

**993 Inside Family Ties.** Documentary, 60 min., PBS, 10/6/88. A fascinating look behind the scenes at the making of one episode of the series "Family Ties" with the cast (Meredith Baxter, Justine Bateman, Michael J. Fox, Michael Gross, Tina Yothers), creator (Gary David Goldberg), and crew of the series. *Host-Narrator:* Henry Winkler. *Producer-Director:* Michael Hirsh. *Writer:* Joel Lipman.

**994 Intermezzo.** Drama, 60 min., NBC, 11/19/61. A "Theater '62" presentation about a married concert violinist who falls in love with his daughter's music teacher, and their efforts to escape responsibility and find a life together. *Cast:* Ingrid Thulin (Anita Hoffman), Jean-Pierre Aumont (Holger Brandt), Teresa Wright (Margit Brandt), George Voskovec (Thomas Stenborg), Fred Stewart (Dr. Newman), Dorothy Blackburn (Emma). *Music:* Paul Bernard, Eileen Fissler. *Producer:* Fred Coe. *Writer:* Patricia Broderick. *Director:* Ronald Winston.

**995 The International All-Star Festival.** Variety, 60 min., Showtime, 6/81. A music and song benefit for UNICEF; taped in West Germany. *Performers:* Lola Falana, The Harlem Globetrotters, Liza Minnelli, The Muppets, Wayne Newton, Ben Vereen. *Producers:* George Schlatter, Bob Wynn, Don Mischer. *Director:* Ekkehard Bohmer.

**996 An Invitation to Paris.** Variety, 60 min., ABC, 4/27/60. A

musical tour of Paris. *Host:* Maurice Chevalier. *Guests:* Anna Gaylor, Joe Basile's Band, Jean Sablon. *Producer:* Pierre Crenesse. *Writer:* Sidney Slon. *Director:* Jean-Claude Schwartz.

**997 Irving Berlin's America.** Tribute, 75 min., PBS, 3/7/86. A salute to composer Irving Berlin via clips of his music from movies and television shows. *Host:* Sandy Duncan. *Guests:* Patty Andrews, Cab Calloway, Rosemary Clooney, Alice Faye, Mary Martin, Donald O'Connor, President Ronald Reagan, Ginger Rogers. *Producers:* Stephan Chodorov, John Musilli. *Writers:* James Arntz, Joann G. Young. *Director:* Glen DuBose.

**998 Irving Berlin's 100th Birthday Celebration.** Tribute, 2 hrs., CBS, 5/27/88. A star-studded salute to composer Irving Berlin on the occasion of his one hundredth birthday. Taped at Carnegie Hall on 5/11/88. *Guest of Honor:* Irving Berlin. *Guests:* Bea Arthur, Tony Bennett, Leonard Bernstein, Barry Bostwick, Nell Carter, Ray Charles, Rosemary Clooney, Natalie Cole, Billy Eckstein, Michael Feinstein, Marilyn Horne, Madeline Kahn, Garrison Keillor, Shirley MacLaine, Willie Nelson, Jerry Orbach, Frank Sinatra, Tommy Tune, Joe Williams. *Music:* Elliot Lawrence. *Producers:* Don Mischer, Jan Cornell, David Goldberg. *Director:* Walter C. Miller.

**999 Irving Berlin's Salute to America.** Variety, 60 min., NBC, 9/12/51. A musical salute to America by composer Irving Berlin. *Host:* Irving Berlin. *Guests:* Bil and Cora Baird Marionettes, Bill Callahan, Teddy Hale, Kathryn Lee, Tony Martin, Dinah Shore, Margaret Truman. *Orchestra:* Al Goodman. *Producer:* Leo Morgan. *Writers:* Goodman Ace, George Axelrod. *Director:* Grey Lockwood.

## 1000 Is This Goodbye, Charlie Brown? Cartoon, 30 min., CBS, 2/21/83. The trauma that faces the Peanuts gang when it is learned that Linus and his sister Lucy are moving to another community. *Voices:* Kevin Brando, Michael Dockery, Brad Kesten, Angela Lee, Bill Melendez, Jeremy Schoenberg, Stacy Tolkin, Victoria Vargas. *Music:* Steve Rifkin, Judy Munsen. *Producers:* Lee Mendelson, Bill Melendez. *Writer:* Charles M. Schulz. *Director:* Phil Roman.

## 1001 It Can't Happen to Me. Drama, 30 min., Syndicated, 6/79. The problems of teenage drinking as seen through the experiences of Lisa Sears, a very pretty but shy 16-year-old girl who becomes addicted to alcohol when she gives into pressure from a friend. *Cast:* Lisa Gerritsen (Lisa Sears), Vincent Van Patten (Rick Adams), Diana Muldaur (Julie Sears), Ren Woods (Angie). *Music:* Chris Stone. *Producers:* Ellwood Kieser, Michael Rhodes. *Writer:* Lan O'Kun. *Director:* David Moessinger.

## 1002 It Isn't Easy Being a Teenage Millionaire. Comedy-Drama, 60 min., ABC, 3/8/78. When her Aunt Liz gives her a lottery ticket, Melissa Harrington, a 14-year-old girl who feels life is nothing but one dull cycle of school, homework, and babysitting, suddenly finds her world turned upside down when she wins $1 million. The story relates the sudden changes that come over Melissa — caught in the excitement of wealth, publicity, and glamour — and how she learns the meaning of the adage "money isn't everything." Aired as an "ABC Afterschool Special." *Cast:* Victoria Meyerink (Melissa Harrington), Karen Hurley (Katherine Harrington), Bob Hastings (Harry Harrington), Lauri Hendler (Teague Harrington), Susan O'Connell (Aunt Liz), Clark Brandon (Mark Henderson). *Music:* Hoyt Curtin. *Producer:* Joseph Barbera. *Writer:* Jim Inman. *Director:* Richard Bennett.

## 1003 It Must Be Love ('Cause I Feel So Dumb!). Comedy-Drama, 60 min., ABC, 10/8/75. Lisa is a pretty blonde cheerleader and the most popular girl in school. She has a crush on LeRoy, captain of the junior high basketball team. Eric is a boy newly liberated from braces on his teeth, who is attracted to Lisa. Cathy is a shy girl who admires Eric from afar. Cathy shares Eric's interests, has a secret crush on him, but her overtures to him go unnoticed. After a series of bungled attempts to attract Lisa's attention, Eric manages to get a date with her, but disaster again strikes: it begins to rain and Eric does not have enough money for a taxicab. The one-sided romance comes to a halt when Eric's dog is killed by a car and Lisa fails to share his grief. Cathy, however, is full of compassion. While Lisa is unable to understand the impact of the dog's death on Eric's life, Cathy empathizes with him. It is at this moment when Eric realizes that appearances can be deceiving and that one must look beyond the surface to find the true character and worth of his peers. An "ABC Afterschool Special." *Cast:* Alfred Lutter (Eric), Vicki Dawson (Lisa), Denby Olcott (Cathy), Kay Frye (Eric's mother), Michael Miller (Eric's father), P. R. Paul (LeRoy). *Producers:* Arthur Barron, Evelyn Barron. *Writer-Director:* Arthur Barron.

## 1004 It Was a Short Summer, Charlie Brown. Cartoon, 30 min., CBS, 9/27/69. The story finds Charlie and the Peanuts gang recalling the past summer at camp when the boys were pitted against the girls in various sports events. *Voices:* Peter Robbins (Charlie Brown), Pamelyn Ferdin (Lucy), Glen Gilger (Linus), Hilary Momberger (Sally), Bill Melendez (Snoopy). *Music:* Vince Guaraldi. *Music Conductor:* John Scott Trotter. *Producers:* Lee

Mendelson, Bill Melendez. *Writer:* Charles M. Schulz. *Director:* Bill Melendez.

## 1005 It's a Bird, It's a Plane, It's Superman. Musical, 2 hrs., ABC, 2/21/75.

A television adaptation of the Broadway play that spoofs the vulnerability of Superman when he is confronted by the machinations of a mad scientist who psychs the Man of Steel out of his superhuman powers. *Cast:* David Wilson (Clark Kent/Superman), Lesley Ann Warren (Lois Lane), Allen Ludden (Perry White), David Wayne (Dr. Sedgwick), Ken Mars (Max Mencken), Loretta Swit (Sydney Carlton). *Narrator:* Gary Owens. *Music Director:* Fred Werner. *Original Music:* Charles Strouse, Lee Adams. *Musical Book:* David Newman, Robert Benton. *Producers:* Norman Twain, Elliot Alexander. *Writer:* Romeo Muller. *Director:* Jack Regas.

## 1006 It's a Mile from Here to Glory. Drama, 60 min., ABC, 5/5/78.

Early McLaren is self-conscious and insecure because he is shorter than other boys his age. One day he finds recognition and applause when his high school coach discovers his potential as a mile runner. To the surprise of everyone, Early develops an inflated ego and loses sight of the team concept in his single-minded drive for victories and records. Shortly after, near the height of his running career, Early suffers a stinging defeat and, in a daze, walks onto the street where he is struck by a speeding van. Although the prognosis is poor for Early's recovery, the support of his father and friends convinces him that he will run to more meaningful triumphs. An "ABC Afterschool Special." *Cast:* Steve Shaw (Early McLaren), Justin Lord (Billy Patnell), David Haskell (Coach Canepa), James G. Richardson (Dave McLaren), Anne Gee Byrd (Mary Bruce), Woodrow Parfrey (John Moody), Suzy Callahan (Dorothy Kidder). *Music:* Glenn Paxton. *Pro-*

*ducer:* Martin Tahse. *Writer:* Durrell Royce Crays. *Director:* Richard Bennett.

## 1007 It's a Mystery, Charlie Brown. Cartoon, 30 min., CBS, 2/1/74.

Snoopy, Charlie Brown's dog, turns detective to solve the mysterious disappearance of Woodstock's missing nest. *Voices:* Todd Barbee (Charlie Brown), Melanie Kohn (Lucy), Stephen Shea (Linus), Lynn Mortensen (Sally), Donna Forman (Peppermint Patty), Jimmy Ahrens (Marcie), Thomas A. Muller (Pigpen), Bill Melendez (Snoopy). *Music:* Vince Guaraldi. *Producers:* Lee Mendelson, Phil Roman. *Writer:* Charles M. Schulz. *Director:* Phil Roman.

## 1008 It's a Wonderful Tiny Toons Christmas. Cartoon, 30 min., Fox, 12/6/92.

A spoof of *It's a Wonderful Life* wherein a dispirited Buster Bunny wishes he had never been on "Tiny Toons" (a daily series) when he is fired as director of the Acme Acres Christmas Pageant. As in the film, Buster receives a visit from his guardian angel and is shown what life at Acme Acres would have been like without him. *Voices:* John Kassir (Buster Bunny), Tress MacNeille (Babs Bunny), Joe Alaskey (Plucky Duck), Danny Cooksey (Montanna Max), Dan Castellaneta (Harvey), Cree Summer (Elmyra), Don Messick (Hamton), Kath Sougi (Sneezer), Frank Welker (Furrball), Rob Paulsen (Arnold), Gail Matthius (Shirley), Greg Burson (Porky Pig), Valri Bromfield (Fran). *Producer:* Steven Spielberg. *Writers:* Sherri Stoner, Deanna Oliver. *Director:* Jon McClenahan.

## 1009 It's an Adventure, Charlie Brown. Cartoon, 60 min., CBS, 5/16/83.

A series of vignettes that highlight the various themes used to showcase the Peanuts characters (for example, love, responsibility, friendship). *Voices:* Jason Castellano, Michael Dockery, Gerald Goyette, Jr., Joel Graves, Johnny Graves, Brent Hauer, Brian Jackson, Angela Lee, Jenny Lewis, Jason Muller, Earl Reilly, Brad Schachter. *Music:* Ed Bogas, Desiree Goyette. *Producers:* Lee Mendelson, Bill Melendez. *Writer:* Charles M. Schulz. *Directors:* Bill Melendez, Phil Roman, Sam Jaimes.

**1010 It's Arbor Day, Charlie Brown.** Cartoon, 30 min., CBS, 3/16/76. The chaos that results when the students of Birchwood School decide to observe Arbor Day and beautify the world. *Voices:* Dylan Beach (Charlie Brown), Sarah Beach (Lucy), Gail M. Davis (Sally), Stuart Brotman (Peppermint Patty), Greg Felton (Schroeder), Liam Martin (Linus), Michelle Muller (Freida), Bill Melendez (Snoopy). *Music:* Vince Guaraldi. *Producers:* Lee Mendelson, Bill Melendez. *Writer:* Charles M. Schulz. *Director:* Phil Roman.

**1011 It's Christmas Time Again, Charlie Brown.** Cartoon, 30 min., CBS, 11/27/92. The sequel to "A Charlie Brown Christmas" finds Charlie struggling to raise money to buy his girlfriend a present; Sally rehearsing for her big role in the Christmas play; and Peppermint Patty struggling to get her over-the-holidays homework done before the big day. *Voices:* Lindsay Bennish, John Grass, Mindy Ann Martin, Bill Melendez, Sean Mendelson, Marne Patterson, James E. Smith, Brittany Thornton. *Music:* Vince Guaraldi. *Producer:* Lee Mendelson. *Writer:* Charles M. Schulz. *Director:* Bill Melendez.

**1012 It's Flashbeagle, Charlie Brown.** Cartoon, 30 min., CBS, 4/16/84. The Peanuts first animated musical special in which Snoopy, Charlie Brown's pampered beagle, fancies himself as a great dancer and proceeds to make dancing history. *Voices:* Stacy Ferguson, Gary Goren, Desiree Goyette, Gini Holtzman, Keri Houlihan, Brett Johnson, Bill Melendez. *Music:* Ed Bogas, Desiree Goyette. *Producers:* Lee Mendelson, Bill Melendez. *Writer:* Charles M. Schulz. *Director:* Bill Melendez.

**1013 It's Howdy Doody Time—A 40 Year Celebration.** Variety, 2 hrs., Syndicated, 11/87. A music and comedy celebration of the "Howdy Doody" show (NBC, 1947–60), on the occasion of its fortieth anniversary. Clips from the series are interspersed with new antics of the Doodyville gang. *Cast:* Bob Smith (Buffalo Bob Smith), Lew Anderson (Clarabelle), Bill LeCornec (Chief Thunderthud), Nick Nicholson (Cornelius Cobb), Louise Vallance (Story Princess), Bob Smith (Voice of Howdy Doody). *Guests:* Milton Berle, Johnny Carson, Dick Clark, Gary Coleman, Gary Collins, Monty Hall, Pee Wee Herman, Perry King, Meredith MacRae, Jerry Mathers, Mary Ann Mobley, John Ritter. *Producers:* Nick Nicholson,, E. Roger Muir. *Writers:* David Lawrence, Aubrey Solomon. *Director:* Dennis Rosenblatt.

**1014 It's in the Closet . . . It's Under the Bed.** Documentary, 30 min., Syndicated, 10/87. The program examines, via film clips, the role of monsters in movies. *Host-Narrator:* Edward Mulhare. *Executive Producer:* Richard Jones. *Producer:* Tak Nakamori.

**1015 It's Magic, Charlie Brown.** Cartoon, 30 min., CBS, 4/28/81. Snoopy's misadventures when he becomes interested in magic and performs as "The Great Houndini"—much to the objections of the Peanuts gang when they become the subjects of his misguided magic. *Voices:* Michael Mandy (Charlie Brown), Brent Hauer

Music brought them together.
Her song tore them apart.
Why should she apologize when...

**IT'S ONLY**
*Rock 'n' Roll*

Guest starring:
David Jones & Carole King

(abc)
THE AFTERSCHOOL
SPECIAL
TOMORROW 4:00 PM ⑦ ⌷
Set your VCR. Watch it with your family.

Ad for "It's Only Rock 'n' Roll"

(Peppermint Patty), Casey Carlson (Paula), Christopher Donohoe (Schroeder), Kristen Fullerton (Sally), Sydney Penny (Lucy), Bill Melendez (Snoopy). *Music:* Ed Bogas, Judy Munsen. *Producers:* Lee Mendelson, Bill Melendez. *Writer:* Charles M. Schulz. *Director:* Phil Roman.

## 1016 It's No Crush, I'm in Love.

Drama, 60 min., ABC, 9/21/83. Ann Cassidy is a teenage high school girl who thinks television soap opera star Zak Whittier is the absolute perfect man and that teenage boys are silly and immature. On the first day of class Ann falls head over heels in love with David Angelucci, her new English teacher— and a Zak look-alike. The story follows Ann's whirlwind campaign to do everything she can to be near David. Aired as an "ABC Afterschool Special." *Cast:* Cynthia Nixon (Ann Cassidy), Mark LaMura (Zak Whittier/David Angelucci), Julie Cohen (Susannah Siegel-

baum), Tod Graff (Robby Pols), Jean Debaer (Mrs. Cassidy), Danga Lee (Chrissy). *Theme Song Writer and Vocalist,* "It's No Crush, I'm in Love": Lesley Gore. *Producer:* Frank Doelger. *Writer:* Judy Engles. *Director:* Mark Cullingham.

## 1017 It's Only Rock 'n' Roll.

Drama, 60 min., ABC, 3/21/91. An "ABC Afterschool Special" that focuses on artistic freedom and the responsibility that goes with it when a storm of controversy swirls around a gifted high school musician (Hallie) after she writes lyrics that are perceived as suggestive. *Cast:* Alison Bartlett (Hallie Angelisi), William McNamara (Johnny DuMont), Carole King (Johanna Martin), Carolyn Kava (Hallie's mother), Lewis Van Bergen (Hallie's father). *Producer:* Denise Kasell. *Writer:* Gordon Rayfield. *Director:* Allen Coulter.

## 1018 It's the Easter Beagle,

**Charlie Brown.** Cartoon, 30 min., CBS, 4/9/74. The story focuses on the Peanuts gang as they prepare for the Easter Beagle, a mythical dog who magically appears to hand out candy and decorated eggs on Easter Sunday morning. *Voices:* Todd Barbee (Charlie Brown), Melanie Kohn (Lucy), Stephen Shea (Linus), Linda Ercoli (Peppermint Patty), Lynn Mortensen (Sally), Jim Ahrens (Marcie), Bill Melendez (Snoopy). *Music:* Vince Guaraldi. *Producers:* Lee Mendelson, Bill Melendez. *Writer:* Charles M. Schulz. *Director:* Phil Roman.

**1019  It's the Girl in the Red Truck, Charlie Brown.** Cartoon, 60 min., CBS, 9/27/88. An unusual Charlie Brown special that mixes live action with animation and for the first time does not focus on the normal Peanuts characters. The story, set in the Arizona desert, focuses on Snoopy's brother, Spike, and the trials and tribulations of puppy love when he falls for a pretty aerobics instructor (Jenny), who drives a red truck. *Voices:* Jill Schulz (Jenny), Greg Deason (Jeff), Molly Boice (Molly), Jason Riffle (Charlie Brown). *Music:* Paul Rodriquez. *Producer:* Charles M. Schulz. *Writers:* Charles M. Schulz, Monte Schulz. *Director:* Walter C. Miller.

**1020  It's the Great Pumpkin, Charlie Brown.** Cartoon, 30 min., CBS, 10/27/66. The saga of Linus's vigil in a pumpkin field, where he eagerly awaits the arrival of the Great Pumpkin, a mythical being who is supposed to give toys to good girls and boys. *Voices:* Peter Robbins (Charlie Brown), Sally Dryer (Lucy), Christopher Shea (Linus), Cathy Steinberg (Sally), Bill Melendez (Snoopy). *Music:* Vince Guaraldi. *Producers:* Lee Mendelson, Bill Melendez. *Writer:* Charles M. Schulz. *Director:* Bill Melendez.

**1021  It's What's Happening, Baby!** Variety, 90 min., CBS, 6/28/65.

Performances by the top names in rock and roll music. *Host:* Murray the K. *Performers:* Cannibal and the Headhunters, Ray Charles, Bill Cosby, The Dave Clark Five, The Drifters, The Four Tops, Marvin Gaye, Fred Gwynne, Herman's Hermits, Chuck Jackson, Jan and Dean, Tom Jones, Gary Lewis and the Playboys, Little Anthony and the Imperials, Martha and the Vandellas, Johnny Mathis, Patti and the Bluebells, The Righteous Brothers, Johnny Rivers, The Supremes, The Temptations, Dionne Warwick. *Music:* Earl Warren, Onzy Matthews. *Producers:* Robert A. Forrest, Barry Shear. *Director:* Barry Shear.

**1022  It's Your First Kiss, Charlie Brown.** Cartoon, 30 min., CBS, 10/24/77. The story centers on Charlie Brown's anxieties when he is chosen to escort Heather, a little red-haired girl on whom he has a crush, to the annual football Homecoming Queen Dance. *Voices:* Arrin Skelley (Charlie Brown), Laura Planting (Peppermint Patty), Daniel Anderson (Linus), Michelle Muller (Lucy), Ronald Hendrix (Franklin), Bill Melendez (Snoopy). *Music:* Ed Bogas. *Producers:* Lee Mendelson, Bill Melendez. *Writer:* Charles M. Schulz. *Director:* Phil Roman.

**1023  I've Had It Up to Here.** Comedy, 60 min., NBC, 4/3/81. A series of comedy sketches that poke fun at the things that irritate people. *Host:* Steve Allen. *Guests:* Bill Bixby, Bill Dana, Louis Nye. *Performers:* Mimi Kennedy, Robert Ridgely, Victoria Carroll, Ceil Cabot, Warren Fergus, R. G. Brown, Deborah Chinowitz. *Music:* Bob Rozario. *Producers:* Dick Clark, Al Schwartz. *Writers:* Carol Hatfield, Jim Staahl, Jim Bishop, Stan Burns, David Axelrod, Stuart Mills, Jim Fisher. *Director:* Perry Rosemond.

**1024  Jack and the Beanstalk.**

Fantasy, 90 min., NBC, 11/12/56. A musical adaptation of the classic children's story about a poor farm boy named Jack who trades the family cow for some magic beans – and his adventures when he climbs a stalk that grows from those beans. *Cast:* Joel Grey (Jack), Celeste Holm (Mad Maggie), Cyril Ritchard (Peddler), Peggy King (Tillie), Billy Gilbert (Poopledoop), Arnold Stang (Little Giant), Leora Dana (Jack's mother). *Music:* Jerry Livingston. *Singers:* The Ray Charles Chorus. *Writer:* Helen Deutsch.

**1025 Jack and the Beanstalk.**
Fantasy, 60 min., NBC, 2/26/67. A live-action animation adaptation of the children's fairy tale about a poor farm boy's adventures when he climbs a stalk that grows from some magic beans. *Cast:* Bobby Rhia (Jack), Gene Kelly (Peddler), Marian McKnight (Jack's mother), Marni Nixon (Imprisoned Princess), Ted Cassidy (Giant), Cliff Norton (Woggle Bird), Chris Allen (Arnold the Mouse), Dick Beals (Monster Cat). *Music:* Lennie Hayton. *Producers:* William Hanna, Joseph Barbera. *Writers:* Michael Morris, Larry Markes. *Producer-Director:* Gene Kelly.

**1026 Jack Benny Specials (1955–58).** A chronological listing of the variety specials hosted by Jack Benny from 11/3/55 to 4/17/58. The programs are 60 minutes long, broadcast by CBS, and have the following credits in common: *Music:* Mahlon Merrick. *Producer:* Irving Fein. *Writers:* Al Gordon, Hal Goldman, Sam Perrin, Milt Josefsberg. *Director:* Fred DeCordova. Announcing was by Don Wilson.
**1** The Jack Benny Program (11/3/55). *Guests:* Gracie Allen, Gary Crosby, Frankie Laine, Marilyn Maxwell, The Sportsman Quartet.
**2** The Jack Benny Program (1/19/56). *Guests:* George Burns, Shirley MacLaine.

**3** The Jack Benny Program (3/15/56). *Guests:* Elsa Lanchester, Peggy Lee, Fredric March.
**4** The Jack Benny Program (4/8/56). *Guests:* Lois Corbett, Gisele MacKenzie, Dale White, Don Wilson.
**5** The Jack Benny Program (5/6/56). *Guests:* Jimmy Baird, Harry Shearing, Steve Woolton.
**6** The Jack Benny Program (11/1/56). *Guests:* Nanette Fabray, Johnnie Ray.
**7** The Jack Benny Program (1/10/57). *Guests:* Liberace, Rod McKuen, Jayne Mansfield, Vincent Price.
**8** The Jack Benny Program (3/14/57). *Guests:* Hedy Lamaar, Gale Storm.
**9** The Jack Benny Program (4/11/57). *Guests:* Tallulah Bankhead, Julie London, Tommy Sands, Ed Wynn.
**10** The Jack Benny Program (5/9/57). *Guests:* Yvonne DeCarlo, Van Johnson, Vincent Price.
**11** The Jack Benny Program (10/31/57). *Guests:* Carol Channing, Fred MacMurray.
**12** The Jack Benny Program (1/12/58). *Guests:* Margaret Brayton, Charles Herbert, Joseph Kearns, Steve Woolton.
**13** The Jack Benny Birthday Program (2/13/58). *Guests:* Joe Besser, Joseph Kearns, Sheldon Leonard, Henry Rubin, Pierre Watkin, Mary Young.
**14** The Jack Benny Program (3/20/58). *Guests:* Zsa Zsa Gabor, Hermione Gingold, Van Johnson, Patty McCormack.
**15** The Jack Benny Program (4/17/58). *Guests:* Betty Grable, Janis Paige, John Raitt.

**1027 Jack Benny Specials (1959–63).** A chronological listing of the variety specials hosted by Jack Benny from 3/19/59 to 4/7/63. All are 60 minutes in length, broadcast by CBS, and have the following credits in common: *Music:* David Rose. *Producers:* Bud Yorkin (1959), Ralph Levy. *Writers:* Sam Perrin, George Balzer,

Hal Goldman, Al Gordon. *Directors:* Bud Yorkin (1959), Ralph Levy.

**1 The Jack Benny Hour** (3/19/59). *Guests:* Mitzi Gaynor, Bob Hope.

**2 The Jack Benny Hour** (5/23/59). *Guests:* Julie Andrews, Phil Silvers.

**3 The Jack Benny Hour** (a.k.a. "Jack Benny with Guest Stars" 11/7/59). *Guests:* Raymond Burr, The McGuire Sisters, Danny Thomas, Jean VanderPyl.

**4 The Jack Benny Hour** (3/17/60). *Guests:* Polly Bergen, Phil Silvers.

**5 The Jack Benny Hour** (4/7/63). *Guests:* Bob Hope, The Marquis Chimps, Dick Van Dyke, Senor Wences.

## 1028 Jack Benny Specials (1965–74).

A chronological listing of the variety specials hosted by Jack Benny from 11/3/65 to 12/4/74. All are 60 minutes and broadcast by NBC.

**1 The Jack Benny Special** (11/3/65). *Guests:* The Beach Boys, Bob Hope, Elke Sommer. *Music:* Dave Grusin. *Producer-Director:* Ralph Levy. *Writers:* Sam Perrin, George Balzer, Al Gordon, Hal Goldman.

**2 The Jack Benny Christmas Special** (12/1/66). *Guests:* Phyllis Diller, Dick Smothers, Tom Smothers. *Music:* Jack Elliott. *Producer:* Irving Fein. *Writers:* Hal Goldman, Al Gordon, George Balzer. *Director:* Bob Henry.

**3 The Jack Benny Special** (3/20/68). *Guests:* Lucille Ball, Ben Blue, Johnny Carson, Sid Fields, Paul Revere and the Raiders, Benny Rubin, Herb Vigran. *Music Directors:* Earl Brown, Jack Elliott. *Producers:* Irving Fein, Fred DeCordova. *Writers:* Hal Goldman, Al Gordon, Herbert Marks, Milt Josefsberg. *Director:* Fred DeCordova.

**4 Jack Benny's Bag** (11/16/68). *Guests:* Eddie "Rochester" Anderson, Dick Clark, Phyllis Diller, Eddie Fisher, Jack Lemmon, Walter Matthau, Dan Rowan and Dick Martin. *Producers:* Irving Fein, Norman Abbott. *Writers:* Bob Fisher, Arthur Marks, Hilliard Marks, Sam Perrin, Ray

Singer, Earl Brown. *Director:* Norman Abbott.

**5 Jack Benny's Birthday Special** (2/17/69). *Guests:* Eddie "Rochester" Anderson, Ann-Margret, Lucille Ball, Dan Blocker, Dennis Day, Jerry Lewis, Lawrence Welk, Don Wilson. *Producers:* Irving Fein, Fred DeCordova. *Writers:* Gerald Gardner, Dee Caruso, Hilliard Marks, Sam Perrin, George Balzer. *Director:* Fred DeCordova.

**6 Jack Benny's New Look** (12/7/69). *Guests:* Eddie "Rochester" Anderson, George Burns, Gregory Peck, Gary Puckett and the Union Gap, Nancy Sinatra. *Producers:* Irving Fein, Norman Abbott. *Writers:* Al Gordon, Hal Goldman, Hilliard Marks, Sam Perrin, Hugh Wedlock, Jr. *Director:* Norman Abbott.

**7 Jack Benny's 20th Anniversary TV Special** (11/16/70). *Guests:* Eddie "Rochester" Anderson, Lucille Ball, Mel Blanc, Dennis Day, Bob Hope, Mary Livingston, Dean Martin, Frank Nelson, Benny Rubin, Dinah Shore, Frank Sinatra, Red Skelton, Don Wilson. *Producers:* Irving Fein, Stan Harris. *Writers:* Hal Goldman, Al Gordon, Hilliard Marks, Hugh Wedlock, Jr. *Director:* Stan Harris.

**8 Everything You Always Wanted to Know About Jack Benny and Were Afraid to Ask** (3/10/71). *Guests:* Lucille Ball, George Burns, Phil Harris, Dionne Warwick, John Wayne. *Producers:* Irving Fein, Norman Abbott. *Writers:* Al Gordon, Hal Goldman, Hilliard Marks, Hugh Wedlock, Jr., Bucky Shearles. *Director:* Norman Abbott.

**9 Jack Benny's First Farewell Show** (1/18/73). *Guests:* Johnny Carson, Isaac Hayes, Joey Heatherton, Bob Hope, Dean Martin, Lee Trevino, Flip Wilson. *Music Directors:* Jack Elliott, Allyn Ferguson. *Producer-Director:* Norman Abbott. *Writers:* Al Gordon, Hal Goldman, Hilliard Marks, Hugh Wedlock, Jr., Stan Daniels, Tom Tenowich.

**10 Jack Benny's Second Farewell**

**Show** (1/24/74). *Guests:* George Burns, Johnny Carson, Tony De-Franco, Redd Foxx, Harry Morgan, Don Rickles, Dinah Shore, Jack Webb. *Music Directors:* Jack Elliott, Allyn Ferguson. *Producers:* Irving Fein, Norman Abbott. *Writers:* Al Gordon, Hal Goldman, Hilliard Marks, Hugh Wedlock, Jr. *Director:* Norman Abbott.

**Jack Benny's Birthday Special** *see* **Jack Benny Specials**

**Jack Benny's First Farewell Show** *see* **Jack Benny Specials**

**Jack Benny's New Look** *see* **Jack Benny Specials**

**Jack Benny's Second Farewell Show** *see* **Jack Benny Specials**

**Jack Benny's 20th Anniversary TV Special** *see* **Jack Benny Specials**

**1029 Jack Cassidy's St. Patrick's Day Special.** Variety, 60 min., Syndicated, 3/69. A music, song, and comedy salute to St. Patrick's Day. *Host:* Jack Cassidy. *Guests:* Jan Daley, Jackie DeShannon, Fred Finn, Mickie Finn, Mickey Shaughnessy, Randy Sparks and the Backporch Majority, Marie Wilson.

**1030 Jack Frost.** Fantasy, 60 min., NBC, 12/5/80. A Christmas special in which Jack Frost, the Sprite Winter Elf, attempts to rescue his girlfriend, Elissa, from a wicked king. *Voices:* Robert Morse (Jack Frost), Debra Clinger (Elissa), Buddy Hackett (Pardon Me Pete/Story Teller), Paul Frees (Kubla Klaus), Dave Garroway (TV Announcer), Larry Storch (Elissa's father), Dee Stratton (Elissa's mother), Don Messick (Snip), Diana Lyn (Holly). *Music:* Maury Laws, Jules Bass. *Pro-*

*ducer-Directors:* Arthur Rankin, Jr., Jules Bass. *Writer:* Romeo Muller.

**1031 Jack Jones on the Move.** Variety, 60 min., ABC, 4/5/66. Singer Jack Jones's first television special; an hour of music, songs, and comedy. *Host:* Jack Jones. *Guests:* Molly Bee, Tony Bennett, Milton Berle, Joanie Sommers, Shani Wallis. *Music:* Marty Paich. *Producer:* Joe Layton. *Writer:* Robert Emmett. *Director:* Bill Hobin.

**1032 Jack Lemmon — Get Happy.** Variety, 60 min., NBC, 2/25/73. A tribute to composer Harold Arlen. *Host:* Jack Lemmon. *Guests:* The Alan Johnson Dancers, Diahann Carroll, Mama Cass Elliot, Johnny Mathis, Doc Severinsen, Dinah Shore. *Music:* Elliot Lawrence. *Producer:* Joseph Cates. *Director:* Dave Wilson.

**1033 Jack Lemmon in 'S Wonderful, 'S Marvelous, 'S Gershwin.** Variety, 90 min., NBC, 1/17/72. A musical tribute to composers Ira and George Gershwin. *Host:* Jack Lemmon. *Guests:* The Alan Johnson Dancers, Fred Astaire, Linda Bennett, Robert Guillaume, Larry Kent, Ethel Merman, Peter Nero, Leslie Uggams. *Music:* Elliot Lawrence. *Producers:* Joseph Cates, Martin Charnin. *Writer:* Martin Charnin. *Directors:* Walter C. Miller, Martin Charnin.

**1034 Jack Paar Specials.** A chronological listing of the variety specials hosted by Jack Paar. All are 60 minutes in length and broadcast by NBC.

**1 Jack Paar Presents** (4/26/60). *Guests:* Cliff Arquette, Shelly Berman, The James Starbuck Dancers, Alexander King, Elaine May, Mike Nichols, Keely Smith. *Music:* Axel Stordahl. *Producer:* Jack Paar. *Writers:* Paul W. Keyes, Bob Howard. *Director:* Greg Garrison.

**2 A Funny Thing Happened on the**

**Way to Hollywood** (5/14/67). See entry for details.

**3 Jack Paar and a Funny Thing Happened Everywhere** (12/6/67). Jack, seated in a projection room, screens funny moments from old newsreels. *Producer-Writer:* Jack Paar. *Director:* Hal Gurnee.

**4 Jack Paar and His Lions** (9/8/69). The special—produced, written, narrated, and partially filmed by Jack Paar—focuses on his pet lion, Amani, and on the offspring of Elsa (of the *Born Free* feature film) as her cubs arrive at Lion Country Safari in Florida. *Guests:* Miriam Paar, Randy Paar (Jack's wife and daughter).

**5 The Jack Paar Diary** (10/5/70). Amusing vignettes about Europeans and their cars (for example, in the Netherlands, where people have a difficult time keeping cars on the streets—they tend to fall into canals; and in Italy, where the insanity of traffic snarls is seen in Rome). The special was inspired by Jack after he and his wife visited Europe. *Cohost:* Miriam Paar. *Producer-Writer:* Jack Paar. *Director:* Hal Gurnee.

**6 Jack Paar Comes Home** (11/29/86). Jack's return to television (and NBC) with highlights from his former series: "The Tonight Show" (1957–62) and "The Jack Paar Show" (1962–65). *Music:* Charles Green. *Producer-Writer:* Jack Paar. *Director:* Hal Gurnee.

**7 Jack Paar Is Alive and Well** (12/19/87). An hour of clips and reminiscences as Jack recalls memorable moments from his television series and specials of the past. *Guests:* Jackie Mason, Debbie Reynolds, Pat Sajak. *Music:* Charles Green. *Producer-Writer:* Jack Paar. *Director:* Hal Gurnee.

## 1035 The Jackie Gleason Special. Variety, 60 min., CBS, 12/20/70. An hour of music, songs, and comedy, including a revision of "The Honeymooners" with Jackie (Ralph Kramden), Art Carney (Ed Norton),

Sheila MacRae (Alice Kramden), and Jane Kean (Trixie Norton). *Host:* Jackie Gleason. *Guests:* Carlos Bas, Art Carney, Bob Ellis, Peter Gladke, Jane Kean, Sheila MacRae, Johnny Morgan, Greta Randall. *Music:* Sammy Spear. *Producers:* Jack Philbin, Ronald Wayne. *Writers:* Marvin Marx, Walter Stone, Rod Parker. *Director:* Frank Bunetta.

## 1036 The Jackie Gleason Special. Variety, 60 min., CBS, 11/11/73. Jackie's second special (after a three-year absence) that features a variety of skits including a "Honeymooners" episode in which Alice (Sheila MacRae) leaves Ralph (Jackie Gleason) and moves in with Trixie (Jane Kean), leaving Ralph and Norton (Art Carney) to fend for themselves. *Host:* Jackie Gleason. *Guests:* Art Carney, The June Taylor Dancers, Jane Kean, Sheila MacRae, Gary Merrill, Lizabeth Prichett, Greta Van Hagge, Jeanne Wolf. *Music:* Sammy Spear. *Producers:* Jack Philbin, Bob Finkel. *Writers:* Frank Peppiatt, John Aylesworth, Walter Stone, Don Reo, Allan Katz. *Director:* Bill Foster.

## 1037 Jackie Gleason: The Great One. Tribute, 2 hrs., CBS, 9/17/80. A star-studded, clip-rich tribute to Jackie Gleason, focusing mostly on his television work. *Hosts:* John Candy, Art Carney, Jane Curtin, Teri Garr, John Larroquette. *Guests:* Red Buttons, Teresa Ganzel, Marilyn Taylor Gleason, Jane Kean, Sue Ane Langdon, Audrey Meadows, Burt Reynolds, June Taylor, Dick Van Patten. *Music:* Kevin Kiner. *Producers:* Toby Martin, Ellen Krass. *Writers:* Daniel Helfgott, Steve Fisher, Joe Morganstern. *Director:* Daniel Helfgott.

## 1038 James Paul McCartney. Variety, 60 min., ABC, 4/23/73. The program spotlights the post–Beatle music of singer-composer Paul McCartney. *Host:* Paul McCartney. *Guests:*

Linda McCartney, Wings. *Music:* Jack Parnell. *Producers:* Gary Smith, Dwight Hemion. *Director:* Dwight Hemion.

**1039  Jane Eyre.** A listing of the three television specials based on the 1847 novel by Charlotte Brontë. The story of Jane Eyre, an orphan girl, educated at Mr. Brocklehurst's Lowood School, who becomes the governess to Adele, the ward of Edward Rochester, the gruff owner of Thornfield Hall in Mikote, England.
   **1 Jane Eyre** (95 min., NBC, 10/12/39). *Cast:* Flora Campbell (Jane Eyre), Dennis Hoey (Edward Rochester), Effie Shannon (Adele), Daisy Belmore (Grace Poole), Ruth Mattheson (Mrs. Fairfax), Philip Tonge (Mason). *Producer-Director:* Edward Sobol.
   **2 Jane Eyre** (60 min., CBS, 4/27/61). *Cast:* Sally Ann Howes (Jane Eyre), Zachary Scott (Edward Rochester), Leslye Hunter (Adele), Fritz Weaver (Mason), Norah Howard (Grace Poole), Barbara Robbins (Mrs. Fairfax), Laurie Mann (St. John Rivers), Dina Paisner (Bertha), Angela Thornton (Blanche). *Producer-Director:* Marc Daniels. *Writer:* Michael Dyne.
   **3 Jane Eyre** (2 hrs., NBC, 3/24/71). *Cast:* Susannah York (Jane Eyre), George C. Scott (Edward Rochester), Sharon Rose (Adele), Ian Bannen (Rivers), Jack Hawkins (Brocklehurst), Nyree Dawn Porter (Blanche), Rachel Kempson (Mrs. Fairfax), Kenneth Griffith (Mason). *Music:* Johnny Williams. *Producer:* George Schaefer. *Writer:* Jack Pulman. *Director:* Delbert Mann.

**1040  The Jane Morgan Show.** Variety, 60 min., Syndicated, 3/68. An hour of music and songs with singer Jane Morgan. *Host:* Jane Morgan. *Guests:* The Doodletown Pipers. *Music:* Johnnie Spence. *Producer:* Jackie Barnett. *Director:* Tony Charmoli.

**1041  The Jane Powell Show.**

Variety, 60 min., NBC, 4/28/61. A lively hour of music, song, and dance. *Host:* Jane Powell. *Guests:* Art Carney, Steve Lawrence, The Roy Fitzell Dancers, Gwen Verdon. *Music:* David Rose. *Producer:* Robert Wells. *Writers:* John Bradford, Robert Wells. *Director:* Barry Shear.

**1042  Jay Leno's Family Comedy Hour.** Comedy, 60 min., NBC, 11/25/87. A fractured look at the all-American family via a series of sketches. *Host:* Jay Leno. *Guests:* Bea Arthur, Barbara Billingsley, Brian Bonsall, Johnny Carson, Chao-Li-Chi, Don DeFore, John Hancock, Florence Henderson, Susan Ruttan, Anne Schedeen, Dick Van Patten. *Vocal Effects:* Frank Welker. *Music:* Ben Lanzarone, Marvin Silberman, Jack Nelson. *Producers:* Helen Kushnick, Patricia Rickey. *Director:* John Bowab.

**1043  The Jazz Singer.** Drama, 60 min., NBC, 10/13/59. The efforts of Joey Robbins, the son of a showbusiness family, to break tradition (to become a singer) and strike out on his own as a comedian. *Cast:* Jerry Lewis (Joey Robbins), Eduard Franz (Cantor Rabinowitz), Molly Picon (Sarah Rabinowitz), Anna Maria Alberghetti (Ginny Gibbons), Alan Reed (Ed Giddleson), Barry Gordon (Harry). *Producer:* Ernest D. Glucksman. *Writer:* Sampson Raphaelson. *Director:* Ralph Nelson.

**1044  Jean Shepherd on Route 1 and Other Thoroughfares.** Humor, 60 min., PBS, 6/84. A sentimental special in which humorist Jean Shepherd rides a limousine along Route 1 in New Jersey to recall memories of the past and reflect on the changes that have occurred across the thoroughfare. *Host-Narrator:* Jean Shepherd. *Producers:* Al Rose, Calvin Iszard. *Writer:* Jean Shepherd. *Directors:* Stephen Arnesen, Calvin Iszard.

## 1045 Jeeter Mason and the Magic Headset.

Comedy, 30 min., ABC, 10/5/85. Jeeter Mason is a pretty girl about to celebrate her tenth birthday. She receives clothes from her parents, a portable radio with a headset from her older brother, and from her younger brother, who forgot about her birthday, she receives a small rock that he claims is a moon rock. Jeeter tries to throw the rock away, but she finds it in her dancing shoes at an audition the next day. At the audition Jeeter hears a voice through the radio's headset and, suddenly, her feet seem possessed and she dances up a storm. The voice tells Jeeter it is from the rock and being projected through the headset. She also learns that the rock can help her do anything—as long as it is in her best interest. The story follows Jeeter's escapades as she uses the rock to help people—and herself when it comes time for her big violin solo. An "ABC Weekend Special." *Cast:* Kim Hauser (Jeeter Mason), Nancy Walker (Moon Rock's Voice), Lily Nell Warren (Janie Goldsmith), Sally Stark (Mrs. Mason), Jimmy Shea (Kevin Mason), Duncan McNeill (Erik Mason), Kimberly Stern (Wilhelmina Higgins). *Music:* Steve Margoshes. *Producers:* Frank Doelger, Eve Silverman. *Writer:* Bruce Harmon. *Director:* Claude Kerven.

## 1046 The Jerry Lester Special.

Variety, 30 min., CBS, 9/30/63. A program of music and comedy with comedian Jerry Lester. *Host:* Jerry Lester. *Guests:* Richard Hayes, Monique Van Vooren, Lew Wills, Gene Wood. *Producer:* Don Silverman. *Writers:* Gene Wood, Jim Magee. *Director:* Lorne Freed.

## 1047 Jerry Lewis Specials.

A chronological listing of the variety specials hosted by Jerry Lewis. All are 60 minutes in length and broadcast by NBC.

**1 The Jerry Lewis Show** (1/19/57). *Guests:* Georgine Darcy, Ernie Kovacs, Jan Murray, The Norman Luboff Choir, Judy Scott, The Woody Herman Band. *Music:* Nelson Riddle. *Producer:* Ernest D. Glucksman. *Writers:* Arthur Phillips, Harry Crane. *Director:* Dick Weinberg.

**2 The Jerry Lewis Show** (6/8/57). *Guests:* Eydie Gorme, Dick Humphrey, Dan Rowan and Dick Martin, Lori Spencer. *Music:* Nelson Riddle. *Producer:* Jerry Lewis. *Writers:* Harry Crane, Arthur Phillips. *Directors:* Jerry Lewis, Jack Shea.

**3 The Jerry Lewis Show** (11/5/57). *Guest:* Susan Silo. *Music:* Walter Scharf. *Producer:* Ernest D. Glucksman. *Writers:* Mel Tolkin, Neil Simon. *Director:* Jack Shea.

**4 The Jerry Lewis Show** (12/27/57). *Guests:* The Count Basie Orchestra, Sammy Davis, Jr., Ronnie Deauville. *Music:* Walter Scharf. *Producer:* Ernest D. Glucksman. *Writers:* Neil Simon, Mel Tolkin. *Director:* Jack Shea.

**5 The Jerry Lewis Show** (2/19/58). *Guests:* Betty Grable, Sophie Tucker. *Music:* Walter Scharf. *Producer:* Ernest D. Glucksman. *Director:* Jack Shea.

**6 The Jerry Lewis Show** (4/15/58). *Guests:* Everett Sloane, Helen Traubel. *Music:* Walter Scharf. *Producer:* Ernest D. Glucksman. *Director:* Jack Shea.

**7 The Jerry Lewis Show** (10/20/58). *Guests:* Louis Prima, Keely Smith, Helen Traubel, The Wiere Brothers. *Music:* Walter Scharf. *Producer:* Ernest D. Glucksman. *Writers:* Mel Brooks, Danny Simon, Harry Crane, Jerry Lewis. *Director:* Jack Shea.

**8 The Jerry Lewis Show** (12/10/58). *Guests:* Kathleen Freeman, Barbara Granlund, The Harry James Band, Jack Paar, Ziva Rodann, Bobby Van. *Music:* Walter Scharf. *Producer-Director:* Jack Shea. *Writers:* Mel Brooks, Danny Simon, Harry Crane.

**9 The Jerry Lewis Show** (1/16/60). *Guests:* Gary Lewis, Ronnie Lewis, Lionel Newman, Helen Traubel. *Music:* Walter Scharf. *Producer:* Ernest D. Glucksman. *Director:* Jack Shea.

**10 The Jerry Lewis Timex Show**

(4/15/60). *Guests:* Tony Bennett, Allen Funt, Lionel Hampton, Rose Hardaway, The Nitwits Comedy Act. *Music:* Walter Scharf. *Producer:* Ernest D. Glucksman. *Director:* Jack Shea.

**11 The Jerry Lewis Show** (5/22/60). *Guest:* Eddie Fisher. *Music:* Walter Scharf. *Producer:* Ernest D. Glucksman. *Director:* Jack Shea.

**1048 Jerry Reed and Special Friends.** Variety, 2 hrs., Syndicated, 10/82. A music-filled celebrity picnic and concert at Hermitage Landing in Nashville, Tennessee. *Host:* Jerry Reed. *Guests:* Glen Campbell, Jimmy Dean, Vicki Lawrence, Brenda Lee, Louise Mandrell, Seidina Reed, Burt Reynolds, The Statler Brothers, Faron Young. *Music:* Bill Walker. *Producers:* Dick Thall, Jim Owens. *Directors:* Lee H. Bernardi, Mary Hardwicke.

**1049 Jimmy Durante Meets the Lively Arts.** Variety, 60 min., ABC, 10/30/65. A variety outing in which comedian Jimmy Durante explores opera, art, drama, dance, and music. *Host:* Jimmy Durante. *Guests:* Rudolf Nureyev, Roberta Peters, Lyn Seymour, The Shindogs, Max Showalter, Robert Vaughn. *Music:* Harper McKay. *Producers:* Alan Handley, Bob Wynn. *Writers:* Milt Rosen, Jackie Barnett. *Director:* Alan Handley.

**1050 The Jimmy Durante Show.** Variety, 60 min., NBC, 8/9/61. An hour of music, songs, and comedy sketches. *Host:* Jimmy Durante. *Guests:* Bob Hope, Garry Moore, Janice Rule. *Producer-Director:* Norman Jewison. *Writers:* Goodman Ace, Selma Diamond, Jay Burton, Frank Peppiatt.

**1051 The Jimmy McNichol Special.** Variety, 60 min., CBS, 4/30/80. An hour of music, songs, and comedy with James Vincent McNichol (the brother of Kristy McNichol). *Host:*

James Vincent McNichol. *Guests:* Conrad Bain, Jeff Conaway, Jeff Kutash's Dance Machine, Magic Johnson, Kristy McNichol, Donna Pescow, Ricky Schroder, Kurt Thomas. *Music:* George Wyle. *Producers:* Jerry Weintraub, Bob Finkel. *Writers:* Robert Wells, Peter Gallay, Bob Finkel. *Director:* Tony Charmoli.

**1052 The Jo Stafford Show.** Variety, 60 min., CBS, 8/18/63. The program spotlights songs nominated for an Academy Award over the thirty years 1933–63. *Host:* Jo Stafford. *Guests:* James Darren, Bob Hope, The Lionel Blair Dancers, The Polka Dots. *Music Director:* Jack Parnell.

**1053 The Jo Stafford Show.** Variety, 60 min., Syndicated, 9/64 and 10/64. An hour of music and songs with singer Jo Stafford. *Host:* Jo Stafford. *Guests* (9/64): Stanley Holloway, The Lionel Blair Dancers, Robert Morley, The Polka Dots. *Guests* (10/64): Peggy Lee, The Lionel Blair Dancers. *Music Director:* Jack Parnell.

**1054 Joan Baez.** Variety, 60 min., PBS, 12/14/74. A concert by singer Joan Baez. *Host:* Joan Baez. *Producer-Directors:* Leslie Miner, Jim Scalem.

**1055 The Joan Rivers Comedy Hour.** Comedy, 60 min., Showtime, 3/81. A comedy concert by Joan Rivers; taped at the Tropicana Hotel in Las Veas. *Host:* Joan Rivers. *Guests:* Monteith and Rand, Roger and Roger, Barclay Shaw, Siegfried and Roy, The Tropicana Dancers. *Producers:* Ray Katz, Edgar Rosenberg. *Director:* Maurice Abraham.

**1056 The Joe Piscopo New Jersey Special.** Variety, 60 min., ABC, 5/13/86. An hour of music, songs, and comedy (spoofs of television shows) with Joe Piscopo in his first network special. See also "The Joe Piscopo Special" for information on the comedian's first cable special. *Host:* Joe Piscopo. *Guests:* Danny DeVito, Deborah Harmon, Thomas Kean (New Jersey Governor), Eddie Murphy. *Music:* Ralph Schuckett. *Producers:* George Schlatter, Joe Piscopo, John DeBellis. *Writers:* John DeBellis, Paul J. Raley, Joe Piscopo. *Director:* Paul Miller.

## 1057 The Joe Piscopo Special. Variety, 60 min., HBO, 9/22/84.

An hour of music and comedy that spotlights the talents of comedian Joe Piscopo. See also the prior title. *Host:* Joe Piscopo. *Guests:* Joseph Bologna, Anthony Caruso, Jan Hooks, Eddie Murphy. *Music:* Ralph Schuckett. *Producers:* Nancy Jones, Joe Piscopo, John DeBellis. *Writers:* Andy Breckman, John DeBellis, Joe Piscopo, Rocco Urbisci. *Director:* Jay Dubin.

## 1058 John Curry's Ice Dancing. Variety, 75 min., Showtime, 11/80.

A television adaptation of the 1978 Broadway production of "Ice Dancing," that features a combination of the technical qualities of figure skating and the choreographic elements of classical and modern dance. *Hosts:* John Curry, Peggy Fleming. *Guests:* JoJo Starbuck. *Producers:* Les Haber, Ken Weinstock, Michael Steele.

## 1059 The John Davidson Christmas Show. Variety, 60 min., NBC, 12/15/76.

A holiday program of music and songs with John Davidson, his family, and the families of his guests, The Lennon Sisters. *Host:* John Davidson. *Guests:* Diane Lennon, Janet Lennon, Kathy Lennon, Peggy Lennon. *Music:* Jack Elliott, Allyn Ferguson. *Producers:* Dick Clark, Alan Bernard. *Writers:* Phil Hahn, Jonnie Johns. *Director:* Norman Campbell.

## 1060 The John Davidson Christmas Show. Variety, 60 min., ABC, 12/9/77.

A holiday special in which John Davidson and his family step through time to celebrate a nineteenth-century English Christmas. *Host:* John Davidson. *Guests:* Tim Conway, Betty White. *Producer:* Bob Finkel. *Writer:* Herbert Baker. *Director:* Tony Charmoli.

## 1061 John Denver Specials.

A chronological listing of the variety specials hosted by singer John Denver. All are 60 minutes in length except where noted.

**1 The John Denver Show** (ABC, 3/11/74). *Guests:* David Carradine, George Gobel, Lily Tomlin, James Whitmore. *Producers:* Rich Eustis, Al Rogers, Jerry Weintraub. *Writers:* Ray Jessel, Harry Lee Scott, John Boni. *Director:* Bill Davis.

**2 The John Denver Special** (ABC, 12/1/74). *Guests:* Doris Day, George Gobel, Dick Van Dyke. *Music:* Milt Okum. *Producers:* Jerry Weintraub, Rich Eustis, Al Rogers. *Writers:* Ray Jessel, Harry Lee Scott, Rich Eustis, Al Rogers. *Director:* Bill Davis.

**3 An Evening with John Denver** (ABC, 3/10/75). *Guests:* Jacques Cousteau, Danny Kaye. *Music:* Milt Okum. *Producers:* Jerry Weintraub, Rich Eustis, Al Rogers. *Writers:* Ray Jessel, Tom Tenowich, Ed Scharlach, Rich Eustis, Al Rogers. *Director:* Bill Davis.

**4 John Denver's Rocky Mountain Christmas** (ABC, 12/10/75). *Guests:* Valerie Harper, Steve Martin, Olivia Newton-John. *Music:* Milt Okum. *Producers:* Jerry Weintraub, Rich Eustis, Al Rogers. *Writers:* Jim Mulligan, April Kelly, Tom Chapman, David O'Malley, Steve Martin, Al Rogers, Rich Eustis. *Director:* Bill Davis.

**5 John Denver and Friend** (ABC, 3/29/76). *Guest:* Frank Sinatra. *Music:* Nelson Riddle. *Producers:* Jerry Weintraub, George Schlatter. *Writers:* Digby Wolfe, George Schlatter. *Director:* Bill Davis.

**6 The John Denver Special** (ABC, 11/17/76). *Guests:* Dennis Weaver, Joanne Woodward. *Music:* Milt Okum. *Producers:* Jerry Weintraub, Rich Eustis, Al Rogers. *Writers:* Marty Farrell, Ray Jessel, Al Rogers, Rich Eustis. *Director:* Bill Davis.

**7 John Denver — Thank God I'm a Country Boy** (ABC, 3/2/77). *Guests:* Glen Campbell, Johnny Cash, Roger Miller, Mary Kay Place. *Music:* Eddie Karam, Lee Holdridge. *Producers:* Jerry Weintraub, Rich Eustis, Al Rogers. *Writers:* Rich Eustis, Al Rogers. *Director:* Walter C. Miller.

**8 John Denver in Australia** (90 min., ABC, 2/16/78). *Guests:* Robby Benson, Debby Boone, Lee Marvin, John Newcombe, Susan Saint James. *Music:* Glen D. Hardin. *Producers:* Al Rogers, Bill Davis. *Writers:* Phil Hahn, George Geiger, Al Rogers. *Director:* Bill Davis.

**9 John Denver and the Ladies** (ABC, 3/8/79). *Guests:* Erma Bombeck, Valerie Harper, Cheryl Ladd, Cheryl Tiegs, Tina Turner. *Music:* Tommy Oliver. *Producers:* Jerry Weintraub, George Schlatter. *Writers:* Digby Wolfe, George Schlatter. *Director:* Don Mischer.

**10 John Denver's Rocky Mountain Reunion** (ABC, 5/29/79). *Producers:* Jerry Weintraub, Mark J. Stouffer. *Writer:* John P. Gilligan. *Director:* Mark J. Stouffer.

**11 John Denver and the Muppets: A Christmas Together** (ABC, 12/23/80). *Guests:* Jim Henson's Muppets. *Music:* Ray Charles. *Producer:* Bob Finkel. *Director:* Tony Charmoli.

**12 John Denver: Music and the Mountains** (ABC, 4/24/81). *Guests:* James Galway, Itzhak Perlman, Beverly Sills. *Music:* Lee Holdridge. *Producer:* Jacques Urbont. *Director:* Walter C. Miller.

**13 John Denver's Christmas in Aspen** (CBS, 12/19/88). *Guests:* Cassie Denver, The Dickens Singers, Alexander Grotsky, Anne Murray, The Nitty Gritty Dirt Band. *Music:* Milt Okum.

*Producer:* Don Ohlmeyer. *Writer:* Robert Arnott. *Director:* Jim Yukich.

**14 John Denver's Montana Christmas Skies** (CBS, 12/13/91). *Guests:* Clint Black, George Burns (as the voice of God), Patty Loveless, Kathy Mattea. *Music:* Milt Okum. *Producers:* John Denver, Harold Thau, Steve Binder, Kimber Rickabaugh. *Writer:* Steven Pouliot. *Director:* Steve Binder.

## 1062 John Grin's Christmas.

Drama, 60 min., ABC, 12/6/86. A contemporary version of *A Christmas Carol*, which places the Scrooge-like John Grin in a middle-class black community in America. Grin was poor as a child and worked hard to become a wealthy toy manufacturer. He is not generous or helpful to anyone in the neighborhood or to those in his employment. Grin is tough and holidays mean very little to him. One Christmas Eve he is visited by three ghosts who whirl him through a terrifying (and eye-opening) look at the lives around him and the life that is missing within him. *Cast:* Robert Guillaume (John Grin), Alfonso Ribeiro (Rocky), Roscoe Lee Browne (Ghost of Christmas Past), Ted Lange (Ghost of Christmas Present), Geoffrey Holder (Ghost of Christmas Future). *Music:* Mitch Margo, Dennis Dreith. *Producers:* Robert Guillaume, Phil Margo. *Writer:* Charles Eric Johnson. *Director:* Robert Guillaume.

## 1063 John Lennon and Yoko Ono Present the One-to-One Concert.

Variety, 60 min., ABC, 12/15/72. An edited-for-television version of John and Yoko's benefit for the Willowbrook Institution for Retarded Children. Taped at Madison Square Garden in New York City. *Hosts:* John Lennon, Yoko Ono. *Guests:* Roberta Flack, The Plastic Ono Band/Elephant's Memory, Sha Na Na, Stevie Wonder. *Producers:* John Lennon, Yoko Ono. *Director:* Steve Debhardt.

Ad for "John Denver's Montana Christmas Skies"

**1064 John Ritter: Being of Sound Mind and Body.** Variety, 60 min., ABC, 5/4/80. John Ritter in his first television special: an hour of comedy sketches. *Host:* John Ritter. *Guests:* Cathryn Damon, Joyce De-Witt, David Doyle, Howard Hesseman, Vincent Price, Suzanne Somers. *Music:* Jack Elliott. *Producers:* Eric Lieber, Robert Myman. *Writers:* Joe Landon, Bill Richmond, Gene Perret, Bill Vilanch, Jack Burns, Eric Lieber. *Director:* Dave Powers.

**1065 John Ritter, Jacqueline**

**Bissett and Mr. T ... Going Back Home.** Variety, 60 min., ABC, 5/26/84. John Ritter returns to his childhood home in an L.A. suburb; Jacqueline Bissett to her home in England; and Mr. T to his roots in South Chicago, to reflect on their childhood and on their start in showbusiness. *Host:* Michele Lee. *Stars:* Jacqueline Bissett, Mr. T, John Ritter. *Producers:* Sherwin Bash, Dan Cleary, Lee Mendelson. *Writer-Director:* Lee Mendelson.

**1066 John Schneider's Christ-**

**mas Holiday.** Variety, 60 min., CBS, 12/17/83. The star of "The Dukes of Hazzard" in a musical celebration of winter; taped in Sun Valley, Idaho. *Host:* John Schneider. *Guests:* Debbie Allen, Larry Gatlin, Bruce Jenner, Van Johnson. *Music:* Earl Brown. *Producers:* John Schneider, Marty Pasetta. *Writer:* Buz Kohan. *Director:* Marty Pasetta.

**1067 John Wayne: Standing Tall.** Documentary, 65 min., PBS, 3/4/89. A profile of actor John Wayne through clips from his movies and television appearances. *Host-Narrator:* James Arness. *Producers:* JoAnn G. Young, John Musilli. *Writer:* JoAnn G. Young. *Director:* John Musilli.

**1068 Johnny Belinda.** A chronological listing of the four television specials based on the 1940 play by Elmer Harris. The story of Belinda McDonald, a deaf-mute farm girl, and her relationship with Jack Richardson, a young doctor who teaches her to speak through sign language. (The title refers to the son born of Belinda when she is raped by Locky McCormick, a lecherous village resident Belinda kills when he tries to take Johnny, her son, away from her.) Each version changes the main characters' names, with the most drastic being the fourth adaptation (Belinda McAdam is the girl; Bill Richmond is now a Vista volunteer and not a doctor; and the rapist is Kyle Hager, a farmer, who attacks Belinda after a dance).

**1 Johnny Belinda** (CBS, 6/29/55). *Cast:* Katherine Bard (Belinda McDonald), Eddie Albert (Dr. Jack Davidson), James Gavin (Locky McCormick), Tudor Owen ( John McDonald), Maudie Prickett (Maggie McDonald). *Producer-Director:* Fletcher Markle.

**2 Johnny Belinda** ("Hallmark Hall of Fame," NBC, 10/13/58). *Cast:* Julie Harris (Belinda McDonald), Christopher Plummer (Dr. Jack Richardson), Rip Torn (Locky McCormick), Victor

Jory (Black McDonald), Joanna Roos (Aggie McDonald), Betty Lou Holland (Stella Maguire), John Cecil Holm (Sheriff). *Producer-Director:* George Schaefer. *Writer:* Theodore Apstein.

**3 Johnny Belinda** (ABC, 10/22/67). *Cast:* Mia Farrow (Belinda McDonald), Ian Bannen (Dr. Jack Richardson), David Carradine (Locky McCormick), Barry Sullivan (Black McDonald), Ruth White (Aggie McDonald), Carolyn Daniels (Stella Maguire), Louise Latham (Mrs. McKee), Stacy Keach (Dr. Grey). *Producer:* David Susskind. *Writer:* Allen Sloane. *Director:* Paul Bogart.

**4 Johnny Belinda** (CBS, 10/19/82). *Cast:* Rosanna Arquette (Belinda McAdam), Richard Thomas (Bill Richmond), Dennis Quaid (Kyle Hager), Roberts Blossom (John McAdam), Candy Clark (Julie Sayles), Fran Ryan (Aggie), Penelope Windust (Dr. Harris), Mickey Jones (Lowell). *Music:* John Rubinstein. *Producers:* Dick Berg, Malcolm Stewart. *Writer:* Sue Milburn. *Director:* Anthony Page.

**1069 Johnny Carson Discovers Cypress Gardens.** Variety, 60 min., NBC, 9/7/68. Music, songs, and comedy from Florida's Cypress Gardens. *Host:* Johnny Carson. *Guests:* Vikki Carr, Every Mother's Son. *Producers:* Bob Stewart, Chester Feldman. *Writers:* Pat McCormick, Chester Feldman. *Director:* Lou Tedesco.

**1070 Johnny Carson Presents the Sun City Scandals.** Variety, 60 min., NBC, 12/7/70. An hour of music and comedy in which showbusiness veterans performed the material that made them famous. See also the following title. *Host:* Johnny Carson. *Guests:* Gladys Ahern, Will Ahern, Louis Armstrong, Fifi D'Orsay, Billy Gilbert, Wilbur Hall, Edward Everett Horton, Julia Rooney, Benny Rubin, Gloria Swanson. *Producer-Director:* Grey Lockwood. *Writers:* Joe Bigelow, Ed Weinberger, Stan Daniels.

**NEW ONE-HOUR SPECIAL!**

# JOHNNY CARSON'S GREATEST PRACTICAL JOKES

An hour of outrageous surprises! JOHNNY and friends JOAN RIVERS, CARL REINER, TIM CONWAY and ED McMAHON.

**8PM**

Watch them play the hilarious practical jokes! Then...Whoops! Watch as jokers Joan and Ed get the surprises of their lives!

Ad for "Johnny Carson's Greatest Practical Jokes"

## 1071 Johnny Carson Presents the Sun City Scandals '72.

Variety, 60 min., NBC, 3/13/72. A second hour of music and comedy in which showbusiness veterans perform the material that made them famous. *Host:* Johnny Carson. *Guests:* Shelton Brooks, Bette Davis, Sammy Fain, Eddie Foy, Jr., Beatrice Kay, Harry Ruby, Gene Sheldon, The Sun City Cuties, Ethel Waters. *Music:* Milton DeLugg. *Producer-Director:* Grey Lockwood.

## 1072 Johnny Carson Presents The Tonight Show Comedians.

Variety, 60 min., NBC, 11/25/84. Clips and live performances of comics who have appeared on "The Tonight Show." *Host:* Johnny Carson. *Guests:* Bill Cosby, Steve Martin, Joan Rivers. *Music:* Doc Severinsen. *Producer:* John L. McMahon. *Writer:* Michael Barrie. *Director:* Bobby Quinn.

## 1073 Johnny Carson's Greatest Practical Jokes.

Comedy, 60 min., NBC, 11/28/83. Johnny Carson becomes the perpetrator (and victim) of an array of practical jokes (for example, Johnny has Ed McMahon arrested for having a trunk full of NBC office supplies; Joan Rivers is chastised for her jokes about the royal family by a Margaret Thatcher look-alike). *Host:*

Johnny Carson. *Guests:* Tim Conway, Ed McMahon, Carl Reiner, Joan Rivers. *Music:* Doc Severinsen. *Producer:* John L. McMahon. *Director:* Bobby Quinn.

## 1074 Johnny Carson's Repertory Company in an Evening of Comedy.

Comedy, 60 min., NBC, 11/12/69. An hour of comedy sketches that lampoon various aspects of life. *Host:* Johnny Carson. *Guests:* Marian Mercer, George C. Scott, Maureen Stapleton. *Producer:* Rudy Tellez. *Writers:* Johnny Carson, Marshall Brickman, David Lloyd. *Director:* Bobby Quinn.

## 1075 Johnny Cash Specials.

A chronological listing of the country and western variety specials hosted by singer Johnny Cash. All are 60 minutes long, except where noted.

**1 Johnny Cash Ridin' the Rails— The Great American Train Story** (ABC, 11/22/74). *Producers:* Nicholas Webster, Dyann Rivkin. *Director:* Nicholas Webster.

**2 The Johnny Cash Christmas Special** (CBS, 12/6/76). *Guests:* June Carter Cash, Roy Clark, the Reverend Billy Graham, Barbara Mandrell, Tony Orlando. *Music:* Bill Walker. *Producer:* Joseph Cates. *Writers:* Chet Hagan, Frank Slocum, Larry Markes. *Director:* Walter C. Miller.

**3 The Johnny Cash Christmas Special** (CBS, 11/30/77). *Guests:* June Carter Cash, Roy Clark, Jerry Lee Lewis, Roy Orbison, Carl Perkins, The Statler Brothers. *Music:* Bill Walker. *Producers:* Joseph Cates, Marty Klein. *Writers:* Chet Hagan, Frank Slocum. *Director:* Walter C. Miller.

**4 Johnny Cash: Spring Fever** (CBS, 5/7/78). *Guests:* June Carter Cash, Rosanne Cash, Ray Charles, Jessi Colter, Waylon Jennings. *Music:* Bill Walker. *Producer:* Chet Hagan. *Writers:* Frank Slocum, Chet Hagan. *Director:* Walter C. Miller.

**5 The Johnny Cash Spring Special** (CBS, 5/9/79). *Guests:* June Carter Cash, Waylon Jennings, George Jones, Merle Kilgore, Martin Mull, Hank Williams, Jr. *Music:* Bill Walker. *Producers:* Joseph Cates, Marty Klein. *Writers:* Chet Hagan, Frank Slocum. *Director:* Walter C. Miller.

**6 A Johnny Cash Christmas** (CBS, 12/6/79). *Guests:* Tom T. Hall, Andy Kaufman, Anne Murray. *Music:* Bill Walker. *Producers:* Joseph Cates, Marty Klein, Chet Hagan. *Writers:* Chet Hagan, Frank Slocum. *Director:* Walter C. Miller.

**7 Johnny Cash: The First 25 Years** (90 min., CBS, 5/8/80). *Guests:* Roy Acuff, Lamar Alexander, Bill Anderson, Chet Atkins, The Carter Family, Maybelle Carter, June Carter Cash, Jack Clement, David Allen Coe, Daniel Davis, Kirk Douglas, Peter Falk, Larry Gatlin, Tom T. Hall, Sonny James, Waylon Jennings, George Jones, Grandpa Jones, Kris Kristofferson, Brenda Lee, Charlie Louvin, Steve Martin, Anne Murray, The Oak Ridge Boys, Dolly Parton, Johnny Paycheck, Minnie Pearl, Jeannie C. Riley, Earl C. Scruggs, Billy Joe Shaver, Kate Smith, The Statler Brothers, Ray Stevens, The Tennessee Three, Dottie West, Don Williams. *Music:* Bill Walker. *Producers:* Joseph Cates, Marty Klein, Chet Hagan. *Writers:* Frank Slocum, Chet Hagan. *Director:* Walter C. Miller.

**8 A Johnny Cash Christmas** (CBS, 12/3/80). *Cohosts:* Johnny Cash, June Carter Cash. *Guests:* Mac Davis, Larry Gatlin, Jeannie C. Riley. *Music:* Bill Walker. *Producer:* Joseph Cates. *Writer:* Frank Slocum. *Director:* Walter C. Miller.

**9 Johnny Cash and the Country Girls** (CBS, 4/29/81). *Guests:* June Carter Cash, Rosanne Cash, Wilma Lee Cooper, Helen Cornelius, Skeeter Davis, Emmylou Harris, Minnie Pearl, Jeannie C. Riley, Misty Rowe. *Music:* Bill Walker. *Producers:* Joseph Cates, Marty Klein, Chet Hagan. *Writers:*

**Johnny Cash and his wife June Carter**

Frank Slocum, Chet Hagan, Carmen Finestra. *Director:* Walter C. Miller.

**10 Johnny Cash: Christmas in Scotland** (CBS, 12/10/81). *Guests:* Carlene Cash, John Carter Cash, June Carter Cash, Andy Williams. *Music:* Bill Walker. *Producers:* Marty Klein, Joseph Cates. *Writers:* Frank Slocum, Chet Hagan. *Director:* Stan Harris.

**11 Johnny Cash: Cowboy Heroes** (CBS, 5/6/82). *Guests:* John Anderson, Glen Campbell, June Carter Cash, The Oak Ridge Boys. *Music:* Bill Walker. *Producers:* Marty Klein, Joseph Cates. *Writers:* Frank Slocum, Chet Hagan. *Director:* Stan Harris.

**12 Johnny Cash's America** (75 min., HBO, 8/15/82). *Guests:* June Carter Cash, Rodney Crowell, Steve Goodman, John Prine. *Music:* Bob Wooton. *Producers:* Michael Fuchs, Marty Klein. *Writer:* Frank Slocum. *Director:* Stan Harris.

**13 Johnny Cash — A Merry Memphis Christmas** (CBS, 12/7/82). *Guests:* June Carter Cash, Rosanne Cash, Jack Clement, Crystal Gayle, The Mighty Clouds of Joy, Eddie Rabbitt. *Music:* Bill Walker. *Producers:* Marty Klein, Joseph Cates. *Writer:* Frank Slocum. *Director:* Bill Davis.

**14 Johnny Cash Christmas 1983** (CBS, 12/16/83). *Guests:* Anita Carter, Helen Carter, Janette Carter, Joe Carter, June Carter Cash, Merle Haggard, Ricky Skaggs, Joanne Cash Yates. *Music:* Bill Walker. *Producers:* Marty Klein, Joseph Cates. *Writer:* Larry Murray. *Director:* Gilbert Cates.

**15 Johnny Cash: Christmas on the Road** (CBS, 12/7/84). *Guests:* June Carter Cash, Jessi Colter, Waylon Jennings, Kris Kristofferson, Lisa Kristofferson, Connie Nelson, Willie Nelson. *Music:* Arnold Levine. *Producers:* Marty Klein, Joseph Cates. *Writer:* Larry Murray. *Directors:* Joseph Cates, Gilbert Cates.

**16 The Johnny Cash 10th Anniversary Christmas Special** (CBS, 12/10/85). *Guests:* John Carter Cash, June Carter Cash, Rosanne Cash, Larry Gatlin, Jerry Lee Lewis. *Music:* Bill Walker. *Producers:* Marty Klein, Joseph Cates. *Writers:* Frank Slocum, Larry Murray. *Director:* Gilbert Cates.

**1076 Johnny Mathis in the Canadian Rockies.** Variety, 60 min., Syndicated, 12/75. A musical songfest taped in Canada. *Host:* Johnny Mathis. *Guest:* Karen Valentine. *Music:* Jim Barnett, Bob Alcivar, Bob Summers. *Producer:* Jack Sobel. *Writer:* Ken Friedman. *Director:* Clark Jones.

**1077 The Joke and the Valley.** Drama, 90 min., NBC, 5/5/61. The story, set in a rural farming community, tells of a drifter (Davis Tucker) who takes refuge in a barn during a storm and becomes involved in a murder when he finds a body. Aired on the "Hallmark Hall of Fame." *Cast:* Dean Stockwell (Davis Tucker), Thomas Mitchell (Truman Winters), Keenan Wynn (Lambert Giles), Russell Collins (Ed Holt), Leora Thatcher (Lucille), Mildred Trases (Rosella Winters), Logan Ramsey (Andy). *Producer-Director:* George Schaefer. *Writer:* Jerry Bock.

**1078 The Joke's on Mr. Little.** Comedy, 30 min., ABC, 2/6/82. When schoolboys Streeter and Drag learn that their favorite teacher, Miss Kellogg, has been replaced by Lester Little, they devise a plan to get Miss Kellogg back by playing a series of outrageous practical jokes on Mr. Little. The story relates Mr. Little's efforts to teach Streeter and Drag a much deserved lesson. Aired as an "ABC Weekend Special." *Cast:* Richard Sanders (Lester Little), K. C. Martel (Streeter), Georg Olden (Drag), Ned Wertimer (Mayor Pugett), Herb Armstrong (Sheriff Hurley), Nina Shipman (Miss Johnson), Connie Sawyer (Miss Hughes). *Producer:* Robert Chenault. *Writers:* Glen Olson, Rod Baker. *Director:* Harvey Laidman.

**1079 Jonathan Winters Specials.** A chronological listing of four comedy specials hosted by comedian Jonathan Winters. Each 60-minute program, broadcast on NBC, features Jonathan's ability to perform without a script. The first three specials feature the music of Eddie Safronski and are produced and directed by Greg Garrison.

**1 The Jonathan Winters Special** (11/9/64). *Guests:* Noelle Adams, Connie Francis, Mickey Rooney.

**2 The Jonathan Winters Show** (2/1/65). *Guest:* Michael Bentine.

**3 The Jonathan Winters Show** (5/10/65). *Guests:* Steve Allen, Leo Durocher, Anne Meara, Jerry Stiller.
**4 Jonathan Winters Presents 200 Years of American Humor** (1/21/76). *Guests:* Scatman Crothers, David Doyle, Ronny Graham, Mary Gregory, Julie McWhirter. *Music:* George Wyle. *Producers:* George Spota, Bob Henry. *Writers:* Max Wilk, Stephen Spears, Jonathan Winters. *Director:* Bob Henry.

**1080 Josie.** Drama, 30 min., Syndicated, 7/83. The story of Josie Dobbs, a beautiful high school girl with a loose reputation, who learns to overcome her insecurities with the help of a shy, handicapped classmate (Luke). *Cast:* Elizabeth Daily (Josie Dobbs), James Van Patten (Luke Price). *Music:* Richard Lyman. *Producers:* Ellwood Kieser, Michael Rhodes. *Writer:* James E. Mosher. *Director:* Michael Rhodes.

**1081 Journey to Survival.** Drama, 60 min., CBS, 4/6/82. The story of six troubled teenagers who must learn to cope with themselves, nature, and each other when they are enrolled for rehabilitation in a Wilderness Encounter Project. A "CBS Afternoon Playhouse." *Cast:* Ralph Macchio (Tony Barnett), James G. Richardson (Neil Wentworth), Dori Brenner (Cindy Chalmers), Sal Lopez (Cesar Martinez), Larry B. Scott (Luther Jackson), Leon Robinson (Bobby Joe Tucker), David Greenlee (Mark Delman), Grant Gotschall (Andy Grimes). *Music:* Tim Simon. *Producer:* Biff Johnson. *Writer:* Adam Dubov. *Director:* Richard Bennett.

**1082 Joys (A Bob Hope Special).** Comedy, 90 min., NBC, 3/5/76. A comedy mystery in which Bob Hope hires six famous television detectives to solve a series of mysterious disappearances that have been occurring at his home. *Cast:* Bob Hope (Himself), Angie Dickinson (Pepper Anderson), Mike Connors (Joe Mannix), Jim Hutton (Ellery Queen), David Janssen (Harry Orwell), Telly Savalas (Theo Kojak), Abe Vigoda (Phil Fish). *Music:* Les Brown. *Producers:* Bob Hope, Hal Kanter. *Writers:* Ben Starr, Charles Lee, Gig Henry, Harvey Weitzman, Ruth Batchelor, Jeffrey Barron. *Director:* Dick McDonough.

**1083 Jubilee.** Variety, 90 min., NBC, 3/26/76. A musical salute to the one hundredth anniversary of the telephone. *Host:* Bing Crosby, Liza Minnelli. *Guests:* Roy Clark, Eydie Gorme, Joel Grey, Steve Lawrence, Ben Vereen. *Music:* Ian Fraser. *Producers:* Sam Jaffe, Gary Smith. *Writers:* Buz Kohan, Marty Farrell. *Director:* Dwight Hemion.

**1084 The Judds — Across the Heartland.** Variety, 60 min., CBS, 1/16/89. An hour of country and western music with mother and daughter singers Naomi and Wynonna Judd. *Hosts:* Naomi Judd, Wynonna Judd. *Guests:* Ashley Judd, The Judd Boys, Gary Morris. *Producers:* Ken Stilts, Anthony Eaton. *Writer:* Leland Zaitz. *Director:* Anthony Eaton.

**1085 Judy Garland and Her Guests, Phil Silvers and Robert Goulet.** Variety, 60 min., CBS, 3/19/63. An hour of music, songs, and light comedy. *Host:* Judy Garland. *Guests:* Robert Goulet, Phil Silvers. *Music:* Saul Chaplin. *Producer:* Burt Shevelove. *Writer:* Larry Gelbart. *Director:* Charles S. Dubin.

**1086 The Judy Garland Show.** Variety, 90 min., NBC, 9/24/55. Judy Garland's first television special: a 90-minute program of music, songs, and light comedy. *Host:* Judy Garland. *Emcee:* David Wayne. *Guests:* The Escorts, The Goofers, Mitsuko Swanura. *Music:* Jack Cathcart. *Producer:* Sid Luft. *Writer:* John Tackaberry. *Director:* Paul Harrison.

**1087  The Judy Garland Show.**
Variety, 30 min., CBS, 4/8/56. An intimate 30-minute special in which Judy sings songs she has never performed before in public. *Host:* Judy Garland. *Introductions:* Ronald Reagan. *Guests:* Peter Gennaro, Leonard Pennario. *Music:* Nelson Riddle. *Producer:* Sid Luft. *Director:* Richard Avedon.

**1088  The Judy Garland Show.**
Variety, 60 min., CBS, 2/25/62. An hour of music, song, and light comedy. *Host:* Judy Garland. *Guests:* Dean Martin, Frank Sinatra. *Music:* Mort Lindsey. *Producers:* Norman Jewison, Chris Schultz. *Director:* Norman Jewison.

**1089  Judy Garland: The Concert Years.** Documentary, 2 hrs., PBS, 3/22/85. A well-produced and touching special that traces Judy Garland's concert performances, including her television and stage work. *Host:* Lorna Luft. *Guests:* Tony Bennett, Alan King, Mort Lindsey, Sid Luft, Melissa Manchester, Rex Reed, Nelson Riddle. *Producers:* Jac Venza, Joan Kramer. *Writer:* John L. Miller. *Director:* David Heeley.

**1090  The Juggler of Notre Dame.** Drama, 60 min., Syndicated, 12/82. The play, based on a twelfth-century French folk tale, tells of Barnaby Stone, a down-and-out street performer who has only his talents as a juggler to present as a Christmas offering to a statue of the Virgin Mary. (The legend states that when Barnaby offered his only gift, the statue came to life and presented him with the red rose she was carrying.) *Cast:* Carl Carlsson (Barnaby Stone), Patrick Collins (Sparrow), Merlin Olsen (Jonas Wintergreen), Melinda Dillon (Dulcy Wintergreen), Eugene Roche (Father Delaney), James Callahan (Police Officer), Karen Price (Virgin Mary). *Music:* Chris Stone. *Producers:* Ellwood Kieser, Lan O'Kun.

*Writer:* Lan O'Kun. *Director:* Michael Rhodes.

**1091  Julie!** Documentary, 60 min., ABC, 8/24/72. A profile of singer-actress Julie Andrews. *Star:* Julie Andrews. *Music:* Nelson Riddle. *Producer-Director:* Blake Edwards. *Choreography:* Tony Charmoli.

**1092  Julie and Carol at Carnegie Hall.** Variety, 60 min., CBS, 6/11/62. An hour of music and song with Julie Andrews and Carol Burnett. Taped live at Carnegie Hall in New York City. *Hosts:* Julie Andrews, Carol Burnett. *Music:* Irwin Kostel. *Producers:* Bob Banner, Joe Hamilton. *Writers:* Mike Nichols, Ken Welch. *Director:* Joe Hamilton.

**1093  Julie and Carol at Lincoln Center.** Variety, 60 min., CBS, 12/7/71. A sequel to the above special with Julie Andrews and Carol Burnett teaming for an hour of music, song, and comedy at New York's Lincoln Center. *Hosts:* Julie Andrews, Carol Burnett. *Music:* Peter Matz. *Producer:* Joe Hamilton. *Writers:* Bob Ellison, Marty Farrell. *Director:* Dave Powers.

**1094  Julie and Carol: Together Again.** Variety, 60 min., ABC, 12/13/89. A reunion special (see prior two titles) that teams Julie Andrews and Carol Burnett together again for an hour of music, song, and comedy from the Los Angeles Pantages Theater. *Hosts:* Julie Andrews, Carol Burnett. *Music:* Ian Fraser. *Producers:* Jeff Margolis, Ken Welch, Mitzie Welch. *Writers:* Ken Welch, Mitzie Welch, Stan Hart. *Director:* Jeff Margolis.

**1095  Julie and Dick in Covent Garden.** Variety, 60 min., ABC, 4/21/74. An hour of music, songs, and light comedy with Julie Andrews and Dick Van Dyke. *Hosts:* Julie Andrews, Dick Van Dyke. *Guest:* Carl Reiner.

*Music:* Jack Parnell. *Producer:* Blake Edwards. *Writers:* Marty Farrell, Frank Waldman, Dick Hills. *Director:* Blake Edwards.

**1096 Julie and Jackie: How Sweet It Is.** Variety, 60 min., ABC, 5/22/74. Julie Andrews and Jackie Gleason perform in a music-hall setting that pays homage to Jackie Gleason's career. Taped in London. *Hosts:* Julie Andrews, Jackie Gleason. *Producers:* Gary Smith, Dwight Hemion. *Writers:* Bob Ellison, Walter Stone, James Sheldon, Mort Schariman. *Director:* Dwight Hemion.

**1097 Julie Andrews: One Step into Spring.** Variety, 60 min., CBS, 3/9/78. A musical salute to spring. *Host:* Julie Andrews. *Guest:* Alan King. *Music:* Ian Fraser. *Producer:* Bob Banner. *Writer:* Kenny Solms. *Director:* Jeff Margolis.

**1098 The Julie Andrews Show.** Variety, 60 min., NBC, 11/28/65. An hour of music and songs. *Host:* Julie Andrews. *Guests:* Gene Kelly, The New Christy Minstrels. *Music:* Irwin Kostel. *Producer-Director:* Alan Handley. *Writers:* Bill Perksy, Sam Denoff.

**1099 The Julie Andrews Special.** Variety, 60 min., ABC, 11/9/69.

**Julie Andrews**

Music and songs with singers Julie Andrews and Harry Belafonte. *Host:* Julie Andrews. *Guest:* Harry Belafonte. *Music:* Michel Legrand. *Producer-Director:* Gower Champion.

**1100 Julie Andrews: The Sound of Christmas.** Variety, 60 min., ABC, 12/16/87. An hour of Christmas music and songs from Salzburg, Austria. *Host:* Julie Andrews. *Guests:* John Denver, Placido Domingo, The King's Singers. *Music:* Ian Fraser. *Producer:* Nick Vanoff. *Writer:*

Buz Kohan. *Director:* Dwight Hemion.

## 1101 The Julie London Special.
Variety, 60 min., Syndicated,
2/68. An hour of music and songs with
singer Julie London. *Host:* Julie London. *Guests:* Mickie Finn, Chad Stewart and Jeremy Clyde. *Music:* Ralph
Carmichael. *Producer:* Jackie Barnett.
*Director:* Dick Ross.

## 1102 Julie — My Favorite Things.
Variety, 60 min., ABC, 4/18/
75. Music and light comedy as Julie
Andrews sings the songs associated
with her movie career. *Host:* Julie An-
drews. *Guest:* Peter Sellers. *Music:*
Jack Parnell. *Producer:* Bob Wells.
*Writers:* Frank Waldman, Bob Wells,
Blake Edwards. *Director:* Blake Ed-
wards.

## 1103 Julie on Sesame Street.
Variety, 60 min., ABC, 11/23/73. A
musical tour of the children's television
series "Sesame Street." *Host:* Julie Andrews. *Guests:* Perry Como, The Muppets, The Paddy Stone Dancers. *Music:*
Jack Parnell. *Producers:* Blake Edwards, Gary Smith, Dwight Hemion.
*Writers:* Jon Stone, Marty Farrell, Bob
Ellison. *Director:* Dwight Hemion.

## 1104 Junior Miss.
Comedy, 90
min., CBS, 12/20/57. Judy Graves is a
very pretty and imaginative teenage girl
with a knack for involving herself in
and attempting to solve the problems
of others. When Judy mistakenly believes her father (Harry) is having an
affair with his employer's daughter
(Ellen), Judy sets out to resolve the
situation by setting Ellen up with
another man — her Uncle Willis. *Cast:*
Carol Lynley (Judy Graves), Don
Ameche (Harry Graves), Joan Bennett
(Grace Graves), Jill St. John (Lois
Graves), Susanne Sidney (Fuffy
Adams), Paul Ford (J. B. Curtis),
Diana Linn (Ellen Curtis), David
Wayne (Willis Reynolds). *Music:* Bar-
ton Lane. *Producer:* Richard Lewine.

*Writers:* Joseph Stern, Will Glickman.
*Director:* Ralph Nelson.

## 1105 Just a Regular Kid: An AIDs Story.
Drama, 60 min., ABC,
9/9/87. A reality drama about a
16-year-old boy (Kevin) infected with
the AIDS virus from a blood transfu-
sion, and the problems that arise when
it is learned that he has the disease. An
"ABC Afterschool Special." *Cast:*
Christian Hoff (Kevin Casio), Florence
Henderson (Ellen Casio), Ronny Cox
(Jim Casio), Wally Wood (Paul), Cady
McClain (Nicole), Jessica Walter (Dr.
Stern), Catherine MacNeal (Mrs.
Schroeder), Lewis Arquette (Dr.
Kolovson). *Music:* Harold Wheeler.
*Producer:* Diana Kerew. *Writer-Direc-
tor:* Victoria Hochberg.

## 1106 Just Friends.
Variety, 60
min., ABC, 9/13/70. A reunion of the
regular cast from the CBS-television
series "The Smothers Brothers Comedy
Hour" (1967–69). *Hosts:* John Hartford, Jennifer Warnes. *Cast:* Bob Einstein, Pat Paulsen, Kenny Rogers and
the First Edition, Mason Williams.
*Music:* Al Capps. *Producers:* Ken
Kragen, Bill Carruthers. *Writers:* Rick
Mittleman, Mickey Newbury, Kris
Kristofferson. *Director:* Bill Carruthers.

## 1107 Just Like a Woman.
Variety, 60 min., Syndicated, 11/69. A
solo concert performance by singer
Kaye Stevens. *Host:* Kaye Stevens.
*Producer:* Hendrick Booraren. *Pro-
ducer-Director:* Hal Tulchin.

## 1108 Just Pals.
Drama, 60 min.,
CBS, 9/14/82. Jo Davis is a pretty
12-year-old tomboy. She enjoys soccer,
skateboarding, and hanging out with
her best friend, Danny Gordon. When
Jo returns from a summer vacation in
Europe with her parents, she is no
longer a tomboy, but a beautiful
13-year-old young lady. Danny is
stunned — and upset when his best friend

is now more interested in feminine pursuits with her girlfriends rather than playing soccer. The story relates Danny's efforts to put his and Jo's relationship into perspective. A "CBS Afternoon Playhouse." *Cast:* Heather McAdam (Jo Davis), Byron Thames (Danny Gordon), Sandy Lipton (Susan Davis), Terrence O'Connor (Fay Gordon), Arthur Peterson (Mr. Steinmetz), Shelly Juttner (Marie), Marc Gilpin (Ric), Linda Hoy (Teacher), Richard McKenzie (Tom Gordon). *Music:* Scott Wilk. *Producers:* Peter Walz, Bob Johnson, Nick Anderson. *Writer:* H. B. Kay. *Director:* Randa Haines.

**1109 Just Polly and Me.** Variety, 60 min., CBS, 10/8/60. Music, songs, and comedy with Phil Silvers and Polly Bergen. *Hosts:* Polly Bergen, Phil Silvers. *Music:* Luther Henderson. *Producer:* Nick Vanoff. *Writer:* Nat Hiken. *Director:* Coby Ruskin.

**1110 Just the Facts.** Comedy, 60 min., Syndicated, 6/87. A celebration of the 1987 feature film *Dragnet* with clips from the movie and from the source on which it is based—television's "Dragnet" (NBC, 1951–59). *Hosts:* Dan Aykroyd, Tom Hanks. *Narrator:* William Conrad. *Producers:* Robert K. Weiss, Gail Hollenbaugh. *Writer:* Rick Sublett. *Director:* Suzanne McCafferty.

**1111 Just Tipsy, Honey.** Drama, 60 min., ABC, 3/16/89. An "ABC Afterschool Special" about an alcoholic mother (Carolyn) and the effect her drinking has on her family, especially her teenager daughter, Patty. *Cast:* Joanna Pettet (Carolyn Adams), Ellie Cornell (Patty Adams), Lyman Ward (Chris Adams), Jon Matthews (Dennis), Julie Parrish (Mrs. Frazier), Erin O'Leary (Robin), LaRita Shelby (Rosemary), Hilary Morse (Judy), Jaki Valensi (Amy). *Music:* Misha Segal. *Producer:* Martin Tahse. *Writers:* Linda Bergman, Martin Tahse. *Director:* Robert C. Thompson.

**1112 Juvi.** Drama, 60 min., CBS, 4/21/87. A very harsh and realistic "CBS Schoolbreak Special" about the experiences of Susan Atherton, a very pretty but naive teenage girl who is subjected to the horrors of Juvi (juvenile hall) when her mother falsely accuses her of felonious assault. *Cast:* Traci Lin (Susan Atherton), Karen Petrasek (Farrah Atherton), Khrystyne Haje (Michelle Rourk), Theresa Saldana (Laura Chicone), Joi Martins (Willie Mae Brown), Mariclare Costello (Kate Cummings), Ashlie Walker (Susan, age 4), Christy Edwards (Susan, age 11), Ismael Carlo (Judge Leonard Medina), Kenneth Tigar (Sam Renaldo). *Music:* Jimmie Haskell. *Producers:* Joanna Lee, Don Hultman. *Writer-Director:* Joanna Lee.

**1113 Kaleidoscope.** Variety, 90 min., NBC, 4/24/55. A fast-paced program of music, songs, and comedy sketches. *Performers:* Rod Alexander, Judy Holliday, Bambi Linn, Dick Shawn, Frank Sinatra. *Music:* Charles Sanford. *Producer-Director:* Max Liebman.

**1114 Kate and Anna McGarrigle in Concert.** Variety, 60 min., Syndicated, 6/86. A concert by singers Kate and Anna McGarrigle. *Hosts:* Anna McGarrigle, Kate McGarrigle. *Guests:* Pat Donaldson, Dane Larkin, Gillis Losier, Jane McGarrigle, Maria Muldaur, Linda Ronstadt. *Producer:* Chris Zimmerman. *Director:* Fran Hensler.

**1115 Kate Smith Presents Remembrances of Rock.** Variety, 60 min., Syndicated, 7/73. The program features Kate Smith reprising her past hits, then performing a medley of songs by Neil Diamond, Stephen Schwartz, Jimmy Webb, and Michel Legrand. *Host:* Kate Smith. *Guests:* Dom DeLuise, Florence Henderson, The Kids Next Door, Steve Mandell, The Supremes, Eric Weissberg. *Producers:*

ABC
Mother's Day
Special

KATHIE LEE GIFFORD'S
*Celebration of*
*Motherhood*

With Special Guest Stars
Nell Carter, Barbara Mandrell,
Cindy Williams and a special
appearance by Regis Philbin.
And Mother's Day memories
from Troy Aikman,
Tony Danza, Arsenio Hall,
Michael Jordan, Dolly Parton,
H. Ross Perot, Diane Sawyer,
Arnold Schwarzenegger,
Travis Tritt, Donald Trump,
Barbara Walters and Wynonna.

ⓐⓑⓒ 10:00PM ⑦⑧ ♡

**Ad for "Kathie Lee Gifford's Celebration of Motherhood"**

Don Kirshner, Ray Katz. *Director:* Bill Foster.

## 1116 The Kate Smith Show.

Variety, 60 min., ABC, 4/28/57. An hour of music and songs with singer Kate Smith. *Host:* Kate Smith. *Guests:* The Benny Goodman Orchestra, Gertrude Berg, Edgar Bergen, The Billy Williams Quintet, Boris Karloff, Ed Wynn. *Music:* Jack Miller. *Producer:* Ted Collins.

## 1117 The Kate Smith Show.

Variety, 60 min., Syndicated, 9/69. Music and songs with Kate Smith and her guests. *Host:* Kate Smith. *Guests:* The Charlie Byrd Trio, The Kids Next Door. *Music:* Mitchell Ayres. *Producer:* Jackie Barnett. *Director:* Richard Dunlap.

## 1118 Kathie Lee Gifford's Celebration of Motherhood.

Variety, 60 min., ABC, 5/5/93. A humorous look at motherhood through a series of songs and sketches. *Host:* Kathie Lee Gifford. *Guests:* Nell Carter, Barbara Mandrell, Regis Philbin, Cindy Williams. *Cameos:* Arsenio Hall, Michael Jordan, Wynonna Judd, Dolly Parton, H. Ross Perot, Diane Sawyer, Arnold Schwarzenegger, Travis Tritt, Donald Trump, Barbara Walters. *Music:* David Shire. *Producers:* Kathie Lee Gifford, Lee Miller. *Writers:* Kathie Lee Gifford, Richard Maltby, David Shire. *Director:* Louis J. Horvitz.

## 1119 Keefe Brasselle's Variety Garden. Variety, 60 min., CBS, 9/18/62. Music and songs that recapture the

flavor and atmosphere of America at the turn of the century. *Host:* Keefe Brasselle. *Guests:* Arlene DeMarco, Beatrice Kay, Liberace. *Music:* Sammy Kaye. *Producer:* Jack Philbin. *Writers:* Sydney Zelenka, Will Glickman, Dee Diamond. *Director:* Jerome Shaw.

**1120 Keep in Step.** Musical Comedy, 60 min., CBS, 1/23/59. A special based on "The Phil Silvers Show" (CBS, 1955–59) wherein master sergeant and master schemer Ernest Bilko wheels and deals to put on a musical show for the post. *Cast:* Phil Silvers (Ernest Bilko), Paul Ford (Colonel Hall), Joe E. Ross (Sergeant Rubert Ritzik), Maurice Gosfield (Private Duane Doberman), Herbie Faye (Private Sam Fender), Beatrice Pons (Emma Ritzik), Harvey Lembeck (Corporal Rocco Barbella). *Guests:* Jerry Carter, Sydney Chaplin, Diana Dors. *Music:* Ronny Graham. *Producer:* Edward J. Montagne. *Writers:* Billy Friedberg, Arne Rosen, Coleman Jacoby, Terry Ryan. *Director:* Aaron Ruben, Al De Caprio.

**1121 Keep U.S. Beautiful.** Variety, 60 min., NBC, 4/3/73. An antipollution program of skits and songs that stress the importance of keeping America beautiful. *Host:* Raymond Burr. *Guests:* Edward Andrews, Carol Burnett, Ruth Buzzi, Tim Conway, Sandy Duncan, Redd Foxx, Lena Horne, The Muppets, Carroll O'Connor, Yvonne Wilder. *Producers:* Bob Henry, Patricia Rickey. *Writers:* Herbert Baker, Mike Marmer, Stan Burns, Don Hinkley, Sid Green, Dick Hills, Paul McCauley, Peter Gallay. *Director:* Tim Kiley.

**1122 The Kennedy Center Honors.** A chronological listing of 15 of the programs (1978–92) that honor individuals who throughout their lifetimes have made significant contributions to American culture through the performing arts. Each two-hour special was taped at the Kennedy Center for the Performing Arts in Washington, D.C., and recalls the subject's career through tributes, clips, and stills. George Stevens, Jr., is the producer.

**1 The Kennedy Center Honors** (CBS, 12/5/78). *Honorees:* Marian Anderson, Fred Astaire, George Balanchine, Richard Rodgers, Arthur Rubinstein. *Guests:* Harry Belafonte, Leonard Bernstein, Art Buchwald, President and Mrs. Jimmy Carter, Suzanne Farrell, Florence Henderson, Alberta Hunter, Hal Linden, Mary Martin, Peter Martins, Gregory Peck, Itzhak Perlman, Isaac Stern, Edward Villela.

**2 The Kennedy Center Honors** (CBS, 12/29/79). *Honorees:* Aaron Copland, Ella Fitzgerald, Henry Fonda, Martha Graham, Tennessee Williams. *Guests:* Alan Alda, Jane Alexander, Elizabeth Ashley, Count Basie and His Orchestra, Leonard Bernstein, Art Buchwald, Placido Domingo, Elia Kazan, Gene Kelly, Peggy Lee, Joshua Logan, The Martha Graham Dance Company, Ann Miller, Michael Moriarty, Mickey Rooney, Eric Sevareid, Jean Stapleton, Maureen Stapleton, Joe Williams.

**3 The Kennedy Center Honors** (CBS, 12/27/80). *Honorees:* Leonard Bernstein, James Cagney, Agnes de Mille, Lynn Fontanne, Leontyne Price. *Guests:* Lauren Bacall, Mikhail Baryshnikov, Art Buchwald, President Jimmy Carter, Betty Comden, Donald Graham, Adolph Green, Kitty Carlisle Hart, Zubin Mehta, Pat O'Brien, Jason Robards, Beverly Sills, John Travolta.

**4 The Kennedy Center Honors** (CBS, 12/26/81). *Honorees:* Count Basie, Cary Grant, Helen Hayes, Jerome Robbins, Rudolf Serkin. *Guests:* Mikhail Baryshnikov, Victor Borge, Art Buchwald, Richard Chamberlain, Count Basie and His Orchestra, Ella Fitzgerald, Rex Harrison, Audrey Hepburn, Henry Mancini, Leontyne Price, President and Mrs. Reagan, James Stewart, Meryl Streep, Donald Sutherland, Joe Williams.

**5 The Kennedy Center Honors** (CBS, 12/25/82). *Host:* Walter Cronkite. *Honorees:* George Abbott, Lillian Gish, Benny Goodman, Gene Kelly, Eugene Ormandy. *Guests:* Eddie Albert, Tom Bosley, Betty Buckley, Cyd Charisse, Claudette Colbert, Betty Comden, Adolph Green, Gregory Hines, Eugene Istomin, Van Johnson, Hal Linden, Lionel Hampton and His Orchestra, Leona Mitchell, Yves Montand, Donald O'Connor, Andre Previn, Harold Prince, Eva Marie Saint, Jean Stapleton, Isaac Stern.

**6 The Kennedy Center Honors** (CBS, 12/27/83). *Host:* Walter Cronkite. *Honorees:* Katherine Dunham, Elia Kazan, Frank Sinatra, James Stewart, Virgil Thomson. *Guests:* Mikhail Baryshnikov, Warren Beatty, Art Buchwald, Carol Burnett, Perry Como, Carmen De Lavallade, Agnes de Mille, Geoffrey Holder, John Houseman, Gene Kelly, Elaine Kudo, Burt Lancaster, Arthur Mitchell, Anthony Quinn.

**7 The Kennedy Center Honors** (CBS, 12/25/84). *Host:* Walter Cronkite. *Honorees:* Lena Horne, Danny Kaye, Gian-Carlo Menotti, Arthur Miller, Isaac Stern. *Guests:* Debbie Allen, Art Buchwald, Joan Copeland, Karl Malden, Itzhak Perlman, Roberta Peters, Carl Reiner, Mary Lou Retton, Vin Scully, George Segal, Eli Wallach, Dionne Warwick, John Williams, Efrem Zimbalist, Jr.

**8 The Kennedy Center Honors** (CBS, 12/27/85). *Host:* Walter Cronkite. *Honorees:* Merce Cunningham, Irene Dunne, Bob Hope, Alan Jay Lerner, Frederick Loewe, Beverly Sills. *Guests:* Don Ameche, Mikhail Baryshnikov, Carol Burnett, Chevy Chase, Gloria Dinzel, Rodolfo Dinzel, Kirk Douglas, Robert Goulet, Rex Harrison, Louis Jourdan, Michele Lee, Merce Cunningham Dance Company, Anthony Newley, Liz Robertson, Maureen Stapleton, James Stewart.

**9 The Kennedy Center Honors** (CBS, 12/26/86). *Host:* Walter Cronkite.

*Honorees:* Lucille Ball, Ray Charles, Hume Cronyn, Yehudi Menuhin (violinist), Jessica Tandy, Antony Tudor (choreographer). *Guests:* Bea Arthur, Glen Close, Pam Dawber, Agnes de Mille, Jose Ferrer, Margot Fonteyn, Valerie Harper, Rosemary Harris, Quincy Jones, Hal Linden, Walter Matthau, Robert Stack, Liv Ullmann, Peter Ustinov, Sigourney Weaver.

**10 The Kennedy Center Honors** (CBS, 12/30/87). *Host:* Walter Cronkite. *Honorees:* Perry Como, Bette Davis, Sammy Davis, Jr., Nathan Milstein (violinist), Alan Nikolais (choreographer). *Guests:* Don Ameche, Lucille Ball, Diahann Carroll, Ray Charles, Rosemary Clooney, Hume Cronyn, Jacques d'Amboise, Vic Damone, Ken Howard, Angela Lansbury, Joseph Papp, James Stewart, Jessica Tandy.

**11 The Kennedy Center Honors** (CBS, 12/30/88). *Host:* Walter Cronkite. *Honorees:* Alvin Ailey (choreographer), George Burns, Myrna Loy, Alexander Schneider (violinist), Roger L. Stevens (producer). *Guests:* John Denver, Helen Hayes, Hal Holbrook, Bob Hope, Sen. Edward Kennedy, Nancy Reagan, President Ronald Reagan, Ann Reinking, Bobby Short, Isaac Stern, Tommy Tune, Kathleen Turner, Cicely Tyson, Leslie Uggams.

**12 The Kennedy Center Honors** (CBS, 12/29/89). *Host:* Walter Cronkite. *Honorees:* Harry Belafonte, Claudette Colbert, Alexandra Danilova, Mary Martin, William Schuman. *Guests:* Don Ameche, Larry Hagman, Kelly McGillis, Gregory Peck, Bernadette Peters, Sidney Poitier, Lynn Redgrave, Jerome Robbins.

**13 The Kennedy Center Honors** (CBS, 12/28/90). *Host:* Walter Cronkite. *Honorees:* Dizzy Gillespie, Katharine Hepburn, Rise Stevens, Jule Styne, Billy Wilder. *Guests:* Lauren Bacall, Art Buchwald, Glen Close, Bill Cosby, Tyne Daly, Marilyn Horne, Jack Jones, Angela Lansbury, Jack Lemmon, Hal Linden, Maureen McGovern,

Walter Matthau, Ann Reinking, Jerome Robbins, Tommy Tune.

**14 The Kennedy Center Honors** (CBS, 12/26/91). *Host:* Walter Cronkite. *Honorees:* Roy Acuff, Betty Comden, Adolph Green, Harold and Fayard Nicholas (tap dancers), Gregory Peck. *Guests:* Chet Atkins, Lauren Bacall, Carol Burnett, President George Bush, Keith Carradine, Emmylou Harris, Audrey Hepburn, Gregory Hines, Gene Kelly, Patti LuPone, Bill Monroe, Phyllis Newman, Mike Nichols, Jean Stapleton, Isaac Stern, Steve Wariner.

**15 The Kennedy Center Honors** (CBS, 12/30/92). *Host:* Walter Cronkite. *Honorees:* Lionel Hampton, Paul Newman, Ginger Rogers, Mstislav Rostropovich, Paul Taylor (choreographer), Joanne Woodward. *Guests:* President George Bush, Betty Comden, Sally Field, Aretha Franklin, Herbie Hancock, Gregory Peck, Robert Redford, Tom Selleck.

**1123 Kenny and Dolly: A Christmas to Remember.** Variety, 60 min., CBS, 12/2/84. A program of Christmas music and songs with Dolly Parton and Kenny Rogers. *Hosts:* Dolly Parton, Kenny Rogers. *Music:* Larry Kansler. *Original Songs:* Dolly Parton. *Producers:* Ralph Cohen, Ken Yates. *Writer:* Buz Kohan. *Director:* Bob Giraldi.

**1124 Kenny, Dolly and Willie: Something Inside So Strong.** Variety, 60 min., NBC, 5/20/89. A concert by Kenny Rogers, Dolly Parton, and Willie Nelson. Taped 5/2/89 at the Johnson Space Center in Houston, Texas. *Stars:* Willie Nelson, Dolly Parton, Kenny Rogers. *Announcer:* Lance LeGault. *Music:* Edgar Struble. *Producers:* Ken Kragen, Jeff Wald. *Writer:* Leslie Fuller. *Director:* Tom Trbovich.

**1125 Kenny Loggins in Concert.** Variety, 60 min., HBO, 12/17/83.

The Grammy-winning singer performs a concert from Santa Barbara, California. *Host:* Kenny Loggins. *Music:* Bruce Botnick. *Producers:* Larry Larsen, Vic Kaplan.

**1126 Kenny Rogers in Concert.** Variety, 60 min., HBO, 9/18/83. A concert by singer Kenny Rogers. Taped in March 1983 at the Greensboro Coliseum in North Carolina. *Host:* Kenny Rogers. *Guest:* Sheena Easton. *Producers:* Kenny Rogers, Ken Kragen. *Director:* Jeff Margolis.

**1127 Kenny Rogers: Keep Christmas with You.** Variety, 60 min., CBS, 12/18/92. Christmas songs are coupled with a behind-the-scenes look at a group of youngsters as they prepare to star in Kenny's holiday stage show in Branson, Missouri. *Host:* Kenny Rogers. *Guests:* Boyz II Men, Garth Brooks, Trisha Yearwood. *Producers:* Ken Kragen, Kelly Junkerman. *Writer:* Lan O'Kun. *Director:* Jack Cole.

**1128 The Kenny Rogers Special.** Variety, 60 min., CBS, 4/12/79. An hour of music and songs. *Host:* Kenny Rogers. *Guests:* Ray Charles, Dottie West. *Music:* Bill Justis. *Producers:* Ken Kragen, Stan Harris, Rocco Urbisci. *Director:* Rocco Urbisci.

**1129 Kenny Rogers: Working America.** Variety, 60 min., CBS, 3/27/87. A music and song salute to the working American. *Host:* Kenny Rogers. *Music:* The Kenny Rogers Band. *Producers:* Ken Kragen, Ken Yates, Howard G. Malley. *Writer:* Robert Arnott. *Directors:* Ken Yates, David Hogan.

**1130 The Kid Who Wouldn't Quit — The Brad Silverman Story.** Drama, 60 min., ABC, 9/23/87. The true story about five years in the life of Brad Silverman, a boy with

First Time On Stage Together!

A Once-
In-A-Lifetime
Superstar Summit

Kenny, Dolly, and Willie:
*Something Inside So Strong*

10PM WNBC-TV4 cc

Ad for "Kenny, Dolly and Willie: Something Inside So Strong"

Down's syndrome who struggled to be a regular kid. Aired as an "ABC After-school Special." *Cast:* Marion Ross (Billie Silverman), Shelly Berman (Harold Silverman), K. C. Martel (Brad Silverman; age 13–18), Carl Stephen (Brad; age 10–13), David Fite (Brad, age 5), Milt Kogan (Doctor). *Music:* Roger Bellon. *Producers:* Joanna Lee, Don Hultman. *Writer-Director:* Joanna Lee.

**1131 The Kids from Fame.**
Variety, 60 min., NBC, 3/3/83. Six of the stars from the television series "Fame" perform out of character at Al-

bert Hall in London (where "Fame" is one of England's highest-rated programs). *Host:* George Burns. *Performers:* Debbie Allen, Lee Curreri, Erica Gimpel, Carlo Imperato, Gene Anthony Ray, Lori Singer. *Music:* Barry Fasman. *Producer:* Nicholas Clapp. *Writer:* Draper Lewis. *Director:* Terry Sanders.

**1132 A Killer in Every Corner.** Thriller, 90 min., ABC, 11/19/74. The story of a criminal psychologist who uses humans as guinea pigs to test the behavior patterns of killers. *Cast:*

Joanna Pettet (Sylvia), Patrick Magee (Dr. Carnaby), Eric Flynn (Slattery and Aldridge); also: Don Henderson, Petra Markham, Max Wall. *Music:* Laurie Johnson. *Producers:* Cecil Clarke, John Cooper. *Writer:* Brian Clemens. *Director:* Malcolm Taylor.

## 1133 Killer with Two Faces.
Thriller, 90 min., ABC, 12/3/74. The story of Patty Heron, an American woman who falls in love with an Englishman whose twin is a homicidal maniac. *Cast:* Donna Mills (Patty Heron), Ian Hendry (Terry and Bob Spelling), Roddy McMillan (Fillory), David Lodge (Bradley). *Music:* Laurie Johnson. *Producers:* Cecil Clarke, John Cooper. *Writer:* Brian Clemens. *Director:* John Scholz-Conway.

## 1134 The Killing Game.
Thriller, 90 min., ABC, 2/17/75. The story of Eddie Vallance, a gambler who becomes involved with an eccentric millionaire who will do anything to win a bet. *Cast:* Edd Byrnes (Eddie Vallance), Ingrid Pitt (Ilse), James Berwick (Daddy Burns), Trevor Baxter (Winters), Frank Coda (Purcell), Larry Cross (Tommy Vaughan). *Music:* Laurie Johnson. *Producer:* John Cooper. *Writer:* Brian Clemens. *Director:* Don Leaver.

## 1135 The King and Mrs. Candle.
Musical, 90 min., NBC, 8/22/55. Rupert is the King of Brandovia, a country he rules like a dictator. Lily Candle is his romantic interest, a woman who owns a dancing school. The story relates King Rupert's efforts to adjust to living in a democracy when his subjects revolt and oust him. *Cast:* Cyril Ritchard (King Rupert), Irene Manning (Lily Candle), Joan Greenwood (Irina), Richard Haydn (Bibo), Donald Marye (Zurkin the Fierce), Theodore Bikel (General Korbova), Agnes Doyle (Natasha), Helen Raymond (Mrs. Cornwallis), Raymond Bramley (Mr. Casanby). *Music:* Moose Charlap. *Lyrics:* Chuck Sweeney. *Producer:* Fred Coe. *Writer:* Sumner Locke Elliott. *Director:* Arthur Penn.

## 1136 King Family Specials.
A chronological listing of the variety (music and song) specials starring the King Family. Each are 60 minutes in length. *The King Family:* William King Driggs, Sr., Karleton Driggs, Luise King Rey, Donna King Conkling, Yvonne King Burch, Steve Driggs, Debra Driggs, Phyllis Driggs, Jonathan King Driggs, Barbara Driggs, Tammy Driggs, Todd King Driggs, Don Driggs, Cheryl Driggs, Ray Driggs, Bob Clarke, Lex deAzevedo, Linda deAzevedo, Julie deAzevedo, Carrie deAzevedo, Cameron Clarke, Liza Rey, James Conkling, Candy Conkling Wilson, Donna Alexandra Conkling, Jon Christopher Conkling, Bill Burch, Cathy Cole Green, Jim Green, Susannah Lloyd, Hazel Driggs, Bill Driggs, III, Jon Rey, Ric deAzevedo, Tommy Thomas, Bryan Elliott, Jamie Conkling, Laurette Conkling, Brooke Wilson, Jamie Green. *Music:* Alvino Rey. *Producers:* Yvonne King Burch, Luise King Rey.

**1** The King Family (ABC, 8/29/64).

**2 Thanksgiving with the King Family** (Syndicated, 11/67).

**3 Christmas with the King Family** (Syndicated, 12/67).

**4 Valentine's Day with the King Family** (Syndicated, 2/68).

**5 Easter with the King Family** (Syndicated, 4/68).

**6 Mother's Day with the King Family** (Syndicated, 5/68).

**7 June with the King Family** (Syndicated, 6/68).

**8 Back to School with the King Family** (Syndicated, 9/68).

**9 October with the King Family** (Syndicated, 10/68).

**10 January with the King Family** (Syndicated, 1/69; also known as "The King Family Winter Carnival").

**11 A Holiday Cruise with the King Family** (Syndicated, 3/69; also known as "The King Family in Hawaii").

**12 Backstage with the King Family** (Syndicated, 7/69).
**13 Back Home with the King Family** (Syndicated, 8/69).
**14 The King Family in Washington, D.C.** (Syndicated, 3/71).
**15 The King Family in San Francisco** (Syndicated, 5/71).
**16 The King Family in Atlanta** (Syndicated, 8/71).
**17 Home for Christmas with the King Family** (Syndicated, 12/74).

**1137 King Kong: The Living Legend.** Documentary, 60 min., Syndicated, 8/86. An interesting but somewhat corny look at the cinematic history of King Kong, the legendary screen gorilla who terrorized the beautiful Ann Darrow (Fay Wray) in 1933. Clips from *King Kong* (1933 and 1976), *Son of Kong* (1933), and *Mighty Joe Young* (1949) are interspersed with the comical hosting of Jonathan Winters as he previews Universal City's newest attraction, the King Kong Exhibit. *Host:* Jonathan Winters. *Guests:* Forrest Ackerman, Rick Baker, Charles Grodin, Jenilee Harrison, Anthony Perkins. *Music:* Putter Smith. *Producer:* Arnold Shapiro. *Writer:* Rick Davis. *Director:* Bob Raser.

**1138 King Richard II.** Drama, 2 hrs., NBC, 1/24/54. A television adaptation of the Shakespeare play about a mad king and the deceitful tactics he employs to achieve his goals. Broadcast as a two-hour special during the regular series run on the "Hallmark Hall of Fame." *Cast:* Maurice Evans (King Richard), Sarah Churchill (Queen), Frederic Worlock (John of Gaunt), Kent Smith (Bolingbroke), Bruce Gordon (Thomas Mowbray), Richard Purdy (Duke of Aumerle). *Producer:* Albert McCleery. *Director:* George Schaefer.

**1139 Kismet.** Drama, 90 min., ABC, 10/24/67. A television adaptation of the Edward Knoblock play that tells of a street beggar in ancient Baghdad who falls in love with a princess; and of a prince who falls in love with the beggar's daughter. The title refers to fate. *Cast:* Jose Ferrer (Haji), Anna Maria Alberghetti (Marsinah), George Chakiris (Caliph Abdullah), Barbara Eden (Lalume), Cecil Kellaway (Omar), Hans Conried (The Wazir Mansur), Bern Hoffman (Police chief). *Music and Lyrics:* Robert Wright, George Forrest. *Producer:* Norman Rosemont. *Director:* Bob Henry.

**1140 Kiss Kiss, Kill Kill.** Thriller, 90 min., ABC, 3/11/74. The story of a fortune hunter who marries, then murders, wealthy women. Also known as "A Coffin for the Bride." *Cast:* Michael Jayston (Mark Walker), Helen Mirren (Stella MacKenzie), Michael Gwynn (Oliver Mason), Richard Coleman (Weston), Margaret Courtenay (Claire Jameson), Josephine Tewson (Yvonne), Marcia Fox (Connie). *Music:* Laurie Johnson. *Producers:* Cecil Clarke, John Sichel. *Writer:* Brian Clemens. *Director:* John Sichel.

**1141 Kiss Me, Kate.** Musical, 90 min., NBC, 11/20/58. A musical comedy based on William Shakespeare's *Taming of the Shrew* in which a shrewish exwife (Lilli) tries to win back the love of her former husband (Fred), a stage star who is now in love with an actress (Lois) whom Lilli deplores. Aired on the "Hallmark Hall of Fame." *Cast:* Patricia Morison (Lilli Vanessi), Alfred Drake (Fred Graham), Julie Wilson (Lois Lane), Bill Hayes (Bill Calhoun), Eve Jessaye (Hattie), Paul McGrath (Harrison Howell), Jack Klugman and Harvey Lembeck (Men). *Producers:* Mildred Freed Alberg, George Schaefer. *Writers:* Sam Spewack, Bella Spewack. *Director:* George Schaefer.

**1142 The Klowns.** Variety, 60 min., ABC, 11/15/70. Performances by members of the Ringling Brothers and Barnum and Bailey Circus. *Hosts:* Charlie Callas, Sammy Davis, Jr., Jerry Lewis, Juliet Prowse. *Producers:* Gary Smith, Dwight Hemion. *Writers:* Marty Farrell, Bob Ellison, Marc Richards. *Directors:* Dwight Hemion, Tim Kiley.

**1143 The Kraft All-Star Salute to Ford's Theater.** Variety, 60 min., CBS, 6/12/85. A music, song, dance, and comedy salute to historic Ford's Theater. Sponsored by Kraft Foods. *Hosts:* Linda Evans, John Forsythe. *Guests:* Bobby Berosini's Orangutans, David Copperfield, Robert Guillaume, Delores Hall, Cynthia Harvey, Patti LaBelle, Ronn Lucas, Ricardo Montalban, James Whitmore. *Music:* Stanley Lebowsky. *Producer:* Joseph Cates. *Writer:* Frank Slocum. *Director:* Gilbert Cates.

**1144 Kraft Presents: Jim Henson's "The Christmas Toy."** Comedy, 60 min., ABC, 12/6/86. Kermit the Frog introduces several new Muppet characters in a story that focuses on a group of toys on Christmas Eve as they contemplate the joy they will bring to the children of the Jones family on Christmas morning. Sponsored by Kraft Foods. *Cast:* Jim Henson (Kermit), Dave Goelz (Rugby), Steve Whitmire (Mew), Kathryn Mullen (Apple), Jerry Nelson (Balthazar), Richard Hunt (Belmost), Camille Bonora (Meteora), Brian Henson (Cruiser), Rob Mills (Bleep), Nikki Tilroe (Ding-a-Ling). *Music and Lyrics:* Jeff Moss. *Producers:* Jim Henson, Martin Baker. *Writer:* Laura Phillips. *Director:* Eric Till.

**1145 Kraft Salutes Walt Disney World's 10th Anniversary.** Variety, 60 min., CBS, 1/28/82. A view of Walt Disney World as seen through the eyes of an Indiana family visiting the park in Florida. Sponsored by Kraft Foods. *Cast:* Michele Lee (Mother), Dean Jones (Father), Dana Plato (Daughter), Ricky Schroder (Son), Eileen Brennan (Aunt). *Guests:* Michael Keaton, John Schneider. *Music:* Ian Fraser. *Producers:* Gary Smith, Dwight Hemion. *Writers:* Buz Kohan, Phil May. *Director:* Dwight Hemion.

**1146 The Kraft 75th Anniversary Show.** Variety, 90 min., CBS, 1/24/78. Highlights of radio and television programs sponsored by Kraft Foods. *Host:* Bob Hope. *Guests:* Edgar Bergen, Milton Berle, Roy Clark, Bob Crosby, Alan King, Donna McKechnie, Hal Peary, Leslie Uggams. *Music:* Ian Fraser. *Producers:* Gary Smith, Dwight Hemion. *Writers:* Buz Kohan, Marty Farrell, Jerry Perzigian, Don Siegel. *Director:* Dwight Hemion.

**1147 The Kuklapolitan Easter Show.** Children, 30 min., ABC, 4/10/55. The program, which is actually a "Kukla, Fran and Ollie" special, features a tour of the famed Easter Bunny Plant with Fletcher Rabbitt and his good friend, the Easter Bunny (both hand puppets). *Host:* Fran Allison. *Voices/Puppeteer:* Burr Tillstrom. *Music:* Jack Fascinato. *Music Director:* Rex Maupin. *Producer:* Beulah Zachary. *Writer:* Burr Tillstrom. *Director:* Lewis Gomvatiz.

**1148 Ladies and Gentleman ... Bob Newhart.** Comedy, 60 min., CBS, 2/19/80. Sketches, monologues, and blackouts that spoof contemporary American life. See also the following title. *Host:* Bob Newhart. *Guests:* Marian Mercer, LaWanda Page, Robert Ridgely, Joan Van Ark. *Producers:* Greg Garrison, Lee Hale, Robert Fletcher. *Writers:* Howard Albrecht, Sol Weinstein, Mike Marmer, Bill Box, Bill Daily, Ken Friedman, Goodman Ace. *Director:* Greg Garrison.

## 1149 Ladies and Gentleman ... Bob Newhart, Part II.
Comedy, 60 min., CBS, 5/14/81. A sequel to the previous special; additional spoofs of the contemporary American scene. *Host:* Bob Newhart. *Guests:* Dean Martin, Dick Martin, Marian Mercer, Don Rickles, Robert Ridgely. *Producers:* Greg Garrison, Lee Hale. *Writers:* Howard Albrecht, Bob Newhart, Sol Weinstein, Bill Box, Frank Mula. *Director:* Greg Garrison.

## 1150 Lady in the Dark.
Musical, 90 min., NBC, 9/24/54. A television adaptation of the play by Moss Hart about Liza Elliott, a plain and insecure magazine editor whose psychotic dreams propel her into a world where she is beautiful and in charge of her life. *Cast:* Ann Sothern (Liza Elliott), James Daly (Charley Johnson), Paul McGrath (Kendall Nesbitt), Luella Gear (Maggie Grant), Sheppard Strudwick (Dr. Brooks), Carleton Carpenter (Russell Paxton), Robert Fortier (Randy Curtis), Bambi Linn, Rod Alexander (Dancers). *Music:* Charles Sanford. *Producer:* Max Liebman. *Writers:* William Friedberg, Max Liebman. *Director:* Jeffrey Hayden.

## 1151 Lady Killer.
Thriller, 90 min., ABC, 1/18/73. The story of a young American bride (Jenny) who fears that her British husband (Paul) is plotting to kill her. Also known as "The Death Policy." *Cast:* Barbara Feldon (Jenny Tanner), Robert Powell (Paul Tanner), Jeddie Evans (Mrs. Bradley), T. P. McKenna (Jack Hardisty), Linda Thorson (Toni), Ivor Roberts (Doctor), Ronald Mayer (Minister). *Music:* Laurie Johnson. *Producers:* Cecil Clarke, John Sichel. *Writer:* Brian Clemens. *Director:* Bill Hays.

## 1152 The Lainie Kazan Show.
Variety, 60 min., Syndicated, 10/68. A solo concert by singer-actress Lainie Kazan. *Host:* Lainie Kazan. *Band:* John Hammond (drums), Howard Collins (guitar), Ernie Furtado (bass), Lloyd Morales (drums).

## 1153 Lamp at Midnight.
Drama, 90 min., NBC, 4/27/66. A "Hallmark Hall of Fame" presentation about Galileo Galilei (1564–1642) as he attempts to disprove the church's promulgation that the earth is the center of the universe. *Cast:* Melvyn Douglas (Galileo), David Wayne (Father Firenzuola), Michael Hordern (Cardinal Barberini), Hurd Hatfield (Sagredo Niccolini), Kim Hunter (Polissena), Thayer David (Magini). *Producer-Director:* George Schaefer.

## 1154 Landscape with Waitress.
Drama, 30 min., PBS, 1/5/89. A two-character play set in a New York restaurant. The story relates a customer's (Arthur) thoughts about Rita — the waitress he becomes fascinated with but cannot seem to figure out. *Cast:* John Rothman (Arthur Grainger), Nurit Koppel (Rita), Joseph Zarro (Man at bar; nonspeaking role). *Theme Vocal,* "Can Anyone Explain?": The Ames Brothers. *Music:* Kim Oler. *Producer:* David Massar. *Writer:* Robert Pine. *Director:* Jeffrey Townsend.

## 1155 The Lark.
Drama, 90 min., NBC, 2/10/57. A dramatic retelling of the story of Joan of Arc, the young French girl who was tried for heresy and sorcery before an inquisitional court and later sentenced to be burned at the stake (in 1431). Aired on the "Hallmark Hall of Fame." *Cast:* Julie Harris (Joan of Arc), Boris Karloff (Cauchon), Basil Rathbone (Inquisitor), Eli Wallach (Dauphin), Denholm Elliott (Warwick), Jack Warden (Robert de Baudricourt), Bruce Gordon (Captain La Hire). *Producer-Director:* George Schaefer. *Writer:* James Costigan.

## 1156 Larry Gatlin and the Gatlin Brothers.
Variety, 60 min., ABC, 5/25/81. An edited-for-television

(for length) concert by Larry Gatlin and his brothers. *Hosts:* Larry Gatlin, Rudy Gatlin, Steve Gatlin. *Guests:* Johnny Cash, Roger Miller, Dottie West. *Music:* The Gatlin Brothers Band. *Producers:* Gary Smith, Dwight Hemion, Rita Scott. *Writer:* Chet Hagan. *Director:* Dwight Hemion.

**1157 Las Vegas: An All-Star 75th Anniversary.** Variety, 2 hrs., ABC, 11/29/87. A star-studded salute to Las Vegas on the occasion of its seventy-fifth anniversary. *Hosts:* Dean Martin, Frank Sinatra. *Guests:* Debbie Allen, Red Buttons, Nell Carter, Ray Charles, Sammy Davis, Jr., Gallagher, Shecky Greene, Mary Hart, Engelbert Humperdinck, Tom Jones, Jerry Lewis, The McGuire Sisters, The Oak Ridge Boys, Juliet Prowse, Don Rickles, Wil Shriner, Siegfried and Roy, Pia Zadora. *Announcer:* Gary Owens. *Music:* Dennis McCarthy. *Producers:* George Schlatter, Marty Pasetta. *Writers:* Bruce Vilanch, George Schlatter. *Director:* Marty Pasetta.

**Las Vegas Palace of Stars** *see* **Cinderella at the Palace**

**1158 The Last Bride of Salem.** Thriller, 90 min., ABC, 5/8/74. Jennifer Clifton, her husband, Matt, and their daughter, Kelly, are a happy and carefree family who move to a small village in Salem, Massachusetts. Matt and Kelly change shortly after, and Jennifer realizes that they are being manipulated by diabolic powers housed in a brooding Gothic mansion near their home. The story relates Jennifer's terrifying confrontation with these supernatural forces to save her family. *Cast:* Lois Nettleton (Jennifer Clifton), Bradford Dillman (Matt Clifton), Joni Bick (Kelly Clifton), Paul Harding (Sebastian), Ed McNamara (Seth), Susan Rubis (Grace), Patricia Hamilton (Rebecca), James Douglas (Dr. Glover), Rex Hagon (Master). *Pro-*

*ducer:* Bob Lewis. *Writer:* Rita Lakin. *Director:* Tom Donovan.

**1159 The Last Days of Marilyn Monroe.** Documentary, 90 min., Syndicated, 11/26/85. A British-produced special that attempts to reconstruct the events that led to actress Marilyn Monroe's death on 8/5/62. Guests, film clips, and newsreel footage disclose evidence that Marilyn's reported suicide (drug overdose) was actually a cover-up for murder. *Guests:* Jeanne Carmen, John Danoff, Deborah Gould, Joan Greenson, Eunice Murray, Fred Otash, Tom Reddin, George Smathers, Sam Yorty. *Producers:* George Carey, Ted Landveth. *Writer-Director:* Christopher Olgiati.

**1160 The Last Halloween.** Comedy, 30 min., CBS, 10/28/91. Crystal Falls is a small town that may be celebrating its last Halloween as the Cosmic Candy Factory, which produces the town's supply of sweets, is about to close (the water in the lake that supplies the power is drying up). As the town's children begin trick or treating, four Martians (Gleep, Scoota, Romtu the Great, and Bing), have come to Crystal Falls to replenish their supply of Coobie (candy). The Martians befriend two earth children, Michael and Jeanie, and join them as trick or treaters to obtain candy. When Michael and Jeanie discover that the evil Mrs. Gizborne has been draining the lake because she feels its water holds the secret to eternal youth, the Martians foil her plans and save the lake. In gratitude, the Martians are given all the candy they can take back to Mars. *Cast:* Will Nipper (Michael), Sarah Martineck (Jeanie), Rhea Perlman (Mrs. Gizborne), Richard Moll (Hans), Eugene Roche (Grandpa), Stan Ivar (Hubble), Michael D. Roberts (Accountant), Sean Roche (Sheriff), Grant Gelt (Lou), William Hanna (Narrator). *Voices:* Paul Williams (Gleep), Don Messick (Romtu

**Ad for "The Last Halloween"**

the Great), Frank Welker (Scotta). Bing is non-speaking. *Music:* Bruce Broughton. *Live Action Producer:* David Kirschner. *Computer Animation Producers:* Carl Rosendahl, Brad Lewis. *Writers:* Sean Roche, Savage Steve Holland. *Live Action Director:* Savage Steve Holland. *Computer Animation Director:* Henry Anderson III.

**1161 The Last Hurrah.** Drama, 2 hrs., NBC, 11/16/77. Big-city politics as seen through the experiences of Frank Skeffington, a mayor who, despite his failing health, decides to run for a fourth term. Based on the novel by Edwin O'Connor; broadcast on the "Hallmark Hall of Fame." *Cast:* Carroll O'Connor (Frank Skeffington), Leslie Ackerman (Purdy Cass), John Anderson (Amos Force), Dana Andrews (Roger Shanley), Mariette Hartley (Clare Gardiner), Burgess Meredith (Cardinal Burke), Robert Brown (Nat Gardiner), Patrick O'Neal (Norman Cass), Jack Carter (Sam Weinberg).

*Music:* Peter Matz. *Producer:* Terry Becker. *Writer:* Carroll O'Connor. *Director:* Vincent Sherman.

**1162 A Last Laugh at the 60s.** Comedy, 60 min., ABC, 1/8/70. A music and comedy revue of the 1960s. *Performers:* Don Adams, Richard Benjamin, Carol Burnett, John Byner, Godfrey Cambridge, Buck Henry, Elaine May, Mike Nichols, Pat Paulsen, Richard Pryor, Don Rickles, Mort Sahl, George Schlatter, Allan Sherman, Tiny Tim, Lorene Yarnell. *Producers:* Dan Melnick, Steve Binder. *Writers:* Dick Clair, Jeanna McMahon, Ron Graham. *Director:* Steve Binder.

**1163 The Last Leaf.** Drama, 30 min., Syndicated, 4/84. A television adaptation of the story by O. Henry. Susan Brady is a very sick young girl who believes that when the last leaf of a dying vine is blown away by the winter wind, she will die. The efforts of her sister, Joanna, and of an aging artist, Mr. Verlane, to convince her otherwise, have failed. One night during a fierce storm, Mr. Verlane risks his life to give the girl the one hope she needs to live. The following morning, as Joanna opens the curtains, they are both amazed to see that, despite the storm, one leaf is still clinging to the vine. The sight gives Susan the will to live. As Joanna looks out the window she sees something that Susan does not—a last gush of wind loosens the vine from the wall and the last leaf remains—a painting by Mr. Verlane. *Cast:* Art Carney (Mr. Verlane), Sydney Penny (Susan Brady), Jane Kaczmarek (Joanna Brady), Hermione Baddeley (Landlady), Patrick Billingsley (Doctor). *Theme,* "Susan's Theme": Sonia Eddings Brown. *Music:* Larry Bastian. *Producers:* Cheryl Allen, Jane Gardner. *Writer:* Caryl Lender. *Director:* David Anspaugh.

## 1164  Last of the Curlews.

Cartoon, 60 min., ABC, 10/4/72. A program about respect for wildlife wherein a male Eskimo Curlew, a stately shore bird now believed to be extinct, searches in vain for a mate. Aired as the first "ABC Afterschool Special." *Voices:* Ross Martin (Hunter), Vincent Van Patten (Son). *Narrator:* Lee Vines. *Music:* Hoyt Curtin. *Producers:* William Hanna, Joseph Barbera.

## 1165  The Last Polka. Comedy,

60 min., HBO, 3/14/85. A comical documentary that traces the careers of Josh and Stan Shmenge, a famous Leutonia polka team. Stan and Josh, the children of poor cabbage pickers in Leutonia (on the dark side of the Balkans), appear on HBO for their farewell polka concert. *Cast:* John Candy (Josh Shmenge), Eugene Levy (Stan Shmenge). *Guests:* Robin Duke, Rick Moranis, Catherine O'Hara, Mary Margaret O'Hara. *Narrator:* Dave Thomas. *Music:* Russ Little. *Producer-Writers:* John Candy, Eugene Levy. *Director:* John Blanchard.

## 1166  The Last War. Science

Fiction, 45 min., NBC, 11/10/46. A drama based on Darwin's theory of evolution: how man annihilates himself in a final war and how the animals begin life anew on earth. *Cast:* John McQuade (Monkey), Fay Marlowe (Angel), Vaughn Taylor (Dog). *Also:* Kendall Clark, Walter Coy, Arthur Hunnicutt, Evelyn Peterson, William Post, Jr., Eva Marie Saint, Mary Wilsey. *Producer-Director:* Fred Coe. *Animal Masks:* Richard Smith.

## 1167  The Late Great Me: The Story of a Teenage Alcoholic.

Drama, 90 min., ABC, 11/14/79. Geri Peters is a 15-year-old, small-town girl with few friends and few interests. When David Townsend, a new student, takes a liking to her, Geri decides to keep his attentions by sharing one of his avid pursuits—drinking. The sensitive "ABC Afterschool Special" details her rapid decline and desperate attempts to get help when alcoholism begins to affect her appearance and attitude. *Cast:* Maia Danziger (Geri Peters), Charley Lang (David Townsend), Teri Keane (Ginger Peters), Michael Miller (George Peters), Kaiulani Lee (Mrs. Laine), Al Corley (Jack Peters), Amy DeMayo (Carolyn). *Music:* Jay Smith. *Producers:* Daniel Wilson, Linda Marmelstein. *Writer:* Jan Hartman. *Director:* Anthony Lovell.

## 1168  Late Night with David Letterman 10th Anniversary Special. Variety, 90 min., NBC,

2/6/92. Highlights of ten years of "Late Night with David Letterman." Clips from the series are seen along with performances by guests. Taped at Radio City Music Hall in New York City. *Host:* David Letterman. *Guests:* Bob Dylan, Bill Murray, Paul Shaffer. *Producers:* Jack Rollins, David Letterman, Robert Morton, Frank Gannon. *Writers:* Steve O'Donnell, Garry Mulligan, Larry Jacobson, Bob Burnett, Paul

Simms, Steve Young, Maria Pope, David Letterman, Ken Keeler, Jill Davis. *Director:* Hal Gurnee.

**1169 The Laundromat.** Drama, 60 min., HBO, 4/1/85. Alberta Johnson and Dee Dee Johnson are two troubled women who share the same last name but are not related. They meet at a laundromat in Paris and quickly become friends. The story relates their conversation as they exchange personal histories while coming to terms with the men in their lives. *Cast:* Carol Burnett (Alberta Johnson), Amy Madigan (Dee Dee Johnson), Michael Wright (Shooter Stevens). *Producer:* Scott Bushnell. *Writer:* Marsha Norman. *Director:* Robert Altman.

**1170 Laura.** A listing of the two television adaptations of the three-act play by Vera Caspary and George Sklar. While investigating the murder of Laura Hunt, an advertising executive whose face has been blasted away by a shotgun blast, Detective Mark McPherson becomes fascinated by her portrait, which dominates her apartment. Later, when the presumably murdered woman returns to her apartment (from an unannounced trip), it is discovered that the dead girl was actually a friend of Laura's who had been staying in the apartment. The story relates Mark's efforts to protect Laura from a killer who will now try to correct his mistake.
　**1 Laura** (60 min., CBS, 10/19/55). *Cast:* Dana Wynter (Laura Hunt), Robert Stack (Mark McPherson), George Sanders (Waldo Lydecker), Scott Forbes (Shelby Carpenter). *Producer:* Otto Lang. *Writer:* Mel Dinelli. *Director:* John Brahm.
　**2 Laura** (2 hrs., ABC, 1/24/68). *Cast:* Lee Bouvier (Laura Hunt), Robert Stack (Mark McPherson), George Sanders (Waldo Lydecker), Farley Granger (Shelby Carpenter), Arlene Francis (Anne Treadwell), Edith Dunne (Bessie Clary). *Music:* David Raksin.

*Producer:* David Susskind. *Writers:* Truman Capote, Thomas W. Phipps. *Director:* John Llewellyn Moxey.

**1171 The Lawrence Welk Christmas Special.** Variety, 60 min., Syndicated, 12/84. A holiday program of music and song in which many stars from "The Lawrence Welk Show" (ABC, 1955–71) gather to celebrate Christmas. *Host:* Lawrence Welk. *Announcer:* Bob Warren. *Music:* George Cates. *Producer:* Larry Welk. *Writer:* Bernice McGeehan. *Director:* Michele Jackman.

**1172 Lawrence Welk: Television's Music Man.** Tribute, 60 min., PBS, 3/19/87. A clip-filled tribute to Lawrence Welk, the beloved champagne music leader who was a staple of Saturday night television for 27 years (ABC, 1955–71; Syndicated, 1971–83). *Hosts:* Dianne Lennon, Janet Lennon, Kathy Lennon, Peggy Lennon. *Guests:* Bobby Burgess, JoAnn Castle, George Cates, Ranla English, Myron Floren, Guy Hovis, Jack Imel, Norma Zimmer. *Producers:* Stephan Chadorva, John Musilli, JoAnn Young. *Writer:* JoAnn Young. *Director:* John Musilli.

**1173 Leadfoot.** Drama, 30 min., Syndicated, 12/82. Tommy Russell is a teenage boy and the proud owner of the first car he worked and saved for. The story relates the tragedy that results when a friend sideswipes him and Tommy seeks revenge. *Cast:* Philip McKeon (Tommy Russell), Wendy Smith Howard (Pam), Peter Barton (Murph), K Callan (Pam's mother), Stephen Young (Jordan Russell), Richard Lawson (Officer Venchek), Dennis Dugan (Officer Needham). *Music:* Chris Stone. *Producers:* Ellwood Kieser, Michael Rhodes. *Writer:* Jim McGinn. *Director:* Michael Rhodes.

**1174 Leapin' Lizards, It's Liberace.** Variety, 60 min., CBS, 2/1/

78. Music, songs, and light comedy with Liberace from the Hilton Hotel in Las Vegas. *Host:* Liberace. *Guests:* Vince Cardell, The Chinese Acrobats of Taiwan, Phyllis Diller, Debbie Reynolds, Barclay Shaw. *Music:* Bo Ayars. *Producers:* Bob Banner, Seymour Heller. *Director:* Tony Charmoli.

**1175 Learned Pigs and Fireproof Women.** Variety, 60 min., CBS, 4/19/90. The program explores the world of magic and unusual performers of the past and present. Taped at the Warner Grand Theater in Los Angeles. *Host:* Ricky Jay. *Guests:* Matt Biondi, Elayne Boosler, Shakuntala Devi, John Gaughan, Michael McGiveney, Steve Martin, Michael Moschen, Meagen Riesel, Bruce Schwartz, Jamey Turner. *Producers:* Andrew Solt, Sam Egan. *Writers:* Ricky Jay, Sam Egan, Andrew Solt. *Director:* Michael Lindsay-Hogg.

**1176 The Legend of Firefly Marsh.** Adventure, 30 min., Syndicated, 5/21/88. A young boy and his grandfather attempt to free a sea creature (the Legend of Firefly Marsh) from a marsh when the government decides to fill in the loch that has the creature trapped and unable to return to the sea. *Cast:* Jonas Marlowe (Grandpa Charlie Curtis), Adrian Drake (Kevin Curtis). *Music:* Laraine Claire. *Producers:* Steven Hedstrom, Judith Pollack. *Writer-Director:* Gabe Torres.

**1177 The Legend of Lochnager.** Cartoon, 30 min., ABC, 4/24/93. A fable, written by Charles, Prince of Wales, when he was 21, about a know-it-all Scotsman who leaves civilization for the simple life as a hermit (he retreats to a cave in Lochnager in the Scottish mountains. There he befriends a race of little people called the Gorms, who plant the flowers for Scotland. His efforts to save them from a raging fire are the focal point of the story). Aired

as an "ABC Weekend Special." *Voices:* Robbie Coltrane (Hermit), Nick McArdle, Hannah Gordon, Victoria Bowstead, John Hamilton. *Host-Narrator:* Prince Charles. *Producers:* Christopher Grace, Dave Edwards. *Story:* Prince Charles. *Scripts:* Jocelyn Stevenson, Pamela Hickey, Dennis McCoy. *Director:* Chris Fenna.

**1178 The Legend of Marilyn Monroe.** Documentary, 60 min., ABC, 11/30/66. The life of actress Marilyn Monroe from her childhood sorrows to her adult heartaches and death. *Narrator:* John Huston. *Guests:* Ida Bolander, Jim Dougherty, Lee Strasberg. *Producers:* David L. Wolper, Terry Sanders. *Writer-Director:* Terry Sanders.

**1179 The Legend of Silent Night.** Drama, 30 min., ABC, 12/25/68. The story, set in Austria in 1818, tells of Franz Gruber and how he came to write "Silent Night," one of the most beloved Christmas songs. Based on the story by Paul Gallico. *Cast:* James Mason (Franz Gruber), John Leyton (Pastor Mohr), Claudia Butenuth (Gretchen), Manfred Seipold (Ernst). *Narrator:* Kirk Douglas. *Producer:* Harry Rasky. *Writers:* Christopher Sherwood, Harry Rasky. *Directors:* Daniel Mann, Harry Rasky.

**1180 The Legend of the Beverly Hillbillies.** Comedy, 60 min., CBS, 5/24/93. The program explains what happened to "The Beverly Hillbillies" after the program left the air in 1971. Clips are used to recall the lives of Jed, Elly Mae, and Jethro; in-person interviews tell us that Jed lost his money through Milburn Drysdale's embezzling (Drysdale is now in prison). Jed had some money left and has bought himself a comfortable home. Jethro is now a doctor with a very large family; Elly Mae is single and lives with her beloved critters; and Granny has

**COME AND LISTEN TO A STORY 'BOUT A MAN NAMED JED...**

Take your shoes off and sit a spell with the Clampetts, as we recollect their hilarious past and discover what they've been up to.

THE LEGEND OF

**The BEVERLY HILLBILLIES**

A CBS SPECIAL PRESENTATION

EDDIE ALBERT    MAX BAER    DONNA DOUGLAS    BUDDY EBSEN    EVA GABOR    REBA McENTIRE

and many, many more!

8 PM ⊚2 WCBS-TV

Ad for "The Legend of the Beverly Hillbillies"

passed away. *Host:* Mac Davis. *Guests:* Eddie Albert, Hoyt Axton, Max Baer, Jr., Ray Charles, Roy Davis, Donna Douglas, Buddy Ebsen, Eva Gabor, Reba McEntire, Louis Nye. *Music:* Ray Bunch. *Producers:* Ken Ross, Jay Levey. *Writers:* Al Bendix, Mike Rowe. *Director:* Jay Levey.

**1181 Legend of the Super Heroes — The Roast.** Comedy, 60 min., NBC, 1/25/79. A spoof of "The Dean Martin Celebrity Roasts" wherein an assemblage of superheroes take a ribbing from their archenemies. *Host:*

Ed McMahon. *Cast:* Adam West (Batman), Burt Ward (Robin), Jeff Altman (Weather Wizard), Ruth Buzzi (Aunt Minerva), Charlie Callas (Sinestro), Pat Carroll (Hawkman's Mother), Gabe Dell (Mordru), William Schallert (Retired Man), Brad Sanders (Ghetto Man), Mickey Morton (Solomon Grundy).

**1182 The Legendary Curse of the Hope Diamond.** Drama, 60 min., CBS, 3/27/75. A Smithsonian Institution special that dramatizes the history of the Hope Diamond. *Cast:*

Bradford Dillman (Ned McLean), Samantha Eggar (Evalyn Walsh McLean), Claudine Longet (Marie Antoinette), Martha Scott (Mummsie), Harry Dean Stanton (President Harding), Jim Boles (Albert Fall), Christopher Cary (Lord Hope), Robert Clary (Louis XVI), Lezlie Dalton (May Yohe). *Narrator:* Rod Serling. *Producers:* George Lefferts, Delbert Mann. *Writer:* George Lefferts. *Director:* Delbert Mann.

## 1183  The Leif Garrett Special.

Variety, 60 min., CBS, 5/18/79. An hour of music, songs, and comedy with actor Leif Garrett in his only television special. *Host:* Leif Garrett. *Guests:* Bob Hope, Marie Osmond, Pink Lady, Brooke Shields, Flip Wilson. *Producer-Director:* Bob Henry. *Writers:* Rod Warren, Stephan Spears.

## 1184  Lena Horne: The Lady and Her Music.

Variety, 2 hrs. 10 min., Showtime, 3/15/84. A one-woman show in which singer-actress Lena Horne performs her most popular songs. Based on Miss Horne's Broadway show. *Host:* Lena Horne. *Producer:* Robert Manby. *Director:* Paddy Sampson.

## 1185  The  Leningrad  Ice Show.

Variety, 60 min., CBS, 8/29/78. Performances by ice skaters from the Leningrad Sports Palace. *Hosts:* Harry Morgan, Sally Struthers. *Producers:* Mike Gargiulo, Lothaar Bock. *Writer:* Chuck Horner. *Directors:* Mike Gargiulo, Vern Diamond, Frank Marischka.

## 1186  The  Lennon  Sisters Show.

Variety, 60 min., ABC, 5/6/69. An hour of music and song with the Lennon Sisters in their first and only television special. *Hosts:* Dianne Lennon, Janet Lennon, Kathy Lennon, Peggy Lennon. *Guests:* Jimmy Durante, Bobby Goldsboro. *Music:* Nelson Riddle. *Producers:* Harold Cohen, Bernie Kukoff, Jeff Harris. *Writers:* Jeff Harris, Bernie Kukoff, Elias Davis, David Pollock. *Director:* Grey Lockwood.

## 1187  The Leprechaun's Christmas Gold.

Children, 30 min., ABC, 12/23/81. An animated tale that explores the legend of how the leprechauns brought the Christmas gold to Ireland. *Voices:* Art Carney (Barney Kilakarney), Peggy Cass (Faye Kilakarney), Ken Jennings (Dinty Doyle), Christine Mitchell (Old Mag), Glynis Bier (Child), Michael Moronosk (Child). *Music:* Maury Laws. *Producer-Directors:* Arthur Rankin, Jr., Jules Bass. *Writer:* Romeo Muller.

## 1188  Lesley in Love.

Variety, 60 min., Syndicated, 7/70. A program of love songs with singer Lesley Gore. *Host:* Lesley Gore. *Producers:* Hendrik Booraem, Hal Tulchin. *Director:* Hal Tulchin.

## 1189  Leslie.

Variety, 60 min., ABC, 5/1/68. Music and songs with Leslie Uggams in her only variety special. *Host:* Leslie Uggams. *Guests:* Noel Harrison, Robert Morse, The Young Rascals. *Music:* H. B. Barnum. *Producers:* Saul Ilson, Ernest Chambers.

## 1190  The Less Than Perfect Daughter.

Drama, 60 min., ABC, 1/24/91. An "ABC Afterschool Special" about Melissa Harmon, a high school girl who runs away from home to get away from her mother (Irene), who belittles her. *Cast:* Robin Lively (Melissa Harmon), Jenny O'Hara (Irene Harmon), Andrea Elson (Liz), Michael Pritchard (Michael Peterson), Debbi Morgan (Celia), Ernie Lively (Jack Harmon). *Music:* Lisa Bolen. *Producers:* Terry Kirby, Gilbert Moses. *Writers:* David Villaire, Kat Smith, Gordon Rayfield. *Director:* Gilbert Moses.

*Left to right:* **Dianne, Kathy, Peggy, and Janet Lennon — stars of "The Lennon Sisters Show."**

**1191 Let Me Tell You About a Song.** Variety, 60 min., Syndicated, 11/72. Videotaped highlights of performances by singer Merle Haggard. *Host:* Merle Haggard. *Guests:* Bonnie Owens, The Strangers. *Narrator:* Jefferson Kaye. *Producer-Writer-Director:* Michael P. Davis.

**1192 Let There Be Stars.** Variety, 60 min., ABC, 9/21/49. A program of music, songs, and dances presented as a revue. *Performers:* Patti Brill, Warde Donovan, Roland Dupree, Ward Edwards, Corky Geil, Jane Harvey, Charles Lind, Peter Marshall, Tom Noonan, Thayer Roberts, Dolores Starr. *Producers:* Leighton Brill, William Triz. *Writer:* Nat Linden. *Director:* Richard J. Goggin.

**1193 Let's Celebrate.** Comedy, 75 min., ABC, 11/21/72 (part 1); 11/22/72 (part 2). A late-night program of comedy sketches (broadcast from 11:30

P.M. to 12:45 A.M.). See also "Bedtime Story" for information on the epilogue program (12:45 A.M. to 1:00 A.M.). *Cast:* Susan Browning, Hope Clark, Paul Dooley, Steve Landesberg, Richard Libertini, Terry O'Mara, Austin Pendleton, Tony Roberts. *Producer:* Richard Lewine. *Writers:* Betty Comden, Adolph Green. *Director:* Dave Wilson.

**1194 Liberace with the London Philharmonic Orchestra.** Variety, 60 min., Syndicated, 8/85. A 1983 concert by Liberace that was taped at London's Wembley Centre. *Host:* Liberace. *Leader, London Philharmonic Orchestra:* David Nolan. *Orchestra Conductor:* David Snell. *Producers:* John Fisher, Stewart Morris.

**1195 Liberty Weekend: A Classic Salute to Liberty.** Variety, 2 hrs., ABC, 7/5/86. A classical musical salute to the Statue of Liberty on the occasion of its one hundredth birthday. See also the following two titles. *Host:* Peter Jennings. *Guests:* Placido Domingo, Marilyn Horne, Sherrill Milnes, Leona Mitchell, The New York Choral Artists, The New York Philharmonic Orchestra, Itzhak Perlman, The U.S. Army and Marine Bands. *Music Director:* Zubin Mehta. *Producers:* David L. Wolper, Roone Arledge. *Writer:* Frank Slocum. *Directors:* Kirk Browning, Roger Goodman.

**1196 Liberty Weekend: Closing Ceremonies.** Variety, 4 hrs. 5 min., ABC, 7/6/86. A spectacular finale of music and song to ABC's extended coverage of Liberty Weekend, a commemoration of the Statue of Liberty's centennial. *Host:* Peter Jennings. *Guests:* Frankie Avalon, Fabian Forte, Waylon Jennings, Gene Kelly, Patti LaBelle, Shirley MacLaine, The Manhattan Transfer, Liza Minnelli, Willie Nelson, The Pointer Sisters, Billy Preston, Kenny Rogers, Bobby Rydell,

Elizabeth Taylor, The Temptations, Cicely Tyson. *Music:* Elliot Lawrence. *Producers:* David L. Wolper, Don Mischer. *Writer:* Buz Kohan. *Director:* Don Mischer.

**1197 Liberty Weekend: Opening Ceremonies.** Variety, 3 hrs. 15 min., ABC, 7/3/86. The opening ceremonies of the four-day Statue of Liberty Centennial from New York Harbor. Included: the unveiling of Lady Liberty and the lighting of her torch by President Ronald Reagan; a film on Ellis Island narrated by Kirk Douglas; and a history of the Statue of Liberty narrated by Gregory Peck. *Hosts:* Peter Jennings, Barbara Walters. *Reporters:* David Brinkley, Hugh Downs, Pierre Salinger, James Wooten. *Guests:* Debbie Allen, Mikhail Baryshnikov, Neil Diamond, Jose Feliciano, Kenny Rogers, Frank Sinatra, Elizabeth Taylor. *Music:* Ian Fraser. *Producers:* David L. Wolper, Gary Smith, Dwight Hemion. *Writer:* Buz Kohan. *Director:* Dwight Hemion.

**1198 Lies of the Heart.** Drama, 60 min., CBS, 1/8/91. Jordan Crane is the all–American high school senior. One day he is involved in a hit-and-run accident when he strikes a woman with his car, then flees from the scene. The woman is injured and Jordan tells his father about it. Frank, Jordan's father, tells him to keep quiet about it. The story relates the torment Jordan faces when his conscience begins to bother him and he feels he must face up to his responsibilities. Aired as a "CBS Schoolbreak Special." *Cast:* Christopher Rydell (Jordan Crane), Charles Frank (Frank Crane), Brooke Theiss (Patricia), Jennifer Gatti (Anna Manetti), Tricia O'Neil (Beth Crane). *Music:* Russ Levinson. *Producers:* Steve Tisch, Mireilla Soria. *Writer-Director:* Barra Grant.

**1199 The Life and Adventures of Santa Claus.** Fantasy, 60 min.,

CBS, 12/17/85. An animated holiday special that relates how the traditions of Christmas evolved and how Kris Kringle acquired his immortality from the Great A. K. Based on the novel by L. Frank Baum. Produced in animagic, a computer process that gives "life" to marionettes. *Voices:* Earl Hammond (Santa Claus), Earle Hyman (King Awgwa), Lynne Lipton (Queen Zurline), Larry Kenney (Wind Demon), Robert McFadden (Tingler), Lesley Miller (Necile), Peter Newman (Peter Knook), Alfred Drake (Great A. K.), J. D. Roth (Young Santa Claus). *Music:* Bernard Hoffer. *Producer-Director:* Arthur Rankin Jr., Jules Bass. *Writer:* Julian P. Gardner.

## 1200 Life Goes to the Movies.

Documentary, 3 hrs., NBC, 10/31/76. The Hollywood films and stars of the era 1936–72 are recalled through film clips. Based on the book *Life Goes to the Movies.* *Hosts:* Henry Fonda, Shirley MacLaine, Liza Minnelli. *Music:* Fred Karlin. *Producer:* Jack Haley, Jr. *Writer:* Richard Schickel. *Director:* Mel Stuart.

## 1201 Life Is a Circus, Charlie Brown.

Cartoon, 30 min., CBS, 10/24/80. The story follows Snoopy as he leaves home and joins the circus to be with his lady love, Fifi, a French poodle who performs in a traveling circus. *Voices:* Michael Mandy (Charlie Brown), Brent Hauer (Peppermint Patty), Casey Carlson (Paula), Christopher Donohoe (Schroeder), Earl Reilly (Linus), Kristen Fullerton (Sally), Shannon Cohn (Lucy), Bill Melendez (Snoopy). *Music:* Ed Bogas, Judy Munsen. *Producers:* Lee Mendelson, Bill Melendez. *Writer:* Charles M. Schulz. *Director:* Phil Roman.

## 1202 Life's Most Embarrassing Moments.

A chronological listing of comedy specials that feature the bloopers (outtakes) made by celebrities, politicians, athletes, and news-men. Each program is 60 minutes and aired on ABC. All have the following credits in common: *Theme Music:* The Music Design Group. *Producers:* Alan Landsburg, Woody Fraser. *Writers:* Richard Crystal, Marty Tenney. *Director:* Jerry Kupcinet. The only exception is the first special, which was directed by Woody Fraser.

**1 Life's Most Embarrassing Moments** (4/27/83). *Host:* John Ritter. *Guests:* Cathy Lee Crosby, Phil Esposito, Bob Eubanks, Jim Marshall, Pat O'Brien, Eugene Roche.

**2 Life's Most Embarrassing Moments** (9/18/83). *Host:* Steve Allen. *Announcer:* Johnny Olsen.

**3 Life's Most Embarrassing Moments** (11/10/83). *Host:* Steve Allen.

**4 Life's Most Embarrassing Moments** (2/23/84). *Host:* Steve Allen. *Guests:* Bert Parks, Cassandra Peterson ("Elvira"), Bobby Riggs.

**5 Life's Most Embarrassing Moments** (11/11/84). *Host:* Steve Allen. *Guests:* John Byner, Norman Donaldson, Linda Purl.

**6 Life's Most Embarrassing Moments** (2/17/85). *Host:* Steve Allen. *Guests:* Rene Auberjonois, John Byner, Jane Curtin, Robert Guillaume, Susan Saint James.

**7 Life's Most Embarrassing Moments** (5/5/85). *Host:* Steve Allen. *Guests:* Milton Berle, Mary Cadorette.

**8 Life's Most Embarrassing Moments** (2/1/86). *Hosts:* Steve Allen, Emmanuel Lewis. *Guests:* Sid Caesar, Gary Coleman, Bob Einstein, Peter Scolari.

**9 Life's Most Embarrassing Moments** (5/24/86). *Host:* Steve Allen. *Guests:* Roy Clark, James Noble.

## 1203 The Light Fantastic, or How to Tell Your Past, Present and Maybe Even Your Future Through Social Dancing.

Variety, 60 min., ABC, 2/9/67. A lighthearted look at dancing in the United States. *Hosts:* Lauren Bacall, John

Forsythe. *Music:* Peter Matz. *Producer:* Dee Dee Wood. *Writer:* Arthur Laurents. *Director:* Marc Breaux.

## 1204 Lights, Camera, Monty!

Variety, 60 min., ABC, 4/24/75. An hour of music, songs, and comedy sketches with game show host Monty Hall in his first television special. *Host:* Monty Hall. *Guests:* The Carl Jablonski Dancers, Marty Feldman, Steve Lawrence, Michele Lee, Dianne Lennon, Janet Lennon, Kathy Lennon, Peggy Lennon. *Music:* Harper McKay. *Producer-Director:* Bob Wynn. *Writers:* Bob Arnott, Coslough Johnson, Marilyn Hall.

## 1205 Light's Diamond Jubilee.

Variety, 2 hrs., ABC, CBS, DuMont, NBC, 10/24/54. A four-network celebration of the seventy-fifth anniversary of Thomas Edison's invention of the electric light bulb; two hours of music, songs, and comedy with the top names in showbusiness. *Guests:* Judith Anderson, Lauren Bacall, Walter Brennan, Joseph Cotten, Dorothy Dandridge, Brandon DeWilde, Helen Hayes, Guy Madison, Thomas Mitchell, David Niven, Kim Novak. *Music:* Victor Young. *Producers:* David O. Selznick, Carey Wilson. *Directors:* King Vidor, Christian I. Nyby.

## 1206 Li'l Abner.

Comedy, 30 min., NBC, 9/5/67. Incidents in the lives of the citizens of an Ozark community called Dog Patch. In the story, based on the comic strip by Al Capp, a senator arrives in Dog Patch to investigate the magical charm of Daisy Mae, the most beautiful resident of Dog Patch. *Cast:* Sammy Jackson (Li'l Abner), Jeannine Riley (Daisy Mae), Judy Canova (Mammy Yokum), Jerry Lester (Pappy Yokum), Robert Reed (Senator Henry Cabbage Cod), Larry Mann (Marryin' Sam). *Producer:* Howard Leeds. *Writer:* Al Capp. *Director:* Coby Ruskin.

## 1207 Li'l Abner.

Comedy, 60 min., ABC, 4/26/71. The story finds Al Capp's comic strip characters battling a new threat to Dog Patch: pollution in the form of Deadly Glops. *Cast:* Ray Young (Li'l Abner), Nancee Parkinson (Daisy Mae), Billie Hayes (Mammy Yokum), Billy Bletcher (Pappy Yokum), Dale Malone (Marryin' Sam), Bobo Lewis (Nightmare Alice), Jennifer Narin-Smith (Snow Blight), Inga Neilson (Beautify America), Jackie Kahane (Captain Rickeyback), H. B. Haggarty (Hairless Joe), Tom Solari (Lonesome Polecat). *Music/Lyrics:* Earl Brown, Jimmy Dale. *Producers:* Allan Blye, Chris Bearde. *Writers:* Coslough Johnson, Ted Zeigler, Allan Blye, Chris Bearde. *Director:* Gordon Wiles.

## 1208 Li'l Abner in Dog Patch Today.

Musical, 60 min., NBC, 11/9/78. A musical adaptation of the Al Capp comic strip characters that updates life in the Ozark community of Dog Patch. The story finds Bella Asgood upsetting the annual Sadie Hawkins Day Dance by telling women to chase careers instead of husbands. *Cast:* Stephan Burns (Li'l Abner), Debra Feuer (Daisy Mae), Polly Bergen (Phyllis Shoefly), Kaye Ballard (Bella Asgood), Louis Nye (General Bullmoose), Rhonda Bates (Appassionata), Deborah Zon (Moonbeam McSwine), Susan Tolsky (Mammy Yokum), Cissy Cameron (Mitzi Galore), Diki Lerner (Lonesome Polecat), Charlene Ryan (Stupefyin' Jones), Ben Davidson (Hairless Joe), Candy McCoy (Smokin' Yokum), Prudence Holmes (Sexless). *Producer:* George Schlatter. *Writers:* Digby Wolfe, Billy Barnes. *Director:* Jack Regas.

## 1209 Lily Tomlin Specials.

A chronological listing of the variety specials hosted by comedienne Lily Tomlin. All are 60 minutes in length.

**1 The Lily Tomlin Show** (CBS, 3/16/73). *Guests:* Richard Crenna, Nancy

Dussault, Richard Pryor. *Music:* Dick DeBenedictis. *Producers:* Irene Pinn, Robert H. Precht. *Writers:* Allan Manings, Ann Elder, Karyl Geld, Richard Pryor, John Rappaport, Jim Rusk, Lily Tomlin, Jane Wagner, Rod Warren, George Yanok. *Directors:* Joseph Hardy, Dan Smith.

**2 Lily** (CBS, 11/2/73). *Guests:* Alan Alda, Judith Kahan, Richard Pryor. *Regulars:* Rosalyn Drexler, Bill Gerber, Lorne Michaels, Felix Silla, Richard Tomlin, George Yanok. *Music:* Peter Matz. *Producers:* Irene Pinn, Herb Sargent. *Writers:* Herb Sargent, Rosalyn Drexler, Lorne Michaels, Richard Pryor, Jim Rusk, James R. Stein, Robert Illes, Lily Tomlin, Jane Wagner. *Director:* Bill Davis.

**3 Lily** (ABC, 2/21/75). *Guests:* Valri Bromfield, Richard Dreyfuss, Archie Hahn. *Music:* Peter Matz. *Producers:* Irene Pinn, Jane Wagner, Lorne Michaels. *Writers:* Sybil Adelman, Barbara Gallagher, Gloria Banta, Patricia Nardo, Stuart Birnbaum, Matt Newman, Lorne Michaels, Marilyn Miller, Earl Pomerantz, Lily Tomlin, Jane Wagner. *Director:* John Moffitt.

**4 The Lily Tomlin Special** (ABC, 7/25/75). *Guests:* Betty Beaird, Valri Bromfield, Christopher Guest, Doris Roberts, Bill Zuckert. *Music:* Peter Matz. *Producers:* Irene Pinn, Jane Wagner, Lorne Michaels. *Writers:* Jane Wagner, Lorne Michaels, Ann Elder, Christopher Guest, Earl Pomerantz, Jim Rusk, Lily Tomlin, Rod Warren, George Yanok. *Director:* Jay Sandrich.

**5 Lily — Sold Out** (CBS, 2/2/81). The program focuses on Lily Tomlin as she prepares for a top spot at a Las Vegas nightclub. *Guests:* Paul Anka, Jane Fonda, Harvey Lembeck, Liberace, Melanie Mayron, Audrey Meadows, Dolly Parton, Joan Rivers, Alex Rocco. *Music:* Louis St. Louis. *Producers:* Lily Tomlin, Jane Wagner. *Writers:* Nancy Ordley, Irene Mecchi, Elaine Pope, Ziggy Steinberg, Rocco Urbisci, Rod Warren, Jane Wagner. *Director:* Bill Davis.

**6 Lily for President** (CBS, 5/20/82). A comical farce wherein comedienne Lily Tomlin runs for the office of president of the United States. *Cast:* Lily Tomlin (Herself), Eileen Brennan (Maggie, her wardrobe lady), James Coco (Arthur Davis; Lily's agent), Regis Philbin (TV interviewer), Warren Berlinger (Sid Kogan; the political boss), Penny Marshall (Laverne DeFazio; the factory worker), Jane Fonda (Judy Bernley; a secretary), Linda Lavin (Alice Hyatt; a waitress), Pee Wee Herman (Child educator), James Garner (Bret Maverick; a saloon owner), Sally Field (Beth Barber; a housewife), Howard Duff (General), Scott Baio (Singer), Lily Tomlin (Ernestine/Judith Beasely/Edith Ann/Agnes Angst/Tess the Bag Lady/Holly Oneness). *Music:* Louis St. Louis. *Producers:* Jane Wagner, Rocco Urbisci. *Writers:* Jane Wagner, Ann Elder, Elaine Pope, Ziggy Steinberg, Rocco Urbisci, Rod Warren. *Director:* Bill Davis.

**1210 Linda in Wonderland.** Variety, 60 min., CBS, 11/27/80. Music, songs, and light comedy that spotlight the talents of actress Linda Lavin. *Host:* Linda Lavin. *Guests:* Ron Leibman, Anthony Newley, Lynn Redgrave. *Music:* Ian Fraser. *Producers:* Gary Smith, Dwight Hemion. *Writers:* Ken Welch, Mitzie Welch. *Director:* Dwight Hemion.

**1211 Linda Ronstadt in Concert.** Variety, 60 min., HBO, 5/27/84. A concert by singer Linda Ronstadt that features the music and songs of the big band era. *Host:* Linda Ronstadt. *Music Composer and Arranger:* Nelson Riddle. *Music Performer:* Peter Asher. *Producers:* Ira Koslow, Robert Lombard. *Director:* David Lewis.

**1212 Linda . . . Special.** Documentary, 60 min., Syndicated, 5/91. A look at the film and television career of actress Linda Blair — from her role as a possessed child in *The Exorcist* to her reign as a queen of "B" movies (with such films as *Hell Night, Deadly Sleep, Chained Heat, Red Heat,* and *Savage Streets*). A glimpse of Linda's television career follows (with such work as "Born Innocent" and "A Stranger in Our House") as does a segment dealing with Lnida's sexy film roles (for example, topless in *Chained Heat*) and her photo shoot for a girlie magazine (where she appeared nude and in sexy lingerie). The program concludes with a look at Linda's return to feature films in such "R" rated movies as *Repossessed, Grotesque,* and *Night Patrol. Host-Narrator:* Debbie Milano. *Producer-Writer-Director:* Skip Johnson.

Linda Blair

**1213 Lindsay Wagner — Another Side of Me.** Variety, 60 min., ABC, 11/7/77. The beautiful star of "The Bionic Woman" in a variety special that explores her favorite fantasies. *Host:* Lindsay Wagner. *Guests:* Paul Anka, Michael Brandon, Vincent Price, Avery Schreiber, Vito Scotti. *Music:* Everett Gordon. *Producers:* Ron Samuels, Dick Foster. *Writers:* Tom Egan, Mike Marmer. *Director:* Art Fisher.

**1214 The Lion, the Witch and the Wardrobe.** Cartoon Fantasy, 60 min., CBS, 4/2/79. Four children (Lucy, Susan, Peter, and Edmund), exploring an old country house, step through a wardrobe closet and magically enter Narnia, an enchanting fantasyland of constant winter that is ruled by an ice-hearted witch. The story relates the children's efforts to bring warmth and beauty to Narnia by finding a noble lion called Aslan to defeat the power of the witch. Based on C. S. Lewis's *The Chronicles of Narnia.*

**Lindsay Wagner**

through their own group therapy sessions. Based on the novel by John Neufield; aired as a "Hallmark Hall of Fame." *Cast:* Kay Lenz (Lisa Schilling), Anne Baxter (Margaret Schilling), John Forsythe (William Schilling), Debralee Scott (Mary Nell), Anne Lockhart (Elizabeth), Jamie Smith Jackson (Betsy), Anson Williams (Brian). *Music and Theme,* "Lisa's Theme": Rod McKuen. *Producer:* Bob Banner. *Writer:* Lionel E. Siegel. *Director:* Jeannot Szwarc.

**1216 Little Arliss.** Drama, 30 min., Syndicated, 6/86. The story, set in the old west of the 1800s, relates the efforts of a 12-year-old boy (Arliss Coates) to capture and tame a wild palomino. *Cast:* R. D. Robb (Arliss Coates), Susan Lipton (Judy Anders), Jean Cotlett (Mrs. Coates), Eugene Anthony (Mr. Coates). *Producers:* Tom Robertson, Gene McPherson. *Writer-Director:* Gene McPherson.

**1217 The Little Drummer Boy.** Christmas, 30 min., NBC, 12/23/67. The story, set in ancient times, follows Aaron, the Little Drummer Boy, as he journeys with the three Wise Men to Bethlehem on the eve of the birth of Christ. Based on the song by Katherine Davis, Henry Onorati, and Harry Simeone and filmed by using dimensional stop-motion photography (animating manmade figures). *Voices:*

*Voices:* Beth Porter (The Witch), Rachel Warren (Lucy), Susan Sokol (Susan), Reg Williams (Peter), Simon Adams (Edmund), Stephen Thorne (Aslan), Dick Vosborough (The Professor). *Music:* Michael Lewis. *Producer:* David Connell. *Writers:* Bill Melendez, David Connell. *Director:* Bill Melendez.

**1215 Lisa, Bright and Dark.** Drama, 90 min., NBC, 11/28/73. Lisa Schilling is a teenage girl with two personalities — one bright and cheerful, the other depressing and strange. The story relates the efforts of Lisa's three friends (Betsy, Elizabeth, and Mary Nell) to help her overcome her problem

Jose Ferrer (Haramed), Teddy Eccles (Aaron), Paul Frees (Ali/Other voices). *Narrator:* Greer Garson. *Vocals:* The Vienna Boys Choir. *Producer-Director:* Arthur Rankin, Jr., Jules Bass. *Writer:* Romeo Muller.

**1218 The Little Drummer Boy, Book II.** Christmas, 30 min., NBC, 12/13/76. A sequel to the previous title that finds Aaron, the Little Drummer Boy, journeying with the Three Wise Men after the birth of Christ to "spread the word" of a new savior. *Voices:* Zero Mostel (Brutus), David Jay (Aaron), Allen Swift (Melchior), Ray Owens (Simeon), Robert McFadden (Plato). *Narrator:* Greer Garson. *Producer-Directors:* Arthur Rankin, Jr., Jules Bass. *Writer:* Romeo Muller.

**1219 Little Ears: The Velveteen Rabbit.** Children, 30 min., PBS, 3/10/85. The charming story of a plush velveteen rabbit that is loved so much by a little boy that it becomes real. Told via narration over still drawings. *Narrator:* Meryl Streep. *Music:* George Winston. *Producer:* Clay Stites. *Director:* Mark Sotnick.

**1220 The Little Foxes.** Drama, 90 min., NBC, 12/16/56. A taut drama of a desperate Southern family in the post–Civil War days. Based on the play by Lillian Hellman; aired on the "Hallmark Hall of Fame." *Cast:* Greer Garson (Regina Giddens), Franchot Tone (Horace Giddens), Sidney Blackmer (Benjamin Hubbard), E. G. Marshall (Oscar Hubbard), Peter Kelly (Leo Hubbard), Lauren Gilbert (Mr. Marshall), Georgia Burke (Addie), Mildred Trases (Alexandra Giddens). *Producer-Director:* George Schaefer. *Writer:* Robert Hartung.

**1221 Little Lulu.** Comedy, 30 min., ABC, 11/4/78. The adventures of a pretty but mischievous preteenage girl named Lulu. In the story, broad-

cast as an "ABC Weekend Special," Lulu decides that she and her girlfriends must prove they are not the weaker sex when she discovers that Tubby and his gang are adamantly enforcing a "no girls allowed" rule at their clubhouse. See also "The Big Hex of Little Lulu." *Cast:* Lauri Hendler (Little Lulu), Annrae Walterhouse (Gloria), Kevin King Cooper (Tubby), Robbie Rist (Iggie), Tim Reid (Tillson), Beverly Archer (Ms. Greenfield), Lulu Baxter (Annie), Billy Jacoby (Alvin), Toy Newkirk (Diane), Nita Di Giampaolo (Maria). *Music:* Tommy Leonetti. *Producers:* Robert Chenault, Ann Elder, Cindy Leonetti. *Writers:* Ann Elder, Cindy Leonetti. *Director:* Arthur Lubin.

**1222 The Little Mermaid.** Fantasy, 30 min., CBS, 2/4/74. When she saves the life of a drowning prince, a beautiful mermaid discovers a feeling she has never known before: love. The animated story relates her efforts to give up the languid and painless limbo of her mortal undersea world for an immortal soul through human love, suffering, and selfless works. Based on the fable by Hans Christian Andersen. *Narrator:* Richard Chamberlain. *Music:* Ron Goodwin. *Producers:* Christine Larocque, Murray Shostak. *Writer:* Christine Larocque. *Director:* Peter Sander.

**1223 Little Miss Perfect.** Drama, 60 min., CBS, 1/13/87. A "CBS Schoolbreak Special" about the eating disorder bulimia. The program shows how the disorder can start—and how it can be treated—through a teenage girl, Debbie Welker, who develops the disease due to an inability to adjust to her mother's recent remarriage. *Cast:* Mary Tanner (Debbie Welker), Diane Baker (Ellen Summers), Pat Peterson (Steve), April Lerman (Cindy Greco), Lisa Arrick (Melissa Eric), Robert Colbert (Grant Summers), Thelma Houston (Ms. Bonner). *Music:* Charles Bernstein. *Producers:* Sam Strangis, Alan

L. Gansberg. *Writer:* Alan L. Gansberg. *Director:* Marsha Mason.

## 1224 Little Moon of Alban.

Drama, 90 min., NBC, 3/24/58. The story is set in Ireland in 1919 and concerns the relationship between a naive young Irish nursing sister (Brigid Mangan) and her cynical patient, a gravely wounded British officer (Kenneth Boyd). Aired on the "Hallmark Hall of Fame"; see the following title also. *Cast:* Julie Harris (Brigid Mangan), Christopher Plummer (Kenneth Boyd), Barry Jones (Dr. Clive), Frank Conroy (Father Curran), George Peppard (Dennis Walsh), Mildred Trases (Sister Barbara), Pamela Flanagan (Sister Martha Kevin), Tom Clancy (Patch Keegan), Elspeth March (Sister Servant). *Producer-Director:* George Schaefer. *Writer:* James Costigan.

## 1225 Little Moon of Alban.

Drama, 90 min., NBC, 3/18/64. A restaged "Hallmark Hall of Fame" presentation of the previous title (which see for story). *Cast:* Julie Harris (Brigid Mangan), Dirk Bogarde (Kenneth Boyd), Ruth White (Mrs. Mangan), Alan Webb (Dr. Clive), Stephen Brooks (Dennis Walsh), Katherine Hynes (Sister Servant), Liam Redmond (Father Curran). *Producer-Director:* George Schaefer. *Writer:* James Costigan.

## 1226 Little Women.

A chronological listing of the television adaptations of Louisa May Alcott's *Little Women*. The story, set in Concord, Massachusetts, relates the progression of the four March sisters—Meg, Jo, Beth, and Amy—from girls to women during the late 1800s. Their romances and tragedies are the focal point of the drama.

**1 Little Women** (60 min., NBC, 12/22/39). *Cast:* Molly Pearson (Marmee March), Joanna Post (Meg March), Flora Campbell (Jo March), Frances Reid (Beth March), Joyce Arling (Amy March), Robert Conners (Jonathan March), Charles Bryant (Theodore Lawrence), Wilton Graff (Friedrich Bhaer), Linda Kane (Hannah). *Producer-Director:* Edward Sobol. *Writer:* Marian DeForest.

**2 Little Women** (70 min., NBC, 12/29/45). *Cast:* Gene Blakely, Dorothy Emery, Margaret Hayes, Fran Lee, Madeline Lee, Ruth Masters, Peter Press, Tom Seidel, Charles Thompson, Billie Lou Watt. *Producer-Director:* Ernest Colling.

**3 Little Women** (60 min., CBS, 12/16/49). *Cast:* Kim Hunter (Meg March), Meg Mundy (Jo March), Patricia Kirkland (Beth March), June Lockhart (Amy March), Frances Starr (Margaret "Marmee" March), Bill Lipton (Jonathan March), Will Hare (Theodore Lawrence), Karl Malden (Friedrich Bhaer), Ruth McDevitt (Kathryn March), Kathryn Grill (Hannah). *Producer:* Garth Montgomery. *Writer:* Ellis Marcus. *Director:* Marc Daniels.

**4 Little Women** (2 hrs., CBS, 12/18/50 and 12/25/50). *Cast:* Mary Sinclair (Meg March), Nancy Marchand (Jo March), June Dayton (Beth March), Lois Hall (Amy March), Peg Hillias (Margaret March), Richard Purdy (Jonathan March), Henry Bernard (Theodore Lawrence), Kent Smith (Friedrich Bhaer), Una O'Connor (Hannah), John Baragrey (John Brooks). *Producer:* Worthington Miner. *Writer:* Sumner Locke Elliott. *Director:* Lela Swift.

**5 Little Women** (60 min., NBC, 12/25/56). *Cast:* Diane Jergens (Meg March), Judith Braun (Jo March), Adrienne Ulmer (Beth March), June Ashton (Amy March), Irene Hervey (Margaret March), Alexander Lockwood (Jonathan March), William Traylor (Theodore Lawrence), Peter Hanson (Friedrich Bhaer). *Producer:* Albert McCleery. *Writer:* Elaine Ryan.

**6 Little Women** (60 min., CBS, 10/16/58). *Cast:* Florence Henderson (Meg March), Jeannie Carson (Jo

March), Margaret O'Brien (Beth March), Zina Bethune (Amy March), Rise Stevens (Margaret March), Joel Grey (Theodore Lawrence), Bill Hayes (John Brooks), Roland Winters (Mr. Lawrence). *Music Director:* Hal Hastings. *Orchestrations:* Don Walker. *Music and Lyrics:* Richard Adler. *Producer:* David Susskind. *Writer:* Wilson Lehr. *Director:* William Corrigan. *Note:* This adaptation is a musical version of the book.

**7 Little Women** (60 min., NBC, 12/14/76). *Cast:* Anna Aragno (Meg March), Susan Hendl (Jo March), Susan Pilarre (Beth March), Judith Fugate (Amy March), Joanne Woodward (Marmee March), Bart Cook (Jonathan March), Nolan T'sani (Theodore Lawrence), Edward Villella (John Brooks), David Richardson (Teacher). *Producer:* George Heinemann. *Writer:* June Reig. *Director:* Sid Smith. *Note:* The above is a ballet version of the novel. *Also:* Three additional versions appeared: two series and one television movie. A British series, syndicated to the United States in 1971, featured Angela Down as Jo, Janina Faye as Amy, Jo Rowbottom as Meg, and Sarah Craze as Beth. A two-part, four-hour television movie appeared on NBC, with Susan Dey as Jo, Meredith Baxter Birney as Meg, Ann Dusenberry as Amy, and Eve Plumb as Beth. A second series ran on NBC (2/8/79 to 3/8/79) with Jessica Harper as Jo, Susan Walden as Meg, Ann Dusenberry as Amy, and Eve Plumb as Melissa Jane Driscoll (in the television movie Beth, the frail sister, dies; she is replaced by Melissa for the series).

**1227 The Littlest Angel.** Musical, 90 min., NBC, 12/6/69. A musical adaptation of Charles Tazwell's Christmas story about a boy's efforts to adjust to heaven. Aired on the "Hallmark Hall of Fame." *Cast:* Johnnie Whitaker (Michael), Fred Gwynne (Patience), E. G. Marshall (God), Cab Calloway (Gabriel), Tony

Randall (Democritus), Connie Stevens (Flying Mistress), John McGiver (Angel of Peace), George Rose (Sycopomp), James Coco (Father), Evelyn Russell (Mother). *Music:* Lan O'Kun. *Producers:* Lan O'Kun, Lester Osterman. *Writers:* Lan O'Kun, Patricia Gray. *Director:* Joe Layton.

**1228 Live Dead!** Music, 60 min., Showtime, 1981. An edited-for-television (for length) version of a concert by the rock group The Grateful Dead at Radio City Music Hall in New York City. *Hosts:* Tom Davis, Al Franken. *Producers:* John Scher, Richard Loren. *Director:* Len Dell'-Amico.

**1229 Live from the Lone Star.** Variety, 60 min., Syndicated, 7/82. Performances by country and western artists; taped at the Lone Star Café in New York City. *Host-Announcer:* Mike Fitzgerald. *Guests:* Bo Diddley, Levon Helm, Johnny Paycheck. *Producer:* David Bergman. *Director:* Paul Harris.

**1230 Liza.** Variety, 60 min., NBC, 6/29/70. An hour of music, songs, and light comedy. *Host:* Liza Minnelli. *Guests:* Anthony Newley, Randy Newman, Michael J. Pollard, Jimmy Webb. *Producer-Director:* Steve Binder. *Writer:* Fred Ebb.

**1231 Liza in London.** Variety, 90 min., HBO, 5/17/86. The program, taped at the London Palladium on March 20, 1986, features Liza Minnelli's return engagement, performing to a packed house—as she did once before, on November 8, 1964 (at age 18), with her mother, Judy Garland. *Host:* Liza Minnelli. *Guests:* Fred Ebb, Lorna Luft. *Music:* Bill LaVorgna. *Producers:* Elliot Wiseman, Don Mischer. *Writer:* Fred Ebb. *Director:* Don Mischer.

**1232 Liza Minnelli in Sam Found Out: A Triple Play.** Variety, 60 min., ABC, 5/31/88. Three one-act plays that feature Liza Minnelli and a special guest star. The stories revolve around the words "Sam Found Out." (1) Sam Found Out, Act 1. A stark drama about a prostitute (Liza Minnelli who helps the police get the goods on her sadistic pimp (Ryan O'Neal). (2) Sam Found Out, Act 2. A comedy about a tap-dance teacher (Liza Minnelli) trying to cope with the affections of a klutzy student who has a crush on her. With Louis Gossett, Jr., Marilyn Cooper, and Joseph Sciari. (3) Sam Found Out, Act 3. A musical drama about a couple, Norma (Liza Minnelli) and Johnny (John Rubinstein), whose impending marriage is jeopardized by her friend Sam (a jealous dog). *Music:* Marvin Hamlisch. *Producers:* Alexander H. Cohen, Fred Ebb. *Writer, Act 1:* Lanford Wilson. *Writers, Act 2:* Terrence McNally, Wendy Wasserstein. *Writers, Act 3:* John Kander, Fred Ebb. *Director:* Piers Haggard.

**1233 Liza with a Z.** Variety, 60 min., NBC, 9/10/72. A one-woman concert by singer-actress Liza Minnelli. *Host:* Liza Minnelli. *Music:* Jack French. *Producer:* Kenneth Utt. *Writers:* Fred Ebb, John Kander. *Director:* Bob Fosse.

**1234 Lola.** Variety, 60 min., ABC, 12/18/75, 1/29/76, 3/9/76, 3/23/76. A series of four variety specials starring singer-dancer Lola Falana. *Guests* (12/18/75): Muhammad Ali, Hal Linden. *Guests* (1/29/76): Bill Cosby, Dinah Shore. *Guests* (3/9/76): Redd Foxx, Dick Van Dyke. *Guests* (3/23/76): Art Carney, Dennis Weaver. *Regulars:* Peter Cullen, Lois January, Richard Kiel, Murray Langston, Jimmy Martinez, Pat Morita, Marilyn Sokol, Willie Tyler. *Music:* H. B. Barnum. *Producers:* Allan Blye, Bob Einstein. *Writers:* Allan Blye, Bob Einstein, Alan Thicke, George Burditt, Rick Kellard. *Director:* John Moffitt.

**1235 Long Day's Journey into Night.** Drama, 3 hrs., ABC, 3/10/73. A television adaptation of the Broadway play by Eugene O'Neill which relates one day in the life of the Tyrone family—a long hot day in August 1912 when the Tyrones torture one another with suppressed truths. *Cast:* Sir Laurence Olivier (James Tyrone), Constance Cummings (Mary Tyrone), Dennis Quilley (James Tyrone, Jr.), Ronald Pickup (Edmund Tyrone), Maureen Lipman (Cathleen Tyrone). *Producer:* Cecil Clarke. *Writers:* Michael Blakemore, Peter Wood. *Director:* Peter Wood.

**1236 A Look at the Light Side.** Variety, 60 min., NBC, 4/26/69. A look at people at play as captured on film in various parts of the country. *Host:* Bill Dana. *Music:* The New York Rock and Roll Ensemble, Jefferson Airplane. *Producer-Director:* Al Wasserman. *Writer:* Bill Dana, Al Wasserman.

**1237 Look Back in Darkness.** Thriller, 90 min., ABC, 5/27/75. The story of a blind pianist who seeks revenge on the man who was responsible for the loss of his sight. Also known as "The Next Voice You See." *Cast:* Bradford Dillman (Sam Kay), Catherine Schell (Julie), Geoffrey Chater (Hastings), Ray Smith (Ben Tamplin), Terence Sewards (Alan Richards), Holly Palance (Susie Kay). *Music:* Laurie Johnson. *Producer:* Ian Fordyce. *Writer:* Terence Feely. *Director:* Robert Tronson.

**The Lorax** *see* **Dr. Seuss' The Lorax**

**1238 Loretta.** Variety, 60 min., Syndicated, 4/85. A concert by country and western singer Loretta Lynn. Taped at Harrah's in Reno, Nevada. *Host:* Loretta Lynn. *Music:* Bruce Frazier. *Producers:* David Skepner, Alan Nadohl. *Director:* Gene Weed.

## 1239 Loretta Lynn in the Big Apple. Variety, 60 min., NBC, 11/8/82. A concert benefit for the National Committee for the Prevention of Child Abuse. Taped at the Majestic Theater in New York City. *Host:* Loretta Lynn. *Guests:* Debbie Allen, Peter Allen, Judd Hirsch, Jennifer Holliday, Conway Twitty. *Music:* Bill Walker. *Producer-Writer:* James Lipton. *Director:* Sid Smith.

## 1240 Loretta Lynn: The Lady ... The Legend. Variety, 60 min., NBC, 11/16/81. A salute to Loretta Lynn on the occasion of her twentieth year as a country and western entertainer. *Host:* Loretta Lynn. *Guests:* Crystal Gayle, Howard Hesseman, The Oak Ridge Boys, Sissy Spacek, Ernest Tubb. *Music:* Bill Walker. *Producers:* James Lipton, Mike Gargiulo. *Writers:* Rod Warren, James Lipton. *Director:* Tim Kiley.

## 1241 Lost in Death Valley. Drama, 60 min., CBS, 4/19/80. Darlene, Bob, Barbara, Sam, and Oliver are members of a high school marching band. They are returning home when their small charter plane develops engine trouble. The plane crash-lands in the searing heat of Death Valley, California, one of the hottest places in the world. The pilot (Jim) is badly hurt and the five kids are totally unprepared for the killing desert heat. The story relates their struggle for survival until help arrives. Filmed on location. *Cast:* Leslie Winston (Darlene), Bennett Liss (Bob), Teri Lyn Taylor (Barbara), David Knell (Sam), Mark Miyama (Oliver), Guy Boyd (Jim), Barbara Tarbuck (Marion), Paul Kent (Jeremy). *Music:* Glenn Paxton. *Producer:* Lawrence Jacobson. *Writer-Director:* Stephen Gyllenhaal.

## 1242 The Lou Rawls Show. Variety, 60 min., Syndicated, 2/71. An hour of music and songs. *Host:* Lou Rawls. *Guests:* Duke Ellington, Stanley Myron Handleman, Freda Payne. *Producers:* Burt Rosen, David Winters, Murray Chercover. *Writers:* Neal Marshall, Sandy Baron. *Directors:* Ernest D. Glucksman, Jorn Winther.

## 1243 The Lou Rawls Special. Variety, 60 min., ABC, 4/21/77. Music and songs with singer Lou Rawls and his guests. *Host:* Lou Rawls. *Guests:* Lola Falana, Crystal Gayle. *Producers:* Dick Clark, Bill Lee. *Writers:* Robert Illes, James Stein. *Director:* Barry Glazer.

## 1244 The Louis Jourdan Timex Special. Variety, 60 min., NBC, 11/11/59. A program of music, songs, and comedy sponsored by Timex watches. *Host:* Louis Jourdan. *Guests:* Xavier Cugat, Bobby Darin, Abbe Lane, Jerry Lewis, Jane Morgan. *Music:* Nelson Riddle. *Producer:* Lawrence White. *Writers:* Mel Tolkin, Sydney Zelenka, Lyn Duddy. *Director:* Frank Satenstein.

## 1245 Louise Mandrell: Diamonds, Gold and Platinum. Variety, 2 hrs., Syndicated, 6/83. The program spotlights singer Louise Mandrell as she takes a tuneful trip through the history of music (from the roaring twenties to the disco era). *Host:* Louise Mandrell. *Guests:* Janie Frickie, Lee Greenwood, Barbara Mandrell, Irlene Mandrell, Tony Orlando, Jerry Reed, Johnny Rivers, T. G. Shepherd, Jim Stafford, Danny Thomas. *Music:* Bill Walker. *Producers:* Reg Dunlap, Jim Owens, Jack Regas. *Writers:* Bill and Pat Galvin. *Director:* Jack Regas.

## Love, Andy *see* Andy Williams Specials

## 1246 The Love Boat Fall Preview Special. Variety, 60 min., ABC, 9/17/83. Clips of ABC's fall 1983 television season are showcased as the crew of "Love Boat" host an elaborate party

to welcome new and returning stars to the ABC schedule. *Hosts:* Fred Grandy, Bernie Kopell, Ted Lange, Gavin Mac-Leod, Lauren Tewes, Jill Whelan. *Special Guests:* Maureen McGovern, Rita Moreno. *Guests:* Ursula Andress, Scott Baio, Priscilla Barnes, Douglas Barr, Christine (Christina) Belford, Pamela Bellwood, Tom Bosley, James Brolin, T. K. Carter, Susan Clark, Joan Collins, Marshall Colt, Bert Convy, Nathan Cook, Cathy Lee Crosby, James Darren, Bette Davis, Linda Evans, Lou Ferrigno, John For-sythe, Richard Gilliland, Missy Gold, Robert Guillaume, Dorian Harewood, Pamela Hensley, Christopher Hewett, Lee Horsley, Daniel Hugh-Kelly, Madeline Kahn, Alex Karras, Brian Keith, Richard Kline, Emmanuel Lewis, Heather Locklear, Lee Majors, Jayne Meadows, Ricardo Montalban, Erin Moran, Ben Murphy, James Naughton, James Noble, Holly Pal-ance, Jack Palance, Ethan Phillips, Markie Post, Stefanie Powers, Bill Randolf, John Ritter, Marion Ross, Connie Sellecca, William Shatner, Lionel Stander, Inga Swenson, Heather Thomas, Gordon Thomson, Robert Wagner, Carlene Watkins, Henry Winkler, Alfie Wise, Adrian Zmed. *Music:* Bob Rozario. *Producer:* Ernest Chambers. *Writer:* Bob Booker. *Director:* Jack Regas.

## 1247 Love Is ... Barbara Eden. Variety, 60 min., ABC, 12/15/72. A look at the many sides of love through music, song, and comedy. *Host:* Barbara Eden. *Guests:* Tim Con-way, Robert Goulet, Charley Pride, The Ray Charles Singers. *Music:* Ray Charles. *Producers:* Saul Ilson, Ernest Chambers. *Writers:* Saul Ilson, Ernest Chambers, Marty Farrell, Bob Gar-land, George Yanok. *Director:* Nor-man Campbell.

## 1248 Love Is Funny. Comedy, 60 min., NBC, 10/16/60. A series of comedy sketches based on the trials and

tribulations of love. *Host:* Art Linklet-ter. *Guests:* Zsa Zsa Gabor, Betty Gar-rett, Jimmie Rodgers, Alan Young. *Music:* Bob Walters. *Producer:* Henry Jaffe. *Writers:* Glenn Wheaton, Elroy Schwartz, John Guedel. *Director:* Bob Henry.

## 1249 A Love Letter to Jack Benny. Tribute, 2 hrs., NBC, 1/5/81. An affectionate remembrance of come-dian Jack Benny via film clips from his series and specials. *Hosts:* George Burns, Johnny Carson, Bob Hope. *Music:* Jack Elliott. *Producers:* Irving Fein, Fred DeCordova. *Writers:* Hal Goldman, Hugh Wedlock, Jr. *Direc-tor:* Norman Abbott.

## 1250 Love, Life, Liberty and Lunch. Comedy, 60 min., ABC, 5/18/76. The overall title for four original plays. (1) "Natasha Kovolina Pipishin-sky" (written by Murray Schisgal). Lawrence (Alan Arkin), a wealthy businessman, decides to forsake his riches for the love of Natasha (Kay Mazzo), a beautiful ballerina. (2) "The Quiet War" (written by Neil Simon). A retired Russian admiral (Peter Ustinov) and general (Zero Mostel) meet in a park to relive the thrill of battle in a sit-down war of words. (3) "Word of Mouth" (written by Herb Gardner). Jack (Alan King), a middle-aged den-tist, decides to take a bigger bite out of a world he feels is passing him by. Ben: Christopher Hewett. (4) "Swordsplay" (written by Peter Ustinov). An Ameri-can officer (Dick Shawn) and his British counterpart (Cyril Ritchard), decide on a unique way of ending the Revolu-tionary War — by dueling to the death. *Producers:* Alan King, Rupert Hitzig, Herb Sargent. *Director:* Peter Ustinov.

## 1251 Love! Love! Love! Vari-ety, 60 min., NBC, 2/8/72. A "Hall-mark Hall of Fame" presentation that salutes young love through music and song. *Host:* Robert Wagner. *Guests:* Mac Davis, Helen Reddy. *Music:* David

Gates, James Griffin, Mike Butts. *Producers:* Bob Banner, Dick Foster. *Writer:* David Hamilton. *Director:* Sterling Johnson.

### 1252 Love, Sex ... and Marriage.

Comedy, 60 min., ABC, 5/11/83. A satirical look at love as seen through the eyes of two Manhattan singles who meet, date, fall in love, and attempt to live with each other's idiosyncracies. *Cast:* Marlo Thomas (Her), Charles Grodin (Him), Renee Taylor (Her friend), Michael Tucker (His friend), Jane Hoffman (Her mother), Gene Saks (Psychiatrist), Bill Lazarus (Taxi driver). *Narrator:* Phil Donahue. *Music:* Danny Goldberg. *Producers:* Marlo Thomas, Don Mischer. *Writer:* Charles Grodin. *Director:* Gene Saks.

### 1253 The Lucille Ball Comedy Hour.

Comedy, 60 min., CBS, 4/19/64. A play within a play about Bonnie Barton, a female television studio head, and her attempts to cast Bob Hope as the star of a special about an ideal couple. *Cast:* Lucille Ball (Bonnie Barton), Bob Hope (Bob Hope/Bill Barton), Gale Gordon (Mr. Harvey), Jack Weston (Cash), Max Showalter (Walter), John Dehner (Mr. Henderson), William Lanteau (Potter). *Music:* Jerry Fielding. *Producers:* Jess Oppenheimer, Edward H. Feldman. *Writer:* Richard Powell. *Director:* Jack Donohue.

### 1254 The Lucille Ball Special.

Comedy, 60 min., CBS, 11/21/77. An hour of comedy sketches with Lucille Ball and her cast from "The Lucy Show" (Vivian Vance and Gale Gordon). *Host:* Lucille Ball. *Guests:* Steve Allen, Lillian Carter, Ed McMahon, Mary Wickes. *Music:* Mort Stevens. *Producers:* Lucille Ball, Gary Morton. *Writers:* Madelyn Davis, Bob Carroll, Jr. *Director:* Marc Daniels.

### 1255 A Lucille Ball Special Starring Lucille Ball and Dean Martin.

Comedy, 60 min., CBS, 3/1/75. A series of comedy skits that revolve around Lucy Collins, a woman who walks hand in hand with trouble. *Cast:* Lucille Ball (Lucy Collins), Dean Martin (Himself), Jackie Coogan (Gus Mitchell), Bruce Gordon (Max Vogel), Joey Forman (Eddie), Gino Conforti (Antonio), Paul Picerni (Packy West). *Music:* Nelson Riddle. *Producers:* Lucille Ball, Gary Morton. *Writer:* Bob O'Brien. *Director:* Jack Donohue.

### 1256 A Lucille Ball Special Starring Lucille Ball and Jackie Gleason.

Comedy, 60 min., CBS, 12/3/75. A trilogy of one-act plays in which Lucille Ball and Jackie Gleason play three different couples facing marriage crises. *Stars:* Lucille Ball, Jackie Gleason. *Music:* Nelson Riddle. *Producers:* Lucille Ball, Gary Morton. *Writers:* Renee Taylor, Joseph Bologna. *Director:* Charles Walters.

### 1257 A Lucille Ball Special: What Now Catherine Curtis?

Drama, 60 min., CBS, 3/30/76. Three one-act plays that relate the experiences of Catherine Curtis, newly divorced after twenty years of marriage, as she attempts to begin a new life for herself. *Cast:* Lucille Ball (Catherine Curtis), Art Carney (Walter), Joseph Bologna (Peter). *Music:* Nelson Riddle. *Producers:* Lucille Ball, Gary Morton. *Writers:* Sheldon Keller, Lynn Roth. *Director:* Charles Walters.

### 1258 Lucy and Desi: A Home Movie.

Documentary, 2 hrs., NBC, 2/14/93. Lucille Ball and Desi Arnaz are recalled through interviews, stills, and film clips (including never-before seen home movies). *Hosts:* Desi Arnaz, Jr., Lucie Arnaz. *Producers:* Laurence Luckinbill, Lucie Arnaz. *Writer-Director:* Laurence Luckinbill.

### 1259 Lucy Comes to Nashville.

Variety, 60 min., CBS, 11/19/78.

**Lynda Carter**

Comedy mixes with country and western music as comedienne Lucille Ball clowns and sings with established country stars. *Host:* Lucille Ball. *Guests:* Lynn Anderson, Tom T. Hall, Barbara Mandrell, Ronnie Milsap, Mel Tillis. *Music:* Bill Walker. *Producers:* Gary Smith, Dwight Hemion. *Director:* Dwight Hemion.

**1260 Lucy in London.** Comedy, 60 min., CBS, 10/24/66. A musical comedy that relates Lucille Ball's escapades as she visits London. *Host:* Lucille Ball. *Guests:* The Dave Clark Five, Wilfrid Hyde-White, Anthony Newley, Peter Wyngarde. *Music:* Irwin Kostel. *Producers:* Lucille Ball, Steve Binder. *Writers:* Pat McCormick, Ron Friedman. *Director:* Steve Binder.

**1261 Lynda Carter: Body and Soul.** Variety, 60 min., CBS, 3/16/84. A musical variety hour in which singer-actress Lynda Carter traces the influences that helped shape her versatile career. *Host:* Lynda Carter. *Guests:* Eddie Rabbitt, Ben Vereen. *Music:* Johnny Harris. *Producers:* Lynda Carter, Don Mischer. *Writer:* Robert Arnott. *Director:* Don Mischer.

**1262 Lynda Carter: Encore.** Variety, 60 min., CBS, 9/16/80. A lavish hour of music and songs that is a sequel to "Lynda Carter's Special." *Host:* Lynda Carter. *Guests:* Merle Haggard, Tom Jones, John Phillips, Donald Young. *Music:* Johnny Harris. *Producer:* Ron Samuels. *Writer:* Jeffrey Barron. *Director:* Stan Harris.

**1263 Lynda Carter: Street Lights.** Variety, 60 min., CBS, 3/5/82. A celebration of the electrifying rhythm of street music. *Host:* Lynda Carter. *Guests:* George Benson, Tony Orlando, Frank Stallone. *Music:* Johnny Harris. *Producers:* Ron Samuels, Stan Harris. *Writer:* Jeffrey Barron. *Director:* Stan Harris.

**1264 Lynda Carter's Celebration.** Variety, 60 min., CBS, 5/11/81. A lively hour of music, songs, and dances in which Lynda Carter entertains with some of her showbusiness friends. *Host:* Lynda Carter. *Guests:* Ray

Charles, Chris Evert Lloyd, Jerry Reed. *Music:* Johnny Harris. *Producers:* Ron Samuels, Stan Harris. *Writer:* Jeffrey Barron. *Director:* Stan Harris.

**1265 Lynda Carter's Special.** Variety, 60 min., CBS, 1/12/80. Actress Lynda Carter's first television special; a lavish hour of music, songs, and dances. *Host:* Lynda Carter. *Guests:* Richard Rizzo, Kenny Rogers, Leo Sayer. *Music:* Johnny Harris. *Producers:* Ron Samuels, Saul Ilson. *Writer:* Jeffrey Barron. *Director:* Stan Harris.

**1266 Lyndon Johnson.** Drama, 90 min., PBS, 4/8/87. Actor Laurence Luckinbill portrays the thirty-sixth president in a monologue that recalls LBJ's rise in politics. Based on the biography by Merle Miller. *Producer:* David Susskind. *Writer:* James Prideaux. *Director:* Charles Jarrott.

**1267 M and W Men and Women.** Variety, 60 min., ABC, 5/19/88. An exploration of the contemporary world that seeks out the fascinating, glamorous, surprising, and puzzling. Based on M and W magazines. *Hosts:* Christy Ferer, Fawn Hall, Ronald Reagan, Jr., Jane Seymour, Danny Sullivan, Katie Wagner. *Music:* Bobby McFerrin. *Producers:* Don Mischer, JoAnn Goldberg, David Goldberg. *Writers:* Anne Winn, Garrett Brown. *Director:* Don Mischer.

**1268 Mac Davis Specials.** A chronological listing of the variety specials hosted by country and western entertainer Mac Davis. All are 60 minutes long and broadcast by NBC.
**1 I Believe in Music** (11/24/73). *Guests:* Rita Coolidge, Danny Davis, Doug Kershaw, Kris Kristofferson, Anne Murray, The Nashville Brass, Patti Page, Charlie Rich, Earl Scruggs. *Music:* Bill Walker. *Producer:* Joseph Cates. *Writer:* Chet Hagan. *Director:* Walter C. Miller.

**2 The Mac Davis Special** (11/13/75). *Guests:* Liza Minnelli, Neil Sedaka. *Music:* Mike Post. *Producers:* Sandy Gallin, Jack Haley, Jr., Marty Farrell. *Writers:* Marty Farrell, Jeremy Stevens. *Director:* Steve Binder.
**3 The Mac Davis Christmas Special** (12/14/75). *Guests:* Roy Clark, Peggy Fleming. *Music:* Mike Post. *Producer:* Sandy Gallin. *Writers:* Marty Farrell, Jeremy Stevens. *Director:* Steve Binder.
**4 The Mac Davis Christmas Special ... When I Grow Up** (12/15/76). *Guests:* Richard Thomas, Raquel Welch. *Music:* Mike Post. *Producers:* Gary Smith, Dwight Hemion. *Writers:* Buz Kohan, Alan Thicke. *Director:* Steve Binder.
**5 Mac Davis ... Sounds Like Home** (4/26/77). *Guests:* George Carlin, Tom Jones, Dolly Parton, Donna Summer. *Music:* Vernon Ray Bunch. *Producers:* Raymond Katz, Sandy Gallin. *Writers:* Buz Kohan, Rod Warren. *Director:* Dwight Hemion.
**6 Mac Davis ... I Believe in Christmas** (12/7/77). *Guests:* Engelbert Humperdinck, Shields and Yarnell, David Soul. *Music:* Vernon Ray Bunch. *Producers:* Raymond Katz, Sandy Gallin. *Writers:* Bill Dyer, Robert Shields. *Director:* Steve Binder.
**7 You Put Music in My Life** (5/11/78). *Guests:* Art Carney, KC and the Sunshine Band, Donna Summer. *Producers:* Sandy Gallin, Raymond Katz. *Writers:* Paul Pumpian, Ed Hider, Rod Warren. *Director:* Art Fisher.
**8 Mac Davis's Christmas Odyssey: Two Thousand and Ten** (12/12/78). *Guests:* Ted Knight, Bernadette Peters. *Music:* Mike Post. *Producers:* Gary Smith, Dwight Hemion. *Writer:* Buz Kohan. *Director:* Dwight Hemion.
**9 Christmas Special ... With Love, Mac Davis** (12/24/79). *Guests:* Dolly Parton, Kenny Rogers, Robert Urich. *Music:* Vernon Ray Bunch. *Producers:* Lennie Katz, Sam Gower. *Director:* Stan Harris.
**10 The Mac Davis 10th Anniversary Special: I Still Believe in Music** (5/20/

80). *Guests:* Tom Jones, Dean Martin, Liza Minnelli, Anne Murray, Olivia Newton-John, Dolly Parton, Donna Summer, Raquel Welch. *Music:* Vernon Ray Bunch. *Producers:* Sandy Gallin, Raymond Katz, Ken Ehrlich. *Writer:* Ken Ehrlich. *Director:* Tom Trbovich.

**11 Mac Davis — I'll Be Home for Christmas** (12/23/80). *Guests:* Linda Gray, Melissa Manchester, Mills Watson. *Music:* Robert Frazier. *Producers:* Sandy Gallin, Raymond Katz. *Writers:* Ken Ehrlich, Marty Farrell. *Director:* Tom Trbovich.

**12 The Mac Davis Christmas Special** (12/14/81). *Guests:* The Commodores, Andre Crouch, The Pointer Sisters. *Music:* Robert Frazier. *Producer:* Raymond Katz. *Writer:* Ken Ehrlich. *Director:* Walter C. Miller.

**13 The Mac Davis Special: The Music of Christmas** (12/23/83). *Guests:* Gladys Knight and the Pips, Barbara Mandrell, Ronnie Milsap. *Music:* Vernon Ray Bunch. *Producer:* Sandy Gallin. *Writer:* Ken Ehrlich. *Director:* Walter C. Miller.

**1269 Macbeth.** Drama, 2 hrs., NBC, 11/28/54. Macbeth, a young Scottish thane, believes he is destined to be king. With his wife's plotting he commits the murders necessary to fulfill that destiny. Based on the tragedy by William Shakespeare and broadcast as a two-hour special during the regular series run of the "Hallmark Hall of Fame." See also the following title. *Cast:* Maurice Evans (Macbeth), Dame Judith Anderson (Lady Macbeth), Staats Cotsworth (Banquo), House Jameson (King Duncan), Richard Waring (MacDuff). *Producer:* Albert McCleery. *Director:* George Schaefer.

**1270 Macbeth.** Drama, 2 hrs., NBC, 11/20/60. A second "Hallmark Hall of Fame" adaptation of the play by William Shakespeare. See the prior entry for story. *Cast:* Maurice Evans (Macbeth), Dame Judith Anderson

(Lady Macbeth), Michael Hordern (Banquo), Ian Bannen (Macduff), Felix Aylmer (Doctor), Malcolm Keen (Duncan), George Ross (Porter), Jeremy Brett (Malcolm), William Hutt (Ross). *Music:* Richard Mathieson. *Producer-Director:* George Schaefer. *Writer:* Richard Addinsell.

**1271 The McLean Stevenson Show.** Variety, 60 min., NBC, 11/20/75. An hour of music, songs, and comedy sketches. *Host:* McLean Stevenson. *Guests:* Mary Jo Catlett, Brion James, Philip Simms, Ken Stein, Raquel Welch, Edward Winter. *Producer:* Gene Lesser. *Writers:* Jim Fritzell, Everett Greenbaum, McLean Stevenson. *Director:* John Moffitt.

**1272 The Mad, Mad, Mad, Mad World of the Super Bowl.** Comedy, 2 hrs., NBC, 1/8/77. A series of comedy sketches that spoof the game of football. *Hosts:* Kate Jackson, Joe Namath, Jaclyn Smith. *Guests:* Steve Allen, Foster Brooks, Ruth Buzzi, Charlie Callas, George Carlin, Charo, Pat Cooper, Irwin Corey, Norm Crosby, Rodney Dangerfield, Jamie Farr, Rosey Grier, Harvey Korman, Ed McMahon, Dick Martin, Anne Meara, Pat Morita, Dan Rowan, Jerry Stiller, Rip Taylor, Fred Travalena, Jimmie Walker, Jonathan Winters, Henny Youngman. *Music:* Jack Elliott, Allyn Ferguson. *Producer:* Perry Rosemond. *Writers:* Marc London, Paul Pumpian, Harvey Weitzman, Terry Hart. *Director:* Tim Kiley.

**1273 Madame in Manhattan.** Comedy, 60 min., Showtime, 5/81. A comedy concert by Wayland Flowers and his puppet, Madame. Taped at Manhattan's Grand Finale Club. *Hosts:* Wayland Flowers and Madame. *Guests:* David Dukes, Alice Ghostley, Anita Gillette, Henny Youngman. *Producers:* Ellen Krass, Phyllis Teitler. *Writer:* Wayland Flowers. *Director:* Thomas Grasso.

**1274 Maddie's Waltz.** Drama, 30 min., Syndicated, 4/93. A bittersweet drama about a middle-aged woman (Maddie) who relives her youth and marriage to a handsome young charmer (Clyde) when he suddenly comes back into her life. *Cast:* Michael Learned (Maddie Louise Wagner), John Cullum (Clyde Fenner), Ed Asner (George Wagner). *Music:* Steve Schoenberg. *Producers:* Andrew Shulman, Elizabeth Cheng. *Writer:* Shirley Ann Grau. *Director:* Jerry Kirschenbaum.

**1275 Maggie's Secret.** Drama, 60 min., CBS, 4/10/90. A "CBS Schoolbreak Special" about a teenage girl (Maggie) and her efforts to cope with an alcoholic mother (Frances) and father (Jack). *Cast:* Joanne Vannicola (Maggie Kingston), Mimi Kuzyk (Frances Kingston), Joseph Bottoms (Jack Kingston), Nathaniel Moreau (John Kingston), Jaimz Woolvett (Jason), Michael Caruana (Dr. Davidson). *Music:* Anne Bourne. *Producer:* Alan Landsburg. *Writers:* Ellen Lantz-Burke, Judith Reeves, Garfield Stevens. *Director:* Al Waxman.

**1276 The Magic Boy's Easter.** Drama, 60 min., Syndicated, 4/15/90. A very sick boy, facing an operation, dreams he is the helper of Mordechai, a magician in ancient Jerusalem. When the boy learns of Jesus and his ability to heal the sick, he begins a journey to find him—a journey that gives the boy the courage to face his operation when he awakens. *Cast:* Bernie Kopell (Mordechai), Chris Demetral (The Magic Boy), Anne Marie McEvoy (Joanna), Lori Lethin (Mother), Kenneth Livingston Taylor (Doctor), Len Birman (Lazarus), Robert Miller (Jesus). *Music:* Garry Schyman. *Producer:* Don David Schroeder. *Writer:* Richard Wendley. *Director:* John Meredyth Lucas.

**1277 A Magic Garden Christ-** **mas.** Children, 60 min., Syndicated, 12/81. Carole Demas and Paula Janis, the stars of "The Magic Garden" television series, revive their roles for a special wherein Carole and Paula, and puppets Sherlock and Flap, celebrate the Christmas season through songs, stories, and sketches. *Cast:* Carole Demas (Carole), Paula Janis (Paula). *Voices:* Cary Antebi (as Sherlock the Squirrel and Flap the Bird). *Music:* Paula Janis, Alex Demas. *Producer-Writers:* Carole Demas, Paula Janis. *Director:* Lenore Bode.

**1278 The Magic Million.** Documentary, 40 min., NBC, 6/7/49. The ceremonies surrounding RCA's production of its one millionth television picture tube. Broadcast from RCA's tube plant in Lancaster, Pennsylvania, where a behind-the-scenes look at how picture tubes are made was also shown. *Narrator:* Ben Grauer. *Guest:* Frank Folson (RCA president).

**1279 The Magic of David Copperfield.** A chronological listing of the variety specials hosted by illusionist David Copperfield. All are 60 minutes and broadcast by CBS. David Copperfield hosted each show, except where noted otherwise.

**1 The Magic of David Copperfield** (10/27/78). *Guests:* Carl Ballantine, Valerie Bertinelli, Sherman Hemsley. *Music:* George Wyle. *Producer:* Joseph Cates.

**2 The Magic of David Copperfield II** (10/24/79). *Guests:* Loni Anderson, Valerie Bertinelli, Bill Bixby, Robert Stack. *Music:* George Wyle. *Producers:* Joseph Cates, David Copperfield.

**3 The Magic of David Copperfield III** (10/27/80). *Music:* George Wyle. *Producers:* David Copperfield, Joseph Cates.

**4 The Magic of David Copperfield IV** (10/26/81). *Guests:* Susan Anton, Catherine Bach, Barnard Hughes, Elaine Joyce, Audrey Landers, Jason Robards. *Music:* George Wyle. *Pro-*

*ducers:* Joseph Cates, David Copperfield. *Director:* Sid Smith.

**5 The Magic of David Copperfield V** (4/8/83). *Guests:* Morgan Fairchild, Lynn Griffin, Michele Lee, Eugene Levy, William B. Williams. *Music:* George Wyle. *Producers:* Sid Smith, Bruce Haywood. *Writer:* David Cole. *Director:* David Copperfield.

**6 The Magic of David Copperfield VI** (4/6/84). *Guests:* Ricardo Montalban, Heather Thomas, Bonnie Tyler. *Music:* George Wyle. *Producers:* Joseph Cates, Kevin Bright. *Writers:* Gary Bormet, Frank Slocum. *Directors:* Jeff Margolis, David Copperfield.

**7 The Magic of David Copperfield VII** (3/8/85). *Host:* Angie Dickinson. *Star:* David Copperfield. *Guests:* Teri Copley, Peggy Fleming. *Music:* George Wyle. *Producers:* Joseph Cates, Kevin Bright. *Writer:* Gary Bormet. *Directors:* Paul Miller, David Copperfield.

**8 The Magic of David Copperfield VIII ... In China** (3/14/86). *Host:* Ben Vereen. *Star:* David Copperfield. *Music:* George Wyle. *Producers:* Joseph Cates, Kevin Bright. *Writer:* Gary Bormet. *Directors:* Stan Harris, David Copperfield.

**9 The Magic of David Copperfield IX: The Escape from Alcatraz** (3/13/87). *Host:* Ann Jillian. *Star:* David Copperfield. *Announcer:* Ed Herlihy. *Producers:* Joseph Cates, David Copperfield. *Writer:* Gary Bormet. *Directors:* Gary Halvorson, David Copperfield.

**10 The Magic of David Copperfield X: The Bermuda Triangle** (3/12/88). *Guests:* Lisa Hartman, Dawn Marie Swatchick. *Producers:* Joseph Cates, David Copperfield. *Writer:* Gary Bormet. *Director:* David Copperfield.

**11 The Magic of David Copperfield XI** (3/3/89). *Guest:* Emma Samms. *Producers:* Gregory Sills, Jeff Ross. *Writer:* Seth Kotkin. *Directors:* Michael Dimich, David Kotkin.

**12 The Magic of David Copperfield XII** (3/30/90). *Producer:* Gregory Sills. *Writers:* Seth Kotkin, Ted Blumberg.

*Directors:* Michael Dimich, David Kotkin.

**13 The Magic of David Copperfield XIII: Mystery on the Orient Express** (4/9/91). *Guest:* Jane Seymour. *Producers:* Chris Giordano, Gregory Sills. *Writer:* Seth Kotkin. *Directors:* Michael Dimich, David Kotkin.

**14 The Magic of David Copperfield XIV: Flying ... "Live the Dream"** (3/31/92). *Guest:* James Earl Jones. *Producers:* Sherrie Castleberry, Wylleen May. *Writer:* Seth Kotkin. *Directors:* Michael Dimich, David Kotkin.

**15 The Magic of David Copperfield XV: Fires of Passion — This Time His Life Is on the Line** (3/30/93). *Guest:* Wayne Gretzky. *Producers:* David Copperfield, Sherrie Castleberry. *Writer:* Seth Kotkin. *Directors:* Michael Dimich, David Kotkin.

**1280 The Magic Planet.** Fantasy, 60 min., ABC, 3/17/83. While exploring outer space, an astronaut's NASA space capsule is hit by an asteroid. The craft crash-lands on a strange planet, where the astronaut immediately wins the heart of the beautiful Queen of the Outerworld People. Shortly after, the astronaut is confronted by Fraze, the evil leader of the rival Underworld who covets the Queen's hand in marriage. After an altercation between the two suitors, Fraze is banished from the Outerworld. Furious, Fraze abducts the Queen and takes her to his underworld kingdom. A sympathetic sorcerer approaches the grief-stricken astronaut and gives him a pair of magic skates. The story, which unfolds through the language of movement by ice skaters, tells of the astronaut's efforts to reclaim his beloved Queen. *Cast:* Toller Cranston (Astronaut), Wendy Burge (Queen), Brian Pockar (Fraze). *Guests:* Sandra Bezic, Val Bezic, The George Faison Dancers, Vanessa Harwood, Ann Jillian, Ricky O'Neill, Deniece Williams. *Narrator:* William Shatner. *Music:* Paul Hoffert. *Producers:* Mace Neufeld, David

Ad for "The Magic of David Copperfield XIII: Mystery on the Orient Express"

Acomba. *Writer:* Toller Cranston. *Director:* David Acomba.

## 1281 Magic with Mary Martin.

Variety, 60 min., NBC, 3/29/59. The first of two specials, broadcast on the same day, to feature Mary Martin in an hour of music and song. See also "Music with Mary Martin" for information on her evening program ("Magic with Mary Martin" was her Easter Sunday daytime show). *Host:* Mary Martin. *Music-Lyrics:* Linda Melnick, Mary Rodgers. *Producer:* Richard Halliday. *Director:* Vincent J. Donehue.

## 1282 Magic with the Stars.

Variety, 2 hrs., NBC, 1/17/82. Hollywood celebrities assist magicians in a program of magic and illusion. *Hosts:* Loni Anderson, Robert Guillaume, Jaclyn Smith, Orson Welles. *Magicians:* Harry Anderson, Carlton and Company, David Copperfield, The Fantasy Factory, The Great Tomson, Norm Nielson, Richiardi. *Guests:* Scott Baio, Barbi Benton, Cathy Lee Crosby, Tony Curtis, Dom DeLuise, Erik Estrada, Linda Evans, Morgan Fairchild, Norman Fell, Jack Klugman, Pam Long, Martin Mull, Vincent Price, Cindy Williams. *Music:* George Wyle. *Producers:* Joseph Cates, David Copperfield. *Writers:* Frank Slocum, Gary Bormet. *Director:* Walter C. Miller.

## The Magical Music of Burt Bacharach *see* Burt Bacharach Specials

## 1283 The Magical Mystery Trip Through Little Red's Head.

Cartoon, 60 min., ABC, 5/15/74. An animated musical odyssey into the human mind. Two youngsters (Carol and Larry), reduced to microscopic size, travel through Little Red's head (as in "Little Red Riding Hood") to see how the mind works. An "ABC After-school Special." *Voices:* Diane Murphy (Carol), Ike Eisenmann (Larry), Sarah Kennedy (Little Red), Lennie Weinrib (Timer), Joan Gerber (Mother). *Music:* Dean Elliott.

## Magnavox Presents Frank Sinatra *see* Frank Sinatra Specials

## 1284 The Magnificent Yankee.

Drama, 90 min., NBC, 1/28/65. The story, based on Emmet Lavery's Broadway biography, traces the Washington years of Supreme Court Justice Oliver Wendell Holmes. Broadcast on the "Hallmark Hall of Fame." *Cast:* Alfred Lunt (Oliver Wendell Holmes), Lynn Fontanne (Fanny Dixwell Holmes), Robert Emhardt (Henry Adams), James Daly (Oliver Wister), Brenda Forbes (Mary), Nan McFarland (Ellen Jones), William Griffis (Teddy Roosevelt). *Producer-Director:* George Schaefer. *Writer:* Robert Hartung.

## 1285 Make Believe Marriage.

Drama, 60 min., ABC, 2/14/79. An "ABC Afterschool Special" in which ten high school seniors, for a course in modern marriage, "get married," get jobs, have babies, and deal with divorce to experience what real married life would be like. *Cast:* Alexa Kenin (Penny Costanzo), James Carroll (Gary Simmons), Janina Mathews (Gail Cooper), Larry Keith (Mr. Webster), Bea Bevis (Rosie Bieberman), Lonny Proce (Danny Dawson), David Paymer (Ralph), Amy DeMayo (Sarah), Jane Cecil (Mrs. Frederick), Marilyn Rockafellow (Mrs. Webster). *Music:* John Morris. *Producers:* Linda Gottlieb, Evelyn Barron. *Writer:* Jeffrey Kindley. *Director:* Robert Fuest.

## 1286 Make 'Em Laugh.

Comedy, 60 min., CBS, 11/25/79. Performances by various comedians. *Host:* Tom Bosley. *Guests:* George Carlin, Norm Crosby, Phil Foster, The Hudson

Brothers, Chuck McCann, Jim Mc-George, Pam Myers, Soupy Sales, Robert Shields, Skiles and Henderson, Rip Taylor. *Music:* Hal Heidi. *Producers:* Robert Arnott, Sid Smith. *Writer:* Robert Arnott. *Director:* Sid Smith.

**1287 Make Mine Red, White and Blue.** Variety, 60 min., NBC, 9/9/72. A musical salute to America. *Host:* Fred Astaire. *Guests:* Bob Crane, The Fifth Dimension, The Jimmy Joyce Singers, Michele Lee, The Tom Hansen Dancers. *Music:* David Rose. *Producers:* David L. Wolper, Warren V. Bush. *Writers:* Ed Haas, Jack Lloyd. *Director:* Bill Hobin.

**1288 Making "Gorillas in the Mist."** Documentary, 30 min., Syndicated, 9/16/88. A behind-the-scenes look at the making of the film *Gorillas in the Mist* (about Dian Fossey and her attempts to save the mountain gorillas from extinction). *Host-Narrator:* Jason Robards. *Guest:* Sigourney Weaver (portrays Dian in the film). *Producers:* Arnold Glimcher, Jon Peters, Robert Nixon, Karen Kelly Klopp. *Director:* Robert Nixon.

**1289 The Making of a Model.** Documentary, 60 min., ABC, 10/26/88. A behind-the-scenes look at the world of modeling as seen through the eyes of the models, photographers, agents, and others involved in the industry. *Host:* Cheryl Tiegs. *Guests:* Lisa Baker, Nina Blanchard, Walter Chin, Cindy Crawford, Michael Flutie, Eileen Ford, Jerry Ford, Lacey Ford, Rachel Hunter, Milla Jovovich, Elle McPherson, Anthony Mazzolla, Herb Pitts, Monique Pollard, Courtney Powell, Mike Rheinhardt, Irene Selvagni, Greg Stephens. *Narrator:* Bill Ratner. *Producers:* Carol Sherman, Eric Schotz. *Writers:* Lou DeCosta, Bryce Zabel. *Directors:* Robert Kirk, Eric Schotz.

**1290 The Mama Cass TV Program.** Variety, 60 min., ABC, 6/26/69. A program of music, songs, and comedy with singer Mama Cass Elliot. *Host:* Mama Cass Elliot. *Guests:* Barbara Bain, Buddy Hackett, Martin Landau, Joni Mitchell, John Sebastian, Mary Travers. *Producers:* Chuck Barris, Saul Turtletaub, Bernie Orenstein. *Writers:* John Brent, Severn Darden, Gordon Farr, Carl Gottlieb. *Director:* Sid Smith.

**1291 Man and Superman.** Comedy, 90 min., NBC, 11/25/56. John Tanner is a bachelor; his efforts to remain single, despite the endless attempts of his ward, Ann Whitefield, to find him a wife, are the focal point of this "Hallmark Hall of Fame" presentation, adapted from the play by George Bernard Shaw. *Cast:* Maurice Evans (John Tanner), Joan Greenwood (Ann Whitefield), Malcolm Keen (Roebuck Ramsden), Chet Stratton (Octavius), Edith King (Mrs. Whitefield), Sylvia Short (Violet), Douglas Watson (Hector Malone, Jr.), Patricia Moore (Maid), Ian Martin (Henry Starker). *Producer-Director:* George Schaefer.

**1292 The Man in the Dog Suit.** Comedy, 60 min., NBC, 1/8/60. Oliver Walling is a Milquetoast man who is constantly being degraded. One day he rents a dog suit for a costume party and finds he can face the world while wearing it. The story relates his efforts to find the same courage without wearing the dog costume. *Cast:* Art Carney (Oliver Walling), Celeste Holm (Martha Walling), Orson Bean (Tony Roberts), Hiram Sherman (Henry Stoddard), Jessie Royce Landis (Mrs. Stoddard), Neva Patterson (Eileen Stoddard), Lawrence Weber (George Stoddard). *Producer:* David Susskind. *Writer:* Robert Emmett. *Director:* Henry Kaplan.

**1293 The Man in the Moon.** Variety, 60 min., NBC, 4/16/60. A music and comedy special in which the Man in the Moon comes down to earth to tour the United States. *Man in the Moon:* Andy Williams. *Performers:* Diahann Carroll, Jester Hairston, Lisa Kirk, Cloris Leachman, Bambi Linn, James Mitchell, Tony Randall. *Music:* David Rose. *Producer:* Robert Wells. *Writers:* Mel Brooks, Robert Wells. *Director:* Barry Shear.

## 1294  Man, Myths and Titans.

Documentary, 60 min., Syndicated, 6/81. The program traces the legends of the ancient Titans of Greek mythology. Narration is coupled with clips from various films, especially *Clash of the Titans*, to show how modern man has re-created the ancient gods. *Host-Narrator:* Burgess Meredith. *Guest:* Ray Harryhausen. *Producers:* Ronald Saland, Mark Schneider. *Writer:* Carroll O'Connor. *Director:* Mark Schneider.

## 1295  The Man Who Came to

**Dinner.** Comedy, 60 min., NBC, 10/13/54. The story of Sheridan Whiteside, an irascible and insulting author who comes to a friend's home for dinner, breaks his hip — and drives everyone batty while nursing himself back to health. Based on the Broadway play by George S. Kaufman and Moss Hart. *Cast:* Monty Woolley (Sheridan Whiteside), Sylvia Field (Mrs. Stanley), Howard St. John (Mr. Stanley), ZaSu Pitts (Miss Preen), Frank Tweddell (John), Margaret Hamilton (Sarah), Merle Oberon (Maggie Cutler), Buster Keaton (Dr. Bradley), Joan Bennett (Lorraine Sheldon), Bert Lahr (Banjo). *Music:* David Broekman. *Producer:* Martin Manulis. *Writer:* Ronald Alexander. *Director:* David Alexander.

## 1296  The Man Who Came to

**Dinner.** Comedy, 90 min., NBC, 11/29/72. A "Hallmark Hall of Fame" adaptation of the Broadway play by George S. Kaufman and Moss Hart. See the prior title for story. *Cast:* Orson Welles (Sheridan Whiteside), Lee

Remick (Maggie), Joan Collins (Lorraine), Peter Haskell (Bert), Edward Andrews (Stanley), Don Knotts (Dr. Bradley), Mary Wickes (Nurse), Marty Feldman (Banjo), Kim Braden (June). *Producer-Writers:* Bill Persky, Sam Denoff. *Director:* Buzz Kulik.

## 1297  Mandy's Grandmother.

Drama, 30 min., Syndicated, 5/80. The tender story of the relationship that develops between a young girl (Mandy) and her grandmother when they meet for the first time. *Cast:* Maureen O'Sullivan (Grandmother), Amy Levitan (Mandy), Kathryn Walker (Susan), Philip Carlson (Mandy's father), Christopher Erickson (Paulie), Yvette Deas (Sharon), Rosetta LeNoire (Librarian). *Music:* Linda Schreyer. *Producer:* Brabara Bryant. *Writer:* Mary Ryan Munisteri. *Director:* Andrew Sugarman.

## 1298  Manhattan      Tower.

Musical, 90 min., NBC, 10/27/56. The romantic adventures of a young couple (Stephen and Julie) who meet and fall in love while visiting New York City. *Cast:* Peter Marshall (Stephen), Helen O'Connell (Julie), Phil Harris (Billy), Edward Everett Horton (Noah), Cesar Romero (Mambo teacher), Ethel Waters (Sunday School teacher), Hans Conried (Village artist), Tommy Farrell (Tommy). *Music:* Gordon Jenkins. *Producers:* Elliott Lewis, Gordon Jenkins. *Writer:* Gordon Jenkins. *Director:* Boris Sagal.

## 1299  The  Many  Faces  of

**Comedy.** Comedy, 60 min., ABC, 12/4/73. A rapid-fire laugh-a-thon tracing the origins and varied manifestations of humor, past and present. *Host:* Alan King. *Guests:* Milton Berle, George Burns, Godfrey Cambridge, Angie Dickinson, Nancy Dussault, Totie Fields, Don Knotts, Steve Landesberg, Rich Little, Howard Morris, Danny Thomas, Henny Youngman. *Music:* Norman Paris. *Producer:*

Howard Morris. *Writers:* Howard Albrecht, Sol Weinstein, Norman Steinberg, Alan Uger, Jon Boni, George Yanok, Herb Sargent, Alan King. *Director:* Bill Hobin.

**The Many Moods of Perry Como** see **Perry Como Specials**

**1300 The Many Sides of Don Rickles.** Variety, 60 min., ABC, 9/17/70. An hour of madcap comedy that spotlights the versatile talents of insult master Don Rickles. *Host:* Don Rickles. *Guests:* Don Adams, Robert Goulet, Ann Morgan Guilbert, Harvey Korman. *Music:* Jack Elliott. *Producer-Director:* Bud Yorkin. *Writers:* Pat McCormick, Jack Riley, Kenny Solms, Gail Parent.

**1301 The Many Sides of Mickey Rooney.** Variety, 60 min., CBS, 3/31/60. Mickey Rooney's many talents are spotlighted from singer and comedian to dancer and dramatic actor. *Host:* Mickey Rooney. *Guests:* Gloria DeHaven, Joey Forman, Edith Leslie, Howard McNear, Dick Winslow. *Producers:* Jack Donohue, Red Doff. *Writers:* Elon Packard, Harry Winkler, Sid Silvers. *Director:* Jack Donohue.

**1302 The March of Dimes Benefit Show.** Variety, 60 min., CBS, 1/22/49. A program of music, songs, and comedy for the benefit of the March of Dimes. *Guests:* David Atkinson, Shirley Booth, Sondra Deel, Henry Fonda, Betty Jane Watson. *Music:* Ray Bloch. *Producer:* Barry Wood. *Director:* Kingman T. Moore.

**1303 The March of Dimes Fashion Show.** Variety, 60 min., CBS, 1/27/48. The first televised benefit for the March of Dimes; a celebrity fashion show to aid the National Foundation for Infantile Paralysis. See also the prior title. *Commentator:* Gil Fates.

*Guests:* John Conte, Nanette Fabray, Judy Holliday, Kim Hunter, June Lockhart, Basil Rathbone, George Sanders, Gloria Swanson. *Producer:* Frances Buss. *Writer:* Inez Robs. *Directors:* Lester Gaba, Eleanor Lambert.

**1304 Marco Polo.** Musical, 90 min., NBC, 4/14/56. A musical chronicle of Marco Polo, the thirteenth-century Venetian traveler, as he journeys from land to land as an emissary of the Mongol emperor Kublai Khan. *Cast:* Alfred Drake (Marco Polo), Doretta Morrow (Girl), Arnold Moss (Niccolo), George Mitchell (Maffeo), Paul Ukena (Kublai Khan), Beatrice Kraft (Dancer), Harold Vermilyea (Baron of Tibet). *Music:* Clay Warnick, Mel Pahl. *Producers:* Max Liebman, Bill Hobin. *Writers:* William Friedberg, Neil Simon. *Director:* Max Liebman.

**1305 Marilyn: Something's Got to Give.** Documentary, 60 min., Fox, 12/13/90. A profile of actress Marilyn Monroe with a focus on her last film, *Something's Got to Give*, which, for some time, was considered destroyed due to the rumors that Marilyn's performance was weak and uninspired. *Narrator:* Henry Schipper. *Producer:* Bill Knoedelseder. *Writer:* Henry Schipper.

**1306 Marineland Carnival.** Variety, 60 min., CBS, 3/29/64. A tour of Marineland of the Pacific as seen through the eyes of television's "Beverly Hillbillies." *Cast:* Tom and Dick Smothers (Tour Guides), Buddy Ebsen (Jed Clampett), Irene Ryan (Granny), Donna Douglas (Elly Mae Clampett), Max Baer, Jr. (Jethro Bodine), Cliff Norton (Man). *Music:* Les Brown. *Producer:* Bill Gammie. *Writers:* Charles E. Andrews, Bill Gammie. *Director:* Bob Lehman.

**1307 Marineland Carnival.** Variety, 60 min., CBS, 4/18/65. An insider's view of the Marineland Carnival as seen through the eyes of television's Munster family as they visit Marineland of the Pacific. *Cast:* Fred Gwynne (Herman Munster), Yvonne DeCarlo (Lily Munster), Al Lewis (Grandpa), Pat Priest (Marilyn Munster), Butch Patrick (Eddie Munster). *Guests:* Jane Aul, Sid Gould, The New Christy Minstrels, Zale Parry. *Music:* Les Brown. *Producer:* Charles Andrews. *Writers:* Charles Andrews, Bill Gammie. *Director:* Bob Lehman.

## 1308 Marlene Dietrich: I Wish You Love. Variety, 60 min., CBS, 1/13/73. A solo performance by actress Marlene Dietrich as she adapts her acclaimed 1967 one-woman Broadway show to television. *Host:* Marlene Dietrich. *Music Director:* Stan Freeman. *Music Arranger:* Burt Bacharach. *Producer:* Alexander H. Cohen. *Director:* Clark Jones.

## 1309 Marlo Thomas and Friends in Free to Be ... You and Me. Variety, 60 min., ABC, 3/11/74. The program, aimed primarily at children, relates music, songs, stories, and poems, all designed to teach children to be their individual selves. *Host:* Marlo Thomas. *Guests:* Alan Alda, Harry Belafonte, Mel Brooks, Rita Coolidge, Billy DeWolfe, Roberta Flack, Rosey Grier, Dustin Hoffman, Michael Jackson, Kris Kristofferson, Robert Morse, Tom Smothers, Cicely Tyson, Dionne Warwick. *Music:* Stephen Lawrence. *Producers:* Marlo Thomas, Carole Hart. *Directors:* Bill Davis, Alan Alda, Fred Wolf.

## 1310 Marlo Thomas in Acts of Love — And Other Comedies. Comedy, 60 min., ABC, 3/16/73. An unusual comedy special, consisting of six sketches based on the predicament of men and women trying to find common ground on which to base relationships. *Host/The Girl:* Marlo Thomas.

*Guests:* Rae Allen, Stephanie Braxton, Art Garfunkel, Bill Lazarus, Stella Longo, Peggy Pope, Linda Rubinoff, Jean Stapleton, Michael Vale, Gene Wilder. *Music:* Peter Matz. *Producers:* Gary Smith, Dwight Hemion. *Writers:* Renee Taylor, Joseph Bologna. *Director:* Dwight Hemion.

## 1311 Marriage — Handle with Care. Comedy, 60 min., CBS, 12/2/59. A series of sketches that spoof the contrasting ideas of courtship and marriage throughout the world. *Host:* Sid Caesar. *Guests:* Gower Champion, Marge Champion, Jose Ferrer, Connie Francis, Audrey Meadows. *Music:* Ted Cappy. *Producer:* Leo Morgan. *Writers:* Mel Tolkin, Mel Brooks, Sydney Zelenka. *Director:* Jerome Shaw.

## 1312 Marty Robbins: Super Legend. Tribute, 2 hrs., Syndicated, 8/86. A salute to the Grammy-winning country and western singer (1925–82). *Host:* John Schneider. *Guests:* Roy Acuff, Bobby Allison, Little Jimmy Dickens, Ralph Emery, Larry Gatlin, Merle Haggard, Brenda Lee, Barbara Mandrell, Faron Young. *Music:* Bill Walker. *Producers:* Richard C. Thrall, Steve Womack. *Writers:* Bill Galvin, Pat Galvin. *Director:* Steve Womack.

## 1313 Marvin Hamlisch: They're Playing My Song. Variety, 60 min., Showtime, 1981. Composer Marvin Hamlisch performs the songs associated with his career. *Host:* Marvin Hamlisch. *Guests:* Gladys Knight, Priscilla Lopez, Johnny Mathis, Liza Minnelli, Carly Simon. *Producers:* Ken Weinstock, Les Haber.

## 1314 Mary Hart Presents Love in the Public Eye. Variety, 60 min., Syndicated, 3/17/90. Celebrities appear and comment on the pressures of constantly being in the public eye. *Host:* Mary Hart. *Guests:* Roseanne Arnold, George Burns, Emilio

Estefan, LaToya Jackson, Janet Jones, Vice President Dan Quayle. *Music:* Tim Truman. *Producers:* Mary Hart, Burt Sugarman. *Writer:* Susan Michaels. *Director:* Clay Harrison.

## 1315 The Mary Martin Show.

Variety, 60 min., NBC, 4/3/66. A musical salute to the spring of 1966. *Host:* Mary Martin. *Guests:* The Radio City Music Hall Rockettes. *Music:* Jay Blackton. *Producer-Director:* Gower Champion.

## 1316 Mary Tyler Moore: The 20th Anniversary Show. Com-

edy, 90 min., CBS, 2/18/91. An anniversary show that reunites original cast members of "The Mary Tyler Moore Show" (1970–77) for a look at some of the most memorable moments from the series. *Host:* Mary Tyler Moore. *Guests:* Ed Asner, Valerie Harper, Cloris Leachman, Gavin MacLeod, Betty White. *Producers:* Jack Haley, Jr., James L. Brooks, Allan Burns, Ed Weinberger, Marcia Lewis. *Writers:* Phil Savenick, Laurie Jacobson, Marcia Lewis. *Director:* Jack Haley, Jr.

## 1317 Mary's Incredible Dream. Variety, 60 min., CBS, 1/22/

76. An unusual special in which the vivacious Mary Tyler Moore acts out her wildest fantasies. *Host:* Mary Tyler Moore. *Cast:* Mary Tyler Moore (Angel/Devil/Woman), Ben Vereen (Devil/Noah/Man), Doug Kershaw (Adam/Devil/War), Arthur Fiedler (The Maestro), The Manhattan Transfer (Angels/Devils/Onlookers). *Music:* Ray Pohlman. *Producer:* Jack Good. *Directors:* Gene McAvoy, Jaime Rogers.

## 1318 Mathnet: The Case of the Swami Scam. Children, 60

min., PBS, 1/8/90. A primetime special based on the recurring segment, "Mathnet," on the series "Square One TV." The spoof of "Dragnet" follows

mathematicians Kate Monday and George Frankly—math sleuths from the L.A.P.D.—who travel to New York City to solve the case of a swami who is swindling retired lawyers out of their money. *Cast:* Beverly Leech (Kate Monday), Joe Howard (George Frankly), James Earl Jones (Captain), Neal Ben-Ari (Swami River), Ron Frazier (F. Lee Bully), Michael Lombard (Percy Mason), Louis Zorichi (Marvin Belly), Mary Watson (Officer Debbie Williams). *Music:* John Rodby. *Producer:* David D. Connell. *Writers:* David D. Connell, Jim Thurman. *Director:* Charles S. Dubin.

## 1319 A Matter of Time.

Drama, 60 min., ABC, 2/11/81. An Emmy Award–winning "ABC Afterschool Special" about Lisl Gilbert, a teenage girl who discovers strength she never knew she had when she is forced to deal with the terrifying fact that her mother (Jean) is dying of cancer. *Cast:* Karlene Crockett (Lisl Gilbert), Rosemary Forsyth (Jean Gilbert), Kate Zentall (Samantha Canby), Wayne Heffley (Louis Gilbert), Carrie Freeman (Jane Allerton), Lisa Jane Persky (Jo Dayton), Rob Lowe (Jeff Bartlett). *Producer:* Martin Tahse. *Writer:* Paul W. Cooper. *Director:* Arthur A. Seidelman.

## 1320 A Matter of Trust: Billy Joel in the USSR. Variety, 90 min.,

ABC, 6/15/88. A chronicle of the singer's visit to the Soviet Union with his wife (Christie Brinkley), his daughter (Alexa Ray), and his music. *Host:* Billy Joel. *Band:* Billy Joel (vocals, keyboard, guitar), Liberty DeVito (drums), Doug Stegmeyer (bass), Dave LeBolt (keyboards), Russell Javors (acoustic and electric guitars), Mark Rivera (sax), Kevin Dukes (electric guitar), Peter Hewett, George Simms (background vocals). *Producer:* Frank Weber. *Director:* Martin Bell.

"**Mathnet: The Case of the Swami Scam.**" James Earl Jones *(front),* Beverly Leech, Mary Watson, Joe Howard *(back, left to right).*

**1321 The Maurice Chevalier Show.** Variety, 90 min., NBC, 12/4/55. Music, song and light comedy with French entertainer Maurice Chevalier. *Host:* Maurice Chevalier. *Guests:* Pat Carroll, Jeannie Carson. *Music:* Charles Sanford. *Producer-Director:* Max Liebman.

**1322 The Maurice Chevalier Special.** Variety, 60 min., NBC, 5/20/56. A lively program of music, song, and dance. *Host:* Maurice Chevalier. *Guests:* Polly Bergen, Stanley Holloway,

Michel Legrand, Chita Rivera. *Music:* Charles Sanford. *Producers:* Max Liebman, Bill Hobin. *Director:* Max Liebman.

## 1323 Maurice Chevalier's Paris. Variety, 60 min., NBC, 3/6/57.

A musical tour of Paris with the remembrances of French entertainer Maurice Chevalier. *Host:* Maurice Chevalier. *Producer:* Ted Mills. *Writers:* Stephen White, Ted Mills, Maurice Chevalier. *Director:* Andrew Marton.

## 1324 Mayday! Mayday!

Drama, 30 min., ABC, 4/12 and 4/19/86. Following a plane crash that traps their father in the wreckage and immobilizes their mother with a broken leg, youngsters Allison and Mark Parker set out to find help. The tense story relates their journey across the rugged terrain of the High Sierras to find help for their parents. An "ABC Weekend Special." *Cast:* Heather McAdam (Allison Parker), Brad Savage (Mark Parker), Hersha Parady (Janice Parker), Don Fenwick (Lou Parker), Frank Aletter (Walt Thompson), John Anderson (Curtis George). *Producer:* Tom Armistead. *Writers:* Jim Carlson, Terrence McDonnell. *Director:* Robert Chenault.

## 1325 Me and Dad's New Wife. Drama, 60 min., ABC, 2/18/76.

An "ABC Afterschool Special" about Nina Beckwith, a 12-year-old girl who is struggling to accept her parents' divorce — and the recent remarriage of her father, George, to her new math teacher, Dolores. *Cast:* Kristy McNichol (Nina Beckwith), Melendy Britt (Dolores Beckwith), Ned Wilson (George Beckwith), Beatty Beaird (Charlotte Beckwith), Lance Kerwin (Buzz), Leif Garrett (Roger). *Producer:* Daniel Wilson. *Writers:* Pat Nardo, Gloria Banta. *Director:* Larry Elikann.

## 1326 Me and Mr. Stenner.

Drama, 60 min., CBS, 6/2/81. The story of Abigail O'Neill, an 11-year-old girl, as she attempts to accept the man (Peter Stenner) her soon-to-be divorced mother (Lillian) intends to marry. A "CBS Afternoon Playhouse." *Cast:* April Gilpin (Abigail O'Neill), David Ogden Stiers (Peter Stenner), Bobbie Faye Ferguson (Lillian O'Neill), Frederick Tully (Frank O'Neill), Bubba Larramore (Jeff Stenner), Joseph William Galt (Luke Stenner). *Producer:* Alan Landsburg. *Writer:* Corey Blechman. *Director:* Sigmund Neufeld, Jr.

## 1327 Meet Cyd Charisse.

Variety, 60 min., NBC, 12/29/59. An hour of music, song, and comedy that spotlights the talents of actress-singer Cyd Charisse. *Host:* Cyd Charisse. *Guests:* Eve Arden, Tony Martin, James Mitchell. *Music:* Tutti Camarata. *Producer:* Hubbell Robinson. *Choreography:* Eugene Loring.

## 1328 Meet Marcel Marceau.

Variety, 60 min., Syndicated, 9/67. The program spotlights the genius of mime Marcel Marceau. *Host:* Marcel Marceau. *Producers:* Mal Klein, Wally Sherwin, Bob Searls. *Writer-Director:* Wally Sherwin.

## 1329 Meet Me in St. Louis.

Musical, 2 hrs., CBS, 4/26/59. A romantic musical comedy about a turn-of-the-century St. Louis family who face a crisis when they discover they must leave Missouri and move to New York City. *Cast:* Tab Hunter (John Truett), Jane Powell (Esther), Walter Pidgeon (Alonzo), Jeanne Crain (Rose Smith), Patty Duke (Tootie), Myrna Loy (Anna), Lois Nettleton (Lucille), Ed Wynn (Grandfather), Reta Shaw (Katey), Ginger McManus (Agnes). *Music:* Franz Allers. *Producer:* David Susskind. *Writers:* Irving Brecher, Fred P. Finkehoffe. *Director:* George Schaefer.

275. 1337. Men Who Rate a "10"

## 1330 Melina Mercouri's Greece.
Variety, 60 min., ABC, 5/3/65. An hour of music, song, and talk as actress Melina Mercouri tours her home country of Greece. *Host:* Melina Mercouri. *Music:* Stavros Xarhakos. *Producers:* Norman Baer, Philip D'Antoni. *Writers:* Max Wilk, Jacovos Campanellis. *Director:* Clifford Owens.

## 1331 Melody of Hate.
Thriller, 90 min., ABC, 9/30/75. The story of an opera singer whose plans for remarriage are complicated by the husband she thought was dead. Also known as "Nightmare for a Nightingale." *Cast:* Susan Flannery (Anna Cartell), Keith Baxter (Tony), Stuart Damon (Anna's fiancé), Sydney Tafler (Anna's manager), Ronald Leigh-Hunt (Giles), Theresa Cahill (Anna's singing voice), Richard Lewis (Tony's singing voice). *Music:* Laurie Johnson. *Producer:* Ian Fordyce. *Writer:* Brian Clemens. *Director:* John Scholz-Conway.

## 1332 The Member of the Wedding.
Drama, 90 min., CBS, 6/12/58. The drama, set in Georgia in 1945, tells of Frankie Adams, a 12-year-old girl who cannot wait to grow up and become a woman, and of her fears of losing her brother, who is about to marry. Based on the play by Carson McCullers. See also the following title. *Cast:* Collin Wilcox (Frankie Adams), Claudio McNeil (Bernie), Dennis Kohler (John Henry), Larry Wilcox (Jarvis), Stanley Greene (T. J. Williams), Jo Hurt (Mrs. West), Claire Griswold (Janice), Catherine Ayres (Sis Laura). *Producers:* David Susskind, Robert Mulligan. *Writers:* Jacqueline Babbin, Audrey Gellen. *Director:* Robert Mulligan.

## 1333 The Member of the Wedding.
Drama, 2 hrs., NBC, 12/20/82. A second television adaptation of the play by Carson McCullers. See the prior title for story. *Cast:* Dana Hill (Frankie Adams), Pearl Bailey (Bernice), Howard E. Rollins, Jr. (Honey), Benjamin Bernouy (John Henry), Dwier Brown (Jarvis Adams), Lane Smith (Mr. Adams), Sherry Hursey (Janice), Bill Cobbs (T. T.). *Producers:* David Rintels, Paul Waigner. *Writer:* Carson McCullers. *Director:* Delbart Mann.

## 1334 Memories of M*A*S*H.
Retrospective, 90 min., CBS, 11/25/91. A look back at the series "M*A*S*H" (CBS, 1972–83), with clips and interviews with cast members. *Host:* Shelley Long. *Guests:* Alan Alda, G. W. Bailey, Linda Bloodworth-Thomason, Gary Burghoff, William Christopher, Dr. Walter Dishell, Charles S. Dubin, Jamie Farr, Mike Farrell, Larry Gelbart, Larry Linville, Burt Metcalfe, Harry Morgan, Gene Reynolds, Wayne Rogers, McLean Stevenson, David Ogden Stiers, Loretta Swit. *Producers:* Gene Reynolds, Burt Metcalfe, Michael Hirsh. *Writer-Director:* Michael Hirsh.

## 1335 Memories Then and Now.
Documentary, 60 min., CBS, 8/8/88. A nostalgic look at the places, people, and events that shaped our past. *Hosts:* Candice Bergen, Teri Garr, Martin Mull, Suzanne Pleshette, Victoria Principal, John Ritter, Dennis Weaver. *Guests:* Jim Henson, Daphne Maxwell Reid, Tim Reid. *Producer-Writer-Director:* Robert Guenette.

## 1336 Men at Work in Concert.
Variety, 60 min., HBO, 3/10/84. A concert by the rock group Men at Work. *Men at Work:* John Rees, Colin Hay, Ron Strykert, Jerry Speiser, Greg Ham. *Producers:* Russell Deppeler, George Paige. *Director:* Bruce Gowers.

## 1337 Men Who Rate a "10."
Variety, 60 min., NBC, 10/7/80. A look at the men women feel are attractive. A sequel to "Women Who Rate a 10." *Hosts:* Barbara Eden, Brooke Shields, Gloria Swanson. *Guests:* Barbi Benton,

Greg Evigan, Wayland Flowers, Annette Funicello, Zsa Zsa Gabor, Jayne Kennedy, Abbe Lane, Marilyn McCoo, Lee Meriwether, Rick Nelson, Randi Oakes, Teddy Pendergrass, Rudy Vallee. *Music:* Bob Rozario. *Producers:* Dick Clark, Al Schwartz. *Writer:* Rod Warren. *Director:* Barry Glazer.

### 1338 A Menace Called Dennis.

Comedy, 30 min., ABC, 6/22/93. A look at the making of the 1993 feature film *Dennis the Menace.* The program shows how Hank Ketchum created the character (based on his own mischievous son) and its evolution from comics to television to the movies. The story itself revolves around the attempts of Walter Matthau (who played Mr. Wilson) to explain how the movie was made—despite the antics of Dennis. *Host:* Walter Matthau. *Guests:* Mason Gamble (Dennis), Lea Thompson (Alice Mitchell), Joan Plowright (Mrs. Wilson), Nick Castle (the director), John Hughes (writer), Hank Ketchum (creator). *Producer-Writer-Directors:* John Pattyson, Michael Meadows.

### 1339 Merman on Broadway.

Variety, 60 min., NBC, 11/24/59. Actress Ethel Merman recalls the music and songs associated with her Broadway career. *Host:* Ethel Merman. *Guests:* Tab Hunter, Fess Parker, Tom Poston, Bobby Sherwood. *Music:* Jack Kane. *Producer:* Roger Edens. *Writers:*

**"Men Who Rate a '10'."** Hosts *(left to right)***: Barbara Eden, Gloria Swanson, and Brooke Shields.**

A. J. Russell, Joe Bigelow. *Director:* Greg Garrison.

### Merry Christmas, Fred, from the Crosbys *see* Bing Crosby Specials

### 1340 Merry Christmas from the Grand Ole Opry.

Variety, 60 min., ABC, 12/14/79. A program of Christmas music and songs from the Grand Ole Opry in Nashville. *Hosts:* Loni Anderson, Robert Urich. *Guests:* Larry Gatlin, Wendy Holcombe, Barbara Mandrell, Louise Mandrell, Ronnie Milsap, The Statler Brothers. *Music:* Bill Walker. *Producers:* Gary Smith, Dwight Hemion. *Writers:* Buz Kohan, Chet Hagan. *Director:* Dwight Hemion.

## 1341 Merry Christmas Land.
Children, 50 min., NBC, 12/19/47. A pioneering television Christmas special in which a group of children meet Santa Claus, see store decorations, and visit fairyland candy castles. *Host:* Frank Luther. *Announcer/Tour Guide:* Ray Forrest. *Producer-Director:* Harold Keith. *Technical Director:* Alfred Jackson.

## 1342 Merry Christmas ... With Love, Julie. Variety, 60 min.,
Syndicated, 12/79. A holiday program of music and songs as singer Julie Andrews celebrates Christmas. *Host:* Julie Andrews. *Guests:* Alice Ghostley, Joel Grey, Rich Little, Jimmy Stewart. *Music Director:* Nelson Riddle. *Special Musical Material:* Dick Williams. *Producer:* Nick Vanoff. *Writers:* Jack Burns, Jay Burton, George Bloom. *Director:* Bill Davis.

## 1343 The Merry Widow.
Operetta, 90 min., NBC, 4/9/55. Sonia Sadoya is a wealthy young widow who is being romanced by Prince Danilo, a womanizing Marsovian embassy attaché who is courting Sonia in hopes of using her fortune to restore his country's empty treasury. Sonia's efforts to convince Danilo that she is penniless — and still acquire his marriage proposal — are the focal point of the story. *Cast:* Anne Jeffreys (Sonia Sadoya), Barry Sullivan (Prince Danilo), Edward Everett Horton (Barton Zelta), Helena Bliss (Valencienne), Jack Russell (Lieutenant Nicholas), John Conte (Georges), Bambi Linn and Rod Alexander (Dancers). *Music:* Charles Sanford. *Producer-Director:* Max Liebman. *Writers:* William Friedberg, Neil Simon, Will Glickman.

## 1344 Merv Griffin and the Christmas Kids. Variety, 60 min.,
Syndicated, 12/73. A celebration of Christmas with child stars. *Host:* Merv Griffin. *Child Stars:* Randy Gray, Leland Greenwald, Mary Elizabeth Mc-

Donough, Kim Richards, Rodney Allen Rippy, The Robert Mitchell Boys Choir, Eric Scott, Ricky Segall. *Music:* Mort Lindsey. *Producer:* George Moynihan. *Director:* Kirk Alexander.

## 1345 Merv Griffin's New Year's Eve Special. Variety, 60
min., Syndicated, 12/31/91. Merv Griffin welcomes in 1992 with a 19-piece orchestra, singing, and dancing from his Resorts Casino Hotel in Atlantic City, New Jersey. *Host:* Merv Griffin. *Guests:* Eva Gabor, Jack Sheldon, The Temptations, Toni Tennille. *Music:* Mort Lindsey. *Producers:* Merv Griffin, John P. Belisle. *Director:* Dick Carson.

## 1346 Merv Griffin's St. Patrick's Day Special. Variety, 60
min., Syndicated, 3/68. A musical celebration of St. Patrick's Day. *Host:* Merv Griffin. *Guests:* The Clancy Brothers and Tommy Makem, Sandy Duncan, John Huston, Burl Ives, Jimmy Joyce, Ella Logan, John Wayne. *Music:* Mort Lindsey. *Producers:* George Moynihan, Bob Shanks. *Writer:* Bob Shanks. *Director:* Kirk Alexander.

## 1347 Merv Griffin's Sidewalks of New England. Variety, 60 min.,
Syndicated, 12/68. A musical tour of New England. *Host:* Merv Griffin. *Guests:* Agnes de Mille, Aretha Franklin, Paul Revere and the Raiders. *Music:* Mort Lindsey. *Producer:* George Moynihan. *Director:* Kirk Alexander.

## 1348 Michael Jackson ... The Legend Continues. Docu-
mentary, 60 min., CBS, 1/17/92. A look at singer Michael Jackson's rise to stardom (includes home movies, behind-the-scenes interviews, and interviews with celebrities). *Guests:* Dick Clark, Katharine Hepburn, Quincy Jones, Smokey Robinson, Elizabeth Taylor, Yoko Ono. *Producers:* Michael Jack-

son, Suzanne de Passe, Suzanne Coston, Burl Hechtman. *Director:* George Paige.

## 1349 Michel's Mixed-Up Musical Bird. Drama, 60 min., ABC, 2/15/78.

A true story based on an incident from composer Michel Legrand's childhood. Eugenie is the daughter of Michel Legrand. When Eugenie becomes discouraged because she can not fully recognize the difference between the notes in her piano scales, Michel tells her that by varying the order or intensity of the notes, any number of feelings or images can be conveyed. When he demonstrates by playing "One Note's Song," Eugenie says it reminds her of the sound of a bird. An animated flashback is then used as Michel tells her of finding an injured baby bird in the forest during a summer of his boyhood. He named the bird "One Note" (since that's all the bird could sing) and nursed it back to health. As the bird grew it developed definite musical likes and dislikes and finally "collaborated" with Michel in a musical composition. An "ABC Afterschool Special." *Cast:* Michel Legrand (Himself), Olivia Barash (Eugenie). *Voices:* Michael Barbera (Young Michel), Rita Lynn (Madame Footy), Hal Smith (Professor Latouche). *Music:* Michel Legrand. *Lyrics:* John Bradford. *Producers:* Nat Shapiro, David H. DePatie, Friz Freleng. *Writers:* Dick Robbins, Duane Poole. *Live Action Director:* Michel Legrand. *Animation Directors:* Tom Yakutis, Brad Case, Gerry Chiniquy.

## 1350 The Mickey Rooney Show. Comedy, 60 min., CBS, 3/31/60.

Various sketches that spotlight the talents of comedian Mickey Rooney. *Host:* Mickey Rooney. *Guests:* Victor Borge, Art Carney, Gloria DeHaven. *Music:* Robert Emmett Dolan. *Producer-Director:* Jack Donohue. *Writers:* Elon Packard, Harry Winkler, Sid Silvers.

## 1351 The Mickie Finn Special. Variety, 60 min., Syndicated, 6/71.

An hour of music and song set against a gay nineties motif with singer-guitartist Mickie Finn and her husband, pianist Fred Finn. *Hosts:* Fred Finn, Mickie Finn. *Guests:* The Accents, Arte Johnson, Forrest Tucker. *Music:* The Mickie Finn Band. *Producer:* Bob Finkel.

## 1352 The Mickie Finns Finally Present How the West Was Lost. Variety, 60 min., Syndicated, 7/75.

A music and comedy salute to the American cowboy. *Hosts:* Fred Finn, Mickie Finn. *Guests:* Foster Brooks, Charlie Callas, Rob Reiner, Diana Trask. *Narrators:* Dale Evans, Roy Rogers. *Music:* Larry Cansler. *Producer-Director:* Alan Handley. *Writer:* John Bradford.

## 1353 Mighty Moose and the Quarterback Kid. Drama, 60 min., ABC, 2/1/76.

Alex "Mighty Moose" Novak is a lineman for the Los Angeles Rams who agrees to become a substitute coach for a little league football team (the Jets) while he is recovering from an injury. The Jets are quarterbacked by Benny Singleton, a 12-year-old who would rather be a photographer than a football player. Benny's father, however, is determined that his son will become a great professional passing ace, consistent with his own unfulfilled dreams. The story relates Alex's attempts to help father and son by arranging for Mr. Singleton to quarterback for the L.A. Rams. While the pros are in a scrimmage game, he comes to understand his son's reluctance to play, and Benny begins to have a better understanding of his father. An "ABC Afterschool Special." *Cast:* Alex Karras (Alex Novak), Brandon Cruz (Benny Singleton), Dave Madden (Coach Puckett), Joseph Mascolo (Mr. Singleton), Nancy Puthuff (Suzy), Peter Horton (Morris), Charles Everett

**Fred Finn** *(left)* **and Mickie Finn, hosts of "The Mickie Finn Special."**

(L. J.). *Music:* Glen Ballard. *Producers:* Alex Karras, Harry Bernsen. *Writers:* Gerald Gardner, Kay Cousins Johnson. *Director:* Tony Frangakis.

**1354 Mike and Pearl.** Variety, 60 min., Syndicated, 3/68. An hour of music and songs with singers Mike Douglas and Pearl Bailey. *Hosts:* Pearl Bailey, Mike Douglas. *Music:* Ellie Frankel. *Producer:* Roger Allen. *Writer:* Bunny Briggs. *Director:* Ernest Sherry.

**1355 The Mike Douglas Christmas Special.** Variety, 60 min., Syndicated, 12/69. A holiday program of music and songs. *Host:* Mike Douglas. *Guests:* Bob Elliott, The First Edition, Ray Goulding, Patti Page, Kenny Rogers. *Music:* Ellie Frankel. *Producer:* Eric Leiber. *Writers:* Tom Whedon, David Axelrod. *Director:* David Barnhizer.

**1356 The Million Dollar Incident.** Comedy, 60 min., CBS, 4/21/61. A Jackie Gleason comedy special in which Jackie, playing himself, is kidnapped and held for a $1 million ransom. The story relates Jackie's efforts to escape. *Cast:* Jackie Gleason (Himself), Everett Sloane (Mr. Bannister), Jack Klugman (Charles), Peter Falk (Sammy), William Redfield (Philbin), Harvey Lembeck (Eddy), Millette Alexander (Lee Bevins), Salome Jens (Sheila), Barnard Hughes (Mr. Wallace). *Producer:* Gordon Duff. *Writers:* A. J. Russell, Sydney Zelenka, Walter Stone. *Director:* Norman Jewison.

**1357 Milton Berle Specials.** A chronological listing of the variety specials hosted by comedian Milton Berle. All are 60 minutes except where noted.
  **1 Uncle Miltie's Christmas Party** (NBC, 12/25/50). *Guests:* James Little,

The Martin Brothers, Lauritz Melchior, Manuel Perez, Marita Perez, Martha Raye. *Orchestra:* Al Goodman. *Producer:* Irving Gray. *Writers:* Hal Collins, Jay Burton, Bobby Gordon, Buddy Arnold, Woody Kling. *Director:* Arthur Knorr.

**2 Uncle Miltie's Easter TV Party** (NBC, 3/28/51). *Guests:* Jan Bart, Joan Edwards, Excess Baggage, Joe Jackson, Fatso Marco, Alan Schackner, Sid Stone, the Wong Troupe. *Orchestra:* Al Goodman. *Producer:* Irving Gray. *Director:* Arthur Knorr.

**3 The Milton Berle Special** (NBC, 10/11/59). *Guests:* Barbara Heller, Peter Lawford, Danny Thomas, Lana Turner. *Producer:* Milton Berle. *Writers:* Milt Josefsberg, Marty Klein, Hal Goldman, Dan Shapiro, Hal Golden. *Director:* Greg Garrison.

**4 The Milton Berle Special** (NBC, 11/1/59). *Guests:* Desi Arnaz, Lucille Ball, Marion Colby, Lloyd Corrigan, Cyril Delvanti, Nancy Kulp, George Macready, Mike Mazurki. *Producer:* Irving Starr. *Writer:* Lou Derman. *Director:* Desi Arnaz.

**5 The Milton Berle Special** (NBC, 3/9/62). *Guests:* Jack Benny, Lawrence Harvey, Lena Horne, Janis Paige. *Music:* Les Brown. *Producer:* William O. Harbach. *Writers:* Herb Sargent, Harry Crane, Stan Drebin, Milt Josefsberg, Dan Shapiro. *Director:* Barry Shear.

**6 Milton Berle's Mad Mad Mad World of Comedy** (90 min., ABC, 1/9/75). *Guests:* Don Adams, Albert Brooks, Hal Kanter, Flip Wilson. *Producer:* Jack Haley, Jr. *Writer:* Stan Davis. *Director:* Jim Washburn.

**Milton Berle's Mad Mad Mad World of Comedy** *see* **Milton Berle Specials**

**1358 Minnelli on Minnelli.** Documentary, 60 min., PBS, 3/18/87. An affectionate tribute to filmmaker Vincente Minnelli by his daughter, Liza. Includes clips from his many

films. *Host:* Liza Minnelli. *Music:* Henry Mancini. *Producers:* Jack Haley, Jr., David Niven, Jr. *Writer-Director:* Richard Schickel.

**1359 Minsky's Follies.** Comedy, 60 min., HBO, 7/2/82. The program recalls the golden age of vaudeville through burlesque-like comedy routines. *Hosts:* Phyllis Diller, Stubby Kaye, Rip Taylor. *Guests:* Bill Cook, Ann Dane, Brandi Doran, Jolly Jovers, Greg Lewis, Rosalind Moreland, Bob Paris, Charles Vespia. *Music:* Jon Charles. *Producers:* Barry Ashton, Wolf Kochmann, Ken Gibson, James Rich, Jr. *Director:* Michael Watt.

**1360 The Miracle Babies of Sea World.** Variety, 60 min., ABC, 6/11/89. A look at the exhibits at Sea World in San Diego, San Antonio, and Orlando. Also known as "Sea World's Miracle Babies and Friends." *Hosts:* Joanna Kerns, Danny Pintauro. *Music:* Lenny Stack. *Producers:* Dick Clark, Gene Weed, Al Schwartz, Robert Arthur. *Writer:* Robert Arthur. *Director:* Gene Weed.

**1361 Miracle on 34th Street.** A chronological listing of the three television specials based on the 1947 story by Valentine Davies. Kris Kringle is a kindly old gentleman who comes to the aid of advertising manager Doris Walker and agrees to play Santa Claus in the Macy's Thanksgiving Day Parade. Kris so impresses Doris and her young daughter, Susan, that Doris offers him a job as a Macy's department store Santa. The classic story relates the problems that occur when Kris claims he is the real Santa Claus. (The third version changes the Doris Walker character to Karen Walker, and Doris's boyfriend, Fred Gailey, to Bill Schaffner).

**1 Miracle on 34th Street** (60 min., CBS, 12/14/55). *Cast:* Thomas Mitchell (Kris Kringle), Teresa Wright (Doris

Walker), Macdonald Carey (Fred Gailey), Sandy Descher (Susan Walker), Ray Collins (Judge Harper), Hans Conried (Mr. Shellhammer), Dick Foran (Thomas Mara), Whit Bissell (Dr. Pierce), Don Beddoe (R. H. Macy), Herbert Heyes (Mr. Gimble), Herb Vigran (Postal Clerk). *Producer:* Jules Bricken. *Director:* Robert Stevenson.
**2 Miracle on 34th Street** (60 min., NBC, 11/27/59). *Cast:* Ed Wynn (Kris Kringle), Mary Healy (Doris Walker), Peter Lind Hayes (Fred Gailey), Susan Gordon (Susan Walker), Orson Bean (Dr. Sawyer), Loring Smith (Mr. Shellhammer), Hiram Sherman (R. H. Macy), William Post, Jr. (Mr. Gimble), John Gibson (Judge Harper). *Producer:* David Susskind. *Writer:* Harry Mulheim. *Director:* William Corrigan.
**3 Miracle on 34th Street** (2 hrs., CBS, 12/14/73). *Cast:* Sebastian Cabot (Kris Kringle), Jane Alexander (Karen Walker), David Hartman (Bill Schaffner), Suzanne Davidson (Susan Walker), Roddy McDowall (Dr. Sawyer), Jim Backus (Mr. Shellhammer), David Doyle (R. H. Macy), Roland Winters (Adam Gimble), Tom Bosley (Judge Harper), Conrad Janis (Dr. Pierce). *Music:* Sid Ramin. *Producer:* Norman Rosemont. *Writer:* Jeb Rosenbrook. *Director:* Fielder Cook.

**1362 Mirror, Mirror, Off the Wall.** Comedy-Drama, 60 min., NBC, 11/21/69. When Max Maxwell, a writer with a sinking reputation, publishes a dirty book under the pen name N. Y. Rome, he finds immediate success and a problem—schizophrenia. The story relates Max's attempts to cope with his alter ego, Rome, when he suddenly appears and becomes visible only to Max. *Cast:* George C. Scott (Max/Rome), Maureen Stapleton (Ruthie Maxwell), David Burns (Linkoff), John McGiver (Brock), Ziva Rodann (Elena). *Producers:* M. J. Rifkin, Murray Chercover. *Writer:* David Shaw. *Director:* Fielder Cook.

**1363 Mirror of Deception.** Thriller, 90 min., ABC, 5/12/75. A young woman's efforts to learn the whereabouts of her two roommates—who never returned from answering the same employment ad. Also known as "Good Salary—Prospects—Free Coffin." *Cast:* Kim Darby (Helen Terrick), James Maxwell (Carter), Keith Barron (Charley), Julian Glover (Gifford), Susan Dury (Babs Bryant), Janina Faye (Wendy), John Abineri (Inspector Bruff). *Music:* Laurie Johnson. *Producers:* Cecil Clarke, Ian Fordyce. *Writer:* Brian Clemens. *Director:* John Scholz-Conway.

**1364 Miss Kline, We Love You.** Drama, 90 min., ABC, 2/27/74. Shortly after her divorce, a shy schoolteacher (Melanie Kline) acquires a job teaching children in the pediatrics ward of a hospital in the hopes of putting her life back together again. Melanie previously taught in a conventional school setting and is overwhelmed at the emotional challenge posed by the youngsters, some of whom are terminal cases. Slowly she begins to earn their trust and affection and helps to dispel some of the feelings of hopelessness and abandonment that pervade their lives. She is also drawn out by the children and comes to perceive a new meaning to life. The story relates the difficult decision Melanie soon faces—choosing between her work at the hospital or a second marriage. *Cast:* Patty Duke (Melanie Kline), John Astin (Dr. Irv Kellerman), June Dayton (Lisa Foyerman), Fred Beir (Alex Markham), Josh Albee (Lexie), Cindy Fisher (Tracy), Jerry Daniels (Dr. Artunian), Mia Bendixsen (Maryanne), Christopher Hanks (William). *Producers:* Wes Kenney, Wendy Charles. *Writer:* George Lefferts. *Director:* Wes Kenney.

**1365 Miss Switch to the Rescue.** Cartoon, 30 min., ABC, 1/16 and

1/23/81. One stormy night while reading, Rupert Brown and Amelia Daly are interrupted by an unexpected visit from a mysterious old woman. The woman gives Rupert a box and tells him that it contains a puzzle that only he can solve. Upon opening the box, Rupert and Amelia find a ship inside a bottle with a tiny man as its passenger. When Rupert removes the cork from the bottle, he releases Mordo, an evil warlock, who kidnaps Amelia and disappears. With nowhere else to turn, Rupert calls on Miss Switch, a good witch, for help. The story relates their efforts to rescue Amelia from Mordo. Aired as a two-part "ABC Weekend Special." *Voices:* Janet Waldo (Miss Switch), Eric Taslitz (Rupert Brown), Nancy McKeon (Amelia Daly), Hans Conried (Mordo), Hal Smith (Caruso), June Foray (Old Woman), Anne Lockhart (Barmaid), Alan Dinehart (Pirate). *Music:* Dean Elliott. *Producers:* Joe Ruby, Ken Spears. *Writer:* Sheldon Stark. *Director:* Charles A. Nichols.

**Mitzi** *see* **Mitzi Gaynor Specials**

**Mitzi: A Tribute to the American Housewife** *see* **Mitzi Gaynor Specials**

**1366 Mitzi Gaynor Specials.** A chronological listing of the variety specials hosted by singer-dancer Mitzi Gaynor. All are 60 minutes in length.
**1 Mitzi** (NBC, 10/14/68). *Guests:* Joan Gerber, George Hamilton, Phil Harris, Jack Riley. *Music:* Peter Matz. *Producers:* Jack Bean, Bob Henry. *Writers:* Larry Hovis, Ann Elder. *Director:* Bob Henry.
**2 Mitzi's Second Special** (NBC, 10/20/69). *Guests:* The Four Fellows, Ross Martin, Eddie Ryder. *Music:* Peter Matz. *Producers:* Jack Bean, James Loren. *Writers:* Larry Hovis, Ann Elder. *Director:* Richard Dunlap.

**3 Mitzi ... The First Time** (CBS, 3/28/73). *Guests:* Ken Berry, Mike Connors, Dan Dailey. *Music:* Dick DeBenedictis. *Producers:* Jack Bean, Lee Miller. *Writers:* Jerry Mayer, Stanley Ralph Ross. *Director:* John Moffitt.
**4 Mitzi: A Tribute to the American Housewife** (CBS, 1/10/74). *Guests:* Ted Knight, Cliff Norton, Jerry Orbach, Suzanne Pleshette, Jane Withers. *Producers:* Jack Bean, Lee Miller. *Writers:* Jerry Mayer, Charlotte Brown. *Director:* Tony Charmoli.
**5 Mitzi and a Hundred Guys** (CBS, 3/24/75). *Guests:* Jack Albertson, Marty Allen, Steve Allen, Tige Andrews, Ken Berry, Carl Betz, Bill Bixby, Tom Bosley, Bob Crane, Bill Dana, Clifton Davis, James Farentino, Christopher George, Andy Griffith, Monty Hall, Bob Hope, Ross Hunter, Dean Jones, Tom Kennedy, Ted Knight, Michael Landon, Rich Little, Allen Ludden, Jim McKrell, Gavin MacLeod, Monte Markham, Peter Marshall, Ross Martin, Strother Martin, Greg Morris, Leonard Nimoy, Louis Nye, William Shatner, Lyle Waggoner. *Producers:* Jack Bean, Mort Green. *Writer:* Jerry Mayer. *Director:* Tony Charmoli.
**6 Mitzi ... Roarin' in the 20s** (CBS, 3/14/76). *Guests:* Ken Berry, Linda Hopkins, Carl Reiner. *Music:* Bill Byers. *Producers:* Jack Bean, Harry Waterson. *Writer:* Jerry Mayer. *Director:* Tony Charmoli.
**7 Mitzi ... Zings into Spring** (CBS, 3/29/77). *Guests:* Roy Clark, Wayne Rogers. *Music:* Marvin Laird. *Producer:* Jack Bean. *Writer:* Jerry Mayer. *Director:* Tony Charmoli.
**8 Mitzi ... What's Hot, What's Not** (CBS, 4/6/78). *Guests:* John McCook, Gavin MacLeod. *Music:* Jerry Hill. *Producer:* Jack Bean. *Writer:* Jerry Mayer. *Director:* Tony Charmoli.

**Mitzi ... Roarin' in the 20s** *see* **Mitzi Gaynor Specials**

**Mitzi . . . The First Time** see **Mitzi Gaynor Specials**

**Mitzi . . . What's Hot, What's Not** see **Mitzi Gaynor Specials**

**Mitzi . . . Zings into Spring** see **Mitzi Gaynor Specials**

**1367 Mom and Dad Can't Hear Me.** Drama, 60 min., ABC, 4/5/78. Charlotte Meredith is a beautiful 15-year-old girl with many friends. Charlotte is also the daughter of deaf parents and afraid that her friends will ridicule her if they discover that her mother and father communicate through sign language. The story, broadcast as an "ABC Afterschool Special," relates how Charlotte learns to appreciate the special kind of family she comes from when her friends do find out and accept them as they do her. *Cast:* Rosanna Arquette (Charlotte Meredith), Priscilla Pointer (Mrs. Meredith), Stephen Elliott (Dan Meredith), Wendy Rastatter (Joyce), Eric Scott (David), Noelle North (Alice), David Hollander (Hughie), Susan Myers (Martha). *Music:* Joe Weber. *Producers:* Daniel Wilson, Fran Sears. *Writers:* Irma Reichert, Daryl Warner. *Director:* Larry Elikann.

**1368 Mom's on Strike.** Comedy, 60 min., ABC, 11/14/84. When Ellie Skinner, a loving housewife, fails to get other family members to assume household responsibilities, she pitches a tent on the front lawn and goes on strike against her family. The story relates the chaos that arises as Ellie walks a picket line and her near helpless family attempt to fend for themselves. An "ABC Afterschool Special." *Cast:* Mary Kay Place (Ellie Skinner), Stephen Keep (Michael Skinner), Yeardley Smith (Jenny), George Gaynes (The Commander), Jenny Rebecca Dwier (Marcia), Jonathan Ward (Ben), Timmy Geissler (Jack), Lauren Tom (Sarah), Jean Debaer (Tiffany), Jere Burns (Hal). *Producer:* Diana Kerew. *Writer:* Judy Engles. *Director:* Joan Darling.

**Mondo Beyondo** see **Bette Midler's Mondo Beyondo**

**1369 Monsanto Night Specials.** A chronological listing of the variety specials sponsored by the Monsanto Corporation. All are 60 minutes in length and syndicated.

**1 Monsanto Presents Mancini** (3/71). *Host:* Henry Mancini. *Guests:* Roberta Flack, Elton John, Johnny Mathis, Andy Williams, Meredith Wilson. *Music:* Henry Mancini. *Producer-Writer-Director:* Art Fisher.

**2 Monsanto Presents Mancini** (8/71). *Host:* Henry Mancini. *Guests:* Jose Feliciano, Rosey Grier, Claudine Longet, Nancy Wilson. *Music:* Henry Mancini. *Producer-Writer-Director:* Art Fisher.

**3 Monsanto Presents Mancini** (12/71). *Host:* Henry Mancini. *Guests:* Hoagy Carmichael, Bing Crosby, Michael Landon, Sergio Mendes and Brasil '77, Carla Thomas. *Music:* Henry Mancini. *Producer-Writer-Director:* Art Fisher.

**4 Monsanto Night Presents Burl Ives** (6/72). *Host:* Burl Ives. *Guests:* Jimmy Durante, The Golddiggers, Roger Miller. *Producer:* Jack Sobel. *Director:* Clark Jones.

**5 Monsanto Night Presents Jose Feliciano** (12/72). *Host:* Jose Feliciano. *Guests:* Carol Lawrence, The Mike Curb Congregation. *Producer:* Jack Sobel. *Director:* Clark Jones.

**6 Monsanto Night Presents Robert Goulet and Carol Lawrence** (11/73). *Hosts:* Robert Goulet, Carol Lawrence. *Producer:* Jack Sobel. *Writer:* Ron Friedman. *Director:* Clark Jones.

**1370 Monte Carlo, C'est La Rose.** Variety, 60 min., ABC, 3/6/68. A musical tour of the principality of

Monaco. *Host:* Princess Grace. *Guests:* Gilbert Becaud, The David Winters Dancers, Terry-Thomas. *Producers:* Jack Haley, Jr., Roger Gimbel. *Writers:* Frank Peppiatt, John Aylesworth. *Director:* Michael Pfleghar.

## 1371 Monteith and Rand.

Comedy, 60 min., Showtime, 10/79. The comedy team of Monteith and Rand star in a special sparked by the duo's original skits, sketches, and improvisational comedy. Taped at the Ed Sullivan Theater in New York. *Hosts:* John Monteith, Suzanne Rand. *Producer:* James Lipton.

## 1372 Monty Hall's Variety Hour. 

Variety, 60 min., ABC, 8/7/76. An hour of music, songs, and comedy with the host of the television game show "Let's Make a Deal." *Host:* Monty Hall. *Guests:* Edward Asner, Cloris Leachman, Minnie Ripperton, Robert Shields and Lorene Yarnell. *Music:* David Rose. *Producers:* Bill Hobin, Jack Weston, Ken Shapiro. *Writers:* Ken Shapiro, Fred S. Fox, Seaman Jacobs, Arthur Phillips, Alan Metter, Charles Isaacs. *Director:* Bill Hobin.

## 1373 The Moon and Sixpence. 

Drama, 90 min., NBC, 10/30/59. The story of Charles Strickland, an aging stockbroker who deserts his family to pursue a career as an artist. Based on the 1925 novel by William Somerset Maugham. The novel was first adapted to television via "The Somerset Maugham Theater" on April 30, 1951, with Lee J. Cobb and Olive Deering as Charles and Amy Strickland. *Cast:* Sir Laurence Olivier (Charles Strickland), Geraldine Fitzgerald (Amy Strickland), Judith Anderson (Tiare), Hume Cronyn (Dirk Stroeve), Jessica Tandy (Blanche Stroeve), Jean Marsh (Ata), Cyril Cusak (Dr. Coutras), Murray Matheson (MacAndrew), Denholm Elliott (Writer). *Producer-Director:* Robert Mulligan. *Writer:* S. Lee Pogostin.

## More of the Best of the Hollywood Palace *see* The Best of the Hollywood Palace

## 1374 The Morey Amsterdam Show. 

Variety, 2 hrs., CBS, 12/31/48. A music and comedy celebration to welcome in the new year (1949). *Host:* Morey Amsterdam. *Guests:* Carole Coleman, Dorothy Collins, Danny Daniels, Larry Douglas, The Tally Beatty Dancers, The Three Stooges. *Music:* Raymond Scott. *Producers:* Barry Wood, Paul Feegay. *Director:* Kingman T. Moore.

## 1375 The Mort Sahl Special. 

Variety, 60 min., NBC, 1/22/60. Performances by established artists and new talent discoveries. *Hosts:* Eddie Cantor, Mort Sahl. *Guests:* Vicki Bennet, Marc Breaux, The Buzz Miller Dancers, Norman and Dean, Swen Swenson, Frankie Vaughn. *Music:* Peter Matz. *Choreography:* Bob Hurget.

## 1376 The Moscow Circus. 

Variety, 60 min., ABC, 12/18/88. Highlights of the Moscow Circus, which was on tour in the United States at the time of taping. *Host:* Mark-Linn Baker. *Producers:* Joseph Cates, Scott Sanders. *Writer:* Frank Slocum. *Director:* Joseph Cates.

## 1377 Motown Merry Christmas. 

Variety, 60 min., NBC, 12/14/87. A program of Christmas music and songs presented in the Motown music style. *Host:* Philip Michael Thomas. *Guests:* Natalie Cole, Desiree Coleman, Lola Falana, Redd Foxx, Darlene Love, Carrie McDowell, Stephanie Mills, The Pointer Sisters, Smokey Robinson, Ronnie Spector, The Temptations, Marsha Warfield. *Music:* Howard Wheeler. *Producers:* Suzanne de Passe, Susan Coston, Lee Miller. *Writers:* Stephen Pouliot, Rita Cash. *Director:* Jeff Margolis.

**1378 Motown 30: What's Going On?** Variety, 2 hrs., CBS, 11/26/90. A celebration of the Motown sound and music and the artistry of African-American performers. *Guests:* Debbie Allen, Michael Bolton, Tracy Chapman, The Four Tops, Marla Gibbs, Gladys Knight, Patti LaBelle, Dawnn Lewis, Smokey Robinson, Sinbad, Meshach Taylor, Denzel Washington, Damon Wayans, Keenen Ivory Wayans, Stevie Wonder. *Producers:* Suzanne de Passe, Don Mischer. *Writers:* Buz Kohan, Rita Cash, Suzanne de Passe. *Director:* Don Mischer.

**1379 A Mouse, a Mystery and Me.** Christmas, 30 min., NBC, 12/13/87. When a young boy (Stevie) witnesses the kidnapping of a department store Santa (Joey), he enlists the aid of his friend Jill, a mystery book writer, to find Santa. Jill—who ghostwrites for Alex, a detective mouse (animated)—takes the case and helps Stevie rescue Santa and expose the corrupt department store manager. *Cast:* Donald O'Connor (Voice of Alex), Dick Van Patten (Joey), Darcy Marta (Jill), Bobby Becken (Stevie), Lloyd Bochner (Sam Hill), Dinah Gaston (Amy). *Music:* Patricia Cullen. *Producers:* Joe Ruby, Ken Spears, Tony Allard. *Writers:* Harvey Bullock, Everett Greenbaum. *Director:* Randy Bradshaw.

**1380 The Mouse and the Motorcycle.** Fantasy, 30 min., ABC, 11/8 and 11/15/86. Ralph is a talkative mouse who lives in a hole in the wall at the Mountain View Inn. When a young boy named Keith and his family come to stay at the inn, Ralph becomes fascinated with Keith's toy motorcycle—so much so that he reveals himself to Keith. Keith allows Ralph to sit on the motorcycle. When Ralph makes sounds like a running car, the motorcycle begins to move. The story relates Ralph's adventures in and around the inn with the motorcycle. Before Keith leaves, he gives Ralph the shiny red motorcycle to keep as his own. Ralph appears in dimensional animation. The "ABC Weekend Special" is based on the book by Beverly Cleary. See also "Ralph S. Mouse" and "Runaway Ralph." *Cast:* Ray Walston (Matt), Mimi Kennedy (Mrs. Gridley), Philip Waller (Keith Gridley), John Byner (Man with dog), Helene Udy (Maid), Mary Jo Catlett (Woman). *Voices:* Evan Richards (Ralph), Zelda Rubinstein (Mother Mouse), Billy Barty (Uncle Lester), Keri Houlihan (Suzy). *Music:* David Mansfield. *Producer:* George McQuilkin. *Live Action Director:* Ron Underwood. *Animation Producer-Director:* John Matthews.

**1381 The Mouseketeers Reunion.** Variety, 60 min., NBC, 11/23/80. The program reunites 31 of the original "Mickey Mouse Club" Mouseketeers for an hour of song, dance, and reminiscences. *Host:* Paul Williams. *Mouseketeers:* Sherry Alberoni, Sharon Baird, Billie Jean Beanblossom, Bobby Burgess, Lonny Burr, Tommy Cole, Johnny Crawford, Dennis Day, Eileen Diamond, Dickie Dodd, Mary Espinosa, Bonni Lynn Fields, Annette Funicello, Darlene Gillespie, Judy Harriett, Cheryl Holdridge, Linda Hughes, Bonnie Lou Kern, Charley Laney, Larry Larsen, Cubby O'Brien, Karen Pendleton, Lynn Ready, Mickey Rooney, Jr., Tim Rooney, Mary Lou Sartori, Michael Smith, Ronnie Steiner, Margene Storey, Doreen Tracy, Don Underhill. *Music:* Peter Matz. *Producers:* Ron Miziker, Phil May. *Director:* Tom Trbovich.

**1382 The Movie Palaces.** Documentary, 30 min., PBS, 7/9/87. A nostalgic look at the history of the movie theater—the "palaces" of the 1920s and 1930s that were architectural treasures designed to showcase the films of the day. *Host-Narrator:* Gene

Kelly. *Guests:* Mary Bishop, Gaylord Carter, Charles Lee. *Producer:* Karen Loveland. *Writer-Director:* Lee R. Bobker.

## 1383 A Movie Star's Daughter. Drama, 60 min., ABC, 10/10/79.

An "ABC Afterschool Special" about Dena McKain, the pretty but shy daughter of a famous movie star (Hal McKain) and her experiences in a new school when she discovers that her new friends are accepting her only because she has a famous father. *Cast:* Trini Alvarado (Dena McKain), Frank Converse (Hal McKain), Marcia Rodd (Barbara McKain), Laura Dean (Alison), Alexa Kenin (Geri). *Music:* Brad Fiedel. *Producer:* Linda Gottlieb. *Director:* Robert Fuest.

## 1384 Movin' with Nancy.

Variety, 60 min., NBC, 12/12/67. A fast-paced musical tour of California. Also known as "The Nancy Sinatra Show." See also the following title. *Host:* Nancy Sinatra. *Guests:* The David Winters Dancers, Sammy Davis, Jr., Lee Hazelwood, Dean Martin, Frank Sinatra. *Music:* Billy Strange. *Producer-Director:* Jack Haley, Jr. *Writer:* Tom Mankiewicz.

## 1385 Movin' with Nancy on Stage. Variety, 60 min., CBS, 4/4/71.

A sequel to the prior title. Taped highlights of Nancy Sinatra's Las Vegas nightclub act. *Host:* Nancy Sinatra. *Guests:* The Osmond Brothers, Don Randi, Billy Strange. *Music Director:* Billy Strange. *Producers:* Robert H. Precht, Hugh Lambert. *Director:* John Moffitt.

## 1386 Mr. Broadway. Musical,

90 min., NBC, 5/11/57. A musical biography of George M. Cohan—actor, producer, playwright, songwriter, and dancer. The story focuses on his days in vaudeville when he, his mother, father, and sister performed as "The Four Cohans." *Cast:* Mickey Rooney (George

M. Cohan), James Dunn (Jerry Cohan), Roberta Sherwood (Ella Cohan), Gloria DeHaven (Josie Cohan), June Havoc (Trixie Friganza), Eddie Foy, Jr. (Joe Summerhalter), Robert Ellenstein (Sam Harris), Arny Freeman (Jerry Armstrong), Bobby Mariano (George as a boy), Patricia Mariano (Josie as a girl). *Narrator:* Garry Moore. *Music:* George Bassman. *Producer-Director:* Sidney Lumet. *Writers:* Sam Spewack, Bella Spewack.

## 1387 Mr. Dickens of London.

Drama, 60 min., ABC, 12/12/67. While alone in the London home of novelist Charles Dickens, a tour guide is stunned when the ghost of Dickens appears to her. When the spirit finds that so little of his beloved nineteenth century remains, he takes her (and viewers) through his books to compensate for the passing years. *Cast:* Michael Redgrave (Charles Dickens), Juliet Mills (Guide). *Producer:* Jules Power. *Writer:* Joseph Hurley. *Director:* Barry Morse.

## 1388 Mr. Halpern and Mr. Johnson. Drama, 60 min., HBO, 6/3/83.

The conversation between two elderly men who meet at the funeral of Florence Halpern—the wife of Mr. Halpern and the close friend of Mr. Johnson—two men who were unknown to each other and now gather to discuss their relationship with Florence. *Cast:* Laurence Olivier (Joseph Halpern), Jackie Gleason (Ernest Johnson). *Producers:* Mort Abrahams, Edie Landeau, Ely Landeau. *Writer:* Lionel Goldstein. *Director:* Alvin Rakoff.

## 1389 Mr. Mergenthwirker's Lobblies. Comedy-Mystery, 75 min.,

NBC, 9/22/46. Mr. Mergenthwirker is a reporter for a small-town newspaper, and he is assisted by a group of invisible pixies who appear and speak only to him. The pixies, who appear to Mr. Mergenthwirker because he is pure of heart, help him solve a series of murders in a three-act whodunit. *Cast:* Vaughn Taylor (Mr. Mergenthwirker), Vinton Hayworth (Editor), John McQuade (Legman), Maurice Manson (Publisher), Philip Robinson (Photographer), Patricia Shay (Staffer). *Also:* Everett Gammon, Frank Harris, Robert Lieb, Ed Mannery, Jack Sloane. *Producers:* Fred Coe, Howard Cordery. *Writers:* Nelson Bond, David Kent. *Director:* Fred Coe.

**1390 Mr. Porter of Indiana.** Variety, 60 min., ABC, 8/17/60. An hour of music and songs with Cole Porter and his guests. *Host:* Cole Porter. *Guests:* Dick Haymes, Heidi Krall, June Valli. *Music Director:* Glenn Osser.

**1391 Mr. Roberts.** Comedy, 2 hrs. 10 min., NBC, 3/19/84. A live television adaptation of the stage play by Thomas Heggen and Joshua Logan. The story, set aboard the U.S. Navy cargo ship *Reluctant* during World War II, follows the efforts of Lieutenant Douglas Roberts as he tries to convince his mean-spirited skipper to transfer him to combat duty. *Cast:* Robert Hays (Lt. Douglas Roberts), Charles Durning (Captain), Howard Hesseman (Doc), Kevin Bacon (Ensign Pulver), Marilu Henner (Nurse Girard), Charley Lang (Dolan), Joe Pantoliano (Insigna), Tyler Tyhurst (Mannion), Bruce Wright (Wiley), John Walcutt (Lindstrom). *Producers:* David Rintels, Paul Waigner. *Director:* Melvin Bernhardt.

**1392 Mrs. Miniver.** Drama, 90 min., CBS, 1/7/60. A television adaptation of the novel by Jan Struther about the effects of World War II on the Minivers, a family of five who live in a small English town. *Cast:* Maureen O'Hara (Mrs. Miniver), Leo Genn (Clem Miniver), Paul Roebling (Vin Miniver), Peter Lazer (Toby Miniver), Joan Terrace (Judy Miniver), Cathleen Nesbitt (Lady Beldon), Juliet Mills (Carol Beldon), Ian Martin (Mr. Ballard), Beulah Garrick (Gladys), George Turner (Mr. Foley), Ronald Long (Vicar). *Producer:* David Susskind. *Writer:* George Baxt. *Director:* Marc Daniels.

**1393 MTV: Music Television's 10th Anniversary.** Tribute, 60 min., ABC, 11/27/91. A salute (by ABC) to cable television's MTV station on the occasion of its tenth anniversary on the air. *Hosts:* Kim Basinger, Cher, Tom Cruise, Mel Gibson, Spike Lee. *Guests:* Aerosmith, Michael Jackson, Madonna, George Michael, R. E. M. *Producers:* Doug Herzog, Judy McGrath, Joel Gallen.

**1394 The Muhammad Ali Variety Special.** Variety, 60 min., ABC, 9/13/75. World heavyweight boxing champion Muhammad Ali hosts a program of celebrity performances and appearances by former sports greats. *Host:* Muhammad Ali. *Guests:* The Captain and Tennille, Howard Cosell, Aretha Franklin, Gabe Kaplan, Betty White, Flip Wilson. *Sports Guests:* Henry Armstrong, Carmen Basillo, Billy Conn, Jackie Fields (boxers), Don Budge, Pancho Gonzales, Aletha Gibson, Nancy Chaffee Kiner, Gussie Morgan (tennis stars), Jim Brown, Tom Harmon, Sid Luckman (football stars), Buster Crabbe (Olympic swimmer), Satchel Paige (baseball star), Florence Chadwick (swam the English Channel), Mel Patton (Olympic track team), Sammy Lee, Patty McCormick (diving champs). *Music:* J. J. Johnson. *Producers:* Clarence Avant, Bob Finkel. *Writers:* Herbert Baker, Bob Finkel. *Director:* Stan Lathan.

**1395 Muhammad Ali's 50th Birthday Celebration.** Variety, 2 hrs., ABC, 3/1/92. A benefit for the United Negro College Fund, coupled with an all-star birthday celebration for boxer Muhammad Ali on the occasion of his fiftieth birthday. Taped at the Wiltern Theater in Los Angeles. *Guest of Honor:* Muhammad Ali. *Guests:* Dan Aykroyd, Howard Cosell, Billy Crystal, Tony Danza, Ella Fitzgerald, The Four Tops, Dustin Hoffman, Whitney Houston, Magic Johnson, Little Richard, The Pointer Sisters, Raven-Samone, Diana Ross, Arnold Schwarzenegger, Sinbad, Sylvester Stallone, Blair Underwood. *Producer:* George Schlatter. *Writer:* Buz Kohan. *Director:* Louis J. Horvitz.

### 1396 A Muppet Family Christmas. Variety, 60 min., ABC, 12/16/87. Jim Henson's Muppet creations from "Sesame Street" and "Fraggle Rock" gather at Fozzie's house for an hour of Christmas music, songs, and comedy. *Cast:* Gerry Parkes (Doc), Carroll Spinney (Big Bird). *Muppet Voices:* Dave Goelz, Jim Henson, Jerry Juhl, Jerry Nelson, Frank Oz, Karen Prell. *Music:* Eric Robertson. *Producers:* Jim Henson, Diana Birkenfield, Martin G. Baker. *Writer:* Jerry Juhl. *Director:* Peter Harris.

### 1397 The Muppets: A Celebration of 30 Years. Variety, 60 min., CBS, 1/21/86. A thirtieth anniversary celebration of Jim Henson's Muppets. Includes clips from the Muppet movies and television shows (including "Sam and Friends," a local program that first brought the Muppets to television in 1956). *Host:* Kermit the Frog (voice of Jim Henson). *Music:* Jon Charles, (The Other) Ray Charles. *Producer:* Andrew Solt. *Writer:* Jerry Juhl. *Director:* Peter Harris.

### 1398 The Muppets at Walt Disney World. Variety, 60 min., NBC, 5/6/90. While attending a Frog Festival, the Muppets decide to take a break and see Walt Disney World. The story relates the efforts of a security guard (Charles Grodin) to find the Muppets and get them back to the festi-

val. *Guests:* Charles Grodin, Raven-Samone. *Muppet Voices:* Dave Goelz, Jim Henson, Richard Hunt, Jerry Nelson, Frank Oz, Steve Whitmire. *Music:* Phil Ramone. *Writers:* Jim Henson, Diana Birkenfield, Martin G. Baker. *Director:* Peter Harris.

### 1399 The Muppets Celebrate Jim Henson. Tribute, 60 min., CBS, 11/21/90. A tribute to the memory of Jim Henson by his creations, the Muppets. *Guests:* Harry Belafonte, Carol Burnett, John Denver, Frank Oz, Steven Spielberg. *Muppet Performers:* Kevin Clash, Kathy Cullen, Dave Goelz, Richard Hunt, Jerry Nelson, Frank Oz, Carroll Spinney, Steve Whitmire. *Music:* Larry Grossman. *Producers:* Don Mischer, Martin G. Baker, David J. Goldberg. *Writers:* Jerry Juhl, Sara Luckinson, Bill Prady. *Director:* Don Mischer.

### 1400 The Muppets Go to the Movies. Comedy, 60 min., ABC, 5/20/81. A re-creation of the Muppets' favorite moments from various films. *Guests:* Dudley Moore, Lily Tomlin. *Host:* Kermit the Frog (voice of Jim Henson). *Music:* Larry Grossman. *Producers:* Jim Henson, David Lazar. *Writers:* Jerry Juhl, Chris Langan. *Director:* Peter Harris.

### 1401 Murder at NBC (A Bob Hope Special). Comedy, 60 min., NBC, 10/19/66. A departure from Bob Hope's usual variety format wherein Bob plays a mad scientist who invents a nuclear chemical that is capable of shrinking the United States. *Host/Dr. Van Smirtch:* Bob Hope. *Guests:* Don Adams, Milton Berle, Red Buttons, Johnny Carson, Jack Carter, Bill Cosby, Wally Cox, Jimmy Durante, Dick Martin, Don Rickles, Soupy Sales, Dick Shawn, Jonathan Winters. *Music Director:* Les Brown.

### 1402 Murder Is a One-Act Play. Thriller, 90 min., ABC, 5/21/74.

The story of a psychopath who taunts the cast members of his favorite television soap opera. Also known as "Death of Sister Mary." *Cast:* Robert Powell (Rook), Jennie Linden (Sister Mary), George Maharis (Mark), Joan Hawthorne (Mother Superior), Anthony Newlands (Tony), Windsor Davies (Detective Moore). *Music:* Laurie Johnson. *Producer:* Cecil Clarke. *Writer:* Brian Clemens. *Director:* Robert D. Cardona.

**1403 Murder Motel.** Thriller, 90 min., ABC, 5/26/75. The story of a brother and sister, fleeing with stolen money, who find the perfect refuge—in a hotel that caters to murder. *Cast:* Robyn Millan (Kathy), Ralph Bates (Mike Spencer), Anne Rutter (Helen), Patrick Tull (Terry), Roscoe Hallam (John), June Watson (Petra). *Music:* Laurie Johnson. *Producers:* Cecil Clarke, Ian Fordyce. *Writer:* Brian Clemens. *Director:* Malcolm Taylor.

**1404 Murder on the Midnight Express.** Thriller, 90 min., ABC, 1/7/75. The story of Helen Marlow, a young American girl who innocently becomes involved in a spy plot during a train journey through England. Also known as "Night Is the Time for Killing." *Cast:* Judy Geeson (Helen Marlow), James Smillie (Bob Mallory), Charles Grey (Hillary Vance), Milos Kivek (Ivan Malov), Alister Williams (Barkly). *Music:* Laurie Johnson. *Producers:* Cecil Clarke, John Cooper. *Writer:* Brian Clemens. *Director:* John Cooper.

**1405 Music by Cole Porter.** Variety, 60 min., NBC, 11/25/65. A tribute to Cole Porter and his music. *Guests:* Nancy Ames, Maurice Chevalier, The Dick Williams Singers, Robert Goulet. *Music Director:* Nick Perito.

**1406 Music City News Top Country Hits of the Year.** Variety, 2 hrs., Syndicated, 8/81. A presentation of the top 15 country and western hits of 1980 (according to a poll by the *Music City News*). *Hosts:* Jim Stafford, Tanya Tucker. *Guests:* Rex Allen, Jr., Chet Atkins, Roger Bowling, Christy Chase, Lacey J. Dalton, Mickey Gilley, Tom T. Hall, George Jones, Johnny Lee, Eddie Rabbitt, The Statler Brothers, Conway Twitty, Don Williams, Tammy Wynette. *Music:* Bill Walker. *Producers:* Walter Barrett, Steve Womack, Jim Owens. *Writers:* Bill and Pat Galvin. *Director:* Lee H. Bernardi.

**1407 Music in the Mississippi Mood.** Variety, 60 min., Syndicated, 4/82. A tuneful cruise down the Mississippi River aboard the steamboat *Mississippi Queen*. *Host:* Glen Campbell. *Guests:* Rita Coolidge, John Hartford, Arte Johnson, Sonny Terry and Brownie McGhee, Tanya Tucker.

**1408 The Music Makers: An ASCAP Celebration of American Music.** Variety, 90 min., PBS, 10/16/87. A salute to the American Society of Composers, Authors, and Publishers (ASCAP) with performances of the society's most beloved songs. *Performers:* Patti Austin, Tony Bennett, Gary Chryst, Glen Close, Judy Collins, Robert Guillaume, Marvin Hamlisch, Richie Havens, Henry Mancini, The Oak Ridge Boys, Jeffrey Osborne, Bernadette Peters, Melinda Roy, Randy Travis, Andy Williams, Peter Yarrow. *Music:* Ian Fraser. *Producers:* Jack Venza, Alan Bergman, Marilyn Bergman. *Writer:* Frank Slocum. *Director:* Phillip Byrd.

**1409 The Music of Gershwin.** Variety, 90 min., NBC, 5/12/56. A musical salute to composer George Gershwin. *Performers:* Toni Arden, The Art Van Damme Quintet, The Ballerinas Diana, Tony Bennett, The Bob Hamilton Trio, Peter Conlow, Alfred Drake, Richard Hayman, Eugene List,

Robert Maxwell, Ethel Merman, Harrison Muller, Patricia Wilde. *Music:* Charles Sanford. *Producers:* Max Liebman, Bill Hobin. *Director:* Max Liebman.

## 1410  The Music of Your Life.

Variety, 60 min., Syndicated, 2/85. An entertaining program that recalls memorable songs from the past. *Host:* Toni Tennille. *Guests:* Andy Gibb, Johnny Mathis, Donald O'Connor, Patti Page. *Music:* Joey Carbone. *Theme Vocalist,* "The Music of Your Life": Toni Tennille. *Theme Writer:* Barry Manilow. *Producers:* Bob Banner, Stephen Pouliot. *Writers:* Jeffrey Barron, Stephen Pouliot. *Director:* Kip Walton.

## 1411  Music with Mary Martin. Variety, 60 min., NBC, 3/29/54.

An hour of music and songs. The second of two specials to feature Mary Martin and broadcast in a single day. See also "Magic with Mary Martin." *Host:* Mary Martin. *Music:* John Lesko. *Producer:* Richard Halliday. *Writer:* Mary Rodgers. *Director:* Vincent J. Donehue.

## 1412  Musical Comedy Tonight. Variety, 90 min., PBS, 2/11/81.

Hit numbers from Broadway plays are restaged via four plays from *Finian's Rainbow* (1947), *South Pacific* (1949), *Sweet Charity* (1966), and *Lady in the Dark* (1941). *Host:* Sylvia Fine Kaye. *Guests:* Annette Charles, Richard Crenna, Nancy Dussault, Sergio Franchi, Bonnie Franklin, Danny Kaye, Burton Lane, Jack Lemmon, Joshua Logan, Juliet Prowse, Lynn Redgrave, Larry Storch. *Music:* Peter Matz. *Producer-Writer:* Sylvia Fine Kaye. *Director:* Tony Charmoli.

## 1413  Musical Comedy Tonight. Variety, 90 min., PBS, 11/22/85. Guest artists re-create great moments from Broadway plays. *Host:*

Sylvia Fine Kaye. *Guests:* Eddie Albert, Christine Andreas, Gregg Burge, Florence Henderson, Patti LaBelle, Donna McKechnie, Roberta Peters, Dick Van Dyke. *Music:* Peter Matz. *Producer-Writer:* Sylvia Fine Kaye. *Director:* Stan Harris.

## 1414  My Dad Can't Be Crazy, Can He? Drama, 60 min., ABC, 9/14/89. An "ABC Afterschool Special" about schizophrenia that focuses on Nick Karpinsky, a high school sophomore who is trying to cope with the increasingly bizarre behavior of his father (Jack). *Cast:* Loretta Swit (Wanda Karpinsky), Don Murray (Jack Karpinsky), Will Wheaton (Nick Karpinsky), Christian Jacobs (Danny), Sadie Kratzig (Lois), Judith Jones (Karen), Fran Bennett (Nurse Etting). *Music:* Earl Rose. *Producers:* Joanna Lee, Karen S. Shapiro. *Writer-Director:* Joanna Lee.

## 1415  My  Dad  Lives  in  a Downtown  Hotel. Drama, 60 min., ABC, 11/28/73. The impact of divorce on an innocent victim: the child (Joey Grant) who cannot comprehend why his parents (Joe and June) are permanently separating. An "ABC Afterschool Special." *Cast:* Beau Bridges (Joe Grant), Margaret Blye (June Grant), Ike Eisenmann (Joey Grant), Diane Civita (Receptionist), Claudio Martinez (Bobby), Betty Bresler (Lady on Bus), Dermott Downs (Tommy). *Producer:* Gerald I. Isenberg. *Writers:* Stephen Karpf, Elinor Karpf. *Director:* Jeremy Kagan.

## 1416  My  Dear  Uncle  Sherlock. Comedy, 30 min., ABC, 4/16/77. When the police arrest the wrong man for the robbery of a wealthy, old recluse, Joey Trimble, a 12-year-old boy who has developed powers of deductive reasoning playing Sherlock Holmes with his uncle, decides to set matters straight. The story relates his efforts as

he teams with his uncle "Sherlock" George to find the real culprit. Aired as an "ABC Weekend Special." *Cast:* Robbie Rist (Joey Trimble), Royal Dano (Uncle George), John Karlen (Bill Leggett), Vaughn Armstrong (Officer Gilligan), Inga Swenson (Mrs. Trimble), John Carter (Mr. Trimble). *Producers:* Allen Ducovny, William Beaudine, Jr. *Writer:* Manya Starr. *Director:* Arthur H. Nadel.

## 1417 My Dissident Mom.
Drama, 60 min., CBS, 1/14/87. A "CBS Schoolbreak Special" about Kathy Sanders, a discontented housewife who finds a new meaning to life when she undertakes a cause — demonstrating against a nuclear weapons company. *Cast:* Annie Potts (Kathy Sanders), Martin Sheen (Joe Sanders), Alexandra Powers (Laura), Lukas Haas (Mike), John Randolph (General Norman), Paula Irvine (Liz). *Producers:* Sally Hill, Barry Dantscher. *Writer:* Barry Dantzscher. *Director:* Matt Clark.

## 1418 My Father the Clown.
Drama, 30 min., Syndicated, 10/87. A tender story that focuses on a teenage girl (Amy), embarrassed by her father's profession as a circus clown, as she struggles to understand and communicate with him. *Cast:* Kim Hauser (Amy Fisher), Bob Marvin (Robert Fisher), Jennifer Rudin (Amy's mother), Kara Riemann (Jill), Frances Hecht (Gretchen), Eugene Oakes (Tom Miller). *Producers:* Tom G. Robertson, Gene McPherson. *Writer-Director:* Gene McPherson.

## 1419 My First Swedish Bombshell.
Comedy, 30 min., Syndicated, 11/85. The story of an awkward 14-year-old boy (Harry) and his attempts to impress Ingrid, a beautiful Swedish exchange student, who will be living with his family for the summer. *Cast:* Cheryl Arutt (Ingrid), Jonathan Marc Sherman (Harry), Hilary Matthews

(Laura), Manny Jacobs (Harry's father), Jeanna Michaels (Harry's mother). *Music:* Steve Hoskins, Rob Reider. *Producers:* Tom G. Robertson, Gene McPherson. *Writer:* Steve Spiegel. *Director:* Gene McPherson.

## 1420 My Mom's Having a Baby.
Drama, 60 min., ABC, 2/16/77. A friendly pediatrician (Dr. Lendon Smith) helps nine-year-old Petey Evans, whose mother is pregnant, and his two friends (Kelly and Oscar) to understand the facts of human reproduction. The "ABC Afterschool Special" features the birth of an actual baby — the child of Candace Farrell, who plays Petey's mother. *Cast:* Dr. Lendon Smith (Himself), Shane Sinutko (Petey Evans), Rachel Longaker (Kelly), Jarrod Johnson (Oscar), Candace Farrell (Anne Evans), Ed Rombola (Petey's father), Karen Glow Carr (Nurse), Dodo Denney (Receptionist). *Music:* Dean Elliott. *Producers:* David H. DePatie, Friz Freleng. *Writers:* Susan Fichter Kennedy, Elaine Evans Rushnell. *Director:* Larry Elikann.

## 1421 My Mother Was Never a Kid.
Drama, 60 min., ABC, 3/18/81. Victoria Martin, a pretty high school girl with a knack for finding trouble, believes no one understands her (that she just happens to be there when things happen), especially her superperfect mother (Felicia) — a woman Victoria contends was never a kid. One day, when she is sent home for smoking on school grounds, Victoria has an argument with her mother and storms out of the house. While riding a New York subway train to a friend's house, Victoria falls and hits her head. Upon awakening she discovers that she has been sent back in time to the 1940s. As she leaves the subway station, she meets and befriends a young girl her own age — a girl she discovers is always in trouble, always complaining that adults do not understand her — and that

this michievous girl named Cici is actually the girl who will grow up to be her mother! The charming story relates Victoria's adventures in the 1940s — and when she again falls and is sent back to 1981, her understanding that perhaps her mother has been right and she has been at fault. An "ABC Afterschool Special." *Cast:* Mary-Beth Manning (Victoria Martin), Holland Taylor (Felicia Martin), Rachel Longaker (Felicia as a teenager), Elizabeth Ward (Nina Martin), Jane Lowry (Esther Drew), Gale Myron (Steffi), Judith Grimley (Betty). *Music:* Brad Fiedel. *Producers:* Linda Gottlieb, Doro Bachrach. *Writer:* Jeffrey Kindley. *Director:* Robert Fuest.

## My Name Is Barbra *see* Barbra Streisand Specials

### 1422 My Past Is My Own.
Drama, 60 min., CBS, 1/24/89. A "CBS Schoolbreak Special" about two black teenagers who are transported back in time to the 1960s to experience first hand racial prejudice in a small Georgia town. *Cast:* Whoopi Goldberg (Mariah Johnston), Allison Dean (Kerry), Phil Lewis (Justin), C. C. H. Pounder (Renee), Thalmus Rasulala (Marshall), William Allen Young (the Reverend Jordan), Geoffrey Blake (Dexter), Gloria Carlin (Frances), Laurena Wilerson (Brianne). *Music:* Joe Sample, Steve Tyrrell. *Producers:* Bradley Wigor, Joseph Mauer. *Writer:* Alan Gansburg. *Director:* Helaine Head.

### 1423 My Three Angels. Comedy, 90 min., NBC, 12/8/59. While repairing the roof of shopkeeper Felix Ducotel's home on Christmas Eve, three convicts overhear that the family is facing several crises. The story relates the efforts of the convicts (Alfred, Jules, and Joseph) to resolve the Ducotels' problems so they may have a merry Christmas. *Cast:* Walter Slezak (Joseph), Barry Sullivan (Jules), George

Grizzard (Alfred), Henry Daniell (Henri Ducotel), Carmen Matthews (Emily Ducotel), Will Kuluva (Felix Ducotel), Diana Millay (Mary Louise Ducotel). *Producers:* Hubbell Robinson, Bretaigne Windust. *Writers:* Sam Spewack, Bella Spewack. *Directors:* Bretaigne Windust, Gordon Rigsby.

### 1424 Mystery at Fire Island.
Mystery, 60 min., CBS, 11/27/81. While vacationing at a beachfront retreat on New York's Fire Island, a young girl (Dash) and her cousin (Jess) hear unconfirmed reports that their friend, Mike, an old angler, is missing and asumed to have drowned. Unconvinced about the police reports on the expert fisherman, the 12-year-old sleuths set out to find Mike. A "CBS Mystery Theater" presentation. *Cast:* Beth Ehlers (Dash Littlewood), Eric Gurry (Jess), Barbara Bryne (Blanche Guizot), Frank Converse (Dan Alexander), Edward Seaman (Mike O'Brien), Jamey Sheridan (George), Ken Walsh (Sergeant Hawkins), Daniel Keyes (Mr. Thompson). *Music:* Richard Peaslee. *Producers:* James Startz, Doro Bachrach. *Writers:* Carolyn Miller, Daryl Warner. *Director:* Robert Fuest.

### 1425 Nadia — From Romania with Love. Variety, 60 min., CBS, 11/23/76. A behind-the-scenes look at Nadia Comaneci in the first entertainment coproduction between the United States and Romania. *Host:* Flip Wilson. *Star:* Nadia Comaneci. *Music:* Everett Gordon. *Producers:* Dick Foster, Monte Kay. *Writers:* Tom Egan, Dumitru Udrescu. *Directors:* Dick Foster, Sterling Johnson.

### 1426 Nags. Drama, 30 min., Syndicated, 5/87. The story of a teenage girl (Cindy) and her efforts to get her father to stop smoking cigarettes. *Cast:* Lara Jill Miller (Cindy Hughes), Joe Hamer (Mr. Hughes), Jenna Michaels (Mrs. Hughes), Corey Carrier (Martin), Jim Matthews (Doctor). *Music:*

Steve Hoskins. *Producer-Writer-Director:* Gene McPherson.

**1427 Narc.** Drama, 30 min., Syndicated, 2/88. A very powerful drama about responsibility as seen through the experiences of a popular high school girl (Annie) who prevents the school's football captain from driving when drunk and is later shunned by her friends when he is suspended. The story focuses on Annie as she struggles to cope with the situation that results and about the doubts she has over whether or not she did the right thing. *Cast:* Talia Paul (Annie Merritt), Amy Locane (Karen), Todd Louiso (Jake). *Also:* Christie Budig, Bob Elkins, Carol Lorenz, Larry Schwartz. *Music:* Dennis Betz. *Producers:* Tom G. Robertson, Gene McPherson. *Writer-Director:* Gene McPherson.

**1428 The Nashville Palace.** Variety, 60 min., ABC, 10/25/80. Performances by country and western entertainers. *Host:* Roy Clark. *Guests:* Catherine Bach, Mickey Gilley, Andy Griffith, George Lindsey, Barbara Mandrell, The Oak Ridge Boys, Misty Rowe. *Announcer:* Slim Pickens. *Music:* Charlie McCoy. *Producer:* Sam Louvollo. *Writers:* Barry Adelman, John Aylesworth, Phil Hahn, Sheldon Keller. *Director:* Stan Harris.

**1429 Nashville Remembers Elvis on His Birthday.** Tribute, 90 min., NBC, 1/8/78. A salute to Elvis Presley on the occasion of his forty-third birthday. *Host:* Jimmy Dean. *Guests:* Chubby Checker, Larry Gatlin, Merle Haggard, The Jordanaires, Jerry Lee Lewis, Ronnie McDowell, Roy Orbison, Carl Perkins, Charlie Rich, Tanya Tucker, Dottie West. *Cameos:* Jack Albertson, Bill Bixby, Edith Head, Gary Lockwood, Mary Ann Mobley, Sheree North, Arthur O'Connell, Nancy Sinatra, Stella Stevens. *Music:* Bill Walker. *Producers:* Joseph Cates, Gilbert Cates.

*Writer:* Frank Slocum. *Director:* Ivan Cury.

**1430 The Nashville Sound of Boots Randolph.** Variety, 60 min., Syndicated, 3/71. A program of country and western music with singer Boots Randolph. *Host:* Boots Randolph. *Guests:* Pete Fountain, Jonah Jones, The Nashville Strings. *Music:* Bill Walker. *Producers:* Roy A. Smith, Bill Williams. *Writers:* Bill Wingard, Jim Carlson. *Director:* Tom Jacobson.

**1431 The Natalie Cole Special.** Variety, 60 min., CBS, 4/27/78. An hour of music and songs with Natalie Cole in her first television special. *Host:* Natalie Cole. *Guests:* Stephen Bishop, Earth, Wind and Fire, Johnny Mathis. *Music:* Nelson Riddle. *Producers:* Dick Clark, Kevin Hunter. *Writer:* Robert Arthur. *Director:* Tim Kiley.

**1432 National Kids' Quiz.** Quiz, 60 min., NBC, 1/28/78. Children, aged 8 to 13, are asked questions about themselves and their relationships with family and friends. *Host:* Michael Landon. *Producers:* Sonny Fox, Jane Norman, Jack Kuney. *Director:* Jack Kuney.

**1433 The National Love, Sex and Marriage Test.** Quiz, 90 min., NBC, 3/5/78. Home viewers are asked questions regarding male-female relationships. Celebrity guests appear and give their opinions. *Hosts:* Suzanne Somers, Tom Snyder. *Guests:* Marty Allen, Jim Backus, Phyllis Diller, Bonnie Franklin, George Gobel, Don Knotts, Ann Landers, Vicki Lawrence, Audra Lindley, Greg Mullavey, Lynn Redgrave, Della Reese, Barbara Rhoades, Joan Rivers, Misty Rowe, Debralee Scott, Abe Vigoda, Jo Anne Worley. *Producer:* Norman Sedawie. *Writers:* Ruben Carson, Michael Kagan, Norman Sedawie, Karyl Miller. *Director:* Joel Tator.

**1434 The National Memorial Day Concert.** Variety, 90 min., PBS, 5/27/90. A musical celebration of Memorial Day. *Host:* E. G. Marshall. *Guests:* Rosemary Clooney, Colleen Dewhurst, James Earl Jones. *Announcer:* Paul Anthony. *National Symphony Orchestra Conductor:* Erich Kunzel. *Producers:* Jerry Colbert, Walter C. Miller. *Director:* David Deutsch.

**1435 National Off the Wall People's Poll.** Comedy, 60 min., NBC, 11/24/84. A tongue-in-cheek salute to surveys with hilarious answers to outrageous questions. *Hosts:* Liberace, Sarah Purcell. *Guests:* Joan Collins, Vince Edwards, Tab Hunter, Peter Isacksen, Barry Manilow, Tiny Tim. *Announcer:* John Harlan. *Music:* Bill Royce. *Producer:* Woody Fraser.

**1436 The Nativity.** Christmas, 30 min., Syndicated, 12/82. Yuletide celebrations from Rome, London, and New York City are introduced by Princess Grace of Monaco (taped in July 1982). *Host:* Princess Grace of Monaco. *Guest:* Placido Domingo. *Narrator:* Cary Grant. *Music:* Robert Cornford. *Producer:* Frank O'Connor. *Writers:* James E. Mosher, Mike Sharkey. *Director:* Barry Chattington.

**1437 Naughty Marietta.** Comic Opera, 90 min., NBC, 1/15/55. Seeking to avoid an unwanted, prearranged marriage, Marietta D'Altena, an Italian countess, stows away aboard a ship bound for New Orleans. Before reaching her destination, the ship is seized by pirates. She is rescued by Dick Warrington, an American captain with whom she falls in love. Being content with a soldier's life, he wants nothing to do with marriage. Her efforts to change his mind are the focal point of the opera by Victor Herbert and Rida Johnson Young. *Cast:* Patrice Munsel (Marietta D'Altena), Alfred Drake (Dick Warrington), John Conte (Lieu-

tenant Governor Le Grange), Gale Sherwood (Yvonne), Don Driver (Louis D'Arc), Robert Gallagher (Ship captain), William LeMessena (Rudolfo). *Music:* Charles Sanford. *Producers:* Max Liebman, Bill Hobin. *Writers:* Neil Simon, Will Glickman, William Friedberg. *Director:* Max Liebman.

**1438 Naughty Negligee Nights.** Variety, 60 min., Unaired (Produced in 1987). The program, set in a nightclub, features eight negligee-clad girls stripping, then performing a specialty dance. The audience votes for the best dancer. The girls, credited only by a first name are: Greta, LeAnna, Natalie, Stephanie, Vanity (not the singer-actress), Chris, Venus, and Twalia. *Host:* Bobby Gaylir. *Guest:* Vic Dunlop. *Producers:* Ron Le Vanson, Anthony Christopher. *Director:* Mark Wolfson.

**1439 The NBC All-Star Hour.** Variety, 60 min., NBC, 9/16/85. A preview of NBC's fall 1985 schedule with its stars introducing clips from the programs. *Guests:* Bea Arthur, Robert Blake, Thom Bray, Nell Carter, Bill Cosby, Ted Danson, Michael J. Fox, Soleil Moon Frye, Erin Gray, David Hasselhoff, Joel Higgins, Bob Hope, Don Johnson, Betty Kennedy, Perry King, David Letterman, Patricia McPherson, Richard Moll, Joe Penny, George Peppard, Rhea Perlman, Charlotte Rae, Rick Schroder, Lisa Whelchel. *Music:* Bob Rozario. *Producer:* Peter Calabrese. *Writers:* Doug Steckler, Ken Welch, Mitzie Welch, Mason Williams. *Director:* Don Mischer.

**1440 NBC All-Star Stay in School Jam.** Variety, 30 min., NBC, TNT, Nickelodeon, 2/9/91. A three-network simulcast from the Charlotte, North Carolina, Coliseum, where 20,000 Charlotte area public school students from grades four through nine are honored by celebrities for maintaining perfect attendance records. *Hosts:* Marv Albert, Bob Costas, Julie

Bob appears before a congressional committee of comedians. The big question is— What did Bob know and when did he ad-lib it?

**TOP SECRET GUESTS**
in surprise cameo appearances.

Scheduled to appear:

**Tony Randall    Milton Berle    Danny Thomas    Jack Carter    Elyse Hall as Fawn Dawn**

**ALL-NEW ALL-STAR SPECIAL!**
**8:30PM WNBC-TV4**

Ad for "NBC Investigates Bob Hope"

Moran, Ahmad Rashad, Pat Riley. *Guests:* Mayim Bialik, Tempestt Bledsoe, The Boys and Heavy D, Michael Jordan, Kid 'n' Play, Curley Neal, Will Smith.

## 1441 The NBC Family Christmas Party. Variety, 60 min., NBC, 12/13/82. Cast members from various NBC series gather for a celebration of Christmas. *Performers:* Debbie Allen, Ed Begley, Jr., Ken Berry, David Birney, Meredith Baxter Birney, Tauren Blacque, Barbara Bosson, Dean Butler, Nell Carter, Nicholas Colasanto, Gary Coleman, Lee Curreri, Ted Danson, Tony Danza, Danny DeVito, Rene Enriquez, Erik Estrada, Norman Fell,

Melissa Gilbert, Anita Gillette, Erin Gray, Charles Haid, David Hasselhoff, Joel Higgins, Geri Jewell, Kaleena Kiff, Valerie Landsburg, Howie Mandel, Vicki Lawrence, Ketty Lester, Shelley Long, Peter Marshall, Keil Martin, Edward Mulhare, Rhea Perlman, Charlotte Rae, Lynn Redgrave, Mark Russell, Ricky Schroder, James Sikking, Lori Singer, Morgan Stevens, Leslie Uggams, George Wendt, Tina Yothers. *Special Guest:* George Burns. *Music:* Jack Elliott. *Producer:* Robert H. Precht. *Writer:* Bob Arnott. *Director:* Walter C. Miller.

## 1442 NBC Follies of 1965. Variety, 60 min., NBC, 11/27/64. An all-star musical comedy revue. *Host:* Steve Lawrence. *Guests:* The Bitter End Singers, Nipsey Russell, Jill St. John, Allan Sherman. *Producer:* George Schlatter. *Writers:* Arnie Rosen, Coleman Jacoby. *Director:* Sid Smith.

## 1443 NBC Investigates Bob Hope. Comedy, 60 min., NBC, 9/17/87. A departure from the usual Bob Hope specials, this program spoofs the Iran-Contra Hearings, Colonel Oliver North, and his secretary, Fawn Hall. As he begins his fiftieth year with NBC, Bob is accused of biting the network hand that feeds him by selling his jokes to cable television, diverting funds, and, with his secretary, Fawn Dawn, shredding the evidence. The program

then goes to the hearings room where Bob is cross-examined by the Network Committee. *Cast:* Bob Hope (Himself), Tony Randall (Mr. LaTort), Milton Berle (Mr. Fox), Jack Carter (Mr. Perret), Danny Thomas (Mr. Mills), Elyse Hall (Fawn Dawn), Peter Leeds (Mr. Leeds). *Guests:* Army Archerd, George Burns, Phil Donahue, Fred Dryer, Stepfanie Kramer, Michael Landon, Louis Nye, Gary Owens, Tom Selleck, Brandon Tartikoff. *Announcer:* John Harlan. *Music:* Les Brown. *Producers:* Bob Hope, Elliott Kozak. *Writers:* Fred S. Fox, Seaman Jacobs, Robert L. Mills, Robert Arthur, Martha Bolton, Jeffrey Barron. *Director:* Bob Henry.

**1444 NBC's 60th Anniversary Celebration.** Variety, 3 hrs., NBC, 5/12/86. A spectacular three-hour, star-studded look at six decades of radio and television broadcasting. The program features clips from many NBC series, coupled with live appearances by NBC stars and lavish production numbers. *Hosts:* Milton Berle, Nell Carter, John Chancellor, Angie Dickinson, Barbara Eden, Michael J. Fox, Bryant Gumbel, Deidre Hall, Bob Hope, Michael Landon, Merlin Olsen, Jack Paar, Jane Pauley, Pat Sajak, Dinah Shore. *Guests:* Steve Allen, Fran Allison, Harry Anderson, Bea Arthur, Gene Barry, Tom Brokaw, Pierce Brosnan, Raymond Burr, Red Buttons, Sid Caesar, Macdonald Carey, Johnny Carson, Nell Carter, Connie Chung, Dick Clark, Robert Conrad, Robert Culp, Ted Danson, Don DeFore, Hugh Downs, Nanette Fabray, Kim Fields, Arlene Francis, Soleil Moon Frye, Marla Gibbs, George Gobel, Lorne Greene, Valerie Harper, Julie Harris, David Hasselhoff, Ed Herlihy, Don Johnson, Perry King, Jack Klugman, Hope Lange, Shari Lewis, Hal Linden, Shelley Long, Norman Lloyd, Gloria Loring, Rue McClanahan, Peter Marshall, Dick Martin, Mitch Miller, Edwin Newman, Donald O'Connor, Merlin Olsen, Jack Paar, Patti Page, Bert Parks, George Peppard, Rhea Perlman, Sarah Purcell, Charlotte Rae, John Ratzenberger, Gene Rayburn, Martha Raye, Carl Reiner, Joan Rivers, Doris Roberts, Dan Rowan, Ricky Schroder, Doc Severinsen, Bob Smith, Robert Stack, Craig Stevens, Robert Vaughn, Betty White, Jane Wyatt, Robert Young. *Music:* Elliot Lawrence. *Producers:* Alexander H. Cohen, Hildy Parks. *Writer:* Hildy Parks. *Director:* Clark Jones.

**1445 Neil Diamond: Hello Again.** Variety, 60 min., CBS, 5/25/86. An hour of music and songs with singer Neil Diamond. *Host:* Neil Diamond. *Guests:* Carol Burnett, Stevie Wonder. *Neil Diamond Band:* Richard Bennett, Vince Charles, King Errisson, Tom Hensley, Alan Lindgrin, Linda Press, Reine Press, Doug Rhoni. *Music Directors:* Alan Lindgrin, Tom Hensley. *Producers:* Sandy Gallin, Gary Smith, Dwight Hemion, Kenny Solms. *Writers:* Kenny Solms, Ann Elder, Tom Perew. *Director:* Dwight Hemion.

**1446 The Neil Diamond Special.** Variety, 60 min., NBC, 2/21/77. A concert by singer Neil Diamond from the Greek Theater in Los Angeles. *Host:* Neil Diamond. *Producers:* Jerry Weintraub, Gary Smith, Dwight Hemion. *Writer:* Buz Kohan. *Director:* Dwight Hemion.

**1447 The Neil Diamond Special: I'm Glad You're Here with Me Tonight.** Variety, 60 min., NBC, 11/17/77. A concert by Neil Diamond from Woburn Abbey in England. *Host:* Neil Diamond. *Producers:* Jerry Weintraub, Art Fisher. *Writer:* Rod Warren. *Director:* Art Fisher.

**1448 Neil Sedaka Steppin' Out.** Variety, 60 min., NBC, 9/17/76. Music and songs with Neil Sedaka in his first telvision special. *Host:* Neil

Sedaka. *Guests:* David Brenner, Bette Midler. *Music:* Artie Butler. *Producers:* Saul Ilson, Ernest Chambers. *Writers:* Ed Scharlach, James Ritz, Saul Ilson, Ernest Chambers. *Director:* Art Fisher.

**1449 Neither Are We Enemies.** Drama, 90 min., NBC, 3/13/70. The play, set in Judea, centers on two characters: the Hebrew Judge Joseph of Arimathea and his son Jonathan, both of whom are troubled by the Roman occupation of their land. Aired on the "Hallmark Hall of Fame." *Cast:* Van Heflin (Joseph), Kristoffer Tabori (Jonathan), J. D. Cannon (Pontius Pilate), Ed Begley (Annas), Kate Reid (Deborah), Leonard Frey (Judas). *Producer:* Jacqueline Babbin.

**1450 Nell Carter – Never Too Old to Dream.** Variety, 60 min., NBC 3/22/86. The program, set in a club that opens a speakeasy and closes as a disco, salutes music from the jazz age to the age of Aquarius. *Host:* Nell Carter. *Guests:* Harry Anderson, The Four Tops, Phylicia Rashad. *Music:* Bruce Miller. *Producers:* Joel Thurm, Don Mischer. *Writer:* Buz Kohan. *Director:* Don Mischer.

**1451 Nestor, the Long-Eared Christmas Donkey.** Cartoon, 30 min., ABC, 12/3/77. Two thousand years ago a donkey named Nestor is born. While Nestor has warm, brown eyes, he also has long, floppy ears that trip him up and make him an object of jokes by the other stable animals. Shortly after Nestor is driven from his home by his angry owner, who considers him worthless, Nestor is confronted in the wilderness by Tillie, who sees the beauty in his heart and leads him to a very special assignment: to take Mary and Joseph to the little town of Bethlehem. It is through this mission that Nestor discovers a meaning for his life. *Voices:* Brenda Vaccaro (Tillie), Eric Stern (Nestor), Linda Gary (Nes-

tor's mother), Paul Frees (Olaf), Don Messick (Soldier), Iris Rainer and Shelly Hines (Girl donkeys). *Narrator/ Singer:* Roger Miller. *Music:* Maury Laws. *Producers:* Arthur Rankin, Jr., Jules Bass. *Writer:* Romeo Muller.

**1452 Night Dreams.** Variety, 90 min., NBC, 8/2 and 8/9/75. A two-part (each 90 min.) late night (1–2:30 A.M.) program of music and songs. *Guests* (8/2/75): The Spinners, 10 C. C., B. J. Thomas, Tanya Tucker. *Guests* (8/9/75): Freddy Fender, Hamilton, Joe Frank and Reynolds, Little Richard, Rod Stewart, Three Dog Night. *Producers:* Syd Vinnedge, Art Fisher. *Director:* Art Fisher.

**1453 Night of 100 Stars.** Variety, 3 hrs., ABC, 3/8/82. An elaborate, star-studded benefit for the Actors' Fund of America; taped on February 14 at New York's Radio City Music Hall. *Guests:* Jane Alexander, Peter Allen, Steve Allen, June Allyson, Don Ameche, Loni Anderson, Susan Anton, Lucie Arnaz, Bea Arthur, Edward Asner, Christopher Atkins, Lauren Bacall, Catherine Bach, Pearl Bailey, Martin Balsam, Priscilla Barnes, Warren Beatty, Harry Belafonte, Tony Bennett, Milton Berle, Theodore Bikel, Tom Bosley, Barry Bostwick, Danielle Brisebois, George Burns, Ellen Burstyn, James Caan, James Cagney, Diahann Carroll, Nell Carter, Dick Cavett, Richard Chamberlain, Carol Channing, Cher, Dick Clark, Joan Collins, James Coco, Peter Cook, Bud Cort, Howard Cosell, Cathy Lee Crosby, Christopher Cross, Arlene Dahl, The Dance Theater of Harlem, Bette Davis, Robert DeNiro, Danny DeVito, Colleen Dewhurst, Joyce DeWitt, Placido Domingo, The Doobie Brothers, Alfred Drake, Sandy Duncan, Nancy Dussault, Linda Evans, Douglas Fairbanks, Jr., Morgan Fairchild, Lola Falana, Peter Falk, Alice Faye, Jose Ferrer, Peggy Fleming, Jane Fonda, John Forsythe, Phyllis Frelich,

Eva Gabor, Anthony Geary, Andy Gibb, Melissa Gilbert, Lillian Gish, Ruth Gordon, Princess Grace, Farley Granger, Linda Gray, Rocky Graziano, Joel Grey, Charles Grodin, Harry Guardino, Robert Guillaume, Larry Hagman, The Harlem Globetrotters, Valerie Harper, Julie Harris, Helen Hayes, Florence Henderson, Doug Henning, Judd Hirsch, Celeste Holm, Lena Horne, Ken Howard, Barnard Hughes, Kate Jackson, Anne Jeffreys, Ann Jillian, Van Johnson, James Earl Jones, Diane Keaton, Howard Keel, Gene Kelly, Richard Kiley, Alan King, Robert Klein, Jack Klugman, Ted Knight, N.Y. Mayor Edward Koch, Burt Lancaster, Frank Langella, Linda Lavin, Michael Learned, Michele Lee, Janet Leigh, Jack Lemmon, David Letterman, Hal Linden, John V. Lindsay, Gina Lollobrigida, Priscilla Lopez, Dorothy Loudon, Myrna Loy, Joel McCrea, Gavin MacLeod, Penny Marshall, Mary Martin, James Mason, Marcello Mastroianni, Ethel Merman, Dina Merrill, Ann Miller, Liza Minnelli, Anna Moffio, Dudley Moore, Mary Tyler Moore, Paul Newman, Leonard Nimoy, Jerry Orbach, Al Pacino, Gregory Peck, Anthony Perkins, Christopher Plummer, Jane Powell, Stefanie Powers, Robert Preston, Victoria Principal, Anthony Quinn, Radio City Music Hall Rockettes, Charlotte Rae, Tony Randall, Robert Reed, Christopher Reeve, Lionel Richie, Jason Robards, Pernell Roberts, Cliff Robertson, Ginger Rogers, Mickey Rooney, John Rubinstein, Jane Russell, Isabel Sanford, John Schneider, Ricky Schroder, George Segal, William Shatner, Brooke Shields, Sylvia Sidney, Alexis Smith, Allison Smith, Rick Springfield, Maureen Stapleton, Robert Sterling, James Stewart, Beatrice Straight, Lee Strasberg, Donald Sutherland, Lynn Swann, Elizabeth Taylor, Daniel J. Travanti, Cicely Tyson, Liv Ullmann, Peter Ustinov, Ben Vereen, Jack Warden, Orson Welles, Robin Williams, Henry Winkler. *Announcer:* Les Marshack. *Music Director:* Elliot Lawrence. *Musical Staging:* Albert Stevenson. *Producers:* Albert H. Cohen, Hildy Parks. *Writer:* Hildy Parks. *Director:* Clark Jones.

## 1454 Night of 100 Stars II.
Variety, 3 hrs., ABC, 3/11/85. A star-studded sequel to "Night of 100 Stars" (see prior title) that is a celebrity benefit for the Actors' Fund of America. Taped at Radio City Music Hall in New York City. *Guests:* Debbie Allen, Harry Anderson, Ann-Margret, Lucie Arnaz, Edward Asner, Tracy Austin, Scott Baio, Lucille Ball, Drew Barrymore, Anne Baxter, Shari Belafonte-Harper, Marisa Berenson, Valerie Bertinelli, David Birney, Meredith Baxter Birney, Jacqueline Bisset, Bob and Ray, Laura Branigan, Lloyd Bridges, Morgan Brittany, Charles Bronson, Pierce Brosnan, Yul Brynner, Carol Burnett, George Burns, Ellen Burstyn, Red Buttons, Michael Caine, Dyan Cannon, Diahann Carroll, Lynda Carter, Nell Carter, Marge Champion, Carol Channing, Dick Clark, Petula Clark, Dabney Coleman, Joan Collins, Bert Convy, Cathy Lee Crosby, Billy Crystal, Tyne Daly, William Daniels, Tony Danza, Olivia de Havilland, Robert DeNiro, Colleen Dewhurst, Angie Dickinson, Richard Dreyfuss, Sandy Duncan, Charles Durning, Nancy Dussault, Linda Evans, Nanette Fabray, Morgan Fairchild, Peggy Fleming, John Forsythe, Michael J. Fox, Anthony Franciosa, David Frost, Soleil Moon Frye, Teri Garr, Lillian Gish, Linda Gray, Gene Hackman, Mark Hamill, Julie Harris, Lisa Hartman, David Hasselhoff, Florence Henderson, Dustin Hoffman, Lena Horne, Lee Horsley, Beth Howland, Kate Jackson, Van Johnson, Elaine Joyce, Danny Kaye, Linda Lavin, Michele Lee, Janet Leigh, Hal Linden, Heather Locklear, Ali MacGraw, Gavin MacLeod, Burgess Meredith, Donna Mills, Mary Tyler Moore, Melba Moore, Anne

Murray, Jim Nabors, Bob Newhart, Donald O'Connor, Jennifer O'Neill, Jack Palance, Bert Parks, Bernadette Peters, Sidney Poitier, Jane Powell, Priscilla Presley, Robert Preston, Vincent Price, Juliet Prowse, Charlotte Rae, Tony Randall, Chita Rivera, Pernell Roberts, Ginger Rogers, Jill St. John, Jane Seymour, William Shatner, Brooke Shields, Dinah Shore, Jaclyn Smith, Gloria Steinem, James Stewart, Heather Thomas, Richard Thomas, Mel Torme, Lana Turner, Leslie Uggams, Robert Urich, Joan Van Ark, Dick Van Dyke, Gwen Verdon, Robert Wagner, Raquel Welch, Billy Dee Williams, Henny Youngman, Stephanie Zimbalist. *Music Director:* Elliot Lawrence. *Special Musical Material and Lyrics:* Buz Kohan. *Producers:* Alexander H. Cohen, Hildy Parks. *Writer:* Hildy Parks. *Director:* Clark Jones.

**1455 99 Ways to Attract the Right Man.** Comedy, 60 min., ABC, 5/7/85. A satirical look at the world of the unattached woman as she goes through her life looking for "Mr. Right." *Hosts:* Tony Danza, Susan Lucci. *Guests:* Brian Bradley, Lois Bromfield, Tracy Cabot, Judy Carter, Dr. Irene Kasorla, Maureen Murphy, Dr. Ruth Westheimer. *Music Directors:* Wendy Fraser, Stacy Widelitz. *Producers:* Ernest Chambers, Woody Fraser. *Writers:* Elayne Boosler, Ernest Chambers. *Director:* Woody Fraser.

**1456 The 1957 Rocket Review.** Variety, 30 min., ABC, 11/8/56. A short review featuring music, songs, and dances. *Host:* John Daly. *Guests:* The 4 Chordettes, Great Gray, Bill Hayes, Bonnie Murray. *Producer-Writer:* Lee Cooley. *Director:* Matt Harlib.

**1457 1968 Hollywood Stars of Tomorrow.** Variety, 60 min., ABC, 1/27/68. Performances by new talent discoveries. *Host:* Gene Kelly.

*Producer:* Roger Gimbel. *Writer:* Will Glickman. *Director:* Dean Whitmore.

**1458 90210 Behind the Scenes.** Documentary, 30 min., Fox, 5/26/93. A personal look at the cast members of the series "Beverly Hills, 90210." *Host:* Katie Wagner. *Guests:* Gabrielle Cateris, Shannen Doherty, Jennie Garth, Brian Austin Green, Luke Perry, Jason Priestley, Tori Spelling, Ian Ziering. *Producer:* Paul Waigner. *Writer:* Nina Tuo. *Director:* Jason Priestley.

**1459 Ninotchka.** Comedy, 90 min., ABC, 4/20/60. The story of a Soviet government official (Ninotchka) who finds love and romance while in Paris on an assignment to barter jewels for farm machinery. *Cast:* Maria Schell (Lena Yakushova/Ninotchka), Gig Young (Leon Dolga), Zsa Zsa Gabor (Grand Duchess Swana), Mischa Auer (Buljanoff), Leon Belasco (Michael Iranoff), Anne Meara (Anna), Marcel Hillaire (Mercier). *Producer:* David Susskind. *Writer:* Roger Hirson. *Director:* Tom Donovan.

**1460 No Greater Gift.** Drama, 60 min., ABC, 9/11/85. Nick and Keith are two boys who become friends during an illness that makes them hospital roommates. After Nick accepts the fact that his disease is fatal, he makes a decision to become an organ donor to save his friend's life. His efforts to convince his opposing father that his decision is the right one is the focal point of this "ABC Afterschool Special." *Cast:* Ajay Naidu (Nick Santana), Zero Hubbard (Keith Williams), Betty Thomas (Dr. Mary Lewis), Reni Santoni (Mario Santana). *Music:* Jim Dunne. *Producers:* Ron Howard, Norman G. Brooks. *Writers:* Josef Anderson, Anson Williams. *Director:* Anson Williams.

**1461 No Man's Valley.** Cartoon, 30 min., CBS, 9/12/83. When a

**Ad for "90210 Behind the Scenes"**

construction crew begins building on the sanctuary of a rare breed of California condors, the birds feel their lives are threatened. The story relates their efforts to find No Man's Valley—a place where they can live in peace. *Voices:* Arnold Stang (Fred Firmwing), Richard Deacon (Nobody Panda), Desiree Goyette (Pat the Pigeon). *Music:* Desiree Goyette, Ed Bogas. *Producers:* Lee Mendelson, Phil Howort, Bill Melendez. *Writers:* Chris Brough, Frank Buxton. *Director:* Bill Melendez.

**1462 No Means No.** Drama, 60 min., CBS, 10/18/88. A "CBS Schoolbreak Special" about date rape. The program examines the issue as seen through the eyes of the victim (Megan), her attacker (Doug), and Megan's older brother (Michael). *Cast:* Dana Barron (Megan Wells), Chad Lowe (Michael Wells), Lori Loughlin (Sally), Jim Marshall (Doug Simpson), Bonnie

Bedelia (Mrs. Wells), Al White (Coach Sanders), Kat Green (Blanche), Rachel Jacobs (Nellie), Manfred Melcher (Bob), Harry Johnson (Mr. Simpson). *Music:* Jed Feurer. *Producers:* Martin Sheen, William Greenblatt. *Writer-Director:* Jeffrey Auerbach.

**1463 Norman Rockwell: An American Portrait.** Documentary, 60 min., PBS, 11/25/87. A tribute to the illustrator (1894–1978) whose sentimental and hopeful works appeared on magazine covers. His legacy is recalled through his works and the memories of his colleagues. *Host-Narrator:* Mason Adams. *Guests:* Erma Bombeck, Ellen Goodman, Jean Shepherd. *Music:* Van Dyke Parks. *Producers:* Greg Andorfer, Mary Rawyson. *Writer:* Mary Rawyson. *Director:* Marcie Setlow.

**1464 Not Guilty!** Thriller, 90 min., ABC, 7/16/74. The story of a young executive and his attempts to prove that he is not guilty of murdering his wife. *Cast:* Christopher George (Bernard Peel), Derek Bond (Maycroft), Richard Todd (George Tulliver), Dinsdale Landen (Mathew Earp-Tomson), Edward Hardwicke (Gifford). *Music:* Laurie Johnson. *Producer:* John Sichel. *Writer:* Brian Clemens. *Director:* Robert D. Cardona.

**1465 Notorious.** Drama, 60 min., NBC, 12/10/61. The story, set in Brazil in 1945, relates the efforts of a U.S. government agent to report on the activities of the Nazi underground in Rio de Janeiro. Aired on "Theater '62." *Cast:* Joseph Cotten (Alex Sebastian), Barbara Rush (Alicia Huberman), George Grizzard (James Devlin), Cathleen Nesbitt (Madame Sebastian), Edward Andrews (Captain Prescott), Fred Scollay (Wilhelm Rossner), Peter Von Zerneck (Emil Hupka). *Producer:* Fred Coe. *Writer:* Sumner Locke Elliott. *Director:* Jack Smight.

**1466 The Notorious Jumping Frog of Calaveras County.** Comedy, 30 min., ABC, 9/19/81. A modern adaptation of the Mark Twain classic in which Jimmy Smiley, a young scoundrel with a passion for wagering, challenges Skip Burnett, the new kid in town, to a bicycle race. Jimmy wins, but his unorthodox path to victory infuriates his friends, Buddy Sanders and Mary Lou Thompkins. After observing Jimmy's latest escapade, Miss Fletcher, Jimmy's teacher, calls on the young gambler to read "The Notorious Jumping Frog of Calaveras County." Jimmy's mind quickly devises a plan to hold a frog-jumping contest. The story relates the outcome when Jimmy falls prey to his own kind of sting. Aired as an "ABC Weekend Special." *Cast:* Billy Jacoby (Jimmy Smiley), Steven Spencer (Skip Burnett), Mara Alexander (Mary Lou Thompkins), Derek Wells (Buddy Sanders), Juanita Moore (Miss Fletcher), Owen Bush (Farmer Parsons). *Producer-Director:* Robert

Chenault. *Writers:* Glen Olson, Rod Baker.

**1467 The Nunundaga.** Drama, 30 min., ABC, 12/3 and 12/10/77. The moving, dramatic story of a fictional Indian tribe (the Nunundaga) as they struggle for survival in a hostile world. Aired as an "ABC Weekend Special." *Cast:* Ned Romero (Painted Bear), Guillarmo San Juan (Snake Eyes), John War Eagle (One Feather), Monika Ramirez (Wind Song), Joe Renteria (Low Wolf), Victoria Racimo (Star Fire), Emelio Delgado (White Bull), Madeline Taylor Holmes (Yellow of the Fire). *Music:* Andrew Belling. *Producer:* Edgar J. Scherick. *Writer:* I. C. Rapoport. *Director:* John Llewellyn Moxey.

**1468 The Nut House.** Comedy, 60 min., CBS, 9/1/64. A series of rapid-fire, burlesque-like skits that spoof the American scene. *Host:* Kathy Kersh. *Guests:* Ceil Cabot, Jane Connell, Fay DeWitt, Andy Duncan, Don Francks, Tom Holland, Adam Keefer, Muriel Landers, Marilyn Lovell, Mara Lynn, Len Maxwell, Jack Sheldon, Alan Sues. *Music:* Jerry Fielding. *Producers:* Bill Scott, Bob Ward. *Writers:* Robert L. Arbogast, George Atkins, Allan Burns, Chris Hayward, Art Keane, Jack S. Margolis, Lloyd Turner, Bob Wood. *Director:* Charles S. Dubin.

**1469 Of Mice and Men.** Drama, 2 hrs., ABC, 1/31/68. The unusual relationship between two migrant workers: George, wry and earthly, and Lennie, a powerful giant with the mind of a child. The drama, based on the novel by John Steinbeck, plunges the good-natured pair into a conflict with a ranch owner's vicious, belligerent son and his beautiful, slatternly wife. *Cast:* George Segal (George), Nicol Williamson (Lennie), Will Geer (Candy), Don Gordon (Curley), Joey Heatherton (Curley's wife), Donald Moffat (Slim), Moses Gunn (Crooks), James Hall (The

Boss), Dana Elcar (Carlson), John Randolph (Whit). *Producer:* David Susskind. *Writer:* John Hopkins. *Director:* Ted Kotcheff.

**1470 Of Thee I Sing.** Musical, 90 min., CBS, 10/24/72. A television adaptation of the 1931 Broadway musical by George Gershwin about John P. Wintergreen, a presidential candidate with an irresistible platform based on silver linings and love. *Cast:* Carroll O'Connor (John P. Wintergreen), Jack Gilford (Alexander Throttlebottom), Cloris Leachman (Mary Turner), Michele Lee (Diana Devereaux), Jim Backus (Robert F. Lyons), Jesse White (Matthew Fulton), David Doyle (Francis X. Gilhooley), Herb Edelman (Louis Lippman), Paul Hartman (Chief Justice), Shirley Kirkes (Miss Benson), Ted Knight (News commentator), Jeannine Riley (Hotel chambermaid). *Music Director:* Peter Matz. *Music Adaptation:* Artie Malvin. *Lyrics:* Ira Gershwin. *Producers:* Arne Rosen, George Sunga. *Writers:* Arne Rosen, Don Hinkley, Woody Kling. *Director:* Dave Powers.

**1471 Off-Hollywood.** Comedy, 90 min., NBC, 1/14/78. A series of comedy skits that satirize contemporary California society. *Cast:* Glenn Daniels, Susan Elliot, Cyndy James-Reese, Dizzy Lowell, Chase Newhart, Lorna Patterson. *Producer:* Ken Belsky. *Writers:* Vic Dunlop, Chase Newhart, David Garber, Marty Farrell, Kevin Hartigan. *Director:* Sterling Johnson.

**1472 Oh! Baby, Baby, Baby** .... Comedy, 90 min., ABC, 12/5/74. The story of Stacy and Rick Stoner, a young married couple whose lives and marriage are overwhelmed, confused, and eventually strengthened by the prospect of becoming parents of quintuplets. *Cast:* Judy Carne (Stacy Stoner), Bert Convy (Rick Stoner), King Moody (Dr. Fisher), Henry Corden (Dr. Roth), Boni Enten (Gwen),

Parley Baer (Dr. Burkeholder), Reva Rose (Mrs. Hoffman), Reta Shaw (Mrs. Tusher), Laura Kaye (Ms. Phillips), Dodo Denney (Mrs. Cook). *Producers:* Alan Landsburg, Laurence D. Savadore. *Writer:* Ruth Brooks Flippen. *Director:* Howard Morris.

**1473 Oh, Boy! Babies!** Children, 60 min., NBC, 10/5/81. A lighthearted story about sixth-grade boys who are given an unusual course in infant care (using real babies during their lessons) to help them learn the importance of their nurturing instincts in becoming caring adults and responsible parents. *Cast:* Matthew Kolmes (Matt), Claude Brooks (Claude), Aramis Estevez (Aramis), Philip Ross (Philip), J. D. Roth (J. D.), Ward Saxton (Ward), Nita Novy (Janet), Chip Zien (Jake), Fran Brill (Kaye). *Music:* Stephen Lawrence. *Producers:* Bruce Hart, Carole Hart. *Writers:* Bruce Hart, Carole Hart, Sherry Coben. *Director:* Gail Frank.

**1474 The Old Maid and the Thief.** Opera, 60 min., NBC, 3/16/49. A television adaptation of Gian-Carlo Menotti's comic operetta about a man-hungry old maid and a thief who happens to cross her path and with whom she falls in love. *Cast:* Marie Powers (Old Maid), Norman Young (Thief). *Also:* Virginia MacWatters, Ellen Paul. *Producer:* Roger Englander. *Writer-Director:* Gian-Carlo Menotti.

**1475 The Oldest Living Graduate.** Drama, 2 hrs., NBC, 4/7/80. The story, set in a small Texas prairie town in 1962, follows old Colonel J. C. Kincaid's efforts to keep a lakefront tract of land he loves so much from his son Floyd, a businessman who wants to develop it. The title is derived from the fact that J. C. Kincaid is the only surviving member of a local military academy. *Cast:* Henry Fonda (J. C. Kincaid), George Grizzard (Floyd Kincaid), Cloris Leachman (Maureen),

John Lithgow (Clarence), Harry Dean Stanton (Mike Tremaine), Penelope Milford (Martha Ann), David Ogden Stiers (Major), Timothy Hutton (Cadet), Allyn Ann McLerie (Mrs. Hampton). *Producer:* Gareth Davis. *Writer:* Preston Jones. *Director:* Jack Hofsiss.

**Olivia** *see* **Olivia Newton-John Specials**

**1476 Olivia Newton-John Specials.** A chronological listing of the variety specials hosted by singer-actress Olivia Newton-John. All are 60 minutes in length.
    **1 A Special Olivia Newton-John** (ABC, 11/17/76). *Guests:* Rona Barrett, Tom Bosley, Lynda Carter, Elliott Gould, Ron Howard, Rock Hudson, Lee Majors, Nancy Walker. *Music:* Lee Rittenour. *Producers:* Lee Kramer, Scott Mullaney. *Writer:* Alan Thicke. *Director:* Jeff Margolis.
    **2 Olivia** (ABC, 5/17/78). *Guest:* Andy Gibb. *Music:* Dennis McCarthy. *Producers:* Lee Kramer, Steve Binder. *Writers:* Alan Thicke, Steve Binder, Susan Elliot. *Director:* Steve Binder.
    **3 Olivia Newton-John's Hollywood Nights** (ABC, 4/14/80). *Guests:* Karen Carpenter, Dick Clark, Andy Gibb, Elton John, Gene Kelly, Ted Knight, Toni Tennille, Tina Turner. *Music:* Lee Rittenour. *Producers:* Lee Kramer, Alan Thicke. *Writer:* Alan Thicke. *Director:* Jeff Margolis.
    **4 Olivia Newton-John: Let's Be Physical** (ABC, 2/8/82). *Music:* John Farrah. *Producer:* Scott Mullaney. *Choreographer:* Kenny Ortega. *Director:* Brian Grant.
    **5 Olivia Newton-John in Concert** (HBO, 1/23/83). *Music:* Tom Scott. *Producers:* Roger Davies, Christopher Smith. *Director:* Brian Grant.
    **6 Olivia Newton-John in Australia** (HBO, 7/30/88). *Producers:* Paul Raphael, Brian Grant. *Writers:* Brian Grant, Bruce Walmsley. *Director:* Brian Grant.

**1477 The Olsen Twins Mother's Day Special.** Variety, 60 min., ABC, 5/5/93. The six-year-old twins from "Full House" (Mary Kate and Ashley Olsen) host a program of music, comedy, and song for their mother and mothers everywhere. *Hosts:* Mary Kate and Ashley Olsen. *Guests:* Kim Alexis, Tim Allen, Mark Curry, Kid 'n' Play, Joey Lawrence, Jerry Van Dyke. *Music:* Lenny Stack. *Producers:* Dick Clark, Robert Thorne, Al Schwartz. *Writer:* Barry Adelman. *Director:* Gary Halvorson.

**1478 Omnibus.** Variety, 60 min., ABC, 12/28/80, 4/19/81, 7/19/81. A series of three specials that update the old television series of the same title (1952–61) to present culture in an entertaining form. *Host:* Hal Holbrook. *Music:* Peter Matz. "Omnibus" *theme:* William Goldstein. *Producers:* Martin Starger, Eric Lieber. *Writer:* Leonard Harris. *Director, 12/28/80:* Bill Davis. *Director, 4/19/81:* Alan Smithee. *Director, 7/19/81:* Bob Mischer.

**1479 On Borrowed Time.** Comedy, 90 min., NBC, 11/17/57. A television adaptation of the play by Paul Osborn about a grandfather, not ready to meet his maker, who chases death away (Mr. Brink), seeking more time to raise his orphaned grandson (Pud). Aired on the "Hallmark Hall of Fame." *Cast:* Ed Wynn (Gramps), Claude Rains (Mr. Brink), Beulah Bondi (Granny), Dennis Kohler (Pud), Margaret Hamilton (Aunt Demetria), Dorothy Eaton (Susan), Larry Gates (Dr. Pilbean). *Producer-Director:* George Schaefer. *Writer:* James Costigan.

**1480 On Location with Rich Little.** Comedy, 60 min., HBO, 9/17/82. A showcase for comedian Rich Little and his array of comic impersonations. *Host:* Rich Little. *Music:* Robert E. Hughes. *Producers:* Rich Little, Ken

Kragen. *Writer:* Rich Little. *Director:* Trevor Evans.

**1481 On Stage with Barbara McNair.** Variety, 60 min., Syndicated, 1/70. Music and songs with singer Barbara McNair and her guests. *Host:* Barbara McNair. *Guests:* Duke Ellington, Carlton Johnson. *Music:* Ralph Carmichael. *Producer:* Jackie Barnett. *Director:* Norman Sedawie.

**1482 On Stage with Maurice Chevalier.** Variety, 60 min., Syndicated, 8/70. A one-man show with French entertainer Maurice Chevalier. *Host:* Maurice Chevalier. *Music:* Ralph Carmichael. *Producer:* Jackie Barnett. *Director:* John Robins.

**1483 On Stage with Phil Silvers.** Variety, 60 min., Syndicated, 11/68. Comedy and songs with comedian Phil Silvers and his guests. *Host:* Phil Silvers. *Guests:* The Lionel Blair Dancers, Barbara McNair. *Music:* Jack Parnell. *Producer:* Jackie Barnett. *Director:* Tony Charmoli.

**1484 On the Flip Side.** Musical Comedy, 60 min., ABC, 12/7/66. The problems that befall Carlos O'Connor, a has-been singer who is saved from obscurity when Angie, a beautiful spirit, and her quartet, the Celestials, are assigned to make him a star once again. *Cast:* Rick Nelson (Carlos O'Connor), Joanie Sommers (Angie), Donna Jean Young (Juanita), Will MacKenzie (Jerome), Lada Edmund, Jr. (Irene), Murray Roman (Hairy Eddie), Tyrone Cooper, Steve Perry, Jeff Siggins (Celestials). *Music:* Burt Bacharach. *Lyrics:* Hal David. *Music Directors:* Peter Matz, Jimmie Haskell. *Producer:* Richard Lewine. *Writer:* Robert Emmett. *Director:* Joe Layton.

**1485 On the Town with Tony Bennett.** Variety, 60 min., Syndicated, 1/83. Music and songs taped at various New York City locales. *Host:* Tony Bennett. *Producers:* Danny Bennett, Dennis Paget. *Writer:* C. W. Lukas. *Director:* Vincent Scarza.

**1486 On the Two a Day.** Variety, 30 min., NBC, 5/9/49. A re-creation of the music, song, and comedy of vaudeville. *Cast:* The Elm City Four, Jackie Gleason, Pat Harrington, Jr., Red Ingle's Natural Seven, Elaine Stritch, Karen Teddler. *Orchestra:* Harry Sosnik. *Producer:* Vic McLeod. *Directors:* Vic McLeod, Vince Curran.

**1487 On Tour.** Variety, Showtime, 1979. A series of four concerts by top stars, taped on location during the respective performer's tour. *Producer:* Chuck Braverman.
  **1 On Tour: Frankie Valli** (70 min., 1/79). Taped live in New York's Central Park.
  **2 On Tour: Willie Nelson** (90 min., 2/79). Taped live at Lake Tahoe.
  **3 On Tour: Crystal Gayle and Ray Stevens** (105 min., 3/79). Taped at the Opryland Hotel in Nashville.
  **4 On Tour: Roy Clark and the Oak Ridge Boys** (90 min., 4/79). Taped at the Frontier Hotel in Las Vegas.

**1488 On Tour with Lawrence Welk.** Variety, 60 min., Syndicated, 1/85. Music and songs with bandleader Lawrence Welk. *Host:* Lawrence Welk. *Guests:* Ava Barber, Dick Dale, Kathie Sullivan. *Announcer:* Joseph Campanella. *Music Director:* George Cates. *Producers:* Jack Immel, Larry Welk. *Writer:* Bernice McGeehan. *Director:* James Balden.

**1489 Once the Killing Starts.** Thriller, 90 min., ABC, 1/7/74. The story of a professor who attempts to dispose of his wife after he falls in love with another woman. *Cast:* Patrick O'Neal (Michael Lane), Patricia Donahue (Elizabeth Page), Angharad Rees (Stella Mason), Michael Kitchen (George Newton). *Music:* Laurie Johnson. *Producer:* John Sichel. *Writer:* Brian Clemens. *Director:* John Scholz-Conway.

## 1490 Once Upon a Brothers Grimm.

Children, 2 hrs., CBS, 11/23/77. Jacob and Wilhelm Grimm were brothers who collected legends that became world-famous fairy tales. The special presents eight of the brothers' most famous stories. *Cast:* Dean Jones (Jacob Grimm), Paul Sand (Wilhelm Grimm), Betsy Beard (Wood Nymph), Sorrell Booke (King of Hesse), Arte Johnson (Selfish and Mean), Ruth Buzzi (Queen Astrid). *Music:* Mitch Leigh. *Lyrics:* Sammy Cahn. *Producers:* Bernard Rothman, Jack Wohl. *Writer:* Jean Holloway. *Director:* Norman Campbell.

**The Stories:**

(1) "The Bremen Town Musicians." *Cast:* Don Correia (The Ass), Joe Giamalva (The Rooster), Gary Morgan (The Hound), Maria Pogge (The Cat).

(2) "Cinderella." *Cast:* Stephanie Steele (Cinderella), Corinne Conley (Fairy Godmother), John McCook (Prince Charming), Gordon Connell (Driver).

(3) "Hansel and Gretel." *Cast:* Mia Bendixsen (Gretel), Todd Lookinland (Hansel), Edie McClurg (Esmerelda), Chita Rivera (Gingerbread Lady).

(4) "The Frog Prince." *Cast:* Teri Garr (Princess), Ken Olfson (The King).

(5) "Little Red Riding Hood." *Cast:* Susan Silo (Little Red Riding Hood), Cleavon Little (Wolf), Dean Jones (Grandmother).

(6) "The King with Eight Daughters." *Cast:* Dan Tobin (Prime Minister), Clive Revil (Rumpelstiltskin).

(7) "The Mazurka." *Cast:* The Los Angeles Ballet Company (Dancers).

(8) "Sleeping Beauty." *Cast:* Joanna Kirkland (Sleeping Beauty), John Clifford (Prince).

## 1491 Once Upon a Christmas Time.

Musical, 60 min., NBC, 12/9/59. When a group of Vermont villagers want to welcome the town's orphan children to their homes for Christmas, the stern Miss Scugg refuses to let them leave her orphanage. The story relates the efforts of the townspeople to change Miss Scugg's mind and provide a merry Christmas for the children. Based on Paul Gallico's *The Thirteenth Orphan.* *Cast:* Claude Rains (John Woodcutter), Margaret Hamilton (Miss Scugg), Charlie Ruggles (Mayor), Kate Smith (Beth), Patty Duke (Lori), Pat Henning (Ezra), Ronnie Robertson (Ronnie). *Music Director:* Kenyon Hopkins. *Songs:* Al Stallman, Robert Allen. *Choral Director:* Harry Simeone. *Producer:* Jack Philbin. *Writer:* A. J. Russell. *Director:* Kirk Browning.

## 1492 Once Upon a Mattress.

Musical, 90 min., CBS, 6/3/64. A spoof of the Hans Christian Andersen fable *The Princess and the Pea,* wherein Winnifred Woebegone, a girl who lives in a bog, attempts to win the heart of Dauntless the Drab, a prince whose mother strives to keep him from marrying. See the following title also. *Cast:* Carol Burnett (Winnifred Woebegone), Joe Bova (Dauntless the Drab), Jane White (Queen Agravain). *Also:* Jack Fletcher, Bill Hayes, Shani Wallis. *Music:* Mary Rodgers. *Producers:* Bob Banner, Joe Hamilton. *Writers:* Jay Thompson, Marshall Barer, Dean Fuller. *Directors:* Joe Layton, Dave Geisel.

## 1493 Once Upon a Mattress.

Musical, 90 min., CBS, 12/12/72. A restaging of the prior title (which see for story) with Carol Burnett recreating the role that made her famous. *Cast:* Carol Burnett (Winnifred Woebegone), Ken Berry (Dauntless the Drab), Jane White (Queen Agravain), Jack Gilford (King Sextimus), Bernadette Peters (Lady Larken), Wally Cox (Jester), Siv Aberg (Princess), DoDo Denny (Lady Agatha), Ron Husmann (Sir Harry), Sid Kane (Lord Hamble), Billy Beck (Wintel Wamba).

*Music Director:* Peter Matz. *Music and Lyrics:* Mary Rodgers, Marshall Barer. *Producers:* Joe Hamilton, Bob Wright. *Writers:* Marshall Barer, Jay Thompson, Dean Fuller. *Director:* Dave Powers.

## 1494 Once Upon a Midnight Dreary. Children, 60 min., CBS, 10/21/79.

Three stories of the supernatural geared to children: *The Legend of Sleepy Hollow, The House with a Clock in Its Walls,* and *The Ghost Belonged to Me.*

"The Legend of Sleepy Hollow" (by Washington Irving) depicts what happens when a meek schoolteacher encounters what he believes to be the infamous Headless Horseman, who has terrorized the New England countryside. *Cast:* Rene Auberjonois (Ichabod Crane), Pamela Brown (Katrina), Guy Boyd (Brom Bones), Robert Foster (Horseman).

"The House with a Clock in Its Walls" (by John Bellairs) tells of Jonathan Barnavelt and his young nephew, Lewis, who live in an old Victorian house which hides a clock containing plans for the destruction of the world. *Cast:* Severn Darden (Jonathan Barnavelt), Michael Brick (Lewis), Mary Betten (Selena), Pat Peterson (Tarby).

"The Ghost Belonged to Me" (by Richard Peck) tells the story of the spirit of a young girl who comes back from the dead to save a busload of children headed for a disaster. *Cast:* Alexandria Johnson (Ghost), Christian Berrigan (Alexander), Jessica Lynn Pennington (Blossom), Wayne Heffler (Bus driver). *Host:* Vincent Price. *Producers:* Diane Asselin, Paul Asselin. *Writer:* Kimmer Ringwald. *Director:* Nell Cox.

## 1495 Once Upon a Time ... Is Now the Story of Princess Grace. Documentary, 90 min., NBC, 5/22/77.

A look at the life and career of Princess Grace of Monaco (a.k.a. Grace Kelly). *Host:* Lee Grant. *Music:* Ron Grainer. *Producers:* William Allyn, Sandra Smith Allyn, David Lunney. *Director:* Kevin Billington.

## 1496 Once Upon an Easter Time. Fantasy, 60 min., CBS, 4/18/54.

A salute to the spiritual rebirth of spring and the Easter season. Gwen Verdon is featured in an Easter parade dance number and Bobby Clark stars in a dramatic vignette about a boy who eats a forbidden Easter egg and is magically transported into a world of fantasy. In his home town people appear as symbols of good and evil; the boy (Jimmy) becomes part of the battle between these conflicting forces. *Cast:* Bobby Clark (Pell), Doretta Morrow (Sally), Gwen Verdon (Cathy), Pud Flanagan (Jimmy), Pat Harrington (Prime Minister), Ruth McDevitt (Grandma), Bobby May (Turtle), Glen Burris (The Boy Friend). *Producers:* William Dozier, Martin Manulis. *Writers:* Leon Leonidoff, Reginald Lawrence, Arnold Horwitt. *Director:* Byron Paul.

## 1497 One Deadly Owner. Thriller, 90 min., ABC, 11/6/73.

The story of Helen Cook, a British photographer's model, who becomes involved in a murder when the car she purchases takes her against her will to the scene of a crime. *Cast:* Donna Mills (Helen Cook), Jeremy Brett (Peter Tower), John Lacey (Laurence Payne), Freddy Green (Robert Morris). *Music:* Laurie Johnson. *Producer:* Cecil Clarke. *Writer:* Brian Clemens. *Director:* John Fordyce.

## 1498 One Hour in Wonderland. Variety, 60 min., NBC, 12/25/50.

Walt Disney's first venture into television. An hour of live performances and highlights from Disney cartoon classics. The Christmas Day special is the first television program to be produced by a major studio, and was budgeted far beyond anything that had previously aired. Sponsored by Coca-Cola. See also "The Walt Disney Christmas Show" for information on the sequel special. *Host:* Walt Disney. *Guests:* Kathryn Beaumont, Edgar Bergen, Hans Conried, Bobby Driscoll. *Music:* Paul Smith. *Producer-Writer:* Bill Walsh.

**1499 100 Years of America's Popular Music.** Variety, 2 hrs., NBC, 4/27/81. A star-studded celebration of American music. *Host:* George Burns. *Guests:* Eydie Gorme, Gregory Hines, Steve Lawrence, Henry Mancini, Paul Simon, Sarah Vaughan. *Guest Orchestras:* Jon Charles, Jack Elliott, Don James, Peter Matz, Nan Schwartz, Tori Zito. *Announcer:* William B. Williams. *Producers:* Danny Arnold, Jack Elliott. *Writers:* Herbert Baker, James T. Maher. *Director:* Stan Harris.

**1500 100 Years of Golden Hits.** Variety, 2 hrs., NBC, 7/19/81. An all-star cast salutes the recording industry in a program taped in 1978. The show is built around the invention of the phonograph (in 1877) and how music has progressed over the past 100 years. *Cast:* William Windom (Thomas Edison/Host), John Davidson (Ed/Co-Host). *Performers:* Glen Campbell, George Carlin, Johnny Cash, June Carter Cash, Sandy Duncan, Marilyn Horne, KISS, Gladys Knight, Don McLean, Gordon MacRae, Henry Mancini, Ethel Merman, The Mills Brothers, Johnnie Ray, Sha Na Na, Andy Williams. *Music:* Ray Charles. *Producers:* Pierre Cossette, Buz Kohan, Walter C. Miller. *Writers:* Buz Kohan, Rod Warren, Ed Hider. *Director:* Walter C. Miller.

**1501 One More Hurdle.** Drama, 60 min., NBC, 4/10/84. The story of Donna Marie Cheek, a 20-year-old college journalism student, in her own true-life story about her struggle to become the first black member of

the U.S. Olympic Equestrian team. *Cast:* Donna Marie Cheek (Herself), William Marshall (Don Cheek), Saundra Sharp (Calista Cheek), Paul Lukather (Stan), Ernest Harden, Jr. (Steve Cheek), Clyde Jones (Gary Cheek). *Music:* Nicholas Simone. *Producers:* Norman G. Brooks, Fern Field Brooks. *Writer:* Jim Tisdale. *Director:* Neema Barnette.

**1502 One More Time.** Variety, 60 min., ABC, 4/8/68. Performances by the top names in pop music. *Host:* Wayne Newton. *Performers:* Charlie Barnet, Louis Bellson, Les Brown, Tennessee Ernie Ford, Louis Jourdan, Frankie Laine, The Mills Brothers, Johnnie Ray, Kay Starr. *Music Directors:* Paul Weston, Count Basie. *Producers:* George Schlatter, Carolyn Raskin. *Writers:* Don Reo, Allan Katz.

**1503 One More Time.** Variety, 60 min., CBS, 1/10/74. Music and comedy stars from the past and present perform their own special material. *Performers:* Patty Andrews, Pearl Bailey, Pat Boone, George Burns, Carol Channing, George Gobel, The Jackson Five, The June Taylor Dancers, The Mills Brothers, The Pointer Sisters, Gene Sheldon, Tiny Tim. *Music:* Nelson Riddle. *Producers:* George Schlatter, Carolyn Raskin. *Writers:* Don Reo, Allan Katz. *Director:* Marty Pasetta.

**1504 One Night Stands.** Documentary, 60 min., ABC, 11/28/67. A behind-the-scenes look at the grind of touring with a band. *Guests:* The Fifth Dimension, Woody Herman, Johnny Rivers. *Music:* Woody Herman. *Producer-Writer:* Stephen Fleischman. *Director:* Aram Awkian.

**1505 One of a Kind.** Drama, 60 min., ABC, 9/27/78. An "ABC Afterschool Special" that tackles the subject of child abuse. Carrie Williams is a young mother with a rebellious daughter named Lizzie, and mother and daughter seem to fight constantly. Lizzie resents being left alone all day to run their beachfront concession stand while her mother is out working. Carrie resents Lizzie's need for her attention and the girl's desire to join her friends for some fun and sun on the beach. Soon resentment leads to anger and arguments and finally to blows as Lizzie feels unloved and unwanted and Carrie wonders why she is burdened with an ungrateful child. One day a wandering puppeteer sets up a Punch and Judy show on the beach. The make-believe slaps and insults become painfully real to Lizzie as she realizes she is a victim of child abuse from an overworked mother who does not even realize she is guilty of it. The story relates Lizzie's efforts to stand up for herself and not become her mother's puppet. *Cast:* Diane Baker (Carrie Williams), Stephanie Brown (Lizzie Williams), Ken Hill (Ellie), Patrick Finnegan (Sonny), Olive Abbott (Mrs. Cohen), Charlie Gold (Mr. Cohen), Federico Montoya (Dancer). *Music:* Maurice Jarre. *Producer:* Diane Baker. *Writers:* Marjorie L. Sigley, Harry Winer. *Director:* Harry Winer.

**1506 The $1,000 Bill.** Comedy, 30 min., ABC, 5/17/86. Henry Cooper is a timid young insurance salesman. One day he finds a large sum of money and lets the cash go to his head. He tells off his boss, quits his job, and impulsively decides to marry his fiancée. The story relates Henry's efforts to make amends when he discovers that his newfound security consists of counterfeit $1,000 bills. Aired as an "ABC Weekend Special." *Cast:* Donny Most (Henry Cooper), Richard Deacon (Albert French), Charles Lane (Walter Becker), Dawn Jeffory (Susie Carson), Gary Springer (Dan Michaels), Owen Bush (Amos). *Music:* Tommy Leonetti. *Producer:* Robert Chenault. *Writer:* David Frelman. *Director:* Ed Abroms.

**1507 One Too Many.** Drama, 60 min., ABC, 10/23/84. A compelling "ABC Afterschool Special" about teenage drinking and driving as seen through the experiences of Eric, a high school student whose drinking leads to tragic results. *Cast:* Mare Winningham (Beth), Michelle Pfeiffer (Annie), Lance Guest (Tim), Val Kilmer (Eric), Gerry Black (Interrogator). *Producers:* Frank Doelger, Mark Gordon. *Writer:* Bruce Harmon. *Director:* Peter Horton.

**1508 One Touch of Venus.** Musical Comedy, 90 min., NBC, 8/28/55. While in a museum of modern art, Rodney Hatch, a barber, places the engagement ring he bought for his girlfriend, Molly, on the finger of the statue of Venus. Magically, the statue comes to life. Learning of Rodney's love for Molly, Venus banishes her to the North Pole and sets out to win the reluctant Rodney's love. Finally, when Venus does win Rodney's love—but realizes what a dull life she will have—she returns to being a statue. Molly, returned from exile, breaks her engagement to Rodney. Shattered, Rodney returns to worship the statue of Venus. The story concludes with Rodney meeting a girl who resembles the statue. Based on the musical by S. J. Perelman and Owen Nash (from F. Anstey's story *The Tainted Venus*). *Cast:* Janet Blair (Venus), Russell Nype (Rodney Hatch), George Gaynes (Whitelaw Savory), Laurel Shelby (Molly Grant), Mort Marshall (Taxi Black), Iggie Wolfington (Stanley), Adina Rice (Mrs. Kramer), Mildred Trases (Mrs. Moats). *Music:* Gino Smart. *Producer:* Jack Rayel. *Writer:* John Gerstad. *Director:* George Schaefer.

**1509 Only a Scream Away.** Thriller, 90 min., ABC, 2/18/74. The story of Samantha Miller, a beautiful newlywed who is beset by a series of inexplicable accidents. *Cast:* Hayley Mills (Samantha Miller), Gary Collins

(Howard Heston), Liza Meredith (Joyce Carey), David Warbeck (Robert Miller), Candida Brown (Samantha as a girl), Ronald Mayer (Dr. Lambert), Jonathan Elsom (John Stratford), Jeremy Bulloch (Tom Manners). *Music:* Laurie Johnson. *Producer:* Cecil Clarke. *Writer:* Brian Clemens. *Director:* Peter Jeffries.

**1510 Open House.** Variety, 60 min., CBS, 5/23/48. An all-star variety salute to welcome WCAU-TV in Philadelphia as a CBS affiliate. *Guests:* Robert Benedict, Patricia Bright, Shaye Cogan, Johnny Desmond, Gil Fates, Edward R. Murrow, Horace Shaw, Frank Stanton, Ed Sullivan. *Music:* The Tony Mottola Trio. *Producer:* Jerry Danzig. *Writer-Directors:* Ace Ochs, Fred Rickey.

**1511 Opening Night.** Comedy, 60 min., CBS, 9/24/62. A series of sketches and blackouts that feature stars from various CBS programs. *Stars:* Lucille Ball, Jack Benny, Andy Griffith, Garry Moore, Danny Thomas. *Announcer:* Don Wilson. *Music:* Paul Weston. *Producer:* Burt Shevelove. *Writer:* Larry Gelbart. *Director:* Sid Smith.

**1512 Opening Night: U.S.A.** Variety, 60 min., CBS, 12/25/72. Videotaped highlights of opening nightclub acts in Las Vegas. *Stars:* Milton Berle, Sammy Davis, Jr., The Fifth Dimension, Debbie Reynolds. *Producers:* Jack Naylor, Sid Smith. *Writer:* Louis Solomon. *Directors:* Sid Smith, Charles W. Liotta.

**1513 Operation Entertainment.** Variety, 60 min., NBC, 9/20/54. A tribute to the soldiers in greasepaint; the many members of showbusiness who gave their services and time to the USO during World War II and the Korean War. *Hosts:* George Meany, General Matthew B. Ridgeway. *Guests:* The Bell Sisters, Ray Bolger, Jack Car-

son, Jerry Colonna, Eddie Fisher, Connie Haines, Jack Haley, William Holden, Bob Hope, Danny Kaye, Terry Moore, Pat O'Brien, Tyrone Power, Ronald Reagan, Debbie Reynolds, Edward G. Robinson, Tony Romano, Dinah Shore, Danny Thomas, Patti Thomas, Audrey Totter, Keenan Wynn. *Music Directors:* Robert Armbruster, Von Dexter. *Producers:* Robert Welch, William Kayden. *Writer:* Glenn Wheaton. *Director:* William Bennington.

**1514 Opryland Celebrates America's Music.** Variety, 60 min., Syndicated, 3/24/88. A country and western salute to 200 years of American music. *Hosts:* Frankie Avalon, Barbara Mandrell. *Guests:* Arte Johnson, Bobby Jones, The New Life Country Singers, Minnie Pearl, Charley Pride, Randy Travis. *Music:* Bill Walker. *Producers:* Ed Stone, Bob Wynn. *Writer:* Jim McGinn. *Director:* Bob Wynn.

**1515 Opryland U.S.A.** Variety, 60 min., NBC, 10/22/73. A salute to American music. Taped at Opryland in Nashville. *Host:* Petula Clark. *Guests:* Tennessee Ernie Ford, Melba Moore, Wayne Newton, The Tom Hanson Dancers. *Music:* Bill Walker. *Producer-Director:* Bob Wynn. *Writers:* Bob Booker, George Foster.

**1516 Opryland U.S.A., 1975.** Variety, 60 min., NBC, 5/14/75. Music, songs, and comedy from the Opryland U.S.A. music-theme park in Nashville, Tennessee. *Hosts:* Sandy Duncan, Dennis Weaver. *Guests:* Jonelle Allen, Jim Stafford, Tanya Tucker. *Music:* Bill Walker. *Producers:* Bob Wynn, Ray Canady, Irving Waugh. *Writer:* Bob Arnott. *Director:* Bob Wynn.

**1517 The Original Rompin' Stompin' Hot and Heavy, Cool and Groovy All-Star Jazz Show.**

Variety, 60 min., CBS, 4/13/76. A history of jazz music, featuring performances by its top artists. *Host:* Dionne Warwick. *Guests:* Count Basie, Stan Getz, Dizzy Gillespie, Lionel Hampton, Herbie Hancock, Gerry Mulligan, Max Roach, Joe Williams. *Music:* Chico O'Farrell. *Producers:* Ron Kass, Gary Keys. *Writers:* Gary Keys, Edward Gant. *Director:* Jerome Schnur.

### 1518 Oscar Presents John Wayne and the War Movies.
Documentary, 2 hrs., ABC, 11/27/77. The program traces the history of World War II as depicted in motion pictures. *Host:* John Wayne. *Guests:* Jeff Bridges, Louise Fletcher, Walter Matthau, Brenda Vaccaro. *Music:* Nelson Riddle. *Producer:* Alan Landsburg. *Writer:* Charles Champlin. *Director:* Mel Stuart.

### 1519 Oscar's Best Actors.
Documentary, 60 min., ABC, 5/23/78. A look at the careers of fifty men who have won the Academy Award for Best Actor. *Hosts:* William Holden, Gene Kelly, Marsha Mason, John Wayne. *Producer-Director:* Howard W. Koch. *Writers:* William Ludwig, Leonard Spigelgass.

### 1520 The Osmond Brothers Special.
Variety, 60 min., ABC, 5/26/78. Music, songs, and comedy with the Osmond Brothers and their guests. *Hosts:* Alan Osmond, Jay Osmond, Merrill Osmond, Wayne Osmond. *Guests:* Crystal Gayle, Andy Gibb, Bob Hope, Jimmie Walker. *Music:* Bob Rozario. *Producers:* The Osmond Brothers, Art Fisher. *Writers:* James Parker, Michael Kagan. *Director:* Art Fisher.

### 1521 The Osmond Family Christmas Special.
Variety, 60 min., NBC, 12/15/80. A yuletide celebration with the Osmond family. *Hosts:* Donny Osmond, Marie Osmond.

*Guests:* Greg Evigan, Peggy Fleming, Doug Henning, The Osmond Family. *Music:* Bob Rozario. *Producers:* Wayne Osmond, Jay Osmond, Jerry McPhie. *Writers:* Bob Arnott, Ronny Graham, Walter C. Miller. *Director:* Walter C. Miller.

### 1522 The Osmond Family Thanksgiving Special.
Variety, 60 min., NBC, 11/26/81. A Thanksgiving celebration with the Osmond family. *Hosts:* Donny Osmond, Marie Osmond. *Guests:* The Don Crichton Dancers, Anthony Geary, The Osmond Family, Lorna Patterson. *Music:* Bob Rozario. *Producers:* Alan Osmond, Merrill Osmond, Jerry McPhie. *Writers:* Bob Arnott, Ronny Graham, Walter C. Miller. *Director:* Walter C. Miller.

### 1523 The Osmonds Special.
Variety, 60 min., CBS, 11/20/74. Music and songs with the Osmond Brothers and Marie. *Hosts:* Alan Osmond, Donny Osmond, Jay Osmond, Jimmy Osmond, Marie Osmond, Merrill Osmond, Wayne Osmond. *Guests:* Isaac Hayes, Andy Williams. *Music:* Earl Brown. *Producers:* Raymond Katz, Allan Blye, Chris Bearde. *Writers:* Chris Bearde, Allan Blye. *Director:* Jeff Margolis.

### 1524 The Other Broadway.
Variety, 60 min., Syndicated, 1/79. A London nightclub act by George Burns (monologues) and Abbe Lane (songs). *Hosts:* George Burns, Abbe Lane. *Music:* George Wilkins. *Producer-Director:* Rick Gardner.

### 1525 Otherwise Known as Sheila the Great.
Drama, 30 min., ABC, 3/23/91. An "ABC Weekend Special" about a 10-year-old girl named Sheila and her efforts to overcome her two worst fears—dogs and swimming—when her mother enrolls her in a camp for the summer. *Cast:* Leah Foster (Sheila), Stacey Moseley (Mouse), Cammy Peterson (Sondra), Shondi

Jones (Jane), David Rudman (Marty), Catherine Featherstone (Libby), Sheryl Simms-Foster (Mom), Stephen Bradley (Dad). *Producers:* Judy Blume, George Cooper. *Writer:* Judy Blume. *Director:* Lawrence Blume.

## 1526 Our Kids and the Best of Everything. Variety, 60 min., ABC, 6/21/87.

Celebrity parents and their children relate what is best for children (for example, recalling an experience and relating how the problem was resolved). *Hosts:* Joan Lunden, Alan Thicke. *Guests:* Debbie Allen, Danny DeVito, Joe Namath, Harriet Nelson, Joe Piscopo, Phylicia Rashad, Nancy Reagan, Geraldo Rivera, Dr. Benjamin Spock, Pia Zadora. *Music:* Mitch Kerper. *Producers:* Michael Krauss, Jay Rubin. *Writers:* Janice Kaplan, Ellen Steinberg, Sue Castle. *Director:* David Grossman.

## 1527 Our Town. A chronological listing of the three television adaptations of the play by Thornton Wilder.

A stage manager introduces the audience to the people of Grover's Corners, a small town in New Hampshire. It is a morning in May 1901 when Emily Webb, daughter of the newspaper editor, and George Bibbs, a doctor's son, fall in love. Three years later George and Emily marry; in 1911, Emily dies giving birth. The story relates Emily's feelings about life when she accepts a celestial offer to relive one day in her life. In addition to the three specials that follow, "Our Town" has also been seen as a segment of the following series: "Robert Montgomery Presents" (NBC, 4/10/50) with Burgess Meredith (Stage Manager) and Jean Gillespie (Emily); and "Pulitzer Prize Playhouse" (ABC, 12/1/50) with Edward Arnold (Stage Manager) and Betty Caulfield (Emily).

**1 Our Town** (90 min., NBC, 9/19/55). *Cast:* Frank Sinatra (Stage Manager), Eva Marie Saint (Emily Webb), Paul Newman (George Gibbs), Ernest

Truex (Dr. Gibbs), Sylvia Field (Mrs. Gibbs), Paul Hartman (Mr. Webb), Peg Hillias (Mrs. Webb), Carol Venzie (Mrs. Soames). *Music:* Nelson Riddle. *Producer:* Fred Coe. *Writer:* David Shaw. *Director:* Delbert Mann.

**2 Our Town** (90 min., NBC, 11/13/59). *Cast:* Art Carney (Stage Manager), Kathleen Widdoes (Emily Webb), Clint Kimbrough (George Gibbs), Bibi Osterwald (Mrs. Gibbs), Dana Elcar (Dr. Gibbs), Jerome Kilty (Mr. Webb), Mary Van Fleet (Mrs. Webb), Ginger MacManus (Rebecca Gibbs), Martha Greenhouse (Mrs. Soames). *Producer:* David Susskind. *Writers:* Jacqueline Babbin, Audrey Gellen. *Director:* Jose Quintero.

**3 Our Town** (2 hrs., NBC, 5/30/77). *Cast:* Hal Holbrook (Stage Manager), Glynnis O'Connor (Emily Webb), Robby Benson (George Gibbs), Ned Beatty (Dr. Gibbs), Sada Thompson (Mrs. Gibbs), Barbara Bel Geddes (Mrs. Webb), Ronny Cox (Mr. Webb), Elizabeth Cheshire (Rebecca Gibbs), Charlotte Rae (Mrs. Soames). *Producers:* Saul Jaffe, George Schaefer. *Director:* George Schaefer.

## 1528 Out of Step. Musical Drama, 60 min., ABC, 10/10/84.

Lisa Williams and Patti DiAngelo are teenage girls who are also best friends. Lisa is spirited and confident with a natural flair for dance. Patti is hardworking but less self-assured about her musical abilities. The story relates a problem each girl has and her attempts to overcome it: Lisa, when she auditions for and wins a job as a dancer (her lack of formal training soon becomes a source of deep frustration for her); and Patti, whose lack of self-confidence becomes an obstacle when she prepares for a music scholarship in classical piano. An "ABC Afterschool Special." *Cast:* Terry Donahoe (Lisa Williams), Johann Carlo (Patti DiAngelo), Laura Dean (Cheryl), Charlie McGowen (Tony), Veanne Cox (Robin Miller), Bambi Jordan (Laurie Michaels). *Pro-*

*ducers:* Carol Caruso, Frank Doelger. *Writers:* Michael Duncan, Richard Glatzer. *Director:* Jeffrey Hornaday.

### 1529 Out of Time. Drama, 60 min., NBC, 1/29/85.

While exploring a secret room in their barn, two youngsters, 13-year-old Bridget and her 9-year-old brother, Martin, discover an old sea chest that contains the personal belongings of Otto Frommer, an ancestor believed to be a nineteenth-century villain from Maryland. Without warning, Bridget and Martin are hurled from their home in Frederick County, Maryland, to 1851 Maryland via a time warp to learn the truth about Otto: in reality he was an avid abolitionist who bought slaves in order to free them. After learning the truth, the children are returned to 1985. *Cast:* Amy Locane (Bridget Frommer), R. D. Robb (Martin Frommer), Adam Baldwin (Otto Frommer), Dion Anderson (Taggert), Doug Tillett (Cedric Chamberlain), Katy Fannon (Anna), Hans Karem (Pastor). *Music:* Richard Brier. *Producer-Writers:* Ruth Pollack, Ira Klugerman, Patrick Prentice. *Director:* Michael Schweitzer.

### 1530 Over the Limit. Drama, 60 min., ABC, 3/22/90.

An "ABC Afterschool Special" about the dangers of teenage drinking and driving and the disaster that results when the two are mixed. *Cast:* Michael St. Gerard (Bobby Stewart), Keith Coogan (Matt), Lisanne Falk (Karen), Michael Lombard (Mr. Stewart), Ellen Hamilton Latzen (Casey), Tony LoBianco (Officer Abbott). *Theme performer,* "Get Up": R. E. M. *Music:* Robbie Kondar. *Producers:* Karen S. Shapiro, Gilbert Moses. *Writer:* Todd Strasser. *Director:* Nancy Cooperstein.

### 1531 Packy. Drama, 30 min., Syndicated, 4/87.

The story of a pushy theatrical agent (Packy Rowe) with a poor self-image who dies and goes to meet his maker — a God without a lot of razzmatazz. *Cast:* Jack Klugman (Packy Rowe), Bob Newhart (God), Steve Franken (Interviewer), Larry Gelman (Benny Wilkes). *Music:* Lan O'Kun. *Producers:* Ellwood E. Kieser, Mike Rhodes, James Moser. *Writer:* Lan O'Kun. *Director:* Jay Sandrich.

### 1532 Painting Churches. Drama, 90 min., PBS, 5/19/86.

A poignant story about a young artist (Mags) who returns home after a long absence to paint a portrait of her parents: a now senile father (Gardner) and a constantly complaining mother (Fanny). *Cast:* Roxanne Hart (Mags Church), Donald Moffat (Gardner Church), Sada Thompson (Fanny Church). *Music:* Conrad Susa. *Producers:* Phyllis Geller, David Loxton. *Writer:* Tina Howe. *Director:* Jack O'Brien.

### 1533 Pajama Tops. Comedy, 2 hrs., Showtime, 3/18/83.

The story, set in a villa in Deauville, France, follows the misadventures of George Chauvinet, the man of the house, as he struggles to conceal the presence of his mistress, the Parisian bombshell Babette Latouche, from his unsuspecting wife, Yvonne. *Cast:* Pia Zadora (Babette Latouche), Robert Klein (George Chauvinet), Susan George (Yvonne Chauvinet). *Producers:* Michael Brandman, Iris Merlis, Deborah Oppenheimer. *Writers:* Mawby Green, Ed Feilbert. *Director:* Rob Iscove.

### 1534 Panama Hattie. Comedy, 60 min., CBS, 11/10/54.

While in Panama, Hattie Maloney, a member of the singing and dancing Canal Zone Girls, meets and falls in love with Nick Bullett, the scion of a wealthy Philadelphia family. The story relates Hattie's efforts to impress the eligible Mr. Bullett, despite the differences their social positions create. Based on the musical by Herbert Fields and B. G. DeSylva. *Cast:* Ethel Merman (Hattie Maloney), Ray Middleton (Nick Bullett), Art Carney (Woozy), Jack E.

**Pia Zadora, star of "Pajama Tops"**

Leonard (Windy), Karin Wolfe (Gerry), Betty O'Neill (Mildred Carstairs), Neil Hamilton (Charles Randolph), Joseph Macauley (Bartender). *Music:* Buster Davis. *Producers:* Martin Manulis, Jule Styne. *Writer:* Ronald Alexander. *Director:* David Alexander.

**1535 Panorama.** Variety, 90 min., NBC, 2/26/56. A fast-paced series of comedy skits coupled with music and songs. *Host:* Imogene Coca. *Guests:* Rod Alexander, Eileen Barton, The Bil and Cora Baird Puppets, Alan Dale, Johnny Desmond, Robert Gallagher, Bill Hayes, Bambi Linn, Tony Randall. *Music:* Charles Sanford. *Producers:* Max Liebman, Bill Hobin. *Director:* Max Liebman.

**1536 Papa and Me.** Drama, 60 min., NBC, 2/10/76. A tender drama about the relationship between a young boy (Joseph) and his elderly grandfather (Papa D'Amico). *Cast:* Joseph

Mascolo (Papa D'Amico), Matthew Laborteaux (Joseph), Renata Vanni (Nana), Paul Picerni (Dominick), Dimitra Arliss (Lily), Robert Ginty (Father McKenna), Rhoda Gemignani (Aunt Olga), Lou Tiano (Uncle Al). *Producers:* George A. Heinemann, Michael McLean. *Writers:* William P. D'Angelo, Harvey Bullock, Ray Allen. *Director:* William P. D'Angelo.

**1537 Parade of Stars.** Variety, 2 hrs., ABC, 5/22/83. Celebrities perform in a benefit for the Actor's Fund charity in a program that recalls vaudeville's golden age. *Guests:* Eddie Albert, Debbie Allen, Edward Asner, Lauren Bacall, Milton Berle, George Burns, David Cassidy, Dick Cavett, Carol Channing, Michael Davis, Pam Dawber, Sandy Duncan, Bonnie Franklin, Jack Gilford, Gregory Hines, Ann Jillian, Larry Kent, Richard Kiley, Jack Klugman, Linda Lavin, Michele Lee, Dorothy Loudon, Lee

Meriwether, Christopher Plummer, Tony Randall, Ann Reinking, Jean Stapleton, Daniel J. Travanti, Gwen Verdon, James Whitmore, Shelley Winters, Michael York. *Announcer:* Lee Marshack. *Music:* Alexander H. Cohen. *Producer-Writer:* Hildy Parks. *Director:* Clark Jones.

### 1538 The Paradine Case.

Drama, 60 min., NBC, 3/11/62. A "Theater '62" presentation about a lawyer (Arthur Keane) who falls in love with his client—a woman (Maddalena Paradine) accused of murdering her husband. *Cast:* Richard Basehart (Arthur Keane), Viveca Lindfors (Maddalena Paradine), Boris Karloff (Sir Simon Flaquer), Robert Webber (Andre Latour), Bramwell Fletcher (Horfield), Tom Helmore (Farrell). *Producer:* Fred Coe. *Writer:* Robert Goldman. *Director:* Alex March.

### 1539 Paradise.

Comedy, 60 min., CBS, 3/12/74. The story of a couple who decide to get away from it all and spend their vacation on a tropical island paradise—and the misadventures that arise when the problems they left behind suddenly turn up as unexpected baggage. Also known as "One Night in Paradise." *Cast:* Renee Taylor (Marilyn/Carmel/Madelaine/Woman on Beach), Joseph Bologna (David/Biff/Tony/Nick), Ruth Buzzi (Roberta), Broderick Crawford (Patsy), Ted Knight (Dickie), Tama Leao (Fire Dancer). *Music:* Fotu Leao. *Producer-Directors:* Charles Grodin, Bill Foster. *Writers:* Renee Taylor, Joseph Bologna.

### 1540 The Paragon of Comedy.

Comedy, 60 min., Showtime, 4/21/84. Various skits that highlight the talents of comedian John Paragon. *Host:* John Paragon. *Guests:* Sandy Helberg, Suzanne Kent, JoAn Leizman, Edie McClurg, Tress MacNeille, John Moody, Cassandra (Elvira) Peterson, Paul (Pee Wee Herman) Reubens. *Producers:* Oliver Nelson, Judy Simon. *Writers:* John Paragon, Edie McClurg, Paul Reubens. *Director:* Wayne Orr.

### 1541 Paris in the Springtime.

Musical Comedy, 90 min., NBC, 1/21/56. Set in Paris, the story relates the romantic misadventures of a tap dancer (Steven) who becomes involved with two women: Josie, his former partner, now a nightclub dancer, and Jeannie, the manager of a theater group. *Cast:* Dan Dailey (Steven), Helen Gallagher (Josie), Gale Sherwood (Jeannie), Jack Whiting (Felix), Carleton Carpenter (Go-Go), Marcel Hillaire (Marcel). *Music:* Charles Sanford. *Producers:* Max Liebman, Bill Hobin. *Writers:* Neil Simon, William Friedberg. *Director:* Max Liebman.

### 1542 The Parsley Garden.

Drama, 30 min., ABC, 3/27/93. A television adaptation of the William Saroyan short story about an Armenian-American boy (Al) growing up in a small town (Fresno, California, in 1938). The simple story involves Al's efforts to acquire a hammer by working for it at Clemmer's Five and Dime. An "ABC Weekend Special." *Cast:* Adrienne Barbeau (Lucy; Al's mother), Christopher Miranda (Al), Tom Bosley (C. W. Clemmer), Curtis Armstrong (Tom), Vivian Luchessi (Leeza). *Narrator:* James Earl Jones. *Music:* Robert Irving. *Producers:* Adam Bleibtren, Faye Nuell. *Writer-Director:* Hank Saroyan.

### 1543 Passion and Memory.

Documentary, 60 min., PBS, 5/11/86. A retrospective on the careers of five black film pioneers: Stepin Fetchit, Hattie McDaniel, Bill "Bojangles" Robinson, Dorothy Dandridge, and Sidney Poitier. *Host-Narrator:* Robert Guillaume. *Guest:* Richard Widmark. *Music:* George Winston. *Producer-Director:* Roy Campanella, Jr. *Writers:* Roy Campanella, Jr., Christopher Koefoed.

**1544  Pat Benatar in Concert.**
Variety, 60 min., HBO, 11/5/83. A concert by the Grammy-winning rock star. Taped at Veterans Memorial Coliseum in New Haven, Connecticut. *Host:* Pat Benatar. *Music:* Neil Geraldo. *Producers:* Rick Newman, Richard Fields. *Director:* Marty Callner.

**1545  Pat Boone and Family.**
Variety, 60 min., ABC, 4/8/78. Songs and skits that revolve around daily happenings in the Boone household: parents Pat and Shirley and their daughters, Cherry, Lindy, Debby, and Laury. Guest stars are woven into the happenings: Dick Van Patten (a tennis playboy houseguest), Parker Stevenson (who makes his singing debut with Debby with the song "You and Me" in a romantic dating sketch), Fran Ryan (as the Boones' housekeeper, Maggy), Perry Lang (as Joey, the bartender at Pat's favorite watering hole, the Milky Way Bar) and Greg Lewis (as Grady, the neighbor). *Host:* Pat Boone. *Guests:* Perry Lang, Greg Lewis, Fran Ryan, Parker Stevenson, Dick Van Patten. *Music:* George Wyle. *Producers:* Jerry Weintraub, Bernard Rothman, Jack Wohl. *Writers:* Burt Styler, Adele Styler. *Director:* Perry Rosemond.

**1546  Pat Boone and Family Christmas Special.** Variety, 60 min., ABC, 12/8/79. A holiday celebration with Pat Boone and his family (his wife, Shirley, and their daughters, Cherry, Lindy, Debby, and Laury). *Host:* Pat Boone. *Guests:* Rosemary Clooney, Norman Fell, The Hudson Brothers, Audra Lindley. *Music:* George Wyle. *Producers:* Bernard Rothman, Jack Wohl. *Director:* Jack Regas.

**1547  Pat Boone and Family Easter Special.** Variety, 60 min., ABC, 4/15/79. An Easter celebration with Pat Boone and his family (his wife, Shirley, and their daughters,

Cherry, Lindy, Debby, and Laury). *Host:* Pat Boone. *Guests:* John Byner, Katherine Helmond, Ted Knight. *Music:* George Wyle. *Producers:* Jerry Weintraub, Bernard Rothman, Jack Wohl. *Director:* Jack Regas.

**1548  Pat Paulsen for President.** Comedy, 60 min., CBS, 10/20/68. The program relates comedian Pat Paulsen's mock campaign for president of the United States. Adapted from a series of skits on "The Smothers Brothers Comedy Hour." *Cast:* Pat Paulsen (The Candidate), Henry Fonda (The Narrator). *Producers:* Tom Smothers, Ken Kragen. *Writers:* Cecil Tuck, John Barrett, Mason Williams, Allan Blye. *Director:* Robert Collins.

**1549  The Patriots.** Drama, 90 min., NBC, 11/15/63. The story, set in the 1790s, relates the clash between Thomas Jefferson (who believes in the new constitution) and Alexander Hamilton (who opposes it) and its effect on the nation's future (having just been established as an independent nation). Based on the play by Sidney Kingsley and broadcast on the "Hallmark Hall of Fame." *Cast:* Charlton Heston (Thomas Jefferson), John Fraser (Alexander Hamilton), Howard St. John (George Washington), Peggy Ann Garner (Patsy), Frank Schofield (James Madison), Michael Higgins (James Monroe), Laurinda Barrett (Mrs. Hamilton), John Karlen (Ned). *Producer-Director:* George Schaefer. *Writer:* Robert Hartung.

**1550  The Patti LaBelle Show.** Variety, 60 min., NBC, 11/28/85. A Thanksgiving special of music and songs with singer Patti LaBelle and her guests. *Host:* Patti LaBelle. *Guests:* Bill Cosby, Amy Grant, Cyndi Lauper, Luther Vandross. *Music Directors:* Gene Page, Bud Ellison. *Producers:* Sandy Gallin, Armstead Edwards, Sid Krofft, Marty Krofft. *Writers:* Buz Kohan, Lorne Frohman, Paul Mooney,

Tom Perew, Carl Wolfson. *Director:* Steve Binder.

## 1551 The Patti Page Premiere Party Show. Variety, 30 min., NBC, 11/2/55. A program of music and songs with singer Patti Page in her first television special. *Host:* Patti Page. *Guests:* Perry Como, Gene Nelson, Franklin Pangborn, The Ray Charles Singers, Ben Wrigley. *Orchestras:* Mitchell Ayres, Joe Reisman. *Producer:* Harry Auger. *Writers:* Jimmy Shirl, Ervin Drake, Bud Burston. *Director:* Bill Colleran.

## 1552 Paul Anka in Monte Carlo. Variety, 60 min., CBS, 8/27/78. A musical variety hour taped in Monte Carlo. *Host:* Paul Anka. *Guests:* Suzanne Somers, Donna Summer. *Music:* Mike Barone. *Producer-Director:* Marty Pasetta. *Writer:* Buz Kohan.

Patti Page

## 1553 Paul Anka ... Music My Way. Variety, 60 min., ABC, 4/25/77. An hour of music and songs taped at the Hollywood Palladium. *Host:* Paul Anka. *Guests:* Natalie Cole, Dr. Buzzard's Original Church Band, St. Paul's Baptist Church Choir. *Music:* John Harris. *Producer-Direc-* *tor:* Marty Pasetta. *Writer:* Buz Kohan.

## 1554 Paul Lynde Specials. A chronological listing of the comedy specials hosted by comedian Paul Lynde. All are 60 minutes in length and broadcast by ABC.

**1 The Paul Lynde Comedy Hour (11/6/75).** *Guests:* Jack Albertson, The Osmond Brothers, Barbara Rhoades, Robbie Rist, Nancy Walker, Fred Willard. *Music:* Jack Elliott, Allyn Ferguson. *Producer:* Jack Burns. *Writers:* George Yanok, Bob O'Brien, Alan Thicke, Michael Weinberger, Laura Levine, Ann Elder, Paul Lynde. *Director:* Tony Charmoli.

**2 The Paul Lynde Halloween Special** (10/29/76). *Guests:* Tim Conway, Margaret Hamilton, Billie Hayes, Florence Henderson, Roz Kelly, Betty White. *Music:* Artie Butler. *Producers:* Raymond Katz, Sandy Gallin. *Writers:* Sol Weinstein, Howard Albrecht, Ron Pearlman, Ronny Graham. *Director:* Sid Smith.

**3 The Paul Lynde Comedy Hour** (4/23/77). *Guests:* Tom Biener, R. G. Brown, LeVar Burton, April Kelly, Cloris Leachman, Tony Randall, Felix Silla. *Music:* Eddie Karam. *Producers:* Raymond Katz, Sandy Gallin. *Writers:* Chet Dowling, Sandy Krinski, April Kelly, George Geiger, David Letterman, Jim Mulligan. *Director:* Sid Smith.

**4 The Paul Lynde Comedy Hour** (5/20/78). *Guests:* Harry Morgan, Juliet Prowse, Brenda Vaccaro. *Music:* Alf Clausen. *Producers:* Raymond Katz, Sandy Gallin. *Writer:* Stan Hart. *Director:* Jim Washburn.

**5 Paul Lynde at the Movies** (3/24/79). A comic look at movies as seen through the eyes of Paul Lynde (as movie buff Maurice Darlyrimple). *Guests:* Gary Coleman, Vicki Lawrence, Robert Urich, Betty White. *Music:* Peter Matz. *Producers:* Raymond Katz, Sandy Gallin. *Writers:* Sheldon Keller, Bryan Blackburn, Robert Casey Keller, Howard Albrecht. *Directors:* Joe Layton, Sheldon Keller.

**6 Paul Lynde Goes M-A-A-A-AD.** *Guests:* Charo, Vicki Lawrence, Marie Osmond. *Music:* Bob Rozario. *Producers:* Raymond Katz, Sandy Gallin. *Writers:* Stan Hart, Larry Siegel. *Director:* Joe Layton.

**1555 Paul McCartney Live in the New World.** Variety, 2 hrs., Fox, 6/15/93. A concert by Paul McCartney from the Blockbuster Video Pavilion in Charlotte, North Carolina. McCartney draws songs from his complete repertoire, including classic Beatles songs as well as songs from his *Off the Ground* album. *Host:* Paul McCartney. *Band:* Linda McCartney (vocals/keyboard), Robbie McIntosh (lead guitar), Hamish Stuart (rhythm, bass guitar), Paul Wickens (keyboard), Blaire Cunningham (drums). *Producer:* Steve J. Swartz. *Director:* Aubrey Powell.

**1556 The Paul Simon Special.** Variety, 60 min., NBC, 12/8/77. The singer-composer performs his own compositions. *Host:* Paul Simon. *Guests:* Chevy Chase, Art Garfunkel, Charles Grodin, Lily Tomlin. *Producer:* Lorne Michaels. *Writers:* Paul Simon, Lorne Michaels, Chevy Chase, Charles Grodin, Lily Tomlin, Tom Davis. *Director:* Dave Wilson.

**1557 Pavarotti and Friends.** Variety, 60 min., ABC, 3/29/82. Music and songs with opera star Luciano Pavarotti. *Host:* Luciano Pavarotti. *Guests:* Jacqueline Bisset, John McEnroe, Fernando Pavarotti, Richard Thomas, John Williams. *Music:* Emiloa Romahna. *Producers:* Herbert Breslin, Gary Smith, Dwight Hemion. *Writer:* Buz Kohan. *Director:* Dwight Hemion.

**1558 The Peapicker in Piccadilly.** Variety, 60 min., NBC, 11/24/69. Music and comedy from London's Piccadilly Palace that features the antics of singer-comedian Tennessee Ernie Ford. *Host:* Tennessee Ernie Ford. *Guests:* Davy Jones, Harry Secombe, Terry-Thomas. *Music Directors:* Jack Parnell, Derek Scott, Jack Fascinato. *Producers:* Digby Wolfe, Bob Wynn. *Writers:* Bob Wynn, Digby Wolfe, Sheldon Keller. *Director:* Bob Wynn.

## 1559 The Pee Wee Herman Show. Comedy, 60 min., HBO, 9/11/81.

The story, set in Pee Wee's Playhouse, spoofs children's shows of the 1950s via puppets, jokes, cartoons, and assorted weird characters who just happen to drop by. *Cast:* Paul Reubens (Pee Wee Herman), Phil Hartman (Kap'n Karl), Tito Larriva (Hammy), Nicole Panter (Susan), Lynne Stewart (Miss Yvonne), John Moody (Mailman Mike), John Paragon (Jambi), Edie McClurg (Hermit Hattie), Monica Ganas (Mrs. Jelly Donut), Brian Seff (Mr. Jelly Donut), JoAn Leizman (Joan). *Music:* Jay Condom. *Producers:* Paul Reubens, Marty Callner. *Writers:* Paul Reubens, Bill Stein, Marty Callner, Lynne Stewart, Phil Hartman, John Paragon, Edie McClurg. *Director:* Marty Callner.

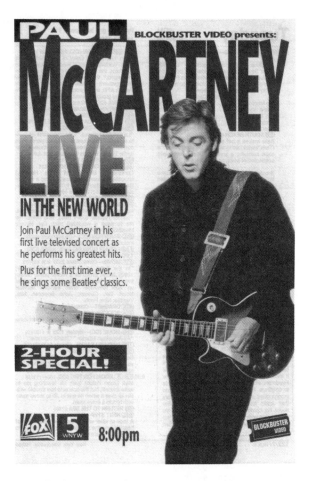

Ad for "Paul McCartney Live in the New World"

## 1560 Pee Wee's Playhouse Christmas Special. Comedy, 60 min., CBS, 12/21/88.

A primetime special based on the Saturday morning series, "Pee Wee's Playhouse," in which Pee Wee and the gang prepare to celebrate Christmas. *Cast:* Paul Reubens (Pee Wee Herman), Larry Fishburne (Cowboy Curtis), Suzanne Kent (Mrs. Rene), William Marshall (King of Cartoons), John Paragon (Jambi), Lynne Stewart (Miss Yvonne), Aaron Fletcher (Santa Claus), Kevin Carlson (Clockey). *Music:* Van Dyke Parks. *Producers:* Paul Reubens, Steve Binder. *Writers:* John Paragon, Paul Reubens. *Director:* Wayne Orr, Paul Reubens.

## 1561 Pee Wee's Ragtime Band. Drama, 30 min., Syndicated, 10/29/88.

The story of a teenage girl (Penelope) and her efforts to raise the spirit of her town (Aurora) by organizing a marching band for a Fourth of July celebration. *Cast:* Victoria Lennon (Penelope; nicknamed Pee Wee), Sylvia Davis (Granny), Bob Lipka

(Poppa), Robert Michael Morris (Mayor Baldridge). *Producer-Writer-Director:* Tom Robertson.

## 1562 Peek-a-Boo: The One and Only Phyllis Dixey. Drama, 1 hr. 45 min., PBS, 8/6/79. A musical drama based on the life of Phyllis Dixey, a British stripper of the 1930s and 1940s. *Cast:* Lesley-Anne Down (Phyllis Dixey), Christopher Murney (Jack Tracey), Jacqueline Tong (Judy), Michael Elphick (Wallace Parnell), Phyllis Dresser (Gretchin Franklin). *Music:* Alfred Ralston, Patrick Hodge. *Producer-Director:* Michael Tuchner. *Writer:* Philip Purser.

## 1563 Peeping Times. Comedy, 60 min., NBC, 1/25/78. A spoof of television news magazine shows. *Cast:* Alan Oppenheimer (Miles Rathbone), David Letterman (Dan Cochran), Sharon Spelman (Eva Braun), Ron Carey (Monk), Michael Fairman (Mayor of Ewell), Murphy Dunne (Dr. Burnett), J. J. Barry (Angelo Bertinelli). *Producers:* David Frost, Marvin Minoff. *Writers:* Bill Richmond, Gene Perret, Robert Illes, James Stein, Christopher Guest, Rudy DeLuca, Barry Levinson. *Directors:* Rudy De-Luca, Barry Levinson.

## 1564 Peggy Fleming Specials.
A chronological listing of the variety specials hosted by precision ice skater Peggy Fleming. All are 60 minutes in length.
**1 The Peggy Fleming Show** (NBC, 11/24/68). *Guests:* Richard Harris, Gene Kelly, Robert Paul, Spanky and Our Gang. *Music:* Marty Paich. *Producer-Director:* Robert Scheerer. *Writer:* Bob Wells.
**2 Peggy Fleming at Madison Square Garden** (NBC, 11/30/69). *Guests:* Jose Feliciano, The Ice Follies. *Producers:* Bob Banner, Clark Jones. *Writer:* Bruce W. Blythe. *Director:* Clark Jones.
**3 Peggy Fleming at Sun Valley** (NBC,

1/24/70). *Guests:* Pete Barbutti, Karen Carpenter, Richard Carpenter, Jean-Claude Killy, Hugh Smith, Bill Thomas. *Producers:* Bob Banner, Dick Foster. *Director:* Sterling Johnson.
**4 To Europe with Love** (NBC, 1/23/72). *Guests:* Willy Bictak, Paul Sibley, Andy Williams. *Producers:* Bob Banner, Dick Foster. *Director:* Sterling Johnson.
**5 Peggy Fleming Visits the Soviet Union** (NBC, 10/28/73). *Guests:* The Kirov Ballet, Vladimir Luzin, The Moscow Circus, Moscow's Civic Ballet, The Obrazsova Theater. *Producers:* Bob Banner, Dick Foster. *Director:* Sterling Johnson.
**6 Peggy Fleming with Holiday on Ice at Madison Square Garden** (CBS, 10/26/76). *Guests:* The Holiday on Ice Skaters, The Muppets, Andy Williams, Mark Wilson. *Music:* Paul Walberg. *Producer:* Bob Banner. *Director:* Steve Binder.

## 1565 The Peggy Lee Special.
Variety, 60 min., Syndicated, 5/66. An hour of songs with singer Peggy Lee. Also known as "Something Special: Peggy Lee." *Host:* Peggy Lee. *Guest:* Jean "Toots" Thielemans. *Music:* Ralph Carmichael. *Producer:* Jackie Barnett. *Director:* Dick Ross.

## 1566 Peking Encounter.
Drama, 60 min., Syndicated, 8/82. The romance between an American tourist (Susan) visiting Peking, China, and the Chinese musician (Tony) she meets and falls in love with. *Cast:* Diana Canova (Susan), Teneyck Swackhamer (Tony), June Lockhart (Emily), Mason Adams (Clyde Hawthorne), Shi Yong (Symphony conductor), Chen Chong (Guide). *Producers:* Robert Halmi, Cecile Tang. *Writer:* Cecile Tang. *Director:* E. W. Swackhamer.

## 1567 Penn and Teller: Don't Try This at Home! Variety, 60 min., CBS, 11/23/90. Illusionists Penn and Teller perform feats of illusion and

explain how they are done. *Hosts:* Penn and Teller. *Guests:* Jane Curtin, Victoria Jackson. *Producers:* Bernie Brillstein, Brad Grey, Scott Sanders. *Writers:* Penn Jillette, Teller, Mike Armstrong, Eddie Gorodetsky. *Director:* John Moffitt.

**1568 The People Next Door.** Drama, 90 min., CBS, 10/15/68. The story traces the slow destruction of a family by the generation gap, drugs, and a lack of understanding of each other. *Cast:* Lloyd Bridges (Arthur), Kim Hunter (Gerrie), Deborah Winters (Maxie), Peter Galman (Artie), Fritz Weaver (David), Phyllis Newman (Tina), Nehemiah Persoff (Dr. Salazar), Don Scardino (Sandy). *Producer:* Herbert Brodkin. *Writer:* J. P. Miller. *Director:* David Greene.

**1569 The People's Command Performance.** Variety, 2 hrs., CBS, 4/7/77. Performances by entertainers selected through a public opinion survey. *Hosts:* George Burns, Bernadette Peters. *Performers:* The Ace Trucking Company, George Benson, Edgar Bergen, LeVar Burton, George Carlin, Carol Channing, The Doobie Brothers, Nancy Dussault, Redd Foxx, Robert Goulet, Loretta Lynn, Don Rickles, Beverly Sills, Red Skelton, Dionne Warwick, Paul Williams. *Special Music:* Artie Malvin. *Music Directors:* Jack Elliott, Allyn Ferguson. *Producers:* Bob Stivers, Bernard Rothman, Jack Wohl. *Writer:* Herbert Baker. *Director:* Walter C. Miller.

**1570 The Perfect Date.** Comedy-Drama, 60 min., ABC, 4/19/90. An "ABC Afterschool Special" about a high school basketball star (Steven) and the mishaps that occur when he lines up a date with his idea of the perfect girl (Bernice). *Cast:* Richard Murphy (Steven Sanders), Lycia Naff (Bernice), James Sutorius (Mr. Sanders), Marnie Mosiman (Mrs. Sanders), Jason Kristopher (Carl), Alison Elliott (Cindy),

Terri Ivens (Iola), Emily Schulman (Anna), Jim Calvert (Dewey). *Music:* Ross Levinson. *Producer:* Joseph Stern. *Writer:* Josef Anderson. *Director:* Kristoffer Siegel-Tabori.

**1571 Perfectly Frank.** Variety, 60 min., Showtime, 1/82. A musical tribute to composer Frank Loesser (whose credits include *Guys and Dolls, The Most Happy Fella,* and *How to Succeed in Business Without Really Trying*). *Performer:* Cloris Leachman. *Producers:* Beth Trachtenberg, Steve Novick, Kenny Solms. *Writer:* Kenny Solms. *Director:* Peter LeDonne.

**1572 Perry Como Specials.** A chronological listing of the variety specials hosted by singer Perry Como. All are 60 minutes in length.

**1 The Perry Como Special** (NBC, 10/3/63). *Guests:* June Allyson, George Burns, Cyd Charisse, The Ray Charles Singers, Allan Sherman. *Announcer:* Frank Gallop. *Music:* Mitchell Ayres. *Producer-Director:* Bob Henry.

**2 The Perry Como Special** (NBC, 10/29/64). *Guests:* Anne Bancroft, Victor Borge, Stanley Holloway, The Ray Charles Singers. *Announcer:* Frank Gallop. *Music:* Nick Perito. *Producer-Director:* Bob Henry.

**3 The Perry Como Christmas Show** (NBC, 12/21/64). *Guests:* Angela Lansbury, Bob Newhart. *Announcer:* Frank Gallop. *Music:* Nick Perito. *Producer-Director:* Bob Henry. *Writer:* Goodman Ace.

**4 The Perry Como Show** (NBC, 2/4/65). *Guests:* Shirley Jones, The Ray Charles Singers, Danny Thomas. *Announcer:* Frank Gallop. *Music:* Nick Perito. *Producer-Director:* Bob Henry.

**5 The Perry Como Thanksgiving Show** (NBC, 11/22/65). *Guests:* Gertrude Berg, The Lennon Sisters, Bobby Vinton. *Announcer:* Frank Gallop. *Music:* Nick Perito. *Producer-Director:* Bob Henry.

**6 The Perry Como Christmas Show**

(NBC, 12/20/65). *Guests:* Roberta Peters, Jackie Vernon. *Announcer:* Frank Gallop. *Music:* Nick Perito. *Producer-Director:* Bob Henry.
**7 The Perry Como Springtime Special** (NBC, 3/28/66). *Guests:* The Danny Daniels Dancers, Liza Minnelli, Tommy Steele, Burr Tillstrom. *Announcer:* Frank Gallop. *Music:* Nick Perito. *Producer-Director:* Bob Henry. *Writer:* Goodman Ace.
**8 Perry Como's Summer Show** (NBC, 4/25/66). *Guests:* Jack Burns, The Danny Daniels Dancers, John Davidson, Ella Fitzgerald, Avery Schreiber, Caterina Valente. *Announcer:* Frank Gallop. *Music:* Nick Perito. *Producer-Director:* Bob Henry. *Writer:* Goodman Ace.
**9 The Perry Como Thanksgiving Special** (NBC, 11/21/66). *Guests:* The Danny Daniels Dancers, Angela Lansbury, Bob Newhart. *Announcer:* Frank Gallop. *Music:* Nick Perito. *Producer-Director:* Bob Henry. *Writer:* Goodman Ace.
**10 The Perry Como Christmas Show** (NBC, 12/19/66). *Guests:* Anne Meara, Anna Moffio, Jerry Stiller, Senor Wences. *Announcer:* Frank Gallop. *Music:* Nick Perito. *Producer-Director:* Bob Henry. *Writer:* Goodman Ace.
**11 The Perry Como Winter Show** (NBC, 1/25/67). *Guests:* Nancy Ames, Eddy Arnold, Jerry Atkins, The Danny Daniels Dancers, The Ray Charles Singers. *Announcer:* Frank Gallop. *Music:* Nick Perito. *Producer-Director:* Bob Henry.
**12 The Perry Como Valentine Special** (NBC, 2/22/67). *Guests:* Jack Burns, Frances Langford, The Ray Charles Singers, Avery Schreiber. *Announcer:* Frank Gallop. *Music:* Nick Perito. *Producer-Director:* Bob Henry. *Choreographer:* Danny Daniels.
**13 The Perry Como Springtime Show** (NBC, 4/17/67). *Guests:* George Carlin, The Ray Charles Singers, Nancy Wilson. *Announcer:* Frank Gallop. *Music:* Nick Perito. *Producer-Director:* Bob Henry. *Writer:* Goodman Ace.

**14 The Perry Como Special** (NBC, 5/22/67). *Guests:* Monique Leyrac, Oscar Peterson, Don Rice. *Music:* Nick Perito. *Producer-Director:* Bob Henry.
**15 The Perry Como Christmas Show** (NBC, 12/1/68). *Guests:* Don Adams, Carol Burnett, The Young Americans. *Music:* Nick Perito. *Producer-Director:* Bob Henry. *Writers:* Bill Angelos, Buz Kohan.
**16 The Many Moods of Perry Como** (NBC, 2/22/70). *Guests:* Nancy Sinatra, Flip Wilson. *Music:* Nick Perito. *Producer:* Bob Finkel. *Writers:* Bill Angelos, Buz Kohan, Ann Elder, Jeffrey Mayer. *Director:* Marty Pasetta.
**17 Perry Como's Winter Show** (NBC, 12/9/71). *Guests:* The Bob Sidney Dancers, Art Carney, The Establishment, Mitzi Gaynor. *Music:* Nick Perito. *Producers:* Bob Finkel, Buz Kohan, Bill Angelos. *Writers:* Bill Angelos, Buz Kohan, Jeffrey Mayer. *Director:* Marty Pasetta.
**18 Perry Como's Winter Show** (NBC, 12/4/72). *Guests:* Art Carney, Joey Heatherton, The Muppets, The Ray Charles Singers, The Robert Sidney Dancers. *Music:* Nick Perito. *Producers:* Bob Finkel, Saul Turteltaub, Bernie Orenstein. *Writers:* Saul Turteltaub, Bernie Orenstein. *Director:* John Moffitt.
**19 Perry Como's Winter Show** (NBC, 12/10/73). *Guests:* Jack Burns, The Establishment, Avery Schreiber, Sally Struthers. *Music:* Nick Perito. *Producer:* Bob Finkel. *Writers:* Bob Wells, Johnny Bradford, Lorne Michaels. *Director:* Tony Charmoli.
**20 The Perry Como Sunshine Show** (CBS, 4/10/74). *Guests:* Marie Osmond, Debbie Reynolds. *Music:* Nick Perito. *Producer-Director:* Nick Vanoff. *Writers:* Frank Peppiatt, John Aylesworth, Jay Burton.
**21 Perry Como's Summer of '74** (CBS, 9/12/74). *Guests:* Michele Lee, Paul Lynde, Jimmie Walker. *Music:* Ray Charles. *Producer-Director:* Nick Vanoff. *Writers:* Bob Ellison, Jay Burton, Mort Scharfman.

**22 The Perry Como Christmas Show** (CBS, 12/17/74). *Guests:* Karen Carpenter, Richard Carpenter, Peggy Fleming, Rich Little. *Music:* Nick Perito. *Producers:* Perry Como, Nick Vanoff. *Writer:* Herbert Baker.

**23 Como Country ... Perry and His Nashville Friends** (CBS, 2/17/75). *Guests:* Chet Atkins, Danny Davis and the Nashville Brass, Donna Fargo, Loretta Lynn, Charley Pride, Charlie Rich. *Music:* Ray Charles. *Producer:* Joseph Cates. *Writer:* Marty Farrell. *Director:* Walter C. Miller.

**24 Perry Como's Springtime Special** (CBS, 3/27/75). *Guests:* Pat Boone, Bob Newhart, Olivia Newton-John. *Music:* Nick Perito. *Producer:* Bob Finkel. *Writer:* Herbert Baker. *Director:* Jack Regas.

**25 Perry Como's Lake Tahoe Holiday** (CBS, 10/28/75). *Guests:* Suzy Chaffee, Bob Hope, Billie Jean King, Anne Murray. *Music:* Nick Perito. *Producers:* Bob Banner, Dick Foster. *Writer:* Bryan Joseph. *Director:* Sterling Johnson.

**26 Perry Como's Christmas in Mexico** (CBS, 12/15/75). *Guests:* The Captain and Tennille, Vikki Carr. *Music:* Nick Perito. *Producers:* Bob Banner, Stephen Pouliot. *Writer:* Nick Castle, Jr. *Director:* Sterling Johnson.

**27 Perry Como's Hawaiian Holiday** (NBC, 2/22/76). *Guests:* George Carlin, Petula Clark, Don Ho. *Music:* Nick Perito. *Producers:* Bob Banner, Dick Foster. *Writer:* Nick Castle, Jr. *Director:* Dick Foster.

**28 Perry Como's Spring in New Orleans** (NBC, 4/7/76). *Guests:* Leslie Uggams, Dick Van Dyke. *Music:* Nick Perito. *Producers:* Bob Banner, Stephen Pouliot. *Writer:* Alan Baker. *Director:* Stephen Pouliot.

**29 Perry Como in Las Vegas** (NBC, 9/11/76). *Guests:* Ann-Margret, Rich Little. *Music:* Nick Perito. *Producers:* Bob Banner, Stephen Pouliot. *Writer:* Jim Mulligan. *Director:* Kip Walton.

**30 Perry Como's Christmas in Aus-** tria (NBC, 12/13/76). *Guests:* Senta Berger, Sid Caesar. *Music:* Nick Perito. *Producers:* Bob Banner, Stephen Pouliot. *Writer-Director:* Stephen Pouliot.

**31 Perry Como's Music from Hollywood** (ABC, 3/28/77). *Guests:* Sandy Duncan, Shirley Jones, Hal Linden, Henry Mancini. *Music:* Nick Perito. *Producer-Director:* Bob Henry. *Writer:* George Yanok.

**32 Perry Como's Olde English Christmas** (ABC, 12/14/77). *Guests:* Petula Clark, John Curry. *Music:* Nick Perito. *Producer-Director:* Yvonne Littlewood.

**33 Perry Como's Easter by the Sea** (ABC, 3/22/78). *Guests:* Debby Boone, Kenny Rogers. *Music:* Nick Perito. *Producers:* Bob Banner, Stephen Pouliot. *Writer:* Jim Mulligan. *Director:* David Acumba.

**34 The Perry Como Springtime Special** (ABC, 4/9/79). *Guests:* Pam Dawber, Bernadette Peters. *Music:* Nick Perito. *Producer:* Bob Banner. *Director:* Russ Petranto.

**35 Perry Como's Christmas in New Mexico** (ABC, 12/14/79). *Guests:* Michele Lee, Sara Litzsinger, The Peppercorn Players Puppets, The St. Patrick's Cathedral Choir. *Music:* Nick Perito. *Producers:* Stan Braddock, Jeff Margolis. *Writer:* Rod Warren. *Director:* Jeff Margolis.

**36 Perry Como's Bahama Holiday** (ABC, 5/21/80). *Guests:* Daryl Dragon, Loretta Swit, Toni Tennille. *Music:* Nick Perito. *Producers:* Bob Banner, Stephen Pouliot. *Writer:* Stephen Pouliot. *Director:* Sterling Johnson.

**37 Perry Como's Christmas in the Holy Land** (ABC, 12/13/80). *Guest:* Richard Chamberlain. *Music:* Nick Perito. *Producers:* Bob Banner, Stephen Pouliot. *Writer:* Stephen Pouliot. *Director:* Sterling Johnson.

**38 Perry Como's Spring in San Francisco** (ABC, 5/10/81). *Guests:* Larry Gatlin, Cheryl Ladd. *Music:* Nick Perito. *Producers:* Bob Banner, Stephen Pouliot. *Writers:* Sterling

Julia Migenes, George Strait, Perry Como, and Angie Dickinson of "The Perry Como Christmas Special."

Johnson, Stephen Pouliot, Harry Crane. *Director:* Sterling Johnson.

**39 Perry Como's French-Canadian Christmas** (ABC, 12/21/81). *Guests:* Debby Boone, Andre Gagnon, Dorothy Hamill. *Music:* Nick Perito. *Producers:* Bob Banner, Stephen Pouliot. *Writer:* Stephen Pouliot. *Director:* Jeff Margolis.

**40 Perry Como's Easter in Guadalajara** (ABC, 4/13/82). *Guests:* Charo, Ann Jillian. *Music:* Nick Perito. *Producers:* Bob Banner, Stephen Pouliot. *Writer:* Stephen Pouliot. *Director:* Jeff Margolis.

**41 Perry Como's Christmas in Paris** (ABC, 12/18/82). *Guests:* Angie Dickinson, The Notre Dame Boys Choir, Line Renaud. *Music:* Nick Perito. *Producers:* Bob Banner, Stephen Pouliot. *Writers:* Phil Kellard, Stephen Pouliot. *Director:* Kip Walton.

**42 Perry Como's Christmas in New York** (ABC, 12/17/83). *Guests:* Michele Lee, Sara Litzsinger. *Music:* Nick Perito.

*Producer:* Jeff Margolis. *Writer:* Rod Warren. *Director:* Jeff Margolis.

**43 Perry Como's Christmas in England** (ABC, 12/15/84). *Guest:* Ann-Margret. *Music:* Nick Perito. *Producer-Director:* Jeff Margolis. *Writer:* Rod Warren.

**44 Perry Como: Las Vegas Style** (Syndicated, 5/85). *Guests:* Ann-Margret, Rich Little. *Music:* Nick Perito. *Producers:* Bob Banner, Stephen Pouliot. *Writer:* Jim Mulligan. *Director:* Kip Walton.

**45 Perry Como's Christmas in Hawaii** (ABC, 12/14/85). *Guests:* Marie Osmond, Burt Reynolds. *Music:* Nick Perito. *Producer-Director:* Don Mischer. *Writer:* Buz Kohan.

**46 The Perry Como Christmas Special** (ABC, 12/6/86). *Guests:* Angie Dickinson, Julia Migenes, The San Antonio Symphony Orchestra and Master Singers, George Strait. *Music:* Nick Perito. *Producer-Director:* Bob Wynn. *Writer:* Jim McGinn.

**1573 Peter Marshall Salutes the Big Bands.** Variety, 60 min., Syndicated, 8/81. A salute to the big band era. *Host:* Peter Marshall. *Guests:* Tex Beneke, Ray Eberle, Paula Kelly, The Modernaires, Helen O'Connell, Jack Sperling. *Music:* Al Peligrini. *Producers:* Peter Marshall, Bill Armstrong. *Director:* Bob Cawley.

**1574 Peter Pan.** Musical Fantasy, 2 hrs., NBC, 3/7/55. The adventures of Peter Pan, the boy who never grew up, and his exploits with the Darling children (Wendy, John, and Michael) in Never Land, where they are menaced by the evil Captain Hook and his pirates. Based on the 1904 play by Sir James M. Barrie. See also the following three titles. *Cast:* Mary Martin (Peter Pan), Cyril Ritchard (Captain Hook/George Darling), Margalo Gillmore (Mary Darling), Kathleen Nolan (Wendy Darling), Robert Harrington (John Darling), Joseph Stafford (Michael Darling), Hellen Halliday (Liza), Joe E. Marks (Smee), Sondra Lee (Tiger Lily), David Bean (Slightly), Ann Connolly (Wendy as an adult), Paris Theodore (Nibs), Frank Lindsay (Noodles), Joan Tewkesbury (Ostrich), Norman Shelly (Crocodile). *Music Director:* Louis Adrian. *Music Supervisor:* Harry Sosnik. *Music:* Mark Charlap, Jule Styne. *Lyrics:* Adolph Green, Carolyn Leigh, Betty Comden, Sumner Locke Elliott. *Producers:* Richard Halliday, Fred Coe. *Director:* Jerome Robbins.

**1575 Peter Pan.** Musical Fantasy, 2 hrs., NBC, 1/9/56. A second television adaptation of Sir James Barrie's fantasy. A live, color, restaged version of the prior title. *Cast:* Mary Martin (Peter Pan), Cyril Ritchard (Captain Hook/Mr. Darling), Margalo Gillmore (Mrs. Darling), Kathleen Nolan (Wendy Darling), Michael Allen (John Darling), Tommy Halloran (Michael Darling), Hellen Halliday (Liza), Norman Shelly (Nana the dog/Crocodile), Joe

E. Marks (Smee), Sondra Lee (Tiger Lily). *Music:* Mark Charlap, Jule Styne. *Lyrics:* Carolyn Leigh, Betty Comden, Adolph Green. *Incidental Music:* Trude Rittman, Elmer Bernstein. *Producer-Stager-Choreographer:* Jerome Robbins.

**1576 Peter Pan.** Musical Fantasy, 2 hrs., NBC, 12/8/60. A third staging of the Barrie classic (this time in color and on videotape). See first title for storyline. *Narrator:* Lynn Fontanne. *Cast:* Mary Martin (Peter Pan), Cyril Ritchard (Captain Hook/Mr. Darling), Maureen Bailey (Wendy Darling/Jane), Margalo Gillmore (Mrs. Darling), Sondra Lee (Tiger Lily), Joey Trent (John Darling), Kent Fletcher (Michael Darling), Jacqueline Mayro (Liza), Joe E. Marks (Smee), Norman Shelly (Nana/Crocodile), Edmund Gaines (Slightly), William Snowden (Curly), Richard Watt (Lion), Joan Tewkesbury (Ostrich), Peggy Maurer (Wendy; grown up), Frank Lindsay (Noodles). *Music Arranger:* Albert Sendry. *Music:* Mark Charlap, Jule Styne. *Music Conductor:* John Lesko. *Lyrics:* Carolyn Leigh, Betty Comden, Adolph Green. *Producers:* Richard Halliday, Dick Linkrous. *Writer:* Sumner Locke Elliott. *Director:* Vincent J. Donehue.

**1577 Peter Pan.** Musical Fantasy, 2 hrs., NBC, 12/12/76. Television's fourth adaptation of the 1904 play. See also the prior three titles. Aired as a "Hallmark Hall of Fame" production. *Cast:* Mia Farrow (Peter Pan), Danny Kaye (Captain Hook/Mr. Darling), Virginia McKenna (Mrs. Darling), Paula Kelly (Tiger Lily), Briony McRoberts (Wendy Darling), Ian Sharrock (John Darling), Adam Stafford (Michael Darling), Peter O'Farrell (Nana/Crocodile), Jerome Watts (Slightly), Nicky Lyndhurst (Tootles), Adam Richens (Nibs), Michael Deeks (Curly), Tony Sympson (Smee), Joe Melia (Starkey), Jill Gascione (Wendy; older), Linsey Baxter (Jane). *Narrator:*

Sir John Gielgud. *Music Director:* Ian
Fraser. *Music and Lyrics:* Anthony
Newley, Leslie Bricusse. *Producers:*
Gary Smith, Dwight Hemion. *Writers:*
Jack Burns, Andrew Birkin. *Director:*
Dwight Hemion.

**1578 The Petrified Forest.**
Drama, 90 min., NBC, 5/30/55. The
story of Alan Squire, a drifter who becomes involved with Gabby Maple, the
daughter of the owner of an Arizona
diner, and a gang of escaped convicts,
led by Duke Mantee, as they seize the
diner for a hideout. Based on the play
by Robert Emmett Sherwood. "The
Petrified Forest" was also seen as a segment of "Robert Montgomery Presents" (NBC, 10/23/50) with Robert
Montgomery (Alan), Joan Lorring
(Gabby), and Herbert Rudley (Duke);
and "Celanese Theater" (ABC, 2/20/52)
with David Niven (Alan), Kim Hunter
(Gabby), and Lloyd Gough (Duke).
*Cast:* Henry Fonda (Alan Squire),
Lauren Bacall (Gabby Maple), Hum-
phrey Bogart (Duke Mantee), Paul
Hartman (Jason Maple), Jack Warden
(Boze), Richard Jaeckel (Ruby), Nata-
lie Schafer (Mrs. Chisholm), Richard
Gaines (Mr. Chisholm), Jack Klugman
(Jackie), Joseph Sweeney (Gramps),
Steve Ritch (Lineman), Dick Elliott
(Commander). *Music:* Harry Sosnik.
*Producers:* Fred Coe, William Nichols.
*Director:* Delbert Mann.

**1579 Petula.** Variety, 60 min.,
NBC, 4/9/68. A charming hour of
music and songs. The program created
a nationwide controversy when, during
a song, Petula Clark held the arm of
her guest, Harry Belafonte. For a white
to touch a black on television was considered taboo at the time and much
criticism and controversy resulted from
Miss Clark's innocent gesture. *Host:*
Petula Clark. *Guest:* Harry Belafonte.
*Producers:* Steve Binder, Yvonne Littlewood. *Writers:* Allan Blye, Mason
Williams, Gordon Farr, Steven Stern.
*Director:* Steve Binder.

**1580 Petula.** Variety, 60 min.,
ABC, 12/9/70. Music and songs from
Caesar's Palace in Las Vegas. *Host:*
Petula Clark. *Guests:* The Everly
Brothers, David Frost, Peggy Lee,
Dean Martin, The Mike Sammes
Singers, The Paddy Stone Dancers.
*Music:* Jack Parnell. *Producer:* Gary
Smith. *Writers:* Herb Sargent, Bob
Ellison. *Director:* Dwight Hemion.

**1581 The Phenomenon of
Benji.** Documentary, 30 min., ABC,
5/4/78. A behind-the-scenes look at
Benji, the canine star of motion pic-
tures. *Guests:* Edgar Buchanan, Mere-
dith MacRae, Charlie Rich. *Producers:*
Joe Camp, Richard Baker. *Writers:*
Joe Camp, Dan Witt, Richard Baker.
*Director:* Stan Harris.

**1582 Phil Collins—No Jacket
Required.** Variety, 60 min., HBO,
9/28/85. Highlights of singer Phil Collins's 1985 concert from Reunion Arena
in Dallas. *Host:* Phil Collins. *Producers:* Bob Hart, Tony Smith, Peter
Flattery. *Director:* Jim Yukich.

**1583 Phil Silvers in New
York.** Variety, 60 min., CBS, 9/9/63.
Music, songs, and comedy sketches set
against the background of New York
City. *Host:* Phil Silvers. *Guests:* Carol
Haney, Carol Lawrence, Jules Mun-
shin. *Producer:* Nat Hiken. *Writers:*
Billy Friedberg, Nat Hiken, Charles
Sherman. *Director:* Greg Garrison.

**1584 Phil Silvers on Broad-
way.** Variety, 60 min., CBS, 5/13/58.
A music and comedy revue of current
(1958) Broadway shows. *Host:* Phil
Silvers. *Guests:* Georgann Johnson,
The June Taylor Dancers, Gloria
Krieger, William Redfield. *Music
Directors:* Hal Hastings, Ralph Burns.
*Producer:* Allan Sherman. *Writers:*
Will Glickman, Joe Stein, Allan Sher-
man. *Director:* Bill Hobin.

## The Phil Silvers Pontiac Special: Keep in Step *see* Keep in Step

**1585 The Philadelphia Story.** Comedy, 60 min., CBS, 12/8/54. The story of a reporter (Mike Connor) and a photographer (Liz Imbrie) assigned to cover the fashionable wedding of wealthy Tracy Lord to the snobbish George Kittredge, and the problems that arise when Tracy has second thoughts about George and announces that she still loves her first husband, Dexter Haven. Based on the play by Philip Barry. In addition to the title that follows, "The Philadelphia Story" was also adapted to television as a segment of "Robert Montgomery Presents" (NBC, 12/4/50) with Leslie Nielsen (Mike), Barbara Bel Geddes (Tracy), and Richard Derr (Dexter). *Cast:* Richard Carlson (Mike Connor), Neva Patterson (Liz Imbrie), Dorothy McGuire (Tracy Lord), Charles Winninger (Willie Tracy), John Payne (Dexter Haven), Mary Astor (Margaret Lord), Jane Sutherland (Dinah Lord), Dick Foran (George Kittredge). *Music:* David Broekman. *Producer:* Martin Manulis. *Writer:* Philip Barry, Jr. *Director:* David Alexander.

**1586 The Philadelphia Story.** Comedy, 90 min., NBC, 12/7/59. A second special adaptation of the Broadway play by Philip Barry. See the prior title for storyline. *Cast:* Christopher Plummer (Mike Connor), Ruth Roman (Liz Imbrie), Diana Lynn (Tracy Lord), Gig Young (Dexter Haven), Don DeFore (George Kittredge), Mary Astor (Margaret Lord), Gaye Huston (Dinah Lord), Alan Webb (Seth Lord), Leon Janney (Sidney Kidd). *Producers:* David Susskind, Fielder Cook. *Writers:* Jacqueline Babbin, Audrey Gellen. *Director:* Fielder Cook.

**1587 Piaf.** Drama, 74 min., The Entertainment Channel, 9/6/82. A dramatic retelling of the life of Edith Piaf, called France's "Little Sparrow," who led a life full of controversy and scandal, yet became a vivid symbol of love, courage, and survival to the world. Based on the Broadway play. *Cast:* Jane Lapotaire (Edith Piaf), Zoe Wanamaker (Toine), David Leary (Emcee/Manager), Peter Friedman (Papa Leplee), Nicholas Woodeson (Emil), Jean Smart (Marlene), Robert Christian (Eddie), Stephen Davies (Pierre), Sherry Steiner (Nurse). *Music:* Michael Dansicker. *Producer:* Bill Siegler. *Writer:* Pam Gems. *Director:* Gary Halvorson.

**1588 The Picture of Dorian Gray.** Drama, 60 min., CBS, 12/6/61. The story of Dorian Gray, a man unaffected by age or sin, whose portrait, painted by artist Basil Hallward, constantly changes, reflecting his scandalous life. Based on the novel by Oscar Wilde. See the following title also. *Cast:* Sir Cedric Hardwicke (Narrator), John Fraser (Dorian Gray), Louis Hayward (Basil Hallward), George C. Scott (Lord Henry Wotton), Susan Oliver (Susan Vane), Robert Walker, Jr. (James Vane), Carrie Nye (Felicia), Margaret Phillips (Pamela). *Producers:* David Susskind, Jacqueline Babbin. *Writers:* Jacqueline Babbin, Audrey Gellen. *Director:* Paul Bogart.

**1589 The Picture of Dorian Gray.** Drama, 3 hrs., ABC, 4/23 and 4/24/73. A second television adaptation of the novel by Oscar Wilde. See the previous title for storyline. *Cast:* Shane Briant (Dorian Gray), Charles Aidman (Basil Hallward), Nigel Davenport (Sir Henry Wotton), Fionnuala Flanagan (Felicia), John Karlen (Alan Campbell), Linda Kelsey (Beatrice), Vanessa Howard (Sybil Vane), Dixie Marquis (Madame De Ferrol). *Music:* Robert Cobert. *Producer:* Dan Curtis. *Writer:* John Tomerlin. *Director:* Glenn Jordan.

## 1590 The Pied Piper of Hamelin. Musical, 90 min., NBC, 11/26/57.

A musical adaptation of the German legend about a town infested with rats, and of a wanderer who uses his magical flute to lure the rodents out of the town of Hamelin. *Cast:* Van Johnson (Pied Piper), Claude Rains (Mayor), Lori Nelson (Maria), Kay Starr (Mother), Jim Backus (King's Emissary), Doodles Weaver (First Counselor), Stanley Adams (Second Counselor), Rene Kroper (Paul). *Music Director:* Pete King. *Music:* Eduard Grieg. *Lyrics:* Hal Stanley, Irving Taylor. *Producer:* Hal Stanley. *Director:* Bretaigne Windust.

## 1591 The Pinballs. Drama, 60 min., ABC, 10/26/77.

Carlie, Thomas J., and Harvey are three children from varying backgrounds who now live in a foster home (the Masons). Carlie is very pretty but tough and argumentative and cannot adjust to her latest stepfather. Thomas J. was abandoned as a baby and raised by two elderly ladies who are also twins. He was sent to the foster home when the twins were hospitalized. Harvey is a bright and sensitive boy who was deserted by his mother when she left to join a commune. The moving "ABC Afterschool Special" relates the children's efforts to adjust to a new home and tries to answer a question raised by Carlie— "Can three foster children ever find the family love and happiness they need? Or will it always be 'pinballs'—tossed here, there, everywhere, always under someone else's care?" *Cast:* Kristy McNichol (Carlie Higgins), Johnny Doran (Harvey), Sparky Marcus (Thomas J.), Priscilla Morrill (Ramona Mason), Walter Brooke (Mr. Mason), Jacque Lynn Colton (Mrs. Harris), Barry Coe (Harvey's father). *Producer:* Martin Tahse. *Writer:* Jim Inman. *Director:* Richard Bennett.

## 1592 Pinocchio. A chronological listing of the three television adaptations of the classic children's story by Carlo Collodi. The simple story of a wooden boy (Pinocchio) from his creation by a lonely toymaker (Gepetto) to his search for truth, courage, and unselfishness—the elements he needs to become a real boy.

**1 Pinocchio** (60 min., NBC, 10/13/57). *Cast:* Mickey Rooney (Pinocchio), Walter Slezak (Papa Gepetto), Fran Allison (Fairy Queen), Stubby Kaye (Town Crier), Jerry Colonna (Jolly Coachman), Martyn Green (Fox), Sondra Lee (Gepetto's cat), Matt Mattox (Fox's friend). *Music Director:* Glenn Osser. *Music:* Alec Wilder. *Lyrics:* William Engvick. *Producer-Writer-Director:* Yasha Frank.

**2 Pinocchio** (60 min., NBC, 12/8/68). *Cast:* Peter Noone (Pinocchio), Burl Ives (Gepetto), Anita Gillette (Blue Fairy), Mort Marshall (Cat), Jack Fletcher (Cat), Ned Wertimer (Farmer Whale), Charlotte Rae (Rosa Whale), Pierre Epstein (Weasel). *Music:* Walter Marks. *Producer:* Richard Lewine. *Writer:* Ernest Kinoy. *Director:* Sid Smith. *Note:* Aired on the "Hallmark Hall of Fame."

**3 Pinocchio** (90 min., CBS, 3/27/76). *Cast:* Sandy Duncan (Pinocchio), Danny Kaye (Gepetto), Flip Wilson (The Fox), Liz Torres (The Cat), Gary Morgan (Candlewick), Clive Revill (Coachman), Don Correa (First Bad Boy), Roy Smith (Second Bad Boy). *Music Director:* Eddie Karam. *Songs:* Billy Barnes. *Producer:* Bernard Rothman. *Writer:* Herbert Baker. *Directors:* Sid Smith, Ron Field.

## 1593 Pinocchio's Christmas. Cartoon, 60 min., ABC, 12/3/80.

A sequel to the Carlo Collodi classic that finds Pinocchio, the wooden boy, searching for the perfect Christmas gift for his Papa Gepetto. *Voices:* Todd Parker (Pinocchio), George S. Irving (Gepetto), Alan King (Fire Eater). *Other Voices:* Timothy Blake, Patricia Bright, Diane Leslie, Robert McFadden, Gerry Matthews, Ray Owens,

Allen Swift. *Music:* Maury Laws. *Lyrics:* Julian P. Gardner. *Producer-Directors:* Arthur Rankin, Jr., Jules Bass. *Writer:* Romeo Muller.

**1594 P. J. and the President's Son.** Drama, 60 min., ABC, 11/10/76. A contemporary drama based on the Mark Twain classic *The Prince and the Pauper*, wherein P. J., the son of a middle-class Washington, D.C., family, and Preston, the son of the president of the United States, switch places for a few days after a chance encounter reveals they are exact look-alikes. Aired as an "ABC Afterschool Special." *Cast:* Lance Kerwin (P. J./Preston), Irene Tedrow (Grandma McNutly), Laurence Haddon (Mr. Nolan), Patti Cohoon (Tina), Peter Brandon (The President), Jane Brandon (First Lady), Fritz Feld (The Chef), Rosalind Chao (Ambassador's Daughter), Carol Worthington (Reporter). *Music:* Joe Weber. *Producer:* Fran Sears. *Writer:* Thomas Baum. *Director:* Larry Elikann.

**1595 A Place at the Table.** Drama, 60 min., NBC, 3/20/88. A story about hunger in America as seen through the eyes of Rachel Singer, a young girl who learns that a classmate (Charlie) and his family are literally going hungry when the boy's father loses his job. *Cast:* Susan Dey (Beth Williams), Jenny Lewis (Rachel Singer), Luke Haas (Charlie Williams), David Morse (Tom Williams), Jean Smart (Susan Singer), Jandi Swanson (Emily Williams), Matthew Newmark (Kevin), Christopher Burton (Andrew), Lindsey Fisher (Karen). *Music:* Nan Schwartz. *Producers:* Joan Barnett, Alan Landsburg. *Writer:* E. H. Guest. *Director:* Arthur Allan Siedelman.

**1596 A Place to Die.** Thriller, 90 min., ABC, 4/18/75. A tale of devil worship in a picturesque English village, involving a doctor and his American bride. *Cast:* Alexandra Hay (Tessa), Bryan Marshall (Bruce), Lila

Kaye (Bess), Sally Stephens (Jill). *Music:* Laurie Johnson. *Producer:* Cecil Clarke. *Writer:* Terence Feely. *Director:* Peter Jeffries.

**1597 Placido Domingo Sings Zarzuela!** Variety, 60 min., PBS, 4/2/86. Grand opera star Placido Domingo and Spain's Antologia de la Zarzuela (a touring company) perform excerpts from some of Spain's most tuneful operettas. Taped at Madison Square Garden in August 1985. *Host:* Ricardo Montalban. *Star:* Placido Domingo. *Announcer:* Peter Allen. *Orchestra:* Jose DeFelipe. *Producers:* Mel Howard, David Lown. *Writer:* Gary Lipton. *Director:* Kirk Browning.

**1598 Placido Domingo ... Stepping Out with the Ladies.** Variety, 60 min., ABC, 5/14/85. An hour of music and song with opera star Placido Domingo as he tours Manhattan with his female guests. *Host:* Placido Domingo. *Guests:* Susan Anton, Patti LaBelle, Marilyn McCoo, Maureen McGovern, Stefanie Powers, Juliet Prowse, Leslie Uggams. *Music:* Elliot Lawrence. *Producers:* Alexander H. Cohen, Paul Miller, Hildy Parks. *Writer:* Hildy Parks.

**1599 Play It Again, Charlie Brown.** Cartoon, 30 min., CBS, 3/28/71. Through Lucy's meddling, Schroeder, the gifted pianist, is booked to play his toy piano for the PTA. The story relates his efforts to please an audience that is expecting a rock concert from a boy who is strictly a Beethoven fan. *Voices:* Chris Inglis (Charlie Brown), Pamelyn Ferdin (Lucy), Stephen Shea (Linus), Danny Hjelm (Schroeder), Hilary Momberger (Sally), Linda Mendelson (Frieda), Kip DeFaria (Peppermint Patty), Bill Melendez (Snoopy). *Music:* John Scott Trotter. *Producers:* Lee Mendelson, Bill Melendez. *Writer:* Charles M. Schulz. *Director:* Bill Melendez.

**1600 Play It Again, Uncle Sam.** Variety, 60 min., ABC, 10/1/75. A musical salute to American history. *Host:* Gloria Loring. *Guests:* Sammy Cahn, Bob Hope, Henry Mancini, Tom Smothers. *Producer-Writer:* Alan Thicke. *Director:* Larry Lancit.

**1601 Playboy's Playmate Party.** Variety, 90 min., ABC, 5/12/77. A lavish party at the Playboy Mansion West to introduce the 1977 Playmate of the Year. *Host:* Dick Martin. *Guests:* Steve Bluestein, Jay Leno, Barbara Mandrell, Johnnie Taylor. *Producers:* Hugh Hefner, Michael Trikilis. *Director:* Jack Regas.

**1602 Playboy's 25th Anniversary Celebration.** Variety, 60 min., ABC, 5/7/79. A salute to *Playboy* magazine on the occasion of its twenty-fifth anniversary. Includes comments from celebrities and clips from Hugh Hefner's series, "Playboy After Dark" (Syndicated, 1969). *Hosts:* James Caan, Tony Curtis, George Plimpton. *Guests:* Ray Bradbury, Chevy Chase, Bill Cosby, Hugh Hefner, Buck Henry, Bill Russell, Carl Sandburg. *Music:* Don Randi. *Producers:* Hugh Hefner, Edward L. Rissien. *Producer-Writer-Director:* Marshall Flaum.

**1603 Plaza Suite.** Comedy, 2 hrs., HBO, 12/31/82. The first of two adaptations of the Neil Simon comedy about events in the lives of three couples who, at different times, stayed at the same suite (719) of the Plaza Hotel in New York City. See the following title also. (1) "A Visitor from Mamaroneck." The story of Sam and Carol Nash, a married couple who return to the Plaza Hotel to celebrate their twenty-third wedding anniversary. (2) "A Visitor from Hollywood." A Hollywood producer (Jessie) returns to New York to seduce an old girlfriend (Muriel). (3) "A Visitor from Forest Hills." A family faces a sudden crisis

when their daughter decides not to get married moments before her wedding at the Plaza Hotel. *Cast:* Lee Grant (Karen Nash; story 1. Muriel Tate; story 2. Claire Hubley; story 3), Jerry Orbach (Sam Nash; story 1. Jessie Kiplinger; story 2. Roy Hubley; story 3), Julie Garfield (Mimsie Hubley; story 3). *Producers:* Richard H. Frank, Maria Govons, Harvey Medlinsky. *Writer:* Neil Simon. *Director:* Harvey Medlinsky.

**1604 Plaza Suite.** Comedy, 2 hrs., ABC, 12/3/87. A second television adaptation of the play by Neil Simon. See the prior title for storyline information. *Cast:* Carol Burnett (Karen Nash; story 1. Muriel Tate; story 2. Claire Hubley; story 3), Hal Holbrook (Sam Nash; story 1), Dabney Coleman (Jessie Kiplinger; story 2), Richard Crenna (Roy Hubley; story 3), Erin Hamilton (Mimsie Hubley; story 3). *Music:* Peter Matz. *Producers:* Carol Burnett, Kenny Solms, George Sunga. *Writer:* Neil Simon. *Directors:* Roger Beatty, Kenny Solms.

**1605 Please Don't Hit Me, Mom.** Drama, 60 min., ABC, 9/20/81. While baby-sitting for eight-year-old Brian Reynolds, teenager Nancy Parks discovers that Brian is a battered child. The story relates Nancy's attempts to help Brian's divorced mother (Barbara) realize that she is abusing her son— without jeopardizing her close relationship with Brian's older brother, Michael. Aired as an "ABC Afterschool Special." *Cast:* Patty Duke (Barbara Reynolds), Nancy McKeon (Nancy Parks), Lance Guest (Michael Reynolds), Sean Astin (Brian Reynolds), Deena Freeman (Judy). *Music:* John Anderson. *Producers:* Virginia L. Carter, Fern Field. *Writer:* Jeri Taylor. *Director:* Gwen Arner.

**1606 Plimpton! Did You Hear the One About ...?** Comedy, 60 min., ABC, 4/2/71. An hour of comedy in which George Plimpton learns the ropes of being a comedian. *Host:* George Plimpton. *Guests:* Steve Allen, Woody Allen, Milton Berle, Jack Carter, Dick Cavett, Phyllis Diller, David Frye, Buddy Hackett, Bob Hope, Marc London, David Panich, Phil Silvers, Jonathan Winters. *Producer-Director:* William Kronick. *Writers:* George Plimpton, William Kronick.

## 1607 Plimpton! Showdown at Rio Lobo. Variety, 60 min., ABC, 12/16/70. A behind-the-scenes look at the filming of western movies. *Host:* George Plimpton. *Guests:* Jack Elam, Victor French, David Huddleston, Joe Namath, John Wayne. *Producer-Director:* William Kronick. *Writers:* George Plimpton, William Kronick.

## 1608 Plimpton! The Man on the Flying Trapeze. Variety, 60 min., ABC, 2/9/71. A behind-the-scenes look at circus life as actor George Plimpton attempts to master the flying trapeze. *Host:* George Plimpton. *Producer-Director:* William Kronick. *Writers:* George Plimpton, William Kronick.

## 1609 The Pointer Sisters. Variety, 60 min., Syndicated, 7/82. A concert by the Pointer Sisters. Taped before a live audience in March 1982. *Hosts:* The Pointer Sisters (Anita, June, and Ruth). *Producers:* Steve Derris, William McKenna. *Director:* Bob McKinnon.

## 1610 The Pointer Sisters in Paris. Variety, 60 min., Showtime, 9/14/85. A concert by the Grammy-winning group the Pointer Sisters. *Hosts:* Anita, June, and Ruth Pointer. *The Band:* Joe Mumford (guitar), Jim Ingle (drums), Eric McKain (percussion), Don Boyett (bass), Marc Ritter, Greg Whelchel (piano). *Producer:* Anthony Eaton. *Director:* David Mallet.

## 1611 The Pointer Sisters — Up All Nite. Variety, 60 min., NBC, 1/23/87. Music and songs from various Los Angeles night spots. *Hosts:* June, Anita, and Ruth Pointer. *Guests:* Whoopi Goldberg, The McGuire Sisters, Bruce Willis. *Music:* Ray Bunch. *Producer-Director:* Don Mischer.

## 1612 The Polly Bergen Special. Variety, 60 min., Syndicated, 12/69. An hour of music and songs. *Host:* Polly Bergen. *Guests:* The Fifth Dimension, The Pearce Sisters. *Music:* Johnnie Spence. *Producer:* Jackie Barnett. *Director:* Tony Charmoli.

## 1613 Polly Parker's Party. Variety, 30 min., NBC, 11/22/47. A fashion show coupled with variety performances (at the end of a fashion lineup to give models a chance to change). *Host:* Helen Parrish. *Guest:* Jeanne Palmer (model). *Producer:* Lee Cooley. *Director:* Edward Sobol.

## 1614 The Popeye Valentine Special: Sweethearts at Sea. Cartoon, 30 min., CBS, 2/14/79. The story finds Olive Oyl boarding the Valentine's Day Sweetheart Cruise and seeking a new beau after Popeye forgets her on Valentine's Day. Popeye's efforts to salvage his love life — thwarted by the evil Sea Hag, who has her own designs on Popeye — are the focal point of the program. *Voices:* Jack Mercer (Popeye), Marilyn Schreffler (Olive Oyl/Sea Hag), Allan Melvin (Bluto), Daws Butler (Wimpy), Ginny McSwain (Jeep). *Music:* Hoyt Curtin. *Producers:* William Hanna, Joseph Barbera. *Writers:* Tom Daganais, John V. Hanrahan. *Director:* Oscar Dufau.

## 1615 The Poppy Is Also a Flower. Drama, 2 hrs., ABC, 4/22/66. A special, produced by the United Nations, that is an attempt to make the public aware of the drug problem and

how nations are attempting to stamp out the growth of poppies, a flower that is the source of heroin. The program itself focuses on the UN's efforts to trace a contraband opium shipment. Also known as "Poppies Are Also Flowers." *Cast:* Angie Dickinson (Linda Benson), E. G. Marshall (Collier Jones), Yul Brynner (Colonel Saleem), Stephen Boyd (Agent Benson), Senta Berger (Singer), Rita Hayworth (Monique Marco), Trevor Howard (Sam Lincoln), Trini Lopez (Himself), Marcello Mastroianni (Inspector Mosca), Anthony Quayle (Captain Vanderbilt), Gilbert Roland (Serge Marco), Omar Sharif (Dr. Rad), Eli Wallach (Happy Locaino). *Host:* Grace Kelly. *Music:* Georges Auric. *Producers:* Edgar Rosenberg, Del Tenney. *Writer:* Jo Eisinger. *Director:* Terence Young.

**1616 Portrait of a Teenage Shoplifter.** Drama, 60 min., CBS, 12/1/81. One day, while shopping in a boutique with friends, Karen Hughes finds that one girlfriend has stashed stolen clothing in her shoulder bag. The experience entices Karen to conduct subsequent shoplifting sprees. The story relates the consequences that occur when Karen is caught and arrested. Aired on "The CBS Afternoon Playhouse." *Cast:* Maureen Teffy (Karen Hughes), Laura Dean (Trisha Marcus), Allen Fawcett (Pete Crawford), Marisa Marcell (Alice Hughes), Tom Quinn (Sam Hughes), Jessica Cain (Cheryl). *Music:* Elliot Lawrence. *Producers:* Sonny Grosso, Larry Jacobson. *Writers:* Todd Kessler, Deborah Baker. *Director:* William P. D'Angelo.

**1617 Portrait of Grandpa Doc.** Drama, 30 min., ABC, 11/5/77. Grandpa Doc is a gentle and loving man who can see, respect, and encourage the wonder in a child's eyes. He now lives only in the memories of those whose lives he touched. Bruce is a young artist preparing an exhibition which will be a tribute to his Grandpa Doc, who treated him as an individual, not just a child, encouraging his appreciation of beauty and guiding his observation of the color and variety of life. The story follows Bruce from boy to man as he prepares his exhibit to assure that his Grandpa Doc will always be remembered. Aired as an "ABC Weekend Special." *Cast:* Melvyn Douglas (Grandpa Doc), Bruce Davison (Bruce as a man), Keith Blanchard (Bruce as a boy), Barbara Rush (Bruce's mother), Anne Seymour (Bruce's grandmother). *Music:* Charles Albertine. *Producer:* Diane Baker. *Writer-Director:* Randal Kleiser.

**1618 Portrait of Nancy Wilson.** Variety, 60 min., Syndicated, 3/72. An hour of music and songs with singer Nancy Wilson. *Host:* Nancy Wilson. *Guests:* John Bunch, Billy Eckstine, Sarah Vaughan. *Orchestra:* Robert Farnon. *Producers:* Philip Jones, Peter Frazer-Jones. *Director:* Peter Frazer-Jones.

**1619 Portrait of Petula.** Variety, 60 min., NBC, 4/7/69. An hour of international music and song (filmed on location in Paris, London, New York, and Switzerland). *Host:* Petula Clark. *Guests:* Sacha Distel, Ron Moody, Andy Williams. *Music:* Michel Colombier. *Producers:* Alan Handley, Bob Wynn. *Writers:* Sheldon Keller, Gordon Farr. *Director:* Alan Handley.

**1620 Possession.** Thriller, 90 min., ABC, 4/12/73. The story of a newlywed couple who purchase a country house with a reputation for being haunted. *Cast:* Joanna Dunham (Penny Burns), John Carson (Ray Burns), James Cossins (Kellet), Hilary Hardiman (Cecily Rafting), Richard Aylen (Inspector Miles). *Music:* Laurie Johnson. *Producer:* Cecil Clarke. *Writer:* Brian Clemens. *Director:* John Cooper.

**1621 The Power and the Glory.** Drama, 90 min., CBS, 10/29/

61. The story of a dissolute, alcoholic priest caught in the 1930 Mexican Revolution against the Catholic church, who is pursued by a Communist police lieutenant determined to kill him. Based on the novel by Graham Greene. *Cast:* Sir Laurence Olivier (Priest), George C. Scott (Police Lieutenant), Roddy McDowall (Mestizo), Martin Gabel (Police Chief), Julie Harris (Maria), Keenan Wynn (Bootlegger), Patty Duke (Coral), Fritz Weaver (Schoolmaster), Mildred Dunnock (Spinster). *Music:* Laurence Rosenthal. *Producer:* David Susskind. *Writer:* Dale Wasserman. *Director:* Marc Daniels.

## 1622 Power and the Presidency. Drama, 60 min., CBS, 4/24/74.

An historical special that incorporates actors, animation, dance, and graphic effects based on authentic historical material to provide a visual impression of the growing power of six presidents: George Washington, Andrew Jackson, James K. Polk, Abraham Lincoln, William McKinley, and Theodore Roosevelt — and the times in which they governed. *Cast:* Bob Terhune (George Washington), Carl Saxe (George Clinton), Clyde Hudkins (Robert Livingston), David Sharpe (Mr. Oates), Jerry Brown (Coachman), Alan Wyatt (Andrew Jackson), Chuck Hayward (Nicholas Biddle), Buff Brady (Indian Chief). *Narrator:* George C. Scott. *Music:* Lee Holdridge. *Producer:* Jack Willis. *Writer:* Craig Gilbert. *Director:* Jerome Rosenfeld.

## 1623 A Prairie Home Companion. Variety, 2 hrs., PBS, 4/26/86.

A video version of National Public Radio's "A Prairie Home Companion" (which began in 1974). The program, set in Lake Wobegone, Minnesota, presents music and the homespun humor of author, humorist, and singer Garrison Keillor. *Host:* Garrison Keillor. *Guests:* Chet Atkins, Philip Brunelle, Johnny Gimble, Jean Redpath. *Radio Program Regulars:* Peter Ostroushko,

Howard Mohr, Peter Eklund. *Music:* The Butch Thompson Trio. *Producer-Writer:* Garrison Keillor. *Director:* Thomas Schlamme.

## 1624 Premiere: Inside the Summer Blockbusters. Variety, 60 min., Fox, 6/3/89.

A behind-the-scenes look at the making of four 1989 summer movies: *Indian Jones and the Last Crusade, Batman, The Abyss,* and *Lethal Weapon 2. Host:* Mark Harmon. *Guests:* Kim Basinger, Richard Donner, Harrison Ford, Al Giddins, Ed Harris, Michael Keaton, Jon Peters, Steven Spielberg. *Producers:* Susan Lyne, Michael Meadows. *Writer:* Michael Meadows.

## 1625 The Presidential Inaugural Gala. Variety, 2 hrs., CBS, 1/19/89.

A lavish party for newly elected President George S. Bush. *Guests:* Nell Carter, Walter Cronkite, Clint Eastwood, Crystal Gayle, Julio Iglesias, Cheryl Ladd, Loretta Lynn, Dina Merrill, Chuck Norris, The Oak Ridge Boys, Roberta Peters, Arnold Schwarzenegger, Frank Sinatra, Randy Travis, Tommy Tune. *Music:* Peter Matz. *Producers:* Joseph Canzeri, Don Mischer. *Writer:* Buz Kohan. *Director:* Walter C. Miller.

## 1626 The Presidential Inaugural Gala. Variety, 2 hrs., CBS, 1/19/93.

Showbusiness celebrities honor newly elected President Bill Clinton and his wife Hillary. *Guests:* Ron Carter, Judy Collins, Bill Cosby, Aretha Franklin, Randy Goodrum, Herbie Hancock, James Earl Jones, Jack Lemmon, Wynton Marsalis, Kenny Rogers, Barbra Streisand, Grover Washington, Jr., Trisha Yearwood. *Producers:* Harry and Linda Bloodworth-Thomason, Gary Smith. *Writer:* Buz Kohan. *Director:* Dwight Hemion.

## 1627 The Price. Drama, 90 min., NBC, 2/3/71.

The story, set in a

condemned Manhattan brownstone, is a graphic portrait of bitter memories as seen through the eyes of two brothers — a cop and a surgeon — who reunite after 16 years of separation to sell off the family heirlooms. Based on Arthur Miller's 1968 Broadway play. Aired on the "Hallmark Hall of Fame." *Cast:* George C. Scott (Victor), David Burns (Solomon), Barry Sullivan (Walter), Colleen Dewhurst (Esther). *Producer:* David Susskind. *Writer:* Arthur Miller. *Director:* Fielder Cook.

**1628 Princess.** Drama, 30 min., Syndicated, 4/80. Laurie "Princess" Marshall is a seemingly well-adjusted teenager from an apparently ideal family. Suddenly, her world begins to fall apart when her parents plan to divorce. Her attempts to understand the situation are the focal point of the program. *Cast:* Lenora May (Laurie Marshall), Corinne Michaels (Stephanie Marshall; her mother), Richard Jaeckel (Mark Marshall; her father), Jeff Parker (Tony Marshall; her brother), Melissa Sue Anderson (Mary Beth; her friend), Eugene Roche (Paul; a friend). *Music:* Charles Stone, Richard Rand. *Producers:* Ellwood Kieser, Michael Rhodes, Judy Greenberg. *Writer:* Jim McGinn. *Director:* Michael Rhodes.

**1629 Private Affairs.** Drama, 60 min., ABC, 10/26/89. An "ABC Afterschool Special" about a teenage girl (Madeline) who accidentally discovers that her father is having an affair with her mother's best friend. Her efforts to resolve the problem without breaking up her family are the focal point of the story. *Cast:* Kerri Green (Madeline Green), Kay Lenz (Bonnie Green), Dean Butler (Matthew Green), Amy Lynne (Lindy), Christopher Daniel Barnes (Boyd), Elizabeth Savage (Doreen), Michael Warren (Dr. Hawkins), Nancy Kulp (Aurora), Lynne Thigpen (Mrs. Meeks). *Music:* Jonathan Wolff. *Producers:* Brenda Wilson, Karen S. Shapiro. *Writers:* Neal Baer, Brenda Wilson. *Director:* Neal Baer.

**1630 Private Eye, Private Eye.** Comedy, 60 min., CBS, 3/8/61. A series of comedy sketches that spoof the television private detective. *Host:* Ernie Kovacs. *Guests:* Edie Adams, Pat Carroll, Hans Conried. *Music:* Charles Sanford. *Producer:* Max Liebman. *Writers:* Will Glickman, Sydney Zelenka, Lucille Kallen. *Director:* Barry Shear.

**1631 Promenade.** Variety, 90 min., NBC, 5/22/55. A program of music, dances, songs, and comedy sketches. *Host:* Tyrone Power. *Guests:* Rod Alexander, Barbara Baxley, The Bil and Cora Baird Puppets, Janet Blair, Zachary Charles, Judy Holliday, George Irving, Bambi Linn, Jack Russell, Herb Shriner, Kay Starr. *Music:* Charles Sanford. *Producer-Director:* Max Liebman.

**1632 Pssst! Hammerman's After You!** Comedy, 60 min., ABC, 1/16/74. The story follows sixth grader Mouse Fawley's "run for his life" when he calls the school bully, Marv Hammerman, an ape man and becomes number one on the rough guy's most wanted list. The heart of the program is Mouse's learning of what self-respect is all about when he stops running and decides to confront the bully. Aired as an "ABC Afterschool Special." *Cast:* Christian Juttner (Mouse Fawley), Lance Kerwin (Ezzie), Jim Sage (Marv Hammerman), Jay W. McIntosh (Mrs. Fawley), Penny Santon (Mrs. Casino), Jack Manning (Mr. Stein), Ann D'Andrea (Margy). *Producer:* Martin Tahse. *Writer:* Bob Rodgers. *Director:* Jack Regas.

**1633 Puff and the Incredible Mister Nobody.** Cartoon, 30 min., CBS, 5/17/82. A sequel to "Puff the Magic Dragon" that finds Puff the Magic Dragon and a young boy named

Terry journeying to the World of Fanterverse to find Terry's imaginary friend, Mister Nobody. Focal point of the story is Puff's efforts to make Terry see his own creative abilities and encourage his self-confidence. Based on the song "Puff the Magic Dragon" by Peter Yarrow and Leonard Lipton. *Voices:* Burgess Meredith (Puff), David Mendenhall (Terry), Diana Dumpis, Joan Gerber, Bob Holt, Billy Jacoby, Hal Smith, Robert Ridgely. *Music:* Peter Yarrow, David Campbell. *Producers:* Robert L. Rosen, Kevin Hunter, Peter Yarrow, Romeo Muller. *Writer:* Romeo Muller. *Director:* Fred Wolf.

**1634 Puff the Magic Dragon.** Cartoon, 30 min., CBS, 10/30/78. Jackie Draper is a shy and withdrawn young boy who is afraid to face new situations. The story follows Jackie as he and Puff the Magic Dragon journey to the magic land of Honahlee where Jackie's encounters with an array of amazing creatures help him overcome his fears. Based on the song "Puff the Magic Dragon" by Peter Yarrow and Leonard Lipton. See also "Puff and the Incredible Mister Nobody." *Voices:* Burgess Meredith (Puff), Phillip Tanzini (Jackie), Robert Ridgely (Pirate/Pieman/Sneeze), Maitzi Morgan (Mother/Star), Peter Yarrow (Father), Regis Cordic (Bald doctor), Frank Nelson (Tall doctor), Charles Woolf (Short doctor). *Music:* Peter Yarrow, David Campbell. *Producers:* Kevin Hunter, Robert L. Rosen, Peter Yarrow, Romeo Muller. *Writer:* Romeo Muller. *Directors:* Charles Swenson, Fred Wolf.

**1635 A Punt, a Pass and a Prayer.** Drama, 90 min., NBC, 11/20/68. A "Hallmark Hall of Fame" presentation about Johnny Aragon, a pro quarterback who was injured during a game, as he attempts to make a comeback after a two-year absence. *Cast:* Hugh O'Brian (Johnny Aragon), Shelly

Novak (Barney), Don DeFore (Baker), Betsy Palmer (Nancy), Ralph Meeker (Wally), Nancy Dussault (Millie), Bert Freed (Pete). *Producer:* Robert Hartung. *Writer:* David Mark. *Director:* Tom Donovan.

**A Purex Dinah Shore Special** *see* **Dinah Shore Purex Specials**

**1636 Pygmalion.** Comedy, 90 min., NBC, 2/6/63. A phonetics professor (Henry Higgins) tries to transform Eliza Doolittle, a cockney London flower girl, into a refined duchess within three months (to win a bet with Colonel Pickering, a linguistic expert). Based on the play by George Bernard Shaw and broadcast on the "Hallmark Hall of Fame." *Cast:* Julie Harris (Eliza Doolittle), James Donald (Henry Higgins), John Williams (Colonel Pickering), Gladys Cooper (Mrs. Higgins), George Rose (Alfred P. Doolittle), Dorothy Sands (Mrs. Pearce), John D. Irving (Fred Eynsford-Hill), Valerie Cossart (Mrs. Eynsford-Hill), Mildred Trases (Clara Hill). *Producer-Director:* George Schaefer. *Writer:* Robert Hartung.

**A Quarter Century of Bob Hope on Television** *see* **Bob Hope Specials**

**1637 A Question About Sex.** Drama, 60 min., ABC, 9/13/90. An "ABC Afterschool Special" about Shauna Kelly, a high school girl who takes a stand and begins a campaign for sex education at her school. *Cast:* Tracey Gold (Shauna Kelly), Cindy Pickett (Joanne Kelly), Kristen Dattilo (Allison Street), Derek Randall (Ron). *Music:* Misha Segal. *Producers:* Sue Steinberg, Mark Hufnail. *Writer:* Courtney Flavin. *Director:* Tom Skerritt.

**1638 Radio City Music Hall at Christmas Time.** Variety, 60

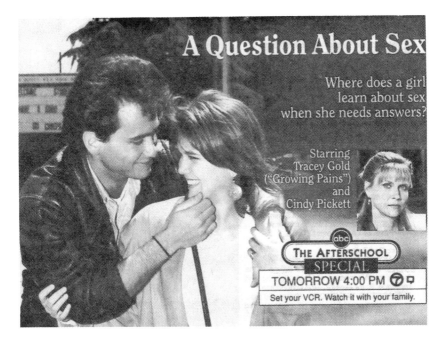

**Ad for "A Question About Sex"**

min., NBC, 12/11/67. A Yuletide program of music and songs from Radio City Music Hall in New York City. *Performers:* The Corps de Ballet, The Doodletown Pipers, The Rockettes. *Music:* Gordon Wiles. *Producer-Director:* George Schlatter.

## 1639 The Rag Tag Champs.

Comedy-Drama, 60 min., ABC, 3/22/78. The Arborville Recreation League is a sandlot baseball team managed by a scrappy 14-year-old named Jake Wrather. Lenny Johnson is Jake's uncle and guardian, a bachelor musician whose schedule of night work and day sleeping keeps him from coaching the team and may cost him the custody of the boy. The "ABC Afterschool Special" relates Jake's efforts to change Lenny's ways so he can coach the team and remain with him. *Cast:* Larry B. Scott (Jake Wrather), Glynn Turman (Lenny Johnson), Madge Sinclair (Mrs. Bradbury), Shannon Terhune (Cindy Franks), Guillermo San Juan (Tony

DeVito), Chris Petersen (Pat McCleod), John Durren (Mr. McCleod), Jacque Lynn Colton (Mrs. Fulton). *Producer:* Robert Chenault. *Writer:* E. Jack Kaplan. *Director:* Virgil W. Vogel.

## 1640 Raggedy Ann and Andy in the Great Santa Claus Caper.

Cartoon, 30 min., CBS, 11/30/78. A Christmas tale wherein Raggedy Ann and Andy and their sheep dog, Raggedy Arthur, battle the villainous Alexander Graham Wolf, who plans to take over Santa's workshop and turn it into a modernized factory where everything is for sale. *Voices:* June Foray (Raggedy Ann), Daws Butler (Raggedy Andy), Les Tremayne (Alexander Graham Wolf). *Music:* Earl Robinson. *Producer-Writer-Director:* Chuck Jones.

## 1641 Raggedy Ann and Andy in the Pumpkin Who Couldn't Smile. Cartoon, 30 min., CBS, 10/31/

79. Raggedy Ann and Andy's efforts to cheer up a lonely pumpkin. *Voices:* June Foray (Raggedy Ann/Aunt Agatha), Daws Butler (Raggedy Andy), Les Tremayne (Pumpkin). *Music:* Earl Robinson. *Producer-Writer-Director:* Chuck Jones.

**1642 Rainbow of Stars.** Variety, 60 min., NBC, 4/17/62. A series of variety acts and ice skating performances set against the background of Rockefeller Center in New York City. *Host:* Carol Lawrence. *Guests:* Dick Button, Al Hirt, The Rockettes, Nancy Walker. *Music:* Harry Sosnik. *Producer-Director:* Clark Jones. *Writers:* George Foster, Saul Ilson.

**1643 The Rainmaker.** Drama, 2 hrs. 15 min., HBO, 10/22/82. A romantic drama, set in the 1920s at the drought-stricken farm of the Currys, that focuses on Bill Starbuck, an enterprising man who offers them their only hope: for $100 in advance he will make it rain within 24 hours. *Cast:* Tommy Lee Jones (Bill Starbuck), Tuesday Weld (Lizzy Curry), Lonny Chapman (H. C. Curry), James Cromwell (Noah Curry), William Katt (Jimmy Curry). *Producer:* Marcia Govons. *Writer:* N. Richard Nash. *Director:* John Frankenheimer.

**1644 A Rainy Day.** Drama, 40 min., PBS, 6/10/81. A sensitive portrait of the strained relationship between Stephanie Cramer, a successful but unhappy actress, and her overbearing mother. *Cast:* Mariette Hartley (Stephanie Cramer), Collin Wilcox (Stephanie's mother), Erik Holland (Stephanie's father), Robert Walden (Stephanie's manager), Don Keefer (the Reverend). *Producer-Writer-Director:* Beth Brickell.

**1645 Ralph S. Mouse.** Children, 30 min., ABC, 2/16 and 2/23/91. The third of three specials about Ralph S. Mouse, a dimensionally animated

mouse (see also "The Mouse and the Motorcycle" and "Runaway Ralph"). The story is set at the Mountain View Inn where Ralph lives in a hole in the wall with his family, and describes Ralph's adventures at the inn and with his human friend, Ryan, when he accompanies him to school one day (where Ralph must avoid capture by the custodian and run an obstacle course when he gets Ryan into trouble by speaking in class). An "ABC Weekend Special." *Cast:* Ray Walston (Matt), Robert Oliveri (Ryan), Karen Black (Miss Kirkenbocker), Kimmy Robertson (Emma Spritz), Jacob Kenner (Brad), Lou Cuttell (William Minch), Britt Leach (Mr. Costa), John Clark Matthews (Voice of Ralph). *Music:* Steve Kohn. *Producers:* George McQuilkin, John Clark Matthews. *Writer:* Joe S. Landon. *Director:* Thomas G. Smith.

**1646 Randy Newman at the Odeon.** Variety, 60 min., Showtime, 12/8/83. A concert by singer Randy Newman from New York's Odeon Restaurant. *Host:* Randy Newman. *Producers:* Lorne Michaels, Janis Signorelli. *Director:* Michael Lindsay-Hogg.

**1647 The Ransom of Red Chief.** Comedy, 60 min., NBC, 8/16/59. Seeking what they believe will be an easy stake for them to journey to California, two drifters (Billy and Sam) kidnap a young boy (Johnny) who envisions himself as a fearless Indian named Red Chief. The story relates the problems that befall Billy and Sam when they discover the boy enjoys being kidnapped and that the only way to get rid of him is to pay his father (Ebenezer Dorset) to take him off their hands. Based on the story by O. Henry. See also the following title and "The Revenge of Red Chief." *Cast:* William Bendix (Billy Driscoll), Hans Conried (Sam Snyder), Teddy Rooney (Red Chief), Russell Collins (Ebenezer Dorset). *Producer:* David Susskind. *Writer:* Phil Reisman. *Director:* Alvin Rakoff.

**1648 The Ransom of Red Chief.** Comedy, 30 min., ABC, 10/22/77. A second special adaptation of the novel by O. Henry. See the prior title for storyline information. Aired as an "ABC Weekend Special." *Cast:* Strother Martin (Billy), Jack Elam (Sam), Patrick J. Petersen (Red Chief), William Mims (Ebenezer Dorset). *Music:* Tommy Leonetti. *Producer:* Robert Chenault. *Writers:* Jim Carlson, Terrence McDonnell. *Director:* Jeffrey Hayden.

**1649 Raquel.** Variety, 60 min., ABC, 11/23/80. Elegant production numbers tied into a whimsical story about a beautiful star who yearns to escape from her obnoxious agent and find an elite corner of paradise in New York City. *Cast:* Raquel Welch (The Star), James Coco (The Agent), Mickey Rooney (Cabbie), Douglas Fairbanks, Jr. (God). *Music:* Peter Matz. *Producers:* Andre Weinfeld, Gareth Davis. *Writers:* Raquel Welch, Andre Weinfeld. *Director:* Tony Charmoli.

**1650 Rare Silk.** Variety, 60 min., PBS, 7/8/87. A musical concert by the group Rare Silk. *Hosts:* Rare Silk (Gale Gillaspe, Mary Lynn Gillaspe, Marguerite Jeanute, Todd Berry). *The Band:* Jim Ridl, Michael Berry, Pete Hofneger. *Producers:* John Beyer, Terry Hinrich. *Director:* John Beyer.

**1651 The Ray Bolger Show.** Variety, 60 min., NBC, 6/4/57. The program re-creates the music, songs, and comedy of Broadway. *Host:* Ray Bolger. *Guests:* Kay Armen, Vivian Blaine, George Jessel, Muriel Landers. *Music Director:* David Rose.

**1652 Ray Charles: 50 Years of Music, Uh-Huh!** Tribute, 90 min., Fox, 10/6/91. A celebrity gathering for musician-singer Ray Charles on the occasion of his fifty years of making music. The show was taped on September 19 in Pasadena, California, for the Starlight and Starbright Pavilion foundations, nonprofit organizations that grant wishes and provide special entertainment to seriously ill children. The "Uh-Huh" in the title refers to Ray's catchphrase as a spokesman for Pepsi Cola. *Hosts:* Whoopi Goldberg, Quincy Jones, Robert Townsend. *Special Guest:* Ray Charles. *Guests:* Michael Bolton, Tevin Campbell, Bill Cosby, Gloria Estefan, James Ingram, Paul McCartney, Michael McDonald, Willie Nelson, Randy Travis, Stevie Wonder. *Producer:* Ray Charles, Jr., Gregory H. Willenborg.

**1653 The Ray Conniff Christmas Special.** Variety, 60 min., Syndicated, 12/71. Christmas songs and music with bandleader Ray Conniff. *Host:* Ray Conniff. *Guests:* The Pixiekin Puppets, The Ray Conniff Singers, Alan Young. *Music Director:* Ray Conniff.

**1654 The R.C.A. Thanksgiving Show.** Variety, 2 hrs., NBC, 11/25/48. A live holiday program of music, songs, and comedy. *Host:* Wendell Niles. *Guests:* Eddy Arnold, The Deep River Boys, Betty Keane, Jean Keane, Jane Pickens, Bill Robinson, Helen Ryan, Eve Young. *Announcer:* Joe Mulchill. *Music Directors:* Walbert Brown, Cleveland Aires. *Producers:* Warren Wade, Vic McLeod.

**1655 R.C.A. Victor Gallery of Stars.** Variety, 60 min., NBC, 6/15/57. Performances by artists signed by RCA Victor Records (enlarged album covers were used to introduce the talent). *Host:* Vaughn Monroe. *Guests:* The Bob Hamilton Trio, Martha Carson, Georgia Gibbs, The Lane Brothers, Julius LaRosa, Tony Martin,

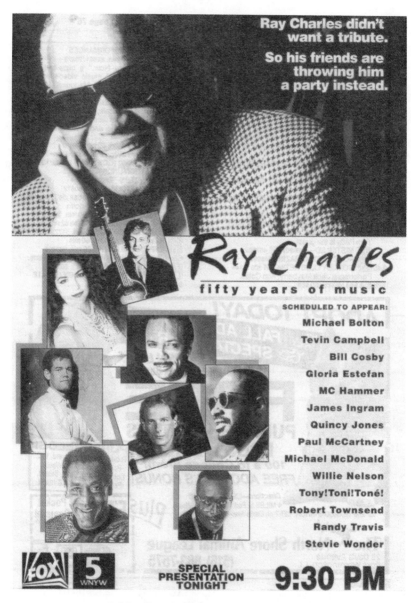

Ad for "Ray Charles: Fifty Years of Music"

Jaye P. Morgan. *Producer-Director:* Joe Cates. *Writer:* Ervin Drake.

**1656 The Real Patsy Cline.** Tribute, 60 min., Syndicated, 8/87. An affectionate tribute to country singer Patsy Cline (1932–63) by her friends and colleagues. *Narrator:* Johnny Koval. *Guests:* Owen Bradley, Charlie Dick, Julian Dick, Harlan Howard, Loretta Lynn, Carl Perkins, Sylvia, Mel Tillis, Dottie West. *Music:* Scott

Humphrey. *Producers:* Daniel McLellan, Kent L. Ford, Paul Gross. *Writers:* Ritchie York, Mark Hall. *Director:* Mark Hall.

## 1657 Really Raquel.

Variety, 60 min., CBS, 3/8/74. An hour of music and song featuring actress Raquel Welch. *Host:* Raquel Welch. *Music:* Jack Elliott, Allyn Ferguson. *Producers:* Ron Talsky, Joe Layton. *Writer:* Charlotte Brown. *Director:* Dave Wilson.

## 1658 Rebecca.

Drama, 60 min., NBC, 4/8/62. The story of an unsophisticated girl who marries a prominent country gentleman and the problems that ensue when the husband is dominated by the memory of his first wife (Rebecca). Based on the book by Daphne DuMaurier and broadcast on "Theater '62." *Cast:* James Mason (Maxim de Winter), Joan Hackett (Second Mrs. de Winter), Nina Foch (Mrs. Danvers), Lloyd Bochner (Jack Favall), Murray Matheson (Fred Crawley). *Producer:* Fred Coe. *Writer:* Ellen M. Violett. *Director:* Boris Sagal.

## 1659 The Red Goose Kid's Spectacular.

Children, 90 min., ABC, 8/25/56 (first special), 10/6/56 (second special). The program, sponsored by Red Goose Shoes, features a visit to the St. Louis Zoo and interviews with the trainers. Also included are skits and documentary film footage of wild animals. *Host:* Johnny Olsen. *Assistants:* Andy Andrews, Red Colbin, Arlene Dalton, Tom Lockhard. *Producers:* Lee Cooley, John Weber. *Writer:* Lee Cooley. *Director:* Matthew Harlib.

## 1660 The Red Room Riddle.

Mystery, 30 min., ABC, 2/5/83. As part of a club initiation, Bill Slocum and Todd Burton are taken to an old mansion and asked to report on what they find inside the house. Late that night Bill and Todd are led to a glowing red room and trapped by a ghost named Jamie Bly. The story relates Bill's and Todd's efforts to solve the riddle of the red room in order to escape. Aired as an "ABC Weekend Special." *Cast:* Billy Jacoby (Billy Slocum), Nicholas Gilbert (Todd Burton), Christian Hoff (Jamie Bly), Sandra Caron (Maid/Old woman), Peter Brocco (Caretaker), David Wiley (Butler). *Music:* John Cacavas. *Producer-Director:* Robert Chenault. *Writer:* Stephen Manes.

## 1661 Red Skelton Specials.

A chronological listing of the comedy specials hosted by Red Skelton. All are 60 minutes in length.

**1 The Red Skelton Revue** (CBS, 7/21/54). *Guests:* The Ames Brothers, Tony Curtis, Liberace, The Redettes, The Sahara Hotel Line Chorus Girls. *Music:* Lud Gluskin. *Producers:* Jack Donohue, Doug Whitney. *Writers:* Al Gordon, Hal Goldman, Martin A. Ragaway. *Director:* Jack Donohue.

**2 The Red Skelton Chevy Special** (CBS 10/9/59). *Guests:* James Arness, Rhonda Fleming, Lionel Hampton, Burl Ives, Tommy Sands. *Music:* David Rose. *Producers:* Cecil Barker, Seymour Berns. *Writers:* Sherwood Schwartz, Al Schwartz, Dave O'Brien, Red Skelton. *Director:* Seymour Berns.

**3 The Red Skelton Timex Special** (CBS, 11/30/60). *Guests:* William Demarest, George Raft, Bobby Rydell, Dinah Shore, Frank Sinatra. *Music:* David Rose. *Producer:* Cecil Barker. *Writers:* Hal Goldman, Larry Klein, Red Skelton. *Director:* Seymour Berns.

**4 Red Skelton's Christmas Dinner** (HBO, 12/14/82). A holiday special in which Freddy the Freeloader and his equally impoverished friend, the Professor, struggle to scrape together money for a Christmas dinner in a fancy restaurant. *Cast:* Red Skelton (Freddy the Freeloader), Vincent Price (Professor Humperdue), Jack Duffy (Santa Claus), Tudi Wiggins (Mrs. Wiberspoon), Louis Negin (Maitre d'), Michelle Peruich (Michelle), Ian Keith

(Tommy). *Music:* Ian Bernard. *Producer:* Riff Markowitz. *Writer:* Red Skelton. *Director:* John Trent.

**5 Red Skelton's Funny Faces** (HBO, 5/29/83). A one-man show featuring Red Skelton in a series of his most famous comedy bits. *Music:* Jimmy Dale. *Producer:* Mitchell Blanchard. *Writer:* Red Skelton. *Director:* John Blanchard.

**6 Red Skelton: A Royal Performance** (HBO, 4/22/84). Red Skelton's solo performance for the British royal family at the Albert Hall in England. *Music:* The Lord Anthony Colwyn Orchestra. *Producers:* Kent Walwin, Riff Markowitz, Lewis Chesler. *Writer:* Red Skelton. *Director:* Ken Griffin.

**Marilyn Monroe**

Andy Williams. *Music Directors:* Harry James, Axel Stordahl.

### Red Skelton's Christmas Dinner *see* Red Skelton Specials

### Red Skelton's Funny Faces *see* Red Skelton Specials

### 1662 The Redd Foxx Special.
Variety, 90 min., ABC, 4/4/78. Comedy skits that spotlight the comedic talents of Redd Foxx. *Host:* Redd Foxx. *Guests:* Susan Anton, Red Buttons, Lorne Greene, Bill Saluga, Rip Taylor, Slappy White. *Producers:* Allan Blye, Bob Einstein. *Director:* Donald Davis.

### 1663 Remember How Great?
Variety, 60 min., NBC, 2/9/61. A review of the hit songs of the 1950s. *Host:* Jack Benny. *Guests:* Connie Francis, The McGuire Sisters, Juliet Prowse,

### 1664 Remembering Groucho.
Documentary, 30 min., ABC, 9/2/77. A tribute to Groucho Marx, featuring clips from his movies of the 1930s. *Host:* Harry Reasoner. *Guest:* Dick Cavett. *Producers:* Elliot Bernstein, Arthur Holch.

### 1665 Remembering Marilyn.
Documentary, 60 min., ABC, 5/8/88. A celebration of the enduring fame of Marilyn Monroe, featuring rare film footage and interviews with celebrities. *Host:* Lee Remick. *Guests:* Robert Mitchum, Gloria Steinem, Susan Strasberg, Robert Wagner. *Music:* Kevin Kiner. *Producers:* Andrew Solt, Syd Vinnedge, Susan F. Walker, Harry Arends. *Writer:* Theodore Strauss. *Director:* Andrew Solt.

**1666 Return Engagement.**
Drama, 90 min., NBC, 11/17/78. The
story of Dr. Emily Loomis, a professor
of ancient history whose secret past —
that of a song-and-dance woman —
comes to light when she becomes in-
volved with one of her students (Stew-
art Anderman). Aired on the "Hall-
mark Hall of Fame." *Cast:* Elizabeth
Taylor (Dr. Emily Loomis), Joseph
Bottoms (Stewart Anderman), Allyn
Ann McLerie (Florence), Peter Donat
(George), James Ray (Keith). *Music:*
Arthur B. Rubinstein. *Producers:*
Mike Wise, Franklin Levy. *Writer:*
James Prideaux. *Director:* Joseph
Hardy.

**1667 The Return of the
Smothers Brothers.** Variety, 60
min., NBC, 2/16/70. An hour of music
and comedy that marks the return of
the Smothers Brothers to television
following cancellation of their weekly
CBS series. *Hosts:* Dick Smothers, Tom
Smothers. *Guests:* Glen Campbell,
Alex Drier, Bob Einstein, Peter Fonda,
David Steinberg, Fred Wayne. *Pro-
ducers:* Tom Smothers, Don Van Atta.
*Writers:* David Steinberg, Tom
Smothers. *Director:* Tim Kiley.

**1668 Reunion in Vienna.**
Comedy, 90 min., NBC, 4/4/55. While
in Vienna on a holiday, Elena Krug, the
happily married wife of a psychiatrist,
meets Rudolf Maximillian, an old flame
who is now the archduke of Austria.
The story, in which Greer Garson
makes her dramatic television debut,
relates the problems that arise when
Elena realizes she still loves Rudolf.
*Cast:* Greer Garson (Elena Krug),
Brian Aherne (Rudolf Maximillian),
Robert Flemyng (Dr. Anton Krug),
Peter Lorre (Poffy), Lili Darvas
(Countess Von Stainz), Herbert Berg-
hof (Count Von Stainz), Cathleen Nes-
bitt (Frau Lucher), Nehemiah Persoff
(Strup), Tamara Daykarhanova
(Kathie). *Music:* Harry Sosnik. *Pro-
ducers:* Fred Coe, Jean Dalrymple.

*Writer:* David Shaw. *Director:* Vincent
J. Donehue.

**1669 The Revenge of Red
Chief.** Comedy, 30 min., ABC, 12/15/
79. A sequel to "The Ransom of Red
Chief" (see entry) wherein drifters Sam
and Billy again encounter the boy called
Red Chief — this time while attempting
to fleece a drought-stricken town of
$2,000 with a phony rainmaking
machine. Aired as an "ABC Weekend
Special." *Cast:* Jack Elam (Sam), Noah
Beery (Bill), Patrick J. Petersen (Red
Chief), Alan Hale (Mayor). *Producer:*
Robert Chenault. *Writers:* Jim Carl-
son, Terrence McDonnell. *Director:*
Larry Elikann.

**1670 Revenge of the Nerd.**
Comedy, 60 min., CBS, 4/19/83. Bertram Cummings is a very bright student
at Masters High School. His lack of
style has made him an object of ridicule
among his classmates. All is fine with
Bertram until his arch nemesis, Mike
Godey, makes fun of his unrequited
affection for one particular classmate,
Louise Baker. Deciding that he has
been on the receiving end long enough,
Bertram puts his intelligence to work
and, with the help of his good friend,
Dalton, fashions a high-tech scheme of
vengeance against his tormentors (only
to learn that revenge can be bittersweet
at best). Aired on the "CBS Afternoon
Playhouse." *Cast:* Manny Jacobs (Ber-
tram), Christopher J. Barnes (Dalton),
Sarah Inglis (Louise), Robert Weiler
(Mike), Brian Lima (Dennis), April
Lerman (Andrea), Herb Downer (Mr.
Barnes), Jean Debaer (Mrs. Mead).
*Music:* Steven Margoshes. *Producers:*
Frank Doelger, Bob Keeshan, Jim
Hirschfeld. *Writer:* John McNamara.
*Director:* Ken Kwapis.

**1671 Rex Harrison's Son,
Noel.** Variety, 60 min., Syndicated,
7/70. Music, songs, and comedy with
actor Noel Harrison and his guests.

*Host:* Noel Harrison. *Guests:* Stefanie Powers, Mickey Rooney, Marie Wilson. *Producers:* Hendrik Booraem, Hal Tulchin. *Director:* Hal Tulchin.

**1672 Rich Little Specials.** A chronological listing of the comedy specials hosted by impressionist Rich Little. All are 60 minutes in length.

**1 The Rich Little Show** (NBC, 9/3/75). *Guests:* George Burns, Glen Campbell, Sandy Duncan, Peter Marshall. *Music:* Robert E. Hughes. *Producers:* Jerry Goldstein, Rich Eustis, Al Rogers. *Writers:* Barry Blitzer, Ron Clark, Rudy DeLuca, Ray Jessel, Jack Kaplan, Jim Mulligan. *Director:* Walter C. Miller.

**2 Rich Little's Washington Follies** (ABC, 5/13/78). *Guests:* Tom Bosley, Robert Guillaume, Suzanne Somers, Dick Van Patten. *Music:* Bob Hughes. *Producers:* Jerry Goldstein, Saul Ilson. *Writers:* Hal Goldman, Jeffrey Barron, Wayne Kline, Saul Ilson. *Director:* Stan Harris.

**3 The Rich Little Special** (HBO, 7/7/82). *Guests:* Thom Bresh, Julie McWhirter. *Music:* Robert E. Hughes. *Producer-Director:* Marty Callner. *Director:* Rich Little.

**4 Rich Little's A Christmas Carol** (HBO, 12/9/82). A one-man show in which Rich Little portrays all the characters in a comical adaptation of Charles Dickens's *A Christmas Carol.* *Music:* Jerry Toth. *Producer:* Norman Sedawie. *Writer:* Rich Little. *Director:* Trevor Evans.

**5 The Rich Little Special** (HBO, 12/31/82). A solo performance of impressions. *Orchestra:* Ray Price. *Producers:* Rich Little, Ken Kragen. *Writer:* Rich Little. *Director:* Lee H. Bernhardi.

**6 Rich Little's Robin Hood** (HBO, 3/2/83). A one-man show in which Rich Little portrays showbusiness personalities as characters from Sherwood Forest in a comical retelling of the Robin Hood legend. *Music:* Dave Woods. *Producers:* Rich Little, Ken

Kragen. *Writers:* Rich Little, Mel Bishop. *Director:* Trevor Evans.

**7 Rich Little—Come Laugh with Me** (HBO, 7/29/84). *Guest:* Julie McWhirter. *Music:* Paul Mann. *Producer:* Norman Sedawie. *Writers:* Rich Little, Frank Mula. *Director:* Trevor Evans.

**8 Rich Little and a Night of 42 Stars** (HBO, 11/16/85). A spoof of the network television special "Night of 100 Stars," wherein Rich Little presents a showcase for 42 stars. *Music:* Robert Hughes. *Producers:* Gary Smith, Dwight Hemion. *Writer:* Rich Little. *Director:* Dwight Hemion.

**Rich Little's A Christmas Carol** *see* **Rich Little Specials**

**Rich Little's Robin Hood** *see* **Rich Little Specials**

**1673 The Richard Pryor Special?** Comedy, 60 min., NBC, 5/5/77. An hour of comedy with Richard Pryor in his first television special. *Host:* Richard Pryor. *Guests:* Maya Angelou, John Belushi, Mike Evans, Shirley Hemphill, LaWanda Page, Tim Thomerson, Glynn Turman. *Producers:* Burt Sugarman, Bob Ellison. *Writers:* Richard Pryor, Bob Ellison, Rocco Urbisci, Paul Mooney, Alan Thicke. *Director:* John Moffitt.

**1674 The Richard Pryor Special.** Comedy, 60 min., NBC, 5/11/82. Skits that poke fun at contemporary society. *Host:* Richard Pryor. *Guests:* Maya Angelou, John Belushi, Mike Evans, Yvonne Mooney, Laurie Washington, Dick Williams. *Music:* H. B. Barnum. *Producer:* Burt Sugarman. *Writers:* Richard Pryor, Bob Ellison, Rocco Urbisci, Alan Thicke, Paul Mooney. *Director:* John Moffitt.

**1675 Rickles.** Comedy, 60 min., CBS, 11/19/75. Various comedy skits with the master of insults. *Host:* Don Rickles. *Guests:* Don Adams, James Caan, Michael Caine, Jose Ferrer,

Arthur Godfrey, Elliott Gould, Jack Klugman, Michele Lee, Jack Palance, Otto Preminger, Loretta Swit. *Music:* Bobby Kroll. *Producers:* Joseph Scandore, Barry Shear. *Writer:* Harriet Baker. *Director:* Barry Shear.

**1676 The Right Man.** Comedy-Drama, 60 min., CBS, 10/24/60. A review of presidential campaigns and the gimmicks used to attract voters. *Host:* Garry Moore. *Cast:* Edward G. Robinson (Teddy Roosevelt), Thomas Mitchell (Grover Cleveland), Richard Boone (Abraham Lincoln), Art Carney (Franklin Delano Roosevelt), Tom Bosley (Throttlebottom), Celeste Holm (Victoria Woodhull), Paul Ford (Perfect Candidate), Martin Gabel (William Jennings Bryan), Alan Bunce (Al Smith), John Alexander (Wendell Wilke), David Doyle (Fulton). *Music:* George Kleinsinger. *Producer-Writer:* Fred Freed. *Director:* Burt Shevelove.

**1677 Ringling Brothers and Barnum and Bailey Clown College's 20th Anniversary.** Variety, 60 min., CBS, 2/17/88. The world of clowns is explored in a program that celebrates the twentieth anniversary of the world-famous circus's clown college. *Host:* Dick Van Dyke. *Guests:* Michael Davis, Lou Jacobs, Frosty Little, Tammy Parrish. *Music:* Jerry Bilik. *Producers:* Kenneth Feld, Joe Layton. *Writer:* Turk Pipkin. *Director:* Gary Halvorson.

**1678 Ringo.** Variety, 60 min., NBC, 4/26/78. A take-off on *The Prince and the Pauper* wherein Ringo Starr plays himself, a rock star and his lookalike Ognir Rrats, an average guy who has absolutely nothing to do with the music business. The story relates their misadventures when they change places for a day. *Cast:* Ringo Starr (Himself/Ognir Rrats), Angie Dickinson (Police Woman), John Ritter (Marty), Carrie Fisher (Markene), Art Carney (Ognir's father), Vincent Price (Dr. Nancy),

Mike Douglas, George Harrison (Themselves). *Music:* Jimmy Webb. *Producers:* Robert Meyrowitz, Peter Kauff, Alan Steinberg. *Writers:* Neil Israel, Paul Proft. *Director:* Jeff Margolis.

**1679 The Rivalry.** Drama, 90 min., NBC, 12/12/75. A television adaptation of the famous 1858 Lincoln-Douglas Debates (in which Abraham Lincoln debated Stephen Douglas, his opponent for a U.S. Senate seat, over the issue of slavery). Aired on the "Hallmark Hall of Fame." *Cast:* Arthur Hill (Abraham Lincoln), Charles Durning (Stephen Douglas), Hope Lange (Mrs. Douglas). *Music:* Mauro Bruno. *Producer:* Duane C. Bogie. *Writers:* Donald Carmosant, Ernest Kinoy. *Director:* Fielder Cook.

**1680 Robbers, Rooftops and Witches.** Children, 60 min., CBS, 4/20/82. Washington Irving, America's first internationally successful author, is at Sunnydale, his idyllic 24-acre estate abutting the Hudson River in Tarrytown, New York, when he sees three youngsters playing a game. Irving is amused by their childish behavior and feels it may have the making of a short story. He tells the audience the genesis of this work. To illustrate his remarks, three short stories are dramatized.

1 "The Chaparral Prince" (by O. Henry) tells of Hondo Bill, a notorious but good-natured outlaw who rescues an overworked 11-year-old girl (Lena) from a mean innkeeper (Mrs. Maloney). *Cast:* John Shea (Hondo Bill), Tamara Jones (Lena), Grayson Hall (Mrs. Maloney), James Greene (Jeb), Maurice Copeland (Fritz).

2 "Antaeus" (by Borden Dean) tells of a 12-year-old Alabama boy (T. J.), newly arrived in New York City (during the 1940s), as he and a group of neighborhood kids attempt to start a garden on the roof of an abandoned factory. *Cast:* Stephen Miller (T. J.),

Claude Brooks (Chris), Jarrod Ross (Peter), Brendan Ward (Rusty), John Bennes (Janitor).

3 "Invisible Boy" (by Ray Bradbury) concludes the anthology with a story about an eccentric old woman who plans to keep her visiting nephew (Charlie), who can't wait to return home, with her by enticing him with hocus-pocus to make him invisible. *Cast:* Kate Reid (Aunt), Christian Slater (Charlie). *Host:* Tom Aldredge (as Washington Irving). *Music:* Dick Hyman. *Producers:* Frank Doelger, Elaine Halpert Sperber. *Writer:* Bruce Harmon. *Director:* Mark Cullingham.

### 1681 The Robert Goulet Special. Variety, 60 min., Syndicated, 11/68. An hour of music and songs. *Host:* Robert Goulet. *Guests:* Tommy Cooper, Lainie Kazan, The Lionel Blair Dancers, The Michael Sammes Singers, The Peddlers. *Music:* Jack Parnell. *Producer:* Jackie Barnett. *Director:* Dick Ross.

### 1682 Robert Klein on Broadway. Comedy, 60 min., HBO, 7/26/86. A comedy concert by Robert Klein. Taped in June 1986 at New York's Nederlander Theater. *Host:* Robert Klein. *Singers:* Betsy Bircher, Chrissy Faith, Norma Jean Wright. *Dancers:* Pamela Blasetti, Diana Laurenson, Amelia Marshall, Barbara Yeager. *Performers:* Joanne Bayes, Fyvush Finkel, David Jasse, Elaine Keesack, Billy Longo, Peggy Miley, Jeff Traghta, Stu Trivax, Jennifer Leigh Warren, George Wolf. *The Robert Klein Orchestra:* Michael Boone, Dave Ratajezak, Bob Rose, Jim Saporeto, Stan Schwartz. *Producers:* Robert Klein, Joseph Cates. *Writer:* Robert Klein. *Director:* Thomas Schlamme.

### 1683 The Robert Klein Show. Comedy, 60 min., NBC, 5/30/81. A program of sketches, monologues, and music with comedian Robert Klein in his first television special. *Host:* Robert

Klein. *Guests:* Marvin Braverman, The Charlie Daniels Band, Judd Hirsch, Bob Kaliban, Andrea Martin, Arnold Stang. *Music:* Louis St. Louis. *Producers:* Jack Rollins, Joseph Cates. *Writers:* Tony Geiss, Robert Klein, Joseph Bailey. *Director:* Stan Harris.

### 1684 The Robert Klein Show. Comedy, 60 min., NBC, 7/31/81. Various comedy sketches that poke fun at everyday life. *Host:* Robert Klein. *Guests:* Jane Curtin, Rodney Dangerfield. *Music:* Joe Raposo. *Producers:* Joseph Cates, John Gilroy. *Writers:* Robert Klein, David Axelrod. *Director:* Tom Trbovich.

### 1685 The Robert Q. Lewis Christmas Show. Variety, 60 min., CBS, 12/22/49. A holiday program of music, songs, and light comedy. *Host:* Robert Q. Lewis. *Guests:* The DeMarco Sisters, Jane Marshall, Doretta Morrow, Byron Palmer, Bill Skipper. *Music:* Ray Bloch. *Producer:* Barry Wood.

### 1686 Robert Shaw's Christmas Festival. Variety, 90 min., PBS, 12/24/88. Christmas music and songs with orchestra leader Robert Shaw. *Host:* Robert Shaw. *Guests:* The Georgia Symphony Orchestra and Chorale. *Producers:* Bill Johnstone, Philip Byrd. *Director:* Philip Byrd.

### 1687 Robert Young and the Family. Comedy, 60 min., CBS, 3/10/71. A series of sketches that satirize family life in America. *Host:* Robert Young. *Guests:* Beau Bridges, Eric Chase, Cynthia Eilbacher, Lee Grant, Barry Hamilton, Julie Sommars, Lurene Tuttle, Dick Van Dyke, Jack Warden, William Windom. *Music:* Alexis De Azevedo. *Producer-Director:* Bud Yorkin. *Writers:* Rob Reiner, Phil Mishkin, Michael Elias, Frank Shaw, David Pollock, Elias Davis.

**1688 Roberta (A Bob Hope Special).** Musical, 90 min., NBC, 9/19/58. A television adaptation of the Broadway play by Jerome Kern and Otto Harbach. The story of John Kent, a former all–American halfback who inherits Roberta's, his late aunt Minnie's fashion boutique, and the romance that blossoms between him and Stephanie, his aunt's assistant, an exiled Russian princess. See the following title also. *Cast:* Howard Keel (John Kent), Anna Maria Alberghetti (Stephanie), Bob Hope (Huckelberry Haines), Janis Paige (Scharwenka), Sara Dillon (Sophie Tate), Lilli Valenti (Aunt Minnie). *Music:* Les Brown. *Producer:* Jack Hope. *Writers:* Mort Lachman, Bill Larkin, Lester White, John Rapp, Charles Lee, Norman Sullivan. *Directors:* Dick McDonough, Ed Greenberg.

**1689 Roberta (A Bob Hope Special).** Musical, 90 min., NBC, 11/6/69. A restaged version of the previous title, which see for storyline information. *Cast:* John Davidson (John Kent), Michele Lee (Stephanie), Bob Hope (Huckelberry Haines), Janis Paige (Scharwenka), Laura Miller (Sophie Tate), Ann Shoemaker (Aunt Minnie), Irene Hervey (Mrs. Teale), Eve McVeagh (Anna). *Music:* Les Brown. *Producer:* Bob Hope. *Writers:* Mel Tolkin, Lester White, Charles Lee, Gig Henry, Bill Larkin, Mort Lachman. *Director:* Dick McDonough, John Kennedy.

**1690 Roberta Flack ... The First Time Ever.** Variety, 60 min., ABC, 6/19/73. An hour of music and song with Roberta Flack in her first television special. *Host:* Roberta Flack. *Guests:* Seals and Crofts, The Toni Basil Dancers. *Producers:* Bill Lee, Hank Saroyan.

**1691 Robin Hood: The Myth, the Man, the Movie.** Documentary, 60 min., CBS, 6/13/91. The program explores the legend of Robin Hood as a tie-in with the release of the 1991 motion picture *Robin Hood, Prince of Thieves. Host:* Pierce Brosnan. *Guest:* Kevin Costner. *Producers:* Mike Meadows, John Pattyson.

**1692 Robin Williams: An Evening at the Met.** Comedy, 60 min., HBO, 10/11/86. A concert by Robin Williams from New York's Metropolitan Opera House. *Host:* Robin Williams. *Producers:* Buddy Morra, Larry Brezner, David Steinberg. *Writer:* Robin Williams. *Director:* Bruce Gowers.

**1693 A Rock 'n' Roll Christmas.** Variety, 60 min., Fox, 12/11/88. A holiday special of live performances and film sequences in which rock and pop stars perform Christmas songs. *Host:* Denny Miller. *Guests:* Pat Benatar, The Fabulous Thunderbirds, Little Richard, John Cougar Mellencamp, Eddie Money. *Producers:* Bonnie Peterson, Jim Milio. *Writer:* Jim Milio. *Director:* Malcolm Leo.

**1694 The Rock 'n' Roll Show.** Variety, 30 min., ABC, 5/4 and 5/11/57. A two-part special that presents performances by the top names in rock and roll music. *Host:* Alan Freed. *Guests:* Edie Adams, Martha Carson, Charles Gracie, Ivory Joe Hunter, Sal Mineo, Guy Mitchell, June Valli, Andy Williams. *Music-Producer-Writer-Director:* Alan Freed.

**1695 Rock the House.** Variety, 30 min., NBC, 5/14/90. A high energy program of dances (choreographed by The Dance Possey) and rap songs from Young MC (Marvin Young) and Kid 'N Play (Mark Eastmond, Christopher Martin, Christopher Reid). *Hosts:* Mecca Dyas, Lisa Kellogg, Romeo Rich. *Music Director:* Richard Gibbs. *Producers:* Don Mischer, Bernie Brillstein, Brad Grey. *Director:* Don Mischer.

Ad for "Rock the House"

## 1696 The Rod McKuen Special. Variety, 30 min., NBC, 5/10/69. A solo concert by singer Rod McKuen. *Host:* Rod McKuen. *Music:* Arthur Greenslade. *Producer:* Lee Mendelson. *Director:* Marty Pasetta.

## 1697 Rodgers and Hart Today. Variety, 60 min., ABC, 3/2/67. A tribute to composer Richard Rodgers and lyricist Lorenz Hart with performances of their songs in a contemporary style. *Host:* Petula Clark. *Guests:* Count Basie, Bobby Darin, The Doodletown Pipers, The Mamas and the Papas, Diana Ross and the Su-premes. *Music:* Quincy Jones. *Producer:* Richard Lewine. *Director:* Bill Davis.

## 1698 Rodney Dangerfield: Exposed. Comedy, 60 min., ABC, 3/3/85. A variety of comedy sketches that satirize Rodney's endless problems with life. *Host:* Rodney Dangerfield. *Guests:* Dick Butkus, Morgan Fairchild, Harvey Korman, Bubba Smith. *Regulars:* Bernadette Birkett, Marvin Braverman, Jim Erving, Mark King, Dorothy Van, Lucy Webb, Paul Wilson. *Music:* Peter Matz. *Producers:* Estelle Endler, Rick Hawkins, Liz Sage.

*Writers:* Rodney Dangerfield, Rick Hawkins, Liz Sage, Jeffrey Barron, Greg Fields, Dennis Snee, Brian Roy.

## 1699 Rodney Dangerfield: It's Not Easy Bein' Me. Comedy, 60

min., HBO, 9/6/86. A special, produced independently of program number 1701, that presents an hour of comedy with Rodney Dangerfield and his guests. *Host:* Rodney Dangerfield. *Guests:* Jeff Altman, Roseanne Barr, Sam Kinison, Bob Nelson, Jerry Seinfeld, Robert Townsend. *Producer:* Kathy Lymberopoulos. *Writer:* Rodney Dangerfield. *Director:* Walter C. Miller.

## 1700 The Rodney Dangerfield Show: I Can't Take It No More.

Comedy, 60 min., ABC, 11/29/83. Various comedy sketches that feature Rodney Dangerfield's efforts to cope with life. *Host:* Rodney Dangerfield. *Guests:* Angie Dickinson, Donna Dixon, Andy Kaufman, Harold Ramis, Robert Urich. *Music:* Jack Elliott. *Producers:* Estelle Endler, Ed Simmons, Sid Stone. *Writers:* Rodney Dangerfield, Liz Sage, Ed Simmons, Dennis Snee. *Director:* Sidney Miller.

## 1701 The Rodney Dangerfield Special: It's Not Easy Bein' Me.

Comedy, 60 min., ABC, 5/12/80. Comedy skits that revolve around the world of comedian Rodney Dangerfield, a world, Rodney says, where "It's not easy bein' me." *Host:* Rodney Dangerfield. *Guests:* Rex Benson, Aretha Franklin, Steven Kampmann, Bill Murray, Valerie Perrine. *Music:* Peter Matz. *Producers:* Estelle Endler, Harold Ramis. *Writers:* Rodney Dangerfield, Harold Ramis, Elayne Boosler, Steven Kampmann, Stanley Myron Handelman, Brian Doyle Murray, Lennie Ripps. *Director:* Walter C. Miller.

## 1702 Roger Rabbit and the Secrets of Toon Town. Docu-

mentary, 60 min., CBS, 9/13/88. A behind-the-scenes look at the making of *Who Framed Roger Rabbit.* The program also features an interesting look at prior attempts to combine live action with animation. *Host:* Joanna Cassidy. *Guests:* Mel Blanc, Charles Fleischer (Voice of Roger Rabbit), Friz Freleng, Chuck Jones, Gene Kelly, Mae Questel, Steven Spielberg, Kathleen Turner, Dick Van Dyke, Robert Zemeckis. *Music:* Alan Silvestri. *Producers:* Frank Marshall, Kathleen Kennedy. *Writers:* William Rus, Michael Greer, Frank Marshall.

## 1703 Rolling Stone Magazine: The 10th Anniversary.

Variety, 2 hrs., CBS, 11/25/77. The top names in music perform in honor of *Rolling Stone* magazine's tenth anniversary. *Guests:* Richard Baskin, Chief Ed Davis, Yvonne Elliman, Ben Fong-Torres, Art Garfunkel, Teri Garr, Richie Havens, Gladys Knight and the Pips, Patti LaBelle, The Lester Wilson Dancers, Jerry Lee Lewis, Mike Love, Melissa Manchester, Steve Martin, Jim Messina, Bette Midler and the Harlettes, Keith Moon, Ted Neeley, Billy Preston, Martin Sheen, Phoebe Snow, Sissy Spacek, Lesley Ann Warren, Jimmy Webb. *Theme Music:* Jimmy Webb. *Music Director:* Jack Nitzsche. *Producers:* Janna Wenner, Steve Binder. *Writers:* Ben Fong-Torres, Steve Martin, David Felton, Mason Williams, Bill Angelos, Don Clark, Susan Clark. *Director:* Steve Binder.

## 1704 Rolling Stone Magazine: 20 Years of Rock and Roll.

Variety, 2 hrs., ABC, 11/24/87. A celebration of *Rolling Stone* magazine's twentieth anniversary with clips of performers and music it has covered over the past two decades. *Host:* Dennis Hopper. *Guests:* David Bowie, George Clinton, Aretha Franklin, Jerry Garcia, George Harrison, Cyndi Lauper, Paul McCartney, Randy Newman, Smokey Robinson, Grace Slick, Tina Turner, Neil Young. *Music:* Peggy

Sandvig. *Producers:* Janna Wenner, Lorne Michaels. *Writers:* Peter Elbing, Steve Muscarella. *Director:* Malcolm Leo.

## 1705 The Romance of Betty Boop. Cartoon, 30 min., CBS, 3/20/85.

Betty Boop, the sexy innocent with big eyes and a shapely body, brunette split curls, and a high squeaky voice, was the 1920s and 1930s Depression-era symbol of optimism and determination. In her first television special, the jazz-age bombshell is living in a one-room, walk-up flat in New York City (1939) and holding down two jobs: shoe clerk by day and toe-tapping nightclub performer at a speakeasy owned by Mischa Bubbles. Betty is being romanced by her dutiful boyfriend, Freddie the Iceman, but dreams about marrying Waldo Van Lavish, a millionaire. Songs of the era are interwoven into the story. *Voices:* Desiree Goyette (Betty Boop), Sandy Kenyon (Mischa Bubbles), Seth Allen (Freddie), Derek McGrath (Waldo), George Wendt (Johnny Throat), Marsha Meyers (Beverly), John Stephenson (Announcer). *Music:* Desiree Goyette, Ed Bogas. *Producers:* Bruce L. Paisner, Lee Mendelson, Bill Melendez. *Writer:* Ron Friedman. *Director:* Bill Melendez.

## 1706 Romeo and Juliet. Ballet, 30 min., NBC, 6/17/48.

Shakespeare's classic story of ill-fated lovers is performed to the music of Prokofiev's *Romeo and Juliet* and Tchaikovsky's *Romeo and Juliet Overture. Cast:* Eleanore Chapin (Juliet), Douglas Moppert (Romeo). *Also:* Ray Gaintner, Will Inglis, Daniel Perna, Audrea Price. *Producer-Director:* Paul Nickell. *Choreographer:* Eleanore Chapin.

## 1707 Romeo and Juliet on Ice. Ballet, 60 min., CBS, 11/25/83.

International ice skating star Dorothy Hamill opens the program by relating Shakespeare's story of ill-fated lovers to a group of young people. The story dissolves into skating sequences and finally an elaborate ballet on ice. *Cast:* Dorothy Hamill (Juliet), Brian Pockar (Romeo), Toller Cranston (Tybalt), Suzanne Russell (Nurse), Richard O'Neil (Friar Laurence), Michael Shinniman (Mercutio), Val Bezic (Paris), Gord Crossland (Capulet). *Conductor of the London Symphony Orchestra:* Andre Previn. *Producers:* Gary Smith, Dwight Hemion, Rob Iscove. *Choreographer:* Rob Iscove. *Director:* Dwight Hemion.

## 1708 Romp. Variety, 60 min., ABC, 4/21/68.

Music, songs, and comedy skits filmed on location in Europe, Japan, and California. *Hosts:* Michele Lee, Ryan O'Neal. *Guests:* Steve Allen, Joey Bishop, Harpers Bizarre, Michael Blodgett, James Darren, Sammy Davis, Jr., Richard Dreyfuss, Jimmy Durante, Barbara Eden, Liberace, Sonny Tufts. *Producer-Director:* Al Burton. *Writers:* Chris Bearde, Rob Reiner, David L. Lander, Mike Greer, Rich Goren.

## 1709 Rookie of the Year. Drama, 60 min., ABC, 10/3/73.

Sharon Lee is a pretty 11-year-old girl who loves baseball and plays the game better than most boys. She serves as equipment manager for a team and triggers controversy among players, parents, and school officials when Coach Shafer gives her a chance to play on his all-boys team. While Sharon is in seventh heaven, she receives cool treatment from other girls, the coach faces expulsion, and the team is dubbed "Shafer's Sissies." The "ABC Afterschool Special" explores the issue of sex discrimination as Sharon, both hurt and bewildered, tries to do the one thing she loves most—play baseball. *Cast:* Jodie Foster (Sharon Lee), Ned Wilson (Coach Shafer), Dennis McKiernan (Mark), David Perkins (Charlie), Steve Gustafson (Ralph), Barbara Andres (Mrs. Lee), Ken Kimmins (Mr. Lee), Victoria Dawson (Laura), Timmy Smith (Matt),

David Perkins (Charlie), Joey Marvel (Kenny). *Music:* George Craig. *Producer:* Daniel Wilson. *Writer:* Gloria Banta. *Director:* Lawrence S. Elikann.

**1710 The Room.** Drama, 60 min., PBS, 12/26/87. A television adaptation of British playwright Harold Pinter's cryptic one-act drama about five strange people who reside in a dreary London rooming house. *Cast:* Linda Hunt (Mrs. Hudd), Donald Pleasence (Mr. Kidd), David Hemblen (Mr. Hudd), Annie Lennox (Clarissa Sands), Julian Sands (Mr. Sands), Abbott Anderson (Mr. Riley). *Music:* Judith Gruber-Steitzer. *Producers:* Scott Bushnell, Robert Alda. *Writer:* Harold Pinter. *Director:* Robert Alda.

**1711 The Rosalind Russell Show.** Variety, 90 min., NBC, 10/6/59. A musical revue that traces the changes in showbusiness over the years. Rosalind Russell's only television special. *Host:* Rosalind Russell. *Guests:* Polly Bergen, Maurice Chevalier, Eddie Foy, Jr., Eddie Hodges, Ernie Kovacs, Jack Parr, Kate Smith. *Music:* Harry Sosnik. *Producers:* Hubbell Robinson, Jess Oppenheimer. *Writer:* Larry Gelbart. *Director:* Kirk Browning.

**1712 Rosalinda.** Comedy, 90 min., NBC, 7/23/56. The comic story of a romantic quadrangle involving the beautiful Rosalinda, her jealous but philandering husband Mr. Eisenstein, their charming maid Adele, and a tenant named Alfredo. *Cast:* Jean Fenn (Rosalinda), Cyril Ritchard (Mr. Eisenstein), Lois Hunt (Adele), Thomas Hayward (Alfredo), Robert Wright (Falke), Sig Arno (Prince Orlofsky), Ralph Dumke (Frank), The Wiere Brothers (Frosh/Frish/Frush). *Producer-Director:* Bob Banner.

**1713 The Roseanne Barr Show.** Comedy, 55 min., HBO, 9/19/87. A comedy concert by Roseanne

Barr (now Roseanne Arnold), as she pokes fun at the traditional roles of women, including a series of sketches built around the family. *Host:* Roseanne Barr. *Cast:* Tom Arnold, Lois Bromfield, Heather Hopper, Erica Horn, Steve Morris. *Music:* Kevin Kiner. *Producers:* Syd Vinnedge, Tony Scotti. *Writers:* Roseanne Barr, Rocco Urbisci, Bill Petland. *Director:* Rocco Urbisci.

**1714 The Rosey and Buddy Show.** Cartoon, 30 min., ABC, 5/15/92. An animated special based on characters created by Roseanne Arnold and her husband Tom. The characters, Rosey and Buddy, are a fun-loving couple who drive around the country in a recreational vehicle. They drive into Cartoonland and try to free some famous cartoon characters (e.g., Droopy Dog, Tom and Jerry, Strawberry Shortcake) who are being held prisoner by power-hungry weasels. *Voices:* Roseanne Arnold (Rosey), Tom Arnold (Buddy). *Producers:* Roseanne and Tom Arnold. *Writers:* Buddy Sheffield, Leo Benvenuti, Leslie Fuller, Steve Rudnick, Sam Greenbaum, Ron Friedman, Becky Hartman, David N. Weiss, Drew Ogier. *Director:* Larry Jacobs.

**1715 Rowan and Martin Bite the Hand That Feeds Them.** Variety, 60 min., NBC, 1/14/70. Comedy skits in which Rowan and Martin poke fun at their livelihood—television. *Hosts:* Dan Rowan, Dick Martin. *Guests:* Carol Burnett, Sammy Davis, Jr., Ray Kellogg, Sally Mills, Joanna Ray, Dick Smothers, Tom Smothers, Gary Walberg. *Producers:* Dan Rowan, Dick Martin. *Writers:* Gordon Wiles, Ed Simmons, Bill Richmond, Ed Haas, Terry Richmond, Terry Ryan, George Sunga. *Director:* Gordon Wiles.

**1716 The Rowan and Martin Special.** Variety, 60 min., NBC, 9/13/73. Vaudeville-style music, songs, and

**Ad for "Rowan and Martin's Laugh-In 25th Anniversary"**

comedy sketches. *Hosts:* Dick Martin, Dan Rowan. *Guests:* Edward Asner, Harry Belafonte, Ernest Borgnine, Jack Carter, Glenn Ford, Redd Foxx, Ruby Keeler, Kent McCord, Martin Milner, Bob Newhart, Dolly Parton, Cathy Rigby, Porter Wagoner, Jimmie Walker. *Producer:* Paul W. Keyes.

*Writers:* Marc London, Paul W. Keyes, David Panich, Allan Katz, Don Reo. *Director:* Bill Foster.

**1717 Rowan and Martin's Laugh-In 25th Anniversary.** Comedy, 2 hrs., NBC, 2/7/93. High-lights of "Rowan and Martin's Laugh-

In," which ran on NBC from 1968 to 1973. Dan Rowan and Dick Martin were the hosts and regulars included Goldie Hawn (the giggling ding-a-ling lady), Lily Tomlin (the nasal telephone operator), Ruth Buzzi (the frumpy matron), Arte Johnson (the lecherous Tyrone), Jo Anne Worley (the shrill-voiced extrovert), Gary Owens (the announcer), and Judy Carne (the Sock-It-to-Me Girl). Former cast members appear to reflect on the series. *Announcer:* Gary Owens. *Producer-Writer-Director:* George Schlatter.

## 1718 Roy Acuff — 50 Years the King of Country Music. Variety, 2 hrs., NBC, 3/1/82. A salute to Country Music Hall of Famer Roy Acuff through recollections, film clips, and songs. *Host:* Minnie Pearl. *Special Guest:* Roy Acuff. *Guests:* Bill Anderson, Eddy Arnold, Chet Atkins, Gene Autry, Larry Gatlin, Crystal Gayle, Don Gibson, Emmylou Harris, Barbara Mandrell, Dolly Parton, Ronald Reagan, Kenny Rogers, Ernest Tubb, Hank Williams, Jr. *Music:* Bill Walker. *Producers:* Joseph Cates, Chet Hagan. *Writers:* Frank Slocum, Chet Hagan. *Director:* Walter C. Miller.

## 1719 The Royal Family. Comedy, 60 min., CBS, 9/15/54. An adaptation of the Broadway play by George S. Kaufman and Edna Ferber about the life and times of the Cavendishes, America's number one family of the theater. *Cast:* Claudette Colbert (Julie Cavendish), Helen Hayes (Fanny Cavendish), Fredric March (Tony Cavendish), Nancy Olson (Gwen Cavendish), Charles Coburn (Oscar Wolfe). *Music:* David Broekman. *Producer:* Martin Manulis. *Writer:* Ronald Alexander. *Director:* Paul Nickell.

## 1720 The Royal Follies of 1933. Musical Comedy, 60 min., NBC, 12/11/67. A spoof of the movie musicals of the 1930s. When he is unable to escape the constant barrage of women seeking to marry him, Prince Wolfgang, the rich bachelor prince of a tiny kingdom, flees his country by stowing away on a ship bound for America. While on board ship he takes refuge with the cast of a Broadway-bound show. The story focuses on his efforts to help his newly adopted family when gangsters threaten to halt the show unless they pay for protection. *Cast:* Danny Thomas (Prince Wolfgang), Hans Conried (Van Plinkle), Eve Arden (Thelda Cunningham), Kurt Kaszner (Hansie), Shirley Jones (Peggy Ruby), Gale Gordon (Anthony Baxter), Ken Berry (Skip), Jackie Joseph (Suzie), Bob Hope (Makeup man). *Narrator:* Johnny Carson. *Music:* Earle Hagen. *Producer-Director:* Alan Handley.

## 1721 Royal Variety Performance. Variety, 90 min., ABC, 1/3/73. A variety benefit, taped at the London Palladium, for the British Olympic team. *Hosts:* Dick Martin, Dan Rowan. *Guests:* Liza Minnelli, Roger Moore, Des O'Connor, The Osmonds, Lily Tomlin. *Music:* Jack Parnell. *Producers:* Gary Smith, Dwight Hemion. *Director:* Dwight Hemion.

## 1722 Rudolph the Red-Nosed Reindeer. Christmas, 60 min., NBC, 12/64. The story, based on the song of the same title by Johnny Marks, recounts the tale of how Rudolph, the reindeer with the illuminated red nose, helps save Christmas by guiding Santa's sleigh through a very bad storm on Christmas Eve. The action is provided by the use of puppets seemingly brought to life through the technique of dimensional animation (animagic). The program is a holiday tradition and after a run of eight years on NBC made its debut on CBS on 12/8/72. *Voices:* Burl Ives (Sam the Snowman/Host-Narrator), Billie Richards (Rudolph), Paul Soles (Hermy the Elf), Larry D. Mann (Yukon Cornelius), Stan Francis (Santa Claus), Janet Orenstein (Clarice).

*Orchestrations:* Maury Laws. *Music and Lyrics:* Johnny Marks. *Producers:* Arthur Rankin, Jr., Jules Bass. *Writer:* Romeo Muller. *Director:* Larry Roemer.

**1723 Rudolph's Shiny New Year.** Christmas, 60 min., ABC, 12/10/76. The story follows Rudolph, the Red-Nosed Reindeer, as he embarks on a mission for Santa: finding Happy, the Baby New Year, who has run away from Father Time; if not found, there will be no New Year and December 31st will remain forever. *Voices:* Red Skelton (Father Time/Narrator), Billie Richards (Rudolph), Frank Gorshin (Sir Tent Worthree), Morey Amsterdam (One Million), Paul Frees (Santa Claus), Hal Peary (Big Ben). *Music:* Maury Laws. *Producer-Directors:* Arthur Rankin, Jr., Jules Bass. *Writer:* Romeo Muller.

**1724 Ruggles of Red Gap.** Musical, 90 min., NBC, 2/3/57. The comic escapades of Alfred Ruggles, the British butler to Egbert Floud, a cattleman in the wild frontier town of Red Gap, as he attempts to adjust to life in America (having been won by Egbert from his owner, the Earl of Brinstead, in a poker game). Based on the *Saturday Evening Post* story by Harry Leon Wilson. *Cast:* Michael Redgrave (Alfred Ruggles), David Wayne (Egbert Floud), Imogene Coca (Effie Floud), Jane Powell (Clementine), Peter Lawford (Lord George Vane-Brinstead), Paul Lynde (Charles Belknap-Jackson), Joan Holloway (Klondike Kate), Hal Linden (Man). *Music Director:* Buddy Bregman. *Music/Lyrics:* Jule Styne, Leo Robin. *Producer:* Charles Friedman. *Writer:* David Shaw. *Director:* Clark Jones.

**1725 Run, Don't Walk.** Drama, 60 min., ABC, 3/14/81. Following a fall from a horse, 18-year-old Samantha Anderson finds that she is paralyzed from the waist down. After spending a year in a special school to help her resume a normal life, Samantha refuses to admit to herself that she will always be in a wheelchair. The story relates the changes that occur in her life when she befriends a young teacher (Sue Jinkins) and discovers that she is capable of more in life than she expected. Aired as an "ABC Afterschool Special." *Cast:* Toni Kalem (Samantha Anderson), Dee Wallace (Sue Jinkins), Scott Baio (Johnny Jay), Jim McKrell (Ted Anderson), Rosemary Prinz (Beth Anderson), Bruno Kirby (Official), Sheila Frazier (Betty Ross), Hal Williams (Mr. Carter). *Producers:* Ervin Zavada, Henry Winkler. *Writer:* Durrell Royce Crays. *Director:* John Herzfeld.

**1726 Run, Rebecca, Run!** Drama, 60 min., PBS, 7/8/76. While taking pictures aboard a motor boat, a young girl (Rebecca) loses control and is swept down a raging river. Rebecca manages to maneuver the boat to a nearby island where she is taken captive by Manuel Cortez, an escaped political prisoner from South America. The story, set in Australia, relates her efforts to escape. *Cast:* Simone Buchanan (Rebecca Porter), Henri Szeps (Manuel Cortez), Mary Severne (Rebecca's mother), John Stanton (Rebecca's father), Dawn Blay (Officer Kelly). *Music:* Simon Walker. *Producer:* Gene Scott. *Writer:* Charles Stamp. *Director:* Peter Maxwell.

**1727 Runaway Ralph.** Children, 30 min., ABC, 10/29 and 11/5/88. A sequel to "The Mouse and the Motorcycle" (see entry). When Ralph, the talkative mouse, feels he is not appreciated by his family at the Mountain View Inn, he decides to run away on his motorcycle. After traveling for some time, he finds himself at the Happy Acres Camp. There he is rescued from a cat by a boy named Garfield. Feeling he can now have a pet, the lonely Garfield places Ralph in a cage. The story relates Ralph's efforts to escape and return home. Aired as an "ABC Weekend Special." *Cast:* Fred Savage (Garfield), Conchata Ferrell (Aunt Jill), Sara Gilbert (Steffie), Kellie Martin (Karen), Summer Phoenix (Lana), Anne Bloom (Garfield's mother), Ray Walston (Matt), Bruce French (Garfield's father), Hal Smith (Night clerk), John Matthews (Voice of Ralph). *Music:* Steven Kohn. *Producers:* George McQuilkin, John Matthews. *Writer:* Malcolm Marmorstein. *Director:* Ron Underwood.

**1728 Runaway to Glory.** Drama, 30 min., Syndicated, 6/87. The story, set in 1912, tells of an eight-year-old girl (Molly) and her grandfather (Sven) who prove their worthiness when they foil a bank robbery. *Cast:* Cara Prentice (Molly), Pat Cranshaw (Grandpa Sven), Ken Strunk (Papa), Rebecca Shouse (Mama), Charlie Payne (Jim), Bob Norris (Gus). *Producers:* Thomas G. Robertson, Gene McPherson. *Writer-Director:* Gene McPherson.

**1729 The Runaways.** Drama, 60 min., ABC, 3/27/74. Cindy Britton is a 17-year-old girl and a diabetic who is suffering emotional conflicts caused by her widowed mother's planned remarriage. Unable to cope with the situation, Cindy runs away from home. On the road she befriends a 12-year-old boy named Francis. The "ABC Afterschool Special" relates their efforts to help one another as they struggle for survival in a big city. *Cast:* Belinda Balaski (Cindy Britton), Claudio Martinez (Francis), Patricia Blair (Louise Britton), Anthony Eisley (John Turner), William Bryant (Detective), Moosie Drier (Freddie). *Producer:* Bill Schwartz. *Writer:* Clyde Ware. *Director:* John Florea.

**1730 Russian Roulette.** Comedy, 60 min., NBC, 11/17/65. A spoof of the cold war as seen through the experiences of Les Haines, a comedian

bound for Moscow, who becomes involved in a sticky international situation involving an American pilot captured by the Russians. A Bob Hope Special. *Cast:* Bob Hope (Les Haines), Jill St. John (Janie Douglas), Don Rickles (Lenny), Victor Buono (Grebb), Harold J. Stone (Borgman), Leon Askin (Chunky Russian), Leon Belasco (Thin Russian). *Music:* Les Brown. *Producers:* Jack Laird, Harry Tugend, David Lachman. *Writers:* Bob Hope, Burt Styler, Albert E. Lewin. *Director:* David Butler.

**1731 Saga of Sonora.** Musical, 60 min., NBC, 5/3/73. A musical fantasy about Sonora, a ghost town of the old west, that comes to life to relive the adventures of a singing villain with a lust for gold. *Hosts-Narrators:* Dale Evans, Roy Rogers. *Cowboy Narrator:* Don Adams. *Cast:* Zero Mostel (Villain), Vince Edwards (Sheriff), Sam Jaffe (Prospector), Lesley Ann Warren (Prospector's daughter), Jill St. John (Town's wicked lady), George Gobel (Town drunk), Frankie Avalon (Stagecoach driver), Cass Elliot (Saloon girl), George Kirby (Bartender), Carl Ballantine (Town banker), Kenny Rogers and the First Edition (Ghostly balladeers). *Music:* Larry Cansler. *Producers:* Burt Rosen, David Winters. *Writers:* Bernard Rothman, Jack Wohl. *Director:* Marty Pasetta.

**1732 St. Joan.** Drama, 2 hrs., NBC, 12/4/67. A "Hallmark Hall of Fame" adaptation of George Bernard Shaw's provocative drama that traces the life of Joan of Arc—from her first attempt to save France from the English to her court trial and burning at the stake. *Cast:* Genevieve Bujold (Joan of Arc), Roddy McDowall (Charles), Maurice Evans (Bishop Cauchon), James Donald (Richard), James Daly (Jack Dunois), Theodore Bikel (Robert de Baudricourt), Raymond Massey (Inquisitor), Leo Genn (Archbishop of Rheims), David Birney

(Ladvenie), George Rose (Chaplain). *Producer-Director:* George Schaefer. *Writer:* Robert Hartung.

## 1733 A Salute to America's Pets. Variety, 60 min., ABC, 6/13/91.
Celebrities salute their pets. The program also features a tribute to Lassie. *Hosts:* Rick Dees, Mary Frann, Marla Gibbs, Alex Trebek. *Guests:* Nina Blackwood, Dick Clark, Angie Dickinson, Bob Hope, Lily Tomlin, Betty White. *Producers:* Bob Hope, Linda Hope, Loreen Arbus. *Writers:* Jeffrey Barron, Steve Kunes. *Director:* Sid Smith.

## 1734 A Salute to Lady Liberty. Variety, 2 hrs., CBS, 7/8/84. A
star-studded salute to the Statue of Liberty as she undergoes restoration after standing in New York Harbor for 98 years. *Guests:* Byron Allen, Betty Buckley, Ray Charles, The Charlie Daniels Band, The Dallas Cowboys Cheerleaders, John Denver, Kirk Douglas, Linda Gray, Louis Jourdan, Emmanuel Lewis, Liza Minnelli, Tony Orlando, Marie Osmond, Anthony Quinn, Kenny Rogers, Brooke Shields, Frank Sinatra, Ben Vereen, Vanessa Williams. *Music:* Johnny Harris. *Producers:* George Schlatter, Bob Wynn. *Writers:* Rod Warren, George Schlatter. *Directors:* Bob Wynn, Danny Gomez, Jeff Simon.

## 1735 A Salute to Sir Lew— The Master Showman. Tribute,
60 min., ABC, 6/13/75. The New York Chapter of the National Academy of Television Arts and Sciences honors the master showman Sir Lew Grade. *Guests:* Dave Allen, Julie Andrews, Tom Jones, John Lennon, Peter Sellers. *Music:* Milton DeLugg. *Producer:* Dick Schneider. *Writer:* Joseph Scher. *Director:* Dwight Hemion.

## 1736 A Salute to Stan Laurel.
Tribute, 60 min., CBS, 11/23/65. A salute to comedian Stan Laurel (of the comedy team of Laurel and Hardy). *Host:* Dick Van Dyke. *Guests:* Lucille Ball, Fred Gwynne, Danny Kaye, Buster Keaton, Harvey Korman, Tina Louise, Audrey Meadows, Bob Newhart, Gregory Peck, Cesar Romero, Phil Silvers. *Music:* David Rose. *Producers:* Henry Jaffe, Seymour Berns. *Writers:* Charles Isaacs, Hugh Wedlock, Allan Manings. *Director:* Seymour Berns.

## 1737 A Salute to Television's 25th Anniversary. Variety, 90
min., ABC, 9/10/72. The outstanding moments from 25 years of television broadcasting, with clips from some 400 shows. *Guests:* Judith Anderson, Russell Arms, James Arness, Lucille Ball, Milton Berle, Sid Caesar, George Chakiris, Jimmy Durante, Dave Garroway, Lorne Greene, Florence Henderson, Bob Hope, Snooky Lanson, Gisele MacKenzie, Harry Reasoner, George C. Scott, Rod Serling, Dinah Shore, Dick Smothers, Tom Smothers, Ed Sullivan, John Wayne, Eileen Wilson, Robert Young, Efrem Zimbalist, Jr. *Producers:* Bob Finkel, Marty Pasetta. *Writers:* Bob Wells, John Bradford, Lennie Weinrib. *Director:* Marty Pasetta.

## 1738 A Salute to the American Theater. Variety, 60 min., CBS,
12/6/59. A salute to Broadway with a focus on the many contributions it has made in the cause of freedom of expression and antidiscrimination. *Host-Narrator:* Franchot Tone. *Guests:* Ossie Davis, Dorothy Fields, Louis Lotito, Art Lund, Claudia McNeill, Phyllis Newman, Robert Preston, Shepard Traube, Eli Wallach. *Producers:* Jack Juney, Elliott Baker. *Writer:* Elliott Baker. *Director:* John Desmond.

## 1739 Samantha Smith Goes to Washington. Documentary, 60
min., Disney, 2/19/84. Samantha Smith,

**Samantha Smith**

the Wonderful World of Children. Variety, 60 min., ABC, 2/1/66. Sammy Davis, Jr., and a group of children perform songs, comedy sketches, and dances. *Host:* Sammy Davis, Jr. *Producer:* Stan Greene. *Writers:* Bill Angelos, Allan Kohan. *Director:* Dick Schneider.

**1742 Sammy Davis, Jr., in Europe.** Variety, 60 min., Syndicated, 12/69. Highlights of Sammy Davis, Jr.'s overseas concert tour. *Host:* Sammy Davis, Jr. *Guests:* Charles Aznavour, Maurice Chevalier. *Producer-Director:* Helga Liesendahl.

the young girl who won America's hearts with her dream of world peace, visits a school in Washington, D.C., and asks fellow 11-year-olds what questions they want to ask of presidential hopefuls (candidates at the time were the Rev. Jesse Jackson, Reubin Askew, and John Glenn). *Host:* Samantha Smith. *Producers:* Arnold Shapiro, Jean O'Neill, Gerald Rafshoon.

**1740 Sammy and His Friends.** Variety, 60 min., ABC, 11/25/65. An hour of music and songs. *Host:* Sammy Davis, Jr. *Guests:* Count Basie and His Orchestra, Joey Heatherton, Frank Sinatra. *Producer:* Joe Hamilton. *Director:* Clark Jones.

**1741 Sammy Davis, Jr., and**

**1743 The Sammy Davis, Jr., Special.** Variety, 60 min., NBC, 2/18/65. An hour of music, songs, and light comedy. *Host:* Sammy Davis, Jr. *Guests:* Billy Daniels, Lola Falana, Peter Lawford, Mike Silva. *Music:* George Rhodes. *Producer:* Sammy Davis, Jr. *Director:* Hal Tulchin.

**1744 Sammy Davis, Jr.'s 60th Anniversary Celebration.** Tribute, 2 hrs. 30 min., ABC, 2/4/90. A star-studded salute to Sammy Davis, Jr., on the occasion of his sixtieth year in show business. *Host:* Eddie Murphy. *Special Guest:* Sammy Davis, Jr. *Guests:* Debbie Allen, Anita Baker, Diahann Carroll, Nell Carter, Bill Cosby, Tony Danza, Clint Eastwood, Lola Falana, Ella Fitzgerald, Goldie Hawn, the Rev. Jesse Jackson, Michael Jackson, Quincy

Jones, Shirley MacLaine, Dean Martin, Gregory Peck, Richard Pryor, Frank Sinatra, Mike Tyson, Stevie Wonder. *Announcer:* Dick Tufeld. *Music:* Glen Roven. *Producers:* George Schlatter, Jeff Margolis, Buz Kohan. *Writers:* Buz Kohan, George Schlatter. *Director:* Jeff Margolis.

**1745 Sandy.** Variety, 60 min., CBS, 6/9/67. Music, songs, and dances with Canadian singer Sandy O'Neill. *Host:* Sandy O'Neill. *Guests:* Natalie Butko, Jeff DeBenning, Anthony George, Gordie Tapp. *Producer-Director:* Dave Thomas. *Writer:* Chris Bearde.

**1746 The Sandy Duncan Show.** Variety, 60 min., CBS, 11/13/74. An hour of music, songs, and comedy sketches. *Host:* Sandy Duncan. *Guests:* Valorie Armstrong, John Davidson, Gene Kelly, Paul Lynde. *Music:* Jack Parnell. *Producers:* Gus Schirmer, Gary Smith. *Writers:* Marty Farrell, Jack Burns, Karyl Geld, Alan Thicke. *Director:* Dwight Hemion.

**1747 Sandy in Disneyland.** Variety, 60 min., CBS, 4/10/74. A musical tour of Disneyland in Southern California. *Host:* Sandy Duncan. *Guests:* Ernest Borgnine, Ruth Buzzi, John Davidson, Lorne Greene, The Jackson Five, Ted Knight, Doc Severinsen. *Music:* Eddie Karam. *Producers:* Marty Pasetta, Bernard Rothman, Jack Wohl. *Writers:* George Bloom, Gary Ferrier, Audrey Tadman, Bernard Rothman, Jack Wohl. *Director:* Marty Pasetta.

**1748 Santa Claus Is Comin' to Town.** Christmas, 60 min., ABC, 12/70. The program relates how the legend of Santa Claus originated, and answers such other questions as why he wears a red suit, why he leaves presents, why he comes down the chimney, and why he lives in the North Pole. It begins with Tanta Kringle finding an abandoned baby boy. The boy, named Kris Kringle, grows up in Rainbow River Valley and learns how to make toys, which are supposed to be distributed to the good children of Sombertown. However, because Sombertown is over the mountain — and in the path of the dreaded Winter Warlock — the Kringle Elfs are unable to deliver their toys. When older, Kris begins delivering the toys but is soon declared an outlaw by the mean Burgermeister who has come to hate toys and forbids toys in Sombertown. With the help of Jessica, the schoolteacher he befriends (and later marries), Kris begins sneaking into Sombertown to deliver his toys (via chimneys). To escape the Burgermeister, Kris, Jessica, and the Kringle family move to the North Pole where Kris establishes his base and decides to limit his toy deliveries to only one night a year, the most holy night, Christmas Eve. Repeated annually at Christmas time. *Voices:* Fred Astaire (S. D. Kluger; the postman and narrator), Mickey Rooney (Kris Kringle), Robie Lester (Jessica), Keenan Wynn (Winter Warlock), Joan Gardner (Tanta Kringle), Paul Frees (Burgermeister). *Music:* Maury Laws. *Producer-Directors:* Arthur Rankin, Jr., Jules Bass. *Writer:* Romeo Muller.

**1749 Santa Claus: The Making of the Movie.** Variety, 60 min., ABC, 12/24/87. A behind-the-scenes look at the making of the 1987 feature film *Santa Claus: The Movie* (with Dudley Moore). *Guests:* Sheena Easton (who performs the song "Christmas All Over the World"), Dudley Moore. *Narrator:* Ted Maynard. *Music:* Henry Mancini. *Producers:* Ilya Salkind, Pierre Spengler. *Writer:* Lain Johnstone. *Director:* Danny Huston.

**1750 Santabear's First Christmas.** Cartoon, 30 min., ABC, 11/22/86. A young bear, swept away from his family at the North Pole by an ice floe, is found and befriended by a young girl. Shortly after, when the girl's kindly old grandfather becomes ill, the bear attempts to help by gathering firewood to cook food and keep the grandfather warm. As the bear searches in vain for wood, he meets Santa Claus and expresses a wish for firewood for Christmas. So impressed by the bear's unselfish request, Santa grants his wish and recruits him to help deliver toys to the woodland animals. *Narrator:* Kelly McGillis. *Music:* Michael Hedges. *Producers:* Christopher Campbell, Mark Sottnick. *Writer:* Tom Roberts. *Director:* Mark Sottnick.

## 1751 Santiago's America.

Drama, 60 min., ABC, 2/19/75. A sequel to "Santiago's Ark" (see next title for information). Santiago, the Puerto Rican boy with dauntless ambition, wins an essay contest and is invited to attend the Young American Continental Congress in Los Angeles as the New York delegate. The prize, however, does not include the cost of transportation and Santiago's parents cannot afford to finance the trip. Not willing to forego the honor he has won, Santiago seeks the help of his friend John, the junkman, and, with the help of some friends, they fix up a dilapidated taxi and raise enough money for Santiago to begin his trip. The story relates Santiago's motor trip across the United States as he and John head for California. Aired as an "ABC Afterschool Special." *Cast:* Ruben Figueroa (Santiago), Marc Jordan (John), Alex Colon (Carlos), Carmen Maya (Santiago's mother), Rene Enriquez (Santiago's father), Gloria Irizzary (Teacher), Bill Duke (Mr. Sands). *Music:* Keith Avedon. *Producer-Writer-Director:* Albert Waller.

## 1752 Santiago's Ark. Drama,

60 min., ABC, 12/6/72. Santiago is a 14-year-old Puerto Rican boy with imagination and ambition who lives in New York's Spanish Harlem. The story, broadcast as an "ABC Afterschool

Special," relates Santiago's efforts to build a sailing ship and man the helm of the vessel in the lake in Central Park. See the sequel story, "Santiago's America." *Cast:* Reuben Figueroa (Santiago), Carmen Maya (Santiago's mother), Rene Enriquez (Santiago's father), Marcus Ticotin (Stevie), Bill Duke (Mr. Sands), Alex Colon (Carlos). *Producer-Writer-Director:* Albert Waller.

## 1753 Sara's Summer of the Swans. Drama, 60 min., ABC, 10/2/

74. Sara Godfrey is a pretty redheaded 14-year-old girl who feels she is too tall and awkward. She is having a terrible summer caring for her younger brother (Charlie) and living in the shadow of her older, glamorous sister (Wanda). Sara's parents are away on business and Sara is living with her Aunt Willie, whom she feels has no interest in her and fails to understand her problems. Sara's only joy is her refuge at the nearby lake; a secret area where she enjoys watching and feeding the swans. Her world changes one day when Charlie tries to find Sara's secret refuge and becomes lost. Sara's quick thinking and the help and friendship offered by a teenage boy named Joe Melby open the doors which allow Sara to see the world and herself in a better light after she saves Charlie's life (he had fallen in a ravine in the woods). The touching coming-of-age story was broadcast as an "ABC Afterschool Special." *Cast:* Heather Totten (Sarah Godfrey), Christopher Knight (Joe Melby), Priscilla Morrill (Aunt Willie Godfrey), Eve Plumb (Gretchen Wyant), Betty Ann Carr (Wanda Godfrey), Reed Diamond (Charlie Godfrey), Doney Oatman (Mary). *Producer:* Martin Tahse. *Writer:* Bob Rodgers. *Director:* James B. Clark.

## 1754 Satins and Spurs. Musi-

cal, 90 min., NBC, 9/12/54. A romantic comedy about a beautiful rodeo queen (Cindy) who falls in love with a magazine reporter. *Cast:* Betty Hutton (Cindy), Guy Raymond (Tex), Josh Wheeler (Dick), Edwin Phillips (Ollie), Kevin McCarthy (Tony), Neva Patterson (Ursula), Genevieve (Chanteuse). *Music Director:* Charles Sanford. *Music Arranger/Composer:* Henry Mancini. *Music/Lyrics:* Jay Livingston, Ray Evans. *Producers:* Max Liebman, Bill Hobin. *Writers:* William Friedberg, Max Liebman. *Director:* Charles O'Curran.

**1755 Saturday Night Live Goes Commercial.** Comedy, 90 min., NBC, 2/10/91. A compilation of commercial parodies from the series "Saturday Night Live." *Hosts:* Victoria Jackson, Kevin Nealon. *Producers:* Lorne Michaels, Al Franken, James Downey. *Writers:* Al Franken, James Downey. *Director:* James Signorelli.

**1756 Saturday's Children.** Drama, 60 min., CBS, 2/25/62. The romantic adventures of Bobby Halevy, a stenographer who pursues a lover instead of a husband, fearing marriage and its related hardships would not be right for her. Based on the play by Maxwell Anderson. *Saturday's Children* (which refers to people who must work for a living) was also adapted to television as a segment of "The Lux Video Theater" (CBS, 10/2/50) with Joan Caulfield (Bobby), John Ericson (Rims), and Eileen Heckart (Florrie); and on "Celanese Theater" (ABC, 3/10/52) with Shirley Standee (Bobby), Mickey Rooney (Rims), and Patricia Bright (Florrie). *Cast:* Inger Stevens (Bobby Halevy), Cliff Robertson (Rims O'Neil), Lee Grant (Florrie Sands), Ralph Bellamy (Mr. Halevy), Doro Merande (Mrs. Gorlick), Katherine Meskill (Mrs. Halevy), Ted Beniades (Willie Sands). *Music:* Alfredo Antonini. *Music Director:* George Leinsinger. *Producer:* Leland Hayward. *Writer:* Robert Emmett. *Director:* Tom Donovan.

**1757 The Savage Curse.**

Thriller, 90 min., ABC, 2/25/74. The story of an American (Robert Stone) who journeys to England to find his missing brother and his involvement with the people of a strange village where his brother was last seen. Also known as "Kiss Me and Die." *Cast:* George Chakiris (Robert Stone), Jenny Agutter (Dominie Lanceford), Anton Diffring (Jonathan Lanceford), John Sharpe (Jack Woodbridge), Stephen Grief (Ben Groom), Sue Robinson (Jenny), Peggy Sinclair (Miss Faversham). *Music:* Laurie Johnson. *Producer-Director:* John Sichel. *Writer:* Terence Feely.

**1758 Save the Planet: A CBS/Hard Rock Special.** Variety, 60 min., CBS, 4/20/90. Music and comedy segments that celebrate Earth Day. Taped at the Hard Rock Cafe in Los Angeles. *Hosts:* Bobcat Goldthwait, Katey Sagal. *Celebrity Guests:* Paula Abdul, Sandra Bernhard, Cher, Alice Cooper, Billy Idol, James Earl Jones, Quincy Jones, Tom Petty. *Performers:* Fine Young Cannibals, Red Hot Chili Peppers, Taylor Dane and M. C. Hammer.

**1759 The Scoey Mitchlll Show.** Variety, 60 min., Syndicated, 4/72. Music, songs, and comedy skits with comedian Scoey Mitchlll. *Host:* Scoey Mitchlll. *Guests:* The Carlton Johnson Dancers, Jim Erving, Damita Jo Freeman, Buddy Hackett, Dave Reeves, Dorothy Van, Nancy Wilson. *Music:* Ralph Carmichael. *Producer:* Kenny Spaulding. *Director:* Marc Breslow.

**1760 Screamer.** Thriller, 90 min., ABC, 11/12/74. The story of a young woman (Nicola) who fears she is being stalked by a rapist. *Cast:* Pamela Franklin (Nicola Stevens), Frances White (Virna), Donal McCann (Jeff), Jeff Holt (The Man), Peter Howell (Dr. Ward), Derek Smith (Inspector). *Music:* Laurie Johnson. *Producer:* John

Cooper. *Writer:* Brian Clemens. *Director:* Shaun O'Riordan.

## 1761 Scrooge's Rock 'n' Roll Christmas. Musical, 30 min., Syndicated, 12/84. A young girl's efforts to help a Scrooge-like character celebrate a musical Christmas in southern California. *Cast:* Jack Elam (Scrooge), Lee Benton (Girl). *Music Performers:* The Association, Bobby Goldsboro, Mike Love, Mary MacGregor, Paul Revere and the Raiders, Merrilee Rush, Three Dog Night, Dean Torrance. *Producers:* Rex Sparger, Bob Franchini. *Writer:* Rex Sparger. *Director:* Bob Franchini.

## 1762 Scruffy. Cartoon, 30 min., ABC, 10/4, 10/11, 10/18/80. An animated drama inspired by the true story of a stray dog that received wide public attention when her tale was told in the newspapers. The dog was rescued from an overcrowded pound and saved from death when a reporter adopted her (Scruffy). The dog's story appeared in print and Scruffy became a symbol of all homeless creatures doomed by the uncertainty of their future. The story inspired an outpouring of love that made her a national heroine. In this "ABC Weekend Special," Scruffy's adventures unfold in a three-part story that follows her search for her original owners. *Voices:* Alan Young (Narrator), Nancy McKeon (Scruffy), June Foray (Duchess), Hans Conried (Tibbles), Mike Bell (Butch). *Producers:* Joe Ruby, Ken Spears. *Writer:* Sheldon Stark. *Director:* Charles A. Nichols.

## 1763 The Sea World/Busch Gardens Summer Celebration. Variety, 60 min., CBS, 6/9/93. The program honors young people who have made an effort to protect the environment. *Hosts:* Deidre Hall, Ann Jillian. *Guests:* Dick Clark, Stefanie Powers, Betty White. *Music:* Lenny Stack. *Producer:* Dick Clark. *Writer:* Barry Adelman. *Director:* Gene Weed.

## 1764 Sea World's All-Star Lone Star Celebration. Variety, 2 hrs., CBS, 6/18/88. Music and songs coupled with performances by animals at Sea World in San Antonio, Texas. *Hosts:* Patrick Duffy, Marie Osmond. *Guests:* Morgan Fairchild, Farrah Fawcett, Freddy Fender, Katherine Helmond, John Hillerman, Waylon Jennings, Trini Lopez, Barbara Mandrell, Jaclyn Smith, George Strait, Willie Tyler and Lester. *Music:* Tom Bruns. *Producers:* Dick Clark, Gene Weed, Al Schwartz. *Writer:* George Stalle. *Director:* Gene Weed.

## 1765 The Search for Haunted Hollywood. Documentary, 2 hrs., Syndicated, 10/27/89. The program explores the haunted areas of Hollywood (for example, a hotel where Marilyn Monroe's image is seen in a mirror; a field where a woman's spirit has been seen; and the spirits of Hollywood backlots). *Host:* John Davidson. *Guests:* Harry Blackstone, Jr., Norm Crosby, Pat McCormick, Patrick Macnee, Paul Williams. *Music:* Robert Sabellico. *Producers:* Lance Thompson, David MacKenzie. *Writers:* Pat McCormick, Dan Goldman. *Director:* Arthur Forrest.

## 1766 Seasonal Differences. Drama, 60 min., ABC, 12/2/87. An "ABC Afterschool Special" about two friends, one Catholic, one Jewish, who learn to accept each other's seasonal differences when a controversy erupts over a public school's decision to display the Nativity scene at Christmastime. *Cast:* Megan Follows (Dana Sherman), Timothy Owen (Mark Davis), Melba Moore (Mrs. Verady), Uta Hagen (Omi), Frank Whaley (Jeff Dillon), Jonathan Tiersten (Jason), Gabrielle Carteris (Leslie Merrill), Mara Hobel (Vanessa), Joan Kaye (Mrs. Sherman). *Music:* Elliot Sokolow. *Producers:* Tom G. Robertson, Peggy Doyle, Mary Kelly. *Writer:* D. J. McHale. *Director:* Tom G. Robertson.

## 1767 Season's Greetings — An Evening with John Williams and the Boston Pops Orchestra.

Variety, 60 min., NBC, 12/23/88. A yuletide program of Christmas music and songs that was taped on December 21, 1988, at Boston's Symphony Hall and features John Williams conducting the Boston Pops Orchestra. *Host:* John Williams. *Guests:* The Boston Boys Choir, John Candy, Roberta Flack, Reba McEntire, Andy Williams. *Producers:* Don Ohlmeyer, Linda Jonsson. *Writer:* Robert Arnott. *Director:* Don Ohlmeyer.

## 1768 Season's Greetings from the Honeymooners.

Christmas, 2 hrs., Syndicated, 11/85. "The Honeymooners" (Ralph and Alice Kramden and their friends Ed and Trixie Norton) celebrate the holidays with clips first seen on "The Jackie Gleason Show" in the 1950s. *Host:* Jackie Gleason (Ralph Kramden). *Guests:* Art Carney (Ed Norton), Audrey Meadows (Alice Kramden), Joyce Randolph (Trixie Norton). *Music:* Kevin Kiner. *Producer-Writer:* Andrew Solt, Susan F. Walker. *Director:* Andrew Solt.

## 1769 The Second Barry Manilow Special.

Variety, 60 min., ABC, 2/24/78. A sequel to "The Barry Manilow Special" (see title). An additional hour of music and songs. *Host:* Barry Manilow. *Guest:* Ray Charles. *Producers:* Miles Lourie, Barry Manilow, Ernest Chambers. *Writers:* Ernest Chambers, Barry Manilow. *Director:* George Schaefer.

## 1770 The Second City 25th Anniversary Special.

Comedy, 60 min., HBO, 4/13/85. A celebration of Second City, the famous Chicago-based improvisational comedy troupe, on the occasion of its twenty-fifth anniversary. The program features illustrious graduates appearing in skits. *Hosts:* Ed Asner, David Susskind. *Performers:* Alan Arkin, Jim Belushi, Shelly Berman, Danny Breen, John Candy, Joe Flaherty, Mary Gross, Tim Kazurinsky, Robert Klein, Shelley Long, Andrea Martin, Harold Ramis, Betty Thomas, Dave Thomas, George Wendt, Fred Willard. *Music:* Fred Kaz. *Producers:* Andrew Alexander, Bernard Shalins. *Director:* John Blanchard.

## 1771 The Secret Life of T.K. Dearing.

Drama, 60 min., ABC, 4/23/75. A touching story that focuses on the relationship between a preteen girl (Theresa Dearing, who is known as T. K.) and her grandfather, a free soul with whom she shares adventures. Aired as an "ABC Afterschool Special." *Cast:* Jodie Foster (T. K. Dearing), Eduard Franz (Grandpa Kindermann), Leonard Stone (Walter Dearing), Zoe Karant (Ruth Dearing), Brian Wood (Potato Tom), Robin Stone (Alice), Brian Part (Dugger), Tierre Turner (Jerry). *Music:* George Craig. *Producer:* Daniel Wilson. *Writer:* Bob Rodgers. *Director:* Harry Harris.

## 1772 The Secret of Charles Dickens.

Drama, 60 min., CBS, 4/16/78. The special is actually a play within a play, wherein actress Valerie Bertinelli portrays herself as well as Mamie, the teenage daughter of English novelist Charles Dickens. The story begins with Valerie arriving in London to play Mamie on a television program. Through her portrayal, the viewer is shown the creativity of Dickens's writing and how Mamie comes to an appreciation of her father as a man and an author. The program marks the first dramatic role for Valerie Bertinelli, and also a rare American television appearance for Alan Badel, a distinguished British actor. *Cast:* Valerie Bertinelli (Herself/Mamie Dickens), Alan Badel (Charles Dickens), Elizabeth Spriggs (Kate), Linda Polan (Georgina), Richard Wilson (TV Director), Luke Batchelor (Sidney), Michael

Mannion (Henry), Benjie McKie (Edward). *Producers:* Daniel Wilson, Linda Marmelstein. *Writer:* Lee Kalcheim. *Director:* Sheldon Larry.

## 1773 The Secret World of Kids.
Children, 60 min., NBC, 10/27/59. Children discuss various aspects of life with celebrities. *Host:* Art Linkletter. *Guests:* Ann Blyth, Angela Cartwright, Richard Nixon, Vincent Price, Jon Provost, Teddy Rooney. *Producers:* Hubbell Robinson, Paul Henning. *Writer:* Paul Henning. *Director:* Dick Wesson.

## 1774 The Secret World of Og.
Cartoon, 30 min., ABC, 4/30, 5/7, 5/14/83. While five children (Penny, Pamela, Patsy, Peter, and Pollywog) are playing, an elf-like creature named Og saws his way up through the floor of their playhouse, helps himself to some comic books, and returns to his world. When Pollywog goes through the hole, the other children follow him. The children enter the enchanting underground world of small, green people who love games of make-believe. The story relates the children's adventures as they search for the way back to their world. Aired as an "ABC Weekend Special." *Voices:* Fred Travalena (Og), Noelle North (Penny), Josh Rodine (Peter), Marissa Mendenhall (Pamela), Julie McWhirter (Pollywog), Brittinay Wilson (Patsy), Janet Waldo (Mother). *Producer:* Doug Paterson. *Writer:* Mark Evanier. *Director:* Geoff Collins.

## 1775 The Secret World of the Very Young.
Children, 60 min., CBS, 9/12/84. The often baffling world of the preschooler is explored through humor, music, and dramatic vignettes. *Hosts:* Shelley Duvall, John Ritter. *Guests:* Ruth Gordon, Geri Jewell, Emmanuel Lewis, Joan Lunden, Annette O'Toole, Lou Rawls, Nancy Morgan, John Ritter, Dick Smothers, Tom Smothers, Sally Struthers, Mr. T, Ben Vereen. *Music:* Tommy Goodwin. *Pro-*

*ducers:* Tom Griffin, Joe Bascal. *Writers:* David Axelrod, Joe Landon. *Director:* Sterling Johnson.

## 1776 The Sensational, Shocking, Wonderful Wacky 70s.
Variety, 2 hrs., NBC, 1/4/80. A look back at the people, events, music, and trends of the 1970s. *Hosts:* Sonny Bono, Dick Clark. *Guests:* Woody Allen, Bill Bixby, Art Buchwald, Carol Burnett, Roy Clark, Brandon Cruz, Faye Dunaway, Henry Fonda, Jane Fonda, Leif Garrett, Crystal Gayle, Valerie Harper, Hugh Hefner, Sherman Hemsley, Kate Jackson, Diane Keaton, Evel Knievel, Ted Knight, Shirley MacLaine, Barry Manilow, Steve Martin, Paul Newman, Olivia Newton-John, Isabel Sanford, David Sheenan, Carly Simon, Rod Stewart, Toni Tennille. *Music:* Lenny Stack. *Producers:* Dick Clark, Al Schwartz. *Director:* Jeff Margolis.

## 1777 Sentimental Swing: The Music of Tommy Dorsey.
Variety, 90 min., PBS, 8/15/87. A concert by the new Tommy Dorsey Orchestra with songs and music reminiscent of the big band sound (1940s) of Tommy Dorsey. *Host:* Mel Torme. *Guests:* Jack Jones, The L.A. Voices, Maureen McGovern. *Announcer:* John Harlan. *Music Director:* Buddy Morrow.

## 1778 Separate Tables.
Drama, 2 hrs., HBO, 3/14/83. Two one-act plays that explore bittersweet relationships at an English seaside resort. Based on Terence Rattigan's one-act plays *Table by the Window* and *Table Number Seven.* Taped in England. *Cast:* Julie Christie (Anne Shankland/Sybil Railton-Bell), Alan Bates (John Malcolm/Major Pollock), Claire Bloom (Miss Cooper), Irene Worth (Mrs. Railton-Bell), Sylvia Barter (Lady Matheson), Bernard Archard (Mr. Flower), Susannah Fellows (Jean Tanner), Kathy Staff (Mabel), Brian Deacon (Charles Stratton). *Music:* Phil Smith. *Producers:* Mort Abrahams, Edie Landau, Ely Lan-

dau. *Writer:* Julie Trevelyn-Oman. *Director:* John Schlesinger.

## 1779 Sgt. Pepper: It Was 20 Years Ago Today. Documentary,

2 hrs., PBS, 11/11/87. A British-produced program that attempts to explain what the late 1960s counterculture was all about. The program recalls Sgt. Pepper's Lonely Hearts Club Band and attributes it to the beginning of a mini-renaissance in music and attitude. Rare film clips, concert footage, and recent interviews are used to heighten the program. *Guests:* Peter Coyote, Peter Fonda, Allen Ginsberg, George Harrison, Abbie Hoffman, Dr. Timothy Leary, Paul McCartney, George Martin. *Producers:* Rod Caird, Simon Albury, John Sheppard. *Research-Writer:* Colin Bell. *Director:* John Sheppard.

## 1780 Sesame Street ... 20 and Still Counting. Variety, 60

min., NBC, 4/7/89. A look at the history of "Sesame Street," the PBS program for children, on the occasion of its twentieth year on the air. *Host:* Bill Cosby. *Guests:* Ray Charles, Placido Domingo, Jim Henson and the Muppets. *Music:* Joe Raposo. *Producers:* Jim Henson, Dulcey Singer. *Writers:* Judy Fraudenberg, Tony Geiss. *Director:* Peter Harris.

## 1781 The Seven Dials Mystery. Mystery, 2 hrs. 30 min., Syndi-

cated, 4/16/81. The story, based on the 1929 novel by Agatha Christie, relates the exploits of Lady Eileen "Bundie" Brent, an amateur sleuth, as she attempts to solve a murder that gets her involved with a secret British society known as the Seven Dials. *Host:* Peter Ustinov. *Cast:* Cheryl Campbell (Lady Eileen Brent), John Gielgud (Marquis of Caterham), James Warwick (Jimmy Thesiger), Lucy Gutteridge (Lorraine Wade), Sarah Crowden (Helen), Tom Belaney (Terrence O'Rourke), Lynne

Ross (Nancy), Robert Longden (Gerry Wade), Rula Lenska (Countess Radzsky), Leslie Sands (Sir Oswald Coote), Harry Andrews (Superintendent Battle). *Music:* Joseph Horovitz. *Producers:* Tony Wharmby, Jack Williams. *Director:* Tony Wharmby.

## 1782 The Seven Wishes of a Rich Kid. Comedy, 60 min., ABC,

12/5/79. Calvin Brundage is a rich but lonely boy. One day, while watching television, a genie appears on Calvin's television screen and offers him seven wishes — which he uses in all the wrong ways to impress Melanie, a girl on whom he has a crush. Aired as an "ABC Afterschool Special." *Cast:* Butterfly McQueen (Genie), Robbie Rist (Calvin Brundage), Cynthia Nixon (Melanie Gamble), Christopher Hewett (Runcible). *Music:* Brad Fiedel. *Producers:* Linda Gottlieb, Doro Bachrach. *Writer:* Jeffrey Kindley. *Director:* Larry Elikann.

## 1783 The Seven Wishes of Joanna Peabody. Comedy-Drama,

60 min., ABC, 9/9/78. While watching television, a fairy godmother (Aunt Thelma) appears on the television screen of 12-year-old Joanna Peabody and offers her seven wishes ("I'm your official Special Spirit, come from the Special Spirit to watch over you and give you something nice"). The story relates Joanna's misadventures as she struggles over the prospect of what to wish for (and learns an important lesson about herself, life and the love of others). Aired as an "ABC Afterschool Special." *Cast:* Butterfly McQueen (Aunt Thelma), Star-Shemah (Joanna Peabody), Garrett Morris (Frank), Starletta DuPois (Mother), Loretta Greene (Duvelle), Angelo Hunter (Bubba), Deborah Malone (Malta June), Sandra Phillips (Mrs. Mulberry). *Music:* Score Productions. *Producer:* Doro Bachrach. *Writer-Director:* Stephen Foreman.

## 1784 The Seven Wonders of the Circus World. Variety, 60 min., CBS, 10/7/88. Highlights of the best acts from circuses around the world. *Host:* Harry Anderson. *Music:* Bob Gerardi. *Producer-Director:* Francois Bronett, Joseph Cates.

## 1785 The 75th Anniversary of Beverly Hills. Variety, 60 min., ABC, 2/26/89. A star-studded salute to Beverly Hills on the anniversary of its founding 75 years ago. *Host:* Merv Griffin. *Guests:* Scott Baio, Joan Collins, Angie Dickinson, Clint Eastwood, Linda Evans, John Forsythe, Whoopi Goldberg, Charlton Heston, Jack Klugman, Stepfanie Kramer, Robin Leach, Shelley Long, Dudley Moore, Richard Mulligan, Gregory Peck, Tom Selleck, Frank Sinatra, James Stewart, Mel Torme, Henry Winkler. *Music:* Tom Chase, Steve Rucker. *Producers:* George Schlatter, Jack Haley, Jr. *Writers:* Samuel R. Roth, George Schlatter, Jack Haley, Jr. *Director:* George Schlatter.

## 1786 76 Men and Peggy Lee. Variety, 60 min., CBS, 4/14/60. Music and songs with singer Peggy Lee and 76 male guests. *Host:* Peggy Lee. *Guests:* The Chad Mitchell Trio, The Newport Youth Band, Mel Torme, The Vagabonds, The Yale Glee Club. *Music:* Robert Emmett Dolan. *Producer-Directors:* Abe Burrows, Perry Lafferty. *Writers:* George Foster, Jay Burton.

## 1787 Sex Symbols: Past, Present and Future. Documentary, 60 min., Syndicated, 5/87. The program explores America's fascination with sex symbols. Through interviews and film clips, the sex symbols of the past, present, and future are examined. See also the next title. *Host:* Melissa Sue Anderson. *Guests:* Ana Alicia, Carroll Baker, Cathy Lee Crosby, Ted Danson, Christina Ferrer, Valerie Harper, Jenilee Harrison, Mary Hart, Telma Hopkins, Stacy Keach, Lorenzo Lamas, Bob Mackie, Donna Mills, George Peppard, Cheryl Tiegs, Shannon Tweed, Dennis Weaver. *Music:* John Fuller, Scott Reynolds. *Producers:* Louis Rudolph, David Marmel. *Writer:* Haig Mackey. *Director:* Benjamin Young.

## 1788 Sex Symbols II. Documentary, 60 min., Syndicated, 8/87. A sequel to the above special that again looks at stars with sex appeal (including Marilyn Monroe, Ann-Margret, Tom Cruise, Don Johnson, and Donna Mills). *Host:* Jenilee Harrison. *Music:* John Fuller, Scott Reynolds. *Producers:* Louis Rudolph, David Marmel. *Writer:* Haig Mackey. *Director:* Benjamin Young.

## 1789 Shadows and Light. Variety, 60 min., Showtime, 12/80. A concert by singer Joni Mitchell. *Host:* Joni Mitchell. *Guests:* Jaco Pastorius, The Persuasions. *Producers:* Elliot Rabinowitz, Larry Johnson. *Director:* Joni Mitchell.

## 1790 The Shaman's Last Raid. Drama, 60 min., ABC, 11/19/75. An "ABC Afterschool Special" about an Apache brother and sister (Ebon and Melody) who gain a new perspective on what it means to be an Indian in the modern world when they receive a visit from their great-grandfather, a medicine man who is called the Shaman. It all begins when a motion picture company plans to use their home town as the setting for a western movie. The town becomes a staging ground for a conflict between the romance of the old tradition (as represented by the Shaman) and the realities of the new Apache life (embodied by Melody and Ebon). A raid by the Shaman on the movie company's cattle serves to reinforce in each family member the most important and positive aspects of their differing frames of reference. *Cast:* Ned Romero (Chief Red Eagle), Dehl Berti (the Shaman), Monika Ramirez

(Melody Strong), Oscar Valdez (Ebon Strong), Gina Alvarado (Mrs. Strong), Angus Duncan (Woodley), Clay Tanner (Wrangler). *Music:* Neiman Tillar. *Producer:* John Kubichan. *Writers:* Tom August, Helen August. *Director:* Wes Kenney.

**1791 Shangri-La.** Drama, 90 min., NBC, 10/24/60. A television adaptation of James Hilton's *Lost Horizon*, it is a story of five men, lost in the Himalayas after their plane crashes, who stumble upon Shangri-La, a paradise on earth. Aired on the "Hallmark Hall of Fame." *Cast:* Claude Rains (High Lama), Richard Basehart (Conway), Marisa Pavan (Lo-Tsen), Gene Nelson (Robert), Alice Ghostley (Mrs. Brinklow), Helen Gallagher (Lise), John Abbott (Chang), James Vallatine (Mallinson). *Music:* Harry Warren. *Producer-Director:* George Schaefer. *Writers:* Jerome Lawrence, Robert E. Lee.

**1792 The Shani Wallis Show.** Variety, 60 min., Syndicated, 9/70. An hour of music and songs with singer Shani Wallis. *Host:* Shani Wallis. *Guests:* Buddy Rich, The Righteous Brothers. *Music:* Ralph Carmichael. *Producer:* Jackie Barnett. *Director:* John Robins.

**1793 The Shape of Things.** Variety, 60 min., CBS, 10/19/73. A satirical revue by, with, and about women. *Performers:* Phyllis Diller, Lee Grant, Valerie Harper, Lynn Redgrave, Joan Rivers, Brenda Vaccaro. *Guests:* Wilt Chamberlain, Jack Klugman, Bobby Riggs. *Producers:* George Schlatter, Carolyn Raskin. *Directors:* Carolyn Raskin, Lee Grant.

**1794 Shari Lewis, Ed McMahon: Bearly in the Parade.** Children, 60 min., NBC, 11/25/76. A one-hour network special based on characters from the syndicated (1975) "Shari Show." Shari Lewis is the human assistant manager of the Bearly Broadcasting Company, a television station run by puppets. In the story Mr. Bearly, the president, fantasizes about marching in a parade with Ed McMahon and Shari Lewis. *Host:* Shari Lewis. *Guest:* Ed McMahon. *Music:* Milton DeLugg. *Puppeteers:* Shari Lewis, Ron Martin. *Voices:* Shari Lewis, Ron Martin, Mallory Tarcher. *Producer-Director:* Dick Schneider. *Writers:* Jaie Brashar, Jeremy Tarcher.

**1795 She Drinks a Little.** Drama, 60 min., ABC, 9/23/81. An "ABC Afterschool Special" that dramatizes the impact of an alcoholic mother on her family. The story follows the efforts of the daughter (Cindy) to cope with the situation and convince her mother (Mariam) to seek professional help. The drama stresses the role of Alateen, a national organization that helps teenagers with alcoholic parents. *Cast:* Amanda Wyss (Cindy Scott), Bonnie Bartlett (Mariam Scott), Elliot Jaffe (Brett Scott), Peg Stewart (Esther Sharrigan), Anna Garduno (Sherrie Bergman), Kathryn Greer (Janelle Andrews), Jack Manning (Mr. Sharrigan). *Music:* Glenn Paxton. *Producer:* Martin Tahse. *Writer:* Paul W. Cooper. *Director:* Arthur Allan Seidleman.

**1796 Sheena Easton — Act 1.** Variety, 60 min., NBC, 3/24/83. A stylish variety hour that features the Scottish-born singer in her first network television special. *Host:* Sheena Easton. *Guests:* Johnny Carson, Al Jarreau, Kenny Rogers. *Music:* Peter Matz. *Producers:* Dek Arlen, Jill Arlen, Gary Smith, Dwight Hemion. *Writer:* Buz Kohan. *Director:* Dwight Hemion.

**1797 Sheena Easton — Live at the Palace.** Variety, 60 min., HBO, 4/15/83. A concert by the beautiful Scottish performer; taped live at the Hollywood Palace Theater. *Host:* Sheena Easton. *Musicians:* Jeff Carpenter, Ian Lynn, Jerry Moffat, Gary

**Carol Burnett and Shirley MacLaine from "Shirley MacLaine: If They Could See Me Now"**

Twig, Bob Jenkins. *Backup Vocalists:* Alan Carvel, Jackie Rowe, Peter Zoran. *Producers:* Bob Hart, Valerie Robins, David Hillier. *Director:* David Hillier.

**1798 She's a Good Skate, Charlie Brown.** Cartoon, 30 min., CBS, 2/25/80. The story focuses on Peppermint Patty as she attempts to prepare for a figure skating competition under the eagle eye of her coach — Charlie's beagle dog, Snoopy. *Voices:* Arrin Skelley (Charlie Brown), Patricia Ann Patts (Peppermint Patty), Debbie Miller (Lucy), Scott Beach (Linus), Bill Melendez (Snoopy), Jason Serinus (Woodstock), Casey Carlson (Paula). *Music:* Ed Bogas, Judy Munsen. *Producers:* Lee Mendelson, Bill Melendez. *Writer:* Charles M. Schulz. *Director:* Phil Roman.

**1799 The Shirley Bassey Show.** Variety, 60 min., Syndicated, 9/68. A solo concert performance by singer Shirley Bassey. *Host:* Shirley Bassey. *Music:* Ralph Carmichael. *Producer:* Jackie Barnett. *Director:* Tony Charmoli.

**1800 The Shirley Bassey Special.** Variety, 60 min., Syndicated, 5/69. An hour of music and songs. *Host:* Shirley Bassey. *Guests:* Laurindo Almedia, Noel Harrison. *Music:* Johnnie Spence. *Producer:* Jackie Barnett. *Director:* Tony Charmoli.

**1801 The Shirley Bassey Special.** Variety, 60 min., Syndicated, 7/81. Music and songs with Shirley Bassey and her guests. *Host:* Shirley Bassey. *Guests:* Michel Legrand, Dusty Springfield. *Music:* Arthur Greensalde. *Producer-Director:* Stewart Morris.

**1802 Shirley MacLaine Specials.** A chronological listing of the variety specials hosted by actress Shirley MacLaine. All are 60 minutes except where noted.
**1 Shirley MacLaine: If They Could See Me Now** (CBS, 11/28/74). *Guest:* Carol Burnett. *Music:* Donn Trenner. *Producer:* Robert Wells. *Writers:* Robert Wells, John Bradford, Cy Coleman. *Director:* Robert Scheerer.
**2 The Shirley MacLaine Special: Where Do We Go from Here?** (CBS, 3/12/77). *Music:* Donn Trenner. *Pro-*

*ducer:* George Schlatter. *Writer:* Digby Wolfe. *Director:* Tony Charmoli.

**3 Shirley MacLaine at the Lido** (CBS, 5/20/79). Shirley's concert from the Lido De Paris, a fashionable night spot on the Champs Elysées. (The European version of this special features the topless Bluebell Girls.) *Guests:* Les Bluebell Girls, Tom Jones. *Music:* Billy Byers, Nick Perito.

**4 Shirley MacLaine . . . Every Little Movement** (CBS, 5/22/80). *Guests:* Dean Martin, Kurt Thomas. *Music:* Ian Fraser. *Producers:* Gary Smith, Dwight Hemion. *Writer:* Buz Kohan. *Director:* Dwight Hemion.

**5 Shirley MacLaine: Illusions** (CBS, 6/24/82). *Guest:* Gregory Hines. *Music:* Peter Matz. *Producers:* Don Mischer, Buz Kohan. *Writer:* Buz Kohan. *Director:* Don Mischer.

**6 Shirley MacLaine** (90 min., Showtime, 2/11/85). *Dancers:* Gerri Reddick, Mark Reina, Larry Vickers, Toni Yuskis. *Musicians:* Rick Marvin, John Smith, John Spooner. *Music Director:* Jack French. *Producer-Director:* Don Mischer. *Writers:* Buz Kohan, Larry Grossman.

**1803 Shirley Temple's Storybook: The Legend of Sleepy Hollow.** Drama, 60 min., NBC, 3/5/58. A special presentation of Shirley Temple's regular series ("Shirley Temple's Storybook") to mark her dramatic acting debut on television. An adaptation of the Washington Irving story about the residents of Sleepy Hollow and the efforts of a love-sick schoolteacher (Ichabod Crane) to impress Katrina, the village beauty. *Cast:* Shirley Temple (Katrina Van Tassel), John Ericson (Brom Bones), Jules Munshin (Ichabod Crane), Russell Collins (Alpheus), Fred Essler (Baltus Van Tassel). *Narrator:* Boris Karloff. *Music:* Vic Mizzy. *Producer-Director:* Paul Bogart. *Writer:* Norman Lessing.

**1804 Shoot-In at NBC (A Bob Hope Special).** Comedy, 60 min., NBC, 11/8/67. A comical blend of *High Noon* and high camp wherein Bob Hope attempts to arrange a showdown between cowpunchers and punchliners when cowboys take over television and force comedians off the air. *Host:* Bob Hope. *Guests:* Don Adams, Steve Allen, Jack Carter, Wally Cox, Bill Dana, James Drury, Bobbie Gentry, Jack Kelly, Doug McClure, Cameron Mitchell, Don Rickles, Dale Robertson, Danny Thomas. *Music:* Les Brown. *Producers:* Mort Lachman, Jack Hope.

**1805 The Shooting.** Drama, 60 min., CBS, 6/1/82. Billy Lee Daniels and Jesse and Amos Cotter are three boys who live in Carversville, Missouri, during the Depression. One day the boys decide to go hunting (Jesse has taken his father's old rifle without permission). When the boys spot a turkey in some corn stubble, Billy Lee and Jesse fire. Young Amos races off to retrieve the bird, only to return to tell them that he found the body of a man, apparently killed by their errant shots. The story focuses on some of the responsibilities and consequences of using a gun as the boys come to realize what they have done. Aired as a "CBS Afternoon Playhouse." *Cast:* Lance Kerwin (Billy Lee Daniels), Gavin Muir (Jesse Cotter), Will Wheaton (Amos Cotter), Woodrow Parfrey (Will), John Quade (Toad), Ivy Bethune (Woman), Michael Greene (Simon Kitwell), Lynn Redgrave (Sarah Cotter), Barry Primus (Andrew Cotter). *Music:* John Cacavas. *Producers:* S. Bryan Hickox, Jay Daniel, Michael Ray Rhodes. *Writer:* Josef Anderson. *Director:* Michael Ray Rhodes.

**1806 Show Biz.** Variety, 90 min., NBC, 10/9/55. The program traces the art of music and comedy from the early days of vaudeville to present-day (1955) video. *Host:* Art Linkletter. *Guests:* Rosemary Clooney, Dennis Day, Sid Fields, Jack Fisher, Jay C.

Flippen, Paul Gilbert, Arnold Goodwin, Buster Keaton, Eartha Kitt, Bert Lahr, Mara Lynn, Groucho Marx, Melinda Marx, Evelyn Russell, Herb Vigran, Snag Werris. *Music:* Gordon Jenkins. *Producers:* Ernest D. Glucksman, Roy Montgomery. *Writers:* Ken Englund, Ed Tyler, Snag Werris, Dorothy Sacks, Lou Haber. *Director:* Dick McDonough.

**1807 A Show Business Salute to Milton Berle.** Variety, 60 min., NBC, 12/4/73. A music and comedy salute to Mr. Television (Milton Berle) on the occasion of his sixtieth year in showbusiness. *Host:* Sammy Davis, Jr. *Special Guest:* Milton Berle. *Guests:* Lucille Ball, Jack Benny, Kirk Douglas, Redd Foxx, Jackie Gleason, Bob Hope, Jack Lemmon, Walter Matthau, Jan Murray, Carroll O'Connor, Don Rickles, Henny Youngman. *Music:* Quincy Jones. *Producers:* Bernie Kukoff, Jeff Harris. *Writers:* Don Reo, Allan Katz, Bill Box, Stanley Davis. *Director:* Grey Lockwood.

**1808 Show of the Year.** Variety, 2 hrs. 30 min., NBC, 6/10/50. A star-studded variety spectacular for the benefit of cerebral palsy sufferers. *Host:* Milton Berle. *Guests:* Desi Arnaz, Lucille Ball, Mindy Carson, Jinx Falkenberg, Eddie Fisher, Jerry Lewis, Clem McCarthy, Tex McCrary, Dean Martin, The Martin Brothers, Robert Merrill, Jan Murray, Janis Paige, Jane Pickens, Verna Raymond, Sid Stone, George Tapps, Henny Youngman. *Music:* Allen Roth. *Producers:* Irving Gray, Bill Garden. *Director:* Arthur Knorr.

**1809 The Showoff.** Comedy, 60 min., CBS, 2/2/55. An adaptation of the Broadway play by George Kelly about Aubrey Piper, an egotistical, loud-mouthed show-off and dreamer who attempts to impress others with his big ambitions, while at the same time preserving his self-respect. *Cast:* Jackie Gleason (Aubrey Piper), Thelma Ritter (Mrs. Fisher), Cathy O'Donnell (Amy Fisher), Alice Ghostley (Clara Hyland), Carleton Carpenter (Joe Fisher). *Music:* David Broekman. *Producer:* Martin Manulis. *Writer:* Ronald Alexander. *Director:* Sidney Lumet.

**1810 The Sid Caesar, Imogene Coca, Carl Reiner, Howard Morris Special.** Comedy, 60 min., CBS, 4/5/67. The program reunites Sid Caesar, Imogene Coca, Carl Reiner, and Howard Morris, the former costars of "Your Show of Shows," for an hour of outlandish comedy sketches. *Music:* Charles Sanford. *Producer:* Jack Arnold. *Writers:* Mel Brooks, Sam Denoff, Bill Persky, Carl Reiner, Mel Tolkin. *Director:* Bill Hobin.

**1811 The Sid Caesar Special.** Variety, 60 min., CBS, 10/21/59. An hour of music, song, and comedy. *Host:* Sid Caesar. *Guests:* Gisele MacKenzie, Audrey Meadows, Tony Randall. *Producer:* Leo Morgan. *Writers:* Mel Tolkin, Mel Brooks, Sydney Zelenka. *Director:* Frank Bunetta.

**1812 Siegfried and Roy.** Variety, 60 min., NBC, 2/1/80. An hour of illusions with magicians Siegfried and Roy. *Host:* Eddie Albert. *Guests:* Loni Anderson, Lola Falana, The Lido De Paris Dancers. *Music:* Bill Newkirk. *Producers:* Irving Feld, Kenneth Feld, Art Fisher, Frank Brill. *Director:* Art Fisher.

**1813 Silent Mouse.** Christmas, 60 min., PBS, 12/10/88. The charming tale of how the Christmas song "Silent Night" came to be written through the efforts of a mouse who loved music. *Host-Narrator:* Lynn Redgrave. *Cast:* Gregor Fisher (Franz Gruber), Jack McKenzie (Joe Mohr), Carl Maraucher (Bill McCue), Mary Riggans (Franz's wife), John Moore (King's Choirmaster). *Music:* John Moore. *Producer-*

*Director:* Robin Crichton. *Writer:* Jocelyn Stephenson.

**1814 Sills and Burnett at the Met.** Variety, 60 min., CBS, 11/25/76. Beverly Sills and Carol Burnett in an hour of music and song from the Metropolitan Opera House in New York City. *Hosts:* Carol Burnett, Beverly Sills. *Music:* Peter Matz. *Producer:* Joe Hamilton. *Writers:* Kenny Solms, Gail Parent. *Director:* Dave Powers.

**1815 Simon and Garfunkel.** Variety, 60 min., CBS, 11/30/69. A concert by Paul Simon and Art Garfunkel. *Hosts:* Art Garfunkel, Paul Simon. *Producers:* Paul Simon, Art Garfunkel, Chuck Grodin. *Director:* Chuck Grodin.

**1816 Simon and Garfunkel in Concert.** Variety, 90 min., HBO, 2/4/83. Simon and Garfunkel's reunion concert; taped before 500,000 fans in New York's Central Park in September 1981. *Hosts:* Art Garfunkel, Paul Simon. *Musicians:* David Brown, Peter Carr, John Eckart, Steve Gadd, Anthony Jackson, Bob Mounsey, Jerry Niewood, Grady Tate, Richard Tee, Dave Tofani. *Orchestra:* David Matthews. *Producers:* Lorne Michaels, Joe Signorelli. *Director:* Michael Lindsay-Hogg.

**1817 Sinatra.** Documentary, 60 min., CBS, 11/16/65. The program explores the life of Frank Sinatra through film clips and interviews with friends and family. See also "Frank Sinatra Specials." *Host:* Walter Cronkite. *Guests:* Frank Sinatra, Jr., Nancy Sinatra. *Producer-Director:* Don Hewitt. *Writer:* Andy Rooney.

**Sinatra and Friends** *see* **Frank Sinatra Specials**

**Sinatra: Concert for the Americas** *see* **Frank Sinatra Specials**

**Sinatra: The First 40 Years** *see* **Frank Sinatra Specials**

**Sinatra: The Main Event** *see* **Frank Sinatra Specials**

**Sinatra: The Man and His Music** *see* **Frank Sinatra Specials**

**1818 Sinbad and Friends.** Comedy, 60 min., ABC, 12/28/91. An hour of comedy sketches and monologues with comedian Sinbad. *Host:* Sinbad. *Guests:* Kim Coles, Bill Cosby (as the voice of God), Laura Hayes, Heavy D and the Boyz. *Music:* Everette Harp. *Producers:* Sinbad, Mark Adkins. *Director:* Chuck Vinson.

**Sing America Beautiful** *see* **Tennessee Ernie Ford Specials**

**Singer Presents Elvis** *see* **Elvis**

**1819 Singer Presents Hawaii Ho.** Variety, 60 min., NBC, 5/27/68. Music and light comedy from Hawaii with singer Don Ho in his first television special. Sponsored by Singer Sewing Machines. *Host:* Don Ho. *Producers:* Ed Brown, Sid Smith. *Director:* Sid Smith.

**1820 The Singers.** Variety, 60 min., ABC, 5/11/68. A profile of singers Aretha Franklin and Gloria Loring who perform songs associated with their careers. *Hosts:* Aretha Franklin, Gloria Loring. *Producer-Writer:* Steve Fleischman.

**1821 The Singing Cowboys Ride Again.** Tribute, 60 min., Syndicated, 11/82. A salute to the singing cowboys, the heroes of the western films of the 1930s, 1940s, and 1950s (for example, Gene Autry, Roy Rogers and Dale Evans). *Host:* John Ritter. *Guests:* Gene Autry, Roy Rogers, Jimmy Wakely. *Music:* Carl Cotner. *Theme*

*Vocalist,* "The Singing Cowboys": Jerry Scoggins. *Producer:* Arnold Shapiro. *Writers:* Arnold Shapiro, Carol L. Fleisher, Robert Niemack. *Director:* Arnold Shapiro.

**1822 Sisters in the Name of Love.** Variety, 60 min., HBO, 7/12/86. A pop music concert by Gladys Knight, Patti LaBelle, and Dionne Warwick. Taped at the Aquarius Theater in Hollywood. *Hosts:* Gladys Knight, Patti LaBelle, Dionne Warwick. *Music:* H. B. Barnum. *Producers:* Gladys Knight, Bob Henry, Bubba Knight. *Writers:* Marty Farrell, Paul Mooney. *Director:* Bob Henry.

**1823 6 RMS RIV VU.** Comedy, 90 min., CBS, 3/17/74. An adaptation of the Broadway play about Anne Miller and Paul Freeman, two married strangers who meet in an empty apartment and have an affair. (The title refers to a six-room Manhattan apartment with a Riverside Drive view.) *Cast:* Carol Burnett (Anne Miller), Alan Alda (Paul Freeman), Millie Slavin (Janet Friedman), Lawrence Pressman (Richard Miller), Maureen Silliman (Pregnant woman), Francine Beers (Woman in 4A), Jose Ocasio (Eddie). *Music:* Peter Matz. *Producers:* Joe Hamilton, Robert Wright. *Writer:* Bob Randall. *Directors:* Clark Jones, Alan Alda.

**1824 Sixty Years of Seduction.** Documentary, 2 hrs., ABC, 5/4/81. A montage of film clips that recall Hollywood's greatest stars in their most glamorous moments—from the 1920s to the 1970s; 60 years of romance on the screen. *Hosts:* Angie Dickinson, James Garner, Victoria Principal, Robert Urich. *Narrator:* Paul Frees. *Producers:* Scott Garen, John Brice. *Writer:* Buz Kohan. *Director:* Jeff Margolis.

**1825 The Skating Rink.** Drama, 60 min., ABC, 2/5/75. A realis-

tic story about a boy (Tuck Faraday) who struggles to rise above his handicap of stuttering by developing his skills as an accomplished skater. Aired as an "ABC Afterschool Special." *Cast:* Stewart Petersen (Tuck Faraday), Rance Howard (Myron Faraday), Devon Ericson (Lilly Degley), Betty Beaird (Ida Faraday), Jerry Dexter (Pete Degley), Cynthia Eilbacher (Elva Grimes), Tara Talboy (Karen Faraday), Sparky Marcus (Tuck as a young boy). *Music:* Glenn Paxton. *Producer:* Martin Tahse. *Writer:* Bob Rodgers. *Director:* Larry Elikann.

**1826 The Skin of Our Teeth.** Comedy, 2 hrs., NBC, 9/11/55. A television adaptation of the play by Thornton Wilder about the Antrobuses, a family fraught with problems, but who always manage to come through the worst by the skin of their teeth. *Cast:* Helen Hayes (Mrs. Antrobus), Mary Martin (Sabrina Antrobus), George Abbott (Mr. Antrobus), Hellen Halliday (Gladys), Florence Reed (Fortune teller), Frank Silvera (Mr. Tremayne). *Producer:* Fred Coe. *Writer:* Ellen M. Violett. *Directors:* Alan Schneider, Vincent J. Donehue.

**1827 Skinflint.** Musical Comedy, 2 hrs., NBC, 12/18/79. A country and western version of Dickens's *A Christmas Carol.* The story, set in a small Tennessee town, follows one day in the life of Cyrus Flint, a stingy banker who comes to realize his faults one Christmas Eve. *Cast:* Hoyt Axton (Cyrus Flint), Mel Tillis (Dennis Pritchett), Lynn Anderson (Laura Pritchett), Barbara Mandrell (Emmy Flint), Larry Gatlin (Roger Flint), Tom T. Hall (Jacob's Ghost), Martha Raye (Ghost of Christmas Past), Daniel Davis (Ghost of Christmas Present), Dottie West (Annabelle Williams), Julie Gregg (Joan), David Bond (Ghost of Christmas Future), Stephen Lutz (T. J. Pritchett), Carol Swabrick (Mrs. Abby), Byron Webster (Mr.

Abby). *Music/Lyrics:* Mel Mandel, Norman Sachs, Aaron Schroeder. *Producers:* Joseph Cates, Gilbert Cates. *Writer:* Mel Mandel. *Director:* Marc Daniels.

**1828 Sleeping Beauty.** Ballet, 90 min., NBC, 12/12/55. The narrated story of a beautiful princess who is put under a sleeping spell by a wicked fairy; and of a prince who attempts to awaken her by bestowing a kiss. Performed by the Sadler's Wells Ballet company of England (now called the Royal Ballet). *Cast:* David Wayne (Harlequin, the narrator), Margot Fonteyn (Princess Aurora), Michael Somes (Prince Florimund), Frederick Ashton (Wicked Fairy), Beryl Grey (Lilac Fairy), Rowena Jackson (Fairy of the Golden Vine), Jada Rowland, Dennis Kohler, Edmund Gaynes (Children). *Music:* Robert Irving. *Producer:* Sol Hurok. *Narrative Writer:* John Van Druten. *Director:* Clark Jones.

**1829 Sleeping Beauty.** Ice Ballet, 60 min., PBS, 12/6/87. An ice ballet based on Charles Perrault's classic fairy tale about a handsome prince who awakens Sleeping Beauty with a kiss. Choreographed to Tchaikovsky's score. *Cast:* Rosalynn Sumners (Sleeping Beauty), Robin Cousins (Prince), Patricia Dodd (Good Fairy), Shaun McGill (Evil Fairy), Nathan Birch (King Florestan), Catherine Foulkers (Queen Guinevere), Stephen Pickavance (Archbishop), Karen Barber (Fairy), Amber Baker (Baby). *Narrator:* Merlin Olsen. *Music Director of the London Symphony Orchestra:* Bramwell Tovey. *Choreographer:* Lars Lubovitch, Patricia Dodd.

**1830 Sleepwalker.** Thriller, 90 min., ABC, 10/7/75. The story follows a young woman's efforts to end a recurring nightmare in which she sees a young man stab an older man. *Cast:* Darleen Carr (Katey Summers), Ian

Redford (Barnstable), Robert Beatty (Katey's father), Elaine Donnelly (Esme), Michael Kitchen (Ian), Basil Lord (Parsons). *Music:* Laurie Johnson. *Producer:* Cecil Clarke. *Writer:* Brian Clemens. *Director:* Alan Gibson.

**1831 The Slowest Gun in the West.** Comedy, 60 min., CBS, 7/29/63. When Fletcher Bissell III, a spineless coward known as the Silver Dollar Kid, arrives in the lawless town of Primrose, Arizona, the citizens elect him as their sheriff when they find that no self-respecting bad guy will shoot him (fearing to lose his reputation). The story relates the bad guys' efforts to rid their lives of Bissell and get down to their usual nasty business by hiring Chicken Farnsworth, a gunman as cowardly as the sheriff, to gun Bissel down. *Cast:* Phil Silvers (Fletcher Bissell III), Jack Benny (Chicken Farnsworth), Bruce Cabot (Nick Nolan), Ted DeCorsia (Blark Bart), Jack Elam (Ike Dalton), Jean Willes (Kathy McQueen), Parley Baer (Collingswood), Tom Fadden (Jed Slocum), Gina Gillespie (Girl), Jeanne Bates (Wife), Paul Lukas (Jack Dalton), Jack Albertson (Carl Dexter), Marion Ross (Elsie May), Kathie Brown (Lulu Belle), Lee Van Cleef (Sam Bass), Robert J. Wilke (Butcher Blake). *Producers:* William Frye, Nat Hiken. *Writer:* Nat Hiken. *Director:* Herschel Daugherty.

**1832 The Small Miracle.** Drama, 90 min., NBC, 4/11/73. A "Hallmark Hall of Fame" presentation about a spirited boy who believes that his sick pet donkey will be cured if he can take it to the crypt of St. Francis of Assisi. *Cast:* Mario Della Cava (Pepino), Raf Vallone (Father Superior), Vittorio De Sica (Father Domico), Guidarino Guidi (Salesman), Jan Larrson, Paolo Marco (Guards). *Producer:* Duane C. Bogie. *Writers:* John Patrick, Arthur Dales. *Director:* Jeannot Szwarc.

**Leslie Uggams, Mariette Hartley, and Rich Hall hosts of "Small World."**

**1833 Small World.** Variety, 60 min., NBC, 3/7/82. The program spotlights the talents, abilities, and opinions of children. *Hosts:* Rich Hall, Mariette Hartley, Leslie Uggams. *Guests:* Dr. Lee Salk, Leo Surgess, Vic Tayback. *Announcer:* Charlie O'Donnell. *Music:* Roy Prendergast. *Pro-* *ducers:* David L. Wolper, Bob Shanks. *Writer:* Marc London. *Director:* Don Mischer.

**1834 The Smokey Robinson Show.** Variety, 60 min., ABC, 12/18/ 70. Music and songs with singer Smokey Robinson. *Host:* Smokey

Robinson. *Guests:*
Diana Ross and the
Supremes, Fran Jeff-
ries, The Miracles,
The   Temptations,
Stevie      Wonder.
*Music:* Ralph Car-
michael. *Producer:*
Jackie Barnett. *Direc-
tor:* Kip Walton.

**1835 The
Smothers
Brothers Comedy
Hour: The 20th
Reunion.** Variety,
60 min., CBS, 2/3/88.
A nostalgic program
that reunites the cast
of "The Smothers
Brothers   Comedy
Hour" (CBS, 1967–69)
for an hour of clips
that recall the best
moments from the
series. *Hosts:* Dick
Smothers,      Tom
Smothers. *Cast Mem-
bers:* Glen Campbell,
Bob Einstein, Leigh
French, John Hart-
ford, Pat Paulsen, The Ron Poindexter
Dancers, Jennifer Warnes. *Announcer:*
Roger Carroll. *Music:* Larry Cansler.
*Producers:* Howard G. Malley, Ken
Kragen. *Writers:* Mason Williams,
Robert Arnott. *Director:* David Gross-
man.

Tom and Dick Smothers hosts of "The Smothers Brothers Comedy Hour: The 20th Reunion."

(Frieda), Bill Melendez (Snoopy).
*Music/Lyrics:* Richard M. Sherman,
Robert Sherman. *Music Conductor:*
Don Ralke. *Producers:* Lee Mendel-
son, Bill Melendez. *Writer:* Charles M.
Schulz. *Director:* Bill Melendez.

**1837 Snoopy—The Musical.**
Cartoon, 60 min., CBS, 1/29/88. An
animated version of the play in which
the Peanuts gang share their secrets,
hopes, and dreams in a program of
song and dance. *Voices:* Cameron
Clark (Snoopy), Sean Colling (Charlie
Brown), Tiffany Billings (Lucy), Kristi
Baker (Patty), Jeremy Miller (Linus),
Ami Foster (Sally). *Music/Lyrics:* Larry
Grossman, Hal Hackaday. *Music Director:* Desiree Goyette. *Music Con-
ductors:* Lenny LeCroix, Ed Bogas.

**1836 Snoopy, Come Home.**
Cartoon, 90 min., CBS, 11/5/76. An ex-
panded Charlie Brown Special (from
the usual 30 minutes) in which Snoopy,
Charlie's pampered beagle, leaves home
to find his original owner. *Voices:*
Chad Webber (Charlie Brown), Robin
Kohn (Lucy), Stephen Shea (Linus),
David Carey (Schroeder), Christopher
Defaria (Peppermint Patty), Johanna
Baer (Lila), Hilary Momberger (Sally),
Linda Ercoli (Clara), Linda Mendelson

*Producers:* Lee Mendelson, Bill Melendez. *Writer:* Charles M. Schulz. *Director:* Sam Jaimes.

## 1838 Snoopy's Getting Married, Charlie Brown. Cartoon, 30 min., CBS, 3/20/85.

Snoopy's adventures are told when he is struck by Cupid's arrow and falls in love with a pretty poodle named Jan-Viev. The program introduces Spike, Snoopy's brother. *Voices:* Brett Johnson (Charlie Brown), Jeremy Schoenberg (Linus), Danny Colby (Schroeder), Gini Holtzman (Peppermint Patty), Stacy Ferguson (Sally), Keri Houlihan (Marcie), Heather Stoneman (Lucy), Carl Steven (Pigpen/Franklin), Bill Melendez (Snoopy), Dawn S. Leary (Sally, singing). *Music:* Judy Munsen. *Producers:* Lee Mendelson, Bill Melendez. *Writer:* Charles M. Schulz. *Director:* Bill Melendez.

## 1839 Snoopy's Musical on Ice. Variety, 60 min., CBS, 5/24/78.

An ice skating revue featuring the Peanuts characters created by Charles M. Schulz. *Hosts:* Peggy Fleming, Charles M. Schulz, Judy Sladky (as Snoopy). *Skaters:* Pat Baker, Skip Baster, Lisa Carey, Chris Harrison, Dan Henry, Lisa Illsley, Mary Ellen Kinsey, Karen Kresge, Suzanna Leduc, Julie Lockhart, Robert Lockhart, Vicki Lockhart, Amy Schulz, Robert Steiner, David Thomas, Atoy Wilson. *Music:* Eg Bogas, Judy Munsen. *Producers:* Charles M. Schulz, Lee Mendelson, Warren Lockhart. *Writer:* Charles M. Schulz. *Director:* Walter C. Miller.

## 1840 Snoopy's Reunion. Cartoon, 30 min., CBS, 5/1/91.

A program about Snoopy, the pampered beagle, recalling his birth, his early "childhood," and how he and Charlie Brown met. *Voices:* Philip Shafran (Charlie Brown), Josh Weiner (Linus), Megan Parlen (Lila), Bill Melendez (Snoopy/Woodstock), Laurel Page (Lila's mother). *Producers:* Lee Mendelson,

Bill Melendez. *Writer:* Charles M. Schulz. *Director:* Sam Jaimes.

## 1841 The Snow Goose. Drama, 60 min., NBC, 11/15/71.

The story, set on the marshes of England's Essex coast, tells of a withdrawn, deformed artist (Philip), an orphaned teenage girl (Frith), and an injured snow goose that brings them together. Based on the novel by Paul Gallico and broadcast on the "Hallmark Hall of Fame." *Cast:* Richard Harris (Philip Rhayader), Jenny Agutter (Frith), Ludmilla Nova (Jane), Freda Bamford (Postmistress), Noel Johnson (Captain), William Marlowe (Soldier). *Producer:* Frank O'Connor. *Writer:* Paul Gallico. *Director:* Patrick Garland.

## 1842 Snowman. Cartoon, 30 min., HBO, 12/22/88.

Shortly after he builds a snowman, a young boy is amazed to see his creation come to life. Later that night, the snowman and the boy share a series of adventures, the most thrilling of which is the boy meeting Santa Claus. Voices and sound effects are not used. Music is incorporated to convey all emotions. *Music:* Howard Blake. *Producers:* Iain Harvey, John Coates. *Storyboard:* Dianne Jackson, Hilary Auduc, Joanna Fryer. *Director:* Dianne Jackson.

## 1843 So Help Me, Aphrodite. Musical, 60 min., NBC, 5/31/60.

An original musical, written especially for television, about Sally, a waitress who refuses to marry, hoping instead to make her dreams of becoming famous a reality. *Cast:* Nanette Fabray (Sally), Tony Randall (Ernest), Jean-Pierre Aumont (Louis), Stubby Kaye (Joe), Robert Strauss (Frank), Peter Leeds (Charlie). *Music:* Jack Regas. *Lyrics:* Danny Arnold. *Music Director:* Axel Stordahl. *Producer:* Hubbell Robinson.

## 1844 Sojourner. Drama, 60 min., CBS, 3/30/75.

An historical drama based on the life of Sojourner Truth, a

freed slave who became an active abolitionist when President Lincoln signed the Thirteenth Amendment to the Constitution. *Cast:* Vinnette Carroll (Sojourner Truth), Frances Sternhagen (Harriet Beecher Stowe), Anthony Chisholm (Ned), Robert Dryden (Esquire Chip), Minnie Gentry (Sophia), Lawrence Jacobs (Peter), Damien Leake (Jamie), Fred Stuthman (Abraham Lincoln), Thurman Scott (Frederick Douglass). *Music:* Lee Holdridge. *Producers:* Joel Heller, Lois Bianchi. *Writer:* Bill Gunn. *Director:* Peter Levin.

**1845 Soldier Boys.** Drama, 60 min., CBS, 10/20/87. A "CBS Schoolbreak Special" about a small town New Jersey police chief's investigation into a group of high school boys whose fascination with war games has gone from fantasy to reality (when a classmate is found stabbed). *Cast:* James Earl Jones (Detective Robb), William McNamara (Jay Medford), Charlie Walsh (Tom Strickland), Frank Whaley (Scott McNichol), James G. McDonald (Vance Tabor), Jordana Levine (Michelle), J. Allen Suddeth (Detective Sealy). *Music:* Peter Harris. *Theme:* Bruce Hornsby. *Producers:* Frank Doelger, Roberta Rowe. *Writer:* Paul Cooper. *Director:* Daniel Taplitz.

**1846 Soldier in Love.** Drama, 90 min., NBC, 4/26/67. A biographical drama based on the lives of John and Sarah Churchill. Aired on the "Hallmark Hall of Fame." *Cast:* Claire Bloom (Queen Anne), Jean Simmons (Sarah Churchill), Keith Michell (John Churchill), Basil Rathbone (Duke of York), Roy Poole (Cadogan). *Music:* Bernard Green. *Producer-Director:* George Schaefer. *Writer:* Jerome Ross.

**1847 Soldiers in Greasepaint.** Variety, 60 min., NBC, 4/26/60. A music and comedy tribute to the USO (United Service Organizations). *Host:* Bob Crosby. *Guests:* Don Adams, Jane Adams, The Modernaires. *Music:* Tutti Camarata. *Producer:* Hubbell Robinson.

**1848 Someday You'll Find Her, Charlie Brown.** Cartoon, 30 min., CBS, 10/30/81. Charlie Brown's endless search to find his latest heartthrob: an unknown girl he saw cheering (in a crowd of 80,000 people) during the final moments of a televised football game. *Voices:* Nicole Eggert, Jennifer Gaffin, Bill Melendez, Ed Reilly, Melissa Strawmeyer, Grant Wehr. *Music:* Ed Bogas, Judy Munsen. *Producers:* Lee Mendelson, Bill Melendez. *Writer:* Charles M. Schulz. *Director:* Phil Roman.

**1849 Someone at the Top of the Stairs.** Thriller, 90 min., ABC, 9/21/73. The story of Chrissie Morton and Jill Pemberton, two beautiful American girls whose lives are threatened by the inhabitants of an eerie Victorian mansion. *Cast:* Donna Mills (Chrissie Morton), Judy Carne (Jill Pemberton), Gary Masters (Francis Wallis), Aletha Charlton (Mrs. Oxney), Scott Forbes (Mr. Patrick), Alan Roberts (Jonathan Patrick), Laura Collins (Sally Thurston), Brian McGrath (Elgar). *Music:* Laurie Johnson. *Producer:* Cecil Clarke. *Writer:* Brian Clemens. *Director:* John Sichel.

**1850 Sometimes I Don't Love My Mother.** Drama, 60 min., ABC, 10/13/82. The story of a teenage girl (Dallas Davis) who struggles to cope with her mother's (Ellen) sudden and complete dependence on her following the death of her father. An "ABC Afterschool Special." *Cast:* Melinda Culea (Dallas Davis), Pat Elliot (Ellen Davis), Ruth Warwick (Eva), Vicky Dawson (Jen), Claudette Sutherland (Vi Waters), Ron Parady (Dr. Saunders), Barton Heyman (Bill Waters). *Music:* Elliot Lawrence. *Producers:* Ken Greengrass, Marilyn Olin, Phil Lawrence.

*Writers:* Daryl Warner, Carolyn Miller. *Director:* Alex Grashoff.

## 1851 Song and Dance. Variety,

15 min., NBC, 9/4/46. An unusual special (only 15 minutes long) of music, songs, and dances. *Host:* Diane Courtney. *Guests:* The Corsairs, Ronnie and Ray. *Producer-Director:* Edward Sobol.

## 1852 Song of Myself. Drama,

60 min., CBS, 3/9/76. An historical drama based on the life of America's great epic poet, Walt Whitman. *Cast:* Rip Torn (Walt Whitman), David Hooks (Walt's father), Betty Henritze (Walt's mother), Thomas Hulce (Edward Whitman), Ron Faber (George Whitman), Brenda Currin (Hannah Whitman), James Rebhorn (Ira Smith), Brad Davis (Peter Doyle), James Cahill (Henry Clapp), Suzanne Grossman (Adah Isaacs Mencken), William Newman (President Lincoln), Leo Chimino (Thomas Eakins). *Music:* Lee Holdridge. *Producers:* Joel Heller, Robert Markowitz. *Writer:* Jan Hartman. *Director:* Robert Markowitz.

## 1853 The Songwriter's Hall of Fame. Variety, 2 hrs., CBS, 6/22/

89. Music performers salute members of the Songwriter's Hall of Fame. *Hosts:* Anita Baker, Dick Clark. *Guests:* Gregory Abbott, Paula Abdul, Lee Adams, Michael Bolton, Leslie Bricusse, Linda Elder, Crystal Gayle, Lee Greenwood, Whitney Houston, Freddie Jackson, Quincy Jones, Patti LaBelle, Marilyn McCoo, Melissa Manchester, Liza Minnelli, Gary Morris, Anthony Newley, Jeffrey Osborne, K. T. Oslin, Buster Poindexter, Lou Rawls, Ann Reinking, Tommy Tune, Dwight Yoakam. *Music Director:* Elliot Lawrence. *Orchestrations:* Torrie Zito, Don Sebesky, Lanny Meyers, James Lawrence, Jack Cortner. *Producers:* Al Masini, Sam Riddle. *Writer:* Bob Arnott. *Director:* Louis J. Horvitz.

## 1854 Sonja Henie's Holiday on Ice. Variety, 90 min., NBC, 12/22/

56. A color special that features music, songs, comedy, and the ice skating skills of Sonja Henie. *Host:* Art Linkletter. *Performers:* Sonja Henie, Alan Jenkins, Al Kelly, Ernie Kovacs, Julius LaRosa, Jaye P. Morgan. *Music:* Harry Sosnik. *Producer:* Perry Cross.

## 1855 Sophia! Documentary, 60

min., ABC, 10/23/68. Actress Sophia Loren recalls her life and road to stardom in Italy. *Host:* Sophia Loren. *Guests:* Vittorio DeSica, Stanley Kramer, Merwyn LeRoy, Omar Sharif. *Narrator:* Joseph Campanella. *Music:* Jack Tillar. *Producers:* Robert Abel, Mel Stuart. *Writers:* Mel Stuart, Robert Abel, David Settzer. *Director:* Mel Stuart.

## 1856 Sophia Loren in Rome.

Variety, 60 min., ABC, 11/12/64. A program of music and recollections as actress Sophia Loren tours her adopted city of Rome (born a Neapolitan, but Roman by choice). *Host:* Sophia Loren. *Guest:* Marcello Mastroianni. *Music:* John Barry. *Producers:* Norman Baer, Philip D'Antoni. *Writers:* Basilo Franchina, Sheldon Reynolds. *Director:* Sheldon Reynolds.

## 1857 Sorry, Wrong Number.

Drama, 30 min., CBS, 1/30/46. The story of an invalid woman who overhears a murder plot on the telephone, then desperately seeks help — unaware that she is the intended victim. *Cast:* Mildred Natwick (The Woman), Wayne Gordon, Esther Sommers, Ruth Gilbert, Gilbert Mack, Dulcie Cooper, Maxine Stuart, Dayton Lummis, Ruth Ford. *Producers:* John Houseman, Lucille Fletcher. *Writer:* Lucille Fletcher. *Directors:* John Houseman, Nick Ray, Frances Buss, Lucille Hudleburg.

## 1858 Sorry, Wrong Number.

Drama, 30 min., CBS, 1/8/50. An early

experimental color special by CBS in an attempt to market its ill-fated color-wheel process. A one-character story in which an invalid woman overhears a murder plot on the telephone then tries to get help, unaware that she is the intended victim. *Cast:* Meg Mundy (The Woman). *Producer-Director:* Fred Rickey.

## 1859 The Sound and the Scene. Variety, 60 min., Syndicated, 10/69. An hour of music and songs. *Host:* Bobbie Gentry. *Guests:* Ferlin Husky, Brenda Lee, Don Meredith, Charlie Pride, Joe Tex. *Producers:* Robert Klein, Michael Gargiulo. *Writer:* Ted Bergan. *Director:* Michael Gargiulo.

## 1860 The Sound of the 60s. Variety, 60 min., NBC, 10/9/61. The sights and sounds that are closely associated with the way Americans live. *Host:* John Daly. *Guests:* Art Carney, Vic Damone, Gogi Grant, Pat Harrington, Jr., Andre Previn, Tony Randall. *Music:* Harry Sosnik. *Producer-Writer:* Dory Schary. *Director:* William A. Graham.

## 1861 The Sounds of Christmas Eve. Variety, 30 min., NBC, 12/24/73. A program of Christmas music, songs, and readings. *Host:* Doc Severinsen. *Guests:* Victor Buono, Henry Mancini, the St. Charles Borromeo Church Choir. *Musical Arrangements:* Tommy Newsom. *Producer-Director:* Dick Schneider. *Writer:* Shelly Cohen.

## 1862 The Sounds of Home. Variety, 60 min., ABC, 7/6/60. A musical concert, set against the background of the Civil War, that details the love of a Southern belle for her beau, who has gone off to war. *Cast:* Dorothy Collins (Mary Lee Harrison), James Hurst (William Devereaux), Bruce McKay (Scott Harrison), Shannon Bolin (Eulalia Harrison), Carol Bruce (Vi-

dalia), Patty Lee (Mary Lee as a girl). *Music Director:* Glenn Osser.

## 1863 The Sounds of Summer. Variety, 90 min., ABC, 5/30/93. Previews of the album releases, movies, and concert tours scheduled for the summer of 1993 (aired at 1:30 A.M.). *Hosts:* Neneh Cherry, Billy Dean, Mike Love. *Guests:* The Beach Boys, David Bowie, Vince Gill, The Grateful Dead, Van Halen, Whitney Houston, Billy Idol, Janet Jackson, Def Leppard, Arnold Schwarzenegger, Travis Tritt, Tina Turner, Trisha Yearwood, Dwight Yoakam. *Producer:* David Saltz.

## 1864 Soup and Me. Comedy, 30 min., ABC, 2/4/78. Soup and Rob are a modern-day Tom Sawyer and Huck Finn, two boys with a zest for adventure and a genius for trouble. The story relates one day in their lives — a day wherein they get caught skinny-dipping in a chilly pond, dressing like girls to avoid a bully, and destroying a Halloween party with an out-of-control doll carriage that is carrying a gigantic pumpkin. See also the following title. Aired on the "ABC Weekend Special." *Cast:* Christian Berrigan (Soup), Shane Sinutko (Rob), Mary Margaret Patts (Janice), Frank Cady (Mr. Sutter), Kathleen Freeman (Mrs. Stetson), Owen Bush (Delivery man). *Music:* Tommy Leonetti. *Producer:* Robert Chenault. *Writer:* Mark Fink. *Director:* Dennis Donnelly.

## 1865 Soup for President. Comedy, 30 min., ABC, 11/18/78. A sequel to the prior title, which again focuses on the antics of two mischievous boys named Soup and Rob. The story relates the campaign for school president that Soup and Rob wage against Janice Riker, Soup's opponent, the toughest kid in school. Aired as an "ABC Weekend Special." *Cast:* Christian Berrigan (Soup), Shane Sinutko (Rob), Mary Margaret Patts (Janice Riker), Annrae Walterhouse

(Norma Jean Bissell), Florida Friebus (Miss Kelly), Frank Cady (Mr. Sutter). *Music:* Tommy Leonetti. *Producer:* Robert Chenault. *Writer:* Mark Fink. *Director:* Larry Elikann.

### 1866 The Soupy Sales Show.
Comedy, 60 min., CBS, 8/30/70. Outrageous comedy sketches geared to Soupy's burlesque-style humor. *Host:* Soupy Sales. *Guests:* Tommy Boyce, Bobby Hart, Paula Kelly, Art Metrano, Dave Shelley, Yvonne Wilder, Carol Worthington. *Music:* Don Ellis. *Producers:* Robert H. Precht, Perry Cross. *Writers:* Herbert Baker, Ed Hider, Jack Hanrahan, Phil Hahn. *Director:* John Moffitt.

### 1867 A Special Anne Murray Christmas.
Variety, 60 min., CBS, 12/9/81. A program of Christmas music and songs with singer Anne Murray. *Host:* Anne Murray. *Guests:* Kris Kristofferson, The Men of the Deep. *Music:* Rick Wilkins. *Producers:* Gary Smith, Dwight Hemion. *Writer:* Alan Thicke. *Director:* Dwight Hemion.

### A Special Bill Cosby Special
*see* Bill Cosby Specials

### A Special Bob Hope Special
*see* Bob Hope Specials

### 1868 A Special Carol Burnett.
Variety, 2 hrs., CBS, 3/29/78. A special airing for the last episode of "The Carol Burnett Show"; two hours of highlights from the series (CBS, 1967–78). *Host:* Carol Burnett. *Regulars:* Tim Conway, The Ernest Flatt Dancers, Vicki Lawrence. *Music:* Peter Matz. *Producers:* Joe Hamilton, Ed Simmons. *Director:* Dave Powers.

### 1869 A Special Eddie Rabbitt.
Variety, 60 min., CBS, 3/24/83. An hour of music and songs with singer Eddie Rabbitt. *Host:* Eddie Rabbitt. *Guests:* Anne Murray, Donna Summer,

Lesley Ann Warren. *Music:* Vernon Ray Bunch. *Producers:* Syd Vinnedge, Tony Scotti. *Writers:* Rod Warren, Steve Binder. *Director:* Steve Binder.

### 1870 The Special Gentry One.
Variety, 60 min., Syndicated, 11/70. Music and songs with singer Bobbie Gentry. *Host:* Bobbie Gentry. *Guests:* The Great Speckled Bird, John Hartford, Richie Havens, Biff Rose, Ian Tyson, Sylvia Tyson. *Producers:* Tony Charmoli, Bernard Rothman. *Writer:* Bernard Rothman. *Director:* Tony Charmoli.

### 1871 A Special Gift.
Drama, 60 min., ABC, 10/24/79. Peter Harris is a 14-year-old boy with a special gift, the ability to dance ballet. The story relates his efforts to pursue his talent, despite his father's disapproval. Aired as an "ABC Afterschool Special." *Cast:* Stephen Austin (Peter Harris), Bill Sorrells (Carl Harris), Alice Hirson (Grace Harris), Kene Holliday (Coach), Al Eisenmann (George). *Music:* Glenn Paxton. *Producer:* Martin Tahse. *Director:* Arthur Seidelman.

### 1872 A Special Kenny Rogers.
Variety, 60 min., CBS, 12/15/81. Music and songs as Kenny Rogers returns to his home town of Crockett, Texas. *Host:* Kenny Rogers. *Guests:* Ray Charles, The Oak Ridge Boys, Dottie West. *Music:* Bill Justis. *Producers:* Ken Kragen, Stan Harris, Rocco Urbisci. *Writers:* Rick Kellard, Bob Comfort, Cort Casady, Rocco Urbisci. *Director:* Stan Harris.

### 1873 A Special London Bridge Special.
Musical, 60 min., NBC, 5/7/72. A musical fantasy that follows the meeting and courtship of a young couple. Taped in London and in Lake Havasu City, Arizona, the site of the transplanted London Bridge. *Cast:* Tom Jones (Boy), Jennifer O'Neill (Girl). *Guests:* Karen Carpenter, Richard Carpenter, Kirk Douglas, Hermione

Gingold, Elliott Gould, Rudolf Nureyev. *Cameos:* Chief Dan George, Lorne Greene, Charlton Heston, Engelbert Humperdinck, George Kirby, Michael Landon, Jonathan Winters. *Music Directors:* Johnnie Spence, Marvin Hamlisch. *Producers:* Burt Rosen, David Winters. *Writers:* Marty Farrell, Marc Ray, Ronnie Cass, David Ross. *Director:* David Winters.

**A Special Olivia Newton-John** *see* **Olivia Newton-John Specials**

**1874 Spell of Evil.** Thriller, 90 min., ABC, 10/11/73. The story of a medieval witch who returns to present-day England in the form of Clara Pantan to avenge the wrongs done to her in the past. *Cast:* Diane Cilento (Clara Pantan), Edward DeSouza (Tony Mansell), Jeremy Longhurst (George Matthews), Jennifer Daniel (Liz), Linda Cunningham (Suzy), David Belcher (Dr. Peterson), Peg Lye (Caretaker), Patricia Kneale (Mrs. Marshall). *Music:* Laurie Johnson. *Producer:* Cecil Clarke. *Writer:* Terence Feely. *Director:* John Sichel.

**1875 Spellbound.** Drama, 60 min., NBC, 2/11/62. A "Theater '62" presentation about a psychiatrist (Constance Peterson) as she tries to help a young amnesiac (J.B.) prove that he is not guilty of murder. *Cast:* Maureen O'Hara (Constance Peterson), Hugh O'Brian (J.B.), Oscar Homolka (Dr. Burlov), Paul McGrath (Dr. Murchism), Tim O'Connor (Lieutenant Cooley), Dan Morgan (Sergeant Gillespie), Alfred Leberfeld (Sheriff Collins). *Producer:* Fred Coe. *Writer:* Sumner Locke Elliott. *Director:* Paul Bogart.

**1876 The Spencer Tracy Legacy: A Tribute by Katharine Hepburn.** Documentary, 90 min., PBS, 3/10/86. The program recalls the life and career of Spencer Tracy as seen through clips from his films and the eyes of his coworkers and friends, especially Katharine Hepburn, who was closely associated with Tracy. *Host:* Katharine Hepburn. *Guests:* Joan Bennett, Garson Kanin, Stanley Kramer, Angela Lansbury, Joseph L. Mankiewicz, Lee Marvin, Sidney Poitier, Burt Reynolds, Mickey Rooney, Frank Sinatra, John Sturges, Elizabeth Taylor, Susie Tracy, Robert Wagner, Richard Widmark, Joanne Woodward. *Music:* John Adams. *Producers:* George Page, David Heeley, Joan Kramer. *Writer:* John L. Miller. *Director:* David Heeley.

**1877 The Spiral Staircase.** Mystery, 60 min., NBC, 10/4/61. The story focuses on Helen Warren, a beautiful mute girl, who becomes the target of a mysterious killer who preys on young, handicapped women. Based on the screenplay by Mel Dinelli; broadcast on "Theater '62." *Cast:* Elizabeth Montgomery (Helen Warren), Gig Young (Stephen Warren), Eddie Albert (Albert Warren), Lillian Gish (Mrs. Warren), Edie Adams (Blanche), Jeffrey Lynn (Dr. Parry), Frank McHugh (Constable Williams), Jean-Pierre Aumont (Man). *Producer:* Fred Coe. *Writer:* Robert Goldman. *Director:* Boris Sagal.

**1878 Sports Illustrated: The Making of the Swimsuit Issue.** Documentary, 50 min., HBO, 2/9/89. A behind-the-scenes look at the making of the *Sports Illustrated* twenty-fifth anniversary swimsuit issue. The program also profiles the individual girls whose pictures appear in the issue. *The Models:* Carol Alt, Christie Brinkley, Rachel Hunter, Mara Can Hurz, Kathy Ireland, Elle MacPherson, Stephanie Seymour, Yvette Sylvander, Yvonne Sylvander, Cheryl Tiegs, Kara Young. *Music:* Matt Kadowitz. *Producers:* Susan Froemke, Albert Maysles. *Directors:* Albert Maysles, Dyanna Taylor.

**Ad for "Spy Magazine Hit List"**

**1879 Spotlight.** Variety, 90 min., NBC, 3/21/56. A program of music, songs, and comedy sketches designed to spotlight the talents of comedian Jimmy Durante. *Host:* Jimmy Durante. *Guests:* Jack Buchanan, Pat Carroll, Jeannie Carson, Sonja Henie. *Music:* Charles Sanford. *Producer:* Max Liebman. *Producer-Director:* Bill Hobin.

**1880 Spring Break Reunion.** Variety, 2 hrs., Syndicated, 8/87. A beach party of music and songs from Fort Lauderdale, Florida. *Hosts:* Frankie Avalon, Connie Stevens. *Guests:* The Drifters, Jan and Dean, Stephanie Karis (Car rental agent), Rick Rawitz (Mr. Nichols), Del Shannon, Rick Shaw (as the D.J.), The Ventures. *Producers:* Frankie Avalon, Grant H. Gravitt. *Writers:* Bob

O'Brien, Ed Freeman. *Director:* Vincent Scarza.

**1881 Spring Holiday.** Variety, 30 min., CBS, 3/21/56. A music and comedy salute to spring. *Host:* Tony Martin. *Guests:* Polly Bergen, Cyd Charisse, Jack E. Leonard. *Announcer:* Tony Marvin. *Music:* Bert Farber. *Producer:* Milton Douglas. *Director:* Byron Paul.

**1882 The Spy Magazine Hit List.** Variety, 60 min., NBC, 12/21/92. The irreverent *Spy* magazine spoofs the 100 most annoying and alarming people and events of 1992 (for example, Madonna, Woody Allen, John Gotti, and Ross Perot). *Host:* Julia Louis-Dreyfus. *Guests:* David Alan Grier, Mary Tyler Moore, Wayne Newton,

Harry Shearer. *Producers:* Kurt Andersen, Bob Kaminsky, Peter Kaminsky. *Director:* Paul Miller.

## 1883 Spy Magazine Presents How to Be Famous. Variety, 60 min., NBC, 4/18/90. *Spy* magazine's examination of America's fascination with celebrities and the world in which they live. *Host:* Jerry Seinfeld. *Guests:* Dick Cavett, Victoria Jackson, Ricardo Montalban, Joe Namath, Harry Shearer, Dick Smothers, Tom Smothers. *Producers:* Kurt Andersen, E. Graydon Carter, Thomas L. Phillips, Bob Kaminsky, Peter Kaminsky. *Writers:* Kurt Andersen, E. Graydon Carter, Bruce Handy, Paul Simms. *Director:* Paul Miller.

## 1884 SST: Screen, Stage, Television. Documentary, 60 min., ABC, 5/7/89. A behind-the-scenes look at various aspects of Hollywood, the Broadway stage, and television. *Host:* Robert Guillaume. *Correspondent:* Greg Jackson. *Producers:* Harry Moses, Robert Guillaume, Allan Maraynes. *Theme:* Marvin Hamlisch.

## 1885 Stage Door. Drama, 90 min., NBC, 3/28/48. A television adaptation of the play by George S. Kaufman and Edna Ferber. A look at backstage Broadway life as seen through the experiences of Terry Randall, a dedicated but unemployed actress who resides at a theatrical boarding house called the Footlights Club. See also the following title. *Cast:* Louisa Horton (Terry Randall), Harvey Stephens (David Kingsley), Mary Anderson (Kaye Hamilton), John Forsythe (Keith Burgess), Enid Markey (Judith Canfield), Mary Alice Moore (Jean Maitland). *Producer:* Theresa Helburn. *Director:* Edward Sobol.

## 1886 Stage Door. Drama, 60 min., CBS, 4/6/55. A television adaptation of the 1936 Broadway play by George S. Kaufman and Edna Ferber.

See the prior title for storyline information. *Cast:* Diana Lynn (Terry Randall), Peggy Ann Garner (Kaye Hamilton), Dennis Morgan (David Kingsley), Rhonda Fleming (Jean Maitland), Nita Talbot (Judith Canfield), Charles Drake (Keith Burgess), Elsa Lanchester (Mrs. Orcutt), Jack Weston (Larry Westcott), Virginia Vincent (Bernice), Victor Moore (Adolph). *Producer:* Felix Jackson. *Writer:* Gore Vidal. *Director:* Sidney Lumet.

## 1887 Stan Freberg Presents Chinese New Year. Comedy, 60 min., ABC, 2/4/62. A series of skits that satirize contemporary television, especially tasteless commercials. *Host:* Stan Freberg. *Guests:* Sterling Holloway, Mike Mazurki, Frances Osborne, Patti Regan, Ginny Tiu, Gloria Wood. *Producer-Director:* Jack Donohue. *Writer:* Stan Freberg.

## Stand By for HNN *see* Bob Hope Specials

## 1888 The Standard Oil Anniversary Show. Variety, 90 min., NBC, 10/13/57. A music and comedy celebration of the seventy-fifth anniversary of the Standard Oil Company of New Jersey. *Hosts:* Brandon DeWilde, Tyrone Power. *Guests:* Art Buchwald, Gower Champion, Marge Champion, Jimmy Durante, Duke Ellington, Eddie Mayehoff, Sid Miller, Donald O'Connor, Jane Powell, Ronald Seale, Kay Thompson. *Music:* George Bassman. *Producer-Director:* Greg Garrison.

## 1889 Stanley, the Ugly Duckling. Cartoon, 30 min., ABC, 5/1/82. When he is rejected by his parents, Stanley, the misfit in a family of four ducks, sets out to discover where he belongs. The story relates Stanley's search for identity and the important lesson he learns about liking himself and accepting the virtues and faults that

make him unique. Originally aired as a primetime special; repeated as an "ABC Weekend Special" on 2/4/84. *Voices:* Susan Blu (Stanley), Jack DeLeon (Nathan), Wolfman Jack (Eagle One). *Other Voices:* Brian Cummings, Rick Dees, Julie McWhirter, Lee Thomas. *Music:* Artie Butler. *Producers:* Steve Binder, John Wilson. *Writers:* Norman L. Martin, Lee Pockriss. *Director:* John Wilson.

## 1890 The Star-Crossed Romance of Josephine Cosnowski.
Comedy-Drama, 60 min., PBS, 3/6/85. A moment from the past of humorist Jean Shepherd as he recalls an incident from his childhood in Hohnman, Indiana, in the 1950s: his intoxication with anything Polish, especially Josephine Cosnowski, the new girl in the neighborhood. *Cast:* Jean Shepherd (Ralph; adult), Peter Kowanko (Ralph; teenager); Katherine Kahmi (Josephine Cosnowski), George Coe (Ralph's father, "The Old Man"), Barbara Bolton (Ralph's mother), Jay Ine (Randy), William Lampley (Flick), Peter Gaffey (Archie), Jean Solbes (Helen), William Lynch (Josephine's father). *Producer:* Olivia Tappan. *Writer:* Jean Shepherd. *Director:* Leigh Brown.

## 1891 A Star Spangled Celebration.
Variety, 3 hrs., ABC, 7/4/87. A music and comedy celebration of Independence Day 1987. *Host:* Oprah Winfrey. *Cohost:* Robert Urich. *Guests:* Kareem Abdul-Jabbar, Alabama, Peter Allen, Tony Bennett, Carol Burnett, Richard Chamberlain, Chubby Checker, Angie Dickinson, Steve Driscoll, Steve Guttenberg, Jennifer Holliday, Loretta Lynn, Barbara Mandrell, Bernadette Peters, Lee Remick, The Rockettes, Suzanne Somers, Yakov Smirnoff, Malcolm-Jamal Warner, Dwight Yoakam. *Music:* Lenny Stack. *Producers:* Marty Pasetta, Vince Maynard. *Writer:* Richard A. Steel. *Director:* Marty Pasetta.

## 1892 A Star Spangled Celebration.
Variety, 2 hrs., ABC, 7/3/88. A musical celebration of Independence Day 1988. *Hosts:* Patrick Duffy, Joanna Kerns. *Guests:* Kareem Abdul-Jabbar, Glen Campbell, Angie Dickinson, Earth, Wind and Fire, Steve Guttenberg, John Hartford, John James, Kool & The Gang, Rob Lowe, The Osmond Brothers and The Osmond Boys, The Pointer Sisters, Restless Heart, Run-DMC, Scott Valentine, Michael Winslow, Pia Zadora. *Music:* Nick Perito. *Producers:* Marty Pasetta, Vince Maynard. *Writer:* Elise Pasetta. *Director:* Marty Pasetta.

## 1893 A Star Spangled Country Party.
Variety, 60 min., Showtime, 4/26/84. A country and western tribute to the U.S. Navy. Taped aboard the USS *Constellation* in San Diego Harbor. *Host:* Hank Williams, Jr. *Guests:* Alabama, Earl Thomas Conley and the ETC Band, Gus Hardin, Waylon Jennings, Mel McDaniel, Sylvia. *Producer-Director:* Marty Pasetta.

## 1894 Star Tour Australia.
Variety, 60 min., Syndicated, 6/86. A view of the land down under as seen through the eyes of a group of American celebrities who are touring Australia. *Celebrities:* Ed Asner, Chet Atkins, Barry Bostwick, Ben Gazzara, Florence Henderson, Marion Ross, Connie Stevens. *Producers:* Louis Rudolph, David Marmel. *Director:* Jeff Androsky.

## The Starmakers *see* Bob Hope Specials

## 1895 The Stars and Stripes Show.
A chronological listing of five variety specials that celebrate Independence Day.
**1 The Stars and Stripes Show** (90 min., Syndicated, 7/71). *Host:* Bob Hope. *Guests:* Phyllis George, Mickey Mantle, The New Christy Minstrels,

Dale Robertson, Kay Starr, Chill Wills. *Music:* Les Brown. *Producers:* Lee Allen Smith, Dick Schneider. *Writer:* Daniel Marks. *Director:* Bill Thrash.

**2 The Stars and Stripes Show** (60 min., NBC, 7/4/72). *Host:* Bob Hope. *Guests:* Ed McMahon, The Strategic Air Command Band, Chill Wills. *Music:* Les Brown. *Producer:* Lee Allen Smith. *Director:* Dick Schneider.

**3 The Stars and Stripes Show** (60 min., NBC, 7/3/73). *Hosts:* Tennessee Ernie Ford, Bob Hope. *Guests:* Anita Bryant, Lou Rawls, Doc Severinsen, The Strategic Air Command Band, The U.S. Army Chorus. *Music:* Les Brown. *Producer:* Lee Allen Smith. *Writer:* Dennis Marks. *Director:* Dick Schneider.

**4 The Stars and Stripes Show** (60 min., NBC, 7/3/75). *Guests:* Anita Bryant, John Davidson, Bob Hope, Charley Pride, Juliet Prowse. *Producer:* Lee Allen Smith. *Writer:* Barry Downes. *Director:* Bill Thrash.

**5 The Stars and Stripes Show** (2 hrs., NBC, 6/30/76). *Host:* Tennessee Ernie Ford. *Guests:* Anita Bryant, Mike Douglas, Frank Gorshin, Ed McMahon, Chita Rivera, Kate Smith, Dionne Warwick. *Music:* Milton De-Lugg. *Producer:* Lee Allen Smith. *Writer:* Barry Downes. *Director:* Bill Thrash.

**1896 Stars in the Eye.** Variety, 60 min., CBS, 11/13/52. Performances by stars from CBS programs (the title refers to CBS's logo, the eye). *Cast:* Gracie Allen, Eve Arden, Desi Arnaz, Lucille Ball, Jack Benny, George Burns, Cass Daley, William Frawley, Jody Gilbert, Gale Gordon, Florence Halop, Marvin Kaplan, Cathy Lewis, Art Linkletter, The Sportsman, Bob Sweeney, Vivian Vance, Elena Verdugo, Margaret Whiting, Marie Wilson, Alan Young. *Music:* Lud Gluskin. *Producer:* Robert Forward. *Director:* Parke Levy.

**1897 The Stars Salute Israel**

**at 30.** Variety, 2 hrs., ABC, 5/8/78. A star-studded celebration for Israel on the occasion of its thirtieth anniversary. *Guests:* Anne Bancroft, Mikhail Baryshnikov, Debby Boone, Pat Boone, Sammy Davis, Jr., Kirk Douglas, Henry Fonda, Hermione Gingold, Kate Jackson, Gabe Kaplan, Gene Kelly, Alan King, Billie Jean King, Barry Manilow, Dean Martin, Millicent Martin, Zubin Mehta, Paul Newman, Bernadette Peters, Jean Stapleton, Barbra Streisand, Sally Struthers, Cicely Tyson, Ben Vereen, John Williams, Flip Wilson, Henry Winkler, Joanne Woodward. *Producers:* James Lipton, Charles Fishman, Marty Pasetta. *Director:* Marty Pasetta.

**1898 Starstruck.** Drama, 60 min., ABC, 10/14/81. Alicia Marin is a talented young performer and songwriter who dreams of becoming a famous singer. During her high school summer vacation, Alicia acquires a job as a singer and waitress in a coffeehouse — on the same day her mother (Inez) arranges for her to take a job as an apprentice bookkeeper in the factory where she works. Inez is hardworking and opposes Alicia pursuing a songwriting career. Alicia, however, convinces her mother to let her work the two jobs since the hours do not conflict. Alicia's work as a bookkeeper impresses her boss, who offers to send her to college if she will give up her music career and devote herself to bookkeeping. Shortly after, when Alicia sees for the first time the conditions under which her mother works, she realizes the sacrifices her mother has made and why her mother wants her to have a secure job. The story relates Alicia's dilemma: to be loyal to her mother's wishes or fulfill her dream of becoming a star. Aired as an "ABC Afterschool Special." *Cast:* Trini Alvarado (Alicia Marin), Joanna Merlin (Inez Marin), Lee Curreri (Steve), Miriam Colon (Yolanda), Anna Maria Horsford (Jessica), Jay O. Sanders (Mr. Miller),

Francine Beers (Mrs. Kvares), Rita Karin (Mrs. Reuben), Terry Layman (Warren Adler). *Music/Lyrics:* Lynn Ahrens. *Producers:* Diana Kerew, Patrick McCormick. *Writer:* Marisa Gioffre. *Director:* Claude Kerven.

**1899 State Fair America.** Variety, 2 hrs., CBS, 9/10/77. Highlights of the activities of four state fairs: The Allentown Fair (Allentown, Pennsylvania), Cheyenne Frontier Days (Cheyenne, Wyoming), the San Luis Obispo Fair (Paso Robles, California), and the Illinois Fair (Peoria, Illinois). *Guests:* Lynn Anderson, Roy Clark, Billy Davis, Jr., Steven Ford, Gabe Kaplan, Alan King, Robert Klein, Hal Linden, Mary MacGregor, Marilyn McCoo, Mel Tillis, Jimmie Walker. *Music:* Jack Elliott, Allyn Ferguson. *Producers:* Bernard Rothman, Jack Wohl. *Writers:* Aubrey Tadman, Garry Ferrier. *Director:* Jeff Margolis.

**1900 State Fair, U.S.A.** Variety, 2 hrs., Syndicated, 9/81. Two 60-minute specials that were syndicated in the same month and presented highlights of two state fairs: the Illinois State Fair in Peoria (first special) and the California State Fair. *Hosts:* Irlene Mandrell, Dick Van Patten. *Guests* (first special): Air Supply, Sister Sledge. *Guests* (second special): Jim Stafford, Tina Turner. *Announcer:* John Harlan. *Producers:* Jeff Simmons, Carolyn Raskin, Mort Libow. *Director:* Carolyn Raskin.

**1901 The Statlers' Christmas Present.** Variety, 90 min., Syndicated, 12/20/86. A program of Christmas music and songs with the Statler Brothers. *Hosts:* The Statler Brothers. *Guests:* Gene Autry, Crystal Gayle, Merle Haggard, Carol Lawrence, Roger Miller. *Music:* Bill Walker. *Producers:* Richard C. Thrall, Bill Galvin. *Writers:* Bill Galvin, Pat Galvin, Don Reid. *Director:* Steve A. Womack.

**1902 The Steeler and the Pittsburgh Kid.** Drama, 60 min., NBC, 11/15/81. An unusual special inasmuch as it is based on a 1981 television commercial (for Coca-Cola in which football star Mean Joe Greene is given a coke by a loyal fan, a young boy, after a tough game). Adapting this premise, "The Steeler and the Pittsburgh Kid" tells of a nine-year-old boy (Nick Smith) who learns about values, discipline, and relationships when he is temporarily adopted by Mean Joe Greene, defensive tackle of the Pittsburgh Steelers, and his teammates (who, in turn, are affected and inspired by the boy's love of football). *Cast:* Joe Greene (Himself), Henry Thomas (Nick Smith), Lonny Chapman (Coach Chuck Noll), Franco Harris (Himself), Harvey Martin (Monster Man), Hugh Gorrian (Arnie), Jim Brinson (Robbins), Norma Moore (Mom), John Martin (Parisi). *Music:* Peter Matz. *Producers:* Philip Barry, Joe Boston. *Writer:* I. C. Rapoport. *Director:* Lou Antonio.

**1903 Step on the Gas.** Comedy, 60 min., CBS, 10/19/60. Skits that spoof drivers and driving in America. *Cast:* Rod Alexander, Pat Carroll, Hans Conried, Jackie Gleason, Shirley Jones, Shari Lewis. *Music:* Charles Sanford. *Producers:* Max Liebman, Bill Hobin. *Director:* Bill Hobin.

**1904 Steve and Eydie Celebrate Irving Berlin.** Variety, 90 min., NBC, 8/22/78. A salute to the music of Irving Berlin. *Hosts:* Eydie Gorme, Steve Lawrence. *Guests:* Carol Burnett, Sammy Davis, Jr., Oscar Peterson. *Producers:* Steve Lawrence, Gary Smith, Dwight Hemion. *Writer:* Harry Crane. *Director:* Dwight Hemion.

**1905 Steve and Eydie: On Stage.** Variety, 60 min., NBC, 9/16/73. A concert by Steve Lawrence and

Eydie Gorme from Caesar's Palace in Las Vegas. *Hosts:* Eydie Gorme, Steve Lawrence. *Guests:* Lucille Ball, Sergio Mendes and Brasil '77. *Music:* Nick Perito. *Producers:* Steve Lawrence, Marty Pasetta. *Director:* Marty Pasetta.

**1906 Steve and Eydie: Our Love Is Here to Stay.** Variety, 60 min., CBS, 11/27/75. A musical variety hour that highlights the music of George Gershwin. *Hosts:* Eydie Gorme, Steve Lawrence. *Guest:* Gene Kelly. *Music:* Nick Perito. *Producers:* Gary Smith, Dwight Hemion. *Writers:* Harry Crane, Marty Farrell. *Director:* Dwight Hemion.

**1907 Steve Lawrence and Eydie Gorme from This Moment on ... Cole Porter.** Variety, 60 min., ABC, 3/10/77. A musical tribute to composer Cole Porter. *Hosts:* Eydie Gorme, Steve Lawrence. *Guests:* Bob Hope, Ethel Merman. *Music:* Jack Parnell. *Producers:* Gary Smith, Dwight Hemion. *Writers:* Buz Kohan, Harry Crane. *Director:* Dwight Hemion.

**1908 Steve Martin Specials.** A chronological listing of the variety specials hosted by comedian Steve Martin. All are 60 minutes and broadcast on NBC.

**1 Steve Martin—A Wild and Crazy Guy** (11/22/78). *Guests:* Milton Berle, George Burns, Johnny Cash, Bob Hope, Strother Martin. *Producer:* Joseph Cates. *Writers:* Steve Martin, Michael Elias, Alan Metter, Jack Handey. *Director:* Gary Weis.

**2 Steve Martin: Comedy Is Not Pretty** (2/14/80). *Guests:* Marty Allen, Steve Allen, Will Alpert, Joan Collins, Richard Deacon, Joyce DeWitt, Phil Foster, Peter Graves, Meredith MacRae, Louis Nye, Carl Reiner, Dick Schapp. *Music:* John McEuen. *Producers:* John McEuen, Joseph Cates. *Director:* Joseph Cates.

**3 Steve Martin's Best Show Ever** (11/25/81). *Guests:* The American String Quartet, Dan Aykroyd, John Belushi, Lauren Hutton, Bill Murray, Laraine Newman, Lynn Redgrave, Paul Shaffer. *Music:* Howard Shore. *Producer:* Lorne Michaels. *Writers:* James Downey, Al Franken, Max Ross, Tom Davis. *Director:* Dave Wilson.

**4 Steve Martin's The Winds of Whoopie** (2/6/83). *Guests:* David Brenner, Bill Cosby, Antonio Fargas, Ron Leibman, Ed McMahon, Strother Martin, Gilda Radner, Burt Reynolds, Doc Severinsen. *Producers:* Steve Martin, Ken Suddleston. *Director:* Alan Metter.

**Steve Martin's Best Show Ever** *see* **Steve Martin Specials**

**Steve Martin's The Winds of Whoopie** *see* **Steve Martin Specials**

**1909 Stevie Nicks in Concert.** Variety, 60 min., HBO, 8/9/83. A solo concert by Stevie Nicks, a former singer with the group Fleetwood Mac. *Host:* Stevie Nicks. *Music:* Jimmy Lovine. *Producers:* Irving Azoff, Marty Callner, Greg Sills. *Director:* Marty Callner.

**1910 Stoned.** Drama, 60 min., ABC, 11/12/80. A harsh "ABC Afterschool Special" about drug addiction. The story follows its effects on Jack Melon, a shy boy who retreats into the world of marijuana as a way of acquiring friendship, and its consequences when his thinking becomes impaired and he is unable to deal with a situation in which his brother's life is in his hands. *Cast:* Scott Baio (Jack Melon), Vinnie Bufano (Mike Melon), Largo Woodruff (Felicity), Jack Finch (Teddy), Steve Monarque (Alan), John Herzfeld (Doug), Ira Elliott (Glen). *Music:* Gary Anderson. *Producer:* Linda Gottlieb. *Writer-Director:* John Herzfeld.

**1911 Stood Up.** Drama, 60 min., ABC, 12/6/90. An "ABC Afterschool Special" that attempts to teach teenagers about responsibility and the law. Becky and Garrett are high school sweethearts who make a date for the senior prom. Becky buys an expensive dress and is excited about prom night until she is stood up by Garrett. When she is unable to return the dress, she files a suit in small claims court against Garrett to recover the cost of the dress. When an overcrowded court calendar means a long wait, Becky elects to have her case tried by her high school "Street Law" class. The story relates the trial. *Cast:* Lucy Deakins (Becky Noonan), Spike Alexander (Garrett), Jan Miner (Mrs. Abbott), Adam LeFevre (Becky's father), Ellen Parker (Becky's mother), William Murray Weiss (Kyle Noonan), Royana Black (Michele), Kimberly Payne Williams (Vanessa), Geoffrey Owens (Teacher). *Producers:* Aviva Slesin, Nancy Kanter. *Writers:* Peg Haller, Bob Schneider. *Director:* Aviva Slesin.

**1912 Stooge Snapshots.** Documentary, 60 min., Syndicated, 1984. A profile of the men who played The Three Stooges: Moe Howard, Jerome "Curly" Howard, Shemp Howard, Larry Fine, Joe Besser, and Curly Joe DeReta. *Narrator:* Steve Allen. *Guests:* Edward Bernds, Elaine Diamond, Julie Gibson, Jock Mahoney, Leonard Maltin, Emil Sitka, Ellwood Ullman, Jules White, Paul Winchell. *Music:* Doug Scharf. *Producers:* Forrest P. Gill, Mark S. Gilman. *Writer-Director:* Mark S. Gilman, Jr.

**1913 Stop, Thief!** Drama, 60 min., CBS, 4/22/76. An historical drama about the fall of the notorious William Marcy "Boss" Tweed, a grand sachem of New York's Tammany Hall who held absolute power in the city's Democratic organization and thus controlled politics and patronage. The story shows how the vigorous free press — particularly the scathing political cartoons of Thomas Nast in *Harper's Weekly* and a series of exposés in the *New York Times* blew the lid off the biggest scandal in New York City's history. *Cast:* Howard Da Silva (Boss Tweed), Brad Davis (Thomas Nast), Jack Bittner (Peter Sweeny), Frederick Rolf (Mayor Oakey Hall), Hannah McKay (Sarah Nast), Addison Powell (John Jacob Astor), Jim Harder (James Watson), David Tress (James O'Brien), Richard Waring (Fletcher Harper), Patrick Horgan (Louis Jennings), Ed Holmes (George Jones), Hansford Rowe (John Harper), John Cecil Holm (James Harper). *Music:* Lee Holdridge. *Producers:* Joel Heller, Lois Bianchi. *Writer:* Terry Southern. *Director:* William F. Claxton.

**1914 A Storm in Summer.** Drama, 90 min., NBC, 2/6/70. The story of a hostile old man (Herman Washington) who becomes the reluctant foster father of a young, angry black child (Abel). Aired as a "Hallmark Hall of Fame" special. *Cast:* Peter Ustinov (Herman Washington), N'Gai Dixon (Abel Shaddick), Peter Bonerz (Stanley), Marlyn Mason (Gloria Ross), Penny Santon (Mrs. Gold), Frances Robinson (Mrs. Parker). *Producer-Director:* Buzz Kulik. *Writer:* Rod Serling.

**1915 The Story of Christmas.** Variety, 60 min., NBC, 12/22/63. A yuletide program of song and pageant. Christmas carols from many lands are performed, along with an animated story of the Nativity by artist Eyvind Earle (and based on the Gospel according to St. Luke). The program also introduces a new Christmas song by Roger Wagner (music) and Charles Tazewell (lyrics) called "Little Grey Donkey." *Host:* Tennessee Ernie Ford. *Performers:* The Sheets Twins, The Roger Wagner Chorale. *Orchestra:* Roger Wagner. *Producer-Director:* William N. Burch.

## 1916 The Strange Case of Dr. Jekyll and Mr. Hyde. Drama, 2 hrs. 30 min., ABC, 1/7/68. An adaptation of the novel by Robert Louis Stevenson. The story, set in London in 1885, tells of the experiences of Henry Jekyll, a dedicated physician who develops a potion that changes human personality and transforms him into Edward Hyde, an evil murderer. See also "Dr. Jekyll and Mr. Hyde." *Cast:* Jack Palance (Dr. Jekyll/Mr. Hyde), Leo Glenn (Dr. Lanyon), Denholm Elliott (Devlin), Oscar Homolka (Dr. Stryke), Billie Whitelaw (Gwyn), Tessie O'Shea (Tessie O'Toole), Torin Thatcher (Sir John Turnbull), Gillie Fenwick (Ivy Peterson). *Music:* Robert Cobert. *Producer:* Dan Curtis. *Writer:* Ian McLellan-Hunter. *Director:* Charles Jarrett.

## 1917 Strange Interlude. Drama, 4 hrs. 30 min., PBS, 1/18, 1/19, 1/20/88. A television adaptation of the nine-act play by Eugene O'Neill tells of a woman (Nina Leeds) haunted by the memories of the untimely death of her fiancé (Gordon) in World War I and the effect Gordon had on the lives of a group of people. *Cast:* Glenda Jackson (Nina Leeds), Ken Howard (Sam Evans), David Dukes (Dr. Ned Darnell), Edward Petherbridge (Charley Marsden), Jose Ferrer (Professor Leeds), Rosemary Harris (Mrs. Evans), Julie Eccles (Madeline Arnold), Kenneth Branaghi (Gordon Evans), Elizabeth Kelly (Mary). *Music:* Richard Rodney Bennett. *Producers:* Robert Enders, Philip Barry. *Writer:* Robert Enders. *Director:* Philip Barry.

## 1918 The Strawberry Blonde. Musical Comedy, 60 min., NBC, 10/18/59. A musical adaptation of the Broadway play *One Sunday Afternoon* by James Hogan. The story relates the attempts of a dentist (Biff Grimes) to get even with the man (Hugo Barnstead) who put him in jail and married his sweetheart (Virginia Brush, the straw-

berry blonde of the title). The play, under the title "One Sunday Afternoon," has also been telecast as a segment of the following series: "Ford Theater" (CBS, 5/16/49) with Burgess Meredith (Biff), Francesca Bruning (Amy), and Hume Cronyn (Hugo); "Prudential Playhouse" (CBS, 3/13/51) with Richard Carlson (Biff) and June Lockhart (Amy); "Broadway Television Theater" (local New York, 12/8/52) with Jack Warden (Biff), Mimi Kelly (Amy), and Jimmy Sheridan (Hugo); "Kraft Television Theater" (ABC, 11/11/54) with Frank Albertson (Biff), Valerie Cossart (Amy), and John Shellie (Hugo); and "Lux Video Theater" (NBC, 1/31/57) with Gordon MacRae (Biff), Mary Healy (Amy), and Peter Lind Hayes (Hugo). *Cast:* David Wayne (Biff Grimes), Janet Blair (Amy Lind), Eddie Bracken (Hugo Barnstead), Dolores Dorn-Heft (Virginia Brush), Iggie Wolfington (Snapper). *Host:* Edgar Bergen. *Producer:* David Susskind. *Writer:* George Baxter. *Director:* William Corrigan.

## 1919 A String of Beads. Drama, 60 min., ABC, 2/7/61. The story of Gloria Winters, a young woman who buys a string of cultured pearls and the complications that ensue when she wears them to a lavish party and is mistaken for a woman of great wealth. *Cast:* Jane Fonda (Gloria Winters), George Grizzard (Joey Raymond), Chester Morris (Walter Harmon), Louisa Horton (Ruth Harmon). *Producer-Director:* Fielder Cook. *Writer* (adapted from the William Somerset Maugham story): Steven Gethers.

## 1920 Strippers. Documentary, 45 min., HBO, 3/23/83. The program explores the art of the striptease via the lives of the world's most famous strippers: Lydia Thompson, Josephine Baker, Gypsy Rose Lee, Little Egypt, Carrie Farrell, and Sally Rand. The special, which contains nudity, incor-

porates rare film clips, still photo-
graphs, and recreations to tell the story
of how the striptease began and how it
prospered. *Cast:* Julie Miller (Lydia
Thompson), Christina Kumi Kimball
(Josephine Baker), Deborah Bartlett
(Gypsy Rose Lee), Christine Busini
(Little Egypt), Cynthia S. Lee (Carrie
Farrell), Janet Kinsman (Sally Rand).
*Narrator:* Gwen Verdon. *Music:* Scott
Salmon. *Producers:* Richard Barclay,
Gary Monet. *Writer:* Coleman Jacoby.
*Director:* Robert Deubel.

**1921 Stubby Pringle's Christ-
mas.** Drama, 60 min., NBC, 12/17/78.
The story of Stubby Pringle, a lonesome cowboy with a generous heart
who brings some Christmas happiness
to an impoverished homesteader (Jolene Henderson), her sick husband,
and two small children. A "Hallmark
Hall of Fame" presentation. *Cast:*
Beau Bridges (Stubby Pringle), Julie
Harris (Jolene Henderson), Edward
Binns (Red), Kim Hunter (Mrs.
Harper), Strother Martin (Old Hollander), Chill Wills (Janitor). *Music:*
Garry Sherman. *Producer:* Gilbert
Cates. *Writer:* James Lee Barrett. *Director:* Burt Brinckerhoff.

**1922 Student Court.** Drama,
60 min., CBS, 4/24/85. A "CBS Schoolbreak Special" about student courts,
which are "in session" in various cities
around the United States. The story
focuses on Jennifer Johnson, a 15-year-
old girl who is caught shoplifting and
who chooses to face a jury of her peers
in Student Court rather than risk
spending time in juvenile hall by appearing in Juvenile Court. *Cast:* Katy
Kurtzman (Jennifer Johnson), Nina
Shipman (Mrs. Johnson), Julie Jeter
(Susan), Moosie Drier (Danny), Eric
Brown (Ed), Lisa Fong (May Kim),
Veronica Redd (Mrs. Carlisle), David
Greenlee (Ollie), Julie Dolan (Jane),
Garin Bougie (Mike), Eric Wallace
(Jonas), Glenn Michael Miller (Bailiff).
*Producers:* Robert Chenault, Cynthia

Chenault. *Writers:* Adam Rodman,
Arthur Heineman. *Director:* Robert
Chenault.

**1923 The Sullivan Years: A
Tribute to Ed.** Retrospective, 60
min., CBS, 2/2/75. Film and videotaped
highlights of 23 years of "The Ed
Sullivan Show." *Host:* Dick Cavett.
*Producer:* Robert Precht. *Director:*
Russ Petranto.

**1924 Summer in New York.**
Variety, 60 min., CBS, 6/30/60. Music,
songs, and comedy sketches set against
the background of New York City.
*Host:* Phil Silvers. *Guests:* Maurice
Gosfield, Carol Haney, Carol Law-
rence, Jules Munshin, Joe E. Ross.
*Music:* Luther Henderson. *Producer:*
Nat Hiken. *Writers:* Nat Hiken, Billy
Friedberg, Charles Sherman. *Director:*
Greg Garrison.

**1925 Summer Solstice.** Drama,
60 min., ABC, 12/30/81; HBO, 10/9/82;
Syndicated, 11/82. The story, set in
Wyoming, explores the 50-year mar-
riage of Joshua and Margaret Turner—
from their first meeting on a Cape Cod
beach to the present. The title refers to
the longest day of summer. *Cast:*
Henry Fonda (Joshua Turner), Myrna
Loy (Margaret Turner), Stephen Col-
lins (Young Joshua), Lindsay Course
(Young Margaret), Patricia Elliott
(Emily), Elisa Erali (Lucy), Michael
Simmons (Toby), Jo Henderson (Mrs.
Burnside), Thomas Ruisinger (Mr.
Burnside), Marcus Smythe (Ranger).
*Music:* John Nagy. *Producer:* Bruce
Marson. *Writer:* Bill Phillips. *Director:*
Ralph Rosenblum.

**1926 Summer Switch.** Comedy, 60 min., ABC, 9/19/84. As he is
about to leave for Los Angeles on a
business trip, movie executive Bill Andrews wishes he could be like his son,
Ben, who has nothing to do but play.
At that exact moment, as Ben wishes he
could be more like his father (who he

believes has a much easier life), it happens—their souls change bodies. The story relates their misadventures as they learn some insightful lessons about each other's way of life, including the importance of moral values. An "ABC Afterschool Special." *Cast:* Robert Klein (Bill Andrews), Scott Schwartz (Ben Andrews), Margo Skinner (Ellen Andrews), Anna Maria Horsford (Stephanie Marshak), Lenora May (Annabel Andrews), Knowl Johnson (Duck Levine), Rex Everhart (Captain Splasher Wilking). *Music:* Gil Goldstein. *Producers:* Frank Doelger, Carol Polakoff. *Writer:* Bruce Harmon. *Director:* Ken Kwapis.

## 1927 Sunday Funnies. Variety,
60 min., NBC, 5/8/83. Musical numbers, sketches, and blackouts based on comic strip characters. *Host:* Loni Anderson. *Cast:* Judith Cohen (Broomhilda), Dick Butkus (Tank McNamara), Milt Oberman (Crock), Paul Willson (Frank), Martin Ferrero (Ernest), Ed Barth (Conrad). *Regulars:* Murphy Dunne, Lois Faraker, Lisa Freeman, Desiree Goyette, Michael Harrington, Joanna Lee, Christopher Prince, Paul Ventura. *Music/Lyrics:* Desiree Goyette. *Music Arranger/Conductor:* Tim Simon. *Producers:* Lee Mendelson, Frank Buxton. *Writers:* Gary Jacobs, Lee Mendelson, Steven Michelle, Tom Moore, Jr., Marty Nadler, Bob Sand, Dennis Rinsler, Mark Warren. *Director:* Frank Buxton.

## 1928 Sunday in the Park with George. Musical Drama, 2 hrs. 30 min., Showtime, 2/18/86. A television adaptation of the Broadway play by Stephen Sondheim and James Papine about Georges Seurat (1859–91), a French artist who created the celebrated canvas *A Sunday Afternoon on the Island of La Grande Jatte* (which shows a group of Parisians enjoying a day in the park). *Cast:* Mandy Patinkin (Georges Seurat), Bernadette Peters (Dot/Marie), Dana Ivey (Yvonne/Naomi), Charles Kimbrough (Jules/Greenberg), Mary D'Arcy (Celeste/Elaine), Barbara Bryne (Blair Daniels/Old lady), Chris Groenendaal (Louis/Billy), Judith Moore (Nurse/Mrs. Harriet), William Parry (Boatman/Redmond), Brent Spiner (Franz/Dennis), Nancy Opel (Freida/Betty). *Music/Lyrics:* Stephen Sondheim. *Book:* James Lapine. *Music Director:* Paul Gemignani. *Producers:* Michael Brandman, Emmanuel Azenberg. *Director:* Terry Hughes.

## 1929 Sunday in Town. Ballet,
90 min., NBC, 10/10/54. The overall title for two mini-ballets: "The Filling Station" (which relates one day's incidents in a typical American filling station) and "The Waitress" (about a waitress whose dream becomes a reality when she delivers food to a ballet group during rehearsal and is asked to become a part of the troupe). *Hosts:* Steve Allen, Dick Shawn. *Cast:* ("The Filling Station"): Janet Reed (Rich girl), Jacques D'Amboise (Mac), Todd Balender (Rich boy), Robert Barnett (Truck driver), Walter Gregory (Motorist), Shawn O'Brien (Motorist's wife), Ronald Colton (State trooper); ("The Waitress"): Judy Holliday (Waitress), Ballet Group: Janet Reed, Jacques D'Amboise, Todd Balender, Robert Barnett, Shawn O'Brien, Ronald Colton, Edith Brozak, Walter Georgov, John Marida. *Music:* Charles Sanford. *Producers:* Max Liebman, Bill Hobin. *Director:* Max Liebman.

## 1930 Sunday Night at the London Palladium. Variety, 60 min., Syndicated, 11/73. Music and songs from the London Palladium theater in England. *Host:* Jim Dale. *Guests:* Petula Clark, Rudolf Nureyev, Merle Park, Bryn Phillips, The Tiller Girls. *Music:* Jack Parnell. *Producers:* Bill Ward, Jon Schoffield. *Writers:* Sid Colin, Dick Vosburgh. *Director:* Jon Schoffield.

## 1931 Super Comedy Bowl 1.
Comedy, 60 min., CBS, 1/10/71. A comical spoof of the Super Bowl, its fans and its players. See also the following title. *Host:* Lucille Ball. *Guests:* Carol Burnett, Judy Carne, Tina Cole, Norm Crosby, Jack Gilford, Teresa Graves, Rosey Grier, Charlton Heston, Marty Ingels, Arte Johnson, Alex Karras, Jack Lemmon, Art Metrano, Joe Namath, Pat O'Brien, Charles Nelson Reilly, Jill St. John, Alan Sues, Leslie Uggams, John Wayne, Dave Willock. *Producer-Director:* Marty Pasetta. *Writers:* Saul Turteltaub, Bernie Orenstein, Gordon Farr, Arnold Kane.

## 1932 Super Comedy Bowl 2.
Comedy, 60 min., CBS, 1/12/72. A sequel to the above title; a spoof of football players and their fans. *Host:* Jack Lemmon. *Guests:* Mike Connors, Norm Crosby, Tony Curtis, Teresa Graves, David Hartman, David Huddleston, Arte Johnson, Jack Klugman, Burt Lancaster, Sue Ane Langdon, Dick Martin, Walter Matthau, Paul Newman, Charles Nelson Reilly, Burt Reynolds, Dan Rowan, Kurt Russell, Jill St. John, Ronnie Schell, George C. Scott, Karen Valentine, Jo Anne Worley. *Producers:* Saul Turteltaub, Bernie Orenstein, Marty Pasetta. *Writers:* Gordon Farr, Arnold Kane, Elias Davis, David Pollock, Saul Turteltaub, Bernie Orenstein. *Director:* Marty Pasetta.

## 1933 Super Night at Forrest Hills.
Variety, 60 min., CBS, 9/9/77. A music and comedy salute to the sport of tennis. Taped at the West Side Tennis Club in Forrest Hills, New York. *Hosts:* Sammy Davis, Jr., Sandy Duncan, Andy Williams. *Guests:* Arthur Ashe, Tracy Austin, Foster Brooks, Buddy Hackett, Lainie Kazan, The Keane Brothers, Alan King, Billie Jean King, Ethel Merman, Ilie Nastase, Virginia Wade. *Music:* Alan Copeland. *Producers:* Pierre Cossette, Marty Pasetta. *Writers:* Buz Kohan, Aubrey Tadman, Garry Ferrier. *Director:* Marty Pasetta.

## 1934 Super Night at the Super Bowl.
Variety, 90 min., CBS, 1/8/77. A music and comedy salute to Super Bowl XI from Pasadena, California. *Hosts:* Sammy Davis, Jr., Elliott Gould, Andy Williams. *Guests:* Jack Albertson, Johnny Bench, Natalie Cole, Angie Dickinson, Joe Frazier, Phyllis George, Ken Norton, Roger Owens, Charley Pride, Don Rickles, Sha Na Na, O. J. Simpson, John Wayne. *Music:* George Wyle. *Producers:* Pierre Cossette, Marty Pasetta. *Writer:* Buz Kohan, Alan Thicke, Pat McCormick. *Director:* Marty Pasetta.

## 1935 Super Night at the Super Bowl.
Variety, 60 min., CBS, 1/24/87. A live music and comedy salute to the Super Bowl. *Host:* Patrick Duffy. *Guests:* Lucie Arnaz, The Beach Boys, Ruth Buzzi, Tim Conway, Eric Dickerson, Gladys Knight and the Pips, John Madden, Barbara Mandrell, The Miami Sound Machine, Joe Namath, Tony Papenfuss, William Sanderson, Pat Summerall, John Voldstad. *Announcer:* Ed Herlihy. *Music:* Dennis McCarthy. *Producers:* Pierre Cossette, Marty Pasetta. *Writers:* Jeffrey Barron, Robert Arnott. *Director:* Marty Pasetta.

## 1936 Super Picnic '87.
Variety, 90 min., Syndicated, 9/87. A music and comedy salute to George Burns. Taped at Arrowhead Stadium in Kansas City, Missouri. *Host:* Mary Hart. *Special Guest:* George Burns. *Guests:* Harry Blackstone, Larry Gatlin and the Gatlin Brothers, Rich Little, Mary Wilson and the Supremes. *Music:* David Diggs. *Producers:* Michael Choate, Ed Rheinhart, Thomas F. Julian III. *Writer:* Ray Reese. *Director:* Al Footnick.

## 1937 Supergirl: The Making of the Movie.
Documentary, 60

min., ABC, 12/29/85. A fascinating behind-the-scenes look at the making of the motion picture *Supergirl*. *Host:* Faye Dunaway. *Guests:* Peter O'Toole, Helen Slater, Jeannot Szwarc, Brenda Vaccaro, Simon Ward. *Narrator:* Ted Maynard. *Music:* Jerry Goldsmith. *Producers:* Ilya Salkind, Timothy Burrell. *Writer-Director:* Peter Hollywood.

## 1938 Superman's 50th Anniversary: A Celebration of the Man of Steel. Tribute, 60 min., CBS, 2/29/88. A fiftieth-anniversary celebration of Superman, featuring skits and clips from the movie and television series. *Host:* Dana Carvey. *Guests:* The Amazing Kreskin, Tom Davis, Al Franken, Hal Holbrook, Jan Hooks, Jack Larson, Noel Neill, John Randolph, Christopher Reeve, Robert Vaughn, Fred Willard. *Skit Cast:* Fred Willard (Finn Howard), John Randolph (Morton Simon), Robert Vaughn (Ross Webster), Jackson Beck (Announcer), Marcia Harden (Marcia Connolly), Robert Smigel (Brainwave), Anthony Bishop, Woody Romoff, Brad Sullivan (Thugs). *Music:* Hal Willner. *Producers:* Lorne Michaels, Jon Peters, Mary Salter, Rosie Shuster. *Writers:* Adam Greene, Bruce McCulloch, Rosie Shuster, Robert Smigel. *Director:* Robert Boyd.

## 1939 Supermom's Daughter. Drama, 60 min., ABC, 2/18/87. Noelle Crandall is a brilliant 17-year-old high school student who excels in science. When she receives a scholarship to MIT she refuses to accept it, wanting to pursue her own dream of becoming a nursery schoolteacher. The story, broadcast as an "ABC Afterschool Special," focuses on the conflict that arises when her desires conflict with those her mother, Donna, has set for her—to become a successful businesswoman. *Cast:* Marisa Tomei (Noelle Crandall), Barbara Bosson (Donna Crandall), Cynthia Mace (Lucy Bard), Vicky Richardson (Karen), Ray Baker (Dr.

Thomas Crandall), Donna Vivino (Kendall Bard), Robert Oliveri (Paul Bard), Bobby Leslie (Josh). *Music:* Gil Goldstein. *Producers:* Diana Kerew, Carol Polakoff. *Writer:* Jeanne Betancourt. *Director:* Joan Darling.

## 1940 Superstars and Their Moms. Variety, 60 min., ABC, 5/3/87. A Mother's Day special in which celebrities appear with their mothers to relate incidents from their pasts. *Hosts:* Carol Burnett, Carrie Hamilton. *Guests:* Debbie Allen, Cher, Bill Cosby, Whitney Houston, Phylicia Rashad, John Ritter, Tom Selleck, Cybill Shepherd, Robin Williams. *Music:* Lenny Stack. *Producers:* Dick Clark, Georgia Holt, Phyllis Quinn. *Writers:* Ann Elder, Barry Adelman. *Director:* Al Schwartz.

## 1941 Superstars and Their Moms. Variety, 60 min., ABC, 5/1/88. A pre–Mother's Day special in which celebrities honor their mothers. *Host:* Carol Burnett, Carrie Hamilton. *Guests:* Kirk Cameron, Richard Dreyfuss, Farrah Fawcett, Barbara Mandrell, Irlene Mandrell, Louise Mandrell, Arnold Schwarzenegger, Lily Tomlin. *Music:* Lenny Stack. *Producers:* Dick Clark, Georgia Holt. *Writers:* Ann Elder, Barry Adelman. *Director:* Al Schwartz.

## 1942 Suzanne. Variety, 60 min., Syndicated, 5/87. Actress Suzanne Somers displays her singing and dancing talents in segments based on her nightclub act. *Host:* Suzanne Somers. *Music:* Artie Butler. *Producers:* Chris Bearde, Alan Hamel, Lee Miller. *Writer:* Bob Logan, Chris Bearde. *Director:* Lee Miller.

## 1943 The Suzanne Somers Special. Variety, 60 min., CBS, 2/22/82. Actress Suzanne Somers in her first television special; an hour of music, songs, and comedy taped aboard the

**Suzanne Somers**

aircraft carrier USS *Ranger* in San Diego Bay. *Host:* Suzanne Somers. *Guests:* Gladys Knight and the Pips, Marie Osmond, Flip Wilson. *Music:* Artie Butler. *Producers:* Alan Hamel, Art Fisher. *Writer:* Brian Vance. *Director:* Art Fisher.

**1944 The Suzanne Somers Special.** Variety, 60 min., CBS, 1/3/83. Music, songs, dances, and comedy routines with Suzanne Somers entertaining American troops overseas in Germany. *Host:* Suzanne Somers. *Guests:* Susan Anton, The Pointer Sisters, Jonathan Winters. *Music:* Artie Butler. *Producers:* Alan Hamel, Art Fisher. *Writer:* Bruce Valance. *Director:* Art Fisher.

**1945 Svengali and the Blonde.** Musical Comedy, 90 min., NBC, 7/30/55. The story of a beautiful artist's model (Trilby) who is transformed into a great singer by Svengali, a musical genius who possesses strange hypnotic powers. Based on the 1894 romance novel *Trilby* by George du Maurier. This novel was first seen on television as a segment of "Studio

One" (CBS, 9/11/50) with Priscilla Gillette as Trilby and Arnold Moss as Svengali. *Cast:* Ethel Barrymore (Narrator), Carol Channing (Trilby O'Farrell), Basil Rathbone (Svengali), Russell Arms (William Bagot), Nancy Kulp (Honorine), Mitzi McCall (Clo-Clo), Franklin Pangborn (Theater Manager). *Music/Lyrics:* Alan Handley, Charles Gaynor. *Producer-Writer-Director:* Alan Handley.

**1946 The Swan.** Comedy, 60 min., CBS, 6/9/50. A romantic comedy about the problems of a prearranged marriage as seen through the experiences of an aristocratic princess (Alexandra) and the heir apparent to the throne (Albert)—people who marry only because royal heritage demands they do so. *Cast:* Grace Kelly (Princess Alexandra), George Keane (Prince Albert), Alfred Ryder (Dr. Nicholas Agi), Dennis Hoey (Father Hyacinth), Jane Hoffman (Princess Beatrix), Leopoldine Konstantine (Princess Maria Dominica). *Producer:* Donald David. *Writer:* Melville C. Baker. *Director:* David Pressman.

**1947 Sweeney Todd.** Musical, 2 hrs. 19 min., The Entertainment Channel, 9/12/82. A television adaptation of the Broadway show about Sweeney Todd, a London barber who delights in killing his customers, and Mrs. Lovett, "the worst pastry chef" in London, who helps him dispose of the evidence as "meat pies." Based on the 1970 play by Christopher Bond (suggested by the 1847 play by George Dibbin Pitt); book by Hugh Wheeler. *Cast:* George Hearn (Sweeney Todd), Angela Lansbury (Mrs. Lovett), Cris Groenendall (Anthony Hope), Sara Woods (Beggar woman), Edmund Lyndeck (Judge Turpin), Betsy Joslyn (Johanna), Calvin Remsberg (The Beadle), Ken Jennings (Tobias Ragg), Michael Kalinyea (Jonas Fogg). *Music/Lyrics:* Stephen Sondheim. *Music Director:* Paul Gemigani. *Music Conductor:* Jim

Coleman. *Orchestra:* Jonathan Tunich. *Producers:* Ellen Kass, Archer King, Bonnie Burns. *Director:* Terry Hughes.

**1948 The Swimsuit Edition.** Fashion, 30 min., Syndicated, 8/87. An array of beautiful women model the latest in swimwear off the coast of Hawaii. Inspired by the *Sports Illustrated* swimsuit edition. *Hosts:* Kathy Ireland, Shawn Weatherly. *Producers:* Mark Anderson, Steve Klayman, Ralph Howard. *Director:* Steve Klayman.

**1949 Swing into Spring.** Variety, 60 min., CBS, 4/10/59. A musical salute to the spring of 1959. *Performers:* William Curly, Ella Fitzgerald, Benny Goodman, Lionel Hampton, Peggy Lee, Matt Mattox, Andre Previn. *Producer:* Lawrence White. *Writers:* Maurice Zolotow, David Geisel.

**1950 Swing Out, Sweet Land.** Variety, 90 min., NBC, 4/8/71. A musical event that traces America's growth. *Host:* John Wayne. *Guests:* Ann-Margret, Lucille Ball, Jack Benny, Dan Blocker, Johnny Cash, Roy Clark, Bing Crosby, Phyllis Diller, Lorne Greene, Celeste Holm, Bob Hope, Michael Landon, Dean Martin, Dick Martin, Ross Martin, Greg Morris, David Nelson, Rick Nelson, Hugh O'Brian, Dan Rowan, William Shatner, Red Skelton, Tom Smothers, Leslie Uggams, Dennis Weaver. *Music:* Dominic Frontiere. *Producers:* Nick Vanoff, William O. Harbach, Paul W. Keyes. *Writer:* Paul W. Keyes. *Director:* Stan Harris.

**1951 The Swingin' Singin' Years.** Variety, 90 min., NBC, 3/8/60. A nostalgic special that recalls the music and songs of the 1940s. *Host:* Ronald Reagan. *Guests:* Jack Fina, Woody Herman, Eddy Howard, Vaughn Monroe, Jo Stafford, Dinah Washington. *Music Director:* Tutti

Camarata. *Orchestrations:* Woody Herman, Stan Kenton, Freddy Martin. *Producers:* Hubbell Robinson, Gil Rodin. *Writers:* Tom Waldman, Frank Waldman. *Director:* Barry Shear.

**1952 The Swingin' Years.** Variety, 60 min., NBC, 2/9/60. The program recalls the music of the big band era. *Host:* Ronald Reagan. *Guests:* Count Basie, Gene Krupa, Guy Lombardo, Helen O'Connell, Anita O'Day. *Music:* Tutti Camarata. *Producers:* Hubbell Robinson, Gil Rodin. *Writers:* Frank Waldman, Tom Waldman. *Director:* Barry Shear.

**1953 The Swinging Scene of Ray Anthony.** Variety, 60 min., Syndicated, 5/68. An hour of music and songs with bandleader Ray Anthony. *Host:* Ray Anthony. *Singers:* The Bookends. *Music:* Ray Anthony. *Producers:* Lawrence Riport, Milton Lehr. *Director:* Milton Lehr.

**1954 Swiss Family Robinson.** Adventure, 60 min., NBC, 10/12/58. The adventures of the Robinsons, a Swiss family shipwrecked on a deserted island, as they struggle for survival. Based on the novel by Johann Wyss. *Cast:* Walter Pidgeon (Father), Laraine Day (Mother), Patty Duke (Lynda), Dennis Hopper (Fritz), Dennis Kohler (Ernest). *Producer:* Alex March. *Writer:* M. L. Davenport. *Director:* William A. Graham.

**1955 Taking a Stand.** Drama, 60 min., ABC, 1/19/89. A fact-based "ABC Afterschool Special" about racism. The story focuses on a white teenage boy (Matthew) who sees and reports a racist incident—and the torment he is subjected to by his classmates when he is asked to testify in court and refuses to change his position. *Cast:* Betty Buckley (Louise Robinson), Timothy Collins Griffin (Matthew Robinson), Jane Adams (Ellie Robinson), Dan Lauria (D. A.),

Joe Aufiery (Earl), Michael Beach (Jake), Scott Allegrucci (Glenn), Margaret Devine (Cathy Owens), Steven Culp (Bob Anderson). *Music Composers:* Keith Herman, Betty Buckley. *Producer:* Frank Doelger. *Writer:* Bruce Harmon. *Director:* Sandy Smolan.

**1956 A Tale of Four Wishes.** Drama, 60 min., CBS, 11/8/81. Jane is a pretty 13-year-old girl who feels that the whole world is against her. She is an habitual daydreamer who constantly wishes for good things to happen. The story relates the changes that occur in her life when she meets Skeeter, a gentle storyteller whose tales help Jane to understand that action, patience, and flexibility can make something good happen when mere wishing never will. Aired on "The CBS Library." *Cast:* Tracey Gold (Jane), Rick Nelson (Skeeter), Bibi Osterwald (Grandmother), Judy Farrell (Mother), Bob Ross (Father), Chad Krentzman (Daniel), Seeley Ann Thumann (Margaret). *Producer:* Nick Bosustow. *Writer:* George Arthur Bloom. *Director:* Seth Pinsker.

**1957 The Talent Scouts Program.** Variety, 60 min., NBC, 2/23/60. Performances by the undiscovered professional talent of well-known celebrities. Also known as "Talent Search." *Host:* Dave Garroway. *Guests:* Joan Crawford, Colleen Dewhurst, Ethel Merman, Maureen O'Hara, Richard Rodgers, Tommy Sands, Joanie Sommers, Phil Wallace. *Music:* Harry Sosnik. *Producers:* Irving Mansfield, Peter Arnell, William Nichols. *Director:* Grey Lockwood.

**Talent Search** *see* **The Talent Scouts Program**

**1958 Tales from Muppetland.** Comedy, 60 min., ABC, 4/10/70. The story of Cinderella, the mistreated girl who becomes a beautiful princess for one night, is told with the help of the Muppets, the fanciful creations of Jim Henson. *Host:* Kermit the Frog (Voice of Jim Henson). *Cast:* Belinda J. Montgomery (Cinderella), Robin Ward (Prince Charming), Joyce Gordon (Fairy Godmother), Pat Galloway (Stepmother). *Music:* Jack Parnell. *Producer-Director:* Jim Henson. *Writers:* Jon Stone, Tom Whedon.

### 1959 Taming of the Shrew.

Comedy, 90 min., NBC, 3/18/56. A television adaptation of the play by William Shakespeare about a father's efforts to marry off his beautiful and rich but vile and violent-tempered daughter (Katherine); and the efforts of Petruchio, who is seeking her money, to court and tame the tempestuous Katherine. Aired on the "Hallmark Hall of Fame." *Cast:* Lilli Palmer (Katherine), Maurice Evans (Petruchio), Diane Cilento (Bianca), Philip Bourneuf (Baptista), John Colicos (Lucentio), Douglas Watson (Hortensio), Jerome Kilty (Grumio), Robinson Stone (Vincentio), Ronald Long (Biondello). *Music:* Lehman Engle. *Producer:* Maurice Evans. *Writer:* William Nichols. *Director:* George Schaefer.

### 1960 Tanya Tucker ... Hot!

Variety, 90 min., Showtime, 7/81. The sultry singer in a concert that showcases her wide range of songs from country and western to hard-driving rock. Taped at the Roxy nightclub in Los Angeles. *Host:* Tanya Tucker. *Producer:* Roger Galloway.

### 1961 Tappin'.

Documentary, 60 min., Syndicated, 1/8/89. The program, which presents a behind-the-scenes look at the making of the film *Tap*, also explores the history of tap music in films. *Hosts:* Sammy Davis, Jr., Gregory Hines. *Guests:* Buddy Briggs, Suzanne Douglas, Gene Kelly, Steve Marfin. *Producers:* Les Mayfield, George Zaloom. *Writers:* Fax Bahr, John Pace. *Director:* Fax Bahr.

### 1962 Tattle: When to Tell on a Friend.

Drama, 60 min., ABC, 10/26/88. Maggie, Colleen, Sandy, and Linda are high school students who have been best friends since childhood. The girls attend Roosevelt High and are members of the swim team. The team is riding high and on the way to the state finals. Everything changes when Colleen asks the other girls to try cocaine. Maggie and Linda refuse and leave, but Sandy decides to try it. Soon they are both hooked. As their condition worsens, Maggie tries talking to them, but it is to no avail. Feeling that she has to do something, Maggie tells their swim coach. Sandy admits she needs help, but Colleen insists she does not have a drug problem. The friendship ends—as does the story—rather abruptly. Although Maggie has been labeled a tattle-tale, she feels that what she did was right. She and Linda are still friends, but Linda refuses to associate with Colleen and Sandy. Sandy, desperately in need of a friend, finds a true one in Maggie when Maggie tells her that she will help her through the long road to recovery. Colleen's fate is unknown. After a bitter confrontation with Maggie for telling the coach, it is only learned that Colleen ran away from home. Sandy thinks it was with a seedy drug pusher, but she, along with Maggie, Colleen's parents, and the police, cannot find her. An "ABC Afterschool Special." *Cast:* Allison Smith (Maggie), Tammy Lauren (Colleen McNeil), Amy Benedict (Sandy), Marisol Rodriquez (Linda), Katharine Ross (Maggie's Mother), Bibi Besch (Coach), Charles Siebert (Mr. McNeil), Zachary Bostrom (Teddy), April Brotherton (Cindy), Luke Edwards (Jack), Connie Mercede (Donna Mitchell). *Music:* Harold Wheeler. *Producers:* Carol Polakoff, Diana Kerew. *Writer:* Jeanne Betancourt. *Director:* Gabrielle Beaumont.

### 1963 Taxi.

Drama, 60 min., NBC, 2/2/78. A two-character, original tele-

**TATTLE:**
**When to tell**
**on a friend**
The story of the fine line
that sometimes exists
between friendship
and betrayal.

Starring Katharine Ross
and Allison Smith
("Kate and Allie")

THE AFTERSCHOOL
*Special*

TOMORROW 4:00 PM ⑦ ♫
Set your VCR.
Watch it with your family.

Ad for "Tattle: When to Tell on a Friend." Pictured, *left to right*: Amy Benedict, Allison Smith, Marisol Rodriquez and Tammy Lauren.

vision play about the conversation between a taxicab driver and his passenger. Aired on the "Hallmark Hall of Fame." *Cast:* Martin Sheen (Taxi driver), Eva Marie Saint (Passenger). *Producers:* Stan Parlan, Joseph Hardy. *Writer:* Lanford Wilson. *Director:* Joseph Hardy.

**1964 Teacher, Teacher.**
Drama, 90 min., NBC, 2/5/69. A "Hallmark Hall of Fame" presentation about three people: Hamilton Cade, a tutor struggling to rebuild a teaching career that has been shattered by drinking; Charles Carter, a disillusioned soul who works as a handyman because he believes there is no demand for black commercial pilots; and Freddie, a retarded youngster they are both trying to reach. *Cast:* David McCallum (Hamilton Cade), Ossie Davis (Charles Carter), Billy Shulman (Freddie), George Grizzard (Putnam), Anthony Jones (Joey). *Producer:* George Lefferts. *Writer:* Allan Sloane. *Director:* Fielder Cook.

**1965 Teahouse of the August Moon.** Comedy, 90 min., NBC, 10/26/62. The story, set on the Japanese island of Okinawa at the end of World War II, follows the U.S. Army's efforts to introduce American culture to the natives of the village of Tobiki. (The title refers to the elegant teahouse that serves the natives.) Based on the play by John Patrick and broadcast on the "Hallmark Hall of Fame." *Cast:* John Forsythe (Captain Fishby), David Wayne (Sakini), Paul Ford (Colonel Wainwright Purdy), William LeMessena (Captain McLean), Fred Kareman (Sergeant Gregovitch), Yuki Shimoda (Mr. Sumata), Armand Alzamora (Mr. Omura), William Hansen (Mr. Oshira), Osceola Archer (Woman in jeep). *Producer-Director:* George Schaefer. *Writer:* Robert Hartung.

**1966 Tears of Joy, Tears of Sorrow.** Documentary, 60 min., ABC, 11/28/86. The program recalls unforgettable moments from television, sports, news, and films that have touched the heart (for example, a 1969 Eastman Kodak commercial that depicted the real-life reunion of a returning Vietnam War soldier with his family and girlfriend; and Hallmark's Christmas Wish commercial that had a lonely little girl asking Santa Claus for her father's love). *Host:* John Forsythe. *Music:* Dan Slider, Harry Eagle. *Producer-Writers:* David Horowitz, Robert Guenette.

### 1967 The Ted Knight Musical Comedy Variety Special. Variety, 60 min., CBS, 11/30/76. Music, songs, and comedy skits with Ted Knight in his only television special. *Host:* Ted Knight. *Guests:* Edward Asner, Rue McClanahan, Fred MacMurray, Ethel Merman, Phil Silvers, Loretta Swit. *Music:* Peter Matz. *Producers:* Ned Shankman, Bob Finkel. *Writers:* Herbert Baker, Mike Marmer, Stan Burns. *Director:* Sid Smith.

### 1968 Teddy Pendergrass in Concert. Variety, 60 min., HBO, 9/11/82. A concert by rock star Teddy Pendergrass. *Host:* Teddy Pendergrass. *Producers:* Peter Abbey, Mike Mansfield. *Director:* Mike Mansfield.

### 1969 Teen Father. Drama, 60 min., ABC, 10/22/86. An "ABC Afterschool Special" about Roy Thomas and Maria Torres, teenagers whose lives are changed forever when Maria gives birth to their baby and they face the harsh realities of unwed parenthood. *Cast:* Corey Parker (Roy Thomas), Christine Langer (Maria Torres), Don Auspitz (John Torres), Janis Dardaris (Mrs. Torres), Emmanuelle LaSalle (Patricia), Rick Barnard (Stan), Jean DeBaer (Ellen), Gene Crane (Father Ruelle). *Producer:* Fran Sears. *Writer:* Jeanne Betancourt. *Director:* Kevin Hooks.

### 1970 Teenage America: The Glory Years. Documentary, 60 min., CBS, 5/23/86. A look at the evolution of the American teenager over the past 50 years as depicted in real life, in film, and on television. *Host:* John Ritter. *Music:* Peggy Sandvig. *Producer:* Bonnie Peterson. *Writers:* Steve Muscarella, David Oyster, Malcolm Leo. *Director:* Malcolm Leo.

### 1971 Tele Theater. Variety, 30 min., NBC, 9/14/47. A mixed bag of variety performances by mostly unknown entertainers. *Performers:* The Briants, The Hartmans, Jumbo, Kitty Kallen, The Mack Triplets, The Minevitch Harmonica Rascals, Rosario and Antonio. *Producer-Director:* Edward Sobol. *Technical Director:* Al Protzman.

### 1972 Television Symphony. Music, 60 min., CBS, 3/20/48. The first network broadcast of a symphony orchestra over television. The one-hour special features the Philadelphia Orchestra under the direction of Eugene Ormandy. *Host:* Carl McDonald. *Guest:* William Paley. *Music Director:* Eugene Ormandy. *Producer:* Norris West.

### 1973 Television's Greatest Commercials. A chronological listing of the four specials that presented a montage of some of television's most memorable commercials over the past 30 years. All are 60 minutes and broadcast by NBC.

**1 Television's Greatest Commercials** (5/25/82). *Hosts:* Tim Conway, Ed McMahon. *Music:* William Goldstein. *Producers:* John J. McMahon, Scott Garen. *Writers:* Jack Weinstein, James Andrew Hall. *Director:* Scott Garen.

**2 Television's Greatest Commercials II** (11/7/82). *Hosts:* Mariette Hartley, Ed McMahon. *Music:* William Goldstein. *Producers:* Joie Albrecht, Scott Garen. *Writer:* Percy Lockwood. *Director:* Scott Garen.

**3 Television's Greatest Commercials III** (5/8/83). *Hosts:* Mariette Hartley, Ed McMahon. *Music:* William Gold-

**Ad for "Television's Greatest Commercials"**

stein. *Producers:* John J. McMahon, Joie Albrecht, Scott Garen. *Writers:* Buz Kohan, Joie Albrecht, Scott Garen. *Director:* Scott Garen.

**4 Television's Greatest Commercials IV** (11/26/83). *Hosts:* Ann Jillian, Ed McMahon. *Music:* William Goldstein. *Producers:* John J. McMahon, Joie Albrecht, Scott Garen. *Writers:* Buz Kohan, Scott Garen, Joie Albrecht. *Director:* Scott Garen.

**1974 Tell Me on a Sunday.**
Musical, 60 min., Syndicated, 4/80. A one-woman concert, created expressly for television, in which Marti Webb portrays a young English girl living in New York and whose bittersweet love affairs are chronicled through song. *Host:* Bill Boggs. *Star:* Marti Webb. *Music:* Andrew Lloyd Webber. *Lyrics:* Don Black. Music performed by the London Philharmonic Orchestra.

**1975 Telly ... Who Loves Ya, Baby?** Variety, 60 min., CBS, 2/18/76. Music, songs, and comedy sketches with Telly Savalas in his first variety special (the title refers to Telly's catchphrase, "Who Loves Ya, Baby?" from his series "Kojak"). *Host:* Telly Savalas. *Guests:* Diahann Carroll, Barbara Eden, Cloris Leachman. *Music:* Marvin Laird. *Producers:* Howard W. Koch, Marty Pasetta. *Writer:* Buz Kohan. *Director:* Marty Pasetta.

**1976 The Tempest.** Comedy-Drama, 90 min., NBC, 2/3/60. A television adaptation of the William Shakespeare play about a former duke (Prospero) and his daughter (Miranda) who become rulers of an enchanted island when the duke is usurped from his throne by his brother, Antonio, and set adrift at sea. Complications set in when, years later, Antonio, now the king of Naples, comes to the island for a visit—unaware that Prospero is its ruler. Broadcast on the "Hallmark Hall of Fame." *Cast:* Maurice Evans (Prospero), Lee Remick (Miranda), Richard Burton (Caliban), Roddy McDowall (Ariel), Tom Poston (Tinculo), Liam Redmond (Gonzalo), Ronald Radd (Stephano), William H. Bassett (Ferdinand), Geoffrey Lumb (Alonso), Paul Ballantyne (Sebastian). *Music:* Lehman Engel. *Producer-Director:* George Schaefer. *Writer:* John Edward Friend.

**1977 Ten Little Indians.** Mystery, 60 min., NBC, 1/18/59. A television adaptation of the novel by Agatha Christie about ten people, summoned to a deserted house on the coast of England, who are taunted by an unknown voice that accuses each of them of murder—then sets out to kill each one of them. Also known as "And Then There Were None." *Cast:* Nina Foch (Vera Claythorne), Barry Jones (Judge Wargrave), Kenneth Haigh (Philip Lombardi), Rommey Brent (Dr. Armstrong), Peter Bathurst (General MacKenzie), Valerie French (Emily Brent), Chandler Cowles (Arthur Marston), James Kenny (Blore), George Turner (Rodgers). *Producer:* David Susskind. *Writer:* Phil Reisman, Jr. *Director:* Paul Bogart.

**1978 Tender Places.** Drama, 30 min., Syndicated, 4/87. The effects of a divorce on a family as seen through the eyes of a young boy (Eric). The story was written by a 13-year-old boy. *Narrator:* Don Wescott. *Cast:* Jean Stapleton (Josephine), Frederick Koehler (Eric), Deborah Hedwall (Mary), Barry Nolan (Paul). *Music:* Mason Daring. *Producer:* Janet Krause. *Writer:* Jason Brown. *Director:* Fred Barzyk.

**1979 Tennessee Ernie Ford Meets King Arthur.** Comedy, 60 min., NBC, 5/10/60. When a clause in his contract forces him to become a guinea pig of a scientist demonstrating a time machine on television, singer-comedian Tennessee Ernie Ford is whisked back in time—to England and the days of King Arthur. The story, adapted from *A Connecticut Yankee in King Arthur's Court* by Mark Twain, relates Ernie's adventures as he attempts to find his way back to the present (1960). *Cast:* Tennessee Ernie Ford (Himself), Vincent Price (Sir Boris), Alan Young (Clarence), Alan Mowbray (King Arthur), Robert Emhardt (Professor), John Dehner (Commentator), Addison Richards (Doctor), Danny Arnold (Fricke). *Producers:* Hubbell Robinson, Roland Kibbee. *Writer:* Roland Kibbee. *Director:* Lee J. Cobb.

**1980 Tennessee Ernie Ford Specials.** A chronological listing of the variety specials hosted by singer Tennessee Ernie Ford. All are 60 minutes and broadcast by NBC.

**1 Tennessee Ernie Ford Meets King Arthur** (5/10/60). See entry for details.

**2 The Tennessee Ernie Ford Special** (12/3/67). *Guests:* Andy Griffith, Don Knotts, Diana Ross and the Supremes, Danny Thomas. *Music:* Jack Fascinato. *Producers:* George Schlatter, Carolyn Raskin. *Writers:* Sheldon Keller, Digby Wolfe. *Director:* Dean Whitmore.

**3 The Tennessee Ernie Ford Special** (11/16/68). *Guests:* Lucille Ball, The Golddiggers, Andy Griffith. *Producers:* Greg Garrison, Don Van Atta. *Director:* Robert Sidney.

**4 Sing America Beautiful** (5/19/71). *Guests:* Diahann Carroll, Arlene Golonka, The Smothers Brothers, Danny Thomas. *Producers:* Digby Wolfe, Bob Wynn. *Writers:* Tommy Koch, Bob Ornott, James R. Stein, Robert Illes, Digby Wolfe. *Director:* Bob Wynn.

**5 Tennessee Ernie Ford's White Christmas** (12/23/72). *Guests:* Lynn Anderson, Mac Davis, Claudine Longet, The Mike Curb Congregation, Lou Rawls. *Music:* Jack Fascinato. *Producers:* Roy A. Smith, Bill Williams. *Writers:* Bud Wingard, Jim Carlson. *Director:* Joseph Hostettler.

**6 Tennessee Ernie's Nashville–Moscow Express** (1/8/75). Highlights of a series of country and western concerts taped in September 1974 in the USSR. *Guests:* The Beriozka Troupe, Sandi Burnett. *Producer-Director:* Bob Wynn. *Writer:* Howard Leeds.

## 1981 Tennessee Williams' South. Documentary, 80 min., PBS, 12/14/76. The program explores the South as depicted in plays by Tennessee Williams. Excerpts from his plays are presented to heighten the story. *Host:* Tennessee Williams. *Performers:* John Colicos, Colleen Dewhurst, Burl Ives, Maureen Stapleton, Jessica Tandy, Michael York. *Producer-Director:* Harry Rasky. *Writer:* Tennessee Williams.

## 1982 The Terrible Secret. Drama, 60 min., ABC, 3/7/79. One foggy night while driving home, a teenage girl named Bobbie Marston hits a paper boy with her van. Scared and not knowing what to do, she drives him to the hospital, but flees without reporting the incident to the police. Though the accident was not her fault (the boy ran in front of her van), she fears someone will discover her "terrible secret." The story portrays her torment—until her conscience gets the better of her and she turns herself in. Aired as an "ABC Afterschool Special." *Cast:* Linda Adams (Bobbie Marston), Michael Biehn (Seth), Inga Swenson (Mrs. Mar-

ston), Laurence Haddon (Mr. Marston), Dawn Jeffory (Lola Marston), Peggy Rae (Mrs. Atwater), John Waldron (Boy). *Music:* Glenn Paxton. *Producers:* Daniel Wilson, Fran Sears. *Writer:* George Malko. *Director:* Larry Elikann.

## 1983 Terrible Things My Mother Told Me. Drama, 60 min., ABC, 1/20/88. A tender "ABC Afterschool Special" about the impact of emotional child abuse as seen through the experiences of Julia Flemming, a 16-year-old girl who longs for the affections of her mother (Eleanor), but seems to receive nothing but verbal abuse. *Cast:* Katherine Kamhi (Julia Flemming), Beth Howland (Eleanor Flemming), Ita De Marco (Katie Flemming), Ian Zeiring (Randy Forrester), Stephen James (Tom Bacharan), Carol Goodheart (Mary Forrester), Stephanie Winters (Beth). *Music:* Brent Havens. *Producer:* Susan Rohrer. *Writer:* Chris Whitesell. *Director:* Susan Rohrer.

## 1984 Terror from Within. Thriller, 90 min., ABC, 3/3/75. The story of Abby Stevens, a visitor to an artist's colony who is haunted by visions and voices that tell her of a murder. Also known as "Won't Write Home, Mom—I'm Dead." *Cast:* Pamela Franklin (Abby Stevens), Ian Bannen (Frank Dean), Suzanne Neve (Beryl Whittaker), Oliver Tobias (Alan Smerdon), Lesley North (Janet Sadler), Dallas Adams (Douglas Sadler). *Music:* Laurie Johnson. *Producers:* Cecil Clarke, Ian Fordyce. *Writer:* Dennis Spooner. *Director:* James Ormerod.

## 1985 Testing Dirty. Drama, 60 min., ABC, 10/18/90. An "ABC Afterschool Special" that explores the issue of mandatory drug testing programs in high schools with a focus on a student (Will) who tests positive—but is not using drugs and has not used them. *Cast:* Christopher Daniel Barnes (Will), Lisa

Dean Ryan (Carla), Alley Mills (Linda), A Martinez (Emanuel Jensen), Art Le-Fleur (Mr. Stone). *Music:* Peter Melnick. *Producer:* Diane Asselin. *Writer:* Bruce Harmon. *Director:* Lynn Hamrick.

### 1986 Texaco Command Performance. 
Variety, 60 min., NBC, 9/19/57. A salute to comedian Ed Wynn on the anniversary of his fifty-fifth year in showbusiness. Sponsored by Texaco Gasoline. *Hosts:* Alfred Drake, Oscar Hammerstein II, Keenan Wynn. *Special Guest:* Ed Wynn. *Guests:* Rod Alexander, Steve Allen, Ralph Bellamy, Mimi Benzell, Janet Blair, Billie Burke, Jill Corey, Beatrice Lillie, Bambi Linn, Jack Palance. *Music:* Paul Weston. *Producer:* Ezra Stone. *Director:* Charles S. Dubin.

### 1987 Texaco Command Performance. 
Variety, 60 min., NBC, 11/23/57. A musical tribute to Ethel Barrymore. Sponsored by Texaco Gasoline. *Special Guest:* Ethel Barrymore. *Guests:* Roy Campanella, Claudette Colbert, Joseph Cotten, Leo Durocher, Dolores Gray, Fred Haney, David Niven, Casey Stengel, Orson Welles. *Music:* Paul Weston. *Producer-Director:* Burt Shevelove. *Writer:* Ralph Blane.

### 1988 Texaco Star Parade I. 
Variety, 60 min., CBS, 6/4/64. A program of music and songs based on the musical compositions of composer Meredith Wilson. Sponsored by Texaco. See the following title also. *Hosts:* Meredith Wilson, Rini Wilson. *Guests:* Sergio Franchi, Caterina Valente, The Young Americans. *Music:* Frank De-Vol. *Producers:* Meredith Wilson, George Schlatter. *Writers:* Saul Ilson, Keith Fowler. *Director:* Bill Hobin.

### 1989 Texaco Star Parade II. 
Variety, 60 min., CBS, 7/28/64. A sequel to the above special. An additional hour of music and songs based on the works of Meredith Wilson. *Hosts:* Meredith Wilson, Rini Wilson. *Guests:* Vikki Carr, Jack Jones. *Music:* Harry Zimmerman. *Producers:* Meredith Wilson, George Schlatter. *Writers:* Saul Ilson, Keith Fowler. *Director:* Dwight Hemion.

### 1990 Texaco Star Theater: Opening Night. 
Variety, 90 min., NBC, 9/11/82. A music and song salute to the American musical theater. *Performers:* Debbie Allen, Steve Allen, Ken Berry, Carol Burnett, Sammy Davis Jr., Pam Dawber, Placido Domingo, Zsa Zsa Gabor, Robert Guillaume, Ann Jillian, Ethel Merman, Joe Namath, Donald O'Connor, Bernadette Peters, Charles Nelson Reilly, John Schneider, Loretta Swit. *Music:* Bill Byers. *Producers:* Marty Pasetta, Kenny Solms. *Writers:* Ann Elder, Fritz Holt, Kenny Solms. *Director:* Marty Pasetta.

### 1991 Texas 150 — A Celebration. 
Variety, 2 hrs., ABC, 4/28/86. A star-studded celebration for the Lone Star State on the occasion of its one hundred fiftieth birthday. *Guests:* Ana Alicia, Gene Autry, Johnny Cash, Van Cliburn, Lydia Cornell, Walter Cronkite, Mac Davis, Jimmy Dean, Sam Donaldson, Sandy Duncan, Morgan Fairchild, Larry Gatlin, Phyllis George, Katherine Helmond, John Hillerman, Jennifer Holliday, Tommy Lee Jones, Kris Kristofferson, Tom Landry, Johnny Lee, Steve Martin, Don Meredith, The Mighty Clouds of Joy, Gary Morris, Michael Martin Murphy, Martina Navratilova, Willie Nelson, Dennis Quaid, Phylicia Rashad, Ginger Rogers, Jaclyn Smith, Sissy Spacek, Roger Staubach, B. J. Thomas, Tommy Tune, The University of Texas Marching Band. *Music:* James Gaeterer, Paul Kelly. *Producers:* William Carruthers, Bill Starnes, Joseph Cates. *Writers:* Chet Hagan, Frank Slocum. *Director:* Joseph Cates.

## 1992 A Thanksgiving Reunion with the Partridge Family and My Three Sons. Variety, 60 min., ABC, 11/25/77.

Cast members from the series "The Partridge Family" and "My Three Sons" gather to celebrate Thanksgiving with clips from their respective series. *Hosts:* Shirley Jones, Fred MacMurray. *Partridge Family Members:* Danny Bonaduce, David Cassidy, Suzanne Crough, Susan Dey, Shirley Jones. *My Three Sons Members:* Tina Cole, Tim Considine, William Demarest, Beverly Garland, Don Grady, Barry Livingston, Stanley Livingston, Fred MacMurray, Meredith MacRae, Ronne Troup. *Music:* Lenny Stack. *Producers:* Dick Clark, Al Schwartz. *Writers:* Bob Sand, Bo Kaprall. *Director:* Perry Rosemond.

## 1993 The Thanksgiving Treasure. Drama, 90 min., CBS, 11/18/73.

The second of four specials about life in Nebraska in the 1940s, as seen through the experiences of the Mills family (see also "Addie and the King of Hearts," "The Easter Promise," and "The House Without a Christmas Tree"). The story follows Addie Mills, the 11-year-old daughter of widower James Mills, as she attempts to befriend Mr. Rhenquist, a bitter old man who is an enemy of her gruff father. (The title is derived from Addie's experiences, winning Rhenquist's friendship just before Thanksgiving, as she cares for his horse, Treasure.) *Cast:* Jason Robards (James Mills), Lisa Lucas (Addie Mills), Mildred Natwick (Grandmother Mills), Barnard Hughes (Mr. Rhenquist), Kathryn Walker (Miss Thompson), Larry Reynolds (Uncle Will), Kay Hawtrey (Aunt Nora), Cec Linder (Aaron Burkhart). *Producer:* Alan Shayne. *Writer:* Eleanor Perry. *Director:* Paul Bogart.

## 1994 The Thanksgiving Visitor. Drama, 60 min., ABC, 11/28/68.

A sequel to "A Christmas Memory" (see title) and a second autobiographical drama by novelist Truman Capote. The story, set in rural Alabama, tells of Buddy (Capote as a boy) and his Aunt Sookie and their efforts to provide a happy Thanksgiving for each other. The title refers to Odd Henderson, an older boy who delights in taunting Buddy—and whom Sookie has invited to dinner. *Cast:* Geraldine Page (Aunt Sookie), Michael Kearney (Buddy), Hansford Rowe (Odd Henderson). *Music:* Meyer Kupferman. *Producer-Director:* Frank Perry. *Writer:* Eleanor Perry.

## 1995 That Funny Fat Kid. Drama, 30 min., Syndicated, 5/86.

The dangers of dieting as seen through the experiences of Tony DeLuca, an overweight teenager who seeks quick weight loss by stealing his sister's diet pills. *Cast:* Chris Russo (Tony DeLuca), Kaye Ballard (Maria DeLuca), Paul Palmisono (Mr. DeLuca), Kristin Stephens (Kim), Sarah Simon (Theresa). *Music:* Dave Wayne. *Producers:* Tom G. Robertson, Gene McPherson. *Writer-Director:* Tom G. Robertson.

## 1996 That Second Thing on ABC. Comedy, 60 min., ABC, 3/8/78.

A sequel to "That Thing on ABC" (see title) that features performances by new comedy talents. *Guests:* Dr. Joyce Brothers, Bert Parks, Danielle Spencer, Dick Van Patten. *Performers:* Irv Burton, Judy Carter, Denny Evans, Shelley Long, Andrea Martin, Mandy Patinkin, Tim Thomerson, Paul Tracey, Deborah Zon. *Producers:* Bernie Kukoff, Jeff Harris. *Writers:* Bo Kaprall, Bob Sand, Valri Bromfield, Terry Hart, Jim Brecher, Scott McGibbon. *Director:* Tony Mordente.

## 1997 That Thing on ABC. Comedy, 60 min., ABC, 1/4/78.

An hour of fast-paced comedy featuring new comedy talent. See also "That Second Thing on ABC." *Guests:* Bill Bixby,

Cheryl Ladd, John Ritter, John Cameron Swayze, Henny Youngman. *Performers:* Judy Carter, Denny Evans, Shelley Long, Andrea Martin, Mandy Patinkin, Will Porter, Paul Tracey, Marsha Warfield, Deborah Zon. *Music:* Peter Matz. *Producers:* Bernie Kukoff, Jeff Harris. *Writers:* Bernie Kukoff, Jeff Harris, Valri Bromfield, Ray Taylor, Allyn Warner. *Director:* Tim Kiley.

## 1998 That Was the Year That Was. Comedy, 60 min., ABC, 1/4/73.

A satirical review of 1972. *Hosts:* Jack Burns, Avery Schreiber. *Guests:* Art Buchwald, William F. Buckley, Jr., David Frost, George S. Irving. *Music:* Dick Hyman. *Producer:* Charles Andrews. *Writers:* Gary Belkin, David Axelrod, Tony Geiss, Thomas Meehan. *Director:* Arthur Forrest.

## 1999 That Was the Year That Was. Comedy, 90 min., NBC, 12/26/76.

A satirical review of the major events of 1976. *Hosts:* Blythe Danner, Buck Henry, Robert Klein, Brenda Vaccaro. *Guests:* James Coco, William Daniels, Ruth Gordon, Tammy Grimes, Estelle Parsons, Rex Reed, Gloria Steinem. *Music:* Joe Raposo. *Producers:* Irv Wilson, Herman Rush, Burt Shevelove, Frank Badami. *Writers:* Tony Geiss, Tom Meehan, Art Buchwald, Jules Pfeiffer, Gloria Steinem, Lynn Roth, Jonathan Reynolds, Harvey Jacobs. *Director:* Don Mischer.

## 2000 That's What Friends Are For. Variety, 2 hrs., CBS, 4/17/90.

A musical celebration that marks the fifteenth anniversary of Arista Records. *Hosts:* Lauren Bacall, Chevy Chase, Jane Curtin, Michael Douglas, Whoopi Goldberg, Melanie Griffith. *Guests:* Air Supply, Burt Bacharach, Eric Carmen, Taylor Dane, The Four Tops, Jennifer Holliday, Whitney Houston, Alan Jackson, Kenny G, Melissa Manchester, Barry Manilow,

Carly Simon, Patti Smith, Lisa Stansfield, Milli Vanilli, Dionne Warwick. *Music:* Leon Pendarois. *Producers:* Clive Davis, Scott Sanders. *Writers:* Bob Schaetzle, Bruce Vilanch. *Director:* Bruce Gowers.

## 2001 Theater '62. Anthology, 60 min., NBC, 10/4/61 to 4/8/62.

A series of specials commemorating the film legacy of producer David O. Selznick. Each of the titles is adapted from one of his films. See the following titles for details: "The Farmer's Daughter," "Intermezzo," "Notorious," "The Paradine Case," "Rebecca," "Spellbound," and "The Spiral Staircase." *Host:* Jinx Falkenberg.

## 2002 There Shall Be No Night. Drama, 90 min., NBC, 3/17/57.

A "Hallmark Hall of Fame" presentation about an Hungarian family caught up in the Soviet invasion of their country in 1956. Based on the Broadway play. *Cast:* Charles Boyer (Dr. Kurloy Valkay), Katherine Cornell (Miranda Valkay), Ray Walston (Dave Corween), Bradford Dillman (Eric Valkay), Theodore Bikel (Uncle Vlahos), Phillis Love (Katalin Tor), Karel Stepanek (Major Rutowski), Val Avery (Gus Shuman), Gerald Hiken (Frank Olmstead). *Producer-Director:* George Schaefer. *Writer:* Morton Wishengrad.

## 2003 There Were Times, Dear. Drama, 60 min., PBS, 6/3/87.

A sensitive reality drama about the effects Alzheimer's disease (a brain disorder) has on one family. *Cast:* Shirley Jones (Susanne Millard), Len Cariou (Bob Millard), Cynthia Eilbacher (Jenny Reed), Mark Harrison (Tom Reed), Judith Barsi (Molly Reed), Dana Elcar (Don Mason), Claudette Nevins (Carrie Mason), Nancy Malone (Louise), Steve Franken (Harry). *Special Guest:* Bob Hope (spokesman for Alzheimer's disease). *Music:* Jay Gruska. *Producers:* Linda Hope, Nancy

Malone. *Writer:* Harry Cauley. *Director:* Nancy Malone.

## 2004 There's No Time for Love, Charlie Brown. Cartoon, 30 min., CBS, 3/11/73. A hectic day in the life of the Peanuts gang is recalled through essay tests, Peppermint Patty's crush on Charlie, and a misguided field trip. *Voices:* Chad Webber (Charlie Brown), Stephen Shea (Linus), Robin Kohn (Lucy), Kip DeFaria (Peppermint Patty), Hilary Momberger (Sally), Jimmy Ahrens (Marcie), Todd Barbee (Franklin), Jeff Bailey (Schroeder), Bill Melendez (Snoopy). *Music:* Vince Guaraldi. *Producers:* Lee Mendelson, Bill Melendez. *Writer:* Charles M. Schulz. *Director:* Bill Melendez.

## 2005 They Said It with Music: Yankee Doodle to Ragtime. Variety, 2 hrs., CBS, 7/4/77. A salute to American songwriters. *Hosts:* Bernadette Peters, Tony Randall, Jason Robards, Jean Stapleton, Flip Wilson. *Guests:* Ladd Anderson, Robert Babb, Teddy Buckner, Tammi Bula, Michael Dees, Art Evans, Donna Fein, Tammy Glenn, Bill Lee, Jay Meyer, Thurl Ravenscroft, Vi Redd. *Music:* Fred Karlin. *Producers:* Goddard Lieberson, Bob Henry. *Writers:* Max Wilk, Goddard Lieberson. *Director:* Bob Henry.

## 2006 Think Pretty. Musical Comedy, 60 min., NBC, 10/2/64. The story of Fred Adams, a former dancer who is now the owner of a record company, and his efforts to sign comedian Mickey Marshall as a client—despite the fact that his rival, Tony Franklin, is seeking the same man for her record company. *Cast:* Fred Astaire (Fred Adams), Barrie Chase (Tony Franklin), Louis Nye (Mickey Marshall), Roger Perry (Dan Corbin), Linda Foster (Lori Adams), Reta Shaw (Head nurse), Edward Mallory (Quinn Randall), Eddie Ryder (Shelley), Jack Bernardi (Patient). *Producer:* Richard Lewis. *Writers:* Garry Marshall, Jerry Belson. *Director:* Jack Arnold.

## 2007 The Third Barry Manilow Special. Variety, 60 min., ABC, 5/23/79. An hour of music and songs with singer Barry Manilow. See also "The Barry Manilow Special" and "The Second Barry Manilow Special." *Host:* Barry Manilow. *Guest:* John Denver. *Music:* Jimmie Haskell. *Producer-Writers:* Ernest Chambers, Barry Manilow. *Director:* Don Mischer.

## The Third Bill Cosby Special *see* Bill Cosby Specials

## 2008 35 Years of Magic Disneyland. Documentary, 60 min., Syndicated, 7/4/90. A fascinating look at the history of the Disneyland theme park in California through film clips from its past. *Host:* Harry Anderson. *Producer:* Brad Lachman. *Writer:* Turk Pipkin. *Director:* Gary Halvorson.

## 2009 The 36 Most Beautiful Girls in Texas. Variety, 60 min., ABC, 9/24/78. Music, songs, and comedy with the Dallas Cowboys Cheerleaders. *Host:* Hal Linden. *Guests:* Billy Crystal, Melinda Naud, Charles Nelson Reilly, Joey Travolta. *Producers:* Merrill Grant, John Hamlin, Bob Wynn. *Writer:* Bob Arnott. *Director:* Bob Wynn. *Cheerleaders Director:* Suzanne Mitchell.

## 2010 33⅓ Revolutions Per Monkee. Variety, 60 min., NBC, 4/14/69. An hour of music, songs, and comedy with the rock group The Monkees. *Hosts:* Mickey Dolenz, Davy Jones, Mike Nesmith, Peter Tork. *Guests:* Brian Auger, The Buddy Miles Express, The Clara Ward Singers, Fats Domino, Julie Driscoll, Jerry Lee Lewis, Little Richard. *Producers:* Ward Sylvester, Jack Good, Art Fisher.

*Writer:* Jack Good, Art Fisher. *Director:* Art Fisher.

## 2011 This Is America, Charlie Brown. Cartoon, 30 min. (each segment), CBS, 10/21/88 to 5/23/89. A series of eight animated specials that take Charlie Brown back in time (and into the future) to discover the events that shaped the nation. The episodes: "The Mayflower Voyagers" (10/21/88), "The Birth of the Constitution" (10/28/88), "The Wright Brothers at Kitty Hawk" (11/4/88), "The NASA Space Station" (11/11/88), "The Building of the Transcontinental Railroad" (2/10/89), "The Great Inventors" (3/10/89), "The Smithsonian and the Presidency" (4/19/89), and "The Music and Heroes of America" (5/23/89). *Voices:* Bud Davis, Ami Foster, Keri Houlihan, Christina Lange, Bill Melendez, Jason Mendelson, Jeremy Miller, Chuck Olson, Jason Riffle, Hal Smith, Frank Welker. *Music:* Dave Brubeck. *Producers:* Lee Mendelson, Bill Melendez. *Writers:* Charles M. Schulz, Lee Mendelson. *Directors:* Evert Brown, Sam Grimes.

## 2012 This Is Garth Brooks. Variety, 60 min., NBC, 1/17/92. An hour of country and western music and songs with singer Garth Brooks in his first television special. Includes behind-the-scenes concert footage and highlights of performances at Reunion Arena in Dallas, Texas. *Host:* Garth Brooks. *Producers:* Bud Schaetzle, Martin Fischer. *Director:* Bud Schaetzle.

## 2013 This Is Michael Bolton. Variety, 60 min., NBC, 10/28/92. Videotaped highlights of singer Michael Bolton's concert at Chicago's historic Arie Crown Theater. *Host:* Michael Bolton. *Band:* Joey Melotti (keyboards), Chris Camozzi (guitar), Schuyler Deale (bass), Mugs Cain (drums), Joe Turano (sax). *Backup Vocals:* Pat Hawk, Vann Johnson,

Janie Liebart. *Music Director:* Joey Melotti. *Orchestra:* David Foster. *Producers:* Bud Schaetzle, Michael Bolton, Louis Levin. *Director:* Bud Schaetzle.

## 2014 This Is Your Life 30th Anniversary Special. Tribute, 2 hrs., NBC, 2/26/81. A review (via film clips) of the series "This Is Your Life" (NBC, 1952–61) on the occasion of its thirtieth anniversary. *Hosts:* Ralph Edwards, David Frost. *Producers:* Ralph Edwards, David Frost, Andy Friendly. *Writers:* Frank Buxton, Ed Haas, Andy Friendly. *Director:* Bruce Gowers.

## 2015 This Time It's Personal—Jaws: The Revenge. Documentary, 30 min., Syndicated, 7/17/87. A behind-the-scenes look at the making of the film *Jaws: The Revenge.* The program also explores the great white shark and people's fears of sharks. *Guests:* Mitchell Anderson, Michael Caine, Lorraine Gary, Lance Guest, Diane Hatfield, Jordan Klein, Dr. John McCosker, Pete Romano, Joseph Sargent, Mario Van Peebles, Lynn Whitfield, Karen Young. *Producers:* George Zaloom, Les Mayfield. *Writer-Director:* William Rus.

## 2016 This Time Next Year. Comedy-Drama, 75 min., NBC, 9/14/47. A fantasy tale that revolves around an aristocratic Southern politician with a 50-year dream to build a monument to the Confederacy that will outshine Grant's Tomb. *Cast:* John Becker, Kendall Clark, Percy Helton, Mary Alice Moore, Leona Powers, Vaughn Taylor, Frank Thomas, Frank Wilson. *Producer-Director:* Fred Coe. *Remote Director:* Garry Simpson.

## 2017 This Will Be the Year That Will Be. Comedy, 60 min., ABC, 1/5/73. A satirical prediction of what will happen in the months that follow this January 1973 broadcast.

*Hosts:* Jack Burns, Avery Schreiber. *Guests:* Selma Diamond, Kelly Garrett, Dick Gautier, Nita Talbot. *Music:* Dick Hyman. *Producer:* Charles Andrews. *Writers:* Gary Belkin, Tony Geiss, Thomas Meehan. *Director:* Arthur Forrest.

## 2018 Those Fabulous Clowns.

Documentary, 40 min., HBO, 2/4/84. A nostalgic look at the history of clowns — from real-life clowns to the vaudeville and movie comedians. *Host-Narrator:* Richard Kiley. *Theme Vocal,* "Be a Clown": Liza Minnelli. *Producers:* Richard Barclay, Robert Deubel, Gabey Monet. *Director:* Coleman Jacoby.

## 2019 Those Wonderful TV Game Shows.

Documentary, 60 min., NBC, 2/27/84. A nostalgic look at some of the game shows that have been broadcast on television over the past thirty years. *Host:* Carl Reiner. *Guests:* Ralph Edwards, George Fenneman, Monty Hall, Betty White. *Announcers:* Don Pardo, Rod Roddy. *Music:* Bob Alberti. *Producers:* Eric Ellenbogen, Andrew Solt. *Writers:* Peter Tomarken, Andrew Solt. *Director:* Andrew Solt.

## 2020 Three for the Girls.

Comedy-Drama, 90 min., CBS, 11/5/73. The overall title for three one-act plays. "Raincheck," the first story, a drama, focuses on a husband and wife who decide to get a divorce after 16 years of marriage; the second story, "Clothes Make the Girl," is a musical comedy about a man from a small town who is shocked to see his daughter acting in a nude play; and "Sonny Boy," the concluding play, comically relates the efforts of a son to tell his mother that he is moving to another state. *Cast:* ("Raincheck"): Carroll O'Connor (Husband), Lee Remick (Wife); ("Clothes Make the Girl"): Carroll O'Connor (Father), Barbara Sharma (Judy, the daughter), Nancy Walker (Ida), T. J. Sullivan (Peter); ("Sonny Boy"): Carroll O'Connor (Son), Joan Blondell (Mother). *Music:* Marvin Hamlisch. *Producer:* Robert H. Precht. *Writer:* "Raincheck": Carroll O'Connor; "Clothes Make the Girl": Fred Ebb, John Kander; "Sonny Boy": Rob Reiner, Phil Mishkin. *Director:* Bob LaHendro.

## 2021 Three for Tonight.

Variety, 60 min., CBS, 6/22/55. A showcase for dancers Marge and Gower Champion and singer Harry Belafonte as they perform material associated with their careers. *Hosts:* Harry Belafonte, Gower Champion, Marge Champion. *Guests:* Betty Benson (vocalist), The Voices of Walter Schumann. *Music Director:* Walter Schumann. *Music Conductor:* Richard Pribor. *Producer:* Paul Gregory. *Writer:* William Nichols. *Director:* Gower Champion.

## 2022 Three in One.

Comedy-Drama, 90 min., NBC, 2/5/60. The overall title for the one-act plays featuring Art Carney. "A Pound on Demand" tells of an inebriated workman who attempts to get money from his Post Office account; "Where the Cross Is Made" relates a man's efforts to get his father, a sea captain, committed to a mental institution; and "Red Peppers" relates the trials and tribulations of a constantly bickering English music-hall team. *Cast:* (**"A Pound on Demand"**): Art Carney (Sammy), Myron McCormick (Jerry); (**"Where the Cross Is Made"**): Art Carney (Nat), Frank Conroy (Captain Isaiah Bartlett), Frances Sternhagen (Sue); (**"Red Peppers"**): Art Carney (George Pepper), Elaine Stritch (Lily Pepper). *Producers:* Robert Alan Arthur, David Susskind. *Writers:* (**"A Pound on Demand"**): Sean O'Casey; (**"Where the Cross Is Made"**): Eugene O'Neill; (**"Red Peppers"**): Noel Coward. *Director:* Tom Donovan.

## 2023 The Three Musketeers.

Adventure, 2 hrs., CBS, 11/30 and 12/1/

60. The story, set in Paris during the 1620s, relates the adventures of D'Artagnan, an expert swordsman and head of the King's Musketeers (Athos, Aramis, and Porthos). The focal point of the adaptation of the novel by Alexandre Dumas is the musketeers' efforts to save the court of King Louis XIII from Cardinal Richelieu, who desperately seeks to become ruler. *Cast:* Maximilian Schell (D'Artagnan), Barry Morse (Athos), Tim O'Connor (Aramis), John Colicos (Porthos), Vincent Price (Richelieu), Felicia Farr (Constance), George Macready (King Louis XIII), Patricia Cutts (Milady de Winter), Thayer David (DeTreville), Polly Rowles (Mme. de Guisse), Joan Tetzel (Queen Anne), Mark Lenard (Jusac). *Producers:* David Susskind, Jacqueline Babbin. *Writer:* George Baxter. *Director:* Tom Donovan.

### 2024 The Tim Conway Special.

Comedy, 60 min., CBS, 3/17/70. A fast-paced hour of comedy skits and blackouts. *Host:* Tim Conway. *Guests:* Carol Burnett, Joe Flynn, Harvey Korman, Danny Thomas. *Music:* Harry Zimmerman. *Producer:* Joe Hamilton. *Writers:* Arne Rosen, Stan Burns, Mike Marmer. *Director:* Dave Powers.

### 2025 Time for Elizabeth.

Comedy-Drama, 60 min., NBC, 4/24/64. After working 28 years for the Snowdrift Washing Machine Company, Ed Davis decides to quit and enjoy life. The story, which marks the first dramatic appearance of Groucho Marx and his wife, Kathryn Eames, follows the efforts of Ed and his wife, Kay, as they move to Florida to enjoy retirement. *Cast:* Groucho Marx (Ed Davis), Kathryn Eames (Kay Davis), Eden Marx (Vivian Morgan), Carole Wells (Aime), John Considine (Richard Coburn), Roland Winters (Walter Schaffer). *Producer-Director:* Ezra Stone. *Writer:* Alex Gottlieb.

### 2026 Time Out for Ginger.

Comedy, 60 min., CBS, 10/6/55. Following a speech in which Harold Carol advocates freedom of individuality, his tomboyish daughter, Ginger, decides to join the school's all-male football team. The story relates Harold's efforts to stand by his daughter's decision, despite opposition from all concerned, and Ginger's growth from tomboy to young woman. *Cast:* Jack Benny (Howard Carol), Janet Parker (Ginger Carol), Ruth Hussey (Agnes Carol), Gary Crosby (Eddie Davis), Ronnie Burns (Tommy Carol), Edward Everett Horton (Ed Hoffman), Mary Wickes (Lizzie), Fred Keating (W. J. Archer). *Producer-Director:* Ralph Levy. *Writers:* Hugh Wedlock, Howard Snyder, Jack Tackaberry.

### 2027 Time Remembered.

Drama, 90 min., NBC, 2/7/61. A sentimental "Hallmark Hall of Fame" presentation about a prince (Albert) and the grief he bears for Leocadia Gordi, his lost love, a beautiful ballerina who died three years earlier. *Cast:* Christopher Plummer (Prince Albert), Edith Evans (Duchess), Janet Munro (Amanda), Barry Jones (Lord Hector), Sybil Bowan (Mme. Rensada), Sig Arno (Ferdinand), Paul Hartman (Landlord). *Producer-Director:* George Schaefer. *Writer:* Theodore Apstein (based on a play by Patricia Moyes).

### 2028 Time Travel: Fact, Fiction and Fantasy.

Documentary, 60 min., Syndicated, 7/85. The program explores the imaginative dimensions of time travel and the way Hollywood has presented the subject (via film clips). *Host-Narrator:* Michael J. Fox. *Music:* Phil Davis. *Producers:* Bob Gale, Suzanne McCafferty, Gale Hollenbaugh. *Writer:* Rick Sublett. *Directors:* Gale Hollenbaugh, Suzanne McCafferty.

### 2029 The Timex All-Star Jazz Show I.

Variety, 60 min., NBC, 12/30/57. Performances by jazz musicians.

Sponsored by Timex watches and billed as "The first sponsored jazz concert on TV." *Host:* Steve Allen. *Performers:* Louis Armstrong, Dave Brubeck, June Christy, Cozy Cole, Duke Ellington, Bobby Hackett, Woody Herman, Gene Krupa, Carmen MacRae, Jack Teagarden. *Producer:* Larry White. *Writer:* George T. Simon. *Director:* Dwight Hemion.

## 2030 The Timex All-Star Jazz Show II.
Variety, 60 min., CBS, 4/30/58. A second concert by jazz musicians; sponsored by Timex watches. *Host:* Garry Moore. *Performers:* Henry "Red" Allen, Louis Armstrong, The Gerry Mulligan Quartet, Lionel Hampton, Gene Krupa, Jaye P. Morgan, Marty Napoleon, George Shearing. *Producers:* Lawrence White, Bill Hobin. *Writer:* George T. Simon. *Director:* Bill Hobin.

## 2031 The Timex All-Star Jazz Show III.
Variety, 60 min., CBS, 11/10/58. A third jazz concert sponsored by Timex watches. *Hosts:* Hoagy Carmichael, Bob Crosby. *Performers:* Louis Armstrong, Bob Crosby's Wildcats, Chico Hamilton and His Quintet, Lionel Hampton, Gene Krupa, Les Brown and His Orchestra, Jaye P. Morgan, Anita O'Day. *Producers:* Lawrence White, Garth Dietrick, Marshall Stone. *Writer:* George T. Simon. *Director:* Garth Dietrick.

## 2032 The Timex All-Star Jazz Show IV.
Variety, 60 min., CBS, 1/7/59. Performances by jazz musicians and sponsored by Timex watches. The last in a series of four specials. *Host:* Jackie Gleason. *Performers:* Cat Anderson, Louis Armstrong, Harry Carney, Vic Dickenson, Duke Ellington, Dizzy Gillespie, Bobby Hackett, Johnny Hodges, Jo Jones, Gene Krupa, Ruth Olay. *Producers:* Lawrence White, Bill Hobin. *Writer:* George T. Simon. *Director:* Bill Hobin.

## 2033 Timex Presents Love from A to Z.
Variety, 60 min., NBC, 4/30/74. An hour of music and songs with Liza Minnelli and Charles Aznavour. Sponsored by Timex watches. *Hosts:* Charles Aznavour, Liza Minnelli. *Producers:* Burt Rosen, Ernest Glucksman. *Writer:* Donald Ross. *Director:* Mel Stuart.

## 2034 Tin Pan Alley Today.
Variety, 60 min., NBC, 10/11/67. An hour of music, songs, and comedy. *Host:* George Burns. *Guests:* Nancy Ames, Dick Cavett, Harpers Bizarre, Sergio Mendes and Brasil '66, Tony Tanner, Dionne Warwick. *Producers:* Gary Smith, Dwight Hemion. *Writers:* Frank Peppiatt, John Aylesworth, Jack Burns, Pat McCormick. *Director:* Dwight Hemion.

## 2035 Tina Turner: Break Every Rule.
Variety, 60 min., HBO, 3/14/87. Rock singer Tina Turner performs songs from her album *Break Every Rule*. *Host:* Tina Turner. *Guests:* Robert Cray, Max Headroom. *Band:* James Ralston (guitar-vocalist), Jack Bruno (drums), Bob Feit (bass guitar), Laurie Weisfeld (guitar), Gary Branacle (sax). *Music Directors:* Alan Clark, John Hudson. *Producers:* Roger Davies, Jacqui Bylord. *Director:* David Mallet.

## 2036 Tina Turner in Concert.
Variety, 60 min., HBO, 6/8/85. A concert by rock star Tina Turner from England's Birmingham Stadium. *Host:* Tina Turner. *Guests:* Bryan Adams, David Bowie. *Band:* Jack Bruno (drums), Tim Capello (keyboards, sax and percussion), Bob Feit (bass guitar), Kenny Moore (piano), James Ralston (lead guitar), James West-Oram (guitar). *Producers:* Jacqui Bylord, Roger Davies. *Director:* David Ballard.

## 2037 The Tiny Tree.
Christmas, 30 min., CBS, 12/18/77. One spring, a lonely little girl, prevented by

an accident from running and playing with other children, moves with her family into a farmhouse near a small whispering pine (the tree of the title). As the days pass, the forest animals and the pine tree befriend the girl. Together they begin to share the joys of the seasons. Then winter comes. Just days before Christmas, a fierce snowstorm isolates the farm from the town, where the little girl's presents are waiting. The story relates the efforts of the animals and especially the tree to make the holiday joyous for the little girl and her family. *Voices:* Buddy Ebsen (Squire Badger, the narrator), Paul Winchell (Turtle), Allan Melvin (Hawk), Janet Waldo (Little Girl/Lady Bird), Stephen Manley (Boy Bunny/Girl Raccoon), Frank Welker (Father Bird/Groundhog/Beaver/Mole). *Theme Vocalist,* "When Autum Comes" and "To Love and Be Loved": Roberta Flack. *Music:* Dean Elliott. *Producers:* David H. DePatie, Friz Freleng. *Producer-Writer-Director:* Chuck Couch.

## 2038 Tiptoe Through TV.
Comedy, 60 min., CBS, 5/5/60. Comedy sketches that spoof the medium of television. *Host:* Sid Caesar. *Guests:* Gene Barry, Charlton Heston, Audrey Meadows, Paul Reed, Chita Rivera. *Music:* Charles Sanford. *Producer:* Leo Morgan. *Writers:* Mel Brooks, Mel Tolkin, Sydney Zelenka. *Director:* Jerome Shaw.

## To Europe with Love *see* Peggy Fleming Specials

## 2039 To the Queen! A Salute to Elizabeth II.
Documentary, 60 min., ABC, 6/11/77. An informal look at the reign of Queen Elizabeth II and England's royal family. *Host:* Peter Jennings. *Guests:* Peter Cook, Jean Marsh, Dudley Moore, Jackie Stewart. *Producers:* Elliot Bernstein, Gary Herman, Penelope Fleming. *Writer:* Harvey Jacobs. *Director:* Jack Sameth.

## 2040 Today at 35.
Variety, 60 min., NBC, 1/31/87. A thirty-fifth anniversary celebration of "The Today Show" (which premiered 1/14/52) via clips and present-day interviews with former regulars. *Hosts:* Bryant Gumbel, Jane Pauley. *Guests:* Frank Blair, Tom Brokaw, John Chancellor, Hugh Downs, Betty Furness, Joe Garagiola, Jim Hartz, Jack Lescoulie, Edwin Newman, John Palmer, Willard Scott, Gene Shalit, Barbara Walters, Sylvester "Pat" Weaver. *Producers:* Steve Friedman, Marty Ryan, Cliff Kappler. *Director:* George Paul.

## 2041 Today at 40.
Variety, 60 min., NBC, 1/14/92. A celebration of the fortieth birthday of "The Today Show," with current and former anchors sharing their reminiscences from their time on the program. *Hosts:* Katie Couric, Bryant Gumbel. *Guests:* Tom Brokaw, John Chancellor, Faith Daniels, Hugh Downs, Joe Garagiola, Jane Pauley, Willard Scott, Gene Shalit, Barbara Walters, Sylvester "Pat" Weaver. *Producers:* Steve Friedman, Jim Ackerman. *Director:* Bucky Gunts.

## 2042 Together with Music.
Variety, 60 min., CBS, 10/22/55. A showcase that highlights the talents of Mary Martin and Noel Coward. Also known as "Two for Tonight." *Hosts:* Noel Coward, Mary Martin. *Music:* Peter Matz. *Producers:* Lance Hamilton, Charles Russell, Richard Lewine. *Writer-Directors:* Noel Coward, Jerome Shaw.

## 2043 The Tom and Dick Smothers Show.
Variety, 60 min., NBC, 11/1/80. An hour of topical comedy skits, music, and songs with the Smothers Brothers. *Hosts:* Dick Smothers, Tom Smothers. *Guests:* The Flying Karamazov Brothers, Nicolette Larson, Martin Mull, Pat Paulsen, Tom Watts, Fred Willard. *Producers:* Tom Smothers, Dick Smothers, Art Fisher.

*Writers:* Mason Williams, John Barrett, Bob Gardiner, Don Novello, Carl Gottlieb. *Director:* Art Fisher.

## 2044 Tom Jones Specials. A

chronological listing of the variety specials hosted by singer Tom Jones. All are 60 minutes and have the following credits in common: musical direction by Johnnie Spence, and produced and directed by Jon Scoffield.

**1 The Tom Jones Special** (ABC, 5/15/71). *Guests:* Paul Anka, Frank Gorshin, The Mike Sammes Singers, The Norman Maen Dancers, Dusty Springfield.

**2 The Tom Jones Special** (ABC, 6/17/71). *Guests:* Eloise Laws, Liberace, The Mike Sammes Singers, The Norman Maen Dancers.

**3 The Tom Jones Special** (ABC, 7/8/71). *Guests:* Dave Edmunds, The Mike Sammes Singers, The Muppets, The Norman Maen Dancers, Connie Stevens.

**4 The Tom Jones Special** (ABC, 7/15/71). *Guests:* Lulu, The Mike Sammes Singers, The Norman Maen Dancers, Tom Paxton, Nicol Williamson.

**5 The Tom Jones Special** (ABC, 7/22/71). *Guests:* Charley Pride, Big Jim Sullivan, Jimmy Tarbuck.

**6 The Tom Jones Special** (Syndicated, 10/71). *Guests:* The Ace Trucking Company, Lonnie Donegan, Don Ho, Dusty Springfield.

**7 The Tom Jones Christmas Special** (Syndicated, 12/71). *Guests:* Judy Collins, David Frye, Millicent Martin, The Welsh Treorchy Male Choir.

## 2045 Tommy — The Who.

Concert, 2 hrs., Fox, 9/13/89. A twentieth anniversary celebration of the rock opera *Tommy* and its performers, The Who. Taped on August 24 at the Universal Amphitheater in Los Angeles. *Host:* Howard Hesseman. *Guests:* Phil Collins, Billy Idol, Elton John, Patti LaBelle, Steve Winwood. *Announcer:* David James. *Producers:* Bob

Meyrowitz, Bill Curbishley, Steve Rosendorf, Peter Kauff, Michael Pillot. *Director:* Larry Jordan.

## 2046 Tonight at 8:30. Comedy-

Drama, 90 min., NBC, 10/18/54. The overall title for three one-act plays by Noel Coward. The first story, "Red Peppers," relates incidents in the life of Lily Pepper, a petulant, caustic-tongued housewife. In the second story, "Still Life," Laura Jesson, a respected English housewife, faces a crisis when she finds herself in love with another man; and in "Shadow Play," the final story, Victoria Gayforth, a socially impeccable wife, relives her courtship (via a dream sequence) in an attempt to understand why her husband is divorcing her. The special marks the television debut of Ginger Rogers. *Cast:* (**"Red Peppers"**): Ginger Rogers (Lily Pepper), Martyn Green (George Pepper), Philip Coolidge (Bert Bentley), Louis Hector (Mr. Edwards), Estelle Winwood (Mabel Grace); (**"Still Life"**): Ginger Rogers (Laura Jesson), Trevor Howard (Alec Harvey), Philip Bourneuf (Albert Godby), Lucie Lancaster (Myrtle Bagot), Ilka Chase (Dolly Messiter), Robert Shawley (Stanley); (**"Shadow Play"**): Ginger Rogers (Victoria Gayforth), Gig Young (Simon Gayforth), Margaret Hayes (Martha Cunningham), John Baragrey (Michael), Diana Herbert (Lena), Will West (Hodge). *Music:* Carmen Dragon. *Producers:* Otto Preminger, Fred Coe. *Writer:* Noel Coward. *Directors:* Otto Preminger, John Bloch.

## 2047 Tonight in Samarkand.

Drama, 60 min., NBC, 3/24/61. A live and taped drama that tells of the love of a circus magician for a beautiful lion tamer and his efforts to help her escape a disastrous prediction foretold by a crystal ball. (The title refers to an ancient legend that if a man is frightened on the street by a woman he believes to be dead, he flees to the safety of a kingdom called Samarkand.) *Cast:* Janice

Rule (Nerica), James Mason (Sourab), Betsy Von Furstenberg (Therese), Martin Gabel (Massourbe), Paul Valentine (Angelo), Frank Milan (Paul), Margaret Hayes (Leontine), William Le-Messena (Poliakoff). *Producer-Director:* Garry Simpson. *Writer:* William Kendall Clark.

### 2048 Tonight Preview. Variety, 30 min., NBC (Closed Circuit), 8/27/54. A sneak preview of "The Tonight Show" with Steve Allen as host (NBC, 9/27/54 to 1/25/57). The program, not broadcast to the general public (only to NBC-owned and -operated stations and their advertising agencies), was actually a sales party for agency representatives for the forthcoming "Tonight Show." *Host:* Sylvester "Pat" Weaver. *Guests:* Steve Allen, Arlene Francis, Dave Garroway.

### 2049 The Tonight Show Anniversary Specials. A yearly series of speicals in which Johnny Carson, the king of late-night television, hosts a retrospective of clips from "The Tonight Show" (usually covering the prior year, but clips from earlier shows are also seen). Johnny's long-time friends, Ed McMahon and Doc Severinsen, cohost. The specials, broadcast in primetime by NBC, are produced by Fred DeCordova and directed by Bobby Quinn. Johnny served as host of "The Tonight Show" from 10/1/62 to 5/22/92.

**The Specials:** 10/1/76 (2 hrs., 14th anniversary show); 9/30/77 (2 hrs., 15th anniversary show); 10/2/78 (2 hrs., 16th anniversary show); 9/29/79 (2 hrs., 17th anniversary show); 10/2/80 (2 hrs., 18th anniversary program); 9/27/81 (2 hrs., 19th anniversary program); 10/3/82 (2 hrs., 20th anniversary special); 10/3/83 (2 hrs., 21st anniversary show); 10/1/84 (2 hrs., 22nd anniversary program); 9/30/85 (2 hrs., 23rd anniversary special); 9/25/86 (90 min., 24th anniversary show); 10/1/87 (90 min., 25th anniversary special); 10/6/88 (90 min., 26th anniver-

sary program); 9/28/89 (90 min., 27th anniversary show); 9/27/90 (90 min., 28th anniversary program); 10/3/91 (90 min., 29th and final anniversary special).

### 2050 Tonight with Belafonte. Variety, 60 min., CBS, 12/10/59. An hour of folk songs with Harry Belafonte. *Host:* Harry Belafonte. *Guests:* Bonnie McGee, Odetta, Sonny Terry. *Music:* Robert Corman. *Producers:* Phil Stein, George Charles. *Director:* Norman Jewison.

### 2051 Tony Bennett Specials. A chronological listing of the variety specials hosted by singer Tony Bennett. Tony Bennett hosted each show, except where noted otherwise.

**1 The Tony Bennett Show** (60 min., ABC, 10/20/66). *Guest:* Frank Sinatra. *Music:* David Rose. *Producers:* Gary Smith, Dwight Hemion. *Director:* Dwight Hemion.

**2 The Tony Bennett Special** (60 min., Syndicated, 12/67). Highlights of Tony Bennett's nightclub act. Taped at The Empire Room of New York's Waldorf Astoria Hotel. *Host:* Clay Cole. *Star:* Tony Bennett. *Music Director:* John Bunch.

**3 Tony Bennett in Waikiki** (60 min., Syndicated, 3/71). *Guests:* Ruby Braff, Don Costa, Joey Heatherton, Bernie Leighton. *Music:* Jack Parnell. *Producers:* Jack Sobel, Clark Jones. *Writer:* Jack Lloyd. *Director:* Clark Jones.

**4 The Tony Bennett Super Special from London** (60 min., Syndicated, 12/71). *Guests:* John Bunch, Robert Farnon, the London Philharmonic Orchestra. *Philharmonic Orchestra Conductor:* John Bunch. *Producer:* Derek Boulton. *Director:* Yvonne Littlewood.

**5 Tony Bennett—This Is Music** (60 min., Syndicated, 6/73). *Guests:* John Bunch, Billy Eckstine, Sarah Vaughan. *Orchestra:* Robert Farnon. *Producers:* Philip Jones, Peter Frazer-Jones. *Director:* Peter Frazer-Jones.

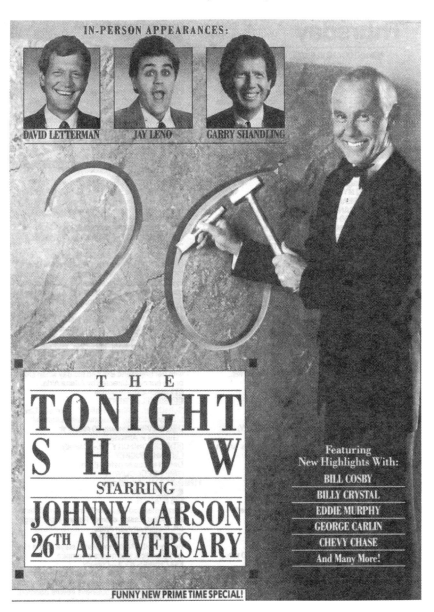

**Ad for "The Tonight Show 26th Anniversary Special"**

**6  Tony Bennett in London** (60 min., Syndicated, 8/74). *Guest:* The London Philharmonic Orchestra. *Producer:* Derek Boulton. *Director:* Peter Frazer-Jones.

**2052  The Tony Martin Special.** Variety, 60 min., Syndicated, 9/70. An hour of music, songs, and comedy with singer Tony Martin. *Host:* Tony Martin. *Guests:* Mary Lou

Collins, Rich Little, Bobby Vinton. *Producer:* Jackie Barnett. *Director:* Tony Charmoli.

## 2053 Tony Randall's All-Star Circus. Variety, 60 min., NBC, 6/19/81. Highlights of the Stockholm (Sweden) International Circus. *Host:* Tony Randall. *Producers:* Francois Bronett, Elizabeth Wennverg. *Writer:* Frank Slocum. *Director:* Joseph Cates.

## 2054 The Toothpaste Millionaire. Comedy, 60 min., ABC, 11/27/74. When Rufus Mayflower, a 12-year-old boy, discovers that toothpaste has skyrocketed to 79 cents a tube, he refuses to buy it and decides to fight inflation by manufacturing his own and selling it for 35 cents a jar. The story relates the problems that befall Rufus when business begins to boom and he is challenged by the bigger toothpaste companies and by the city, state, and federal government for violation of packaging and marketing rules and regulations. An "ABC Afterschool Special." *Cast:* Tierre Turner (Rufus Mayflower), Shelly Juttner (Kate MacKinstrey), David Pollack (Oscar Hobarth), Wright King (Joe Smiley), Helena Hatcher (Mrs. Mayflower), Reuben Collins (Mr. Mayflower). *Music:* Charles Bernstein. *Producers:* Irv Wilson, Harold Schneider, Ronald Rubin. *Writer:* Ronald Rubin. *Director:* Richard Kinon.

## 2055 Top Flight. Documentary, 60 min., CBS, 10/27/87. A salute to the U.S. Air Force on the occasion of its fortieth birthday. The program, a history of aviation, is highlighted by clips from various feature films. *Host-Narrator:* William Shatner. *Music:* James McVay. *Producers:* Arnold Shapiro, Carol L. Fleischer. *Writer-Director:* Carol L. Fleischer.

## 2056 Top Secret TV. Comedy, 60 min., NBC, 8/22/93. A collection of clips and outtakes from television programs from around the world. *Host:* Fred Roggin. *Music:* Anthony Marinelli. *Producers:* Fred Roggin, Phil Olsman. *Director:* Phil Olsman.

## 2057 Torn Between Two Fathers. Drama, 60 min., ABC, 4/20/89. An "ABC Afterschool Special" about a child custody case (that of a teenage girl who, after her mother's death, becomes the object of a custody battle between her natural father and her stepfather). *Cast:* Elizabeth Bliss (Debbie Jensen), Richard Kendall (Tim), Carl Weintraub (Peter), Pat Benatar (Donna), Susannah Blinkoff (Angela Morris), Susan Blakely (Jennifer), Melissa Watson (Jody), Patricia Ponton (Linda). *Music:* Richard Belis. *Producer:* Nancy Weaver Nixon. *Writer:* Penny DuPont. *Director:* Richard Masur.

## 2058 Tots, Tweens and Teens. Children, 30 min., DuMont, 9/2/48. A fashion show for children that is actually a 30-minute commercial for Macy's Department Store as it displays its fall wardrobe for teenagers and children. The program features the puppet Oky-Doky (created by Raye Copelan) commentating and plugging Macy's new 6 percent buying plan. *Host-Narrator:* Wendy Barrie. *Voice of Oky-Doky:* Dayton Allen. *Producer-Director:* Raymond E. Nelson.

## 2059 Tough Girl. Drama, 60 min., ABC, 10/28/81. When she is arrested for being in a stolen van with a cargo of drugs, Renie Lake, a city street-hardened teenage girl, is removed from her mother's custody in the city and placed in the temporary care of her father (Russell), his second wife (Marlene), and Marlene's hostile (to Renie) teenage daughter (Gretchen). The story relates Renie's experiences as she moves to the suburbs, struggles to break out of her tough shell, and win the acceptance of Marlene and Gretchen. An "ABC Afterschool Spe-

Traci Lords depicted in an ad from her last adult film.

Winston to change its ways and use organic insect killers. *Cast:* Keith Coogan (Eric Nelson), Elizabeth Franz (Cecile Nelson), Brian Smiar (John Nelson), Donna Haley (Hannah), Amelia Campbell (Ida), Richard Kuss (Carl), James Mathers (Benjamin), David Carpenter (Dan Prescott), Matthew Kimbrough (Sheriff), Walter Flanagan (Bill Benton), Nicholas Sadler (Billy Dryer). *Producer:* Frank Doelger. *Writer:* Bruce Harmon. *Director:* Helen Whitney.

**2061 Traci ... Then and Now.** Documentary, 30 min., Syndicated, 11/92. A profile of actress Traci Lords, a beautiful adult film queen (1984–87) turned mainstream actress. Traci, born on May 7, 1968, began her X-rated career with the 1984 film *What Gets Me Hot* and made her last one, *Traci ... I Love You,* in 1987. The program next explores Traci's legitimate career, beginning with her television debut on "Wiseguy" in 1988 and ending with a look at her feature films (which include "Not of This Earth," "Shock 'Em Dead," and "Intent to Kill"). *Host-Narrator:* Debbie Milano. *Guests:* Christy Canyon, Ginger Lynn. *Producer:* Nora Louise Kuzma.

cial." *Cast:* Karin Argoud (Renie Lake), Bibi Besch (Marlene), Lin McCarthy (Russell), Kristina Sorenson (Gretchen), Sally Kemp (Janet), Anne Seymour (Dr. Bancroft), Gregory Koppel (Jan Redner), William Bramley (Judge), Susan Vickery (Denise). *Music:* Al Allen. *Producer:* Martin Tahse. *Writer:* Paul W. Cooper. *Director:* Robert C. Thompson.

**2060 A Town's Revenge.** Drama, 60 min., ABC, 11/30/89. A reality-based "ABC Afterschool Special" about a teenage boy (Eric) and his efforts to persuade the farming town of

**2062 Travels with Charley.** Drama, 60 min., NBC, 3/17/68. A partial adaptation of the novel by John

Steinbeck, which depicts one man's odyssey across the United States (the television adaptation of the book covers only the scenic wonders from New England to California). *Narrator:* Henry Fonda. *Music:* Rod McKuen. *Vocals:* Glenn Yarbrough. *Producers:* Lee Mendelson, Walt DeFaria, Sheldon Fay, Jr. *Writer-Directors:* Walt DeFaria, Sheldon Fay, Jr.

**2063 Travels with Flip.** Variety, 60 min., NBC, 10/13/75. A tour of the United States with comedian Flip Wilson as he visits Los Angeles, San Francisco, Hawaii, Nashville and Boley, Oklahoma, and Atlanta. *Host:* Flip Wilson. *Guests:* Muhammad Ali, Loretta Lynn. *Producers:* Monte Kay, Lee Mendelson, Chuck Barbee. *Writer:* Lee Mendelson. *Director:* Lee Mendelson, Chuck Barbee.

**2064 The Treasure of Alpheus T. Winterborn.** Drama, 60 min., CBS, 12/26/81. A story about a boy (Anthony Munday) and his efforts to unravel a series of cryptic clues to find a supposed treasure. Aired as a "CBS Children's Mystery Theater" Special. *Cast:* Keith Mitchell (Anthony Munday), Dody Goodman (Miss Eells), Keith McConnell (Sherlock Holmes), Laurie Main (Dr. Watson), Matthew Tobin (Hugo Philpotts), Al Lewis (Mr. Garginfermer). *Music:* Don Heckman. *Producers:* Paul Asselin, Diane Asselin. *Writer:* Kimmer Ringwald. *Director:* Murray Golden.

**2065 A Tribute to Elton John and Bernie Taupin.** Tribute, 60 min., ABC, 12/12/91. Top recording artists perform songs made famous by the songwriting team of Elton John and Bernie Taupin. *Host:* Sylvester Stallone. *Guests:* The Beach Boys, Eric Clapton, Phil Collins, George Michael, Sinead O'Connor, Sting, Tina Turner, The Who. *Producers:* Jonathan Bendis, David Levin. *Writer:* David Ben-

jamin Wain. *Director:* Jonathan Bendis.

**2066 A Tribute to Jack Benny.** Tribute, 60 min., CBS, 12/29/74. A look at the life of comedian Jack Benny. *Host-Narrator:* Charles Kuralt. *Guests:* Eddie "Rochester" Anderson, Mel Blanc, Dennis Day, Danny Kaye, Don Wilson. *Producer:* Leslie Midgley. *Writer:* Charles Kuralt.

**2067 A Tribute to John Lennon.** Tribute, 2 hrs., Syndicated, 12/7/90. A remembrance of John Lennon by performances of his most famous songs (e.g., "Ticket to Ride," "Born in the USSR," "Nowhere Man," "Isolation," "Working Class Hero," and "Give Peace a Chance"). *Host:* Michael Douglas. *Guests:* David Bowie, Ray Charles, Joe Cocker, Natalie Cole, Terence Trent D'Arby, Dave Edmonds, Lou Gramm, Hall and Oates, Michael Jackson, Billy Joel, Elton John, Lenny Kravitz, Cyndi Lauper, Sean Ono Lennon, Paul McCartney, Kylie Minogue, Roy Orbison, Ringo Starr, Dave Stewart, U2. *Music:* Anne Dudley conducting the Royal Liverpool Philharmonic Orchestra.

**2068 A Tribute to "Mr. Television" Milton Berle.** Variety, 60 min., NBC, 3/26/78. A star-studded salute to comedian Milton Berle, who is fondly called "Mr. Television" (his 1948 series, "Texaco Star Theater," was responsible for the sales of many millions of television sets when the medium was brand new in 1948). *Special Guest:* Milton Berle. *Guests:* Lucille Ball, Joey Bishop, George Carlin, Johnny Carson, Angie Dickinson, Kirk Douglas, Bob Hope, Gabriel Kaplan, Gene Kelly, Kermit the Frog, Donny Osmond, Marie Osmond, Gregory Peck, Carl Reiner, Don Rickles, Frank Sinatra, Marlo Thomas, Flip Wilson. *Producers:* Jerry

Frank, Bill Carruthers. *Writer:* Marty Farrell. *Director:* Bill Carruthers.

**2069 A Tribute to Ricky Nelson.** Documentary, 60 min., Syndicated, 5/87. A tribute to singer Ricky Nelson with highlights of his career, including rare or never-before-seen film footage. *Hosts:* Gunnar and Matthew Nelson. *Guests:* Fats Domino, John Fogerty, Waylon Jennings, Kris Kristofferson, Roy Orbison, Carl Perkins, Sam Phillips. *Producers:* Greg McDonald, Edward LaBuick, Jeffrey Krandorf, Paul Rose. *Writers:* Jeffrey Krandorf, Paul Rose. *Directors:* Taylor Hartford, T. V. Grosso.

**2070 A Tribute to Sam Kinison.** Tribute, 60 min., Fox, 5/23/93. The late comic (1953–92) is honored by his fellow comics. Also included are clips from his movie and television appearances. *Guests:* Jim Carrey, Rodney Dangerfield, Carl Labove, Pauly Stone, George Wallace, Robin Williams. *Music:* Dennis McCarthy. *Producers:* Bill Kinison, Walter C. Miller. *Director:* Walter C. Miller.

**2071 A Tribute to Woody Guthrie and Leadbelly.** Musical Tribute, 60 min., PBS, 12/5/88. A tribute to Woody Guthrie and Huddie "Leadbelly" Leadbetter, singer-songwriters who were first to give America a conscience (for example, Woody Guthrie with the song "This Land Is My Land"). *Guests:* Arlo Guthrie, Emmylou Harris, Little Richard, John Cougar Mellencamp, Willie Nelson, Pete Seeger, Bruce Springsteen, Sweet Honey in the Rock, Taj-Mahal, U2. *Music:* Don Devito. *Producers:* Peter Wagner, Jim Brown, Harold Leventhal. *Director:* Jim Brown.

**2072 The Trini Lopez Show.** Variety, 60 min., Syndicated, 10/68. An hour of music, songs, and comedy with singer Trini Lopez. *Host:* Trini Lopez. *Guests:* Georgia Brown, Frank Gorshin. *Music:* Jack Parnell. *Producer:* Jackie Barnett. *Director:* Tony Charmoli.

**2073 Trouble River.** Adventure, 30 min., ABC, 11/12 and 11/19/77. The story, set in the early days of the Pacific Northwest, relates the adventures of a boy (Dewey) and his grandmother as they ride a makeshift raft down a dangerous river to escape from a group of renegades. An "ABC Weekend Special." *Cast:* Nora Denney (Grandma), Michael LeClair (Dewey), Geno Silva (Indian), Mike Howden (Mr. Dragan), Hal England (Mr. Martin), Jay W. MacIntosh (Mrs. Martin). *Music:* Glenn Paxton. *Producer:* Martin Tahse. *Writer:* Larry Bischof. *Director:* Roger Flint.

**2074 The Trouble with Grandpa.** Drama, 30 min., Syndicated, 3/81. The relationship between a 17-year-old girl (Dorie) and her 70-year-old grandfather — two lonely people, both dependent upon each other — both afraid of facing the future. *Cast:* Meg Tilly (Dorie), Elisha Cook (Grandfather), Millie Perkins (Dr. Langley), Lee Lucas (Paul). *Music:* Chris Stone. *Producers:* Ellwood Kieser, Michael Rhodes. *Writer:* Lan O'Kun. *Director:* Michael Rhodes.

**2075 The Trouble with Mother.** Drama, 30 min., Syndicated, 9/79. The story of Patricia Benson, a traditional homemaker who must defend her position as a wife and mother to her 13-year-old feminist daughter, Laurie. *Cast:* Sandy Dennis (Patricia Benson), Jennifer Benson (Laurie Benson), Amy Palmer (Judy Benson), Robert Elkins (Herb Benson). *Producers:* Ellwood Kieser, Tom Robertson. *Writer-Director:* Tom Robertson.

**2076 The Trouble with People.** Comedy, 60 min., NBC, 11/12/72. The overall title for five short sketches by Neil Simon. "The Greasy Diner" tells of a couple who enter a diner, take one look around, and wish they had never entered; "The Man Who Got a Ticket" relates the frustrations of a driver who is issued 369 summonses by a confused computer; "The Night Visitor" relates the efforts of a detective to catch an elusive prowler; Ben and Ernie are "The Office Sharers," friends who have worked side by side for eight years without an argument until . . . ; and the final story, "Double Trouble," tells of a husband who wrenches his back while closing the window for his wife who has the chills. *Cast:* (**"The Greasy Diner"**): James Coco (Husband), Dena Dietrich (Wife), Doris Roberts (Waitress); (**"The Man Who Got a Ticket"**): George C. Scott (Driver), Elaine Shore (Police Woman); (**"The Night Visitor"**): Renee Taylor (Lure), Joseph Campanella (Detective); (**"The Office Sharers"**): Gene Wilder (Ernie), Jack Weston (Ben); (**"Double Trouble"**): Alan Arkin (Husband), Valerie Harper (Wife). *Music:* Neal Hefti. *Producers:* Neil Simon, Danny Simon. *Writer:* Neil Simon. *Directors:* Danny Simon, Dave Wilson.

## 2077 The True Meaning of Christmas. Fantasy, 60 min., Syndicated, 12/88. A yuletide special that explores Christmas via the legends and superstitions that surround the feast day. Special effects are used to follow a young boy (Chris) as he experiences the history of Christmas. *Cast:* Martha Gibson (Befana), Eric Hebert (Chris). *Also:* Douglas Campbell, Kitty Carruthers, Peter Carruthers, Robin Cousins, Toller Cranston, Arthur Gibson, Christopher Kadai, Shelley MacLeod, John Raitt, Shelley Jaclyn Stevens. *Music:* Marvin Dolgay. *Producers:* Donald Davis, Paul Palmer. *Writers:* Jack Bond, Paul Palmer. *Director:* David Acomba.

## 2078 Truman at Potsdam. Drama, 90 min., NBC, 4/8/76. A "Hall-

mark Hall of Fame" presentation that dramatizes the July 1945 summit meeting between Harry Truman, Joseph Stalin, and Sir Winston Churchill to determine the fate of a defeated Germany and lay the groundwork for a peace conference. *Cast:* Ed Flanders (Harry S Truman), Jose Ferrer (Joseph Stalin), John Houseman (Winston Churchill), Barry Morse (Secretary of State Byrnes), Alexander Knox (Secretary of War Stimson), Dennis Burgess (Eden). *Producer:* David Susskind. *Writer:* Sidney Carroll. *Director:* George Schaefer.

## 2079 The Tube Test. Trivia, 60 min., ABC, 11/28/90 and 3/18/91. A quiz that tests viewers' knowledge of television from the 1950s to the 1990s. Clips are used to illustrate questions. *Host:* Alan Thicke. *Producer-Director:* Susan Winston, Dan Funk. *Writers:* Phyllis Cannon, Todd Thicke, Susan Winston, Dan Funk.

## 2080 The Turn of the Screw. Drama, 90 min., NBC, 10/20/59. A television adaptation of the 1950 novel by Henry James about a governess (Miss Giddens) and her efforts to protect a young girl (Flora) and her brother (Miles) from a spirit who seeks to possess them. The program marks the American television debut of Ingrid Bergman. "The Turn of the Screw" was also seen as a segment of "Omnibus" (2/13/55, with Geraldine Page as Miss Giddens) and on "Matinee Theater" (9/30/57, with Sarah Churchill in the title role). *Cast:* Ingrid Bergman (Miss Giddens), Alexandra Wagner (Flora), Hayward Morse (Miles), Isabel Elsom (Mrs. Grose), Paul Stevens (Peter Quint), Laurinda Barrett (Miss Jessel). *Music:* David Amron. *Producers:* Hubbell Robinson, John Frankenheimer. *Writer:* James Costigan. *Director:* John Frankenheimer.

## 2081 TV: The Fabulous '50s. Variety, 90 min., NBC, 3/5/78. A clip-

filled, nostalgic look at the programs America watched during the 1950s. *Hosts:* Lucille Ball, David Janssen, Michael Landon, Mary Martin, Dinah Shore, Red Skelton. *Producers:* Henry Jaffe, Draper Lewis, David Lawrence. *Writers:* Draper Lewis, David Lawrence. *Director:* Jonathan Lucas.

## 2082 TV's Funniest Commercials. Variety, 60 min., ABC, 2/3/93.

A look at humorous commercials that have aired nationally, regionally, and in foreign countries. *Host:* Patrick Duffy. *Producers:* Woody Fraser, Bonnie Karrin. *Writer:* Woody Fraser. *Director:* Lawrence Einhorn.

## 2083 TV's Funniest Game Show Moments. Variety, 60 min.,

ABC, 5/10/84 and 1/15/85. A look at humorous, embarrassing, and unexpected moments from thirty years of television game shows. *Host:* William Shatner. *Guests* (5/10/84): Bob Barker, Bill Cullen, Richard Dawson, Mark Goodson, Gene Rayburn; (1/15/85): Steve Allen. *Announcer:* Johnny Olsen. *Music:* The Music Design Company. *Producers:* Mark Goodson, Gil Fates. *Director:* Paul Alter.

## 2084 'Twas the Night Before Christmas. Cartoon, 30 min., CBS,

12/8/74. The story, adapted from Clement Moore's poem "A Visit from St. Nicholas," follows the efforts of the citizens of Junctionville to discover who wrote an unsigned letter to the editor of the local paper denouncing Santa Claus as a myth, and right the wrong so Santa will pay his yearly visit to the children of Junctionville. *Voices:* Tammy Grimes (Albert Mouse), John McGiver (Mayor), George Gobel (Father Mouse). *Other Voices:* Patricia Bright, Scott Firestone, Robert McFadden, Allen Swift, Christine Winter. *Music:* Maury Laws, Jules Bass. *Producer-Directors:* Arthur Rankin, Jr., Jules Bass. *Writer:* Jerome Coopersmith.

## 2085 'Twas the Night Before Christmas. Comedy-Drama, 60

min., ABC, 12/7/77. A warm and humorous look at how one American family celebrated Christmas in the 1890s as seen through the experiences of the Cosgrove family. The story focuses on Clark Cosgrove, a nervous man who, after a long day at work, is in no mood for a Christmas Eve with noisy children, gabby in-laws, uninvited guests, and an irksome cat. The program shows how his frazzled nerves become visions of sugar plums by the magic of "'Twas the Night Before Christmas." *Cast:* Paul Lynde (Clark Cosgrove), Anne Meara (Nellie Cosgrove), Foster Brooks (Edmund Butler), Martha Raye (Elvira Butler), Alice Ghostley (Mildred Cosgrove), Howard Morris (Heinrich Kotzebue), George Gobel (Nathaniel Terwilliger), Anson Williams (James Hewitt), Susan Page (Sarah Cosgrove), Tiffany Ann Francis (Nancy Cosgrove), Rachel Jacobs (Mary Beth Cosgrove), Sparky Marcus (Clarkie Cosgrove), Tommy Crebbs (Elias Cosgrove). *Music:* Vernon Ray Bunch. *Producers:* Raymond Katz, Sandy Gallin, Joe Layton, Ken Welch, Mitzie Welch. *Writers:* Dick Clair, Jenna McMahon. *Director:* Tim Kiley.

## 2086 Twelfth Night. Comedy,

90 min., NBC, 12/15/57. The story of a girl (Viola) who poses as a boy—and the complications that ensue when another girl (Olivia) becomes infatuated with her, thinking she is a boy. Based on the play by William Shakespeare and broadcast on the "Hallmark Hall of Fame." *Cast:* Piper Laurie (Viola), Rosemary Harris (Olivia), Maurice Evans (Malvolio), Dennis King (Sir Toby Belch), Max Adrian (Sir Andrew), Howard Morris (Fester), Lloyd Bochner (Orsino), Alice Ghostley (Maria), Gregory Morton (Antonio). *Music:* Lehman Engel. *Producer-Director:* George Schaefer. *Writer:* William Nicholas.

**2087 Twelve Star Salute.** Variety, 60 min., ABC, 12/9/61. A music and comedy salute to the work of the Federation of Jewish Philanthropies. *Host:* Danny Kaye. *Guests:* Anna Maria Alberghetti, Lucille Ball, Benny Goodman, Morton Gould, Charlton Heston, Eartha Kitt, Tony Martin, Mitch Miller, Jan Peerce, Edward G. Robinson. *Producer:* Hi Brown.

**2088 Twentieth Century.** Comedy, 90 min., CBS, 4/7/56. A television adaptation of the play by Charles Millholland about a bankrupt theatrical producer (Oscar Jaffe) who schemes to sign Lily Garland, a famous movie star he molded (from a clerk named Mildred Plotka), to an exclusive contract and recover his theatrical fortunes. (The title refers to the Twentieth Century, a famed passenger train of the 1930s, where the action takes place.) The "Twentieth Century" was first seen on television as a segment of "Ford Theater" (CBS, 10/7/49), with Fredric March as Oscar and Lili Palmer as Lily. *Cast:* Orson Welles (Oscar Jaffe), Betty Grable (Lily Garland), Keenan Wynn (Owen O'Malley), Ray Collins (Oliver Webb), Olive Sturgess (Mrs. Lockwood), Gage Clark (Matthew Clark), Steve Terrell (Grover Lockwood). *Producer-Director:* Arthur Schwartz. *Writer:* Robert Buckner.

**2089 Twenty-Four Hours in a Woman's Life.** Drama, 60 min., CBS, 3/20/61. The story of an elderly woman who recalls one day in her life—when, as a young woman, she tried to reform a gambler and failed. *Cast:* Ingrid Bergman (Clare Lester), Rip Torn (Paul Winter), John Williams (Stevens), Lili Darvas (Louise), Jerry Orbach (Cristol), Cynthia Latham (Mildred Lester). *Producers:* Lars Schmidt, Gordon Duff. *Writer:* John Mortimer. *Director:* Silvio Narizzano.

**2090 Twiggy in New York.** Documentary, 60 min., ABC, 4/27/67.

The program reviews a day in the life of Leslie Hornby, the beautiful, slim fashion model nicknamed Twiggy, as she visits New York City for a fashion shoot. *Host:* Twiggy. *Producer-Director:* Bruce Stern.

**2091 Twigs.** Comedy-Drama, 90 min., CBS, 3/6/75. A comedy of four one-act plays in which Carol Burnett portrays three sisters and their feisty old Irish Catholic mother, each with a heartwarming and often hilarious story to tell. Based on the Broadway play. See also the following title. *Cast:* Carol Burnett (Emily/Celia/Dorothy/Mother), Alex Rocco (Frank), Edward Asner (Phil), Conrad Bain (Swede), Pat Hingle (Lou), Jack Gilford (Ned), Liam Dunn (Pa), Gary Burghoff (Clergyman). *Music:* Peter Matz. *Producers:* Joe Hamilton, Robert Wright. *Writer:* George Furth. *Directors:* Alan Arkin, Clark Jones.

**2092 Twigs.** Comedy-Drama, 2 hrs. 20 min., The Entertainment Channel, 11/7/82. A second television adaptation of the Broadway play with Cloris Leachman playing three sisters and their feisty mother, each of whom has a story to tell. See the prior title also. *Cast:* Cloris Leachman (Emily/Celia/Dorothy/Mother), Jack Callahan (Frank), Tony Mockus (Phil), Ralph Foody (Swede), Ward W. Ohrman (Lou), Frank Smith (Ned), George Womack (Pa), Weldon Boyce Bleiler (Clergyman). *Producers:* Sarah Frank, Bonnie Burns. *Writer:* George Furth. *Director:* Scott Steinberg.

**2093 Two of a Kind: George Burns and John Denver.** Variety, 60 min., ABC, 3/30/81. A two-man show featuring the comedy of George Burns and the songs of John Denver. *Hosts:* George Burns, John Denver. *Announcer:* Dick Tufeld. *Music:* Sid Feller. *Producers:* Jerry Weintraub, Don Siegel. *Writer:* Buz Kohan. *Director:* Stan Harris.

## 2094 Two Teens and a Baby.
Drama, 60 min., CBS, 1/21/92. A "CBS Schoolbreak Special" about a middle-aged couple (Emily and Paul) who become the parents of a baby and the adjustments a baby sister demands on the lives of her two teenage brothers (Brian and Chris). *Cast:* Sandy Faison (Emily Lance), Robert Picardo (Paul Lance), Jim Calvert (Brian Lance), Brice Beckham (Chris Lance), Maureen Flannigan (Sherie; Brian's girlfriend). *Music:* Dan Slider. *Producer:* Mike Kellin. *Writer:* Carol Starr Schneider. *Director:* David J. Eagle.

## 2095 The 2,000 Year Old Man.
Cartoon, 30 min., CBS, 1/11/75. A television adaptation of the Carl Reiner–Mel Brooks comedy routine about a 2,000-year-old man who relates his past experiences when he is interviewed by a modern-day reporter. *Voices:* Carl Reiner (Interviewer), Mel Brooks (2,000-Year-Old Man). *Music:* Mort Garson. *Producer-Director:* Leo Salkin. *Writers:* Carl Reiner, Mel Brooks.

## 2096 The Ultimate Stuntman: Dar Robinson.
Tribute, 60 Min., ABC, 11/30/87. A tribute to Dar Robinson, a daring Hollywood stuntman whose stunts, engineered for safety, often broke world records. Clips (and a behind-the-scenes look at his most famous stunts) are shown. *Host-Narrator:* Chuck Norris. *Guests:* Gary Busey, Cathy Lee Crosby, Mel Gibson, Timothy Hutton, Burt Reynolds, Robert Urich. *Music:* Al Kasha, Michael Lloyd. *Producers:* Gary Benz, William Kronick. *Writer-Director:* William Kronick.

## 2097 Umbrella Jack.
Drama, 30 min., Syndicated, 4/86. The friendship between a young boy (Billy) and an eccentric old war veteran called Umbrella Jack. *Cast:* John Carradine (Umbrella Jack), Joey Lawrence (Billy), Donna Wandrey (Billy's mother), Tom McGowan (Billy's father). *Producer:* Tom G. Robertson. *Writer:* William P. Berke. *Producer-Director:* Gene McPherson.

## 2098 Unauthorized Biography: Jane Fonda.
Documentary, 2 hrs., Syndicated, 10/24/88. An in-depth examination of the life and career of actress Jane Fonda. *Host:* Barbara Howar. *Guests:* Peter Fonda, Shirlee Fonda, Brooke Hayward, Katharine Hepburn, Roger Vadim, John Wright. *Music:* Tom Wagner. *Producers:* Mark Monsky, Peter O. Almond. *Writer:* Barbara Howar. *Director:* John Parsons-Peditto.

**Uncle Miltie's Christmas Party** *see* **Milton Berle Specials**

**Uncle Miltie's Easter TV Party** *see* **Milton Berle Specials**

## 2099 Uncle Tim Wants You!
Variety, 60 min., CBS, 9/17/77. A music and comedy salute to the U.S. armed forces. *Host:* Tim Conway. *Guests:* Bernadette Peters, Jonathan Winters. *Music:* Peter Matz. *Producer:* Joe Hamilton. *Writers:* Bill Richmond, Gene Perret, Roger Beatty, Tim Conway, Jonathan Winters. *Director:* Dave Powers.

## 2100 Uncommon Women and Others.
Drama, 90 min., PBS, 5/24/78. A television adaptation of the play by Wendy Wasserstein about the graduates of an exclusive women's college who meet seven years later to discuss their life and loves. *Cast:* Swoosie Kurtz (Rita), Jill Eikenberry (Kate), Meryl Streep (Leilah), Ellen Parker (Muffet), Alma Cuervo (Holly), Ann McDonough (Samantha), Cynthia Herman (Susie), Anna Levine (Carter). *Narrator:* Alexander Scourby. *Producers:* Jac Venza, Phyllis Geller. *Directors:* Steven Robman, Merrily Mossman.

## 2101 The Unexpurgated Benny Hill Show.
Comedy, 60 min., HBO, 8/6/82. A compilation of risqué, adult-oriented comedy skits produced especially for cable television. *Host:* Benny Hill. *Regulars:* Bella Emberg, Roger Finch, Hill's Angels, Henry McGee, Ken Sedd, Bob Todd, Sue Upton, Jack Wright. *Music:* Ronnie Aldrich. *Vocalists:* The Ladybirds. *Producer-Director:* Dennis Kirkland. *Writer:* Benny Hill.

## 2102 The Unforgivable Secret.
Drama, 60 min., ABC, 2/10/82. Following her "remarriage," Karen Dunoway decides to tell her 15-year-old daughter, Angela, a long-hidden secret: that she was never married when Angela was born and that her father is unaware of her birth. The news shatters Angela, who had believed that Karen had divorced her father because he was always away from home. When Angela learns that her father lives in a small New England town where a close friend also lives, Angela arranges a visit so that she may possibly meet her father. The story relates Angela's search—and her struggles over a decision: whether or not to tell Frank Caruso (her father) that she is his daughter. An "ABC Afterschool Special." *Cast:* Barbara Feldon (Karen Dunoway), Amanda Plummer (Angela Dunoway), Danny Aiello (Frank Caruso), Steve Vinovich (Larry Brandon), Jo Lynn Sciarro (Carole), Lois Smith (Margaret), Ken Albrecht (Robert Gray). *Music:* Elliot Lawrence. *Producers:* Ken Greengrass, Marilyn Olin, Lynn Ahrens. *Writer:* Durrell Royce Crays (based on the novel *Tell Me No Lies* by Hila Colman). *Director:* Alex Grashoff.

## 2103 United We Stand.
Variety, 2 hrs., Syndicated, 9/11/88. A lavish celebration of the 1988 Summer Olympic Games in Seoul, Korea. *Hosts:* Loretta Swit, Johnny Yune. *Guests:* Sheena Easton, Bob Hope, Julio Iglesias, Jermaine Jackson, Rich Little, The Miami Sound Machine, Brooke Shields. *Announcer:* John Harlan. *Music:* Morton Stevens. *Producers:* Jihee Cho, Johnny Yune, Igo Kantor, Marlee Dailey. *Director:* Louis J. Horvitz.

## 2104 Uptown.
Variety, 2 hrs., NBC, 5/30/80. A tribute to a New York City landmark—Harlem's famed Apollo Theater. *Guests:* Jack Albertson, Bunny Briggs, Cab Calloway, Natalie Cole, Gladys Knight, Lou Rawls, Nipsey Russell, Doc Severinsen, Sandman Sims, Ben Vereen, Flip Wilson. *Music:* Phil Moore. *Producers:* Gary Smith, Dwight Hemion. *Writers:* Harry Crane, Marty Farrell. *Director:* Dwight Hemion.

## 2105 Uptown Comedy Express.
Comedy, 60 min., HBO, 5/9/87. The program showcases new comedy talent (largely black performers). Taped at the Ebony Showcase in Los Angeles. *Host:* Eddie Murphy. *Guests:* Mark Corey, Arsenio Hall, Chris Rock, Clint Smith, Barry Sobel, Robert Townsend, Marsha Warfield. *Music:* The Bus Boys. *Producers:* Clint Smith, Mark Corey. *Writers:* Ilunga Adell, Mark Oberman. *Director:* Russ Petranto.

## 2106 US Against the World.
Game, 2 hrs., NBC, 9/7/77. Celebrities from the United States, Great Britain, and "the rest of the world" compete in various athletic games at the University of California in Los Angeles. See also the next title. *Hosts:* Jack Klugman, Ed McMahon, Don Rickles. *U.S. Team:* Linda Blair, Dan Haggerty, Gabriel Kaplan (captain), Kristy McNichol, Rob Reiner, Susan Saint James, Suzanne Somers, Flip Wilson. *British Team:* Roger Daltry, Richard Dawson, Marty Feldman (captain), Susan George, Andy Gibb, Olivia Hussey, Jane Seymour, Bill Shoemaker, Twiggy. *Rest of the World Team:* Susan Blakely, LeVar Burton, Susan

Clark, Britt Ekland, Rich Little (captain), Sergio Mendes, Michael Ontkean, Elke Sommer. *Producers:* Howard Katz, Rudy Tellez. *Producer-Director:* Don Ohlmeyer.

## 2107 US Against the World II. Game, 2 hrs., NBC, 9/9/78.

A sequel to the above title wherein celebrities from the United States challenge stars from the World Team in various athletic events. Taped at Magic Mountain amusement park and at College of the Canyons in Valencia, California. *Hosts:* Gabriel Kaplan, Ted Knight, Ed McMahon. *U.S. Team:* Scott Baio, Valerie Bertinelli, Gary Burghoff, Dick Clark, Joyce DeWitt, Erik Estrada, Melissa Gilbert, Dan Haggerty, Cloris Leachman, Kristy McNichol, Dick Van Patten, Jimmie Walker. *World Team:* Sivi Aberg, LeVar Burton, Oleg Cassini, Britt Ekland, Fionnuala Flanagan, Rich Little, Dudley Moore, Paul Nicholas, Victoria Principal, Jane Seymour, William Shatner, Bo Svenson. *Producers:* Howard Katz, Carolyn Raskin, Craig Tennis. *Director:* Jim Cross.

## 2108 U.S. Treasury Salutes. Variety, 30 min., ABC, 12/6/48.

Music and songs designed to assist in the post–World War II U.S. bond drive. The special is the first simulcast of a radio and television program over the Midwest Television Network. *Host:* Skip Farrell. *Guests:* June Browne, The Honeydreamers. *Announcer:* Wayne Griffin. *Music:* Rex Maupin. *Producer-Director:* Jack Gibney.

## 2109 The U.S.A. Music Challenge. Variety, 60 min., ABC, 6/2/92.

Professional musicians, chosen in contests held across the country, perform their material in hopes of winning a recording contract. *Host:* Malcolm-Jamal Warner. *Guests:* David Faustino, Jennie Garth, Victoria Jackson. *Performers:* Wendy Ingram, Mike Kochevar, Matt Mattheiss, Charlotte Moore, Patti Russo, Will Wheaton, Jr. *Bands:*

Bus Stop, Phil Bono and the Innocents, Sugar Shack. *Producers:* Al Schwartz, Arthur Smith. *Writer:* Barry Adelman. *Director:* Jeff Margolis.

## 2110 Valentine's Second Chance. Drama, 30 min., ABC, 1/29/77.

Jimmy Valentine is a reformed safecracker with a new status as a solid citizen, but detective Ben Price suspects Valentine of having a shady background and being responsible for a series of recent burglaries involving safecracking. When a young boy (Joe Willie) is accidentally locked in a bank safe that is equipped with a time lock, Valentine is torn between retaining his new image (and possibly his freedom) or risking arrest to open the safe and save the boy. Valentine comes to the rescue. Having witnessed the entire scene, Price gives up the chase and provides "Valentine's Second Chance." An ABC Weekend Special." *Cast:* Ken Berry (Jimmy Valentine), Greg Morris (Ben Price), Sean Marshall (Joe Willie), Elizabeth Baur (Annabel), Ham Larson (Fergus), Max Showalter (Mr. Dawson), Burke Byrnes (Sheriff). *Music:* Ray Ellis. *Producers:* Allen Ducovny, William Beaudine, Jr. *Writer:* Alvin Boretz. *Director:* Hollingsworth Morse.

## 2111 Valley Forge. Drama, 90 min., NBC, 12/3/75.

A television adaptation of Maxwell Anderson's 1934 play about George Washington's efforts to maintain his troops during the harsh winter of 1777–78. Aired on the "Hallmark Hall of Fame." *Cast:* Richard Basehart (George Washington), Harry Andrews (General William Howe), Simon Ward (Major Andre), Victor Garber (Lafayette), Michael Tolan (Tench), David Dukes (Cutting), Josef Sommer (Varnum), Nancy Marchand (Auntie), Woodrow Parfrey (Minto). *Music:* Vladimir Selinsky. *Producer:* Walt DeFaria. *Writers:* Donald Carmorant, Ernest Kinoy. *Director:* Fielder Cook.

## 2112 Van Dyke and Company. Variety, 60 min., NBC, 10/30/75. Various comedy sketches tailored to the talents of Dick Van Dyke. *Host:* Dick Van Dyke. *Guests:* Richard Kiel, Lynne Lipton, Ken Mars, Mary Tyler Moore, Carl Reiner, Tina Turner. *Music:* Lex de Azevedo. *Producers:* Byron Paul, Allan Blye, Bob Einstein. *Writers:* Dick Van Dyke, Allan Blye, Bob Einstein, George Burditt, Robert Illes, Steve Martin, James Stein, Rick Mittleman. *Director:* Art Fisher.

## 2113 Vanities. Comedy, 90 min., HBO, 3/15/81. A nostalgic story that follows the lives of Mary, Joanne, and Kathy, three Texas cheerleaders, from high school in 1963 to their post-college reunion in 1974. *Cast:* Shelley Hack (Mary), Meredith Baxter Birney (Joanne), Annette O'Toole (Kathy). *Producers:* Allan Baumrucker, Norman Twain. *Writer:* Jack Heifner. *Director:* Gary Halvorson.

## 2114 Vanity Fair. Drama, 2 hrs., CBS, 1/12 and 1/13/61. A television adaptation of the novel by William Thackeray about Becky Sharpe, an amoral adventuress in nineteenth-century London. The play was also adapted to television as "Becky Sharpe" ("Philco Television Playhouse," NBC, 3/27/49), with Claire Lucas as Becky. *Cast:* Diane Cilento (Becky Sharpe), Jack Gwillim (Lord Steyne), John Colicos (Rawdon Crawley), Laurie Main (Joseph Sedley), Jeanette Sterke (Amelia Sedley), Cathleen Nesbitt (Miss Crawley), Denholm Elliott (Lieutenant Dobbin), Christina Pickles (Lady Jane). *Producer:* Robert Costello. *Writer:* Roger Hirson. *Director:* Tom Donovan.

## 2115 Variety. Variety, 90 min., NBC, 1/30/55. A potpourri featuring music, songs, comedy, and a jazz production of Gilbert and Sullivan's comic opera, *HMS* Pinafore. *Performers:* The Bil and Cora Baird Puppets, Pat Carroll, Perry Como, Buddy Hackett, Bill Hayes, Kitty Kallen, Jack Russell, Herb Shriner. *Music:* Charles Sanford. *Producers:* Max Liebman, Bill Hobin. *Director:* Max Liebman.

## 2116 Variety '77: The Year in Entertainment. Variety, 90 min., CBS, 1/9/78. The program recalls the top entertainment stories and names of 1977 as recorded in *Variety* magazine. *Hosts:* Telly Savalas (Television segment), Valerie Perrine (Movies), Alan King (Nightclubs), Dionne Warwick (Music), Sada Thompson (Theater). *Music:* Nelson Riddle. *Producers:* Jack Watson, Ernest Chambers. *Writers:* William Box, Ernest Chambers. *Director:* Stan Harris.

## 2117 Variety: The World of Show Biz. Variety, 60 min., CBS, 6/20/60. An hour of music, songs, and comedy. *Host:* Sid Caesar. *Guests:* Gene Barry, Audrey Meadows, Howard Morris, Chita Rivera. *Music:* Charles Sanford. *Producer:* Leo Morgan. *Writers:* Mel Tolkin, Mel Brooks, Sydney Zelenka. *Director:* Jerome Shaw.

## 2118 The Vaudeville Show. Variety, 30 min., CBS, 12/10/53. Performances by former vaudeville entertainers. *Host-Announcer:* Art Fleming. *Guests:* Bunny Briggs, the Cycling Villeaves, Juanita Hall, Gil Lamb, Russell Swann. *Orchestra:* Glenn Osser. *Producer:* Fred Heider. *Director:* Baron Trenner, Jr.

## 2119 Verna: U.S.O. Girl. Drama, 90 min., PBS, 1/25/78. A television adaptation of the short story by Paul Gallico about Verna, a Chicago dancer who dreams of becoming a star, despite her complete lack of talent. *Cast:* Sissy Spacek (Verna), Sally Kellerman (Maureen), Howard Da Silva (Eddie), William Hurt (Walter). *Producers:* Ronald F. Maxwell, Jac

Venza. *Writer:* Albert Innaurato. *Director:* Ronald F. Maxwell.

## 2120 Ver-r-r-ry Interesting.

Comedy, 60 min., NBC, 3/18/71. A series of sketches and blackouts hosted by the German soldier Arte Johnson created for "Rowan and Martin's Laugh-In" (the title refers to the soldier's catchphrase). *Host:* Arte Johnson. *Guests:* Bing Crosby, Billy DeWolfe, Joe Flynn, Nancy Kulp, Peter Marshall, Elke Sommer. *Producers:* Saul Ilson, Ernest Chambers. *Writers:* Ron Friedman, Coslough Johnson, Arte Johnson, Saul Ilson, Ernest Chambers. *Director:* Bill Foster.

## 2121 The Very Best of the Ed Sullivan Show. Variety, 2 hrs., CBS,

2/17/91. Film and videotaped highlights from "The Ed Sullivan Show" (CBS, 1948–71). *Host:* Carol Burnett. *Guests:* Ella Fitzgerald, Will Jordan, Alan King, Carol Lawrence, Jackie Mason, Michelle Phillips. *Producer:* Andrew Solt. *Writer:* Peter Elbling. *Director:* Andrew Solt.

## 2122 A Very Delicate Matter.

Drama, 60 min., ABC, 11/10/82. While at the summer camp where she is a counselor, 17-year-old Kristin Sorenson grows lonely and depressed because her boyfriend (Greg) has not written to her. On her birthday her loneliness leads to an intimate encounter with another counselor. When Kristin returns home she and Greg resolve their misunderstanding. Later, the boy from camp calls Kristin to tell her that a recent medical exam revealed he had gonorrhea on the night they were intimate. The story relates Kristin's fears about having a medical exam and telling Greg that she may have passed the disease onto him. Aired as an "ABC Afterschool Special." *Cast:* Lori-Nan Engler (Kristin Sorenson), Zach Galligan (Greg Pscharapolus), Marta Kober (Cookie Platt), John Didrichsen (Eddie Burak), Grant Aleksander (Larry Milligan), Valorie Armstrong (Caroline Sorenson), Andreas Katsulas (Zachary Pscharapolus), Alma Cuervo (Dr. Riccardo). *Music:* Steven Margoshes. *Producer:* Frank Doelger. *Writer:* Marissa Gioffre. *Director:* Claude Kerven.

## 2123 The Very First Glen Campbell Television Special.

Variety, 60 min., NBC, 9/16/73. An hour of music and song with singer Glen Campbell in his first television special. Sponsored by Chevrolet. *Host:* Glen Campbell. *Guests:* Burt Reynolds, Dick Smothers, Tom Smothers, Sonny and Cher. *Music:* Jack Parnell. *Producers:* Gary Smith, Dwight Hemion. *Director:* Dwight Hemion.

## 2124 Very Good Friends.

Drama, 60 min., ABC, 4/6/77. Thirteen-year-old Kate and her 11-year-old sister, Joss, are not only sisters but also best friends. Joss is an irrepressible scamp and loves horses. Her dream to own a horse becomes a reality when she uses her birthday money to rent a horse for a week. During one of the happiest times of her life, Joss meets with a fatal accident. The tragedy shatters Kate and leaves her grieving bitterly. The story focuses on Kate as she tries to understand what has happened and put it into perspective. Aired as an "ABC Afterschool Special." *Cast:* Melissa Sue Anderson (Kate), Katy Kurtzman (Joss), Pamela Nelson (Mother), William H. Bassett (Father), Sparky Marcus (Tootie), Anne Seymour (Mrs. Pemberthy), William Lanteau (Essig), Montana Smoyer (Mrs. Essig), Joshua Davis (Harry). *Producer:* Martin Tahse. *Writer:* Arthur Heinemann. *Director:* Richard Bennett.

## 2125 A Very Merry Cricket.

Cartoon, 30 min., ABC, 12/14/73. A sequel to "The Cricket in Times Square" (see title). Harry (a cat) and Tucker (a mouse) are dismayed by the lack of Christmas spirit about them. The two reminisce about a previous time when Chester, the Connecticut cricket, made violin-like music with his wings and caused a sensation at Forty-Second Street and Broadway in New York City. The story relates their efforts to "bring goodwill" to men by recruiting the help of their friend Chester. Violinist Israel Baker performs the music for Chester. *Voices:* Les Tremayne (Chester C. Cricket/Harry the Cat), Mel Blanc (Tucker the Mouse/ Alley Cat). *Producer-Writer-Director:* Chuck Jones.

## 2126 A Very Special Occasion. Variety, 60 min., Syndicated, 9/67. A concert by singers Vikki Carr and Jack Jones. *Hosts:* Vikki Carr, Jack Jones. *Music:* Jerry Fielding. *Producer-Director:* Johnny Bradford.

## 2127 Victor Borge Specials.
A chronological listing of the variety specials hosted by Victor Borge, the comical wizard of the keyboard. All are 60 minutes long.
**1 Victor Borge's Comedy in Music I** (CBS, 6/14/56). *Music:* Budddy Bregman. *Producer:* Jerome Shaw. *Writer:* Victor Borge. *Director:* Robert Mulligan.
**2 Victor Borge's Comedy in Music II** (CBS, 12/11/56). *Music:* Buddy Bregman. *Producer:* Jerome Shaw. *Writer:* Victor Borge. *Director:* Robert Mulligan.
**3 Victor Borge's Comedy in Music III** (CBS, 2/9/58). *Guests:* Rod Alexander, Bambi Linn, Doretta Morrow. *Music:* Luther Henderson, Jr. *Producer:* Victor Borge. *Writers:* Jack Douglas, Victor Borge, Henry Morgan. *Director:* Jack Smight.
**4 Victor Borge's Comedy in Music IV** (CBS, 11/29/58). *Guest:* Alicia Markova. *Music:* Axel Stordahl. *Producer:* Jack Smight. *Writers:* Victor Borge, M. Andre Popp. *Director:* Jack Smight.
**5 The Victor Borge Special** (NBC, 2/18/60). *Guest:* Jane Powell. *Music:* Walter Scharf. *Producer:* Herbert

Wells. *Writer:* Bill Box. *Director:* Barry Shear.
**6 The Victor Borge Show** (NBC, 3/18/ 60). *Guests:* Jane Powell, Elliott Reid. *Music:* Walter Scharf. *Producers:* Lawrence White, Joseph Cates. *Writers:* Larry Markes, Eddie Lawrence, Robert Hilliard, Ben Joelson, Art Baer. *Director:* Joseph Cates.
**7 The Victor Borge Show** (ABC, 10/6/60). *Guests:* Leonid Hambro, Mike Wallace, Shiko Yagi, Izumi Yukimura. *Music:* Walter Scharf. *Producers:* Lawrence White, Joseph Cates. *Writers:* Larry Markes, Eddie Lawrence, Ben Joelson, Art Baer, Robert Hilliard. *Director:* Joseph Cates.
**8 Victor Borge's 20th Anniversary Show** (CBS, 9/27/61). *Guest:* Hermione Gingold. *Music:* Luther Henderson, Jr. *Producer:* George Schlatter. *Writers:* Charles Isaacs, Walt Canter, Mike Marmer, Victor Borge, Jay Burton. *Director:* Mike Gargiulo.

## 2128 Victoria Regina. Drama, 90 min., NBC, 11/30/61. A series of vignettes that trace the life of England's Queen Victoria—from 18-year-old princess to queen. Based on the play by Laurence Houseman and broadcast on the "Hallmark Hall of Fame." *Cast:* Julie Harris (Queen Victoria), James Donald (Prince Albert), Basil Rathbone (Disraeli), Felix Aylmer (Lord Melbourne), Pamela Brown (Duchess of Kent), Isabel Jeans (Mistress of the Robes), Louis Edmonds (Prince Ernest), Sorrell Booke (James), Geoffrey Lumb (Archbishop). *Producer-Director:* George Schaefer. *Writer:* Robert Hartung.

## 2129 Victory. Drama, 90 min., NBC, 4/8/60. A television adaptation of the novel by Joseph Conrad about a recluse (Axel Heyst) who comes to realize he cannot hide from life when he comes to the aid of a stranded entertainer (Alma) being pursued by two evil men. *Cast:* Art Carney (Axel Heyst),

Lois Smith (Alma), Eric Portman (Mr. Jones), Oscar Homolka (Mr. Schomberg), Ruth White (Mrs. Schomberg), Richard Harris (Ricardo), Ira Petina (Madame Elvira). *Producer:* David Susskind. *Writer:* Michael Dyne. *Director:* Daniel Petrie.

**2130 The Vikki Carr Show.** Variety, 60 min., Syndicated, 6/69. An hour of music and songs with singer Vikki Carr. *Host:* Vikki Carr. *Guests:* The New Christy Minstrels. *Music:* Ralph Carmichael. *Producer:* Jackie Barnett. *Director:* Dean Whitmore.

**2131 Viva Miami: The Night of Supersounds.** Variety, 60 min., CBS, 1/21/89. A program of Latin music and songs from a Miami, Florida, nightclub that salutes the Super Bowl. *Host:* Herb Alpert. *Guests:* Julio Iglesias, Cheech Marin, Willie Nelson, Linda Ronstadt, Carlos Santana. *Producers:* Ken Ehrlich, David Saltz, Jeff Ross. *Writer:* Ken Ehrlich. *Director:* Louis J. Horvitz.

**2132 Vivien Leigh: Scarlett and Beyond.** Documentary, 45 min., PBS, 5/7/90. A tribute to Vivien Leigh (1913–67), the actress who played what is considered the greatest role in movie history: Scarlett O'Hara in 1939's *Gone with the Wind.* Clips from some of Vivien's 30 films are seen, as are rare photos and home movies of her childhood in India. *Host-Narrator:* Jessica Lange. *Guests:* Elizabeth Ashley, Claire Bloom, Douglas Fairbanks, Jr., John Gielgud, Kim Hunter, Garson Kanin. *Music:* Michael Bacon.

**2133 Wait Until Dark.** Drama, 2 hrs., HBO, 12/29/82. A television adaptation of the play by Frederick Knott about Suzy Hendrix, a young blind girl who is victimized by a psychopathic killer and two desperate convicts when they invade her apartment seeking a musical doll filled with illegal drugs. Suzy's battle of wits against the thugs is the focal point of the story. *Cast:* Katharine Ross (Suzy Hendrix), Edward Winter (Sam Hendrix), Stacy Keach (Harry Roat), Natalie May (Gloria), Joshua Bryant (Mike Talman), David Leisure (Policeman), Robin Gammell (Sergeant Carlino). *Music:* Lalo Schifrin. *Producers:* Sanford Greenberg, Paul Heller. *Director:* Barry Davis.

**2134 The Walt Disney Christmas Show.** Variety, 60 min., CBS, 12/25/51. A Yuletide program of music, live performances (featuring Disney characters), and film clips from Disney films. A sequel to "One Hour in Wonderland" (see entry), Walt Disney's first venture into television. *Host:* Walt Disney. *Guests:* Don Barclay, Hans Conried, Sharon Disney, Bobby Driscoll, Kathryn Driscoll. *Music:* Phil Smith. *Producer-Writer:* Bill Walsh. *Director:* Robert Florey.

**2135 Walt Disney . . . One Man's Dream.** Documentary, 2 Hrs., CBS, 12/12/81. The program focuses on the life and achievements of Walt Disney, one of the legendary giants of American creativity, a visionary genius who, after revolutionizing the art of motion-picture animation, went on to create a magical entertainment empire that has enthralled countless millions all over the world. *Host:* Michael Landon. *Guests:* Mac Davis, Marie Osmond, Carl Reiner, Dick Van Dyke, Ben Vereen. *Cast:* Christian Hoff (Young Walt Disney), Charles Aidman (Mark Twain), Jan Hoff (Roy Disney), Lawrence Guy (Elias Disney), Frances Bain (Flora Disney), Kathleen MacNaighton (Ruthie). *Cameos:* Julie Andrews, Mikhail Baryshnikov, Walter Cronkite, Beverly Sills, Andy Warhol. *Music:* Ian Fraser. *Producers:* Gary Smith, Dwight Hemion. *Writers:* John McGreevey, Stan Hart, Mitzie Welch. *Director:* Dwight Hemion.

## 2136 Walt Disney World Celebrity Circus. Variety, 60 min., NBC, 11/27/87. A program of music, songs, and comedy from the circus at EPCOT Center at Walt Disney World in Florida. *Host:* Tony Randall. *Guests:* Allyce Beasley, Lisa Bonet, Kim Fields, Jim Varney, Malcolm-Jamal Warner. *Music:* Bruce Healy. *Producer:* Marty Pasetta. *Writers:* Bruce Bilane, Tom Perew. *Director:* Marty Pasetta.

## 2137 Walt Disney World's 15th Birthday Celebration. Variety, 2 hrs., ABC, 11/9/86. A music and comedy salute to Walt Disney World in Florida on the occasion of its fifteenth anniversary. *Hosts:* Bea Arthur, Betty White. *Guests:* Air Supply, Diahann Carroll, Ray Charles, The Charlie Daniels Band, The Everly Brothers, Charlton Heston, Gladys Knight and the Pips, Emmanuel Lewis, The Monkees, Dolly Parton. *Announcer:* Jack Wagner. *Music:* Dennis McCarthy. *Producers:* Brad Lachman, Marty Pasetta. *Writers:* Jeffrey Barron, Bob Arnott, David Forman, Ken Welch, Mitzie Welch. *Director:* Marty Pasetta.

## 2138 Wanted: The Perfect Guy. Comedy-Drama, 60 min., ABC, 10/1/86. Ellie Coleman is divorced and tired of the singles scene. Although Ellie tells her son, Danny, that she is happy, Danny is worried that in fact she is lonely. With the help of his friend, Melanie, Danny hatches a scheme to secretly place ads in the personal column of a local magazine. The story relates Danny's and Melanie's efforts to arrange a date for Ellie without her knowledge when they believe they have found "Mr. Right." Originally titled "Wanted: A Man for Mom." Aired as an "ABC Afterschool Special." *Cast:* Madeline Kahn (Ellie Coleman), Ben Affleck (Danny Coleman), Pam Potillo (Melanie), Keith Szarabajka (Peter Desmond), Melanie Mayron

(Sue), Candy Trabucco (Candy). *Music:* Jonathan Sheffler. *Producer:* Milton Justice. *Writer:* Mary Willis. *Director:* Catlin Adams.

## 2139 The War Between the Classes. Drama, 60 min., CBS, 10/22/85. In an attempt to give his students a better understanding of socioeconomic groups, a high school social studies teacher (Mr. Molner) divides his class into three color groups (blue, green, and orange) with each color representing a different economic class. The story relates what happens as each group behaves according to the rules of his or her own status. A "CBS Schoolbreak Special." *Cast:* Kale Brown (Mr. Molner), Jan Gan Boyd (Amy), Don Michael Paul (Adam), Robert Ito (Mr. Sumida), Paul Winfield (Mr. Bateman), Tanja Lynne Lee (Jana), Missy Francis (Tina), Cindi Eyman (Gale), Begona Plaza (Carol). *Producers:* Frank Doelger, Mark R. Gordon, Alan C. Blomquist. *Writer:* Paul W. Cooper. *Director:* Michael Toshiyuki Uno.

## 2140 The Wave. Drama, 60 min., ABC, 10/4/81. A compelling "ABC Afterschool Special" about a high school experiment in mind control. While studying Nazi Germany, a student asks "How could the Germans sit back while the Nazis slaughtered people all around them?" To answer the question, Burt Ross, their teacher, provides a psychological game for his students based on a strict code of behavior that stresses a feeling that an individual is part of something that is more important than himself: a movement. Soon the game becomes real—and turns the school into an aggressive, regimental and regressive fascist state—the Wave. *Cast:* Bruce Davison (Burt Ross), Lori Lethin (Laurie), John Putch (David), Johnny Doran (Robert), Pasha Gray (Amy), Wesley Pfenning (Christy), Larry Keith (Saunders). *Music:* John Addison. *Producers:* Virginia Carter, Fern Feld. *Writer:*

Johnny Dawkins. *Director:* Alex Gras-hoff.

## 2141 The Way They Were.

Variety, 2 hrs., Syndicated, 2/81. A music and comedy reunion of celebrity graduates from Northwestern University. *Guests:* Claude Akins, Ann-Margret, Richard Benjamin, Candice Bergen, Robert Conrad, Nancy Dussault, Penny Fuller, Sheldon Harnick, Charlton Heston, Ron Husmann, Martha Hyer, Carol Lawrence, Cloris Leachman, Patricia Neal, Jerry Orbach, Paula Prentiss, Charlotte Rae, Robert Reed, Tony Roberts, McLean Stevenson, Peter Strauss. *Announcer:* Dick Tufeld. *Music:* Larry Grossman, Sheldon Harnick. *Producers:* Bob Banner, Gerald Freedman. *Writer:* Marty Farrell. *Directors:* Clark Jones, Tim Kiley.

## 2142 Wayne and Garth's Saturday Night Live Music a Go-Go.

Music, 2 hrs., NBC, 2/21/93. A compilation of clips featuring performances by musical guests from the past 17 seasons of NBC's "Saturday Night Live" series. *Hosts:* Mike Myers (Wayne), Dana Carvey (Garth). *Producer:* Lorne Michaels.

## 2143 The Wayne Newton Special.

Variety, 60 min., NBC, 9/28/74. Singer Wayne Newton's first television special: an hour of music, songs, and light comedy. *Host:* Wayne Newton. *Guests:* Farrah Fawcett, Robert Goulet, Carol Lawrence, Lee Majors, Barbara Mandrell, Freda Payne, Burt Reynolds. *Producers:* Henry Jaffe, Bob Booker, George Foster. *Writers:* George Yanok, George Foster, Bob Brooks, Howard Albrecht, Sol Weinstein. *Director:* Harold Tulchin.

## 2144 The Wayne Newton Special.

Variety, 60 min., ABC, 5/19/82. Music and songs from both New York and Las Vegas. *Host:* Wayne Newton. *Guest:* Lauren Bacall. *Music:* Don Vincent. *Producer:* Bob Finkel. *Writers:* Herbert Baker, Bob Finkel. *Director:* Tony Charmoli.

## 2145 W. C. Fields Straight Up.

Documentary, 90 min., PBS, 3/4/86. A profile of William Claude Dukenfield (1880–1946), better known as W.C. Fields, one of the screen's greatest comedians. *Narrator:* Dudley Moore. *Guests:* Madge Blake, Harry Caplan, Ron Fields, Will Fowler, Everett Freeman, Gloria Jean, Leonard Maltin, Joseph L. Mankiewicz. *Producers:* Robert B. Weide, Ron Fields. *Writers:* Joe Adamson, Ron Fields. *Director:* Joe Adamson.

## 2146 We Interrupt This Season.

Comedy, 60 min., NBC, 3/26/67. A music and comedy spoof of television. *Performers:* Dennis Allen, Arthur Alpert, Sudie Bond, MacIntyre Dixon, Charlotte Fairchild, John Heffernan, Nagle Jackson, Paul Larson, Paul Melton, Bernadette Peters, Maggie Peters, Jamie Ross, Virginia Vestoff. *Songs:* William Roy. *Producer:* Thomas Hammond. *Writers:* Arthur Alpert, Dee Caruso, Richard Craven, Tony Geiss, Clark Gesner, Tony Hendra, Nick Ullett, Lucille Kallen, Treva Silverman. *Director:* Lynwood King.

## 2147 We the People 200: The Constitutional Gala.

Variety, 2 hrs. 5 min., CBS, 9/17/87. A music, comedy, and song tribute to the Constitutional Convention's September 17, 1787, vote that approved the Constitution. Taped in Philadelphia. *Host:* Walter Cronkite. *Guests:* Ned Beatty, Lloyd Bridges, Dorian Harewood, Patti LaBelle, Rich Little, Marilyn McCoo, Barry Manilow, E. G. Marshall, Walter Matthau, The Mormon Tabernacle Choir, Sandi Patti, Gregory Peck, George Peppard, Stefanie Powers, John Ritter, Wayne Rogers, Eli Wal-

Ad for "We the People 200: The Constitutional Gala"

lach, Fritz Weaver. *Music:* Ian Fraser. *Producers:* Gary Smith, Michael B. Seligman. *Writer:* Buz Kohan. *Director:* Dwight Hemion.

**2148 We the Women.** Docu-mentary, 60 min., CBS, 3/17/74. An historical special that utilizes dramatic vignettes, animation, puppetry, and historical film footage to trace the history of women in America from the *Mayflower* to the 1970s. *Host-Narrator:*

Mary Tyler Moore. *Cast:* Geraldine Fitzgerald (Carrie Chapman Catt), Vinnette Carroll (Sojourner Truth), Kathleen Widdoes (Anne Bradstreet), Sasha Von Scherler (Elizabeth Cady Stanton), Leora Dana (Susan B. Anthony), Anne Meacham (Sarah Grimke), Maeve McGuire (Angelina Grimke), Carmen Matthews (Lucretia Mott), Carol Kane (Susannah White), Michael Edwards (Harry Burn), Barry Ford (Thomas Jefferson), Dennis Helfend (William Lloyd Garrison). *Music:* Lee Holdridge. *Producers:* Jack Kuney, Lois Bianchi. *Writer:* Eve Merriam. *Puppeteer:* Steve Hansen. *Animation:* Jerome Rosenfeld. *Director:* Jack Kuney.

## 2149 Welcome Home, America. 

Tribute, 2 hrs., ABC, 4/14/91. A tribute to the armed forces and honoring 50 years of service by the USO (United Service Organizations). *Guests:* Debbie Allen, President George Bush, Nell Carter, Secretary of Defense Dick Cheney, Blake Clark, Tony Danza, John Forsythe, Lee Greenwood, Merle Haggard, Bob Hope, Joanna Kerns, Roger Moore, Tony Orlando, The Pointer Sisters, Kenny Rogers, General Norman Schwarzkopf, Tom Selleck, Brooke Shields, Frank Sinatra, Victoria Tennant, Lindsay Wagner, Paul Williams, James Woods. *Producers:* George Schlatter, Bob Wynn. *Director:* Jeff Margolis.

## 2150 Welcome Home, Jellybean. 

Drama, 60 min., CBS, 3/27/84. Feeling that their mentally retarded daughter, Geraldine, has spent enough time in an institution (where she has been since birth) Margery and Ted Oxley decide it is time she came home to live. The sensitive "CBS Schoolbreak Special" depicts the havoc, humor, breakup, and growth of family members as they learn to love and accept Geraldine, fondly called "Jellybean." *Cast:* Dana Hill (Geraldine Oxley), Deborah May (Margery Oxley), Burke

Byrnes (Ted Oxley), Christopher Collet (Neil Oxley), Irene Tedrow (Miss Bowring), Basil Hoffman (Mr. Rasmussen), Vince Howard (Mr. Parrish), Courtney Gains (Joe), Beau Dremann (Beef). *Music:* James Di Pasquale. *Producers:* Harry Ackerman, Cynthia Cherbak. *Writer:* Cynthia Cherbak. *Director:* Robert Mandel.

## 2151 The West That Never Was. 

Documentary, 60 min., Syndicated, 3/87. A tribute to the American western film, with a focus on several western stars (William S. Hart, Ken Maynard, Hoot Gibson, Harry Carey, Tim McCoy, Roy Rogers, Gene Autry, John Wayne, Randolph Scott, Tex Ritter, Buck Jones and William Boyd). *Narrator:* Tony Thomas. *Music:* Hans J. Salter. *Producer-Writer-Director:* Tony Thomas.

## 2152 What a Nightmare, Charlie Brown. 

Cartoon, 30 min., CBS, 2/23/78. The program relates the nightmare Snoopy has following Charlie Brown's unsuccessful efforts to make a sled dog out of him. The dream sequence places the pampered beagle in the Arctic, where he finds himself harnessed to a team of snarling huskies. The story relates Snoopy's efforts to work up the courage to face the huskies and help pull the sled. *Voices:* Liam Martin (Charlie Brown), Bill Melendez (Snoopy). *Music:* Ed Bogas. *Producers:* Lee Mendelson, Bill Melendez. *Writer:* Charles M. Schulz. *Director:* Phil Roman, Bill Melendez.

## 2153 What Are Friends For? 

Drama, 60 min., ABC, 3/19/80. The story of Amy Warner, shy, insecure, and soft-spoken, and Michelle Mudd, outgoing, outspoken, and outrageous, two 12-year-old girls who swear eternal loyalty to one another out of a common bond: both are only children and victims of divorce. An "ABC Afterschool Special." *Cast:* Melora Hardin (Amy Warner), Dana Hill (Michelle Mudd),

Host Dick Van Patten *(center)* and guests Angela Cartwright *(left)* and Irish McCalla *(right)* from the 1981 special "Whatever Became Of...?"

Susan Adams (Mrs. Warner), Tasha Zemrus (Nora), Sally Kemp (Mrs. Mudd), Michael Currie (Dr. Mudd), Ellie Tompkins (Diane). *Music:* Glenn Paxton. *Producer:* Martin Tahse. *Writer:* Durrell Royce Crays. *Director:* Stephen Gyllenhaal.

## 2154 What Gap?

Comedy, 60 min., ABC, 9/9/68. The story of a square who learns to accept what is really happening through a girl he meets in San Francisco. *Cast:* Wally Cox (The Square), Ann Prentiss (The Girl). *Producers:* Aaron Beckwith, David Yarnell. *Writers:* Bruce Yarnell, David Kane.

## 2155 What Have We Learned, Charlie Brown?

Cartoon, 30 min., CBS, 5/30/83. A Memorial Day tribute that recalls the time Charlie Brown, Peppermint Patty, and Linus were exchange students in France and experienced a ghostly reenactment of the Allies' landing on Omaha Beach on June 6, 1944. *Voices:* Michael Dockery, Brad Keston, Bill Melendez, Monica Parker, Jeremy Schoenberg, Stacy Heather Tolkin, Victoria Vargas. *Music:* Judy Munsen. *Producers:* Lee Mendelson, Bill Melendez. *Writer:* Charles M. Schulz. *Director:* Bill Melendez.

## 2156 Whatever Became Of ...?

Human Interest, 60 min., ABC, 10/25/81. A current update on the lives of celebrities from the past: Irish McCalla, Angela Cartwright, Jay North, Rusty Hamer, Danny Bonaduce, Margaret O'Brien, Ursula Andress, Brigitte Bardot, The Monkees, Elizabeth Ray, Mark Spitz, Lisa Loring, Mason Reese, Spanky McFarland, Danny Thomas, Barbara Hale, Bobby Sherman, Paul Winchell, Alan Young, Janet Pilgrim (*Playboy* magazine's first Playmate).

*Host:* Dick Van Patten. *Guests:* Angela Cartwright, Phyllis Diller, Donna Dixon, Barbara Hale, Rusty Hamer, Richard Lamparski, Irish McCalla, Adam Rich. *Theme Vocal,* "Whatever Became Of?": Bobby Sherman. *Producers:* Dick Clark, Al Schwartz. *Writers:* Robert Arthur, Carol Hatfield. *Director:* Jeff Margolis.

## 2157 Whatever Became Of

**...?** Human Interest, 60 min., ABC, 9/26/82. A sequel to the prior title, which updates the lives of past celebrities: Sandra Dee, Virginia Mayo, George Montgomery, Mamie Van Doren, Fanne Foxe, Deborah Walley, Jane Withers, Sheila James, Jackie Coogan, Brandon Cruz, Johnny Whitaker, Kathryn Grayson, Terry Moore, Patty Andrews, The Silhouettes. *Host:* Gavin MacLeod. *Guests:* Bill Bixby, Melanie Chartoff, Morgan Fairchild, Richard Lamparski. *Producers:* Dick Clark, Al Schwartz. *Writer:* Robert Arthur. *Director:* Al Schwartz.

## 2158 What's a Museum for, Anyway?

Children, 60 min., CBS, 1/16/78. The program introduces young people to the treasures to be found not only in the National Gallery of Art in Washington, D.C., but in museums throughout the country. *Host:* Gabriel Kaplan. *Guests:* J. Carter Brown (Director of the National Gallery of Arts), Joan Mondale (wife of Vice President Walter Mondale), Soupy Sales. *Producers:* Robert F. Stolfi, Lester Gottlieb, Burt Shevelove. *Writer:* Thomas H. Baum. *Director:* Sid Smith.

## 2159 What's Up, America.

Comedy, 60 min., NBC, 8/24/71. Sketches and blackouts that satirize the contemporary American scene. *Host:* Jackie Cooper. *Performers:* Ernest Borgnine, Tom Bosley, Phil Leeds, Paul Lynde, Marian Mercer, Lee H. Montgomery, John Ritter, Bill Zuckert. *Producer-Director:* Greg Garrison.

*Writers:* Stan Daniels, Ed Weinberger, Rod Parker.

## 2160 Whatta Year . . . 1986.

Variety, 60 min., ABC, 12/29/86. An entertaining look at the best songs, moments, television shows, personalities, and movies of 1986. *Hosts:* Justine Bateman, Ron Reagan. *Guests:* George Burns, Angie Dickinson, Quincy Jones, Ben E. King, Joan Lunden, Henry Mancini, Joe Namath, Geraldo Rivera, Smokey Robinson, O. J. Simpson, Bruce Willis. *Music:* Glenn Roven. *Producers:* Dick Clark, Jeff Margolis, Barry Adelman. *Director:* Jeff Margolis.

## 2161 When Jenny, When?

Drama, 30 min., Syndicated, 7/80. The story focuses on a very pretty high school girl (Jenny) who masks her loneliness with promiscuity. *Cast:* Maureen McCormick (Jenny), Clark Brandon (Brad), Jeff East (Rob), Olivia Cole (Karen), Joanne Romero (Laura), Bob Tory (Tom), Tom Borquze (Billy). *Music:* Dick Halligan. *Producers:* Ellwood Kieser, Mike Rhodes. *Writer:* Lan O'Kun. *Director:* Ted Post.

## 2162 When Television Was Live.

Documentary, 2 hrs., CBS, 4/28/77. A clip-filled look at television's golden age—the era of live programming and quality dramas in the 1950s. *Host:* Charles Kuralt. *Producers:* Perry Wolff, Max Wilk, Judith Hole. *Writer:* Perry Wolff.

## 2163 When the West Was Fun: A Western Reunion.

Variety, 60 min., ABC, 6/5/79. A star-studded, clip-filled salute to the golden age of television westerns (the 1950s and 1960s). *Host:* Glenn Ford. *Guests:* Michael Ansara, Neville Brand, John Bromfield, Peter Brown, Pat Buttram, Rod Cameron, Chuck Connors, Jackie Coogan, Johnny Crawford, Linda Cristal, Ken Curtis, Dale Evans, Alan

Hale, Jr., Ty Hardin, Will Hutchins, John Ireland, Dick Jones, Jack Kelly, Harry Lauter, John McIntire, Guy Madison, Clayton Moore, Jeanette Nolan, Slim Pickens, Denver Pyle, Roy Rogers, John Russell, The Sons of the Pioneers, Milburn Stone, Larry Storch, Lee Van Cleef, Terry Wilson, X Brands, Tony Young. *Announcer:* Dick Tufeld. *Music:* Ray Ellis. *Producer:* Brad Marks. *Director:* Walter C. Miller.

## 2164 When We Were Young: Growing Up on the Silver Screen. Documentary, 95 min., PBS, 12/7/89. A nostalgic, clip-rich look at children in movies and on television. *Host:* Maureen Stapleton. *Guests:* Angela Cartwright, Jackie Cooper, Darryl Hickman, Roddy McDowall, Spanky McFarland, Hayley Mills, Dick Moore, Margaret O'Brien, Tommy Rettig, Mickey Rooney, Dean Stockwell, Jane Withers. *Producers:* Glenn DuBose, James Arntz, Shelley Spencer. *Writers:* James Arntz, Katherine Mc-Millan. *Director:* Dick Carter.

## 2165 Where Do Teenagers Come From? Drama, 60 min., ABC, 3/5/80. A sequel to "My Mom's Having a Baby" (see entry) wherein Kelly, Pete, and Oscar, now teenagers, seek advice about puberty from their friend, pediatrician Lendon Smith. An "ABC Afterschool Special." *Cast:* Rachel Longaker (Kelly), Shane Sinutko (Pete), Jarrod Johnson (Oscar), Stephanie Steele (Julie), Dr. Lendon Smith (Himself). *Music:* Doug Goodwin, Eric Rodgers. *Producers:* David DePatie, Friz Freleng, Robert Chenault. *Director:* Larry Elikann.

## 2166 Where the Girls Are. Variety, 60 min., NBC, 4/23/68. A potpourri of flashy photography, comedy sketches, and music geared to the male pursuit of the American girl. *Host:* Noel Harrison. *Guests:* Don Adams,

The Association, The Byrds, Cher, Professor Irwin Corey, Barbara McNair. *Producers:* Burt Rosen, Al Burton. *Writers:* Saul Turteltaub, Bernie Orenstein, Chris Bearde, Leigh Chapman. *Director:* David Winters, Gordon Wiles.

## 2167 Which Mother Is Mine? Drama, 60 min., ABC, 9/26/79. An "ABC Afterschool Special" about a 16-year-old foster girl (Alexandria) and the turmoil she faces when her natural mother (Jill) returns to take her away from her adoptive parents (Marion and Tom). *Cast:* Melissa Sue Anderson (Alexandria Benton), Marion Ross (Marion Dennis), Bruce Kirby (Tom Dennis), Shannon Terhune (Jill Benton), Eric Scott (Eric), Virginia Capers (Judge Atherton). *Music:* Glenn Paxton. *Producer:* Martin Tahse.

## 2168 Whitney Houston: This Is My Life. Variety, 60 min., ABC, 5/6/92. Music and memories with singer Whitney Houston. Highlights of her European concert tour are intercut with reflections by Whitney, her mother, Cissy (a gospel singer), and Kevin Costner (her costar in the film *The Bodyguard*). *Host:* Whitney Houston. *Guests:* Kevin Costner, Cissy Houston. *Music:* Ricky Minor. *Producers:* Whitney Houston, John Houston, Cissy Houston, Anthony Eaton. *Writer-Director:* Anthony Eaton.

## 2169 Who Has Seen the Wind? Drama, 2 hrs., ABC, 2/19/65. When they are forced from their home in the aftermath of World War II, the Radeks, a family of three, take refuge aboard a tramp steamer. The story, set 12 years later, relates their experiences as they await the papers that will free them from their shipbound prison. Produced by the United Nations. *Cast:* Maria Schell (Maria Radek), Theodore Bikel (Josef Radek), Veronica Cartwright (Kiri Radek), Stanley Baker (Janos), Edward G. Robinson (Captain),

**Ad for "Whitney Houston: This Is My Life"**

Goose), Frankie Avalon (Jack), Nancy Sinatra (Jill), Fred Clark (William H. Berry), Margaret Hamilton (Mother Hubbard), Dick Martin (Simon), Dan Rowan (Pieman), Dick Shawn (King Cole), Joanie Sommers (Bo Peep), Scooter Jolley (Little Boy Blue), Stuart Getz (Billy). *Music:* Sherman Edwards. *Lyrics:* Ruth Batchelor. *Producer:* Frank Peppiatt. *Director:* Peter Gennaro.

Gypsy Rose Lee (Proprietress), Victor Jory (Peraltor), Paul Richards (Father Aston), Simon Oakland (Inspector), Lilia Skala (Nun). *Music:* John Green. *Theme Vocal,* "Who Has Seen the Wind?": Nancy Wilson. *Producer-Director:* George Sidney. *Writer:* Don M. Mankiewicz.

## 2170 Whoopi Goldberg—Direct from Broadway. Comedy, 60 min., HBO, 1/20/85. An explicit (vulgar language) one-woman comedy concert by comedienne Whoopi Goldberg. *Host:* Whoopi Goldberg. *Producers:* Sandy Gallin, Barry Josephson. *Writer:* Whoopi Goldberg. *Director:* Thomas Schlamme.

## 2171 Who's Afraid of Mother Goose? Musical, 60 min., ABC, 10/13/67. When William H. Berry, the head of the board of education, decides to ban Mother Goose as a bad influence on children, he is visited by the storybook lady and transformed into a young boy. The story relates Mother Goose's attempts to prove him wrong by taking him on a trip through her domain. *Cast:* Maureen O'Hara (Mother

## 2172 Why, Charlie Brown, Why? Cartoon, 30 min., CBS, 3/16/90. A departure from the usual Charlie Brown specials wherein the Peanuts gang receive a real lesson in life when a close friend (Janice) develops a form of bone cancer called leukemia. *Voices:* Kaleb Henley (Charlie Brown), Brandon Stewart (Linus), Olivia Burnette (Janice), Adrienne Stiefel (Sally), Jennifer Banks (Lucy), Bill Melendez (Snoopy). *Music:* Judy Munsen. *Producers:* Lee Mendelson, Bill Melendez. *Writer:* Charles M. Schulz. *Director:* Sam Jaimes.

## 2173 Why Didn't They Ask Evans? Mystery, 3 hrs., Syndicated, 5/21/85. A stylish television adaptation of the 1935 whodunit by Agatha Christie. The story follows the efforts of two people, Lady Frances Derwent, and her foil, Bobby Jones, as they attempt to solve the death of a man—whose last words to them were "Why Didn't They Ask Evans?"—they find along the Welsh coast. *Cast:* Francesca Annis (Frances Derwent), James Warwick (Bobby Jones), Eric Porter (Dr. Nicholson), Lee Lawson (Roger Bas-

sington), Madeline Smith (Moria Nicholson), John Gielgud (the Reverend Jones), Connie Booth (Sylvia Bassington), Rowland Davies (Dr. George Arbuthnot), Rose Pratt (Doris Hare), Elaine Wells (Nurse Fletcher), Annette Robinson (Julie), Debbie Armstrong (Mary), Alan Carstairs (Roy Boyd). *Host:* Peter Ustinov. *Music:* Joseph Horovitz. *Producers:* Tony Wharmby, Jack Williams. *Directors:* John Davies, Tony Wharmby.

## 2174 The Wickedest Witch.

Comedy, 30 min., NBC, 10/30/89. When Avarissa, an evil witch, fails to commit enough dastardly deeds, she is banished to an underground kingdom beneath Ohio to rule over creatures called Greevils (half reptile, half gameshow contestant). The story relates Avarissa's efforts to return to her prior life by making an innocent child commit a despicable act. *Cast:* Rue McClanahan (Avarissa), Jackie Gayle (The Great Schtick), Paul Fusco (Ersatz), Ronn Lucas (Sammy), Raffi DiBlasio (Lewis). *Narrator:* Burgess Meredith. *Music:* Alf Clausen. *Producers:* Bernie Brillstein, Al Lowenstein, Paul Fusco. *Writers:* David Cohan, Roger Schulman. *Director:* Steve Dubin.

## 2175 The Wide Open Door.

Drama, 90 min., ABC, 4/20/67. The story of Jill and Jane Marriott, beautiful twins with a penchant for crime, and their efforts to rob a well-stocked jewelry store. *Cast:* Honor Blackman (Jane and Jill Marriott), Tony Randall (Inspector Berry/Geoffrey Judge), Reginald Gardiner (Uncle Andrew), Bernard Fox (Jock), Leon Ames (Gray), Richard Haydn (Whitey). *Producer-Director:* Franklin Schaffner. *Writer:* T. E. B. Clarke.

## 2176 Wild Women Don't Sing the Blues.

Documentary, 60 min., PBS, 2/26/89. A profile of five blues singers (Ma Rainey, Bessie Smith, Ethel Waters, Alberta Hunter, and Ida Cox), pioneers who worked the high-class night spots and hole-in-the-wall honkytonks between 1910 and 1930. *Narrator:* Vinie Burrows. *Producers:* Carol Doyle, Van Valkenburgh, Christine Dall. *Writer-Director:* Christine Dall.

## 2177 The Wildest West Show of the Stars.

Variety, 2 hrs., CBS, 5/27/86. The program features celebrities performing various rodeo acts and competing in wild west contests (for example, gun draw, sharpshooting) for the sheer fun the sport offers. *Hosts:* James Coburn, Dennis Weaver. *Guests:* Army Archerd, Dirk Benedict, Linda Blair, Amanda Blake, The Buckboard Ranch Hands, Rory Calhoun, Kirk Cameron, Glen Campbell, Danny Cooksey, Alex Cord, Bo Derek, William Devane, Jamie Farr, Rhonda Fleming, Robert Fuller, Deidre Hall, Steve Kanaly, Joey Lawrence, Patricia McPherson, Jennifer O'Neill, Markie Post, Peter Reckell, Paul Reubens, Alfonso Ribeiro, Melody Rogers, Tracy Scoggins, Alan Thicke, Red Dog Webber, Tammy Wynette. *Music:* Jon Charles. *Producers:* Bob Stivers, Bob Finkel. *Writer:* Bunny Stivers. *Director:* Tony Charmoli.

## 2178 Will Rogers—Look Back in Laughter.

Documentary, 60 min., HBO, 4/25/87. A comical tribute to folk humorist Will Rogers (1879-1935). *Hosts:* Dan Aykroyd, Chevy Chase, Rodney Dangerfield, Harold Ramis, Robin Williams. *Narrator:* Harold Ramis. *Music:* Jack Tillar. *Producers:* Harold Ramis, Malcolm Leo, Hildegard Duane, Bonnie Peterson. *Writer:* Bennett Tramer. *Director:* Malcolm Leo.

## 2179 Will Rogers' U.S.A.

Drama, 60 min., CBS, 3/9/72. A television adaptation of the nationally acclaimed one-man show with James Whitmore utilizing the words of the legendary humorist Will Rogers. *Cast:*

James Whitmore (Will Rogers). *Music:* Tommy Morgan. *Producer:* George Spota. *Director:* Clark Jones.

**2180  William.** Variety, 60 min., ABC, 1/3/73. The only variety presentation of the "ABC Afterschool Special": an hour of music, comedy, and drama that celebrates William Shakespeare's life and attempts to introduce the bard to children. Taped in London. *Performers:* Lynn Redgrave, Simon Ward. *Readings:* Sir John Gielgud, Sir Ralph Richardson. *Vocalist:* Paul Jones. *Producer:* Alexander H. Cohen. *Director:* Ian McNaughton.

**2181  Willie Nelson: The Big Six-O.** Variety, 2 hrs., CBS, 5/22/93. An all-star concert to honor Willie Nelson on the occasion of his sixtieth birthday. *Guest of Honor:* Willie Nelson. *Guests:* Edie Bricknell, Ray Charles, Bob Dylan, Emmylou Harris, B. B. King, Kris Kristofferson, Bonnie Raitt, Paul Simon, Travis Tritt. *Music:* Don Was. *Producers:* Stanley M. Brooks, Mark Rothbaum. *Writer:* Turk Pipkin. *Director:* Jim Yukich.

**2182  Willie Nelson's Picnic.** Variety, 2 hrs., Syndicated, 6/87. A country and western concert to aid farmers in the United States (as part of Farm Aid). *Host:* Claude Akins. *Featured Performer:* Willie Nelson. *Guests:* Alabama, Catherine Bach, Charles Haid, Don Johnson. *Music Supervision:* Robin Wren. *Producers:* Willie Nelson, Steve Sterling, Richard Kimball, Robin Wren. *Directors:* Steven Callahan, Henry Capshaw, Jonathan Wacks.

**2183  Wilson's Reward.** Drama, 60 min., Syndicated, 1/84. A television adaptation of the short story by William Somerset Maugham about Martha James, a 1920s West Indies missionary, as she tries to reform Ginger Ted Wilson, an intoxicated womanizer. *Host:* Patrick O'Neal. *Cast:*

Sandy Dennis (Martha James), Gerald S. O'Loughlin (Ginger Ted Wilson), Fred Morsell (Van Den Hoag), Rosemarie Vis (Young girl), Lois Dia Donales (Wilson's mate), Mark Soper (the Reverend James), Wilfred Depal (Houseboy). *Music:* Dick York. *Producer:* Robert Halmi. *Writer:* Bernard Eismann. *Director:* Patrick O'Neal.

**2184  Wind in the Wire.** Variety, 60 min., ABC, 8/25/93. Country singer Randy Travis performs songs from his new album, *Wind in the Wire,* in a story about the making of a western movie (wherein Randy is the star). *Star-Narrator:* Randy Travis. *Guests:* Chuck Norris, Lou Diamond Phillips, Denver Pyle, Charles Nelson Reilly, Burt Reynolds, Dale Robertson. *Music:* Bobby Goldsboro. *Producers:* Elizabeth Travis, Lib Hatcher. *Writers:* James Brooks, Jim Shea. *Director:* Jim Shea.

**2185  Window Shade Revue.** Variety, 35 min., NBC, 8/25/46. A series of songs and sketches based on vaudeville routines. The title refers to the program's opening: a window shade is opened to reveal the cast (who perform behind two windows). *Cast:* Maxine Barrett, Lillian Cornell, Paul Gordon, Harold Lang, Lou Nelson, Bibi Osterwald, Carl Ravazza. *Producer-Director:* Ronald Oxford. *Writer:* Robert Mayberry.

**2186  The Winged Colt.** Fantasy, 30 min., ABC, 9/10, 9/17, 9/24/77. A three-part "ABC Weekend Special" about a mysterious colt that is born with wings. The birth takes place on a ranch owned by a former movie stuntman called Uncle Coot. Charles, Coot's nephew, names the colt Comet and believes that one day it will fly. Coot refuses to believe it—until the colt actually flies. The story relates their escapades as they try to keep the colt's secret, despite the animal's tendency to fly off in search of adventure. *Cast:* Slim

Pickens (Uncle Coot), Ike Eisenmann (Charles), Keenan Wynn (Hiram the Hermit), Jane Withers (Mrs. Minney), Frank Cady (Mr. Minney). *Music:* Tommy Leonetti. *Producer:* Robert Chenault. *Writer:* Jim Inman. *Director:* Larry Elikann.

### 2187  The Wings of the Dove.

Drama, 2 hrs., Syndicated, 7/81. A television adaptation of the novel by Henry James about the effect of Europe on the Americans of his day who went there in search of enlightenment, romance, and excitement. The story opens to reveal that Kate Croy is secretly in love with Merton Densher, an impoverished journalist of whom Kate's guardian, Maud Lowder, would strongly disapprove. While on a tour of Europe, Susan Stringham, an old friend of Maud's, and her companion, Milly Theale, stop off in London to visit Maud. When Kate discovers that Milly is ill and may not have long to live, she persuades Merton to pretend to be interested in her — to brighten her last few days — but to also gain some of her vast wealth by the way of legacy. The tale unfolds to relate what happens to Kate and Merton's relationship when Merton genuinely falls in love with Milly. *Cast:* Elizabeth Spriggs (Maud Lowder), Betsy Blair (Susan Stringham), Suzanne Bertish (Kate Croy), Lisa Eichhorn (Milly Theale), John Castle (Merton Densher), Rupert Frazer (Lord Mark), Alan Rowe (Sir Luke Strett), Gino Melvazzi (Eugenio). *Producer:* Alan Shallcross. *Writer:* Denis Constanduros. *Director:* John Gorrie.

### 2188  Winnie the Pooh, and Christmas Too.

Cartoon, 60 min., ABC, 12/14/91. It is Christmas time in the Hundred Acre Wood and all is not calm: the letter written by the animal residents to Santa went undelivered by Winnie the Pooh. To make up for his mistake, Pooh pretends to be Santa Claus and heads out on Christmas Eve with a sleigh-load of gifts for the animals. *Voices:* Jim Cummings (Winnie the Pooh), John Fiedler (Piglet), Paul Winchell (Tigger), Ken Sansom (Rabbit), Edan Gross (Christopher Robin), Peter Cullen (Eeyore). *Producer:* Ken Kessel. *Writers:* Mark Zaslove, Karl Geurs. *Directors:* Ken Kessel, Jamie Mitchell.

### 2189  Winnie the Pooh and the Honey Tree.

Cartoon, 30 min., NBC, 3/10/70. Winnie the Pooh's challenge: to lose weight by giving up his favorite food — honey. His struggle to keep on his diet is the focal point of this story adapted from A. A. Milne's children's books. *Voices:* Sterling Holloway (Winnie the Pooh), Howard Morris (Gopher), Bruce Reitherman (Christopher Robin), Hal Smith (Owl), Ralph Wright (Eeyore), Barbara Luddy (Kanga). *Producer:* Walt Disney Animation. *Writers:* Larry Clemmons, Xavier Atencio, Vance Gerry, Ralph Wright, Ken Anderson, Dick Lucas. *Director:* Wolfgang Reitherman.

### 2190  The Winning Hand.

Variety, 2 hrs., Syndicated, 3/85. A program of country and western music from the Tennessee Performing Arts Center in Nashville. *Hosts:* Johnny Cash, Dolly Parton. *Announcer:* T. Tommy Cutrarer. *Music:* Bill Walker. *Producers:* Richard C. Thrall, Jack Thompson, Fred Foster. *Writers:* Fred Foster, Jack Thompson. *Director:* Bob Finkel.

### 2191  Winston  Churchill.

Drama, 90 min., PBS, 6/18/86. A one-man show in which Robert Hardy, portraying Winston Churchill (1874–1965), mixes anecdotes and witticisms with frank and sometimes painful recollections as he reflects on a variety of personal and political topics. *Cast:* Robert Hardy (Winston Churchill). *Host:* Sir John Gielgud. *Producers:* David Susskind, Diana Loptook, Charles Jarrott. *Writer:* James C. Humes. *Director:* Charles Jarrott.

**2192 Winterset.** Drama, 90 min., NBC, 10/26/59. A television adaptation of the play by Maxwell Anderson about a man (Mio Romagna) and his attempts to clear the name of his father, who was executed for a murder he did not commit. Aired on the "Hallmark Hall of Fame." *Cast:* Don Murray (Mio Romagna), Piper Laurie (Mirianna), George C. Scott (Trock), Charles Bickford (Judge Gaunt), Martin Balsam (Garth), George Mathews (Shadow). *Producer-Director:* George Schaefer. *Writer:* Robert Hartung.

## 2193 The Wish That Changed Christmas.

Cartoon, 30 min., CBS, 12/20/91. Ivy is a young girl who lives in Miss Shepherd's Home for Orphan Girls. She desperately wants a family and, believing that she has a grandmother, she sets out to find a home for the holidays. The story relates her search and how her wish to find love comes true on Christmas Eve when she crosses the path of a lonely and childless couple (the Joneses) who are desperately seeking a child. *Voices:* Brittany Thornton (Ivy), Beverly Garland (Miss Shepherd), Paul Winfield (Mr. Smith), Jonathan Winters (Abracadabra), Marc Robinson (Peter). *Music:* Normand Roger. *Producers:* Frank Getchell, Marjorie Kalins. *Writer:* Romeo Muller. *Director:* Catherine Margerin.

## 2194 Witches, Warlocks and Wizards.

Documentary, 30 min., Syndicated, 10/87. The program examines the history of witchcraft via film clips, photos, and drawings. *Host-Narrator:* Jonathan Harris. *Producers:* Richard Jones, Tak Nakamori. *Writer-Director:* Richard Jones.

## 2195 With All Deliberate Speed.

Drama, 60 min., CBS, 6/16/76. An historic dramatization of the original school desegregation case that led the Supreme Court to bar racial segregation in American schools on May 17, 1954. *Cast:* Paul Winfield (the Reverend J. A. DeLaine), John Randolph (Judge Waites Waring), Jay Garner (Mr. McCord), Joe Seneca (Levi Pearson), Marlena Lustik (Elizabeth Waring), Fernita Martin (Mattie DeLaine), Martin Mayhew (Jesse DeLaine), Keith Allen (Billy Hamilton), Sandra Rackley (Mary Oliver), Ronald O. Davis (Bishop Crane), Ethel Ayler (Carlene Simmons). *Music:* Lee Holdridge. *Producers:* Joel Heller, Robert Markowitz. *Writers:* Bill Badalato, Jan Hartman. *Director:* Robert Markowitz.

## 2196 With Love, Sophia.

Variety, 60 min., ABC, 10/25/67. Actress Sophia Loren conducts a musical fantasy tour of her world. *Host:* Sophia Loren. *Guests:* Tony Bennett, Marcello Mastroianni, Peter Sellers, Jonathan Winters. *Music:* Leslie Bricusse. *Producers:* Jack Haley, Jr., Roger Gimbel. *Writer:* Sheldon Keller. *Director:* Michael Pfleghar.

## 2197 The WJZ-TV Inaugural.

Variety, 4 hrs. 37 min., ABC, 8/10/48. The ABC-TV network is launched with New York station WJZ-TV (now WABC-TV) and stations in Philadelphia and Washington, D.C., hosting a lavish program of music, songs, and vaudeville performances. The New York segment is broadcast from the Palace Theater in Manhattan. *Guests:* James Barton, Ray Bolger, Buck and Bubbles, Carlton Emmy's Mad Wags, Allen Funt and his "Candid Microphone" (the pre–"Candid Camera" title), Beatrice Lillie, Pat Rooney, Sr., Gus Van, Willie West and McGinty, Paul Whiteman and His Orchestra. *Producers:* Paul Mowrey, Burk Crotty. *Palace Theater Producer:* Larry Puck. *Technical Supervisor:* George Milne.

## 2198 The Woman in White.

Mystery, 60 min., NBC, 5/23/60. The

story, set in Victorian England (1800s) tells of a mysterious ghost-like woman who intervenes in the lives of two sinister villains who are plotting to gain control of an innocent girl's fortune. Aired on "The Dow Hour of Great Mysteries" and based on the novel by Wilkie Collins. *Cast:* Siobhan McKenna (Marion Halcombe), Walter Slezak (Count Fosco), Robert Flemyng (Sir Percival Glyde), Arthur Hill (Walter Hartright), Lois Nettleton (Laura and Anne Catherick), Rita Vale (Countess Fosco), Catherine Proctor (Mrs. Vesey). *Host:* Joseph N. Welch. *Producer:* Robert Saudek. *Writer:* Frank Ford. *Director:* Paul Nickell.

### 2199  Woman of the 21st Century. Documentary, 60 min., CBS, 10/19/89. Women in various fields are profiled to show the benefits of fitness. The program is also known as "Women of the 21st Century" (the title that appears in *TV Guide;* "Woman" is the screen title). *Host:* Rachel McLish. *Narrator:* Mary Gregory. *Cast:* Heather Schell (Gymnast), Gino D'Auri (Guitarist), Linda Vallejo (Flamingo Dancer), Jessie Larken (Woman with children), Sharon Ferrol, Carla Earle, Monique Darcel Leonard (Dancers), Rave Hollitt, Michelle "Mimi" Hitzman, Diana Dennis, Sandra Blackie, Joni Bowing (Women at gym), Mike Kirton, Laszlo Bene, Oleg Spector (Thugs). *Music:* Johnny Harris. *Producers:* Ron Samuels, Alfred Kelman. *Writers:* Ron Samuels, Arthur Kelman. *Director:* Arthur Kelman.

### 2200  The  Woman  Who Willed a Miracle. Drama, 60 min., ABC, 2/9/83. The true story of a severely retarded infant, deserted by his parents, and given small odds for survival by medical experts, who receives a chance at life when he is adopted by May Lemke, a woman whose loving faith and devotion give the child a future. An Emmy Award–winning "ABC Afterschool Special." *Cast:* Cloris Leachman (May Lemke), James Noble (Dr. Edwards), Fran Bennett (Nurse Matthews), Bruce French (Dr. Vince), M. Emmet Walsh (Joe Lemke), Rosemary Murphy (Gladys), Lief Green (Leslie). *Producers:* Dick Clark, Preston Fischer, Joanne A. Curley, Sharron Miller. *Writer:* Arthur Heinemann. *Director:* Sharron Miller.

### 2201  The Women. Comedy, 90 min., NBC, 2/7/55. A television adaptation of the 1936 Broadway play by Clare Boothe Luce about the devastating effects a rumor has on a happily married housewife when she believes her husband is seeing a pretty salesgirl. *Cast:* Shelley Winters (Crystal Allen), Paulette Goddard (Sylvia Fowler), Ruth Hussey (Marcy Haimes), Mary Astor (Nancy Blake), Nancy Olson (Peggy Day), Mary Boland (Countess de Lage), Valerie Bettis (Miriam Aarons), Cathleen Nesbitt (Mrs. Moorehead), Nita Talbot (Olga), Bibi Osterwald (Edith Potter), Pat Carroll (Gym teacher), Pamela Lawrence (Saleslady), Jada Rowland (Little Mary), Mary Michael (Maggie), Nan McFarland (Miss Watts), Sybil Baker (Jane), Paula Bauersmith (Lucy), Helen Raymond (Mrs. Wagstaff), Brett Somers (Cigarette girl), Sara Mead (Helen). *Producers:* Max Gordon, Fred Coe. *Writer:* Sumner Locke Elliott. *Director:* Vincent J. Donehue.

### 2202  The Women of Country. Variety, 2 hrs., CBS, 5/6/93. A salute to the women of country music via live performances and clips of concert footage. *The Women:* Suzy Bogguss, Mary-Chapin Carpenter, Emmylou Harris, Wynonna Judd, Patty Loveless, Loretta Lynn, Kathy Mattea, Lorrie Morgan, Anne Murray, Pam Tillis, Tanya Tucker, Michelle Wright, Tammy Wynette, Trisha Yearwood. *Music:* The American Music Shop Band (Mark O'Connor, Jerry Douglas, Brent Mason, Gary Smith, Harry Stin-

**Tonight, 70 of country's biggest female stars join together.**

Tammy Wynette

Anne Murray

Mary-Chapin Carpenter

EmmyLou Harris

Loretta Lynn

Trisha Yearwood

Wynonna

**Past concert footage, interviews and live performances, featuring: Suzy Bogguss • Naomi Judd • Brenda Lee Linda Ronstadt • Tanya Tucker • Kitty Wells and many more!**

the 𝒲OMEN of COUNTRY

A CBS SPECIAL PRESENTATION

8PM ☻2WCBS-TV

son, Glenn Worf). *Producers:* Bud Schaetzle, Martin Fischer, Douglas Forbes. *Writer:* Robert Okormon. *Director:* Bud Schaetzle.

## 2203 Women Who Rate a "10."
Variety, 60 min., NBC, 2/15/81. A look at the women whom men consider to be a perfect "10." See also "Men Who Rate a 10." *Hosts:* Erik Estrada, Morgan Fairchild, Howard Hesseman. *Guests:* Maud Adams, Lois Areno, Candi Brough, Randi Brough, Cathy Lee Crosby, Sheila DeWindt, Donna Dixon, Britt Ekland, Barbra Horan, Ann Jillian, Victoria Johnson, Judy Landers, Linda McCullough, Maureen Murphy, Victoria Principal, Sherilyn Wolter. *Announcer:* Casey Kasem. *Music:* Fred Werner. *Producers:* Marvin Minoff, Robert Guenette. *Writers:* Sheldon Keller, Jerry Russell. *Director:* Mark Warren.

## 2204 Wonderful Town.
Musical, 2 hrs., CBS, 11/30/58. The romantic adventures of Ruth and Eileen Sherwood, two sisters who arrive in New York's Greenwich Village from Columbus, Ohio, seeking fame and fortune — Ruth as a writer and Eileen as an actress. Based on the *My Sister Eileen* stories by Ruth McKenney. *Cast:* Rosalind Russell (Ruth Sher-

wood), Jacqueline McKeever (Eileen Sherwood), Joseph Buloff (Mr. Appopolous), Dort Clark (Chick Clark), Sydney Chaplin (Robert Baker), Michelle Burke (Helen), Jordan Bentley (The Wreck), Cris Alexander (Frank Lippencott), Jean Carrons (Violet), Jack Fletcher (Nightclub patron). *Music Director:* Lehman Engel. *Music:* Leonard Bernstein. *Lyrics:* Betty Comden, Adolph Green. *Producers:* Joseph Fields, Robert Fryer. *Writers:* Joseph Fields, Jerome Choldoron. *Director:* Mel Ferber.

## 2205 The Wonderful World of Aggravation. Comedy, 60 min., ABC, 11/15/72.

A series of sketches and blackouts based on the things that annoy people in their everyday lives. *Host:* Alan King. *Guests:* Ron Carey, Lee Grant, The Joy People, Jack Klugman, Tony Randall, Timmie Rodgers, Larry Storch. *Producers:* Alan King, Herb Sargent, Bob Ellison. *Writers:* Herb Sargent, Bob Ellison, Norman Barasch, Carroll Moore, John Boni, Sue Haven, Norman Steinberg, Alan King, Alan Uger. *Director:* Dave Wilson.

## The Wonderful World of Burlesque *see* Danny Thomas Specials

## 2206 The Wonderful World of Girls. Variety, 60 min., NBC, 1/14/70.

A music, song, and comedy salute to the girls of the world. *Host:* Barbara Eden. *Guests:* Ruth Buzzi, Diane Davis, Chanin Hale, Barbara Heller, Kay Medford. *Music:* Les Brown. *Producer:* Greg Garrison. *Director:* Danny Daniels.

## 2207 The Wonderful World of Jack Paar. Variety, 60 min., NBC, 1/26/60.

A casual hour of music, song, and chatter. *Host:* Jack Paar. *Guests:* Betty Bruce, Alice Pearce, Harry Mimmo, Pat Suzuki, Jonathan Winters.

*Music:* Jose Melis. *Producers:* Hubbell Robinson, Jack Paar. *Writers:* Paul W. Keyes, Bob Howard, Jack Douglas, Dick Maury. *Director:* Greg Garrison.

## 2208 The Wonderful World of Jonathan Winters. Variety, 60 min., NBC, 10/31/70.

An hour of comedy tailored to the talents of comedian Jonathan Winters. *Host:* Jonathan Winters. *Producers:* George Spota, Rupert Hitzig. *Writers:* Max Wilk, Jeremy Stevens, Fred Halliday, Jonathan Winters, Carole Hart, Bruce Hart.

## 2209 The Wonderful World of Pizzazz. Variety, 60 min., NBC, 3/18/69.

A music and comedy look at the world of fashion—past, present, and future. *Hosts:* Michele Lee, Carl Reiner. *Guests:* The Cowsills, Harpers Bizarre, Pat Paulsen. *Music:* Perry Botkin, Jr. *Producers:* Lee Mendelson, Walt DeFaria. *Writers:* Lee Mendelson, Larry Markes, Charles Einstein. *Director:* Walt DeFaria.

## 2210 The Woody Allen Special. Variety, 60 min., NBC, 9/21/69.

A series of sketches built around the weird and wacky world of Woody Allen, "the underweight champion of the underdog." Woody's first television special. *Host:* Woody Allen. *Guests:* Candice Bergen, The Fifth Dimension, the Rev. Billy Graham, The Robert Herget Dancers. *Music:* Elliot Lawrence. *Producers:* Jack Rollins, Charles H. Jaffe. *Writers:* Woody Allen, Marshall Brickman, Mickey Rose. *Directors:* Woody Allen, Alan Handley.

## 2211 A Word from Our Sponsor. Variety, 60 min., NBC, 10/1/92.

A look at memorable commercials from 40 years of television (including foreign television commercials, special effects in commercials, and the changing role of women in television commercials). *Hosts:* Crystal Bernard, Phil Hartman. *Producer:* Brad Lach-

**Ad for "A Word from Our Sponsor"**

man. *Writers:* William Marich, Rich Ross. *Director:* Michael Dimitch.

**2212 Words to Live By.**
Drama, 60 min., CBS, 1/10/89. A "CBS Schoolbreak Special" about freedom of speech. The fact-based story of two high school students who are suspended for distributing an underground newspaper judged obscene by the school board. *Cast:* Christopher Gartin (Danny), Ricky Paull Golden (Phil), Barbara Bosson (Kathy), Amy Benedict (Sarah), Michael Fairman (Sinclair), Robert Harper (Bird), Ken Jenkins (Lawyer), Anne Gee Byrd (Stacy), Natalia Nogulich (Tina), William Frankfather (Mr. Beale). *Music:* Misha Segal. *Producers:* Bradley Wigor, Joseph Mauer, Dale White. *Writer:* Rick Doehring. *Director:* Bradley Wigor.

**2213 Working for Peanuts.**
Drama, 50 min., HBO, 4/8/87. The romantic story of a beer vendor at a ballpark (Jeffrey) and a beautiful rich girl (Melissa) who meet, fall in love—then discover their respective backgrounds will prevent them from living

happily together. *Cast:* Carl Marotte (Jeffrey Mead), Jessica Steen (Melissa), Shawn Thompson (Rick), August Schellimber (Louis Mead), John Hempell (Al), Elvia Mia Hoover (Mrs. Riley). *Producers:* John Brunton, Ian Paterson. *Writer:* Marisa Gioffre. *Director:* Martin Lavut.

### 2214 The World Famous Moscow Circus. Variety, 60 min., CBS, 7/22 and 7/29/77. A two-part special that presents highlights of the Moscow Circus in the USSR. *Host* (Part 1): William Conrad. *Host* (Part 2): Shirley Jones. *Producers:* Lothar Bock, Charles Andrews. *Writer:* Charles Andrews. *Director:* Ian Smith.

### The World of Bob Hope *see* The Bob Hope Special (5/14/79)

### 2215 The World of James Bond. Documentary, 60 min., NBC, 11/26/65. A behind-the-scenes look at James Bond, filmdom's indestructible British secret agent. *Narrator:* Alexander Scourby. *Producer-Writer-Director:* Jack Haley, Jr.

### 2216 A World of Love. Variety, 60 min., CBS, 12/22/70. A program of Christmas music and songs that salute children all over the world. *Hosts:* Bill Cosby, Shirley MacLaine. *Guests:* Julie Andrews, Harry Belafonte, Richard Burton, Florence Henderson, Audrey Hepburn, Barbra Streisand. *Music:* Elliot Lawrence. *Producer:* Alexander H. Cohen. *Writer:* Hildy Parks. *Director:* Clark Jones.

### 2217 The World of Magic. Variety, 60 min., NBC, 12/26/75. An hour of magic and illusions with magician Doug Henning. *Host:* Bill Cosby. *Star:* Doug Henning. *Guests:* Gene Kelly, Julie Newmar. *Music:* Tom Pierson. *Producer:* David Susskind. *Writer:* Marty Farrell. *Director:* Walter C. Miller.

### 2218 The World of Maurice Chevalier. Documentary, 60 min., NBC, 2/22/63. A review of the life of French entertainer Maurice Chevalier. *Narrator:* Alexander Scourby. *Producer-Director:* Eugene S. Jones. *Writer:* Joseph Liss.

### 2219 The World of Sophia Loren. Documentary, 60 min., ABC, 2/27/62. The program follows the beautiful Italian actress through a typical day in her life. *Host:* Sophia Loren. *Guests:* Art Buchwald, Vittorio DeSica, Anthony Perkins. *Narrator:* Alexander Scourby. *Music:* Robert Emmett Dolan. *Producer-Director:* Eugene S. Jones. *Writer:* Joseph Liss.

### 2220 World's Fair Spectacular. Variety, 60 min., ABC, 4/29/65. A musical tour of the 1965 New York World's Fair. Highlights include visits to the various national pavilions, a performance by the Hell Drivers of the Auto Thrill Show, acrobatics by Mexico's daring Flying Eagles of Papantla, and samples of traditional African dances by Watusi tribesmen. *Hosts:* Gordon MacRae, Sheila MacRae. *Guests:* Al Hirt and his sextet, The New Christy Minstrels. *Producer-Director:* Gil Cates.

### 2221 The World's Funniest Commercial Goofs. Comedy, 60 min., ABC, 11/17/83, 11/20/84, 11/24/85. A look at comical outtakes from television commercials. *Hosts:* Robert Guillaume, Emmanuel Lewis. *Music:* Evan Greenspan. *Producers:* Alan Landsburg, Merrill Grant, David Auerbach. *Writers* (11/17/83): Bob Booker, Jeffrey Barron. *Writer* (11/20/84): Robert Arnot. *Writers* (11/24/85): Jack Wohl, Phil Hahn, Donna Brown. *Director* (11/17/83 and 11/24/85): Arthur Forrest. *Director* (11/20/84): Dick Feldman.

### 2222 The Worst Witch. Comedy, 75 min., HBO, 10/22/86. The story

follows a clumsy teenage girl (Mildred) as she struggles to pass her courses (at Miss Cackle's International Academy for Witches) and become a full-fledged witch. Filmed in England. *Cast:* Diana Rigg (Miss Hardbroom), Charlotte Rae (Miss Cackle), Fairuza Balk (Mildred Hubble), Tim Curry (The Grand Wizard), Sue Elliott (Delilah), Kate Buckley (Donna), Leila Marr (Pixie Brown), Tara Stevenson (Gloria), Julia Magle (Bubble Toil), Amy Shindler (Spinne Webb). *Theme Vocal,* "Growing Up Isn't Easy": Bonnie Langsford. *Producers:* Louis Rudd, Hilary Heath, Colin Shindler. *Writer:* Jill Murphy. *Director:* Robert Young.

## 2223 The Wrong Way Kid.

Comedy-Drama, 60 min., CBS, 3/15/ 83. A look at adolescence as seen through the experiences of Chris, a young boy who seems to do everything wrong. Through the efforts of a 203-year-old bookworm (seen in animated form), Chris is shown scenes from books and made to understand that his apparent run of bad luck is merely a part of adolescence. A "CBS Schoolbreak Special." *Cast:* Dick Van Dyke (Father/Librarian/Old Man), Keith Mitchell (Chris), Derek Barton (Falling Man). *Voices:* June Foray, Stan Freberg, Melanie Gaffin, Joan Gerber, Wayne Hall, Don Messick, Jason Naylor, Arnold Stang. *Music:* Larry Wolff. *Producer:* Nick Bosustow. *Writer:* George Arthur Bloom. *Live Action Director:* Lawrence Levy. *Animation Director:* Sam Weiss.

## 2224 Yabba Dabba Doo!

Documentary, 60 min., CBS, 10/12/79. A behind-the-scenes look at the animated world of characters created by the team of William Hanna and Joseph Barbera. (Their characters include Yogi Bear, Huckleberry Hound, The Flintstones, Quick Draw McGraw, and Scooby-Doo.) *Host:* Bill Bixby. *Guest:* Daws Butler (voice for many Hanna-Barbera characters). *Music:* Hoyt Cur-

tin. *Producers:* William Hanna, Joseph Barbera, Robert Guenette. *Writer:* Len Janson. *Director:* Robert Guenette.

## 2225 Yabba Dabba Doo! The Happy World of Hanna-Barbera.

Documentary, 2 hrs., CBS, 11/24/77. A look at the animated world of characters created by William Hanna and Joseph Barbera over the past 20 years (which include such characters as The Flintstones, The Jetsons, Huckleberry Hound, Yogi Bear, Josie and the Pussycats, Penelope Pitstop, Quick Draw McGraw, and Scooby-Doo). *Hosts:* Gene Kelly, Cloris Leachman, Jonathan Winters. *Guest:* Lorne Greene. *Producers:* William Hanna, Joseph Barbera, Marshall Flaum. *Writer-Director:* Marshall Flaum.

## 2226 Yankee Doodle Cricket.

Cartoon, 30 min., ABC, 1/16/75. A sequel to "The Cricket in Times Square" and "A Very Merry Cricket" (see titles) wherein Chester C. Cricket and his pals, Harry the Cat and Tucker the Mouse, recall their ancestors' contribution to America's struggle for independence. *Voices:* Les Tremayne (Chester), Mel Blanc (Harry), June Foray (Tucker). *Music Director:* Dean Elliott. *Violinist:* Israel Baker. *Producer-Writer-Director:* Chuck Jones.

## 2227 The Year of the Gentle Tiger.

Drama, 60 min., CBS, 11/23/79. Following the death of his estranged wife, a social-climbing executive (Hamilton) finds himself the guardian of his son (Keni), and embarrassed by the fact of having to raise him. The story relates the boy's efforts to win his father's love and acceptance (which he does when Keni enters the judo competition in the Junior Olympics). A "CBS Schoolbreak Special." *Cast:* Lance LeGault (Hamilton), Keenan Shimizu (Keni), Tony Candell, Jr. (Angelo), Jeff Edmond (Tommy), George Harris (Coach),

Karen Anthony (Sally), Henry Calvert (Brewster). *Producer:* Lawrence Jacobson. *Writers:* Dennis Kane, Barney Cohen. *Director:* Dennis Kane.

## 2228 The Year Without a Santa Claus. Christmas, 60 min., ABC, 12/10/74. An animated musical fantasy that revolves around Santa Claus's disenchantment over the lack of holiday spirit and his threat to cancel his traditional Christmas Eve sleigh ride (his mind is changed when he finds that there are still people who have not lost the Christmas spirit). *Voices:* Mickey Rooney (Santa Claus), Shirley Booth (Mrs. Santa), Dick Shawn (Snowmiser), George S. Irving (Heatmiser), Robert McFadden (Jingle Bells), Bradley Bolke (Jangle Bells), Rhoda Mann (Mother Nature), Colin Duffy (Ignatius Thistlewhite), Ron Marshall (Mr. Thistlewhite), Christine Winter (Blue Christmas girl). *Music:* Jules Bass, Maury Laws. *Producer-Directors:* Arthur Rankin, Jules Bass. *Writer:* William Keenan.

## 2229 Yearbook: Class of 1967. Variety, 60 min., CBS, 5/21/85. A musical special that looks back at the high school and college graduating classes of 1967 and the music, fads, fashions, heroes, and events of the era. *Hosts:* Lyle Alzado, Natalie Cole, Patrick Duffy, Betty Thomas. *Guests:* Judy Collins, The Four Tops, Barry Livingston, Stanley Livingston ("My Three Sons"), Frankie Valli and the Four Seasons. *Producer:* Ken Ehrlich. *Writers:* Ken Ehrlich, Jay Grossman. *Director:* Stan Harris.

## 2230 The Yeoman of the Guard. Operetta, 90 min., NBC, 4/10/57. A television adaptation of the Gilbert and Sullivan operetta about a greedy family who frame a rich relative (the dashing Colonel Fairfax) in an attempt to acquire his wealth. Aired on the "Hallmark Hall of Fame." *Cast:*

Alfred Drake (Jack Point), Celeste Holm (Phoebe Merry II), Bill Hayes (Colonel Fairfax), Barbara Cook (Elsie), Henry Calvin (Wilfred Shadbolt), Robert Wright (Sir Richard), Murial O'Malley (Dame Carruthers), Marjorie Gorden (Kate), Norman Atkins (Sergeant Merry II). *Music:* Franz Allers. *Producer-Director:* George Schaefer. *Writer:* William Nichols.

## 2231 Yes Virginia, There Is a Santa Claus. Christmas, 30 min., ABC, 12/6/74. The time is 1897. Virginia O'Hanlon is eight years old and the only child among her skeptical friends who still believes in Santa Claus. Strong in her faith, Virginia tries every source for the answer. Finally, Virginia writes to the editor of the *New York Sun* to ask "Is there a Santa Claus?" The editor's response assuring little Virginia that Santa does exist became one of the most famous editorials in newspaper history. *Voices:* Jim Backus (Narrator), Courtney Lemmon (Virginia O'Hanlon), Susan Silo (Miss Taylor), Billie Green (Billie), Sean Manning (Specs), Tracy Belland (Mary Lou), Christopher Wong (Arthur), Vickey Ricketts (Amy), Arnold Moss (Sergeant Muldoon), Herb Armstrong (Officer Riley). *Theme Vocal,* "Yes Virginia, There Is a Santa Claus": Jimmy Osmond. *Producers:* Burt Rosen, Bill Melendez, Mort Green. *Writer:* Mort Green. *Director:* Bill Melendez.

## 2232 Yogi Bear's All-Star Comedy Christmas Caper. Cartoon, 30 min., CBS, 12/21/82. An animated adventure in which Yogi Bear and his friend, Boo Boo Bear, leave Jellystone Park to experience Christmas in the city. *Voices:* Daws Butler (Yogi Bear/Quick Draw McGraw/Huckleberry Hound/Snagglepuss/Hokey Wolf/Snooper/Blabber/Auggie Doggie/Mr. Jinks/Wally Gator), Don Messick (Boo Boo/Ranger Smith/Pixie), John Stephenson (Doggie

Daddy/Butler/Announcer/Mr. Jones/ First zookeeper), Hal Smith (Sergeant/ Mrs. Jones/P.A. Voice), Janet Waldo (Lady in the street), Jimmy Weldon (Yakky Doodle/Second zookeeper), Allan Melvin (Magilla Gorilla/Chief Blake/Murray), Henry Corden (Fred Flintstone/Policeman), Mel Blanc (Barney Rubble/Bulldog/Security guard), Georgi Irene (Judy Jones). *Music:* Hoyt Curtin. *Producers:* William Hanna, Joseph Barbera, Art Scott. *Writer:* Mark Evanier. *Director:* Steve Lumley.

## 2233 You Can't Do That on Television. Comedy, 90 min., ABC, 9/12/68.

A series of fast-paced comedy sketches considered risqué at the time, that test the limits of television censorship. *Host:* Al Hamel. *Performers:* David Aster, Melendy Britt, Ann Elder, Bonnie Scott, McLean Stevenson, Billy Van, Robert Wagner. *Producer-Director:* Bill Davis.

## 2234 You Can't Take It with You. Comedy, 2 hrs., CBS, 5/16/79.

A television adaptation of the 1936 Moss Hart and George S. Kaufman Broadway play about two people in love and the totally outrageous night when both families meet for the first time. *Cast:* Art Carney (Grandpa Vanderhof), Blythe Danner (Alice Sycamore), Jean Stapleton (Penny Sycamore), Beth Howland (Essie), Barry Bostwick (Tony), Harry Morgan (Mr. De Pinna), Robert Mandan (Kirby), Eugene Roche (Paul), Paul Sand (Ed), Marla Gibbs (Rheba), Ken Mars (Kolenkhov), Polly Holliday (Mrs. Kirby), Joyce Van Patten (Gay), Tim Reid (Donald), Mildred Natwick (Olga). *Music:* Arthur B. Rubinstein. *Producers:* Paul Bogart, Lindsay Law. *Director:* Paul Bogart.

## 2235 You Don't Look 40, Charlie Brown. Cartoon, 60 min., CBS, 2/2/90.

A nostalgic look at the great moments from 40 years of Charlie Brown and the Peanuts gang in the comics and 25 years on television. *Host:* Michele Lee. *Guests:* David Benoit, Cathy Guisewite, B. B. King, Bill Melendez, Charles M. Schulz. *Music:* Vince Guaraldi, Desiree Goyette, David Benoit, Dave Grusin, Dave Brubeck. *Vocals:* Desiree Goyette, Cam Clarke, Joey Scarbury. *Producers:* Lee Mendelson, Bill Melendez. *Writer-Director:* Lee Mendelson.

## 2236 You Gotta Start Somewhere. Drama, 30 min., CBS, 12/8/77.

The true story of Philip Gilbert, an 11-year-old Indian boy who established a special school for Indian children in Rapid City, South Dakota. (When his grammar school curriculum ignored his Indian heritage, he went about organizing his fellow students, obtaining an abandoned building, and convincing the local school board that his mother and uncle should teach this special school for Indian children so they could learn about their background. The school proved successful and has been moved from its humble beginnings to a place of prominence on the Pine Ridge Reservation outside Rapid City.) *Cast:* Panchito Gomez (Philip Gilbert), Dimitra Arliss (Madonna Gilbert), Van Williams (Ted Means), Parley Baer (Mr. Painter), Bill Quinn (Mr. Smith), David Yanez (Howard), Danny Agrella (Arnold), Eric Greene (Keith). *Music:* Richard LaSalle. *Producer:* Bob Birnbaum. *Writers:* Lois Peyser, Arnold Peyser. *Director:* William P. D'Angelo.

**You Put Music in My Life** *see* **Mac Davis Specials**

## 2237 Young at Heart Comedians. Comedy, 60 min., Showtime, 9/11/84.

A reunion of seven of comedy's most respected veteran performers (who display their now classic material). *Host:* David Brenner. *The*

*Comics:* Carl Ballantine, Shelly Berman, Norm Crosby, Jackie Gayle, George Gobel, Jackie Vernon, Henny Youngman. *Producers:* Oliver Wilson, Michael Fowles, Judy Simon. *Director:* Howard Storm.

## 2238 Your All Time Favorite Songs. Variety, 60 min., CBS, 11/29/64.

A Thanksgiving special in which songs, selected by a *Reader's Digest* poll, are performed. The favorite songs are: "Begin the Beguine," "Some Enchanted Evening," "As Time Goes By," "Sentimental Journey," "Tonight," "I Left My Heart in San Francisco," "Night and Day," "Greensleeves," "Summertime," "Autumn Leaves," "Exodus," "Stardust," "Old Man River," "Moon River," "Tea for Two," and "You'll Never Walk Alone." *Hosts:* Eydie Gorme, Al Hirt, Dean Martin. *Producer:* Roger Gimbel. *Choral Director:* Dick Williams. *Director:* Dwight Hemion.

## 2239 You're a Good Man, Charlie Brown. Musical, 90 min., NBC, 2/9/73.

A television adaptation of the off–Broadway musical in which the Peanuts gang philosophizes on everything from Charlie Brown's less than successful baseball team to Snoopy's endless antics. Aired on the "Hallmark Hall of Fame." *Cast:* Wendell Burton (Charlie Brown), Bill Hinnant (Snoopy), Mark Montgomery (Schroeder), Barry Livingston (Linus), Noelle Matlovsky (Peppermint Patty), Ruby Persson (Lucy). *Producers:* Lee Mendelson, William L. Lockhart. *Writer:* Charles M. Schulz. *Director:* Walter C. Miller.

## 2240 You're a Good Sport, Charlie Brown. Cartoon, 30 min., CBS, 10/28/75.

The story finds Charlie Brown, the famous sports failure, competing against Peppermint Patty and the Masked Marvel (alias Snoopy) in a charity motor-cross race. *Voices:* Dun-

can Watson (Charlie Brown), Liam Martin (Linus), Stuart Brotman (Peppermint Patty), Gail M. Davis (Sally), Jimmy Ahrens (Marcie), Melanie Kohn (Lucy), Bill Melendez (Snoopy). *Music:* Vince Guaraldi. *Producers:* Lee Mendelson, Bill Melendez. *Writer:* Charles M. Schulz. *Director:* Phil Roman.

## 2241 You're in Love, Charlie Brown. Cartoon, 30 min., CBS, 2/9/67.

Charlie Brown's attempts to acquire the affections of the red-haired girl who sits in front of him in class. *Voices:* Peter Robbins (Charlie Brown), Sally Dryer (Lucy), Christopher Shea (Linus), Gail DeFaria (Peppermint Patty), Cathy Steinberg (Sally), Ann Altieri (Violet), Bill Melendez (Snoopy). *Music:* John Scott Trotter. *Producers:* Lee Mendelson, Bill Melendez. *Writer:* Charles M. Schulz. *Director:* Bill Melendez.

## 2242 You're Not Elected, Charlie Brown. Cartoon, 30 min., CBS, 9/23/76.

Charlie Brown's disastrous campaign against Linus for the presidency of the sixth grade at the Birchwood School. *Voices:* Chad Webber (Charlie Brown), Stephen Shea (Linus Van Pelt), Robin Kohn (Lucy Van Pelt), Todd Barbee (Russell Anderson), Hilary Momberger (Sally), Linda Ercoli (Violet), Brian Karanjian (Schroeder), Bill Melendez (Snoopy). *Music:* Vince Guaraldi. *Producers:* Lee Mendelson, Bill Melendez. *Writer:* Charles M. Schulz. *Director:* Bill Melendez.

## 2243 You're the Greatest, Charlie Brown. Cartoon, 30 min., CBS, 3/19/79.

Charlie Brown's attempts to win the most demanding event in the Junior Olympics: the decathlon. *Voices:* Arrin Skelley (Charlie Brown), Daniel Anderson (Linus), Patricia Ann Patts (Peppermint Patty), Michelle Muller (Lucy), Casey Carlson (Paula),

Scott Beach (Sally), Tim Hall (Schroeder), Bill Melendez (Snoopy). *Music:* Ed Bogas, Judy Munsen. *Producers:* Lee Mendelson, Bill Melendez. *Writer:* Charles M. Schulz. *Director:* Phil Roman.

**2244 You're the Top.** Variety, 90 min., CBS, 10/6/56. A panoramic celebration of Cole Porter's career. *Host:* Cole Porter. *Guests:* Louis Armstrong, George Chakiris, Bing Crosby, Dorothy Dandridge, Sally Forrest, Peter Lind Hayes, Mary Healey, Shirley Jones, George Sanders. *Music:* David Rose. *Producer-Director:* Robert Alton. *Writer:* Herbert Baker.

**2245 Yummy, Yummy, Yummy.** Variety, 60 min., Syndicated, 6/69. A solo concert performance by singer Julie London. *Host:* Julie London. *Band:* Don Overberg (guitar), Milton Hiatom (bass), Carl Fontana (trombone), Mousie Alexander (drums).

**2246 Yves Montand on Broadway.** Variety, 60 min., NBC, 5/11/62. Music and songs with French entertainer Yves Montand. *Host:* Yves Montand. *Guests:* Polly Bergen, Helen Gallagher, John Raitt, Bobby Van. *Music Director:* Harry Sosnik.

**2247 Zack and the Magic Factory.** Comedy, 30 min., ABC, 1/10 and 1/17/81. When his parents leave for their European vacation, Zachary Dabble is sent to live with his eccentric Aunt Daisy. Soon Zach discovers that Daisy runs the Dabble Magic Factory and is facing eviction for unpaid bills. The story relates Zach's efforts to help

Daisy raise the money she needs to save the factory. Aired as an "ABC Weekend Special." *Cast:* Jimmy Gatherum (Zachary Dabble), Jane Withers (Daisy Dabble), Olivia Barash (Jenny), Janet MacLachlan (Eve Harrington), Tom Williams (Mario the Great), Robert Lussier (Mr. Stuple). *Music:* John Cacavas. *Producer:* Robert Chenault. *Writers:* Ann Elder, Cindy Leonetti. *Director:* Ernest Pintoff.

**2248 Zero Hour.** Comedy, 60 min., ABC, 5/1/67. An outrageous hour of comedy skits, featuring the unique talent of Zero Mostel. *Host:* Zero Mostel. *Guests:* Sudie Bond, Barney Martin, Marian Mercer, Josh Mostel, John Pleshette. *Producers:* Gary Smith, Dwight Hemion. *Writers:* John Aylesworth, Ian Hunter, Pat McCormick, Jack Burns, Avery Schreiber, Mel Brooks. *Director:* Dwight Hemion.

**2249 The Zertigo Diamond Caper.** Mystery, 60 min., CBS, 5/31/83. Following the theft of the 564-carat, white Zertigo diamond from a museum where his mother (Maggie) arranged the security, blind 12-year-old Jeffrey Brenner attempts to help his detective father (Jack) solve the case and clear his mother. Aired on the "CBS Afternoon Playhouse." *Cast:* Adam Rich (Jeffrey Brenner), Jane Elliot (Maggie Brenner), David Groh (Jack Brenner), Emory Bass (Charles Emerson III), Jeffrey Tambor (Nick Alessio), Carole Cook (Florence Dumont), Soon-Tech Oh (James Wong), Scanlon Gail (Matthew Kerkorian). *Producers:* Diane Asselin, Paul Asselin. *Writers:* David Hoffman, Leslie Daryl Zerg. *Director:* Paul Asselin.

# INDEX

*References are to entry numbers.*

Borquze, Tom 2161
Bosley, Tom 4, 30, 124, 604, 865, 866, 1122, 1246, 1286, 1361, 1366, 1453, 1476, 1542, 1672, 1676, 2159
Bosson, Barbara 1441, 1939, 2212
Boston, Joe 1902
Bostrom, Zachary 1962
Bostwick, Barry 998, 1453, 1894, 2234
Bosustow, Nick 988, 1956, 2223
Boswell, Connee 923
Botkin, Perry, Jr. 2209
Botnick, Bruce 1125
Botsford, Sara 855
Bottoms, Joseph 160, 1275, 1666
Bouchard, Bruce 901
Bougie, Garin 1922
Boulais, Jean Pierre 976
Bouler, Richard 519
Boules, Paul 797
Boulton, Derek 2051
Bourneuf, Philip 730, 1959, 2046
Bouvier, Lee 1170
Bova, Joe 1492
Bowab, John 1042
Bowan, Sybil 2027
Bowen, John 250
Bowen, Dennis 726
Bowie, David 213, 488, 489, 1704, 1863, 2036, 2067
Bowing, Joni 2199
Bowker, Bob 463
Bowker, Judy 595
Bowles, Peter 593
Bowling, Roger 1406
Bowman, Roger 978
Bowstead, Victoria 1177
Box, Bill 499, 565, 566, 567, 1148, 1149, 1807, 2116, 2127
Boxcar Willie 430
Boxleitner, Bruce 160
Boy George 232, 465
Boyce, Tommy 1866
Boyd, Jan Gan 2139
Boyd, Guy 1241, 1494
Boyd, Jimmy 958
Boyd, Robert 1938
Boyd, Stephen 856, 891, 1615
Boyer, Charles 2002

Boyett, Don 1610
Boyz II Men 77, 1127
Bracken, Eddie 121, 769, 878, 1918, 2159
Bradbury, Ray 1602
Braden, Kim 1296
Bradford, Johnny (John) 138, 537, 729, 766, 825, 1041, 1349, 1352, 1572, 1737, 1802, 2126
Bradley, Brian 1455
Bradley, Ed 820
Bradley, General Omar 623
Bradley, Owen 1656
Bradley, Stephen 1525
Bradshaw, Randy 1379
Brady, Buff 1622
Brady, Jordan 790
Braff, Ruby 2051
Brahm, John 1170
Branacle, Gary 2035
Branaghi, Kenneth 1917
Brand, Jolene 645
Brand, Neville 2163
Brandis, Diane 802
Brandman, Michael 151, 194, 222, 494, 905, 1533, 1928
Brando, Kevin 1000
Brandon, Clark 1002, 2161
Brandon, Jane 1594
Brandon, Julie 941
Brandon, Michael 1213
Brandon, Peter 174, 726, 911, 1594
Brands, X 2163
Branigan, Laura 76, 1454
Brannum, Lumpy 811
Brashar, Jaie 1794
Brasselle, Keefe 1119
Braun, Judith 1226
Braverman, Chuck 1487
Braverman, Marvin 1683, 1698
Braxton, Stephanie 1310
Bray, Thom 1439
Brayton, Margaret 1026
Breaux, Marc 213, 315, 417, 506, 533, 1203, 1375
Brecher, Irving 1329
Brecher, Jim 1996
Breckman, Andy 1057
Breen, Danny 1770
Bregman, Buddy 23, 825, 1724, 2127

Bregman, Tracy 394, 789
Brennan, Eileen 721, 1145, 1209
Brennan, Stephen 901
Brennan, Walter 480, 485, 1205
Brenner, David 75, 1448, 1908, 2237
Brenner, Dori 1081
Brent, Earl 724
Brent, Jason G. 408
Brent, John 1290
Brent, Rommey 1977
Brenton, Larry 580
Bresh, Thom 1672
Bresler, Betty 1415
Breslin, Herbert 1557
Breslin, Patricia 124
Breslow, Marc 1759
Bresnahan, Don 813
Brett, Jeremy 1270, 1497
Brevard, Aleshia 347
Brewer, Teresa 776
Brian, Jeb 304, 305
Briant, Shane 1589
Brice, John 1824
Brice, Monty 232
Brick, Michael 1494
Brickell, Beth 1644
Bricken, Jules 1361
Brickman, Marshall 1074, 2210
Bricknell, Edie 2181
Bricusse, Leslie 1577, 1853, 2196
Bridges, Alan 250, 457
Bridges, Beau 86, 292, 581, 590, 1415, 1687, 1921
Bridges, Jeff 82, 1518
Bridges, Lloyd 343, 394, 823, 1454, 1568, 2147
Bridges, Todd 160, 161, 394, 811
Brier, Richard 1529
Briggs, Buddy 1961
Briggs, Bunny 1354, 2104, 2118
Briggs, David 436
Bright, Kevin 1279
Bright, Patricia 1510, 1593, 1756, 2084
Brightman, Sarah 821
Brill, Charlie 294
Brill, Fran 1473
Brill, Frank 1812
Brill, Leighton 1192
Brill, Patti 1192

*Television Specials*